HANDBOOK OF LATIN AMERICAN STUDIES: No. 48

A Selective and Annotated Guide to Recent Publications in Art, Folklore, History, Language, Literature, Music, and Philosophy

VOLUME 49 WILL BE DEVOTED TO THE SOCIAL SCIENCES: ANTHROPOLOGY, ECONOMICS, EDUCATION, GEOGRAPHY, GOVERNMENT AND POLITICS, INTERNATIONAL RELATIONS, AND SOCIOLOGY

EDITORIAL NOTE: Comments concerning the *Handbook of Latin American Studies* should be sent directly to the Editor, *Handbook of Latin American Studies*, Hispanic Division, Library of Congress, Washington, D.C. 20540.

HANDBOOK OF LATIN AMERICAN STUDIES: NO. 48

HUMANITIES

Prepared by a Number of Scholars
for the Hispanic Division of The Library of Congress

Edited by DOLORES MOYANO MARTIN

1986

UNIVERSITY OF TEXAS PRESS Austin

International Standard Book Number 0-292-73041-1
Library of Congress Catalog Card Number 36-32633
Copyright © 1988 by the University of Texas Press
Printed in the United States of America

Requests for permission to reproduce material from this work should be sent to
Permissions, University of Texas Press,
Box 7819, Austin, Texas 78713-7819.

First Edition, 1988

IN MEMORIAM

CHARLES GIBSON (August 12, 1920–August 22, 1985)

Contributing editor to the *Handbook of Latin American Studies* for more than 20 years (1952–78), member and finally Chairman of its Advisory Board (1965–79), Charles Gibson died on August 22, 1985, in Keeseville, New York. His untimely death at the age of 65 removed from our midst a staunch friend and advisor of the Hispanic Division of the Library of Congress as well as one of the most distinguished scholars of Latin America of his generation.

My friendship with Gibson dated from 1948 when we met as graduate students from different universities working on our doctoral dissertations in the same collections, at the University of Texas Library and at the Archivo General de la Nación in Mexico City. Gibson was already a published author, his M.A. thesis *The Inca concept of sovereignty* (1948) having been issued by the University of Texas Press. He completed his Ph.D. at Yale in 1950 under the direction of George Kubler. At Yale he met Howard F. Cline, then an instructor, who in 1952 would become the second Chief of the Hispanic Division of the Library of Congress. The fruitful collaboration of Gibson and Cline would lead to the development of the new field of ethnohistory. Throughout the 1950s, 1960s and 1970s, Gibson continued to work closely with as well as to advise the Chiefs and staff of the Hispanic Division on many projects. His section on Mexican history in the *Handbook* set the highest standards and continues to serve as a model of selectivity, fairness and good writing.

Gibson's many publications such as *Tlaxcala in the sixteenth century* (1952) and his monumental *The Aztecs under Spanish rule* (1964) reordered the research priorities for a generation of colonial historians. Much of today's best work on the post-Conquest Indian experience whether in Mesoamerica or South America owes much to the pioneering research of Charles Gibson.

His academic career began at the University of Iowa where he spent 16 years, after which he moved to the University of Michigan in 1965. He would remain in Ann Arbor until his premature retirement for reasons of health. Throughout the years, Gibson devoted much of his time and effort to professional associations. He served as Chairman of the Conference on Latin American History (1952), Associate Managing Editor of the *Hispanic American Historical Review* (1955–60), and member of the Board of Editors of *The American Historical Review* (1973–75). In 1977, he received the highest accolade accorded to a United States historian when he was elected President of the American Historical Association.

Despite his many intellectual achievements and the honors that he received, Gibson remained throughout his life a gentle man of exceptional modesty. He was never too busy to respond to students or fellow scholars with advice and suggestions that were invariably thoughtful and useful. Those of us who had the good fortune to know him or work with him have suffered an incalculable loss.

Robert A. Potash
University of Massachusetts, Amherst

CONTRIBUTING EDITORS

HUMANITIES

Jean A. Barman, *University of British Columbia*, HISTORY
Roderick J. Barman, *University of British Columbia*, HISTORY
María Luisa Bastos, *Lehman College-CUNY*, LITERATURE
Judith Ishmael Bissett, *Miami University, Ohio*, LITERATURE
David Bushnell, *University of Florida*, HISTORY
D. Lincoln Canfield, *Southern Illinois University at Carbondale*, LANGUAGES
Sara Castro-Klarén, *The Johns Hopkins University*, LITERATURE
Donald E. Chipman, *North Texas State University, Denton*, HISTORY
Flora Clancy, *University of New Mexico, Albuquerque*, HISTORY
S.L. Cline, *University of California, Santa Barbara*, HISTORY
Don M. Coerver, *Texas Christian University*, HISTORY
Michael L. Conniff, *University of New Mexico, Albuquerque*, HISTORY
René de Costa, *University of Chicago*, LITERATURE
Edith B. Couturier, *National Endowment for the Humanities*, HISTORY
Joseph T. Criscenti, *Boston College*, HISTORY
Ethel O. Davie, *West Virginia State College*, LITERATURE
Ralph E. Dimmick, *Organization of American States*, LITERATURE
Leonard Folgarait, *Vanderbilt University*, ART
Fernando García Núñez, *University of Texas at El Paso*, LITERATURE
Magdalena García Pinto, *University of Missouri, Columbia*, LITERATURE
Naomi M. Garrett, *West Virginia State College*, LITERATURE
Jaime Giordano, *State University of New York at Stony Brook*, LITERATURE
Cedomil Goić, *University of Michigan*, LITERATURE
Richard E. Greenleaf, *Tulane University*, HISTORY
Oscar Hahn, *University of Iowa*, LITERATURE
Michael T. Hamerly, *Latin American Bibliographic Foundation*, HISTORY
John R. Hébert, *Library of Congress*, BIBLIOGRAPHY AND GENERAL WORKS
Carlos R. Hortas, *Hunter College*, LITERATURE
Regina Igel, *University of Maryland, College Park*, LITERATURE
Randal Johnson, *University of Florida*, FILM
Djelal Kadir, *Purdue University*, LITERATURE
Norma Klahn, *Columbia University*, LITERATURE
Pedro Lastra, *State University of New York at Stony Brook*, LITERATURE
Asunción Lavrin, *Howard University*, HISTORY
Suzanne Jill Levine, *University of Washington*, LITERATURE
Maria Angélica Guimarães Lopes, *University of South Carolina, Columbia*,
  LITERATURE
William Luis, *Dartmouth College*, LITERATURE
Murdo J. MacLeod, *University of Florida*, HISTORY
Wilson Martins, *New York University*, LITERATURE

Robert J. Mullen, *University of Texas at San Antonio*, ART
José Neistein, *Brazilian American Cultural Institute, Washington*, ART
Julio Ortega, *University of Texas at Austin*, LITERATURE
José Miguel Oviedo, *University of California, Los Angeles*, LITERATURE
Colin Palmer, *University of North Carolina, Chapel Hill*, HISTORY
Vincent C. Peloso, *Howard University*, HISTORY
Anne Pérotin-Dumon, *Kent State University*, HISTORY
Richard A. Preto-Rodas, *University of South Florida, Tampa*, LITERATURE
René Prieto, *Southern Methodist University*, LITERATURE
Jane M. Rausch, *University of Massachusetts-Amherst*, HISTORY
Daniel R. Reedy, *University of Kentucky*, LITERATURE
James D. Riley, *Catholic University of America*, HISTORY
Rubén Ríos Avila, *University of Puerto Rico*, LITERATURE
Frank Salomon, *University of Wisconsin, Madison*, HISTORY
John F. Scott, *University of Florida*, ART
Rebecca J. Scott, *University of Michigan*, HISTORY
Nicolas Shumway, *Yale University*, LITERATURE
Blanca G. Silvestrini, *University of Puerto Rico*, HISTORY
Susan M. Socolow, *Emory University*, HISTORY
Saúl Sosnowski, *University of Maryland, College Park*, LITERATURE
Robert Stevenson, *University of California, Los Angeles*, MUSIC
Juan Carlos Torchia-Estrada, *Organization of American States*, PHILOSOPHY
Kathryn Waldron, *New York University*, HISTORY
George Woodyard, *University of Kansas*, LITERATURE
Thomas C. Wright, *University of Nevada, Las Vegas*, HISTORY
Winthrop R. Wright, *University of Maryland, College Park*, HISTORY
George Yudice, *Hunter College*, LITERATURE

SOCIAL SCIENCES

Amalia Alberti, *Cornell University*, SOCIOLOGY
G. Pope Atkins, *United States Naval Academy, Annapolis*, INTERNATIONAL RELATIONS
Roderic A. Camp, *Central College, Pella, Iowa*, GOVERNMENT AND POLITICS
Lyle Campbell, *State University of New York at Albany*, ANTHROPOLOGY
William L. Canak, *Tulane University*, SOCIOLOGY
Manuel J. Carvajal, *Florida International University*, ECONOMICS
César Caviedes, *University of Florida*, GEOGRAPHY
Donald V. Coes, *University of Illinois, Urbana*, ECONOMICS
Lambros Comitas, *Columbia University*, ANTHROPOLOGY
David W. Dent, *Towson State College*, GOVERNMENT AND POLITICS
Clinton R. Edwards, *University of Wisconsin, Milwaukee*, GEOGRAPHY
Everett Egginton, *University of Louisville*, EDUCATION
Gary S. Elbow, *Texas Tech University*, GEOGRAPHY
Damián Fernández, *Colorado College*, INTERNATIONAL RELATIONS
James W. Foley, *University of Miami, Coral Gables*, ECONOMICS
Michael J. Francis, *University of Notre Dame*, INTERNATIONAL RELATIONS
Roberto Frisancho, *University of Michigan*, ANTHROPOLOGY
Edmundo F. Fuenzalida, *Stanford University*, SOCIOLOGY
Daniel W. Gade, *University of Vermont*, GEOGRAPHY

William R. Garner, *Southern Illinois University at Carbondale*, GOVERNMENT AND POLITICS
Norman Hammond, *Rutgers University, New Brunswick*, ANTHROPOLOGY
Ann Hartness, *University of Texas at Austin*, BIBLIOGRAPHY AND GENERAL WORKS
Mostafa Hassan, *Florida International University*, ECONOMICS
Kevin Healy, *Inter-American Foundation*, SOCIOLOGY
Jonathan Hill, *University of Georgia*, ANTHROPOLOGY
Mario Hiraoka, *Millersville State College*, GEOGRAPHY
James Howe, *Massachusetts Institute of Technology*, ANTHROPOLOGY
W. Jerald Kennedy, *Florida Atlantic University*, ANTHROPOLOGY
Thomas J. LaBelle, *University of Pittsburgh*, EDUCATION
Barbara Deutsch Lynch, *Cornell University*, SOCIOLOGY
Scott Mainwaring, *University of Notre Dame*, GOVERNMENT AND POLITICS
Markos Mamalakis, *University of Wisconsin, Milwaukee*, ECONOMICS
Tom L. Martinson, *Auburn University*, GEOGRAPHY
Betty J. Meggers, *Smithsonian Institution*, ANTHROPOLOGY
Ernesto Migliazza, *Gaithersburg, Md.*, ANTHROPOLOGY
Andrew M. Modelski, *Library of Congress*, GEOGRAPHY
Raúl Moncarz, *Florida International University*, ECONOMICS
William Norris, *Oberlin College*, SOCIOLOGY
Lisandro Pérez, *Florida International University*, SOCIOLOGY
Jorge F. Pérez-López, *U.S. Department of Labor*, ECONOMICS
Roger N. Rasnake, *Goucher College*, ANTHROPOLOGY
Steve C. Ropp, *University of Wyoming*, GOVERNMENT AND POLITICS
Jorge Salazar-Carrillo, *Florida International University*, ECONOMICS
Stephen M. Smith, *The Pennsylvania State University*, ECONOMICS
Barbara L. Stark, *Arizona State University*, ANTHROPOLOGY
Dale Story, *University of Texas at Arlington*, INTERNATIONAL RELATIONS
Andrés Suárez, *University of Florida*, GOVERNMENT AND POLITICS
Paul Sullivan, *Yale University*, ANTHROPOLOGY
Simon Teitel, *Inter-American Development Bank*, ECONOMICS
Antonio Ugalde, *University of Texas at Austin*, SOCIOLOGY
Miguel Urrutia, *Inter-American Development Bank*, ECONOMICS
Robert E. Verhine, *Universidade Federal da Bahia, Salvador, Brazil*, EDUCATION
Carlos H. Waisman, *University of California, San Diego*, SOCIOLOGY
Gary W. Wynia, *University of Minnesota*, GOVERNMENT AND POLITICS

Foreign Corresponding Editors

Lino G. Canedo, *Franciscan Academy, Bethesda, Md.*, COLONIAL HISTORY
Marcello Carmagnani, *Università degli Studi di Torino, Italy*, ITALIAN LANGUAGE
Krystian Complak, *Wrocław University, Wrocław, Poland*, POLISH SOCIAL SCIENCE MATERIAL
Magnus Mörner, *Göteborgs Universitet, Sweden*, SCANDINAVIAN LANGUAGES
Ulrich Menge, *Ibero-Amerikanisches Institut, Berlin, Federal Republic of Germany*, GERMAN LANGUAGE
Hasso von Winning, *Southwest Museum, Los Angeles*, GERMAN MATERIAL ON MESOAMERICAN ARCHAEOLOGY

Special Contributing Editors

Robert V. Allen, *Library of Congress*, RUSSIAN LANGUAGE
Marie-Louise H. Bernal, *Library of Congress*, SCANDINAVIAN LANGUAGES
Georgette M. Dorn, *Library of Congress*, GERMAN AND HUNGARIAN LANGUAGES
George J. Kovtun, *Library of Congress*, CZECH LANGUAGE
Norine I. Vicenti, *Library of Congress*, DUTCH LANGUAGE

CONTENTS

EDITOR'S NOTE

I. GENERAL AND REGIONAL TRENDS

Themes in this volume can be divided among: a) continuing subjects, those that have been constant throughout the last three or four volumes of the *Handbook*; b) emerging subjects, those appearing for the first time; and c) declining subjects, those no longer commanding the same interest as in past volumes.

Among the first category is the continuing interest in Mexican and Brazilian art of the 20th century, countries which, once again, lead all others in the number of publications on the subject (p. 36 and p. 42). Scholarly interest in Spanish American literature of the colonial period is even more noticeable in this *Handbook* than in previous volumes (p. 392). Studies of the Mexican-US border continue to attract as much attention as in the past (p. 148). Two Latin American writers that elicit the same interest as in previous years are Colombia's Nobel Prize winning author Gabriel García Márquez (p. 448), and that perennial favorite, the Peruvian philosopher José Carlos Mariátegui (p. 626). Dominant themes in Dominican prose fiction are still the Trujillo dictatorship and the US occupation of the island (p. 435), subjects that also preoccupy the island's historians as is evident from the publication of a very important documentary collection on US-Dominican relations during that time (p. 185). That works by and about women continue to command attention is apparent in Mexican history (p. 127), in critical studies of and works by female writers (p. 385), and in Central American feminist poetry (p. 482). In Argentina, historical studies of the post-1930 and contemporary period continue to attract the most attention (p. 307).

Among the second category or emerging themes that are becoming dominant, one should note the remarkable popularity of Latin American films, studies of which have been growing at such a pace over the last ten years "that it is now virtually impossible to keep up with all relevant publications." (p. 59). Indeed, ten years ago when we published the first FILM section in *HLAS 38* our bibliography was the first comprehensive one on the subject. Now, our contributing editor's chief concern is how to be selective rather than comprehensive given the vast number of publications on Latin American film that are appearing in Latin America, the US, Europe, and other areas of the world. The extraordinary increase in the number of publications on the Caribbean is evident in this volume in which the Caribbean history section, previously compiled by two historians, now requires four: two for the Hispanic Caribbean, one of the British Commonwealth area and another for the French, Dutch and Danish islands (p. 184). As in history, there has been a notable increase in the literature and poetry of the French Caribbean (p. 574). The growing interest of French publishers in the region is exemplified by the number of new editions of classics on the former French Caribbean colonies (p. 187). Interest in the history of disease and epidemics is once again evident in this volume (p. 128). Evident too is the growing fascination with the past and future roles of the Catholic Church in the region, the Church as an institution that both reflects and affects socioeconomic and political change (p. 127 and p. 285). Indeed, interest in the controversial doctrine known as theology of liberation and the political role that the Catholic Church should or should not play in the region continues unabated (p. 625). We are pleased to note that a country neglected in past volumes of *HLAS* is finally receiving from historians the attention it deserves: in this volume there are more than twice the number of works on Ecuadorian history than were annotated in *HLAS 42* and *HLAS 44* (p. 269). French scholars are among those most responsible for the upsurge of interest in Ecuador; especially noteworthy are their studies of the nation's historical geography during both the colonial and republican periods (p. 223). As in the case of Ecuador, peoples and periods unrecognized by scholars are finally commanding the necessary attention. Favorite subjects of research such as the Incas are receding into the background to be examined in "secondary roles" as either antagonists or rivals of long-neglected ethnic groups which "now attract the liveliest research" (p. 87). And finally, a vigorous *polémica* has erupted about the origins of Caribbean and Colombian "Spanish Creoles," notably Papiamentu and Palenquero: Are they the offspring of an African *lingua franca* or a dialectical derivation of colonial Spanish? (p. 357).

Among the third category, themes that are declining or topics that are commanding less interest than in the past, is the study of the independence period of Spanish America (p. 256). The decline of interest in this subject, noted in previous *Handbooks*, is especially evident in this volume, the last one to include a separate section on the Independence period. As of *HLAS 50*, independence studies will be apportioned according to country and annotated by the historian of its national period. Studies that deal with the overall independence movement will be assigned to the historian responsible for the general history of Latin America. Declines are also evident in Brazilian literature in which the "voices of protest" in poetry are "less numerous than in past years" (p. 554), and in literary criticism in which there is a "clear decline of interest in theory" (p. 565). A trend away from theory is also discernible in studies of contemporary Spanish American art (p. 37). Colonial studies of the River Plate region are also declining, especially as of this *Handbook* (p. 225). We also note a sharp decrease in literary criticism of Ecuadorian and Bolivian authors (p. 446). The decline in studies of the Mexican *hacienda*, noted in previous *Handbooks*, is compensated in this volume by the growing scholarship on the interrelation of Mexico's land, its ownership and cultivation (p. 127).

Despite economic difficulties affecting Latin America, the publishing business continues to issue outstanding works. Splendid achievements deserving mention are Mexican publications of precolumbian codices and other documentary sources basic for the study of Mesoamerican ethnohistory (p. 79) as well as the monumental series of 23 volumes devoted to the history of the Mexican Revolution (p. 147). Like Mexico, Venezuela ought to be commended for publishing a high-quality documentary collection on the nation's modern history (item 2904 and p. 262). Also issued in Venezuela is "the publishing event of the decade" (p. 400), the 24-volume complete works of Andrés Bello (item 5125). Like government agencies in Mexico and Venezuela, those in Brazil also play a major role in editing and publishing the nation's historic and artistic patrimony. FUNARTE, Brazil's Fundação Nacional de Arte, "sponsored the most lavish music publication series of the decade," on the works of Brazilian composer José Maurício Nunes Garcia (1767–1830), "the Afro-Brazilian father of the nation's music" (p. 596). Many celebrated collections of Brazilian short stories long out of print have also been reissued (p. 543). Publications of translations of Latin American literature continue to attract so much attention that they became "the main focus of the New Latin American Poetry Conference (Oct. 1985) sponsored by the Colorado Endowment for the Arts" (p. 583).

As we noted in *HLAS* 47 (p. xvii), the reestablishment of liberal democracy throughmost of South America (the exceptions being Chile, Paraguay and Surinam) has resulted in a remarkable publishing renaissance. Most notable are works that attempt to restore material or subjects that were censored or suppressed during the dictatorships. This is especially true in Argentina where many works of fiction explore and examine the violence that afflicted the nation as well as the Falklands/Malvinas War (p. 464). A remarkable novel that deals with both phenomena is Rodolfo Fogwill's *Los pichy-cyegos* (item 5603). In Cuba, where the repression and exile of writers continue, authors who remain in the island must write what the government regards as "acceptable" fiction (p. 434). Nevertheless, the Cuba government's official *Dictionary of Cuban literature* which excluded dissident wriers in its first volume appears to have relented somewhat in the second volume: rather than making dissident writers "disappear" as before, vol. 2 includes them but "with 'clarifying' notations" (p. 433).

Finally, we should note the extraordinary growth of the Spanish American theatre of the last years. The contributor to this volume notes a record number of 200 plays! (p. 523). This boom reflects not only the freedom of expression re-introduced by elected governments after years of censorship but the fascination of Latin Americans with the modern theatre, especially with its potential for dramatizing and expressing the extraordinary variety of the region's culture and political concerns.

II. OBITUARIES

ROBERTO ETCHEPAREBORDA (1923–1985)

On April 9, 1985, Roberto Etchepareborda died of heart failure in Fairfax, Virginia. A contributing editor to the Argentine history of the national period, Etchepareborda's first contribution to *HLAS 44* appeared in 1982, his last one to *HLAS 46*, in 1984. Under his editorship, the Argentine history section grew in volume and sophistication reflecting not only his exceptional knowledge of the field but his persistent tracking of valuable articles and monographs inaccessible through ordinary channels. Born in Milan, Italy, where his father served as a diplomat, Etchepareborda was schooled in Europe and Argentina where he received a doctorate from the University of Buenos Aires. After graduation, he pursued parallel careers in both history and politics becoming a prominent member of the Argentine Radical Party as well as its principal historian. One of his major contributions was the compilation and editorship of the multivolume *Hipólito Yrigoyen: pueblo y gobierno* (1956). He held public office as federal legislator, President of the Buenos Aires City Council, Governor of the Province of Buenos Aires, Director of the Argentine National Archives, Minister of Foreign Relations, and Argentine Ambassador to India.

Government service notwithstanding, Etchepareborda's first vocation was history. Among the numerous books he published, we should single out *Zeballos y la política exterior argentina del 90* (1968), *Historia de las relaciones internacionales argentinas* (1978), and *Tres revoluciones: 1890, 1893, 1905* (1968), for which he received the 1970 Argentine National Book Award. His third vocation, after history and government service, was teaching. He is fondly remembered by the faculty and students of various institutions where he taught: Universidad del Sur, Bahía

Blanca, Argentina; University of North Carolina, Chapel Hill; The American University and The Johns Hopkins School for Advanced International Studies, Washington D.C.

He was a close friend and advisor of the Hispanic Division of the Library of Congress. He played an important part in obtaining the funding of the third edition of the *National Directory of Latin Americanists,* compiled and edited at the Library of Congress under the direction of the Chief of the Hispanic Division, the late William E. Carter. Etchepareborda was also instrumental in obtaining the grant money to microfilm the Gabriela Mistral Papers, a project jointly sponsored by the Organization of American States and the National Library of Chile, and carried out by the Library of Congress.

Etchepareborda's last accomplishment was the compilation of the most comprehensive bibliographic study of the Falkland/Malvinas controversy, a work that is yet to be published. Those of us who had the privilege to work with him will miss his devotion to the field and the enthusiasm he brought to the performance of his tasks.

DONALD ROBERTSON (1919–1984)

On October 18, 1984, Donald Robertson died after a brief illness in New Orleans, Louisiana. A contributor to the Spanish American colonial art section of the *Handbook* for more than 15 years, Robertson submitted his first contribution to *HLAS 24* in 1962, his last to *HLAS 38* in 1976. During his tenure, the *Handbook's* section developed into a major guide to a rapidly expanding field, the variety and sophistication of which was reflected in Robertson's erudite annotations. During the period he served as our contributor, Robertson evolved into a leading scholar in precolumbian and Spanish American colonial art. The recipient of the first History of Art Ph.D. in Mesoamerican Studies ever awarded in the US (Yale, 1956), Robertson went on to author several outstanding works in the field: *Mexican manuscript painting of the early colonial period: the metropolitan schools* (1959), a fundamental contribution to the study of Mexican Indian codices, and *Precolumbian architecture* (1963), another seminal contribution that has been translated into several languages and published in various countries. He was also a contributor to the monumental study *Handbook of Middle American Indians,* edited by Howard F. Cline at the Hispanic Division of the Library of Congress; to the *Propylaen Kunstgeschichte's* precolumbian volume; and to *Ancient Oaxaca* and *The cloud people,* significant works on the Indians of South Central Mexico. At the time of his death, Robertson was in the process of editing *The Codex Tulane,* an early colonial painted manuscript that portrays the history of the Mixtec Indians. A professor of art history at Newcomb College, Tulane University in New Orleans, Robertson was the recipient of numerous awards as well as of the deserved scholarly recognition of his peers and the gratitude and affection of his students.

III. CHANGES IN VOLUME 48

Art

Flora S. Clancy, University of New Mexico, Albuquerque, was responsible for preparing the section on Precolumbian Art, Folk Art, and Popular Art. As of this *Handbook,* the section on the colonial art of Spanish America has been subdivided into: 1) General, Middle America and the Caribbean still prepared by Robert J. Mullen, University of Texas, San Antonio; and 2) South America, a new section that will be compiled by John F. Scott, University of Florida, Gainesville.

Film

In *HLAS 42* (p. xvii) we explained the reasons for alternating Folklore and Film in the Humanities volume of the *Handbook*. As noted therein, this volume carries the Film section; the next humanities volume, *HLAS 50*, will carry the next Folklore section.

History

As stated above, the major change in history is the extraordinary increase in the quantity and quality of works on the Caribbean, a change that explains why there are now four rather than two contributing editors who canvass materials on the region: Rebecca J. Scott, University of Michigan, and Blanca G. Silvestrini, University of Puerto Rico, who cover the Hispanic Caribbean are assisted by Colin A. Palmer, University of North Carolina, Chapel Hill, who is responsible for materials on the British Commonwealth Caribbean, and Anne Pérotin-Dumon, Kent State University, who will cover works on the former French, Dutch, and Danish islands.

The increase in the number of history works published on Colombia, Venezuela, and Ecuador led to the division of this section as well. As of this *Handbook*, Winthrop R. Wright, University of Maryland, College Park, will annotate only materials on Venezuela. The literature on Colombia and Ecuador will be covered by Jane M. Rausch, University of Massachusetts, Amherst.

Joseph T. Criscenti, Boston College, prepared the section on Argentine history of the 19th and 20th centuries.

Literature

Sara Castro-Klarén, The Johns Hopkins University, canvassed materials for the General section. René Prieto, Southern Methodist University, prepared the section on Central American prose fiction. María Luisa Bastos, City University of New York, annotated novels and short stories for the three River Plate countries. Suzanne Jill Levine, University of Washington, compiled the section on Translations into English from the Spanish and Portuguese.

Table of Contents

As of *HLAS 47*, the table of contents of the *Handbook* was expanded to feature not merely the major disciplinary and regional breakdowns as had been customary (e.g., I. HISTORY, A. SPANISH SOUTH AMERICA, 1. INDEPENDENCE) but *all* subsection headings within such major breakdowns wherever they appear (e.g., 1. INDEPENDENCE, a. General, b. Bolivariana, c. Gran Colombia, d. Peru, e. Alto Peru, f. Chile, and g. Río de la Plata). The reasons for the expansion of the *Handbook*'s table of contents are directly related to the reduction of its subject index and are set forth in *HLAS 47* (p. xxi) as well as in the next paragraph.

Subject Index

As stated in previous volumes, the policy of the *Handbook*'s subject index is to use the Library of Congress Subject Headings as much as possible but when necessary to adapt them to terms that predominate in the literature as familiar and useful ones to Latin Americanists. In this volume, the geographic index terms have been restored and include city, state, and regional geographic names. Cross references (i.e., "see also" terms) are again eliminated from the *Handbook* but subject terms have remained the same to insure consistency with previous volumes and to facilitate research. For related subject terms, readers should consult the *Library of Congress Subject Headings* and the subject indexes of previous volumes of the *Handbook*. Subject headings which appear in our expanded table of contents will no longer appear in the subject index. The expanded table of contents which now reflects *all* subsection headings and/or breakdowns wherever they appear in a *Handbook* volume should make for easier access and facilitate research.

Finally, we would like to acknowledge the invaluable assistance of Fehl Cannon, a Librarian and Cataloging Editor at the Library of Congress, for his assistance in the compilation of the subject index of this volume.

Other Changes

Changes in the editorial staff of the *Handbook*, the administrative officers of the Library of Congress, and membership in the Advisory Board are reflected in the title pages of the present volume.

Dolores Moyano Martin

BIBLIOGRAPHY AND GENERAL WORKS

JOHN R. HEBERT, *Acting Chief, Hispanic Division, The Library of Congress*

GENERAL BIBLIOGRAPHIES

1 *Bibliografía Latinoamericana.*
UNAM, Centro de Información Científica y Humanística. No. 1, 1983 [and] No. 2, Pts. 1/2, 1984–. México.
Multi-indexed listing of publications on Latin America from two separate sources of information. Pt. 1 of the semestral publication provides access to publications by Latin Americans in foreign journals, and pt. 2 provides access to periodical articles on Latin America by non-Latin Americans. Includes separate subject, author, institutional, and key-word indexes.

2 **Bibliography of Latin American and Caribbean Bibliographies: annual report, 1983–1984.** Compiled and edited by Lionel V. Loroña. Madison: SALALM Secretariat, Memorial Library, Univ. of Wisconsin, 1984. 34 p.: indexes. (Bibliography and reference series; 11)
Report calls attention to recent bibliographies on Latin American topics. The intent was to include all bibliographies published either as monographs or as articles during 1982–83, however, due to publishing or reporting delays, items published two to three years earlier are included. More than 350 items are recorded. Entries are arranged alphabetically under broad subject areas; provides author and subject indexes.

3 **Ingram, Kenneth E.** Jamaica. Santa Barbara, Calif.: Clio Press, 1984.
369 p., 1 leaf of plates: ill., indexes, map (World bibliographical series; 45)
Author utilizes primarily contemporary books and journal articles to offer a bibliographic overview of Jamaica. Over 1,180 annotated entries are arranged alphabetically by author within broad subject chapters treating the history, geography, economy, politics, culture, customs, religion, and social organization of the country. Includes author, title, and subject indexes.

4 **Jordan, Alma** and **Barbara Comissiong.**
The English-speaking Caribbean: a bibliography of bibliographies. Boston: G.K. Hall, 1984. 411 p.: indexes (Reference publications in Latin American studies)
Over 1,400 items appear in this useful annotated bibliography, covering bibliographies produced to April 1981 about the lands and peoples of the former British Caribbean territories, both island and mainland. Individually numbered entries are arranged alphabetically by author, under broad subjects, with form and country subdivisions. Under each subject a section with works covering the area in general precedes sections on the countries. Gives library location of items reviewed and includes name and subject indexes.

5 **United Nations. Economic Comission for Latin America (ECLA).** Sistema de información bibliográfica: uso de hojas de trabajo (HDB y HAC) y tarjeta de registro bibliográfico (TRB). Santiago: UN, 1984. 169 p.: bibl., forms (Manual de procedimiento; 1)
Provides instruction to those creating bibliographic entries on the computer. Includes information on the technical aspects of the Bibliographic Information System of CEPAL, basic concepts utilized, and tagging information for computer generated bibliographies.

NATIONAL BIBLIOGRAPHIES

6 *Anuario Bibliográfico Hondureño.*
Biblioteca Nacional de Honduras, Dirección General de Cultura, Ministerio de Cultura y Turismo. 1981/1983–. Tegucigalpa.

Provides a listing by year of the monographic output in Honduras in 1981, 1982, and 1983. Lists a total of 72 publications in 1981, 39 in 1982, and 60 in 1983.

7   *Anuario Bibliográfico Uruguayo.* Biblioteca Nacional. 1985–. Montevideo.

Lists in alphabetical order 751 monographic and 726 periodical titles published in 1985 in Uruguay. Monographs are arranged into disciplines; the most popular fields for study are the social sciences, language and literature, and history. Separate listings for books by foreign authors published in Uruguay, periodicals published in the country but edited by foreign institutions, and periodical publications by international organizations in Uruguay appear. Includes an alphabetical index of authors, entities, and editors.

8   *Anuario Bibliográfico Uruguayo.* Suplemento. Biblioteca Nacional. 1984–. Montevideo.

Listing of an additional 119 monographs, 77 journals, and other periodicals and foreign authors' books and periodicals that appeared in 1984 and came to the attention of the National Library after the 1984 annual was published. Provides separate periodical and author indexes.

9   Kallsen, Margarita. Paraguay: cinco años de bibliografía, 1980–1984. Asunción: Cromos, 1986. 145 p.: indexes (Serie Bibliografía paraguaya, 0257–7070; 4)

Lists over 1400 titles for the years indicated and includes an additional 174 titles for 1985. Materials are arranged in alphabetical order by author, with separate subject and author indexes. Also lists official publications, individual journal numbers, and publications about Paraguay published outside of the country.

SUBJECT BIBLIOGRAPHIES

Bibliografía del teatro hispanoamericano contemporáneo, 1900–1980. See item **6060.**

10   Blanes Jiménez, José and **Gonzalo Flores.** Bibliografía referida al trópico cochabambino. La Paz: Ediciones CERES, 1982. 163 p.: indexes (Serie Estudios regionales; 4. Serie Documentos CERES)

Lists 687 citations of works related to the Cochabamba dept. Arranged in alphabetical order by author with subject and geographic indexes. The bibliography reflects the growing area of new colonization in Bolivia, the tropical region of Cochabamba, especially Chapare. Useful compilation of records on a developing area.

Buve, Raymondh Th.B. Bibliografía básica para la historia de las Antillas Holandesas y Suriname. See item **2325.**

11   Celma, Cécile. Guide des sources disponibles sur la Révolution de St. Domingue en Guadeloupe, Guyane, Haïti, Martinique: 1787–1794. Fort de France: Assn. des archivistes bibliothécaires [et] documentalistes francophones de la Caraïbe, 1985. 60 p., 2 p. of plates: indexes, maps.

Provides bibliographic information on printed materials relating to the Haitian revolution as reported in the French Antilles. Includes publications on the impact of the Revolution in Martinique, Guadeloupe, Haiti, and Guyane. Institutional locations of the publications in the French Antilles are given. Lists 346 publications in alphabetical order by author. Also includes a chronological index by author.

12   Centro de Documentación INIES. Nicaragua revolucionaria: bibliografía, 1979–1984. Managua: INIES: Coordinadora Regional de Investigaciones Económicos y Sociales, 1984. 140 p. (Cuadernos de pensamiento propio. Serie Bibliografía; 1)

Select list of publications on Nicaragua following the 1979 overthrow of Somoza. Items are arranged by subject with large sections related to agriculture, regional development, economy, communications, military, politics, natural resources, religion, Sandinismo, society, and general topics. Includes author and acronym indexes. Provides list of official and non-official Nicaraguan publications and author and acronym indexes.

13   Centro de Información y Documentación (CIDOC). Bibliografía sobre los indígenas guayamíes de Panamá (LNB/L, 324/325, marzo/abril 1983, p. 79–122, appendices, bibl.)

Lists articles and monographs on the subject of the Panamanian guayamíes in alphabetical order by author. Writings on the neighboring bokotá, teribe, and bribrí groups also appear. Subject entries are given for each item.

14 Fuentes para la historia de la Ciudad de México, 1810–1979. v. 1, Siglo XIX. v. 2, Siglo XX. Coordinación de Alejandra Moreno Toscano y Sonia Lombardo de Ruiz. México: INAH, 1984. 2 v.: bibl., indexes

Fine contribution provides references to various materials on the study of the development of the city of Mexico since 1810. Separate chapters are devoted to a listing of 19th-century plans of the city, descriptions, traveler accounts, periodicals published between 1805 and 1910, census accounts, and 20th-century publications describing the city in this century. Provides a greatly augmented revision of the work prepared by the Seminario de Historia Urbana of INAH's Depto. de Investigaciones Históricas in 1972. Over 1,500 additional publications were added to the bibliography on the development of the city, with access to over 2,050 citations. Includes a subject index.

15 Guzmán Navarro, Arturo. Fuentes documentales para el estudio del siglo XIX panameño (LNB/L, 336/337, marzo/ abril 1984, p. 90–98)

Bibliographical essay which describes the contents of various archival materials in Colombia, England, US, and Spain related to the 19th-century history of Panama.

16 Lipton Stein, Mateo. Guía bibliográfica nacional sobre tecnologías apropiadas. Cochabamba, Bolivia: Centro de Información y Documentación para el Desarrollo Regional: Editorial Arol, 1984. 320 p.: table.

Provides information on holdings of materials on appropriated technology located in Bolivian institutions. Each citation is presented in several arrangements, including by subject, title, and author. Gives names of the centers involved in the study, a glossary of acronyms, and a table of the subjects.

Luzuriaga, Gerardo. Bibliografía del teatro ecuatoriano, 1900–1982. See item **6091.**

17 Mauro, Frédéric. Recent works on the political economy of Brazil in the Portuguese empire (LARR, 19:1, 1984, p. 87–105)

Bibliographical essay focuses on Brazil as a Portuguese possession between 1500 and 1800 as described in publications since 1970.

Author provides a useful introduction to the literature on various fields of colonial history and suggests that a reader could utilize only the contemporary publications on the subject and still attain a "very complete knowledge of the subject."

18 Merlino, Rodolfo and **Alicia C. Quereilhac.** Acerca de los estudios andinos en la Argentina (CBC/RA, 2:1, julio 1984, p. 265–282, bibl.)

Describes 25 publications appearing between 1967 and 1981 on aspects of the Argentine Andean region.

19 Newton, Velma. Civil rights with special reference to the Commonwealth Caribbean: a select bibliography. Cave Hill, Barbados: Institute of Social and Economic Research (Eastern Caribbean), Univ. of the West Indies, 1981. 110 leaves: index (Occasional bibliography series; 7)

Lists bibliographic materials on human and civil rights held by the Libraries of the Univ. of the West Indies at Cave Hill, Barbados. Includes references to the fundamental rights provisions of Commonwealth Caribbean constitutions, a select list of other statutory provisions, judgments of Commonwealth Caribbean superior courts, reports of groups such as the Minority Rights Groups, textbooks, newspaper items, and a selection of periodical literature. Contains 890 items with separate author and country indexes.

20 Orduña Rebollo, Enrique. Bibliografía iberoamericana de administración local. Caracas: Asociación Venezolana de Cooperación Intermunicipal; Madrid: Instituto de Estudios de Administración Local, 1983. 813 p.: indexes.

Listing of over 10,100 publications, monographs and articles, on variant themes related to local administration, enhanced by the presence of separate author, geographic, and subject indexes. Over 160 journal titles were reviewed for the compilation of this publication. Some of the themes treated include the history of local administration, theory of local administration, legal texts and municipal laws, planning, services, urbanism, local taxes, and the relation between the local administration and the State or other governmental entities.

21 Pôrto, Angela; Lilian de A. Fritsch; and Sylvia F. Padilha. Processo de modernização do Brasil, 1850–1930: economia e sociedade; uma bibliografia. Rio de Janeiro: Fundação Casa de Rui Barbosa: Biblioteca CREFISUL, 1985. 364 p.: indexes.

Over 2,000 annotated entries, organized topically and indexed by subject, author, and title. Extremely useful for specialists. [R. Barman]

22   United Nations. Economic Commission for Latin America (ECLA). Office for the Caribbean. Transport bibliography. Sponsored by UNESCO, Division of the General Information Programme. Port of Spain?: The Office, 1982? 53 p.: indexes.

One of three bibliographies by the UN/ECLA subregional office for the Caribbean in response to a set of priorities identified by the member governments of the Caribbean Development and Cooperation Committee as being crucial to economic development. Prepared from information provided by the participating centers of the Caribbean Information System for Socio-Economic Planning. Documents produced since 1970 appear with abstracts in many cases. Subject, title, author, and geographic location indexes included.

23   Welch, Thomas L. Bibliografía de la literatura uruguaya. Prólogo de Val T. McComie. Washington: Biblioteca Colón, OEA, 1985. 502 p., 1 plate: indexes (Serie de documentación e información; 10)

Lists 9,329 titles of literary works including criticism, interpretation, history of literature, poetry, essays, novels, short stories, and theater. Publication is divided into three parts: individual works in alphabetical order by author, names, and title indexes.

COLLECTIVE AND PERSONAL BIBLIOGRAPHIES

Becco, Horacio Jorge. Simón Bolívar, el libertador, 1783–1830. See item **2846.**

Brazil. Biblioteca Nacional. Seção de Promoções Culturais. Lima Barreto, 1881–1922: catálogo da exposição comemorativa do centenário de nascimento. See item **6350.**

Reeve, Richard. Selected bibliography: 1949–1982. See item **5243.**

24   Restrepo Manrique, Daniel. Bibliografía del historiador don José Manuel Restrepo (ACH/BHA, 70:740, enero/marzo 1983, p. 255–270, bibl.)

Annotated bibliography of the publications of this early 19th-century Colombian historian, government official, and patriot. Publications are presented in several sections devoted to historical works, geographical descriptions, governmental reports, political and agricultural publications, and translations.

25   Rojas, Nicholas W. Bibliografía crítica selecta de Mario Monteforte Toledo (RIB, 36:1, 1986, p. 29–38)

Describes 24 critical studies on the literary work of the Guatemalan author, Mario Monteforte Toledo.

LIBRARY SCIENCE AND SERVICES

26   Agudo Guevara, Alvaro. A study of public library users in some countries of Latin America and the Caribbean. Paris: General Information Programme [and] UNISIST, UNESCO, 1984. 59 p.: tables (PGI-84/WS/23)

Contains an analysis of data obtained by survey and the conclusions drawn. Survey and its limited results should be useful for a better understanding of the situation of services and for guidance in planning the growth of public library services in the region. Survey was taken in 1982 in anticipation of a regional meeting on the present situation and strategies for development of public library services in Latin America and the Caribbean held in Caracas in Oct. 1982, organized by UNESCO, the Autonomous National Library and Library Services Institute in Venezuela, the Regional Centre for Book Development in Latin America and the Caribbean (CERLAL), and the International Federation of Library Associations and Institutions (IFLA).

27   Conference of the Association of Caribbean University and Research Libraries, *13th, Caracas, 1982.* Información y desarrollo en el Caribe: documentos oficiales. Caracas: ACURIL, 1983. 224 p.: bibl., ill.

Contains the papers of the 13th ACURIL conference. Specific papers deal with themes of resource development, national systems of information, communications network development between Latin

America and Caribbean universities, Caribbean information system for economic and social development planning, CERLAL, and OAS programs.

28   Conference of the Association of Caribbean University and Research Libraries, *17th, St. Croix, 1986.* Continuing education for librarians in the Caribbean. Fort-de-France: Univ. des Antilles-Guyane; Montréal, Canada: Univ. de Montréal, 1987. 194 p.

Includes the papers presented at the 17th ACURIL meeting in St. Croix, Virgin Islands, May 4–10, 1986, on such themes as continuing education in library schools in the Caribbean, role of institutions in continuing education, role of associations in continuing education for librarians, and future prospects for continuing education for librarians in the Caribbean.

29   Gleaves, Edwin S. and **Rocío Herrera.** La investigación en las escuelas de bibliotecología y ciencias de la información en América Latina y Norteamerica: perspectivas históricas, modelos de cooperación y bibliografía (Revista Interamericana de Bibliotecología [Univ. de Antioquia, Escuela Interamericana de Bibliotecología, Medellín, Colombia] 6 : 1/2, 1983, p. 19–69, bibl.)

This article, presented in several parts by each author, reviews the current status of library science and information science schools in Latin America and the US, detailing their characteristics, cooperative programs, and courses offered for the educator and the student. Includes an annotated bibliography of didactic materials.

30   Index to the SALALM papers, 1956–1980. Edited by Barbara G. Valk. Los Angeles, Calif.: SALALM, 1984. 51 p. (Bibliography and reference series; 12)

Provides access to nearly 500 printed working papers and annual reports that appeared in the first 25 years of SALALM (1956–80). Lists separate subject and author sections in the index.

31   Mathes, W. Michael. Santa Cruz de Tlatelolco: la primera biblioteca académica de las Américas. México: Secretaría de Relaciones Exteriores, 1982. 101 p.: bibl., ill., index (Archivo histórico diplomático mexicano. Cuarta epoca; 12)

Brief history of the library of the impe-

rial college of Santa Cruz de Tlatelolco (1536–71), the center of ethnographic and linguistic study at the college (1572–1605), the catalog of that library (1535–1600), and the imprint and printers of books in the library's collections. Provides separate listing of titles in the library of Fray Juan de Zumárrage (Bishop of Mexico).

32   Villa, Oscar Jorge and **Alicia Fernández.** Libros, lecturas y bibliotecas durante la colonia y la revolución artiguista (UBN/R, 23, dic. 1983, p. 7–39)

Authors provide a rambling account of the development of libraries and book printing in Latin America with particular references to the La Plata region.

ACQUISITIONS, COLLECTIONS, AND CATALOGS

33   Academia Nacional de la Historia, Venezuela. Departamento de Publicaciones. Catálogo: Departamento de Publicaciones: 3 agosto 1958–3 agosto 1983. Caracas: La Academia, 1983. 519 p.: ill., indexes.

Describes each catalog of the Venezuelan historical academy's publication office with separate references to publications on the 150th anniversary of independence by Manuel Pérez Vila, Venezuelan colonial history by Santiago Gerardo Suárez, and national history, monographic studies, minor books, bibliographies, and archives described by R.J. Lovera de Sola. Includes author and title indexes.

34   Archives de la Martinique. Bibliographie relative aux Antilles: ouvrages appartenant aux cotes C et D, selon l'ancien cadre de classement des Archives départementales. Fort-de-France: Archives départementales de la Martinique, 1978 [i.e. 1982]. 1 v.: facsim.

Provides useful bibliographic information on sources for the study of the French Antilles.

35   Banco Central del Ecuador. Archivo Histórico. Fondo Jijón y Caamaño. v. 1. Preparación de Milton Luna Tamayo y Patricio Ordóñez Chiriboga. Quito: Centro de Investigación y Cultura, El Banco, 1983–1984. 1 v.: bibl., ill., indexes, port. (Catálogos del Archivo Histórico; 2)

Vol. 1 describes the miscellaneous documents segment of the large Jijón y Caamaño collection in the possession of the Banco Central del Ecuador. The documents' section contains nearly 13,000 pieces grouped in 72 vols. and 980 folders covering the period 1543–1914. Items in the collection concern the Revolution of the Alcabalas y Estancos, the Tupac Amaru uprising, the revolutionary process of Aug. 10, the war for independence, the formation and demise of Gran Colombia, and various events in the Republic's national period. Vol. 2 was not available at press time.

36   Banco Central del Ecuador. Archivo Histórico. Fondo Neptalí Bonifaz. Preparación de Lucía Suárez Pasquel. Quito: Centro de Investigación y Cultura, El Banco, 1983–1984. 2 v.: bibl., ill., indexes (Catálogos del Archivo Histórico; 1, 4)

Two-volume work serves as an introductory description to the valuable 20th-century personal collection of one of the founders of the Banco Central del Ecuador and prominent Ecuadorean political figure and developer, Neptalí Bonifaz. His collection is described in five distinct series. Vol. 1 contains references to family documents, personal papers, and documents of the Banco Central. Vol. 2 contains political documents and papers related to the family hacienda, Guachalá. Each volume has separate general and illustration indexes.

37   Brazil. Superintendência do Desenvolvimento do Nordeste. Ministerio do Interior. Catálogo de publicações da SUDENE, 1970–80. Recife: SUDENE, 1983. 132 p.: indexes.

Lists publications by subject; includes a separate author index. Contains 1,251 publications covering mainly socioeconomic topics.

38   Cardona, Luis Antonio. A selected directory of audio-visual materials on Puerto Rico and the Puerto Ricans. Foreword by Antonia Pantoja. Bethesda, Md.: Carreta Press, 1984. 56 p.

Lists in alphabetical order by title 120 motion pictures and 55 filmstrips on Puerto Rico and the Puerto Ricans on the island and in the US. Primary sources for the text was the Library of Congress, the National Archives, the Community Education Division of Puerto Rico's Dept. of Education, the Cen-

tro de Estudios Puertorriqueños of CUNY. Work is part of a larger publication by the author, *A manifest of Puerto Rican materials: an annotated bibliography II* (Bethesda, Md.: Carreta, 1985).

39   Feldman, Lawrence H. El Archivo Eclesiástico de Guatemala (CIRMA/M, 6:9, junio 1985, p. 170–177)

Provides a description of the primarily colonial period documents found in the ecclesiastical archives in Guatemala City. Information brings up to date the description of the archives since the appearance of Lino Gómez Canedo's *Los archivos de la historia de América* (Mexico: Editorial Cultural, 1961).

40   France. Archives nationales. Guide des sources de l'histoire de l'Amérique latine et des Antilles dans les archives françaises. Paris: Les Archives, 1984. 711 p., 8 p. of plates: appendices, bibl., col. ill.

An impressive and valuable guide to the archives of France related to Latin America and the Caribbean. Brief descriptions of the contents of the Archives nationales, the departmental and communal archives, and various missionary and private archives are provided. Also lists holdings of the printed materials archives which contain 18th to 20th century official publications. Provides list of governmental officials from 17th to the present century, who were involved in Latin American affairs, including the names of representatives of France in each Latin American nation. Necessary addition to any reference collection. For historian's comment, see item **2339**.

41   Guzmán Navarro, Arturo. Presencia de Panamá de documentos de la Sección II del Archivo General de Indias, en Sevilla (LNB/L, 342/343, sept./oct. 1984, p. 56–71)

Provides a selective sampling of the contents of the 61 *legajos* of the Second Section (Contaduría General) in the Archivo General de Indias that is retained in the Univ. of Panama. Materials relate to the colonial history and fiscal matters of Panama.

42   Ingram, Kenneth E. Sources for West Indian studies: a supplementary listing, with particular reference to manuscript sources. Zug, Switzerland: Inter Documentation Co., 1983. 412 p.: index.

Provides brief descriptions of manuscript sources for the study of the West Indies found in public and private collections in England, Wales, Scotland, Northern Ireland, Ireland, Holland, Denmark, Barbados, Jamaica, St. Kitts, Trinidad, and Australia. Includes extensive general index.

43 Instituto de Desenvolvimento de Pernambuco. Catálogo de publicações do CONDEPE, 1952–1982. Recife: Governo do Estado de Pernambuco, Secretaria de Planejamento, El Instituto, CONDEPE, 1982. 56 leaves.
Lists 482 publications by the Pernambucan development institute. Items are listed in alphabetical order by author.

Inventaris van de colectie prenten tekeningen, kaarten en foto's van de Evangelische Broedergemeente te Zeist, ca. 1700–1982. See item 2351.

Inventaris van het archief van het Zendingsgenootschap der Evangelische Broedergemeente te Zeits: Zeister Zendingsgenootschap, 1792–1962. See item 2352.

44 Moss, Alan. Acquisitions guide to Barbados. St. Michael, Barbados: Univ. of the West Indies, 1986. 52 p.
Author provides information on bookstores and other sources for the purchase of Barbadian publications as well as the private and public sector publishers on the island. Listing of periodical titles and their publishers completes the information provided. Useful first hand information on the book trade in Barbados by one of the island's most well known bibliographer and acquisitions specialist.

Relatórios dos Presidentes da Província de São Paulo, 1836–1889: coleção microfilmada pelo Plano Nacional de Microfilmagem de Periódicos Brasileiros: pesquisa, descrição catalográfica, catálogo coletivo e notas informativas. See item 3508.

45 Yale University. Library. Guide to Latin American pamphlets from the Yale University Library: selections from 1600–1900. v. 1, Mexico: subject guide, A–Im. v. 2, Mexico: subject guide, In–Z. v. 3, Mexico: author/title guide. v. 4, Mexico: chronological guide. v. 5, Peru: subject guide. v. 6, Peru: author/title & chronological guide. v. 7, Miscellaneous guide. Edited by Lofton Wilson. Compiled by Lisa Browar, Anna Fernicola, and Miryam A. Ospina. New York: Clearwater Publishing Co., 1985. 7 v.

Lists over 9,600 pamphlets in the collections of Yale Univ. Library pertaining primarily to Mexico and Peru. Entries appear under subject headings, alphabetically by author and title, and chronologically. Guide was prepared to complement the Clearwater Publishing Co.'s microfiche edition of *Latin American pamphlets from the Yale University Library.*

REFERENCE WORKS AND RESEARCH

46 Bloch, Thomas. Regional sources of economic and social information on Central America (LARR, 20:2, 1985, p. 142–147)
Survey identifies the major periodical publications in Central America that contain data and information on the economic and social conditions of the countries of the region. Publications are divided into categories of statistics, newsletters, economic and political reports, journals, and bibliographies.

47 Cavazos Garza, Israel. Diccionario biográfico de Nuevo León. Monterrey, México: Univ. Autónoma de Nuevo León, 1984. 2 v. (540 p.): bibl., ill.
Listing of notables from throughout the history of Nuevo León, Mexico. Selection criteria are not provided. Biographies appear in alphabetical order.

48 Consumer markets in Central America. London: Euromonitor, 1984. 220 p., 1 leaf of plates: ill.
Statistical information for each country includes a summary of social and economic information on such aspects as population, geography, labor, the economy, resources, industrial output, major companies, wages and prices, standard of living, consumer expenditure, media and advertising, tourism, and mass media. Provides country by country survey of major consumer markets. Includes information on Mexico and Panama.

49 Consumer markets in Latin America. London: Euromonitor, 1984. 407 p., 1 leaf of plates: map.
For each country surveyed provides a summary of social and economic information with statistics and commentary on such aspects as population, geography, labor, the

economy, resources, industrial output, major companies, wages and prices, standard of living, consumer expenditure, media and advertising, tourism, and mass media. Also includes major consumer markets, giving imports and sales in foodstuffs, alcohol, tobacco, cosmetics, pharmeceuticals, textile goods, furnishings, electrical goods, and automobiles. Useful reference tool relying on printed statistical information, in the most part, for the statistics given. Information given is for South America, not Latin America. A complementary volume on Central America includes Mexico (see item 48).

50 Contents of Periodicals on Latin America. Institute of Interamerican Studies, Univ. of Miami. Vol. 3, No. 1, Winter 1986–. Coral Gables, Fla.

This issue reproduces the tables of contents of nearly 60 journals containing articles related to Latin America. With the exception of one title, the journals given publish materials in the social sciences.

Costa, Eunice R. Ribeiro. Indice de arquitetura brasileira, 1971–1980. See item **486.**

Daniel, Neptune. Dissertations de littérature haïtienne. See item **6481.**

Diccionario de la literatura cubana. See item **5434a.**

51 Dicionário histórico-biográfico brasileiro, 1930–1983. Coordenação de Israel Beloch e Alzira Alves de Abreu. Rio de Janeiro: Editora Forense Universitária: FGV, Centro de Pesquisa e Documentação de Historia Contemporânea do Brasil: FINEP, 1984. 4 v.

Major work published by the Center for Research and Documentation of Contemporary Brazilian History of the Getúlio Vargas Foundation to commemorate the first centenary of Vargas's birth in 1883. Contains 4,493 entries of which 3,741 are biographic. Over 750 thematic articles deal with institutions, events, concepts, and legal matters important during the Vargas era and afterwards. Focus of the work is political, with emphasis on individuals who exerted influence or held office at the national level. For historian's comment, see item **3453.**

52 The Directory of Caribbean personalities in Britain and North America. Edited by Roy Dickson. Kingston: Gleaner Co., 1985. 333 p., 1 leaf of plates: map, ports.

Contains biographical descriptions of Caribbean personalities, not only those born in the Caribbean but also descendants from the English speaking Caribbean. Identifies individuals in the US, Canada, and Britain, in individual geographical sections. Gives brief sketch of the various English speaking entities of the Caribbean area.

53 Directory of information units in Jamaica: libraries, archives and documentation services. Kingston: National Council on Libraries, Archives and Documentation Services, 1986. 200 p.: index.

Provides information on the contents and services of the national library, public libraries, educational institution libraries (university, post-secondary, high school, and specialized schools), special libraries, and the Jamaica Archives and Records Dept. A total of 171 libraries are described in this impressive survey.

54 Elkin, Judith Laikin. Latin America's Jews: a review of sources (LARR, 20:2, 1985, p. 124–141)

Provides access to a selected number of monographs, articles, and dissertations that describe the Jewish experience in Latin America. Separate sections describe materials on the Jews in Argentina, Brazil, Chile, Costa Rica, Cuba, the Dominican Republic, Mexico, Netherlands Antilles, and Paraguay.

Fernández, José B. and Roberto G. Fernández. Indice bibliográfico de autores cubanos: diáspora, 1959–1979 = Bibliographical index of Cuban authors: diaspora, 1959–1979. See item **5437.**

Foster, David William. Cuban literature: research guide. See item **5440.**

France. Bibliothèque nationale. Département des cartes et plans. Le fonds cubain de la Société de géographie en dépôt au Département des cartes et plans. See item **2340.**

55 Guatemala: a country study. Edited by Richard N. Nyrop. 2nd ed. Washington: Foreign Area Studies, American Univ., 1984. 261 p.: bibl., ill., index, maps (Area handbook series. DA pam; 550–78)

Substantially revises the 1970 first edition of the area handbook on Guatemala. Although following closely the pattern of previous handbooks, this edition contains five separately authored sections on the historical setting, society, economy, government and politics, and national security. Includes separate tables, a selected bibliography, glossary, and a general index.

56 **Guide to the notarial records of the Archivo General de Notarias, Mexico City, for the year 1829 = Guía de los protocolos notariales del Archivo General de Notarias, México, D.F., año 1829.** Compiled by Robert A. Potash, Jan Bazant, and Josefina Z. Vásquez. Amherst, Mass.: Univ. Computing Center, 1982. 301 leaves.

Bilingual guide to the notarial records for 1829 found in the Archivo General de Notarias, Mexico City. This work, documenting records prior to the Reform and providing access to the records of 40 notaries, is divided into two primary sections: 1) a guide to persons and legal entities; and 2) specialized guides to assets, financial transactions, partnerships and companies, and service contracts.

57 **Guide to the notarial records of the Archivo General de Notarias, Mexico City, for the year 1875: part one = Guía de los protocolos notariales del Archivo General de Notarias, México, D.F., año 1875: primera parte.** Compiled by Robert A. Potash, Jan Bazant, and Josefina Z. Vásquez. Amherst, Mass.: Univ. Computing Center, 1984. 473 leaves.

Ambitious work provides access to notarial records for 1875 as part of a project jointly developed at the Univ. of Massachusetts and El Colegio de México. Similar listing of records for 1829 (see item **56**) and 1847 were prepared in separate publications. Scattered dates selected for coverage reflect the project's efforts to facilitate research for the period prior to the Reform, to examine a period of political and fiscal crises (1847), and to test the impact that the adoption of Mexico's first civil code in 1870 had on the kinds of transactions brought before the notaries. Records of 23 notaries appear indexed in this 1875 guide. Publication is divided into two major sections: 1) a guide to persons and legal entities in the guise of a general index to persons, an index to women, an index to foreigners, and an index to religious, commercial, and public entities; 2) specialized guides to assets, financial transactions, partnerships and companies, and service contracts.

58 **Hartmann, Roswith.** Estudios americanistas de Bonn (CBC/RA, 2:1, julio 1984, p. 299–307, bibl.)

Article describes the 11 contributions in the Bonner Amerikanistische Studien/ Estudios Americanistas de Bonn series created in 1971 and published by the Americanist Section of the Institute of Cultural Anthropology at the Univ. of Bonn.

59 **Hilton, Sylvia L.** El americanismo en España, 1982–1983 (IGFO/RI, 43/172, julio/dic. 1983, p. 847–914, bibl.)

Provides a useful and revealing insight into research activities related to the Americas in Spanish institutions. Includes a listing of 480 publications on the Americas published in Spain in 1982 and 1983.

60 **La Infraestructura de información para el desarrollo: América Latina y el Caribe; informe de diagnóstico regional.** Santiago: UN, CEPAL, Centro Latinoamericano de Documentación Económica y Social, 1981. 286 p.: bibl., ill.

Essentially "communications" research of extensive proportions reported country-by-country. Concerned with "information" as a resource and the mechanisms of its transmission. [J.M. Hunter]

61 **Instituto Nacional de Antropología e Historia, *Mexico*. Departamento de Monumentos Prehispánicos.** Indice del Archivo Técnico de la Dirección de Monumentos Prehispánicos del INAH. Compilación de Roberto García Moll. Presentación de Eduardo Matos Moctezuma. México: INAH, La Dirección, 1982. 304 p.: ill., index (Col. científica; 120. Catálogos y bibliografías)

Presents materials in three sections: 1) identifies items in the 241 books that form the archive; 2) contains references to the 1,748 citations by author; and 3) a subject index to the materials in the archive.

62 **Latin American Newsletters, Ltd.** Science and technology in Latin America. Edited by Christopher Roper and Jorge Silva. London: Longman, 1983. 363 p.: ill. (Longman guide to world science and technology; 2)

Resource for researchers, professionals, and businessmen who seek points of reference and contacts in Latin America. All 26 countries of the region are covered individually. Each chapter outlines the organization of science and technology in the country at the governmental, academic, and private industry level.

63 Mitchell, Brian R. International historical statistics: the Americas and Australasia. Detroit, Mich.: Gale Research Co., 1983. 949 p.: bibl.

Provides a wide range of statistical data for the countries of North and South America and Australasia. Main categories of data relate to climate, population, labor, agriculture, industry, trade, transportation, finances, prices, education, and national accounts. Lists sources of data for each country and provides statistical information for the national period, independence to 1975.

64 National directory of Latin Americanists: biographies of 4,915 specialists. Edited by Inge Maria Harman. Compiled in the Hispanic Division of the Library of Congress. 3rd ed. Washington: The Library, 1985. 1011 p.: bibl., indexes.

This third edition brings together in one volume biographic and bibliographic data on 4,915 individuals with specialized knowledge of Latin America. Listed alphabetically by name, entries include specialists from the social sciences, humanities, and pure sciences. Extensive geographic and subject area indexes make this compendium particularly useful as a catalog of current research, teaching, and work related to Latin America. Available from the Superintendent of Documents, GPO, Washington, D.C. 20402, for $34.00, stock no. 030-013-00009-3.

65 Organisation for Economic Cooperation and Development. Development Centre. Répertoire des projet de recherche en matière de développement en Amérique latine = Register of development research projects in Latin America. Paris: L'Organisation, 1984. 831 p.: indexes.

Prepared by CLACSO through questionnaire, work provides a description of research projects in the fields of economics and social development by institution and country. Title of the project, description, research dates, researchers, source of funding, and publications are given. Includes researchers, institutions, and theme of research indexes and a glossary of equivalent terms in Spanish, English, and French.

66 Organization of American States. General Secretariat. Directory of inter-American and other associations in the Americas. Washington: The Secretariat, 1986. 81 p.

Descriptive listing of cultural and informative associations, professional and semi-professional organizations, and fellowship and Latin American studies programs in the US. Entries are arranged in order by individual states. For each institution or association the complete address and telephone number, objectives, membership number, and periodicity of meetings are provided.

67 Publicaciones oficiales de Chile: 1973–1983. Edición de María Teresa Sanz con la colaboración de Manuel Cornejo A. y Héctor Gómez F. Compilación de Manuel Corneja A. *et al.* Santiago: Instituto Profesional de Santiago, Escuela de Bibliotecología y Documentación, 1985. 196 p.: indexes.

Lists publications by agency of the national government, including individual monographs and serials. Serves as an invaluable source of information on Chilean governmental activities during the Pinochet years. Separate agency and author indexes facilitate use. Publication extends information found in Lee Williams's *The Allende years* (Boston: G.K. Hall, 1977).

Raat, W. Dirk. La revolución global de México. See item **2186.**

Rafide, Matías. Diccionario de autores de la Región del Maule: bio-bibliográfico y crítico. See item **5590.**

68 Research guide to Central America and the Caribbean. Editor-in-chief, Kenneth Grieb. Associate editors, Ralph Lee Woodward, Jr., Graeme S. Mount, and Thomas Mathews. Madison: Univ. of Wisconsin Press, 1985. 1 v.: bibl., index.

Collaborative effort involving scholars from the US, Central America, the Caribbean, Canada, and Europe to identify archival resources regarding Central America and Caribbean regions available to historians, and to indicate future directions for research about the regions. Contains 83 articles that describe major archival depositories of research centers and essays that suggest future directions for research.

Rhoades, Duane. The independent monologue in Latin American theatre: a primary bibliography with selective secondary sources. See item **6110.**

69 **South America, Central America, and the Caribbean.** Europa Publications. 1986 [i.e. 1985]–. London.

Excellent reference book contains essays on political and economic problems of the region, lists of research institutes and periodicals, and individual country surveys and directories. Four major essays cover political and economic aspects of the region, including: economic problems, dictatorship and democracy in Latin America; Central America on the international stage; and sovereignty, dependency, and social change in the Caribbean. Detailed directories appear for each country of Latin America and include names, addresses, and descriptions for branches of government, diplomatic representation, judicial system, religion, the press, publishers, radio and television, finance, trade and industry, transport, tourism, atomic power, defense, and education. A corps of 21 British scholars contributed to the publication. In addition to the individual country surveys, a section is devoted to the regional organizations of Latin America. An important reference publication of broad interest to a wide group of users.

70 **Stopford, John M.** The world directory of multinational enterprises, 1982–83. v. 1–2. 2nd, updated and expanded ed. Detroit, Mich.: Gale Research Co., 1982–1983. 2 v.: indexes.

Deals exclusively with firms that control important foreign investments. This second edition (first edition, 1980) profiles 500 major multinational enterprises that account for over 80 percent of the world's stock of direct foreign investment. Sources of data presented are the annual reports of the companies, reports of such companies to the Securities and Exchange Commission of the US, and general publicity. Individual profiles on each company appear in alphabetical order. The third volume of the work will contain a full index of all principal subsidiary companies and name of the parent company listed alphabetically by country of operation.

71 **Tamayo Rodríguez, Carlos.** Notas para el estudio de las publicaciones periódicas en Santiago de Cuba: 1900–1930 (Santiago [Univ. de Oriente, Santiago de Cuba] 49, 1983, p. 125–159, bibl.)

Very useful listing of journals and newspapers published in Santiago de Cuba between 1900 and 1930. Equally important is the brief history of publishing in Cuba that precedes the annotated listing.

71a **Uruguay. Ministerio de Industria y Energía. Unidad Asesora de Promoción Industrial.** Compendio de informaciones básicas, bibliografía y fuentes de información. Montevideo: El Ministerio, 1981. 146 p.: index.

Intended to aid the preparation of market studies related to industrial and other developmental projects of the Uruguayan economy. Attempts to provide a uniform terminology for various economic functions as well as a listing by function of particular entities.

72 **World armies.** Edited by John Keegan. 2nd ed. Detroit, Mich.: Gale Research Co., 1983. 688 p.: ill.

Provides useful historical and current information on the armies in each country of Latin America and the Caribbean: history, strength, role in society, recent operations, organizations, recruitment, reserves, and equipment and arms industries of/or related to the army. Includes an extensive section on the Brazilian army.

73 **Zubatsky, David S.** An international bibliography of cumulative indices to journals publishing articles on Hispanic languages and literatures: first supplement (AATSP/H, 67: 3, Sept. 1984, p. 383–393, bibl.)

This bibliography is a supplement to an article on the subject that appeared in *Hispania* (58, March 1975). Lists reviews of general cultural interest, bulletins and memoirs of major learned institutions and societies when they include language and/or literature sections, and literary, critical, and philological journals. Pertinent items appear under country listings.

Zuleta, Emilia de. Relaciones literarias entre España y la Argentina. See item **5689.**

GENERAL WORKS

74 **Cubitt, David J.** The Latin American model for area studies programmes (ATSP/VH, 32:2, Autumn 1983, p. 47–51)

Brief overview of Latin American studies development in Great Britain since the 1960s. A gradual acceptance of the interdisciplinary approach became increasingly favorable in the 1970s.

75   El Uruguay de nuestro tiempo: 1958–1983. v. 1, Economía: la hora del balance [de] Alicia Melgar y Walter Cancela. Montevideo: Centro Latinoamericano de Economía Humana: 1983. 1 v.: bibl., graphs, ill., indexes.

This work, outgrowth of a celebration of the 25th anniversary of the Centro Latinoamericano de Economía Humana (CLAEH), contains 10 articles which focus on distinct aspects of the past quarter century of Uruguay's history. Articles address themes of the economy, the international scene, sports and society, the population, political parties, the future of social sciences, letters, agriculture, the arts, and the State. Includes wide range of indexes and graphs.

NEW SERIAL TITLES

76   Anuario de Políticas Exteriores Latinoamericanas. Grupo Editor Latinoamericana. 1984–. Buenos Aires.

This impressive overview of the foreign relations of Latin America contains separately authored articles on the foreign relations of each country of South and Central America and selected entities in the Caribbean. A total of 30 articles appear including works on the regional powers (i.e., Brazil, Mexico, Venezuela); the Caribbean; the Andean nations; Central America; the Cono Sur; and on regional themes such as SELA, US-Latin America, USSR-Latin America, and Europe-Latin America relations. Work is the initial contribution compiled by the Programa de Seguimiento de las Políticas Exteriores Latinoamericanas (PROSPEL) of the Centro de Estudios de la Realidad Contemporánea (CERC), Academia de Humanismo Cristiano, Santiago, Chile. Journal is produced by the Grupo Editor Latinoamericano, Sarmiento 1474, 1042 Buenos Aires, Argentina, and edited by Heraldo Muñoz. Valuable addition to the literature on Latin American foreign relations.

Historia Latinoamericana en Europa. See item **1785.**

Historias. See item **1897a.**

77   Indice Hispanoamericano de Ciencias Sociales. Indizar. Vol. 1, No. 1, enero/feb. 1985–. Bogotá.

Bimonthly publication cites articles on Latin America that appear in 188 journals published in the Americas and Europe. Items are in alphabetical order by author arranged under broad subject categories. Publication is available for an annual subscription rate of $95.00, from Indizar, Carrera 10, No. 19–65, Of. No. 901C, Bogotá, Colombia.

78   Lading Meizhou yanjiu/Latin American Studies/Studios LatinoAmericanos. Latin American Institute, Chinese Academy of Social Sciences. No. 1, Feb. 1986–. Beijing.

Bimonthly journal published by the Latin American Institute of the Chinese Academy of Social Sciences. Formerly published as *Lading Meizhou congkan/ Latin American Review/Revista Americana Latina* which began publication in 1979 and terminated with the consecutive issue No. 33 (No. 6, Dec. 1985). Contains articles on Latin American politics, economics, international relations, scientific and technological development, culture and education, modern history, social ideology, as well as academic activities, book reviews, and library information, including such items as: Seminar of Chinese Assn. of Latin American Historical Studies and the meeting of the Chinese National Assn. of Spanish, Portuguese and Latin American Libraries Studies. Promotes academic exchanges between China and Latin America. Articles include reports on the Chinese in Latin America and Latin American relations with China. Sources used include books and publications by Chinese authors on Latin American history and affairs. [Robert Dunn]

Revista de Historia. See item **2377.**

Revista del Archivo Nacional de Historia, Sección del Azuay. See item **2617.**

79   La Revista del Centro de Estudios Avanzados de Puerto Rico y El Caribe. No. 1, julio/dic. 1985–. San Juan.

Biannual publication includes articles on all phases of Puerto Rican and Caribbean history and culture. In addition to articles on precolumbian inhabitants of the region, includes articles on the history of slavery in Mexico, architecture of San Juan, historical documents, and popular arts and the 19th-century independence movements in the Caribbean. Interspersed throughout the publication are literary contributions such as short stories, poetry, and literary criticism. For further information, write to the editor, Ricardo E. Alegría, Apartado de Correos S-4427, Viejo San Juan, P.R. 00904. For historian's review, see item **2378**.

80 **UNISA Latin American Report.** Univ. of South Africa, Centre for Latin American Studies. Vol. 3, No. 1, March 1987–. Pretoria.

Third issue of biannual journal of the Univ. of South Africa's Latin American program contains a variety of articles on contemporary issues in Latin American affairs. Several articles relate to Africa and Latin America relations such as Brazil and Angola and low-cost housing in Latin America and models for South Africa. Over half of the articles are translations from various Latin American journals. For further information, write to the Executive Editor, *UNISA Latin American Report*, P.O. Box 392, 0001 Pretoria, Republic of South Africa.

JOURNAL ABBREVIATIONS BIBLIOGRAPHY AND GENERAL WORKS

AATSP/H Hispania. American Assn. of Teachers of Spanish and Portuguese, Univ. of Cincinnati. Cincinnati, Ohio.

ACH/BHA Boletín de Historia y Antigüedades. Academia Colombiana de Historia. Bogotá.

ATSP/VH Vida Hispánica. Assn. of the Teachers of Spanish and Portuguese. Wolverhampton, U.K.

CBC/RA Revista Andina. Centro Bartolomé de las Casas. Cusco, Perú.

CIRMA/M Mesoamérica. Centro de Investigaciones Regionales de Mesoamérica. Antigua, Guatemala.

IGFO/RI Revista de Indias. Instituto Gonzalo Fernández de Oviedo [and] Consejo Superior de Investigaciones Científicas. Madrid.

LARR Latin American Research Review. Univ. of North Carolina Press *for the* Latin American Studies Assn. Chapel Hill.

LNB/L Lotería. Lotería Nacional de Beneficencia. Panamá.

RIB Revista Interamericana de Bibliografía/Inter-American Review of Bibliography. Organization of American States. Washington.

UBN/R Revista de la Biblioteca Nacional. Ministerio de Educación y Cultura. Montevideo.

ART

SPANISH AMERICA
Precolumbian Art, Folk Art, and Popular Art

FLORA S. CLANCY, *Associate Professor of Art History, University of New Mexico, Albuquerque*

THIS SEEMS TO BE A PERIOD of revision rather than redefinition as reflected in the publications dealing with the Ancient New World as well as in the studies of popular and folk art. Nonetheless, by "reading between the lines" one perceives that revisionist thinking is laying the basis for just such a reformation and redefinition. This may be most clearly apprehended in the cultural ethnography of the popular and folk arts in the New World.

Often structural, and indeed Marxist, in approach, these ethnographic and social studies range from monographic descriptions for the practice and social context of a particular craft (items **294, 299,** and **301**), catalogs of craft-designs (items **298, 300,** and **305**), rescue attempts to put into writing and image (photographs) craft and folk traditions eroded by the modern world (items **290, 296, 297, 302, 305,** and **308**), and careful efforts to systematize methodology and to define and differentiate the various components of popular and folk craft traditions (items **286, 291,** and **292**). In concert, these published works proclaim the validity of their subject matter as a major aspect of mankind's activity and worthy of careful attention by philosophers and anthropologists (items **291, 292,** and **305**). The effort is clearly towards a redefinition of what is the proper subject matter for the study of mankind. Except for the study of textiles, interestingly enough (items **289, 293, 295, 296, 303,** and **304**), this field of study is almost completely dominated by Latin American scholars. Unfortunately, the rawness of the paper and printing industry in many Latin American countries produces pamphlets and books whose forms belie their content.

Only a few efforts (item **288**) have been made towards interpreting the meanings contained by the works labeled folk or popular arts. One exception, "Text and Textile: Language and Technology in the Arts of the Quiche Maya," by Barbara and Dennis Tedlock (item **304**), is indicative of one kind of reformation or redefinition we might expect to see in the future. Ethnography and linguistics form the bases of their study, but these methods are fused to create a larger and more synthetic point of view from which we grasp the complexity (and pleasure) of the ways meaning can be achieved.

Interdisciplinary efforts are common. They are most evident in the symposia, catalogs, and published works devoted to the ancient cultures of the Americas. Usually scholars of various disciplines are asked to focus their skills on one problematic theme (items **253, 258, 261, 263, 264, 275**) or an archaeological site (item

268, 276, and **277**) to create multiple points of view from which to understand the problem. The point being made here, is that the disciplines are not synthesized or fused, as suggested by the Tedlocks' article, but added to one another.

Perhaps it is due to the social and political upheavals in many parts of Central America, hampering excavations and research especially in the Maya area and forcing archaeologists to work in Belize and in the northern (Mexican) lowlands of the Yucatan peninsula, that there has been a recent emphasis placed on the postclassic period in Mesoamerica (items **257** and **258**). The question of revision versus reformation is eloquently touched upon in *Late Lowland Maya civilization,* edited by Jeremy Sabloff and E. Wyllys Andrews V. (item **257**). Not going so far as reforming our vision of the postclassic Maya, it clearly demonstrates in its collected papers and overview essays that the authors think redefinition is soon to follow. Rekindled interest in the late postclassic can also be seen in the work being inspired by the important excavations (1978–81) of the Templo Mayor of Tenochtitlán (modern day Mexico City) (items **271, 272,** and **273**).

The few attempts that have been made to provide explanatory overviews of a particular subject or area in Ancient America, such as the revised edition of Sylvanus Morley's classic work, *The Ancient Maya* (item **260**), edited and extensively annotated by Robert Sharer, include new information provided by recent ethnographic, archival, or archaeological work, but do not attempt to reformulate traditional points of view in light of this new information (items **254, 258a,** and **282**). In general the effort is to revise our interpretation of data rather than to reform or redefine our use of the data. This is especially true of the many works that deal specifically with iconographic meaning (items **255, 256, 259, 265, 266, 268, 269, 272, 273, 274, 275, 276,** and **277**). Pablo Gamboa Hinestrosa's formal and contextual analyses of the sculpture of San Agustín is a welcome exception (item **278**), because his ultimate concerns for meaning are iconological and therefore arrived at by a more synthetic approach (see as well items **267, 270,** and **274**).

PRECOLUMBIAN
General

Boglár, Lajos and **Tamás Kovács.** Indian art from Mexico to Peru. See *HLAS* 47:252.

Gordon, Michael W. The Third World and the protection of national patrimony: oil, art and orchid. See *HLAS* 47:255.

251 Landa Abrego, María Elena. Simbolismo en el arte. Puebla, México: Univ. Autónoma de Puebla, 1980. 41 p.: ill.
　　Catalog of precolumbian works of art in foreign (non-Mexican) collections.

252 Masterpieces of Pre-columbian art from the collection of Mr. and Mrs. Peter G. Wray: an exhibition at the André Emmerich Gallery, from April 11 to May 12, 1984. New York: The Gallery: Perls Galleries, 1984. 1 v.: bibl., map, col. plates.
　　Illustrated catalog of an exhibition jointly mounted by the André Emmerich and Perls Galleries. Very little information accompanies the beautifully photographed pieces from the collection of Mr. and Mrs. Peter Wray.

253 Las Representaciones de arquitectura en la arqueología de América. v. 1, Mesoamérica. Coordinador, Daniel Schávelzon. México: UNAM, Coordinación de Extensión Universitaria, 1982. 1 v.: bibl., ill.
　　Collection of essays by various authors that treat images of architecture rather than architecture itself. A question posed by the editor is why, when compared to actual architectural forms, those found in imagery have much greater variety. Useful compendium includes new material presented by several authors.

PRECOLUMBIAN
Mesoamerica: General

254 Dickey, Thomas; Vance Muse; and Henry Wiencek. The god-kings of Mexico. Chicago: Stonehenge, 1982. 176 p.: bibl., col. ill., index (Treasures of the world)

Overview of the history of five precolumbian cultures: Olmec, Maya, Teotihuacan, Mixtec, and Aztec. It is for the cultural tourist with an interest in beautiful objects and lurid text that is, nonetheless, based on fact.

255 Fuente, Beatriz de la. Figura humana olmeca de jade (IIE/A, 13:52, 1983, p. 7–19, bibl., ill.)

Stylistic and iconographic analysis of small, masked figure carved in jadeite. Author considers provenience as this piece is now in a private collection. For archaeologist's comment, see *HLAS 47:384.*

256 Labbé, Armand J. Religion, art, and iconography: man and cosmos in prehispanic Mesoamerica. Including a catalog of an exhibition "People of the sun: man and cosmos in pre-Christian Middle America." With special contributing scholarship (in order of essay) by Hasso von Winning, Dieter Dutting, L.R.V. Joesink-Mandeville. Santa Ana, Calif.: Bowers Museum Foundation, 1982. 80 p.: bibls., ill. (some col.).

Catalog with introduction, essays on religious iconography, special essays, and entries. Aztec iconography is presumed to explain all of Mesoamerican imagery. Nonetheless, the essays are written with care and obvious sympathy.

257 Late Lowland Maya civilization: classic to postclassic. Edited by Jeremy A. Sabloff and E. Wyllys Andrews V. Albuquerque: Univ. of New Mexico, 1986. 526 p.: bibl., ill., index (School of American Research Advanced Seminar series. A School of American Research book)

As the edited volume for the School of American Research Advanced Seminar, "After the Fall: New Perspectives on the Postclassic Period in the Maya Lowlands" (1982), this book provides the definitive overview of what is now known from recent research into the post 800 AD era of the entire Maya lowlands, as well as provocative new work that suggests future directions of research rethinking.

258 The Lowland Maya postclassic. Edited by Arlen F. Chase and Prudence M. Rice. Austin: Univ. of Texas Press, 1985. 352 p.: bibl., ill., indexes.

Collection of essays, most of which were written in 1979 from the American Anthropological Assn. meetings in Cincinnati, Ohio. The collective effort presents new research, containing essential information and important insights for the relatively new concerns about the postclassic period.

258a Miller, Mary Ellen. The art of Mesoamerica: from Olmec to Aztec. New York: Thames & Hudson, 1986. 240 p.: ill. (some col.)

One of the better of the many surveys of precolumbian art and architecture. It is especially welcome because it is clearly written and takes some of the latest scholarly thinking into account.

259 Miller, Virginia E. A reexamination of Maya gestures of submission (UCLA/JLAL, 9:1, Summer 1983, p. 17–38, bibl., ill.)

Well written article representing an enormous amount of research that does not, as yet, come to any definite conclusions.

260 Morley, Sylvanus Griswold and George W. Brainerd. The ancient Maya. Revised by Robert J. Sharer. 4th ed. Stanford, Calif.: Stanford Univ. Press, 1983. 708 p.: bibl., ill., index.

Extensive revision has brought this classic work up to date without distorting Morley's personal vision of the ancient Maya. For archaeologist's comment, see *HLAS 47:321.*

261 Painted architecture and polychrome monumental sculpture in Mesoamerica: a symposium at Dumbarton Oaks, 10th to 11th October, 1981. Edited by Elizabeth Hill Boone. Washington: Dumbarton Oaks Research Library and Collection, 1985. 186 p., 8 p. of plates: bibls., ill. (some col.)

Symposium papers, published by Dumbarton Oaks, are devoted to an important, but seldom studied aspect of precolumbian art and architecture: color. The assembled authors provide the best overview of this subject that has been published to date.

Pasztory, Esther. The function of art in Mesoamerica. See *HLAS 47:322.*

263 **Ritual human sacrifice in Meso-
america: a conference at Dumbarton
Oaks, October 13th and 14th, 1979.** Elizabeth
P. Benson, organizer. Elizabeth H. Boone, edi-
tor. Washington: Dumbarton Oaks Research
Library and Collection, 1984. 247 p.: bibls., ill.

Authors vary in their ability to handle
the frightening and difficult topic of human
sacrifice. Still, as an interdisciplinary overview, the volume is informative and useful.
For archaeologist's comment, see *HLAS
47:328.*

264 **Maya: treasures of an ancient civilization.** Edited by Charles Gallenkamp
and Regina Elise Johnson. Photos by Stuart
Rome. New York: Harry N. Abrams, Inc.; Albuquerque, N.M.: The Albuquerque Museum, 1985. 240 p.: bibl., ill. (some col.),
index, maps.

Valuable catalog for its text as well as
its beautifully photographed images of Maya
art. Features several works of art not previously published. One of its biggest contributions is bringing to general attention the
massive problems surrounding the looting
and illegal exportation of ancient art. Text
by: F.S. Clancy, C.C. Coggins, T.P. Culbert,
C. Gallenkamp, P.D. Harrison, J. Sabloff.

PRECOLUMBIAN
Mesoamerica: Mexico

265 **Alvarez A., Carlos.** Las esculturas de
Teotenango (UNAM/ECN, 16, 1983,
p. 233–264, bibl., ill.)

Stylistic and comparative analysis of
the sculptures of Teotenango for the purposes
of establishing a chronology and definition of
the late to post-classic styles in Central Mexico. For archaeologist's comment, see *HLAS
47:341.*

266 **Foncerrada de Molina, Marta.** Los murales de Cacaxtla: muerte en la guerra
(JGSWGL, 20, 1983, p. 537–562, ill.)

Foncerrada treats these beautiful murals as synthetic and logical expressions of
their time and place. Proposing that Cacaxtla
was inhabited by a mixture of Mexican and
Maya peoples (the Olmec-Xicalancas), she
demonstrates that the murals, as synthesis of
Mexican and Maya, represent the beginnings
of the post-classic idea of sacred war.

267 **Gandelman, Claude.** Problemas de lo
non finito en el arte mexicano: sobre
una cabeza totonaca del Museo Antropológico de Jalapa, México (IIE/A, 13:52,
1983, p. 59–68, ill.)

Welcome effort to understand the iconology (rather than the iconography) of a
work of Totonac sculpture. For archaeologist's
comment, see *HLAS 47:385.*

268 **Greene Robertson, Merle.** The sculpture of Palenque. v. 2, The early building of the Palace and the wall paintings.
Princeton, N.J.: Princeton Univ. Press, 1985.
1 v.: ill., photos.

Vol. 2 of ambitious project to compile
a photographic record of the remarkable art
of Palenque, a precolumbian site in modern-
day Chiapas. By illustrating drawings along
with photographs, these volumes become
very useful (as well as beautiful) research
tools. The text is a mixture of informative archaeological data and careful interpretation.
For vol. 1, see *HLAS 47:387.*

269 **Gutiérrez Solana, Nelly.** Sobre un
fémur con grabados perteneciente a la
cultura mexica (IIE/A, 13:52, 1983, p. 47–58,
bibl., ill.)

Iconographic study that tries to place
the function and images of an engraved bone
into the context of what is known about
Mexica solar sacrificial rites.

270 **Kubler, George.** Portales con columnas-
serpiente en Yucatán y el altiplano
(IIE/A, 13:52, 1983, p. 21–45, ill., tables)

Formal analysis that suggests the serpent columns of Yucatan could be used as
chronological markers. For archaeologist's
comment, see *HLAS 47:310.*

271 **Matos Moctezuma, Eduardo.** Una
visita al Templo Mayor de Tenochi-
titlán. México: INAH, 1981. 77 p.: bibl., ill.,
plates.

Short, but well written, description of
the construction history and symbolism of
the Templo Mayor of Tenochtitlán. The information comes from the most recent and
most important excavations (1978–1981) of
this Aztec monument. For archaeologist's
comment, see *HLAS 47:432.*

Mullen, Robert J. Santa María Tiltepec: a
masterpiece of Mixtec vernacular architecture. See item **341.**

272 **Nicholson, Henry B.** and **Eloise Quiñones Keber.** Art of Aztec Mexico: treasures of Tenochtitlán. Washington: National Gallery of Art, 1983. 188 p.: bibl., ill.
This catalog is a testimony to the sculptural brilliance of the Aztec. The excellent scholarship evident in the accompanying texts makes this beautifully produced book a model for achieving the didactic and aesthetic functions required of exhibition catalogs. For archaeologist's comment, see *HLAS 47:442.*

273 **Pasztory, Esther.** Aztec art. New York: Harry N. Abrams, 1983. 335 p.: bibl., ill., index.
Beautiful illustrations enhance a scholarly text. Author creates an informative and very useful overview of Aztec art and culture. For archaeologist's comment, see *HLAS 47:448.*

274 **Smith, Virginia Grady.** Izapa relief carving: form, content, rules for design, and role in Mesoamerican art history and archaeology. Washington: Dumbarton Oaks Research Library and Collection, 1984. 103 p.: bibl., ill. (Studies in precolumbian art and archaeology; 27)
This is one of the more successful attempts to explain a precolumbian art through structural analysis. Unfortunately, the illustrations are fragmented details of the monuments and are difficult to use with the text.

275 **von Winning, Hasso.** La procesión de los teomamaque: notas sobre la iconografía de la cerámica moldeada de Veracruz (IIE/A, 13:51, 1983, p. 5–11, bibl., plates)
By noting the manner of figural delineation, gesture, and various costume and regalia features, the author makes a good case that a particular series of classic molded vases represent a ritual procession associated with the precolumbian ballgame.

PRECOLUMBIAN
South America

Castillo Venero, Carlos. Cuzco: patrones de asentamientos. See item 374.

276 **Culturas precolombinas: Chancay.** Lima: Banco de Crédito del Perú, 1982. 180 p.: bibl., ill. (some col.) (Col. Arte y tesoros del Perú)

Book is part of monographic series on Peruvian precolumbian cultures. A group of thematic essays by various authors create a somewhat disjointed, but at times, poetic text for this beautifully illustrated volume.

277 **Culturas precolombinas: Paracas.** Lima: Banco de Crédito del Perú, 1983. 189 p.: bibl., ill. (some col.) (Col. Arte y tesoros del Perú)
Volume on the arts of Paracas is beautifully illustrated. Devotes special attention to many color photographs of the famed textiles found in the necropolis. Essays by different authors recount history of the site and various efforts to understand the meaning of the Paracas images.

278 **Gamboa Hinestrosa, Pablo.** La escultura en la sociedad agustiniana. Bogotá: Ediciones CIEC; Univ. Nacional de Colombia, Depto. de Historia, Facultad de Ciencias Humanas, 1982. 217 p.: bibl., ill.
Careful and insightful analysis of the sculptures from San Agustín, Colombia. To date, this is one of the better efforts to understand their sculptural context and form, and meanings that can be deducted from their artistic traits.

Hemming, John. Monuments of the Incas. See *HLAS 47:824.*

279 **Mostny Glaser, Grete** and **Hans Niemeyer Fernández.** Arte rupestre chileno. Santiago: Depto. de Extensión Cultural, Ministerio de Educación, 1983. 146 p.: ill. (some col.) (Serie El patrimonio cultural chileno. Col. Historia del arte chileno; 8)
Lucid description and analysis of Chilean rock art organized by location, style and technique. Of interest is the technique, *geoglifo,* of large images imposed on the landscape and similar in concept to the better known Nazca lines of Peru.

280 **Museo Chileno de Arte Precolombino.** Platería araucana. Santiago: El Museo, 1983. 85 p.: bibl., ill. (some col.)
Beautiful photographs enhance this catalog of the Walter Reccius Collection. Includes useful explanatory text.

281 **Puppo, Giancarlo.** Arte argentino antes de la dominación hispánica. Presentación de Alberto Rex González. Buenos Aires: Hualfin Ediciones Edicolor, 1979. 273 p.: bibl., ill. (some col.)

Author uses photographic essay that shows precolumbian Argentine sculpture as works of art rather than as artifacts, in order to demonstrate that little will be done for the nation's archaeological history until the aesthetic qualities of such art are acknowledged. Includes extraordinary and evocative images.

282 Stierlin, Henri. L'art Inca et ses origines: de Valdivia à Machu Picchu. Fribourg, Switzerland: Office du livre, 1983. 224 p.: bibl., ill. (some col.), index.

General history of precolumbian high cultures in South America from earliest artifacts of preceramic period to Incaic arts practiced at the time of the conquest. It is well organized and beautifully illustrated. Author believes that the basic themes known for Incaic life and culture underly the preceding, as well as the peripheral, cultures in South America. For archaeologist's comment and English translation, see *HLAS 47:611.*

283 I Tesori della terra di Atahualpa: Ecuador dalla preistoria agli Inca. Venezia, Italy: Centro di cultura, Palazzo Grassi: Marsilio, 1982. 192 p.: bibl., ill. (some col.)

Catalog for an exhibition of Ecuadorian, precolumbian art (Venice, Centro di Cultura di Palazzo Grassi, 1982). Includes didactic essays and photographs of the objects arranged by cultures and more or less chronologically.

284 Truel, Juana. Los textiles precolombinos y su conservación. Lima: Proyecto Regional de Patrimonio Cultural, PNUD, UNESCO, 1979? 37 p., 29 p. of plates: ill. (some col.)

Careful description of methods used for the conservation of precolumbian textiles at the Museo Nacional de Antropología y Arqueología in Cuzco. Text supplies the *how* of conservation as well as impassioned reasons *why* conservation must take place. Provides historical overview of textiles world wide as well as precolumbian, but the chapters on the New World are the most interesting and specific.

285 Zamora, R. Musée d'art précolombien de Santiago du Chili (ARCHEO, 199, fev. 1985, p. 20–29, ill.)

Honorific essay describes patronage and works of this museum. Includes interesting pictoral display of precolumbian chronology for Mesoamerica and South America.

POPULAR AND FOLK
General

286 Acevedo, Esther. A propósito de esa olla convertida en "arte popular" (*in* Mexican art of the 1970s: images of displacement. Edited by Leonard Folgarait. Nashville, Tenn.: Vanderbilt Univ., 1984, p. 29–36, appendices)

Author rejects stylistic grounds for defining the term "arte popular." By analyzing a year's worth of journal articles on "arte popular," she demonstrates the chaotic and changing social conditions that make a set definition almost impossible.

287 El Arte efímero en el mundo hispánico. México: UNAM, Instituto de Investigaciones Estéticas, 1983. 389 p., 57 p. of plates: bibl., ill. (Estudios de arte y estética, 0185–1748; 17)

Consists of 15 papers presented at an international colloquium on various ephemeral arts primarily in Mexico: Aztec military costume and ritual; Baroque fiestas and poetry; 19th-century fireworks, bullfights, triumphal arches, ladies' fashion, Afro-Cuban dances; more recent Mexican bourgeois dances; and avant-garde happenings throughout Latin America. Most papers have commentaries by leading Latin American cultural and art historians. [J.F. Scott]

288 Cerny, Charlene. Thoughts on anonymity and signature in folk art (SAR/P, 90:1, Spring 1984, p. 34–37, ill.)

Short but intelligent essay on the subject.

289 Herbenar Bossen, Laurel. Huipeles, tzutes and molas: context and coincidence in Central American textiles (CRI/CR, 13:4, 1984, p. 31–33)

More critical than clarifying review essay about A.P. Rowe's book on Guatemalan textiles (see *HLAS 46:1067*) and Mary Helms's *Cuna molas and Coclé art forms* (Philadelphia, Penn.: Institute for the Study of Human Issues, 1981).

290 Luján Muñoz, Jorge. El artesano tradicional y su papel en la sociedad contemporánea. Guatemala: Sub-Centro Regional de Artesanías y Artes Populares, 1983. 40 p.

In this sociological overview of traditional arts (crafts), author considers their disruption and disappearance; their "politics" of preservation; and what the future might hold.

291 Rodríguez Rouanet, Francisco. Breve introducción al estudio de las artesanías populares de Guatemala. Guatemala: Sub-Centro Regional de Artesanías y Artes Populares, 1983. 51 p., 9 leaves of plates: bibl., ill . (Col. Artesanías populares; 4)

This little book represents an effort to rationalize and define the studies of popular art.

292 Villa, Eugenia. Consideraciones generales acerca del objeto artesanal (PUJ/UH, 12:19, enero/junio 1983, p. 19–36, bibl.)

Author tries to define by social context the very human activity of crafting objects for everyday use. An effort to create a conceptual overview is made by focusing less on the object as art than on the contexts of the maker and the eventual use of the object.

POPULAR AND FOLK
Middle America and the Caribbean

Aguilar Arrivillaga, Eduardo. Estudio de la vivienda rural en Guatemala. See *HLAS* 47:5061.

293 Anawalt, Patricia Rieff. Prehispanic survivals in Guatemalan dress (SAR/P, 90:1, Spring 1984, p. 12–19, ill.)

Less interested in the survival of prehispanic costume traits, author presents evidence for what kind of Spanish influence occurred, and how these influences were integrated into native clothing.

294 Camposeco M., José Balbino. La cestería de la aldea Cerro Alto, San Juan Sacatepéquez, Guatemala. Guatemala: Sub-Centro Regional de Artesanías y Artes Populares, 1983. 16 leaves, 13 leaves of plates: ill. (Col. Artesanías populares; 3)

Structural, sociological investigation of the means of production and distribution for basket-making in the region of San Juan Sacatepéc, Guatemala.

295 Casagrande, Louis B.; Walter F. Morris, Jr.; and Suzanne Baizerman. The art and meaning of Chiapas ceremonial brocade (SAR/P, 90:1, Spring 1984, p. 28–33, ill.)

Descriptive list of meanings com-

monly attributed to certain brocade designs. No effort is made to analyze the meanings.

296 Fisher, Nora. Beyond boundaries: highland Maya dress (SAR/P, 90:1, Spring 1984, p. 4–11, ill.)

Nostalgic review of highland Maya costumes and weaving techniques.

297 Heckadon Moreno, Stanley. Pintores del ambiente popular (LNB/L, 344/345, nov./dic. 1984, p. 93–100, ill.)

Focusing on the brilliantly decorated buses of Panama, author describes this "tradition," and muses about its disappearance in the face of modernization.

298 Martinique d'antan: le costume = Martinique in olden time: the local dress. 2ème ed. Fort-de-France?: LEP Dillon, Annexe St. Joseph, 1983. 31 p., 4 folded leaves of plates: ill.

Interesting little book that supplies patterns as well as instructions for making the traditional female costumes of Martinique: *la grand'robe, la gaule,* and *le jupe et chemise.*

299 Morales, Liliana. La artesanía del cobre en Chiantla. Guatemala: Sub-Centro Regional de Artesanías y Artes Populares, 1984. 111 p.: ill. (Col. Tierra adentro; 3)

Sociological analysis of the copper craft-industry in the town of Chiantla, Guatemala (Huehuetenango). Author focuses on the processes of production and the economics of the craft.

300 Morales Hidalgo, Italo. U cayibal atziak = Imágenes en los tejidos guatemaltecos = Images in Guatemalan weavings. Guatemala: Ediciones Cuatro Ahau, 1982. 108 p.: all ill.

Catalog of embroidery and weaving designs found in modern textiles of Guatemala. Identifies designs by their conventional names, and includes short introduction.

Mosquera, Gerardo. Exploraciones en la plástica cubana. See item **408.**

301 Müller, Florencia. Estudio de la cerámica hispánica y moderna de Tlaxcala-Puebla. México: INAH, Depto. de Salvamento Arqueológico, 1981. 81 p.: bibl., ill. (some col.) (Col. científica; 103. Arqueología)

Necessary and well conceived analysis of ceramic-types that range from the conquest to the present. More studies like this one would be welcome.

302 Parker, Ann and **Avon Neal.** *Los ambulantes*: the itinerant photographers of Guatemala. Photos by Ann Parker. Text by Avon Neal. Cambridge, Mass.: MIT Press, 1982. 149 p.: plates.

Book offers a nostalgic, poetic, and somewhat superficial account of the itinerant photographers of highland Guatemala. Nonetheless, the subject matter is new and the area, if studied, could yield rich artistic and sociological insights.

303 Sayer, Chloë. Costumes of Mexico. Austin: Univ. of Texas Press; London: British Museum Publications, 1985. 240 p.: bibl., ill. (some col.), index.

Nicely illustrated historical account of Mexican costume uses primary documents, eyewitness accounts, works of art that illustrate costume, and ethnographic sources.

304 Tedlock, Barbara and **Dennis Tedlock.** Text and textile: language and technology in the arts of the Quiche Maya (UNM/JAR, 4:2, Summer 1985, p. 121–146)

This study provides the type of reformation or redefinition one looks foward to. Authors use ethnography and linguistics in order to establish a large perspective about the complexity and beauty of meaning and ways it can be achieved.

305 Terán, Silvia. Artesanías de Yucatán. Fotos, Christian Rasmussen. Mérida, México: PESIP, Arte y Comunicación; México: Dirección General de Culturas Populares, SEP, 1981. 85 p.: ill.

Authors consider each type of craft practiced today in Yucatán, and provide locations of workshops, description of varieties of craftsmanship and ways of accomplishing them.

POPULAR AND FOLK
South America

306 Arte indígena de Venezuela: Sala Mendoza, Fundación Eugenio Mendoza, Caracas, 6 de noviembre-3 de diciembre, 1983. Caracas: Ministerio de Estado para la Cultura, Fundación para el Desarrollo de la Cultura (FUDECO), 1983. 164 p.: bibl., ill.

Illustrated catalog of art and artifacts made by the tribal peoples of Venezuela. The most impressive for their diversity and imagination are pieces of the Piaroa tribe.

El Arte textil en Bolivia. See *HLAS 47:1418*.

Boh, Luis Alberto and **Annie M. Granada.** Apuntes sobre evolución histórica y tipológica de la vivienda popular urbana en el Paraguay. See *HLAS 47:5177*.

Escobar, Ticio. Una interpretación de las artes visuales en el Paraguay. See item 362.

307 Exposición de artesanías tradicionales de la Argentina. Buenos Aires: Presidencia de la Nación, Secretaría de Cultura, Centro Cultural Las Malvinas, 1982. 29 p., 23 p. of plates: ill. (some col.)

Didactic catalog organized by various media with which the craft traditions in Venezuela are practiced. Series of descriptive essays are followed by photographs, some of which show the production or use of the craft-object.

308 López Antay, Joaquín. Don Joaquín, testimonio de un artista popular andino. Edición de Mario Razzeto. Lima: Instituto Andino de Artes Populares, Sede Nacional del Perú, 1982. 177 p., 12 p. of plates: bibl., ill. (some col.)

Recorded remembrances of Don Joaquín (i.e., a "popular" artist from the highlands of Peru) are of interest for many reasons: ethnographic, historic, artistic, etc. But it is the tone, the philosophy, and the humanity of the artist that creates the real value of this book.

Colonial: General, Middle America and the Caribbean

ROBERT J. MULLEN, *Associate Professor of Art History, The University of Texas at San Antonio*

THE NUMBER OF ARTICLES AND BOOKS now being published on the colonial art and architecture of Latin America is such that a division of labor was introduced in this volume of the *Handbook*. As of *HLAS 48*, John F. Scott, Univ. of Florida, will serve as contributing editor for the colonial art of Spanish South America.

Even in the more limited perspective of Middle America and the Caribbean, the numbers of works published are imposing (19 books, 31 articles) while the variety of topics researched is unprecedented. Architecture and painting continue as favorite topics while new ones include biographies, votive figures, arms and armor, silver, bullrings, registries, lienzos, iconographies, technical analyses, and the social impact of vernacular architecture.

A new approach in the study of portraiture is apparent in articles on self-portraits and donor portraits discovered among the persons attending the principal figure (items **349** and **350**). And one article reveals the surprise of discovering a Luis Juárez oil in Quebec (item **338**). The technical analysis of oil painting in New Spain (item **319**), examining chemistry, framing, themes, and iconography, is an absolute "must" for those interested in restoration, curators or dealers.

Research on architecture, religious and civil, is largely concentrated on 16th-century Mexico. Noteworthy examples are the vernacular architecture of Tasco (item **334**), the distinctive portal/portería arrangement of the Franciscan conventos in the Yucatan (item **317**), and the monographs on the Palace of Cortés in Cuernavaca, the Hospital de Jesús (founded by Cortés) in Mexico City, and the former Franciscan church and convento in Huejotzingo (items **316, 322,** and **347**). In that same category, but addressing the 19th century, is the book on the transformation of the interior of Puebla's cathedral from the Renaissance-Baroque style to neoclassicism (item **327**).

Moving to Guatemala there is a well documented account of the three cathedrals which once graced the original capital in Antigua (item **353**). Other exemplary instances of documentary research offer new insights into casas reales or official residences (item **324**), construction details of Mexico's original cathedral as of 1584 and 1585 (item **352**) and the likelihood that there were two Conchas, one a well known painter, the other an architect engaged in the 16th-century construction of Mexico's first cathedral (item **326**). Three articles take an affirmative approach to the question of "indigenous influence" on the architecture-sculpture composite during the 16th century (items **331, 333,** and **341**).

Another group of studies that ought to be singled out because of their unusual subject matter are studies of topics one seldom has the chance to review at the same time: a book that examines nine rarely seen but clearly illustrated *lienzos* (item **343**); a volume (566 p.) that depicts and answers everything (it would seem) on the art of the silversmiths of the New World (item **310**), an extraordinary accomplishment; the first known full study of Cuba's colonial, mostly 18th-century architecture, represents another prodigious feat (item **357**); books on 16th-century furniture of Mexico are rare but what makes the one annotated below unusual are its illustrations of furniture reproduced from codices (item **328**); and finally, a classic in Spanish, Toussaint's *Arte colonial en México* (item **348**) has been reissued as the fourth edition.

A number of other significant books, not annotated below deserve special mention. George Kubler's well known *Mexican architecture of the sixteenth century* (Westport, Conn.: Greenwood Press, 1972, 1 v.: bibl., ill.) has at long last, been translated into Spanish. The architecture and cultural heritage of colonial Chiapas, an area only occasionally studied, are finally available in Sidney D. Markman's *Architecture and urbanization in colonial Chiapas, Mexico* (Philadelphia, Pa.: American Philosophical Society, 1984, 443 p.: bibl., ill., index [Memoirs series, 0065–9738; 153]). Vol. 2, *Art of the colonial period* of the set *Handbook of Latin American Art* (Santa Barbara, Calif.: ABC-Clio Information Services, 1986, 1 v.: indexes) edited by Joyce Waddell Bailey and published in Jan. 1986, provides "complete bibliographic data on books, articles, anthologies, catalogs, and reports (including unpublished material) on Latin American art. Citations appear in the language origin (English, Spanish, Portuguese, French, German, Italian, Russian, or other)." Harper & Row's *Art and time in Mexico: from the conquest to the Revolution* (New York: Harper & Row, 1985, 284 p.: bibl., ill. (some col.), index, map [Icon editions]) contributes a venture seldom undertaken in the US by a non-university press. Its text is by Elizabeth Wilder Weisman and photographs by Judith Hancock Sandoval. Described as an "introduction" to Mexican colonial architecture and sculpture, the book covers the "whole range, from the grand to the vernacular."

A few institutional facts need updating. The Research Center for the Arts renamed as Research Center for the Arts and Humanities is now the Research Center for the Visual Arts. It is still located at the Univ. of Texas at San Antonio (Director, Jacinto Quirarte) and its focus remains the Iberian-American world. The Assn. for Latin American Art (ALAA) continues to function as part of the College Art Assn.'s annual meetings. Sessions concerning the Hispanic Arts are now appearing with some regularity on the agenda of the annual meetings of the Society of Architectural Historians and in the periodic gatherings of the International Congress of the History of Art.

In this final introductory essay as contributing editor, one completes a decade of service for the *Handbook*. It is heartening to be able to note that the number of scholars researching Latin American art has increased significantly. Nevertheless, comprehensive studies of Viceregencies are still lacking as are regional studies. A work that partly fills this void is *Art and time in Mexico*. Since one has often deplored this gap, it seems appropriate to conclude by noting that this contributing editor has completed a manuscript, now under review, on the architecture and sculpture of colonial Mexico written for the student, traveler, and interested layman.

GENERAL

309 Bouysse Cassagne, Thérèse. Une histoire entre la métaphore et la métonymie: réflexiones autour d'un livre de Teresa de Mesa, *Iconografía y mitos indígenas en el arte* (UTIEH/C, 44, 1985, p. 9–20)

Appreciative structuralist review of ideas on "mestizo" art and its bicultural meanings contained in a book by Teresa Gisbert. Indian culture is believed to be more clearly expressed in art than in writing. [J.F. Scott]

Estudios sobre la ciudad iberoamericana. See item **1783**.

310 Fernández, Alejandro; Rafael Munoa; and Jorge Rabasco. Enciclopedia de la plata española y virreinal americana. Prólogo de José Manuel Cruz Valdovinos. Madrid: Asociación Española de Joyeros, Plateros y Relojeros Federación Española de Anticuarios y Almonedistas, 1984. 566 p.: bibl., ill.

Volume catalogs about 2,000 pieces from the 14th to the 20th centuries (566 p.). Organized into three parts: 1) concerns metals, laws, technical aspects, origins in Spain (p. 1–96); 2) covers Spanish pieces by marks (alphabetized and illustrated), silversmiths (location and name) with hundreds of high quality illustrations which describe and identify by mark and locale (p. 97–496); and 3) deals with Viceregency pieces from the Americas organized as in pt. 2 (p. 497–536). Spanish silversmiths: 54 p.; New Spain silversmiths: 6 p. Extensive bibliography, excellent research, compilation and presentation. An extraordinary work of scholarship.

311 Heredia Moreno, María del Carmen. Unas piezas de orfebrería hispanoamericana en Navarra (IIE/A, 13:51, 1983, p. 59–71, plates)

After noting that Spain is rich in silver pieces from the Americas, author examines, in terms of style and influence, those in Navarra. Fine illustrations.

312 Museo de las Casas Reales, *Santo Domingo*. Sala de Armas: catálogo. Edición al cuidado de Moisés de Soto David. Santo Domingo: El Museo, 1983. 83 p.: bibl., ill.

Permanent collection of arms, armor, swords from Europe, Africa, Asia and the Americas from 15th to 19th centuries. Hundreds of items are illustrated, dated and described.

313 Simposio internazionale sul Barocco latino americano, *Roma, 1980*. Simposio internazionale sul Barocco latino americano. Roma: Istituto italo-latino americano, 1982. 1 v.: bibl., ill. (some col.)

Major conference (Rome, 1980) on the Latin American Baroque consists of 41 short papers by major figures from Latin America and Europe (none from North America). They cover primarily architecture, beginning with philosophy and ending with sculpture with only passing references to painting. Introductory group of plates do not relate to the papers' topics which are not illustrated. [J.F. Scott]

314 Wyrobisz, Andrzej. La ordenanza de Felipe II del año 1573 y la construcción de ciudades coloniales españolas en la América (PAN/EL, 7, 1980, p. 11–34)

Intelligent and well-researched summary of the literature concerning colonial Spanish city planning which was finally codified in 1573 in the Laws of the Indies. [J.F. Scott]

MEXICO

315 Amerlinck de Corsi, María Concepción. Arquitectos y plazas de toros en Nueva España (JGSWGL, 20, 1983, p. 393–408, ill.)

Story of bullrings in Mexico City from mid 16th-century to 1821. Includes plans. Unusual.

316 Báez Macías, Eduardo. El edificio del Hospital de Jesús: historia y documentos sobre su construcción. México: UNAM, 1982. 164 p., 42 p. of plates: ill., ports. (Monografías de arte; 6)

Much needed study on this building used as hospital since its founding in 1528. Also known as Purísima Concepción. Complete documentation from 16th century to present with a chapter per century. Includes 42 illustrations, many of them paintings (e.g., portraits of Hernán and Martín Cortés).

317 Bretos, Miguel A. Fray Juan de Mérida y los portales franciscanos de Yucatán (UY/R, 25:148, oct./dic. 1983, p. 140–155, ill.)

Calls attention to hitherto unrecognized features of 16th-century Franciscan architecture in Yucatan. The innovation is an arched portal serving as portería for the convento and also as vestibule of the church.

318 Carrillo Azpeitia, Rafael. El arte barroco en México desde sus inicios, hasta el esplendor de los siglos XVII y XVIII. México: Panorama Editorial, 1982. 162 p.: bibl., ill. (Col. Panorama)

Well presented and beautifully illustrated pocket-size "survey" of the 17th and 18th centuries in Mexico, commonly called "Baroque." One of a series.

319 Carrillo y Gariel, Abelardo. Técnica de la pintura de Nueva España. 2a ed. México: UNAM, 1983. 203 p., 92 p. of plates: ill.

Four chapters deal with: 1) color and chemical analyses of materials; 2) painting of surfaces and frames; 3) historical context and themes; and 4) iconography, backgrounds, morphology of hands and feet. Required reading for restorationists and curators.

320 Castro Morales, Efraín. Los cuadros de castas de la Nueva España (JGSWGL, 20, 1983, p. 671–690, ill.)

Traces literary and pictorial origins of castes (castas) to early 18th century. Illustrates 12 "cuadras de castas" (in various locations in Mexico).

321 Castro Morales, Oliva. La Casa de Mangino en la ciudad de Puebla (JGSWGL, 20, 1983, p. 437–447, ill.)

Full analysis of "one of the most notable" civil colonial structures preserved in the city of Puebla. Begun in early 18th century, restored in 1788. Plans, sections, photos.

322 Chanfón Olmos, Carlos. El Castillo-Palacio de Don Hernando Cortés en Cuernavaca (JGSWGL, 20, 1983, p. 299–319, ill.)

Detailed historical and architectural account of structure in Cuernavaca known as the Palace of Cortés. Illustrations of growth stage in 16th century clearly demonstrate its original function as a castle (military) palace. It was restored in 1974 to give it that character (after extensive earlier modifications). Important addition to our knowledge of 16th-century civil architecture.

323 Díaz, Marco. La arquitectura doméstica en Atlixco (JGSWGL, 20, 1983, p. 377–392, ill.)

Reviews plans, growth and changes of a group of domestic structures from 17th to 20th centuries. Shows many variations with expressive use of materials. Cites possible influence on religious architecture of artisans involved in these structures.

324 Dyckerhoff, Ursula. La reedificación de las "casas reales" de Huejotzingo, 1640 (JGSWGL, 20, 1983, p. 409–436, appendices)

"Casas reales" refers to official residences of representatives of Spanish crown. Masterful research on this little known class of colonial architecture, at one time quite prevalent. Extensive documentation.

325 Estrada de Gerlero, Elena. El programa pasionario en el Convento Franciscano de Huejotzingo (JGSWGL, 20, 1983, p. 643–662, ill.)

Mural depicting a group of flagellants (a religious society whose processions are associated with Holy Thursday) was discovered during the recent restoration of the former Franciscan church (now museum) in Huejotzingo.

326 Fernández, Martha. El matrimonio de Andrés de Concha (IIE/A, 13 : 52, 1983, p. 85–99)

Examines theory that there were two Conchas, one a painter, the other an architect, active in Mexico (1568–1615). On the basis of a 1583 matrimonial document, author opts for two persons. The architect served as Maestro Mayor of Mexico's cathedral (1596–1601).

327 García Zambrano, Angel Julián. El remodelado interior de la Catedral de Puebla, México, 1850–1860. Mérida, Venezuela: Univ. de los Andes, Consejo de Desarrollo Científico, Humanístico y Tecnológico, Comisión de Estudios Humanísticos, 1984. 207 p.: bibl., ill.

Detailed account of transformation of Puebla's cathedral interior from Renaissance/Baroque to neoclassical style, principally in 19th century. A definite contribution to our understanding of the latter century. Good photos.

328 Gómez de Orozco, Federico. El mobiliario y la decoración en la Nueva España en el siglo XVI. México: UNAM, Instituto de Investigaciones Estéticas, 1983. 111 p., 15 p. of plates: ill. (Estudios y fuentes del arte en México; 44)

Describes the kind of furniture one would have found in various rooms in various kinds of 16th-century buildings. Illustrations (good) are drawings derived from codices. Documented inventories. A most unusual work that will appeal to both specialist and layman. Good scholarship.

329 González Galván, Manuel. Asian influences in the colonial art of the Americas (in International Congress of Human Sciences in Asia and North Africa, 30th, Mexico, 1976. Asia and colonial Latin America. Edited by Ernesto de la Torre. México: El Colegio de México, 1981, p. 141–144)

Discusses the question of Chinese (or Philippine) influence on Mexico, a provocative but untested concept: several items proposed by author as purely Asian origin have precolumbian antecedents (e.g., Aztec use of tissue paper and Tarascan craft of lacquered wood). [J.F. Scott]

330 González Galván, Manuel. *Epifanía Guadalupana* (JGSWGL, 20, 1983, p. 663–670, ill.)

Painting in cathedral of Morelia shows unusual iconography of the three Magi offering their gifts to the Virgin of Guadalupe. Author asks if this is another possible manifestation of universal salvation of the Americas.

331 Gussinyer A., Jordi. Influencias precolombinas en la distribución y desarrollo de la primera arquitectura colonial en el centro de Chiapas (INAH/A, 1 : 55, 1976/1977, p. 5–34, bibl., ill., plates)

Pursues theme that indigenous, precolumbian influence on colonial architecture is most evident in the type, use, and handling of materials. Less influence can be detected in ornamental details and monumental scale of church structures. Insightful study with excellent illustrations that include plans.

332 Gutiérrez, Ludivina. Monumentos coloniales de Xalapa. México: UNAM, Instituto de Investigaciones Estéticas, 1981. 54 p., 50 p. of plates: bibl., ill. (Cuadernos de historia del arte; 17)

Monograph on city of Jalapa (near Veracruz) concentrates on its architecture from 16th through 19th centuries. Reports historical data on non-existent structures of the San Francisco convento and hospital. Devotes separate chapter to sculpture and paintings. Includes some 50 (poor) illustrations.

333 Landa Abrego, María Elena. Presencia de simbología indígena en una capilla posa del siglo XVI (JGSWGL, 20, 1983, p. 637–642, ill.)

Discusses representation of the prehispanic metaphor of flower and song as the only true aspect of life in the sculpture on one of Huejotzingo's posas.

334 Lombardo de Ruiz, Sonia. Arquitectura religiosa marginada en el siglo XVI: un estudio de caso (JGSWGL, 20, 1983, p. 331–376, ill., tables)

Thorough typological investigation of 16th-century churches (not conventos) in the area of Tasco. Illustrates impact of Spanish culture, particularly architectural, on an otherwise "marginal area." Draws a comparative analysis of more than 100 aspects among 23 churches. Exemplary research.

335 López Cervantes, Gonzalo. Porcelana oriental en la Nueva España (INAH/A, 1 : 55, 1976/1977, p. 65–82, bibl., ill.)

Consists of literary references to and commercial records of oriental ceramics in New Spain. Description of fragments. Brief history of Chinese ceramics (1368–1912).

336 Markman, Sidney D. El espacio longitudinal y los frontispicios "escenográficos" de las iglesias de los pueblos indígenas de Chiapas (CIRMA/M, 4 : 5, junio 1983, p. 109–127, bibl., ill., maps)

Contends that churches in the pueblos have a particular significance in the formation of social structure in the New World. In this their importance is quite different from the metropolitan churches where style analyses are more applicable.

337 Martínez del Río, Marita. Un retrato de Doña Leona Vicario a los cinco años (IIE/A, 13 : 52, 1983, p. 117–121, ill.)

Group portrait by Domingo Ortiz shows Don Gaspar Martín Vicario with two children of his first marriage, his second wife and their daughter, age five, Doña María Leona. Detailed description.

338 Moura Sobral, Luis de. Un cuadro de Luis Juárez en la Catedral de Québec (IIE/A, 13 : 51, 1983, p. 21–23, plates)

Contends this large oil "Imposición de la Casulla a San Ildefonso" (i.e., Vestiture of . . .), now in Quebec's Cathedral, is not the work of Zurbarán, as attributed, but of Luis Juárez.

339 Moyssén Echeverría, Xavier. Los dibujos de arquitectura de Justino Fernández. México: UNAM, Instituto de Investigaciones Estéticas, 1982. 1 portfolio: 10 leaves, 29 leaves of plates.

Short biography of this former distinguished director of Mexico's Instituto de Investigaciones Estéticas. Describes his long involvement with preservation of colonial architecture. Includes 29 drawings, superbly reproduced, that attest to his deep appreciation of architecture, the basis of many of his writings.

340 Moyssén Echeverría, Xavier. La pintura flamenca, Rubens y la Nueva España (JGSWGL, 20, 1983, p. 699–706, ill.)
Traces influence of Flemish painters, especially Rubens, on colonial artists of Mexico.

341 Mullen, Robert J. Santa María Tiltepec: a masterpiece of Mixtec vernacular architecture (IIE/A, 13:51, 1983, p. 45–58, ill., plates)
Despite 17th-century carved dates (and Mixtec word), contends church is 16th-century masterpiece of *tequitqui*. Links sculptural details with prehispanic symbols of the sacred, including a possible allusion to Eight Deer, the Mixtec cultural hero. A new approach to the troublesome question of "indigenous influence."

342 Museo Nacional de las Intervenciones, Mexico. Churubusco: colecciones de la Iglesia y Ex-Convento de Nuestra Señora de los Angeles. Edición a cargo de Efraín Castro M. y Armida Alonso L. México: INAH, 1981 [i.e. 1982]. 300 p.: bibl., ill., indexes (Serie de catálogos de la Dirección de Monumentos Históricos; 1)
In 1981 the church and former convent of Nuestra Señora de los Angeles was designated as the Museo Nacional de las Intervenciones. A history of the two structures precedes the catalog of collections in each one. The catalog provides diagrams and examines every painting and statue in the church's eight retablos. Includes high quality photos with many details and signatures. There are illustrations of hundreds of oils, sculptures, and ex-votos. Thoroughly researched and admirably presented study.

343 Oettinger, Marion. Lienzos coloniales: una exposición de pinturas de terrenos comunales de México, siglos XVI–XIX. México: UNAM, Instituto de Investigaciones Antropológicas, 1983. 61 p.: bibl., ill.
Detailed information on nine *lienzos* (paintings) of boundaries of community properties in Oaxaca, Puebla, Mexico, and Guerrero. A most extraordinary exhibition and catalog. Provides succinct account of prehispanic manuscripts and colonial *lienzos* including their characteristics. All nine *lienzos* are illustrated.

344 Reyes-Valerio, Constantino. La pintura mural del siglo XVI en México (JGSWGL, 20, 1983, p. 629–635)
Analyzes four new aspects of mural paintings in 16th-century Mexico.

345 Ruiz Gomas C., José Rogelio. La Capilla del Señor de Contreras en El Carmen de San Angel y las pinturas de Luis Juárez (IIE/A, 13:52, 1983, p. 101–115, ill.)
Investigates relationships between retablos and paintings, especially those four attributed to Luis Juárez in the reopened (1942) capilla with those lost in 1935, when the original was destroyed by fire. Speculates if the four were the same as those described by Toussaint.

346 Ruiz Gomas C., José Rogelio. El pintor Antonio Rodríguez y tres cuadros desconocidos (IIE/A, 13:51, 1983, p. 25–36, plates)
Brings to light three paintings by this neglected 17th-century Mexican artist. Biographic details. Analyzes style, color, relative importance. Good illustrations.

347 Salas Cuesta, Marcela. La iglesia y el convento de Huejotzingo. México: UNAM, Instituto de Investigaciones Estéticas, 1982. 144 p., 20 p. of plates: bibl., ill. (Cuadernos de historia del arte; 18)
Monograph in two parts: 1) historical records (48 p.) and thorough architectural study (47 p.); and 2) treatment of atrio, exterior walls, façade, plan, interior, lateral doors, convento, posas, style, *tequitqui* reliefs. Describes 10 retablos. Includes 20 illustrations (fair). This complex was one of the most important of the 16th century. When last visited it was a museum, both church and convento.

348 Toussaint, Manuel. Arte colonial en Mexico. 4a ed. México: UNAM, Instituto de Investigaciones Estéticas, 1983. 303 p., 316 p. of plates: bibl., ill. (some col.), indexes.
Fourth ed. of classic, seminal work, first published in 1948. The translated version (E. Wilder Weismann) was published by the Univ. of Texas Press, Austin, in 1966. There are slight differences between the two. The English version has many more footnotes (research since 1948) and sharper illustrations. The Spanish text has more illustrations and separate indexes for persons and

places. Both have a few color plates. It is still, and is likely to remain, the basic work on Mexico's colonial arts (all of them).

349 Vargas Lugo, Elisa. Una pintura desconocida del siglo XVII (JGSWGL, 20, 1983, p. 691–698, ill.)

Hitherto unknown painting of St. Anthony of Padua, in parish church of Ozumbilla (state of Mexico), by anonymous artist shows influence of Juárez and Rodríguez. Author dates painting to mid-17th century. Calls attention to portrait of young girl (donor?) in lower right (includes close-up photo).

350 Vargas Lugo, Elisa. El retrato de donantes y el autorretrato en la pintura novohispana: notas para el estudio de la pintura colonial de retrato (IIE/A, 13:51, 1983, p. 13–20, plates)

Initial analysis of self-portraits of artists discovered among groups of persons in religious paintings. Compares their characteristics to portraits of donors found in religious paintings. Fascinating scholarship. Convincingly illustrated.

351 Zaldívar Guerra, Sergio. El Cabillito (JGSWGL, 20, 1983, p. 501–509, ill.)

Artistic and historic examination of bronze equestrian statue of Charles IV by Manuel Tolsá. Emphasizes its most recent relocation in Mexico City.

352 Zavala, Silvio. Una etapa en la construcción de la Catedral de México, alrededor de 1585 (JGSWGL, 20, 1983, p. 321–330)

New documentation on large payments made in 1584 and 1585 for "la fábrica" of Mexico's original cathedral (torn down in 1626) possibly signifies alteration from wood *artesonado* ceiling to vaulted bays and dome over crossing. Includes names of numerous artisans.

CENTRAL AMERICA AND THE CARIBBEAN

353 Amerlinck de Corsi, María Concepción. Las catedrales de Santiago de los Caballeros de Guatemala. México: UNAM, 1981. 199 p., 38 p. of plates: ill. (some col.) (Monografías de arte; 4)

Well documented account of Antigua's three cathedrals, all destroyed by earthquakes. Their ruins were used to build San Jose's parish church. Discusses many new facts. Vivid chronicle that reveals the economic, institutional, and technical problems encountered in this major undertaking.

354 Polanco Brito, Hugo Eduardo. Exvotos y "milagros" del Santuario de Higüey. Santo Domingo: Ediciones Banco Central, 1984. 162 p., 42 leaves of plates: bibl., ill. (some col.), index.

History of votive figures precedes those described in this most famous santuario. Includes copious illustrations, many in color. Objects are categorized, typed and some are dated by reason of a 1738 inventory. Patron (and statue) is Nuestra Señora de Altagracia.

355 Rodas Estrada, Haroldo. Arte e historia del Templo y Convento de San Francisco de Guatemala. Fotografías, Mauro Calanchina. Guatemala: Dirección General de Antropología e Historia, 1981. 242 p., bibl., ill., photos (Publicación extraordinaria. Serie Historia del arte)

Brief account of Franciscans in Guatemala and their first convento in Antigua (destroyed) followed by extensive study of San Francisco in Guatemala City. Begun towards end of 18th century, the building was in neoclassic style. Restored. Attached museum (Fray Francisco Vázquez) includes many colonial works such as three Villalpando oils as well as 19th-century pieces. Many photos are of varying quality.

356 Velarde, Oscar. Notas sobre la platería religiosa colonial panameña (LNB/L, 336/337, marzo/abril 1984, p. 75–89, ill.)

Examines some of the better pieces of colonial silver (mostly religious in origin) that remain in Panama. Good pictures with dimensions.

357 Weiss, Joaquín E. La arquitectura colonial cubana. v. 1, Siglos XVI/XVII. v. 2, Siglo XVIII. La Habana: Instituto Cubano del Libro: Editorial Letras Cubanas, 1973–1979. 2 v.: bibl., ill.

Here "colonial" means 18th century. After an historical sketch of the island, there is a chapter on style (generally Baroque, says the author). Describes basic traits of homes, civil, military, and religious buildings (plans, portals, walls, etc.). Provides historical analysis of all major buildings in Havana and other cities of Cuba (over 100 p.). Includes 267 b/w illustrations (fair quality) as well as plans and details. It is, to my knowledge, the first complete treatment of Cuba's 18th-century architecture. A monumental undertaking of inestimable value.

358 **Zea Flores, Carlos Enrique.** Historia y descripción de la iglesia de Santo Do-

mingo de Guatemala. Guatemala: Cenaltex, 1984. 110 p.: bibl., ill.

Provides separate histories of church and convento, both begun in 1541 and severely damaged in 1773. Relocated to present site in Guatemala in 1778. Provides full description of latter structure, including its many sculptures.

Colonial: South America

JOHN F. SCOTT, *Associate Professor of Art History, University of Florida, Gainesville*

AS OF THIS VOLUME OF THE *HANDBOOK*, works on the colonial art of South America will be listed in a separate section and no longer annotated together with the colonial art of the rest of Spanish America. This division of labor is the result of the extraordinary number of works on Mexican colonial art being published these days which by themselves make up almost an entire art section of this volume (see p. 23–29).

Unlike Mexico, where basic information on major monuments has already been established, equivalent data is still being compiled in South America. Much remains to be accomplished before a comprehensive view of artistic developments can be made on a regional, national or—very far off indeed—a hemispheric level.

The great majority of titles received at the Library of Congress and canvassed by this contributing editor consist of works reporting archival and physical facts of colonial architecture with relatively little stylistic interpretation or comparison with other monuments in the same area. Needless to say, such gathering of basic information about the construction stages and modifications of structures is a prerequisite for interpretive studies. Therefore, one must applaud such efforts, especially the coordinated program underway in Argentina, where the Academia Nacional de Bellas Artes is conducting a survey of regional architecture (item **367**), another of art works (item **365**), and compiling all documentation on the Manzana de las Luces in Buenos Aires (item **366**). Similar efforts underway in Colombia are exemplified by the catalogs of the colonial town of Mompós (item **368**) and the historic Villa de Leyva zone (item **371**). And in Ecuador, the dean of that nation's colonial art historians has published an inventory of Quito's ecclesiastical architecture (item **383**). Although useful, none of these works give any sense of the aesthetic significance of the structures being surveyed, compiled, or studied. One exception is the book by Ramón Gutiérrez on the Cathedral of Santiago del Estero in Argentina (item **364**) which discusses the historical priority and significance of the cathedral's Salomonic columns. Given the paucity of such works, one should note that an unpublished Master's thesis not seen by this reviewer does attempt the first nationwide coverage of colonial architecture and ornament since Harold E. Wethey's survey of the 1950s (see *HLAS 15: 580*): María Ortuzar's *Non-Spanish influences in the development of the architecture and ornament in the Viceroyalty of Peru: 16th to 18th centuries* (Flinders Univ., South Australia, 1985). Finally, the collected works by the best art historians active in South America today the "dynamic duo" of Mesa and Gisbert, have appeared under one cover: *Arquitectura andina* (item **377a**). Despite the lack of a continuously flowing text, the book is an important contribution that ought to be acquired by interested individuals and libraries.

In spite of the numerical dominance of architectural studies in the field of South American colonial art, those few publications which do examine the representational arts make significant additions to our knowledge. The documentation of the Lima Mannerists by Chichízola Debernardi (item **375**), based on his doctoral dissertation, consists of an excellent and much needed summary. One hopes that this promising scholar of the *arte culto* of Peru will continue to publish, especially on the enigmatic Lima School of the Baroque age, a group of artists which grew out of the seeds planted by the Italian Jesuit Mannerists he so ably examined in his first work. Another author, Francisco Corti (item **360**), uses exemplary art historical methodology to show that a pair of Valencian retablos previously listed as 14th-century pieces by the Argentine museum housing them should be dated two centuries later. A wide range of Indian, folk, and high art from Paraguay is brilliantly presented and organized by Ticio Escobar (item **362**). One looks forward to his analysis of 20th-century materials expected in vol. 3.

Two symposia annotated did not live up to expectations. The Rome meeting devoted to the Latin American Baroque (item **313**) perhaps had too much pomp and too many people involved to be as productive as it could have been. Although the scholarly credentials of many participants were impeccable, their short presentations mostly about their own previous contributions reduced to a minimum the opportunity to present new research or to illustrate unpublished works. Mexico's Instituto de Investigaciones Estéticas (item **287**) held a symposium on ephemeral art, a welcome break from more traditional topics. Nevertheless, the subjects that were discussed hardly merited the attention that was devoted to them and served only to suggest the range of topics still to be investigated.

ARGENTINA AND PARAGUAY

360 Corti, Francisco. Dos tablas valencianas en Santa Fe (UNL/U, 95, enero/abril 1980, p. 125–141, ill.)

Good, focused, art-historical analysis of two early retablo painted panels from Valencia, Spain, now found in the Galisteo Museum of Santa Fe, Argentina. Representing the Annunciation and the Visitation, they now have been carefully dated to the first quarter of the 16th century.

361 Díaz de Raed, Sara. Santiago del Estero: títulos, distinciones, preeminencias. Santiago del Estero, Argentina: El Liberal, 1983. 93, 5 p.: bibl., ill.

More an ecclesiastical history than a history of art; for example, the photo of the Cathedral is identified as 16th century, whereas the text makes evident it is 19th, but does not discuss its neoclassic style.

362 Escobar, Ticio. Una interpretación de las artes visuales en el Paraguay. v. 1–2. Asunción: Centro Cultural Paraguayo Americano, 1982–1984. 2 v.: bibl., ill. (Col. de las Américas; 1–2)

In spite of inexpensive publication and medium-quality illustrations, this book by a college anthropology and philosophy professor offers a refreshing look at the various arts of Paraguay seen from both local and international perspectives. Covers Indian arts, both precolumbian and ethnographic, colonial and 19th-century folk and high arts but not architecture. Vol. 2 will deal with this century. Likeable and readable with good documentary support from previous scholars like Josefina Plá, whom Escobar may replace as the most capable Paraguayan art historian/critic.

363 Gómez-Perasso, José Antonio. Interpretación de estructuras en arqueología histórica: sitio Trinidad, Itapúa,

Paraguay. Asunción: Arte Nuevo Editores, 1984. 1 v.: bibl., ill. (Ensayos de arqueología paraguaya; 2)

Plans of 18th-century mission of Trinidad in southeastern Paraguay and excavations serve to document stone tools used in the *casas de indios* that were clustered around the church.

364 Gutiérrez, Ramón. La Iglesia Catedral de Santiago del Estero: apuntes para su historia arquitectónica (IHAAER/B, 17:27, 1982, p. 135–181, ill.)

Analysis of the history of construction of this Cathedral in north-central Argentina which began with the first mud-wall seat of the Diocese (1570) and culminated with the Baroque stone church (1678–86). Known only through descriptions and sketches, this Cathedral may be the first building in the Americas to use Salomonic columns on its façade. Abandonment and subsequent collapse of the structure led to a new parochial church in neoclassic style (1868–76).

365 Patrimonio artístico nacional: inventario de bienes muebles. Buenos Aires: Academia Nacional de Bellas Artes, 1982. 1 v.: ill. (some col.)

First of a national project of the Argentine academy documenting works of sculpture, painting, and furniture considered to have any artistic merit, listed by city within this province. Each object is described, dated by century and attributed by region of origin; about half are illustrated, some in color.

366 Soulés, María I. *et al.* Manzana de las Luces: Iglesia de San Ignacio, XVII–XX. Buenos Aires: Instituto de Investigaciones Históricas de la Manzana de las Luces Jorge E. Garrido, 1983. 152 p.: bibls., ill.

Continues documentation of historic block in downtown Buenos Aires, focusing this time primarily on the Jesuit church of San Ignacio, built primarily between 1722–34, and discussed by Soulés and Gurrido, with a significant examination of the retablos inside by Héctor Schenone.

367 Viñuales, Graciela María. La Ciudad de Salta y su región. Buenos Aires: Academia Nacional de Bellas Artes, 1983. 177 p.: bibl., ill. (Estudios de arte argentino; 2)

Vol. 2 in monographic series (vol. 1, Jujuy) on Argentine art, sponsored by Academia Nacional de Bellas Artes, on regional centers and their architecture. Handsome book gives settlement history of Salta, general description of its urban fabric, and quick summary of important individual buildings. Includes excellent b/w plates but lacks complete documentation (location, date, size). Few end notes are too brief to serve as reference resources.

COLOMBIA AND VENEZUELA

368 Corradine Angulo, Alberto. Santa Cruz de Mompox: estudio morfológico y reglamentario. 2a ed. Bogotá: Corp. Nacional de Turismo, 1982. 166 p., 13 folded leaves of plates: bibl., ill.

Architect's catalog of buildings and design motifs of beautiful colonial town of Mompós in northern riverine Colombia lacks understanding of stylistic development of architecture in the Western world.

369 Gil Tovar, Francisco. Historia y arte en el Colegio Mayor del Rosario. Fotografías, Luis Mila y Archivo del Colegio Mayor del Rosario. Bogotá: Ediciones Rosaristas, 1982. 197 p.: bibl., ill. (some col.)

Homage to Bogotá's premier prep school, located on the corner of the main plaza and founded in 1654, written by Colombia's best colonial art historian, but marred by a disjointed text, split among history, analyses of 30 major art works, and a b/w catalog of painting, sculpture, and decorative arts.

370 Rivero, Manuel Rafael. Memorias y fantasías de algunas casas de Caracas. Caracas: Academia Nacional de la Historia, 1980. 178 p.: bibl. (El Libro menor; 8)

Cheap paperback, without illustrations or maps, contains gossipy histories of various important buildings in Caracas (e.g., Bolívar's home, colonial governor's residence, home of dictator Páez, Santa Rosa church complex, and government house).

371 Téllez, Germán and Ernesto Moure. Villa de Leyva, Sáchica: zona histórica, estudio analítico y reglamentario. Bogotá: Corp. Nacional de Turismo, 1982. 89 p.: ill.

Careful examination includes measured drawings of each building in the historic zone of north-central Colombia. Documents major periods (colonial, republican, contemporary) and architectural value, but shows marked prejudice in favor of simple vernacular structures over historicizing styles.

Zapatero, Juan Manuel. Historia de las fortalezas de Santa Marta y estudio asesor para su restauración. See item **2686.**

PERU, ECUADOR AND BOLIVIA

372   Azevedo, Paulo O.D. de. Cusco, ciudad histórica: continuidad y cambio. S.l.: Proyecto Regional de Patrimonio Cultural, PNDU, UNESCO: Promoción Editorial Inca S.A., 1982. 177 p.: ill.

Brazilian architect who specializes in restoration attempts to trace the evolution of the city of Cuzco, Peru, from its role as the capital of the Inca Empire through the colonial era up to the present. Work's value is reduced by over-reliance on secondary sources and very cheap publication.

373   Bernales Ballesteros, Jorge. Las pinturas murales de la Quinta del Prado (IRA/B, 12, 1982/1983, p. 29–39, ill., photos)

Continues investigation of history of painting in Lima (begun 1979) by examining murals in "Quinta del Prado," constructed as a recreational center in 1762 but now in ruins. Photos of murals are fair. [R.J. Mullen]

374   Castillo Venero, Carlos. Cuzco: patrones de asentamientos. Lima: Colegio de Arquitectos del Perú, 1983. 152 p.: bibl., ill. (Col. Bienales de arquitectura)

Publication of architect's 1970 thesis for National Engineering Univ. of Lima, illustrated with his own drawings. Includes good summary of others' analysis of settlement patterns in Cuzco area, from precolumbian formative through colonial period.

375   Chichízola Debernardi, José. El manierismo en Lima. Lima: Pontificia Univ. Católica del Perú, Fondo Editorial, 1983. 243 p., 47 leaves of plates: ill. (some col.), photos.

Based on author's doctoral dissertation (Univ. of Seville, 1975). Excellent scholarly text documents relationship of Seville and Lima during the late 16th-early 17th centuries, focusing especially on carved wooden

choir stalls and the paintings of four Italian Jesuits: Bitti, Pérez de Alesio, Medoro, and Morón. Fine art historical analysis marred by poor photographs, including blurry and inaccurate color.

Descalzi, Ricardo. La Real Audiencia de Quito: claustro de los Andes. See item **2694.**

Estabridis Cárdenas, Ricardo. El grabado colonial en Lima. See item **2741.**

376   Kennedy Troya, Alexandra and **Alfonso Ortiz Crespo.** Convento de San Diego de Quito: historia y restauración. Quito: Museo del Banco Central del Ecuador, 1982. 365 p.: bibl., ill. (some col.)

Primary documentation and history obtained from Franciscan archives, of a major work of architecture. Depicts its 1978 restoration in fine photos, both b/w and color, but sculpture and painting are poorly covered.

377   Martínez Borrero, Juan. La pintura popular del Carmen: identidad y cultura en el siglo XVIII. Cuenca, Ecuador: Centro Interamericano de Artesanías y Artes Populares, 1983. 271 p.: bibl., ill. (some col.), index.

Important complete publication of significant late 18th-century mural painting from major nunnery in Cuenca, Ecuador. Painting reveals life at various levels of society, analyzed from a Marxist perspective. Also analyzes Chapel of Susudel (1752), 92 km south of Cuenca.

377a   Mesa, José de and **Teresa Gisbert.** Arquitectura andina, 1530–1830: historia y análisis. La Paz: Embajada de España en Bolivia, 1985. 376 p., 104 p. of plates: bibl., ill., indexes (Col. Arzans y Vela)

Cheaply printed compilation of major articles of the last 20 years (1965–83) by the most capable pair of art historians of South America, including five unpublished studies. Covers Spanish Viceroyalty of Peru, from Bogotá to northwest Argentina, focusing on highlands of Peru and Bolivia (their homeland), but including one study of Antigua Guatemala. Subjects include Italian Renaissance pattern books and their impact, especially in circular architectural plans and San Ignacio de Bogotá; atriums and posas and open chapels in the Andes; Baroque retablos and their impact on façades; the "mestizo style" and its manifestation in the 18th century; and neoclassic architecture in Bolivia.

378 **Mesa, Jose de** and **Teresa Gisbert.** La platería monumental en la región del Lago Titicaca: el frontal (UB/HC, 6, oct. 1984, p. 87–101, ill.)

Documentation of 18th-century silver frontispieces to altars in Puno dept., Peru, and La Paz dept., Bolivia.

379 **Rojas Silva, David V.** "El León y la Sierpe:" una alegoría andina del siglo XVIII (SBH/HC, 5, abril 1984, p. 49–62, ill.)

Iconographic analysis of painted cloth which portrays a mythological battle between a lion (puma) and a dragon (winged serpent), representing two branches of the surviving Inca royalty, from which the Tupac Amaru rebellion arose in 1782. The cloth was painted no more than 10 years later.

380 **San Cristóbal, Antonio.** El retablo de la Concepción en la Catedral de Lima (PMNH/HC, 15, 1982, p. 91–108)

Documentary evidence from the Archivo General de la Nación, Lima, proves that this retablo, previously attributed to various named joiners (and inexplicably not illustrated with the article), was done by Asencio de Salas (1654–56).

381 **Stastny M., Francisco.** *Jardín Universitario* y *Stella Maris*: invenciones iconográficas en el Cuzco (PMNH/HC, 15, 1982, p. 141–160, ill.)

Technical discussion of fine points of Marian iconology which was employed in Cuzco-School painting from the latter 17th century and continued into the 18th as a means of political infighting between the Univ. of San Antonio Abad and some religious orders.

382 **Tord, Luis Enrique.** Templos coloniales del Colca-Arequipa. Presentación de Fernando Belaúnde Terry. Lima: Industrial Papelera Atlas, 1983. 168 p.: bibl., ill. (chiefly col.), index.

Sumptuous publication with good color photographs of 16 very provincial churches in the "mestizo style" of southern Peru, associated with the Collagua Indians. Historian author provides poor documentation and dating about buildings and no measured drawings.

383 **Vargas, José María.** La Iglesia y el patrimonio cultural ecuatoriano. Quito: Ediciones de la Univ. Católica, 1982. 149 p., 24 leaves of plates: bibl., ill. (some col.), photos.

Inventory by the dean of colonial Ecuadorian art historians of the architecture of Quito arranged by building and its contents. Focuses on documents rather than forms or styles, with very little discussion of sculpture and painting found within. Photos are mediocre and unrelated to the text.

384 **Viñuales, Graciela** and **Ramón Gutiérrez.** Arquitectura en Moquegua (PMNH/HC, 15, 1982, p. 69–89)

Historical data, from 16th century to present, of major buildings in this city in southern Peru. Outlines activities of Jesuits, Mercerdarians, Franciscans. [R.J. Mullen]

19th and 20th Centuries

LEONARD FOLGARAIT, *Assistant Professor of Fine Arts, Vanderbilt University*

THE LITERATURE ON MEXICAN ART annotated for this volume of *HLAS* is once again the most numerous with 17 works. Next in order of frequency are Colombia with six contributions, Argentina with five, and Chile, Nicaragua, and Venezuela with two each. These totals are representative of trends noted over the last five years and do not indicate any geographical shift. The single surprise is Nicaragua, the focus of so much attention in recent years as noted in other sections of *HLAS*. Much less than expected has been published on the modern art of this nation, even taking into account the fact that research there is logistically complicated and hazardous outside of major cities.

Among works on the art of Mexico published in recent years, one should single out two studies, one devoted to José Clemente Orozco (item **389**) and another to Juan O'Gorman (item **403**). The result of original research, both works provide a general reassessment of the importance of these artists. Finally, a number of works annotated below concern very current Mexican art, a subject that is usually neglected (see items **387, 392, 394, 398, 401,** and **402**).

With regard to other Spanish American countries, one should single out a major contribution: the comprehensive biography of Cuban surrealist Wifredo Lam by Antonio Núñez Jiménez (item **409**), a work in which the balancing of material history vis-à-vis the subjectivities of aesthetics is exemplary.

Another notable publication is James Findlay's *Modern Latin American art: a bibliography* (item **386**), a compilation in which the clear selection criteria as well as the overall organization make it a most efficient reference tool. One can safely predict that this work will become a much consulted source.

To conclude, one can state that among works annotated below, the overall trend is toward documentation and away from theoretically based methodology. There is much emphasis in accumulating facts and images, a sort of archaeological gathering for which there is a great need at present. Nevertheless, such a tendency developing in a vacuum for its own sake can easily deteriorate into a cult of the art object per se, dressing it up for the art market. Thus, a rigorous application of revisionist methodology is required to counteract the meaningless stockpiling of art information for information's sake. It will interesting to anticipate if, how and when such an application develops.

GENERAL

385 Bienal Nacional de Artes Visuales, 2nd, Caracas, 1983. Segunda Bienal Nacional de Artes Visuales. Caracas: Museo de Arte Contemporáneo de Caracas, 1983. 127 p.: ill., photos (Catálogo; 61)

Consists of 127 artists of every medium whose representative works are documented with photographs. Also includes photos of artists themselves, brief biographical chronology, and in most cases, an extended statement of purpose. Well organized and presented research tool.

Estudios sobre la ciudad iberoamericana. See item **1783**.

386 Findlay, James A. Modern Latin American art: a bibliography. Westport, Conn.: Greenwood Press, 1983. 301 p.: index (Art reference col., 0193–6867; 3)

Over 2,000 entries are arranged first by country and then by medium. Entries include exhibition catalogs but due to self-imposed limitations, the bibliography does not include monographs or articles on individual artists. Nevertheless, this is a very important work, chiefly because of its otherwise comprehensive coverage. Highly recommended.

MEXICO

387 Acha, Juan. Hersúa: obras/escultura, persona/sociedad. México: UNAM, Coordinación de Humanidades, 1983. 207 p.: bibl., ill. (some col.)

Book of mixed quality about one of the major Mexican sculptors of recent times. Despite author's very subjective and impressionistic writing, the book has two chapters that are historically rigorous, one on the political course of Mexican society (1940–82), and another on sculpture produced during that time. Includes excellent color photos and a welcome and detailed biographical chronology.

388 Bolívar en México: Museo Nacional de Historia, Castillo de Chapultepec, 24 de julio/31 octubre. México: El Museo, 1983. 35 p.: ill. (some col.)

Real value of this catalog lies in the essay and illustrations concerning the Fernando Leal mural on the subject of Bolívar in the Anfiteatro Bolívar, painted in 1930–42. Rarely do we see and read such a clear exposition of a muralist's working methods.

389 Cardoza y Aragón, Luis *et al.* Orozco: una relectura. Presentación de Octavio

Rivero Serrano. México: UNAM, Instituto de Investigaciones Estéticas, 1983. 255 p., 68 p. of plates (some folded): bibl., ill. (some col.), index.

Eight Orozco specialists update scholarship on the centennial of the artist's birth. As expected, essays are of the congratulatory sort, welcoming the opportunity to celebrate Orozco's work and personality. Only the essays by Azuela, Eder, and Barnitz rise above this level to offer critical revisionism. Provides very good collection of new documents and illustrations of rarely seen works.

390 Covantes, Hugo; María Eugenia Rodríguez; and Esther Vázquez Ramos. El grabado mexicano en el siglo XX, 1922–1981. México: Orbe Impresora, 1982. 256 p., 112 p. of plates: bibl., ill., index.

Valuable research tool is divided into a sensible essay on the subject, a long and detailed chronology, many biographical profiles, a section on technique, and a short but pertinent bibliography. Although mediocre, the illustrations complement well the data contained in this most useful book.

391 Cuevas, José Luis. Marzo, mes de José Luis Cuevas: presencia del artista en México y en el extranjero. México: M.A. Porrúa, 1982. 57 p.: bibl., film., ill. (some col.)

In March of 1982, over 1,000 recent works by Cuevas were exhibited in various galleries in Mexico City and abroad (Barcelona, Milan, San Diego, to name only a few). This catalog documents the events, features a deeply subjective essay by Jorge Ruiz Dueñas, includes some excellent reproductions, and a very complete list of the artist's exhibitions, prizes, and illustrated books. Most important is an extensive bibliography.

392 Deffis Caso, Armando. Oficio de arquitectura: práctica profesional en México. México: Editora Serantes, 1981. 189 p.: ill., photos, plans.

This is probably the best overview of current architectural practice in Mexico. Over 90 projects of every category, including planning, are included with complete statistical documentation, photographs, plans, and descriptive essays. Book provides ample and detailed information, ready for incorporation into historical or theoretical contexts.

393 Fernández, Justino. El arte del siglo XIX en México. 3a ed. México: UNAM,

1983. 256 p., 214 p. of plates: bibl., ill. (some col.)

Third ed. of 1962 classic. Although it is still the most complete treatment of the period, the reader should be warned of the by now rather dated methodology. As author states: "I insist that this book . . . consider a selection of art works from a critical sensibility, in order to perform my own historical interpretation." Includes best collection of illustrations (22 color and 343 b/w) of such materials available in one book. Scant but useful notes and bibliography.

394 Folgarait, Leonard. Murals and marginality in Mexico City: the case of Arte Acá (Art History [Routledge & K. Paul, London] 9:1, March 1986, p. 55–76, ill.)

The ghetto of Tepito in Mexico City has recently been the subject of an attempted "reconstruction," a massive material and cultural transformation directed by city planners. Citizens of Tepito, a few of whom formed the group Arte Acá at this time, saw this plan as a threat to the survival of the ghetto and resisted its implementation. The murals produced by Arte Acá can be explained as signs of a marginalized society asserting itself politically against its own elimination.

395 Homenaje a Juan O'Gorman, 1905–1982: Palacio de la Antigua Escuela de Medicina, junio-agosto 1983. México: UNAM, Coordinación de Extensión Universitaria, 1983. 47 p.: ill. (some col.)

Catalog of important exhibition that affirms O'Gorman's position as being at the center rather than the periphery of 20th-century Mexican art. Especially revealing are his architectural projects that demonstrate how he spanned a pluralistic spectrum from precolumbian revivals to uncompromising modernism. Informative essays provide good account of his development.

396 La Iconografía en el arte contemporáneo: coloquio internacional de Xalapa. México: UNAM, 1982. 248 p., 31 p. of plates: ill. (Estudio de arte y estética; 16)

Nine essays of mixed quality range from considerations of the philosophy of creativity to serious archaeology of prehispanic influences on modern Mexican muralism. Especially noteworthy are the essays by Ida Rodríguez Prampolini, Xavier Moyssen, and

Beatriz de la Fuente. Of special interest are the commentaries after each essay.

397 José Clemente Orozco: antología crítica. Recopilación con comentarios de Teresa del Conde. México: UNAM, Instituto de Investigaciones Estéticas, 1982 [i.e. 1983]. 158 p., 1 leaf of plates: bibl., port (Cuadernos de historia del arte; 13)

Most valuable collection of documents about the central issues of Orozco's work. Many items have been unavailable before. Introductory essay is lucid and straightforward. The only disappointment is a rather cursory bibliography.

398 Mexican art of the 1970s: images of displacement. Edited and with an introduction by Leonard Folgarait. Nashville: Center for Latin American and Iberian Studies, Vanderbilt Univ., 1984. 67 p.: ill. (Monographs on Latin American and Iberian studies; 1)

This introduction and six essays (J.A. Hellman, A. Pérez Gómez, H. Escobedo, E. Acevedo, M. Benavídez and K. Vozoff, and C.J. Mora) seek to define the historical context for and the development of five different modes of art production during the 1970s in Mexico and in Los Angeles. Methodologies are derived from political science, social history, autobiography, material culture, and journalism/oral history. This anthology only begins the serious work of filling a large gap in the bibliography for this subject.

399 Morais, Frederico. Mathias Goeritz. México: UNAM, Coordinación de Humanidades, Laboratorio de Experimentación en Arte Urbano, 1982. 159 p.: bibl., ill. (some col.), index.

Useful treatment of German-born artist consists of short, non-analytical text, most biographical. Updated bibliography is followed by over 200 good illustrations. Still, a truly rigorous work on Goeritz as yet to be done. This slim treatment merely holds the old pattern, but is welcome as a practical reference.

400 Moreno, Salvador. El pintor Antonio Fabrés. México: Instituto de Investigaciones Estéticas, UNAM, 1981. 226 p.: bibl., ill. (some col.) (Monografías. Serie mayor; 3)

Fabrés was instrumental in promoting academic realism in Mexico in the second half of the 19th century. It is his crucial role

in this context which is charted by this book. The biographical essays are short and sensible. Of real interest are many letters from the artist to those in his circle. Well illustrated, especially in regard to his little known sculpture.

401 Paz, Octavio. Pintura mexicana contemporánea (VUELTA, 83:7, nov. 1983, p. 52–54)

Catalog essay to the exhibit *Ocho pintores mexicanos* (Madrid, Nov. 1983). Paz attempts to explain Mexican modernism as an outgrowth of and reaction to modernist developments in Paris and New York. Rather than analyze the works on display, he poses and answers the question that interests him: "Can one be an artist of one's own time and country when that country is Mexico?"

402 Ponce, José Bernardo. José Luis Cuevas, ¿genio o farsante?: charlas con el polémico pintor. México: Signos, 1983. 125 p. (Col. Papiro. Serie Entrevistas)

This book pits an astute journalist and a proud and "polemical" artist against each other. The 26 short sections range in subject from pure aesthetics to pure politics, but mostly a provocative mix of the two. This is must reading for Cuevas scholars and for anyone interested in how expressionism of this sort finds its rationale in Mexico.

403 Rodríguez Prampolini, Ida. Juan O'Gorman: arquitecto y pintor. México: UNAM, 1982. 258 p., 29 p. of plates: ill. (some col.)

Rather than apply the traditional narrative biography format, author presents nine short essays, dealing with special aspects of O'Gorman's architecture and painting. Book's second half is devoted to the artist's writings and to a generous selection of illustrations of work in every genre. Important and necessary book, but conspicuously lacking in documentation and bibliography.

404 Rodríguez Prampolini, Ida. El surrealismo y el arte fantástico de México. 2a ed. México: UNAM, Instituto de Investigaciones Estéticas, 1983. 133 p., 142 p. of plates: bibl., ill. (some col.)

Very welcome reissue of 1969 original. Author's writing is noted for its clear and deliberate development of ideas in and through history. Offers long explanation of European sources that is persuasive and precise. This is a model of Mexican art historical scholarship, although the bibliography is by now outdated.

CENTRAL AMERICA
Nicaragua

405 Arellano, Jorge Eduardo. Aportes a la historia del arte en Nicaragua. Managua: Ediciones del *Boletín Nicaragüense de Bibliografía y Documentación,* 1982. 120, 87 p.: bibls., ill.

Book's last third is devoted to the modern period. Coverage is encyclopedic in method, touching on as many developments as possible in a few pages. Although superficial out of necessity, the writing is clear, to the point, and well documented. Illustrations are poor, but the bibliography is substantial and up-to-date.

406 Traba, Marta. Mirar en Nicaragua (El Pez y la Serpiente [Editorial Unión, Managua] 25, invierno 1981, p. 27–86)

As author notes in her introduction, Nicaraguan 20th-century painting has been ignored systematically by most "comprehensive" treatments of Latin American art. Author's approach is within the context of contemporary poetry and activities of vanguard magazines, an inter-disciplinary perspective that effectively traces the motives of Nicaragua's modernist culture.

THE CARIBBEAN
Cuba

407 Juan, Adelaida de. Las artes plásticas en Cuba socialista (*in* La Cultura en Cuba socialista. La Habana: Editorial Letras Cubanas, 1982, p. 35–62)

Author's two main theses are: 1) that after the 1959 Revolution, Cuba's various media experienced extraordinary formal changes as compared to the past; and 2) that graphics and the cinema in particular emerged with particular assertiveness. After setting the political context for post-revolutionary cultural production, the essay surveys major figures and movements in an encyclopedic fashion. Includes much important material.

408 Mosquera, Gerardo. Exploraciones en la plástica cubana. La Habana: Letras Cubanas, 1983. 472 p. (Col. Espiral)

Mostly a personalized account of recent Cuban art, the book also digresses often and with good results to the art of the island's first inhabitants and to contemporary folk art. Commentary is concise and full of historical data. Includes several chapters on individual artists, such as Flavio Garciandia and Tomás Sánchez. No illustrations.

409 Núñez Jiménez, Antonio. Wifredo Lam. La Habana: Editorial Letras Cubanas, 1982. 280 p.: bibl., port.

This is the definitive biography of Lam, the story of a politicized artist over and above considerations of the development of his art. Author's approach is correct given his subject's life of intense and constant commitment. Despite the inevitable political bias of some sections, the narrative is very serviceable. Includes special section (30 p.) with long bibliography and complete exhibition history.

SOUTH AMERICA
Colombia and Venezuela

410 Artes gráficas. Coordinación de Gloria Peña de Kahn. Bogotá: Litografía Arco, 1983. 77 leaves, 77 leaves of plates: ill. (some col.) (Panorama artístico colombiano; 4)

Large and sumptuous book is vol. 4 of the monographic series *Panorama artístico colombiano.* Features 77 artists with separate entries including critical essay, short biography, and large, well-printed reproductions. Well balanced selection serves as an excellent introduction to its subject.

411 Goldberg, Mariano. Guía de edificaciones contemporáneas en Venezuela: trabajo de ascenso en el escalafón universitario. v. 1, Caracas. Caracas: Facultad de Arquitectura y Urbanismo, Univ. Central de Venezuela, 1980. 1 v.: bibl., ill.

Essentially a source book of facts and images, it includes profiles of more than 150 building projects. Drawings, photographs, technical information, and brief descriptions accompany each entry. Important primary source material for researchers.

412 Grau, Enrique. Enrique Grau. Curador de la exposición y director de la investigación, Germán Rubiano Caballero. Bogotá: Centro Colombo-Americano: Fondo Cultural Cafetero, 1983. 168 p.: appendices, bibl., ill. (some col.)

Exhibit catalog that transcends that category as the single best treatment of this major Colombian artist. Achieves its intended comprehensiveness by presenting a broad sample of the many media treated by Grau. Each period in his life is well researched and explained by straightforward essays. Appendices list every document related to Grau's life and work. Includes well selected bibliography and high quality illustrations.

413 Samper Pizano, Daniel; Juan Acha; and Jesse Fernández. Negret: uno, dos y tres. Bogotá: Italgraf, 1983. 290 p.: ill. (some col.), photos, ports.

Curious combination of overly intimate and indulgent hero-worship with valuable information and documentation on this important modernist Colombian sculptor. The critical writing is dreamy and vague, but the abundance of documentary photos and illustrations of his work make this a key book on this subject.

414 Rubiano Caballero, Germán. Escultura colombiana del siglo XX. Bogotá: Fondo Cultural Cafetero, 1983. 203 p., 80 p. of plates: bibls., ill., index (Ediciones Fondo Cultural Cafetero; 17)

Traditionally minded and sympathetic account of its subject. No special appeal apart from its utility as a solid research tool. Several interesting indexes include a list of the artist's sculpture prizes awarded since 1940.

La Vivienda multifamiliar: Caracas, 1940–1970. See *HLAS* 47:3509.

Peru and Chile

415 Aguiló M., Osvaldo. Propuestas neo-vanguardistas en la plástica chilena: antecedentes y contexto. Santiago: Centro de Indagación y Expresión Cultural y Artística (CENECA), 1983. 40, 1 p., 9 leaves of plates: bibl., ill. (Documento de trabajo; 27)

Book includes very important essay tracing the development and eventual disappearance of the "neo-vanguardistas" in Chile (1970–82). Examined in the context of the political upheavals of the same period, these artistic works are presented as specialized manifestations of an entire culture of political commitment. The only such treatment of this subject, this book should be read by all those interested in the topic.

Campos Narduccim, Mariano. La Iglesia de la Preciosa Sangre: aproximación al centenario de su edificación. See item **3120**.

416 Carvacho Herrera, Víctor. Historia de la escultura en Chile. Santiago: Editorial Andrés Bello, 1983. 328 p.: bibl., ill. (some col.), index.

Work has all the virtues and problems of a survey treatment. The historical scope is from pre-history to present, and the excellent illustrations are well chosen. In spite of the intent to generalize, the writing is very instructive. It establishes a coherent historical context and is straightforward in description and analysis.

Chambi, Martín. Martín Chambi: fotografía del Perú, 1920–1950. See item **3028**.

417 Rodríguez Cobos, Luis. Arquitectura limeña: paisajes de una utopía. Lima: Colegio de Arquitectos del Perú, 1983. 98 p.: bibl., ill. (Col. bienal)

Interesting examination by decades of neoclassic and modern architecture in Lima, featuring several revivals of colonial and pre-columbian styles, marred by cheap publication and gritty photos. [J.F. Scott]

Schweitzer Lopetegui, Angela *et al.* Recuperación de patrimonio turístico: Cerro Santo Domingo de Valparaíso. See *HLAS* 47:5162.

Argentina, Paraguay and Uruguay

418 Blinder, Olga; Josefina Plá; and Ticio Escobar. Arte actual en el Paraguay, 1900–1980: antecedentes y desarrollo del proceso en las artes plásticas. Asunción: Ediciones IDAP, 1983. 195 p.: ill.

Includes three long historical essays by the authors that are sensible and synthetic. Includes illustrations of more than 100 works in several media, 14 critical essays by other contributors reprinted from original sources, and chronological biographies. Well organized and relevant volume.

Boronat, J. Yolanda and Marta R. Risso. Román Fresneda Siri: un arquitecto uruguayo. See item **3351**.

419 Escultores argentinos del siglo XX.
v. 5. Buenos Aires: Centro Editor de
América Latina, 1982. 1 v.: bibls., ill. (some
col.), plates (col. and b/w)

Large volume features 16 sculptors.
Each artist is covered by a long critical essay,
narrative and chronological history, testimonials, bibliography, and many excellent
b/w and color plates. The writing is rigorous
and aimed at a straightforward historical
presentation.

420 Fotógrafos argentinos del siglo XX.
Buenos Aires: Centro Editor de América Latina, 1982. 256 p.: bibls., ill. (some
col.)

Highlights 10 photographers who have
worked since mid-century. Each entry includes critical essay, artist's statement, short
biography, notes, and bibliography. Professional, well produced volume, it will interest
scholars of photography and photographic
criticism.

421 Nessi, Angel Osvaldo. El arte en La
Plata y su resonancia nacional
(UNLP/R, 26, 1979/1980, p. 95–107, bibl.,
ill.)

Short but articulate essay traces the
development of painting and graphics since
the 1920s. At once objectively encyclopedic
and wryly critical, the author covers a lot of
ground and issues, such as the difference between public and private patronage, the dark
intricacies of the art market, and differences
between nationalism and folklorism. A
meaty and pleasurable read.

422 Perazzo, Nelly. El arte concreto en la
Argentina en la década del 40. Buenos
Aires: Ediciones de Arte Gaglianone, 1983.
211 p.: bibls., ill. (some col.)

In Argentina in the 1940s, *arte concreto* was a hybrid version of modernism.
The story of its strategies to adopt and adapt
the European avant-garde tradition makes for
interesting reading. Book balances the questions of nationalism vs. internationalism
with tact. Includes many documentary
photographs and long bibliography.

423 Rodríguez, Ernesto B. Visiones de
la escultura argentina. Buenos Aires:
Academia Nacional de Bella Artes, 1983.
105 p.: ill.

Although very general in both writing
and illustrations and not designed for the specialized researcher, this is a useful work for
library collections.

424 Squirru, Rafael F. Arte argentino hoy:
una selección de 48 artistas. Buenos
Aires: Ediciones de Arte Gaglianone, 1983.
201 p.: ill. (some col.) (Col. Unión Carbide)

Primarily a source book, this volume
includes entries on 48 artists of different media. Entries consist of short critical essay,
hand-scripted statement by the artist (many
illegible, a silly tribute to "subjectivity"),
short biography, and large single, excellent
color reproductions. Data and images are
very useful, but the criticism does not get beyond blandness.

BRAZIL

JOSÉ M. NEISTEIN, *Executive Director, Brazilian-American Cultural Institute*

THE OVERWHELMING MAJORITY OF BOOKS reviewed for this *HLAS* volume
are devoted to 20th-century Brazilian art. There are, however, many titles of great
interest on other periods and topics. Annotated below are books whose permanent
record value was determined because of scholarly, iconographical, cultural, or historical reasons.

Questions concerning heritage, modernity, and power are discussed in items
434 and **437**. *História geral da arte no Brasil* (item **432**) is the best study of its kind
to date, and will appeal both to art historians and the general public. The exhibition *Tradição e ruptura* (item **436**) presents a unique, all encompassing view. There

is also a compilation of essays on the controversies of craftsmanship in contemporary society (item **435**). Two books offer a good—if at times somewhat incomplete—view of the sources and development of Catholic sacred art in Brazil (items **427** and **433**). With the exception of Germain Bazin's classic (item **439**), now published in Portuguese and updated, most publications on the colonial art of Brazil included below are somewhat lacking in scholarship.

The still neglected 19th century is represented by a fine monograph on Belmiro de Almeida (item **450**) and a good study of Veiga Valle (item **451**), a lesser known but remarkable *santos* maker from Goiás. Other works on the 19th-century studies are included because of their reproductions.

Despite their proliferation, very few publications on 20th-century Brazilian art are of true scholarly interest. The majority bear witness to the diversity of the nation's modern art, and attest to the continually rising level of the printing craft in Brazil, an improvement that can be attributed both to technological advances and to the large support of private foundations and business. Some, though, succeed in writing both fine printing and scholarship. Examples of this trend are books such as: *Ismael Nery, 50 anos depois* (item **465**), *Sérgio de Camargo* (item **455**), *Tempos de Guerra* (item **456**), *Mario Zanini e seu tempo* (item **454**), and *Menotti del Picchia* (item **464**).

Several fine monographs on architecture included below focus on different aspects and periods of building in Brazil. A work that should be singled out as a "tour de force" is *A Arquitetura da imigração alemã* in Rio Grande do Sul (item **491**). Another study of Rio Grande do Sul is item **484**. Also worthwhile are an examination of the architecture of the city of São Paulo (item **492**) and a work on the impact that Le Corbusier's presence had on Brazil (item **485**)

Cecília Meireles's drawings of Brazilian folklore will constitute a revelation for younger generations (item **475**). Two major folk artists are also the subject of intense study: Antônio de Oliveira (item **476**) and Guarany (item **479**).

The long overdue Museu Afro-Brasileiro (item **496**) has finally been established and is now open to the public.

Only four books on photography are annotated below, but all are relevant because of their comprehensiveness or particular focus (items **480, 481, 482,** and **483**). Under the subheading "Miscellaneous," are grouped publications as varied and stimulating as *Comunicação, notícias de Cabral à informática* (item **499**), the contribution of Italian painters to art in Brazil (item **509**), and a book that celebrates the 35th anniversary of the *Museu de Arte de São Paulo*. The most important institution of its kind in Latin America and one of the most active in Brazil, the Museum's commemoration is of great significance because of the institution's cultural contribution to the nation and to Latin America as a whole (items **502** and **508**). Finally, there is a splendid book about João Marino's collection which can serve as a very fine introduction to the past and present art of Brazil (item **506**).

REFERENCE AND THEORETICAL WORKS

425 Amaral, Aracy A. Arte para quê?: a preocupação social na arte brasileira, 1930–1970: subsídio para uma história social da arte no Brasil. São Paulo: Nobel, 1984. 435 p.: bibl., facsims., ill.

Main subjects: the dilemma of art's dysfunction; emergence of political consciousness in the artistic milieu; the 1940s as a dividing line; post-war generation; experience of printmaking clubs; realism vs. abstraction and the impact of São Paulo's Biennial; polemics on the social function of architecture; the 1960s: from art that serves the community to art of galleries. Includes extensive bibliography, many *facsimiles*, and b/w reproductions. Comparative chronology: Brazil, Latin America, other continents.

426 Andrade, Mário de. A imagem de Mário: textos extraídos da obra. Introdução de Telê Porto Ancona Lopez. Rio de Janeiro: Edições Alumbramento, 1984. 181 p.: bibl., ill. (some col.), ports. (some col.)

Includes texts, iconography, and a broad biographical sketch of the intellectual leader of his generation, a source of inspiration to subsequent generations in Brazil. The artist appears in his many incarnations as poet, novelist, art critic, literary critic, ethnologist, musicologist, collector, cultural leader, and one of the protagonists of the "Week of Modern Art" in 1922. Based on documentation drawn from the Mário de Andrade Archive, Univ. of São Paulo. A sensitive and well informed team led by Telê Ancona Lopez has issued this excellent self-portrait of the multiple Mários.

427 Artistas de Pernambuco. José Cláudio, comp. Recife: Governo de Pernambuco, 1982. 221 p.: bibl., ill.

Introductory text underscores the point that the presence of Dutch artists in 17th-century Pernambuco constitutes a new chapter in Brazilian art rather than an episode of Dutch art abroad. Also discusses Portuguese, English, French, and German 18th- and 19th-century artists. Book makes clear the great variety and significance of 20th-century Pernambuco's contribution to Brazilian art. Identifies these artists and includes their work but without description or analysis. B/w reproductions only.

428 Canabrava, Ilka. As imagens do povo e o espaço vazio da arte/educação: um estudo sobre Antônio Poteiro. Brasília: Senado Federal, 1984. 150 p.: bibl., ill. (some col.), ports. (some col.)

Work that explores how to develop artistic education within formal education. Human social reality becomes whole and establishes an interaction net when such reality is expressed. Author checks her theory through "a case study:" the ceramist and naïve painter Antônio Poteiro (e.g., relationship to reality, his life, aspects of his creativity, paintings and sculpture, his contribution to education). Author assumes Poteiro's paintings and sculpture are material represen-

tations of his poetic work. She did research in his studio, interviewed him, recorded and photographed his output (1977–81). Towards end she asks: "Shouldn't school preserve in each child the magic, intuitive, creative background, ultimately the poetic sensibility?" Bibliography. English abstracts.

429 Do simbolismo aos antecedentes de 22: Fundação Casa de Rui Barbosa, Rio de Janeiro, Sala de Exposições, 1° de outubro a 3 de novembro de 1982: Secretaria de Estado da Cultura e do Esporte do Paraná, Universidade Federal do Paraná, Sala Miguel Bakun, 17 de novembro a 12 de dezembro de 1982. Curitiba: A Secretaria, 1982. 62 p.: bibl., ill. (some col.)

Examines the "Week of Modern Art" of 1922 from the perspective of the dissolution of symbolist renovation. Illustrates visual aspects of symbolism and the "decadent" poets in order to show where and how Modernism connects with them. An interesting thesis that is not well articulated.

430 Etzel, Eduardo. Arte sacra, berço da arte brasileira. Fotografias e desenhos de Manuel Grau Fontova. São Paulo: Melhoramentos: Instituto Nacional do Livro, Fundação Nacional Pró-Memória, 1984. 256 p.: bibl., ill. (some col.)

Study covers virtually all religious art of the Roman Catholic Church in Brazil. Also includes special chapters on the contribution of blacks to religious folk art. Author's main point: such religious art is the basis of all Brazilian art. Etzel conducted research throughout Brazil. Includes bibliography, many drawings and reproductions in color and b/w.

431 Guia dos bens tombados: Minas Gerais. Coordenação e pesquisa, Wladimir Alves de Souza. Prefácio de Tancredo Neves. Rio de Janeiro: Expressão e Cultura, 1984. 447 p.: bibl., ill.

Guide to the state's landmarks opens with alphabetical listing of main sites and monuments. Architecture, sculpture, palaces, fountains, ornaments, farms and farm houses, markets, landscapes and cityscapes are illustrated by several artists with pen-and-ink drawings. Provides detailed description of major landmarks. Minas's highest percentage of Brazil's historical and artistic landmarks, protected by federal, state, and municipal laws, constitutes one of the richest concentrations in the country. Includes preface by late President Tancredo Neves concerning the conservation and revitalization of this wealth, and a historical introduction by Alcídio Mafra de Souza. Glossary and bibliography.

432 História geral da arte no Brasil. Walter Zanini, coordenação e direção editorial. Cacilda Teixeira da Costa, pesquisa, assistência editorial e coordenação técnica. Marília Saboya de Albuquerque, pesquisa e assistência editorial. São Paulo: Instituto Walther Moreira Salles: Fundação Djalma Guimarães, 1983. 2 v. (1116 p.): bibl., ill. (some col.), indexes.

This splendid team of 16 highly qualified scholars and designers deserves much credit for this work, the most complete overall view of and introduction to the history of art in Brazil to date. Two lavishly illustrated volumes cover the following art periods and styles: pre-colonial (including archaeology); Indian works; 16th to beginning of the 19th centuries: Mannerism, Baroque and rococo; 17th century and Dutch Brazil; painters of Count Nassau-Siegen; 19th century; transition and beginning of 20th century; artnouveau, Modernism, eclecticism and industrialism; contemporary art; contemporary architecture; photography; industrial design; visual communication; Afro-Brazilian works; crafts; art and education. Highly recommended.

433 Museu de Arte Sacra de São Paulo. O Museu de Arte Sacra de São Paulo. Editor, Antônio de Oliveira Godinho. Texto de Carlos A.C. Lemos, João Marino, José Geraldo Nogueira Moutinho. Fotografias, Romulo Fialdini. São Paulo: Banco Safra, 1983. 269 p.: ill. (some col.)

One of the very finest of its kind in Brazil, and for that matter one of the finest anywhere, this Museum houses a collection of more than 10,000 pieces. Most represent the history of Roman Catholic religious art in Brazil, from the early 16th to late 19th centuries. Also includes many European examples. A special feature of this handsomely printed book is the reproduction of pieces permanently on display (e.g., over 500). Detailed catalog. List of donors. Many color reproductions.

434 Produzindo o passado: estratégias de construção do patrimônio cultural.

Organização de Antônio Augusto Arantes. São Paulo: Brasiliense: Secretaria de Estado da Cultura, Conselho de Defesa do Patrimônio Histórico, Arqueológico, Artístico e Turístico do Estado (CONDEPHAAT), 1984. 225 p.: bibl.

Collection of papers and discussions drawn from seminar (São Paulo, Aug. 1983) devoted to theoretical principles of preservation and to transmission of a cultural heritage, in the Brazilian context. Of special interest are the following works: "Revitalização da Capela de São Miguel Paulista," "A Casa das Retortas," "Ouro Preto e Mariana," and "O Caso Pelourinho." They concern values and the modern interpretation of the past which are in conflict with the contemporary world and its pressures.

435 Ribeiro, Berta G. *et al*. O artesão tradicional e seu papel na sociedade contemporânea = The traditional artisan and his role in contemporary society. Rio de Janeiro: FUNARTE, Instituto Nacional do Folclore, 1983. 253 p.: bibl.

Award-winning essays deal with: Why and for whom are Indian handicrafts made?; craftsmanship, tradition and social change, a study based on the "art of gold" in Juazeiro do Norte, Brazil; rethinking handicrafts: some considerations; the beauty of everyday life; the traditional artisan and his role in contemporary society; a study of the Karajá ethnozoology: Aruanã masks. Main issues are: the dilemma of native craftsmen of traditional products whose traditions may be the wane and the consumption of these products, both domestic and foreign.

436 Tradição e ruptura: síntese de arte e cultura brasileiras, novembro 1984- janeiro 1985. Organização de João Marino. São Paulo: Fundação Bienal de São Paulo, 1984. 308 p.: chiefly ill. (some col.)

Unique exhibition assembled more than 600 pieces and thoroughly succeeds in demonstrating its purpose: creativity in Brazil, from archaeological art to the 20th century. Covers every important period, virtually all major names, and even anonymous representative pieces. Also includes European Brasiliana. Every single object is reproduced in the catalog, a book of historical and artistic value in itself. A splendid team of collectors, scholars, and technicians orchestrated by João Marino made it all possible.

Excellent texts. Fine quality of reproductions and printing. Title suggests a national art style that went through many *rupturas* but managed to preserve traditional components.

437 Zílio, Carlos; João Luiz Lafetá; and Lígia Chiappini Moraes Leite. Artes plásticas. São Paulo: Brasiliense, 1982. 267 p.: bibl. (O Nacional e o popular na cultura brasileira)

Critical examination of the notion that the "power of the State in Brazil is historical power *par excellence*." Of particular interest is Carlos Zílio's "Da Antropofagia à Tropicália," an essay which examines how Modernism overcame the inferiority complex of Brazilian art in two stages, first by leading to a dynamic interaction between Western and Brazilian cultures, and secondly by the challenge of anti-establishment art such as Hélio Oiticica's and Ferreira Gullar's. A contribution to understanding what constitutes anti-art, starting with "Parangolé e Penetráveis." Main point is to determine how the avant-garde, artistic or political, can be two in one.

COLONIAL PERIOD

438 Barbosa, Waldemar de Almeida. O Aleijadinho de Vila Rica. Belo Horizonte: Editora Itatiaia; São Paulo: Editora da Univ. de São Paulo, 1985. 94 p., 24 p. of plates: bibl., ill. (some col.) (Col. Reconquista do Brasil; 3:1)

Incorporation of Indians and blacks into colonial society was a concern of the Portuguese. As Jaime Cortesão said decades ago, "The Baroque in Minas, in spite of its Portuguese origins, is one of the highest original expressions of Brazilian art." This biography of Aleijadinho although enriched with new details is not a substantial study. Congonhas is examined minutely (Prophets and Stations of the Cross) but no original contribution is made. Nevertheless, work draws together polemical sources and serves as a good reference.

439 Bazin, Germain. A arquitetura religiosa barroca no Brasil. v. 1, Estudo histórico e morfológico. v. 2, Repertório monumental, documentação fotográfica, índice geral. Revisão técnica e atualização, em colaboração com o autor, por Mário Barata. Tradução de Glória Lúcia Nunes. Rio de Janeiro: Editora Record, 1983. 2 v.: bibl., ill., index.

Brazilian Portuguese edition of 1956 French original. Updated with technical revisions. A classic of Brazilian art history. Includes preface by Germain Bazin. Much has been written about this standard work. A must in any bibliography of the field. Includes nearly 200 b/w photographs as well as plans, drawings, and plates.

440 Lisboa, Antônio Francisco. Passos da paixão: o Aleijadinho. Fotos de Claus Meyer. Texto de Rodrigo José Ferreira Bretas. Comentários de Myriam Andrade Ribeiro de Oliveira. Rio de Janeiro: Edições Alumbramento, 1984. 128 p.: bibl., col. ill.

Monograph devoted to Aleijadinho's complex of sculptures in Congonhas do Campo (i.e., 60 odd polychrome wood sculptures and 12 prophets in soapstone) regarded by many as the artist's masterpiece and one of the highlights of colonial art in the New World. Includes biographical notes on José Ferreira Bretas's "Biographical Sketches" about Aleijadinho, published in 1858, notes on the images, and beautiful color photographs, mostly close-ups.

441 Mueller, Bonifácio. O Convento de Santo Antônio do Recife: esboço histórico, 1606–1956. 2a ed. Recife: Prefeitura da Cidade do Recife, Secretaria de Educação e Cultura, Conselho Municipal de Cultura, Fundação de Cultura Cidade do Recife, 1984. 179 p., 14 leaves of plates: bibl., ill. (Col. Monumentos do Recife; 2)

Monograph originally written to commemorate the 350th anniversary of one of the finest examples of Luso-Brazilian Franciscan architecture. After author's death, splendid sets of Portuguese and Dutch tiles (from the 1640s) were discovered in the convent. Included in this second edition, these tiles as well as the tile panels in Recife's Santo Antônio Convent are among the best in Brazil. Text discusses the building's history, architecture, tiles, and paintings as well as its social and political vicissitudes throughout the centuries. Welcome edition since the first has long been out of print.

442 Museu da Inconfidência. Textos de Rui Mourão e Francisco Iglésias. Rio de Janeiro: FUNARTE, 1984. 159 p.: bibl., ill. (some col.) (Col. Museus brasileiros; 7)

Good introduction to the first major Brazilian museum to be established far from the Atlantic, an institution closely related to the history of Minas Gerais and Ouro Preto in particular. The building itself is one of Brazil's greatest colonial structures. The collection assembles religious and secular art works, furniture, and crafts from the 18th and 19th centuries as well as works by Aleijadinho and Manuel da Costa Ataíde.

19th CENTURY

443 Bardi, Pietro Maria. Miguel Dutra, o poliédrico artista paulista: Itú 1810-Piracicaba, 1875. São Paulo: Museu de Arte de São Paulo Assis Chateaubriand, 1981. 110 p.: col. ill., ports.

Illustrations of life in 19th-century São Paulo province are very rare. Among such unusual items are Miguelzinho Dutra's watercolors, most of them in the Museu Paulista. The latter together with Museu de Arte de São Paulo organized this unique show of Dutra's naïve realism. A self-taught artist, he was also a pioneer who organized the first Museum of the State of São Paulo in Piracicaba, no longer in existence. Includes excellent text and many color reproductions.

444 Cotrim, Alvaro. Pedro Américo e a caricatura. Rio de Janeiro: Edições Pinakotheke, 1983. 82 p.: ill., ports (Série especial. Col. História da pintura brasileira; 7)

A lesser known aspect of Pedro Américo's production is caricature. Mostly psychological views of his contemporaries and himself, his caricatures appeared in *A Comédia social* (Rio, ca. 1870–73). He and his paintings were, in turn, the object of caricatures by others. Author defines his approach as a "digressão otimista." Text emphasizes relationship between Pedro Américo's caricature, his life and contemporary events. Includes many reproductions of his work and of related artists, published as well as unpublished.

445 Debret, Jean Baptiste. J.B. Debret: aquarelas. São Paulo: Governo Democrático do Estado de São Paulo, Secretaria de Estado da Cultura, 1984. 91 p.: col. ill.

Debret is one of the most important creators of historical and social images of Brazil in the first half of the 19th century.

After arriving with the French Artistic Mission, invited by Dom João VI to Brazil, he stayed and worked in the country (1816–31), publishing later in France (1834–39) a small—and now very rare—monumental three-volume in-folio edition of 156 lithographs of drawings and watercolors (e.g., landscapes, architecture, and many aspects of Brazilian society of that period). This catalog commemorates the sesquicentennial of that publication, with many color reproductions, including watercolors which are part of the seldom seen collection of the Marquesses of Bonneval in São Paulo, and other major collections in Brazil.

446 Francisco, Nagib. João Batista da Costa, 1865–1926. Rio de Janeiro: Edições Pinakotheke, 1984. 132 p.: ill. (some col.) (Série Prata; SP-11)

Welcome monograph about landscape painter from the state of Rio, active during a neglected period, the latter part of the 19th and first decades of the 20th centuries. Batista da Costa, a pioneer in the exploration of Brazil's interior as a pictorial theme, was a "pantheistic and lyric" artist as well as member of a group (i.e., Parreiras, Visconti, Belmiro de Almeida, Pedro Alexandrino, etc.) which was Brazil's answer to the School of Barbizon. Not receptive to the Impressionists, Batista da Costa was more of a romantic realist. Includes critical excerpts by various authors and many color reproductions.

447 Lacombe, Lourenço Luís and **Alvaro Cotrim.** Museu Imperial. Petrópolis: O Museu; Rio de Janeiro: Colorama, 1982. 124 p.: ill. (some col.), ports.

The Museum's exhibits attest to an entire period of Brazil's history that runs from the First Empire's and predecessors' neoclassicism to the last Monarchy's Victorianism. The collections feature taste in furnishings, *objets d'art*, portraits, crowns and jewels, insignias, miniatures, photographs, documents and diaries, Brazilian and European artifacts. Includes notes on the principal Braganças, Brazil's royal and imperial family.

448 Machado, Arnaldo. Aspectos de marinha na obra de João Zeferino da Costa. Rio de Janeiro: A. Machado, 1984. 69 p.: bibl., ill. (some col.)

Focuses on J.Z. da Costa's large mural paintings (1898) in Rio's Candelária Church.

Dominant theme (three out of six) is the seascape (e.g., "The Departure," "The Tempest," "The Arrival"), the finest of this genre in Brazilian painting. Includes many illustrations but text is more of a chronicle than an artistic appraisal. A good reference work on the subject is the classic *150 anos de pintura de marinha na história da arte brasileira: 1790–1945*.

449 Mello Júnior, Donato. Pedro Américo de Figueiredo e Melo, 1843–1905: algumas singularidades de sua vida e de sua obra. Rio de Janeiro: Edições Pinakotheke, 1983. 81 p.: bibl., ill. (Série especial. Col. História da pintura brasileira; 6)

Pedro Américo is among Brazil's most important 19th-century painters, together with Vítor Meireles and Almeida Júnior. Like them, he was a man of humble birth who studied at Rio's Academia Imperial das Belas Artes, and later at Paris's Ecole des beaux arts, under Ingres. A disciple of classicism, romanticism, and realistic traditions, Pedro Américo's major works are "Batalha do Avaí" and "Grito do Ipiranga." Study provides little analysis but offers well researched biography and reproductions of lesser known b/w drawings.

450 Reis Júnior, José Maria dos. Belmiro de Almeida, 1858–1935. Rio de Janeiro: Edições Pinakotheke, 1984. 120 p.: bibl., ill. (some col.), index (Série Prata; SP-10)

Belmiro led the way towards the modernization of Brazilian painting. An artist without ties to the "Week of Modern Art," he studied at Rio's former Imperial Academy of Fine Arts and worked in Paris (1884) and Rome (1890) where he absorbed Impressionism, Pointillism, and Post Impressionism. He was much influenced by Seurat and Cézanne but also experimented with Cubism. After returning to Brazil, he immersed himself in local subjects, drawing newspaper illustrations and painting realistic portraits. An "impertinent humorist" with a critical approach to social life, he was also interested in history. Excellent monograph that includes many illustrations and reproductions.

451 Salgueiro, Heliana Angotti. A singularidade da obra de Veiga Valle. Goiânia: Univ. Católica de Goiás, Vice-Reitoria Administrativa, Div. Gráfica e Editorial, 1983. 502 p., 84 p. of plates: bibl., ill. (some col.)

Veiga Valle (b. 1806, Goiás), member of a socially prominent family and a judge, turned out to be one of Brazil's finest *santos* makers. The only known "high-born" practitioner of this Brazilian religious art, he was a classicist who carefully created his sculptures from choice of wood to final polish. This monograph is an excellent contribution to the appreciation of this artist, practically rediscovered in the 1940s. Includes minute examination of many pieces, overall evaluation, bibliography, and b/w and color reproductions.

20th CENTURY

452 Araújo, Emanoel. O construtivismo afetivo de Emanoel Araújo. Prefácio de P.M. Bardi. Introdução de C.P. Valladares. Texto de Jacob Klintowitz. Salvador: Odebrecht; São Paulo: Raízes, 1983. 174 p.: bibl., ill. (some col.)

Book conceived to accompany Araújo's show at the São Paulo Art Museum (1981) emphasizes his woodpainted sculpture. Valladares stresses the impact of Araújo's background as a craftsman (i.e., carpenter at age nine, typesetter, architecture student, printmaker) on his art. As a painter and printmaker, he assimilated Cubism, Afro-Brazilian traditions, etc. developing a universal sense of form and a personal sense of color—both in his figurative and constructivist-abstract periods. Splendid edition includes excellent study by Klintowitz, with enriching texts by Jorge Amado, Mario Barata, Joaquim Cardozo, Walmir Ayala, etc.

453 Bento, Antônio. Sergio Telles. Introdução de Gaston Diehl. Rio de Janeiro: L. Christiano Editorial; Lausanne, Switzerland: Bibliothèque des arts, 1983. 275 p.: bibl., ill. (some col.), index.

Gaston Diehl's introduction is less concerned with fitting Telles into a modern "school," than with examining his personality, background, influences, artistic strength and his Brazilian idiom that incorporated European traditions. Dorival's text underscores tropical features in Telles's art, his "japonisme," and influences of Matisse and Vlaminck. Bento analyzes paintings produced in Brazil, Portugal, Argentina, France, and Japan. Includes drawings and prints. Reproductions are excellent.

454 Brill, Alice. Mário Zanini e seu tempo: do Grupo Santa Helena ás bienais. São Paulo: Editora Perspectiva, 1984. 202 p.: bibl., ill., ports (Col. Debates; 187. Arte)

Author's point of departure: the 1922 "Week of Modern Art" was only consolidated in the 1930s and 1940s, thanks to such groups as "Família Artística Paulista" and "Grupo Santa Helena." Descendants of Italian immigrants, these groups consisted mostly of working-class artisans who struggled between figurative art and abstraction until they found their own idiom. Zanini's long neglected contribution is finally recognized by this study. Author's thorough research notes Cézanne's influence, the period's relevant political issues and affinities with De Fiori and Volpi in landscapes and human figures. Includes bibliography and many b/w reproductions.

455 Camargo, Sérgio de. Sérgio de Camargo. São Paulo: Unibanco; Rio de Janeiro: Museu de Arte Moderna do Rio de Janeiro, 1981. 62 p.: ill., photos.

This major Brazilian sculptor, an artist of clear affinities (Brancusi, Arp, Vantongerloo) and personal style, began working with cylindrical reliefs in wood (International Prize, 3rd Paris Biennial, 1963) then with Carrara marble in varied tower-like white structures of superb craftsmanship and subtle geometry. Includes excellent text by Casimiro Xavier de Mendonça and Ronaldo Brito, many good photographs of the artist's works by Romulo Fialdini, and curriculum.

456 Ciclo de exposições sobre arte no Rio de Janeiro. v. 6, Tempos de guerra: Hotel Internacional: pensão mauá. Curador, Frederico Morais. Rio de Janeiro: Galeria de Arte BANERJ, 1986. 134 p.: ill., photos.

As a result of World War II, more than 20 European, Japanese, and US artists came to Rio in the 1940s. Their living quarters became places frequented by young Brazilian artists (e.g., Hotel Internacional). Their impact was considerable as this publication demonstrates in an exploration of the roots of contemporary Brazilian art. Catalog covers two retrospective exhibitions of this period (135 works). Includes many texts, photographs, b/w reproductions, statements by and short biographies of several artists from both shows.

456a Di Cavalcanti, Emiliano. Desenhos de Di Cavalcanti na coleção do MAC. Coordenação de Aracy Amaral. São Paulo: Univ. de São Paulo, Museu de Arte Contemporânea, 1985. 223 p.: bibl., ill. (some col.)

Collection of Di Cavalcanti's drawings at the Univ. of São Paulo's Museum of Contemporary Art, probably the most comprehensive of its kind, allows one to appreciate the breadth and depth of this major Brazilian artist's graphic creativity. Donated by him to the university in 1952, the collection is especially strong in the 1920s-40s, very relevant and creative decades indeed. Competent team under the leadership of Aracy Amaral has produced a splendid volume with many color and b/w reproductions, numerous and varied texts, and extensive bio-bibliography with iconography.

457 Fang, Chen-Kong. Fang. Organização de Glaucia S. Cohn, J. Peter Cohn. Analise crítica de Theon Spanudis. Tradução de Idle Maksoud. São Paulo: Dan Galeria, 1984. 144 p.: ill. (some col.)

Author examines Fang's Chinese background to the meaning of his art. Devotes much space to the conflict between oriental subtlety and spiritual expression vs. Western crude realism in order to trace Fang's natural predilection for the figurative over the abstract, a tendency underscored in his diaries. Fang (b. 1931, Tung Cheng, China) emigrated in 1951, studied with Takaoka, and developed into one of Brazil's finest painters of recent years (e.g., seascapes, landscapes, still lifes— with life, as author notes—animals, intriguing puppet theaters).

458 Gotlib, Nádia Battella. Tarsila do Amaral. São Paulo: Brasiliense, 1983. 113 p.: bibl., ill., ports (Encanto radical; 25)

Seminal artist of modern Brazilian painting, Tarsila opened the way for the "Pau-Brasil" and "Antropofagia" movements and introduced Cubism to Brazil. She also "rediscovered" Brazil by using primary colors and pinks, integrating rural and architectural elements, expressing political and social issues of the 1930s, and, in a very unmistakably personal way, establishing a Brazilian pictorial idiom. A stunning beauty as a woman, she was also courageous and emancipated, an individual ahead of her times. Concise, intelligent, informative introduction to the artist, book includes chronology and few b/w reproductions.

459 Ianelli, Arcangelo. Ianelli: forma e cor: exibição "Ianelli, 40 Anos de Pintura:" Museu de Arte Moderna, Rio de Janeiro, setembro 1984. Textos de Frederico Morais e Juan Acha. São Paulo: s.n., 1984? 52 p.: bibl., col. ill.

Commemorates Ianelli's 40 years as a painter summed up by Acha as combining "the ideal of all times, and the most probable of our times." Morais notes that "the artist reached his peak, . . . by seeking the ultimate in sensibility, the excitement that derives from the innermost aspect of painting . . . a spiritual pleasure." Includes fine color reproductions, biography, and bibliography.

460 Klintowitz, Jacob. Brasil, a arte de hoje = Brazil, the art of today. São Paulo: Galeria São Paulo, 1983. 96 p., 2 leaves of plates: ill. (some col.)

Private gallery emphasizes how in Brazil the practice of showing, discussing, stimulating, promoting, discovering, and documenting art is largely the purview of private enterprise. Artists of contrasting backgrounds handled by this gallery are featured. Seriousness and vitality were sole criteria for selection. Klintowitz writes about the 12 artists noting their issues, media, aesthetic, and historical perspectives: Nicola, Flemming, Flexor, Tozzi, Barrio, Gerchman, Shoko, Pedrosa, Szpigel, Vallauri, Matuck, Zaidler.

461 Klintowitz, Jacob. Mestres do desenho brasileiro: 27 artistas representativos = Masters of Brazilian drawing: 27 representative artists. São Bernardo do Campo: Volkswagen do Brasil, 1983. 219 p.: ill. (some col.)

Discusses nature of drawing and compares it to photography, noting how the former does not document but "fulfills man's acute need to express and register his emotions." Most Brazilian artists featured in this beautiful anthology are great masters of figurative art, working in various media and exemplifying some of the finest Brazilian art trends in this century. Excellent quality color and b/w reproductions.

462 Lee, Wesley Duke. Wesley Duke Lee. Texto relatado de Cacilda Teixeira da Costa. Rio de Janeiro: MEC, FUNARTE, 1980. 56 p.: ill. (some col.) (Arte brasileira contemporânea)

The year 1952 which Lee spent at New York's Parsons School of Design was crucial in that he learned how to work in various media and assimilated the new Bauhaus revival. Upon his return, he greatly affected the course of Brazil's avant garde and the style of younger generations. Other influences on Lee were Paul Klee, Marcel Duchamp (1965), and his own development of magical realism after working with Karl Plattner in São Paulo. His interview with Cacilda Teixeira da Costa includes many notable statements. Includes chronology, many reproductions and essential color and b/w photographs.

463 Martins, Carlos. Carlos Martins. Textos de Frederico Morais e Wilson Coutinho. Projecto e produção gráfica de Editora Ex Libris. Fotos do artista e de seu ateliê de Ana Teóphilo. São Paulo: Galeria Luisa Strina; Pôrto Alegre: Cambona Centro de Arte; Rio de Janeiro: Arteespaço Escritório de Arte, 1985. 1 v.: ill. (some col.), photos.

Fine publication by contemporary Brazilian artist is a miniature gem. Text focuses on Martins's art as being "nítido, preciso, espetacular" and "intimismo mínimo." Includes 10 b/w etchings, 19 variations of a watercolored print on silver in their original small oval size, as well as photographs of artist, his studio and short biography.

464 Menotti del Picchia. O gedeão do modernismo, 1920–22. Introdução, seleção e organização de Yoshie Sakiyama Barreirinhas. Rio de Janeiro: Civilização Brasileira; São Paulo: Secretaria de Estado da Cultura, 1983. 374 p.: bibl. (Col. Vera Cruz; 346)

Together with Anita Malfatti, Tarsila do Amaral, Mário and Oswald de Andrade, Menotti del Picchia—also a poet—is an essential figure for understanding the development of Modernism in Brazil. Under his own name and pseudonyms of Hélios and Aristophanes, Menotti wrote for *Correio Paulistano* before, during and after the "Week of Modern Art" (1920–22), nearly 900 social chronicles which discussed the impact of the new art and literature. This excellent anthology features his most relevant pieces on polemics. The serial *Correio Paulistano* constitutes a major primary source for research into Brazilian Modernism.

465 Nery, Ismael. Ismael Nery, 50 anos depois. Equipe da exposição e livro, Aracy Amaral *et al.* São Paulo: Museu de Arte Contemporânea, Univ. de São Paulo, 1984. 277 p.: bibl., ill. (some col.)

The extraordinary Ismael Nery, one of Brazil's major 20th-century artists, impressed his contemporaries as "a comet" that vanishes after a quick and sensational trajectory. The Surrealism he pioneered in Brazil, although concurrent with its sway in Europe, was very independent in its expression. This excellent catalog features his most comprehensive retrospective to date covering exhibits at Rio's Petite Galerie (1966) and São Paulo's Art Museum (1974). Includes important essays by Mário de Andrade, Murilo Mendes, Jorge de Lima, Mário Barata, Mário Pedrosa, Clarival Valladares, Senir Lourenço Ferandez, Aracy Amaral, Antônio Bento, Giuseppe Baccaro, Luiz Munari, Pedro Nava, Aníbal Machado and Chaim José Harmer; very good reproductions of paintings, drawings and other media; photographs; chronology; bibliography; and list of exhibitions.

466 Ostrower, Fayga. Exposição retrospectiva de Fayga Ostrower: obra gráfica, 1944–1983: Museu Nacional de Belas Artes, Rio de Janeiro, outubro de 1983. Text by Antônio Bento *et al.* Rio de Janeiro: MNBA: MEC, Secretaria da Cultura, Fundação Nacional Pró-Memória, 1983. 58 p.: bibl., ill. (some col.)

Catalog of major retrospective of leading contemporary artist. Various texts complement one another but the artist's own statement sums up her life in art and opens new possibilities. Reproductions and description are in chronological order.

467 Prado, Vasco. Vasco Prado. Textos de Manoel Sarmento Barata e Marc Berkowitz. Fotos de Luiz Carlos Felizardo. Coordenação de José Rolim Valença. Pôrto Alegre: Museu de Arte do Rio Grande do Sul; São Paulo: Companhia Iochpe de Participações, 1984. 84 p.: bibl., ill. (some col.)

Monograph commemorates artist's 70th birthday. His statement reaffirms his commitment to figurative art as well as to constant experiment with form. One of Brazil's finest sculptors, Prado works with wood, stone, metals, clay, and acrylic, and ranges from the neoclassical to modern figurative art. Includes text by several artists and critics, documentary photographs of Prado at work in Porto Alegre, and retrospective color and b/w photographs of his works.

468 Sant'Anna, Affonso Romano de. Estória dos sofrimentos, morte e res-

surreição do Senhor Jesus Cristo na pintura de Emeric Marcier. Rio de Janeiro: Edições Pinakotheke, 1983. 66 p.: bibl., ill. (some col.) (Série especial. Col. História da pintura brasileira; 3)

Marcier is a Catholic painter who "paints *his* passion, starting with the Passion of Christ." A Protestant critic and poet, the author tries to capture Marcier's *passion*, an attempt that makes for a fascinating encounter between two Christian cultures of 20th-century Minas Gerais. Because Marcier is not especially mystical, the poet also speaks of the passion of the flesh as well as of God, the Devil, Swedenborg, Boehme, Eliade. Influenced by Piero della Francesca, Masaccio, Giotto, and Tiepolo, Marcier conceived his *passions* in eight series (1952–83) that transmitted the light of Europe into that of Minas Gerais. Many good reproductions.

469 Scliar, Carlos. Carlos Scliar. Prefácio de Pietro Maria Bardi. Fotografias de Jeferson Silva. Edição de Emanoel Araújo. São Paulo: Raízes, 1983. 175 p.: bibl., film., ill. (some col.), photos.

The novelist Moacyr Scliar, a cousin of the artist, reminisced about the family's history, tracing the roots of Carlos's art to Jewish Ukranian pogroms and the stricken existence of those who landed in Porto Alegre around the turn of the century. Beautifully printed book includes many photographs, retrospective and critical texts by several intellectuals, color and b/w reproductions along with photographs of biographical interest, resumé, iconography, and filmography.

470 Scliar, Carlos. Desenhos: 1940/49. v. 1, 1940/43. v. 2, Feb. 1944; Feb. 1945. v. 3, 1944/47. v. 4, 1947/49. Belo Horizonte: Oficina Goeldi, 1983. 4 v. in 5: ill.

Set of *facsimiles* (1940–49) introduced by Scliar who reminisces on earliest and more decisive influences on his drawings (e.g., portraits, 1940–43), war experiences in Italy as soldier (1944–45), and life in Paris (1947–49). Very fine art book; a collector's item.

471 Silva, Orlando da. Poty, o artista gráfico. Curitiba: Fundação Cultural de Curitiba, 1980. 145 p.: chiefly ill.

Important Brazilian expressionist, illustrator, and printmaker (1940s-late 1960s) who strongly influenced younger generations of artists. Best examples of his drawings, woodblock prints, and lithographs are reproduced in this deluxe edition. Includes very good introductory text.

472 Tarsila. Tarsila. São Paulo: Art Editora: Círculo do Livro, 1983? 24 p., 48 p. of plates: ill. (some col.) (Grandes artistas brasileiros)

Concise, handsome book provides the essence of Tarsila, both in texts and reproductions (1921–29) from academic to daring canvases. Decisive ones that established a modern pictorial idiom in Brazil were "A Negra," "São Paulo," "Morro da Favela," "Vendedor de Frutas," "Abaporu," and "Antropofagia." Murilo Mendes once noted that "in the 1920s Tarsila captured the *caipira* spirit of São Paulo and Minas through European techniques transposing onto her canvases the purest blue, violet pink, intense yellow, singing green . . . discovering the animal side of plants, and giving visual expression to Tupi and African magic."

473 Trevisan, Armindo. Escultores contemporâneos do Rio Grande do Sul. Pôrto Alegre: Pontifícia Univ. Católica do Rio Grande do Sul, 1983. 159 p.: bibl., ill. (some col.)

Although some of Brazil's most expressive modern sculptors are from Rio Grande do Sul, there are very few studies of their sculpture. A most welcome work of historical and critical insight, this monograph fills in the gap very well. It covers less famous but worthy sculptors of the younger generation as well as primitive ones such as Guma.

FOLK ART

474 Maia, Isa. O artesanato da renda no Brasil. João Pessoa: Univ. Federal da Paraíba (UFPb), 1980. 131 p.: bibl., ill., photos.

Overview of lace-making in Brazil examines origins (Azores Islands), describes basic types (e.g., Renascença, Labirinto, Filé, Rendendê), draws technical and artistic comparisons, notes main areas of production (12 states), and discusses social and economic aspects. Text by several contributors. Includes many photographs.

475 Meireles, Cecília. Batuque, samba, and macumba: drawings of gestures and rhythm, 1926–1934. Rio de Janeiro:

FUNARTE, Instituto Nacional do Folclore, 1983. 105 p.: bibl., facsims., ill. (some col.)

It is little known that Cecília Meireles, among the greatest Portuguese poets, also pioneered Brazilian folk studies and produced some gifted ethnographic drawings. This publication makes available her otherwise inaccessible shows in Brazil (1933) and Portugal (1935). Splendid collection of china-ink drawings, pastels, and watercolors depict *samba, carnaval, macumba* in all their richness, variety, and sensuousness. Includes facsimiles of contemporary press accounts, very good introduction, and texts. Recommended high quality book.

476 Oliveira, Antônio de. O mundo encantado de Antônio de Oliveira. Rio de Janeiro: FUNARTE, Instituto Nacional do Folclore, 1983. 112 p.: bibl., ill., photos (O Artista popular e seu meio; 1)

A shoemaker and tailor before becoming one of Brazil's greatest folk artists, Oliveira pioneered hand-made and electronically powered wooden toys. Only later in life did he carve and paint hundreds of figurines embodying aspects of Brazilian history as well as folk traditions, legends, etc. Includes useful autobiography and artist's statements as well as b/w photos of his best works. Very fine monograph.

477 Pardal, Paulo. Carrancas do São Francisco. 2a ed. rev. e ampliada. Rio de Janeiro: Serviço de Documentação Geral da Marinha, 1981. 204 p.: appendix, bibl., ill. (some col.), index.

Among the most interesting and creative manifestations of Brazilian folk art of ancient origin are the prow figures of boats along the São Francisco River. Some *carrancas* are attributed to Guarany (see item **479**), famous folk artist who is the subject of a special chapter. Compares São Francisco River *carrancas* to "learned" prow figures of other cultures. Includes special appendix on the "Comité international pour l'étude des figures de proue," (Paris, 1977), overview of subject since antiquity, many photos, color and b/w drawings, and bibliography.

478 Sobreira, Geová. Xilógrafos do Juazeiro. Apresentação de Eduardo Diatahy Bezerra de Menezes. Fortaleza: Edições Univ. Federal do Ceará: PROED, 1984. 128 p.: ill.

Origins of string literature woodcuts, among the most expressive manifestations of folk culture in Brazil, are not well known. This work explores such roots by gathering information from artists who live in the Northeast, 19th-century statements, and 20th-century scholarship (e.g., historians, social scientists, art historians). Includes illustrations of past and present examples. A contribution to knowledge of the topic.

479 Valladares, Clarival do Prado and **Paulo Pardal.** Guarany: 80 anos de carrancas. Rio de Janeiro: Berlendis & Vertecchia Editores, 1981. 90 p.: ill.

Valladares's trip along the São Francisco River covers its history, folk traditions, religious celebrations (some of medieval origin), and archaic/classical patterns introduced by Jesuits and Franciscans. Considers *carrancas* or prow figures from a Jungian perspective to form part of mankind's "underground soul." Most *carrancas* (1900s-70s) analyzed were created by this remarkable folk artist Guarany, a descendant of river boatmen, who was a singular towering personality in a mostly anonymous tradition.

PHOTOGRAPHY

480 Ferrez, Gilberto. A fotografia no Brasil: 1840–1900. 2a ed. Rio de Janeiro: FUNARTE: Fundação Nacional Pró-Memória, 1985. 248 p.: bibl., ill., indexes, ports. (História da fotografia no Brasil; 1)

Leading authority on Brazilian photography offers overall history representing 40 years of work. Unlike equivalent histories of Europe and the US, there appear to be few vistas and panoramas of Brazil in daguerreotype, even if the level of Brazilian photographers was high. Such gaps make it difficult to determine whether there was a national style. Devotes chapter to Marc Ferrez, offers remarkable glimpses into 19th-century Brazil, discusses rare reproductions, includes technical glossary, bibliography, and indexes (general and of leading photographers).

481 Ferrez, Gilberto. O Rio antiguo do fotógrafo Marc Ferrez: paisagens e tipos humanos do Rio de Janeiro, 1865–1918. Prefácio de Pedro Nava. São Paulo: J. Fortes Engenharia: Editora Ex Libris, 1984. 221 p.: ill.

Like a "poet painter," Marc Ferrez's classic photographs subtly capture Rio's

change from Portuguese to French influence to US type megalopolis (1865–1918). His images cover architecture, nature, and people in a comprehensive visual document which is both *saudade* and fine art. Artist's grandson contributes a biographical, historical, and technical study. Superb edition.

482 O Retrato brasileiro: fotografias da coleção Francisco Rodrigues, 1840–1920. Textos de Gilberto Freyre, Fernando Ponce de Leon, Pedro Vasquez. Rio de Janeiro: FUNARTE, Núcleo de Fotografia: Fundação Joaquim Nabuco, Depto. de Iconografia, 1983. 98 p.: ill., index, ports.

Remarkable selection of portraits (12,000 during 1840–1920) of people from all strata of 19th-century Brazilian society, particularly Pernambuco. They exemplify many techniques: daguerreotypes, ambrotypes, irontypes, cartes de visite, images on metal, glass and paper. One of the best photography collections in Brazil. Provides historical account by F. Ponce de Leon and Pedro Vasquez and provocative essay by Gilberto Freyre "Por uma Sociofotografia," as well as index of photographers.

483 Teixeira, Evandro. Evandro Teixeira: fotojornalismo. Texto de Carlos Drummond de Andrade, Antônio Callado, Otto Lara Resende. Rio de Janeiro: Editora JB, 1982. 120 p.: chiefly ill.

Representative selection of 20 years of work as photographer for *Jornal do Brasil*, this is a book about "an art form in its own right: photojournalism." The world of the street seen through Teixeira's eyes and lenses (e.g., scenes of violence, political demonstrations, humor, grotesqueries, etc.). Text by Carlos Drummond de Andrade, Antônio Callado and Otto Lara Resente. B/w photographs. A record of social history and art.

CITY PLANNING, ARCHITECTURE, AND LANDSCAPE ARCHITECTURE

484 A Arquitetura no Rio Grande do Sul. Organização de Günter Weimer. Pôrto Alegre: Mercado Aberto, 1983. 224 p.: bibl., ill., photos (Série Documenta; 15. História)

Essays about many aspects of Rio Grande do Sul's architecture. Titles: "A Habitação Subterrânea: uma Adaptação Ecológica," "O Espaço Urbano e a Arquitetura

Produzidos pelos Sete Povos das Missões," "Arquitetura Luso-Brasieira," "A Arquitetura Rural da Imigração," "Estruturas Sociais Gaúchas e Arquitetura," "Arquitetura Moderna," and "Arquitetura Espontânea no Rio Grande do Sul." Illustrated by b/w photographs.

485 Bardi, Pietro Maria. Lembrança de Le Corbusier: Atenas, Itália, Brasil. Prefácio de Alexandre Eulálio. Tradução de Ana Carboncini e Leda Maria Figueiredo Ferraz. São Paulo: Nobel, 1984. 171 p.: bibl., ill. (some col.)

Eulálio emphasizes importance of Le Corbusier as well as that of Alexis Verger and Blaise Cendrars in the development of 20th-century Brazilian architecture. Le Corbusier's 1923 visit to Rio and subsequent ones through 1962 were seminal. Includes many of his drawings, paintings, plans, manuscripts, lectures, letters (e.g., correspondence with Paulo Prado, 1929–38), sketches and photos of buildings. Also discusses Lúcio Costa, Warchavchik, Rino Levi, Flávio de Carvalho, Oscar Niemeyer and other Brazilian architects. Important historical *mise-au-point*.

486 Costa, Eunice R. Ribeiro. Indice de arquitetura brasileira, 1971–1980. Brasília: MEC, Secretaria da Educação Superior, Subsecretaria de Desenvolvimento da Educação Superior; São Paulo: Univ. de São Paulo, Faculdade de Arquitetura e Urbanismo, Biblioteca, 1982. 313 p.

Vol. 1 covered 1950–70, this sequel covers 1971–80, as well as indexation to specialized and related publications (1971–80). Introduction notes both volumes make up a "catalog-dictionary." Authors and subjects are arranged alphabetically. Subjects appear according to form, function, medium, time and place, affinity, opposition and use. Although not easily accessible, this is still a very useful reference.

487 Daher, Luiz Carlos. Flavio de Carvalho: arquitetura e expressionismo. São Paulo: Projeto, 1982. 114 p.: ill.

Author perceives Expressionism as did Mário de Andrade in 1934: "a trend in modern art in which all elements are submitted to the artist's personal expression." Flávio de Carvalho (1899–1973) was a Renaissance personality whose architecture was realized only exceptionally. His never built São Paulo Government Palace was Brazil's first large scale Modernistic project (1927). Notes indirect parallels with Fritz Lang's 1926 film "Metropolis." Examines relationship to dance, murals, and sculpture. Includes clippings, blueprints, and photographs from archives and discusses projects, art, and writings of later years.

488 Ferrez, Gilberto. Raras e preciosas vistas e panoramas do Recife, 1755–1855. Recife: Núcleo de Editoração Nacional, Fundação Pró-Memória, 1984. 66 p.: bibl., ill.(some col.) (Col. pernambucana; 2a fase)

In contrast to the wealth of the Dutch pictorial record of 17th-century Recife and Olinda, Portuguese and/or Brazilian 18th-century maps and vistas are rare. Recently discovered *prospectivas* made by Portuguese military engineers and Jesuits, published in this welcome contribution, reveal the look of these places after the Dutch departed. Includes illustrations and technical details of these *prospectos* as well as few rare French, German, and English drawings, gouaches, watercolors, and lithographs of the period. Comprehensive text by Gilberto Ferrez. Excellent color and b/w reproductions and bibliography.

489 Klintowitz, Jacob and Rômulo Fialdini. Fortalezas históricas do Brasil. Texto de Jacob Klintowitz. Fotografia de Rômulo Fialdini. São Paulo: Rhodia, 1983. 160 p.: col. ill.

Examines impressive Brazilian historical forts, circumstances under which they were built, transplanted Portuguese architectural traditions, and different perceptions of war in the New World. Also discusses, aesthetic solutions, proportions, complexity, variety, solid craftsmanship, and integration with nature. Handsome, comprehensive publication includes old color drawings and reproductions, new technical blueprints and plans. Discusses Dutch and French influences and includes illustrations of representative examples.

490 Mello Neto, Ulysses Pernambucano de. O Forte das Cinco Pontas: um trabalho de arqueologia histórica aplicado à restauração do monumento. Recife: Prefeitura da Cidade do Recife, Secretaria de Educação e Cultura, Fundação de Cultura Cidade do Recife, 1983. 143 p., 30 p. of plates: bibl., ill. (Col. Monumentos do Recife; 1)

This fort, first built by the Dutch in the 17th century in *taipa* (mud), was rebuilt by the Portuguese in stone after the 1654 Pernambucan restoration. One of the finest architectural examples of its kind in Brazil, this fort was restored after careful archaeological research. Monograph details the process both historically and technically.

Reconstituição da memória estatística da Grande São Paulo. See *HLAS 47:5300.*

491 Weimer, Günter. A arquitetura da imigração alemã: um estudo sobre a adaptação da arquitetura centro-européia ao meio rural do Rio Grande do Sul. Porto Alegre: Univ. Federal do Rio Grande do Sul; São Paulo: Livraria Nobel, 1983. 296 p.: bibl., ill., photos, plans.

This is the best scholarly monograph on the subject. Examines the transplantation of German architecture to Rio Grande do Sul by 19th-century immigrants, their regional origins (e.g., Westfalia, Pomerania, and Franconia), particular styles, rural adaptation and eventual recreation of a *teuto-gaúcha* architecture. Also discusses historical, sociological, and theoretical aspects. Includes many photos, drawings, plans and blueprints (for comparative purposes), and bibliography.

492 Xavier, Alberto; Carlos Lemos; and Eduardo Corona. Arquitetura moderna paulistana. São Paulo: Pini, 1983. 251 p.: ill.

Modern architecture, as defined by author, began in Brazil sometime in 1907 but in the city of São Paulo only as of 1927. Examines 211 projects chronologically (1927–77), discussing each with text and illustrating it with blueprints and photographs. Underscores influences of foreign and Rio's architecture, importance of Vilanova Artigas in pioneering a "Paulista" style, and architects before and after World War II. Principal structures include lodgings, banks, commercial buildings, cultural centers, exhibition halls and museums, stadiums, apartment buildings, industries, public buildings, hospitals, schools and homes. Best book of its kind to date.

AFRO-BRAZILIAN AND INDIAN TRADITIONS

Dorta, Sonia Ferraro. Paríkó: etnografia de um artefato plumário. See *HLAS 47:1232.*

493 Habitações indígenas. Organização de Sylvia Caiuby Novaes. São Paulo: Livraria Nobel: Univ. de São Paulo, 1983. 196 p.: bibl., ill.

Concerned with the indigenous architecture of Brazil, this book presents a group of essays, each by different authors with different points of view. All are based in structural methodology, and several try to achieve a larger sense of cultural meaning from the architectural plans and forms. [F. Clancy]

494 Herança: a expressão visual do brasileiro antes da influência do europeu. Planejamento, coordenação e textos de José Rolim Valença. Concepção, produção, diagramação e fotografias de Bruno Furrer. São Paulo: Empresas Dow, 1984. 152 p.: chiefly ill. (some col.)

The major value of this book lies in its photographs of the little known rock art of Brazil. Recorded are astounding images of complexity, abstract conceptions, and graphic beauty. [F. Clancy]

495 Indios del Brasile: culture che scompaiono: Curia del Senato al Foro Romano, settembre 1983-gennaio 1984. Coordinamento catalogo, Fausto Zevi. Testi, Patrizia Andreasi *et al.* Roma: De Luca, 1983. 161 p., 11 p. of plates: bibl., ill. (some col.)

Catalog of major exhibition of art and artifacts of Brazilian Indian cultures form important Italian collections, Rio's Museu Nacional, and the B.G. Ribeiro and R. Marinho collections. Includes scholarly texts, descriptions and classification as well as b/w and color reproductions. A relevant reference work.

496 Museu Afro Brasileiro. Textos de Luiz Fernando Macedo Costa, Yêda Pessoa de Castro. Fotos de Artur Viana e Raimundo Bandeira. Salvador: O Museu, 1983. 41 p.: ill. (some col.), photos.

The establishment of this museum emphasizes the importance of blacks in the sociocultural make-up of Brazilians. In addition to many African and Afro-Brazilian objects, the collection has Carybé's "Mural of the Orixás," a very significant contemporary work inspired by Afro-Brazilian traditions. The museum also features many photographs.

497 Museu do Estado de Pernambuco. Coleção culto-afro brasileiro: um testemunho do xangô pernambucano. Equipe técnica, coordenação, pesquisa, análise e textos dos verbetes de Raul Lody. Subcoordenação, pesquisa e análise de Eva Auxiliadora Salvador Vasconcelos. Assistentes, Marluce Câmara Azevedo, Icléa Braga Mascarenhas, Anita da Silva Pequeno. Recife: Governo do Estado de Pernambuco, Secretaria de Turismo, Cultura e Esportes, 1983. 110 p.; bibl., ill.

Organized by types of objects, the art and paraphernalia of the Pernambuco Xango are illustrated and described. The range of the catalog (and exhibit) is extensive and essentially ethnographic in approach. [F. Clancy]

MISCELLANEOUS

498 A Arte rupestre no Estado do Minas Gerais: a região de Lagoa Santa. Belo Horizonte: Fundação Centro Tecnológico de Minas Gerais (CETEC), 1982. 1 portfolio (21 p., 9 leaves of plates): bibl., col. ill., photos (Série de publicações técnicas, 0100–9540; SPT-009)

For two million years, prehistoric man drew in caves images of hunting, birth, sexuality, the natural and supernatural. Lagoa Santa in Minas Gerais is a very important example of this art. Discusses: art and prehistoric man; art of the Lagoa Santa area; methodology used for such study; contributions of the Centro Tecnológico de Minas Gerais to such methodology. Features photographs not of the actual panels, which are enormous, but of smaller scale models in mixed media (paint, plastic, clay, etc.) prepared as accurately as possible by Maria Irene and Silva Gaia (1980–82). Includes bibliography.

499 Bardi, Pietro Maria. Comunicação, notícias de Cabral à informática. São Paulo: Banco Sudameris Brasil, 1984. 107 p.: bibl., ill. (some col.) (Arte e cultura; 7)

Commentator P.M. Bardi raises journalism to an art form in this view of Brazil's cultural evolution, a process examined by Gilberto Freyre in his classic *Casa grande de senzala*. In a dashing attempt to "define" Brazil through a mosaic of improbable but tangible details, Bardi combines many disparate elements (e.g., commercial ads, drawings, maps, engravings, photographs, official documents, ceremonies, artifacts, newspapers, menus, bank checks, Afro-Brazilian and indigenous pieces, industrial artifacts, etc.). Excellent printing and color reproductions.

500 Berger, Paulo. A tipografia no Rio de Janeiro: impressores bibliográficos, 1803–1900. Rio de Janeiro: Cia. Industrial de Papel Pirahy, 1984. 226 p.: bibl., col., ill., index.

Despite isolated examples in 18th-century Recife and Rio, tipography did not begin in Brazil until officially established by Dom João VI in Rio (1808). Discusses and illustrates 19th-century books published in Rio. Excellent introduction to the art of book printing in the former capital of the Brazilian Empire.

501 O Comércio e suas profissões: imagens, Brasil 1500/1946. Editoração, texto e projeto gráfico de Arthur Bosisio Júnior. Pesquisas de Jaury Nepomuceno de Oliveira e A. Bosisio Jr. Rio de Janeiro: Serviço Nacional de Aprendizagem Comercial, Depto. Nacional, Div. de Planejamento, Coordenadoria de Divulgação e Promoções, 1983. 127 p., 5 p.: bibl., ill.

Illustrates great variety of trades throughout the centuries. Also provides excellent overall view of Brazilian commercial images in many media, emphasizing lithographs, photography, commercial design, and classified ads.

502 A Cultura nacional e a presença do MASP. Referências de Pietro Maria Bardi. São Paulo: FIAT do Brasil: Fondazione Giovanni Agnelli, 1982. 122 p.: ill. (some col.)

Emphasizes importance of São Paulo's Art Museum (MASP) in Brazil's cultural life. MASP attracted students who eventually became professors that taught the relationship of aesthetics to everyday life and the importance of combining different periods and cultures, as well as understanding political and social contexts. The museum organized exhibitions, lectures, and courses in design, gardening, fashion, music, photography, and cinema. New approaches were opened for artistic expression. Among exhibitors and teachers were Max Bill, Calder, Neutra, Le Corbusier, Nervi and Brest. Highlights MASP's exhibits in foreign countries, one of the most exciting and original being "A Mão do Povo Brasileiro," a show that covered all of Brazilian folk art.

503 Fundação Maria Luisa e Oscar Americano. São Paulo: s.n., 1980. 76 p.: ill. (some col.)

Established in 1974, the Foundation

has one of the largest collections of paintings of Brazil by Frans Post. Although other great modern Brazilian artists are represented, the colonial and imperial periods loom large (e.g., furnishings, *objets d'art*, memorabilia). The beautiful park surrounding the foundation building was landscaped by Otávio Teixeira Mendes.

504 Ilustradores do Brasil. v. 1. São Paulo: Conceito Editora Técnica, 1983? 1 v.: col. ill.

First work of its kind organized by "Clube dos Ilustradores do Brasil." Assembles works, chiefly in color, by dozens of illustrators, mostly club members. Great variety reveals unevenness of such commercial artists. Some works approach art, others ressemble caricature, some are creative and innovative, others conventional and mediocre. The range is impressive. Includes names and addresses of illustrators but no basic information on their output.

505 Machado, Paulo Affonso de Carvalho. Antigüidades do Brasil. Rio de Janeiro: O Autor, 1983? 318 p.: ill.

Despite author's generalized definition of *antigüidades* as "all antiques that embellished the houses of our grandparents," his guide book provides good information and illustrates foreign pieces as well as those made in Brazil under European influence (e.g., Portuguese, French, English, Dutch, German) but modified by local taste and materials (e.g., wood, stone). Covers furniture, *objets d'art*, *objets de vertu*, and religious artifacts in many areas of Brazil, from 16th to 19th centuries. Comprehensive introduction to a rich and varied subject.

506 Marino, João. Coleção de arte brasileira. São Paulo?: O Autor, 1983. 319 p.: bibl., ill. (some col.)

João Marino's collection of Brazilian art includes some of the country's finest pieces in colonial and pre-Portuguese native art. The Marinos' São Paulo home was designed to display them. João Hermes Pereira's essay discusses Brazilian collectors and their importance. João Marino, a fine scholar himself, wrote the accompanying text which provides an excellent in-depth analysis of his collection (e.g., images, sculpture, paintings, furniture, artifacts, pewter, silver, bronzes, ceramics, contemporary art). Several 16th- and 17th-century São Paulo terracottas and

pieces by Aleijadinho are most notable. Deluxe, bilingual edition includes beautiful graphic design by Emanoel Araújo, splendid reproductions, and bibliography.

507 Museu de Arte da Bahia. Museu de Arte da Bahia. Salvador: O Museu, 1982 or 1983. 52 p.: ill. (some col.)

Although the collections are much older, Bahia's Art Museum was first located at Solar Pacífica Pereira (1930–45), then at Solar Góes Calmon (1946–82), and is now at the restored Palácio da Vitória. There it combined several major private collections, mostly from Bahia, of painting, sculpture, furniture, *objets d'art* and ceramics. Pieces range over time and are from many countries. Includes color and b/w reproductions.

508 Museu de Arte de São Paulo Assis Chateaubriand. A pinacoteca do MASP: de Rafael a Picasso. Editor, Pietro Maria Bardi. São Paulo: Banco Safra, 1982. 222 p.: ill. (some col.), photos.

Book conceived to celebrate the 35th anniversary of São Paulo's Art Museum (MASP), an institution that owns the most important collection of Western art in Latin America. Bardi, who amassed this remarkable collection under the leadership of Assis Chateaubriand, a highly intelligent press tycoon, reminisces about the early days and decisive years after World War II, etc. Also discusses many activities that made and make MASP a living museum both in its old and new locations. Collection pieces are reproduced and discussed. Includes general catalog at the end and many documentary photographs.

509 Pintores italianos do Brasil. São Paulo: Governo do Estado de São Paulo, Secretaria de Estado da Cultura, 1982. 136 p.: bibl., col. ill., ports.

Catalog of important exhibition (April 1982) of paintings by ca. 150 Italian painters who lived in Brazil in the 20th century. Neither living Italian nor Brazilian artists of Italian extraction are included. Those who are were anonymous but influential as teachers of several generations. Some made names for themselves (e.g., Eliseu Visconti, Facchinetti, Gobbis, Oswald, Perissinoto). Includes biographies and bibliography.

510 *Revista do I.H.G.G.B.* Instituto Histórico e Geográfico Guarujá-Bertioga.

Nos. 13/14, 1981/1982-. Guarujá-Bertioga, Brazil.

Special issue devoted to three cities of São Paulo state: Cananéia, Iguape, and Iporanga. Covers their history, geography, folklore, legends, architecture, and art. Notes government and public concern for places officially registered as landmarks. Cananéia and Iguape were established in the early 1500s, and Iporanga in 1750s. All three became centers of attention because of their gold. Discusses and illustrates their civilian and religious architecture.

511 Visconti, Eliseu. Eliseu Visconti e a arte decorativa: uma exposição. Organização de Irma Arestizaba. Rio de Janeiro: PUC: FUNARTE, 1982. 157, 3 p.: bibl., ill. (some col.)

The great painter Eliseu Visconti played a crucial role in developing Brazil's modern and industrial design. Major exhibition shows his involvement in functional and decorative objects, light and iron fixtures, graphic arts, ceramics and glass, ex-libris, stamps, and emblems. Includes chronology and biography, color and b/w reproductions as well as excellent texts based on thorough research.

JOURNAL ABBREVIATIONS
ART

ARCHEO Archeologia. Paris.

CIRMA/M Mesoamérica. Centro de Investigaciones Regionales de Mesoamérica. Antigua, Guatemala.

CRI/CR Caribbean Review. Caribbean Review, Inc. Miami, Fla.

FIU/CR See CRI/CR.

IHAAER/B Boletín del Instituto de Historia Argentina y Americana Emilio Ravignani. Univ. Nacional de Buenos Aires. Buenos Aires.

IIE/A Anales del Instituto de Investigaciones Estéticas. Univ. Nacional Autónoma de México. México.

INAH/A Anales de Antropología e Historia. Instituto Nacional de Antropología

e Historia, Secretaría de Educación Pública. México.

IRA/B Boletín del Instituto Riva-Agüero. Pontificia Univ. Católica del Perú. Lima.

JGSWGL Jahrbuch für Geschichte von Staat, Wirtschaft und Gesellschaft Lateinamerikas. Köln, FRG.

LNB/L Lotería. Lotería Nacional de Beneficencia. Panamá.

PAN/EL Estudios Latinoamericanos. Polska Akademia Nauk [Academia de Ciencias de Polonia], Instytut Historii [Instituto de Historia]. Warszawa.

PMNH/HC Historia y Cultura. Museo Nacional de Historia. Lima.

PUJ/UH Universitas Humanistica. Pontificia Univ. Javeriana, Facultad de Filosofía y Letras. Bogotá.

SAR/P El Palacio. School of American Research, Museum of New Mexico [and] the Archaeological Society of New Mexico. Santa Fe.

UB/HC Historia y Cultura. Univ. Boliviana Mayor de San Andrés, Instituto de Estudios Bolivianos, Sección Cultura. La Paz.

UCLA/JLAL Journal of Latin American Lore. Univ. of California, Latin American Center. Los Angeles.

UNAM/ECN Estudios de Cultura Náhuatl. Univ. Nacional Autónoma de México, Instituto de Historia, Seminario de Cultura Náhuatl. México.

UNL/U Universidad. Univ. Nacional del Litoral. Santa Fe, Argentina.

UNLP/R Revista de la Universidad Nacional de La Plata. La Plata, Argentina.

UNM/JAR Journal of Anthropological Research. Univ. of New Mexico, Dept. of Anthropology. Albuquerque.

UTIEH/C Caravelle. Univ. de Toulouse, Institut d'Etudes hispaniques, hispano-américaines et luso-brésiliennes. Toulouse, France.

UY/R Revista de la Universidad de Yucatán. Mérida, México.

VUELTA. Vuelta. México.

FILM

RANDAL JOHNSON, *Associate Professor of Portuguese, University of Florida*

IT HAS NOW BEEN TEN YEARS since the first Film section appeared in *HLAS 38*. In the five sections published since then, including this one, two have dealt with individual countries (*HLAS 39* on Cuba, *HLAS 44* on Brazil), and three have been general bibliographies covering all countries in Latin America. As in the previous general section (*HLAS 40*), the bibliography annotated below is organized by country following a general section that includes items that deal with two or more countries or with issues that affect Latin American cinema as a whole. Five countries—the Dominican Republic, El Salvador (insurgent), Guatemala, Haiti, and Nicaragua—are represented for the first time.

Interest in Latin American cinema has mushroomed over the last ten years, to the extent that it is now virtually impossible to keep up with all relevant publications. The present section, by no means all inclusive, constitutes a selection of materials regarded as the most significant per country. I would refer the interested reader to two other bibliographies which have appeared in recent years, Julianne Burton's *The New Latin American cinema: an annotated bibliography of sources in English, Spanish, and Portuguese, 1950–1980* (item **852**) and Robert Scott's unannotated "Bibliography of Latin American Cinema" (item **961**), which includes only English-language sources. Those two sources, plus the five *HLAS* annotated bibliographies, no doubt constitute the most complete listing of materials available anywhere. Although some duplication is inevitable, I have attempted to avoid repetition to the extent possible.

The single most important item annotated below is the collective volume *Les Cinémas de l'Amérique latine, pays par pays: l'histoire, l'économie, les structures, les auteurs, les oeuvres* (item **954**). Organized by Guy Hennebelle and Alfonso Gumucio-Dagrón, it provides the most complete view of Latin American cinema available in any language. One can only hope for an English translation in the near future.

Also deserving special recognition are the works of Argentine critic José Agustín Mahieu, a resident of Spain, who has written on virtually all Latin American countries. His articles, especially those published in *Cuadernos Hispanoamericanos*, represent a knowledgeable and informative introduction to the theories, practices, problems and accomplishments of Latin American cinema (items **957, 958, 973, 974, 1035, 1036, 1056, 1077, 1078, 1079, 1080** and see also *HLAS 40:970* and *HLAS 44:1038–1039*).

One must recognize as especially significant as well the first comprehensive evaluations of work by Chilean film-makers in exile (item **1037**), the increased interest in film activity in Nicaragua either by foreigners such as García Márquez (item **1095**), Lilienthal (item **1096**), Littín (item **1097**), and Skármeta (item **1100**), or experiments by Nicaraguans themselves (items **1094, 1098,** and **1099**), and works about film production in the rebel-held zones of El Salvador (item **1072**).

The reader will notice that many items are devoted to the Brazilian cinema, a quantitative preponderance partly due to the great strides that cinema has made in international markets since the 1978 release of *Dona Flor e seus dois maridos* in the US. In addition, there is a fairly large number of film researchers in Brazil, both in and outside universities, who are investigating virtually all aspects of film production, including the relationship between cinema and the State (item **1025**), regional cinemas (items **998** and **1001**), and popular film genres (item **993**). Since his untimely death in 1981, two volumes by Glauber Rocha (item **1026** and **1027**) have appeared, along with a number of studies of his films (items **1004** and **1033**). A fairly large number of screenplays have also been published in recent years (items **986**, **987, 999, 1006, 1019, 1024, 1026, 1028, 1029, 1031a,** and **1032**), making the researcher's task somewhat easier, at least with regards to those specific films.

At least three more books have appeared recently in the US: Johnson's *Cinema Novo x 5* (item **1008**), Mora's *Mexican cinema* (item **1084**), and Schnitman's *Latin American film industries* (item **960**), with additional volumes promised for the near future. The Schnitman volume is required reading for anyone seriously interested in Latin American cinema. An increasing number of academic journals and more popular publications have dedicated space to Latin American cinema, with *JumpCut: a Review of Contemporary Media, Cineaste,* and *Film Quarterly* leading the way. In 1984 and 1985, *JumpCut* published two special sections focusing primarily on Cuban and Central American cinema.

Internationally speaking, the annual Latin American Film Festival in Havana has become a meeting place for film-makers and critics from many countries and has, by its very nature, generated a vast amount of critical work (e.g., items **953** and **956**).

GENERAL

951 Alexander, William. Class, film language, and popular cinema (JumpCut [Berkeley, Calif.] 30, March 1985, p. 45–48)

Discussion of the way in which some Latin American film-makers have freed themselves from class values and made films as weapons in revolutionary struggle. Focuses specifically on Jorge Sanjinés's *The principal enemy* (1973) and Tomás Gutiérrez Alea's *Memories of underdevelopment* (1968).

952 Burton, Julianne. The New Latin American cinema: an annotated bibliography of sources in English, Spanish, and Portuguese, 1960–1980. New York: Smyrna Press, 1983. 80 p.

Updated version of author's bibliography of English-language publications on Latin American cinema. Includes section on books in Portuguese and Spanish and organizes articles according to country and director. Essential research tool. For bibliographer's comment, see *HLAS 46:16.*

953 Cine, literatura, sociedad. Selección y prólogo de Ambrosio Fornet. La Habana: Editorial Letras Cubanas, 1982. 275 p.: bibl., index.

Collection of papers presented at the 2nd Festival Internacional del Nuevo Cine Latinoamericano (Havana, 1980). Divided into: 1) Palabra e Imagen: la tensión subyacente; 2) Literatura y Cine: hacia un lenguaje común; 3) La Crítica y su Función Social: una encrucijada; and 4) Otras Voces, Otros Ambitos: la tradición del contexto. Representado are some of the leading voices of Latin American film criticism such as Miguel Torres, Tomás Pérez Turrent, Oswaldo Capriles, Lino Miccichè, and Julianne Burton. Excellent, if uneven.

954 Les Cinémas de l'Amérique latine, pays par pays: l'histoire, l'économie, les structures, les auteurs, les oeuvres. Ouvrage collectif établi sous la direction de Guy Hennebelle et Alfonso Gumucio-Dagrón. Avec le concours de Paulo Antonio Paranagua et René Prédal. Préface de Manuel Scorza. Avant-propos d'Edouard Bailby et de Louis Marcorelles. Paris: Lherminier, 1981. 543 p.: bibl., film., ill., index (Le Cinéma et son histoire)

This richly illustrated collective work constitutes the most complete study of Latin American cinema in a single volume in any language. Includes in-depth analyses of the historical development of the cinema in virtually all Latin American countries. Essential research tool. Highly recommended.

955 Cobo, Juan. El cine latinoamericano: problemas del desarrollo (URSS/AL, 4[52], 1982, p. 87–120, ill.)
Round-table discussion on Latin American cinema held at the 12th Moscow Film Festival. Major themes: general situation and importance of Latin American cinema, relationship between the national and regional, role of documentary films in developing national film industries, and problem of film distribution and consumption. Participants: Pastor Vega (Cuba), Miguel Littín (Chile), Geraldo Sarno (Brazil), Ciro Durán (Colombia), Carlos Vicente Ibarra (Nicaragua), Sérgio Oljóvich (Mexico) and several Soviet film-makers.

956 Davis, Lisa and **Sonia Rivera.** La patria, el dólar y la pantalla o cómo hacer cine en América Latina: una mesa redonda (AR, 10:37, 1984, p. 10–17, ill.)
A reconstructed round-table discussion on the current situation of Latin American cinema. Participants include Marcela Fernández Violante (Mexico), Ramiro Lacayo (Nicaragua), Beatriz Palacios (Bolivia), Edgardo Pallero (Argentina), Jorge Sanjinés (Bolivia), Geraldo Sarno (Brazil), Humberto Solás (Cuba), Manoel Sorto (El Salvador), and Mónica Vásquez (Ecuador). Ideological questions and strategies of production and distribution are the main focus of the participants' comments.

957 Mahieu, José Agustín. Algunas aproximaciones al cine iberoamericano actual (CH, 381, marzo 1982, p. 648–660)
Based on observations of a Spanish festival (Huelva, 1981), Mahieu examines differences and identities between Spanish and Latin American cinemas before turning to the general situation of film production in Argentina, Bolivia, Brazil, Mexico, and Venezuela. Informative, if superficial.

958 Mahieu, José Agustín. Cine iberoamericano: otras voces y otros ámbitos (CH, 356, feb. 1980, p. 392–402)
Continuing his survey of Latin American cinema begun in *Cuadernos Hispano-* *americanos* (No. 340, oct. 1978), Mahieu discusses the situation in Bolivia, Peru, Uruguay, Paraguay, and Central America, countries without the strong cinematic tradition of Brazil, Argentina, and Mexico but ones that have found ingenious ways to overcome common difficulties. As always, his remarks are insightful and well informed.

959 Paranaguá, Paulo Antonio. La nouveau cinéma latino-américain: entre la répression des dictatures et la tutelle étatique (OSPAAAL/T, 2:35, 1981, p. 120–130)
Survey of the birth and evolution of the new Latin American cinema, focusing on resistance, repression, and the benefits and pitfalls of State intervention in national film industries. Main question posed is "Une cinématographie dépendante serait-elle condamnée à être, ou bien à la merci de la production étrangère dominante, ou bien à l'ombre de la protection envahissante des Etats?"

960 Schnitman, Jorge A. Film industries in Latin America: dependency and development. Norwood, N.J.: Ablex Pub. Corp., 1984. 134 p.: bibl., indexes.
Well researched study of film industry development in Latin America seen in the context of its dependency on advanced industrial powers. Includes individual chapters on Argentina and Mexico, Brazil, Chile, and Bolivia, and analysis of the general situation facing all Latin American cinemas. Although recent developments in some countries, such as Brazil and Argentina, date the analysis, it is nonetheless an intelligent piece of work and an essential research tool.

961 Scott, Robert. Bibliography of Latin American cinema (JumpCut [Berkeley, Calif.] 30, March 1985, p. 59–61)
Possibly the most complete bibliography of English-language sources on Latin American cinema. Divided by country. Very useful and highly recommended as research tool.

962 Shatunóvskaya, Irina. El cine latinoamericano de hoy (URSS/AL, 9[33], 1980, p. 120–129, ill., plates)
Brief discussion of films shown at the 6th Three Continents Film Festival (Tashkent, USSR). Author praises Cuban cinema's continued attempt to discuss pressing social issues while at the same time criticizing the commercialism of films from Mexico, Brazil,

and Argentina. Looks at the situation of Chilean cinema and its exiled film-makers and problems faced by Latin American cinema generally.

963 Shatunóvskaya, Irina. Tashkent-82: las cinematografías nacionales en lucha (URSS/AL, 12[60] dic. 1982, p. 89–105, ill.)

Reflections on the achievements of Latin American cinema written on the occasion of the 7th Tashkent Festival (USSR), with special attention given to films of Nicaragua, El Salvador, Colombia, Mexico, and Bolivia. Also discusses use of historical themes, image of the working class, and role of the individual in society in a number of different films. Informative.

964 Twenty-five years of the new Latin American cinema. Edited by Michael Chanan. London: British Film Institute: Channel Four Television, 1983. 40 p.: film.

"Dossier" published to accompany two special showings of Latin American films in London. Brings together English translations of such seminal writings as Fernando Birri's "Cinema and Underdevelopment," Glauber Rocha's "The Aesthetics of Hunger," Solanas and Getino's "Towards a Third Cinema," and García Espinosa's "For an Imperfect Cinema." Chanan's introduction is taken from his documentary *New cinema of Latin America*. Useful as classroom text.

965 West, Dennis. Latin American film studies: some recent anthologies (LARR, 18:1, 1983, p. 179–188)

Review essay discusses 18 books and booklets on Latin American cinema (1975–80) that consist of: film scripts, didactic manuals on how to use film in the classroom, Mexican cinema, Chilean cinema, Cuban cinema, and works dealing with Latin American cinema generally. No in-depth analysis given the number of works covered but a useful essay nonetheless.

966 Woll, Allen L. The Latin image in American film. Rev. ed. Los Angeles: UCLA, Latin American Center Publications, 1980. 128 p., 12 p. of plates: ill. (UCLA Latin American studies; 50)

Highly informative look at Hollywood's stereotypes of Latin America and its people. Analyzes films such as ¡*Viva Villa!*, *Flying down to Rio*, and *Juárez*. Useful.

ARGENTINA

967 Bortnik, Aída and **Mario Reynoso.** Guiones cinematográficos: *La isla; Allá lejos y hace tiempo*. Selección y prólogo de Jorge Miguel Couselo. Buenos Aires: Centro Editor de América Latina, 1981. 242 p. (Capítulo. Biblioteca argentina fundamental; 96)

Aída Bortnik's screenplay of Alejandro Doria's *La isla* (1979) and Mario Reynoso's screenplay of Miguel Antín's *Allá lejos y hace tiempo* (1978), the latter based on a book by Guillermo Enrique Hudson.

968 Carreras, María Elena de las. Cine argentino, 1980–1983 (CRIT, 58:1941, 11 abril 1985, p. 126–130, bibl.)

Examines political cinema during the last four years of military rule in Argentina, noting a gradual increase in political themes coinciding with a quantitative decrease in film production. Special attention given to Miguel Pérez's *La república perdida* and Héctor Oliveira's *No habrá más penas ni olvido* (both 1983), the only explicitly political films of the period.

969 Couselo, Jorge Miguel et al. Historia del cine argentino. Buenos Aires: Centro Editor de América Latina, 1984. 190 p.: appendices, bibl., ill. (some col.)

Richly illustrated history focuses primarily on commercial film-making in Argentina from the silent period until 1983. Although it does provide some essential information about State support of the film industry as well as the necessary historical overview, it reads like a rather superficial succession of names and titles. As appendices, it includes a good chronology of Argentine cinema and a list of prizes won in international festivals.

970 España, Claudio and **Miguel Angel Rosado.** Medio siglo de cine: Argentina Sono Film, S.A.C.I. Buenos Aires: Editorial Abril: Heraldo del Cine, 1984. 345 p.: bibl., film., ill. (some col.), index.

Commemoration of 50 years of activity of Argentina Sono Film, founded in 1932 by Angel Bautista Mentasti. Responsible for the first sound film in the country (*Tango!*, 1933) and for hundreds of films in the last half century, the production company is essential for a complete understanding of Argentine cinema. The book presents the company's history, with comments on all its films and hundreds of illustrations. Appendices provide a complete filmography with technical information and a list of awards won by the company's films. Important document for studying the history of Argentine cinema.

971 Ferreira, Carlos. Por un cine libre. Buenos Aires: Corregidor, 1983. 135 p.

Impassioned defense of freedom of expression and opposition to all forms of censorship. Although author briefly discusses Torre Nilsson and other film-makers, the volume would be much stronger if it provided statistics or other documentation concerning censorship in Argentina.

972 Getino, Octavio. Notas sobre cine argentino y latinoamericano. México: Edimedios, 1984. 160 p.: bibl.

Collection of essays and interviews published during author's exile from his native Argentina (1976–1983). Examines precarious economic and political situation of Argentine cinema after the coup d'état of 1976, discusses his own career (*La hora de los hornos*, etc.), reviews development of concept of Third Cinema, and looks at problems facing Latin American cinema in general. Excellent.

973 Mahieu, José Agustín. Literatura y cine en Latinoamérica (CH, 367/368, enero/feb. 1981, p. 299–309)

Brief panorama of relationship between literature and film in Latin America focusing specifically on national and international works adapted to the screen in Argentina.

974 Mahieu, José Agustín. Revisión crítica del cine argentino: 1960–1980 (CH, 373, julio 1981, p. 173–187)

Knowledgeable discussion of major tendencies of Argentine political cinema, focusing specifically on the work of the Grupo Cine Liberación (Getino, Solanas, etc.) and the Grupo Cine de la Base (Gleizer). Useful.

975 Martín, Jorge Abel. Los films de Armando Bó con Isabel Sarli. Buenos Aires: Corregidor, 1981. 174 p.: film., ill. (Serie mayor)

Examines highly successful careers of director Armando Bó and actress Isabel Sarli

based on extensive interviews with Bó. Includes synopses of 29 films they made.

976 Ortiz, Mecha. Mecha Ortiz. Textos recopilados, testimonios y notas de Salvador D. D'Anna y Elena B. de D'Anna. Buenos Aires: Editorial Moreno, 1982. 430 p., 1 leaf of plates: ill.

Richly illustrated autobiography intercut with interviews and testimonials from theater and film professionals. Celebrates the career of one of Argentina's most famous actresses. A personal look at the development of commercial cinema in that country.

977 Vallejo, Gerardo. Un camino hacia el cine. Buenos Aires: El Cid Editor, 1984. 251 p.: ill. (Col. Estudios interdisciplinarios)

Written in exile, this autobiographical account discusses not only the films and experiences of its author, director of *El camino hacia la muerte del Viejo Reales* (1968), both in Argentina and in exile, but also essential questions of film analysis and production. Looks at author's involvement in Fernando Birri's Instituto de Santa Fe and relates his experiences with Solanas and Getino. Excellent, personal look at film-making in Argentina and at the situation of Latin American film-makers in exile. Includes as an epilogue a letter from Birri.

978 Vanossi, Jorge. El cine argentino (*in* Pirovano, Ignacio *et al.* Arte y cultura en la Argentina. Buenos Aires: Editorial de Belgrano, 1977, p. 129–150)

Two separate interviews on Argentine cinema with directors Manuel Antín and Leopoldo Torre Nilsson. Antín sees the situation at the time (1977) in bleak terms because film-makers are forced to "luchar contra la falta de capitales, contra la censura y a veces contra el mismo público," while Torre Nilsson sees a lack of "generational continuity." Both directors discuss censorship, State support of the industry, and the relationship of Argentine cinema and the public. Useful.

BOLIVIA

979 Gumucio Dagrón, Alfonso. Breve historia del cine boliviano (UV/PH, 24, oct./dic. 1977, p. 29–45, plates)

Excellent, informative survey (up to 1976) of the historical evolution of the Bolivian cinema, reviews writing on the subject as well as films themselves. Devotes special attention to early pioneers Luis G. Castillo and Arturo Posnansky, 1920s film-makers Pedro Sambarino and José María Velasco Maidana, and, of course, Jorge Sanjinés and the 1960s Ukamau group. Important.

980 Gumucio Dagrón, Alfonso. Historia del cine boliviano. México: Filmoteca, UNAM, 1983. 327 p.: bibl., ill., indexes (Documentos de Filmoteca; 5)

This most extensive study of Bolivian cinema to date is divided into: 1) 1904–38; and 2) 1938–82. Discusses both early and more recent films in some depth, looking not only at filmic texts themselves, but also at behind-the-scenes aspects of film production and political intentions of more recent film-makers (e.g., Sanjinés). Excellent.

981 Mesa Gisbert, Carlos D. El cine boliviano según Luis Espinal. La Paz: Editorial Don Bosco, 1982. 209 p., 15 p. of plates: ill., ports. (Col. Cinestudios; 5)

Homage to the late critic, screenwriter, and director Luis Espinal consists of three parts: 1) Espinal's critical and cinematic activity; 2) overview of Bolivian cinema and film criticism; and 3) short anthology of Espinal's writings on Bolivian cinema, including essays on Jorge Sanjinés and Antonio Eguino. Good and useful view of problems and solutions of film-making in Bolivia.

982 Soria Gamarra, Oscar. Chuquiago: guión del film. La Paz: Editorial Don Bosco, 1977. 96 p., 4 leaves of plates: ill. (Col. Cine boliviano; 1)

Narrative that served as basis for the screenplay of Antonio Eguino's Chuquiago (1977).

983 Soria Gamarra, Oscar. Mi socio: guión cinematográfico. Cochabamba, Bolivia: Editorial Los Amigos del Libro, 1982. 85 p., 2 p. of plates: ill. (Col. Cine y teatro)

Narrative screenplay of Paolo Agazzi's film about the friendship between a truck driver and a young boy. Written by one of the major figures of the Ukamau group.

984 West, Dennis. Film and revolution in the Andes (UCSB/NS, 8, 1982, p. 517–521)

Insightful analysis of Jorge Sanjinés's

1971 El enemigo principal focusing on dramatic and narrative structures, the director's political intentions and theory, and major thematic elements. Favorable but at the same time critical.

BRAZIL

985 Avellar, José Carlos. Imagem e som, imagem e ação, imaginação. Rio de Janeiro: Paz e Terra, 1982. 192 p.: ill. (Col. Cinema; 13)

Compilation of journalistic film reviews by one of Brazil's leading critics. Although most deal with foreign films, the volume does include analyses of such Brazilian films as Miguel Borges's Pecado na sacristia (1975), João Ramiro Mello's O sósia da morte (1975), and Zelito Viana's Os condenados (1974), among others.

986 Back, Silvio. República Guarani x. Rio de Janeiro: Paz e Terra, 1982. 116 p.: bibl., film., ill. (Col. Cinema; 14)

This is what director Back calls a "non-script" of his 1981 film República Guaraní or "uma reflexão em voz alta sobre o filme, a inconfidência de suas intenções mais recônditas livremente alinhavadas pelo autor." An interesting document on the work of a prolific, regional Brazilian film-maker.

987 Barreto, Lima. O cangaceiro. Fortaleza: Edições Univ. Federal do Ceará, 1984. 163 p.: ill. (Col. Quadro a quadro; 2)

Script of Lima Barreto's award-winning 1953 film which revitalized the cangaceiro theme in Brazilian cinema. Provides camera scale and movements in addition to complete dialogue.

988 Barros, José Tavares de. Sobre o cinema mineiro (in Seminário sobre a Cultura Mineira, 2nd, Belo Horizonte, Brazil, 1979. Periódo contemporâneo. Belo Horizonte: Conselho Estadual de Cultura de Minas Gerais, 1980, p. 75–91)

Within the context of external and internal dependency, author examines difficulties of producing films in the Brazilian state of Minas Gerais outside of the dominant Rio-São Paulo axis. Article focuses on the tenacity of film-makers such as Humberto Mauro, Higino Bonfioli, and Francisco de Almeida Fleming, and provides a historical overview of film production in the state.

989 Bernardet, Jean Claude. Piranha no mar de rosas. São Paulo: Nobel, 1982. 135 p.

Collection of texts by one of Brazil's leading and most controversial film critics (1976–82). Includes lucid analysis of Glauber Rocha's *A idade da terra* (1980), and considerations of such diverse topics as erotic films, Venezuelan cinema, historical themes, and television commercials. As always, Bernardet must be read by students of Brazilian cinema.

990 Borges, Luiz Carlos Ribeiro. 1960–1980 [i.e. Mil novecentos e sesenta-mil novecentos e oitenta]: o cinema à margem. Campinas: Papirus Livraria Editora, 1984. 72 p. (Col. Krisis)

Short book examines dominant tendencies in Brazilian cinema (1960–80) in an attempt to explain the concept of marginality in that cinema. Presents overview of birth and evolution of Cinema Novo within its historical context, reevaluates the late 1960s underground movement, and discusses the 1970s-80s thematic multiplicity. Concludes, not surprisingly, that the insistence on the portrayal of marginality represents a sense of solidarity of film-makers with the disenfranchised segments of Brazilian society.

991 Burton, Julianne. The politics of aesthetic distance: *São Bernardo* (Screen [Society for Education in Film and Television, London] 24:2, March/April 1983, p. 30–53)

Highly perceptive study of Leon Hirszman's 1972 film, based on the homonymous novel by Graciliano Ramos. Focuses on the film's modes of representation. Best analysis of the film to date in any language.

992 Carlos Ortiz e o cinema brasileiro na década de 50. Pesquisa e seleção de textos, Carlos Eduardo Ornelas Berriel. São Paulo: Depto. de Informação e Documentação Artísticas, Centro de Documentação e Informação sobre Arte Brasileira Contemporânea, 1981. 97 p.: ill. (Cadernos; 8)

Volume in homage to Carlos Ortiz, important Brazilian film critic of the 1950s, includes anthology of his writings, interview on his work, and screenplay of his film *Alameda da saudade, 113* (1950). Essential for understanding the critical and ideological dimensions of Brazilian cinema prior to Cinema Novo.

993 Catani, Afrânio Mendes and **José I. de Melo Souza.** A chanchada no cinema brasileiro. São Paulo: Brasiliense, 1983. 98 p.: film., ill. (Tudo é história; 76)

Brief but well researched study of the *chanchada* (light musical comedy), which reigned supreme in Brazil from the 1940s through the 1950s. Discusses the genre's roots, relation to Vargas's Estado Novo, major practitioners (e.g., Watson Macedo), and ultimate decline. Informative introduction to the subject.

994 Cine jornal brasileiro: Departamento de Imprensa e Propaganda, 1938–1946. Organização de Maria Rita Galvão *et al.* São Paulo: Fundação Cinemateca Brasileira, s.d. 188 p.: plates.

Richly illustrated catalog of the Fundação Cinemateca Brasileira's holdings of government newsreels produced by Getúlio Vargas's infamous DIP. Potentially important research tool for historians.

995 Cinemateca imaginária: cinema & memória. Rio de Janeiro: Empresa Brasileira de Filmes (EMBRAFILME), 1981. 160 p.: ill.

Focuses on important question of preservation of the national cinematic heritage and important role played by *cinematecas*. One section summarizes discussions held at Simpósio sobre o Cinema e a Memória do Brasil (Rio de Janeiro, Aug. 1979).

996 Cronologia cinematográfica brasileira, 1898–1930. 2a ed. Rio de Janeiro: Cinemateca, Museu de Arte Moderna, 1979. 122, 6 leaves: bibl.

Filmography of early Brazilian cinema. Although admittedly incomplete, covering probably no more than 40 percent of national production (1898–1930), it represents an important step toward the establishment of a definitive filmography of Brazilian cinema.

997 Csicsery, George. Individual solutions: an interview with Héctor Babenco (Film Quarterly [Univ. of California, Berkeley] 36:1, Fall 1982, p. 2–15)

Director Babenco talks about the production of his 1981 film, *Pixote*.

999 Farias, Roberto. *Pra frente Brasil*: história, roteiro e diálogos. Baseado no argumento *Sala escura* de Reginaldo Faria e Paulo Mendonça. Rio de Janeiro: Alhambra, 1983. 86 p.: ill.

Screenplay of Farias's controversial 1982 film about an innocent man who is arrested, tortured, and murdered by the repressive apparatus of Brazil's military government.

1000 O Filme curto. Edição de Carlos Roberto Rodrigues de Souza. São Paulo: Prefeitura do Município de São Paulo, Secretaria Municipal de Cultura, Depto. de Informação e Documentação Artísticas (IDART), Centro de Pesquisa de Arte Brasileira, 1980. 2 v.: bibl., film., indexes, ports. (some col.) (Pesquisa; 1)

Survey of problems of production, distribution and exhibition of short films in São Paulo. Describes production companies, interviews directors, and includes filmographies and archive holdings. Also focuses on the role of the film school at the Univ. of São Paulo and on State subvention of short films. Wide-ranging but somewhat disorganized research tool.

1001 Galdino, Márcio da Rocha. Minas Gerais: ensaios de filmografia. Belo Horizonte: Prefeitura de Belo Horizonte, Secretaria Municipal de Cultura e Turismo, 1984? 430 p.: bibl., ill.

First systematic historical survey of film production in the Brazilian state of Minas Gerais (1903–83). Provides synopses and technical information on hundreds of films as well as extensive bibliography. Valuable contribution toward establishing a complete filmography of Brazilian cinema.

1002 Galvão, Maria Rita Eliezer and **Jean-Claude Bernardet.** Cinema, repercussões em caixa de eco ideológica: as idéias de "nacional" e "popular" no pensamento cinematográfico brasileiro. São Paulo: Brasiliense, 1983. 266 p.: bibl., film. (O Nacional e o popular na cultura brasileira)

Historical review of the notions of "national" and "popular" as they have evolved along with the development of Brazilian cinema. Provides important information about ideological debates prior to 1960, in addition to a critical evaluation of Cinema Novo. Essential.

1003 Gerber, Raquel. O cinema brasileiro e o processo político e cultural, de 1950 a 1978: bibliografia e filmografia crítica e seletiva, ênfase no Cinema Novo e Glauber Rocha com entradas na área da política e da cultura: texto introductório, "O processo cinemanovista," notas sobre a história e

filmes. Rio de Janeiro: Empresa Brasileira de Filmes (EMBRAFILME), 1982. 290 p.

Bibliography of books, film reviews, and journalistic articles concerning cinematic production (1950–78), focuses primarily on Glauber Rocha's work. Organized chronologically and by thematic area but difficult to consult. Good index would be helpful.

1004 Gerber, Raquel. O mito da civilização Atlântica: Glauber Rocha, cinema, política e a estética do inconsciente. Petrópolis: Vozes, 1982. 288 p.: bibl., plates.

Psychoanalytical study of Glauber Rocha's films based on author's Master's thesis.

1005 Gomes, Paulo Emílio Salles. Crítica de cinema no *Suplemento literário.* Rio de Janeiro: Editora Paz e Terra: Empresa Brasileira de Filmes (EMBRAFILME), 1982. 2 v.: ill., index (Col. Cinema; 9)

Compilation in two substantial volumes of the late Gomes's film criticism, originally published in *O Estado de São Paulo* (1956–65). Essays deal with both Brazilian and foreign cinemas and include such seminal pieces as "Uma Situação Colonial?" and "O Dono do Mercado." Essential work for understanding the thought of one of Brazil's most influential film critics.

1006 Guizzo, José Octávio. *Alma do Brasil:* o primeiro filme nacional de reconstituição histórica, inteiramente sonorizado. Campo Grande: O Autor, 1984. 115 p.: bibl., ill., photos.

Book describes and documents the production of the first feature-length film made in the state of Mato Grosso (1932). Includes interviews with producer Alexandre Wulfes, director Líbero Luxardo, and main actor and actress, and reproduces correspondence, newspaper clippings, and photographs of the film.

1007 Johnson, Randal. Brazilian Cinema Novo (Bulletin of Latin American Research [Oxford Microfilm Pub., Oxford, England] 3:2, 1984, p. 95–106)

Critical look at Cinema Novo's evolution over the last 25 years discusses its political intentions, attitude toward industrial models, and relationship to the State as well as accomplishments and contradictions.

1008 Johnson, Randal. Cinema Novo x 5: masters of contemporary Brazilian film. Austin: Univ. of Texas Press, 1982. 246 p.: index, plates (Latin American monographs; 60)

Auteur study of films by five major exponents of Cinema Novo: Joaquim Pedro de Andrade, Carlos Diegues, Ruy Guerra, Glauber Rocha, and Nelson Pereira dos Santos.

1009 Johnson, Randal. Film, television, and traditional folk culture in *Bye bye Brasil* (Journal of Popular Culture [Bowling Green State Univ., Bowling Green, Ohio] 18:1, Summer 1984, p. 121–132, plates)

Analysis of Carlos Diegues's 1980 film.

1010 Johnson, Randal. Literatura e cinema: *Macunaíma* do modernismo na literatura ao Cinema Novo. São Paulo: Thomaz A. Queiroz, 1982. 1 v.

Comparative analysis of Mário de Andrade's 1928 novel *Macunaíma* and Joaquim Pedro de Andrade's 1969 adaptation of that novel as seen within the context of literary modernism and Cinema Novo, respectively.

1011 Johnson, Randal. Nelson Rodrigues as filmed by Arnaldo Jabor (UK/LATR, 16:1, Fall 1982, p. 15–18, plates)

Analysis of Jabor's *Toda nudez será castigada* (1973) and *O casamento* (1975), both of which are based on works by playwright/novelist Nelson Rodrigues.

1012 Johnson, Randal. Popular cinema in Brazil (Studies in Latin American Popular Culture [Dept. of Modern Language, New Mexico State Univ., Albuquerque] 3, 1984, p. 86–96)

Discussion of three tendencies in Brazilian films which are produced independently of the state agency, Embrafilme: the Trapalhões comedy team's children's films, Amâcio Mazzaropi's rural morality plays, and the *pornochanchada.*

1013 Johnson, Randal. State policy toward the film industry in Brazil. Austin: Univ. of Texas, Office for Public Sector Studies, Institute of Latin American Studies, 1982. 11 p. (Technical papers series; 36)

Overview of the relationship between cinema and the State in Brazil.

1014 Johnson, Randal. *Vidas secas* and the politics of filmic adaptation (IL, 3:15, Jan./March 1981, p. 4–18)

Analysis of Nelson Pereira dos Santos's 1963 adaptation of Graciliano Ramos's 1938 classic novel *Vidas secas.*

1015 Johnson, Randal and Robert Stam. Recovering popular emotion: an interview with Leon Hirszman (Cineaste [New York] 13:2, 1984, p. 20–23, 58, plates)

Director Hirszman discusses his *Eles não usam black-tie* (1981) on the occasion of its release in New York.

1016 Leal, Wills. O Nordeste no cinema. João Pessoa: Univ. Federal de Paraíba, FUNAPE, Editora Universitaria; Salvador: Univ. Federal da Bahia, 1982. 133 p.: bibl.

Superficial look at films dealing with, but not necessarily produced in, Brazil's Northeast. Includes essays on Nelson Pereira dos Santos's *Vidas secas,* Walter Lima Jr.'s *Menino de engenho,* Glauber Rocha's *Deus e o diabo na terra do sol,* Geraldo Sarno's *Viramundo,* as well as on the documentary in general and films dealing with *cangaceiros.* Epilogue by Jean-Claude Bernardet.

1017 Luccas, Celso and Beatriz de Chavagnac. Cinema ambulante. São Paulo: Global Editora, 1982. 99 p.: ill. (Cinetexto)

Documentation of attempt to create an alternative, "itinerant" circuit of film exhibition in Brazil using Celso Luccas and José Celso Martinez Correia's *25,* which was made in Mozambique. Poetic and cinematic collage.

1018 Munerato, Elice and Maria Helena Darcy de Oliveira. As musas da matinê. Rio de Janeiro: Edições Rioarte, 1982. 105 p.: ports.

Cogent and informative analysis of the role and image of women in Brazilian cinema. Concludes, not surprisingly, that the portrayal of women has often been less than progressive and that they have historically been underrepresented behind the cameras. Useful.

1019 Nadotti, Nelson and Carlos Diegues. *Quilombo:* roteiro do filme e crônica das filmagens. Rio de Janeiro: Achiamé, 1984. 204 p., 20 p. of plates: ill.

Sometimes fascinating diary-like account of the production of Carlos Diegues's *Quilombo* (1984). Includes complete script, interview with Diegues, song lyrics, film's technical data, and biographical information about crew members.

1020 Nascimento, Hélio. Cinema brasileiro. Pôrto Alegre: Mercado Aberto, 1981. 120 p. (Série Revisão; 5)

Panorama of Brazilian cinema, including chapters on early pioneers, the *chanchada*, Vera Cruz, and such directors as Anselmo Duarte, Nelson Pereira dos Santos, Glauber Rocha, Joaquim Pedro de Andrade, Héctor Babenco, and Arnaldo Jabor. Attempt to cover so much in such short a space results in a superficial work.

1021 Nobre, F. Silvia. Inventário do cinema brasileiro: bibliografia. Fortaleza: Gráfica Editorial Cearense, 1978. 256 p.

Annotated bibliography of books and articles dealing with Brazilian cinema. Although not comprehensive, a useful research tool.

1022 Oroz, Silvia. Carlos Diegues: os filmes que não filmei. Rio de Janeiro: Rocco, 1984. 182 p.: bibl., index, plates.

In this extended interview, director Diegues discusses all of his feature-length films up to *Bye bye Brasil* (1980). Includes newspaper reports on *Quilombo* (1984), which had not been completed at the time of the interview, as well as credit information on all films. Interesting.

1023 Osiel, Mark. Bye bye boredom: Brazilian cinema comes of age (Cineaste [New York] 14:1, 1985, p. 30–35)

Despite the title, which implies that Brazilian film-making prior to Sônia Braga was boring in its totality, this is an informative, critical look at the current situation of the film industry in the country.

1024 Peixoto, Mário. A alma, segundo Salustre. Rio de Janeiro: Empresa Brasileira de Filmes (EMBRAFILME), 1983. 100 p., 5 leaves of plates: ill.

A descriptive "screenplay" written in the 1950s by film-maker, novelist, and poet Mário Peixoto, whose *Limite* (1930) is a classic of Brazilian avant-garde cinema. Unfortunately, Peixoto was unable to film this work, which is closely related to *Limite* in its theme and aesthetics.

1025 Ramos, José Mário Ortiz. Cinema, estado e lutas culturais: anos 50/60/70. Rio de Janeiro: Paz e Terra, 1983. 176 p. (Col. Cinema; 16)

Sometimes lucid analysis of the complex and contradictory relations between cinema and the State in Brazil (1950–80). Tends to see such relations as inherently negative and cooptive, which is clearly simplistic. Nonetheless, an important contribution to the literature on the subject.

1026 Rocha, Glauber. Roteiros do Terceyro Mundo. Organização de Orlando Senna. Rio de Janeiro: Alhambra: Empresa Brasileira de Filmes (EMBRAFILME), 1985. 466 p., 32 p. of plates: ill.

Complete screenplays of all of the late Rocha's features preceded by first treatments of all those made in Brazil, including *A Idade da terra*. Important source for studying the work of the undisputed leader of Cinema Novo.

1027 Rocha, Glauber. O século do cinema. Rio de Janeiro: Editorial Alhambra: Empresa Brasileira de Filmes (EMBRAFILME), Secretaria de Cultura, MEC, 1983. 255 p.

Writings by late Rocha on foreign cinemas, divided into uneven parts: 1) Hollywood; 2) Neo-Realism; and 3) the Nouvelle Vague. Important collection for understanding theoretical concerns and evolution of the person many consider Brazil's greatest film-maker.

1028 Serran, Leopoldo. Duas histórias para cinema: roteiros. Rio de Janeiro: Editôra Nova Fronteira, 1981. 191 p.: ill.

Serran's screenplays of Antônio Calmon's *Revólver de brinquedo* and Bruno Barreto's *Amor bandido*. Indication of the increasing professionalization of screenwriters in Brazil.

1029 Silva, Aguinaldo and Joaquim Vaz de Carvalho. Luz del fuego. Rio de Janeiro: Editôra Codecri: Morena Produções de Arte, 1982. 130 p.: plates.

Complete screenplay of David Neves's 1982 film, preceded by documents and interviews concerning the controversial real-life person whose life is the basis of the film.

1030 Souza, Carlos Roberto de. A fascinante aventura do cinema brasileiro. Rev. e aum. São Paulo: Fundação Cinemateca Brasileira, 1981. 104 p.: bibl.

Short book, originally published as two lengthy essays in *O Estado de São Paulo* (25 Oct. and 2 Nov. 1975), provides an excellent and insightful panorama of Brazilian film history from the beginnings until 1980 (in its updated version). Deals with both well known (Cinema Novo) and little known (e.g., Guelfo Andaló) aspects of Brazilian cinema. Recommended.

1031 Stam, Robert. Slow fade to Afro: the black presence in Brazilian cinema (Film Quarterly [Univ. of California, Berkeley] 36:2, Winter 1982/1983, p. 16–32, plates)

Excellent analysis of the image and role of blacks in Brazilian cinema, concentrating not only on racial stereotypes, but also on black participation in film production. Recommended.

1031a Tendler, Sílvio. *Caliban apresenta Jango*: um filme de Sílvio Tendler. Texto de Maurício Dias. Pôrto Alegre: L&PM Editores, 1984. 118 p.: bibl., ports.

Text of Sílvio Tendler's 1984 film about the late Brazilian president João Goulart, deposed by the military in 1964. Important documentary and important document, despite the director's somewhat exaggerated idealization of his subject.

1032 Viany, Alex. *Agulha no palheiro*. Fortaleza: Univ. Federal do Ceará, 1983. 232 p.: plates (Col. Quadro a quadro. Roteiros cinematográficos; 1)

Complete script of Viany's 1952 film, preceded by a chronological biography of the director, two statements by him, and short reviews by Matos Pacheco and Salvyano Cavalcânti de Paiva.

1033 Xavier, Ismail. Sertão mar: Glauber Rocha e a estética da fome. São Paulo: Brasiliense: Empresa Brasileira de Filmes (EMBRAFILME), Secretaria da Cultura, MEC, 1983. 172 p.: plates.

Lucid critical analysis of the "aesthetic of hunger" as expressed primarily in Glauber Rocha's *Barravento* (1962) and *Deus e o diabo na terra do sol* (1964), with comparative analyses of Anselmo Duarte's *Pagador de promessas* (1962) and Lima Barreto's *O cangaceiro*. These fascinating close readings constitute what is clearly the best book on Rocha to date. Highly recommended.

CHILE

1034 Coad, Malcolm. Rebirth of Chilean cinema (INDEX, 9:2, April 1980, p. 3–8, plates)

Informative account of repression and destruction of the Chilean film industry by the Pinochet regime, its censorship policies, activities of exiled directors such as Miguel Littín, and the few films made inside the country since 1973. The new Chilean cinema does exist, but its center of activity remains outside of Chile.

1035 Mahieu, José Agustín. El breve resplandor del cine chileno (CH, 346, abril 1979, p. 198–208)

Informative look at the evolution of Chilean cinema from the 1940s and creation of the State-supported Chile Films to the more politicized production of the 1960s and early 1970s with such film-makers as Miguel Littín, Aldo Francia, Raúl Ruiz, and Patricio Guzmán. Does not discuss films made in exile after the overthrow of Salvador Allende.

1036 Mahieu, José Agustín. Cine iberoamericano: los cuadros vivientes o hipótesis de Raúl Ruiz (CH, 360, junio 1980, p. 647–656)

First in series of studies of Latin American film-makers looks at the work of Chilean Raúl Ruiz, who continued his career in Europe after being exiled from his native land after Salvador Allende's overthrow. Concludes with brief excerpts from Ruiz's own writings on film. Good introduction to his work both in Chile and abroad.

1037 Pick, Zuzana M. El exilio chileno y su cine, 1973–1983 (AR, 10:37, 1984, p. 22–25, ill.)

In the first 10 years since Salvador Allende's violent overthrow, Chilean film-makers in exile have produced some 155 films, an unprecedented phenomenon in the history of world cinema. Pick's article is an informative, if superficial, overview of this production.

1038 Re-visión del cine chileno. Directora de la investigación, Alicia Vega. Ayudantes, Ignacio Agüero *et al*. Santiago: Editorial Aconcagua: Centro de Indagación y Expresión Cultural y Artística, 1979. 391 p.: 16 leaves of plates: bibl., ill. (Col. Lautaro)

Formalist analysis of seven Chilean

features (including Miguel Littín's *El chacal de Nahueltoro*) and seven documentaries (including Patricio Guzmán's *Primer año*). Unlike most studies of Latin American cinema, these analyses isolate the films from their sociopolitical context and focus on the articulations of their cinematic language. While such analysis is important, it is insufficient to provide a complete understanding of the films in question.

COLOMBIA

1039 Alvarez, Carlos. Una década de cortometraje colombiano, 1970–1980. S.l.: *Revista Arcadia va al Cine*, between 1982 and 1984. 110 p. (Borradores de cine; 1)

Book is an amputated version of what was originally planned and written as an extensive survey of short film production in Colombia (1970–80). Introductory essay outlines question of production financing during the period, especially after the implementation of the 1974 *sobreprecio* program. Subsequent chapters list production companies, directors, photographers, and themes.

1040 Duque N., Lizandro. Algunas claves para abordar los problemas del cine en Colombia (*in* El Nuevo pensamiento colombiano. Bogotá: FEDELCO, 1977, p. 99–146)

In this extensive article, Duque argues that the failure of Colombian cinema to develop satisfactorily can only be understood when seen within the context of the neo-colonial nature of Colombian society. After describing early consolidation of US and French film industries (with Edison and Pathé, respectively), author discusses the historical evolution of film in Colombia, showing at every step the reasons for its underdevelopment. Excellent.

1041 Martínez Pardo, Hernando. Historia del cine colombiano. Bogotá: Librería y Editorial América Latina, 1978. 472 p.: bibl., ill., indexes.

Knowledgeable and extensive history of Colombian cinema and its struggle for survival (1898–1976). Discusses major companies, directors, and legislation as well as the structure of the distribution and exhibition sectors. Excellent.

1042 Valverde, Umberto. Reportaje crítico al cine colombiano. Bogotá: Editorial Toronueva, 1978. 355 p., 5 leaves of plates: ill.

Collection of interviews with leading figures of Colombian cinema (e.g., Carlos Alvarez, Luis Alfredo Sánchez, Jorge Silva, Martha Rodríguez). Includes extensive discussion of production of short subjects under the government's *sobreprecio* program as well as independent and "marginal" filmmaking. Preceded by overview essay by Valverde. Excellent introduction to problems faced by the still incipient Colombian film industry.

CUBA

1043 Branly, Robert. La juventud en la producción fílmica cubana (UEAC/GC, 167, mayo 1978, p. 23–24)

Short article argues that youth has been a constant thematic element in Revolutionary Cuban cinema, exemplifying his argument with a descriptive chronology of the theme in both documentary and feature films. Superficial.

1044 Burton, Julianne. El reto de masividad en la cultura popular cubana: una conversación con Julio García Espinosa (AR, 8 : 29, 1982, p. 31–37, plates)

Interview in which film-maker García Espinosa, recently named Cuban Vice-Minister of Culture, discusses the creation of the ministry and its support of popular culture. Also examines use of popular culture in films such as *Las aventuras de Juan Quin Quin* and *Cuba baila*. Also available in English in *Studies in Latin American Popular Culture* (1, 1982, p. 216–224)

1045 Bykova, Irina S. Cuba: el cine y la revolución (URSS/AL, 2, 1977, p. 156–173)

Informative and highly favorable panorama of the birth, evolution, and accomplishments of Revolutionary Cuban cinema. Discusses documentary as well as fiction films, with special attention given to the work of documentarist Santiago Alvarez and films such as Gutiérrez Alea's *Historias de la Revolución* (1960), Humberto Solás's *Lucía* (1968) and *Cantata de Chile* (1976), and Sergio Giral's *El otro Francisco* (1975).

1046 Bykova, Irina S. Kino Kuby = Cuban cinema. Moskva: Iskusstvo, 1984. 150 p., 48 p. of plates: bibl., film., ill.

Guide to Cuban cinema includes short section of biographical entries for film directors. Publisher serves as leading Soviet channel for serious discussion of world art. [R.V. Allen]

1047 Chanan, Michael. Toward a systematic classification of Cuban documentary: *cine testimonio* and *cine didáctico* (AR, 10:37, 1984, p. 26–31, ill.)

British film-maker and scholar Chanan presents some conclusions of his study of the history and nature of the Cuban documentary, critically analyzing categories that have frequently been used to classify such films. As the title indicates, he concentrates primarily on the notions of "testimonial" and "didactic" cinema.

1048 Chijona, Gerardo. El cine cubano, hecho cultural de la Revolución (*in* La Cultura en Cuba socialista. La Habana: Editorial Letras Cubanas, 1982, p. 215–229)

Good overview of birth and evolution of Revolutionary Cuban cinema focusing on general tendencies, purposes, and achievements rather than individual films or directors. Sees the whole of that cinema (fiction and documentary features, short subjects, newsreels, and animated films), as "la expresión de un arte revolucionario que conjugando la eficacia política e ideológica con la calidad estética, contribuye desde su campo a la tarea de descolonización cultural . . ."

1049 García, A.M. El cine en Cuba (AR, 4:3/4, Spring 1978, p. 74–76)

Report on the visit of the New York-based Antonio Maceo Brigade to ICAIC (Cuban film agency) in the form of a brief overview of the major themes, tendencies, and accomplishments of Revolutionary Cuban cinema.

1050 García Espinosa, Julio. Una imagen recorre el mundo. La Habana: Editorial Letras Cubanas, 1979. 106 p. (Col. Crítica)

Collection by leading Cuban film and cultural theorist. Includes his seminal essay "Por un Cine Imperfecto" and the one which gives the volume its title, as well as discussions of the role of intellectuals and the situation of Latin American cinema generally. Important.

1051 García Espinosa, Julio. Meditaciones sobre el cine imperfecto: quince años después (AR, 10:37, 1984, p. 8–9, ill.)

Cuban film-maker and president of ICAIC (Cuba's film agency) reconsiders and updates his seminal concept of an "imperfect

cinema." Finding his conclusions in the 1969 piece still valid, he discusses the relationship of a Third World cinema to its audience, questions of artistic "quality," and how underdeveloped countries should see themselves and their cultural production in the broader context of advanced capitalism.

1052 Ginsberg, Judith. From anger to action: the avenging female in two *Lucías* (UA/REH, 14:1, enero 1980, p. 131–138)

Compares portrayal of women in José Martí's novel *Lucía Jérez* (1885) and in first segment of Humberto Solás's three-part *Lucía* (1969). Ginsberg argues that while women represent a passive, negative presence in Martí's novel, roles are reversed in the film and Lucía becomes a symbol of the oppressed Cuban people and their desire for liberation. Welcome addition to the literature on Solás's film and the Cuban penchant for historical and literary revision.

1053 Gutiérrez Alea, Tomás. Dialéctica del espectador. La Habana: Unión de Escritores y Artistas de Cuba, 1982. 74 p.: bibl. (Cuadernos de la revista *Unión*; 13)

Seminal essay which "nos enfrenta al mundo de relaciones entre el arte cinematográfico y el espectador. Las convenciones y fórmulas a las que está condicionado el gran público, los intereses de la burguesía en contradicción con los del proletariado, el choque, en fin, entre una sociedad de consumo y una sociedad de revolución." English translation of this monograph published in *JumpCut* (Berkeley, Calif., 29, Feb. 1984, p. 18–21; 30, March 1985, p. 48–53).

1055 Lesage, Julia. Creating history (Jump-Cut [Berkeley, Calif.] 30, March 1985, p. 53–58)

Impressive critical analysis of Sergio Giral's *El otro Francisco*.

1056 Mahieu, José Agustín. El cine cubano (CH, 348, junio 1979, p. 638–647)

After brief remarks on the history of Cuban cinema prior to 1959, Mahieu provides a lucid panorama of cinematic accomplishments since the Revolution. Mentions many films, both documentary and fiction, but analyzes none in depth. As usual, author is well informed and his work is a useful introduction to the topic at hand.

1057 Michaels, Albert L. Revolutionary cinema and the self-reflections on a disappearing class (UCLA/JLAL, 4:1, 1978, p. 129–134)

Superficial and often simplistic analysis of Tomás Gutiérrez Alea's *Memorias del subdesarrollo* (1968).

1058 Paz, Senel. Hasta cierto punto: entrevista a Tomás Gutiérrez Alea (AR, 10:37, 1984, p. 44–47, ill.)

Director Gutiérrez Alea talks about his *Hasta cierto punto* (1983), which deals, like Sara Gómez's *De cierta manera* (1974–77), with machismo and relationships between men and women in a revolutionary context.

1059 Rivero, Angel. El brigadista: entrevistas con Octavio Cortázar, Salvador y Patricio Wood (RYC, 70, junio 1978, p. 14–20, plates)

An interview with director Octavio Cortázar and actors Salvador and Patricio Wood about Cortázar's *El brigadista* (1977), which deals with the 1961 literacy campaign in Cuba. They discuss its process of production as well as its social and cultural importance.

1060 Rodríguez Alemán, Mario. La sala oscura. La Habana: Unión de Escritores y Artistas de Cuba, 1982. 2 v.: films., ill. (Contemporáneos)

These two volumes bring together film reviews by author published in Cuban periodicals since the Revolution. Although dealing almost exclusively with foreign films, the essays provide an interesting Cuban perspective on commercial and artistic film-making in the US and Europe.

1061 20 [i.e. Veinte] años de cine cubano. La Habana: Ministerio de Cultura, Centro de Información Cinematográfica, Sección de Publicaciones, 1979. 56 p.: film., ill.

Commemorative booklet of the first 20 years of Revolutionary Cuban cinema. Includes list of some of the 227 awards won in international festivals and a filmography of documentarist Santiago Alvarez.

1062 West, Dennis. One way or another = *De cierta manera*: reviewing the Cuban movie (CRI/CR, 8:3, Summer 1979, p. 42–48, plates)

Insightful review of Sara Gómez's *De cierta manera* (1974) focuses on narrative technique, the mixture of documentary and fictional modes of discourse, and the film's major themes.

DOMINICAN REPUBLIC AND HAITI

1063 Charles, Christophe. Pour une bio-filmographie du réalisateur: une interview accordée a Christophe Charles par Rassoul Labuchin (IFH/C, 158/159, juin/sept. 1983, p. 77–81, ill.)

Interview with Haitian director Rassoul Labucine emphasizes the film *Anita*, which, according to Labuchin, has more to do with magic realism and the aesthetic propositions of his own literary works than with, for example, the political films of Bolivian Jorge Sanjinés.

1064 Desquiron Cardozo, Lilas; Henri Micciollo; and Rassoul Labuchin. Debat télévisé sur *Anita* (IFH/C, 158/159, juin/sept. 1983, p. 127–134, ill.)

Transcription of a debate televised in 1981 concerning Labuchin's *Anita* in which the director describes the film's origin, production process, reception in Haiti, and major themes and symbols.

1065 Labuchin, Rassoul. La femme haitienne dans le cinéma (IFH/C, 158/159, juin/sept. 1983, p. 139–145, ill.)

Brief historical survey of the portrayal of women in Haitian cinema beginning with the country's first feature, *Et moi je suis belle* (Jean Dominique, 1962). Also mentioned are Bob Lemoine's *Olivia* and Labuchin's own *Anita*.

1066 Lafontant Médard, Michaëlle. Analyse thématique du film *Anita* de Rassoul Labuchin: selectionne au Festival de Lille en 1981, Premier Prix Coral au 3e Festival du Nouveau Cinéma Latino Américain de La Havane, Cuba, en 1981 (IFH/C, 158/159, juin/sept. 1983, p. 85–101)

Detailed study of Labuchin's 1980 film focuses on its poetic use of ideological and narrative montage, its major themes, and its political militancy. According to author, *Anita* has as its purpose "Enseigner l'anti-imperialisme aux enfants de o à 77 ans!"

1067 Lafontant Médard, Michaëlle. Le cinéma en Haiti de 1899 à 1982 vu à travers le film des événements (IFH/C, 158/159, juin/sept. 1983, p. 11–61, ill.)

Short history of Haitian cinema ranging from first films exhibited in the country and their reception by the Port-au-Prince public to local production in the early

1980s (e.g., *Anita, Joumankole*). Includes discussion of newsreel production in the 1920s, strong US presence, and development of the exhibition sector. Good overview.

1068 Lafontant Médard, Michaëlle. La presse et *Anita* (IFH/C, 158/159, juin/sept. 1983, p. 105–122, ill.)

Edited collection of reviews of Labuchin's *Anita* (1980), published in the international press.

1069 Sáez, José Luis. Historia de un sueño importado: ensayos sobre el cine en Santo Domingo. Santo Domingo: Ediciones Siboney, 1983. 211 p.: appendix, bibl., ill. (Col. Contemporáneos; 5)

Critical look at the historical development of film culture in the Dominican Republic, book discusses implantation of the exhibition sector early in the century (first film was exhibited in 1900) and traces irregular local production (1915–81), including both commercial and alternative modes of film-making. As the title suggests, Dominican cinema has not developed due in part to the massive presence of US films in its domestic market. Appendix provides historical chronology of the cinema in Santo Domingo. Useful.

1070 Sáez, José Luis. La prensa de celuloide: lecciones de periodismo cinematográfico. Santo Domingo: Editora de la Univ. Autónoma de Santo Domingo (UASD), 1983. 328 p.: bibl., ill. (Publicaciones; 322. Col. Arte y sociedad; 11)

Practical-theoretical guide to the production of newsreels and documentaries. Historical survey briefly examines Latin American "cine contra-información," but emphasizes European, Soviet, and North American film-makers and theorists. Concludes with anthology including excerpts from Fernando Solanas's *Cine, cultura y descolonización* and Santiago Alvarez's "La Noticia a través del Cine."

GUATEMALA AND EL SALVADOR

1071 Davis, Lisa and Sonia Rivera. Guatemala: hacia la victoria: conversación con Arturo Arias y María Vázquez (AR, 10:37, 1984, p. 32–35, ill.)

Interviews with film-maker Vázquez and writer Arias, who collaborated on the script of Gregory Nava's *El Norte*. Although Arias primarily addresses Guatemala's political situation, Vázquez discusses the creation of the Colectivo de la Cinematografía de Guatemala and its role in the opposition movement.

1072 Ryan, Susan. Behind rebel lines: filmmaking in revolutionary El Salvador (Cineaste [New York] 14:1, 1985, p. 16–21)

Interviews with Paolo Martin of the Radio Venceremos Film Collective and José Ponce of the Film Institute of Revolutionary El Salvador.

1073 Solís, Daniel. Betamax and super-8 in revolutionary El Salvador: una entrevista (JumpCut [Berkeley, Calif.] 29, Feb. 1984, p. 15–18)

Interview with Daniel Solís on the use of small formats in the revolutionary struggle in El Salvador.

MEXICO

1074 Franco Sodja, Carlos. Lo que me dijo Pedro Infante. México: Editores Asociados, 1977. 120 p.: ill. (Poetas y compositores contemporáneos)

Personal, anecdotal look at one of Mexico's greatest singers and film stars.

1075 García, Gustavo. El cine mudo mexicano. México: Martín Casillas Editores: Cultura, SEP, 1982. 76 p.: ill., ports (Col. Memoria y olvido: imágenes de México; 9)

Book that aspires to integrate the "cine de entonces (1896–1930) en la cultura cotidiana, en las oscilaciones del gusto y el poder en los años más conflictivos, vitales y creativos del país." Text provides overview of film-making during the silent era and is interspersed with beautiful b/w photos of the period.

1076 Hermosillo, Jaime Humberto. La pasión según Berenice. México: Editorial Katún, 1981. 125 p., 17 leaves of plates: ill. (Col. Libro de bolsillo. Serie Arte-cine; 7)

Screenplay of Hermosillo's cinematic portrait of a woman who, in the words of José de la Colina, "se ahoga espiritualmente tanto en el círculo familiar como en la 'suave patria' mexicana de nuestros días."

1077 Mahieu, José Agustín. El cine mexicano: una curiosa aventura (CH, 347, mayo 1979, p. 409–421)

Insightful introduction to "el cauda-loso, caótico y desigual cine mexicano." Mahieu outlines the long history of Mexican cinema, discussing its accomplishments, shortcomings, and current problems. Devotes special attention to Fernando de Fuentes, Emilio Fernández and his cinematographer Gabriel Figueroa, and the *ranchero* genre.

1078 Mahieu, José Agustín. Feminine types and stereotypes in Mexican and Latin American cinema (UNESCO/CU, 8:3, 1982, p. 83–92)

Informative look at the image of women in Latin American cinema devotes special attention to well known actresses (e.g., Libertad Lamarque, Argentina; María Félix, Mexico; and Ninón Sevilla, Spain). As title indicates, author focuses on types and stereotypes, especially the *femme fatale*, perverse man-eaters, ultimately submissive revolutionaries, and irreproachable sweethearts. Also briefly discusses women behind the camera such as Brazil's Carmen Santos and Tizuka Yamasaki. Mahieu concludes, not surprisingly, that women have been woefully underrepresented in the cinematic production process.

1079 Mahieu, José Agustín. Nuevos apuntes sobre el cine mexicano (CH, 350, agosto 1979, p. 397–409)

Informative article discusses tendency of early Mexican cinema to concentrate on documentary forms and historical themes, especially the Revolution, and on attempts since the 1970s to create an aesthetically and politically innovative cinema. Finally, he looks at the role of the Univ. of Mexico's film school in training new directors with new ideas. Useful, despite some minor factual errors.

1080 Mahieu, José Agustín. El período mexicano de Luis Buñuel (CH, 358, abril 1980, p. 156–172)

Informative panorama of Spanish filmmaker Buñuel's cinematic activities in Mexico (1946–65). After giving special attention to the classic *Los Olvidados* (1953), author discusses Buñuel's comedies and, especially, his black humor in films such as *Ensayo de un crimen* (1955).

1081 Mistron, Deborah E. The role of Pancho Villa in the Mexican and American cinema (Studies in Latin American Popular Culture [Dept. of Modern Languages, New Mexico State Univ., Albuquerque] 2, 1983, p. 1–3)

Compares the image of Pancho Villa created by Mexican and American cinemas. Argues that American films stress his violent nature and ignore positive aspects, while Mexican cinema uses his image to glorify the Revolution. Informative.

1082 Montiel Pagés, Gustavo. El charro en el cine (ARMEX, 23:200, marzo 1976, p. 58–63, photos)

Brief but critical examination of the image of the "charro" in Mexican cinema. As author acerbically notes: "más vale arquetipo ineficaz para el bolsillo mercenario, que posibilidades de renovación flotando."

1083 Mora, Carl J. Mexican cinema in the 1970s (*in* Mexican art of the 1970s: images of displacement. Edited by Leonard Folgarait. Nashville, Tenn: Vanderbilt Univ., 1984, p. 37–44)

After lengthy summary of the history of Mexican cinema, Mora looks at the revival of the industry and the "new wave" that appeared under the administrations of Luis Echeverría (1970–76) and José López Portillo (1976–82). Briefly discusses government policy toward the cinema during this period and examines films such as Felipe Cazal's *Canoa* (1975), Alejandro Galindo's *El juicio de Martín Cortés* (1973). Informative.

1084 Mora, Carl J. Mexican cinema: reflections of a society, 1896–1980. Berkeley: Univ. of California Press, 1982. 287 p.: bibl., film., ill.

Despite Mexico's proximity to the US, Mexican cinema has historically received little attention in this country outside of specialized markets. Mora's book, the first major study of the subject published in English, traces the development of commercial Mexican cinema (1896–1980), concentrating not only on major genres and directors, but also on the sometimes nefarious role of film industry unions and on increasing State intervention. Author sometimes lacks a sufficiently critical vision of his subject. Includes extensive filmography.

1085 Mosier, John. Marcela Fernández Violante on Mexican cinema (Studies in Latin American Popular Culture [Dept. of Modern Languages, New Mexico State Univ., Albuquerque] 2, 1983, p. 182–189)

The director, questionably described by Mosier as "the most important woman director working in Latin America," discusses the general situation of Mexican cinema as well as her own films, including *De todos modos Juan te llamas* (1975) and *Misterio* (1980).

1086 Notas para la historia del cine en México, 1896–1925. Compilación de Helena Almoina. México: Filmoteca, UNAM, 1980. 2 v.: ill. (Col. Documentos de Filmoteca; 1)

Compilation of periodical articles traces early development of Mexican cinema. Useful as a research tool, but could use an index.

1087 Ramírez, Gabriel. El cine yucateco. México: Filmoteca, UNAM, 1980. 89 p.: bibl., index (Col. Documentos de Filmoteca; 3)

History of cinema in Yucatán, primarily Mérida (1897–1930). More informative than analytical.

1088 Reachi, Santiago. La Revolución, Cantinflas y JoLoPo, José López Portillo. 2a ed. México: Editores Asociados Mexicanos, 1982. 232 p.: port.

Memoirs of the founder of Posa Films and long-time friend and partner of comic actor Mario Moreno, Cantinflas. Of anecdotal interest.

1089 Revueltas, José. Tierra y libertad: guión cinematográfico. México: Ediciones Era, 1981. 180 p. (Obras completas; 23)

Unfilmed screenplay by writer Revueltas.

1090 Reyes, Aurelio de los. Cine y sociedad en México, 1896–1930. v. 1, Vivir de sueños, 1896–1920. México: UNAM: Cineteca Nacional, 1981. 1 v.: bibl., ill.

Richly illustrated and thoroughly documented history of Mexican cinema (1900–20). Author argues that documentary films, especially of the Revolution, were superior to fiction films of the period. Traces increasing control of Mexico's domestic film market by US distributors and corresponding decline of national production in the second decade of the century. Important work.

1091 Reyes, Aurelio de los. Los contemporáneos y el cine (IIE/A, 13:52, 1983, p. 167–186)

Interesting discussion of the attitude of the group of Mexican writers known as "Los Contemporáneos" toward the cinema, with special attention given to Xavier Villaurutia, Gilberto Owen, and Enrique González Rojo, authors who experimented with cinematic elements in their style. Important contribution toward the study of the relationship between literature and film in Mexico.

1092 Reyes, Aurelio de los. Los orígenes del cine mexicano, 1896–1900. México: Fondo de Cultura Económica, 1983. 248 p., 8 p. of plates: bibl., ill. (SEP/80; 56)

Detailed look at the first four years of cinema in Mexico, discusses not only the beginnings of exhibition and production, but also the press's and public's reaction to the cinematic "novelty." Important contribution to the study of film history in Mexico.

1093 Rulfo, Juan. El gallo de oro y otros textos para cine. Presentación y notas de Jorge Ayala Blanco. México: Ediciones Era, 1980. 134 p., 12 leaves of plates: film., ill. (Biblioteca Era)

Three texts written by Rulfo for the cinema: *El gallo de oro* (as yet unfilmed), *El despojo* (the basis of a short by Antonio Reynoso, 1960), and *La fórmula secreta* (medium-length film by Rubén Gámez, 1964).

NICARAGUA

1094 Cine obrero sandinista (Cuadernos de Comunicación Alternativa [Centro de Integración de Medios de Comunicación Alternativa (CIMCA), La Paz] 1, mayo 1983, p. 23–28)

Description of activities of the Super-8 workshop of the Central Sandinista de Trabajadores which was part of an unprecedented attempt in Latin American cinema to create a working-class cinema. The workshop grew out of the Campaña de Alfabetización Económica and "abrió la posibilidad de que los trabajadores contaran indefinidamente con un instrumento propio de expresión." Informative and useful, especially for a study of alternative modes of cinematic production.

1095 García Márquez, Gabriel. Alsino y el cóndor (NMC/N, 4:9, abril 1983, p. 163–165, ill.)

Brief but interesting description of the production in Nicaragua of Chilean director Miguel Littín's award-wining *Alsino y el cóndor.*

1096 Lilienthal, Peter. Después de Nicaragua seré otro (NMC/N, 2:4, enero/marzo 1981, p. 165–168, ill.)

Interview with German director Lilienthal about the production of his *La insurrección* (Der Aufstand, 1979), which documents the Sandinista struggle for León during the anti-Somoza revolution.

1097 Littín, Miguel. Alsino y la realidad mágica nicaragüense (NMC/N, 4:9, abril 1983, p. 161–162, ill.)

Short interview with exiled Chilean film-maker Littín about *Alsino y el cóndor,* which was nominated for an Oscar for best foreign film in 1982.

1098 Ramírez, John. Introduction to the Sandinista documentary cinema (AR, 10:37, 1984, p. 18–21, ill.)

Overview of the birth and evolution of the post-Somoza documentary in Nicaragua, focusing especially on the creation and activities of INCINE (Instituto Nicaragüense de Cine), which produces newsreels as well as political and educational documentaries. The objective of the documentation process is "to serve the interests of development, which is to say independence from the effects of imposed economic, cultural and psychological dependency."

1099 Shatunóvskaya, Irina. El nacimiento del cine nacional (URSS/AL, 7[43], 1981, p. 92–96, ill.)

Informative survey of the activities of Nicaragua's film institute (INCINE) from its founding in 1979 through its first year and a half of work. Nicaraguan cinema was in fact born with INCINE.

1100 Skármeta, Antonio. *La insurrección*: gambito nicaragüense de film y novela (NMC/N, 2:4, enero/marzo 1981, p. 157–164, ill.)

Writer Skármeta discusses the theoretical and practical differences between literary and cinematic communication based on his experience in collaborating with Peter Lilienthal on the script of *La insurreción* and the subsequent writing of a novel based on the script.

VENEZUELA

1101 Aguirre, Jesús M. and **Marcelino Bisbal.** El nuevo cine venezolano. Caracas: Editorial Ateneo de Caracas, 1980. 170 p.: bibl., ill., ports.

Discussion of the Venezuelan film industry from 1975 (when the government first implemented significant measures of financial support) to the present. Discusses structures of the industry's various sectors, government intervention, and problems resulting from the industry's bureaucratization. Important work written by two editors of the journal *Comunicación.*

1102 Hippolyte, Nelson. El cine nacional: víctima de intereses creados (Prueba [Escuela de Comunicación Social, Univ. Central de Venezuela, Caracas] 17, 20 mayo 1976, p. 6–7, plates)

Brief overview of the (under)development of Venezuelan cinema, which has long struggled against the indifference of the State and the hostility of distributors and exhibitors, whose interests have historically been tied to foreign cinema.

1103 Izaguirre, Rodolfo. Cine venezolano: largometrajes. Caracas: Fondo Editorial Cinemateca Nacional, Fondo de Fomento Cinematográfico, 1983. 163 p.: films., ill.

Catalog of feature-length films produced in Venezuela (1973–83). Provides technical data, synopses in Spanish and English, and short filmography of each director.

1104 Izaguirre, Rodolfo. Rómulo Gallegos y el cine (CONAC/RNC, 39:232, julio/agosto 1977, p. 32–45)

Former Venezuelan president and novelist Rómulo Gallegos founded a film production company, Avila Films, in 1941, and shortly thereafter wrote and produced *Juan de la Calle.* In this informative article, Izaguirre traces Gallegos's cinematic activity, both in Venezuela and in Mexico, where he spent years of exile writing film scripts. Important look at a little-known aspect of Gallegos's career.

1105 Miranda, Julio E. Cine y poder en Venezuela. Mérida, Venezuela: Univ. de los Andes, Consejo de Publicaciones, Librería Universitaria, 1982. 99 p.

Although title is to an extent misleading since author does not examine the relationship between power and cinema, book does include lucid analyses of Miguel Katz's *Muerte en el paraíso*, Santigo San Miguel's *La casa del paraíso*, and Román Calbaud's *Cangrejo*, as well as interesting discussions of the portrayal of women, the representation of power, and current tendencies of the production of short films in Venezuela.

1106 Valero, Alberto. Aspectos de la historia del cine venezolano (URSS/AL, 12, 1980, p. 98–107)

Superficial look at some key moments in the development of Venezuelan cinema. Lists some of the major films, directors, and themes employed.

JOURNAL ABBREVIATIONS
FILM

AR Areíto. Areíto, Inc. New York.

ARMEX Artes de México. México.

CH Cuadernos Hispanoamericanos. Instituto de Cultura Hispánica. Madrid.

CONAC/RNC Revista Nacional de Cultura. Consejo Nacional de Cultura. Caracas.

CRI/CR Caribbean Review. Caribbean Review, Inc. Miami, Fla.

CRIT Criterio. Editorial Criterio. Buenos Aires.

FIU/CR See CRI/CR.

IFH/C Conjonction. Institut français d'Haïti. Port-au-Prince.

IIE/A Anales del Instituto de Investigaciones Estéticas. Univ. Nacional Autónoma de México. México.

IL Ideologies & Literature. Univ. of Minnesota, Institute for the Study of Ideologies and Literature. Minneapolis.

INDEX Index on Censorship. Writers & Scholars International. London.

LARR Latin American Research Review. Univ. of North Carolina Press *for the* Latin American Studies Assn. Chapel Hill.

NMC/N Nicaráuac. Ministerio de Cultura. Managua.

OSPAAAL/T Tricontinental. Organization for the Solidarity of the Peoples of Africa, Asia and Latin America, Executive Secretariat. Havana.

RYC Revolución y Cultura. Ministerio de Cultura. La Habana.

SBH/HC Historia y Cultura. Sociedad Boliviana de Historia. Editorial Don Bosco. La Paz.

UA/REH Revista de Estudios Hispánicos. Univ. de Alabama, Dept. of Romance Languages, Office of International Studies and Programs. University.

UCLA/JLAL Journal of Latin American Lore. Univ. of California, Latin American Center. Los Angeles.

UCSB/NS New Scholar. Univ. of California, Committee on Hispanic Civilization [and] Center for Chicano Studies. Santa Barbara.

UEAC/GC Gaceta de Cuba. Unión de Escritores y Artistas de Cuba. La Habana.

UK/LATR Latin American Theatre Review. Univ. of Kansas, Center for Latin American Studies. Lawrence.

UNESCO/CU Cultures. UN Educational, Scientific and Cultural Organization. Paris.

URSS/AL América Latina. Academia de Ciencias de la Unión de Repúblicas Soviéticas Socialistas. Moscú.

UV/PH La Palabra y el Hombre. Univ. Veracruzana. Xalapa, México.

VUELTA. Vuelta. México.

HISTORY

ETHNOHISTORY: Mesoamerica

S.L. CLINE, *Associate Professor of History, University of California, Santa Barbara*

PUBLICATION OF CODICES and documentary sources continues to be an important component of the work on Mesoamerican ethnohistory. The two most notable in the first category are *Códice Tudela* (item **1573a**) and the *Lienzo de Tlaxcala* (item **1547**). The facsimile of *Codex Tudela* has ingeniously been made to look like a 16th-century work, with thick, seemingly old paper, complete with holes, ragged edges, and faded ink. The *Lienzo de Tlaxcala*'s oversize format makes the details in the drawings particularly clear. Both publications include extensive analysis and commentary, making these works the definitive editions. Publications of major classic works on the Aztecs have also appeared. Andrews and Hassig's edition of Ruiz de Alarcón's 17th-century text on religious belief (item **1563**) is outstanding, making it the edition to own. Bierhorst's publication of a complete transcription and translation of the *Cantares mexicanos* (item **1513**) is a major addition to the literature. His interpretation of the poems as ghost songs will stir controversy, but his achievement in making available the complete text is important. For local-level Nahuatl documentation, two publications are worth noting. The first is the transcription and German translation of an early 16th-century house-to-house census from the Cuernavaca region (item **1506**). I would urge future translations of such documents to be in Spanish (or possibly English), so that they reach the widest audience. The second local-level collection of Nahuatl documentation worthy of note is the *The Testaments of Culhuacan* (item **1570**), the largest extant collection of wills from the 16th century.

Quite a number of major monographs have appeared, synthesizing large amounts of research on various Mesoamerican groups. Notable for the colonial period are Farriss's work on the Yucatecan Maya (item **1525**), Orellana's on the Tzutujil Maya (item **1556**), Spores's on the Mixtecs (item **1569**), and Warren's on the Tarascans (item **1577**). For the prehispanic period, most important are Zantwijk's intriguing discussion (item **1580**) of Aztec social structure and their perceptions of it, and Duverger's study of the origin of the Aztecs, trying to separate fact from myth (item **1523**).

In the article literature covering the prehispanic period, three subjects merit attention. One which captures both popular and scholarly interest is human sacrifice. A Dumbarton Oaks conference organized around that theme produced a handsome volume (item **1561**). Several popular publications on sacrifice have also appeared in various languages. The second sanguinary topic of interest is Aztec warfare (items **1515**, **1536**, and **1537**). Calendrics also has an enduring following (items **1533**, **1559**, **1565**, and **1572**). For the article literature on the colonial period, analysis of local-level phenomena are most salient. Especially worth noting is Lockhart's analysis of cultural adaptation (item **1548**), Kellogg's discussion of native women before the Spanish courts (item **1541**), Villanueva's piece on native women's role in the colonial economy (item **1576**), and Cline's examination of the Aztec testamentary procedures (item **1516**).

1501 Aguilera, Carmen. Identificación de Topiltzin Quetzalcóatl de Tula (UNAM/ECN, 16, 1983, p. 165–182, bibl., ill.)

Careful analysis of a *Codex Magliabecchiano* figure, proposing an identification of Quetzalcoatl; challenges conclusions of Seler and Nuttall.

1502 Alcina Franch, José. Servidores del ritual y la magia en el medio rural mesoamericano durante el período colonial (RUC, enero 1979, p. 97–127, bibl.)

Valuable study of magic (as opposed to religion) and its specialists among the rural Zapotecs and Mixe.

1503 Anawalt, Patricia Rieff. Memory clothing: costumes associated with Aztec human sacrifice (*in* Ritual human sacrifice in Mesoamerica [see item **1561**] p. 165–193, ill.)

Analysis of four garments associated with sacrifice, focusing on their symbolic meaning, region of origin, and cross-cultural variation.

1504 Anderson, Arthur J.O. Sahagún's *Doctrinal encyclopaedia* (UNAM/ECN, 16, 1983, p. 109–122)

Selections and analyses of some Nahuatl texts; theorizes that they were composed at the Colegio de Santa Cruz for young Nahua students. Welcome addition to the Sahaguntine bibliography.

1505 Andrews, Anthony P. Maya salt production and trade. Tucson: Univ. of Arizona Press, 1983. 173 p.: bibl., index, maps.

Thorough examination of a major commodity of the region, covering the colonial and modern eras with projections to the prehispanic.

1506 Aztekischer Zensus: zur indianischen Wirtschaft und Gesellschaft im Marquesado um 1540: aus dem *Libro de tributos*, Col. ant. ms. 551, im Archivo Histórico, México. Bd. 1, Molotla. Bd. 2, Tepetenchic. Translated into German by Eike Hinz, Claudine Hartau and Marie-Luise Heimann-Koenen. Hannover, FRG: Verlag für Ethnologie, 1983? 2 v. (201, 137 p.): bibl.

Nahuatl transcription and German translation of important early 16th-century census from the Cuernavaca region. Extended analytical introductory essay.

1507 Baus Reed Czitrom, Carolyn. Tecuexes y cocas: dos grupos de la región Jalisco en el siglo XVI. México: INAH, Depto. de Investigaciones Históricas, 1982. 107 p.: bibl., ill. (Col. científica; 112. Serie Etnohistoria)

Simple description of the archaeological and ethnohistorical sources on two Jalisco groups. For archaeologist's comment, see *HLAS 47:353.*

1508 Bierhorst, John. A Nahuatl-English dictionary and concordance to the *Cantares mexicanos* with an analytic transcription and grammatical notes. Stanford, Calif.: Stanford Univ. Press, 1985. 751 p.

Companion volume to item **1513**, with useful dictionary and glossary of 16th-century poetic usage.

1509 Brotherston, Gordon. The sign Tepexic in its textual landscape (IAA, 11:2, 1985, p. 209–251, ill.)

Boldly asserts that "our whole view of Mesoamerican history may be modified as a result of recognizing in Tepexic the provenance of the longest and grandest screenfolds extant, i.e., the narrative on the obverse of the *Codex Vindobonensis Mexicanus I.*"

1510 Brown, Betty Ann. *Ochpaniztli* in historical perspective (*in* Ritual human sacrifice in Mesoamerica [see item **1561**] p. 195–210)

Analysis of an Aztec sacrificial ceremony and its war symbolism; concludes that one function of sacrifice was to recall historic battles and reinforce the Aztec ideological system.

1511 Calvo, Andrea. News of the islands and the mainland newly discovered in India by the Captain of His Imperial Majesty's Fleet. Translated and with notes by Edward F. Tuttle. Culver City, Calif.: Labyrinthos, 1985. 27 p.: ill.

Facsimile of Italian and English translation of a Milanese dissident's translation of Cortés's conquest of Tenochtitlan. English translator's notes compare it to Cortés's original.

1512 Cano, Agustin. Manche and Peten: the hazards of Itza deceit and barbarity. Translated by Charles P. Bowditch and Guillermo Rivera. Additional comments by Adela C. Breton. Edited and with notes by Frank E. Comparato. Culver City, Calif.: Labyrinthos, 1984. 26 p., 3 p. of plates: ill.

Late 17th-century account of unsuccessful expedition. Cano disowns responsibility for the fiasco. Valuable descriptions of various Indian groups.

1513 Cantares mexicanos = Songs of the Aztecs. Translated from the Nahuatl, with an introduction and commentary, by John Bierhorst. Stanford, Calif.: Stanford Univ. Press, 1985. 559 p.: appendix, bibl., ill., index.

Complete transcription and English translation of a major 16th-century Nahuatl manuscript. General introduction is a controversial interpretation of the songs, positing they are ghost songs.

1514 Chimalpahin Cuauhtlehuanitzin, Domingo Francisco de San Antón Muñón. Octava relación: obra histórica de Domingo Francisco de San Antón Muñón Chimalpahin Cuautlehuanitzin. Introducción, estudio, paleografía, versión castellana y notas de José Rubén Romero Galván. México: UNAM, Instituto de Investigaciones Históricas, 1983. 199 p. (Serie de cultura náhuatl. Fuentes; 8)

New translation of the relación which deals primarily with the genealogy of Chimalpahin's grandfather. Helpful introduction with pertinent information on Chimalpahin's work.

1515 Clendinnen, Inga. The cost of courage in Aztec society (PP, 107, May 1985, p. 44–89, ill.)

Brief exploration of the ideology of warfare in Tenochtitlan, especially the socialization of Aztec warriors.

1516 Cline, S.L. A legal process at the local level: estate division in late sixteenth-century Culhuacan (in Five centuries of law and politics in Mexico. Edited by Ronald Spores and Ross Hassig. Nashville, Tenn.: Vanderbilt Univ., 1984, p. 39–53)

Examination of testamentary bequests of colonial Nahuas, pointing out prehispanic precedents and colonial legal procedures.

1518 Los Códices de México: exposición temporal Museo Nacional de Antropología, México, 1979. México: INAH, SEP, 1979. 142 p.: facsims. (some col)

Clearly annotated catalog of a major exhibition of codices; contains number of facsimiles of codices, many in color.

1519 Conrad, Geoffrey W. and Arthur A. Demarest. Religion and empire: the dynamics of Aztec and Inca expansionism. Cambridge, England: Cambridge Univ. Press, 1984. 266 p.: bibl., ill., index (New studies in archaeology)

Thought-provoking comparative study argues that "manipulation of traditional religious concepts and rituals played crucial roles in the rise and fall of the Aztec and Inca empires."

1520 Dahlgren, Barbara et al. Corazón de Cópil. Fotografía, Fernando Robles. México: INAH, 1982. 334 p.: bibl., ill. (some col.)

Presentation that includes brief analysis of 21 16th-century sources dealing with the Templo Mayor. Full-color reproductions make the volume very attractive. Fascinating maps of Mexico-Tenochtitlan.

1521 Demarest, Arthur A. Overview: Mesoamerican human sacrifice in evolutionary perspective (in Ritual human sacrifice in Mesoamerica [see item **1561**] p. 227–247)

Brief review of recent debates on sacrifice; argues that human sacrifice has to be studied holistically within the mainstream of anthropology.

1522 Díaz Infante, Fernando. La educación de los aztecas: cómo se formó el carácter del pueblo mexica. México: Panorama Editorial, 1982. 144 p.: bibl., ill. (Col. Panorama)

Short, nicely done, semi-popular account of Aztec education covering educational structures and teaching methods.

Driever, Steven L. and Don R. Hoy. Población potencial de los mayas durante el período clásico. See *HLAS 47:5063*.

1523 Duverger, Christian. L'origine des Aztèques. Paris: Seuil, 1983. 367 p.,

15 p.: bibl., ill. (Recherches anthropologiques)
Meticulous and insightful analysis of
the myths of origin attempting to separate
fact from fiction.

1524 Edmonson, Munro S. Human sacrifice
in the *Books of Chilam Balam of
Tzimin and Chumayel* (*in* Ritual human
sacrifice in Mesoamerica [see item **1561**]
p. 91–100)
Discussion of ritual murder from the
15th and 16th centuries, linking its occurrence to the *katun* cycles.

**Encuentro Latinoamericano de CEHILA, 9th,
Manaus, Brazil, 1981.** Das reduções latino-
americanas às lutas indigenas atuais. See
HLAS 47:1235a.

1525 Farriss, Nancy Marguerite. Maya society under colonial rule: the collective enterprise of survival. Princeton, N.J.:
Princeton Univ. Press, 1984. 585 p.: bibl., ill.,
index.
Well received monograph on the
Yucatecan Maya based on Spanish sources.
For sociologist's comment, see *HLAS
47:8063.*

1526 Galinier, Jacques. L'homme sans pieds:
métaphores de la castration imaginaire
en Mésoamérique (EPHE/H, 24:2, avril/juin
1984, p. 41–58, ill., table)
Analysis of Otomí castration myths,
attempting to delineate native logic connecting body image and its "cosmic replica."

1527 García de Palacio, Diego. *Letter to the
King of Spain*: being a description of
the ancient provinces of Guazacapan, Izalco,
Cuscatlan, and Chiquimula, in the Audience
of Guatemala, with an account of the languages, customs, and religion of their aboriginal inhabitants, and a description of the
ruins of Copan. Translated and with notes
by Ephraim G. Squier. Edited by Frank E.
Comparato. With additional notes by Alexander von Frantzius and Frank E. Comparato.
Culver City, Calif.: Labyrinthos, 1985. 66 p.:
ill., index.
Detailed 16th-century report on a region of Guatemala. Includes separate descriptions for the various groups and is well
indexed.

1528 Garza, Mercedes de la. Análisis
comparativo de la *Historia de los
mexicanos por sus pinturas* y la *Leyenda

de los soles* (UNAM/ECN, 16, 1983,
p. 123–134)
Suggests that the two texts are based
on the codices, that there is correspondence
between the two, and that independence with
respect to each other is "a confirmation of
the authenticity of the legend."

1529 González Torres, Yólotl. Las aventuras
del alma. México: INAH, 1982.
29 p. (Cuadernos del Museo Nacional de
Antropología)
Brief study of the concept of the soul
among the Aztecs, with comparisons to
other Mesoamerican groups.

1530 González Torres, Yólotl. El sacrificio
humano entre los mexicas. México:
INAH: Fondo de Cultura Económica, 1985.
329 p.: bibl., ill. (Sección de obras de
antropología)
Extensive review of sources on human
sacrifice, places human sacrifices in its religious and political contexts, focusing primarily on the period of Spanish contact.

1531 Gorenstein, Shirley *et al.* Acambaro:
frontier settlement of the Tarascan-
Aztec border. Nashville, Tenn.: Vanderbilt
Univ., 1985. 303 p.: bibl., ill. (Publications in
anthropology; 32)
Mainly concerns archaeology, but has
succinct discussion of Acambaro ethnohistory, concluding that the area was originally a Chichimec settlement conquered
by the Tarascans, subsequently becoming
a multi-ethnic community of strategic
importance.

1532 Graulich, Michel. Myths of paradise
lost in prehispanic central Mexico
(UC/CA, 24:5, Dec. 1983, p. 575–588, bibl.)
Structural analysis of Mesoamerican
creation myths from various regions: views
them as variations on one theme with virtually no Christian influence. Commentary
and response follows.

1533 Graulich, Michel. La structure du
calendrier agricole des anciens mexi-
cains (UEN/LS, 6, 1980, p. 99–113, bibl.)
Attempts to fix the dates of the Aztec
"months" and links the meaning of names
with the agricultural calendar.

1534 Guerrero Castillo, Julian N. and **Lola
Soriano de Guerrero.** Las 9 [i.e. nueve]
tribus aborígenes de Nicaragua. Managua:

s.n., 1982. 154 p.: bibl., ill.
One of the few recent works on the region; based on colonial Spanish chronicles; discusses Caribs, Choroteganos, Niquiranos, among others. Includes a chapter on blacks and zambos.

Hartung, Horst. Alignments in architecture and sculpture of Maya centers: notes on Piedras Negras, Copán, and Chichén Izta. See *HLAS 47:5096.*

1535 Heyden, Doris. Mitología y simbolismo de la flora en el México prehispánico. México: UNAM, Instituto de Investigaciones Antropológicas, 1983. 176 p., 11 p. of plates: bibl., ill. (some col.) (Serie antropológica; 44. Etnohistoria)
Well illustrated monograph on the significance of flowers in Mesoamerican ideology. Includes careful analysis of written and pictorial sources.

1536 Isaac, Barry L. The Aztec 'Flowery War:' a geopolitical explanation (UNM/JAR, 39, 1983, p. 415–432, bibl., table)
Interesting reconsideration of the wars between Tenochtitlan and Tlaxcala, dismissing the ritual element of the conflict and arguing that Tenochititlan was simply unable to win.

1537 Isaac, Barry L. Aztec warfare: goals and battlefield comportment (UP/E, 22, 1983, p. 121–131)
Rejects the view that Aztec warfare primarily aimed toward capture of prisoners; argues that there was large-scale battlefield slaughter.

1538 Izquierdo, Ana Luisa. La educación maya en los tiempos prehispánicos. México: UNAM, Instituto de Investigaciones Filológicas, Centro de Estudios Mayas, 1983. 93 p.: bibl. (Cuaderno; 16)
Brief study based on 16th-century documentation describes educational techniques and general cultural context.

1539 Jones, Grant D. The last Maya frontiers of colonial Yucatan (*in* Spaniards and Indian in southeastern Mesoamerica: essays on the history of ethnic relations. Edited by Murdo J. MacLeod and Robert Wasserstrom. Lincoln: Univ. of Nebraska, 1983, p. 64–91, maps)
Overview of colonial Belize includes interesting discussions of early 17th-century

rebellions and inter-regional trade. Brings to light information on a poorly studied area.

1540 Josserand, J. Kathryn; Maarten E.R.G.N. Jasen; and Angeles Romero. Mixtec dialectology: inferences from linguistics and ethnohistory (Vanderbilt University Studies in Anthropology [Nashville, Tenn.] 31, 1984, p. 141–163)
Analyzes colonial Mixtec records and concludes that in official documents there is no evidence of a single Mixtec dialect imposed on provincial courts and convents.

1541 Kellogg, Susan. Aztec women in early colonial courts: structure and strategy in legal context (*in* Five centuries of law and politics in Mexico. Edited by Ronald Spores and Ross Hassig. Nashville, Tenn.: Vanderbilt Univ., 1984, p. 25–38)
Discusses Mexico City native women's interactions with the Spanish legal system, based on 16th-century lawsuits. Important contribution to understanding the role of women.

1542 Krumbach, Helmut. Schwitzbaddarstellungen und deren Symbole in bilderhandschriften aus Mexiko (DGV/ZE, 107:1, 1982, p. 95–128, ill., plates)
Well illustrated discussion of steambaths as they appear in various codices and the present state of research on the topic.

1543 Leal, Luis. *Los voladores*: from ritual to game (UCSB/NS, 8, 1982, p. 129–142, ill.)
Outlines origins of the flying pole "dance" and its religious significance as reported in colonial chronicles. Notes modern performances.

1544 León-Portilla, Miguel. Los antiguos mexicanos a través de sus crónicas y cantares. México: Fondo de Cultura Económica, 1983. 198 p.: bibl., ill., index (Lecturas mexicanas; 3)
Insightful survey of Nahua culture, based on close reading of Nahuatl chronicles and songs. Provides vision of Nahua culture as the natives saw it and quotes at length from sources.

1545 León-Portilla, Miguel. Conciencia de clase en los textos de los pipiltin: "nobles" del México antiguo (JGSWGL, 20, 1983, p. 175–186)
Enlightening analysis of the

huehuetlatolli shows evidence of class distinctions and class consciousness. Includes information on commoners.

1546 León-Portilla, Miguel. *Cuícatl* y *tlahtolli*: las formas de expresión en náhuatl (UNAM/ECN, 16, 1983, p. 13–108, bibl.)

Excellent study of Nahuatl songs and discourse from the prehispanic tradition, highlighting the social and cultural contexts in which they were produced and preserved.

1547 El Lienzo de Tlaxcala. Edición de Mario de la Torre. Textos de Josefina García Quintana, Carlos Martínez Marín. México: Cartón y Papel de México, 1983. 176 p.: bibl., ill. (some col.), index (Col. CPM)

Magnificent, full-color, oversize publication of major 16th-century pictorial manuscript dealing with the Spanish conquest. Includes extensive commentary in English and Spanish on each drawing.

1548 Lockhart, James. Some Nahua concepts in postconquest guise (History of European Ideas [Oxford, England] 6:4, 1985, p. 465–482)

Superb discussion of cultural adaptation based on local level Nahuatl documentation. Specific examples deal with legal concepts and political organization.

1549 López-Baralt, Mercedes. Tiempo y espacio en Mesoamérica (CH, 397, julio 1983, p. 5–43, bibl., ill., tables)

Compares Nahua and Maya concepts of time and space by using codices, Spanish chronicles, native texts, and stone inscriptions. Concludes that there is cultural unity in Mesoamerica.

1550 Lozoya, Xavier. Sobre la investigación de las plantas psicotrópicas en las antiguas culturas indígenas de México (UNAM/ECN, 16, 1983, p. 193–206, ill.)

Attempts to place in proper cultural context the use of psychotropic plants, rejecting overemphasis on their importance.

1551 Luján Muñoz, Jorge. Investigaciones recientes en etnohistoria de Guatemala (CIRMA/M, 4:5, June 1983, p. 236–252)

Unannotated bibliography, with brief introductory remarks, lists works on Guatemalan ethnohistory (1971–80). Useful for quick reference.

1552 Marjil de Jesús, Antonio; Lázaro de Mazariegos; and Blas Guillén. A Spanish manuscript letter on the Lacandones in the Archives of the Indies at Seville. Translated and with notes by Alfred Marston Tozzer. Additional notes by Frank E. Comparato. Culver City, Calif.: Labyrinthos, 1984. 26 p.: ill., map.

Republication of a late 17th-century manuscript which describes social customs and material culture of Lacandones. Provides insights into Spanish difficulties in Christianizing the Indians.

1553 Martin, Cheryl English. Rural society in colonial Morelos. Albuquerque: Univ. of New Mexico Press, 1985. 255 p.: appendices, bibl., maps, tables.

Fine general regional study with major coverage of Indian populations and their interactions with Spanish haciendas.

1554 Matías Alonso, Marcos. Medidas indígenas de longitud: en documentos de la ciudad de México del siglo XVI. México: Centro de Investigaciones y Estudios Superiores en Antropología Social, 1984. 106 p.: ill. (Cuadernos de la Casa Chata; 94)

Meticulous, highly detailed study of basic longitudinal measures using Nahuatl, Spanish, and glyphic sources.

1555 Musgrave-Portilla, L. Marie. The *nahualli* or transforming wizard in pre- and postconquest Mesoamerica (UCLA/JLAL, 8:1, Summer 1982, p. 3–62, bibl.)

Extensive examination of the *nahualli* with insightful discussion of its function during the colonial period. Changing concept of the *nahualli* can be seen as a microcosm of cultural influence in Mesoamerica. For ethnologist's comment, see *HLAS* 47:962.

1556 Orellana, Sandra Lee. The Tzutujil Mayas: continuity and change, 1250–1630. Norman: Univ. of Oklahoma Press, 1984. 287 p.: bibl., ill., index.

Edifying, in-depth examination of acculturation of this relatively neglected Guatemalan Maya group. Covers prehispanic, colonial and modern periods.

Paddock, John. Lord 5 Flower's family: rulers of Zaachila and Cuilapan. See *HLAS* 47:527.

1557 Pérez-Rocha, Emma. La tierra y el hombre en la Villa de Tacuba durante la epoca colonial. México: INAH, Depto. de

Etnohistoria, 1982. 162, 36 p.: bibl., index, maps, genealogical tables (Col. científica; 115. Etnohistoria)

Important initial study of colonial Tlacopan (Tacuba) includes extensive information on Spanish haciendas and extracts from colonial archival documentation.

1558 *Popul Vuh*: the definitive edition of the Mayan *Book of the dawn of life* and the *Glories of gods and kings*. Translated by Dennis Tedlock. New York: Simon & Schuster, 1985. 380 p.: bibl., ill., index, maps, photos.

Readable new translation of the 16th-century Quichean text; extensive linguistic commentary in the end notes; much data gleaned from a modern Maya informant.

Prem, Hanns J. Das Chronolgieproblem in der autochthonen Tradition Zentralamerikas. See *HLAS 47:528*.

1559 Prem, Hanns J. Las fechas calendáricas completas en los textos de Ixtlilxóchitl (UNAM/ECN, 16, 1983, p. 225–231, bibl., tables)

From analysis and correlation of calendrical data concludes that Ixtlilxochitl's information should be valued more highly.

1560 Relaciones de producción y tenencia de la tierra en el México antiguo. Coordinador, Heinz Dieterich. México: INAH, 1981. 83 p.: bibls., ill. (Col. científica; 99. Etnología)

Collection of articles in the Marxist tradition. Particularly worth noting are Georg Freund's discussion of civil categories of land and Yólotl González Torres's examination of private property concluding that it existed but was not the dominant form.

1561 Ritual human sacrifice in Meso-america: a conference at Dumbarton Oaks, October 13th and 14th, 1979. Organized by Elizabeth P. Benson. Edited by Elizabeth H. Boone. Washington: Dumbarton Oaks Research Library and Collection, 1984. 247 p.: bibl., ill.

Relevant papers presented at this conference are annotated separately in this section (see items **1503, 1510, 1521, 1524, 1562, and 1578**). For archaeologist's comment, see *HLAS 47:328*.

1562 Robicsek, Francis and Donald M. Hales. Maya heart sacrifice: cultural

perspective and surgical techique (*in* Ritual human sacrifice in Mesoamerica [see item **1561**] p. 49–90, ill., photos)

Graphic surgical description of heart removal; postulates change in technique and intermixing of Christianity with prehispanic Maya ritual.

1563 Ruiz de Alarcón, Hernando. Treatise on the heathen superstitions that today live among the Indians native to this New Spain, 1629. Translated and edited by J. Richard Andrews and Ross Hassig. Norman: Univ. of Oklahoma Press, 1984. 406 p.: bibl., facsims., index (The Civilization of the American Indian series; 164)

Careful translation and extensive notes of important 17th-century work make this the definitive scholarly edition.

1564 Sapper, Karl. The Verapaz in the sixteenth and seventeenth centuries: a contribution to the historical geography and ethnography of northeastern Guatemala. Translated by Theodore E. Gutman. Los Angeles: Institute of Archaeology, UCLA, 1985. 53 p., 2 folded leaves of plates: bibls., ill., index (Occasional paper; 13)

English translation of useful 1936 German publication on the situation of the native population in Guatemala.

1565 Siarkiewicz, Marek and Elzbieta Siarkiewicz. Problemas de la correlación de calendarios cristianos y xihuitl solar de los pueblos del altiplano central de México (Ethnologia Polona [Zaklad Etnografii Instytutu Historii Kultury Materialnej Pan, Pazná, Poland] 8, 1982, p. 161–169, bibl., tables)

Contribution to the debate on calendrics and correlation suggests that there existed three different prehispanic native calendars which authors reconstruct and compare to each other and the Julian calendar.

1566 Sisson, Edward B. Recent work on the Borgia Group codices (UC/CA, 24:5, Dec. 1983, p. 653–656, bibl.)

Brief but useful summary of various scholars' recent research on the Borgia Group codices and comparative ceramic data.

1567 Smith, Michael E. El desarrollo económico y la expansión del Imperio Mexica: una perspectiva sistémica (UNAM/ECN, 16, 1983, p. 135–164, bibl., graphs, ill.)

Taking the example of the late prehispanic Valley of Mexico, argues that economic development can best be understood by systems theory and regional analysis, not by a single causal factor.

1568 Smith, Michael E. The role of social stratification in the Aztec empire: a view from the provinces (AAA/AA, 88, 1986, p. 70–91, bibl., charts)

Rejects military coercion as the main integrative force of the Aztec empire, arguing that elites of different polities collaborated, uniting on a class basis.

1569 Spores, Ronald. The Mixtecs in ancient and colonial times. Norman: Univ. of Oklahoma Press, 1984. 263 p.: bibl., ill., index (The Civilization of the American Indian series; 168)

Major contribution to Mixtec ethnohistory. Separate chapters deal with the prehispanic era, Spanish conquest, the colonial economic and religious systems, crime and punishment, and intergroup relations.

1570 The Testaments of Culhuacan. Edited and translated by S.L. Cline and Miguel León-Portilla. Los Angeles: UCLA, Latin American Center Publications, 1984. 281 p. (Nahuatl series; 1. Special studies; 2)

Complete transcription and English translation of the largest extant collection of 16th-century Nahuatl testaments.

1571 Thiemer-Sachse, Ursula. Zum Problem der militärischen Demokratie bei den Azteken zur Zeit der spanischen Eroberung (EAZ, 25, 1984, p. 496–507, bibl.)

Argues that Aztec society was not a military democracy at time of conquest. Dates the rise of a class-based state society during Itzcoatl's reign.

1572 Tichy, Franz. Der Feskalender Sahagún's: Ein echter Soonenkalender? (UEN/LS, 6, 1980, p. 115–137, bibl., ill., tables)

Argues that Sahagún's calendar of religious holidays is a solar calendar citing agrarian content of the calendar, correlations between the calendar and astronomical apparitions, tribute dates, and architectural orientation of temples as evidence.

1573 Tomicki, Ryszard. Sobre la semántica de tres aztecas (Ethnologia Polona [Zaklad Etnografii Instytutu Historii Kultury Materialnej Pan, Poznán, Poland] 8, 1982, p. 111–182, bibl., ill.)

Analysis of the plots of three Aztec creation myths questioning whether the differences in plot correspond to differences in meaning.

Trautmann, Wolfgang. Catálogo históricocrítico de los nombres de lugar relativos a Tlaxcala. See *HLAS 47:5113*.

1573a Tudela de la Orden, José. Códice Tudela. Prólogo de Donald Robertson. Epílogo de Wigberto Jiménez Moreno. Madrid: Ediciones de Cultura Hispánica, Instituto de Cooperación Iberoamericana, 1980. 2 v.: bibl., ill. (Hace quinientos años en América; 1)

Beautiful facsimile edition of an important 16th-century Aztec manuscript especially dealing with the calendar and deities. Full transcription and extensive commentary make this a major contribution.

1574 Veblen, Thomas T. and **Laura Gutiérrez-Witt.** Fuentes documentales y bibliográficas: *Relación de los caciques y número de yndios que hay en Guatemala, 21 de abril de 1572* (CIRMA/M, 4:5, June 1983, p. 212–235)

Transcription of and some introductory remarks on a late 16th-century Spanish document. Worthwhile addition to data on Guatemalan populations.

1575 Villagutierre Soto-Mayor, Juan de. History of the conquest of the province of the Itza: subjugation and events of the Lacandon and other nations of uncivilized Indians in the lands from the Kingdom of Guatemala to the provinces of Yucatan in North America. Translated from the second Spanish edition by Robert D. Wood. Edited and with notes by Frank E. Comparato. Culver City, Calif.: Labyrinthos, 1983. 432 p., 21 p. of plates: bibl., ill., index, folded. map.

First English edition of the 1701 publication. Consists of informative, detailed description of final assault on the Peten Itza. Also includes narratives by some participants in the conquest.

1576 Villanueva, Margaret A. From calpixqui to corregidor: appropriations of women's cotton textile production in early colonial Mexico (LAP, 12:1, Winter 1985, p. 17–40, bibl.)

Argues that domestic labor in weaving was an integral part of the early colonial socioeconomic structure. Highlights the role of women.

Vitale, Luis. Génesis y desarrollo del modo de producción comunal-tributario de las formaciones inca y azteca. See item **1766.**

Vogt, Evon Z. The genetic model revisited: on the origins and development of the Maya. See *HLAS 47:1577.*

Wachtel, Nathan. The Indian and the Spanish conquest. See item **1767.**

1577 Warren, J. Benedict. The conquest of Michoacán: the Spanish domination of the Tarascan kingdom in western Mexico, 1521–1530. Norman: Univ. of Oklahoma Press, 1985. 352 p.: bibl., ill., index.

In-depth study of crucial period of Spanish conquest and consolidation of colonial rule. Offers interesting new interpretation of the role of the *cazonci* casting doubt on his blamelessness.

1578 Wilkerson, S. Jeffrey K. In search of the mountain foam: human sacrifice in eastern Mesoamerica (*in* Ritual human sacrifice in Mesoamerica [see item **1561**] p. 101–132, ill., map, photos)

Marshals ethnohistorical and archaeological evidence to posit a long history of human sacrifice in the Huasteca, but not on the scale of the Aztecs.

1579 Zamora, Elías. La tenencia de la tierra entre los mayas de Guatemala en la época prehispánica: planteamiento de la cuestión y proposición de una tipología (EEHA/AEA, 37, 1980, p. 443–464, ill.)

Stimulating discussion of Maya land tenure, based on colonial documents which suggest prehispanic patterns.

1580 Zantwijk, Rudolf A.M. van. The Aztec arrangement: the social history of pre-Spanish Mexico. Foreword by Miguel León-Portilla. Norman: Univ. of Oklahoma Press, 1985. 345 p.: ill., index (The Civilization of the American Indian series; 167)

Thought-provoking analysis of prehispanic Aztec society, especially stressing the Aztecs' own conception of it.

1581 Zantwijk, Rudolf A.M. van. La ordenación de Tenochititlan: la interrelación de dioses, templos, fechas calendáricas, direcciones y sitios con grupos sociales en la convivencia capitaleña azteca (UEN/LS, 6, 1980, p. 47–98, bibl., ill., tables)

Investigation of the interrelation of time, space, and religion in the 20 *calpullis* of Tenochtitlan. Offers important integration of concepts usually treated separately.

ETHNOHISTORY: South America

FRANK SALOMON, *Associate Professor of Anthropology, University of Wisconsin, Madison*

THE SOUTH AMERICAN THEATER of research seems to be undergoing a period of gradual but fundamental alteration. Long-neglected peoples and periods take center stage, while those durable troupers, the Incas, recede into secondary roles as antagonists to the "ethnic groups," "kingdoms," "chiefdoms," and "confederations" whose colonial transformations now attract the liveliest research. It is not merely the *dramatis personae* that are changing but the spirit which animates the research as well. In both the lowland and Andean areas, some scholars appear ready to confront methodological and theoretical issues which will determine whether or not the hybrid enterprise known as Ethnohistory will evolve from a movement of revindication into a distinctive sustainable pursuit.

The restlessness of ethnohistorians reflects both North American anthropology's search for sociocultural theories giving the culture concept a kinetic, mutable, nonconsensual character, and South American doubts about the usefulness or realism of a discipline that treats native peoples according to axioms (usually structuralist) unrelated to those employed in explaining non-native societies. Researchers who look for ways to handle culture and history as complementary notions, integral to one another, often become interested in "ethno" history *strictu sensu*: the study of how cultures respond to time and change, a concept somewhat analogous to "ethnoscience" (items **1623, 1699, 1709,** and **1753**). The task of studying "how events are ordered by culture (and) how, in that process, the culture is reordered" (Marshall Sahlins's formulation) may have rich potential and novel advantages in the South American context. Such an approach, because it partly defuses the intense local particularism which made highland and lowland studies of the 1960s and 1970s hard to collate, may also quicken dialogue across major regional boundaries. (This agenda was emphasized at 1984, 1985, and 1986 American Anthropological Association symposia on South American cosmologies, so far unpublished). Finally, the newer approach provides a more workable warrant for ethnographic-historical combinations of method (items **1584, 1630,** and **1760**) than did older styles which led researchers to treat extant Andean culture in terms of ill-explained "continuities" and conservatism, or else in terms of a similarly ill-defined process of "destructuration" and "restructuration."

In recent years, historians' deepening acquaintance with mid- and late-colonial Indian societies has undercut the old anthropological image of "communities" as unchanging cells of integrity beseiged by a conflict-ridden "outside" world, and has heightened awareness that conflicts, including major ones like the 1780 Andean rebellions, had sources within native society. Thierry Saignes's *Los Andes orientales: historia de un olvido* and other works growing from his long Bolivian research, and Christine Hunefeldt's *Lucha por la tierra y protesta indígena: las comunidades indígenas del Perú entre colonia y república, 1800–1830* trace them in some depth (see also item **1749**). The dissertations of Thomas Abercrombie (Chicago) and Roger Rasnake (Cornell) identify conflict between kurakal and *cabildo* authorities as a motor of intra-Indian change in colonial Bolivia.

Ethnohistorical-archaeological cooperation is still preached more than practiced, but a Wenner-Gren symposium edited by Shozo Masuda, Izumi Shimada, and Craig Morris led to a dialogue on the diverging offspring of "verticality" (see items **1637, 1646, 1682, 1698, 1706, 1715,** and **1733**). In Inca studies particularly (see items **1519** and **1614** and *HLAS 47:605*), archaeologists have detected new meanings in historically "tired" sources by connecting them with material traces of processes invisible to Spaniards. Less central parts of Tawantinsuyu seem to demand greater efforts to wring coherence from a thinner record (items **1642, 1687, 1736,** and **1747**).

New monographs have deepened our knowledge of the ethnohistory of non-Andean peoples, but other regions still lag behind Andean work in recovering the genesis of events and ideas from the native side; whether this lag can be attributed to source problems or to the lesser growth of the ethnohistorical alliance in lowland studies is not clear. For the Shuar (so-called Jivaro), sophisticated criticism by Anne-Christine Taylor (item **1754**) aids in reading newly recovered sources (items **1684** and **1743**). The Amazon's western reaches continue to attract more ethnohistorical attention (items **1639, 1738, 1750,** and **1770**) than does the Brazilian heartland. Brazilian work remains for the most part a story of things done to, but rarely done by, Indians (items **1592, 1606a, 1620, 1635, 1636, 1643, 1713,** and **1757**). Rausch's meaty *A tropical plain frontier* (item **1708**) and Menezes's sourcebook on Guyanese peoples (item **1669**) open little-known ground in the nothern tier of the continent.

Araucanians fared better than Amazonians. Substantial monographs and a handsome collaborative volume, *Relaciones fronterizas en la Araucanía* (items

1668, 1764, 1765, and 1769), reveal a trend toward a more nuanced sociocultural history of the frontier wars. Several contributions interpret the dynamics and effects of the Araucanians' ad-hoc military confederations (item 1597, 1611, 1612, 1648, and 1744).

A number of editions put less known chronicles into easier circulation, among them Ignacio Prado Pastor's gigantic facsimile of Calancha's Augustinian *Crónica moralizada*. As interest in late colonial natives grows, the Instituto de Cooperación Iberoamericana's bibliophile edition of the richly illustrated Martínez Compañón volumes from Trujillo, Peru, will prove valuable; unfortunately, it is priced beyond most researchers' reach. A cheap reedition of the conquest-era bestseller by Benzoni (item 1594) comes from Guayaquil thanks to the Museo del Banco Central del Ecuador. Ludovico Bertonio's magnificent 1612 Aymara dictionary has been reprinted in Bolivia (item 1595). The Madrid series "Historia 16" promises cheap, reliable editions of many chronicles. Ethnohistorians will probably benefit just as much, however, from the many lesser sources gradually accumulating in print as addenda to articles; these are listed among the materials annotated below.

A number of new works strive for conspectus on the large regional scale. The *Memorias del Primer Simposio Europeo sobre Antropología del Ecuador*, a festschrift for the late Udo Oberem, puts ethnohistoric essays (items 1603, 1634, 1651, 1671, 1677, 1680, 1693, and 1754) in broader anthropological context. *The Cambridge history of Latin America* reflects, at least in its chapter outline, the growing desire among historians to integrate an anthropological perspective (items 1627, 1635, 1636, 1638, and 1681). The English translation of a 1978 *Annales* special issue on the historical anthropology of the Andes (item 1586) comes too late to represent the state of research, but contains valuable works not previously known in English-speaking countries. A variety of mostly tertiary work appears in a three-volume Soviet anthology, *Los pueblos autóctonos de América Latina: pasado y presente* (items 1620, 1628, 1740, 1742, 1746, and 1773). While based on little or no fresh archival and field research, they approach problems of cultural diversity and change with more seriousness than was usual in earlier Marxist scholarship.

Ediciones Abya-Yala, an Ecuadorian publishing house originally concerned with Amazonia, now prints a substantial list of books and pamphlets about the highlands. The Argentine journal *Runa* resumed publication in 1985. Since 1983, *Anthropologica*, published by the Social Sciences Department of Lima's Catholic Univ., has offered a mix of ethnographic and ethnohistorical material.

1582 **Aguiló, Federico.** Una posible pista sobre la presencia de *mitmakunä* en la zona de Pampa Yampara (Historia Boliviana [La Paz] 3:1, 1983, p. 157–171, bibl.)

Parish books (1650–1730) from near Tarabuco show mostly Aymara names but also some which author takes to be Ecuadorian Cañari. Attempts reconstruction of their origin, reproducing fallacies of 1920s "etymological method" and introducing some new ones.

1583 **Aldunate del Solar, Carlos.** El indígena y la frontera (*in* Villalobos, Sergio *et al*. Relaciones fronterizas en la Araucanía.

Santiago: Univ. Católica de Chile, 1982, p. 65–86, ill.)

Distinguishes sharply between the less conflictive establishment of Chilean forts, missions, and farms south of Toltén, and intransigent standoff between Bío Bío and Toltén. Over long run, the latter led to stronger group self-definition and wrested firmer definition of group land rights from the victors.

1584 **Allen, Catherine J.** Patterned times: the mythic history of a Peruvian community (UCLA/JLAL, 10:2, 1984, p. 151–173, bibl.)

In Sonqo, near Cuzco, Quechua speakers explain their origins via myth of cataclysm and replacements. Structurally, study bears common Andean imprint, but archive work (admittedly incomplete) also allows author to identify local problem whose solution the myth provides: ruptures in the ideologically necessary chain of descent that connects *ayllu* with its lands.

Ambaná, tierras y hombres: Provincia de Camacho, Departamento de La Paz, Bolivia. See *HLAS 47:8301.*

1585 Amighetti, Piero *et al.* Antisuyu, ultimo sogno inca. Disegni di Piero Basaglia, Gianluigi Casini, Renzo Zanetti. Traduzioni di Teresa Baldi Guarinoni. Mirano, Italy: Erizzo, 1982. 270 p.: bibl, ill. (Esplorazioni e ricerche; 7)

Eleven authors collaborate in an opulently illustrated coffee table book about the Inca empire's eastern flanks. Contributions by specialists are condensed and prettified.

Andean ecology and civilization. See *HLAS 47:600.*

1586 Anthropological history of Andean polities. Edited by John V. Murra, Nathan Wachtel, and Jacques Revel. Cambridge, England: Cambridge Univ. Press; Paris?: Editions de la Maison des sciences de l'homme, 1986. 383 p.: bibl., ill., map.

Translation of special Andean issue of *Annales* (1978, see *HLAS 42:1592–1593, HLAS 42:1665, HLAS 42:1706, HLAS 42:1727, HLAS 42:1732, HLAS 42:1751,* and *HLAS 42:1758*). Affords sharp (albeit slightly dated) conspectus of recent Argentine, British, Chilean, French, Peruvian, and US ethnohistory and historically-informed ethnography.

1587 Los Araucanos de las pampas en el siglo XIX. Selección y prólogo de Raúl Mandrini. Buenos Aires: Centro Editor de América Latina, 1984. 86 p., 4 p. of plates: bibl., ill. (Historia testimonial argentina; 22. Indígenas y fronteras)

Compact, solidly executed document sampler on the Pehuenche, Ranqueles, Tehuelches under Argentine attack. Includes 1870 narrative of a *nguillatún* ceremony, 1875 visit to Salinero chief, etc. Handy notes and bibliography.

1588 Ares Queija, Berta. Las danzas de los indios: un camino para la evangelización del virreinato del Perú (IGFO/RI, 44:174, julio/dic. 1984, p. 445–463)

Concentrating on the Audiencia de Quito, and briefly quoting unpublished AGI sources, explores Church postures toward the singing dances (*takíes*) at heart of Andean ritual; asks to what degree colonial dances expressed a response to invasion experience.

1588a Argentina indígena: los aborígenes a la llegada de los españoles. Selección y prólogo de Raúl Mandrini. Buenos Aires: Centro Editor de América Latina, 1983. 96 p.: bibl., map (Historia testimonial argentina; 1)

Useful guided tour of main primary sources for all Argentine peoples at contact; includes sketches of authors, bibliographic note, and synoptic introduction.

1589 Arias Palacios, Hugo. Evolución socio-económica del Ecuador: sociedades primitivas y período colonial. Guayaquil, Ecuador: Depto. de Publicaciones, Facultad de Ciencias Económicas, 1980. 310 p.: bibl., ill. (Biblioteca ecuatoriana; 24)

Thinly researched tertiary synthesis (textbook?), written on traditional Marxist outline.

1590 Assadourian, Carlos Sempat. Dominio colonial y señores étnicos en el espacio andino (HISLA, 1, 1983, p. 7–20, bibl.)

Critical synthesis of last decades' findings about native nobility, alerting historians to likelihood that its fate is causal, not epiphenomenal, to main themes of colonial historiography. Urges attention to rise of new native categories: *yanacona, forasteros,* crypto-Indian artisans, etc.

1591 Barnadas, Josep M. Fuentes históricas sobre Mojos jesuita (SBH/HC, 6, 1984, p. 103–114, bibl.)

Short, useful guide to missionary sources, mostly unpublished (ca. 1669-ca. 1782), held in various South American, Spanish archives.

1592 Becker, Itala Irene Basile. El indio y la colonización: charrúas y minuanes. São Paulo: Instituto Anchietano de Pesquisas, 1984. 286 p.: bibl., maps, tables (Pesquisas antropología; 37)

Charrúas and Minuanes, hunting peoples of the Banda Oriental (i.e., Uruguay) became equestrian cattle herders and were crushed much as North American plains peoples. Compiles ample data from printed primary sources, but shreds it to fit an arbitrary outline; method impedes reconstructing social systems or native historic process.

1594 Benzoni, Girolamo. La historia del Mondo Nuovo: relatos de su viaje por el Ecuador, 1547–1550. Traducción en lengua castellana, introducción y notas de Carlos Radicati di Primeglio. 2a ed. Guayaquil, Ecuador: Museo Arqueológico y Pinacoteca, Banco Central del Ecuador, 1985. 135 p.: ill., index.

Reprints Radicatí's 1967 translation of Benzoni's Book III, notable for early eyewitness data on coastal Ecuador. Ample bio-bibliographical introduction observes that now-obscure chronicle was a conquest-era bestseller outside Spain (25 printings before 1650!). Onomastic index.

1595 Bertonio, Ludovico. Vocabulario de la lengua aymara. Cochabamba, Bolivia: Centro de Estudios de la Realidad Económica y Social (CERES): Institut français d'études andines: Museo de Etnografía y Folklore, 1984. 473, 397 p.: bibl. (Serie Documentos históricos; 1. Serie Fuentes primarias; 2. Col. Travaux de l'IFEA; 26)

Facsimile edition of superb colonial dictionary.

1596 Bischof, Henning. Indígenas y españoles en la Sierra Nevada de Santa Marta: siglo XVI (ICA/RCA, 1982/1983, p. 75–124, bibl., ill.)

Useful revised summary in Spanish of author's 1971 *Die spanisch-indianische Auseinandersetzung en der nördlichen Sierra Nevada de Santa Marta: 1501–1600* (see *HLAS 34:1135*).

1597 Boschín, María Teresa and **Lidia Rosa Nacuzzi.** Ensayo metodológico para la reconstrucción etnohistórica: su aplicación a la comprensión del modelo tehuelche meridional. Buenos Aires: Colegio de Graduados en Antropología, 1979. 40 p.: bibl., ill.

Outlines HRAF-like method for itemizing ethnographic data in sources and establishing correlations. Case study concerns social organization and material culture of historic Argentine Araucanians.

1598 Bouysse-Cassagne, Thérèse and **Philippe Bouysse.** Volcan indien, volcan chrétien: à propos de l'éruption du Huaynaputina en l'an 1600: Pérou méridional (SA/J, 70, 1984, p. 43–68)

Volcanic disaster affecting Arequipa appeared to Spanish as a punishment for sins but to Andeans, "le volcan, vielle divinité autochtone, venge les siens et tente d'exterminer les Espagnols; c'est la fin d'un cycle et le commencement d'un autre." Examines European and Andean volcanic lore broadly.

1599 Brundage, Burr Cartwright. Lords of Cuzco: a history and description of the Inca people in their final days. Norman: Univ. of Oklahoma, 1985. 458 p.: ill., maps (Civilization of the American Indian series) Reissue of *HLAS 32:1011*.

1600 Cabeza M., Angel and **Rubén Stehberg.** El cacicazgo de Malloa (Nueva Historia [Asociación de Historiadores Chilenos: World Univ. Service: Institute of Latin American Studies, Univ. of London, London] 3:10, 1984, p. 103–156)

The Pichicobque caciques of Malloa in the "Picunche" or northern Araucanian region ruled 1541–1789. A "colonial tribe" (in Fried's sense, not discussed), this polity proved intermittently effective in fighting forced resettlement.

1601 Caillavet, Chantal. La adaptación de la dominación incaica a las sociedades autóctonas de la frontera septentrional del imperio: Territorio Otavalo, Ecuador (CBC/RA, 3:2, 1985, p. 403–423, bibl.)

Argues that Otavalo, unlike neighboring regions, housed an overarching pre-Inca political unit and that Salomon (see item **1736**) errs in comparing its fate under Inca rule to that of Quito-area polities. Estimates Inca rule to have short and superficial impact.

1602 Caillavet, Chantal. Caciques de Otavalo en el siglo XVI: Don Alonso Maldonado y su esposa (Miscelánea Antropológica Ecuatoriana [Museos del Banco Central del Ecuador, Guayaquil] 2, 1982, p. 38–55, ill.)

Testaments (1606, 1609) from an important north-Ecuadorian aboriginal dynasty itemize regalia, including some prehispanic insignia, and productive assets. Includes full annotated transcriptions with essay emphasizing rules of inheritance.

1603 Caillavet, Chantal. Los grupos étnicos prehispánicos del sur del Ecuador según las fuentes etnohistóricas (in Simposio Europeo sobre Antropología del Ecuador, 1st, 1984. Memorias. Compiladores, Segundo E.

Moreno Yánez y Sophia Thyssen. Bonn, FRG: Instituto de Antropología Cultural, Univ. de Bonn; Quito: Ediciones Abya-Yala, 1985, p. 127–158, bibl., ill.)

Southernmost Ecuador, an ethnohistoric *terra incognita*, yields a few new sources; these identify Chungacaro—the Cuxibamba of the Incas and Loja of the Spanish—as heartland of the Amazonian-derived Palta but also as (possibly Incaic) site of multi-ethnic agricultural colonies.

1604 Caillavet, Chantal. Investigaciones en etnohistoria de (sic) Ecuador (CBC/RA, 2:1, 1984, p. 163–167)

Bibliographic essay emphasizes recent work bearing on native adaptations to north Andean nature and on process of Inca penetration. Assesses prospects for recovery of new primary sources as antidote to stultifying "Velascan" tradition.

Carvalho, José Porfirio F. de. Waimiri Atroari: a historia que ainda não foi contada. See *HLAS 47:1186.*

1605 Castelli G., Amalia and Liliana Regalado de Hurtado. Una versión norteña del origen del Tawantinsuyu (PMNH/HC, 15, 1982, p. 161–183, appendix, bibl.)

Giovanni Anello de Oliva included in his Jesuit history (ca. 1630) a curious myth of the Inca origins, allegedly collected in southern Andes but focused on Ecuadorian coast as home of culture heroes. Offers structural interpretation and reprints text.

1606 Celestino, Olinda. La religiosidad de un noble cañare (sic) en el Valle del Mantaro, siglo XVII: a través de su testamento (IGFO/RI, 44:174, julio/dic. 1984, p. 547–557)

Don Pedro Milachami, *kuraka* of the expatriate Cañaris resident in Wanka territory, recorded in his 1662 testament a series of religious mandates and bequests indicative of elite native styles in worship and of their relevance to colonial governance.

1606a Chaim, Marivone Matos. Aldeamentos indígenas: Goiás, 1749–1811. São Paulo: Livraria Nobel, 1983. 232 p.: appendices, bibl., ill.

Originally published 1974. Pombaline policy attempting to regulate interaction between *sertanistas* and Tupían, Gê peoples, studied via manuscript sources; nine are reproduced as appendices. *Reducción*-like measures emerge clearly but native responses do not.

1607 Chapman, Anne. Drama and power in a hunting society: the Selk'nam of Tierra del Fuego. Cambridge, England: Cambridge Univ. Press, 1982. 201 p.: bibl., ill., index.

Outstanding "memory ethnography" of Selk'nam or Ona, focused on Hain or Kloketen female initiation ceremony, achieves some diachronic depth via restudy of earlier witnesses.

1608 Cock, Guillermo. Sacerdotes o chamanes en el mundo andino (PMNH/HC, 16, 1983, p. 135–146, bibl.)

Argues that *sacerdotes* of Andean shrines in 17th century and earlier behaved like priests of a church-like organization (e.g., full-time practice, bureaucratic transmission), and should not be labeled shamans.

1609 Compilación de crónicas, relatos, y descripciones de Cuenca y su provincia. Edición de Luis A. León. Cuenca: Banco Central del Ecuador, Centro de Investigación y Cultura, 1983. 3 v. (766 p.)

Cuenca, Ecuador, is the successor-city to Incaic Tumipampa and its province the home of the Cañari. Copious selection of sources includes some little-known and hard-to-find items as well as old chestnuts. No index or reference aids.

Conrad, Geoffrey W. and Arthur A. Demarest. Religion and empire: the dynamics of Aztec and Inca expansionism. See item **1519.**

1611 Corregido, Dolores Juliano. Algunas consideraciones sobre el ordenamiento temporo-espacial entre los mapuches (UB/BA, 26:34, 1984, p. 125–152, bibl., ill.)

Overly anecdotal essay charts alleged transformations in structural patterns of Mapuche culture attendant on Spanish conquest and on final political defeat in 1884–85.

1612 Curruhuinca-Roux. Las matanzas del Neuquén: crónica mapuches. Buenos Aires: Plus Ultra, 1984. 320 p.: bibl., ill.

Huilliche author recounts military tactics of surrounding and hunting down Indians. Hunts corralled resistant Araucanian peoples and made them prey to ethnocide or genocide in Argentina's far west.

1614 D'Altroy, Terence and **Timothy K. Earle.** Staple finance, wealth finance, and storage in the Inka political economy (UC/CA, 26:2, 1985, p. 187–206, bibl., ill., tables)

Combining archaeological evidence from Mantaro Valley with document data, argues that functional problems in using state-collected "staple" goods to finance Inca expansion gave rise to a shift toward "wealth" finance and the political distribution of privileged objects: Spondylus, textiles, etc. Intriguing integration of disparate data, with critical comments by specialists.

1615 Dammert Bellido, José. Procesos por supersticiones en la provincia de Cajamarca en la segunda mitad del siglo XVIII (IPA/A, 20, 1984, p. 177–184)

Ecclesiastical trial from Cachén (1784) wrung from Domingo Ramos a confession of sorcery and some information about *mesa* or array of power objects. Accused sought to enchant would-be prosecutors but remainder of social context is obscure.

Davidson, Judith R. El Spondylus en la cosmología chimú. See *HLAS 47:811*.

1616 Dedenbach-Salazar Sáenz, Sabine. Un aporte a la reconstrucción del vocabulario agrícola de la época incaica: diccionarios y textos quechuas del siglo XVI y comienzos del XVII usados como fuentes histórico-etnolingüísticas para el vocabulario agrícola. Bonn, FRG: Seminar für Völkerkunde, Univ. Bonn., 1985. 214 p.: bibl., ill., tables (Bonner Amerikansitische Studien; 14)

Author takes more pains than most dictionary-delvers in handling dialectal, morphological, orthographic diversity encountered on the route to isolable semantic categories. Terms are explained discursively by class rather than listed dictionary-fashion. Helpful reference aid.

1618 Eich, Dieter. Ayllú und Staat der Inka: zur Diskussion der asiatischen Produktionsweise. Frankfurt, FRG: Verlag Klaus Dieter Vervuert, 1982. 311 p.: bibl., ill., tables (Editionen der Iberoamericana Reihe III Monographien und Aufsätze; 11)

Ponderous reworking of familiar primary and secondary sources, attuned to Marx and Marxist literature in general but not to Latin American development of the "Asiatic" theme; misses, for example, Espinoza Soriano's volume on identical topic (see *HLAS 42:1632* and *HLAS 44:1635a*).

Encuentro Latinoamericano de CEHILA, 9th, Manaus, Brazil, 1981. Das reduções latinoamericanas às lutas indigenas atuais. See *HLAS 47:1235a*.

1619 Espinoza Soriano, Waldemar. Los mitimaes salineros de Tarma, Chinchaycocha, y Pasco: siglos XX a.C–XX d.C. (IPA/A, 24, 1984, p. 183–250, bibl.)

Incas probably ratified and reorganized, but did not originate, multi-ethnic clusters of salt refiners around highland salt springs. Refiners enjoyed special advantage up to modern times. Two short documents excerpted (see also item **1704**).

1620 Fáinberg, Lev. Los indígenas de Brasil vistos desde una perspectiva histórica (in Los Pueblos autóctonos de América Latina: pasado y presente. Moscow: Ciencias Sociales Contemporáneos, Academia de Ciencias de la URSS, 1984, t. 2, p. 65–89)

Presents Lathrap-derived argument for complexity and intensive agriculture (e.g., Marajó, Omagua, Tupí) in course of vestpocket four-century historical summary; ends with critique of FUNAI.

1621 Femenias, Blenda. Peruvian costume and European perceptions in the eighteenth century (Dress [Costume Society of America, New York] 10, 1984, p. 52–63, bibl., ill.)

Well illustrated article emphasizes interplay of Inca and European elements expressing rank and ethnicity in clothing. Although 18th century saw resurgence of Inca styles, Túpac Amaru II wore mixed costume.

1622 Fernández, David W. El cabildo indígena de las encomiendas de Guarenas (in Congreso Venezolano de la Historia, 4th, Caracas, 1980. Memoria [see *HLAS 46:2621*] p. 501–514)

Cursory essay on colonial governance in native villages reproduces two documents: a routine 1654 instruction for native magistrates, and part of a 1660 testimony about alleged encomienda abuse.

1623 Flores Galindo, Alberto. Europa y el país de los incas: la utopía andina. Lima: Instituto de Apoyo Agrario, 1986. 89 p.: map.

"Biografía de una idea," namely, the return of the Inca as political messiah, traced from early Andean-born writers through folk theatrical "conquest" dramas, paintings, poems of republican and modern times. Suggestive of "native" ideology's mestizo and hispanic ramifications.

1624 Flusche, Della M. and Eugene H. Korth. Forgotten females: women of African and Indian descent in colonial Chile, 1535–1800. Detroit, Mich.: Blaine Ethridge Publishing, 1983. 112 p.: bibl.

Largely inconclusive despite wide use of primary sources, study notes legal safeguards intended to shelter women, assesses female landholdings, describes female labor, and highlights a few personalities. Among these Beatriz Clara Coya, Inca princess dragged to Chile by Spanish invaders, emerges most clearly.

1625 Forsyth, Donald W. Three cheers for Hans Staden: the case for Brazilian cannibalism (ASE/E, 32 : 1, Winter 1985, p. 17–36, bibl., table)

Detailed refutation of William Arens's attack on Staden's 1557 account of Tupinambá cannibalism. Vindicates Staden's knowledge of Tupí language and demonstrates feasibility of independent confirmation via collation with chronicles of de Léry, Thevet, etc. For ethnologist's comment, see *HLAS 47 : 1239*.

Fundação Instituto Brasileiro de Geografia e Estatística. Divisão de Atlas e Apoio Técnico. Mapa etno-histórico do Brasil e regiões adjacentes. See *HLAS 47 : 5489*.

1626 Garcés, Enrique. Daquilema Rex: biografía de un dolor indio. Quito: Editorial Amanecer, 1983? 159 p.

Reprint of novelized account of an 1871 Quechua revolt around Punín, Ecuador.

1627 Gibson, Charles. Indian societies under Spanish rule (*in* The Cambridge history of Latin America. v. 2, Colonial Latin America [see item 1808] p. 384–422)

Neatly, but conservatively, synthesizes macro-scale factors influencing colonial native conditions. Identifies as crucial determinants: 1) density and organization of preconquest societies; 2) distance from mines, cities; and 3) suitability for estate agriculture.

1628 Goncharov, V. Los indígenas en la revolución liberal de Eloy Alfaro (*in*

Los Pueblos autóctonos de América Latina: pasado y presente. Moscow: Ciencias Sociales Contemporáneas, Academia de Ciencias de la URSS, 1984, t. 2, p. 195–206, bibl.)

In 1895 Ecuador's great coastal-based liberal caudillo marched on the highlands. Quechua peasants of Guamote fought alongside him at Gatazo. His party's involvement with landed interests quickly undid an initially pro-indigenous policy.

González de Santa Cruz, Roque. Pax Christi. See item **2813.**

1629 González Rodríguez, Adolfo. Tasación de Don Diego de Armenteros y Henao en el distrito de Popayán, 1607 (EEHA/HBA, 29, 1985, p. 3–32)

Reproduces *visita*-based tribute quota record from south highland Colombia, focused on question of personal service; despite hispanic and hispano-quechua terminology (e.g., *curicamayo* for gold worker), a pertinent source for groups just beyond Inca frontier.

1630 Grenand, Pierre. Ainsi parlaient nos ancêtres: essai d'ethnologie Wayãpi. Paris: Office de la recherche scientifique et technique d'Outre-mer (ORSTOM), 1982. 408 p.: bibl., ill. (Travaux et documents de l'ORSTOM; 148)

Wayãpi, a Tupí-Guaraní group in French Guiana, have "un mode de repérage dans le temps qui ne ressemble en rien à nos manières de dater." Author has collected local accounts of time and change and, putting them alongside "chronicle of events" seen from outside, notes that Wayãpi dichotomize experience into two separate fields of diachrony. He stops short of erecting theory about their perception of time. Appealing work, pointing toward "ethno-history" in sense analogous to "ethno-science."

1631 Guillén Guillén, Edmundo. Las parcialidades de Hatun Rukana y Laramati en el siglo XVI: la represión de la campaña anticristiana de 1569 y la descripción de sus pueblos en 1586 (Boletín de Lima [Lima] 32, 1984, p. 73–96; 33, 1984, p. 71–82)

Extracts from Albornoz and a 1586 *descripción* published by Jiménez de la Espada, tacked together with interpretative passages, picture part of the area where the *Taki Onqoy* revolt flourished.

1632 Guillén Guillén, Edmundo. Tres documentos para la historia de la guerra de reconquista inca: las declaraciones de Lorenzo Manko y Diego Yuqra Tikona, servidores de Manko Inca Yupanki, y de Francisco Waman Rimachi: testigos presenciales de los sucesos de 1533 a 1558 (IFEA/B, 13:1/2, 1984, p. 17–46, bibl.)

A 1589 deposition of Martín García de Loyola (earlier studied by Guillén in his *Visión peruana de la conquista*) yields more evidence from three native eyewitnesses to events 1553–1558. The testimonies of Diego Yucra Ticona, Francisco Guaman Rimachi, and Lorenzo Mango are held to cast doubt on whether Sayri Tupac ever succeeded to the sovereignty of the Neo-Inca state.

1633 Hartmann, Günther. Zur Demographie des Pau d'Arco-Gebietes, Zentral-Brasilien, im Jahre 1909 (DGV/ZE, 107:2, 1982, p. 259–268, bibl., ill., maps)

Wilhelm Kisseberth's 1908–10 research yielded detailed descriptions of Kayapó dwellings and settlement pattern. Reproduces his field notes on 12 houses, listing inhabitants in *visita* fashion.

1634 Hartmann, Roswith. Un predicador quechua del siglo XVI (*in* Simposio Europeo sobre Antropología del Ecuador, 1st, 1984. Memorias. Compiladores, Segundo E. Moreno Yánez y Sophia Thyssen. Bonn, FRG: Instituto de Antropología Cultural, Univ. de Bonn; Quito: Ediciones Abya-Yala, 1985, p. 291–301, bibl.)

Father Diego Lobato de Sosa, son of conquistador and Inca noblewoman, served Spanish lords of early Quito as bilingual spokesman and tactical advisor in quelling Quijos revolt. His 1592 *memorias* gives 14 witnesses' accounts of Lobato's prowess in persuading and manipulating non-Inca natives.

1635 Hemming, John. Indians and the frontier in colonial Brazil (*in* The Cambridge history of Latin America. v. 2, Colonial Latin America [see item **1808**] p. 501–546)

Well articulated, detailed summary of four poles of pressure on Brazilian peoples: Paulista frontier, inland movement from Bahia, northeastern frontier, and thrust into Amazonia from Maranhão, Pará. Ends with fumbled Pombaline reforms, remarks on Por-

tuguese failure "to record anything about the people they destroyed."

1636 Hemming, John. The Indians of Brazil in 1500 (*in* The Cambridge history of Latin America. v. 1, Colonial Latin America [see item **1808**] p. 119–144)

Tupians sketched through standard sources; scarce Gê evidence eked out with ethnographic analogy; slight coverage of Aruakans and Caribans. Faint historical treatment excused with comments that natives "have presumably changed little during the past five centuries."

1637 Hidalgo Lehuede, Jorge. Ecological complementarity and tribute in Atacama: 1683–1792 (*in* Andean ecology and civilization: an interdisciplinary perspective on Andean ecological complementarity [see *HLAS 47:600*] p. 161–184, bibl.)

Search for money and fragmentation of authority, more than "vertical" diversification, was usual reason for colonial Indians' far-flung extraterritoriality. Nonetheless Atacameños' dispersion "in its formal structure preserve(s) many elements of prehispanic tradition," including loyalty to remote *kurakas*.

1638 Hidalgo Lehuede, Jorge. The Indians of southern South America in the middle of the sixteenth century (*in* The Cambridge history of Latin America. v. 1, Colonial Latin America [see item **1808**] p. 91–118)

Effort to classify and locate groups in southern Andes, Chaco, Argentine pampa and Littoral, and southern Chile. Despite difficult source problems, concentrates on reconstructing social organization and especially political institutions (e.g., dual leadership).

1639 Hudelson, John E. The lowland Quichua as tribe (*in* Political anthropology of Ecuador. Edited by Jeffrey Ehrenreich. Albany: Society for Latin American Anthropology [and] Center for the Caribbean and Latin America, SUNY, 1985, p. 59–79, bibl., maps)

Argues that ethnographic subdivisions of Ecuadorian lowland Quichua ("Quijos," "Canelos") obscure a common historical dynamic, namely "secondary tribe" formation (Fried's sense) rolling eastward from colonial frontier. Botched map mars article.

1640 Hunefeldt, Christine. Lucha por la tierra y protesta indígena: las comunidades indígenas del Perú entre colonia y república, 1800–1830. Bonn, FRG: Seminar für Völkerkunde, Univ. Bonn, 1982. 258 p.: bibl. (Bonner Amerikanistische Studien; 9)

Lacuna of historical knowledge separates Tupac Amaru II from independence wars. Innovative study stresses rural conflict factors that cracked old indigenous order in this period, but also impeded coalescence of class-crossing, region-crossing ethnic consciousness. Intra-native conflict may have helped criollo elite rein in agrarian unrest.

1641 Husson, Jean-Philippe. La poésie quechua dans la chronique de Felipe Waman Puma de Ayala. Paris: L'Hartmattan, 1985. 454 p.: bibl., ill. (Serie Ethnolinguistique amérindienne)

Quechua fragments of greatest "indigenous chronicle" belong to no living dialect and present grave exegetical problems. Meticulous study classifies poems as "spontaneous" (words of author himself), or clerical-influenced, or "ethnographic," and concentrates on the last group. Reading phonological evidence as indicating Waywash-like original tongue, holds that author exploited real vernacular knowledge to authenticate his colonial ideological claims. Severely criticizes recent editions (see *HLAS 44:5092*).

Hux, Meinrado. El indio en la llanura del Plata: guía bibliográfica. See *HLAS 47:35*.

1642 Ibarra Grasso, Dick Edgar. Ciencia en Tihuanaku y el Incario: astronomía y calendarios. La Paz: Editorial Los Amigos del Libro, 1982. 428 p.: ill. (Enciclopedia boliviana)

Copious synthesis of chronicle data on Inca calendars joined somewhat tenuously with archaeological data on remoter times. Argues strenuously for a purely solar calculation of Inca imperial calendar (compare with item **1772**).

1643 Indios no Estado de São Paulo: resistência e transfiguração. São Paulo: Comissão Pró-Indio de São Paulo: Yankatu Editores, 1984. 152 p., 8 p. of plates: bibl., ill., ports.

Partly historical, *engagé* collaboration includes well documented chapters by John Monteiro on Indian enslavement in colonial São Paulo, and by Silvia Helena Simões Borelli on scientific, missionary, and plantation penetration of Kaingang (ca. 1900–20).

1644 Iñigo Carrera, Nicolás. Violence as economic power: the role of the State in creating the conditions for a productive rural system (LAP, 4, 1983, p. 97–113, bibl.)

Depicts "the formation of the working class through the expropriation of the material conditions of existence of the hunting, food-gathering, animal-herding aborigines of the Argentine Chaco" (ca. 1900). Details predatory use of reservations as pools of cheap labor for cotton farming, lumbering, etc.

1645 Jaramillo, Hugo Angel. Pereira: proceso histórico de un grupo étnico colombiano. Pereira, Colombia: Editorial Gráficas Olímpica, 1983. 2 v. (922 p., 51 p. of plates): bibl., ill.

Title notwithstanding, hefty monograph chronicles a Cauca valley municipality (mostly 19th century) with slight attention to ethnic matters or the Quimbaya heritage.

1646 Julien, Catherine J. Guano and resource control in sixteenth-century Arequipa (*in* Andean ecology and civilization: an interdisciplinary perspective on Andean ecological complementarity [see *HLAS 47:600*] p. 185–131, bibl.)

Arequipa housed Lupaqa highlanders (ca. 1567–74) whose lands at Sama probably owed their rich productivity to availability of guano. They supplied Lupaqas' Titicaca-shore homeland. Complex essay explores evidence that Inca intervention and its demise altered settlement, guano procurement.

1647 Krzanowski, Andrzej and Jan Szemiński. La toponimía indígena en la cuenca del Río Chicama, Perú (PAN/EL, 4, 1978, p. 11–51, bibl., maps)

Toponyms of north-Peruvian river system, sorted out by Quechua, Yunka, and unknown linguistic provenience, yield pattern suggesting highland impact of at least two separate waves of Quechua influence. Explores incomplete archaeological correlations.

1648 Landaburu, Roberto E. Los campos del Venado Tuerto. Venado Tuerto, Argentina: Asociación Mutual Venado Tuerto, 1985. 213 p.: ill.

Detailed local history of 1835–76 wars against Araucanians around Venado Tuerto (southern Santa Fé, Argentina) includes some notice of leading native fighters. One-sided military treatment.

1649 Langer, Erick D. Labor strikes and reciprocity on Chuquisaca haciendas (HAHR, 65:2, 1985, p. 255–278, bibl.)

In late 19th, early 20th-century estate peasants suffered acutely from owners' repudiation of reciprocal duties: protection through *compadrazgo*, risk-sharing in crops, supplying of land proportionate to family growth. Strikes in defense of "moral economy" did succeed in preserving a few traditional rights.

1650 Lavallé, Bernard. Las doctrinas de indígenas como núcleos de explotación colonial: siglos XVI–XVII (IPA/A, 16:19, 1982, p. 151–171)

To what experience of Catholicism did mid-colonial folk religion respond? Rich documentation, largely from Quito, shows how regular clergy fought for major missionary parishes and converted them into "empresas familiares" while neglecting minor ones.

1651 Lenz-Volland, Birgit and Martin Volland. Algunas noticias acerca de los caciques de Daule durante el siglo XVII: estudio preliminar (*in* Simposio Europeo sobre Antropología del Ecuador, 1st, 1984. Memorias. Compiladores, Segundo E. Moreno Yánez y Sophia Thyssen. Bonn, FRG: Instituto de Antropología Cultura, Univ. de Bonn; Quito: Ediciones Abya-Yala, 1985, p. 189–200, bibl.)

Examines important native dynasty of Ecuadorian littoral, the Cayches, as reflected in sources from AGI (1600–61). Female *kurakas* figured strongly. Daule chiefs also commanded native coast-guard militia.

1652 Lerche, Peter. Häuptlingstum Jalca: Bevölkerung und Ressourcen bei den vorspanischen Chachapoya, Peru. Berlin, FRG: Dietrich Reimer Verlag, 1986. 229 p.: bibl., ill.

Unit chosen for combined document and field research is a Chacha "chiefdom" of east-slope Andes, traced into the colonial era. Places terraces and architecture in detailed environmental context.

1653 Lorandi, Ana María. Pleito de Juan Ochoa de Zárate por la posesión de los indios ocloyas: ¿un caso de verticalidad étnica o un relicto de archipiélago estatal? (UBAIA/R, 14, 1985, p. 125–144, bibl.)

Puzzling 1556 document shows that Omaguaca native lords claimed ancient dominion over Ocloya, a remote valley. Testimonies suggest likely pre-Inca system of Omaguaca outliers. Ways in which Inca overlay conditioned settlement pattern are partially clarified through comparison with Inca *mitmaq* installation at Cochabamba.

1654 Loza, Carmen Beatriz. Los quirua de los valles paceños: una tentativa de identificación en la época prehispánica (CBC/RA, 2:2, 1984, p. 591–605, bibl, map)

The "Quiruas de Oyune" were a little known category belonging to an "encomienda coquera" of the 1560s. Article explores their possible standing as territorial, ethnic, or occupational group using unpublished sources alongside toponymic and chronicle evidence.

Mabilde, Pierre François Alphonse Booth. Apontamentos sobre os indígenas selvagens da Nação Coroados dos Matos da província do Rio Grande do Sul, 1836–1866. See *HLAS 47:1291.*

1655 MacCormack, Sabine. "The heart has its reasons:" predicaments of missionary Christianity in early colonial Peru (HAHR, 65:3, 1985, p. 443–466)

Penetrating essay reminds us that in conquest era some churchmen thought Andean religion could be evangelized via its own search for divinity, and traces "history of lost opportunity" whereby Andean religion was dogmatically categorized as diabolical error. Comparison with conversion in Roman empire is stimulating.

1656 Magaña, Edmundo. Hombres salvajes y razas monstruosas de los indios kaliña de Surinam (UCLA/JLAL, 8:1, Summer 1982, p. 63–114, bibl., ill., tables)

Profusion of "Plinian" monstrous races in early chronicles, often attributed to European mediaeval lore, can also be connected with American myths of half-human beings. Juxtaposes 54 "mythic tribes" of The Guianas with 23 such recorded in 1980 Kaliña fieldwork. Structural rendering of Kaliña "ethnoethnology" follows.

1657 Mainwaring, Michael James. From the Falklands to Patagonia: the story of a pioneer family. London: Allison & Busby, 1983. 288 p.: bibl., ill., photos.

Diaries of a Scottish settler family of late 19th century, fleshed out with photos and other sources, provide ethnographically naive but vivid account of contact with half-demoralized Tehuelches.

1659 Mannarelli, María Emma. Inquisición y mujeres: las hechiceras en el Perú durante el siglo XVII (CBC/RA, 3:1, 1985, p. 141–156, bibl.)

Both accused witches and their clients were mostly female. Witches were typically young, lower class, unmarried. Witchcraft of basically Mediterranean type, articulated with Andean elements, crossed all ethnic boundaries. Many clients sought to tame and manage male sexual privilege. Oddly ignores Silverblatt's work.

1660 Mannheim, Bruce. *Una nación accoralada*: Southern Peruvian Quechua language planning and politics in historical perspective (Language and Society [Cambridge Univ. Press, Cambridge, England] 13, 1984, p. 291–309, bibl.)

Why have Peruvian hispanophones, enduringly hostile to Quechua as a political language, nonetheless opposed and frustrated several historic attempts to "extirpate" Quechua? Historical discussion of language policy highlights essential constancy of both "extirpationism" and its opponents' critique, ever-repeated through depressing cycle of amnesia and obfuscation.

1661 Márquez Carrero, Andrés. Murachí: un fraude de la colección "Caciques de Venezuela" a la cultura indígena tatuy del estado Mérida (VANH/B, 66:261, marzo 1983, p. 161–165)

Reprimands and corrects a popular history series for erroneously identifying the 16th-century legendary chief Murachi: "es, por tanto, una leyenda tatuy de Mérida y no mirripuy de los predios de El Morro."

1662 Martínez, Eduardo. Cacique García Tulcanaza. Quito: Editora Andina, 1983. 71 p.

Sketchy biography of a Pasto lord who ruled Tulcán (ca. 1600) and was active in the subjection of the western lowland peoples (Barbacoa, etc.).

1663 Martínez Compañón, Baltasar. Trujillo del Perú. Madrid: Instituto de Cooperación Iberoamericana, 1985. 3 v.: col. ill.

Handsome, deluxe facsimile edition of important 18th-century illustrated miscellany from north coastal Peru, with hundreds of color illustrations including many that show popular ceremonial, material culture. Accompanying brochure reprints Porras Barrenechea's comments.

1664 Marzal, Manuel M. La transformación religiosa peruana. Lima: Pontificia Univ. Católica del Perú, 1983. 458 p.: bibl.

Meaty research synthesis, foreshadowed by author's 1977 "hipótesis sobre la aculturación religiosa andina," assembles catechetical sources, "idolatry" trials, diocesan records in support of a stagewise model of how highlanders developed substantially Andean folk Catholicism. Contains paragraph-sized extracts of unpublished sources.

1665 Masferrer Kan, Elio R. Criterios de organización andina, Recuay siglo XVII (IFEA/B, 13:1/2, 1984, p. 47–61, bibl., ill.)

Data from Hernández Príncipe's 1622 visit to the north sierran village of Recuay is structurally interpreted in order to reveal underlying principles (degrees of insider/outsider gender opposition) that endured in the organization of colonial *cofradías*.

1667 Mayer, Enrique. Los atributos del hogar: economía doméstica y la encomienda en el Perú colonial (CBC/RA, 2:2, 1984, p. 557–590, bibl., tables)

Translation of *HLAS 46:1667*.

1668 Méndez B., Luz María. La organización de los parlamentos de indios en el siglo XVIII (*in* Villalobos, Sergio *et al.* Relaciones fronterizas en la Araucanía. Santiago: Univ. Católica de Chile, 1982, p. 107–173, ill.)

Late colonial Araucanians periodically joined non-natives in vast festal gatherings (*parlamentos, juntas*). Collects surprising data on costly feasts, gifts, games by which native leaders and colonial elites conducted mutually manipulative "diálogo fronterizo."

1669 Menezes, Mary Noel. The Amerindians in Guyana, 1803–73: a documentary history. London: Frank Cass, 1979. bibl., ill.

Despite thick haze of missionary and foreign-office mentality, 19th-century documents afford vivid glimpses of Arawak, Carib, Macusi, Waiwai, Warrau cultures. Author, Professor of History at Univ. of Guyana, supplies introductory and connective explanations.

1670 Millones, Luis. Shamanismo y política en el Perú colonial: los curacas de Ayacucho (PUCP/H, 8:2, 1984, p. 131–149, bibl.)

At turn of 18th century, two native lords near Huanta wrangled tenaciously with curates; trial record shows that their loyal following reflected faith in their magical and ritual prowess. Essay suggests economic stress put premium on non-legal sources of leadership.

1671 Minchom, Martin. La economía subterránea y el mercado urbano: pulperos, "indias gateras," y "recatonas" del Quito colonial: siglos XVI–XVII (*in* Simposio Europeo sobre Antropología del Ecuador, 1st, 1984. Memorias. Compiladores, Segundo E. Moreno Yánez y Sophia Thyssen. Bonn, FRG: Instituto de Antropología Cultural, Univ. de Bonn; Quito: Ediciones Abya-Yala, 1985, p. 175–188, bibl.)

The "bazaar economy" conducted by native women and mixed-race vendors, escaping colonial trade regulations, provoked conflict with licensed *pulperos*. But *de facto*, the city relied on flourishing unofficial trade and the far-reaching interethnic network that underlay it. Based on unpublished sources.

1672 Minchom, Martin. The making of a white province: demographic movement and ethnic transformation in the south of the Audiencia de Quito, 1670–1830 (IFEA/B, 12:3/4, 1983, p. 23–29)

Loja, reputed today as largely "white," had black and native population complex enough in late colonial period to escape available categories. A history of "fusion," not of white enclaves, lies below surface homogeneity. Based on unpublished sources.

1673 Miño Grijalva, Manuel. Los cañaris en el Perú (BCE/C, 5:14, sept./dic. 1982, p. 79–131, bibl.)

Reprints *HLAS 42:1677* despite author's acknowledgement of article's inadequacy.

1674 Miño Grijalva, Manuel. Chucuito en 1782: una descripción (CBC/RA, 2:2, 1984, p. 629–636)

Anonymous report on ex-kingdom by Titicaca shore, reproduced in full. "De claro corte borbónico," it emphasizes sources of actual and potential wealth. Also notes that "forsudos y feroces" Lupaqas, despite dispersion far from official villages, coalesce readily to fight whether in rebellion or in His Majesty's service.

1675 Mörner, Magnus. The Andean past: land, societies, and conflicts. New York: Columbia Univ. Press, 1985. 300 p.: bibl., ill., maps.

Economic history predominates, political history follows, and anthropologically informed history runs a poor third in a student-oriented, pleistocene-to-present synthesis.

Morales G., Jorge. and **Gilberto Cadavid Camargo.** Investigaciones etnohistóricas y arqueológicas en el área Guane. See *HLAS 47:750.*

1676 Moreno Yánez, Segundo E. Constitutivos étnicos comunales en la movilización subversiva: las rebeliones indígenas en la comarca de Alausí en el siglo XVIII (Antropología Ecuatoriana [Quito] 2/3, 1984, p. 105–124, bibl.)

Usually native nobles did not join local "Indian" rebellions, but Alausí in central highland Ecuador was an exception. Explores three incidents of insurrection, suggesting that strong cohesion of Alausí *ayllus* is related to ecological demands of their high-altitude lands.

1677 Moreno Yánez, Segundo E. Don Leandro Sepla y Oro, un cacique andino de finales de la colonia: estudio biográfico (*in* Simposio Europeo sobre Antropología del Ecuador, 1st, 1984. Memorias. Compiladores, Segundo E. Moreno Yánez y Sophia Thyssen. Bonn, FRG: Instituto de Antropología Cultural, Univ. de Bonn; Quito: Ediciones Abya-Yala, 1985, p. 223–244, bibl.)

In 1804 the Chimborazo *kuraka* Sepla told Humboldt about a Puruhá-language aboriginal manuscript, lost in fire. Essay details Sepla's career, during which he accumulated titles by denouncing hundreds of Indians "disguised" as mestizos, helping repress three revolts, and organizing earthquake relief.

1678 Moreno Yánez, Segundo E. Traspaso de la propiedad agrícola indígena a la hacienda colonial: el caso de Saquisilí (BCE/C, 4:10, 1981, p. 117–139, tables)

Describes growth of an hacienda (Jesuit, until 1767) near Latacunga, Ecuador, examined via *composición de tierras* sales from late 17th century onward. Detailed account of transactions that gradually detached factors of production from indigenous control.

1679 Mróz, Marcin. Una interpretación numérica de la crónica de Guaman Poma de Ayala (Anthropologica [Univ. Católica del Perú, Depto. de Antropología, Lima] 2, 1984, p. 67–103, bibl., tables)

Argues that Guaman Poma interpreted numeric data from royal *khipu* as longevities and refashioned them into royal chronology (divided in arithmetically equivalent halves) congruent with Christian chronology. Duration of five historic "ages" is correlated to astronomic constants.

1680 Muñoz Bernand, Carmen. Estrategias matrimoniales, apellidos, y nombres de pila: libros parroquiales y civiles en el sur del Ecuador (*in* Simposio Europeo sobre Antropología del Ecuador, 1st, 1984. Memorias. Compiladores, Segundo E. Moreno Yánez y Sophia Thyssen. Bonn, FRG: Instituto de Antropología Cultura, Univ. de Bonn; Quito: Ediciones Abya-Yala, 1985, p. 201–222, bibl., ill.)

"El desprestigio del parentesco entre los campesinos de Pindilig" is reflected in rules allowing one to distance or devalue many links, even consanguinity. Study of parish books (mostly 1858-present) traces shifts in uses of relatedness; holds that shift to Spanish language made prior norms hard to define and apply.

1681 Murra, John V. Andean societies before 1532 (*in* The Cambridge history of Latin America. v. 1, Colonial Latin America [see item **1808**] p. 59–90)

Pointedly programmatic departure from Inca-centered tradition. Emphasizes "ethnic" polities which preceded and outlived Tawantinsuyu, and suggests stresses undergone by Inca State while confronting them. Includes samples of non-chronicle sources; emphasizes intellectual history of field.

1682 Murra, John V. El archipiélago vertical revisited (*in* Andean ecology and civilization: an interdisciplinary perspective on Andean ecological complementarity [see HLAS 47:600] p. 3–14, bibl.)

Originator of the "verticality" concept recalls its genesis (and precursors, notably Condarco Morales), observing that 1970s work did more to delimit its applicability, than to show how "verticality" actually operated. Improved ethnography and the emergence of a mid-colonial "Andean history beyond that which we temporarily call ethnohistory" foretell progress on this score.

1683 Murra, John V. The limits and limitations of the "vertical archipelago" in the Andes (*in* Andean ecology and civilization: an interdiciplinary perspective on Andean ecological complementarity [see HLAS 47:600] p. 15–20)

Translation of HLAS 40:2085.

1684 La Nación shuar: documentación etnohistórica. Edición de Alfredo Costales and Piedad Costales. Quito?: Mundo Shuar, 1977. 85 p.: bibl., ill.

Reprints two new primary sources: a 1775 *Expediente . . . sobre la reducción de los indios infieles de la Misión de Canelos . . .* (a Dominican project) and a 1692 *Autos seguidos por Don Antonio Ormaza . . . sobre la conquista de los gíbaros de Quijos.* Former includes significant face-to-face observation of Shuar *curagas'* behavior.

1685 Naranjo V., Plutarco. Función social de la coca en la América precolombina (BCE/C, mayo/agosto 1981, p. 203–220)

Still under the impression that anthropological study of coca is "defensa del cocainismo," author collects quotations from chronicle to denounce natives "horrenda esclavización" to coca as part of colonial tragedy.

1686 Necker, Louis. La reacción de los guaraníes frente a la conquista española de Paraguay: movimientos de resistencia indígena, siglo XVI (UCNSA/SA, 18:1, 1983, p. 7–29, bibl., maps)

Author argues that marriage alliance between Spaniards and Paraguayan Guaraní owed much to coercion, and that in context of demographic collapse, the demands of their Spanish "in-laws" left Guaraní little choice but to rebel. A list of 23 rebellious incidents (to 1660) emphasizes the seriousness of Guaraní guerrilla threat.

1687 Netherly, Patricia J. The management of late Andean irrigation systems on the north coast of Peru (SAA/AA, 49:2, 1984, p. 227–254, bibl., ill.)

By comparing archaeological and document records, ingenious study shows that "rights to water . . . [were] vested in sociopolitical groups which occupied different hierarchical positions according to the size of the canal." But hydraulic work was organized group by group, without any overarching Wittfogel-style state bureaucracy.

1688 Oberem, Udo. Über den Indianischen Adel im kolonialzeitlichen Ecuador (UEN/LS, 7, 1980, p. 31–41, bibl.)

Short overview of ethnic nobles' role by researcher whose work has brought several Ecuadorian *kuraka* dynasties into focus.

1689 Oberem, Udo. Über die Ausbildung von "hijos de caciques" im frühkolonialen Quito (IAI/I, 10, 1984, p. 341–354, bibl.)

For early dates it is possible to trace certain natives' paths to colonial privilege via their education at special Franciscan colleges. The Henaos, Puentos, other aboriginal dynasties secured power early by accepting bicultural roles.

1690 Onffroy de Thoron, Enrique. America Ecuatorial: su historia pintoresca y política; su geografía y sus riquezas naturales; su estado presente y porvenir. Traducción de Filoteo Samaniego. Quito: Corporación Editora Nacional, 1983. 2 v. in 3 pts. (228, 269 p.): tables (Col. Ecuador. Testimonios de autores extranjeros; 3)

Original publication was Paris, 1866. Extensive travel narrative, with scarce ethnological sensitivity and focus mostly on resources, government.

1691 O'Phelan Godoy, Scarlett. El diario de F.T. Diez de Medina (Historia Boliviana [La Paz] 3:1, 1983, p. 111–121)

Unlike most participants' diaries, Diez de Medina's records civilian point of view on Tupac Catari's 1781 seige of La Paz. Evaluates source's worth for understanding relations with Peruvian rebels, role of cargo crews as vectors of rebellion, and ritual display on battlefield. Text not reproduced.

1692 Ortega, Julio. La corónica de Guaman Poma (SP, 10, 1980, p. 111–115)

Interpretative essay emphasizing "ficción" as an attribute of the text and as a clue to Guaman Poma's posture toward historic experience.

1693 Ortiz de la Tabla Ducasse, Javier. La población ecuatoriana en el siglo XVI: fuentes y cálculos (*in* Simposio Europeo sobre Antropología del Ecuador, 1st, 1984. Memorias. Compiladores, Segundo E. Moreno Yánez y Sophia Thyssen. Bonn, FRG: Instituto de Antropología Cultural, Univ. de Bonn; Quito: Ediciones Abya-Yala, 1985, p. 159–173, bibl.)

Alleges that sources on which Tyrer's account of native population rests do not stand up well to criticism; late ones crib earlier, and some mix data of differing dates. Sketches possible resources for a better count noting that AGI seems to lack Quito encomienda records.

1694 Ortiz de la Tabla Ducasse, Javier. La población indígena del corregimiento de Riobamba, Ecuador, 1581–1605: la visita y numeración de Pedro de León (EEHA/HBA, 25, 1985, p. 1–69, bibl., tables)

Full transcription of summary *visita* (no house-to-house data) from central Ecuador. Essay argues against Tyrer, postulates rising demographic curve to 1605 and suggests tributary ratio of less than 4:1.

1695 Pachón C., Ximena. Los pueblos y los cabildos indígenas: la hispanización de las culturas americanas (ICA/RCA, 23, 1980/1981, p. 297–326, bibl., ill.)

Tertiary synthesis of Bayle, Gibson, and others on origins, function, and range of variation in native village councils established by Spanish.

1696 Parejas Moreno, Alcides. Etnografía de la provincia de Chiquitos, siglo XVI (SBH/HC, 6, 1984, p. 115–123, bibl.)

Very brief review of previously published sources for "Provincia de Xarayes," that is, eastern part of Chiquitos province, modern Santa Cruz.

1697 Parkerson, Phillip T. El monopolio incaico de la coca: ¿realidad o ficción legal? (SBH/HC, 5, abril 1984, p. 1–27)

Translation of *HLAS 46:1687.*

1698 Pease G.Y., Franklin. Cases and variations of verticality in the Southern Andes (*in* Andean ecology and civilization: an interdisciplinary perspective on Andean ecological complementarity [see *HLAS 47:600*] p. 141–160, bibl.)

On the broad canvas of comparison among Andean societies, one sees that Inca practice recognized a diversity of territorial and exchange arrangements which Spanish stereotypes about trade and land tenure obscured. Detailed cases concern Moquegua, mostly late 16th century.

1699 Pease G.Y., Franklin. Mesianismo andino e identidad étnica: continuidades y problemas (BCE/C, 5:13, 1982, p. 57–71, bibl.)

How did Andean rebel ideology evolve from pre-1570 appeal to non-Inca deities, into evocation of pan-Andean Inca sovereignty? A 1667 source from Huancavelica depicts leaders of a native movement arising from fear of enslavement as Inca-like figures a century before Tupac Amaru II.

1700 Pease G.Y., Franklin. El pensamiento mítico. Lima: Mosca Azul Editores, 1982. 235 p. (Biblioteca del pensamiento peruano; 4)

Anthology of primary source excerpts conveying Andean myths, cosmology (e.g., Acosta, Arriaga, Avila, Calancha, Cieza, Guaman Poma, Murúa). Includes interpretative foreword and some modern myths.

1701 Pineda Camacho, Roberto. El rescate de los Tamas: análisis de un caso de desamparo en el siglo XVII (ICA/RCA, 23, 1980/1981, p. 327–363, bibl., tables)

Intriguing combination of colonial and modern ethnographic evidence suggests that Tama, a category of people enslaved by Spaniards in Colombian Amazon and Magdalena valleys, were not an ethnic group but "adopted" captives of neighboring peoples. Analysis bears on interpretation of Páez origin myth about Juan Tama.

1702 Pino Zapata, Eduardo. Pacificación y colonización de la frontera y la Araucanía: pt. 2 (UC/AT, 447, 1983, p. 87–110, bibl.)

Brief notes on incidents around Temuco, more among German and French immigrants than Mapuche (1885–1930).

1703 Platt, Tristan. Liberalism and ethnocide in the Southern Andes (History Workshop [Ruskin College, Oxford, England] 17, Spring 1984, p. 3–18)

Liberal promoters of laws abolishing communal land tenure and colonial-style Indian tributes in mid-19th century Bolivia perceived Indian resistence as irrational. Natives defended old levies as parts of a binding pact embodying ethnic rights. An 1886 Chayanta rebellion serves as exploratory case study.

1704 Pomeroy, Cheryl. El significado de la sal para las culturas andino-ecuatorianas. Quito?: Mundo Andino, 1986. 71 p.: bibl., maps.

Unites ethnographic work at still-used precolumbian salt spring with long diachronic record. Prized for its healthfulness (iodine content), mountain spring salt belonged to a female sphere of labor. Includes quantity estimates of paleotechnic salt production.

Porro, Antônio. Os Omagua do Alto Amazonas: demografia e padrões de povoamento no século XVII. See *HLAS 47:1320*.

1705 Radicati di Primeglio, Carlos. El secreto de la quilca (IGFO/RI, 14:173, enero/junio 1984, p. 11–62, appendices, ill., tables)

Many early sources attest to use of colors to encode non-numeric *khipu* content. Studying four *khipus* and two "wig-caps," author holds that "*cartuchos*" of colored thread wound onto cords exemplify the little-known *qelka* or "writing" of Incas. Speculative essay offers no attempt at decipherment or archaeological context.

1706 Ramírez, Susan. Social frontiers and the territorial base of *curacazgos* (*in* Andean ecology and civilization: an interdisciplinary perspective on Andean ecological complementarity [see *HLAS 47:600*] p. 423–442, bibl.)

"Emically, the *curacazgo* was people. Over time and etically, the *curacazgo* became identified with a given land area." Pre-Toledan data from Peru's north coast show that a lord's vassals could occupy lands outside his territory, including some "rented" ones. Term "*territorialidad salpicada*" obscures distinction between control over land and use of it.

1707 Rappaport, Joanne. History, myth, and the dynamics of territorial maintenance in Tierradentro, Colombia (AES/AE, 12:1, 1985, p. 27–45, bibl., ill.)

Páez have enforced hegemony over their terrain by a variety of ritual and political measures, which "are then incorporated into the body of historical knowledge." Mapped out on the landscape, memories provide mythic exemplars for future action.

1708 Rausch, Jane M. A tropical plain frontier: the llanos of Colombia, 1531–1831. Albuquerque: Univ. of New Mexico Press, 1984. 317 p.: bibl., ill., maps.

Richly researched monograph reconstructs durable frontier society on immense Colombo-Venezuelan grassland. Incursions of Spanish as well as contact between farming peoples (e.g., Achagua) and nomadic Guahibo combined to create complex frontier dynamic, which is closely compared with other frontier zones.

1709 Regalado de Hurtado, Liliana. Un contexto legendario para el origen de los mitmaqkuna y el alcance del prestigio norteño (PUCP/H, 7:2, 1983, p. 255–286, bibl.)

Takes up once again theme of Atahualpa's alleged Quito birth, speculating that it figures in ideology of Inca civil war to fulfill paralellism with mythic Inca-Chanca war.

1710 Regalado de Hurtado, Liliana. De Cajamarca a Vilcabamba: una querella andina (PUCP/H, 8:2, 1984, p. 177–196, bibl.)

Interprets immediate crisis at moment of Pizarran coup d'état in light of subsequent evolution of Inca resistance. Tertiary treatment of well known books.

Reinhard, Johan. Las montañas sagradas: un estudio etnoarqueológico de ruinas en las altas cumbres andinas. See *HLAS 47:608.*

1711 Requena, Francisco. La descripción de Guayaquil por Francisco Requena, 1774. Edición de María Luisa Laviana Cuetos. Sevilla, Spain: Escuela de Estudios Hispano-Americanos de Sevilla, 1984. 132 p.: bibl., ill., index, map (Publicaciones; 229)

Reproduces extensive geographical report with original map and index and new prefatory study by Laviana. Light on ethnographic observation, text does contain scattered clues about "colorados" and other "infieles" as well as vignettes of hispanicized rural mores. Data on crops, markets, military and governmental systems clarifies context of late-colonial native assimilation and flight.

1712 La Revolución de los Túpac Amaru: antología. Edición de Luis Durand Flórez. Lima: Comisión Nacional del Bicentenario de la Rebelión Emancipadora de Túpac Amaru, 1981. 486 p.: bibls.

Collection of 21 interpretative pieces by various hands, a few having ethnographic interest: A. Flores Galindo on rebel "utopia," M.E. Siles S. on Aymara revolts near La Paz, S. O'Phelan G. on internal organization of rebel movements.

1713 Ribeiro, Berta G. O Indio na história do Brasil. São Paulo: Global, 1983. 125 p.: ill. (Historia popular; 13)

Tidy popularization, focused on frontier conflicts and on "o que devemos aos indios" (mostly cultigens). For ethnologist's comment, see *HLAS 47:1334.*

1713a Río, María de las Mercedes del and **Ana María Presta.** Un estudio etnohistórico en los corregimientos de Tomina y Amparaez: casos de multietnicidad (UBAIA/R, 14, 1985, p. 221–245, bibl., ill.)

Like neighboring Cochabamba, Tomina and Yamparáes (Bolivia) show multiple enclaves of "foreigners." Despite difficulty of interpreting post-Toledan record, *mitmaq* and other movements related to warfare with Chiriguanos can be detected. Quotes unpublished sources from Argentine archives.

1714 Romano, Ruggiero. Alrededor de dos falsas ecuaciones: coca buena-cocaína buena; cocaína mala-coca mala (IPA/A, 16:19, 1982, p. 237–252)

Brief, well documented résumé of coca debate. From isolation of cocaine (1860) onward, key deliberations such as 1909 and 1912 international conferences, 1948 UN report, and 1977 US congressional mission, confused properties of coca leaf and cocaine, with grave consequences so far unremedied despite telling evidence. For ethnologist's comment, see *HLAS 47:1408.*

1715 Rostworowski de Díez Canseco, María. Patronyms with the consonant *F* in the *guarangas* of Cajamarca (*in* Andean ecology and civilization: an interdisciplinary perspective on Andean ecological complementarity [see *HLAS 47 : 600*] p. 401–422, bibl.)

Certain Inca-defined *pachacas* around Cajamarca abounded (ca. 1572) in phonologically Yunka patronymics. Author holds they derive not from Inca transplants but from older movements. Same area has *llacuaz* (i.e., "stranger," "pastoralist invader") sector as well, which could derive from highlanders immigrating as early as Huari times. Inconclusive but ingeniously probing essay.

1716 Rostworowski de Díez Canseco, María. Testamento de Don Luis de Colán (PEMN/R, 46, 1982, p. 507–543, bibl.)

Luis de Colán, native lord of Piura on the extreme north coast of Peru, had by 1622 parlayed the salt and fish trade of his non-agricultural people into an estate of rental properties. His commercial net centered on Guayaquil and Quito. Comparison with other *kurakas'* wills (including a newly discovered one from Cajamarca 1591) indicates tendency for succession to exhaust the descendant's generation before passing to that of his children. Two texts reproduced.

1717 Rowe, John Howland. La constitución inca del Cuzco (PUCP/H, 9 : 1, 1985, p. 35–75, bibl.)

Discovery of holographic Cobo text allowed completion of attempt, predating Zuidema's *ceque* system, to render "organización social y ceremonial" implicit in *ceque* lists. Holds that a simple and self-consistent *ceque* system created by Pachacuti Inca was altered by subsequent Incas. Author proposes to reconstruct original by filtering out modifications deductively.

1718 Rowe, John Howland. An interview with John V. Murra (HAHR, 64 : 4, 1984, p. 633–653, bibl.)

Murra's answers concern his experience as combatant, refugee, and scholar, the roots of his ethnohistory (Marxism, British social anthropology, Peruvian colleagues) and his campaign to freshen the sources of ethnohistorical research. Influence of African studies stands out. No exchange of ideas with Rowe.

1719 Rozo Gauta, José. Los muiscas: cultura material y organización sociopolítica. La Habana: Casa de las Américas, 1984. 155 p.: bibl., plates (Col. Nuestros países)

Extensive tertiary treatment defining Chibcha polity, in "stage" terms derived from Marx and Engels. "Dista mucho de ser el clan clásico . . . (está en) el paso del semiestado al estado . . . resultado de las contradicciones de clase."

1720 Saeger, James Schofield. Another view of the mission as a frontier institution: the Guaycuruan reductions of Santa Fe, 1743–1810 (HAHR, 65 : 3, 1985, p. 493–517, bibl.)

On the Chaco frontier, Jesuit missions 1743–67 were invited by Mocobí and Abipón equestrian peoples. Missions, and ex-mission towns after 1767, served both beleaguered Indians and townspeople of Santa Fe as buffer zone against frontier and intra-Indian warfare while permitting commercial penetration.

1721 Saignes, Thierry. "Algún día todo se andará:" los movimientos étnicos en Charcas, siglo XVII (CBC/RA, 3 : 2, 1985, p. 425–450, bibl.)

Stereotyped as era of stable colonialism, 17th century did see flickers of rebellion (e.g., 1623 insurrection in coca-growing *yungas*, shadowy 1613 conspiracies). Attempts to forge alliances across intra-native ethnic lines went together with new, heterodox, sometimes utopian folk religions; their prophets capitalized on hostility to exploitative rule by colonial *kurakas*. Significant emphasis on intra- "Indian" sources of political revolutionism.

1722 Saignes, Thierry. Los Andes orientales: historia de un olvido. Cochabamba, Bolivia: Centro de Estudios de la Realidad Económica y Social: Instituto Francés de Estudios Andinos, 1985. 367 p.: bibl., maps, tables (Travaux de l'Institut. CERES Estudios históricos; 2)

Important contribution on east slope, piedmont of Bolivian Andes. Restores connectedness to aboriginal, Inca and colonial highland history; three essays concern highlanders' (including Kallawayas') presence in valleys, and three others the consequences of non-Indians' efforts at changing settlement pattern. Four of eight studies appear here for first time. All based on wide reading of unpublished sources.

1723 Saignes, Thierry. L'ethnographie missionaire des sauvages: la première description franciscaine des Chiriguano, 1782 (SA/J, 70, 1984, p. 21–42, bibl.)

Author found 1782 narrative of Padre Gerónimo Guillén in Tarija convent archive. Affords clear but superficial ethnographic data. Introductory essay traces Guillén's odd indifference toward Tupian religion to conflicting interests among rival clergy, "pretexte" of Mexican experience.

1724 Saignes, Thierry. L'ethnographie missionaire en Bolivie: deux siècles de regards franciscains sur les Chiriguano, 1782–1980 (*in* Franciscan presence in the Americas. Edited by F. Morales. Potomac, Md.: Academy of American Franciscan History, 1983, p. 345–366, bibl., ill.)

Lists 24 Franciscan accounts of Chiriguano, some still unpublished. Among factors conditioning their viewpoint: disillusionment after failed Mexican apostolic fantasies, frustration in managing acephalous societies, vested interest in "their" Indians' reputation for intractability.

1725 Saignes, Thierry. Las etnias de Charcas frente al sistema colonial, siglo XVII: ausentismo y fugas en el debate sobre la mano de obra indígena, 1595–1665 (JGSWGL, 21, 1984, p. 27–75, bibl., maps, tables)

South highland villages' apparent desolation ca. 1600 may owe less to epidemics, and more to migration, than commonly recognized. New sources allow breakdown of "ausentismo" into varied strategies: flight to Amazonia, manipulated "forastero" movement, residence in vertically dispersed holdings, etc.; points out problems in quantifying and politically analyzing the results.

1726 Saignes, Thierry. Guerres indiennes dans l'Amérique pionnière: le dilemme de la résistance Chiriguano à la colonisation éuropèene, XVIe-XIXe siècles (Histoire économie et sociétés [Paris] 1, 1982, p. 77–103)

Chiriguano resistance and its eventual defeat both arose from a common root: intra-Chiriguano endemic warfare creating demand for alliances. Europeans gradually won upper hand by exploiting it: rich coverage up to 1892.

1727 Saignes, Thierry. Notes on the regional contribution to the *mita* in Potosí in the early seventeenth century (Bulletin of Latin American Research [Oxford Microfilm Publications, Oxford, England] 4 : 1, p. 65–76, bibl., tables)

List compiled by Rafael Ortiz de

Sotomayor, probably after 1610, shows how "obligated" villages paid their *mita* quotas. District of La Plata showed tendency to pay in silver while La Paz and Cuzco villages yielded up manpower. 1617 document listing laborers in Potosí confirms the finding. Spanish version of same appears in *Historiografía y Bibliografía Americanistas* (Sevilla, 28, 1984, p. 47–63)

1728 Saignes, Thierry. Políticas étnicas en Bolivia colonial: siglos XVI–XIX (Historia Boliviana [La Paz] 3 : 1, 1983, p. 1–30) Translation of *HLAS 46 : 1709.*

1729 Saignes, Thierry. Potosí et le sud bolivien selon une ancienne carte (UTIEH/C, 45, 1985, p. 123–128, ill.)

Anonymous early 17th-century map, presented with gazetteer of some 500 toponyms, covers southern half of the Audiencia de Charcas from Tinquipaya south to Lipes. Original is in Bibliothèque Nationale, Paris.

1730 Saignes, Thierry. Sauvages et missionaires: les sociétés de l'Oriente bolivien à travers des sources missionaires récemment éditées (UTIEH/C, 44, 1985, p. 77–89)

Recent printings of sources on the Mojos, Chiquitos, and Chiriguanos bring Bolivia's forest and steppe into clearer view. Programmatically loaded missionary narratives should be compared with more candid, confidential, and still hidden intrachurch correspondence.

1731 Saignes, Thierry and **Carmen Beatriz Loza.** El pleito entre Bartolomé Qhari y los corregidores de Chucuito (SBH/HC, 6, oct. 1984, p. 183–193, tables)

Extracts of a lawsuit ending 1641 (reproduced) show how an heir to the upper-moiety chieftaincy of the Lupaqa, a lakeside Aymara group, fought to reclaim sovereignty and resist the pressures of his *mita*-enforcing role.

1732 Salomon, Frank. Crónicas de lo imposible: notas sobre tres historiadores indígenas peruanos (UN/C, 12, 1984, p. 81–97, bibl., tables) Translation of *HLAS 44 : 1671.*

1733 Salomon, Frank. The dynamic potential of the complementarity concept (*in* Andean ecology and civilization: an interdisciplinary perspective on Andean ecological complementarity [see *HLAS 47:600*] p. 511–531, bibl., table)

Synthetic essay typologizing various complementary mechanisms reported for Andean societies since beginning of "verticality" discussion. "Dynamic potential" refers to their unlike impact on change, growth, and conflict.

1734 Salomon, Frank. The fury of Andrés Arévalo: disease bundles of a colonial Andean shaman (*in* Political anthropology of Ecuador. Edited by Jeffrey Ehrenreich. Albany: Society for Latin American Anthropology [and] Center for the Caribbean and Latin America, SUNY, 1985, p. 83–105, bibl., table)

Arévalo, shaman and enemy of ranching interests in a western Ecuadorian frontier zone (1705), dominated through popular fear of his buried hexes. Testimony at his trial contains details on local magical belief. Essay concerns symbolism of malignity.

1735 Salomon, Frank. The historical development of Andean ethnology (Mountain Research and Development [UN Univ., Tokyo; International Mountain Society, Boulder, Colo.] 5:1, Feb. 1985, p. 78–98, bibl., ill.)

Five-century summary emphasizes social currents giving rise to (or inhibiting) awareness of Andean peoples, contrasting local and external roots of ethnographic inquiry (compare with *HLAS 46:1676*).

1736 Salomon, Frank. Native lords of Quito in the age of the Incas: the political economy of north Andean chiefdoms. Cambridge, England: Cambridge Univ. Press, 1986. 274 p.: bibl., ill., index (Cambridge studies in social anthropology; 59)

Revised English translation of *HLAS 44:1673*.

1737 Salomon, Frank and Susan Grosboll. Names and peoples in Incaic Quito: retrieving undocumented historic processes through anthroponymy and statistics (AAA/AA, 88, 1986, p. 1–4, bibl., ill., tables)

Statistical study of aboriginal names and their components in 1559 *Visita* suggests Quito straddled an aboriginal linguistic divide, and that among both aborigines and *mitmaqkuna* Inca naming attained only modest popularity.

Schmidel, Ulrich. Derrotero y viaje al Río de la Plata y Paraguay. See item **2836**.

1738 Seiler-Baldinger, Annemarie. Indianische Migrationen am Beispiel der Yagua Nordwest-Amazoniens (Ethnologica Helvetica [Berne, Switzerland] 8, 1984, p. 217–267, bibl., ill.)

Located in modern times between Iquitos and Leticia on upper Amazon, Yagua have complex history of migration. Study offers substantial five-century overview of sources, and survey of varied motives for migrating (e.g., mortality taboos, war, shamanic aggresion, ecological stress, slaving, messianism, state encroachment).

1739 Sepúlveda, Jorge and Dagny Haugen. Cowilij, el Yámana. Valparaíso, Chile: Ediciones Universitarias de Valparaíso, 1983. 159 p.: bibl., ill., map.

Ethnographic novel with a subtext of propaganda praising Chilean navy; encounter with Fuegian natives, 1896. Illustrated with old photos and engravings.

1740 Sheinbaum, Lina. Los guaraníes en la historia étnica de Argentina (*in* Los Pueblos autóctonos de América Latina: pasado y presente. Moscow: Ciencias Sociales Contemporáneas, Academia de Ciencias de la URSS, 1984, t. 2, 143–152, bibl.)

"Para los indios argentinos . . . separados por milenios de desarrollo histórico respecto de los europeos," invasion meant transformation by Jesuit coercion, or rural proletarization. Endorses "autoafirmación étnica" as path for surviving Guaraní.

1741 Sherbondy, Jeannette. Una caña guadúa que era adorada (Miscelánea Antropológica Ecuatoriana [Museos del Banco Central del Ecuador, Guayaquil] p. 73–76, bibl., ill.)

"Idolatry" trial (1725) mentions that natives of Palpas, in the Cajatambo province near Lima, offered food and drink to a stalk of *Guadúa angustifolia* probably brought from Guayaquil. It may have been the litter of an important mummy.

1742 Shprintsin, N. Archivos de las expediciones rusas a Sudamérica (*in* Los Pueblos autóctonos de América Latina: pasado y presente. Moscow: Ciencias Sociales Contemporáneas, Academia de Ciencias de la URSS, 1984, t. 2, p. 51–64)

Deals summarily with the Langsdorf expedition to Brazil (1821–29) and at length with a 1914 expedition whose ethnographers,

G. Manizer and F. Fieldstrup, left data on Guaraní, Kaingang, Botocudo, Kadiweu, and other peoples; emphasis on linguistics.

1743 Los Shuar en la historia: Sevilla de Oro y San Francisco de Borja. Edición de Alfredo Costales and Piedad Costales. Quito?: Mundo Shuar, 1978. 174 p.: ill.

Three new primary sources on Spanish "cities" of Quito's Amazonian domains and their "Jivaro" neighbors, dated 1587, 1608, and 1702. Earliest contains native testimony about Ocarigua, Laylagua, other leaders (called "white Indians") during long, successful war against Spaniards.

1744 Silva Galdames, Oswaldo. ¿Detuvo la Batalla de Maule, la expansión inca hacia el sur de Chile? (UC/CH, 3, julio 1983, p. 7–25, bibl., maps)

Taking a cue from Toribio Medina (1882), seeks to distinguish between area of Inca penetration (perhaps to Concepción) and Inca rule (only to Río Maule). Speculates on Inca motives; no new sources.

1745 Smyczek, Malgorzata. El desarrollo territorial del Tawantinsuyu a la luz de la teoría dualista de Tom Zuidema: en base a crónicas españolas escogidas (PAN/EL, 9, 1982/1984, p. 189–210, maps)

Hampered by poor access to books, author limits application of "diarchy" model to data of five well known sources. Collation of Inca kings' alleged conquests with their moiety affiliations in "diarchy" suggests that only *Hanan* moiety rulers conquered afar.

1746 Sózina, S. La herencia de Túpac Amaru (in Los Pueblos autóctonos de América Latina: pasado y presente. Moscow: Ciencias Sociales Contemporáneas, Academia de Ciencias de la URSS, 1984, t. 2, p. 179–194, bibl.)

Short history of great revolt adheres to image of Tupac Amaru as precursor of independence and social rebel. "Vestido con el ropaje incaico y con frases incaicas en los labios," independent Peru nonetheless sacrificed native revolution to bourgeois agenda.

1747 Stahl, Peter. On climate and occupation of the Santa Elena Peninsula: implications of documents for Andean prehistory (UC/CA, 25:3, 1984, p. 351–355)

Refutes Paulsen's 1976 assertion that at contact Ecuadorian coast near Guayaquil was unpeopled. Apt use of chronicle evidence in archaeological context.

1748 Stark, Louisa. The role of women in peasant uprisings in the Ecuadorian highlands (in Political anthropology of Ecuador: perspectives from indigenous cultures. Edited by Jeffrey Ehrenreich. Albany: Society for Latin American Anthropology [and] Center for the Caribbean and Latin America, SUNY, 1985, p. 3–23, bibl.)

Reinterpretation of material on a 1777 revolt in Cotacachi, near Otavalo, presented by Moreno in 1976 (see *HLAS 40:3178*). Attributes women's aggressive posture to fear lest productive males be removed, to women's lesser vulnerability to repression, and to local female independence.

1749 Stavig, Ward A. Violencia cotidiana de los naturales de Quispicanchis, Cañas, y Canchis en el siglo XVIII (CBC/RA, 3:2, 1985, p. 451–468, bibl.)

Quantitative study of mostly intracommunal murder, theft, rape. Killings tended to follow festivals, markets, especially in brawls between different *ayllus* or ethnic groups. "Amor, celos, sexo," however, was most common cause of all.

Stearman, Allyn MacLean. The Yuquí connection: another look at Sirionó deculturation. See *HLAS 47:1350*.

1750 Stocks, Anthony Wayne. Los nativos invisibles: notas sobre la historia y realidad actual de los cocamilla del Río Huallaga, Perú. Lima: Centro Amazónico de Antropología y Aplicación Práctica, 1981. 186 p.: bibl., ill. (Antropológica; 4)

"Invisible" because enmeshed for centuries in Spanish-dominated riverine trade, Tupían Cocamilla still form recognizable collectivity. Chapters 3–6 of dominantly ethnographic book provide unusually detailed history.

Susnik, Branislava. El rol de los indígenes en la formación y en la vivencia del Paraguay. See *HLAS 47:1354*.

1751 Szemiński, Jan. Acerca del significado de algunos de los términos empleados en los documentos relativos a la revolución tupamarista, 1780–1783 (PAN/EL, 8, 1981, p. 65–102, tables)

Combing administrative debris of political repression, author collects terms expressing ideas of hierarchy. Holds that distinguishable hierarchies of *casta*, estate, "culture" (as vs. barbarism), and ethnic group are detectable. *Casta* predominates, but finding is labeled weak because data are largely from hispanophone minority.

1752 Szemiński, Jan. Las generaciones del mundo según Don Felipe Guaman Poma de Ayala (PUCP/H, 7:1, 1983, p. 69–109, bibl., tables)

Argues that the famous "five ages" form part of a larger, less explicit scheme of progressive world order and unification. Adduces tentative reconstructions and holds, against Duviols (see *HLAS 46:1626*), that the "five ages" owe little to medieval European historiosophy. Also published in *Estudios Latinoamericanos* (Warsaw, 9, 1982/1984, p. 89–123).

1753 Taussig, Michael. History as sorcery (Representations [Berkeley, Calif.] 7, Summer 1984, p. 87–109, bibl.)

Ethnohistory is in a sense analogous to ethnoscience: in shamanic lore of the Sibundoy Valley, southern Colombia, events of the past are "experientially appropriated" in the form of magically empowered, efficacious images. Case study concerns image of the Huitoto, victims of rubber-boom atrocities and, in memory, repositories of redemptive power.

1754 Taylor, Anne Christine. La invención del jívaro: notas sobre un fantasma occidental (*in* Simposio Europeo sobre Antropología del Ecuador, 1st, 1984. Memorias. Compiladores, Segundo E. Moreno Yánez y Sophia Thyssen. Bonn, FRG: Instituto de Antropología, Univ. de Bonn; Quito: Ediciones Abya-Yala, 1985, p. 255–267)

The disdainful term *Jívaro* and the self-denomination *Shuar* share etymological root. "*Jívaro*" became exemplars of wicked savagery because their acephalous society struck the Spanish as a frightening conundrum. Missionaries shocked by Shuar "materialism" and tourists who identified head-shrinking with Frankenstein science gave spooky "*Jívaro*" his modern avatars.

1755 Taylor, Anne Christine and Philippe Descola. El conjunto jívaro en los comienzos de la conquista española del Alto Amazonas (Antropología [Pontificia Univ. Católica del Ecuador, Quito] 3, 1984, p. 35–91, bibl., maps)

First published in *Boletín del Instituto Francés de Estudios Andinos* (see *HLAS 44:1680*).

1756 Taylor, Gérald. Un documento de Huarochirí, 1607 (CBC/RA, 3:1, 1985, p. 157–185, bibl., ill.)

Corrected version of significant 1983 *Revista de Indias* article, reproduces Quechua letter by Cristóbal Choquecasa. Text, retracting accusations against Avila, is analyzed philologically: Is Huarochirí manuscript in the Church's "general" version of Quechua, and if so, how much influenced by local tongues? Makers of the text probably used another tongue, either Aru or Quechua I. (For social context, see Antonio Acosta's 1979 article in *Historiografía y Bibliografía Americanistas* [Sevilla]).

1757 Terra, J.E. Catequese e cultura. São Paulo: Loyola, 1982. 54 p. (Bíblia e catequese; 3)

Three historical essays on Jesuit indoctrination of Africans and natives in Brazil, of which one concentrates on "Indios." Lists Jesuit catechetical works in "lingua brasilica" (i.e., Tupí).

Thomas, Georg. Política indigenista dos Portugueses no Brasil, 1500–1640. See *HLAS 47:1357*.

1757a Titu Cussi Yupanqui, Diego de Castro. Ynstruçion del Ynga Don Diego de Castro Titu Cussi Yupangui para el Muy Ilustre Señor el Liçençiado Lope Garçia de Castro, governador que fue destos Reynos del Piru tocante a los negoçios que fue con su Magestad, en su nonbre, por su poder a de tratar: la qual es esta que se sigue, 1570. Introducción de Luis Millones. Lima: Ediciones El Virrey, 1985. 1 portfolio (23, 36 p., 1 folded leaf of plates): bibl., map.

Previously printed (1916, 1973) but little-known text of neo-Inca king's manifesto, a claim for retaining Inca sovereignty under Spanish suzerainty. Introduction comments on peculiarly theatrical discourse and latent Andean context of text produced by Spanish mediation for Spanish eyes.

1758 Torero, Alfredo. El comercio lejano y la difusión del quechua: el caso del Ecuador (CBC/RA, 2:2, 1984, p. 367–402, bibl.)

In 1970s, Torero argued for diffusion of Quechua before Inca times. New essay focuses on Ecuadorian part of problem, holding that coastal Peruvian seafarers and equatorial "merchant Indians" (*mindaláes*) spread a pre-incaic Quechua trade language, and that it underlies peculiarities of later Ecuadorian language. Debate continues in *Revista Andina* (3:1, 1985, p. 107–114).

1759 Torreblanca, Hernando de. Relación histórica de Calchaquí escrita por el misionero jesuita Hernando de Torreblanca en 1695. Versión modernizada, notas y mapas de Teresa Piossek Prebisch. Buenos Aires: Ediciones Culturales Argentinas, Ministerio de Educación y Justicia, Secretaría de Cultura, 1984. 155 p.: bibl., facsims.

Missionary account of Pedro Bohórquez, Andalusian soldier of fortune turned false Inca messiah of the northwest Argentine Calchaquíes. Testifies to native fears of mining as a motor of resistance. Text altered to modern style.

1760 Urton, Gary. Chuta: el espacio de la práctica social en Pacariqtambo, Perú (CBC/RA, 2:2, 1984, p. 7–56, bibl., ill., tables)

In modern Pacariqtambo *chutay*, literally "to stretch out," also means the process of quantifying structurally defined portions of space (e.g., measuring out each *ayllu*'s portion of plaza). Essay has double merit of refining ethnographic analogy to (partly unpublished) primary sources, and of infusing realism about organizational flexibility into structuralist image of village.

1761 Van der Guchte, Maarten. El ciclo mítico andino de la piedra cansada (CBC/RA, 2:2, 1984, p. 539–556, bibl., ill., map)

The "tired stone" figures in chronicles and mythic landscape of many Andean places. It behaves like a person, establishing a "red de relaciones geográficas determinadas por razones de parentezgo." But it becomes human-like at the expense of an injury to nature, which demands restitution.

1762 Vásquez, Socorro. Aproximación a la historia regional de La Guajira: Wayúus y Arijunas, 1900–1935 (PUJ/UH, 12:19, enero/junio 1983, p. 7–17, bibl.)

Holds period in question produced only minor change in Guajira society despite State's aggressively anti-native stance; attributes this to local *modus vivendi* with non-native society, some of whose sectors (notably smugglers) overlapped, and even merged with, Guajira society.

1763 Velasco, Juan de. Historia del Reino de Quito en la América meridional. Edición de Alfredo Pareja Diezcanseco. Caracas: Biblioteca Ayacucho, 1981. 669 p.: bibl.

Much published, eccentric 18th-century history, minus its "natural history" section, with liberal introductory notes. Editor endorses author's competence despite damaging source-critical doubts (see HLAS 42:1748).

1764 Villalobos, Sergio. Tipos fronterizos en el Ejército de Arauco (*in* Villalobos, Sergio et al. Relaciones fronterizas en la Araucanía. Santiago: Univ. Católica de Chile, 1982, p. 175–209, ill.)

Armies that eventually destroyed Araucanian autonomy were themselves partly attuned to Araucanian culture. Refreshingly social-historical treatment of military highlights role of interpreters, *comisarios de naciones* (indirect rule agents), *capitanes de amigos* (military advisors to pro-Chilean native groups).

1765 Villalobos, Sergio. Tres siglos de vida fronteriza (*in* Villalobos, Sergio et al. Relaciones fronterizas en la Araucanía. Santiago: Univ. Católica de Chile, 1982, p. 9–64, ill.)

Synthetic introduction to study of long Araucanian-Chilean struggle, helpful as orientation to other studies in meritorious volume (see items **1583, 1668, 1764,** and **1769**).

1766 Vitale, Luís. Génesis y desarrollo del modo de producción comunal-tributario de las formaciones inca y azteca (UB/BA, 33, 1983, p. 85–117)

Proposes shifting focus of "Asiatic mode" debate from archaic states to pre-State organization, seeking origin of New World State characteristics in emergence of local stratification.

1767 Wachtel, Nathan. The Indian and the Spanish conquest (*in* The Cambridge history of Latin America. v. 1, Colonial Latin America [see item **1808**] p. 207–248)

Compressed treatment of (mostly) Mexican and south Andean information, organized on lines of author's Vision of the vanquished. Argues that Andean peoples retained greater political continuity and developed more counterhegemonic versions of syncretic culture than did Mexicans.

1768 Wood, Robert D. "Teach them good customs:" colonial Indian education and acculturation in the Andes. Culver City, Calif.: Labyrinthos, 1986. 134 p.: bibl., table.

Researched from manuscripts in Bogotá, Quito, Trujillo, Lima, Cuzco, Buenos Aires, and Santiago, rich but curiously old-fashioned monograph details legal and ecclesiastical conduct of schooling for sons of Indian nobles. Sees schools as factor vindicating Spanish rule, regretfully acknowledges incompleteness of acculturating affect.

1769 Zapater, Horacio. La expansión araucana en los siglos XVIII y XIX (*in* Villalobos, Sergio *et al.* Relaciones fronterizas en la Araucanía. Santiago: Univ. Católica de Chile, 1982, p. 87–105, ill.)

Collects eyewitnesses' observations to address sociocultural effects of Huilliche drive toward Atlantic, "Araucanizing" Pehuenche, Puelche, etc. Iron, silver, leather from cows, horses replaced older technologies, created new patterns of relation with non-natives, strengthened hand of chieftains.

1770 Zarzar, Alonso. Relaciones intertribales en el Bajo Urubamba y Alto Ucayali. Lima: Centro de Investigación y Promoción Amazónico, 1983. 124 p.: bibl., ill.

In historic testimony about Piro, Conibo, Cocama (ca. 1570) regional economy was often a matter of "intercambio con el enemigo." Substantial reanalysis of colonial and modern data goes farther than historians do in making explicit problems arising when de facto social system rests on mesh between societies that define themselves as unrelated.

1771 Ziólkowski, Mariusz S. La piedra del cielo: algunos aspectos de la educación

e iniciación religiosa de los príncipes incas (Anthropológica [Pontificia Univ. Católica del Peru, Lima], 2, 1984, p. 45–65, bibl.)

Several chronicles mention that at crisis of succession Incas saw vision of crystal object. Vision is interpreted as "saber supremo," a direct contact with *hanan pacha*, indispensible for ruler.

1772 Ziólkowski, Mariusz S. and Robert M. Sadowski. Los problemas de la reconstrucción de los calendarios prehispánicos andinos (PAN/EL, 9, 1982/1984, p. 45–87, tables)

Hazards in reconstructing Inca calendar arise from 1582 shift to Gregorian reckoning, and from likelihood that Andean calendar itself varied by region and application. Incas employed both a "luni-solar" calendar and a purely solar one.

1773 Zubritski, Yuri. La formación del proletariado quechua (*in* Los Pueblos autóctonos de América Latina: pasado y presente. Moscow: Ciencias Sociales Contemporáneas, Academia de Ciencias de la URSS, 1984, t. 2, p. 207–216, bibl.)

Cites Marx, Engels, Lenin as reminder that "internationalism" of working class does not erase "nationally" diverse makeup. Formation of a specifically Andean proletariat takes place within ethnic framework, at "poles" of capitalist activity. Example: Cotacachi, Quechua textile community in northern Ecuador.

1774 Zuidema, R. Tom. The lion in the city: royal symbols of transition in Cuzco (*in* Animal myths and metaphors in South America. Edited by Gary Urton. Salt Lake City: Univ. of Utah Press, 1985, p. 183–250, bibl., ill.)

Republication of HLAS 46:1747.

HISTORY: GENERAL

DONALD E. CHIPMAN, *Professor of History, North Texas State University*
JAMES D. RILEY, *Professor of History, The Catholic University of America*

THE COLONIAL SECTION CONTAINS a number of items that merit individual recognition. The most important contributions fall into two major categories—topics relating to trade, navigation, and naval defense, and to urban development.

Barbier offers a revisionist assessment of Bourbon reforms and naval expenditure (item **1802**); Castillero Calvo suggests new approaches to the study of commerce and navigation (item **1813**); Pérez-Mallaíno Bueno relates naval policies formulated during the War of Spanish Succession to developments throughout the remainder of the 18th century (item **1843**); Ravina Martín assesses maritime traffic through Cádiz during the reign of Charles II (item **1847**); and Valbuena García (item **1858**) discusses the effect of the 1778 free trade ordinances on the Canary Islands. An overview of work on urban history since 1965 by Borah (item **1804**) deserves careful reading; the defense and fortification of colonial cities by Calderón Quijano (item **1807**) is a seminal work; and the guidelines for founding cities as well as municipal planning by Wyrobisz (item **1862**) is an important study. Also deserving of attention is publication of vol. 2 of a proposed eight on Latin America in the Cambridge History series (item **1808**); an excellent discussion of Indian servitude by González de San Segundo (item **1826**); and two noteworthy contributions on Columbus by Szaszdi (item **1854**) and Watts (item **1860**).

In the independence/19th century period, Anna's article on the breakdown of Spanish Imperial Ethos (item **1863b**) is clearly the outstanding contribution.

The general and 20th-century sections were once again quite small, suggesting a continuing reluctance to deal with theoretical issues or to provide general treatments of subjects. However, the contributions this biennium have shown a considerable improvement. There are few strident theoretical pieces and a salutary tendency to provide a solid evidentiary basis for conclusions. Even pieces which are ideologically committed are for the most part solid contributions that recognize nuances.

The vast majority of works deal with social and economic history. Rather strangely, there are no book-length monographs. There are, on the other hand, a number of good collections of articles which hold together. In the general section, one can point to a volume on family networks by Balmori *et al* (item **1779**) which holds together because of the synthetic articles which open and close it. Political historians also should obtain the Palacio volume on regionalism (item **1794**). In the 20th-century section, the Wirth volume on oil (item **1876**) should not be ignored.

The best items in the general section, however, are articles. The Bauer piece on credit (item **1864**) will become required reading for graduate courses in colonial and 19th-century economic history. Kuznesof and Oppenheimer's article on historiography of the family (item **1786**) contains a very useful bibliography, and the Roxborough piece on approaches to general history (item **1791**) should also be of value to researchers and graduate students alike.

In the 20th-century section, Pablo González Casanova has provided a very ambitious collaborative effort at writing the history of labor movements (item **1874**). Although certainly not the last word, it contains a wealth of useful information. One should also make note of the interviews of historians conducted by the editors of the *Hispanic American Historical Review* (items **1777** and **1796**). These are the type of offerings for which perhaps there is no immediate use but which become more valuable over time.

Finally, Chipman wishes to acknowledge the continuing support of the Faculty Research Committee of North Texas State Univ. and the capable assistance of students Jeri Echeverría and Andrea Mitchell.

GENERAL

1775 Africa in Latin America: essays on history, culture, and socialization. Manuel Moreno Fraginals, editor. Translated by Leonor Blum. New York: Holmes & Meier, 1984. 342 p.: bibl., index.

Collection of 14 essays on various aspects of the African presence in Latin American culture divided into three parts: 1) impact of slave system on culture, resistance to it, and social organization; 2) African heritage in music, language and religion; and 3) cultural nationalism and internationalism. [JDR]

1776 Albert, Bill. South America and the world economy from Independence to 1930. Prepared for the Economic History Society. London: Macmillan, 1983. 96 p.: bibl., index, maps (Studies in economic and social history)

Brief survey of investment and trade in liberal era. Overview of Brazil, Argentina, Peru and Chile. [JDR]

1777 Bakewell, Peter. An interview with François Chevalier (HAHR, 64:3, Aug. 1984, p. 421–442, bibl.)

Another in the ongoing series of *Hispanic American Historical Review* interviews (1984–85). Chevalier talks about his background, influences, interests and feelings about the direction the profession is taking. [JDR]

1778 Balmori, Diana. Family and politics: three generations, 1790–1890 (NCFR/ JFH, 10:3, 1985, p. 247–257)

Examines how family networks influenced politics to further enterprises and family fortunes. Follows the outline of her article (see item **1779**). [JDR]

1779 Balmori, Diana; Stuart F. Voss; and Miles Wortman. Notable family networks in Latin America. Chicago: Univ. of Chicago Press, 1984. 290 p.: bibl., index.

Three prosopographical studies of how families were utilized to form political and economic networks in colonial Central America (Miles Wortman); 19th-century northwestern Mexico (Stuart Voss); and Buenos Aires (Balmori). All are derivative of other works by these authors and since there is no common approach, they stand in isolation. Nevertheless, an excellent theoretical

introduction on family networking and a bibliographic essay on family studies in Latin America tie the volume together. [JDR]

Boersner, Demetrio. Relaciones internacionales de América Latina: breve historia. See *HLAS 47:7012.*

1780 Clayton, Lawrence A. The Bolivarian nations of Latin America. Arlington Heights, Ill.: Forum Press, 1984. 88 p., 8 p. of plates: bibl., index, ill., maps on lining papers (The World of Latin America series)

Brief integrated history of Venezuela, Colombia, Ecuador, Bolivia, and Peru. [JDR]

1781 Dussel, Enrique D. Historia general de la Iglesia en América Latina. t. 1, Introducción general a la historia de la Iglesia en América Latina. Salamanca: Ediciones Sígueme, 1981. 1 v.: bibl., ill., indexes (El Peso de los días; 10)

Vol. 1 of long projected multi-volume history of the Catholic Church offers a general theoretical perspective, an overview of religion in precolumbian times, the process of Christian evangelization, and the Church in the colonial period. More a work of enthusiasm than of scholarship. [JDR]

1782 Dzieje Ameryki Lacińskiej = A history of Latin America. t. 3, 1930–1975/1980. Edited by Ryszard Stemplowski. Warsaw: Książka i Wiedza, 1983. 736 p.: bibl., ill., indexes, maps, tables.

Vol. 3 of major history of Latin America by Polish historians from the Polish Academy of Sciences, represents the most important undertaking in the field of Poland's Latin American studies. This volume contains a list of Latin American heads of state since the establishment of the independent republics up to 1980 as well as a lengthy bibliography. Vol. 1 covers 1750-1870/1880 period, and vol. 2, 1870/1880–1929. [K. Complak]

Elkin, Judith Laikin. A demographic profile of Latin American Jewry. See *HLAS 47:8013.*

1783 Estudios sobre la ciudad iberoamericana. Francisco de Solano, coordinador. 2a ed. ampliada. Madrid: Consejo Superior de Investigaciones Científicas, Instituto Gonzalo Fernández de Oviedo, 1983. 941 p., 48 p. of plates: bibl., ill., index.

Consists of 25 articles on urban history. This second edition (first, 1975) contains inventory of urban plans of Latin

American cities by Jorge Hardoy and Francisco de Solano. [JDR]

1784 Femmes de Amériques. Edition préparée par Claire Pailler and Marie-Cécile Bénassy. Toulouse, France: Univ. de Toulouse-Le Mirail, 1986. 280 p.: bibl. (Travaux; Série B; 11)

Collection of 18 essays presented at the Colloque International (Toulouse, 1985) on women. Authors are historians, anthropologists and literary critics. Subjects range from women in Aztec society to analysis of contemporary novelists and poets. Despite lack of thematic unity, this volume constitutes a worthwhile attempt at examining the multiplicity of historical and literary expressions of Latin American women. [A. Lavrin]

Galenson, David W. The rise and fall of indentured servitude in the Americas: an economic analysis. See item **2341.**

1785 *Historia Latinoamericana en Europa.* Asociación de Historiadores Latinoamericanistas Europeos (AHILA). No. 1, 1986-. Hamburg, FRG.

First issue of journal sponsored by the Assn. of European Historians of Latin America (AHILA) and Univ. of Hamburg's Historisches Seminar. Contains reports on research and publications on Latin America in various countries (e.g., John Fisher on Great Britain, Magnus Mörner on Scandinavia, Antonio Annino on Italy, Raymond Buve on the Low Countries, Hans-Joachim König on West Germany, Ryszard Stemplowski on Poland, Josef Opatrný on Czechoslovakia). Also includes reports on conferences and book reviews of works on Latin America by European historians. [Ed.]

Klein, Hebert S. and **Stanley L. Engerman.** Del trabajo esclavo al trabajo libre: notas en torno a un modelo económico comparativo. See item **2353.**

1786 Kuznesof, Elizabeth and **Robert Oppenheimer.** The family and society in nineteenth century Latin America: an historiographical introduction (NCFR/JFH, 10:3, 1985, p. 215–234, bibl.)

Introductory essay to special issue devoted to the family in Latin America. Reviews themes, issues and methodologies involved in the study of the family in late colonial and 19th-century Latin America and draws comparisons with equivalent literature in Europe and US. Contains good brief bibliography. [JDR]

1787 Lewis, Colin M. The financing of railway development in Latin America, 1850–1914 (IAA, 9:3/4, 1983, p. 255–278, bibl.)

Believes that data will not support interpretation that external funding of railroads was either paramount or dominant in all periods. Until 1880s domestic capital predominated and by 1910, most tracks were government owned. Only in 1880s and 1890s did foreigners take over funding. Although author's argument ignores fact that this was the period when most tracks were built, the study is interesting. [JDR]

1788 Marchán Romero, Carlos. Modelos y corrientes para el estudio de la hacienda latinoamericana (BCE/C, 4:11, sept./dic. 1981, p. 181–242, bibl.)

Intriguing essay compares US and Latin American development. Concludes that Latin American problems are 19th century in origin and relate to the fact that at critical period in late 18th and early 19th centuries, Latin America withdrew from world markets while the US entered them. When Latin America returned, it was greatly weakened and the internal colonial economy had been disrupted. Presentation oddly disjointed and based on older literature. [JDR]

1789 Mauro, Frédéric. Remarques pour une histoire comparée des Amériques: les deux cassures (*in* Unité et diversité de l'Amérique latine. Bordeaux, France: Univ. de Bordeaux III, 1982, t. 1, p. 137–168, bibl.)

Very brief and superficial thoughts on the comparative economic history of the New World. Sees little difference among colonial structures of the New World but substantial divergence after 1830. Attributes this to fact that after independence, Latin American states lost their colonial environment while relations between US and England continued as before. [JDR]

1790 Mörner, Magnus. América Latina en la obra de Magnus Mörner: bibliografía, 1947–1984, homenaje en su 60 aniversario. Stockholm: Instituto de Estudios Latinamericanos de Estocolmo, 1984. 43 p.: ill.

Complete bibliography compiled on the occasion of Mörner's 60th birthday. [JDR]

1790a Otero D'Costa, Enrique. El Dr. Juan Eloy Valenzuela, Subdirector de la Expedición Botánica (ACH/BHA, 70:742, julio/sept. 1983, p. 787–834)

Authoritative though unevenly documented study of significant, often misrepresented figure: priest, publicist, and student of natural science (1756–1834) who was royalist but later accepted patriot victory and was *contertulio* of Bolívar at his parish of Bucaramanga in 1828. [D. Bushnell]

1791 Roxborough, Ian. Unity and diversity in Latin American history (JLAS, 16:1, May 1984, p. 1–26)

Concerns methodological issues involved in the formulation of an adequate theory of Latin American development that is historically sound. Rejects approaches that seek a common thread in these nations' experiences ("Essentialist") or describe common development as a sequence of historical stages ("Modal pattern"). Favors Cardozo and Falleto's "comparative" approach which he regrets is being ignored. [JDR]

Seligson Berenfeld, Silvia. Los judíos en México: un estudio preliminar. See *HLAS* 47:8103.

1792 Sempat A., Carlos. La relación entre el campo y la ciudad en los sistemas económicos latinoamericanos: siglos XVI–XIX (BCE/C, 5:14, sept./dic. 1982, p. 67–77)

Brief interpretive essay on links between country and city, particularly the connection between mining economies and the development of internal markets in the Andean region and Mexico from the 16th through 19th centuries. Superficial and lacking notes and bibliography. [JDR]

1793 Slatta, Richard W. Gauchos, llaneros y cowboys: un aporte a la historia comparada (UB/BA, 26:34, 1984, p. 193–208)

Considers similarities and differences between horsemen and herders in the Americas. Argues that in all three areas they were outcasts with a coherent lifestyle that authorities found suspect. Also that the western cowboy possessed a strong imprint of Spanish traditions derived from Mexican vaqueros. Attributes differences between their cultures to their reaction to change and the social and political climate in which they operated. [JDR]

Trace: travaux et recherche dans les Amériques du centre. See item 1908a.

1794 La Unidad nacional en América Latina: del regionalismo a la nacionalidad. Compilación de Marco Palacios. México: El Colegio de México, Centro de Estudios Internacionales, 1983. 173 p.: bibl.

Generally good collection of papers read at a 1981 seminar on regionalism and national formation at the Colegio de México. Contains six articles by Germán Carrera Damas (Venezuela), José Carlos Chiaramonte (Argentina), René Zavaleta Mercado (Bolivia), Rafael Quintero López (Ecuador), Lorenzo Meyer (Mexico), and Malcolm Deas (Colombia). Palacios provides an introduction. [JDR]

Viñas, David. Indios, ejército y frontera. See item 3323.

1795 Weinberg, Gregorio. Modelos educativos en el desarrollo histórico de América Latina (CPES/RPS, 14:39/40, mayo/dic. 1977, p. 59–123)

Lengthy and interesting interpretation of how models of development in various periods influenced ideas about proper education. Considers various Enlightenment figures in South America emphasizing Argentina; conflicts between liberals and conservatives in the decades following independence particularly in Mexico and Argentina; and plans for popular education in post-Reform Mexico and post-Rosas Argentina. [JDR]

1796 Wilkie, James and Rebecca Horn. An interview with Woodrow Borah (HAHR, 65:3, Aug. 1983, p. 401–441)

Part of series of *Hispanic American Historical Review* interviews with well known historians. Borah discusses his background, research concerns and feelings about his career and the profession. [JDR]

COLONIAL

1797 Abad Pérez, Antolín. Restauración de los colegios misioneros en Hispanoamérica: 1836–1905 (PF/AIA, 42:165/168, enero/dic. 1982, p. 997-1030)

Discusses efforts of Padre Andrés Herrero and others to restore missionary schools throughout Hispanoamérica (1836–1905). Abad Pérez focuses on Bolivian and Peruvian schools and offers a complimentary interpretation of missionary zeal throughout the continent. [DEC]

1798 Albelo Martín, María Cristina. Canarias y los indianos repatriados durante la primera mitad del siglo XIX (*in* Coloquio de Historia Canario-Americana, 4th, Las Palmas, Spain, 1980. Cuarto coloquio de historia canario-americana. Coordinación y prólogo, Francisco Morales Padrón. Las Palmas, Spain: Ediciones del Excelentísimo Cabildo Insular, 1982, p. 513–538, appendix, tables)

Discusses the Canary Islands' economy (1800–50) and effect of repatriation upon population growth and agriculture. Suggests that infusion of New World money during this period was a direct and beneficial result of repatriation. [DEC]

1799 América y la España del siglo XVI: homenaje a Gonzalo Fernández de Oviedo cronista de Indias en el V centenario de su nacimiento, Madrid, 1478. v. 2. Edición preparada por Francisco de Solano y Fermín del Pino. Madrid: Instituto Gonzalo Fernández de Oviedo, 1983. 1 v.: bibl., ill.

Contains 20 interdisciplinary contributions to the general theme of economic and social structure in 16th-century Spain and America. Diverse topics include emigration to the Indies, naval defense, disamortization of lands of military orders, documentation of *bienes de difuntos*, wine traffic to the Indies, urban and rural aspects of Teotihuacán in 1560. [DEC]

1800 Anders, Ferdinand. Die *Historia del Mondo Nuovo* des Girolamo Benzoni und Ihr Weiterwirken bis heute (UEN/LS, 7, 1980, p. 43–50)

Anders thinks that data and ideas in Benzoni's work (1565), drawn heavily from Bartolomé de las Casas (ca. 1560), are too influential even today. Notes particular concern about false impressions of the Spanish conquest and Indian religious life found in copper plate engravings and woodcuts published with an edition of Benzoni by Theodore De Bry (1570). Still reprinted (1950s-70s), the pictures continue to misinform. [DEC]

1802 Barbier, Jacques A. Indies revenues and naval spending: the cost of colonialism for the Spanish Bourbons, 1763–1805 (JGSWGL, 21, 1984, p. 171–188, graphs, tables)

Investigates Bourbon naval expenses and revenues collected from the Indies (1763–1805) in order to evaluate the generally accepted notion that the Spanish State enjoyed the direct benefits of colonialism by drawing funds from the Indies and putting them into naval defense. Concludes that, with the exception of the late Hapsburgs and earliest Bourbons, the naval budget reveals Bourbon reforms to be counterproductive. [DEC]

1803 Blazquez, Adrián. El Padre Las Casas: ¿una primera toma de conciencia de la identidad americana? (*in* Unité et diversité de l'Amérique latine. Bordeaux, France: Univ. de Bordeaux III, 1982, t. 1, p. 259–273)

Examines Las Casas's role in presenting the essence of America to the Old World. His insistence that Indians were rational human beings, his defense of sociopolitical structure in native societies, and his appreciation of New World climate and fertility— while viewed skeptically by many European contemporaries—were in a vein similar to Humboldt's later efforts. [DEC]

1804 Borah, Woodrow. Trends in recent studies of colonial Latin American cities (HAHR, 64:3, Aug. 1984, p. 535–554)

Borah characterizes increase of information on urban history since 1965 as combination of new, sophisticated techniques of data analyses and older, traditional methods, which have expanded historians' concepts of what urban history studies should be. This increase reflects interest in urban areas and greater number of students in higher education. [DEC]

1805 Borrell B., Pedro J. The quicksilver galleons: the salvage of the Spanish galleons Nuestra Señora de Guadalupe and El Conde de Tolosa. Photographs, Federico Schad and Pedro J. Borrell B. Santo Domingo: Underwater Archaeological Recovery Commission, 1983. 122 p.: ill. (some col.), photos.

Brief account of items salvaged by underwater archaeology from two Spanish ships which sunk in 1724 off the coast of Santo Domingo. Good illustrations and photography. [DEC]

1806 Bouza Alvarez, Fernando Jesús and Alfredo Alvar Ezquerra. Apuntes biográficos y análisis de la biblioteca de un gran estadista hispano del siglo XVI: el Presidente Juan de Ovando (IGFO/RI, 14:173, enero/junio 1984, p. 81–139, bibl., tables)

Offers biographical sketch of Juan de Ovando, President of the Council of the Indies (1571–75), and analyzes 351 printed works and manuscripts in Ovando's personal library at the time of his death. Suggests that, although the library was not remarkable for its time, the collection reflects the type of men selected by the Crown for leadership positions. [DEC]

1807 Calderón Quijano, José Antonio. Las defensas indianas en la recopilación de 1680: precedentes y regulación legal. Sevilla, Spain: Escuela de Estudios Hispano-Americanos, 1984. 220 p., 36 p. of plates: bibl., index, plans (Publicaciones, 0210–5802; 294)

Contains brief introduction devoted to historical precedents for defense and fortification of cities as reflected in legal writings and codes of Castille. Second part addresses various topics such as locating, building, provisioning, securing, and munitioning of fortifications in the northern realms of the Indies as specified in *La Recopilación de leyes de Indias.* [DEC]

1808 The Cambridge history of Latin America. v. 1–2, Colonial Latin America. v. 3, From independence to c1870. Edited by Leslie Bethell. Cambridge, England: Cambridge Univ. Press, 1984–1985. 3 v.: bibl., ill., indexes.

Vol. 2 of proposed eight on Latin American history. Major topics on colonial Spanish America and Brazil are covered by 19 specialists and are grouped into Population, Economic and Social Structures, and Intellectual and Cultural Life. In keeping with other Cambridge History series, the "highest standards of collaborative international scholarship" have been observed. This series is a must for college and university libraries. [DEC]

1809 Canedo, Lino Gómez. Los gallegos en América: entre el descubrimiento y la emancipación: algunas notas y un guión provisional para escribir su historia. Santiago de Compostela, Spain: Consellería de Cultura da Xunta de Galicia: Instituto Gallego de Cooperación Iberoamericana, 1982. 174 p.: bibl.

Examines presence of Galicians in the New World from Columbus's expedition through the late 18th century. Canedo cites contributions of Galicians and geographical areas where most Galicians settled. [DEC]

1810 Canedo, Lino Gómez. Mexican sources for the history of the Far East missions

(*in* International Congress of Human Sciences in Asia and North Africa, 30th, Mexico, 1976. Asia and colonial Latin America. Editor, Ernesto de la Torre. Mexico: El Colegio de México, 1981, p. 7–19)

With the New World's discovery, trade between New Spain and the Orient was established. Religion followed trade and commerce from Spain and Mexico to Philippines, China, and Japan. Missionaries left published and unpublished accounts of ecclesiastical expeditions. Author implores students to search Mexican archives, parochial and secular, for materials on missions in the East. [DEC]

1811 Caraci, Ilaria Luzzana. Gli studi Colombiani in Italia e il quinto centenario della scoperta dell'America (SSG/RGI, 91:1, marzo 1984, p. 111–125, bibl.)

Noting that the fifth centennial of Columbus's discovery of America will be in 1992, Caraci calls for an expanded interpretation of the Admiral's voyages. According to the author, new scholarship should include broader discussion of the intellectual and cultural environment of the 1490s as well as Columbus's own view of his explorations. [DEC]

1812 Castillero Calvo, Alfredo. América hispana: aproximaciones a la historia económica. Panamá: Impresora La Nación (INAC), 1983. 97 p., 1 folded leaf of plates: bibl., map.

Broad overview of colonial economic history from a Panamanian perspective. Includes treatment of the Columbian Exchange, difficulties posed by geography for inter-regional commerce, and problems occasioned by adverse winds and currents. Also contains brief observations on the historiography of colonial commerce. [DEC]

1813 Castillero Calvo, Alfredo. Reflexiones para una historia del comercio y la navegación del período colonial (*in* Congreso Venezolano de la Historia, 4th, Caracas, 1980. Memoria [see *HLAS 46:2621*] v. 1, p. 205–258, maps, tables)

While lauding pioneer works of Borah, Carmagnani, Tepaske *et al.*, author suggests avenues and approaches whereby more complete and accurate studies of commerce and navigation in the colonial era may be researched and written. Panama at the crossroads of exchange is the suggested focal point, but the plea is for the all-encompassing big picture. [DEC]

1814 Comas, Juan. Fray Bartolomé, la esclavitud y el racismo (*in* Simposio Nacional de Antropología, Arqueología y Etnohistoria de Panamá, 5th, Panamá, 1974. Actas. Panama: Univ. de Panamá, Centro de Investigaciones Antropológicas e Instituto Nacional de Cultura, Dirección Nacional del Patrimonio Histórico, 1978, p. 369–382, bibl.)

Brief defense of Bartolomé de las Casas against critics who have charged that his attitudes toward blacks brand him as a racist and advocate of slavery. [DEC]

1815 Correia-Alfonso, John. Indo-American contacts through the Jesuit missionaries (*in* International Congress of Human Sciences in Asia and North Africa, 30th, Mexico, 1976. Asia and colonial Latin America. Editor, Ernesto de la Torre. Mexico: El Colegio de México, 1981, p. 45–60)

Author credits Portugal and Jesuit missionaries with transference of inestimable information—geographical, botanical, architectural, medicinal, and cultural—between Latin America and Asia from the 16th to 18th centuries through world-wide exchange of letters and personal travel on Portuguese vessels. Discovery of New World tied previously isolated inhabitants of the world together, with Jesuits performing key role in interchange. [DEC]

1816 Cortés, Santos Rodolfo. La tributación de las castas libres en América, durante la época hispánica (*in* Congreso Venezolano de la Historia, 4th, Caracas, 1980. Memoria [see *HLAS 46:2621*] v. 1, p. 275–334, bibl., tables)

Describes 16th-century attempts by the Spanish Crown to create and impose a tax system on free castes in the colonies. Intense resistance on the part of free castes resulted in the political and fiscal downfall of the system. [DEC]

1817 Cuenca Esteban, Javier. Trends and cycles in U.S. trade with Spain and the Spanish Empire, 1790–1819 (EHA/J, 44:2, June 1984, p. 521–543, graphs, tables)

Analyzes structural and economic factors which accounted for the spectacular gains experienced by the US before the War of 1812. Concludes that trade with Latin America benefitted and buttressed North America's young economy in farming, shipbuilding, and carrying services. [DEC]

1818 Delgado Ribas, Josep M. La emigración española a América Latina durante la época del comercio libre: 1765–1820, el ejemplo catalán (UB/BA, 14:32, 1982, p. 115–137, tables)

Discusses factors which led to growing Catalan emigration (1765–1820). Suggests that commercial interests caused the development of two distinct migratory patterns among Catalans. First began ca. 1750 and settled predominantly in the Caribbean Islands, while second began in the 1770s and terminated in the wealthy colonial parts of Veracruz, Cartagena, and Buenos Aires. [DEC]

1819 Domínguez Compañy, Francisco. Estudios sobre las instituciones locales hispanoamericanas. Caracas: Academia Nacional de la Historia, 1981. 390 p.: bibl. (Biblioteca. Estudios, monografías y ensayos; 10)

Collection of author's previously published studies on municipal government written over 30-year period. Most are general considerations of judicial and administrative topics but selection includes long study of city of La Isabela founded by Columbus and a 1957 bibliography on municipal history. [JDR]

1820 Durán, Juan Guillermo. *Monumenta Catechetica* hispanoamericana: siglos XVI–XVIII. v. 1, Siglo XVI. Buenos Aires: Facultad de Teología, Pontificia Univ. Católica Argentina Santa María de los Buenos Aires, 1984. 744 p.: appendix, bibl., ill., maps, plates.

Substantial volume contains samples of 16th-century catechistic writings. Includes pastoral works (*doctrinas, instrucciones, catecismos, confesionarios, sermonarios*) used in the evangelization of diverse Indian cultures in Santo Domingo, Mexico, and Cartagena. Of particular interest to historians and anthropologists is the varying sophistication of this literature, ranging from ideograms to philosophical treatises, as a reflection of New World exigencies. [DEC]

1821 Engstrand, Iris H.W. The Enlightenment in Spain: influences upon New World policy (AAFH/TAM, 41:4, April 1985, p. 436–444)

Brief summary of 18th-century Bourbon policy, its proponents and its opponents.

In Church-State matters, the divergent views of Franciscan traditionalists and Bourbon regalists are presented as explanation for confrontations between Junípero Serra and the military governors of California. [DEC]

1822 Fall, Yoro K. Las cartas de rumbos y su utilización en los siglos XIV y XV (IFGO/RI, 43:172, julio/dic. 1983, p. 423–437)

Discusses construction and design of maps in use during the 14th and 15th centuries and questions whether their origin was Italian, Arabic, Portuguese or Majorcan. Concludes that magnetic triangulation, developed first by the Majorcans, was essential to map-making through the 17th century. [DEC]

1823 Figueroa Marroquín, Horacio. Enfermedades de los conquistadores. Guatemala: Editorial Universitaria de Guatemala, 1983. 174 p.: bibl., ill. (Col. Estudios universitarios; 25)

Recounts various diseases and ailments mentioned in the literature of the conquest, speculates on origin of smallpox in Mexico, and catalogs medicinal plants used by Guatemalan Indians. [DEC]

1824 García Fuentes, Lutgardo. Licencias para la introducción de esclavos en Indias y envíos desde Sevilla en el siglo XVI (JGSWGL, 19, 1982, p. 1–46, appendices, tables)

Explores 16th-century licensing and introduction of slavery into the New World by the Spanish Crown. Outlines Spanish acquisition of black prisoners from North African conquests and notes Seville's role as the center of slave trade. Tables and appendices suggest that by 1580 the infusion of slavery into the Spanish colonies had reached greater heights than previously suspected. [DEC]

1825 Gelman, Jorge Daniel. Natural economies or money economies?: silver production and monetary circulation in Spanish America, late XVI-early XVII centuries (Journal of European Economic History [Banco di Roma] 13:1, Spring 1984, p. 99–115)

Investigates relationship between production and trade of precious metals from the famed Potosí mines and traces development of a monetized economy in 16th and 17th-century South America. Concludes that the economy was a mixed one in which silver and metallic currency played a major role. [DEC]

1826 González de San Segundo, Miguel Angel. Notas sobre la pervivencia de servicios personales de origen prehispánico y su regulación por el derecho indiano (IGFO/RI, 43:172, julio/dic. 1983, p. 729–795)

Lengthy discussion of Indian servitude in 16th and 17th-century Spanish America. Detailed investigation is limited to the services of indigenous messengers or runners, aboriginal porters, and Peruvian hostelries. Concludes that local work patterns were prehispanic and aborginal rather than having been imposed by the Crown. [DEC]

1827 Guedes, Max Justo. El condicionalismo físico del Atlántico y la expansión de los pueblos ibéricos (IGFO/RI, 43:172, julio/dic. 1983, p. 379–421, maps)

Establishment of sea lanes employed in the expansion of the Iberian nations is related to winds, currents, and the position of intermediate islands. Development of trade routes with the Spanish Indies, Brazil, and the Orient were logically governed by those conditions as well as the experience and seamanship of pilots and navigators. [DEC]

1828 Haring, Clarence Henry. The Spanish Empire in America. San Diego, Calif.: Harcourt Brace Jovanovich, 1985. 371 p.: bibl., index.

Reprint of original 1947 edition (see *HLAS 13:1037* and *HLAS 13:1210*). [DEC]

1829 Izard, Miquel. Reformismo borbónico e insurgencias indianas (JGSWGL, 21, 1984, p. 155–170)

Investigates relationship between 18th-century Bourbon reforms and secessionist sentiment among insurgent Indian groups. After reviewing recent scholarship on Bourbon attempts at reconquest, Izard suggests that expansion of trade and development of a primitive form of capitalism among Indians are factors which contributed to their discontent. [DEC]

1830 Jornadas de Andalucía y América, 2nd, Universidad de Santa María de la Rábida, Spain, 1982. Andalucía y América en el siglo XVI: actas. Edición preparada por Bibiano Torres Ramírez y José Hernández Polomo. Sevilla, Spain: Escuela de Estudios Hispano-Americanos, 1983. 2 v.: bibl., ill. (Publicaciones; 0210–5802; 292)

These substantial volumes contain 44 articles (some with supporting documentation) devoted to the broad topic of Andalusia and America in the 16th century. Originally presented at a conference held at the Univ. of Santa María de la Rábida (March 1982), many of the items relate only tangentially to the region or to the role of Andalusians, and they merit attention as contributions by several distinguished Hispanic scholars. [DEC]

1831 Keen, Benjamin. Recent writing on the Spanish conquest (LARR, 20:2, 1985, p. 161–171)

Brief but excellent analysis of recent trends in the historiography of the Spanish conquest. Keen surveys varying attitudes toward Spaniards and Indians from Prescott, Bourne, and Bolton to the present, and offers review essay of nine books on aspects of the conquest published in the 1980s. [DEC]

1832 Libros y libreros en el siglo XVI. Selección de documentos y paleografía de Francisco Fernández del Castillo. 2a ed., facsim. México: Archivo General de la Nación: Fondo de Cultura Económica, 1982. 14, 607 p.: bibl., ill. (Sección de obras de historia)

Reprint of work originally published in 1914. Excellent preface by Elías Trabulse assesses the historical worth of this compilation of books and book-selling in the 16th century. Diffusion of printed materials, censorship, as well as the impact of Church councils and the Index of Forbidden Literature may be documented. [DEC]

1833 Lobo Cabrera, Manuel. Esclavos indios en Canarias: precedentes (IGFO/RI, 43:172, julio/dic. 1983, p. 515–532, tables)

Outlines purchase and use of New World Indians as slaves in the Canary Islands. More often imported from Spanish rather than Portuguese colonies, these Indians were the cheapest of the slave market. [DEC]

Luján Muñoz, Jorge. Los escribanos en las Indias Occidentales. See item **2240.**

1834 Luna, Lola G. Las amazonas en América (UB/BA, 14:32, 1982, p. 279–305)

Discusses androcentrism in historical scholarship and the Amazon legend as recorded in accounts by early Spanish explorers. Uses the Amazonian model to reflect upon our limited ability to discuss matriarchal societies in history. [DEC]

1835 Marchena Fernández, Juan. Oficiales canarios en el ejército de América: 1700–1810 (in Coloquio de Historia Canario-Americana, 4th, Las Palmas, Spain, 1980. Cuarto coloquio de historia canario-americana. Coordinación y prólogo, Francisco Morales Padrón. Las Palmas, Spain: Ediciones del Excelentísimo Cabildo Insular, 1982, p. 323–343, appendix, tables)

Analyzes service records of 40 Canary islanders who served in the Army of America officer corps (1700–1810). Considers geographical and social origins, length of service, age, marital status and mobility factors. [DEC]

1836 Marchena Fernández, Juan. Oficiales y soldados en el ejército de América. Sevilla, Spain: Escuela de Estudios Hispano-Americanos, 1983. 399 p.: bibl., facsims., ill., index (Publicaciones, 0210–5802; 286)

A detailed study of the 18th-century officer corps in the Americas including military operations, rank distribution, and sociocultural factors. Marchena Fernández presents the military as an important and emerging 18th century institution. [DEC]

1837 Mauger de la Brannière, Gerardo. América: ¿quién la descubrió? Buenos Aires: Editorial Albatros, 1984. 106 p.: bibl., ill., maps.

Broad brush treatment that raises more questions than it answers. Who discovered America, what is discovery, why are some explorers better known than others, and is America fully discovered? [DEC]

1838 Muñoz Pérez, José. Los bienes de difuntos y los canarios fallecidos en Indias: una primera aproximación al tema (in Coloquio de Historia Canario-Americana, 4th, Las Palmas, Spain, 1980. Cuarto coloquio de historia canario-americana. Coordinación y prólogo, Francisco Morales Padrón. Las Palmas, Spain: Ediciones del Excelentísimo Cabildo Insular, 1982, p. 77–132, appendix, bibl.)

Contains brief outline of published works on *bienes de difuntos*, organization of documentation within section *Contratación* of AGI, and evolution of administrative procedure relative to the subject. Analyzes samples of 156 documents (1550–1786) as indicators of material possessions acquired by Canary islanders and their intentions for disposition of them at death. [DEC]

1839 Muro Romero, Fernando. La administración de Indias: de la unidad imperial a la diversidad americana; el tránsito del siglo XVII (*in* Unité et diversité de l'Amérique latine. Bordeaux, France: Univ. de Bordeaux III, 1982, t. 1, p. 275–299)

Summarizes in broad-brush treatment the institutional problems posed by diversity in the Spanish American empire. Imperial policy aimed toward centralization, as initiated by powerful 17th century Spanish *validos*, created clashes and conflicts that augured importantly for the continued preservation of the colonial empire. [DEC]

1840 Muro Romero, Fernando. La reforma del pacto colonial en Indias: notas sobre instituciones de gobierno y sociedad en el siglo XVII (JGSWGL, 19, 1982, p. 47–68)

Describes Spanish reform efforts in the 17th century and their effect upon colonial government. Includes introductory review of recent historiography and suggests that Spanish administrative problems were reflected in the colonies. [DEC]

1841 Peña, Juan de la. De bello contra insulanos: intervención de España en América: Escuela Española de la Paz, segunda generación, 1560–1585: testigos y fuentes. Edición de L. Pereña *et al.* Madrid: Consejo Superior de Investigaciones Científicas (CSIC), 1982. 2 v.: bibl., indexes (Corpus Hispanorum de pace; 9–10)

Examines diverse postures articulated within the Spanish Empire regarding justice or injustice of armed conquest against Indian nations. Years in focus are 1560–85 when official policy evolved toward decisions announced in the ordinances of 1573 and by the Third Mexican Provincial Council. Contains various position papers in Latin text. [DEC]

1842 Pérez de Tudela y Bueso, Juan. *Mirabilis in altis*: estudio crítico sobre el origen y significado del proyecto descubridor de Cristóbal Colón. Madrid: Instituto Gonzalo Fernández de Oviedo, 1983. 429 p., 2 leaves of plates (one folded): bibl, facsims., ill. (Col. Tierra nueva e cielo nuevo; 11)

Discusses numerous themes brought forth by the discovery of the New World. Investigates Columbus's depiction of himself as the "Christ bearer," contemporary thought regarding routes to the Orient, and New World perceptions such as the Amazon myth. [DEC]

1843 Pérez-Mallaína Bueno, Pablo Emilio. Política naval española en el Atlántico, 1700–1715. Sevilla, Spain: Escuela de Estudios Hispano-Americanos, 1982. 486 p., 7 p. of plates: bibl., ill., index (Publicaciones, 0210–5802; 279)

Presents Spanish naval policies during War of Succession and emphasizes financial and military aspects of Spain's transatlantic routes. Maintains that Spain's bitter experience during 1700–15 caused a period of naval restoration in the remainder of the century. [DEC]

1844 Pieter Jacobs, Auke. Pasajeros y polizones: algunas observaciones sobre la emigración española a Indias durante el siglo XVI (IGFO/RI, 43: 172, julio/dic. 1983, p. 439–479, tables)

Discusses types of illegal immigration from Spain (1549–66). Concludes that such immigration was the least expensive and most accessible passage for the less fortunate. [DEC]

1845 Puig, Roberto. El descubrimiento del Nuevo Mundo. 2a ed. corr y aum. Montevideo: Ministerio de Educación y Cultura, 1983. 92 p., 24 p. of plates: bibl., ill.

Despite title, this revised and expanded booklet is devoted exclusively to Columbus memorabilia. Contains useful illustrative material. [DEC]

1846 Ramos, D. et al. La ética en el conquista de América: Francisco de Vitoria y la Escuela de Salamanca. Madrid: Consejo Superior de Investigaciones Científicas (CSIC), 1984. 724 p.: bibl. (Corpus Hispanorum de pace; 25)

A multi-authored examination of the influence of Francisco de Vitoria and the Second Generation Salamanca School on the formulation of Spanish Indian policy. Contains papers presented at a symposium held in Salamanca in 1983 on the topic of "la ética en la conquista de América." [DEC]

1847 Ravina Martín, Manuel. Participación extranjera en el comercio indiano: el seguro marítimo a fines del siglo XVII (IGFO/RI, 43: 172, julio/dic. 1983, p. 481–513, appendices)

Reviews recent bibliography of maritime traffic during the last third of the 17th century and describes commercial contracts which insured against cargo losses. Using 37 archival contracts, Ravina Martín demonstrates that foreign interests monopolized the

maritime market of Cádiz during this period.
[DEC]

**1848 Readings in Latin American history. v.
1, The formative centuries. v. 2, The
modern experience.** Edited by Peter J.
Bakewell, John J. Johnson, and Meredith D.
Dodge. Durham, N.C.: Duke Univ. Press,
1985. 2 v.: bibl.

Collection of 20 articles which according to book's editors are representative of new
approaches and concerns of historians publishing on colonial Latin America in the last
15 years. Materials were selected for beginning students and intended to supplement
standard texts. Major groupings of topics
treat each century of the colonial period and
independence. [DEC]

1849 Rico Linage, Raquel. Las reales com-
pañias de comercio con América: los
órganos de gobierno. Sevilla, Spain: Escuela
de Estudios Hispano-Americanos de Sevilla,
1983. 409 p. (Publicaciones de la Diputación
Provincial de Sevilla. Serie 1a. Sección,
Historia; 24. Publicaciones de la Escuela,
0210–5802; 287)

Discusses the establishment of royal
companies of commerce in the colonies between 1728 and 1803. Organizational aspects
of administration are outlined in detail and
major documents concerning maintenance
and formation are also included. Rico Linage
asserts that the Guipuzcoan Company,
founded in 1728, was the culmination of
commercial development throughout Europe
and that it became the model for successive
Crown companies. [DEC]

1850 Ruiz Rivera, Julián B. La Compañía de
Uztariz, las Reales Fábricas de Talavera
y el comercio con Indias (EEHA/AEA, 36,
1979, p. 209–250, tables)

Study of how the commercial company Uztariz Brothers took over management
(1762–70) of a government industrial monopoly which produced silken and embroidered
silk fabrics. Because of labor and production
problems, the firm was always in trouble. Pt.
1 deals with difficulties and negotiations surrounding the factory; pt. 2 with commerce
with the Indies. [JDR]

1851 Salvador Lara, Jorge. ¡Mañana comienza
nuestra historia . . .! (PAIGH/H, 96,
julio/dic. 1983, p. 7–25)

Text of address delivered on the 490th
anniversary of Columbus's arrival in the New

World at the Instituto Panamericano de
Geografía e Historia. Author proclaims necessity of reflecting together on the significance of this event and calls historians to
join him in the large task of forging an Ibero-
American community. [DEC]

**1852 Simposio Hispanoamericano sobre las
Leyes de Indias, San José, 1981.** Memoria. Selección y ordenamiento, Franco
Cerutti. San José: Instituto Costarricense de
Cultura Hispánica; Madrid: Instituto de Cooperación Iberoamericana, 1984. 303 p.: bibl.,
ill.

Symposium in recognition of the
300th anniversary of publication of the *Recopilación de leyes de Indias* (San José,
1981), devoted its sessions to various aspects
of Derecho Indiano and its development. Includes pertinent papers and formalities observed by Instituto Costarricense de Cultura
Hispánica. [DEC]

Suárez, Santiago Gerardo. Las milicias: instituciones militares hispanoamericanas. See
item **2656.**

1853 Super, John C. The formation of nu-
tritional regimes in colonial Latin
America (*in* Food, politics, and society in
Latin America. Edited by John C. Super
and Thomas C. Wright. Lincoln: Univ. of
Nebraska Press, 1985, p. 1–23)

Interesting study which concludes that
there was considerable mixing of Spanish and
Indian nutritional regimes in the early colonial period. European items such as meat became commonplace in Indian diets and use of
traditional foods was changed in some instances. First section examines changes; second explores forces which shaped and
controlled the changes. [JDR]

1854 Szaszdi Nagy, Adam. Un mundo que
descubrió Colón: las rutas del comercio prehispánico de los metales. Valladolid,
Spain: Casa-Museo de Colón: Seminario
Americanista, Univ. de Valladolid, 1984.
149 p., 4 leaves of plates: bibl., ill. (some col.)
(Cuadernos colombinos; 12)

Edition of Columbian series presents
information on early commercial routes
which Columbus sailed. Of special interest
are the Admiral's descriptions of New World
gold, silver, and jewels. [DEC]

1855 Tardieu, J.P. L'affranchissement des
esclaves aux Amériques espagnoles:

XVIe-XVIIIe siècles (PUF/RH, 544, oct./déc. 1982, p. 341–364)

Analysis of slave emancipation in Spanish America deals with how individual slaves might be freed rather than general emancipation. Tardieu discusses wills, marriages, self-manumission, and conversions to the faith as means of gaining freedom. Stresses, however, that each case was unique and often complicated by circumstances of age and health. [DEC]

1856 Tormo Sanz, Leandro. Some ideas governing relations between the Spanish Indies and the Far Eastern countries during the sixteenth century (in International Congress of Human Sciences in Asia and North Africa, 30th, Mexico, 1976. Asia and colonial Latin America. Editor, Ernesto de la Torre. Mexico: El Colegio de México, 1981, p. 27–43)

Offers opinion that early Hispanic-Asiatic relations were based on principles of universal brotherhood, oneness of human race, and unity without uniformity. Enduring friendship between Spain and the Far East was advocated by both Charles V and Philip II. [DEC]

1857 Torres Santana, Elisa and Manuel Lobo Cabrera. La esclavitud en Gran Canaria en el primer cuarto del siglo XVIII (in Coloquio de Historia Canario-Americana, 4th, Las Palmas, Spain, 1980. Cuarto coloquio de historia canario-americana. Coordinación y prólogo, Francisco Morales Padrón. Las Palmas, Spain: Ediciones del Excelentísimo Cabildo Insular, 1982, p. 5–57, appendices, tables)

Discusses slave trade on Grand Canary Island (1700–25). Reviews history of slavery on the island and considers factors in pricing, sales, and use of slaves in domestic, agricultural, and artisan tasks. [DEC]

1858 Valbuena García, María Antonia. El libre comercio hispano-americano en el Archipiélago Canario, 1778–1785 (Anuario de Estudios Atlánticos [Patronato de la Casa de Colón, Madrid] 28, 1982, p. 417–474)

Discusses effect of 1778 free trade ordinances on the Canary Islands. Valbuena García meticulously details arrival and departure of merchant ships (1778–85) and uses cargo information to discuss agricultural and industrial developments within the archipelago. [DEC]

1859 Vargas, José María. Misioneros españoles que pasaron a la América en el siglo XVI (Revista del Instituto de Historia Eclesiástica Ecuatoriana [Quito] 5/6, 1980, p. 1–205, index)

Chronological listing of Augustinians, Dominicans, Franciscans, Jesuits, Mercedarians, and Carmelites who set sail for the New World from Spain (1493–1600). Indexed by order and name, and by destination. [M.T.Hamerly]

1860 Watts, Pauline Moffitt. Prophecy and discovery: on the spiritual origins of Christopher Columbus's "Enterprise of the Indies" (AHA/R, 90:1, Feb. 1985, p. 73–102, ill., map)

Challenges traditional depiction of Columbus by suggesting that the explorer viewed his expeditions as fulfillment of his calling to Christianize the New World and prepare for the Anti-Christ. Includes useful commentary on related sources, numerous quotations from Columbus and his biographer-son Ferdinand, and adds spiritual dimensions to the famous explorer. [DEC]

1861 Wright, Thomas C. The investiture of bishops and archbishops in Spanish America: protocol and Church-State conflict in the late 1700s (BU/JCS, 25:2, Spring 1983, p. 279–297)

Asserts that investiture of bishops and archbishops in late 18th-century Latin America often resulted in open conflict between civic and religious prelates. Maintains that Carlos IV's policies reflect concern over the conflict and an attempt to avoid it. [DEC]

1862 Wyrobisz, Andrzej. La ordenanza de Felipe II del año 1573 y la construcción de ciudades coloniales españolas en la América (PAN/EL, 7, 1980, p. 11–34)

Good summary of the founding of early cities and towns in Hispanic America and evolution of municipal planning. The 1573 ordinances of Philip II addressed fundamental issues such as sites for coastal and interior settlements, appropriate positioning of public and private structures, location of malodorous industries, width of streets in varying climate, street, and road networks. [DEC]

1863 Zavala, Silvio Arturo. Estudios indianos. 2a ed. México: Colegio Nacional, 1984. 464 p.: bibl., index.

Revised and expanded version of 1948 edition (see *HLAS 15:1448*). [DEC]

INDEPENDENCE AND 19th CENTURY

1863a Andrés Bello: homenage de la UCV. Caracas: Ediciones de Rectorado, Univ. Central de Venezuela, 1982. 607 p.: bibl., facsims., ill., ports.

Good introduction to study of Bello, including both short anthology of his writings and selected writings about him. Among latter are chronology, bibliography, and some inedited writings alongside larger number of previously published essays. They treat him as both literary and political-intellectual figure. [D. Bushnell]

1863b Anna, Timothy E. Spain and the breakdown of imperial ethos: the problem of equality (HAHR, 62:2, May 1982, p. 254–272)

Presents three concepts of empire which enjoyed broad acceptance throughout Spain and her colonies until the 1811 Cortes declared Spaniards on both sides of the Atlantic to be equal. According to Anna, it was this declaration of equality and Spain's failure to implement it which caused the Empire's breakdown. [DEC]

1864 Bauer, Arnold J. The Church in the economy of Spanish America: censos and depósitos in the eighteenth and nineteenth centuries (HAHR, 63:4, Nov. 1983, p. 707–733)

Excellent interpretive article on an ignored topic in Latin American economic and social history. Explains character of *censos* and *depósitos*, sources of Church income and nature of Church involvement in colonial and 19th-century credit system. Draws critical distinction between liens and loans arguing that Church never dominated credit system and while it invested money, it was not a banker in the modern sense. After independence, as the Church's power declined, liens became burdens and republican governments dominated by propertied class, absolved themselves of them. [JDR]

Bergad, Laird W. On comparative history: a reply to Tom Brass. See item **2486.**

Brass, Tom. Coffee and rural proletarianization: a comment on Bergad. See item **2490.**

1865 Carmagnani, Marcello. Emigración italiana en América Latina y el redescubrimiento italiano de Canarias (*in* Coloquio de Historia Canario-Americana,

4th, Las Palmas, Spain, 1980. Cuarto coloquio de historia canario-americana. Coordinación y prólogo, Francisco Morales Padrón. Las Palmas, Spain: Ediciones del Excelentísimo Cabildo Insular, 1982, p. 553–565)

Describes conditions determining Italian understanding of Latin America. Emphasizes work of Paolo Mantegazza described as a key writer who influenced Italian attitudes and disseminated accurate information about Latin America and the Canaries in the late 19th century. [JDR]

1865a González, Margarita. Bolívar y la independencia de Cuba. Bogotá: El Ancora Editores, 1984. 141 p.

Based on limited number of generally familiar sources, reviews changing attitudes of Spanish American revolutionaries toward Cuban question. As for Bolívar, lack of solid commitment to aid Cuba emerges clearly. Nothing original, but coherently presented. [D. Bushnell]

1865b Guerra Martinière, Margarita. Los corsarios insurgentes en la independencia de América: 1808–1824 (IRA/B, 12, 1982/1983, p. 93–136, tables)

Comprehensive and clearly organized overview of revolutionary corsair activity, its effects on Spanish commerce, and Spanish responses, based in part on research in Archivo General de Indias. Slight relative emphasis on Pacific theater. [D. Bushnell]

1866 Hanisch, Walter. La preconización de los obispos de América en 1827 y la actitud de la corte española (IRA/B, 12, 1982/1983, p. 165–190, appendix)

Considers decision of papal consistory of 1827 to appoint six new bishops for the Americas without reference to Madrid, in violation of the Real Patronato, and subsequent diplomatic imbroglio with Spain. Based on file discovered in AGI which is analyzed and presented in full. [JDR]

1866a Kossok, Manfred. Unidad y diversidad de la América española: el caso de la independencia (*in* Unité et diversité de l'Amérique latine. Bordeaux, France: Univ. de Bordeaux, III, 1982, t. 1, p. 301–328, bibl.)

Seemingly careless translation or transcription of original essay, which itself is somewhat schematic. It nevertheless constitutes a systematic look at historical problem of fragmentation of Spanish empire and nature of Creole "nation"-building. Helpful too is bibliography of numerous related writings of author, many hard to locate. [D. Bushnell]

1866b Linares, Julio E. Bolívar, el Congreso Anfictiónico y la soberanía sobre el Canal de Panamá (LNB/L, 328/329, julio/agosto 1983, p. 28–46)

Reedition, in possibly more accessible journal, of *HLAS 44:2811*. [D. Bushnell]

1867 Rama, Carlos M. Historia de las relaciones culturales entre España y la América Latina, siglo XIX. México: Fondo de Cultura Económica, 1982. 350 p.: bibl., index (Sección de obras de historia)

Rather ponderous but very useful consideration of cultural relations between Spain and its former colonies in the 19th century. Includes wealth of detail on attitudes toward the value of the Spanish heritage, role of expatriates, intellectual organizations, writers, book sellers, and publishing industry in transforming attitudes and ultimately reestablishing formal ties. [JDR]

1868 Ridings, Eugene W. Foreign predominance among overseas traders in nineteenth-century Latin America (LARR, 20:2, 1985, p. 3–27, bibl.)

Argues that numerically and economically, foreigners dominated overseas trade in all countries of Latin America except Colombia during the 19th century. Considers reasons for this situation and characteristics of merchant population. Concludes that this fact prevented governments from implementing advice on how to develop and delayed the emergence of local entrepreneurship. Footnotes provide an excellent bibliography of the literature on merchants. [JDR]

1868a Wright, Thomas C. The politics of urban provisioning in Latin American history (*in* Food, politics, society in Latin America. Edited by John C. Super and Thomas C. Wright. Lincoln: Univ. of Nebraska Press, 1985, p. 24–45)

Sweeping overview of problem of urban food supply under changing technological conditions, this essay distinguishes between problems before and after 1870. Early era was characterized by government dominance, both colonial and early republican. Second period gave rise to new export economies, changes in food demand, generated by revival of mining and surge of urbanization. New phase involved pattern of scarcities and importations with increasing state involvement. Analyzes consequences of these patterns for food prices and urban mass politics throughout Latin America and return of government control. Sets out clear guidelines for further research on food related issues in the republican era. [V. Peloso]

20th CENTURY

1869 Brown, Jonathan C. Jersey Standard and the politics of Latin American oil production, 1911–30 (*in* Latin American oil companies and the politics of energy [see item **1876**] p. 1–50)

Evaluates reasons for entering production in Colombia, Mexico, Peru, Venezuela and Argentina; style of operations, relations with local politics, and why it was such a target for nationalists. [JDR]

1870 Chonchol, Jacques. Le poids de l'histoire dans les systèmes agraires de l'Amérique latine (*in* Unité et diversité de l'Amérique latine. Bordeaux, France: Univ. de Bordeaux III, 1982, t. 1, p. 115–135)

Superficial summary of elements of colonial past and late 19th-century development found in the agriculture of industrializing Latin American nations. [JDR]

1871 Dzieje Polonii w Ameryce lacińskiej = A history of the Polish colony in Latin America. Marcin Kula, editor. Warsaw: Zakład Narodowy im. Ossolińskich, 1983. 500 p.: index.

Compilation of historical studies of descendants of Polish emigrants to Latin America, organized geographically by country. Based on sources at the Archives of New Files in Warsaw, records which rarely go beyond 1939. [K. Complak]

1872 Elkin, Judith Laikin. Latin American Jewry today (American Jewish Yearbook [American Jewish Committee, New York] 1985, p. 321–433)

Covers historical factors affecting the Jewish community, character of their life, demography, educational system, and relations with Catholics and Israel. Sees substantial change in recent past and one of major trends in Jewish life, the integration of middle class and intellectuals into mainstream of Latin life. [JDR]

Fagg, John Edwin. Pan Americanism. See
HLAS 47:7028.

1873 Godio, Julio. Historia del movimiento
obrero latinoamericano. v. 1, Anarquistas y socialistas, 1850–1918. v. 2, Nacionalismo y comunismo, 1918–1930.
Caracas: Nueva Sociedad; México: Editorial
Nueva Imagen, 1980–1983. 2 v.: bibl.
  Title is slightly misleading. Vol. 1 emphasizes role of socialism in social movements, and why it failed up to 1930. Vol. 2
explores development of regional confederations and their ideological debates. Mostly
based on official declarations and standard
sources. [JDR]

**1874 Historia del movimiento obrero en
    América Latina.** Coordinación de
Pablo González Casanova. México: Siglo
Veintiuno Editores: Instituto de Investigaciones Sociales, UNAM, 1984. 4 v.: bibl.
(Historia)
  Excellent four-volume, country-by-
country survey traces formation of labor
unions and labor confederations in the countries of Latin America, and Puerto Rico. Although contributors take a leftist orientation, their essays are filled with facts. Vol. 1
covers Mexico and the Spanish Caribbean;
vol. 2, countries of Central America; vol. 3,
Colombia, Venezuela, Ecuador, Peru, Bolivia
and Paraguay; and vol. 4, Brazil, Chile, Argentina and Uruguay. [JDR]

1875 Lapa, José Roberto do Amaral. Histo-
    riografia latino-americano contempo-
rânea: problemática de suas tendencias: um
informe preliminar (Universidade Estadual
Paulista [São Paulo] 1, 1982, p. 7–19, bibl.)
  Brief explanation of general findings of
a survey on research and teaching of history
circulated to selected historians in Latin
America. Concludes that to date there is:
1) little interest in each country on conditions outside of geographical area in which
country is situated; 2) a big gap between
study of colonial period and contemporary
development; and that 3) a uniquely Latin
American historiography has yet to begin to
appear outside of the most developed countries. [JDR]

**1876 Latin American oil companies and the
    politics of energy.** Edited by John D.
Wirth. Lincoln: Univ. of Nebraska Press,
1985. 1 v.: index (Latin American studies
series)

Good collection of six essays and introductory overview of oil production by
John Wirth. Provides a coherent view of the
historical dynamics of the industry in its formative years. Contributors and countries include Brown on Jersey Standard in Latin
America (item **1869**); Solberg on Argentina;
Wirth on Brazil; Durán on Mexico; Lieuwen
on Venezuela; and Saulniers on public policy
(item **1880**). [JDR]

1877 Pike, Frederick B. Latin America and
    the inversion of United States stereo-
types in the 1920s and 1930s: the case of culture and nature (AAFH/TAM, 42:2, Oct.
1985, p. 131–162)
  Thesis that when a strong counterculture is present in US, attitudes toward
Latin America become more favorable because the characteristic image of Latin America is interpreted more favorably. Considers
nature of counterculture movements in
1920s and then makes a leap to argue that
this counterculture is important in understanding the climate in which the Good
Neighbor Policy developed. The problem is
that author does not establish clear connection between attitudes of intellectuals and
policy makers. [JDR]

**1878 Politics and social change in Latin
    America: the distinct tradition.** Edited
by Howard J. Wiarda. 2nd rev. ed. Amherst:
Univ. of Massachusetts Press, 1982. 368 p.:
bibl.
  This edition contains new introduction, new conclusion and one new content
piece added to 15 previous articles. Thesis
unifying the selections is that Latin American political development is generated by a
unique dynamic derived from history and
culture. [JDR]

1879 Rubio Cordón, José Luis. Los movi-
    mientos vertebradores, populistas y
revolucionarios en Iberoamérica (CH, 398,
agosto 1983, p. 343–357, table)
  Brief attempt to classify social movements since 1917. Defines six stages described by the nature of the dependency
present during them and then places the
movements in this context. [JDR]

1880 Saulniers, Alfred H. The state com-
    panies: a public policy perspective (*in*
Latin American oil companies and the poli-
tics of energy [see item **1876**] p. 226–251)
  Concluding overview to item **1876**

which examines issues of concerns surrounding the use of public enterprises to manage oil industries. Suggests that weaknesses noted today are result of government meddling and not inherent flaws in the institutions. Uses other articles in the book for evidence. [JDR]

1880a Sha, Ding. History and present situation of the Chinese in Latin America (Lading Meizhou Congkan [Latin American Review, Peking] 6, Dec. 1985, p. 24–30)

Traces history of overseas Chinese in Latin America. Shows early and relative freedom of entry and later stringent restrictions. Chinese immigrants survived in difficult circumstances and the Chinese government negotiated on their behalf. Concludes with description of recent status of overseas Chinese in Latin America and their organizations. Based on Chinese sources, including monographs and periodicals. [Robert Dunn]

1881 Torrada, Susana. El éxodo intelectual latinoamericano hacia los EE.UU.: 1961–1975 (Migraciones Internacionales en las Américas [Centro de Estudios de Migración: Centro de Estudios de Pastoral y Asistencia Migratoria, Caracas] 1 : 1, 1980, p. 19–39, bibl., tables)

Brief attempt to provide some facts concerning the level and nature of the Latin American "brain drain" to the US. Studies legal immigration only using official documents. Describes regional origins, professions and impact on sending countries. Concludes that laws and economic conditions in US are major determinant of levels of immigration. [JDR]

1882 Varga, Ilona. Los obreros húngaros emigrados en América Latina entre las dos guerras mundiales (PAN/EL, 7, 1980, p. 67–82, table)

Non-statistical study of factors involved in immigration of Hungarian workers to Argentina and Brazil in 1920s and political positions of fraternal organizations they founded until the end of World War II. They were leftist in politics and thus opposed to official Hungarian policy. [JDR]

1883 Viñas, David. Anarquistas en América Latina. México: Editorial Katún, 1983. 203 p.: bibl. (Col. Antología de América Latina; 1)

Rambling and loosely reasoned essay on the impact of anarchism defined vaguely as "rhetoric of the left in Latin cities around 1900." Followed by country-by-country selection of writing by and about the phenomenon. [JDR]

1884 Wilkie, James W. and **Manuel Moreno-Ibáñez.** Latin American food production and population in the era of land reform since the 1950s (in Food, politics and society in Latin America. Edited by John C. Super and Thomas C. Wright. Lincoln: Univ. of Nebraska Press, 1985, p. 65–105, graphs, tables)

Constructs long-term data series on food production for 20 countries (1952–80). Attempts to determine if link exists between domestic food production, population increases and agrarian reform. Concludes that in aggregate, food production did not keep up with population increase, but that there are wide variations from country to country and from year to year. Also on whole, land reform had a positive impact but countries without land reform also posted gains in food production. Thus, no clear trends. [JDR]

MEXICO: GENERAL AND COLONIAL

ASUNCION LAVRIN, *Associate Professor of History, Howard University*
EDITH B. COUTURIER, *National Endowment for the Humanities*

FEW ATTEMPTS TO WRITE long-range works of synthesis covering both the colonial and the independence periods have been published in this biennium. We had already noted the trend towards monographic work in *HLAS 44.* One exception to this pattern is Luis González, who continues to cultivate the art of "extensive microhistory." In lieu of the syntheses, we have a number of volumes containing collections of essays on special topics, or covering one topic for a discretely long period (see items **1919, 1923,** and **1948**). We also note several historiographical essays, which indicate that the task of reexamination and judgement of historical production continue to attract the attention of a few historians (items **1911, 1912, 1914,** and **1922**). On the other hand, the critical assessment of sources, once a flourishing field, has few cultivators today. Works by O'Gorman (item **1979**) and Marchetti (item **1967**) are noteworthy examples of that genre.

Studies of the central core of Mexico continue to prevail, but there is an increased interest in the development of historical research of several sub-regions within the central core. Centers of historical study in cities such as Morelia and Guadalajara have reinforced that trend, and will validate the hope placed on regional history by several distinguished historians of Mexico two decades ago (items **1902** and **1980**). A good example of this new style of history is Cheryl Martin's socioeconomic study of rural society in Morelos (item **1969**). Although in a different vein, Warren's work on the conquest of Michoacán (item **2004**) is partly a regional study and one of the few solid works on the subject of the conquest recently. The number of works written on Yucatán and the South is smaller than in preceding years, but the distinguished book by Nancy Farris on the interplay of the Hispanic and indigenous communities in Yucatán redresses the meager production (item **1525**). The works by Patch, Quezada, and Wasserstrom are also worth mentioning (items **1981, 1985a,** and **2005**).

While a decade ago interest in the history of haciendas was preeminent, today we have a shift to a broader focus of agricultural and rural history. Investigators have begun to explore the network of institutional, social, and even intellectual structures related to land, its ownership, and its cultivation. The works of Martin (item **1969**), Patch (item **1981**), as well as Hassig's study (item **1960**) of the distribution and marketing of agricultural production are good examples of this approach. Romero (item **1990**), Percherón (item **1904**), and Medina Rubio (item **1971**) exemplify other approaches to the economic history of agriculture. Ethnohistorians are also contributing to this shift by emphasizing the history of agricultural-related topics in several specific communities studies (item **1990**).

Family and women are maintaining a discrete place as topics in the literature, strengthened this biennium with the publication of Silvia Arrom's work on the women of Mexico City (item **1885** and also items **1934, 1945, 1962,** and **2018**) and the solid monograph on Sor Juana and her times by Cécile Bénassy (item **1934a**). Of special interest are several studies of the family, which raise important questions, such as the structure and survival of rural families (item **1909**), the issue of concubinage and illegitimacy (item **1940**), the meaning of family law (item **1949**), and matrimonial arrangements (item **2025**).

Although still an undersuscribed field, the history of the Church remains important because of increasing efforts to examine the validity of this institution as a mirror of social and economic issues (items **1963, 1971, 1978, 1997,** and **2001** and **2017**). Particularly welcome are the study of the financial sources of the secular Church in the 16th century by Schwaller (item **1999**) and the collection of essays on the Inquisition by Richard Greenleaf (item **1918a**). In a more traditional vein, the work by Ruiz Zavala on the history of the Augustinian order (item **1907**) is commendable for its breadth and the amount of information gathered. The political implications of unassimilated traditional beliefs is an intriguing theme explored by Serge Gruzinski (item **1959**) in a mentalité work which uses ecclesiastical sources.

Studies of social groups, their interactions in the process of stratification, their interests and activities, have received short shrift in the recent literature. An exceptional work, in a double sense, is the comprehensive work of José de la Peña on the formation of the early colonial elite, a distinguished contribution (item 1982). Also of interest, and at the far end of the colonial years, is the analysis of the activities of the artisans of Mexico City by González Angulo (item 1956) and the alter craftsmen by Tovar de Teresa (item 2002a).

Institutional history is represented by the comprehensive history of education in Guadalajara by Carmen Castañeda (item 1945), a work that incorporates prosopographical elements in the analysis. However, apart of the sources provided by Santoni (item 1995a) and Vila Vilar and Sarabia on the cabildos (item 1910), and Ortiz de la Tabla (item 1972) and Ruiz Rivera (item 1992) on the consulado, no other institution seems to have raised much interest among historians. A special study is that by B. Warren in which, in a special manner, the institution of the encomienda is documented (item 1961).

The labor of either Indians or blacks, women or peasants, is another unrepresented theme. Silvio Zavala, who has become the dean of the studies of Indian labor, has provided some of the best and only examples of this genre in works which closely paraphrase the sources but which have a measurable input of analysis as well (item 2008). Also worth mentioning is Vigueira's study on obraje labor (item 2003a).

Notable topics which have been explored in this past period might be mentioned here. Several attempts to write the history of disease and epidemics (items 1892, 1966, and 1968), Cline's collection of Indian wills is a useful source for the understanding of the process of mixing of Spanish and Aztec cultures (item 1570). Garner's study of prices in the 18th century adds deeper dimensions to the earlier work of Florescano (item 1917), and H. Klein's general picture of the colonial economy will be much quoted in the future (item 1920a). Pérez Herrero's methodological suggestions for the study of prices is thoughtful and helpful (item 1924). Questions of local and imperial conflicts are treated in a number of works including contributions on both the 16th and 18th centuries. Readers should note the works of Alvarado Morales, Archer, and Cummins (items 1929, 1932, and 1950).

In the region of the north and Borderlands, we should note an important article by Weber (item 2036) as much for its perceptive appreciation of North American scholars' work on this region, as for its complete bibliography. María del Carmen Velázquez has contributed several publications of documents. An especially interesting work elucidates the payment of workers and employees on the haciendas which supported the Fondo Piadoso de California (item 2035). The bicentennial commemoration of the death of Fray Junípero Serra has been celebrated by a series of articles about him. Noteworthy are works by Canedo (item 2014) and an issue of the quarterly publication of the Academy of American Franciscan History. Of special interest are the Deeds and Jackson articles (items 2016 and 2020). Some ethnohistorical contributions enrich the offerings for this biennium (items 2009, 2020, and 2028).

One hopes that in the next biennium we will welcome more works of synthesis on a broader scale as well as publications on the quincentennial of the 1492 encounter. Increasing numbers of historians who have been trained or who are working as ethnohistorians should make a substantial contribution to this aim.

GENERAL

1885 Arrom, Silvia Marina. The women of Mexico City, 1790–1857. Stanford, Calif: Stanford Univ. Press, 1985. 384 p.: bibl., ill., index, tables.

Path-breaking book for all Latin American historians of women. Examines women's lives through essays on demography, legal status, employment, marriage and divorce, finding that a "mobilization of women" occurred at the end of the 18th century and continued through the mid-19th century. The phenomenon of *marianismo* was a post-1850 development. Partially parallels current findings in US history. [EBC]

1886 Bazant, Jan. The Basques in the history of Mexico (Journal of European Economic History [Banco di Roma] 12:1, Spring 1983, p. 5–27, ill., map)

Essay by noted economic historian of Mexico analyzes secondary materials about noted Basque families in colonial and early modern Mexico. A contribution to family, economic and institutional history. [EBC]

1887 Canedo, Lino Gómez. Archivos franciscanos de México. 2a ed. México: UNAM: Instituto de Estudios y Documentos Históricos, 1982. 209 p.: ill., index (Serie Guías; 3)

Excellent guide to the Franciscan archives of New Spain by a distinguished historian of the Order. Canedo's judicious and learned historical comments on the collections are just as useful as the index of the holdings itself. [AL]

1888 Chevalier, Michel. México antiguo y moderno. México: Fondo de Cultura Económica, 1983. 444 p.: bibl. (SEP 80; 42)

Translation of French 19th-century work written to support Napoleon III's Mexican take-over. Tries to validate European intervention by highlighting Spain's incompetence and Mexican need for stability. Useful as a statement of imperialist logic. [AL]

1889 Coloquio de Antropología e Historia Regionales, *3rd, Zamora, México, 1981.* Después de los latifundios: la desintegración de la gran propiedad agraria en México. Coordinación de Heriberto Moreno García. Zamora, Mexico: Colegio de Michoacán: Fondo para Actividades Sociales y Culturales de Michoacán, 1982. 359 p.: bibl., ill.

Publication of the Colegio de Michoacán 1981 colloquium proceedings on the theme of the division of latifundia. Covers 18th century to present and contains contributions by almost all the historians who have written on the subject of haciendas and land reform. Although papers vary widely in quality and amount of documentation, they include much valuable material. [EBC]

Commons, Aurea. Desarrollo demográfico de la región central de México, 1519–1980. See *HLAS 47:5086.*

1890 Corcuera de Mancera, Sonia. Entre gula y templanza. México: UNAM, Facultad de Filosofía y Letras, Colegio de Historia, 1981. 261 p., 16 p. of plates: bibl., ill. (Col. Opúsculos. Serie Investigación)

Popularly written and entertaining history of culinary activities in Mexico. Based on primary and secondary sources. Reveals some potentially important facets of social history. [AL]

1891 Enciclopedia de la Iglesia Católica en México. v. 1, A-Benedicto. Director, José Rogelio Alvarez. México: Enciclopedia de México, 1982. 1 v.: ill. (some col.), col. plates.

Vol. 1 of projected encyclopedia of the Catholic Church in Mexico. Covers letters A and B through Benedict XV. Profusely illustrated with color plates, but entries do not adhere to the scope of the work's title. Items such as "Angel" or "Beisan" go beyond expected parameters of Mexico and/or its Catholic Church. Unsigned entries only provide general information for the lay reader. [AL]

1892 Ensayos sobre la historia de las epidemias en México. Compilación de Enrique Florescano y Elsa Malvido. México: Instituto Mexicano del Seguro Social, 1982. 2 v.: bibl., ill. (Col. Salud y seguridad social. Serie Historia)

Collection of 49 essays divided into four major sections: 1) general studies of epidemics that range chronologically from colonial period to 20th century; 2) examination of prehispanic and colonial periods, especially smallpox; 3) discussion of 19th-century epidemics; and 4) 20th-century epidemics. Many essays are local or regional studies. [R.E. Greenleaf]

1893 Flores Caballero, Romeo R. Administración y política en la historia de México. México: Instituto Nacional de Administración Pública (INAP), 1981. 320 p.: bibl.

Well balanced and organized survey of public administration in Mexico from colonial times to the López Portillo administration. Emphasizes post-1876 period. Author is a veteran public administrator. [R.E. Greenleaf]

1894 González y González, Luis. Zamora. 2a ed. Zamora, México: Colegio de Michoacán; México: CONACYT, 1984. 254 p., 12 p. of plates: bibl., ill.

Synthesis of the municipality of Zamora's historical development written in the incomparable style which has made González a legendary figure in Mexico and abroad. Readers will find a great deal of information packed in this charming book which ratifies its author's well-earned reputation of magisterial history-teller. [AL]

1895 Haciendas in central Mexico from late colonial times to the revolution: labour conditions, hacienda management, and its relation to the State. Edited by R. Buve. Amsterdam: Centre for Latin American Research and Documentation, 1984. 307 p.: bibl., ill. (CEDLA incidentele publicaties; 28)

Six substantial papers (two of which have been published earlier) provide a detailed study by Lucas of a hacienda's production and labor (1765–66), another work by Nickel provides new information on prices in early 20th-century Puebla-Tlaxcala, and two last, original papers by Buve and Rendon Garcini analyze the operation of haciendas during the Revolution. Interesting material. [EBC]

1896 Historia de Jalisco. t. 1, Desde los tiempos prehistóricos hasta fines del siglo XVII. t. 2, De finales del siglo XVII a la caída del federalismo. t. 3, De la primera república centralista a la consolidación del Porfiriato. t. 4, Desde la consolidación del Porfiriato hasta mediados del siglo XX. Director, José María Muriá. Guadalajara, México: Gobierno de Jalisco, Secretaría General, Unidad Editorial, 1980–1982. 4 v.: bibl., ill. (some col.)

Historical encyclopedia of Jalisco state under the direction of notable regional historian José María Muriá. Printed in glossy paper and profusely illustrated, these volumes are aimed at the coffee-table luxury market. Nevertheless, they are historically sound and well written, giving a satisfactory account for the general reader. Three of the four volumes concentrate on the post-independence period. [AL]

1897 Historiae variae. Ed. conmemorativa XXV aniversario de la fundación del Departamento de Historia, 1957–1982. México: Univ. Iberoamericana, Depto. de Historia, 1983. 1 v.: bibl.

Mixed festschrift contains articles by Angela Moyana de Guevara on foreign entrepreneurship in 19th-century Baja California, Guadalupe Jiménez on the English press during Mexican independence, Edmundo O'Gorman on Jacques Lafaye's work on the Guadalupan cult, and Elías Trabulse on Fray Diego Rodríguez. [AL]

1897a Historias. Dirección de Estudios Históricos, INAH. 1982-. México.

New journal (address: Apartado Postal 5, 119 México D.F.) publishes interdisciplinary essays on the history of Mexico by well known scholars. Non-academic publication addressed to the educated lay reader but worthwhile reading for academics and graduate students because of the breadth and variety of the contributions. [AL]

1898 Joseph, Gilbert M. From caste war to class war: the historiography of modern Yucatán, c. 1750–1940 (HAHR, 65:1, 1985, p. 111–134)

Able historiographical review of works on Yucatán, especially those produced in the last 25 years. [AL]

1899 León Portilla, Miguel et al. Minería mexicana. México: Comisión de Fomento Minero, 1984. 508 p.: bibl., ill., tables.

Collection of 16 historical essays covering the development of Mexican mining from precolumbian times to the 20th century. Main themes are labor, legislation and production. Among the authors are Miguel León Portilla, Roberto Moreno, José Ruiz de Esparza and María del Refugio González. Work of synthesis and reference. [AL]

1900 Mexico. Archivo General de la Nación. Reales cédulas duplicados. Elaborado por Celia Medina Mondragón. México: AGN, 1982. 140 pages (Serie Guías y catálogos; 64)

Continuation of published guides to

Mexico's Archivo General de la Nación (for earlier issues of this monographic series, see *HLAS 42: 1965*). The 193 volumes of the branch featured in this guide consist of viceregal legislation, from the 16th through 18th centuries, on such diverse topics as labor, religion, food supplies, appointments, taxes, and Indian affairs. No index. [EBC]

1901 Miller, Robert Ryal. Mexico: a history. Norman: Univ. of Oklahoma Press, 1985. 414 p.: bibl., ill., index.

Succinct history of Mexico organized along traditional chronological lines. Easy to read, it shies away from any controversial opinion. For high school and beginners' college courses. [AL]

1902 Morelos: cinco siglos de historia regional. Edición de Horacio Crespo. México: Centro de Estudios Históricos del Agrarismo en México, Univ. Autónoma del Estado de Morelos, 1984. 466 p.: graphs, ill., maps.

Consists of 25 papers presented at conference dedicated to the exploration of the social history of the state of Morelos. Papers are of variable quality but include information on research in progress. [EBC]

1903 Moreno Bonett, Margarita. Nacionalismo novohispano: Mariano Veytia: historia antigua, fundación de Puebla, guadalupanismo. México: UNAM, Facultad de Filosofía y Letras, 1983. 347 p.: bibl., facsims., ill., index, port. (Seminarios)

Historiographical study of the works of Pueblan lawyer and historian Mariano Fernández de Echeverría y Veytia (1718–80), author of precolumbian history of Mexico and history of Puebla, among other works. Commendable analysis of Veytia's production and personality as a historian. [AL]

1904 Percheron, Nicole. Problèmes agraires de l'Ajusco: sept communautés agraires de banlieue de México, XVIe-XXe siècles. México: Centre d'études mexicaines et centraméricaines, 1983. 166 p.: bibl., ill. (Etudes mésoaméricaines, 0378–5726; 8)

Based on extensive and unusually complete historical documentation supplemented by demography, this history of a community in the south of the valley of Mexico begins with the early land grants and continues through 1975. Especially interesting because of the conflicts among hacien-das, peasant proprietors and the village owning communal lands. [EBC]

1905 Pérez Fernández del Castillo, Bernardo. Historia de la escribanía en la Nueva España y el notariado en México. México: UNAM, Instituto de Investigaciones Jurídicas, 1983. 174 p., 12 p. of plates: bibl., ill. (Serie C. Estudios históricos; 15)

History of the office of scrivener in Mexico City through the 20th century. Written by aficionado historian, the organization of the book is difficult to follow. Contains useful information about the internal organization of the institution. [AL]

1906 Recopilación cronológica de datos sobre Comitán de Domínguez. Compilación de María Magdalena del Carmen Argüello Díaz. S.l.: s.n., 1981. 244 leaves, 60 leaves of plates: facsims., ill., ports.

Chronologically arranged data relating to Chiapan town. [R.E. Greenleaf]

1907 Ruiz Zavala, Alipio. Historia de la Provincia Agustiniana del Santísimo Nombre de Jesús de México. México: Editorial Porrúa, 1984. 2 v.: bibl. (Biblioteca Porrúa; 80–81)

Encyclopedic history of the Augustinian Order in Mexico from its foundation through the 20th century. Useful data on the history of chapters, convents, and members of the Order in the colonial period. [AL]

1908 Testimonios históricos guadalupanos. Compilación, prólogo, notas bibliográficas e índices de Ernesto de la Torre Villar y Ramiro Navarro de Anda. México: Fondo de Cultura Económica, 1982. 1468 p.: bibl., index (Sección de obras de historia)

Diverse collection of sources dealing with the apparition of the Virgin of Guadalupe, ranging from a Nahuatl poem to Lizardi's "Auto Mariano." Lengthy bibliography of guadalupan sources. [R.E. Greenleaf]

1908a *Trace: travaux et recherche dans les Amériques du centre.* Centre d'études mexicaines et centraméricaines, Institut de l'Amérique latine. juin 1986-. México.

New journal prepared by French scholars in Mexico, published irregularly. Covers the entire scope of Mexican and Central American history, although the former predominantes. Articles are short and pithy, topics varied and interdisciplinary. Enhanced by maps and illustrations. Welcome publication. [AL]

1909 Tutino, John. Family economies in agrarian Mexico, 1750–1910 (NCFR/JFH, 10:3, Fall 1985, p. 258–271, tables)

Tutino calls attention to the study of family structure and economy of the agrarian poor in an effort to enrich current trends of social history. Posits that the rural poor organized their family economies in many ways to meet the challenge of survival. Uses Jalpa (1866) to support his theories. Welcome shift away from the urban family or large hacienda-owner families, which so far have dominated the literature. [AL]

Vázquez, Josefina Zoraida *et al.* Ensayos sobre historia de la educación en México. See *HLAS 47:4476.*

1910 Vila Vilar, Enriqueta and **María Justina Sarabia Viejo.** Cartas de Cabildos Hispanoamericanos: Audiencia de México. Sevilla, Spain: Escuela de Estudios Hispanoamericanos, 1985. 512 p.: index (Publicaciones; 310)

Index to letters sent by the cabildos of the cities of New Spain to the Crown or the Council of the Indies. Volume covers 1533–1697 and includes cities administered by the Audiencia of Mexico. Key to important historical source, this guide should be very useful to future researchers. [AL]

COLONIAL PERIOD: General

1911 Alberro, Solange and **Serge Gruzinski.** Le Mexique préhispanique et colonial: un bilan provisoire, 1976–1982 (AESC, 38:3, mai/juin 1983, p. 614–627)

Bibliographical review of some of the principal books on Mexican history published 1976–82. [AL]

1912 Benítez Grobet, Laura. La idea de historia en Carlos de Sigüenza y Góngora. México: UNAM, Facultad de Filosofía y Letras, 1982. 148 p.: bibl. (Seminario)

Suggestive study links Sigüenza's concepts of history and science and explains the logic of his thought. Author underlines the writer's modernity and *criollismo.* Able historigraphical essay. [AL]

1913 Cabrera y Quintero, Cayetano. Escudo de armas de México. Escrito para conmemorar el final de la funesta epidemia de matlazáhuatl que asoló a la Nueva España entre 1736 y 1738. Ed. facsim. Estudio histórico y una cronología de Víctor M. Ruiz Naufal. México: Instituto Mexicano del Seguro Social, 1981. 522 p.: bibl., ill., index.

Facsimile edition includes assorted introductory modern materials and author's chronology. Commissioned around the time of the epidemic, the work contains materials on history and treatment of epidemics, history of Mexico City, religious events and worship of Saints and Virgins, as well as accounts of institutions and individuals who tried to assist the sick or to contain the infection. [EBC]

1914 Carmagnani, Marcello. The inertia of Clio: the social history of colonial Mexico (LARR, 20:1, 1985, p. 149–183, bibl.)

Evaluation and discussion of works of social history produced since 1960 which suggest a new periodization and greater concern with developing forms of ethnicity. Commentators indicate some of the difficulties of the new periodization scheme and propose additional categories. Includes comments by Murdo McLeod (p. 167–170), Cheryl English Martin (p. 171–175) and John E. Kicza (p. 176–180), and author's response (p. 181–184). [EBC]

1915 *Claustro de Sor Juana.* Instituto de Estudios y Documentos Históricos. 1980-. México.

Serial publication of the Institute of Documents and Historical Studies based at the Cloister of Sor Juana in Mexico City. Each bimonthly volume is devoted to a specific theme and consists of selected documents from three sources: Mexico's notarial archives, the cloister's documents, and the Vatican's Secret Archives. Some themes chosen for the first 10 volumes are: mayorazgos, women's status, mining, etc. Reproduces both original paleograph and modern versions of the documents in a luxury format. [AL]

1916 Conquista y colonización en México. Recopilación de José María Muriá. México: Fondo de Cultura Económica, 1982. 218 p.: bibl. (SEP/80; 31)

Selection of texts by contemporary historians on the subject of the conquest and colonization. Editor's aim is to make easily accessible to general public the opinion and judgment of eminent historians. Among those included are Luis González, José Miranda and Silvio Zavala. [AL]

1917 Garner, Richard L. Price trends in eighteenth-century Mexico (HAHR, 65:2, 1985, p. 279–325, graphs, tables)
Important work extending Florescano's earlier study of maize prices to other products and additional regions. Uses recent secondary studies, including Garner's own work on Zacatecas, to indicate complexities inherent in the relationship of prices to production and population growth. [EBC]

1918 Goldwert, Marvin. Machismo and conquest: the case of Mexico. Lanham, Md.: Univ. Press of America, 1983. 85 p.: bibl.
Psychohistorical interpretation of Mexico's conquest. In several brief chapters author explains, in Freudian terms, machismo, the conquistador's power, male-female sexuality, the figure of Cortés and other themes. Highly interpretative. [AL]

1918a Greenleaf, Richard E. Inquisición y sociedad en el México colonial. Madrid: J. Porrúa Turanzas, 1985. 325 p.: bibl., index (Col. Chimalistac de libros y documentos acerca de la Nueva España; 44)
Collection of the author's many essays on the Inquisition in New Spain conveniently put together and translated into Spanish. This will make accessible this scholar's work in Spanish America and Spain. [AL]

1919 Historia de la ciencia en México: estudios y textos. v. 1, Siglo XVI: la aparición de un Nuevo Mundo. Fotografías de Ignacio Urquiza. México: CONACYT; Fondo de Cultura Económica, 1984. 1 v.: bibl., ill. (some col.)
Handsomely produced volume with lengthy and informative introductions, contemporary illustrations and well selected extracts from the documents. Of particular interest are sections on the history of medicine, new therapeutic products from America, and metallurgy. [EBC]

1920 Iguíniz, Juan B. Los gobernantes de Nueva Galicia: datos y documentos para sus biografías. 3a ed. Guadalajara, Mé-

xico: Gobierno de Jalisco, Secretaría General, Unidad Editorial, 1981. 190 p.: bibl. (Col. Historia. Serie Documentos e investigación; 4)
Reissue of study first published in 1948 by distinguished historian of New Galicia (Jalisco). Work consists of 38 biographies of colonial governors of New Galicia. Useful reference despite reservations about some of the sources used. [AL]

1920a Klein, Herbert. La economía de la Nueva España, 1680–1809: un análisis a partir de las Cajas Reales (CM/HM, 34:4, abril/junio 1985, p. 561–609, bibl., tables)
Global study of the income produced by the treasury of New Spain, with special attention to the different sources of revenue. Author defines cycles of expansion, stagnation, and depression, assessing the profits rendered by the colony to Spain. Important and useful. [AL]

1921 López, Juan. Cedulario novogalaico. Guadalajara, México: Gobierno de Jalisco, Secretaría General, Unidad Editorial, 1981. 108 p. (Col. Historia. Serie Documentos e investigación; 5)
Index to royal cédulas collected and used by the Audiencia of Guadalajara. Volume covers 1528–1821 period. [AL]

1922 Martínez, Rodrigo. El desarrollo económico novohispano: siglos XVII y XVIII; tendencias historiográficas contemporáneas (Historias [Dirección de Estudios Históricos, INAH, México] 2, oct./dic. 1982, p. 57–70)
Review of main works on Mexico's economic history published in the last 20 years, mostly by non-Mexican historians. [AL]

1922a Martínez Guernica, Armando. De la metáfora al mito: la visión de las crónicas sobre el tianguias prehispánico (CM/HM, 34:4, abril/junio 1985, p. 685–700, bibl.)
Revision of the account of Spanish chroniclers of the functions of indigenous market. Suggests that rather than centers of economic exchange they were foci of ceremonial redistribution of goods. [AL]

1923 Muriel, Josefina. La Orden Jerónima en México. México: Instituto de Estudios y Documentos Históricos, *Claustro de Sor Juana*, 1981. 69 p., 1 leaf of plates: ill. (Serie Cuadernos)

Reissue of chapter from author's book on nunneries first published in 1946. [AL]

1924 Pérez Herrero, Pedro. Comercio y precios en la Nueva España: presupuestos teóricos y materiales para una discussión (IGFO/RI, 44:174, 1984, p. 465–188)

Useful discussion of pros and cons of a variety of sources for the study of trade and prices. Methodologically sound, this work is applicable to other areas of the Spanish Empire. [AL]

1925 Salvucci, Richard. El viejo México colonial y la "Nueva Historia Económica" (HISLA, 1, 1983, p. 89–101, bibl.)

After reviewing important economic studies that exemplify the "New Economic History" as well as more traditional ones, author concludes that both approaches will serve well for future research in Mexican economic history. [AL]

1926 Schell, William. Medieval Iberian traditions and the development of the Mexican hacienda. Syracuse, N.Y.: Maxwell School of Citizenship and Public Affairs, Syracuse Univ., 1986. 117 p.: bibl., index (Foreign and Comparative Studies Program. Latin American series; 8)

Attempt to arrive at a theoretical overview of the origin of the hacienda. Interesting use of secondary materials which might provide new points of departure for understanding the development of the large estate. [EBC]

1927 Seis impresos relativos al establecimiento y gobierno de diversos hospitales navales españoles del siglo XVIII, 1748–1781. Ed. facsim. México: Rolston-Bain, 1983. 112 p. (Col. Documenta Novae Hispaniae, 0821–7777; B-4)

Facsimile edition of six late 18th-century naval hospital rules sent to New Spain to serve as models for Mexican institutions. Information on medical treatment, food and professional administration of medicine are of interest to the social historian. [AL]

Vollmer, Günter. Hispaniae Novae vera descriptia, 1579: zur wirklichkeitstreue einer Mexiko-Karte im Atlas des Abraham Ortelius. See HLAS 47:5116.

1928 Yuste López, Carmen. El comercio de la Nueva España con Filipinas, 1590–1785. México: INAH, Depto. de Investigaciones Históricas, 1984. 98 p.: bibl., ill., maps (Col. científica; 109. Fuentes Historia económica)

New overview study of trade between Mexico and the Phillipines. Registers long-term patterns, but is stronger on late 18th-century information. Good data on bulk of trade and investments of merchants involved in this trade route. [AL]

Central and South

1929 Alvarado Morales, Manuel. La ciudad de México ante la fundación de la Armada de Barlovento: historia de una encrucijada, 1635–1643. México: El Colegio de México, Centro de Estudios Históricos; Río Piedras: Univ. de Puerto Rico, Recinto de Río Piedras, 1983. 284 p.: bibl., index.

Microhistory of 1635–43 period, and role of the cabildo in the set-up of defense plans for the Caribbean region. Stresses confrontation between local and imperial interests. [AL]

1930 Anderson, Rodney D. La familia en Guadalajara durante la independencia y la teoría social de Peter Laslett (UCA/E, 2:4, julio/sept. 1985, p. 75–92, tables)

Study of 1821 Guadalajara census. Comparisons with those of 1811 and 1814 lead author to assume a cautious attitude about transposing Peter Laslett's generalizations on the prevalence of nuclear families to early 19th-century Mexico. Advocates adaptation of his concepts to the Mexican milieu in any future study of family structure. [AL]

1931 Antología de textos sobre la Ciudad de México en el período de la Ilustración, 1788–1792. Compilación de Sonia Lombardo de Ruiz. México: INAH, Depto. de Investigaciones Históricas, 1982. 371 p.: bibl., ill. (Col. científica; 113. Fuentes, historia social)

Consists of two sources for the study of Mexico City towards the end of the 18th century: Discurso sobre la policía de México, attributed to oidor Baltasar Ladrón de Guevara, and a description of the city as an urban complex by Antonio de Alzate, first published in Gaceta de Literatura de México (1780–95). Useful tools for graduate students. [AL]

1932 Archer, Christon I. Banditry and revolution in New Spain (Bibliotheca

Americana [Coral Gables, Fla.] 1:2, Nov. 1982, p. 59–81, maps, table)

Revisionist view of War of Independence emphasizes role of banditry among insurgent forces, and helps to explain the royalists' uncompromising position. [EBC]

1933 Archer, Christon I. The officer corps in New Spain: the martial career, 1759–1821 (JGSWGL, 19, 1982, p. 137–158, tables)

Study surveys changes undergone by the army officers corp in last decades of Spanish dominance. Conflicts among Spanish and Mexican officers, increasing decentralization of power and challenge of the Hidalgo revolt forced a critical change within the army's ruling body. Author makes a good case for his argument. [AL]

1934 Baudot, Georges. Malitzin, l'irrégulière (*in* Femmes des Amériques [see item **1784**] p. 19–29)

Baudot claims that the contemporary national repudiation of Malitzin as a traitor to the Mexican people was not shared by her contemporaries. Despite scarcity of historical tracks, author succeeds in delineating a revised personal profile of this controversial figure. [AL]

1934a Bénassy-Berling, Marie Cécile. Humanisme et religion chez Sor Juana Inés de la Cruz: la femme et la culture au XVIIe siècle. Paris: Editions hispaniques, Publications de la Sorbonne, 1982. 510 p.: bibl., ill., index (Col. thèses, mémoires et travaux; 38)

Admirably researched and written work on Sor Juana Inés de la Cruz and her times. With academic precision and empathy, this global study explores all nuances of Sor Juana's personality and production. It should become the standard reference on the poet nun for many years. [AL]

1935 Bénassy-Berling, Marie-Cécile. Más sobre la conversión de Sor Juana (CM/NRFH, 32:2, 1983, p. 463–471)

Bénassy raises some doubts concerning the generally accepted reasons for the radical change undergone by Sor Juana in the last years of her life. Argues against those who attribute this entirely to Archbishop Aguiar y Seijas's negative influence on the nun. [AL]

1936 Bénassy-Berling, Marie-Cécile. Mineurs ou majeurs?: *las recogidas* dans l'Amérique espagnole coloniale (*in* Femmes des Amériques [see item **1784**] p. 57–67)

Despite title, essay deals with New Spain. Author explains meaning and social purpose of *recogimientos* or retreat houses for impoverished women in colonial Mexico. [AL]

1937 Berthe, Jean-Pierre. Les epidémies au Mexique au XVIe siécle (IAV/AIHM, 35, 1983, p. 257–263)

Author indicates an important work in progress on epidemiology. [EBC]

1938 Borges Morán, Pedro. Expediciones misioneras al Colegio de Querétaro, Méjico: 1683–1822 (PF/AIA, 42:165/168, enero/dic. 1982, p. 809–858)

Provides data on all missionaries who left Spain to populate the Franciscan College of Propaganda Fide in Querétaro. Useful for prosopographic studies. [AL]

1939 Burrus, Ernest J. Alonso de la Vera Cruz, 1584: pioneer defender of the American Indians (ACHA/CHR, 70:4, Oct. 1984, p. 531–546)

Short biographical survey and analysis of main writings of 16th-century Augustinian theologian of New Spain. [AL]

1940 Calvo, Thomas. Concubinato y mestizaje en el medio urbano: el caso de Guadalajara en el siglo XVII (IGFO/RI, 14:173, enero/junio 1984, p. 203–212, tables)

Author calls attention to rates of illegitimacy and concubinage among the different ethnic groups in colonial Guadalajara. He believes that these phenomena are crucial for understanding attitudes about marriage, male-female relationships, and urban mestizaje. Based on demographic samples from 17th-century ecclesiastical sources, this work opens new avenues to study significant social issues in need of further research. [AL]

1940a Calvo, Thomas. Familles mexicaines au XVIIe siècle: une tentative de reconstitution (Annales de demographie historique [Société de démographie historique, Paris] 1984, p. 149–173, tables)

Attempt at family reconstitution based on a marriage sample of the Cathedral Church of Guadalajara, 1666–75. Author provides data on anthroponymic usage, age of marriage, intergenesic intervals and family size. A departure study for this period and area. [AL]

1941 Calvo, Thomas. Japoneses en Guadalajara: "blancos de honor" durante el seiscientos mexicano (IGFO/RI, 43:172, julio/dic. 1983, p. 533–547)

Study discovers and explores the lives and careers of several Japanese migrants to 17th-century Guadajalara describing the how, why and extent of their integration into the social milieu. [AL]

1942 Carabarín Gracia, Alberto. El trabajo y los trabajadores del obraje en la ciudad de Puebla, 1700–1710. Puebla, México: Centro de Investigaciones Históricas y Sociales, Instituto de Ciencias, Univ. Autónoma de Puebla, 1984. 77 p.: bibl. (Cuadernos de la Casa Presno; 1)

Master's thesis partly based on archival but mostly printed sources. Focuses on early 18th-century *obrajes*, especially on the demographics of the labor force. [AL]

1943 Castañeda, Carmen. La educación en Guadalajara durante la colonia, 1552–1821. Guadalajara, México: El Colegio de Jalisco; México: El Colegio de México, 1984. 516 p.: bibl., graphs, ill., index, maps, tables.

Based on extensive archival research, this work covers the institutional history of all educational centers in Guadalajara, from primary schools to the university. It also studies the centers' educational plans and traces a prosopographical outline of students and faculty in higher learning. Serious and richly documented work which will serve as a standard reference for those interested in the history of education. [AL]

1944 Castañeda, Carmen. Una elite de Guadalajara y su participación en la independencia (UCA/E, 2:4, julio/sept. 1985, p. 39–58)

Prosopographic analysis of individuals awarded doctorate degrees at the Univ. of Guadalajara (1792–1810) assesses their reaction to the Hidalgo revolt in their area. Not surprisingly, author confirms that the graduates and their *padrinos* sympathized with the royalists. [AL]

1945 Castañeda, Carmen. La memoria de las niñas violadas (UCA/E, 2:1, oct./dic. 1984, p. 41–56)

Minute analysis of 13 existing cases of child rape in the Audiencia of Guadalajara at-

tempts to determine common characteristics of criminals and victims, circumstances of crime, and how the law and community reacted to it. Interesting blend of prosopography and *mentalité* history. [AL]

1946 Cervantes Bello, Francisco J. La Iglesia y la crisis del crédito colonial en Puebla: 1800–1814 (*in* Banca y poder en México: 1800–1925. Edición de Ludlow Leonor y Carlos Marichal. México: Grijalbo, 1986, p. 51–74)

Contribution to the economic history of Puebla which indicates some effects of the application of the *Consolidación* on a region already in economic difficulties. [EBC]

1947 Chandler, D.S. The *Montepíos* and regulation of marriage in the Mexican bureaucracy, 1770–1821 (AAFH/TAM, 43:1, July 1986, p. 47–68)

Long awaited study of effects of the establishment of government pension system on marriage practices of bureaucrats at all ranks. Article emphasizes the problems of enforcement. [EBC]

1948 La Compañía de comercio de Francisco Ignacio de Yraeta, 1767–1797. t. 1, Cinco ensayos. t. 2, Apéndices. México: Instituto Mexicano de Comercio Exterior: Univ. Iberoamericana, 1985. 2 v.: appendices, bibl., ill. (some col.) (Publicación; 742)

Stimulating collection of essays on one of the most powerful merchants of late colonial New Spain. Family life and commercial activities are thoroughly studied. Documentary appendix with personal business papers and letters are valuable sources for other historians. [AL]

1949 Couturier, Edith B. Women, family and the law (NCFR/JFH, 10:3, Fall 1985, p. 294–304)

During the 18th century, Mexican family law remained almost unchanged despite the fact that ways in which families used the inheritance law changed significantly. Author examines in detail the decline in the use of dowries as well as the role of widows in the administration of family affairs, and suggests that despite the apparent fact of women being less protected by the law in the early 19th century, their position within the family was not affected. [AL]

1950 Cummins, Victoria Hennessey. Imperial policy and Church income: the sixteenth century Mexican Church (AAFH/ TAM, 43, July 1986, p. 87–103)

Discusses historically various sources of income utilized by the secular clergy in an effort to become financially independent, and to compete effectively with the regular clergy both for spiritual services rendered to Indian communities as well as to build their own churches. [EBC]

1951 De cómo vieron y contaron los cronistas de Indias el Descubrimiento y Conquista de Tabasco. Recopilación, edición y prólogo de Manuel González Calzada. México: Consejo Editorial, Gobierno del Estado de Tabasco, 1981. 490 p.: bibl., ill. (Serie Historia; 29)

Fragments from various chroniclers who recounted the earlier stages of the conquest of Mexico. Published with copies of title pages of particular editions used. [EBC]

1952 Dehouve, Danièle. Las separaciones de pueblos en la región de Tlapa: siglo XVIII (CM/HM, 33:4, abril/junio 1984, p. 379–403, bibl., tables)

Meticulous study of different religious and administrative categories of agrarian communities in 18th-century Tlapa (Puebla), stressing varieties of organization patterns and interests. Posits that rather than stability, the indigenous rural communities show persistent patterns of change and disgregation. [AL]

1952a Don Miguel Hidaldo y Don José Antonio Torres en Gudalajara. Edición de Carmen Castañeda. Guadalajara, México: Unidad Editorial, Gobierno de Jalisco, 1985. 57 p.: ill.

First printing of two archival documents of interest for the history of the movement of independence in Guadalajara. One is the *Relación* by Prisciliano Sánchez (1810), and the other is the *Testimonio de . . . Don José Antonio Torres* (1812). They offer two different views of the war: royalist and insurgent, and are put into context by editor Castañeda. [AL]

Farriss, Nancy Marguerite. Maya society under colonial rule: the collective enterprise of survival. See item **1525.**

1953 García-Abásolo, Antonio F. Martín Enríquez y la reforma de 1568 en Nueva España. Sevilla, Spain: Excma. Diputación Provincial de Sevilla, 1983. 382 p., 6

leaves of plates: bibl., ill., index, port. (Publicaciones. Sección Historia. Serie V Centenario del descubrimiento de América; 2)

Extensive coverage of the administration of Viceroy Enríquez, who arrived in New Spain with the intent to enforce a new administrative order designed by Phillip III to strengthen the authority of the Viceroy and the Crown. Author stresses mining, agriculture, the exchequer, society, religion and defense as important aspects of the history of the period. Readable and well documented synthesis of the 1570–80 decade. [AL]

1954 García Ayluardo, Clara. El comerciante y el crédito durante la época borbónica en la Nueva España (*in* Banca y poder en México: 1800–1925. Edición de Ludlow Leonor y Carlos Marichal. México: Grijalbo, 1986, p. 27–50)

Emphasizes importance of commercial as opposed to ecclesiastical sources of credit in late 18th-century Mexico, with particular emphasis on the activities of Antonio Bassoco and other members of the Basque community. [EBC]

1955 García Bernal, Manuela Cristina. García de Palacio y sus Ordenanzas para Yucatán (Temas Americanistas [Cátedra de Historia de América, Univ. de Sevilla] 5, 1985, p. 1–12)

Full text of standard 16th-century policy document for the government of Yucatán. Document is preceded by author's full and meticulous study of García de Palacio and his significance. [AL]

1955a Gonzalbo Aispuru, Pilar. Del tercero al cuarto Concilio Provincial Mexicano, 1585–1775 (CM/HM, 35:1, julio/sept. 1985, p. 5–31, bibl.)

Brief history of the Fourth Provincial Council of New Spain (1771), stressing its agenda and ideological stand as expressions of the concerns of the Bourbon regalist church. [AL]

1956 Gonzáles Angulo Aguirre, Jorge. Artesanado y ciudad a finales del siglo XVIII. México: Fondo de Cultura Económica, 1983. 248 p.: ill. (SEP 80; 49)

Author surveys spatial distribution of crafts, family life, guild regulation, ethnic segregation and litigation among artisan workers in the city of Mexico. Based on guild archival records about artisans, this work is sound and informative. [AL]

1957 Gosner, Kevin. Las elites indígenas en los Altos de Chiapas, 1524–1714 (CM/HM, 33:4, abril/julio 1984, p. 405–423, bibl.)

Warns historians that they "have to learn much from indigenous ideas and their values . . ." Surveys concept of a social elite among communities of Altos de Chiapas and their survival throughout the early and middle colonial period. Reinterprets the 1712 Tzeltal revolt. [AL]

1958 Grobet Palacio, René. El peregrinar de las flores mexicanas: José Mariano Mociño y Losada, 1757–1822. Xalapa, México: Instituto Nacional de Investigaciones sobre Recursos Bióticos, 1982. 100 p., 16 leaves of plates: bibl., ill. (some col.)

General history of Mociño's career as a botanist, and the fate of his plant drawings. Acceptable reproductions of some of them enhance this brief work. [AL]

1959 Gruzinski, Serge. Les hommes-dieux du Méxique: pouvoir indien et société coloniale, XVIe-XVIIIe siècles. Paris: Editions des Archives contemporaines, 1985. 1 v.: index, maps, tables.

Intriguing interpretative study of the preservation and endurance of a Nahua religious mentality embodied in the personalities of several "god-men" (e.g., Emiliano Zapata). Using archival materials on several heterodox indigenous leaders, Gruzinski explores manifestations of power and resistance in religious symbolism. Thought-provoking *mentalité* analysis written in lucid prose. [AL]

1960 Hassig, Ross. Trade, tribute, and transportation: the 16th century political economy of the Valley of Mexico. Norman: Univ. of Oklahoma Press, 1985. 1 v.

Study of the system of agricultural production, market distribution and tribute in central Mexico before and after the Spanish conquest. Author stresses changes and continuities throughout the 16th century. Well conceived and carried-out study of key human and economic factors in the making of a new social order. [AL]

1961 Infante, Juan. La administración de los negocios de un encomendero en Michoacán. Edición e introducción de J. Benedict Warren. México: SEP; Michoacán, México: Univ. Michoacana de San Nicolás de Hidalgo, 1984. 83 p.: folded ill. (Col. cultural; 2)

Transcription of series of letters written (1533–34) by Juan Infante, who had an encomienda in Michoacán, to his mayordomo. Lucid introduction explains the context and indicates salient aspects of business and agriculture in the years after the conquest. [EBC]

1962 Lavrin, Asunción. Aproximación al tema de la sexualidad en el México colonial (UCA/E, 2:1, oct./dic. 1984, p. 23–40, tables)

After surveying religious canons of sexual behavior, as established in colonial confessional treaties, author examines archival sources to find examples of male-female relationships in real life. Concludes that the sexuality of the colonial population was not subject to the thorough control of the Church. Most examples are taken from the Bishopric of Michoacán. [AL]

1963 Lavrin, Asunción. El capital eclesiástico y las elites sociales en Nueva España (Mexican Studies/Estudios Mexicanos [Univ. of California Press, Berkeley] 1:1, Winter 1985, p. 1–28, tables)

Author posits that although availability of credit was not restricted to top members of New Spain's socioeconomic hierarchy, the wealthiest ecclesiastical institutions preferred to lend large amounts of money to members of the top layers of society. Study focuses on the Archbishopric of New Spain in the last decades of the 18th century, stressing that the Church had not, as yet, lost its preeminent role as a leading institution. [AL]

1964 Leiby, John S. Report to the King: Colonel Juan Camargo y Cavallero's historical account of New Spain, 1815. New York: P. Lang, 1984. 215 p.: bibl., ill. (American university studies. Series IX, History; 3)

Translation and annotated edition, including bibliographic footnotes of a Spanish engineer's account of Mexico. The engineer, Camargo, did some research and had considerable knowledge based upon a residence of more than 20 years. Much of the account is a mere listing of different kinds of data and the report lacks interpretation. [EBC]

1965 Lewis, Robert E. El testamento de Francisco López de Gómara y otros documentos tocantes a su vida y obra (IGFO/RI, 14:173, enero/junio 1984, p. 61–79, appendices)

Compact discussion of the biographical data available for historian Francisco López de Gómara. Lewis clarifies some previous confusions and comments on the value of Gómara's will, here published for the first time. [AL]

1965a Long-Solís, Janet. El abastecimiento de chile en el mercado de la ciudad de México-Tenochtitlan en el siglo XVI (CM/HM, 34:4, abril/junio 1985, p. 701–714, bibl.)

Brief survey of the distribution of chile in the city of Mexico, based on printed sources. [AL]

1965b Lozoya, Xavier. José Mariano Mociño: un naturalista mexicano que recorre Nutka, Canada, en el siglo XVIII (CM/HM, 34:1, julio/sept. 1984, p. 114–134, maps, bibl.)

Narrative of Mociño's expedition to Nootka, largely based on the traveler's own account. [AL]

1966 MacLeod, Murdo J. The *Matlazáhuatl* of 1737–8 in some villages in the Guadalajara region (Studies in Social Sciences [West Georgia College, Carrollton] 25, 1986, p. 7–16, tables)

Brief study of circumstances in which a typhus epidemic struck Indian villages in the Guadalajara region. Provides statistical data on deaths and compares this epidemic with better known ones of the 1780s. [AL]

1967 Marchetti, Magda. Hacia la edición crítica de la *Historia* de Sahagún (CH, 396, junio 1983, p. 505–540)

Meticulous appraisal of several versions of Sahagún's *Historia*. Author considers the *Código Florentino* the most authentic of several versions, arguing on its behalf for any possible new edition of this well known work. [AL]

1968 Márquez Morfín, Lourdes. Sociedad colonial y enfermedad: un ensayo de osteopatología diferencial. México: INAH, 1984. 111 p., 1 folded leaf of plates: ill. (Col. científica; 136)

Paleopathological study of bones discovered in the Cathedral of Mexico helps to determine the nature of disease in colonial Mexico. New and interesting attempt to unveil data about health and epidemiology. [AL]

1969 Martin, Cheryl English. Rural society in colonial Morelos. Albuquerque:

Univ. of New Mexico Press, 1985. 255 p.: bibl., index.

Taking the sugar-producing area of Yautepec, author builds a regional study around the themes of sugar production, changing demographic and settlement patterns, landownership, and labor. Backed by sound archival research, this is an apt and satisfactory example of micro-history. [AL]

1970 Martínez Rosales, Alfonso. Fray Nicolás de Jesús María, carmelita descalzo del siglo XVIII (CM/HM, 32:3, enero/marzo 1983, p. 299–348, bibl.)

Biographical essay on a notable preacher and head of his Order in 18th-century Mexico. Interesting example of a rarely cultivated genre. [AL]

1971 Medina Rubio, Arístides. La Iglesia y la producción agrícola en Puebla, 1540–1795. México: Centro de Estudios Históricos, El Colegio de México, 1984. 291 p.: bibl., ill., index.

Using the tithes of the Church in Puebla, author traces the Bishopric's main agricultural products throughout the colonial period. Offers useful data on prices, volume of production and amounts of tithes collected by the Church. Although this is not an agricultural history, but a history of fiscal aspects of agricultural production, the data and generalizations they support will be of use to economic historians. [AL]

1972 Memorias políticas y económicas del Consulado de Veracruz, 1796–1822. Edición y estudio preliminar de Javier Ortiz de la Tabla Ducasse. Sevilla, Spain: Escuela de Estudios Hispanoamericanos de Sevilla, 1985. 320 p.: bibl., index (Publicaciones; 303)

Transcription of 16 reports submitted to the Council of the Indies by the Consulado of Veracruz between its foundation in 1796 and 1822. Introductory study by Ortiz de la Tabla underlines the importance of these sources as testimonies of the socioeconomic concerns of that city's merchant class. [AL]

1973 Menéndez Valdés, José. Descripción y censo general de la Intendencia de Guadalajara, 1789–1793. Estudio preliminar y versión del texto de Ramón Ma. Serrera. Guadalajara, México: Gobierno de Jalisco, Secretaría General, Unidad Editorial, 1980. 161 p.: bibl., col. map (Col. Historia. Serie Estadísticas básicas; 1)

Contains five important sources for the demographic and socioeconomic study of late 18th-century Guadalajara: 1) description of the Intendancy; 2) diary of the royal official in charge of the census and the visit of the Intendancy; 3) map; 4) general census; and 5) corographic description of the area. Ramón Serrera's apt introduction explains the importance of materials that are presented here for the first time. [AL]

1974 Der mexikanische Silberbergbau: 16. und l. Hälfte des 17. Jahrhunderts; Zum Stand der Forschung (UEN/LS, 6, 1980, p. 227–240, tables)

Surveys history and literature of silver mining (1521–1650) with special emphasis on the Taxco and Zacatecas mines as well as the concessions in Sultepec granted to German merchants in Seville. [Joseph Neville]

1975 Mier Noriega y Guerra, José Servando Teresa de. El heterodoxo guadalupano. Estudio preliminar y selección de textos de Edmundo O'Gorman. México: UNAM, Coordinación de Humanidades, 1981. 241 p.: bibl. (Nueva biblioteca mexicana; 83. Obras completas, Servando Teresa de Mier; 3)

Reissue of Mier's discussion of the possibility of the preaching of Christianity in America prior to its discovery by Europe in the 18th century, and his letters to Juan B. Muñoz, chronicler of the Indies, on the Guadalupan worship. Commentaries by Edmundo O'Gorman are helpful. [AL]

1976 Miller, Sara. Francisco Palomino: protector y defensor de los indígenas de Yucatán, 1569–1586 (CIRMA/M, 6:9, junio 1985, p. 133–153, appendix)

Narrative piece traces the career of a 16th-century royal official, based on archival data in Spain. A minor work that contains useful information. [AL]

1976a Miño Grijalva, Manuel. El camino hacia la fábrica en Nueva España: el caso de la *Fábrica de indianillas* de Francisco Iglesias, 1801–1810 (CH/HM, 34:1, julio/sept. 1984, p. 135–148, bibl.)

Drawing on the example of one early textile factory, posits that New Spain was on its way to organizing a capitalist textile industry at the end of the 18th century. [AL]

1977 Miño Grijalva, Manuel. Espacio económico e industria textil: los trabajadores de Nueva España, 1780–1810 (CM/HM,

32:4, abril/junio 1983, p. 524–553, bibl., graph, maps, tables)

Provides new viewpoint on the economic development of late Bourbon Mexico in the transition from a textile industry based on *obrajes* to one based on *telares*. A factor contributing to the change was the increasing emphasis on the production of cotton and declining production of wool. Also discusses regional differences. [EBC]

1978 Morales, Francisco. Pueblos y doctrinas en México, 1623 (PF/AIA, 42:165/168, enero/dic. 1982, p. 941–964)

Reports on two censuses of Indian towns in the Franciscan Province of Santo Evangelio, Archbishopric of Mexico. These documents were the result of a 1623 reassessment for the payment of Franciscan missionaries. The introductory essay is followed by an extract of one of the two documents. [AL]

1979 O'Gorman, Edmundo. La incógnita de la llamada *Historia de los indios de la Nueva España* atribuida a Fray Toribio Motolinía: hipótesis acerca de la fecha, lugar de composición y razón de ser de esa obra, y conjetura sobre quién debió ser el autor y cuál el manuscrito original. México: Fondo de Cultura Económica, 1982. 139 p.: bibl. (Col. Tierra firme)

O'Gorman tries to prove that the *Historia de los indios de Nueva España* could not have been written by Motolinía. Despite his lengthy explanation the subject will remain controversial because of the conjectural nature of O'Gorman's argument. [AL]

1980 Paredes Martínez, Carlos S. et al. Michoacán en el siglo XVI. Morelia, México: Fímax Publicistas, 1984. 444 p., 9 leaves of plates: ill. (Col. Estudios michoacanos; 7)

Four in-depth studies of landownership, taxation, labor and encomienda in 16th-century Michoacán. This useful work will help us revise our notion of institutional adjustment in the post-conquest society of a rural area of New Spain. [AL]

1981 Patch, Robert W. Agrarian change in eighteenth-century Yucatán (HAHR, 65:1, 1985, p. 21–49, maps, tables)

Award-winning article on the agrarian history of Yucatán, establishing the process of change of agricultural properties and production. Author ties geographical factors to internal and external demand, and availability of labor. Concludes that "the major causes of the rise of the hacienda in Yucatan were . . . internal," warning against an uncritical acceptance of "world economy" schemes. [AL]

1982 Peña, José F. de la. Oligarquía y propiedad en Nueva España, 1550–1624. México: Fondo de Cultura Económica, 1983. 308 p.: bibl., index (Sección de obras de historia)

Impressive work on the formation and consolidation of the social elite in Mexico (1550–1624). Author provides information on mercantile activities, use of cabildo positions, marriage strategies and uses of entailment as some of the means used by the new elite to insure its own supremacy. Important contribution to the social and economic history of the mid-colonial years. [AL]

1983 Pérez Zevallos, Juan Manuel. El gobierno indígena en Xochimilco, siglo XVI (CM/HM, 33:4, abril/junio 1984, p. 445–462, bibl.)

Surveys process of superimposition of Hispanic town government over indigenous institutions. Based on the *Ordenanza de Suchimilco* (1553). Author stresses continuity patterns as well as conflicts arising among the indigenous elite throughout the 16th century. [AL]

1984 Pietschmann, Horst. La población de Tlaxcala a fines del siglo XVIII (JGSWGL, 20, 1983, p. 223–238, graphs, tables)

Brief analysis of the 1793 population census of Tlaxcala. Pietschmann presents the original document and explains its most salient features. [AL]

1985 Porras Barrenechea, Guillermo. La provisión de gobernadores interinos de Nueva Vizcaya (UCA/E, 2:3, abril/junio 1985, p. 85–122)

Detailed study of the confrontations between the officials of the Audiencia of Guadalajara and the governors of Nueva Vizcaya in the 16th and 17th centuries. Offers an insight into jurisdictional problems confronting royal officials as well as an intimate and human vision of the politics of administration. [AL]

1985a Quezada, Sergio. Encomienda, cabildo y gubernatura indígena en Yucatán, 1541–1583 (CM/HM, 34:4, abril/junio 1985, p. 662–684, bibl.)

Surveys process of substitution of prehispanic political institutions for Hispanic models in the local government of Yucatecan communities. Towards the end of the 16th century, the authority of the local rulers was seriously undermined. Based on Spanish sources, but well argued. [AL]

1986 Relaciones histórico-geográficas de la gobernación de Yucatán: Mérida, Valladolid y Tabasco. Edición preparada por Mercedes de la Garza *et al.* Paleografía y glosario de arcaísmos y voces poco usuales, María del Carmen León Cázares. Estudio preliminar, Mercedes de la Garza y Ana Luisa Izquierdo. Cuadro de topónimos, nómina de poblados y mapa, Tolita Figueroa. Glosarios de términos indígenas y de americanismos, Ana Luisa Izquierdo. Dibujos, Carlos Ontiveros. México: UNAM, Instituto de Investigaciones Filológicas, Centro de Estudios Mayas, 1983. 1 v.: bibl., facsims., ill., index (Fuentes para el estudio de la cultura maya; 1)

Useful work gathers 52 geographical descriptions of 16th-century Yucatán. Modernized texts of the original reports have been printed alongside facsimile reproductions of the original texts. Glossaries, tables of localities, and a general index facilitate the use of the two volumes. A very valuable reference for mayologists, ethnohistorians and historians of the 16th century. [AL]

1987 Ríos Miramontes, María Teresa. El Arzobispo Monroy: notas para su biografía (PF/AIA, 44:175, julio/sept. 1984, p. 327–350, ill.)

Biography of Archbishop Fray Antonio de Monroy (b. Querétaro, New Spain) who settled in Spain after 1673, where he became General of the Dominican Order and later Archbishop of Santiago de Compostela. [AL]

1988 Rodríguez, Catalina. Comunidades, haciendas y mano de obra en Tlalmanalco, siglo XVIII. Prólogo de Carlos García Mora. México: Biblioteca Enciclopédica del Estado de México, 1982. 202 p., 1 folded leaf of plates: ill. (some col.) (Biblioteca Enciclopédica; 113)

Study of region in the vicinity of Chalco and Amecameca with information about land tenure, economic growth, and rental of lands as well as special emphasis on labor. Contains information from both archival and published sources. [EBC]

1989 Rodríguez Gómez, María Guadalupe. Jalpa y San Juan de los Otates: dos haciendas en el Bajío colonial. León, México: Colegio del Bajío, 1984. 172 p.: bibl., ill.

Excellent case histories based on valuable collections of hacienda documents. Includes material on production, prices, labor supply and the relation between the hacienda and the families that owned them. Useful comparative materials. [EBC]

1990 Romero, María de los Angeles. Evolución económica de la Mixteca Alta: siglo XVII (CM/HM, 32:4, abril/junio 1983, p. 496–523, bibl., graphs, tables)

Historical overview of the regional economy of the Mixteca Alta between the late 16th and late 17th centuries. Author traces several economic cycles experienced by the trade and cattle sectors. Serious effort to reach a synthesis based on archival research. [AL]

1991 Rossell, Cecilia. Cartascuentas: la Real Hacienda en Nueva España, 1557. México: Centro de Investigaciones y Estudios Superiores en Antropología Social, 1984. 302 p.: bibl., ill. (Cuadernos de la Casa Chata; 100)

Work focuses on one 1557–60 *Carta Cuenta* (i.e., account of the gold and silver remittance to Spain). Useful for the careful explanation of the trade system of the period. [AL]

1992 Ruiz Rivera, Julián B. Monopolio del Consulado de México e intrusismo inglés, 1723 (Temas Americanistas [Cátedra de Historia, Univ. de Sevilla] 1, 1982, p. 28–32)

Examines document dated 1723 written by the merchants of the Consulado of the City of Mexico in which they complain about the state of trade and British intrusion in the Spanish commercial system. [AL]

1993 Ruvalcaba Mercado, Jesús. Agricultura colonial y transformación social en Tepeapulco y Tulancingo, 1521–1620 (CM/HM, 33:4, abril/junio 1984, p. 425–444, bibl.)

Novel study of the process of assimilation of agricultural and cattle products by the indigenous communities in central New Spain. Stresses how the new crops affected

the production patterns of individuals and families. [AL]

1994 Salvucci, Linda K. Costumbres viejas, "hombres nuevos:" José de Gálvez y la burocracia fiscal novohispana, 1745–1800 (CM/HM, 33:2, oct./dic. 1983, p. 224–264, bibl., tables)

Substantial contribution to a growing literature on the history of the Bourbon bureaucracy. On the basis of both Mexican and Spanish archives, author suggests a major revision of Priestly's biography of Gálvez. [EBC]

1995 Sánchez de Tagle, Esteban. El regimiento de la Reina: el final de las reformas borbónicas (Historias [Dirección de Estudios Históricos, INAH, México] 2, oct./dic. 1982, p. 42–56, graph)

Theoretical article, based on limited sources, analyzes the familiar connections of the San Miguel El Grande regiment, and finds all of them related. A contribution to family as well as to military and political history. [EBC]

1995a Santoni, Pedro. El cabildo de la Ciudad de México ante las reformas militares en Nueva España, 1765–1771 (CM/HM, 34:3, enero/marzo 1985, p. 389–434, bibl.)

Explains why the cabildo of the city of Mexico opposed the Bourbon introduction of provincial militias. Militias restricted Creole participation and challenged the traditional socioeconomic ranking of the population. [AL]

1996 Schwade, Arcadio. The first diplomatic relations between Japan and Mexico, 1609–1616 (*in* International Congress of Human Sciences in Asia and North Africa, 30th, Mexico, 1976. Asia and colonial Latin America. Editor, Ernesto de la Torre. Mexico: El Colegio de México, 1981, p. 101–109)

Three 17th-century missions to Japan ended in failure. [EBC]

1997 Schwaller, John Frederick. The Cathedral Archive of Mexico (AAFH/TAM, 42:2, Oct. 1985, p. 229–241)

Useful guide to important ecclesiastical archive and microfilm collection of its holdings made by the Mormons. Summary of the archive's organization, which also includes some 19th-century parish records of communities within the Archbishopric. [EBC]

1998 Schwaller, John Frederick. The *Ordenanza del Patronazgo* in New Spain, 1574–1600 (AAFH/TAM, 42:3, Jan. 1986, p. 253–274)

Expanded and revised version of *HLAS 46:2023*. [EBC]

1999 Schwaller, John Frederick. Origins of Church wealth in Mexico: ecclesiastical revenues and Church finances, 1523–1600. Albuquerque: Univ. of New Mexico Press, 1985. 241 p.: bibl., ill., index.

Important contribution to the history of the Church and its relationship to the social and economic development of New Spain in the 16th century. Concentrating upon the secular clergy, this work illuminates the development of chantries and other pious works including the early history of many institutions. Clarifies many aspects of ecclesiastical organization and finance. [EBC]

2000 Schütte, Josef Franz. Don Rodrigo de Vivero de Velasco and Sebastián Vizcaíno in Japan (*in* International Congress of Human Sciences in Asia and North Africa, 30th, Mexico, 1976. Asia and colonial Latin America. Editor, Ernesto de la Torre. Mexico: El Colegio de México, 1981, p. 77–100, bibl.)

Using several key archival sources, author explains the failure of Vizcaíno's attempts to establish trade relations between Spain, New Spain, and Japan in the early 17th century. [AL]

2001 Seed, Patricia. The Church and the patriarchal family: marriage conflicts in sixteenth- and seventeenth-century New Spain (NCFR/JFH, 10:3, Fall 1985, p. 284–293)

Author makes a case for the role of the Catholic Church as supporter of freedom of choice in matrimonial arrangements in 16th- and 17th-century New Spain. Readable piece with straightforward message. [AL]

2002 Super, John C. The provisioning of Mexico City in the late eighteenth century (JGSWGL, 19, 1982, p. 159–182, tables)

Significant contribution to urban history stresses the complexity of wheat and bread production and distribution. Article discusses questions of government regulation, philanthropy, and varieties of distribution systems including the rise of the *pulperos*. [EBC]

The Testaments of Culhuacan. See item 1570.

2002a Tovar de Teresa, Guillermo. Consideraciones sobre retablos, gremios y artífices de la Nueva España en los siglos XVII y XVIII (CM/HM, 34:1, julio/sept. 1984, p. 5–40, bibl.)

Sheds light on the work of artists and craftsmen, their patrons, and the economy of colonial Mexico, using the example of the men who built altarpieces in the city. [AL]

2003 Tributos y servicios personales de indios para Hernán Cortés y su familia: extractos de documentos del siglo XVI. Compilación de Silvio Zavala. México: AGN, 1984. 405 p.: bibl., facsims., indexes.

Zavala gathers here 44 documents or excerpts of documents (1529–96) drawn from judicial suits involving payments in the form of tribute and personal service by Indians in Cortes's estates. Some of these documents have been printed before. [AL]

2003a Vigueira, Carmen. El significado de la legislación sobre mano de obra indígena de los obrajes de paño, 1567–1580 (CM/HM, 35:1, julio/sept. 1985, p. 33–58, bibl.)

Revisionist interpretation of the late 16th century regulatory legislation of *obraje* labor. Refers to prehispanic labor practices and posits that by the end of the century, legislation was moving towards a Castilian model and that labor was salaried, not coerced. [AL]

2004 Warren, J. Benedict. The conquest of Michoacán: the Spanish domination of the Tarascan Kingdom in Western Mexico, 1521–1530. Norman: Univ. of Oklahoma Press, 1985. 352 p.: bibl., ill., index.

Revised English ed. of 1977 Spanish original (see *HLAS 40:2542*). Author has updated several chapters. Finely tuned scholarship covers crucial years of conquest and settlement of Michoacán. [AL]

2005 Wasserstrom, Robert. Spaniards and Indians in colonial Chiapas, 1528–1790 (*in* Spaniards and Indians in southeastern Mesoamerica: essays on the history of ethnic relations. Edited by Murdo J. MacLeod and Robert Wasserstrom. Lincoln: Univ. of Nebraska, 1983, p. 92–106, map, tables)

Socioeconomic history of colonial Chiapas, based on local and Guatemalan archives, indicates still another pattern of exploitation of the native population. Emphasizes development of forms of communal solidarity among the Indians and modifies our views of the 1712 rebellion. [EBC]

Watson, Rodney C. La dinámica espacial de los cambios de población en un pueblo colonial mexicano: Tila, Chiapas, 1595–1794. See *HLAS 47:5117.*

2006 Wobeser, Gisela von. El uso del agua en la región de Cuernavaca, Cuautla, durante la época colonial (CM/HM, 32:4, abril/junio 1983, p. 467–495, bibl., table)
Traces history of the alienation of water rights from villages and ranches to haciendas from technical, legal and political viewpoint. Draws from the archives of the Hospital de Jesús and San Carlos Borromeo in an effort to direct research to the issue of irrigation as well as landownership when analyzing the growth of haciendas. [EBC]

2007 Zavala, Silvio Arturo. Hernán Cortés ante la justificación de su conquista de Tenochtitlán (UY/R, 26:149, enero/marzo 1984, p. 39–61)
Reviews previous studies and contributes to our understanding of the difficult legal and moral problem of conquest. [EBC]

2008 Zavala, Silvio Arturo. El servicio personal de los indios en la Nueva España. t. 1, 1521–1550. t. 2, 1550–1575. México: El Colegio de México, Centro de Estudios Históricos: Colegio Nacional, 1984–1985. 2 v.: bibl., indexes.
Vol. 1 of several that will cover the personal service of Indians in central New Spain. Divided into two categories: 1) service given to settlers; and 2) special services to the Church, public works, Indian communities, etc. This volume follows the sources closely offering important information on the topic. [AL]

North and Borderlands

2009 Anderson, H. Allen. The encomienda in New Mexico, 1598–1680 (UNM/NMHR, 60:4, 1983, p. 353–377, ill., map)
Useful analysis based on published sources and secondary materials notes that encomienda survived longer in New Mexico than in other parts of New Spain and con-

tributed to the Pueblo uprising. Explores dynamics of the relations among Church, Crown, encomienderos both as military men and entrepreneurs, and different groups of Native Americans. [EBC]

2010 Baldwin, Stuart J. A reconsideration of the dating of a seventeenth-century New Mexican document (UNM/NMHR, 59:4, Oct. 1984, p. 411–413)
Suggests that document published by Scholes listing missions in New Mexico must be dated 12 to 14 years later than date assigned by Scholes on the basis of internal evidence. Draws important conclusions from this date change. [EBC]

2011 Boneu Companys, Fernando. Gaspar de Portolá: explorer and founder of California. Translated and revised by Alan K. Brown. Lerida, México: Instituto de Estudios Ilerdenses, 1983. 404 p., 29 leaves of plates (some folded): bibl., ill. (some col.)
Translation of a primarily genealogical biography of Portolá. Includes text of a number of documents about the exploration of California. [EBC]

2012 Brasseaux, Carl A. and **Richard E. Chandler.** The Britain incident, 1769–1770: Anglo-Hispanic tensions in the western Gulf (TSHA/SHQ, 87:4, April 1984, p. 357–370)
Exciting account of the voyage of a group of German and Acadian immigrants to New Orleans which might have involved Britain and Spain in conflict. [EBC]

2013 Burrus, Ernest J. Key sources of Bandalier's history of the Southwest (UNM/NMHR, 60:1, 1985, p. 89–113)
Describes sources and summarizes contents of Bandalier's history of Sonora, Chihuahua, New Mexico and Arizona to 1700. Information about Bandalier's life and methods of research. Promises re-publication of the work by the Jesuit Institute. [EBC]

2014 Canedo, Lino Gómez. Fray Junípero Serra y su noviciado misional en América: 1750–1758 (PF/AIA, 42:165/168, enero/dic. 1982, p. 881–918)
Biographical survey of early years of Fray Junípero Serra, with special emphasis on his missionary work at the Sierra Gorda missions. [AL]

2015 Canedo, Lino Gómez. Las primitivas misiones de Coahuila: la etapa de los franciscanos de Jalisco, 1674–1781 (PF/AIA, 44:175, julio/sept. 1984, p. 261–297, bibl., map)

Surveys establishment of Franciscan missions in Coahuila in the late 17th century, including data on three episcopal visits to the region. Based on archival research and printed missionary chronicles. [AL]

2016 Deeds, Susan. Land tenure patterns in northern New Spain (AAFH/TAM, 41:4, April 1985, p. 446–461)

Review of large body of recent secondary material on rural life observes that the examination of access to water in studying land tenure has been neglected. Author summarizes different ecological factors which led to latifundia, varying motives for debt peonage, development of rancho economy, and the mercantile transformation of agriculture. Valuable and clearly conceived summary which emphasizes the variety of land tenure conditions in the north. [EBC]

Doolittle, William E. Cabeza de Vaca's Land of Maize: an assessment of its agriculture. See *HLAS 47:5090.*

2017 Greenleaf, Richard E. The Inquisition in eighteenth-century New Mexico (UNM/NMHR, 60:1, Spring 1985, p. 29–60)

Interesting survey of the activities of the Inquisition in this northernmost post of colonial Mexico. Highlights the role of the Franciscans as heads of the Holy Office in New Mexico for over two centuries. Rich in information on folk-religious beliefs and practices, social mores, and the tensions between civil and ecclesiastical authorities. [AL]

2018 Gutiérrez, Ramón A. From honor to love: transformations of the meaning of sexuality in colonial New Mexico (*in* Kinship ideology and practice in Latin America. Edited by Raymond T. Smith. Chapel Hill: Univ. of North Carolina, 1984, p. 237–263, bibl., graph)

Study of several subjects related to love, marriage and sexuality in New Mexico from the late 18th through mid-19th centuries. Author notes transformations in the meaning of affective relationships and the changing basis of marital choices. Based on archival sources, this is a solid piece of work on a relatively new subject of research in Mexican history. [AL]

2019 Ives, Ronald L. José Velásquez: saga of a Borderland soldier, northwestern New Spain in the 18th century. Tucson, Ariz.: Southwestern Mission Research Center, 1984. 248 p.: bibl., ill., index.

Biography of an 18th-century Mexican soldier (b. Sonora) who served in the Californias. Written by amateur historian, it is often confusing but the effort to recreate a soldier's life is laudable. [EBC]

2020 Jackson, Robert. Demographic change in northwestern New Spain (AAFH/TAM, 41:4, April 1985, p. 462–479, graphs, tables)

Briefly summarizes recent bibliography on demographic history and then carries out family reconstitution studies of three cases in Pimería Alta, Baja and Alta California. Concludes that stress factors, inherently unhealthy living conditions in missions destroyed Indian populations, while relative isolation of certain groups facilitated their survival. Important article addressing an issue of contemporary interest. [EBC]

2021 John, Elizabeth A.H. Nurturing the peace: Spanish and Comanche cooperation in the early nineteenth century (UNM/NMHR, 59:4, Oct. 1984, p. 345–369, ill.)

Careful and insightful archival examination of both the Texas and New Mexico frontier analyzes alliances and notes differences in Anglo and Hispanic policies, as well as comparing conditions in the two areas. [EBC]

2022 Kelsey, Harry. European impact on the California Indians, 1530–1830 (AAFH/TAM, 41:4, April 1985, p. 494–511)

Overview based on secondary sources. [EBC]

2023 Kessell, John L. Diego de Vargas: another look (UNM/NMHR, 60:1, p. 11–28, ill.)

Important biographical study, based on archival materials, is part of large project on the history of New Mexico from 1680–1710, which will also include publication of Vargas's journals. Article provides a novel perspective on his life. Personal letters have survived. [EBC]

2024 León-Portilla, Miguel. California in the dreams of Gálvez and the achievements of Serra (AAFH/TAM, 41:4, April 1985, p. 428–434)

Urges examination of the work of Gálvez and Serra in tandem rather than in opposition. [EBC]

2025 McCaa, Robert. *Calidad, clase,* and marriage in colonial Mexico: the case of Parral, 1788–90 (HAHR, 64:3, Aug. 1984, p. 477–501, tables)

Analysis of 174 marriages in Parral (1788–90) "to weigh the impact of race; occupational standing and racial drift on nuptial choices." Deals with timing of marriage in the life cycle, match-making policies, concepts of social equality, and class, and how they affected marital choices, especially those of women. [AL]

2026 Mange, Juan Mateo. Diario de las exploraciones en Sonora: *Luz de tierra incógnita.* 3a ed. Hermosillo, México: Gobierno del Estado de Sonora, 1985. 162 p.

Third edition of journal written by a companion of Kino's in 1706 and 1721. Originally published in 1856 and 1921, the new edition makes this document available again. Publication also includes a manuscript of Luis Xavier Velarde dating from 1716. No annotations. [EBC]

2027 Meyer, Michael C. The legal relationship of land to water in northern Mexico and the Hispanic Southwest (UNM/NMHR, 60:1, p. 61–79)

Using archival materials from the north and Borderlands as a laboratory to explore the ways in which different kind of land grants conferred or failed to confer the right to irrigation water, author applies secondary sources and legislation to illuminate important aspects of the history of land tenure. [EBC]

2028 Percheron, Nicole. La pacification des guachichiles et des pames de San Luis Potosí (CDAL, 25, jan./juin 1982, p. 69–94, maps)

Documents gradual loss of identity of two "Chichimec" groups during the 16th and 17th centuries. Trade, subventions, the appropriation of large blocks of land, settlement of other Indian groups, Spaniards and mestizos all contributed to the destruction of Indian civilization. Based on primary sources. [EBC]

2029 Pérez de Ribas, Andrés. Páginas para la historia de Sonora: *Triunfos de nuestra santa fe.* 3a ed. Hermosillo, México:

Gobierno del Estado de Sonora, 1985. 2 v.

Third edition of work originally published in 1645, and a basic source for the history of the northwest. This edition has been carefully printed and should be useful to modern readers. [AL]

2030 Quiñones, Beatriz. La rebelión tepehuana. México: Instituto de Investigaciones Históricas, Univ. Juárez del Estado de Durango, 1984. 98 p.

Brief recounting of the 1616 Tepehuanes revolt in Nueva Vizcaya with heavy Marxist vocabulary. Based on secondary sources, adds little new, except the interpretation. [AL]

2031 Serra, Junípero. Escritos de Fray Junípero Serra. v. 2–5. Edición de P. Salustiano Vicedo. Introducción de Jacinto Fernández-Largo. Petra, Spain: S. Vicedo, 1984. 4 v.: ill. (Publicaciones de Apóstol y civilizador. Col. Petra nostra; 7–10)

Collection consists largely of numerous letters written by Fray Junípero but several memoranda and other documents are also included. Its merit consists in making easily available an important historical source. [AL]

2032 Shipek, Florence C. California Indian reactions to the Franciscans (AAFH/TAM, 41:4, April 1985, p. 480–492, bibl.)

Attempts to explore the mission experience from the Indian viewpoint. Uses older anthropological accounts and interviews. [EBC]

2033 Simmons, Marc. The *Chacón Economic Report* of 1803 (UNM/NMHR, 60:1, 1985, p. 81–88)

Translation and publication of report collected by Veracruz consulado reveals interesting data about New Mexico, arguing that it is not as poor as other *provincias internas*. [EBC]

2034 Velázquez, María del Carmen. La defensa del Virreinato de Nueva España (CM/RE, 3:12, otoño de 1982, p. 45–65)

Summary, without analysis, of various imperial measures undertaken to defend New Spain from attacks both by land and sea. Reminds us of the protective role of Spain as a colonial power. [EBC]

2035 Velázquez, María del Carmen. La frontera norte y la experiencia colonial. México: Secretaría de Relaciones Exteriores, 1982. 238 p.: bibl. (Archivo histórico diplomático mexicano. Cuarta época; 11)

Publication of documents on the formation and government of the *provincias internas* includes brief biographical introductions to the authors of each work. Book includes both manuscripts and excerpts of published documents. Organized in a roughly chronological form with most of the materials dating between 1768–92.

2036 Weber, David J. Turner, the Boltonians, and the Borderlands (AHA/R, 91:1, Feb. 1986, p. 66–81)

Significant historiographical article argues that the followers of Bolton failed to consider the frontier thesis and ignored its implications. Only in the new social history has the frontier been considered as the agent of change in institutions and in human behavior. [EBC]

MEXICO: *19th Century, Revolution and Post-Revolution*

RICHARD E. GREENLEAF, *Director, Center of Latin American Studies, Tulane University*
DON M. COERVER, *Chairman, Department of History, Texas Christian University*

DURING THE LAST BIENNIUM, one of the most ambitious historical projects in recent memory neared completion; the 23-volume *Historia de la Revolución Mexicana* series had seen the publication of 17 of its volumes. The series covers the period from 1910–60 in eight subperiods; 1911–14, 1914–17, 1917–24, 1924–28, 1928–34, 1934–40, 1940–52, and 1952–60. Each subperiod has at least two volumes devoted to it, with each installment the work of a recognized scholar or scholars on the subject and time frame. The project started in 1974 with the assistance of President Luis Echeverría and under the direction of Daniel Cosío Villegas. The first three volumes in the series covering down to 1914 are among the six that remain unpublished. While any such series is bound to suffer from a certain degree of unevenness and imbalance, the *Historia de la Revolución Mexicana* will doubtless serve as a reference point for future scholars of 20th-century Mexico. Annotated below are the following installments in the series: vol. 8, Alvaro Matute's *La carrera del caudillo* (item **2172**); vol. 11, Jean Meyer's *Estado y sociedad con Calles* (item **2175**); vol. 14, Luis González's *Los artífices del cardenismo* (item **2147**); vol. 15, Luis González's *Los días del Presidente Cárdenas* (item **2149**); vol. 16, Alicia Hernández Chávez's *La mecánica cardenista* (item **2157**); vol. 17, Victoria Lerner's *La educación socialista* (*HLAS 44: 2220*); vol. 19, Blanca Torres Ramírez's *México en la Segunda Guerra Mundial* (item **2206**); and vol. 20, Luis Medina's *Civilismo y modernización del autoritarismo* (item **2174**).

The emphasis on regional studies continued undiminished. Thomas Benjamin and William McNellie provide an excellent collection of essays on regional history during the Porfiriato (item **2090**). Two articles by Paul Garner deal with the question of "federalism" in Oaxaca (item **2065** and **2144**). Ian Jacobs furnishes a regional and revisionist interpretation of the Revolution in Guerrero in his *Ranchero revolt: the Mexican Revolution in Guerrero* (item **2161**). Yucatán continues to be a popular location for regional studies: Blanca González R. (item **2068**), Marie Lapointe (item **2076**), Luis Aboites (item **2118**), James Carey (item **2124**), and Ramón Chacón (item **2126**). Jalisco was a distant second as an object of regional study: Mario A. Aldana

Rendón (item **2039**), Carlos Gil (item **2067**), Ann Craig (item **2131**), and Moisés González Navarro (item **2145**).

The boom in border studies tailed-off somewhat but still attracted considerable attention. Veteran border watchers and their studies included Oscar Martínez (item **2171**) and Linda Hall and Don Coerver (items **2129, 2130, 2153,** and **2154**). James Sandos continues his inquiry into crime and revolution (item **2195**), while Manuel Machado provides a valuable insight into a key economic activity on the frontier (item **2169**).

Labor studies accounted for much of the scholarly activity during the last biennium, with output being fairly evenly divided between the 19th and 20th centuries. Porfirian labor developments are examined by Jean-Pierre Bastian (item **2044**), Manuel Ceballos Ramírez (item **2053**), and Lorena Parlee (item **2092**). The important relationship between labor and the government is dealt with in works edited by Victor M. Durand Ponte (item **2134**) and by Pablo González Casanova (item **2128**). The PRI's *Historia documental de la Confederación de Trabajadores de México* (item **2159**) provides a useful collection of documents relating to labor history, while the *Memorias del encuentro sobre historia del movimiento obrero* (item **2140**) is made up of a number of essays covering a broad range of topics relating to strikes and the workers' movements.

Three important historiographical works appeared during the last biennium. Thomas Benjamin and Marcial Ocasio-Meléndez deal with Porfirian historiography in their "Organizing the Memory of Modern Mexico" (item **2049**). Gilbert Joseph sorts out the growing body of literature relating to Yucatán in "From Caste War to Class War: the Historiography of Modern Yucatán" (item **2073**). María de la Luz Parcero provides a broad-ranging, reference-style work on the political historiography of modern Mexico in *Introducción bibliográfica a la historiografía política de México* (item **2091**).

Reprints of earlier publications figured prominently in recent publishing activities. José Fuentes Mares's basic works on Juárez were among those reissued (items **2061** and **2062**). Classic works by Manuel Gamio (item **2063**) and Genaro García (item **2064**) were also reprinted. Works relating to the revolutionary and post-revolutionary periods were also given new life: Antonio Díaz Soto y Gama (item **2136**), Frank Tannenbaum (item **2204**), and José Vasconcelos (item **2210**).

Not falling into any of the above categories but also worthy of note are: Timothy Anna on Iturbide (item **2043**), Mílada Bazant's two articles on education (items **2046** and **2047**), Pedro Santoni's ground-breaking work on the police in the Porfiriato (item **2098**), Paul Vanderwood's study of banditry as business enterprise (item **2109**), Jan de Vos's review of agrarian legislation (item **2112**), and Eugene Wiemers's revisionist views on agricultural credit (item **2116**). For the 20th century, see Alicia Hernández Chávez's study of revolutionary generals as entrepreneurs (item **2158**), Douglas Richmond's controversial interpretation of the Carranza years (item **2189**), and Hans Werner Tobler's analysis of the new revolutionary bourgeoisie (item **2213**).

19th CENTURY

2037 Adame Goddard, Jorge. El pensamiento político y social de los católicos mexicanos, 1867–1914. México: UNAM, 1981. 273 p.: bibl.

Examines the political and social thought of two distinct groups of Catholic thinkers: the "Catholic conservatives" of the Porfirian period who maintained their traditional ideals after the Liberal victory and a new generation of Catholic thinkers who were influenced by the social reformism exemplified by the papal encyclical, *Rerum Novarum*. Work depends heavily on Mexico City newspapers.

2038 Aguirre Sánchez, Evaristo. Remembranzas de Bacubirito. Los Mochis, México: Univ. de Occidente, 1982. 172 p., 24 p. of plates: ill., ports. (Col. Crónica y relato)

Reminiscences of life in a Sinaloan town at the turn of the century. Well illustrated.

2039 Aldana Rendón, Mario A. La cuestión agraria en Jalisco durante el Porfiriato: estructura y luchas agrarias en Jalisco en el siglo XIX: documentos para la cuestión agraria. México: Centro de Estudios Históricos del Agrarismo en México (CEHAM); Guadalajara, México: Univ. de Guadalajara, 1983. 46 p.: bibl. (Col. Investigadores; 6)

Very brief review of Jalisco's agrarian situation during the Porfiriato. Addresses questions of alienation of land and its division on a geographical basis.

2040 Aldana Rendón, Mario A. Jalisco durante la República Restaurada, 1867–1877. Guadalajara, México: Instituto de Estudios Sociales, Univ. de Guadalajara, 1981–1983. 2 v.: bibl. (Col. Aportaciones)

Author attempts to place regional developments in Jalisco within the broader context of developments at the national level. Work is divided into two major sections: 1) deals with legal and political structure in the state, with emphasis on the administrations of Antonio Gómez Cuervo and Ignacio Vallarta; and 2) concerns class struggle, ideology, and education. Vol. 2 will treat the state economy.

2041 Aldana Rendón, Mario A. La rebelión agraria de Manuel Lozada, 1873. México: Fondo de Cultura Económica, 1983. 238 p.: bibl. (SEP/80; 45)

Examination of the complex framework which produced the unsuccessful agrarian revolt led by the supposed conservative, Manuel Lozada. Author describes social and economic conditions that led to the revolt, infighting among various Liberals, separatist tendencies in what will later become Nayarit, and relations between local figures and the central government.

2042 Almaraz, Félix D., Jr. Texas as a Mexican borderland: a review and appraisal of salient events (JW, 24:2, April 1985, p. 108–112)

Review of major developments in Texas as a province in the Mexican Borderlands. Based on secondary sources.

2043 Anna, Timothy E. The rule of Agustín de Iturbide: a reappraisal (JLAS, 17:1, May 1985, p. 79–119)

Revisionist review of the "black legend of Iturbide." Operating on the principle that the historiography of Iturbide was "largely partisan," author answers a series of questions as to why Iturbide became monarch, whether Iturbide's accession was legitimate, what went wrong with the monarchy, and why Iturbide abdicated.

Argüello, Silvia and **Raúl Figueroa E.** El intento de México por retener Texas. See *HLAS* 47:7115.

2044 Bastian, Jean-Pierre. Metodismo y clase obrera durante el Porfiriato (CM/HM, 33:1, julio/sept. 1983, p. 39–71, bibl.)

More ambitious than the title would suggest, this work focuses on the activities of the Missionary Society of the Methodist Episcopal Church. Author describes its establishment in Mexico, opposition it provoked, official support it received, and connection between the spread of Protestantism and Mexico's changing economy. Missionary activity was most successful in those areas being affected by the industrialization process and foreign capital.

2045 Bazant, Jan. Secuestro por infidencia, 1863–1867 (CM/HM, 32:4, abril/junio 1983, p. 554–576, bibl., table)

Author traces Juárez's policy of confiscation of property of those who supported Maximilian's empire. The policy was a direct outgrowth of the Liberal government's financial problems; when financial pressures eased after the overthrow of the Empire, Juárez replaced confiscation with a fine in 1867.

2046 Bazant, Mílada. La enseñaza agrícola en México: prioridad gubernamental e indiferencia social, 1853–1910 (CM/HM, 32:3, enero/marzo 1983, p. 349–388, bibl.)

Excellent review of efforts to develop professional agricultural education from the founding of the first National School of Agriculture in 1853 to the end of the Porfirian period. Efforts in this area peaked during the

Porfiriato with the establishment of rural primary schools, regional agricultural schools, and agricultural experimentation stations. Professional agricultural training fared better (received more money) when under the Ministry of Fomento rather than Public Instruction. The social and economic situation kept interest in such training at a low level.

2047 Bazant, Mílada. La enseñanza y la práctica de la ingeniería durante el Porfiriato (CM/HM, 33:3, enero/marzo 1984, p. 254–297, appendices)

Descriptions of changes in engineering instruction and practice during the development-oriented Porfirian period. Despite much discussion, there were only minimal changes in instruction, and technical training continued to be geared to the theoretical (French influence) rather than to practical application (the growing US influence). Engineering graduates encountered major employment problems.

2048 Beezley, William. El estilo porfiriano: deportes y diversiones de fin de siglo (CM/HM, 33:2, oct./dic. 1983, p. 265–284, bibl.)

Fascinating account of an often neglected aspect of social history—the role and symbol of sports and amusements in society. Author demonstrates that the sports and amusements of the period reflected and also influenced the Porfirian obsession with things foreign. From baseball to bicycling, the sports boom of the 1890s showed a receptiveness to foreigners and foreign influences.

2049 Benjamin, Thomas and Marcial Ocasio-Meléndez. Organizing the memory of modern Mexico: Porfirian historiography in perspective, 1880s-1980s (HAHR, 64:2, May 1984, p. 323–364)

Review and analysis of the historiography of the Porfiriato since the 1880s. There is a discussion of both individual authors and major trends in interpretation. The approach is chronological with the study divided into four periods: 1) 1876–1908; 2) 1908–40; 3) 1940–68; and 4) 1968 to present.

2050 Bermúdez, María Teresa. La docencia en oferta: anuncios periodísticos y escuelas particulares, 1857–1867 (CM/HM, 33:3, enero/marzo 1984, p. 214–253)

Fascinating insight into private education through the analysis of newspaper advertising used by private institutions. Private schools changed their advertising to reflect the rapidly-changing political situation of a chaotic period.

2051 Boils, Guillermo. Las casas campesinas en el Porfiriato. México: M. Casillas Editores: Cultura, SEP, 1982. 74 p., 1 leaf of plates: bibl., ill. (Memoria y olvido—imágenes de México; 5)

Pictorial history of rural housing during the Porfiriato aimed at counterbalancing the urban, middle and upper class bias of similar works.

2052 Bustamante, Carlos María de. Diario histórico de México. t. 3, v. 1, Enero-diciembre 1825. Nota previa y notas al texto, Manuel Calvillo. Edición de Rina Ortiz. México: SEP, INAH, 1982. 1 v.

Latest installment in Bustamante's *Diario* covers 1825. Earlier volumes covered period from Dec. 1822 to Dec. 1824.

2053 Ceballos Ramírez, Manuel. La encíclica *Rerum Novarum* y los trabajadores católicos en la Ciudad de México: 1891–1913 (CM/HM, 33:1, julio/sept. 1983, p. 3–38, appendix, bibl.)

Description of the reaction by Catholic workers to Pope Leo VIII's encyclical *Rerum Novarum*. A growing interest in social action by Catholics combined with the decline of the Porfirian economy led them to promote the creation of Catholic workers' groups, most notably the Unión Católica Obrera. Organizational impetus came primarily from lay leaders rather than the clergy.

2054 Cerutti, Mario. Guerras civiles, frontera norte y formación de capitales en México en años de la Reforma (UB/BA, 33, 1983, p. 223–237)

Somewhat unfocused description of the efforts of the northern caudillo, Santiago Vidaurri, to finance his military needs during 1858–59. Vidaurri seized federal revenues, established special customs posts along the Río Grande, issued his own tariff, and borrowed heavily from merchants in the area. Based primarily on the state archives of Nuevo León.

2055 Cortázar, Connie. The Santa Visita of Agustín Fernández de San Vicente to New Mexico, 1826 (UNM/NMHR, 59:1, Jan. 1984, p. 33–65)

Analysis of the inspection undertaken by Fernández, prebend of the cathedral at Durango and relative of President Guadalupe Victoria. Fernández had the dual mission of reforming the clergy and detecting any pro-Spanish sentiment. While he succeeded in identifying some pro-Spanish priests, he failed in his efforts to reform the clergy.

2056 18 [i.e. Dieciocho] de julio de 1872, muerte del Presidente Benito Juárez. México: Depto. del Distrito Federal, 1983. 158 p.: ill. (Col. Conciencia cívica nacional; 3)

Collection of observations occasioned by the death of Juárez spanning 1872–1972.

2057 Documentos de la relación de México con los Estados Unidos. v. 1, El mester político de Poinsett, noviembre de 1824-diciembre de 1829. Compilador, Carlos Bosch García. México: Instituto de Investigaciones Históricas, UNAM, 1983–1984. 1 v. (Serie documenta; 13)

First volume in a three-volume series covering the time span from 1824–43. Vol. 1 contains lengthy and excellent introduction to the 1824–1829 period and to the documents.

2058 Esparza, Manuel. Padrón general de los habitantes de la Ciudad de Oaxaca, 1842: 450 aniversario, 1532–1982. Oaxaca, México: Central Regional de Oaxaca, INAH, 1981. 224 p.: bibl. (Estudios de antropología e historia; 28)

Complete tax roll for all males between ages 16 and 60 required to pay a head tax in accordance with Santa Anna's decree of 7 April 1842.

2059 Foote, Cheryl J. Selected sources for the Mexican Period, 1821–1848, in New Mexico (UNM/NMHR, 59:1, Jan. 1984, p. 81–89)

Bibliography of secondary works weighted toward the American viewpoint. Contains some sources in Spanish.

2060 Francisco del Paso y Troncoso: su misión en Europa, 1892–1916. Investigación, prólogo y notas de Silvio Zavala. México: UNAM: Instituto de Estudios y Documentos Históricos, 1980. 644 p., 8 p. of plates: appendices, facsims., port. (Biblioteca del Claustro de Sor Juana. Serie Estudios; 1)

Reprint of work first published in 1938 (see *HLAS 4:3094a*).

2061 Fuentes Mares, José. Juárez, el Imperio y la República. México: Editorial Grijalbo, 1983. 357 p., 8 p. of plates: ill.

Combined reprint of author's *Juárez y el Imperio* (1963) and *Juárez y la República* (1963) (see *HLAS 26:530* and *HLAS 28:596a*).

2062 Fuentes Mares, José. Juárez, los Estados Unidos y Europa. Barcelona, Spain: Editorial Grijalbo, 1983. 402 p., 24 p. of plates: ill. (Col. Autores mexicanos)

Combined reprint of author's *Juárez y los Estados Unidos* (1960) and *Juárez y la intervención* (1962) (see *HLAS 24:3895* and *HLAS 26:531*).

2063 Gamio, Manuel. Forjando patria. Prólogo de Justino Fernández. 3a ed. México: Editorial Porrúa, 1982. 210 p., 8 leaves of plates: bibl., ill. (Sepan cuantos; 368)

Reprint of Gamio's classic work first published in 1916.

2064 García, Genaro. Tumultos y rebeliones acaecidos en México. México: Centro de Estudios Históricos del Agrarismo en México (CEHAM), 1981. 261 p. (Documentos para la historia de México)

Installment in the Centro de Estudios Históricos del Agrarismo en México's series of publications of primary documents relating to Mexico's agrarian history. This work is a reprint of vol. 10 of Genaro García's *Documentos inéditos o muy raros para la historia de México*.

2065 Garner, Paul. Federalism and caudillismo in the Mexican Revolution: the genesis of the Oaxaca Sovereignty Movement, 1915–1920 (JLAS, 17:1, May 1985, p. 111–133)

Examines the background of the Oaxaca Sovereignty Movement which he classifies as neither "reactionary" nor "revolutionary" but "federalist." This fact reflected the relationships which had developed between local caudillos as well as between the state government and the central government. Most of the emphasis is on developments during the Porfiriato rather than the post-1910 period (see also item **2144**).

2066 Gay, José Antonio. Historia de Oaxaca. Prólogo de Pedro Vásquez Colmenares. México: Editorial Porrúa, 1982. 568 p.: bibl., index (Sepan cuantos; 373)

Reprint of work first published in 1881.

2067 Gil, Carlos B. Life in provincial Mexico: national and regional history seen from Mascota, Jalisco, 1867–1972. Los Angeles: UCLA Latin American Center, 1983. 220 p.: bibl., graphs, index, tables (UCLA Latin American studies; 53)

Microhistorical study of municipio in Jalisco set against a political framework but mainly concerned with social, economic, and cultural changes. Author concludes that the Porfiriato had a greater impact than the Revolution. Surprisingly little attention to the role of religion and the Catholic Church. Based on local archival sources and interviews.

2068 González R., Blanca et al. Yucatán, peonaje y liberación. Mérida, México: Fonapas-Yucatán, Comisión Editorial del Estado, INAH, 1981. 205 p., 4 p. of plates: bibl., ill.

Collection of essays comparing and contrasting political and economic conditions in Yucatán during the Porfiriato and early years of the Revolution. As might be expected, political elites and henequen dominate the discussion.

2069 Grosso, Juan Carlos. Estructura productiva y fuerza de trabajo: Puebla, 1830–1890. Puebla, México: Centro de Investigaciones Históricas y Sociales, Instituto de Ciencias, Univ. Autónoma de Puebla, 1984. 69 p.: bibl., ill. (Cuadernos de la Casa Presno; 2)

First in a series of studies about the development of the working class in the Puebla region. Focuses on the partial mechanization of the textile industry which was traditional in the area.

2070 Hall, G. Emlen and David J. Weber. Mexican Liberals and the Pueblo Indians, 1821–1829 (UNM/NMHR, 59:1, Jan. 1984, p. 5–32)

Examination of the impact of early Liberal legislation on the communal landholdings of the Pueblo Indians. Although such legislation was aimed at breaking-up the traditional communal landholdings, the Pueblo Indians generally fought a successful legal battle to maintain their communal property. The Liberal effort had come to an end by the late 1820s, not to be revived until the 1850s when the Pueblo Indians were already under US legal jurisdiction.

2071 Hu-DeHart, Evelyn. Yaqui resistance and survival: the struggle for land and autonomy, 1821–1910. Madison: Univ. of Wisconsin Press, 1984. 293 p.: bibl., maps, tables.

Author follows-up her original study of Yaqui efforts at survival in *Missionaries, miners, and Indians* (see *HLAS 44:1956*) with this second installment of a proposed trilogy on the Yaquis. Using a mixture of accommodation, rebellion, and alliance, the Yaquis struggled amidst a complex set of politial, economic, and social problems over which they had little control.

2072 Huerta, David. Las intimidades colectivas. México: Martín Casillas Editores: Cultura, SEP, 1982. 74 p.: ill. (Col. Memoria y olvido—imágenes de México; 4)

Insight into one facet of the cultural history of Mexico at the turn of the century through "poetic postcards."

2073 Joseph, Gilbert M. From caste war to class war: the historiography of modern Yucatán, ca. 1750–1940 (HAHR, 65:1, Feb. 1985, p. 111–134)

Excellent review of recent historiography on modern Yucatán sparked by the growing interest in regional history. Author uses a Yucatecan periodization: 1) 1750–1880, the early expansion of commercial agriculture; 2) 1880–1915, the political economy of monoculture; 3) 1915–40, imported revolution and the crisis of the plantation economy. Also indicates areas of future research.

2074 Kerckvoorde, Mia. Prinses Charlotte van België, keizerin van Mexico, 1840–1927: liefde, eenzaamheid en tragiek rondom een keizerskroon. Gent, Belgium: Het Volk, 1983. 152 p.: bibl., ill.

In-depth biographical study of Empress Carlotta of Mexico, based on royal archives and private letters. Author describes Mexico's political situation leading to the execution of its Emperor Maximilian. Written in a narrative style and very well documented. [N. Vicenti]

2075 Kroeber, Clifton B. Man, land, and water: Mexico's farmlands irrigation policies, 1885–1911. Berkeley: Univ. of California Press, 1984. 288 p., 16 p. of plates: bibl., ill., maps.

Analysis of the unsuccessful Porfirian efforts to develop water and irrigation policies as well as the development projects attempted by the Dept. of Fomento in these areas. Lack of financing and an inefficient legal system undid the few efforts made by the central government to develop and implement such policies.

2076 Lapointe, Marie. Los mayas rebeldes de Yucatán. Zamora, México: Colegio de Michoacán, 1983. 258 p.: bibl., index, maps.

Examination of Mayan rebellion before, during, and after the "caste war." Author focuses on the Mayas *cruzoob*, tracing developments during 1821–1900. Examines the rebel link to British Honduras as well as the impact of the longstanding center vs. periphery conflict in Yucatán. Based on archival sources in Mexico, Belize, and England.

2077 Lecompte, Janet. Manuel Armijo, George Wilkins Kendall, and the Baca-Caballero conspiracy (UNM/NMHR, 59:1, Jan. 1984, p. 49–65)

Revisionist view of Governor Manuel Armijo and his role in the suppression of a military revolt in 1840. Author demonstrates that journalist Kendall's influential account of the affair was inaccurate and biased and that archival sources present a much more favorable view of the governor.

2078 León, Arnaldo de. They called them greasers: Anglo attitudes toward Mexicans in Texas, 1821–1900. Austin: Univ. of Texas Press, 1983. 153 p.: bibl., map.

Examination of the birth and development of Anglo racial thought about Mexicans in 19th-century Texas. Early on Anglo settlers developed a stereotypical view of Mexicans as lazy, unprogressive, immoral, and culturally inferior—an image that was later institutionalized and made part of Texas culture.

2079 León, Nicolás. Correspondencia de Nicolás León con Joaquín García Icazbalceta. Edición de Ignacio Bernal. México: UNAM, Instituto de Investigaciones Antropológicas, 1982. 314 p.: bibl. (Serie antropológica; 43)

Testimonial history of the friendship between two of Mexico's most notable bibliographers. Of historiographical interest. [A. Lavrin]

2080 La Lucha obrera en Cananea, 1906. Eugenia Meyer, coordinadora. México: Secretaría del Trabajo y Previsión Social:

Gobierno del Estado de Sonora: INAH, SEP, 1980. 132 p., 2 p. of plates: bibl., ill.

Useful compilation provides summary of the oft-treated strike of 1906 which the authors place in the regional context of the coming revolution as well as in the general development of the workers' movement. Numerous illustrations.

2081 Macune, Charles W., Jr. The impact of federalism on Mexican Church-State relations, 1824–1835: the case of the state of Mexico (AAFH/TAM, 40:4, April 1984, p. 505–529)

The on-going struggle over Church-State relations took a new turn with the creation of "states" under the federalist constitution of 1824. Author concentrates on the key state of Mexico, describing how federal-state problems influenced Church-State relations. Author concludes that the involvement of the state of Mexico in the ecclesiastical problems between the Church and the central government hindered solution of those problems and contributed to the collapse of the republic in 1835.

2082 Mentz, Brígida von. México en el siglo XIX visto por los alemanes. México: UNAM, 1982. 481 p.: bibl., ill., maps, table.

Work (focused on the 1821–61 period) is not so much a collection of travelers' impressions as a study of the impressions of Mexico conveyed to German readers. Germans received an almost stereotypical image of a Mexico that was potentially wealthy, physically beautiful, but politically unstable. Author examines the effect that this reportage had on German immigration.

2083 Mentz, Brígida von et al. Los pioneros del imperialismo alemán en México. México: Centro de Investigaciones y Estudios Superiores en Antropología Social, 1982. 522 p.: bibl., ill. (Ediciones de la Casa Chata; 14)

Collection of essays on German economic penetration of Mexico during the 19th century. Authors develop a series of topics including the German background, the nature of the German business activity, the success of these economic undertakings, and how the Germans fit into the broader Mexican society. Extensive archival research.

2084 Mertens, Hans-Günther. Wirtschaftliche und soziale Strukturen zentralmexikanischer Weizenhacienda aus dem Tal von Atlixco, 1890–1912. Wiesbaden, FRG: F. Steiner, 1983. 382 p.: tables (Beiträge zur Wirtschafts- und Sozialgeschichte; 26)

Studies in depth the economic and social structure of five wheat-producing haciendas in the Valley of Atlixco through the Porfiriato, when the country witnessed massive modernization and social change. Based on exhaustive documentation and enhanced by excellent tables, this is a major contribution. [G.M. Dorn]

2085 Mexico. Congreso Constituyente.
Diario de las sesiones del Congreso Constituyente de la Federación Mexicana: sesiones del mes de junio y julio de 1824. 2a ed. México: UNAM, Instituto de Investigaciones Jurídicas, 1981. 1 v. (various pagings) (Actas constitucionales mexicanas; 1821–1824; 10. Serie A—Fuentes, b. Textos y estudios legislativos; 51)

Vol. 10 of a monographic series issued by UNAM's Instituto de Investigaciones Jurídicas. Reprints the daily record of the June-July 1824 sessions of the Constitutional Convention of 1824 (first published in 1824). Vols. 8–9 in the series dealt with the April-May 1824 sessions.

2086 Mexico. Congreso de Chilpancingo.
Manuscrito Cárdenas: documentos del Congreso de Chilpancingo, hallados entre los papeles del caudillo José María Morelos, sorprendido por los realistas en la acción de Tlacotepec el 24 de febrero de 1814. Edición facsimilar y paleográfica con un estudio histórico y apéndice documental de Ernesto Lemoine. México: Instituto Mexicano del Seguro Social, 1980. 178 p.: appendix, ill.

Edited collection of documents found in the possession of José María Morelos when captured by royalist forces. Misleading title of collection comes from its original presentation to President Cárdenas in 1936.

2087 Miller, Simon. The Mexican hacienda between the insurgency and the Revolution: maize production and commercial triumph on the temporal (JLAS, 16:2, Nov. 1984, p. 309–336, appendix, tables)

Well organized and researched examination of the maize economy's evolution during the 19th century in *temporal* (rain-fed) areas of the central plateau. Author demonstrates how the cultivation of maize triumphed as a commercial enterprise through the phase-out of the multiple-leasing system

and its replacement by direct cultivation and widespread sharecropping. Although wage costs declined, labor inputs probably increased. This new agrarian organization peaked in the Porfiriato.

2088 Oliva Campos, Carlos. Lázaro Cárdenas y la nacionalización de la industria petrolera en México (Santiago [Univ. de Oriente, Santiago, Cuba] 49, marzo 1983, p. 19–56)

Mediocre review of the political and economic events leading up to the nationalization of the oil industry by Cárdenas in 1938. Based on secondary sources with no new insights or interpretations.

2089 Orozco Linares, Fernando. Porfirio Díaz y su tiempo. México: Panorama Editorial, 1984. 211 p.: ill.

Favorable biography of Díaz meant for general reader. Lacks references, notes, and bibliography.

2090 Other Mexicos: essays on regional Mexican history, 1876–1911. Edited by Thomas Benjamin and William McNellie. Albuquerque: Univ. of New Mexico Press, 1984. 319 p.: bibl., ill., index.

Excellent collection of essays on the Porfirian period covers general topics of regional politics, the rural economy, and social impact of political and economic development. Northern Mexico receives most of the coverage. Includes good bibliographical essay.

2091 Parcero, María de la Luz. Introducción bibliográfica a la historiografía política de México, siglos XIX y XX. México: UNAM, Facultad de Filosofía y Letras, 1982. 347 p.: bibl. (Col. Seminarios)

Useful, reference-style work on the political historiography of modern Mexico. Work is divided into three major sections: 1) historical-political process; 2) political regimes and great crises in the system; and 3) regional historical process. Much of the work is a bibliography divided along the same lines. Coverage almost completely restricted to works in Spanish.

2092 Parlee, Lorena M. The impact of United States railroad unions on organized labor and government policy in Mexico, 1880–1911 (HAHR, 64:3, Aug. 1984, p. 443–475, tables)

Examination of role of US labor unions in the Mexican railroad industry. These unions operated in Mexico, not to organize Mexican workers, but to protect US workers who were employees of Mexican railroads. The presence of US brotherhoods retarded organization of Mexican workers and led to an unlikely alliance between Mexican workers and the Díaz regime, both groups concerned about the foreign role in the industry.

2093 Pérez-Maldonado, Carlos. El segundo Imperio Mexicano: semblanza de Maximiliano y Carlota. Monterrey, México: El Autor, 1980. 82 p.: bibl., ill.

Anecdotal sketches of Maximilian and Carlotta with numerous illustrations.

2094 Randall, Robert W. Mexico's pre-revolutionary reckoning with railroads (AAFH/TAM, 42:1, July 1985, p. 1–28)

While acknowledging the value of studies dealing with the developmental impact of railroads, author is more concerned with personal adaptation to a new technology rather than the impact of the technology. He traces this national effort to "reckon with the railroads" from the original debates over the desirability and feasibility of railroads in the 1830s through the "Mexicanization" program started by Limantour in 1898.

2095 Reina, Leticia *et al.* Las luchas populares en México en el siglo XIX. México: SEP; Cultura, Centro de Investigaciones y Estudios Superiores en Antropología Social, 1983. 522 p.: bibl., chart, ill. (Cuadernos de la Casa Chata; 90)

After introductory remarks concerning methodology, authors describe various forms of popular struggle under four categories: 1) peasant, 1820–1907; 2) textile workers, 1850–1907; 3) miners, 1825–1907; and 4) railway workers, 1870–1908. Work concludes with excellent chronological chart on popular struggles (1820–1908).

2096 Rodríguez O., Jaime E. Down from colonialism: Mexico's nineteenth century crisis. Introduction by Roberto Moreno de los Arcos. Los Angeles: Chicano Studies Research Center Publications, UCLA, 1983. 46 p.: bibl., ill., map (Popular series; 3)

Continuation of the themes the author introduced with Colin MacLachlan in *The forging of the cosmic race* (see *HLAS 44:1865*). Attributes Mexico's decline "from colonial well-being to republican disaster" to economic and psychological factors, with most of the emphasis on the economic.

2097 Sánchez, Joseph P. General Mariano Arista at the Battle of Palo Alto, Texas, 1846: military realist or failure? (JW, 24:2, April 1985, p. 8–21, ill.)

Highly detailed account of the Battle of Palo Alto based on records of a military inquiry into Arista's conduct. Using archival sources, author provides good insight into the Mexican view of the struggle. The Supreme Tribunal of War later exonerated Arista, claiming that the battle was indecisive and that any American advantage was due to superior artillery.

2098 Santoni, Pedro. La policía de la Ciudad de México durante el Porfiriato: los primeros años, 1876–1884 (CM/HM, 33:1, julio/sept. 1983, p. 97–129, bibl.)

Much needed study of the Mexico City police. Author examines various measures taken in the early years of the Porfiriato to upgrade the Federal District police. While there were increases in the number of police and improvements in police organization, the force still suffered from numerous problems at the heart of which was the lax method of recruiting. Based primarily on archival sources and Mexico City newspapers.

2099 Schmitt, Karl. Church and State in Mexico: a corporatist relationship (AAFH/TAM, 40:3, Jan. 1984, p. 349–376)

While acknowledging that there have been sharp breaks in Church-State relations, author maintains that there has been continuity in the underlying relationship based on the concept of a Mexican society as a series of corporate structures regulated by the State.

2100 Schneider, Jürgen. Minería, acuñaciones y comercio exterior de México en la época de la emancipación: 1821–1850 (UEN/LS, 6, 1980, p. 241–299, graphs, tables)

Highly detailed and quantified description of Mexico's foreign trade in the early decades of independence using the production and minting of precious metals as an indicator of the development of the trade. Extensive use of graphs and charts to analyze exports, imports, and relative positions of trading partners. Author seems to have been little handicapped by the "total lack of statistical data" on Mexican trade which he cites for the 1829–56 period.

2101 Sierra Brabatta, Carlos J. 21 [i.e. Veintiuno] de marzo: relación histórica del natalicio del Presidente Juárez. México:

Depto. del Distrito Federal, 1983. 95 p.: bibl. (Col. Conciencia cívica nacional; 1)

Review of various honors bestowed upon Juárez on commemorations of his birthday. Of interest to only the most devoted juaristas.

2102 Simmons, Marc. New Mexico's Spanish exiles (UNM/NMHR, 59:1, Jan. 1984, p. 67–79)

Examination of the effects of the expulsion decrees of 1827 and 1829 on Spaniards residing in the province of New Mexico. Since there were few Spaniards living in the areas, the expulsions had limited impact; the greatest impact was on Church activities where Spaniards made up a large percentage of the clergy.

2103 Sordo Cedeño, Reynaldo. Las sociedades de socorros mutuos, 1867–1880 (CM/HM, 33:1, julio/sept. 1983, p. 72–96, bibl.)

Description of the role of mutual-aid societies with the emphasis on one such society, the "Sociedad del Ramo de Sastrería." The mutual-aid movement went through four distinct phases, beginning in 1864 and peaking in the 1872–76 period. The movement's ideology was a blend of Mexican and European influences, with the ideas of Proudhon particularly influential. Based primarily on Mexico City newspapers.

2104 Tanck de Estrada, Dorothy. Ilustración y liberalismo en el programa de educación primaria de Valentín Gómez Farías (CM/HM, 33:4, abril/junio 1984, p. 463–508, table)

Well organized and researched description of the mixed influences behind the educational reforms introduced by Gómez Farías in 1833. Author treats the Spanish and Mexican antecedents of the reform legislation which in particular reflected the Spanish legislation of 1821 and proposed Mexican legislation of 1823. Author rejects traditional interpretations that the reforms were aimed at destroying a supposed clerical monopoly on education and were inspired primarily by José María Luis Mora.

2105 Torre Villar, Ernesto de la. Testimonios históricos mexicanos en los repositorios europeos: guía para su estudio. México: UNAM: Instituto de Estudios y Documentos Históricos, 1980. 147 p.: bibl. (Biblioteca del claustro. Serie Guías; 1)

Useful guide to Mexican sources in European archives, libraries, and special collections. Most of the work deals with France and Spain.

2106 Tres aspectos de la presencia española en México durante el Porfiriato: relaciones económicas, comerciantes y población. Coordinación de Clara E. Lida. México: El Colegio de México, Centro de Estudios Históricos, 1981. 235 p., 1 folded leaf of plates: bibl., ill., index.

Three aspects examined are general economic relations between Mexico and Spain, Spanish immigration to Mexico, and Mexico City's Spanish population in the early 1880s. Trade between the two countries was quantitatively small but still important. Spanish immigration was generally geared to urban and commercial activity and brought indirect, long-term benefits to Mexico. The analysis of the Spanish population of Mexico City is heavily statistical and based on the Padrón General of 1882.

2107 Valadés, José C. Breve historia de la guerra con los Estados Unidos. 2a ed. México: Editorial Diana, 1980. 220 p.

Reprint of work originally published in 1980 (see *HLAS 44:2124*).

2108 Valadés, José C. El socialismo libertario mexicano: siglo XIX. Prólogo y recopilación de Paco Ignacio Taibo II. México: Univ. Autónoma de Sinaloa, 1984. 174 p.: bibl. (Renovación; 5)

Description of the development of labor organizations (1865–84). The organization of workers is seen as a struggle between a socialist libertarian faction—which was autonomist, federalist, and nonpolitical—against those who are attempting to subordinate the movement to the government. Author is an anarchist labor organizer; the work itelf was written in the 1920s but remained unpublished until recently.

2109 Vanderwood, Paul. El bandidaje en el siglo XIX: una forma de subsistir (CM/HM, 34:1, julio/sept. 1984, p. 41–75)

Author continues his research into law and disorder, treating both the mythic and practical aspects of banditry in 19th-century Mexico. Banditry offered the possibility of personal advancement in a society which had few legal avenues for improvement. An ineffective central government during much of the period encouraged bandits to form alliances with local caudillos, alliances which made it difficult to distinguish among bandits, soldiers, and patriots.

2110 Vázquez, Josefina Zoraida and **Lorenzo Meyer.** México frente a Estados Unidos: un ensayo histórico, 1776–1980. México: El Colegio de México, 1982. 235 p.: bibl., index (Col. México-Estados Unidos)

Two of Mexico's leading historians provide a survey history of relations between Mexico and the US from "the Mexican perspective." Basic theme is the effort of Mexico to defend itself politically, economically, and even militarily against the always more powerful US. Based mainly on secondary sources.

2111 Visión histórica de Ensenada. Coordinación de Angela Moyano de Guevara y Jorge Martínez Zepeda. Mexicali, México: Univ. Autónoma de Baja California (UABC), Centro de Investigaciones Históricas; México: UNAM, 1982.

Collection of essays provides survey history of the city of Ensenada, and to a lesser extent of Baja California, with 19th-century developments receiving the most attention.

2112 Vos, Jan de. Una legislación de graves consecuencias (CM/HM, 34:1, julio/ sept. 1984, p. 76–113, appendices, bibl., tables)

Comprehensive review of legislation and contracts relating to the survey and colonization of vacant lands from passage of the first such law in 1824 to 1910. Most of the attention is on the Porfirian period. Much of the legislation was poorly enforced, if at all, the link between surveying lands and colonizing them being often lost. Concludes that more than two-thirds of the land distributed ultimately wound up in the control of less than 300 landowners.

2113 Walker, David W. Business as usual: the *Empresa del Tabaco* in Mexico, 1837–44 (HAHR, 64:4, Nov. 1984, p. 675–705)

Examination of efforts to revive and maintain the tobacco monopoly, a colonial inheritance, during the early national period. These efforts retarded economic development, heightened political conflict, and

produced little revenue for a central government in constant financial difficulty. Any "profits" from the operation were primarily a result of misappropriation of government properties.

2114 Wasserman, Mark. Capitalists, caciques, and revolution: the native elite and foreign enterprise in Chihuahua, Mexico, 1854–1911. Chapel Hill: Univ. of North Carolina Press, 1984. 232 p.: bibl., index, map

Author examines the triangular relationship involving the regional elite, the national regime, and foreign investors in the key state of Chihuahua. While much attention is devoted to the Terrazas clan, the work skillfully connects regional history with broader themes of development, dependency, and revolution.

2115 Wasserstrom, Robert. Class and society in central Chiapas. Berkeley: Univ. of California Press, 1983. 357 p.: appendix, bibl., glossary, ill., maps.

Revisionist approach amid the growing literature on Chiapas. Author supports a regional, macro-approach as opposed to the widely-used community, micro-approach. Plays down the role of the Maya heritage in favor of the colonial and 19th-century inheritance and discounts the importance of cultural diversity.

2116 Wiemers, Eugene L., Jr. Agriculture and credit in nineteenth-century Mexico: Orizaba and Córdoba, 1822–71 (HAHR, 65:3, Aug. 1985, p. 519–546, graphs, tables)

Revisionist view of the agricultural credit situation. Using extensive archival data, author concludes that access to credit was not restricted to large landholders, that urban housing was the most important method of securing debts, that merchants were the largest source of capital with the Church playing a negligible role, that interest rates often concealed hidden interest charges, that defaults on debts were rare, and that foreclosures were unusual.

2117 Zavala, Lorenzo de. Ensayo histórico de las revoluciones de México desde 1808 hasta 1830. Estudio biográfico del autor por Alfonso Toro. 3a ed. México: Centro de Estudios Históricos del Agrarismo en México (CEHAM), 1981. 2 v.: bibl. (Col. Fuentes para la historia del agrarismo en México)

Reprint of third edition (1918) of

Zavala's classic work. Contains lengthy intro-
duction on Zavala and his works by Alfonso
Toro. Installment in the Centro de Estudios
Históricos del Agrarismo en México series.

REVOLUTION AND POST-
REVOLUTION

2118 Aboites, Luis. La Revolución Mexicana
en Espita, 1910–1940: microhistoria
de la formación del estado de la Revolución.
México: Centro de Investigaciones y Estudios
Superiores en Antropología Social, 1982. 157
p.: bibl. (Cuadernos de la Casa Chata; 62)
Study of the impact of the Revolution
on a Yucatán pueblo. Author focuses on
three processes: 1) freeing of the debt peons
in 1915; 2) activities of the Partido Socialista
del Sureste in 1917; and 3) agrarian reform of
1921. These processes brought about the virtual destruction of the local hacendado class
and began the "vertical incorporation" of
local groups into an emerging national government. Based on local, regional and national archives.

2119 El Agrarismo en Villa. Compilación de
Laura López de Lara. México: Centro
de Estudios Históricos del Agrarismo en
México (CEHAM), 1982. 187 p.: bibl. (Col.
conmemorativa; 7)
Compilation of materials focusing on
Villa's agrarian thought and action. Contains
much information of a general nature on
Villa's career. Part of the "colección con-
memorativa" series published by the Centro
de Estudios Históricos del Agrarismo en
México.

Alvarado, Salvador. El reconstrucción de
México. See *HLAS 47:6041.*

Beato, Guillermo and **Domenico Sindico.**
The beginning of industrialization in Northeast Mexico. See *HLAS 47:3139.*

2120 Beelen, George D. The Harding administration and Mexico: diplomacy by
economic persuasion (AAFH/TAM, 41:2,
Oct. 1984, p. 177–189)
Examination of background leading up
to the Bucareli agreements of 1923. Between
1921–23, the Harding administration followed a policy supported by the State Dept.
which favored oil and land interests. In 1923,
Harding switched to a more flexible approach

favored by Herbert Hoover's Dept. of Commerce aimed at promoting trade.

2121 Binford, Leigh. Political conflict and
land tenure in the Mexican isthmus
of Tehuantepec (JLAS, 17:1, May 1985,
p. 179–200)
Discussion of evolving political
struggle over land tenure centering on the
municipality of Juchitán, Oaxaca. Land tenure was not a major issue in the region until
the construction of an extensive dam and irrigation project in the late 1950s. Disagreement over land tenure finally led to the
formation of a radical local political group
which enjoyed some brief success in challenging the PRI.

2122 Brown, Jonathan C. Why foreign oil
companies shifted their production
from Mexico to Venezuela during the 1920s
(AHA/R, 90:2, April 1985, p. 362–385, ill.,
maps, tables)
Author examines but goes beyond the
traditional political explanation for the shift
(Mexico's nationalistic revolutionary reforms)
to deal with the fundamental economic reason for the transfer: Mexico's loss of competi-
tiveness in an increasingly internationalized
oil market. Based on corporate records as well
as government archives.

2123 Camp, Roderic. The political technocrat in Mexico and the survival of
the political system (LARR, 20:1, 1985,
p. 97–118, tables)
Arguing that the traditional *político*
vs. *técnico* distinction is over-simplified, author analyzes the rise and current role of
what he calls the "political technocrat."
These political technocrats now dominate
the most important federal agencies and constitute an interest group in their own right.
With growing emphasis on technology and
efficient administration, the political technocrats have grown in power and influence at
the same time that the role of the intellectuals in government has declined.

2124 Carey, James Charles. The Mexican
Revolution in Yucatán, 1915–1924.
Boulder, Colo.: Westview Press, 1984. 251 p.:
bibl., index (A Westview replica edition)
Examination of the impact of the
Revolution on Yucatán through the actions
of two principal revolutionary leaders: Sal-
vador Alvarado and Felipe Carrillo Puerto.

Opposition from the well-entrenched local oligarchy and the region's traditional separatism and isolation complicated efforts to introduce major reforms. Should be read in conjunction with Gilbert Joseph's *Revolution from without* (see *HLAS 46:2110*).

2125 Carr, Barry. Mexican communism, 1968–1981: Eurocommunism in the Americas? (JLAS, 17:1, May 1985, p. 201–228)

Examination of the transformation of the Mexican Communist Party (PCM) from the "crisis of 1968" until it ceased to exist as a separate party in 1981, when it joined other leftist parties to form PSUM (the United Socialist Party of Mexico). While the PCM did show certain characteristics of Eurocommunism, such as a more independent foreign policy viewpoint, the leaders of the PCM denied any shift toward Eurocommunism and concentrated on broadening connections with other leftist elements in Mexico.

2126 Chacón, Ramón D. Rural education reform in Yucatán: from the Porfiriato to the era of Salvador Alvarado, 1910–1918 (AAFH/TAM, 42:2, Oct. 1985, p. 207–228)

Examination of efforts to promote rural education from the closing phase of the Porfiriato when progressive planters unsuccessfully sought educational reform for reasons of self interest to the more sweeping and successful reforms under revolutionary Governor Salvador Alvarado. While Alvarado's energy and ideology hastened the creation of rural schools, part of his program's success was due to external factors: Yucatán's isolated geographic position which promoted political stability and a henequen boom which helped to finance the reforms.

2127 Chacón, Ramón D. Salvador Alvarado and the Roman Catholic Church: Church-State relations in revolutionary Yucatán, 1914–1918 (BU/JCS, 27:2, Spring 1985, p. 245–266)

Analysis of an important regional variant in the Revolution's anticlericalism. Alvarado views his anticlerical actions as an essential component in his program to revolutionize Yucatán, closing churches, confiscating religious artifacts, promoting anti-Church demonstrations, setting limits on the number of priests, and reducing the role of the Church in education. Despite the fierce

attack, the Church offered little serious resistance to Alvarado's policies.

2128 La Clase obrera en la historia de México. v. 8, En la Presidencia de Plutarco Elías Calles, 1924–1928. v. 11, Del Avilacamachismo al alemanismo, 1940–1952. Coordinador, Pablo González Casanova. México: Siglo Veintiuno Editores: Instituto de Investigaciones Sociales, UNAM, 1984. 2 v. (247, 291 p.): bibl., ill.

New volumes in the Instituto de Investigaciones Sociales (UNAM) series on the Mexican working class. The basic theme in both volumes is the changing relationship between the State and the labor movement. Vol. 8 focuses on the progressive subordination of the workers' needs to the demands of a government interested in centralizing power. While much attention is devoted to the CROM, the "labor opposition"—the CGT and the Communist Party—also receive extensive coverage. Vol. 11 views the Avila Camacho regime as a transitional period from the pro-labor Cárdenas administration to the "pro-capital" Alemán administration.

2129 Coerver, Don M. and Linda B. Hall. The Arizona-Sonora border and the Mexican Revolution, 1910–1920 (JW, 24:2, April 1985, p. 75–87, ill.)

Examination of the impact of the Mexican Revolution on the "symbiotic relationship" existing between Arizona and Sonora. There is considerable attention to military activities, especially the struggles over the key border towns of Nogales, Naco, and Agua Prieta, but Calles's actions as governor beginning in 1917 are also covered. Based on a variety of primary resources.

2130 Coerver, Don M. and Linda Hall. Texas and the Mexican Revolution: a study in state and national border policy, 1910–1920. San Antonio, Tex.: Trinity Univ. Press, 1984. 167 p.: bibl., ill., index.

Examination of the three-cornered struggle involving the US government, the Texas state government, and the various revolutionary factions in Mexico. Authors conclude that Texas had its own "foreign policy" for much of the period. Extensive use of Mexican, US, and Texas state archives.

2131 Craig, Ann L. The first agraristas: an oral history of a Mexican agrarian reform movement. Berkeley: Univ. of California Press, 1983. 312 p.: appendix, bibl., glossary, map, tables.

Examination of the role of the local peasantry as a pressure group for land reform in the municipio of Lagos de Moreno (Jalisco) in the 1920s and 1930s. Relatively isolated from the military phase of the Revolution, an agrarian movement did not develop until the 1920s and then under urban leadership and with state support. Good description of the legalities of land reform; the analysis of peasant leadership is done in the broader context of Third-World peasant movements.

2132 Cuadernos Americanos. UNAM. Vol. 263, No. 6, nov./dic. 1985–. México.

Entire volume is an *homenaje* to the influential historian-politician-economist Jesús Silva Herzog.

2133 La Cuestión de la tierra. v. 1, 1910–1911. v. 2, 1911–1913. v. 3, 1913–1914. v. 4, 1915–1917. Recopilación de Jesús Silva Herzog. México: Centro de Estudios Históricos del Agrarismo en México (CEHAM), 1981. 4 v.: forms (Col. de folletos para la historia de la Revolución Mexicana. Col. Fuentes para la historia del agrarismo en México)

Four-volume collection of the leading theoreticians of agrarian reform, covering the period from early 1910 to May 1917. Vol. 1, *1910–1911*, contains selections from eight authorities including Oscar Braniff and Andrés Molina Enríquez; vol. 2, *1911–1913*, features selections from Felipe Santibáñez and Luis Cabrera; vol. 3, *1913–1914*, has 12 selections with two offerings by Zeferino Domínguez; vol. 4, *1915–1917*, offers the views of three prominent political figures: Salvador Alvarado, Plutarco Elías Calles, and Vicente Lombardo Toledano.

2134 Las Derrotas obreras, 1946–1952. Coordinación de Víctor M. Durand Ponte. México: UNAM, Instituto de Investigaciones Sociales, 1984. 204 p.

Highly critical account of Alemán's labor and development policies. Various authors of this study accuse Alemán of implementing an interventionist and divisive labor policy aimed at subordinating the workers to the labor and governmental bureaucracies while pursuing an "imperialist" approach to economic development. Authors illustrate these contentions through case

studies of the railroad, petroleum, mining, and electrical workers.

2135 Díaz de Arce, Omar and Armando Pérez Pino. México, revolución y reforma, 1910–1940. La Habana: Editorial de Ciencias Sociales, 1982. 270 p.: bibl., ill. (Historia)

Marxist-Leninist interpretation of the internal and external forces influencing revolutionary development (1910–40) with particular emphasis on the Cárdenas administration. Authors conclude that the revolutionary dynamic led to agrarian reform, a "state capitalism" which served as a counterbalance to foreign capital, a new bourgeoisie interested in a new and more democratic form of development than traditional capitalism, and the restriction of "imperialist domination" of the economy. Authors rely primarily on secondary sources and show little familiarity with the more recent historiography of the Revolution.

2136 Díaz Soto y Gama, Antonio. La revolución agraria del Sur y Emiliano Zapata, su caudillo. México: Centro de Estudios Históricos del Agrarismo en México (CEHAM), 1983. 293 p.: bibl. (Col. conmemorativa; 12)

Reprint of 1960 edition (see also items **2139** and **2183**).

2137 Documentos para la historia del agrarismo en Michoacán. Recopilación de Arnulfo Embriz Osorio y Ricardo León García. México: Centro de Estudios Históricos del Agrarismo en México (CEHAM), 1982. 220 p.: bibl., ill., index, maps, ports. (Col. conmemorativa; 4)

Collection of documents from the 1920s relating to the agrarian movement in Michoacán. Focus is on the region of Ciénega de Zacapu and on one of the leaders of the movement, Primo Tapia, who was assassinated in 1926. There is a good general introduction as well as shorter introductions to most of the documents.

2138 Downes, E. Richard. El préstamo petrolero invisible (CM/HM, 33:2, oct./dic. 1983, p. 183–223, bibl., graph, tables)

After reviewing the attitudes of earlier administrations toward foreign investment, author demonstrates that the often-criticized Alemán followed a policy of "pragmatic nationalism," using domestic capital when possible, restricting foreign investment in certain areas that were historically controversial such as oil and railroads, and encouraging it in some areas especially manufacturing. Alemán thwarted a US effort to link a postwar loan to the return of foreign oil companies, getting instead an "invisible petroleum loan" in the form of a 150 million dollar credit from the Export-Import Bank.

2139 El Ejército campesino del Sur: ideología, organización y programa. Edición de Guadalupe Peña Roja Abraham, Laura López de Lara y Juan Márquez. México: Centro de Estudios Históricos del Agrarismo en México (CEHAM), 1982. 243 p.: bibl. (Col. conmemorativa; 5)

Documentary collection taken from the archives of Jenaro Amezcua (CONDUMEX) and Gildardo Magaña (UNAM). Collection is organized around the following topics: organization of the army, ideology, agrarian politics, economic-social program, and the death of Zapata (see also items **2136** and **2183**).

2140 Encuentro sobre Historia del Movimiento Obrero, *Puebla, México, 1978*. Memorias. v. 3. Puebla, México: Univ. Autónoma de Puebla, 1980. 1 v.: bibl., ill. (Col. Fuentes para el estudio de la historia del movimiento obrero y sindical)

Vol. 3 of the *Memorias* and pt. 2 of theme, "organizaciones y luchas obreras," the work contains 17 essays of varying length and quality covering the 1960s-70s. Most of the attention is on the automobile and metallurgical industries, but topics range from a general discussion of workers' movements to analyses of specific strikes at individual companies.

2141 El Exilio español en México, 1939– 1982. México: Salvat: Fondo de Cultura Económica, 1982. 909 p.: bibl., index.

Collection of essays by and about Spanish exiles who came to Mexico in the wake of the Spanish Civil War. Extensive section devoted to brief biographies of the exiles.

2142 Ferris, Elizabeth G. The politics of asylum: Mexico and the Central American refugees (UM/JIAS, 26:3, Aug. 1984, p. 357–384, bibl.)

Well organized analysis of Mexican policy toward the Central American refugee problem. The Mexican response has varied widely from ignoring the refugees to deporting them secretly. Recent movement is toward a more-restrictive policy. Policy variations reflect the personalist nature of Mexican politics and the declining status of the Mexican economy.

Flores Magón, Ricardo. Artículos políticos, 1910. See *HLAS 47:6061.*

2142a Flores Magón, Ricardo. 1914 [i.e. Mil novecientos catorce], la intervención americana en México. 2a ed. México: Ediciones Antorcha, 1982. 93 p.

The US intervention at Veracruz in 1914 as seen through the pages of Flores Magón's *Regeneración*.

2143 Fuentes Díaz, Vicente. Historia de la Revolución en el Estado de Guerrero. 2a ed. ampliada hasta 1920. México: Instituto Nacional de Estudios Históricos de la Revolución Mexicana, 1983. 202 p.: bibl., ill. (Biblioteca del Instituto; 95)

Revised and expanded edition which takes the revolution in Guerrero through the delahuertista rebellion of 1924.

2144 Garner, Paul. Autoritarismo revolucionario en el México provincial: el carrancismo y el gobierno preconstitucional en Oaxaca, 1915–1920 (CM/HM, 34:2, oct./dic. 1984, p. 238–299, bibl., tables)

Excellent regional study of the failure of carrancismo in Oaxaca. Author demonstrates how efforts to implement "constitucionalismo" in Oaxaca degenerated into "bureaucratic authoritarianism," caused a decline in the economy, and intensified federal-state conflict. The clash between carrancista centralism and traditional Oaxacan federalism led to the "Movement of Oaxaca Sovereignty" (see also item **2065**).

2145 González Navarro, Moisés. La Iglesia y el Estado en Jalisco en vísperas de la rebelión cristera (CM/HM, 33:2, oct./dic. 1983, p. 303–317, bibl.)

Description of the efforts by various Church members to address the problem of agrarian reform in the years immediately before the Cristero rebellion. While there was recognition of the need for agrarian reform, there was widespread opposition to the agrarian reform laws coming out of the Revolution.

2146 González Navarro, Moisés. La obra social de Lázaro Cárdenas (CM/HM, 34:2, oct./dic. 1984, p. 353–374, bibl.)
Examination of Cárdenas's "social policy." Although a broad range of topics are covered (e.g., alcoholism to social security), most of the emphasis is on labor and agrarian reform. Author sees Cárdenas as "conqueror of the hacienda" and his policy as one of "proletarian humanism."

2147 González y González, Luis. Los artífices del cardenismo. México: El Colegio de México, 1979. 273 p.: bibl., ill., index (Historia de la Revolución Mexicana; 14. Período 1934–1940)
One of four volumes in the series (14, 15, 16, 17) dealing with the Cárdenas years. Vol. 14 sets the scene for the actual Cárdenas administration, this installment ending with the presidential election of 1934. Author describes the political, social, and economic situation which Cárdenas was to inherit when he entered the presidency and provides a biographical sketch of Cárdenas to 1934.

2148 González y González, Luis. El Colegio de Michoacán (CM/HM, 32:4, abril/junio 1983, p. 577–596)
Interesting, and often amusing, chronicle of the establishment of the Colegio de Michoacán. More than the story of an educational institution with a brief history, the work offers an excellent insight into problems of decentralization in Mexico where the national capital plays such a dominant role in all activities.

2149 González y González, Luis. Los días del Presidente Cárdenas. México: El Colegio de México, 1981. 381 p.: bibl., ill., index (Historia de la Revolución Mexicana; 15. Período 1934–1940)
One of four volumes dealing with the Cárdenas years (14, 15, 16, 17). Topics examined include the Church-State conflict, labor strife, the split with Calles, and the purge of the callistas. Agrarian reform receives much attention, especially the Laguna region and Yucatán, as does the nationalization of the railroads and the oil industry. Concludes with the presidential election of 1940.

2150 Grindle, Merilee S. Rhetoric, reality, and self-sufficiency: recent initiatives in Mexican rural development (JDA, 19:2, Jan. 1985, p. 171–184, tables)
Evaluation of the Sistema Alimentario Mexicano based on its degree of success and its usefulness as a model for other Third World countries. While the SAM enjoyed short-term success in improving production, it did little to promote rural development and is of doubtful value as a model for other developing countries.

2151 Guillén, Pedro. Fabela y su tiempo: España, Cárdenas, Roosevelt. México: Centro de Estudios Históricos del Agrarismo (CEHAM), 1981. 180 p.: bibl. (Col. Fuentes para la historia del agrarismo en México)
Brief political biography of the famed statesman and collection of correspondence. Focus is on the relationship and correspondence between Fabela and Cárdenas. Part of monographic series issued by Centro de Estudios Históricos del Agrarismo (CEHAM).

2152 Gutiérrez Espíndola, José Luis. Prensa obrera, nación y democracia: crónica de la revista *Solidaridad*, 1937–1980. México: Ediciones El Caballito, 1983. 199 p.: bibl. (Col. Fragua mexicana; 55)
Slightly revised UNAM thesis in journalism and communication. Author traces the evolution (1937–80) of *Solidaridad*, the organ for the electrical workers in their various organizational forms and later for the Movimiento Sindical Revolucionario.

2153 Hall, Linda B. and Don M. Coerver. La frontera y las minas en la Revolución Mexicana, 1910–1920 (CM/HM, 32:3, enero/marzo 1983, p. 389–421, bibl., tables)
Analysis of the impact of revolutionary activity on mining in northern Mexico. Extensive foreign investment made the mines easy targets for the Revolution's anti-foreign sentiments while much of the fighting took place in areas such as Sonora and Chihuahua where mining was significant. Mining activity often shifted to the American side to avoid revolutionary problems. Post-World War I decline in the price of copper exacerbated the miners' miseries.

2154 Hall, Linda B. and Don M. Coerver. Oil and the Mexican Revolution: the southwestern connection (AAFH/TAM, 41:2, Oct. 1984, p. 229–244)
Examination of the connection between the oil industry in the US Southwest and the development of the Mexican oil industry in the first two decades of the 20th

century. Entrepreneurs, geologists, and skilled workers from Texas, Oklahoma, and California, were crucial to the rise of the Mexican oil industry which experienced rapid growth (1910–20) despite revolutionary turmoil. Oil revenues produced new personal fortunes as well as financing much of the revolutionary activity.

2155 Hamilton, Nora. The limits of State autonomy: post-revolutionary Mexico. Princeton, N.J.: Princeton Univ. Press, 1982. 391 p.: appendices, bibl., ill., maps, tables.

Revisionist view of the Cárdenas years. Author describes the problems of introducing reforms in the face of both internal and external opposition, especially the growth of elite economic power. Cárdenas is seen as primarily interested in political peace, promotion of nationalism, and the organization of a working class capable of holding its own against the revolutionary bourgeoisie.

2156 Henderson, Peter V.N. Woodrow Wilson, Victoriano Huerta, and the recognition issue in Mexico (AAFH/TAM, 41:2, Oct. 1984, p. 151–176)

After discussing the evolution of the US policy on recognition to 1913, author contrasts the "traditional" approach of Taft with the "moralistic" approach of Wilson. Wilsonian non-recognition contributed to Huerta's overthrow, but it would have even greater impact when used against other Latin American countries. Although author deals with an oft-treated topic, he provides some interesting insights and interpretations.

2157 Hernández Chávez, Alicia. La mecánica cardenista. México: El Colegio de México, 1980. 236 p.: bibl., ill., index (Historia de la Revolución Mexicana; 16. Período 1934–1940)

One of four volumes in monographic series dealing with the Cárdenas years (14, 15, 16, 17), vol. 16 has some overlap with vol. 15. Author examines Calles's decision to support Cárdenas in 1934 and devotes important chapters to the army and to the CTM, exploring how Cárdenas manipulated the army and blocked Lombardo Toledano's efforts to bring workers and peasants into one giant labor organization.

2158 Hernández Chávez, Alicia. Militares y negocios en la Revolución Mexicana

(CM/HM, 34:2, oct./dic. 1984, p. 181–212, bibl., tables)

Important preliminary study of two basic features of the early years of the Revolution: the regionalization of military power and involvement of military leaders in business activities. Author provides examples of how these leaders used their positions to engage in business operations. Much of the profits of these activities went to meet military and administrative expenses, preventing the rise of a capitalist class of "military-businessmen" (see also item **2213**).

2159 Historia documental de la Confederación de Trabajadores de México. t. 2, 1938–1939. México: Partido Revolucionario Institucional, Instituto de Capacitación Política (PRI/ICAP), 1982. 1 v.: ill., index (Serie Centrales obreras)

Vol. 2 of a documentary history of the CTM; vol. 1 covered 1936–37. Documents relate to such important developments as the expropriation of the foreign-owned oil companies, the establishment of the Party of the Mexican Revolution, the formation of the Latin American Workers' Confederation, and the presidential succession in 1940.

2160 Historia documental de la Confederación Nacional Campesina. t. 1, 1938–1942. México: Partido Revolucionario Institucional, Instituto de Capacitación Política (PRI/ICAP), 1981. 1 v.: ill., index (Serie Centrales campesinas)

Companion piece to earlier documentary works published by PRI's Instituto de Capacitación Política on the Partido Nacional Revolucionario and the Confederación de Trabajadores de México. Documentary collection begins with Cárdenas's decree of 9 July 1935 directing the establishment of the CNC and concludes with the report of Secretary General Graciano Sánchez to the second convention of the CNC in Dec. 1942. Includes lengthy introduction on the history of the relationship between the official party and the peasant movement.

Las Ideas políticas y los partidos en México: historia documental. See *HLAS 47:6070.*

2161 Jacobs, Ian. Ranchero revolt: the Mexican Revolution in Guerrero. Austin: Univ. of Texas Press, 1983. 234 p.: bibl., ill., index, maps. (Texas Pan American series)

Another important work in the growing list of regional and revisionist histories of the Revolution. Author views the Revolution in Guerrero as essentially a revolt of middle-class rancheros who were attracted by the political reforms proposed by Madero and were dismayed by the more radical variations of the Revolution, such as the one taking place in the neighboring state of Morelos. Based on local, state, and national archives.

2162 Johnson, William Weber. Heroic Mexico: the narrative history of a twentieth century revolution. Rev. ed. San Diego, Calif.: Harcourt Brace Jovanovich, 1984. 463 p.: bibl., index.

Revised—but not by much—edition of 1968 work (see *HLAS 32:1670*).

2163 Jrade, Ramon. Inquiries into the Cristero rebellion against the Mexican Revolution (LARR, 20:2, 1985, p. 53–69)

Author examines the growing literature on the Cristero movement and concludes that the vast majority of these works have certain assumptions in common but provide widely divergent interpretations that are often incompatible. These works generally view the rebellion as the culmination of a lengthy Church-State conflict and focus on the religiosity of the participants. Author suggests an alternative approach in which rural rebellion is linked to State-building efforts.

2164 Keremitsis, Dawn. Del metate al molina: la mujer mexicana de 1910 a 1940 (CM/HM, 33:2, oct./dic. 1983, p. 285–302, tables)

Examination of the impact of mechanization on the production of masa and tortillas. Mechanization led to greater involvement by male workers and a sexual division of labor, with women ending up in the lowest-paying jobs. Males dominated the better-paying production jobs while women were found mostly in sales. Growth of the industry led to government regulation, unionization, and loss of union leadership.

Keremitsis, Dawn. Latin American women workers in transition: sexual division of the labor in Mexico and Colombia in the textile industry. See item **2956.**

2165 Knight, Alan. The working class and the Mexican Revolution, c. 1900–1920 (JLAS, 16:1, May 1984, p. 51–79)

Analysis of the interaction between the working class and the Revolution. Author emphasizes that the movement was not a workers' revolution. The working class made a limited contribution to the Revolution and tended to respond to events rather than to shape them. The role of the working class was largely a function of its urban environment and its "immersion in the market."

2166 Krauze, Enrique. Caras de la historia. México: Editorial J. Mortiz, 1983. 195 p. (Cuadernos de Joaquín Mortiz)

Collection of essays dealing with a mixture of general historical problems (the utility of history, objectivity in historical writing, the individual in the historical process) and Mexican-related themes (the liberal-conservative conflict in Mexican historiography, individual studies of "cultural historians" Federico Gamboa, Julio Torri, and José Vasconcelos).

2167 Lajous, Alejandra. El PRI y sus antepasados. México: Martín Casillas Editores, 1982. 58 p.: ill. (Col. Memoria y olvido—imágenes de México; 17)

Pictorial history of the official party in its various manifestations. Text is more informative than other volumes in this series, but the captions may be better than the text.

Lindley, Richard B. Haciendas and economic development: Guadajalara, Mexico at independence. See *HLAS 47:3156.*

2168 Loyo, Engracia. Lectura para el pueblo, 1921–1940 (CM/HM, 33:3, enero/marzo 1984, p. 298–345)

Excellent chronological review of the central government's efforts to provide reading material for the general public. Such figures as José Vasconcelos and Narciso Bassols receive the expected attention, but little space is devoted to the efforts of the Cárdenas administration described as "worthy of a separate study."

2169 Machado, Manuel A., Jr. The north Mexican cattle industry, 1910–1975: ideology, conflict, and change. College Station: Texas A&M Univ. Press, 1981. 152 p., 4 leaves of plates: bibl., ill., tables.

Survey of an industry much influenced by the changing politics of revolutionary Mexico and the international character of its markets. The Revolution's military phase had a devastating effect on the cattle industry which remained in an unsettled condition until the Mexican government recognized the special situation of the northern cattle zone and a joint US-Mexican program was developed to deal with hoof-and-mouth disease.

2170 Martínez, Andrea. La intervención norteamericana, Veracruz, 1914. México: M. Casillas Editores: Cultura, SEP, 1982. 73 p.: ill., index (Col. Memoria y olvido—imágenes de México; 11)

Pictorial history of the US occupation of Veracruz in 1914. Excellent illustrations, mediocre narrative.

2171 Martínez, Oscar Jáquez. Fragments of the Mexican Revolution: personal accounts from the border. Albuquerque: Univ. of New Mexico Press, 1983. 316 p., 34 p. of plates: bibl., ill., map.

Oral history from a variety of sources on the impact of the Revolution on the border. Includes interviews and acccounts of participants in the fighting, border residents, and both Mexican and non-Mexican victims of the Revolution.

2172 Matute, Alvaro. La carrera del caudillo. México: El Colegio de México, 1980. 201 p.: bibl., ill., index (Historia de la Revolución Mexicana; 8. Período 1917–1924)

One of three volumes in the series dedicated to the 1917–24 period. Vol. 8 covers 1919–20, centering on the presidential campaign of 1920. Author describes the emerging alliances that would provide the foundation for the first Obregón regime and depicts Adolfo de la Huerta as a talented politician in his own right.

2173 Medin, Tzvi. El minimato presidencial: historia política del maximato, 1928–1935. México: Ediciones Era, 1982. 176 p.: bibl.

Analysis of methods and mechanisms by which Calles retained power (1928–34). Much of the attention is on Ortiz Rubio who is credited with breaking the political mechanism which permitted the maximato although not actually breaking Calles's grip on power.

2174 Medina, Luis. Civilismo y modernización del autoritarismo. México: El Colegio de México, 1979. 205 p.: bibl., ill., index (Historia de la Revolución Mexicana; 20. Período 1940–1952)

Analysis of domestic politics of the Avila Camacho and Alemán administrations. Basic themes are the subordination of the military and the consolidation of "presidentialism." The power of the federal government expands at the expense of the state and local governments while the president expands his control over the federal government and the official party.

2175 Meyer, Jean A.; Enrique Krauze; and Cayetano Reyes. Estado y sociedad con Calles. México: El Colegio de México, 1977. 371 p.: bibl., ill., index (Historia de la Revolución Mexicana; 11. Período 1924–1928)

One of two volumes in the series devoted to the Calles administration, characterized as a "presidency at war." There is considerable attention to foreign relations, especially with the US. Also covers internal relations with labor, the peasants, and the army, with authors downplaying the role played by Amaro in taming the revolutionary army. Calles's economic policy is seen as promoting capitalism and foreign penetration.

2176 Meyer, Lorenzo. La Revolución Mexicana y las potencias anglosajonas (CM/HM, 34:2, oct./dic. 1984, p. 300–352, bibl.)

Analysis of the interplay among Mexico, the US and Great Britain during the Calles administration. As the "spirit of Bucareli" disappeared, relations between Mexico and the US worsened in 1925, while those with Britain improved leading to formal diplomatic recognition. The moderate British approach was eventually adopted by the US government under pressure from US bankers, leading to the dispatch of Morrow as ambassador.

2177 Miller, Barbara. The role of women in the Mexican Cristero rebellion: las señoras y las religiosas (AAFH/TAM, 40:3, Jan. 1984, p. 303–323)

Author sympathetically examines the role of women—both lay and religious—in the Cristero revolt. Efforts to organize Catholic women had started in the 1920s before the conflict. Most women served in "passive" roles—teaching, nursing, cooking—and returned to their traditional conservative patterns once the fighting had ended.

2178 Moch, Mariana. Mariana de la Revolución. México: L. Boro Editor, 1982. 94 p.

Reminiscences of the Revolution as seen by a child growing up in Mexico City.

2179 Módena, María Eugenia. Pasaporte de culturas: viaje por la vida de un judío ruso en México. México: INAH, 1982. 109 p.: bibl., ill. (Estudios étnicos. Col. científica; 123. Etnología)

Narrowly focused study of Jewish immigration during the 20th century based on interviews and archival sources.

2180 Mumme, Steven P. The Cananea copper controversy: lessons for environmental diplomacy (IAMEA, 38 : 1, Summer 1984, p. 3–22)

Examination of the dependency vs. interdependency debate in US-Mexico relations using the case study of the project to upgrade and expand the Compañía Minera de Cananea's sagging smelter in Sonora. The project provoked a confrontation of interests between a transnational and a US domestic alliance. Author concludes that resolution of the case indicates that a situation of "complex interdependency" exists, at least in environmental issues.

2181 Newell G., Roberto and **Luis Rubio F.** Mexico's dilemma: the political origins of economic crisis. Boulder, Colo.: Westview Press, 1984. 319 p.: appendix, bibl., graphs, tables.

Description of the evolution of a political-economic consensus which provided for political stability and economic development. Authors maintain that the consensus has disappeared as new groups have arisen who are not part of the consensus.

Noticia para la bibliografía anarquista en México. See *HLAS* 47 : 41.

2182 Palabras del exilio. v. 1, Contribución a la historia de los refugiados españoles en México. México: INAH: Librería Madero, 1980. 1 v.: bibl., col. ill, index (Archivo de la Palabra de INAH)

Vol. 1 of INAH's project on Spanish exiles. After a general description of political conditions in Spain and Mexico in the 1930s, the work concentrates on an interview with José Puche Alvarez, prominent exile who held a number of positions in the Spanish Republican government (for vol. 2 of this series, see item **2193**).

2183 Palacios, Porfirio. Emiliano Zapata: datos biográficos e históricos. México: Centro de Estudios Históricos del Agrarismo en México (CEHAM), 1982. 230 p.: bibl. (Col. Investigadores; 4)

Reprint of 1960 edition (see *HLAS* 24 : 3954 and item **2136**).

2184 Primer reparto de tierras del constitucionalismo: Lucio Blanco. México: Centro de Estudios Históricos del Agrarismo en México (CEHAM), 1982. 71 p.: bibl., ill. (Col. conmemorativa; 10)

Collection of 24 documents relating to the political and military career of one of the early proponents of agrarian reform. Introduction provides brief biography of Blanco.

2185 El Proyecto agrario en Vázquez Pallares. México: Centro de Estudios Históricos del Agrarismo en México (CEHAM), 1983. 126 p. (Col. conmemorativa)

Homenaje to the founder and director of the Centro de Estudios Históricos del Agrarismo en México. Contains lengthy section by Vázquez Pallares on agrarianism as well as the expected observations by his friends and associates.

2186 Raat, W. Dirk. La revolución global de México (CM/HM, 32 : 3, enero/marzo 1983, p. 422–448)

The "global revolution" is the growing international interest among professional historians outside of Mexico and the US in the Mexican Revolution. Author focuses on the development of Mexican revolutionary studies since 1960 in both Japan and Europe, with the UK and Germany leading the way.

2187 Reed, John. Villa y la Revolución Mexicana. Reed en México. Edición de Jorge Ruffinelli. México: Editorial Nueva Imagen, 1983. 214 p.: bibl. (Serie Testimonios)

First section of work deals with Reed's life as writer and political activist; second is a collection of Reed's writings on Mexico which did not appear in his classic, *Insurgent Mexico* (see also item **2208**).

2188 Richmond, Douglas W. Confrontation and reconciliation: Mexicans and Spaniards during the Mexican Revolution, 1910–1920 (AAFH/TAM, 41 : 2, Oct. 1984, p. 215–228)

Description of changing relations between Mexicans and Spaniards resident in Mexico, with most of the emphasis on the policies of Carranza. In the early years of the Revolution, the expression of anti-Spanish feelings were permitted. Later, for practical reasons and especially for military considerations, Carranza followed a conciliatory policy toward resident Spaniards and toward Spain.

2189 Richmond, Douglas W. Venustiano Carranza's nationalist struggle, 1893–1920. Lincoln: Univ. of Nebraska Press, 1983. 317 p., 8 p. of plates: bibl., ill., index.

Revisionist, and controversial, analysis of Carranza and his policies. Author stresses Carranza's role as nationalist, reformer, and populist. While a strong case is made for Carranza's nationalism, his commitment to reform and his position as a populist figure are debatable. Well researched study uses extensive archival and printed primary sources.

2190 Robles Gómez, Jorge Alfredo. Huelga tranviaria y motín popular, julio de 1911. Toluca, México: Univ. Autónoma del Estado de México, 1981. 86 p.: bibl., ill. (Col. Lecturas críticas; 2)

Brief chronicle of unsuccessful streetcar workers' strike in Mexico City (July 1911). Based on newspaper accounts (see also item **2191**).

2191 Rodríguez, Miguel. Los tranviarios y el anarquismo en México, 1920–1925. Puebla, México: Centro de Estudios Contemporáneos, Editorial Univ. Autónoma de Puebla, 1980. 261 p.: bibl., ill. (Biblioteca Francisco Javier Clavijero. Serie mayor. Col. Estudios contemporáneos)

With considerable background information on political, social, and economic developments, author traces efforts of streetcar workers to organize for both labor and political purposes. Workers started out as "pillars of anarchosyndicalism" but were progressively neutralized and brought into the emerging official political structure through the CROM-Obregón-Calles connection (see also item **2190**).

2192 Rubín, Ramón. Pedro Zamora: la Revolución sin mística: historia de un violador. Guadalajara, México: Editorial Hexágono, 1983. 186 p.: ill.

Undocumented and anecdotal account of activities of Jaliscan figure described by author as "a guerrilla not a revolutionary." Originally appeared as series of articles in the Guadalajara newspaper, *El Informador.*

2193 Ruiz Funes, Concepción and **Enriqueta Tuñón.** Final y comienzo, el *Sinaia:* Departamento de Estudios Contemporáneos del INAH. México: INAH, SEP: Librería Madero, 1982. 209 p.: 32 p. of plates: bibl., ill. (Palabras del exilio; 2)

Vol. 2 of INAH's project on the history of Spanish refugees in Mexico. Consists of a chronicle of the crossing of the first Spanish refugees on the ship *Sinaia*. Based on a blend of personal interviews, newspaper accounts, and documentary sources. Numerous illustrations, charts, and tables (for vol. 1 of this series, see item **2182**).

2194 Salehizadeh, Mehdi and **Jorge Garza-Adame.** Mexican protectionist policies and their implications for the computer industry (IAMEA, 38 : 1, Summer 1984, p. 85–101, tables)

Review of Mexico's protectionist policies since World War II leading to a discussion of their impact on the computer industry. Most of the emphasis is on policies rather than the computer industry. Somewhat dated by the rapidly changing Mexican economic situation, including the recent IBM decision and Mexico's negotiations to join GATT.

2195 Sandos, James A. Northern separatism during the Mexican Revolution: an inquiry into the role of drug trafficking, 1910–1920 (AAFH/TAM, 41 : 2, Oct. 1984, p. 191–214)

Fascinating study of the role of vice, especially the drug trade, in financing the Revolution and permitting northern separatism. While most of the author's conclusions are speculative, they provide an interesting starting point for additional research. For a related study, see *HLAS 44:2260.*

2196 Schmitt, Karl. Church and State in Mexico: a corporatist relationship (AAFH/TAM, 40 : 3, Jan. 1984, p. 349–376)

While acknowledging that there have been sharp breaks in Church-State relations, author maintains that there has been continuity in their underlying relationship, one based on the concept of a Mexican society as a series of corporate structures regulated by the State.

2197 Silva Herzog, Jesús. Colección *Cuadernos Americanos*: comprensión y crítica de la historia. Mexico: Editorial Nueva Imagen, 1982. 533 p.

Collection of essays which originally appeared in *Cuadernos Americanos* which the author edited for many years. Influential observations on the course of the Revolution by a figure who was important in both describing and determining the Revolution's course.

2198 Sloan, John W. The Mexican variant of corporatism (IAMEA, 38:4, Spring 1985, p. 3–18)

After discussing and defining Latin American corporatism, author examines its most successful variant, Mexico. Differentiating between exclusionary corporatism and inclusionary corporatism, he places Mexico in the latter category. The PRI and the President are at the heart of the corporate structure, demonstrating a flexibility and legitimacy denied most corporate regimes. Familiar territory but a good summary nonetheless.

2199 Smith, Peter H. US-Mexican relations: the 1980s and beyond (UM/JIAS, 27:1, Feb. 1985, p. 91–101, bibl.)

Middle of the road analysis of future US-Mexican relations based on some historical characteristics of the relationship. Author foresees a declining role for bilateral government bargaining and a growing regional role for Mexico as a "newly industrializing country." Concludes that US policymakers would be happiest with a maintenance of the current political system in Mexico.

2200 Story, Dale. Policy cycles in Mexican presidential politics (LARR, 20:3, 1985, p. 139–161, tables)

Using the 1934–82 period, author quantitively analyzes three popular hypotheses about policy cycles in Mexican presidential politics: initial innovations by new administrations, the "pendulum effect," and policy cycles relating to the budget within *sexenios*. Concludes that the first and third hypotheses are valid but that the pendulum effect was not confirmed by his examination.

2201 Strauss Neuman, Martha. El reconocimiento de Alvaro Obregón: opinión americana y propaganda mexicana, 1921–1923. México: UNAM, Facultad de Filosofía y Letras, 1983. 128 p.: bibl. (Seminarios)

Well researched and organized description of the struggle over the recognition of the Obregón regime. US interest groups opposing recognition—especially oil interests—were better organized and financed than those favoring recognition. Initial Mexican propaganda efforts aimed at achieving recognition failed, but recognition was finally extended, primarily because of the economic benefits realized by certain interest groups. Based on archival sources in both the US and Mexico.

2202 Tamayo, Jaime. El movimiento agrario y la revolución maderista, Jalisco, 1910–1913: el movimiento agrario y la Revolución Mexicana; dos momentos cruciales en Jalisco. México: Centro de Estudios Históricos del Agrarismo en México (CEHAM), 1983. 103 p.: bibl. (Col. Investigadores; 7)

One of four volumes from the Centro de Estudios Históricos del Agrarismo en México (CEHAM) dealing with Jalisco's agrarian history. Work tries to counterbalance the "northern bias" and "centralist treatment" of the Revolution's agrarian history by examining the political, economic, social, and geographic factors influencing the agrarian movement in Jalisco during the early years of the Revolution.

2203 Tamayo, Jaime and **Laura Romero.** La rebelión estradista y el movimiento campesino, 1923–1924. México: Centro de Estudios Históricos del Agrarismo en México (CEHAM), 1983. 72 p.: bibl. (Col. Investigadores; 8)

Brief description of unsuccessful revolt led by Gen. Enrique Estrada in conjunction with the larger de la Huerta rebellion of 1923–24. Estrada withdrew recognition from Obregón but did not formally support de la Huerta for the presidency.

2204 Tannenbaum, Frank. Mexico, the struggle for peace and bread. Westport, Conn.: Greenwood Press, 1984. 293 p., 1 folded leaf of plates: index, map.

Reprint of author's classic work first published in 1960 (see *HLAS 16:1013, HLAS 16:1810, HLAS 17:860* and *HLAS 17:948*).

2205 Taracena, Alfonso. José Vasconcelos. México: Editorial Porrúa, 1982. 154 p., 10 leaves of plates: ill., ports. (Sepan cuantos; 386)

Long-time observer and prolific historian of the Revolution provides a stimulating biography of his friend and colleague. Lacks citations and bibliography.

2206 Torres Ramírez, Blanca. México en la Segunda Guerra Mundial. México: El Colegio de México, 1979. 380 p.: bibl., ill., index (Historia de la Revolución Mexicana; 19. Período 1940–1952)

One of four volumes in monographic series devoted to the 1940–52 period. While basically an examination of relations between the US and Mexico within a dependency context, the work is more an analysis of the rationale for Mexican policy. Much attention to foreign and domestic economic activities. Critical of Avila Camacho as being too willing to serve US needs.

2207 Torres Septien, Valentina. Algunos aspectos de las escuelas particulares en el siglo XX (CM/HM, 33:3, enero/marzo 1984, p. 346–377, tables)

Primary focus of work is on Church affiliated-schools (1920–70). Author's conclusions are interesting but hardly surprising; schools studied tend to be elitist or selective, superior to public schools in terms of quality, traditional in their methodology, conservative in their textbooks, and primarily in urban areas.

2208 Tuck, Jim. Pancho Villa and John Reed: two faces of romantic revolution. Tucson: Univ. of Arizona Press, 1984. 252 p.: bibl., ill.

Comparative study of two figures which the author considers as symbols of the romantic tradition in revolution. The fact that the lives of the two actually intersected and that one wrote about the other makes for more than the usual parallel study. Frequently anecdotal and somewhat controversial in its evaluation of leading figures such as Orozco, Huerta, Obregón, and Carranza (see also item **2187**).

2209 Tuñón Pablos, Esperanza. Huerta y el movimiento obrero. México: Ediciones El Caballito, 1982. 116, 2 p.: bibl. (Col. Fragua mexicana; 46)

Author rejects "official historiography" of the Huerta regime, maintaining that Huerta recognized the importance of securing labor support, implemented the most

progressive labor policy (1910–17), and even served as a model for the "collaborationist" approach of later administrations.

2210 Vasconcelos, José. Ulises criollo. La tormenta. México: Fondo de Cultura Económica, 1982. 965 p. (Letras mexicanas. Memorias; 1)

Reprint of 1936 editions (see *HLAS 1:1075*, *HLAS 2:2120* and *HLAS 3:2604–2605*).

Vaughan, Mary K. The State, education, and social class in Mexico, 1880–1928. See *HLAS 47:4475*.

2211 Vela González, Francisco. Diario de la Revolución. t. 2, Enero/octubre de 1914. Monterrey, México: Patronato Universitario de Nuevo León, 1983. 1 v.: bibl. (Serie Historia; 2)

Vol. 2 of proposed three presents daily chronology of revolutionary events from Jan. to Oct. 1914 (vol. 1 covered Feb.-Dec. 1913; see *HLAS 36:2160*).

2212 Velasco-S., Jesús-Agustín. Impacts of Mexican oil policy on economic and political development. Lexington, Mass.: Lexington Books, 1983. 237 p.: bibl., index, tables.

Examination of Mexico's energy policy and its effect on economic and political developments. While author—an advisor to the Mexican government—provides good descriptions of official policies and valuable figures on oil activities, his comparisons between Mexican situation and Iran under the Shah and his laudatory attitude toward José López Portillo as a protector of the interests of the poor are likely to strike readers as ill conceived, if not downright ludicrous.

2213 Werner Tobler, Hans. La burguesía revolucionaria en México: su origen y su papel, 1915–1935 (CM/HM, 34:2, oct./dic. 1984, p. 213–237, bibl.)

Study of the rise of a new revolutionary bourgeoisie and its connection to the new revolutionary ruling elite. Author uses case studies from the Sonoran group (Obregón, Calles, Hill, Rodríguez, and Sáenz) and concludes that the Porfirian upper class essentially survived the Revolution intact and later merged with the new revolutionary bourgeoisie (see also item **2158**).

CENTRAL AMERICA

MURDO J. MACLEOD, *Graduate Research, Professor of History, University of Florida*

POLITICAL STRIFE, CIVIL WARS, and social revolution continue to be leading factors influencing general tendencies in the historical literature of Central America. As a result, trends noted in *HLAS 46* have continued. General research, and especially research on the colonial period, has declined, and the number of works produced in these catogories has fallen off noticeably. Studies of the period since independence, however, have kept up the increased rate noted two years ago.

There are still studies of more traditional themes: the heroes of the wars of independence and of the various civil wars; the presidential acts, accomplishments, and speeches of this or that general or lawyer; the attitudes of the Panamanian elites towards Colombia in the the late 19th century; the Costa Rican civil war of 1948 and its results; and the US-inspired overthrow of President Arbenz of Guatemala in 1954, to name only some of these hardy but somewhat windblown perennials, all continue to receive attention.

The more pointed work, however, is increasing in quantity. Central Americans, and now noticeably North Americans, are searching fairly systematically to discover the historical roots of several modern predicaments. The Nicaraguans—when they take time off from writing about Sandino—are still reevaluating and recasting their history in terms of the new insights provided by the revolution (items **2263** and **2303**). Salvadorans are examining the roles of the military (item **2268**) and the massacres of 1833 and 1932 (items **2274** and **2275**) as clues to the origins of their civil war. Hondurans, fearing US domination and an increase in the militarization of their nation, look for the roots of their national weakness (items **2264, 2272,** and **2293**).

Scholars from the US have been more concerned, logically enough, with the role of outside agents, especially the US, in creating these and other national crises. The books by Conniff on West Indians in Panama (item **2218**); by Dozier on Nicaragua's unique Mosquito Shore, so much influenced by British and US presence (item **2220**); by LaFeber on the US's misguided role in creating the conditions for "inevitable revolutions" (item **2290**); and by Leonard on another variation on the same theme (item **2292**), are all well researched, thorough contributions.

Considerable contributions have been made even on the declining categories mentioned above. Scholars of the colonial centuries who have produced research of the highest quality are: Langenberg on Guatemala City (item **2237**); Lovell on the Cuchumatán Highlands (item **2238**); and Zamora on the 16th-century demographic disaster (item **2252**).

Once again, however, it is the Central American scholars who should be commended above all. That so many of them, working in a wretched research and writing environment, under the most depressing and difficult circumstances, should continue to produce useful and even excellent work, is at once encouraging and inspiring.

GENERAL

2214 Alvarado, Gregorio. San Agustín Acasaguastlán: un pueblo en marcha con un pasado histórico prodigioso y un futuro devenir de muy interesantes perspectivas. Guatemala: EDE, 1982. 141 p.: bibl.

Brief history of village in El Progreso

dept. on the Caribbean slope. Among subjects discussed are its role in the independence movement, cholera epidemic, and various military campaigns and bandit raids which affected this ladino settlement.

2215 Anuario de Estudios Centro-americanos: Historia, Sociedad, Conocimiento. Univ. de Costa Rica, Depto. de Publicaciones. Vol. 10, 1984–. San José.

Important Costa Rican journal continues to maintain its high standards. Historical articles by Rodrigo Quesada, Arturo Taracena, Juan Carlos Solórzano, and Yamileth González cover, in order, Honduran foreign relations, workers confederations in Central America, hacienda and ladinos in Guatemala in the 18th century, and food production in colonial Costa Rica.

2216 Blanco Segura, Ricardo. Historia eclesiástica de Costa Rica: del descubrimiento a la erección de la diócesis, 1502–1850. 2a ed. San José: Editorial Univ. Estatal a Distancia, 1983. 401 p., 19 leaves of plates: bibl., ill., index, map, ports.

First published serially in Costa Rica's *Revista de Archivos Nacionales* (1960), this important but poorly documented Church history appeared in book form in 1967, and is now reissued, without revision or bibliographical updating.

2217 Blanco Segura, Ricardo. 1884 [i.e. Mil ochocientos ochenta y cuatro]: el Estado, la Iglesia y las reformas liberales. San José: Editorial Costa Rica, 1984. 370 p.: bibl., ill., ports.

Study of the Church-State conflict in Costa Rica, which, in 1884, led to the expulsion of the Jesuits and of Archbishop Bernardo Augusto Thiel. Includes most useful chapters on background matters such as the Jesuits in colonial Spanish America, freemasonry in Costa Rica, and intellectual origins of 19th-century Liberalism in Central America.

2218 Conniff, Michael L. Black labor on a white canal: Panama, 1904–1981. Pittsburgh, Pa.: Univ. of Pittsburgh Press, 1985. 221 p.: bibl., ill., index (Pitt Latin American series)

Well written analysis of the role of black West Indians in Panama, beginning before the construction of the Canal, intensifying as some 100,000 people were imported (1904–14) for canal work, and emphasizing

their long struggle against discrimination from both North Americans and Panamanians. West Indians and their descendants, "have been pawns in the long struggle between the United States and Panama . . ." (p. 175), but the process of integration and acceptance has now begun, and Conniff is cautiously optimistic that, with the Panama Canal Treaty out of the way, it will continue.

2219 Conte Porras, Jorge and **Enoch Castillero Calvo.** Santa Ana. Edición oficial, conmemorativa del octogésimo aniversario de la fundación del Banco Nacional de Panamá, 1904–1984. Panamá: Banco Nacional de Panamá, 1984. 158 p.: bibl., ill. (some col.) (Boletín cultural. Biblioteca José Agustín Arango Ch.; 9)

Detailed, illustrated, and affectionate study of the Panamanian barrio of Santa Ana which co-authors hope will evoke the social and political life of urban Panama, especially the 19th-century period when it was part of Colombia. A book of considerable charm.

2220 Dozier, Craig Lanier. Nicaragua's Mosquito shore: the years of British and American presence. University: Univ. of Alabama Press, 1985. 269 p.: bibl., ill., index.

Narrative history of Nicaragua's Mosquito Shore from 16th century to present blends new evidence from British and US diplomatic archives, and accounts by contemporaries, with secondary works. Told from a regional perspective emphasizing the commercial activities of British and Americans in the 19th and 20th centuries. Illustrates weak links of region to the nation. Explores familiar themes of Mosquitia's geographic and cultural isolation. Despite interest by Anglos in its potential as a trans-isthmian route and by the Sandinistas in incorporating it into the nation, the Mosquito Shore's high rainfall and poor soils have hindered efforts to make it economically profitable for export or staple crop production. Well written descriptive synthesis by geographer whose examination of the links between entrepreneurial activities, geopolitical rivalries, and ecological considerations is enhanced by the use of photographs and first-hand accounts.

García Mainieri, Norma. Situación archivística actual en Guatemala. See *HLAS* 47:73.

2221 González García, Yamileth. Desintegración de bienes de cofradías y de fondos píos en Costa Rica, 1805–1845 (CIRMA/M, 5:8, dic. 1984, p. 279–303, tables)

Among factors leading to changes in land tenure structure were attacks on *cofradía* funds and *fondos píos*. As the elites took over many expropriated estates, they laid a base for a future coffee boom.

Gudmundson, Lowell. Estratificación socioracial y económica de Costa Rica, 1700–1850. See *HLAS 47:6130*.

2222 Mejía, Medardo. Historia de Honduras. v. 1. Tegucigalpa: Univ. Nacional Autónoma de Honduras, Editorial Universitaria, 1983. 1 v.: bibl. (Col. Realidad nacional; 8)

General outline, admittedly no more than a survey, this history is projected to encompass five volumes. Vol. 1 covers preconquest period, conquest, colonial centuries, and independence movements.

2223 *Mesoamérica*. Centro de Investigaciones Regionales de Mesoamérica. No. Especial: Honduras, Vol. 6, No. 9, junio 1985-. Antigua, Guatemala.

Special issue devoted to the social sciences and Honduras. Of interest to historians are: Linda Newson on colonial demographics, Gloria Lara Pinto on the culture of the Indians of Comayagua and Sulaco, and William V. Davidson on the Jicaques in the 18th century.

2224 Murphy, James S. Belize at two: keeping its appointments with history (BISRA/BS, 12:1/2, 1984, p. 1–38, appendix, bibl., map)

Recapitulation of the Guatemalan-British dispute over Belize, succinctly and clearly done, with many quotations from appropriate documents.

2225 Pinto Soria, Julio César. Raíces históricas del Estado en Centro América. Guatemala: Editorial Universitaria de Guatemala, 1980. 83 p.: bibl., (Col. Textos; 9)

Author looks for the social and above all economic origins of various Central American states, especially Guatemala, by means of a brief but well documented examination of the colonial period. He contrasts the commercial and administrative capital, Guatemala City, with productive areas such as the indigo zone of El Salvador, and finds, in such contrasts, a main factor in the elite

Creole quarrels of the 19th century, and a cause of the disintegration of the Central American state shortly after independence. Thoughtful and useful study which deserves to be better known.

2226 Prado, Eladio. La Orden Franciscana. Fotografías de 1893, Karla Fernández. 2a ed. San José: Editorial Costa Rica, 1983. 451 p.: bibl., ill. (some col.), ports.

Second edition of traditional history of the Catholic Church, and especially of the Franciscan order, in Costa Rica, from the conquest until the 1920s. From published sources, but comprehensive and informative.

2227 Rubio Sánchez, Manuel. Historia del cultivo de la morera de China y de la industria del gusano de seda en Guatemala. Guatemala: Academia de Geografía e Historia de Guatemala, 1984. 189 p.: bibl., ill. (Publicaciones especial; 28)

Prolific Guatemalan economic historian examines his country's ultimately unsuccessful attempt to establish a silk industry. Introduced in 1797 and again in 1816, silkworms aroused no interest. Finally, in 1836, the priest Juan José Aycinena sent silkworm eggs to his brothers in Guatemala, and by 1839, this elite family had 30,000 bushes. Within six years the mini-boom was over. Lack of expertise, disease in the silkworms, and the growing success of new coffee plantations, killed the infant industry.

2228 Sosa, Juan Bautista and **Enrique J. Arce.** Compendio de historia de Panamá. Edición facsímil de la de 1911 con un estudio preliminar de Carlos Manuel Gasteazoro. Panamá: Editorial Universitaria, 1977. 322 p.: bibl., ill. (Editorial universitaria: Sección Historia: Serie Información general)

Facsimile of the 1911 edition, also published in 1934. Main asset is an excellent introduction (104 p.) to the work by Carlos Manuel Gasteazoro, which places the writers and their times into context with a thoroughly documented study.

2229 Terga, Ricardo. El valle bañado por el Río de Plata: un estudio etnohistórico de los pueblos del Valle Medio del Motagua, desde Morazán hasta Gualán. Guatemala: Tipografía Nacional, 1982. 110 p.: bibl., ill.

New edition of brief and general ethnohistory written by priest who has lived in the central Motagua Valley and Verapaz.

Covers period from 1530 to early 19th-century disappearance of Indian communities. Pt. 1 is ethnographic review; pt. 2 studies process of hispanization and colonization. General thesis is that area is now Hispanic, and dominated by an archaic Spanish culture. Mostly based on standard published sources but also includes some archival research and personal interviews.

2230 Vidal, Manuel. Nociones de historia de Centro América, especial para El Salvador. 10a ed. San Salvador: Ministerio de Educación, Dirección de Publicaciones, 1982. 486 p.: bibl. (Col. Historia; 2)

Tenth edition of standard, elementary text.

2231 Vos, Jan de. La paz de Dios y del Rey: la conquista de la selva lacandona, 1525–1821. México: Fonapas Chiapas, 1980. 521 p.: bibl., maps (Col. Ceiba; 10)

Careful traditional history, beginning with the state of the area before the arrival of Europeans, continuing with early attempts to conquer it, the 100 years of neglect in the 17th century, the conquest of 1695, the decline of the Lacandones, and their partial ethnic and cultural revival recently. Book contains full and useful scholarly apparatus.

COLONIAL

Argueta, Mario R. Guía para el investigador de la historia colonial hondureña: un ensayo temático bibliográfico. See *HLAS* 47:77.

Castillero Calvo, Alfredo. América hispana: aproximaciones a la historia económica. See item **1812.**

2232 Cruz Reyes, Víctor C. Epidemias del siglo XIX en Honduras (CIRMA/M, 6:10, dic. 1985, p. 371–390, table)

Smallpox and cholera were the most frequent epidemics in 19th-century Honduras. Author discusses these diseases, their relationship to the frequent civil wars and times of scarcity, the remarkable spirit of cohesion displayed by many communities, and public health measures taken against these plagues.

2233 Documentos: historia de Honduras. Compilador, Mario Felipe Martínez. Tegucigalpa: Editorial Universitaria, 1983. 1 v. (Col. Documentos; 1)

Consists of variety of colonial primary sources, mostly from Seville's Archive of the Indies, with a few 18th-century documents from Comayagua's ecclesiastical archives. The sources cover many important topics, but their great variety and the compilation's disorganized sequence make them hard to use.

2234 Estudios del Reino de Guatemala: homenaje al profesor S.D. Markman. Editor, Duncan Kinkead. Durham, N.C.: Duke Univ.; Sevilla, Spain: Escuela de Estudios Hispano Americanos, 1985. 201 p., 7 p. of plates: bibl., ill. (Publicaciones; 309)

Articles on colonial Central America by Francisco de Solano, Jorge E. Hardoy, Lawrence H. Feldman, Thomas A. Lee, Jr., David Jickling, Murdo J. MacLeod, Ralph Lee Woodward, Jr., Jorge Luján Muñoz, Carroll Edward Mace, and Antonio Bonet. Introduction discussing Markman's work is by José Antonio Calderón Quijano.

2235 Fonseca Corrales, Elizabeth. Reflexiones en torno a la noción de estructura agraria: su aplicación a la historia colonial del Valle Central de Costa Rica (UNCR/R, No. especial: Simposio: Historia, Problemas y Perspectiva Agraria en Costa Rica, 1985, p. 13–31, bibl.)

Between 1569–1691 a system based on Indian labor and land seizure dominated. Overexploitation of Indian labor was a major cause of population decline, the destruction of this vital element being the main contradiction within the system. This systematic failure led to a new system in the late 17th century, which was flourishing by 1750, one of small holders, family work forces, and subsistence agriculture.

2236 Guzmán Navarro, Arturo. La trata esclavista en el Istmo de Panamá durante el siglo XVIII. Panamá: Editorial Universitaria, 1982 [i.e., 1983]. 7–201 p.: bibl., ill., maps (Sección Historia. Serie Monografía)

Thorough survey of official Panamanian slave imports in the 18th century. Author deals consecutively with the background to this slave trade; French domination (1700–13); the English Asiento and South Sea Company; individual asientos between (1748–66); the Cádiz Company monopoly (1768–77); era of limited free trade; and decadence of the slave trade in the last days of the colonial period. Substantial contribution.

2237 Langenberg, Inge. Urbanisation und Bevölkerungsstruktur der Stadt Guatemala in der ausgehenden Kolonialzeit: eine sozialhistorische Analyse der Stadtverlegung und ihrer Auswirkungen auf die demographische, berufliche, und soziale Gliederung der Bevölkerung (1773–1824). Köln, FRG: Böhlau, 1981. 468 p., 13 leaves of plates: bibl., ill., maps (Lateinamerikanische Forschungen; 9)

Detailed impressive study of the city of Guatemala in the last colonial half century (1773–1824). Langenberg begins with the spatial dimensions and internal layout of the city, then turns to a complex, valuable demographic profile of the inhabitants, continues with a study of ownership and occupations, and concludes with a socioeconomic description which includes corporate, ethnic, and economic status, and social mobility. Very valuable model urban history.

2238 Lovell, William George. Conquest and survival in colonial Guatemala: a historical geography of the Cuchumatán highlands, 1500–1821. Kingston: McGill-Queen's Univ. Press, 1985. 254 p.: bibl., maps.

Outstanding regional study in historical geography. Malthusian in emphasis, the work has new material on the epidemiological shock which resulted from the invasion of the New World by the Old. An interesting case study of the effects of colonialism in an imperial backwater. Excellent notes and bibliography.

Lovell, William George. Landholding in Spanish Central America: patterns of ownership and activity in the Cuchumatán highlands of Guatemala, 1563–1821. See *HLAS 47:5070.*

Lovell, William George. Settlement change in Spanish America: the dynamics of *congregación* in the Cuchumatán highlands of Guatemala, 1541–1821. See *HLAS 47:5071.*

Lovell, William George. To submit and to serve: forced native labor in the Cuchumatán highlands of Guatemala, 1525–1821. See *HLAS 47:5072.*

2239 Luján Muñoz, Jorge. Cambios en la estructura familiar de los indígenas pokomames de Petapa, Guatemala, en la primera mitad del siglo XVI (CIRMA/M, 6:10, dic. 1985, p. 355–370)

By 1562 the preconquest extended

family was destroyed in this village and region. Otherwise little of the disintegration caused elsewhere by economic exploitation, epidemics, and other factors affected Petapa. Interesting case study which will encourage comparative regional enquiry.

2240 Luján Muñoz, Jorge. Los escribanos en las Indias Occidentales. 3a ed. México: UNAM: Instituto de Estudios y Documentos Históricos, 1982. 312 p., 15 p. of plates: bibl., ill. (Serie Estudios; 6)

Current 1982 edition (for 1977 ed., see *HLAS 44:2336*) represents extended coverage in its treatment of scribes in colonial Guatemala. Overall, the works are important legal discourses on the origins of various categories of scribes and their assigned duties in the colonial bureaucracy. Final chapter comments on notarial documents as sources of historical investigation. [D.E. Chipman]

2241 MacLeod, Murdo J. An exorcism in colonial Chiapas: its religious and political meaning (*in* Rocky Mountain Council on Latin American Studies Meeting, Las Cruces, N.M., 1985. Proceedings. Edited by María Telles-McGeagh and Garth M. Hansen. Las Cruces: Center for Latin American Studies, New Mexico State Univ., 1985, p. 20–25)

In 1712 this event had a didactic purpose: it introduced new forms of worship to the local Indian population, and later helped Spaniards rationalize the causes of the 1712 revolt.

2242 MacLeod, Murdo J. Los indígenas de Guatemala en los siglos XVI y XVII: tamaño de la población, recursos y organización de la mano de obra (*in* Población y mano de obra en América Latina. Compilación de Nicolás Sánchez-Albornoz. Madrid: Alianza Editorial, 1985, p. 53–67)

Describes connections between population movements and migrations, the size of labor force, and major categories of work and productivity in colonial Guatemala.

2243 MacLeod, Murdo J. La situación legal de los indios en América Central durante la colonia: teoría y práctica (III/AI, 45:3, julio/sept. 1985, p. 485–504)

Ignored by the imperial government, open frontiers and persistent regionalism led to inconsistent enforcement of colonial laws, and local idiosyncrasies and abuses. Some Indians discovered that the worst effects could be moderated in at least some cases by astute interpretation of the law.

2244 Mencos Franco, Agustín and Carlos Martínez Durán. Estudios históricos sobre Centro América: guerras contra los ingleses y administración de Don Matías de Gálvez. Guatemala: Editorial José de Pineda Ibarra, 1982. 119 p: bibl., ill. (Biblioteca guatemalteca de cultura popular, 15 de septiembre: 113)

Brief accounts of the life of Captain General of Guatemala, later Viceroy of Mexico, Matías de Gálvez, of the seizure of the castle of Omoa by the English, and their attempt to capture a Nicaraguan trans-isthmian route. These events were followed by Gálvez's recapture of the castle and of the island of Roatán.

2245 Pérez Estrada, Francisco. Panorama de la Nicaragua pre-colonial: sector del Pácifico. Managua: Ministerio de Educación, 1982. 109 p.: bibl., ill.

Even Nicaragua's preconquest history, the prologue claims, must be rewritten from a revolutionary perspective. The text is largely composed of extracts from the writings of Gonzalo Fernández de Oviedo, and the interpretations given to these exerpts are *indigenista* and anti-Spanish.

2246 Polo Sifontes, Francis. Nuevos pueblos de indios fundados en la periferia de la Ciudad de Guatemala, 1776–1879. Guatemala: Editorial José de Pineda Ibarra, 1982. 183 p., 8 leaves of plates (some folded): appendix, bibl., ill. (Biblioteca guatemalteca de cultura popular, 15 de septiembre; 112)

When Santiago de Guatemala (now Antigua) was destroyed by an earthquake in 1776, the authorities decided, after bitter debate, to build a new city, Nueva Guatemala de la Asunción, in the Valle de la Ermita. To build and maintain this new city, groups of local Indians were uprooted from their home villages and resettled near the new city. Both the Indians and the Church opposed these forced migrations, and they were never fully completed as planned. More than half the book consists of a very valuable documentary appendix.

2247 Ramos Pérez, Demetrio. Vasco Núñez de Balboa y su "roldanismo" renovado: el proceso de imposición del Extremeño de los Dos Océanos (LNB/L, 346/347, enero/feb. 1985, p. 16–30)

Author uses the case of Balboa to show how and why conquistador captains were removed or elected by their own men.

2248 Reina Valenzuela, José. Historia eclesiástica de Honduras. t. 1, 1502–1600. Tegucigalpa: Tipografía Nacional, 1983. 1 v.: bibl.

Narrative history based on published sources, of the first century of Church activity in colonial Honduras. Standard fare.

2249 Relaciones geográficas del siglo XVI. v. 1, Guatemala. Edición de René Acuña. México: UNAM, Instituto de Investigaciones Antropológicas, 1982. 1 v.: bibl., ill., index (Serie antropológica; 45. Etnohistoria)

Thanks to René Acuña's careful transcription and editing, we have at last a reliable and complete published version of the two 16th-century *relaciones geográficas* on Guatemala: 1) on Zapotitlán (dated 1579); and 2) five documents and map of Santiago Atitlán and its *anexos* (dated 1585). Acuña fleshes out the volume with the following 16th-century accounts: 1) well known letter from *caciques* and *principales* of Santiago Atitlán (1571); *Relación del Obispado de Guatemala* (1572), so entitled by Acuña; three fairly well known *relaciones* on Verapaz (1574, 1575, and 1575?); Diego García de Palacio's *Letter to the King* (1576); and Juan de Pineda's overblown and unreliable 1590s *Avisos* (plus two *anexos*) on the province of Guatemala. Large and reliable corpus of important 16th-century general descriptions all in one volume.

2250 Sanabria Martínez, Víctor. Reseña histórica de la Iglesia en Costa Rica desde 1502 hasta 1850. San José: Depto. Ecuménico de Investigaciones, 1984. 290 p.: bibl.

Traditional, thorough, colonial Church history by cleric emphasizes Franciscans, *visitas* by Nicaraguan bishops, missions to Talamanca and other "unreduced" areas, and the growth of the Costa Rican secular clergy in the 18th century. Draws evidence from familiar published sources.

2251 Taracena Arriola, Arturo. La expedición científica al Reino de Guatemala. Guatemala: Editorial Universitaria de Guatemala, 1983. 153 p.: bibl. (Col. Editorial Universitaria; 63)

Solid history of the Guatemalan part of the Real Expedición Botánica to New Spain (1787–1803). The two scientists, José

Mariano Moziño and José Longinos Martínez, studied matters such as vulcanism, indigo, nitrate deposits, and flora and fauna including the Quetzal.

2252 Zamora, Elías. Conquista y crisis demográfica: la población indígena del occidente de Guatemala en el siglo XVI (CIRMA/M, 4:6, dic. 1983, p. 291–328, graphs, tables)

In a careful review, largely based on research in primary documents, this author elects a middle course between proponents of high and low losses during the demographic collapse of the indigenous population after the Spanish conquest.

2253 Zúñiga C., Edgar. Historia eclesiástica de Nicaragua. v. 1, La cristiandad colonial, 1524–1821. Managua: Editorial Unión, 1982. 1 v.: bibl., index.

Strictly narrative and institutional Church history covers the colonial period. Contains valuable, if sometimes uncritical, biographies of colonial bishops. Promises additional volumes on the national period.

NATIONAL

2254 Acuña Ortega, Víctor Hugo. Clases sociales y conflictos sociales en la economía cafelatera costarricense: productores contra beneficiadores, 1932–1936 (UNCR/R, No. especial: Simposio: Historia, Problemas y Perspectiva Agraria en Costa Rica, 1985, p. 181–205)

This era produced more social conflict than popular myth would propose, and a democracy or near democracy came into existence in spite of exploitation, and, in part, as a result of, not in spite of, class struggles.

2255 Alfaro, Ricardo Joaquín. Esbozos biográficos. Prólogo de Rodrigo Miró. Panamá: Academia Panameña de la Historia, 1982. 159 p.

Panama's Academy of History commemorates the birth centennial of Alfaro by republishing pt. 1 of his well-known biographical sketches of famous fellow countrymen. Briefly discusses 26 Panamanians. Useful as an almanac for 19th- and 20th-century history.

2256 Alvarado Rubio, Mario. Recuento de una polémica: Pellecer-Alvarado, Arévalo-Alvarado, el asesinato del Coronel Arana. Guatemala: IMPREX, 1983. 175 p.

More on an assassination (1949) that has never been fully explained. An avowed *aranista*, author accuses Jacobo Arbenz, Arana's rival for the presidency, of complicity in the murder, and claims that President Arévalo refused to intervene in the gathering crisis, gradually shifting his support from Arana to Arbenz, and failing to pursue vigorously the subsequent investigations. Author published Arévalo's rejoinders, and the tone, while highly polemical, remains polite and reasonable on both sides.

2257 Aranda Barrantes, Jesús. Los excombatientes de 1948–55: ensayo sobre la Guerra Civil, Costa Rica. San José: Unión Grafiset, 1984. 50 p.: ill.

Essay on the Costa Rican civil war which makes a strong effort to reconcile opponents on both sides. Begins with the fraudulent presidential elections of 1944, discusses the fighting in 1948 and the invasion of 1955, and finishes by presenting two narrative accounts from ordinary participants in these events.

2258 Arellano, Jorge Eduardo. Lecciones de Sandino. 2a ed., aum. Managua: Ediciones Distribuidora Cultural, 1983. 127 p.

Prolific writer publishes second expanded edition of his selections from Sandino's writings and speeches. Matters discussed include guerrilla warfare, anti-imperialism, nationalism, the Nicaraguan Atlantic coast, and the need to raise educational levels.

2259 Arévalo Martínez, Rafael. Ecce Pericles: la tiranía de Manuel Estrada Cabrera en Guatemala. 3a ed. San José: Editorial Universitaria Centroamericana, 1983. 794 p. (Col. Séptimo día)

Reissue of the famous novelist's long and somewhat overdrawn picture of the dictatorship of President Manuel Estrada Cabrera of Guatemala.

2260 Arosemena, Justo. Justo Arosemena, patria y federación. Compilación y prólogo de Nils Castro. La Habana: Casa de las Américas, 1977. 485 p.: bibl. (Col. Pensamiento de nuestra América)

Writings of 19th-century pan-Latin American nationalist, who has enjoyed something of a revival in recent years (this compilation published in 1977). Perhaps one of the most modern of the early 19th-century writers in his concerns. Includes his essays on political and moral philosophy, speech against US expansionism, two essays on his outline proposals for a Latin American League or Treaty, and his reflections on early relations between Colombia and Panama.

2261 El Asalto a San Carlos: testimonios de Solentiname: entrevistas a Nubia Aracia *et al.* Managua: Asociación para el Desarrollo Soletiname, 1982. 129 p.: ill.

Interviews with members of the Solentiname Christian community who survived their attack on the Somoza National Guard barracks in San Carlos (Oct. 13, 1977).

2262 Blen, Adolfo. Historia del periodismo. San José: Editorial Costa Rica, 1983. 200 p.: bibl.

Brief basic essays on all newspapers, many ephemeral, published in Costa Rica (1833–76). Some are discussed in fair detail; others seem to merit a few lines of text. Useful compendium for students of political and intellectual history in 19th-century Costa Rica.

2263 Bolaños, Pío. Génesis de la intervención norteamericana en Nicaragua. Managua: Editorial Nueva Nicaragua, 1984. 101 p. (Col. Quinto aniversario)

Seeks to demonstrate that the pro-US and financially corrupt governments—the so-called Conservative restoration—following the overthrow of José Santos Zelaya, especially that of President Adolfo Díaz, prepared the way for US intervention.

2264 Boletín de la Defensa Nacional. Director, Froylán Turcios. Tegucigalpa: Editorial Guaymuras, 1980. 225 p.: bibl. (Col. Talanquera. Documentos y testimonios)

Consists of series of protests published in Honduras vs. the marines' invasion of Tegucigalpa in 1924. Selected from a periodical of the same title published by leading Honduran man of letters at that time. Also includes some interesting documents by Isidro Fabela and others on US intervention in Nicaragua.

2265 Borge, Tomás. Carlos, the dawn is no longer beyond our reach: the prison journals of Tomás Borge remembering Carlos Fonseca, founder of the FSLN. Vancouver, Canada: New Star Books, 1984. 96 p.: appendix, ill.

Elegy, written in prison, about the life and thoughts of one of three founders of the FSLN, killed before the revolution came to power. Includes useful appendix and chronology of Fonseca's life.

2266 Calderón Artieda, Leonor and **Esilda Méndez Robles.** Formación del "Estado" panameño (CSUCA/ESC, 18, sept./dic. 1977, p. 65–74)

Analysis centers on Panama's secession from Colombia, specifically on the 1902 Spooner Bill, the 1903 Declaration of Independence Act and the Hay-Buneau-Varilla Treaty, the 1904 Constitution, and the US Executive Order on the Canal Zone, issued the same year. [A. Ugalde]

2267 Calvo Gamboa, Carlos. León Cortés y su época. San José: Editorial Univ. Estatal a Distancia, 1982. 224 p.: bibl., ill., ports.

Biography of right-wing, authoritarian, Costa Rican president (1936–40), accused of being an anti-semite and a Hitler follower by some, and praised for sound administration and electoral reform by others. He opposed the regimes of Calderón and Picado, and may have been responsible for fraud in the elections of 1944.

2268 Castro Morán, Mariano. Función política del ejército salvadoreño en el presente siglo. San Salvador: Universitaria Centroamericana Editores, 1984. 455 p.: bibl., ill. (Col. Premio nacional. Serie Ensayo; 1)

Military man tries to analyze the armed forces' role in the last 80 plus years of Salvadoran history, hoping that such an analysis will lead to a better understanding of the present crisis and civil war, and how to escape from it. Argues that in the 19th century the army was clearly liberal and reformist, but that in the 20th century it became uncertain and divided, now repressive, now trying to listen to the voice of the people, and thus lost direction. Believes that the army must turn more to fighting internal enemies such as hunger, poverty, and exploitation, and forget some of its more traditional roles such as guarding the frontier. Book contains confused but interesting discussion of an important topic.

2269 Cerutti, Franco. Los Jesuitas en Nicaragua en el siglo XIX. San José: Libro Libre, 1984. 663 p.: appendix, bibl. (Serie histórica)

After a brief visit in 1853, the Jesuit order was readmitted to Nicaragua in 1871, and after a troubled decade of recriminations, accusations, and bitter debate, they were again expelled from the country in 1881. Text is thoroughly footnoted and includes documentation (260 p.) in the lengthy appendix. Thorough job on a minor topic.

2270 Chamorro, Emiliano. El último caudillo: autobiografía. Managua: Ediciones del Partido Conservador Demócrata, 1983. 446 p., 16 p. of plates: ill., ports.

Conservative general, leading opponent of President José Santos Zelaya, the signatory of the Bryan-Chamorro Treaty (which he later sought to amend), President of Nicaragua, and opponent of the Somoza dictatorship, writes a self-justifying autobiography, followed by a touching epilogue by his widow.

2271 Chamorro, Pedro Joaquín. La patria de Pedro: el pensamiento nicaragüense de Pedro Joaquín Chamorro. Managua: *La Prensa*, 1981. 253 p., 12 p. of plates: ill.

Writings and actions of the editor of *La Prensa* and noted anti-Somoza leader, murdered in 1978.

2272 Cruz, Ramón E. La lucha política de 1954 y la ruptura del orden constitucional. Tegucigalpa: Univ. Nacional Autónoma de Honduras, Editorial Universitaria, 1982. 39 p. (Col. Cuadernos universitarios; 28)

Detailed narrative by even-handed Liberal describes the strike and political struggles of 1954 in Honduras.

2273 Cuevas, Alexander. El movimiento inquilinario de 1925. Panamá: Centro de Estudios Latinoamericanos Justo Arosemena, 1980. 24 p.: bibl., ill. (Cuadernos populares; 15)

Story of the 1925 rent riots in Panama City and Colón led by the Liga de Inquilinos. Apparently sensing that it was losing control, the Panamanian government requested help from US troops which occupied Panama City.

2274 Dalton, Roque. Miguel Mármol: los sucesos de 1932 en El Salvador. La Habana: Casa de las Américas, 1983. 267 p. (Col. Nuestros países. Serie Estudios)

First-person, eyewitness account by a Communist of events that led to the anti-Communist and anti-peasant massacres of 1932 in El Salvador by the forces of Gen.

Maximiliano Hernández Martínez. An artisan, Mármol was tortured, survived an execution badly wounded, and witnessed the deaths of many of his comrades. Although simple and full of slang and localisms, the writing is very forceful and effective.

2275 Domínguez Sosa, Julio Alberto. Las tribus nonualcas y su caudillo Anastasio Aquino. San José: Editorial Universitario Centroamericana (EDUCA), 1984. 276 p.: bibl.

Anastasio Aquino led the Nonualcas Indians of El Salvador in an unsuccessful revolt in 1833. The combination of different provinces isolated after independence, their hostility to Guatemala City, traditionalist-liberal rivalries within the confederation, and a deepening economic crisis which antedated independence created anarchy and pressure of various kinds on Indian communities. In fact, independence hurt the Indians by removing the little paternalist protection provided by the Crown. Thus Aquino led the Indians in a race and class war to free them from the exploitation and oppression. Well argued and documented study.

El Salvador, la larga marcha de un pueblo, 1932–82: selección de artículos y entrevistas extraídos de diversos revistas y documentos. See *HLAS 47:6150.*

2276 Escobar Bethancourt, Rómulo. Torrijos, espada y pensamiento. Panamá: Impresora de La Nación, 1982. 122 p.: facsims., maps.

Essays by one of his appointees praising the actions and ideas of the late Panamanian strongman.

2277 Facio, Rodrigo. Obras históricas, políticas y poéticas. Selección y prólogo de Federico Vargas Peralta. San José: Editorial Costa Rica, 1982. 538 p.: bibl. (Obras de Rodrigo Facio; 4)

Vol. 4 of his complete works, this one contains most of his historical, political, and poetical writings. His liberalism, constitutional concerns, interest in Central American union, and university reform, are all thoroughly discussed.

2278 Fallas Monge, Carlos Luis. El movimiento obrero en Costa Rica, 1830–1902. San José: Editorial Univ. Estatal a Distancia, 1983. 438 p.: bibl.

History of the origins of the Costa Rican labor movement. Covers artisan guilds, mutual benefit societies, first small industrial conflicts, workers' role in 19th-century politics, and concludes with the profound economic crisis of the 1890s. It led to the disappearance of many labor organizations, founding of others, and to a new and more active social role on the part of the Church. Complete and important study that integrates such little known agents as imported West Indian workers and strike by Italian immigrants. Ch. 7 consists of important collection of labor laws.

2279 Figueroa Marroquín, Horacio. Biografía del Doctor José Luna Arbizú. Guatemala: Tipografía Nacional, 1983. 148 p.: bibl., facsims., ill., ports. (Col. Guatemala; 7. Serie David Vela; 1)

Biography of important 19th-century Guatemalan physician. Educated in Paris, he played a leading role during the Guatemala cholera epidemics of 1837 and 1857, introducing anasthesia in 1847 and advocating universal smallpox vaccination.

Flores Macal, Mario. Origen, desarrollo y crisis de las formas de dominación en El Salvador. See *HLAS 47:6151*.

2280 Foladori, Guillermo; Charles Hale; and **Edmundo Gordon.** Demografía costeña: notas sobre la historia demográfica y población actual de los grupos étnicos de la costa atlántica nicaragüense. Managua: Centro de Investigaciones y Documentación de la Costa Atlántica, 1982. 58 p., 7 folded leaves of plates: bibl., maps.

Demographic history and survey of the mestizos, Miskitos, Black Caribs, Afro-Creoles, Sumus and Ramas of the Nicaraguan Atlantic coast. The coastal population is much higher than assumed, partly because of undercounting and partly because of the advance of the agricultural frontier. More than half of the inhabitants are mestizo agriculturalists. The agricultural frontier may have reached its eastern limits because of land occupancy and claims by other ethnic groups and the unsuitability of remaining lands.

Gorman, Stephen M. Social change and political revolution: the case of Nicaragua. See *HLAS 47:6190*.

2281 Greene, Graham. Getting to know the general: the story of an involvement. New York: Simon & Schuster, 1984. 249 p.

Account of Greene's visits to Panama under the aegis of Gen. and President Torrijos (1976–80). Greene's view of his friend is almost adulatory but also reveals the personalistic, whimsical, wasteful, disorganized nature of Torrijos and his regime, one that was sincerely patriotic but essentially too incoherent to formulate consistent policies or carry them out over the long haul.

Gudmundson, Lowell. Costa Rica before coffee: occupational distribution, wealth inequality and elite society in the village economy of the 1840s. See *HLAS 47:8127*.

Gudmundson, Lowell. Peasant movements and the transition to agrarian capitalism: freeholding versus hacienda peasantries and agrarian reform in Guanacaste, Costa Rica, 1880–1935. See *HLAS 47:3226*.

Guidos Véjar, Rafael. Ascenso del militarismo en El Salvador. See *HLAS 47:6152*.

2282 Heroísmo de Juan Santamaría: batalla del 11 de abril de 1856, Alajuela, Costa Rica. Recopilación de la Comisión de Investigación Histórica de la Campaña de 1856–1857. San José: Instituto del Libro, Ministerio de Cultura, Juventud y Deportes, 1984. 50 p.: ill. (Serie Rescate; 20)

Documentary collection presents the story of a simple soldier who died like a hero in Rivas, Nicaragua, fighting in the Costa Rican army against William Walker's invading forces (April 11, 1856).

2283 Herrera, Francisco. Los cunas ante la independencia de 1903 (LNB/L, 344/345, nov./dic. 1984, p. 101–109)

After Panama's "independence" from Colombia in 1903, it appeared that some Cuna would have preferred Colombia. The US was concerned because of its preoccupation with the security of a future canal and the Panamanians because of the Cuna's proximity to the Colombian border. Wary of all involved, the Cuna kept to themselves.

2284 Hilje Quirós, Brunilda. Apropiación y distribución de la tierra en Tiralan: 1880–1943 (UNCR/R, No. especial: Simposio: Historia, Problemas y Perspectiva Agraria en Costa Rica, 1985, p. 161–175)

Describes three stages area went through in land tenure and distribution: 1) early one of spare settlement; 2) pioneer settlement; and 3) concentration in few hands as commercial agriculture developed.

Agrarian reformism had little impact on this process.

2285 Instituto de Estudio del Sandinismo.
La insurrección popular sandinista en Masaya. Managua: Editorial Nueva Nicaragua, 1982. 214 p.: bibl., ill. (Col. Tercer aniversario)

Another account of the Sandinista revolt in Masaya (Feb. 1978). Graphic descriptions of the destruction caused by the bombardments of Somoza's National Guard, and of the heroism of local people.

2287 Instituto de Estudio del Sandinismo.
Porque viven siempre entre nosotros: héroes y mártires de la insurrección popular Sandinista en Masaya. Managua: Editorial Nueva Imagen, 1982. 270 p.: facsims., ill., ports. (Col. Tercer aniversario)

Consists of biographies of heroes of national independence from Masaya from Gen. Benjamín Zeledón in 1912 through those killed in the final Sandinista offensive against Somoza.

2288 Instituto de Estudio del Sandinismo.
¡Y se armó la runga!: testimonios de la insurrección popular Sandinista en Masaya. Managua: Editorial Nueva Nicaragua, 1982. 430 p., 15 leaves of plates: ill. (Col. Tercer aniversario)

Story of the anti-Somoza struggle and uprising in Masaya told, in large part, by eyewitnesses and participants. Well illustrated.

2289 Knapp, Herbert. Red, white, and blue paradise: the American Canal Zone in Panama. San Diego, Calif.: Harcourt Brace Jovanovich, 1984. 306 p.: bibl., index.

Colorful, personal view of the history of the Zone, and a fervent, bitter, often emotional justification of its existence, by ex-Zonians.

2290 LaFeber, Walter. Inevitable revolutions: the United States in Central America. New York: Norton, 1983. 357 p.: bibl., index, maps.

Author argues that repression and inequality in the distribution of wealth inevitably breed revolution. US policies of capitalist penetration and military security have so pervasively integrated the Central American region to the US political and economic system and prevented equitable economic development, that the US bears direct responsibility for fomenting the very revolu-

tions it has not been willing to tolerate historically. Although neither author's thesis nor its dependency framework are original, his skillful blending of diplomatic, political, and economic history (based on US sources) makes this an incisive analytical synthesis of the region's recent history. Combining a chronological and country-by-country approach, LaFeber describes how the US established and maintained a system of economic and military pressure to dominate the area. This is labeled neodependency because it is fueled not only by reliance on economic power to make Central American development dependent on US interests, but also by a tendency, less frequently exercised in the rest of Latin America, to use military force to ensure that control. For political scientist's comment, see *HLAS 47:6111.*

2291 Lagos, Agustín. Los pioneros: conversaciones con Doña Rosario S. de Ferrari. Tegucigalpa: s.n., 1983 or 1984. 306 p., 26 p. of plates: bibl., ill.

Conversations with the widow of the pioneer of Honduran radio broadcasting.

2292 Leonard, Thomas M. The United States and Central America, 1944–1949: perceptions of political dynamics. University: Univ. of Alabama Press, 1984. 215 p.: bibl., index.

Following the Good Neighbor era, US policymakers failed to grasp Central America's internal political dynamics, and thus could not pursue a constructive foreign policy in the region. According to this country-by-country analysis, based on an examination of reports by field representatives and State Dept. officials (1944–49), policymakers did not understand the socioeconomic goals of an amorphous middle sector pressing for an end to government by elites. Author argues that Cold War blinkers prevented these officials from supporting proponents of economic modernization and democratic reform, a familiar argument but presented here in more detailed political context. Missing is a precise definition of social categories and an analysis of economic conditions, both of which are necessary to sustain the "middle sector" thesis.

2293 Luque, Chalo. Las revoluciones en Honduras. San Pedro Sula, Honduras: El Autor, 1982. 222 p.: ill. (Memorias de un soldado hondureño; 2)

Vol. 2 of a soldier's unadorned, narrative recollections of military campaigns in Honduras (1932–50). Includes interesting historical details but has little grasp of a larger picture. Shows clearly how such upheavals were dominated by purely personal ambitions, lacked discernible ideological content despite much sloganeering, and were senselessly destructive.

MacCameron, Robert. Bananas, labor and politics in Honduras, 1954–1963. See *HLAS 47:6172.*

2294 Meléndez, Carlos. Juan Santamaría: una aproximación crítica y documental. Alajuela, Costa Rica.: Museo Histórico Cultural Juan Santamaría, 1982. 149 p.: appendix, bibl.

Another study of the humble hero of the Battle of Rivas (April 11, 1856) against Walker's invading filibusters. Provides study of the battle, Santamaría's part in it, extended discussion of the man's positive and negative historical treatment, and bibliography and chronology of his life. Includes valuable documentary appendix and photocopies of important original documents.

2295 Mensajes presidenciales. t. 1, Años 1824–1859. t. 2, Años 1859–1885. t. 3, Años 1855–1906. Compilador, Carlos Meléndez Chaverri. San José: Biblioteca de la Academia de Geografía e Historia de Costa Rica, 1981. 3 v.: bibl.

Consists mostly of presidential messages to congress, national assemblies, and legislatures, a few inaugural and farewell addresses, proclamations, and manifestoes. Valuable for scholars interested in political history, governmental policies, and changing ideologies.

2296 Montúfar y Rivera Maestre, Lorenzo. Francisco Morazán. Prólogo de Rafael Montúfar. 2a ed. San José: Editorial Universitaria Centroamericana, 1982. 196 p. (Col. Rueda del tiempo)

Reasoned but partisan defense of Francisco Morazán, one of the heroes of Central American unity, against various accusations and rumors. Also published in 1982 by Guatemala's Editorial José de Pineda Ibarra.

2297 Morales Henríquez, Viktor. De Mrs. Hanna a la Dinorah: principio y fin de la dictadura somocista; historia de medio siglo de corrupción. S.l.: s.n., 1980? 98 p.: ill.

Describes alleged and presumably some well documented vagaries in the sexual lives of the male Somozas, especially the last of the dynasty. Much of the writing has a strangely puritanical flavor, and its circumlocutions and moralizing are often coy and prurient.

Morris, James A. Honduras: caudillo politics and military rulers. See *HLAS 47:6174.*

2298 Munro, Dana Gardner. A student in Central America, 1914–1916. New Orleans, La.: Middle America Research Institute, Tulane Univ., 1983. 75 p.: bibl., ill., index (Publication; 51)

Brief travelogue by US scholar and diplomat. Munro based these sketches on letters to his parents, and they contain charming and at times perspicacious comments on towns, social groups, social and political relations, and current events. Just 75 years ago, the five nations were more rural, more differentiated, and much more isolated from each other and the outside world.

Newton, Velma. The silver men: West Indian labour migration to Panama, 1850–1914. See *HLAS 47:1098.*

2299 Nogales Méndez, Rafael de. The looting of Nicaragua = El saqueo de Nicaragua. 2a ed. Caracas: Ediciones Centauro, 1981. 357 p.: bibl., ill.

First Spanish edition of this history of recent US-Nicaraguan relations. Emphasizes exploitative nature of US involvement in Nicaragua and Sandino's role.

2300 La Palabra social de los obispos costarricenses: selección de documentos de la Iglesia Católica Costarricense, 1893–1981. Miguel Picado, editor. San José: Depto. Ecuménico de Investigaciones, 1982. 217 p.: bibl., index (Cuadernos DEI; 6)

Consists of letters on Church-State matters and social problems which have preoccupied modern bishops of Costa Rica. Pt. 1 is about Bishop Bernardo Augusto Thiel's debates with the Liberal government and its ministers. Pt. 2, dominated by Bishop Víctor Sanabria M.'s letters, concerns the Church's position on issues such as social security and state health care. (The basic motor was the encyclical *Rerum Novarum*.) Pt. 3, mostly from the 1980s, deals with recent Costa Rican social and economic crisis, and the Church's official position on these matters.

2301 Pallais Lacayo, Mauricio. El periodismo en Nicaragua. v. 1, 1826–1876. Managua: Banco Central de Nicaragua, 1982. 1 v.: bibl., facsims., ill.

More of a catalog than an analytical history, this compendium of 118 newspapers published in these years, many of which were ephemeral, should be of use to historians of literature, politics, and local customs.

2301a Pensamiento antimperialista en Nicaragua: antología. Recopilación del Instituto de Estudios del Sandinismo. Managua: Editorial Nueva Nicaragua, 1982. 363 p.: bibl. (Col. Tercer aniversario)

Collection of documents and commentaries illustrate Nicaragua's long and dogged struggle against outside invasion and especially US domination. Covers 1855 through the 1927 Sandino uprising.

Peters Solórzano, Gertrud. Fuentes para el estudio del comercio de los Estados Unidos con Costa Rica: siglos XIX y XX. See *HLAS 47:108.*

2302 Peters Solórzano, Gertrud. Historia reciente de las grandes empresas cafetaleras: 1950–1980 (UNCR/R, No. especial: Simposio: Historia, Problemas y Perspectiva Agraria en Costa Rica, 1985, p. 241–263, tables)

Dominant as a pressure group, the *cafetaleros* began to lose influence in the 1950s because of the rise of rival pressure groups.

Posas, Mario and **Rafael del Cid.** La construcción del sector público y del Estado nacional en Honduras: 1876–1979. See *HLAS 47:6176.*

2303 Ramírez, Sergio. El alba de oro: la historia viva de Nicaragua. México: Siglo Veintiuno Editores, 1983. 306 p. (Historia inmediata)

Sandinista vice-president and poet studies revolutionary process from a leader's viewpoint. Previously published, some essays are banal, covering familiar territory in a simplistic way, others are clearly repetitive, many are transcribed with heavy rhetoric. Still, some are thoughtful and valuable as they illuminate specific attitudes of the revolutionary leadership.

2304 Ramírez, Sergio. El pensamiento vivo de Sandino. Managua: Editorial Nueva Nicaragua, 1981. 560 p.: bibl.

Another edition of book by the Sandinista vice-president, first published in Costa Rica in 1974, which has become one of the standard texts on Sandino and the Nicaraguan Revolution.

2305 Randall, Margaret. Christians in the Nicaraguan revolution. Translated by Mariana Valverde. Vancouver, Canada: New Star Books, 1983. 207 p.: ill.

Biographical information on and personal interviews with revolutionary Christians, and account of two base communities in the Nicaraguan revolutionary process. Favorable view by Marxist, atheist, and feminist, who seeks a common revolutionary stance uniting liberation theology and Marxism.

La Revolución de Nicaragua. See *HLAS 47:6196.*

2306 Rojas Bolaños, Manuel. Lucha social y guerra civil en Costa Rica, 1940–1948. 2a ed. San José: Editorial Porvenir, 1980. 171, 1 p.: bibl. (Col. Debate)

Reflects Costa Rican continuing preoccupation with the 1948 events. Second edition of Marxist interpretation argues that reformist social democrats, organized under the Liberación Nacional Party since 1951, won the civil war and have fostered capitalist development ever since. Bourgeois capitalism, supported by the petty bourgeoisie and the peasantry, broke the power of the traditional oligarchy, but is now beginning to show signs of systemic exhaustion. Author wonders if the working class is sufficiently organized politically to profit from such exhaustion.

Ropp, Steve C. En espera de un Cavour: la crisis actual y la unificación de Centroamérica. See *HLAS 47:6121.*

Rovira Mas, Jorge. Estado y política económica en Costa Rica, 1948–1970. See *HLAS 47:8138.*

2307 Rubio Sánchez, Manuel. Los mariscales de campo. v. 1, Francisco Cáscara. Guatemala: EDE, 1984. 1 v.: bibl., ill.

First of Rubio's intended biographies of lesser military leaders. An immigrant from Sardinia, Cáscara arrived in Guatemala in 1801 as a corporal in the Spanish forces, and spent his remaining 50 years occupying various military and civil posts. He died as a field marshall in Gen. Carrera's army. Rubio's best efforts do not rescue him from deserved obscurity.

2308 Salas Víquez, José Antonio. La búsqueda de soluciones al problema de la escasez de tierra en la frontera agrícola: aproximación al estudio del reformismo agrario en Costa Rica, 1880–1940 (UNCR/R, No. especial: Simposio: Historia, Problemas y Perspectiva Agraria en Costa Rica, 1985, p. 97–149)

Growing peasant unrest and land invasions caused governments in the first quarter of this century to rethink post-independence land tenure policies. Some landowners sold off surplus land to squatters and tenants. The government forbade further alienation of public land (1913) and began to grant small holdings to poor heads of families. Unfortunately, these were often resold quickly, and there was not enough land available, all of which led to little change in basic land tenure structure.

2309 Samper Kutschbach, Mario. La especialización mercantil campesina en el noroeste del Valle Central, 1850–1900: elementos microanalíticos para un modelo (UNCR/R, No. especial: Simposio: Historia, Problemas y Perspectiva Agraria en Costa Rica, 1985, p. 49–87)

Most of the area's rural population found their level of living to be deteriorating in the late 19th century, although their lands had not been massively expropriated and their labor was not coerced. The market had benefitted larger producers and businessmen.

2310 El Sandinismo: documentos básicos. Recopilación del Instituto de Estudio del Sandinismo. Managua: Editorial Nueva Nicaragua, 1983. 286 p. (Col. Cuarto aniversario)

Documents on the revolutionary hero's actions and thought. Notable are many excerpts from his correspondence with other intellectual and revolutionaries, and a long section (ch. 7) on his impact on other Latin American leaders and intellectuals (e.g., Tristán Maroff, Gabriela Mistral, Agustín Farabundo Martí, Víctor Raúl Haya de la Torre, José Santos Chocano, Rufino Blanco Fombona).

2311 Santacruz Noriega, José. Barrios, el pacificador: gobierno del General Don J. Rufino Barrios. t. 1, 1873–1876. Guatemala: Delgado, 1983. 1 v.: bibl., ill., index (Col. Gobiernos de Guatemala; 2)

Generally favorable vol. 1 of projected multi-volume history of President Justo Rufino Barrios. Narrative history of events, based on official documents, ends with his assumption of the dictatorship in 1876.

2312 Sepúlveda, Mélida Ruth. Harmodio Arias Madrid: el hombre, el estadista y el periodista. Panamá: Editorial Universitaria, 1983. 271 p.: bibl., ports.

Another laudatory biography of a Panamian president. This one (1932–36) continued to have influence after his term, largely through his journalism.

2313 Silva Girón, César Augusto. 12 horas de combate: relato histórico de la batalla del 20 de octubre de 1944. Guatemala: Impreofset Oscar de León Palacios, 1981. 134 p.: ill. (some col.), maps (Col. En busca de autores; 7)

Soldier's account of the overthrow of the Ubico dictatorship, somewhat dampened by a knowledge of what happened to the Guatemalan Revolution in 1954. Maps illustrate routes and tactics used.

2314 Smith, Carol A. El desarrollo de la primacía urbana: la dependencia en la exportación y la formación de clases en Guatemala (CIRMA/M, 5:8, dic. 1984, p. 195–278, graphs, tables)

Very long and important article in which Smith argues that the type of urbanization and the growth of primary cities has not been studied enough in local context, and that these phenomena in general are the result of class relations and class struggle in early capitalist, dependent, export-oriented states.

2315 Soltera, María. Un viaje por Honduras. Traducción de Anita Herzfeld. 2a ed. San José: Editorial Universitaria Centroamericana, 1982. 230 p.: ill. (Col. Viajeros)

Second Spanish edition of *A lady's ride across Spanish Honduras* (London, 1884). Naive and charming account includes interesting material on plans for the first trans-isthmian railroad and on the presidency of Marco Aurelio Soto.

2316 Torres, Edelberto. Sandino. México: Editorial Katún, 1984. 348 p.: bibl., port. (Realidad social; 3)

Yet another biography of Sandino, but

well written and thoroughly documented, and thus more useful than most. However, as author admits, volumes by Gregorio Selser and Sergio Ramírez remain the most definitive.

2317 Torres, Edelberto. Sandino y sus pares. Managua: Editorial Nueva Nicaragua, 1983. 810 p.: bibl. (Biblioteca popular sandinista; 16)

Admits that the book has nothing new to say about Sandino's personality or character, but believes an unvarnished yet heroic account of his life will be of use. Also argues that it helps to place Sandino in a heroic context, and surrounds him with brief biographies of his peers, a motley group including Spartacus, William Tell, Cuauhtémoc, Patrice Lumumba, and Che Guevara.

Vega Carballo, José Luis. Orden y progreso: la formación del Estado nacional en Costa Rica. See *HLAS 47:6137*.

Volio, Marina. Jorge Volio y el Partido Reformista. See *HLAS 47:6139*.

Wasserstrom, Robert. Revolución en Guatemala: campesinos y políticos durante el gobierno de Arbenz. See *HLAS 47:8145*.

2318 Wilson, James. A brief memoir of James Wilson, 1799–1827. Troy, N.Y.: La Tienda el Quetzal, 1983. 6, 165 p.: bibl.

Brief account of young Scottish businessman (d. Belize, Jan. 1827) daily observations in Guatemala and Guatemala City in 1825. Useful for its portrayal of the daily lives of the urban elite.

THE CARIBBEAN, THE GUIANAS AND THE SPANISH BORDERLANDS

REBECCA J. SCOTT, *Associate Professor of History, University of Michigan, Ann Arbor*
COLIN A. PALMER, *Professor of History, University of North Carolina, Chapel Hill*
ANNE PÉROTIN-DUMON, *Assistant Professor of History, Kent State University, Ohio*
BLANCA G. SILVESTRINI, *Professor of History, Universidad de Puerto Rico, Río Piedras*

THE INCREASING VOLUME OF articles and books published both on and in the Caribbean has caused us to redistribute the responsibility for this section, and we now have a contributing editor for Cuba, the Dominican Republic, and the Borderlands (Scott), one for Puerto Rico (Silvestrini), one for the French and Dutch Caribbean (Pérotin-Dumon), and one for the British Caribbean (Palmer). We have divided our introductory discussion accordingly, even though some issues—such as slavery and anti-colonial movements—clearly span these geographical units.

CUBA, THE DOMINICAN REPUBLIC, AND THE SPANISH BORDERLANDS

Despite the fragmentation that often characterizes scholarship on the Caribbean, the study of the social history of the 19th century has offered an opportunity to draw some of this work together, either through explicit comparison or through intentional juxtaposition of case studies. The volume edited by Manuel Moreno Fraginals, Frank Moya Pons, and Stanley Engerman, *Between slavery and free labor: the Spanish-speaking Caribbean in the nineteenth century* (item **2488**), includes articles on economic and social transformations in Cuba, Puerto Rico, and the Dominican Republic, as well as providing synthetic and theoretical essays on the general issue of slave emancipation and post-emancipation sociey. A recent essay by Roberto Marte (item **2527**) also compares patterns of land occupation and economic activity in Cuba and the Dominican Republic from a geographical perspective.

The largest volume of work during this biennium has focused on the 19th and 20th centuries. In both Cuba and the Dominican Republic there has been a proliferation of studies of resistance movements during the 1930s, 1940s, and 1950s. The tone is often hagiographic, but a substantial amount of primary material has been transcribed, photographs have been reproduced, and oral testimonies have been recorded. An important documentary collection on US-Dominican relations during the Trujillo period, edited by Bernardo Vega, complements these works, as do studies by Vega *et al.* on links between the Spanish Civil War and the Caribbean (items **2391, 2573,** and **2584**). In the Cuban case, the focus has generally been on union leaders, student leaders, and the anti-Batista movement. In a very different vein, a translation of Carlos Franqui's tendentious but intriguing memoir of the guerrilla struggle and the early years of the revolution has also appeared (item **2575**).

Work on 19th-century history continues to grow in range and sophistication. Louis Pérez has contributed an essay on land tenure and one on banditry, as well as editing a special number of *Cuban Studies/Estudios Cubanos*. In each case he attempts to link the concerns of political history with those of social history (items **2329, 2536,** and **2537**). Rosalie Schwartz takes a somewhat different perspective on banditry (item **2546**), while several authors look at the social character of the Ten Years War and its aftermath (items **2504, 2524,** and **2538**). Though the second Cuban war for independence has received relatively little attention recently, the period of US occupation has been examined with a greater eye to Cuban initiatives and responses (item **2595**). The debate over Martí continues, with the publication of essays by scholars both within and outside Cuba (see especially item **2553**). Studies and documentary evidence concerning the Dominican Republic in the 19th century appeared in the volume *Between slavery and free labor*, a compilation of essays edited by Tirso Mejía-Ricart G. (item **2385**), and in a volume of statistical and other archival material compiled by Roberto Marte (item **2526**).

Scholarship on slavery in Cuba has expanded to include detailed analyses of slave prices (item **2530**), work on urban slave runaways (item **2501**), and an analysis of the dynamics of the process of slave emancipation (item **2547**). The Editorial Letras Cubanas has published a transcription of the diary of a Cuban professional slave-catcher, providing a useful primary source and an exceptionally vivid picture of slave resistance (item **2510a**).

The early colonial period and the 18th century have been less studied recently, though a series of essays by Allan Kuethe *et al.* provide a careful examination of 18th- and early 19th-century Cuba, with a particular emphasis on Spanish policy-making and Cuban alliances (items **2441, 2442, 2443,** and **2444**). For Santo Domingo, attention has focused on the 16th century, with two useful articles on population (items **2407** and **2408**).

The literature on the Spanish borderlands encompasses familiar topics concerning exploration, diplomacy, and military defense, but also treats such issues as fugitive slaves in Florida in the 17th and 18th centuries (item **2473**), loyalist refugees (item **2478**), and Indian rebellion (item **2477**).

Overall, it was a productive period for the study of the Spanish Caribbean, with new interpretive and comparative work appearing alongside important documentary collections.

PUERTO RICO

In the last decade new research problems and methodological approaches have enriched Puerto Rican historiography. Although some excellent works have been published during the period covered by this volume, in general the thematic breadth of the bibliography does not compare with the historical production reported in the previous *Handbook* volumes. Recent works have focused primarily on the socio-economic and sociopolitical history of Puerto Rico, with an emphasis on the study of local problems. Fernando Picó's *Los gallos peleados* (item **2596**) is a good example of this trend. The author studies the problems of vagrancy and marginality in Puerto Rico during the first 40 years of the 20th century in Utuado, a coffee-producing town in the interior of the island. The contribution of the book rests not only in its topic of study and the questions it addresses, but also in its novel use of local police records as historical sources, opening up a new field of research for the social history of Puerto Rico. Two general books, Fernando Picó's *Historia general de Puerto Rico* (item **2375**) and Lydia Milagros González and Angel G. Quintero-Rivera's *La otra cara de la historia* (item **2344**), are part of the revision of traditional conceptualizations of Puerto Rican history and reflect a more social and economic approach. In *Historia crítica, historia sin coartadas* (item **2342**), Gervasio L. García critically evaluates the state of Puerto Rican historical production in view of the new avenues of research available.

Although some works have been published on 19th-century social and economic history, their quality is far below those reviewed in *HLAS 46*. Emphasis has moved toward the analysis of 20th-century social processes. The study of social movements continues to be an important topic of research, though few historical works have explored, for example, the role of women in these movements or their participation in the work structure. Migration, which seemed to be of much interest in previous years, has not been a major area of publication. Studies on urbanism and historical demography have also diminished, though a series of books of varying quality on the history of towns in Puerto Rico has been completed. Contemporary history seems to lag behind its development elsewhere, and Puerto Rican historical studies continue to be highly isolated from the history of the rest of the Caribbean. Morales Carrión, in his book, *Puerto Rico: a political and cultural history* (item **2365**), tries to place Puerto Rico in the American and Caribbean context at the beginning of the 20th century, but none of the works available analyzes the relationship of Puerto Rico with the rest of the Caribbean islands or its political and economic position in the region.

An important trend in the last two years has been the publication of new historical journals that include monographs on diverse topics. Of particular significance has been the publication of special issues of *Cuadernos de la Facultad de Humanidades* (item **2328**), *La Revista del Centro de Estudios Avanzados de Puerto Rico y el Caribe* (item **2378**), and *Revista de Historia* of the Asociación Histórica Puertorriqueña (item **2377**). Other journals like *Revista de Ciencias Sociales* and the *Revista Jurídica* of the Univ. of Puerto Rico have published historical essays of interest.

FRENCH AND DUTCH CARIBBEAN

The French Caribbean will be the focus of this volume of the *Handbook* but in the next one (*HLAS 50*), we shall concentrate on the Dutch Caribbean. Also, the 17th and 20th centuries will be covered more thoroughly in *HLAS 50*. Although invaluable assistance concerning Dutch Caribbean materials is being provided by Dr. Gert Oostindie (Dept. of Caribbean Studies, Royal Institute of Linguistics and Anthropology, Leiden, The Netherlands), we urge all specialists in the Dutch Caribbean to bring to our attention works in their area which are not easily accessible.

Full-fledged sugar and slave societies of the 18th century continue to attract the most attention and a regional specialization is emerging on St. Domingue. D.

Geggus is systematically studying the slaves of the *plaine du Nord*, where the 1791 revolt took place (item **2430**). J. Cauna summarizes his unpublished monograph on a wealthy planter and merchant family in "Une Réussite de Planteur-Négociant à Saint-Domingue" (item **2418**), and gathers architectural as well as archival evidence of long-term sugar-producing history in the *plaine du Cul-de-Sac* in "Vestiges de Sucreries dans la Plaine du Cul-de-Sac" (item **2419**). Slave populations are also being studied with sophisticated quantitative methods, as in N. Vanony-Frisch's "Les Esclaves de la Guadeloupe à la Fin de l'Ancien Régime" (item **2466**). Slave revolts are another classic theme of 18th-century specialists. For the 1733 revolt in the Danish island of St. John (Virgin Islands), A. Caron and A. Highfield have published French and Danish sources which, being independent but complementary, confirm the facts of what happened (see items **2417** and **2451**). The question of *marronage* is relevant to the St. Domingue/Haitian revolution, and scholars are exploring whether the slave revolt was one of its consequences. D. Geggus examines this question carefully in "On the Eve of the Haitian Revolution: Slave Runaways in Saint Domingue in the year 1790" (item **2431**). Finally, the impact of the French revolution on 18th-century Caribbean revolutions is receiving more attention. A. Pérotin-Dumon's *Être patriote sous les Tropiques* (item **2452**) initiates a revision of the analysis of the revolutionary process in the Lesser Antilles. R.L. Stein has also given us the first biography of the most prominent French emissary in revolutionary St. Domingue, Léger Félicité Sonthonax (item **2461**).

The changing character of 19th-century slave societies is being examined by various scholars. A learned Martinican planter provides an account of the disintegration of one such slave society in Pierre Dessalles's *Journal, 1837–1841* (item **2503**). Several researchers have begun to look into post-emancipation societies and the immigrant labor force, asking, among other things, how different these societies were from the slave societies preceding them. R. Boutin's monograph focuses on demography (item **2489**), while P. Emmer pursues systematic research on indentured Indian immigrants in Surinam in the context of international abolitionist policies (items **2509** and **2510**). Women, finally visible in the scholarship on post-emancipation societies, appear as indentured laborers in P. Emmer's "The Great Escape" (item **2508**) and in O. Krakovitch's articles, both as trial suspects in the Martinican social riots of 1870 and as French convicts deported to the Cayenne penitentiary (items **2521** and **2522**).

The first positive result of interest in the Caribbean among French publishers has been the publication of previously unavailable classics: a second edition of James's *Les Jacobins noirs* was issued by Les Éditions caribéennes (item **2439**), and Karthala published Rémy Bastien's *Les paysan haitien et sa famille* which first appeared in Spanish in 1951 (item **2561**). Impressive research tools have been published by historical societies and university institutions: the *Atlas d'Haïti* by the Centre d'études de géographie tropicale of Bordeaux (item **2319**), and J. Petitjean Roget and E. Bruneau-Latouche's *Personnes et familles à la Martinique au XVIIe siècle* (item **2410**) and B. David's three volumes covering the clergy in *Dictionnaire biographique de la Martinique, 1635–1848* (item **2331**), both from the Société d'histoire de la Martinique.

THE BRITISH CARIBBEAN

The historiography of the British Caribbean continues to undergo considerable methodological refinement. This is particularly the case for the colonial years and specifically for works dealing with slavery and its immediate aftermath. One of the best books to appear on Caribbean slavery in recent years is B.W. Higman's *Slave populations of the British Caribbean, 1807–1834* (item **2517b**). It is a work of great merit and should be consulted by anyone interested in demographic issues and the structure of slavery during the 19th century. Higman's "Terms for Kin in the British West Indian Slave Community: Differing Perceptions of Masters and Slaves" is also a pathbreaking study (item **2350**). Hilary Beckles provides a provocative discussion of the antecedents of black slavery in his "Plantation Production and White 'Proto-Slavery:' White Indentured Servants and the Colonisation of the English West Indies, 1624–1645" (item **2393**). Stephen Fortune's *Merchants and Jews: the struggle for British West Indian commerce, 1650–1750* (item **2397**) is particularly useful for an understanding of the evolution of the colonial economies.

The resistance of slaves to their condition has also received some attention. Michael Craton examines the roles of slaves in creating rebellions in his "The Passion to Exist: Slave Rebellions in the British West Indies, 1630–1832" (item **2327**). His, "We Shall not be Moved: Pompey's Slave Revolt in Exuma Island, Bahamas, 1830" (item **2497**) is a useful discussion of a slave revolt in a marginal colony.

The post-emancipation years have been the focus of increasing scholarly attention. Although no books of distinction have appeared, several very suggestive articles have been published. Swithin Wilmot's "Black Labourers and White Missionaries: Conflict on the Estates of Hanover, Jamaica, 1838–1847" (item **2554**) is one of the best. A number of scholars have also examined the immigration issue and the place of East Indians in society. Peter Fraser's "The Immigration Issue in British Guiana, 1903–1913: the Economic and Constitutional Origins of Racist Politics in Guyana" (item **2576**) is a good example. Kusha Haraksingh writes sensitively about the Indian workers in his "Control and Resistance among Overseas Indian workers: a Study of Labour on the Sugar Plantations of Trinidad, 1875–1917" (item **2349**).

Works published on the 20th century reflect a rising interest in issues relating to social, economic, and political change. Sahadeo Basdeo's *Labour organisation and labour reform in Trinidad, 1919–1939* (item **2558**) examines the rise of a working class movement in that island. The roots of the contemporary crisis in Guyana are addressed by Thomas J. Spinner in *A political and social history of Guyana, 1945–1983* (item **2386**). M. Shahabuddeen describes the role of the sugar industry in the economic and social life of that country and the process of its nationalization (item **2384**). Selwyn Cudjoe's *Movement of the people: essays on independence* (item **2569**) focuses on Trinidad and advocates a complete break with the colonial past. Unsurprisingly, the larger islands and Guyana have commanded the primary attention of most scholars, and this situation is likely to continue.

GENERAL

2319 Atlas d'Haïti. Talence, France: Centre d'études de géographie tropicale (CEGET), CNRS: Univ. de Bordeaux III, 1985. 1 atlas (84 p., 31 leaves of plates): ill. (some col.), index, col. maps.

Handsomely designed and first systematic cartographic study of Haiti. Opening section deals with history (colonization, independence, US occupation). Also includes maps on population, urbanization, economy, communication network, land occupation, administrative divisions, etc. Introduction provides each section with historical as well as quantitative data. Impressive reference which should be in all Latin American collections. [APD]

2320 Benítez, José A. Martí y Estado Unidos. La Habana: Editora Política, 1983. 161 p.: bibl.

Journalistic articles by Cuban author on the US, ostensibly linked to Martí's vision of the country. Interesting as reflection of contemporary perceptions. [RJS]

2321 Blérald, Alain-Philippe. Histoire économique de la Guadeloupe et de la Martinique: du XVIIe siècle à nos jours. Paris: Karthala, 1986. 336 p.: bibl., ill., index, tables (Hommes et sociétés)

Inquiry into the genesis of French Antillean economy, in the light of dependency theory, will replace obsolete economic histories from the 1930s. Deals mainly with post World War II evolution (i.e., of Guadeloupe's integration into a world-capitalist economy, combined with a sustained colonial dependency from the metropolis). Very useful data drawn from French government publications. [APD]

2322 *Boletín del Instituto Duartiano*. Vol. 9, no. 17, dic. 1982-. Santo Domingo.

Special issue consists of essays on Juan Pablo Duarte and other themes of Dominican history. [RJS]

Boucher, Philip and **Gabriel Debien.** Chronique bibliographique de l'histoire des Antilles françaises, 1979–1982. See *HLAS 47:24.*

2323 Brereton, Bridget. A history of modern Trinidad, 1783–1962. Kingston: Heinemann, 1981. 262 p.: bibl., ill., index.

Balanced analysis of the history of Trinidad, and to a lesser extent Tobago, from the 1780s to the achievement of independence in 1962. [CAP]

2324 Brodber, Erna. Oral sources and the creation of a social history of the Caribbean (IJ/JJ, 16:4, Nov. 1983, p. 2–11, bibl., ill.)

Plea for scholars writing about Caribbean societies to use oral sources as supplements to traditional records. [CAP]

2325 Buve, Raymondh Th.B. Bibliografía básica para la historia de las Antillas Holandesas y Suriname (EEHA/HBA, 25, 1981, p. 149–185, bibl.)

Very useful bibliography with mostly Dutch titles dating up to 1978, each receiving a detailed content analysis. [APD]

2326 *Caribe*. Centro de Estudios Avanzados de Puerto Rico y el Caribe. Año 4/5, Nos. 5/6, 1983/84-. San Juan.

Journal published by the students of the Centro de Estudios Avanzados de Puerto Rico y el Caribe. Includes some historical essays and book review section. [BGS]

Carr, Raymond. Puerto Rico, a colonial experiment. See *HLAS 47:6303.*

2327 Craton, Michael. The passion to exist: slave rebellions in the British West Indies, 1650–1832 (UWI/JCH, 13, 1980, p. 1–20)

Reconsideration of author's earlier position that Age of Revolution ideologies (1775–1815) were not influential among British West Indian slaves. Examines roles played by Maroons, unacculturated Africans and Creole slaves in situations conducive to slave rebellions. Concludes that the slaves' ideology was to make or recreate a life of their own. [CAP]

2328 *Cuadernos de la Facultad de Humanidades*. Univ. de Puerto Rico. No. 10, 1983-. Río Piedras.

Special issue devoted to a critical analysis of historical studies in Puerto Rico. Provides valuable information on research resources in Puerto Rican repositories. [BGS]

2329 *Cuban Studies/Estudios Cubanos*. Univ. of Pittsburgh, Center for Latin American Studies, Center for International Studies. Vol. 15, No. 1, Winter 1985-. Pittsburgh, Pa.

Includes four articles and useful research note, linked by themes of ideology, race, and decolonization: Louis A. Pérez, Jr., "Toward a New Future from a New Past: the Enterprise of History in Socialist Cuba;" Rebecca J. Scott, "Class Relations in Sugar and Political Mobilization in Cuba, 1868–1899;" Gerald E. Poyo, "The Anarchist Challenge to the Cuban Independence Movement, 1885–1890;" Harold D. Sims, "Cuban Labor and the Communist Party, 1937–1958;" Susan D. Greenbaum, "Afro-Cubans in Exile: Tampa, Florida, 1886–1984." [RJS]

2330 Daget, Serge. La traite des noirs: travaux récents et voies de recherche (*in* L'Atlantique et ses rivages, 1500–1800: actes du Colloque de l'Association des historiens modernistes des universités, 1983. Bordeaux, France: Presses universitaires de Bordeaux, 1984, p. 103–131, bibl.)

Well informed survey of recent literature, within which French contributions are assessed. Points out two major trends: 1) studies on mentalités and behaviors are now strongly supplementing the established emphasis on econometrics; and 2) a clear distinction is being drawn between two aspects of the slave trade: the European and African. [APD]

2331 David, Bernard. Dictionnaire biographique de la Martinique, 1635–1848: le clergé. Fort-de-France: Société d'histoire de la Martinique, 1984. 3 v.

List of colonial clergy arranged chronologically: vol. 1: 1635–1715; vol. 2, 1716–89; and vol. 3, 1790–1848. Lists more than 1000 clergymen identifying those of French origin and providing detailed biographies of 227. Invaluable research tool on a hitherto neglected topic. Vol. 3 concerns clergy of the whole Lesser Antilles who often sought refuge in Martinique during the revolutionary era. [APD]

2332 Deive, Carlos Esteban. La cultura cristiano islámica medieval y su presencia en Santo Domingo (MHD/B, 11:18, 1983, p. 149–158, bibl.)

Emphasizes significance of Islamic culture in medieval Spain, and traces influence in Santo Domingo. Examines popular customs and legends. [RJS]

2333 Del exilio político dominicano antitrujillista, en Cuba. Recopilación de Justino José del Orbe. Santo Domingo: Editora Taller, 1983. 171 p.: ill.

Recollections of experiences of anti-Trujillo activists in Cuba. Transcribes press clippings, letters, pamphlets. [RJS]

2334 Dodd, David J. Rule-making and rule-enforcement in plantation society: the ideological development of criminal justice in Guyana (UWI/SES, 31:3, 1982, p. 1–35)

Traces development of the criminal justice system in Guyana with special emphasis on its role as protector of the society's elite interests. Although somewhat theoretical in approach, the article does raise some important questions about the independence of the judicial system in contemporary Guyana. [CAP]

2335 Duharte Jiménez, Rafael. Seis ensayos de interpretación histórica. Santiago, Cuba: Editorial Oriente, 1983. 110 p.: bibl.

Interesting essays by young Cuban historian on race, politics, and national identity in 19th- and early 20th-century Cuba. Discusses manumission, free persons of color, officeholding, ideology. [RJS]

2336 Edwards, Melvin Romeo. Jamaican higglers: their significance and potential. Norwich, England: Geo Abstracts for the Centre for Development Studies, Univ. College of Swansea, 1980. 58 p.: bibl. (Monograph/The Centre; 7)

Discusses the significance of the internal marketing operation known as "higglering" in Jamaica and examines it from a historical and sociocultural perspective. Argues that higglers effectively link both peasant and modern economies. For ethnologist's comment, see *HLAS 47:1053*. [CAP]

2337 Etna, Max. Contribution à l'étude de notre patrimoine: sites historiques de Vieux-Habitants. Vieux-Habitants, Guadeloupe: M. Etna, 1981. 31, 2 p.: ill.

Based on original sources, this succinct monograph on one of the oldest colonial settlements in Guadeloupe draws attention to past architectural landmarks. [APD]

2338 Ferreras, Ramón Alberto. Trujillo y su familia. t. 1, Cosas de Patán. Santo Domingo: Editorial del Nordeste, 1984. 1 v.: ill.

Journalistic not scholarly study of the Trujillo family. [RJS]

2339 France. Archives nationales. Guide des sources de l'histoire de l'Amérique latine et des Antilles dans les archives françaises. Paris: Les Archives, 1984. 711 p., 8 p. of plates: appendices, bibl., col. ill.

Long-awaited volume in series of systematic surveys of archival resources in the Western world for the study of the Latin American and Caribbean past. Includes description of French Caribbean archives in the section "Archives départementales." Apart from public archives and manuscript collections, lists government official publications and periodicals of historical interest, private papers, business archives, Church archives. [APD]

2340 France. Bibliothèque nationale. Département des cartes et plans. Le fonds cubain de la Société de géographie en dépôt au Département des cartes et plans. Inventaire par Nicole Simon. Introduction par Michèle Tollis-Guicharnaud. Paris: La Bibliothèque, 1985. 67 p., 6 p. of plates: ill., photos, maps (Etudes Guides et inventaires; 3)

Systematic catalog of the Cuban collection of the prestigious 19th-century French society: manuscripts, maps, photographs, books and periodicals. Reflects the strong interest aroused by the island among European geographers of the last century. [APD]

2341 Galenson, David W. The rise and fall of indentured servitude in the Americas: an economic analysis (EHA/J, 44:1, March 1984, p. 1–26)

Economic analysis of motivations for introducing indentured servitude in North America, its supplanting by slavery and its reemergence in the Caribbean in the period after abolition. Thesis is that its use was related to availability of a population which wished to emigrate but did not have the financial resources to do so. One-sided consideration which while perhaps satisfactory when dealing with US is very weak when examining the Caribbean context. [J.D. Riley]

2342 García, Gervasio L. Historia crítica, historia sin coartadas: algunos problemas de la historia de Puerto Rico. Río Piedras, P.R.: Ediciones Huracán, 1985. 149 p.: bibl. (Col. La Nave y el puerto)

Critical essays on some of the theoretical and thematic problems affecting historical studies in Puerto Rico. Emphasizes the critical examination of political issues and labor history of the late 19th and 20th centuries. Discusses new avenues of research and the need to revise well accepted interpretations. [BGS]

2343 Glasscock, Jean. The making of an island: Sint Maarten—Saint Martin. Wellesley, Mass.: The Author, 1985. 180 p., 8 p. of plates: bibl., ill. (some col.), indexes, maps.

Graceful introduction to this island's past based on interviews with St. Martin's inhabitants. [APD]

2344 González, Lydia Milagros and **A.G. Quintero Rivera.** La otra cara de la historia: la historia de Puerto Rico desde su cara obrera. v. 1, 1800–1925: pt. 1, Album de fotos de la clase obrera puertorriqueña. Río Piedras, P.R.: Cerep, 1984. 1 v.: bibl., ill., photos.

Well researched book which attempts to interpret the history of Puerto Rico from the workers' perspective. Focuses on labor history in Puerto Rico from early 19th to the 20th century. Divided in two parts: 1) photographic essay of living conditions and

struggles of Puerto Rican workers; and 2) three essays that discuss how some of the island's economic problems affected the workers' living and working conditions. [BGS]

2345 Gooding, Earl. The West Indies at the crossroads. Cambridge, Mass.: Schenkman Publishing Co., 1981. 243 p.: bibl., index.

Brief analysis of the history and politics of the British Caribbean with special reference to Trinidad and Tobago, Jamaica and Guyana. Author examines government efforts to effect social and economic changes within the framework of insular nationalisms. [CAP]

2346 Gordon, Shirley C. Caribbean generations: a CXC history source book. Port-of-Spain?: Longman Caribbean; London: Longman Group, 1983. 338 p.: bibl., ill., index.

Useful sourcebook for the study of Caribbean history prepared for secondary school students. [CAP]

2347 Hall, Douglas. The Caribbean experience: an historical survey, 1450–1960. Questions and exercises by David Hall. Kingston: Heinemann Educational Books, 1982. 146 p.: bibl., ill., index, maps (Heinemann CXC history)

Secondary school text prepared by one of the Caribbean's most distinguished historians. Includes exercises for students. [CAP]

2348 Hamilton, Jill. Women of Barbados: Amerindian era to mid 20th century. Foreword by Billie A. Miller. Message from Henry deB. Forde. Bridgetown?: J. Hamilton, 1981? 91 p.: bibl., ill., index.

Superficial discussion of the role of women in Barbadian society. [CAP]

2349 Haraksingh, Kusha. Control and resistance among overseas Indian workers: a study of labour on the sugar plantations of Trinidad, 1875–1917 (UWI/JCH, 14, 1981, p. 1–17)

Sensitive discussion of means by which control was exercised over Indian workers on Trinidad sugar plantations. Rejects argument that Indian workers were preferred over black because of their supposed docility and concludes that the system rendered the Indians controllable. Suggests that cultural resistance and adaptation constituted most persistent forms of resistance by Indian workers. [CAP]

2350 Higman, B.W. Terms for kin in the British West Indies slave community: differing perceptions of masters and slaves (*in* Kinship, ideology and practice in Latin America. Edited by Raymond T. Smith. Chapel Hill: Univ. of North Carolina Press, 1984, p. 59–81, bibl., tables)

Suggestive examination of slave relationship terminology in the British West Indies. Focuses on data available for studying slave kinship patterns from a slave perspective. Underscores difficult methodological problems posed by any such study and provides interesting comparison of slave and master derived relationship terminology. [CAP]

2351 Inventaris van de collectie prenten tekeningen, kaarten en foto's van de Evangelische Broedergemeente te Zeist, ca. 1700–1982. Compiled by C.M.P.F. van den Broek. Utrecht, The Netherlands: Rijksarchief, 1985. 227 p.: ill., index (Inventaris; 46)

Concerns archives of the Moravian Brothers which contain interesting material, particularly iconographic, on Surinam, where they had missions. [APD]

2352 Inventaris van het archief van het Zendingsgenootschap der Evangelische Broedergemeente te Zeits: Zeister Zendingsgenootschap, 1793–1962. Compiled by C.G.W.M. van Hoogstraten. Utrecht, The Netherlands: Rijksarchief, 1985. 203 p.: ill., indexes, maps.

Archives of the Moravian Brothers' Missionary Society contain documents on their missions in Surinam and Paramaribo, particularly towards the end of the 19th and beginning of the 20th centuries. [APD]

2353 Klein, Herbert S. and **Stanley L. Engerman.** Del trabajo esclavo al trabajo libre: notas en torno a un modelo económico comparativo (HISLA, 1, 1983, p. 41–55, bibl., tables)

Schematic analysis of different forms of post-emancipation economies. Primarily concerned with production levels and labor forms. Proposes several models; examines a range of variables; raises useful questions. [RJS]

2354 Kom, Anton de. Nosotros, esclavos de Surinam. La Habana: Casa de las Américas, 1981. 131 p., 20 p. of plates: bibl., ill. (Col. Nuestros países. Serie Estudios)

First Spanish translation of a classic of Surinam anticolonialist literature: this 1930 manifiesto provided the first revisionist history of the colony. [APD]

2355 Labourt, José. Trujillo: seguiré a caballo. Santo Domingo: Ediciones de Taller, 1984. 229 p.: ill. (Biblioteca Taller; 144)

Study by writer and journalist examines Trujillo regime and popular perceptions of Trujillo. Does not provide source notes. [RJS]

2356 López Reyes, Oscar. Historia de los medios de comunicación social de Barahona. Santo Domingo: Taller, 1984. 125 p.: bibl., facsims.

Study by journalist of press and other media of communication in province of Barahona, Dominican Republic. [RJS]

2357 López Reyes, Oscar. Historia del desarrollo de Barahona. S.l.: Servicios Gráficos Integrados, 1983. 271 p.: ill.

Local history, with emphasis on economic development. [RJS]

2358 López Sánchez, José. La doctrina finlaísta: 100 años del descubrimiento de Finlay. La Habana: Ministerio de Cultura, Editorial Científico-Técnica, 1981. 50 p.

Articles emphasize importance of Carlos Finlay's work on transmission of yellow fever to larger issues of contagion. [RJS]

2359 Marie-Sainte, Daniel. Goyave dans l'histoire de la Guadeloupe. S.l.: s.n., 1983. 106 p.: bibl., ill.

Local history of one of the island's oldest sugar-producing areas. Author has gathered sources that document sugar-estate buildings still recognizable in Goyave. [APD]

Marrero Artiles, Leví. Cuba: economía y sociedad. See *HLAS 47:3364.*

2360 Marshall, Bernard. Social stratification and the free coloured in the slave society of the British Windward Islands (UWI/SES, 31:1, March 1982, p. 1–39, bibl.)

Assessment of the nature of social stratification in the Windward Islands and of the interplay between color, class, and legal status. [CAP]

2361 Matos Díaz, Eduardo. Santo Domingo de ayer: vida, costumbres y acontecimientos. Santo Domingo: Editora Taller, 1984. 190 p.: ill. (Biblioteca Taller; 173)

Memoir of early 20th-century public life in the city of Santo Domingo. Illustrated. [RJS]

2362 Mauro, Frédéric. La plantation atlantique: ses structures économiques, 1500–1800 (*in* L'Atlantique et ses rivages, 1500–1800: actes du Colloque de l'Association des historiens modernistes des universités, 1983. Bordeaux, France: Presses universitaires de Bordeaux, 1984, p. 155–179)

Discusses fairly recent studies of aspects of the plantation economy in Brazil and the Caribbean, such as the impact of Brazilian techniques on the development of 17th-century Caribbean sugar as well as 18th-century production trends, interpreted as either growth or decline. [APD]

2363 Monclús, Miguel Angel. El caudillismo en la República Dominicana. Prólogo de Sócrates Nolasco. 4a ed. Santo Domingo: Univ. CETEC, 1983. 161 p., 8 leaves of plates: ports (Col. CETEC; 17. Serie Ensayos; 9)

Biographical sketches of military and political leaders of the Dominican Republic. [RJS]

2364 Montaner, Carlos Alberto. The roots of anti-Americanism in Cuba: sovereignty in an age of world cultural homogeneity (CRI/CR, 13:2, Spring 1984, p. 13–16, 42–46, plate)

Interpretation of Cuban attitudes toward US since 19th century. Sees Cuban nationalism as misguided and contradictory, US intervention as having positive aspects. Essay without footnotes; strongly critical of Fidel Castro. For political scientist's comment, see *HLAS 47:7243.* [RJS]

2365 Morales Carrión, Arturo et al. Puerto Rico: a political and cultural history. New York: W.W. Norton; Nashville: American Assn. for State and Local History, 1983. 384 p.: bibl., ill., index, maps.

Well researched scholarly work, which provides a general overview of Puerto Rican history. Pt. 2, written by Morales Carrión, offers a detailed analysis, based on primary

sources, of the politics of US-Puerto Rican relations during the 20th century. [BGS]

2366 Mota, Francisco. Piratas en el Caribe. La Habana: Casa de las Américas, 1984. 428 p.: bibl., ill. (Col. Nuestros países. Serie Rumbos)

Discussion of piracy, slave trade, and smuggling in the Caribbean from beginnings to the present. Bibliography but no footnotes. Textbook format. [RJS]

2367 Moya Pons, Frank. Historia dominicana. Santo Domingo: Caribe Grolier, 1982. 2 v. (622 p.): bibl., ill. (some col.), index (Cols. dominicanas)

Textbook for secondary and college students, by a capable historian. Combines political with social and economic history of the Dominican Republic. [RJS]

Muñoz, María Elena. Historia de las relaciones internacionales de la República Dominicana. See *HLAS 47:7245.*

2368 Nicholls, David. Los árabes en el Caribe: República Dominicana, Haití y Trinidad (MHD/B, 11:18, 1983, p. 159–177, ill.)

Examines Arab immigration to the Caribbean, beginning in 1880s. Sees relative integration in Santo Domingo; initial hostility in Haiti; later arrival, mixed experiences, and some isolation in Trinidad. [RJS]

2369 Nicholls, David. Haiti in Caribbean context: ethnicity, economy, and revolt. New York: St. Martin's Press, 1985. 282 p.: bibl., index, map.

Collection of essays on issues that have shaped Haitian history, such as economic dependence, rural marginality and protest, the making of "a living ideological past," part of a collective consciousness, 20th-century migrations. Emphasizes color, linguistics and religion as crucial factors. [APD]

2370 Orbe, Justino José del. Mauricio Báez y la clase obrera. Santo Domingo: Taller, 1981. 158 p.: ill. (Biblioteca Taller; 128)

Biography of agricultural union leader and anti-Trujillo activist. Author is former sugar worker, stevedore; autobiographical introduction itself is interesting. Includes transcriptions of contemporary press. Useful. [RJS]

2371 Peña Castillo, Domingo Antonio. Memorias de un revolucionario. Santo Domingo: Editora Alfa y Omega, 1983. 140 p.: ports.

Memoir of anti-Trujillo activist. [RJS]

Pérez, Lisandro. The holdings of the Library of Congress on the population of Cuba. See *HLAS 47:106.*

2372 Pérez, Nancy *et al*. El Cabildo Carabalí Isuama. Santiago, Cuba: Editorial Oriente, 1982. 104 p.: ill, photos.

Study by a team of student researchers who examined the music and history of a largely black "cabildo-comparsa" in the city of Santiago de Cuba. Emphasizes transformations in the institutional structure of the *cabildo*, its function as mutual-aid society and vehicle for anti-colonial conspiracies, and later evolution into a "folkloric" group. Contains transcriptions of songs, archival documents, and photographs of ceremonies and dancers. [RJS]

2373 Pérez Memén, Fernando. La Iglesia y el Estado en Santo Domingo, 1700–1853. Santo Domingo: Editora de la Univ. Autónoma de Santo Domingo, 1984. 706 p.: bibl., ill. (Publicaciones; 330. Col. Historia y sociedad; 61)

Extensive history of the Church in Santo Domingo using primary sources, with attention to political and social context. [RJS]

2374 Pickering, Vernon W. Early history of the British Virgin Islands: from Columbus to emancipation. British Virgin Islands?: Falcon Publications International, 1983. 248 p.: bibls., ill., index, maps, ports.

General and uncritical discussion of aspects of the history of the British Virgin Islands by author who notes that his book does not pretend to be academic or scientific. [CAP]

2375 Picó, Fernando. Historia general de Puerto Rico. Río Piedras, P.R.: Huracán-Academia, 1986. 288 p.: bibl., ill., maps, tables (Col. Huracán academia)

Excellent general history of Puerto Rico that ranges from the 16th to 20th centuries. Incorporates social, economic and political phenomena and deals to a limited extent with Puerto Rico's position in the Caribbean context. Second edition includes additional chapter on changes in social values in contemporary Puerto Rican society within the framework of economic transformations. Includes updated selected bibliography and tables. [BGS]

Price, Richard. First-time: the historical vision of an Afro-American people. See *HLAS 47:1107.*

2376 Ramírez Suero, Matías. Fundación de Barahona. Santo Domingo: Editora Taller, 1983. 337 p.: ill. (Sociedad Dominicana de Geografía. Biblioteca dominicana de geografía y viajes; 18)

Local history by local historian. [RJS]

2377 *Revista de Historia*. Asociación Histórica Puertorriqueña. Año 1, No. 1, enero/junio 1985; No. 2, julio/dic. 1985–. San Juan.

New historical journal explores the social, political, economic, and cultural history of Puerto Rico in essays of high scholarly quality, mostly based on primary sources. Also includes section on "Research Notes and Projects in Progress" and another devoted to reviews of recent books. [BGS]

2378 *Revista del Centro de Estudios Avanzados de Puerto Rico y el Caribe*. No. 1, julio/dic. 1985–. San Juan.

Scholarly journal publishing essays on Puerto Rican literature, history, and anthropology. Includes a section of previously unpublished historical documents. [BGS]

2379 Ripoll, Carlos. José Martí, the United States, and the Marxist interpretation of Cuban history. New Brunswick, N.J.: Transaction Books, 1984. 80 p.: bibl., indexes.

Interpretative essays argue that Martí's view of US and Cuba have been distorted by Marxist scholars. Essentially a polemic against Philip Foner, John Kirk, and the current Cuban government. Contains some interesting analysis of Martí's use of language. [RJS]

2380 Rodríguez Jiménez, Julio César and Rosajilda Vélez Canelo. El precapitalismo dominicano de la primera mitad del siglo XIX, 1780–1850. Santo Domingo: Editora de la Univ. Autónoma de Santo Domingo, 1980. 219 p., 3 leaves of plates: bibl., facsims. (Publicaciones; 285. Col. Historia y sociedad; 40)

Study of Dominican economy and society. Emphasis is on periodization and categorization; uses notarial and other archival materials. [RJS]

2381 Rodríguez Villanueva, Carlos and **Gregorio Villegas Cobián.** Guaynabo: notas para su historia. San Juan: Comité Historia de los Pueblos, 1984. 1 v.: photos, tables.

One of the best volumes in the series, well researched and based on primary sources. Focuses on the social and economic development of the town. [BGS]

2382 Ruz Menéndez, Rodolfo. Dos pueblos hermanos: Yucatán y Cuba (UY/R, 25 : 148, oct./dic. 1983, p. 49–61)

Generalized discussion of links between Yucatán and Cuba. No footnotes. [RJS]

2383 Saint Barthélemy. Aruba, Netherlands Antilles: Litho. O'stad Print., Centro Técnico, 198-? 22 p.: ill.

Light historical essay survey in English and French accompanies charming 19th-century views of Gustavia. [APD]

2384 Shahabuddeen, M. From plantocracy to nationalisation: a profile of sugar in Guyana. Foreword by Shridath S. Ramphal. Georgetown: Univ. of Guyana, 1983. 440 p.: bibl., ill.

Written by lawyer, this book examines the role of sugar in Guyana's economy and society and assesses factors that led to the industry's nationalization. [CAP]

2385 La Sociedad dominicana durante la Segunda República. Tirso Mejía-Ricart Guzmán, editor. Santo Domingo: Editora de la Univ. Autónoma de Santo Domingo, 1982. 399 p.: bibl. (Publicaciones; 308. Historia y sociedad; 53)

Useful collection of essays by Frank Moya Pons, José del Castillo, Roberto Cassá et al., on the 19th- and 20th-century Dominican Republic. Includes analyses of economy, politics, class structure, international relations and culture. [RJS]

2386 Spinner, Thomas J. A political and social history of Guyana, 1945–1983. Boulder, Colo.: Westview Press, 1984. 244 p.: bibl., index, maps.

Discussion of the roots of the economic, social, and political problems confronting contemporary Guyana. [CAP]

2387 Tardo-Dino, Frantz. Le collier de servitude: la condition sanitaire des esclaves aux Antilles françaises du XVIIe au XIXe siècle. Paris: Éditions caribéennes, Agence de coopération culturelle et tech-

nique, 1985. 305 p.: appendices, bibl., tables (Col. Connaissance de la diaspora noire)

Describes slaves' diet, sanitary conditions and diseases. [APD]

2388 Titus, Noel. The Church and slavery in the English-speaking Caribbean. Bridgetown: Caribbean Group for Social and Religious Studies, 1983. 36 leaves: bibl. (CGSRS; 2, 1983)

General discussion of the role of various Christian denominations in ministering to the slave populations of the islands and of the circumstances under which they worked. [CAP]

2389 Torriente, Loló de la. Imagen de dos tiempos. La Habana: Editorial Letras Cubanas, 1982. 223 p. (Col. Crítica)

Reflections on culture and history in Cuba. Discusses artistic trends in social/historical context. [RJS]

2390 Trade, government, and society in Caribbean history, 1700–1920: essays presented to Douglas Hall. Edited by B.W. Higman. Kingston: Heinemann Educational Books Caribbean, 1983. 172 p.: ill., index.

Collection of nine essays presented to historian Douglas Hall on the occasion of his retirement from the Univ. of the West Indies. Written by former students and colleagues, the volume contains useful discussions of the slave trade to Jamaica during the 18th century, domestic service in Jamaica since 1750, a social history of Emancipation Day in Trinidad, etc. [CAP]

2391 Vega, Bernardo. La migración española de 1939 y los inicios del marxismo-leninismo en la República Dominicana. Santo Domingo: Fundación Cultural Dominicana, 1984. 208 p.: bibl., ill.

Careful study of Marxism in the Dominican Republic and effect of Spanish migration to island in 1930s and 1940s. Uses US archival material, press, and interviews. Documented study of intriguing episode. [RJS]

Vila Vilar, Enriqueta. Bibliografía básica para la historia de Puerto Rico. See *HLAS 47 : 48.*

EARLY COLONIAL

2392 Aarons, G.A. Sevilla La Nueva: microcosm of Spain in Jamaica: pt. 1, The historical background; pt. 2, Unearthing the past (IJ/JJ, 16:4, Nov. 1983, p. 37–46, ill.; 17:1, Feb. 1984, p. 28–37, bibl., ill.)

Pt. 1 outlines early history of the foundation of New Seville by the Spaniards. Pt. 2 discusses its history and gives progress report on recent archaeological work in the area's Arawak sites. [CAP]

Alvarado Morales, Manuel. La ciudad de México ante la fundación de la Armada de Barlovento: historia de un encrucijada, 1635–1643. See item **1929.**

2393 Beckles, Hilary. Plantation production and white "proto-slavery:" white indentured servants and the colonisation of the English West Indies, 1624–1645 (AAFH/TAM, 41:3, Jan. 1985, p. 21–45, tables)

Provocative discussion of the manner in which the demands of plantation agriculture changed traditional white indentured servitude with its moral-paternalistic ideology of pre-industrial England, into a type of "proto-slavery" in the West Indies. Beckles maintains that this system preceded the emergence of slavery and provided English planters with the necessary experience for the enslavement of Africans. [CAP]

2394 Beckles, Hilary. Rebels and reactionaries: the political responses of white labourers to planter-class hegemony in seventeenth-century Barbados (UWI/JCH, 15, 1981, p. 1–19)

Pioneering discussion of the opposition of white workers to planter control and domination in Barbados during the 17th century. [CAP]

2395 Borde, Pierre-Gustave-Louis. The history of Trinidad under the Spanish government. v. 1, 1498–1622. v. 2, 1622–1797. Translated by James Alva Bain and A.S. Mavrogordato. Port-of-Spain: Paria Publishing Co., 1982. 2 v.: bibls., ill., 1 folded map.

Republication of work that first appeared in 1876. French Creole Trinidadian author provides interesting insights into the evolution of Trinidadian society. [CAP]

2396 Campbell, P.F. The Church in Barbados in the seventeenth century. St. Ann's Garrison: Barbados Museum and Historical Society, 1982. 188 p.: bibl., ill., index.

Rather superficial treatment of the ecclesiastical history of Barbados. Provides useful biographical sketches of clergymen who served in the island during the period. [CAP]

2397 Fortune, Stephen Alexander. Merchants and Jews: the struggle for British West Indian commerce, 1650–1750. Gainesville: Univ. Presses of Florida, 1984. 1 v.: bibl., index (Latin American monographs; 2nd series, 26)

Fine and richly documented study of British West Indian commerce, with special reference to Barbados and Jamaica. Author focuses on the interplay between trade and production in the island's economic development. Shows that the commercial momentum was, to some extent, directed by Jews. [CAP]

2398 Galenson, David W. Population turnover in the English West Indies in the late seventeenth century: a comparative perspective (EHA/J, 45:2, June 1985, p. 227–235, table)

Quantitative estimates of population persistence among estate managers and owners in Barbados during the late 17th and early 18th centuries. Author finds a low rate of out-migration in the 1670s but a progressive increase in later decades. [CAP]

2399 García de Palacios, Santiago. Sínodo de Santiago de Cuba de 1681. Madrid: Instituto Francisco Suárez; Salamanca: Instituto de Historia de la Teología, 1982. 201 p.: bibl. (Col. Tierra nueva e cielo nuevo; 7. Sínodos americanos; 1)

Facsimile edition of proceedings and rulings of 1681 Synod in Santiago de Cuba. Scholarly introduction. [RJS]

2400 Gil-Bermejo García, Juana. La española: anotaciones históricas, 1600–1650. Sevilla, Spain: Escuela de Estudios Hispanoamericanos, C.S.I.C., 1983. 410 p., 20 p. of plates: bibl., facsims., ill., index (Publicaciones, 0210–5802; 290)

Notes on the social, economic and political history of Hispaniola in the 17th century. Uses, and in some cases transcribes, evidence from the Archivo General de Indias. Deals with issues of population, land use, trade, and administration. [RJS]

2401 Goico Castro, Manuel Jesús. La encomienda y el régimen de la tierra en la Isla Española (in Congreso Venezolano de la Historia, 4th, Caracas, 1980. Memorias [see HLAS 46:2621] v. 2, p. 11–30, bibl.)

General discussion of *encomienda* in Santo Domingo, largely based on secondary sources. [RJS]

2402 Jármy Chapa, Martha de. Un eslabón perdido en la historia: piratería en El Caribe, siglos XVI y XVII. México: UNAM, Coordinación de Humanidades, Centro Coordinador y Difusor de Estudios Latinoamericanos, 1983. 291 p., 1 folded leaf of plates: bibl., col. map (Nuestra América; 6)

Study of piracy, based on secondary and printed primary sources, emphasizes relationship to Spanish colonization. [RJS]

2403 Labat, Jean Baptiste. Nuevo viaje a las islas de la América. Traducción y edición de Manuel Cárdenas Ruiz. Río Piedras: Editorial de la Univ. de Puerto Rico, 1984. 1 v.: bibl., ill., index (Col. caribeña)

Initial effort at translating Labat's work includes only the first year of his residency (1694). Contains observations of flora, fauna, and many aspects of French colonial culture. [D.E. Chipman]

2404 Labat, Jean-Baptiste. Le Père Labat à travers ses manuscrits. Présenté par Marcel Chatillon. Nérac, France: Imprimerie Owen, 1979. 170 p., 2 leaves of plates: ill. (Extrait du *Bulletin de la Société d'histoire de la Guadeloupe*; 40–42)

Provides first critical examination of the Dominican missionary's work, by putting it in the context of both Labat's life and France's complex and changing political situation. [APD]

2405 Mongin, Jean. Lettres du R.P. Mongin: l'évangélisation des esclaves au XVIIe siècle. Présentation de Marcel Chatillon. Aubenas, France: Imprimerie Lienhart, 1984. 136 p. (Extrait du *Bulletin de la Société d'histoire de la Guadeloupe*; 61–62)

First publication of valuable source. Documents missionary methods of the Jesuit order which specialized in slave evangelization and which much influenced Creole culture. Chatillon's introduction offers useful insights on such French Caribbean missions. [APD]

2406 Moscoso Puello, Francisco Eujenio. Apuntes para la historia de la medicina de la Isla de Santo Domingo. Prólogo y notas de Manuel Mañón Arredondo y Vetilio Alfau Durán. San Pedro de Macorís, República Dominicana: Univ. Central del Este, 1983–

1985. 3 v. (470, 447, 548 p.): bibl., ill., indexes, maps, plates (Univ. Central del Este; 46–48. Serie científica; 16–18)

Rich, three-volume compilation of miscellaneous data on medicine in Santo Domingo. Author was medical doctor. Covers pre-colonial period to 18th century, with emphasis on 16th and 17th centuries. Essentially a source book. [RJS]

2407 Moya Pons, Frank. Los trabajadores indígenas y la estructura social de La Española en 1514 (MHD/B, 10:17, 1982, p. 119–138, tables)

Discusses demographic estimates and data on which they are based. Analyzes *repartimiento* of 1514 in detail. Transcribes figures from key 1514 document. Careful essay. [RJS]

2408 Otte, Enrique. La despoblación de La Española: la crisis de 1528 (IAA, 10:3, 1984, p. 241–265, appendix, bibl.)

Detailed examination, based on primary sources, of Spanish efforts to counteract the depopulation of Hispaniola. Sees colonial prohibitions on emigration as ineffectual and lists of emigrés as inaccurate. [RJS]

2409 Petitjean-Roget, Jacques. La société d'habitation à la Martinique: un demi-siècle de formation, 1635–1685. Paris: Honoré Champion, 1980. 852 p.: appendices, bibl., ill., index, maps, tables.

Major work draws from all available archival sources and the author's previous studies. Provides comprehensive portrait of early French settlement in the Lesser Antilles, and revises previous views, especially those concerning demography and material life. Argues that during these 17th-century decades there emerged a Creole culture ignored by most authors who focus on the 18th century. Perceives the brief initial phase as crucial since the coexistence between Carib Indians and European immigrants allowed the latter to adjust to and survive in the new environment. [APD]

2410 Petitjean-Roget, Jacques and Eugène Bruneau-Latouche. Personnes et familles à la Martinique au XVIIe siècle: d'après recensements et terriers nominatifs. t. 1, Documents. t. 2, Dictionnaire. Fort-de-France: Société d'histoire de la Martinique, 1983. 2 v. (729 p.): ill.

First-rate tool for social and economic history of early settlement. Vol. 1 reproduces oldest censuses and land deeds. Preceded by excellent introduction on the making of a plantation society. Vol. 2 lists all names (*patronymes*) and indicates the primary source (mostly civil registers). [APD]

2411 The Rich papers: letters from Bermuda, 1615–1646: eyewitness accounts sent by the early colonists to Sir Nathaniel Rich. Edited by Vernon A. Ives. Transcribed by Ambrose Gosling, Sister Jean Kennedy, and John Adams. Toronto, Canada: Univ. of Toronto Press *for the* Bermuda National Trust, 1984. 413 p.: bibl., ill., index, maps (1 col.)

Collection of documents, known as the Rich Papers, on the early history of Bermuda. Arranged chronologically with explanatory footnotes. [CAP]

2412 Wynter, Sylvia. New Seville and the conversion experience of Bartolomé de las Casas: pt. 1 (IJ/JJ, 17:2, May 1984, p. 25–32, ill.)

Thoughtful analysis of the conversion experience of de las Casas and what author characterizes as his break with the normative reference frame and uniform perception of his fellow Spaniards. Wynter points out that de las Casas's conversion inspired him to oppose all forms of Indian forced labor and to advocate the importation of a limited number of African slaves as a substitute labor force. [CAP]

LATE COLONIAL AND FRENCH REVOLUTIONARY PERIOD

2413 Abénon, Lucien-René. L'évolution de l'habitation de l'Ilet entre 1731 et 1765 d'après deux inventaires (SHG/B, 60:2, 1984, p. 3–12, appendices, tables)

Comparison between two inventories of the same plantation, one from the first half, one from the second half of the 18th century, illustrates the economic boom that took place in Guadeloupe around the middle of the century. [APD]

2414 Abénon, Lucien-René. La révolte avortée de 1736 et la répression du marronage à la Guadeloupe (SHG/B, 55:1, 1983, p. 51–73)

Based on archival sources, shows that slave unrest provided a pretext for slave-hunting expeditions in the then largely unpopulated Grande-Terre, north of Guadeloupe. [APD]

2415 Blérald, Alain-Philippe. L'organisation des finances publiques à la Guadeloupe et à la Martinique sous l'Ancien Régime: contribution à l'étude de l'Etat colonial (SHG/B, 57/58:3/4, 1983, p. 55–81, tables)

Well documented analysis of budget and accounting rules followed by the French colonial administration. [APD]

2416 Butel, Paul. Marchés internationaux, l'Europe et les Antilles (Bulletin du Centre d'histoire des espaces atlantiques [Talence, France] 1, 1984?, p. 9–12)

Useful research report, sets agenda and lists resources for projects on colonial trade between Bordeaux and the Caribbean. [APD]

2417 Caron, Aimery and **Arnold R. Highfield.** The French intervention in the St. John Slave Revolt of 1733–34. Charlotte Amalie, St. Thomas: Bureau of Libraries, Museums, and Archaeological Services, Dept. of Conservation and Cultural Affairs, 1981. 58 p.: bibl., ill., index (Occasional paper; 7)

Introduction to translation of French sources reporting this slave revolt. The document was the result of a French expedition whose intervention was decisive in crushing the revolt. [APD]

2418 Cauna, Jacques. Une réussite de planteur-négociant à Saint-Domingue: les Fleuriau (Bulletin du Centre d'histoire des espaces atlantiques [Talence, France] 2, 1985, p. 151–178)

Based on recent unpublished dissertation. Major contribution: 1) sheds new light on reasons for success and profits of well-managed plantations: slaves were well treated when managers were related to the owners; and 2) illustrates interesting case in which merchant wealth permitted the Club Massiac to play a political role. Very valuable work. [APD]

2419 Cauna, Jacques. Vestiges de sucreries dans le plaine du Cul-de-Sac (IFH/C, 165, avril 1985, p. 29–57, ill.)

Pt. 2 of fascinating tour, conducted by specialist, of one of the richest sugar-producing areas in 18th-century St. Domingue. Based on wealth of original sources, study traces economic policies followed by successive owners of various plantations, the impact of revolutionary events and their aftermath, and the region's architectural heritage. [APD]

2420 Debien, Gabriel and Pierre Pluchon. Trois sucreries de Léogane, Saint-Domingue: 1776–1802 (Bulletin du Centre d'histoire des espaces atlantiques [Talence, France] 2, 1985, p. 71–149, ill., maps)

Detailed description of three sugar-plantations of west St. Domingue. Shows that before sugar was developed, the cultivation of indigo led to the consolidation of small tobacco estates. [APD]

2421 Dessalles, Pierre-François-Régis. Historique des troubles survenus à la Martinique pendant la Révolution. Présenté par Henri de Frémont. Fort-de-France: Société d'histoire de la Martinique, 1982. 471 p., 1 leaf of plates: bibl., ill., indexes.

Detailed account of first two years of Revolution in the island by the earliest Creole historian of Martinique. Includes quotations from numerous original documents. Author, a white Creole judge, reflects on and reports the planters' positions vis-à-vis the Revolution. First publication of long-lost manuscript. [APD]

2422 Di Tella, Torcuato S. La rebelión de esclavos de Haiti. Buenos Aires: Instituto de Desarrollo Económico y Social (IDES), 1984. 118 p.: bibl., ill. (Ediciones del IDES; 2. Col. América Latina)

Sociological reading of the 1791 revolt, based on secondary sources. [APD]

2423 Echevarría, Israel. El primer impreso cubano (UY/R, 25:148, oct./dic. 1983, p. 39–48, bibl.)

Discussion of early Cuban publications, in effort to identify earliest. [RJS]

2424 Fick, Carolyn. Black peasants and soldiers in the Saint-Domingue Revolution: initial reactions to freedom in the South province, 1793–4 (in History from below: studies in popular protest and popular ideology in honour of George Rudé. Edited by Frederick Krantz. Montreal, Canada: Concordia Univ., 1985, p. 243–260)

Drawing from rich sources of the *Comité des colonies* of the French National Convention, examines post-1794 forms of popular resistance in the south of St. Domingue where newly enfranchised slaves op-

posed continuing forced labor on plantations. Fick emphasizes the importance of popular movements among the peasantry which contributed towards the final French defeat. [APD]

2425 Foubert, Bernard. La nourriture des esclaves et la question des vivres sur une grande habitation sucrière à la fin du XVIIIe siècle (Bulletin du Centre d'histoire des espaces atlantiques [Talence, France] 2, 1985, p. 11–36, ill., maps)

Detailed study of subsistence crops, diet, and sanitary conditions of slaves based on archives of wealthy, well run plantation, south of St. Domingue. An important contribution which shows how planter's policy of encouraging slave-farming on small lots to reduce dependency on external supply paved way for transition to small subsistence plantations after slave emancipation. [APD]

2426 Gautier, Arlette. Les esclaves de l'habitation Bisdary, 1763–1817 (SHG/B, 60:2, 1984, p. 13–50, appendices, tables)

Fine, longitudinal study of slave population in one of the biggest sugar plantations. Stresses proportion of Creoles among slaves, and formation of kinship networks that linked half the slaves born at Bisdary in 1763. Appropriately places Guadeloupe slave demography within the context of 18th-century populations of the Western world. [APD]

2427 Gautier, Arlette. Les soeurs de Solitude: la condition féminine dans l'esclavage aux Antilles du XVIIe au XIXe siècle. Paris: Editions caribéennes, 1985. 284, 3 p.: appendices, bibl., ill., maps, tables.

First work of French scholarship that focuses on women slaves. Shows centrality of gender in the building of slave institutions and culture. Draws from large body of literature and archival sources. Argues that masters started encouraging motherhood among slaves well before 19th-century emancipation prospects. Useful contribution that breaks new ground. [APD]

2428 Geggus, David P. The cost of Pitt's Caribbean campaigns, 1793–1798 (The Historical Journal [Cambridge Univ. Press, Cambridge, England] 26:3, 1983, p. 699–706)

Convincingly demonstrates that the British army and navy suffered more casualties than previously estimated while operating in the Caribbean, especially the Lesser Antilles. [APD]

2429 Geggus, David P. Du charpentier au colonel: Jean Kina et la Révolution de Saint-Domingue (SHHG/R, 138, mars 1983, p. 5–23)

Case of elite slave exemplifies black troops in the thousands who fought with Royalists and English, to maintain slavery. Expanded version appeared as "Slave, Soldier, Rebel: the Strange Career of Jean Kina" in the *Jamaican Historical Review* (Kingston, 12, 1980, p. 33–51). [APD]

2430 Geggus, David P. Les esclaves de la plaine du Nord à la veille de la Révolution française: pt. 1, Les équipes de travail sur une vingtaine de sucreries; pt. 2, La sucrerie Baudin au quartier Morin, 1783 (SHHG/R, 135, juin 1982, p. 85–107; 136, sept. 1982, p. 5–32; 144, sept. 1984, p. 15–44)

Systematic study (published in two parts but in three issues) of the north of St. Domingue where the major revolt took place. Pt. 1 (issues Nos. 135–136) offers an in-depth analysis of plantation inventories with systematic data on slaves (e.g., sex, age, ethnicity, skills, mortality, birth). Pt. 2 (issue No. 144) describes the situation of a variety of slaves according to plantation management and economic policy. Exemplary study. [APD]

2431 Geggus, David P. On the eve of Haitian revolution: slave runaways in Saint Domingue in the year 1790 (Slavery and Abolition [Frank Cass, London] 6:3, 1985, p. 112–128)

Geggus continues his systematic explanation of the major slave rebellion of 1791. Uses quantitative treatment based on advertisement for fugitives placed in colonial newspapers in 1790. Draws new distinctions between male/female, Creole/African slaves, plantation newcomers/old-timers, jailed/missing ones, etc. Spectrum that emerges runs from luckiest runaway (Creole colored female) to likeliest to be caught (African black male). Discusses external factors determining under- or over-representation in *marronage* statistics (e.g., rate of slave introduction, ethnic group, etc.). Solid and sophisticated study which revises interpretations of the 1791 revolt as an extension of previous *marronage*. Also appears in *Out of the house of bondage: runaways, resistance and marronage; Africa in the New World*, edited by Gad Heuman (London: Frank Cass, 1986, p. 112–128). [APD]

2432 Geggus, David P. La révolte de Jean Kina à Fort-Royal (SHHG/R, 140, sept. 1983, p. 12–25)

Geggus explores Kina's leadership of an army rebellion, an intriguing case, following his loyalist position in St. Domingue (see item **2429**). [APD]

2433 Hall, N.A.T. Maritime Maroons: *grand marronage* from the Danish West Indies (William and Mary Quarterly [Institute of Early American History and Culture, Williamsburg, Va.] 42:4, Oct. 1985, p. 453–475)

Deals with unresearched aspect of *marronage*. Explores *grand marronage* of males, a constant throughout the history of slavery in Danish West Indies. Discusses area's unsuitable topography for Maroon camps (i.e., flat islands) and proximity of hospitable islands (e.g., Puerto Rico). [APD]

2434 Hall, N.A.T. Slavery in three West Indian towns: Christiansted, Fredericksted and Charlotte Amalie in the late eighteenth and early nineteenth century [i.e. centuries] (*in* Trade, government and society in Caribbean history, 1700–1920: essays presented to Douglas Hall. B.W. Higman, editor. Kingston: Heinemann Educational Books Caribbean, 1983, p. 17–38)

Uses Danish colonial sources to draw precise and suggestive outline of urban slaves (e.g., sex composition, occupational categories), more than half the total urban population. Stresses their interaction with urban freedman, whites, and plantation slaves. [APD]

2435 Hall, Neville. Slaves' use of their free time in the Danish Virgin Islands in the late eighteenth and early nineteenth century [i.e. centuries] (UWI/JCH, 13, 1980, p. 21–43, tables)

Uses Danish colonial sources to examine slave behaviors in non-working activities (e.g., Christian practices, market day, dancing). Such practices serve as indicators of slave culture that resulted from the interplay of African and European elements. [APD]

2436 Hornby, Ove. Kolonierne i Vestindien. Redaktion af Svend Ellehj os Kristof Glamann. Kbenhavn: Politiken, 1980. 394 p.: bibl., ill.

Scholarly volume devoted to history

of Denmark's former West Indian colonies. Reflects current historical thinking and provides objective description of Danish colonial era in what are now the US Virgin Islands. [M.L.H. Bernal]

2437 Howard, Thomas Phipps. The Haitian journal of Lieutenant Howard, York Hussars, 1796–1798. Edited, with an introduction, by Roger Norman Buckley. Knoxville: Univ. of Tennessee Press, 1985. 194 p.: appendix, ill., indexes, tables.

Useful testimony on British military operations in revolutionary St. Domingue as well as on the collapse of the wealthiest 18th-century plantation society. [APD]

2438 Huetz de Lemps, Christian. Les engagés au départ de Bordeaux, fin XVIIe -XVIIIe siècles (in L'Atlantique et ses rivages, 1500–1800: actes du Colloque de l'Association des historiens modernistes des universités, 1983. Bordeaux, France: Presses universitaires de Bordeaux, 1984, p. 133–154, tables)

Impressive first results of work in progress dealing with 13,000 engagés leaving France through Bordeaux. Notes geographical origins and sociological profiles, shows that the engagé institution survived through the 18th century, being chiefly focused on the Caribbean. [APD]

2439 James, C.L.R. Les Jacobins noirs: Toussaint-Louverture et la révolution de Saint-Domingue. Translation, Pierre Naville. Paris: Editions caribéennes, 1983. 375 p.: bibl.

New edition of Pierre Naville's translation of James's classic Black Jacobins includes translations of James's prefaces to successive editions. [APD]

2440 Koest, Françoise. La révolution à la Guadeloupe: 1789–1796. Basse-Terre: Archives départementales; Pointe-à-Pitre, Guadeloupe: Centre départemental de documentation pédagogique, 1982. 1 portfolio: bibl., ill., tables.

Selection of original materials, culled from the Archives of Guadeloupe, documents facets of Guadeloupe's society and the revolutionary process. [APD]

2441 Kuethe, Allan James El ejército criollo y la fidelidad cubana durante la época del Libertador (RO, 30/31, dic. 1983, p. 47–56)

Notes divisions within Creole society in Cuba, failure of Arango y Parreño to ally effectively with militia to obtain restructuring of society during eventful year of 1808. [RJS]

2442 Kuethe, Allan James. El Marqués de Esquilache, Alejandro O'Reilly y las reformas económicas de Carlos III en Cuba (in Congreso Venezolano de la Historia, 4th, Caracas, 1980. Memoria [see HLAS 46:2621] v. 2, p. 117–134)

Sees reforms of Charles III as rooted in needs of imperial security. Argues that Esquilache conceptualized, and O'Reilly modified, reform plans for Cuba, and that policies were favorably received by Cuban elite. Despite subsequent hostility to reforms elsewhere in the empire, Cuban experience lay groundwork for later policies. [RJS]

2443 Kuethe, Allan James and G. Douglas Inglis. Absolutism and enlightened reform: Charles III, the establishment of the Alcabala, and commercial reorganization in Cuba (PP, 109, Nov. 1985, p. 118–143)

Seeks to explain "the processes that led to Spain's achievement in advancing revenue reform" after 1763 by a careful study of the case of Cuba. Traces consultation with Cuban patriciate, extension of commercial prerogatives, stimulus to sugar industry, and blow to Consulado of Cádiz. Emphasizes innovative role of Esquilache, conservatism of Arriaga, and general flexibility of Spanish administration. [RJS]

2444 Kuethe, Allan James and Lowell Blaisdell. The Esquilache government and the reforms of Charles III in Cuba (JGSWGL, 19, 1982, p. 117–136)

Emphasizes role of Esquilache in designing colonial reforms. Discusses military, tax, and commercial policy toward 18th-century Cuba. Based on detailed archival research. [RJS]

2445 Lafleur, Gérard. Relations avec l'étranger des minorités religieuses aux Antilles françaises, XVIIe-XVIIIe s. (SHG/B, 57/58:3/4, 1983, p. 27–44)

Sheds interesting light on spread of Protestant family networks across French and English Caribbean islands which were involved in contraband and diplomacy during French-English wars. [APD]

2446 Loker, Zvi. Jews in the Grand'Anse colony of Saint-Domingue (AJA, 34:1, April 1982, p. 89–97, tables)

Identifies members of Jewish merchant colony in the port of Jérémie and points to their integration into a Catholic environment. [APD]

2447 Loker, Zvi. Were there Jewish communities in St. Domingue—Haiti? (Jewish Social Studies [New York] 45:2, Spring 1983, p. 135–146)

Determines dual origin of St. Domingue's Jewish community by establishing its two emigration points: 1) Bordeaux, France (its "Portuguese Jews"); and 2) Curaçao (its Dutch Jews). [APD]

2448 Louis-Joseph, Christian. Notes sur la rentabilité des sucreries et du commerce colonial à la fin du XVIIe siècle (SHG/B, 57/58:3/4, 1983, p. 45–54)

Reevaluates profitability estimates of sugar trade and plantations. Uses specific examples to criticize accounting methods followed by previous historians. Estimates that much greater profits were made in both sectors. [APD]

2449 Mettas, Jean. Répertoire des expéditions négrières françaises au XVIIIe siècle. t. 1, Nantes. t. 2, Ports autres que Nantes. Édité par Serge et Michèle Daget. Paris: Société d'histoire d'Outre-mer, 1978–1984. 2 v.: bibl., ill., indexes (Nouvelle série. Instruments de travail; 1–2)

Superb reference tool covers history of 18th-century slave trade. Lists every expedition identified in French public archives. Data organized according to: name, tonnage of ship; size of crew and loss of seamen; captain's and ship-owner's name; date, port of registry, and payroll; ports of call and sites of slave-trading; accidents and shipwrecks at sea; number of blacks carried, dead, sold. Highly recommended source for colonial history library collections. [APD]

2450 Palacios, Roberto. Ansia de libertad: documentos relativos a la Revolución Francesa en Curazao y la lucha por la igualdad y libertad de 1791–1800, en el Archivo Nacional de los Países Bajos y en el antiguo Archivo de Curazao que allí reposa (Lantèrnu [Centraal Historisch Archief, Willemstad, Curaçao] 1:1, Feb. 1983, p. 20–27, ill.)

Account of French naval intervention in Curaçao where, author argues, the expedi-

tion was to emancipate the slaves. Based on original sources. [APD]

2451 Pannet, Pierre J. Report on the execrable conspiracy carried out by the Amina Negroes on the Danish island of St. Jan in America, 1733. Translated and edited by Aimery P. Caron and Arnold R. Highfield. Christiansted, St. Croix: Antilles Press, 1984. 23 p.: ill., map.

Publication of English translation of main source on the 1733 slave revolt in St. John's, the report of a French planter established in the island. Introduction establishes that the revolt was caused by severe deterioration of living conditions for slaves, and that it was lead by those born in Africa. [APD]

2451a Pérotin-Dumon, Anne. Ambiguous revolution in the Caribbean: the White Jacobins, 1789–1800 (Historical Reflections/Reflexions historiques [Univ. of Waterloo, Canada] 13:2, 1986, p. 499–515)

Succinct article illuminates strife undergone by French Caribbean society during late 18th and early 19th centuries. Focuses on White Jacobins, restless group of *petit blancs* who were for the most part young, male, poor, unmarried and mobile. Author deftly analyzes basic issues such as colonial vs. Creole, and trade vs. plantation, to settle finally on the *révolution du commerce.* Singularly incisive article. [G.M. Dorn]

2452 Pérotin-Dumon, Anne. Être patriote sous les tropiques: la Guadeloupe, la colonisation et la Révolution, 1789–1794. Basse-Terre: Société d'histoire de la Guadeloupe, 1985. 339 p.: ill. (Bibliothèque d'histoire antillaise; 10)

Using archival materials from both France and the Antilles, author traces relationship between France and Guadeloupe during period of the French Revolution. Emphasizes interactions among events in Europe and the various islands, and ambiguities of the Republican period. Contains thorough scholarly discussion of sources. [RJS]

2453 Pérotin-Dumon, Anne. French America (The International History Review [Univ. of Toronto, Canada] 6, Nov. 1984, p. 551–569, bibl.)

Traces influence of US Revolution and Hispanic-American independence movements on white French Jacobins of the Caribbean within the framework of Peggy Liss's *Atlantic empires* (see HLAS 46:2469). Author synthesizes impact of the two types of revolution in the Americas. Raises provocative questions, such as "What effect did the breakdown of patriarchal power in the 18th century have on the revolutionary movements?" [G.M. Dorn]

2454 Pérotin-Dumon, Anne. Le mal antillais et la Révolution française: des colonies de commerce aux départements d'Outre mer (TM, 41, déc. 1984, p. 1025–1057, bibl.)

Insightful analysis of the political success of the French Revolution's colonial policy which balanced centralized authority with respect for the individual. Abolition of slavery in 1848 and the formation of *départements* in place of the "old colonies" in the French Caribbean led towards peaceful evolution and assimilation, however slow. Author also identifies areas of tension between overseas *départements* and France's central government. Major contribution. [G.M. Dorn]

2455 Pluchon, Pierre. Nègres et juifs au XVIIIe siècle: le racisme au siècle des lumières. Paris: Tallandier, 1984. 313 p.: appendix, bibl.

Uses legal case involving a Jewish master and his black slaves from St. Domingue, to show how principles of the Enlightenment were consistently thwarted by racism, particularly anti-Semitism. [APD]

2456 Ie [i.e. Première] abolition de l'esclavage, février 1794: articles et documents. S.l.: Fondation Schoelcher, 1985. 1 v. (Cahiers; 4, 1985)

Selected publication of original documents on the decree of the French National Convention, and the situation of Guadeloupe, Martinique, St. Lucia, and French Guiana during the French Revolution. Articles by Anne Pérotin-Dumon, Jacques Adélaïde-Merlande, G. Monfret, Liliane Chauleau, and Michel Deveze introduce the documents. [APD]

2457 Price, Richard. First time: the historical vision of an Afro-American people. Baltimore, Md.: Johns Hopkins Univ. Press, 1983. 189 p.: bibl., index, maps (Johns Hopkins studies in Atlantic history and culture)

This study as well as author's other volume annotated below (item **2458**) constitute a masterpiece of combined ethno- and colonial history. Together they recreate a period in the history of the Saramaka who live

in today's Surinam. Here author focuses on oral sources of the colonized descendants of Maroons who gained their freedom from Dutch colonial rule. Author compiles and transcribes the Saramakas' collective memory on this era of wars, history playing a central role in Saramaka culture. For ethnologist's comment, see *HLAS 47: 1107*. [APD]

2458 Price, Richard. To slay a hydra: Dutch colonial perspectives on the Saramaka wars. Ann Arbor, Mich.: Karoma Publishers, 1983. 247 p.: bibl., ill., map, plates.

Complements and enhances preceding item **2457**, by presenting the written records of the colonizers. Culled from Dutch colonial archives and edited by the author, they focus on the last episode of the mid 18th-century Saramaka wars. For ethnologist's comment, see *HLAS 47: 1108*. [APD]

2459 Souty, François J.L. Agriculture et système agricole au Suriname de la fin du XVIIe à la fin du XVIIIe siècle (Revue d'histoire française d'Outre-mer [Société de l'histoire des colonies françaises, Paris] 69:256, 1982, p. 193–224, maps, tables)

First conclusions of comprehensive study underway on Demerara, Essequibo, and Berbice. Well researched and written. Surveys Dutch colonizing process before focusing on agricultural sector (e.g., commodities produced, work-force, plantation management and financing) at time of maximum prosperity and within context of Dutch colonial trade. [APD]

2460 Stein, Robert Louis. The abolition of slavery in the north, west, and south of Saint Domingue (AAFH/TAM, 41:3, Jan. 1985, p. 47–55)

Useful and precise observations about the first abolition of slavery and divergent measures taken in 1794 by the three commissaries of the French National Convention in each region of St. Domingue. [APD]

2461 Stein, Robert Louis. Léger Félicité Sonthonax: the lost sentinel of the Republic. Rutherford, N.J.: Fairleigh Dickinson Univ. Press; London: Associated Univ. Presses, 1985. 234 p.: bibl., index.

Long-awaited rehabilitation of the most influential commissary sent in the 1790s by French revolutionary governments to St. Domingue. Sonthonax was the first to proclaim the abolition of slavery in the New

World. Well written and useful introduction to the complex political process, triggered by the French Revolution, and which led to Haitian independence. Based on archival research. [APD]

2462 Stein, Robert Louis. Revolution, land reform, and plantation discipline in Saint Domingue (PAIGH/H, 96, julio/dic. 1983, p. 173–186)
Using printed sources, Stein shows continuity through 1798 between French revolutionary figures and following Haitian leaders. Both groups sought to maintain large plantations and enforce strict discipline among emancipated slaves. [APD]

2463 Stein, Robert Louis. The revolution of 1789 and the abolition of slavery (Canadian Journal of History [Univ. of Saskatchwan, Saskatoon] 17:3, Dec. 1982, p. 447–467)
History of decree abolishing slavery issued by the French Revolutionary Convention in 1794. Documents process of ratification of initial abolition decree proclaimed six months earlier by one of its commissaries, in north St. Domingue. Fills lacuna in French Revolutionary historiography which has neglected the issue of slavery. [APD]

2464 Stein, Robert Louis. The state of French colonial commerce on the eve of the Revolution (Journal of European Economic History [Banco di Roma] 12, 1983, p. 105–117)
Useful survey in English shows that French colonial commerce at the time was centered in the Caribbean. [APD]

2465 Thésée, Françoise. Les assemblées paroissiales des Cayes à St. Domingue, 1774–1793 (SHHG/R, 40:137, déc. 1982, p. 1–212)
Meticulous use of original source, miraculously saved, which documents proceedings of a colonial parish assembly. Reports on local white politics and institutions during crucial beginning of the Revolution, especially on *petit-blanc* fear of free-colored insurrection in the South. Article reproduces large portions of proceedings and identifies people mentioned therein. Key study for period specialists. [APD]

2466 Vanony-Frisch, Nicole. Les esclaves de la Guadeloupe à la fin de l'ancien régime d'après les sources notariales, 1770–

1789. Aubenas, France: Imprimerie Lienhart, 1985. 165 p.: bibl., graphs, ill., maps, tables (Extrait du *Bulletin de la Société d'histoire de la Guadeloupe*, 63–64)
First computerized treatment of notarial records regarding 8,820 Guadeloupe slaves around 1770–80. Provides much new data for those researching slavery in the French Caribbean. Occupational hierarchy is defined according to gender and race, and includes many mixed-bloods and black Creoles in the top jobs. [APD]

SPANISH BORDERLANDS

2467 Beerman, Eric. Arturo O'Neill: first governor of West Florida during the second Spanish period (FHS/FHQ, 60:1, July 1981, p. 29–41)
Biographical treatment of Irish-born governor of Spanish West Florida. Based on extensive primary materials. [RJS]

2468 De Pratter, Chester B.; Charles M. Hudson; and Marvin T. Smith. The route of Juan Pardo's exploration in the interior southeast, 1566–1568 (FHS/FHQ, 62:2, Oct. 1983, p. 125–158)
Detailed reconstruction of route of Juan Pardo's 16th-century expeditions in what are now South Carolina, North Carolina, and Tennessee. Of relevance both to history of Amerindians encountered and to understanding subsequent expeditions. [RJS]

2469 Din, Gilbert C. War clouds on the Mississippi: Spain's 1785 crisis in West Florida (FHS/FHQ, 60:1, July 1981, p. 51–76)
Discusses diplomatic maneuvering between Spain and US over West Florida immediately after American Revolution. Focuses on Georgia's active effort to take possession of Natchez region, Spanish effort to maintain control. [RJS]

Fernández de Velasco, Manuel. Relaciones España-Estado Unidos y multilaciones territoriales en Latinoamérica. See *HLAS* 47:7029.

2470 Gillaspie, William R. Survival of a frontier presidio: St. Augustine and the subsidy and private contract systems, 1680–1702 (FHS/FHQ, 62:3, Jan. 1984, p. 273–295)

Examines provisioning of St. Augustine in the context of the presidio-mission complex of the Borderlands. Sees subsidy system, in conjunction with private contracts contraband, as key to St. Augustine's survival. [RJS]

2471 Hernández Rodríguez, Germán. La aportación de la isla de La Gomera al poblamiento de la Luisiana (*in* Coloquio de Historia Canario-Americana, 4th, Las Palmas, Spain, 1980. Cuarto Coloquio de Historia Canario-Americana. Coordinación y prólogo, Francisco Morales Padrón. Las Palmas, Spain: Ediciones del Excelentísimo Cabildo Insular, 1982, p. 225–248, appendix, graphs, tables)

Study of role of one of the smaller of the Canary Islands in emigration to Louisiana. Traces local background; uses archival material. [RJS]

2472 Hoffman, Paul E. The Chicora legend and Franco-Spanish rivalry in La Florida (FHS/FHQ, 62:4, April 1984, p. 419–438)

Traces evidence on legend and location of a "New Andalusia" and its effect on 16th-century explorers. [RJS]

2473 Landers, Jane. Spanish sanctuary: fugitives in Florida, 1687–1790 (FHS/FHQ, 62:3, Jan. 1984, p. 296–313)

Careful study of Spanish colonial government's interaction with fugitive slaves. Uses some declarations by fugitive slaves themselves. Draws on primary sources. Effectively conveys dynamic of evolution of policy. [RJS]

2474 Lyon, Eugene. Spain's sixteenth-century North American settlement attempts: a neglected aspect (FHS/FHQ, 59:3, Jan. 1981, p. 275–291)

Argues that Spanish "settlement impulse" has been underestimated. Emphasizes desire for landed estates and northern empire that underlay Florida colonization. Sees lack of control of Indians as key to failure. [RJS]

2475 Marotti, Frank, Jr. Juan Baptista de Segura and the failure of the Florida Jesuit mission, 1566–1572 (FHS/FHQ, 63:3, Jan. 1985, p. 267–279)

Examines "human frailties" of the superior of the Jesuit mission to Florida, and attributes failure of enterprise in large part to them. [RJS]

2476 Molina Martínez, Miguel. La participación canaria en la formación y reclutamiento del batallón de Louisiana (*in* Coloquio de Historia Canario-Americana, 4th, Las Palmas, Spain, 1980. Cuarto Coloquio de Historia Canario-Americana. Coordinación y prólogo, Francisco Morales Padrón. Las Palmas, Spain: Ediciones del Excelentísimo Cabildo Insular, 1982, p. 133–224, appendix, graphs, tables)

Treats 18th-century immigration from Canaries to Louisiana, soon after Spanish acquisition to territory. Sees both military and colonizing aims. Detailed study based on primary sources. Contains lists of colonists and families. [RJS]

2477 Pearson, Fred Lamar, Jr. Timucuan rebellion of 1656: investigation and the civil-religious controversy (FHS/FHQ, 61:3, Jan. 1983, p. 260–280)

Discussion of 17th-century rebellion of Timucuan Indians in Florida. Uses primary sources, including *visita* records. Looks at relationship between colonial governor and Franciscans, gives detailed account of background to revolt. [RJS]

2478 Troxler, Carole Watterson. Loyalist refugees and the British evacuation of East Florida: 1783–1785 (FHS/FHQ, 60:1, July 1981, p. 1–28, tables)

Account of impact on Loyalist refugees from American Revolution of cession of East Florida to Spain. Based on wide range of archival materials, petitions, contemporary press. Describes disruption, banditry, and relocation to the Caribbean and to Nova Scotia. [RJS]

2479 Wilkie, Everett C., Jr. New light on Gálvez's first attempt to attack Pensacola (FHS/FHQ, 62:2, Oct. 1983, p. 195–199)

Discusses Spanish manuscript recently acquired by John Carter Brown Library, that recounts experience of member of fleet of Bernardo de Gálvez in 1780. Translates document, which gives details of expedition and losses. [RJS]

19th CENTURY

2480 Adam, André-Georges. Une crise haïtienne, 1867–1869: Sylvain Salnave. Port-au-Prince: Editions H. Deschamps, 1982 or 1983. 217 p.: bibl., ill.

Fine study of dramatic period in Haitian history, based on archival research. Shows gradual deterioration of the fragile Haitian state and society, leading to financial difficulties and regional wars and an increasingly destabilized President Salnave seeking US support. [APD]

2481 Adélaïde-Merlande, Jacques. Delgrès, ou La Guadeloupe en 1802. Paris: Karthala, 1986. 170 p., 8 p. of plates: bibl., ill.

Standard account of colored and black participants in the army's revolt against the reestablishment of slavery. [APD]

2482 Allahar, Anton L. The Cuban sugar planters, 1790–1820: "the most solid and brilliant bourgeois class in all of Latin America" (AAFH/TAM, 41:1, July 1984, p. 37–57)

Argues that the 19th-century Cuban elite engaged in highly entrepreneurial behavior, was not passive or backward. Based on secondary sources and some published documents. [RJS]

2483 Allahar, Anton L. Merchants, planters, and merchants-become-planters: Cuba, 1820–1868. Toronto, Canada: Dept. of Sociology, Univ. of Toronto, 1983. 28 p.: bibl. (Working paper series, 0226–1774; 42)

Analysis of 19th-century Cuban elite, relying heavily on secondary sources. Argues that a "merchant-become-planter" sector sought abolition and technological advancement. Mechanistic in tone, lacks detailed evidence on merchants and planters that could substantiate thesis. [RJS]

2484 Archambault, Pedro María. Historia de la restauración. 3a ed. Santo Domingo: Editora de Santo Domingo, 1983. 330 p.: bibl., ill. (Col. de cultura dominicana; 49)

Reprint of 1938 narrative history of Restoration period in the Dominican Republic. [RJS]

2485 Armario Sánchez, Fernando. La esclavitud en Cuba durante la regencia de Espartero, 1840–1843 (AATSP/H, 43:153, enero/abril 1983, p. 129–153)

Analyzes British/Spanish relations and issue of slavery and slave trade in Cuba. Uses materials from Archivo Histórico Nacional in Madrid, but fails to incorporate important recent work by David Murray. Discusses the "Turnbull affair" and competing interest groups within Cuba. Argues that Espartero period saw relative willingness on the part of Spain to end slave trade. [RJS]

Armas, Ramón de. El apoyo chileno a la revolución cubana de 1895: apuntes para la historia del internacionalismo revolucionario en América Latina. See item **3109.**

2486 Bergad, Laird W. On comparative history: a reply to Tom Brass (JLAS, 16:1, May 1984, p. 153–156)

Reply to Brass (see item **2490**). Rejects Brass's criticism of Bergad's work on Puerto Rico. Argues that one must distinguish between *potential* and *effective* labor when considering scarcity of labor. Unfree labor found where effective labor scarce. In Puerto Rico, lack of potential labor ultimately led to wage increase. [J.D. Riley]

2487 Betances, Ramón Emeterio. Ramón Emeterio Betances. Selección y prólogo, Haroldo Dilla y Emilio Godínez. La Habana: Casa de las Américas, 1983. 376 p.: bibl. (Col. Pensamiento de nuestra América)

Useful compilation of letters of 19th-century Puerto Rican nationalist. Detailed introduction using archival materials. [RJS]

2488 Between slavery and free labor: the Spanish-speaking Caribbean in the nineteenth century. Edited by Manuel Moreno Fraginals, Frank Moya Pons, and Stanley L. Engerman. Baltimore, Md.: Johns Hopkins Univ. Press, 1985. 294 p.: bibl., ill., index, tables (Johns Hopkins studies in Atlantic history and culture)

Important edited collection, containing an overview essay by M. Moreno Fraginals, a concluding piece by Sidney Mintz, a theoretical article by H.S. Klein and S.L. Engerman, and essays on slavery, abolition, plantation society, immigration, land, and labor by R.J. Scott, F. Iglesias García, F. López Segrera, F.W. Knight, J. Curet, B. Nistal-Moret, A.A. Ramos Mattei, F. Moya Pons, J. del Castillo, and P.E. Bryan. Good introduction to work in progress on the social and economic history of the Spanish Caribbean in the 19th century, and a contribution to several interpretative debates, including those on the causes of abolition, the role of technology in dependent economies, and the formation of rural proletariats. [RJS]

2489 Boutin, Raymond. Petit-Canal: une commune de la Guadeloupe au XIXe siècle. Paris: Editions l'Harmattan, 1983. 221 p.: appendices, bibl., ill., maps, tables.

Rigorous demographic study of one of the island's most important sugar districts. Focuses on post-emancipation period, when the new immigrant labor force was introduced. Argues that neither factor altered the profile of Petit-Canal's population. [APD]

2490 Brass, Tom. Coffee and rural proletarianization: a comment on Bergad (JLAS, 16:1, May 1984, p. 143–152)

Notes problems in article by Bergad which found that coffee produced a rural proletariat in 19th-century Puerto Rico. Uses examples from Colombia, Brazil, Peru, and the Caribbean to argue that when the production of coffee and sugar increased and combined with scarce labor supply, it led to unfree labor. Believes Bergad missed character of coercion in the Puerto Rican system. For Bergad's rejoiner, see item **2486**. [J.D. Riley]

2491 Brereton, Bridget. Sir John Gorrie: a radical Chief Justice of Trinidad, 1885–1892 (UWI/JCH, 13, 1980, p. 45–72)

Useful discussion of a career colonial official who was a social reformer and a strong believer in equal justice for citizens of every class and color. [CAP]

2492 Campbell, Carl C. Missionaries and maroons: conflict and resistance in Accompong, Charles Town and Moore Town, Jamaica; 1837–1838 (JHS/R, 14, 1984, p. 42–58)

Careful analysis of responses of three Maroon communities immediately before and after emancipation to the proselytizing effort of the Church Missionary Society. [CAP]

2493 Campbell, Carl C. The rebel priest: Francis DeRidder and the fight for free coloureds rights in Trinidad, 1825–1832 (UWI/JCH, 15, 1981, p. 20–40)

Analysis of the role of the Reverend Francis DeRidder, a Roman Catholic priest, and his struggle to eliminate discrimination against Trinidad's free colereds. Campbell describes DeRidder's vigorous assault on the political and social attitudes of the Church hierarchy towards coloreds and concludes that he was responsible for sensitizing that body to the aspirations of racially mixed peoples. [CAP]

2494 Cantón Navarro, José. José Martí y los mártires de Chicago (UCLV/I, 75, mayo/agosto 1983, p. 33–45, ill.)

Analysis of José Martí's attitude towards events connected with Haymarket Riot in Chicago. [RJS]

2495 Castañeda Delgado, Paulino and **Juan Marchena Fernández.** Notas sobre la educación pública en Cuba, 1816–1863 (JGSWGL, 21, 1984, p. 265–302, tables)

Study of number and character of primary schools in 19th-century Cuba. Uses census data; examines distinctions of color. [RJS]

2496 Charmant, Rodolphe. La vie incroyable d'Alcius. Port-au-Prince: Ateliers Fardin, 1981. 349 p.: ill.

New edition of biography written by Alcius's descendant in a journalistic style. Illustrates the intensity and extent of political and military conflicts as well as regional tensions that characterized turn-of-the-century Haiti. [APD]

2497 Craton, Michael. We shall not be moved: Pompey's slave revolt in Exuma Island, Bahamas, 1830 (NWIG, 57:1/4, 1983, p. 19–35, bibl.)

Interesting case study of a slave rebellion in what Craton calls the outer margin of the Caribbean plantation sphere. Analyzes the 1830 uprising on the Rolle plantation on the Bahamian island, Exuma, and places it in the broader context of the search by blacks for autonomy. [CAP]

2498 De Verteuil, Anthony. The years of revolt: Trinidad, 1881–1888. Newton, Trinidad: Paria Publishing Co., 1984. 294 p., 20 p. of plates: bibl., ill., ports.

Study of important decade in Trinidad's history and of the revolts that occurred during that time. Focuses on Carnival riots of 1881, Hosay riots of 1884 and the Reform Movement of 1887. [CAP]

2499 Debien, Gabriel. Les biens de Toussaint Louverture (SHHG/R, 139, juin 1983, p. 5–75)

Descriptive list of sources documenting the leader's estate at the time of his arrest (June 1802). [APD]

2500 Delgado Pasapera, Germán. Puerto Rico: sus luchas emancipadoras, 1850–1898. Río Piedras, P.R.: Editorial Cultural, 1984. 609 p.: bibl.

Informative detailed study of the pro-independence struggle in Puerto Rico during the second half of the 19th century. Explores relationship of Puerto Rican politicians with both Cubans and Puerto Rican exiles in New York. [BGS]

2501 Deschamps Chapeaux, Pedro. Los cimarrones urbanos. La Habana: Editorial de Ciencias Sociales, 1983. 55 p.: ill. (Demografía)

Useful study of urban slave runaways in Cuba. Transcribes newspaper announcements; also summarizes physical characteristics appearing in announcements. [RJS]

2502 Despradel i Batista, Guido. Duarte y aporte de la familia Duarte-Diez a la independencia dominicana. Santo Domingo: Publicaciones ONAP, 1984. 60 p.: bibl. (Col. Ensayos; 8)

Florid, hagiographic study of Juan Pablo Duarte y Diez and independence movement in Dominican Republic. [RJS]

2503 Dessalles, Pierre. La vie d'un colon à la Martinique au XIXème siècle. v. 1, Correspondance, 1808–1834. v. 2, Journal, 1837–1841. Édité par Henri de Frémont et Léo Elisabeth. Courbevoie, France: H. de Frémont, 1985. 2 v. (381, 314 p.): appendices, ill., indexes.

Welcome addition to recently published works by Dessalles, member of 19th-century Martinican family of lawyers and planters who were also prolific writers. Pierre's diary documents in a unique fashion social relations and economic difficulties on sugar plantations which were disintegrating on the eve of the abolition of slavery. Invaluable source for social historians of the 19th-century Caribbean. [APD]

2504 Domingo Acebrón, María Dolores. Los hacendados cubanos ante la Guerra de los Diez Años: 1868–1878 (IGFO/RI, 43: 172, julio/dic. 1983, p. 707–727, appendices)

Discussion of different ideological and political groupings during Cuban insurrection of 1868–78. Draws heavily on little-used documentation in Spanish Real Academia de Historia. [RJS]

2505 Domínguez, Jaime de Jesús. Notas económicas y políticas dominicanas sobre el período julio 1865-julio 1886. Santo Domingo: Editora de la Univ. Autónoma de Santo Domingo, 1983–1984. 2 v. (673 p., 6

folded leaves of plates): ill. (Col. Historia y sociedad; 60. Publicaciones; 326)

Examines late 19th-century Dominican Republic, focusing on "renaissance" in sugar industry, *caudillismo*, relationship between subsistence and export sectors. Uses archival sources and press. Detailed, documented study. [RJS]

2506 Elisabeth, Léo. L'abolition de l'esclavage à la Martinique. Fort-de-France: Société d'histoire de la Martinique, 1983. 155 p.: appendix, bibl., index (Mémoires; 5)

Detailed, well documented account of the abolition of slavery in Martinique, after the 1848 French decree. Provides thoughtful interpretation of the role played by free coloreds since the 1820s. Appendix includes significant documents. [APD]

2507 Emmer, Pieter C. Abolition of the abolished: the illegal Dutch slave trade and the mixed courts (*in* The Abolition of the Atlantic slave trade: origins and effects in Europe, Africa and the Americas. Edited by David Eltis, James Walvin and Svend E. Green-Pedersen. Madison: Univ. of Wisconsin Press, 1981, p. 177–192, appendix, map)

Based on archival material. Shows distinct character of abolition of slave trade in the Netherlands (1818) under British pressure. Actual Dutch slave trade was ending by 1818 but continued illegally via foreign (mainly French) ships flying the Dutch flag and directed at Surinam. [APD]

2508 Emmer, Pieter C. The great escape: the migration of female indentured servants from British India to Surinam, 1873–1916 (*in* Abolition and its aftermath: the historical context, 1790–1916. Edited by David Richardson. London: Frank Cass, 1985, p. 245–266, appendices, tables)

Establishes special character and numerical importance of such female migrants as compared to males. Uses Foreign Office records to show that indentured labor may have been easier on females than European free labor. Such migration provided Indian women with opportunities to improve their status, contrary to arguments adduced by Indian males who were nationalists and campaigned against such labor migration. [APD]

2509 Emmer, Pieter C. The importation of British Indians into Surinam—Dutch Guiana—1873–1916 (*in* International labour migration: historical perspectives. Edited by Shula Marks and Peter Richardson. London: Univ. of London, Institute of Commonwealth Studies, 1984, p. 90–111, tables)

Excellent, quantitative study of labor force that replaced slaves, after 1873, on Dutch plantations in the American mainland. Different from slavery in terms of recruitment, indentured service was similar as life and work experience. Author stresses continuity between both types of forced labor. [APD]

2510 Emmer, Pieter C. The meek Hindu: the recruitment of Indian indentured labourers for service overseas, 1870–1916 (in Colonialism and migration: indentured labour before and after slavery. Edited by Pieter C. Emmer. Dordrecht, The Netherlands: Martinus Nijhoff Publishers, 1986, p. 187–207, tables).

Based on yearly reports on Indian immigration, provides quantitative documentation on a recruitment process that leads to revisionist conclusions: 1) unlike slave trade, indentured immigration involved little deception but raised immigrant expectations for a better future; and 2) pressure of Indian nationalists succeeded in ending such emigration, contrary to the wish of immigrants involved. [APD]

2510a Estévez, Francisco. Diario del rancheador. Recopilación de Cirilo Villaverde. La Habana: Editorial Letras Cubanas, 1982. 137 p. (Testimonio)

Transcription of diary of Cuban professional slave-catcher, Francisco Estévez. Covers period 1837–42; was collected by a 19th-century Cuban novelist. Has introduction and annotations. Useful source, providing vivid picture of slave resistance and violence employed to overcome it. [RJS]

2511 Estrade, Paul. Sur les perspectives d'union des Antilles au XIX siècle (in Unité et diversité de l'Amérique latine. Bordeaux, France: Univ. de Bordeaux III, 1982, t. 1, p. 95–111)

Elegant and well written essay on the emergence of the concept of Caribbean unity towards the end of the 19th century. Although the notion was inspired in the writings of de Pradt, Jefferson, Bolívar, and Humboldt, Estrade emphasizes the originality of its complete formulation in the works of such 19th-century Spanish Carib-

bean thinkers as Betances, Hostos, Martí, and Firmin. Based on author's major studies of these figures. [APD]

2512 Fabre, Camille. Dans le sillage de Victor Schoelcher, un préfet apostolique de la Guadeloupe en 1848: Casimir Dugoujon des prêtres de la Sainte-Croix du Mans. Basse-Terre: Société d'histoire de la Guadeloupe, 1983. 1 v. (Notes d'histoire coloniale; 219)

Case study exemplifies small group of clergymen who were abolitionist. They met with hostility, both from others in the colonial Church and the planter elite. Based on archives of religious orders and French public institutions. [APD]

2513 Fallope, Josette. Les esclaves africains à la Guadeloupe en 1848 d'après les registres d'état civil des nouveaux citoyens conservés aux Archives de la Guadeloupe (SHG/B, 57/58:3/4, 1983, p. 3–25, appendix)

Author made quick survey of civil registers for first entries of new citizens. Finds that of those living in sugar-producing areas, 12 percent were born in Africa. Offers sample list of their African names. [APD]

2514 Figueroa, Loida. Puerto Rico y el sueño bolivariano respecto a la América Latina (BNJM/R, 26:1, enero/marzo 1984, p. 9–51)

Reviews Puerto Rican repercussions of independence struggle in Bolivarian theater, then contribution of Puerto Ricans in this century and last toward spreading the Bolivarian ideal of Latin American integration. Author a committed *independentista*, but this is documented scholarly essay. [D. Bushnell]

2515 Gilas, Teresa. Kuba pod okupacją amerykańska, 1899–1902 = Cuba under the US occupation, 1899–1902. Toruń, Poland: Uniw. Mikołaja Kopernika, 1983. 242 p.: bibl.

Well written monograph by Polish historian based on her dissertation. Provides extensive footnotes that rely not only on previous complete bibliography, but on archival documents and the island's leading newspapers at the time. Study gives Cuban view of events. Highly recommended. [K. Complak]

2516 Gómez, Máximo. Obras escogidas. Selección, prólogo y notas de Ambrosio

Fornet. La Habana: Editorial Letras Cubanas, 1979. 260 p.: ill. (Biblioteca básica de literatura cubana)

Selections by Gómez that originally appeared as pamphlets. Contains material on Cuban independence struggle, and a lively introduction by Ambrosio Fornet. [RJS]

González, Margarita. Bolívar y la independencia de Cuba. See item **1865a.**

Gould, Lewis L. The Spanish-American War and President McKinley. See *HLAS* 47:7231.

2517 Green, William A. The perils of comparative history: Belize and the British sugar colonies after slavery (CSSH, 26:1, Jan. 1984, p. 112–119)

Author argues that population density was the key factor determining post-emancipation labor relations in the British West Indies. He takes issue with Nigel Bolland who maintains that labor relations formed a part of an ongoing social system that remained essentially undisturbed by emancipation. [CAP]

2517a Heuman, Gad J. White over brown over black: the free coloureds in Jamaican society during slavery and after emancipation (UWI/JCH, 14, 1981, p. 46–69)

Provides useful discussion of legal and social disabilities confronted by free coloreds in Jamaica in the pre-emancipation period and of their responses to their treatment. Concludes that in spite of continuing discrimination against them, their prospects improved considerably after emancipation. [CAP]

2517b Higman, B.W. Slave populations of the British Caribbean, 1807–1834. Baltimore, Md.: Johns Hopkins Univ. Press, 1984. 781 p.: bibl., ill., index (Johns Hopkins studies in Atlantic history and culture)

Outstanding demographic analysis of the slave populations of the British islands, based primarily on slave registration records. His findings are supported by a wealth of statistical data. [CAP]

2518 Hoogbergen, Wim S.M. De Surinaamse weglopers van de negentiende eeuw. Utrecht, The Netherlands: Centrum voor Caraïbische Studiën, Rijksuniversiteit Utrecht, 1978. 79 p., 3 leaves of plates: bibl., maps (Bronnen voor de studie van Bosneger samenlevingen; 1)

Study about the Maroons of Surinam before emancipation and efforts by their government to scare them into submission and voluntary return to slavery before emancipation went into effect in June 1863. Study based on official correspondence between the Governor of Surinam and military commanders in charge of an expedition to bring the dissenting Maroons under control. [N. Vicenti]

2519 Hungría Morell, Radhamés. La Batalla de las Carreras: victoria decisiva de las armas dominicanas: pts. 1/2 (Historia y Geografía [Museo Nacional de Historia y Geografía, Santo Domingo] 1, 1982, p. 39–46, ill., map; 2, 1983, p. 67–82, ill., map)

Military history of engagement during 1844–56 war between Dominicans and Haitians. [RJS]

2520 Joachim, Benoit. Negocios y burguesía de negocios en Haití en el siglo XIX: 1804–1915 (Boletín de Investigación del Movimiento Obrero [Univ. Autónoma de Puebla, Instituto de Ciencias, Centro de Investigaciones Históricas del Movimiento Obrero, Puebla, México] 3:5, dic. 1982, p. 27–42, ill.)

Applies dependency theory to the Haitian case. More a general interpretation than a research piece. Relates US intervention to the existence of a *comprador* bourgeoisie dependant on foreign capital and unable to develop domestic industry. [APD]

2521 Krakovitch, Odile. "Le bien d'autrui tu ne prendras" ou à Cayenne, pour le vol d'une paire de draps: l'envoi des femmes aux bagnes de Cayenne et de Nouvelle-Calédonie pour vols et escroqueries de 1858 à 1883 (Bulletin d'information des études féministes [Centre d'études féministes, Univ. de Provence, Aix en Provence, France] 13, déc. 1983, p. 61–81, appendices, tables)

Fine statistical study of several thousand women prisoners based on archives of convict prisons. Shows convincingly how economic hardship wrought on women caused most of the petty crimes, later sanctioned by disproportionately harsh decisions of the court. [APD]

2522 Krakovitch, Odile. Le rôle des femmes dans l'insurrection du Sud de la Martinique en septembre 1870 (Nouvelles questions féministes [Editions Tierce, Paris] 910, printemps 1985, p. 35–51)

Based on judicial archives of a trial that repressed participants in a popular, unorganized black revolt. Focuses on female participation and examines humble social origins of the accused (e.g., farmers, seamstresses, servants). Contrasts pettiness of their offenses with merciless sentences passed by the court. Important contribution to our understanding of race, gender, and class relations in Caribbean societies. [APD]

La Rosa, Gabino. El apalencamiento. See *HLAS 47 : 8194.*

2523 Le Riverend, Julio. José Martí, pensamiento y acción. La Habana: Editora Política, 1982. 148 p.: bibl. (Col. de estudios martianos)

Interpretive essays on social and political context of Martí's development, by Cuban economic historian. [RJS]

2524 Lepkowski, Tadeusz. Cuba 1869: desafectos al gobierno e insurrectos (PAN/EL, 9, 1982/1984, p. 125–148)

Interesting analysis of social composition of insurrectionist movement in Cuba, using lists of suspects from Cuban archives. Emphasizes multi-class alliance, including popular and middle class elements, few slaves. Discusses differences among regions, particularly elite character of movement in Camagüey. Important essay. [RJS]

2525 Lucena Salmoral, Manuel. La memoria de Basadre de 1818 sobre comercio y contrabando en el Caribe (JGSWGL, 19, 1982, p. 223–237)

Studies author of early 19th-century memorial presented to Spanish officials concerning trade and contraband, and examines memorial. Transcribes document. [RJS]

2526 Marte, Roberto. Estadísticas y documentos históricos sobre Santo Domingo, 1805–1890. Santo Domingo: Museo Nacional de Historia y Geografía, 1984. 309 p.: bibl., ill. (Serie Documentos; 1)

Useful compendium of statistical and documentary evidence on Haiti and the Dominican Republic in the 19th century. Includes archival material from London and Madrid, as well as extracts from printed sources. [RJS]

2527 Marte, Roberto. Patrones de asentamiento y de afluencia espacial en Santo Domingo y Cuba en el siglo XIX (Historia y Geografía [Museo Nacional de Historia y Geografía, Santo Domingo] 1, 1982, p. 9–38, bibl., graph, tables)

Examines transformations in use of land and patterns of population in 19th-century Cuba and Dominican Republic. Takes geographical/ecological perspective. Traces importance of urban areas, regional differences. Good comparative essay. [RJS]

2528 Métral, Antoine. Histoire de l'expédition des Français à Saint-Domingue sous le consulat de Napoléon Bonaparte, 1802–1803. Introduction de Jacques Adélaïde-Merlande. Paris: Karthala, 1985. 348 p., 12 p. of plates: appendix, ill., map.

Handsome photographic reproduction of original 1825 edition. Métral exemplified French romantics who sympathized with the Haitian cause. Good introduction discusses Métral's sources. The *Histoire* is followed by anonymous *Mémoires* and *Notes* regarding Toussaint-Louverture. [APD]

2529 Morales, Salvador. El bolivarismo de José Martí (UB/BA, 26 : 34, 1984, p. 161–177)

Textual analysis of writings of Martí on Bolívar and Latin American unity. Emphasizes Martí's praise of Bolívar as hero of popular revolution. [RJS]

2530 Moreno Fraginals, Manuel; Herbert S. Klein; and Stanley L. Engerman. The level and structure of slave prices on Cuban plantations in the mid-nineteenth century: some comparative perspectives (AHA/R, 88 : 5, Dec. 1983, p. 1201–1218, charts, graphs)

Study of slave prices in Cuba, based on records in notarial archives. Notes rise in slave prices at mid-century, slight drop in 1860s. Prices somewhat higher for males and for Creoles. Argues that prices suggest that "planters did not anticipate an early end to slavery." Useful data and comparative analysis. [RJS]

2531 Negrón-Portillo, Mariano and Raúl Mayo-Santana. Trabajo, producción y conflictos en el siglo XIX: una revisión crítica de las nuevas investigaciones históricas en Puerto Rico (UPR/RCS, 24 : 3/4, 1985, p. 469–497)

Well written critical essay analyzes contributions and limitations of the "new historiography" on 19th-century Puerto Rico.

Authors discuss trends in recent historical studies and suggest new avenues of research. [BGS]

2532 Nugent, Maria et al. Viajeras al Caribe. Selección, prólogo y notas, Nara Araújo. La Habana: Casa de las Américas, 1983. 548 p.: bibl. (Col. Nuestros países. Serie Rumbos)

Useful compilation, in Spanish translation, of accounts by 19th-century women travelers to the Caribbean, including Maria Nugent, Fredrika Bremer, and Julia Ward Howe, as well as less well known visitors. Introductions and annotations clarify context of visits. [RJS]

2533 Ocasio Meléndez, Marcial E. Río Piedras: notas para su historia. San Juan: Comité Historia de los Pueblos, 1985. 1 v.

Excellent study of Río Piedras's local history. Provides analysis of social and economic forces which transformed the town at the end of the 19th century into a commercial exchange center. [BGS]

2534 El Partido Revolucionario Cubano de José Martí. Compilación y edición, Eva Pedroso del Campo. La Habana: Editora Política, 1982. 89 p.: bibl.

Collection of six essays on Martí, including works by Juan Marinello, Sergio Aguirre, José Antonio Portuondo, Roberto Fernández Retamar, Gonzalo de Quesada, and Martí himself. The emphasis is on Martí's concept of a political party, and on the Cuban Revolutionary Party. Largely exhortatory in tone. [RJS]

2535 Paula, A.F. The "pass the buck" policy of the Dutch government concerning the emancipation of slaves on the island of St. Martin, Dutch-side, in 1848 (Lantèrnu [Centraal Historisch Archief, Willemstad, Curaçao] 1:1, Feb. 1983, p. 9–14, map)

Sophisticated study based on primary sources, shows how emancipation was postponed until the government could indemnify slave-owners, respect for property rights prevailing over the legitimacy of human rights. [APD]

2536 Pérez, Louis A., Jr. Insurrection, intervention, and the transformation of land tenure systems in Cuba, 1895–1902 (HAHR, 65:2, 1985, p. 229–254, table)

Describes economic crisis following

1895–98 war in Cuba. Traces growth of indebtedness, shift in ownership of land, elimination of communal tenure. Sees roots of "dominance of the foreign-owned latifundia" in this period. [RJS]

2537 Pérez, Louis A., Jr. Vagrants, beggars, and bandits: social origins of Cuban separatism, 1878–1895 (AHA/R, 90:5, Dec. 1985, p. 1092–1121)

Interpretive essay based on periodical and archival sources links transformation of Cuban countryside to upsurge in banditry, and in turn to development of separatism. Draws on work of Eric Hobsbawm in analyzing Cuban "social banditry," which Pérez sees as a response to capitalization of agriculture, expropriation of peasant lands, and the dislocation caused by the Ten Years' War. Interesting, provocative article. [RJS]

2538 Pérez Guzmán, Francisco and Rodolfo Sarracino. La Guerra Chiquita, una experiencia necesaria. La Habana: Editorial Letras Cubanas, 1982. 380 p.: bibl.

Discussion of the social and economic environment of anti-colonial agitation in Cuba in 1878–79, and military conflict of 1879. Based on primary as well as secondary sources. [RJS]

2539 Rama, Carlos M. La independencia de las Antillas y Ramón Emeterio Betances. San Juan: Instituto de Cultura Puertorriqueña, 1980. 153 p.: bibl.

Study of the liberation struggles in the Spanish Caribbean region in the mid-19th century, with emphasis on the contribution of Puerto Rican patriot, Ramón Emeterio Betances. Places aspects of Puerto Rican politics in the context of Caribbean history. [BGS]

2540 Rodríguez Demorizi, Emilio. La muerte de Lilís: versos y documentos. Santo Domingo: Editora Taller, 1983. 264 p.: bibl., index (Fundación Rodríguez Demorizi; 18)

Poems, recollections, and documents concerning the 1899 assassination of Gen. Ulises Heureaux of the Dominican Republic. [RJS]

2541 Roig, Pedro. La guerra de Martí. Miami, Fla.: Ediciones Universal, 1984. 259 p.: bibl., ill., ports. (Col. Cuba y sus jueces)

Popular, illustrated, narrative history of the 1895–98 war. Documented, with substantial excerpts from contemporary news-papers and from memoirs. [RJS]

2542 Schmidt, Nelly. Suppression de l'es-clavage, système scolaire et réorgani-sation sociale aux Antilles: les Frères de l'Instruction chrétienne, témoins et acteurs, instituteurs des nouveaux libres (Revue d'histoire moderne et contemporaine [Paris] 31, avril/juin 1984, p. 203–244)

By tracing the establishment of boys' schools in Guadeloupe and Martinique, au-thor uncovers role played by religious orders in the transition from slavery to freedom in Caribbean colonial societies. [APD]

2543 Schoelcher, Victor. Des colonies fran-çaises: abolition immédiate de l'es-clavage. Paris: Culture antillaise, 1984. 577 p.: bibl., ill. (Histoire de l'esclavage; 4)

Photographic reprint of the most fa-mous of Schoelcher's essays in which he compares French and foreign slave processes of gradual emancipation and concludes with a demand for complete and immediate aboli-tion. [APD]

2544 Schoelcher, Victor. Histoire de l'es-clavage pendant les deux dernières années. Paris: Culture antillaise, 1984. 2 v.: bibl., ill. (Histoire de l'esclavage; 2–3)

Collection of Schoelcher's writings on the historical development and political meaning of slavery, based on contemporary parliamentary debates and judicial cases, which he compiled in order to arouse public opinion in favor of abolition. [APD]

2545 Schoelcher, Victor. Vie de Toussaint Louverture. Introduction de Jacques Adélaïde-Merlande. Paris: Karthala, 1982. 453 p.: appendices, ill., maps.

Welcome new edition of the famous abolitionist's last piece of writing. Syn-thesizes what was known about Haiti to-wards the end of the 19th century and in-cludes strong defense of racial equality, at a time when theories of natural racial in-feriority were gaining momentum. [APD]

2546 Schwartz, Rosalie. Bandits and rebels in Cuban independence: predators, pa-triots, and pariahs (Bibliotheca Americana [Coral Gables, Fla.] 1:2, Nov. 1982, p. 91–120, ill., maps)

Examines patterns of outlaw behavior and raises important questions about rela-tionship between banditry and commer-cialization of agriculture in late 19th-century Cuba. Uses consular dispatches, printed sources. Argues that "bandits of the 1880s were very rarely peasants pushed aside by the transition to agrarian capitalism," but con-cludes that the general links between the two phenomena are 'unfathomable.' [RJS]

2547 Scott, Rebecca J. Slave emancipation in Cuba: the transition to free labor, 1860–1899. Princeton, N.J.: Princeton Univ. Press, 1985. 319 p., 12 p. of plates: bibl., in-dex, tables.

Thorough examination of slave eman-cipation in Cuban plantation society that challenges prevailing mono-causal explana-tion that technological changes in sugar pro-duction made slavery unsuitable. Primarily a work of social history, author analyzes dy-namics as slave labor gave way to Chinese contract laborers, *patrocinados*, wage-work-ers. Notes two principal factors in Cuban transition from slavery to freedom: 1) re-gional differences between two modal types (i.e., Matanzas and Santa Clara, where mills were steam-powered and slaves numerous, and Santiago and Puerto Príncipe, where mills were animal-powered and slaves fewer; and 2) metropolitan-colonial interactions over political significance of emancipation. Impeccably researched and argued, Scott's study enriches an already sophisticated literature on 19th-century Spanish Caribbean social and labor history. [APD]

2548 Simmonds, Lorna. Civil disturbances in western Jamaica, 1838–1865 (JHS/R, 14, 1984, p. 1–17, appendix)

Simmonds focuses on civil distur-bances in the western parishes of Jamaica in the years after emancipation. Her definition of civil disturbances is rather broad and in-cludes verbal abuse. She sees the riots as a continuation of the spirit of disaffection that prevailed under slavery. [CAP]

2549 Stewart, Robert. Conflict in the Jamai-can Baptist church: Thomas Dowson and J.M. Phillippo, 1842–1850 (JHS/R, 14, 1984, p. 28–41)

Discussion of bitter conflict between two prominent Baptist missionaries. Author sees controversy as symptom of deeper divi-sions among the Baptists shortly after full emancipation. [CAP]

2550 Trouillot, Hénock. Les ouvriers de La Citadelle et de Sans-Souci (PAIGH/H, 98, julio/dic. 1984, p. 49–68)

Concerns building of famous La Ferriére citadel at beginning of 19th century. Uses new archival sources to revise hitherto accepted version of Emperor Christophe's coercive treatment of labor force, by putting it into context of typical methods of worker mobilization at the time (i.e., harsh but not inhumane). [APD]

2551 Valle Ferrer, Norma. Primeros fermentos de lucha femenina en Puerto Rico (ICP/R, 22:84, julio/sept. 1979, p. 15–19)

Brief summary of some of the struggles for better educational opportunities for Puerto Rican women in the 19th century. [BGS]

2553 Vitier, Cintio. Temas martianos. La Habana: Centro de Estudios Martianos: Editorial Letras Cubanas, 1982. 324 p.: bibl. (Col. de estudios martianos)

Essays by major Cuban scholar of Martí. Discuss literary, philosophical, social, and historical aspects of work, in context of period. Important. [RJS]

2554 Wilmot, Swithin. Black labourers and white missionaries: conflict on the estates in Hanover, Jamaica, 1838–1847 (JHS/R, 14, 1984, p. 18–27)

Assessment of influence of missionaries on black workers in one of Jamaica's western parishes. Argues that workers developed their own leadership and acted independently of the missionaries to get concessions from the planters. [CAP]

20th CENTURY

2555 Acosta Estrella, Emilio. Enrique Blanco, su historia y dramáticas aventuras. Santo Domingo: Editorial del Nordeste, 1983. 389 p.: ill. (some col.)

Amateur historian's account of anti-Trujillo outlaw figure from the Valle del Cibao in the Dominican Republic. [RJS]

2556 Ambursley, Fitzroy and **James Dunkerley.** Grenada: whose freedom? London: Latin America Bureau, 1984. 128 p.: appendix, bibl., ill., maps.

Sophisticated introduction to Grenada's recent history, which stands out from vast journalistic literature devoted to this topic. Focuses on internal dynamics, primarily political, of the 1979 Grenada revolution. Crucial for understanding the US intervention. [APD]

2557 Ameringer, Charles D. The Auténtico Party and the political opposition in Cuba, 1952–57 (HAHR, 65:2, 1985, p. 327–351)

Examines non-violent opposition to Batista. Uses personal archive of Manuel Antonio de Varona, leader of the Auténtico Party during the 1950s. Provides narrative of events; sees achievements and failures of non-insurrectionist opposition as part of context in which Fidel Castro's movement achieved primacy. [RJS]

2557a Annino, Antonio. Dall'insurrezione al regime: politiche di massa e strategie instituzionale a Cuba, 1953–1965. Milano, Italy: Franco Angeli Editore, 1984. 334 p.: bibl., tables.

Italian political scientist addresses two key problems of the Cuban Revolution: growing disharmony between the State and nation, and rise of sporadic, disorganized mass actions. Also considers new post-revolutionary institutions: the party, new financial structure, agrarian system, labor movement, mass actions. Concludes that the State and nation were reunited in Oct. 1965, when the Central Committee of the Cuban Communist Party met and rejected democratic centralism. "New" party delegates were favored over "old" party members. Rather than a "populism of the left," the Cuban process, according to Annino, was the culmination of patterns that gave the regime a unique character in Latin America. Based on analysis of periodical, official, and occasional literature produced in Cuba (1950s–60s) and of the Cuban, American, and European scholarship on the subject, though several important recent studies by US scholars were not taken into consideration. A challenging interpretation that should be read by all students of the Cuban Revolution. [V. Peloso]

2558 Basdeo, Sahadeo. Labour organisation and labour reform in Trinidad, 1919–1939. St. Augustine, Trinidad: Institute of Social and Economic Research, Univ. of the West Indies, 1983. 285 p., 1 p. of plates: ill.

Careful examination of the rise of the

Trinidadian working-class movement after World War I and the struggle to achieve labor reform during the inter-war years. Emphasizes role of the Trinidad Workingmen's Assn. and British Labour Movement in effecting improvements in working conditions in the island. [CAP]

2559 Basdeo, Sahadeo. The role of the British Labour Movement in the development of labour organisation in Trinidad, 1919–1929 (UWI/SES, 30:3, Sept. 1981, p. 21–41, bibl.)

Useful discussion of the impact of the Brtish Labour Movement on working-class organizations in the colony during the post-World War I years. Sees the British Labour Movement as being partly responsible for the politicization of the Trinidad Workingmen's Assn. [CAP]

2560 Basdeo, Sahadeo. The role of the British Labour Movement in the development of labour organisations in Trinidad, 1929–1938 (UWI/SES, 31:1, March 1982, p. 40–73, bibl.)

Basdeo examines impact of the British Labour Movement on public policy towards labor and trade union organization in Trinidad (1929–38). Concludes that the British Labour Movement played an essentially constructive role in Trinidad and succeeded after the 1937 labor disturbances in the colony in getting the British government to implement drastic labor reforms. [CAP]

2561 Bastien, Rémy. Le paysen haïtien et sa famille. Préface de Marcel d'Ans. Paris: ACCT-Karthala, 1985. 217 p.: bibl., maps, tables.

Welcome translation of *La familia rural haitiana: Valle de Marbial* (first published in Mexico, 1951). Written by young Haitian ethnologist who died shortly thereafter. Based on solid fieldwork in poor area of south Haiti, provides a scholarly but sympathetic view of Haitian family-centered culture. Excellent introduction puts this gem in context of a Haitian tradition of exploring national identity in terms of *négritude* and African roots. [APD]

Bellegarde-Smith, Patrick. International relations/social theory in a small state: an analysis of the thought of Dantès Bellegarde. See *HLAS 47:7213.*

Bergad, Laird W. On comparative history: a reply to Tom Brass. See item **2486.**

Bishop, Maurice. Selected speeches, 1979–1981. See *HLAS 47:6249.*

2562 Che, sierra adentro. Compilación de Froilán Escobar y Félix Guerra. La Habana: Unión de Escritores y Artistas de Cuba, 1982. 261 p.: ill. (Girón)

Account of guerrilla struggle in the Cuban sierra. Juxtaposes military documents and recollections of participants. Dramatic and interesting; lacks supporting scholarly apparatus. [RJS]

2563 Cherdieu, Philippe. L'échec d'un socialisme colonial: la Guadeloupe, 1891–1914 (Revue d'histoire moderne et contemporaine [Paris] 31, avril/juin 1984, p. 308–333)

Describes shift in popular political leadership: from mulattoes, whose rising had accompanied early republican regimes, to black socialists linked to the progress of socialists in metropolitan politics. Shows limits and ultimate failure of "colonial socialism." Although it appealed to black racial solidarity, the political agenda of these "colonial socialists" remained entirely subordinated to the Socialist Party of France. [APD]

2564 Cherdieu, Philippe. La rupture Gérault Richard-Légitimus, 1906–1907 (SHG/B, 59:1, 1984, p. 109–134, map, tables)

Page of Guadeloupe political history, centered around one of its major socialist figures, Légitimus. [APD]

2565 Comisión de Historia de la Columna 19 "José Tey." Columna 19 "José Tey." La Habana: Editorial Ciencias Sociales, 1982. 464 p.: bibl., ill., maps, photos, ports. (Historia de Cuba)

History of specific aspects of military conflict between guerrilla forces and Batista's army in 1958 on the Eastern Front. Contains documents and photographs of participants. [RJS]

2566 Conference of Caribbean Historians, 14th, San Juan, 1983. Politics, society, and culture in the Caribbean: selected papers. Edited by Blanca G. Silvestrini. San Juan: Univ. of Puerto Rico, 1983. 273 p.: bibl., ill.

Selected papers of the 14th Conference of Caribbean Historians include three excellent articles on early 20th-century Puerto Rican history: Samuel Silva Gotay "La Iglesia Protestante como Agente de Americanización de Puerto Rico, 1898 -1917;" Fernando Picó "El Impacto de la Invasión Americana en la Zona Cafetalera de Puerto Rico: El Caso de Utuado;" and María Dolores Luque de Sánchez "Las Franquicias: Instrumento de Penetración Económica en Puerto Rico, 1900–1915;" and a fourth paper on the same period by this contributor: Blanca G. Silvestrini "La Política de Salud Pública de los Estados Unidos en Puerto Rico, 1898–1913: Consecuencias en el Proceso de Americanización." [BGS]

2567 Connell-Smith, Gordon. The Grenada invasion in historical perspective: from Monroe to Reagan (TWF/TWQ, 6:2, April 1984, p. 432–445)

Analysis of the US invasion of Grenada in 1983. Argues that it was a modern application of the Monroe Doctrine. Perceives invasion as representing an attempt by the US to reassert its power and influence in Latin America. [CAP]

2568 Corvington, Georges. Port-au-Prince au cours des ans. v. 5, La capitale d'Haïti sous l'occupation, 1915–1922. 2e. ed. Port-au-Prince: Imprimerie H. Deschamps, 1984. 1 v.: bibl.

Corvington continues his chronicle of Port-au-Prince with vol. 5 covering the first years of US occupation. Gracefully written work which contains much valuable information drawn mainly from newspapers. [APD]

2569 Cudjoe, Selwyn Reginald. Movement of the people: essays on independence. Ithaca, N.Y.: Calaloux Publications, 1983. 217 p., 1 leaf of plates: bibl., ill.

Collection of essays that represent what the author calls a "national self examination." Calls for a fundamental break with Trinidad's colonial past and for profound systemic changes. [CAP]

2570 Danache, B. Le Président Dartigenave et les Américains. 2e. ed. Port-au-Prince: Éditions Fardin, 1984. 164 p.: port.

Written by one of the Haitian President's assistants, this defense of Dartiguenave is useful as source material on the period. [APD]

2571 Dávila Santiago, Rubén. El derribo de las murallas y "El Porvenir de Borin-

quen:" los centros de estudios sociales obreros a principios del siglo XX. San Juan: Centro de Estudios de la Realidad Puertorriqueña, 1983. 25 p., 5 p. of plates: bibl., ill. (Cuadernos. Investigación y analysis; 8)

Examines selected literary writings of workers in order to analyze early 20th-century process of proletarianization of Puerto Rican workers. Studies how workers developed *centros de estudios* by themselves in order to discuss theoretical and ideological issues and to reconstruct their own history. Well researched, seminal essay on the topic. [BGS]

2572 Dolz, Mario A. Biografía de una revolución: Cuba de 1925 a 1959. Los Angeles, Calif.: El Autor, 1984. 266 p., 36 p. of plates: ill.

History of participant in Cuban revolution, now resident in US. Modest, non-scholarly work, of interest primarily for personal recollections of author, who participated in early revolutionary tribunals. [RJS]

Los Estados Unidos y Trujillo, año 1946: colección de documentos del Departamento de Estado y de las Fuerzas Armados Norteamericanos. See *HLAS* 47:7227.

2573 Los Estados Unidos y Trujillo, año 1947: colección de documentos del Departamento de Estado y de las Fuerzas Armadas Norteamericanas. Edición de Bernardo Vega. Santo Domingo: Fundación Cultural Dominicana, 1984. 2 v. (1018 p.): bibl., ill., indexes.

Continuation of series of volumes of translated, edited documents from US repositories concerning the Trujillo era. Also includes Dominican materials. Compendious, revealing evidence concerning a complex period in US-Caribbean relations. [RJS]

2574 Ferreras, Ramón Alberto. Cuando la era era era. t. 4, Muertos sin sepultura. 2a ed. Santo Domingo: Editorial del Nordeste, 1980. 224 p.: ill., plates, ports.

Evidence and testimonials concerning resistance to Trujillo. Non-scholarly. [RJS]

2575 Franqui, Carlos. Family portrait with Fidel: a memoir. Translated by Alfred MacAdam. New York: Random House, 1984. 262 p.

Absorbing, polemical, highly tendentious memoir of the early years of the Cuban Revolution. Franqui, a participant in the guerrilla struggle in the sierra, traces what he sees as the abuses of power by Fidel Castro and his allies. His portrait of interactions among the various groups in the new revolutionary government is selective and personalized, but also revealing. [RJS]

2576 Fraser, Peter D. The immigration issue in British Guiana, 1903–1913: the economic and constitutional origins of racist politics in Guyana (UWI/JCH, 14, 1981, p. 19–45)

Author develops argument that economic problems and a shift in the balance of political forces, rather than racial animosities, accounted for controversies surrounding the issue of Indian indentured immigration to British Guiana (1903–13). [CAP]

2577 Gaillard, Roger. Les blancs débarquent. v. 1, La république exterminatrice. v. 4, La république autoritaire. v. 7, La guérilla de Batraville: 1919–1934. Port-au-Prince: Imprimerie Le Natal, 1981–1984. 3 v. (350, 305, 341 p.): bibl., ill., index.

Valuable, detailed narrative political history of Haiti against background of foreign interventions. Vol. 1 describes challenges to presidential power as evidence of Haiti's failure to modernize its State and power structure. Vol. 4 covers emergence of Haitian guerrillas following US 1915 intervention and US dissolution of parliament and introduction of a state of siege. Vol. 7 focuses on battles between US troops and Haitian guerrillas during US occupation and following death of *caco* leader Peralte. Roosevelt's Good Neighbor Policy ended occupation and systematic defeat and elimination of Peralte's generals. Based on interviews, State Dept. documents, newspapers and printed sources. For vol. 2, see *HLAS 38:2881* and for vols. 3 and 5–6, see *HLAS 46:2582–2584*. [APD]

2578 García, Juan Manuel. La matanza de los haitianos: genocidio de Trujillo, 1937. Con epílogo anónimo, La frontera dominicana con Haiti. Santo Domingo: Editora Alfa & Omega, 1983. 243, 182 p.: bibl., ill.

Carefully documented inquiry by journalist. Places massacre in the context of longstanding Dominican concern about Haitian infiltrations of border area. Explains how politicians successfully exploited Dominican xenophobia. [APD]

2579 García Galló, Gaspar M. Jorge. General de las cañas. La Habana: Editora Política, 1983. 220 p., 18 p. of plates: ill., ports.

Third in a series on the life of Jesús Menéndez, communist leader of Cuban sugar workers in the 1930s and 1940s. Based on a range of interviews; hagiographic in tone. Provides biographical details and an account of Menéndez's assassination in 1948. [RJS]

2580 García Oliveras, Julio A. José Antonio Echeverría: la lucha estudiantil contra Batista. La Habana: Editorial Política, 1979 [i.e. 1980]. 373 p.: bibl., ill., photos.

Portrait of evolution of leader of student movement against Batista. Draws on oral history and newspaper accounts; contains contemporary photographs. [RJS]

2581 González Carbajal, Ladislao. El Ala Izquierda Estudiantil y su época. La Habana: Editorial de Ciencias Sociales, 1974. 528 p.: bibl. (Ediciones políticas)

Comprehensive, documented study of Cuban student movement of the 1930s. [RJS]

2582 Grigulevich, Iosif Romual'dovich. Ernesto Che Gevara [sic] i revoliŭtsionnyĭ protsess v Latinskoĭ Amerike = [Ernesto Che Guevara and the revolutionary process in Latin America]. Otvetstvennyĭ redaktor, O.T. Darusenkov. Moskva: Izd-vo Nauka, 1984. 300 p., 1 leaf of plates: bibl., index, port.

Soviet biography of Guevara and study of him as an international revolutionary. Of interest because it was sponsored by the Soviet Academy of Sciences. [R.V Allen]

2583 Homenaje a Juan B. Pérez en el centenario de su nacimiento, 1883–1983. Santo Domingo: Editora TALLER, 1983. 78 p.: ill. (Biblioteca dominicana de geografía e viajes; 17)

Biographical/laudatory essays on jurist and anti-Trujillo exile Juan B. Pérez. [RJS]

2584 Instituto de Historia del Movimiento Comunista y de la Revolución Socialista de Cuba. Cuba y la defensa de la República Española, 1936 -1939. La Habana: Editora Política, 1981. 303 p., 48 p. of plates: bibl., ill., ports.

Recollections by numerous Cuban participants in the International Brigades during the Spanish Civil War. Useful compilation. [RJS]

2585 Judson, Fred. Anti-imperialism in the
Cuban rebel army: the sum of precedents and experiences of armed struggle (NS,
8:16, 1983, p. 75–90)
Traces evolution of anti-imperialism
among Cuban revolutionary forces, particularly during the struggle in the Sierra
Maestra. Sees anti-imperialism as nationalistic, predating Marxism. [RJS]

2586 Lafita, María Luisa. Dos héroes
cubanos en el 5to. Regimiento. La
Habana: Editorial de Ciencias Sociales, 1980.
153 p., 42 p. of plates: ill. (Nuestra historia)
Biographical sketches of two Cubans
who fought first against Machado, then in
the Spanish Civil War. [RJS]

2587 Lluberes Navarro, Antonio. El enclave
azucarero, 1902–1930 (Historia y
Geografía [Museo Nacional de Historia y
Geografía, Santo Domingo] 2, 1983, p. 7–59,
tables)
Examines history of sugar industry in
Dominican Republic (1902–29), characterizing it as an enclave economy. Traces legislation, foreign involvement, tariff policy,
planters' response, labor force. Uses primary
sources. [RJS]

2588 Memorias de la lucha contra la tiranía.
Santo Domingo: Fundación de los
Héroes de Constanza, Maimón y Estero
Hondo, 1982 [i.e. 1983]. 236 p.: ill.
Memoirs and documents reflecting the
activities of anti-Trujillo resistance move-
ment. [RJS]

2589 Mencía, Mario. Time was on our side.
Translation, Cuban Center for Translation and Intepretation (ESTI). La Habana: Editora Política, 1982. 281 p.: ill., indexes,
photos.
Account of time spent by Fidel Castro
and other Moncada attackers in prison in
1950s. Hagiographic, but interesting on the
experiences, readings, and composition of the
revolutionary group. Contains photos and
documents. [RJS]

2590 Nazzari, Muriel. The "women question" in Cuba: an analysis of material
constraints on its solution (UC/S, 9:2,
Winter 1983, p. 246–263)
Discusses efforts to achieve equality
for women in Cuba, and sees persistence
of wage system as obstacle. Argues that
many women remain dependent on wage of a

male; that women constitute a labor reserve;
and that companies are likely to practice job
discrimination. Uses printed sources. [RJS]

2591 Obika, Nyahuma. An introduction to
the life and times of T.U.B. Butler, the
father of the nation. Port-of-Spain: Caribbean
Historical Society, 1983. 219 p.: bibl., ill.
Impressionistic study of the life of one
of Trinidad's foremost labor leaders. [CAP]

2592 Padrón, Pedro Luis. Julio Antonio
Mella y el movimiento obrero. La
Habana: Editorial de Ciencias Sociales, 1980.
303 p.: bibl., ill. (Historia de Cuba)
Biographical study of Cuban student
leader, encompassing discussion of workers'
movement in the early 20th century. Uses
primary sources; approach is somewhat sec-
tarian. [RJS]

2593 Padula, Alfred L. Pan Am in the Caribbean: the rise and fall of an empire
(CRI/CR, 12:1, Winter 1983, p. 24–27,
49–51, ill., map)
Examines case history of US corporation operating in the Caribbean. Notes Pan
Am's lasting role in facilitating Caribbean
migration to the US, but subsequent decline
as a force in region. [RJS]

Payne, Anthony. The Rodney riots in Jamaica: the background and significance of
the events of October 1968. See *HLAS*
47:6281.

2594 Paz Sánchez, Manuel de. Hipótesis en
torno a un desarrollo paralelo de la
masonería canaria y cubana durante el primer tercio del presente siglo: anotaciones
para un estudio (*in* Coloquio de Historia
Canario-Americana, 4th, Las Palmas, Spain,
1980. Cuarto Coloquio de Historia Canario-
Americana. Coordinación y prólogo, Francisco Morales Padrón. Las Palmas, Spain:
Ediciones del Excelentísimo Cabildo Insular,
1982, p. 567–602, ill.)
Detailed analysis of freemasonry in
the Canaries, paralleled with discussion of
lodges in Cuba. Uses both printed and manuscript sources. Traces some direct linkages.
[RJS]

2595 Pérez Concepción, Hebert. Esencia y
forma del Gobierno Interventor Norteamericano en el Departamento Oriental de
Cuba: 1899–1902 (Del Caribe [Casa del
Caribe, Santiago de Cuba] 1:2, 1983, p. 21–
34, bibl.)

Discussion of US occupation government in Cuba, using documents from the Archivo Histórico Provincial of Santiago de Cuba. Emphasizes initiatives of Cubans; transcribes useful materials. Recommended. [RJS]

2596 Picó, Fernando. Los gallos peleados. Río Piedras, P.R.: Ediciones Huracán, 1983. 180 p.: tables.

Correlates economic changes experienced in Puerto Rico in first 40 years of 20th century and problems of social marginality in Utuado, a coffee producing mountain town. Analyzes social class conflicts in the area and political solutions that the dominant local class proposed. Excellent contribution that uses previously unexplored sources and sound methodological approach. [BGS]

2597 Plummer, Brenda Gayle. The metropolitan connection: foreign and semiforeign elites in Haiti, 1900–1915 (LARR, 19:2, 1984, p. 119–142, bibl.)

First valuable and clear installment of a work in progress. Sheds new light on Haiti's economic dependency, by focusing on business community. Documents how disappearing Haitian businessmen were replaced by foreigners in export trade and how they became integrated into the Haitian elite. The Americans' arrival is seen within the general context of growing foreign competition in Haiti. The US successfully achieved hegemony but did not eliminate European trade connections. [APD]

2598 Quintero-Rivera, Angel G. Economía y política en Puerto Rico, 1900–1934: algunos elementos regionales-estructurales del crecimiento azucarero y el análisis de la política obrera (UPR/RCS, 24:3/4, 1985, p. 392–454)

Examines relationship between economic structures and electoral behavior in Puerto Rico. Finds three different types of plantation structures: absentee owned corporations, family enterprise, and Puerto Rican corporations, each with different levels of political participation. [BGS]

2599 Raful, Tony. Movimiento 14 de Junio: historia y documentos. Santo Domingo: Editora Alfa y Omega, 1983. 860 p.: bibl., ill., ports.

Journalistic study of Manolo Tavárez and the 14th of June Movement, an anti-

Trujillo group of the late 1950s and early 1960s. [RJS]

2600 Richardson, Peter. A note on the origins of anti-Castro sentiment: the press treatment of Cuba's war crime trials (JGSWGL, 19, 1982, p. 391–415, tables)

Interesting mainly as a study of the US press, but useful for its chronology of events and perceptions. [RJS]

2601 Rivera Colón, Nilsa. Fajardo: notas para su historia. San Juan: Comité Historia de los Pueblos, 1983. 54 p.: bibl., ill., map, ports.

Brief narrative of Fajardo's history emphasizes early 20th-century social and economic aspects. [BGS]

2602 Roa, Raúl. El fuego de la semilla en el surco. La Habana: Editorial Letras Cubanas, 1982. 512 p.: bibl., index.

Admiring, unfinished biography of early 20th-century Cuban author and revolutionary Rubén Martínez Villena. [RJS]

2603 Rodríguez, Carlos Rafael. Letra con filo. v. 1. La Habana: Editorial de Ciencias Sociales, 1983. 1 v.: bibl. (Política)

Vol. 1 of selected works of major figure in Cuban Communist Party. Includes historical essays on class structure, economic/political analyses from the 1940s and 1950s, and assorted recent political writings. [RJS]

2604 Rodríguez Herrera, Mariano. Ellos lucharon con el Che. La Habana: Editorial de Ciencias Sociales, 1982. 138 p., 21 p. of plates: ill., ports.

Admiring portraits of various comrades-in-arms of Che Guevara, both in Cuba and Bolivia. Not a scholarly work. [RJS]

2605 Rodríguez Julía, Edgardo. Las tribulaciones de Jonás. Río Piedras, P.R.: Ediciones Huracán, 1981. 105 p.: ill. (Col. La Nave y el puerto)

Wonderfully evocative and sensitive portrayal of Luis Muñoz Marín. Contradictions in his political and personal life and his undeniable popular appeal are brought subtly but sharply into profile. Enhances our understanding of Muñoz Marín's central role in the shaping of Puerto Rican history and politics. Exceptionally well written and carefully crafted chronicle with important insights into his political legacy. [C.R. Hortas]

2606 Sánchez, Miguel Angel. Capablanca, leyenda y realidad. La Habana: Unión de Escritores y Artistas de Cuba, 1978. 306, 36 p., 40 p. of plates: ill.

Biography of the famous Cuban chess champion, with discussions of chess technique. [RJS]

Spinner, Thomas J., Jr. Guyana update: political, economic, moral bankruptcy. *HLAS* 47:6267.

2607 Torriente Brau, Pablo de la. Cartas cruzadas. Selección, prólogo y notas de Víctor Casaus. La Habana: Editorial Letras Cubanas, 1981. 602 p. (Testimonio)

Correspondence from and to Cuban opposition figure in exile in New York (1935–36). Provides portrait of political activity, early evaluations of Batista, and analysis of Roosevelt's policies in Latin America. [RJS]

2608 Trías Monge, José. Historia constitucional de Puerto Rico. v. 4. Río Piedras, P.R.: Editorial Universitaria, 1983. 487 p.: bibl., indexes.

Vol. 4, last installment on Puerto Rico's constitutional history and only attempt of its kind. Provides detailed account of efforts by Puerto Rican politicians to modify the island's relationship with the US while restructuring its internal government. Based on primary sources, oral testimonies, and author's first-hand experience in Puerto Rican politics. Outstanding contribution to understanding 20th-century Puerto Rican history. [BGS]

2609 Vargas, José Rafael. ¿Valió la pena el golpe de estado contra Bosch? Santo Domingo: Univ. CETEC, 1983. 317 p.: bibl., ill., ports (Publicaciones; 26. Serie Ensayos; 15)

Compilation of documents concerning the *golpe* against Juan Bosch, particularly pronouncements of participants, newspaper reports, etc. [RJS]

2610 Welch, Richard E., Jr. Herbert L. Matthews and the Cuban Revolution (PAT/TH, 47:1, Nov. 1984, p. 1–18)

Discussion of role of *New York Times* writer who reported on the Cuban Revolution and his subsequent involvement in political controversy. Uses The Herbert L. Matthews Papers at Columbia Univ. and other manuscript sources. [RJS]

2611 Willemsen, Glenn Frank Walter. Koloniale politiek en transformatieprocessen in een plantage-economie: Suriname, 1873–1940. Amsterdam: Kaal, 1980. 356 p.: bibl.

Study about the transformation of Surinam from a plantation economy to one of free enterprise. Examines colonial policies and processes of transformation, pointing to continuing aspects of the plantation system. Well written and documented. [N. Vicenti]

Windt Lavandier, César de. La Segunda Guerra Mundial y los submarinos alemanes en el Caribe. See *HLAS* 47:7256.

Wipfler, William Louis. Poder, influencia e impotencia: la Iglesia como factor sociopolítico en República Dominicana. See *HLAS* 47:6246.

SPANISH SOUTH AMERICA: General

MICHAEL T. HAMERLY, *Latin American Bibliographic Foundation, Redlands, California*

2613 Espinosa Moraga, Oscar. Los Andonaegui de Vizcaya, de Chile y de Argentina. Santiago: Editorial Nascimiento, 1984. 231 p., 12 p. of plates: bibl., ill., ports.

Genealogical study of the Andoneagui Aguirre family of Santiago, the Buenos Aires branch of the same clan, and other parts of the family scattered around Chile. Surpris-

ingly both José de Andonaegui, founder of the Chilean family and his kinsman Gen. José de Andonaegui, Governor of the Río de la Plata, were illegitimate offspring, born in rural Vizcaya. [SS]

2614 Espinoza, Leonardo. Política fiscal de la provincia de Cuenca: reseña histórico-presupuestaria, 1779–1861 (Revista del Archivo Nacional de Historia, Sección del Azuay [Casa de la Cultura Ecuatoriana, Cuenca, Ecuador] 1, 1979, p. 68–103, 213–246)

Quantitative study of public finance and fiscal policy of Cuenca during late colonial, independence, and early national periods. None of Espinoza's findings are surprising but he does provide badly needed data for reconstructing economic history of Ecuador's third largest city and its province. [MTH]

2615 Jaramillo Alvarado, Pío. Historia de Loja y su provincia. 2a ed. Loja, Ecuador: Consejo Provincial de Loja, Depto. de Relaciones Públicas, 1982. 445, 15 p., 8 leaves of plates (some folded): bibl., ill.

Standard history of southernmost province of modern Ecuador. Long out of print and difficult to obtain. Only the illustrations are new. [MTH]

2616 Mörner, Magnus. The Andean past: land, societies, and conflicts. New York: Columbia Univ. Press, 1985. 300 p.: bibl., ill., index.

Thoughtful review of demographic, economic, and social past and present of Ecuador, Peru, and Bolivia. Meets the need for a survey in English of the history of Central Andean countries. Unfortunately the text

does not appear to have been edited or proofed. [MTH]

2617 Revista del Archivo Nacional de Historia, Sección del Azuay. Casa de la Cultura Ecuatoriana, Núcleo del Azuay. No. 1, 1979-. Cuenca, Ecuador.

First issue of new journal on Ecuadorian history, of which five have appeared to date. Apparently intended to be an annual. Each issue publishes two to three articles on various aspects of the history of the southern highlands of Ecuador and several documents from the *fondos* of the Archivo Nacional de Historia, Sección del Azuay. For noteworthy articles in first three issues, see items **2614, 2688, 2692,** and **2711** [MTH]

2617a Sempat Assadourian, Carlos. El sistema de la economía colonial: el mercado interior, regiones y espacio económico. México: Editorial Nueva Imagen, 1983. 367 p.: bibl., ill. (Serie Historia)

First-rate study of the economic "space" encompassing Alto Perú, Chile, and northern Argentina, author concentrates on colonial period, although one section deals with the 19th century. Assadourian tackles with talent and imagination questions of integration of markets, production and circulation of goods, commercial ties and the area's major economic sectors. [SS]

SPANISH SOUTH AMERICA: Colonial Period

MICHAEL T. HAMERLY, Latin American Bibliographic Foundation, Redlands, California
SUSAN M. SOCOLOW, Associate Professor of History, Emory University
KATHY WALDRON, Institute for Historical Research, New York

RECOVERY AND EXPANSION DISTINGUISH the mid from the early 1980s for the most part. Whereas only 193 items appeared on colonial Spanish South America in *HLAS 46*—the least number per issue since *HLAS 36*—230 works are annotated in this *Handbook*—the largest number to date. One telling indicator of the increase in productivity is the unprecedented number of books in English published in the mid 1980s, at least 13: 1) Magnus Mörner, *The Andean past* (item **2616**), a general history of Ecuador, Peru, and Bolivia; 2) Kenneth J. Andrien, *Crisis and decline* (item **2618**), an analysis of the finances of the Viceroyalty of Peru in the 17th century and a reexamination of the "crisis" that is supposed to have prevailed in that century; 3) Robert D. Wood, *Teach them good customs* (item **2627**), a study of Indian education and acculturation by members of the regular clergy throughout Spanish South America; 4) Michael McKinley, *Pre-revolutionary Caracas: politics,* *economy and society, 1771–1811* (item **2646a**); 5) Jane M. Rausch, *A tropical plains frontier* (item **2681**), a history of the llanos of Nueva Granada; 6) Kendall W. Brown, *Bourbons and brandy* (item **2729**), a case study of the impact of the reforms undertaken by the new dynasty on Arequipa and its hinterland; 7) Keith A. Davies, *Landowners in colonial Peru* (item **2737**), a case study of land tenure and its socioeconomic significance in the same district during the Hapsburg era; 8) Scarlett O'Phelan Godoy, *Rebellions and revolts in eighteenth century Peru and Upper Peru* (Köln, FRG: Böhlau Verlag, 1985); 9) Susan E. Ramírez, *Provincial patriarchs* (item **2764**), a case study of "land tenure and the economics of power" in the Lambayeque region; 10) Karen Spalding's long awaited Huarochirí (see *HLAS 46:1721*); 11 and 12) Peter Bakewell, *Miners of the Red Mountain* (item **2766**) and Jeffrey A. Cole, *The Potosí mita, 1573–1700* (item **2767**), which reach different conclusions regarding Indian labor at Potosí itself and the impact of the *mita* on the population of the *altiplano* at large; and 13) C.J. McNappy, *Conquistador without sword* (Chicago: Loyola Univ. Press, 1984), a popular biography of the Jesuit missionary Roque González de Santa Cruz. The increase in productivity was not uniform, however. Whereas half again as many items on Nueva Granada and colonial Venezuela appear in this *Handbook* as in *HLAS 46*, there are about one fifth fewer on the Río de la Plata. And although three times as many works appear on Quito and twice as many on Alto Perú and colonial Chile, registered output on colonial Peru remains about the same.

GENERAL WORKS

The number of truly general studies continues to shrink. The most notable are: Mörner's history of the central Andean countries (item **2616**); Andrien's *Crisis and decline* (item **2618**), which in addition to being a pioneering study of royal revenues, ably synthesizes the now substantial body of literature on economic developments in the Viceroyalty of Peru and its component districts during the 17th century; Carlos Sempat Assadourian's *El sistema de la economía colonial* (item **2617a**), a cogent assessment of economic ties between Alto Perú, Chile, and what is now northwestern Argentina; and Wood's book on acculturation of Indians through education (item **2627**).

VENEZUELA

The publication of basic sources as well as regional studies continues to characterize historical production on colonial Venezuela—so much so that it was not possible to include all of the recent volumes in the monographic series "Fuentes para la historia colonial de Venezuela" in this *Handbook*. Perhaps the most important of the "new" sources in that series are vols. 2–3 of the *Juicios de residencia* (items **2642** and **2643**). Unquestionably important are vols. 2–4 of the "Serie Proyecto hacienda pública colonial venezolana." Vol. 2 is actually a monograph by Eduardo Arcila Farías, Venezuela's leading economic historian, on the finance and trade of the 16th century (item **2639**) as documented by the accounts of the royal fisc (see *HLAS 44:2618* and in this *Handbook*, items **2644** and **2645**). Other excellent monographs are the monumental studies by Lucas Guillermo Castillo Lara on Curiepe (item **2632**) and Panaquire (item **2631**), Miquel Izard's continuing work on the *llaneros* (item **2640** and **2641**), and McKinley's book on *Pre-revolutionary Caracas* (item **2646a**).

NUEVA GRANADA

The works annotated in this *Handbook* are a mixed bag. They consist of popular as well as scholarly monographs, reprints of standard as well as new studies, and a few sources. Almost all of the new works of significance are devoted to particular places, persons, or groups. Perhaps the best of these are: *Cartagena de Indias en el siglo XVI* by María del Carmen Borrego Plá (item **2661**); the four-volume *Historia general de Cartagena* by Eduardo Lemaitre (item **2674**); *Guerra y economía en las haciendas: Popayán, 1780–1830* by Zamira Díaz de Zuluaga (item **2665**); Rausch's book on the llanos (item **2681**); a revisionist biography of Caballero y Góngora by Roberto María Tisnés Jiménez (item **2684**); and the inaugural volume of Luis Carlos Mantilla Ruiz's *Los franciscanos en Colombia* (item **2676**); Apparently the bicentennial of the Mutis expedition has not yet generated much of importance. Nonetheless José Antonio Amaya's *Bibliografía de la Real Expedición Botánica . . .* (item **2660**) is useful. The outpouring on the rebellion of the *comuneros* continues. In addition to Tisnés's book on the archbishop-viceroy, also of interest are the *Documentos para la historia de la insurrección comunera en la provincia de Antioquia* (item **2666**). And Anthony McFarlane breaks new ground by extending Phelan's thesis on that rebellion (see *HLAS 42:2779*) to other manifestations of popular unrest in the 18th century (item **2675**). Also noteworthy is Bernardo Tovar Zambrano's *La colonia en la historiografía colombiana* (item **2685**).

QUITO

The most significant development of the mid 1980s was the massive incursion of the French into Ecuadorian studies. Among the first fruits of their efforts are three works which are important by any criteria: Jean-Paul Deler, *Genèse de l'espace équatorien* (see *HLAS 46:2611*); with Nelson Gómez and Michel Portais, Deler's more recent *El manejo del espacio en el Ecuador* (Quito: Centro de Investigaciones Geográficas, 1983) which reviews the historical geography of the colonial as well as that of the republican period and which constitutes the first of a projected four-volume *Geografía básica del Ecuador*; and issue No. 15 of the serial *Cultura* which is given over to essays and sources on the past of Loja and its province (on the colonial period, see items **2690, 2707, 2713,** and **2715**). Other significant trends are the maturation of Spanish research on the Audiencia of Quito—see especially the studies by Montserrat Fernández Martínez (item **2696**), Antonio Lafuente (item **2700**), María Luisa Laviana Cuetos (items **2702, 2703, 2704,** and **2705**), and Javier Ortiz de la Tabla Ducasse (item **2710**)—and the emergence of a group of younger Ecuadorian scholars, particularly in Cuenca, almost all of whose work is pioneering and is helping to place Ecuadorian scholarship on a much firmer basis. In this *Handbook*, see the studies by Lucas Achig Subia (item **2688**), Manuel Carrasco Vintimilla (item **2692**), Leonardo Espinoza (item **2614**), Fernando Jurado Noboa (items **2698** and **2699**), Manuel Miño Grijalva (item **2695**), and Silva Palomeque (items **2711** and **2712**). The primary organs of diffusion of the *cuencanos* are the publications of the Instituto de Investigaciones Sociales of the Univ. de Cuenca—which are almost impossible to obtain—and the relatively new *Revista del Archivo Nacional de Historia, Sección del Azuay* (item **2617**). Also noteworthy are the historical demographic studies by Martin Minchom, who is British, on Loja (items **1672** and **2707**), and the publication several years ago of a fragment (corresponding to pueblos of the Corregimiento of Otavalo) of the elusive Duque de la Palata census (item **2709**).

PERU

Scholarship on and in Peru continues to mature. This is evident from works as novel as Alberto Flores Galindo and Magdalena Chocano's essay on marital disputes and divorces in late colonial Lima (item **2743**), as fascinating as Claude Mazet's analysis of mortality in 18th-century Lima (item **2757**), monographs as outstanding as Ramírez's *Provincial patriarchs* (item **2764**), and the appearance of a journal transcending country as well as discipline boundaries, the *Revista latinoamericana de historia económica y social*. Topics such as the Spanish conquest, the Church, and the Túpac Amaru rebellion still elicit considerable attention, but new data and fresh light are being brought to bear. Especially interesting are: José Antonio Busto Duthurburu's book on the civil wars (item **2730**); Sabine MacCormack's "The Heart Has Its Reasons" (item **1655**); Leon G. Campbell's articles on banditry and women in the Túpac Amaru rebellion (items **2732** and **2733**); and Scarlett O'Phelan Godoy's proposed typology of native uprisings in the late colonial period (item **2762**). Themes new to Peruvian historiography are emerging. The economic and social role of priests as *doctrineros*, for example, has begun to be scrutinized. In this *Handbook*, see the articles by Antonio Acosta Rodríguez (items **2722** and **2723**), David Cahill (item **2731**), and Christine Hunefeldt (item **2750**). The 17th century has several new devotees, besides Andrien and Davies, Ronald Escobedo Mansilla (items **2739** and **2740**). Recent research has also rescued neglected regions such as the northwest and the southwest from near oblivion. In addition to Ramírez's book, see Lorenzo Huertas Vallejos's *Tierras, diezmos y tributos en el Obispado de Trujillo* (item **2749**) and the quasi-complementary monographs by Davies and Brown on Arequipa and its hinterland (items **2737** and **2729**). And major advances were made in historical demography. Clemencia Aramburú de Olivera and Pilar Remy S.'s *La población del Cuzco colonial* (item **2726**) is as notable and in its own way, as sophisticated as Mazet's study of mortality in Lima.

ALTO PERU

The quality as well as the volume of writing on colonial Bolivia increased in the mid 1980s. But these interrelated developments appear to be the results of the efforts of foreign rather than of national scholars for the most part. The increase in external and the decrease in internal production reflect the growing number of Andeanists in the US and in Europe, especially in France, and the adverse circumstances faced by the majority of Bolivian scholars in recent years. Be that as it may, undoubtedly the most important of the new works on Alto Perú are the previously mentioned books by Bakewell and Cole on Indian labor at Potosí and the *mita* in the 16th and 17th centuries (items **2766** and **2767**), and the pioneering monograph by Enrique Tandeter and Nathan Wachtel on prices in Potosí in the 18th century (item **2780**).

CHILE

Notwithstanding the increase in productivity, historical research on colonial Chile remains slight. Fortunately, what output there has been, continues to be of the high calibre characteristic of Chilean historians. At the risk of being invidious, the most interesting recent contributions are the seminal paper on landed estates by Rolando Mellafe (item **2786**), the demographic studies by Jorge Pinto Rodríguez (items **2788** and **2789**), and vol. 2 of Sergio Villalobos R.'s new approach history of the colonial and national periods (item **2795**). Equally fascinating is the autobiography of Ursula Suárez (1666–1749), a worldly nun (item **2791**).

RIO DE LA PLATA

Most of the recent work on colonial Argentina, Paraguay, and Uruguay is routine. Some interesting studies were produced in the fields of economic and social history, however. The most exciting are the article by Juan Carlos Garavaglia on economic developments in the Viceroyalty of the Río de la Plata in the late 1700s (item **2810**), and his major monograph on the economic history and colonial Paraguay (item **2811**). Although traditional in approach, Hernán Asdrúbal Silva's article on trade between Hamburg and Buenos Aires during the late colonial period is also noteworthy (item **2799**). Far more limited in scope and analysis are three articles by Nelly R. Porro which should also be mentioned because they bridge the traditional field of legal history and the less developed one of social history. Working with cases related to parental opposition to marriage, she provides basic data on marriage law and its application and on the use of the *depósito* as a means of controlling recalcitrant offspring (see items **2824, 2825,** and **2826**). And in a series of articles on the polity and society of Buenos Aires in the 1600s, Eduardo R. Saguier enlightens us to some extent as to what was happening in the port city in the forgotten century. Unfortunately his work is marred by jargon and inappropriate models (see items **2829, 2830, 2831, 2832,** and **2833**).

GENERAL

2618 Andrien, Kenneth J. Crisis and decline: the Viceroyalty of Peru in the seventeenth century. Albuquerque: Univ. of New Mexico Press, 1985. 287 p.: bibl., ill., index, map, tables.

Drawing on substantial monographic literature and royal treasury accounts (Lima's), Andrien argues that although the Viceroyalty of Peru like that of New Spain experienced a crisis in the 17th century, largely after 1660, it was administrative and fiscal rather than demographic or subsistence in nature. Whether or not Andrien turns out to be right, this—his first major work—is a welcome study of a neglected theme of vital importance, the collection and disbursement of royal revenues in greater Peru during the 1600s, and of the official involvement, especially treasury. [MTH]

2619 Bradley, Peter T. The cost of defending a Viceroyalty: Crown revenue and the defense of Peru in the seventeenth century (IAA, 10:3, 1984, p. 267–289, bibl., tables)

Analysis of defense expenditures of Viceroyalty of Peru in the 1600s, and ways in which money was spent. Total came to 51,953,386 pesos or slightly less than half the amount remitted to Spain. [MTH]

2620 Cieza de León, Pedro de. Obras completas. Edición crítica, notas, comentarios e índices, estudios y documentos adicionales de Carmelo Sáenz de Santa María. Madrid: Consejo Superior de Investigaciones Científicas, Instituto Gonzalo Fernández de Oviedo, 1984. 1 v.: indexes (Monumenta hispano-indiana; 2)

Major source on the Indians of the Andes, Spanish discovery and conquest of Tahuantinsuyu, and civil wars between the conquistadores has finally appeared as Cieza de León conceived it or as a single work. Vol. 1, apparently the only one to appear as of 1985, is the first integral edition of the *Crónica del Perú* (i.e., first, second, and third parts). Based on the Seville and Antwerp editions of 1553 and 1554, and on the Escorial and Vatican codices. Vol. 2 will be the first integral edition of the *Guerras civiles*, and vol. 3 will be given over to indices, a biobibliographical study of Cieza de León, and other supplementary materials. Editor is a leading authority on this prince of Andean chroniclers. [MTH]

2621 Cieza de León, Pedro de. Primera parte de la Crónica del Perú. Edición de Manuel Ballesteros. Madrid: Historia 16, 1984. 414 p.: map (Crónicas de América; 4)

Popular edition of the *Primera parte de la Crónica del Perú.* [MTH]

2622 Cieza de León, Pedro de. Primera parte de la Crónica del Perú. Introducción de Franklin Pease G.Y. Nota de Miguel Maticorena E. Lima: Pontificia Univ. Católica del Perú, Fondo Editorial: Academia Nacional de la Historia, 1984. 352 p., 12 p. of plates: bibl., ill., indcxcs (Col. Clásicos peruanos)

Scholarly edition of *Primera parte de la Crónica del Perú*. Based on the original edition (Seville, 1553). [MTH]

2623 Doctrina christiana y catecismo para instrucción de los indios, y de las demás personas que han de ser enseñadas en nuestras sancta fé, con un confessionario, y otras cosas necessarias para los que doctrinan, que se contienen en la pagina siguiente . . . Lima?: Petroperú, 1984? 84 leaves [i.e. 168 p.]

Facsimile edition of first work printed in South America, the *Doctrina christiana* of 1584, an important ethnohistorical and linguistic as well as ecclesiastical source. [MTH]

2624 Morales Alvarez, Juan M. Los extranjeros con Carta de Naturaleza de las Indias durante la segunda mitad del siglo XVIII. Caracas: Academia Nacional de la Historia, 1980. 449 p.: bibl., ill., indexes (Biblioteca de la Academia. Fuentes para la historia colonial de Venezuela; 147)

Ambitious review of Spanish legislation prohibiting foreigners from populating the Americas. Not limited to time period of title, author covers entire colonial period. Concludes that legal restrictions against non-Spaniards eased after 1750. Shifting European alliances, *asientos de negros* granted to the English and commercial partnerships between Spanish and others encouraged inflow of foreigners who later sought to legitimize their status through *cartas de naturaleza*. One-third of monograph is devoted to analysis of 147 individuals who obtained *cartas* but it is not clear how representative this sample is. Much detail is given to provide an accurate definition of foreigners, a term which evolved over time. Well-indexed general study. [KW]

2625 Oviedo Cavada, Carlos. El Arzobispo Pedro Felipe de Azúa: estudio biográfico del "Defensor de los Indios" (UC/AT, 448, 1983, p. 161–204, ill.)

Rescues from quasi-oblivion Chilean born Pedro Felipe de Azúa e Iturgoyen (1693–1754), Auxiliary Bishop and Bishop of Concepción (1740–44) and Archbishop of Santa

Fé de Bogotá (1745–53), who was apparently a remarkable man of God. [MTH]

2626 Szaszdi, Adam. Casa de moneda, mita y factoraje de azogues: instrumentos para el saneamiento monetario en el Virreynato de Lima (*in* Congreso Venezolano de la Historia, 4th, Caracas, 1980. Memoria [see *HLAS 46:2621*] v. 3, p. 207–256)

Detailed review of the problematic history of *plata corriente* or small, irregular pieces of silver, which by the end of the 16th century had most everywhere been replaced by *reales*. [MTH]

2627 Wood, Robert D. "Teach them good customs:" colonial Indian education and acculturation in the Andes. Culver City, Calif.: Labyrinthos, 1986. 134 p., 1 leaf of plates: bibl., ill.

Data laden essay on education and acculturation of Indians, especially by members of the regular clergy, in Spanish South America. [MTH]

VENEZUELA

2628 Armas Chitty, José Antonio de. San Miguel del Batey: poblamiento del siglo XVII. Caracas: Ediciones de la Facultad de Humanidades y Educación, Univ. Central de Venezuela, 1980. 132 p.: bibl.

The *poblador*, Miguel de Urbés and 21 colleagues founded San Miguel del Batey in 1646, one in series of settlements established to solidify Spanish domain over eastern Venezuela. Due to rivalries with neighboring villages, hostile Indians, and Urbés's death, the town disappeared after 12 years. Although limited by lack of sources, author describes life and death of the small town which was probably very representative of many 17th-century communities. A map would be useful. [KW]

2629 Briceño Perozo, Mario. Temas de historia colonial venezolana. Caracas: Academia Nacional de la Historia, 1981. 574 p.: ill. (Biblioteca de la Academia. Fuentes para la historia colonial de Venezuela; 150)

Leading archivist and historian studies important 18th-century archival material in three well documented essays: 1) analyzes 19 judicial proceedings against 1810 revolutionaries contained in Archivo General de la Nación under "Causas de Infidencia;"

2) examines life of José Antonio de Limonta, royal official (1782–1810) who observed and wrote on public financing; and 3) discusses efforts of Pedro José de Olavarriaga (famous for his memoirs) to eliminate illicit commerce, audit royal accounts and compile tributary census during 1720s. [KW]

2630 Castillo Lara, Lucas Guillermo. Apuntes para la historia colonial de Barlovento. Caracas: Academia Nacional de la Historia, 1981. 724 p., 13 leaves of plates: ill. (some col.), indexes (Biblioteca de la Academia. Fuentes para la historia colonial de Venezuela; 151)

Monumental study of Barlovento—fertile plain stretching east from Caracas between two mountain chains and center of slavery—by Venezuela's most prominent regional historian. After analyzing Indian population decline and hacienda consolidation, author turns to fascinating history of Curiepe, town of free blacks established in 1721. Juan del Rosario Blanco, ex-slave and militia captain, fought powerful Blanco Villegas family for royal concession to build town. Fugitive slaves, freed blacks, and refugees from Curaçao gathered together to form unique community. *Hacendados* from adjacent areas feared slave revolt led by Curiepe which did occur during independence. Longstanding enmity of blacks toward *mantuaños* explains why slaves and free blacks favored royalists even after they reneged on emancipation. Well researched monograph of value to all scholars of slavery. [KW]

2631 Castillo Lara, Lucas Guillermo. La aventura fundacional de los isleños: Panaquire y Juan Francisco de León. Caracas: Academia Nacional de la Historia, 1983. 672 p.: bibl., indexes (Biblioteca de la Academia. Fuentes para la historia colonial de Venezuela; 163)

Definitive history of 1749 local revolt led by Juan Francisco de León, Canary Islander, against Basque Compañía Guipuzcoana. Rebellion began as reaction to monopolistic privileges of trading company. Revolt spread to Caracas where local elite gave tacit support. This serious threat to Crown was subdued only in 1755, and León died in prison. Author places uprising within context of isleño history and ongoing conflict between cabildos and royal officials. [KW]

2632 Castillo Lara, Lucas Guillermo. Curiepe: orígenes históricos. Caracas: Biblioteca de autores y temas mirandinos, 1981. 353 p.: bibl. (Col. Juan Rodríguez Suárez; 2)

Shorter version of author's *Apuntes para la historia colonial de Barlovento* (item 2630). Volume eliminates introductory chapters on Barlovento and concentrates on town of Curiepe. [KW]

2633 Castillo Lara, Lucas Guillermo. Intentos para la creación de diócesis en Venezuela en la época colonial (VANH/B, 66:264, oct./dic. 1983, p. 995-1008)

Descriptive article about various attempts by regional cities to become centers of new bishoprics. Venezuela remained under one, Caracas, until 1778 when a new bishopric was erected in Mérida. In 1790, the diocesis of Guayana emerged, incorporating territories of Cuamaná, Barcelona, Margarita, and Trinidad. Article is useful as further demonstration of the competition between regional cities and Caracas. [KW]

2634 Cedulario de las provincias de Venezuela, 1535–1552. v. 2. Caracas: Academia de Ciencias Políticas y Sociales, 1982. 351 p.: indexes (Biblioteca de la Academia. Serie Los Siglos provinciales)

Important collection of 230 *cédulas* relating to Venezuela from 1535-52, many published for the first time. Among the most significant documents are those pertaining to Rodrigo de Bastidas, first bishop, and Juan Pérez de Tolosa, governor. Useful information on Weslers is also given. Over involvement of Crown in more mundane matters is striking. [KW]

2635 Un Censo ganadero en 1791: contribución a la historia de la ganadería en Venezuela. Compilación y estudio de Manuel Pinto C. Caracas: Presidencia de la República, 1980. 244 p.: bibl., ill. (Biblioteca de temas y autores de Anzoátegui; 4)

Reproduces 1791 cattle census conducted by Junta General de Hacendados de Ganados first held in 1789. Junta tried to organize Venezuelan cattle industry and eliminate theft, a growing problem at close of century. Junta established paramilitary squadrons to patrol *llanos* and capture thieves. Census was undertaken to determine each rancher's contribution to support squadrons, based upon number of animals. Ob-

vious desire to understate herd size is not
discussed but census still useful. Brands of
each rancher are reproduced. [KW]

2636 Dávila, Vicente et al. Los comuneros
de Mérida: edición conmemorativa del
bicentenario del movimiento comunero. t. 1,
Estudios. Caracas: Academia Nacional de la
Historia. 1981. 527 p.: bibl., indexes (Biblioteca de la Academia. Fuentes para la historia
colonial de Venezuela; 152)

Seven essays by distinguished scholars
on Venezuelan comunero movement centered
around Mérida. Vicente Dávila, Joseph Pérez,
and Carlos Felice Cardot present background
to revolt in three brief essays, while J.N.
Contreras Serrano reproduces many important documents from participants. Lucas
Castillo Lara shows outbreak of revolt in
Venezuelan town of La Grita in 1779, two
years before the eruption of El Socorro. Reaction to taxes and tobacco monopoly intertwined with long-standing personal feud
between two local personalities, a leading
Creole and administrator of Real Hacienda in
La Grita. Longest essay, almost book length,
is by Carlos Muñoz Oráa who concludes revolt was a popular, anti-colonial movement
anticipating independence. Need to secure
coastal zones spread revolt to Maracaibo and
placed comuneros in contact with English.
Final section by Alí Enrique León provides
useful chronology. By far the best work to
appear on subject. [KW]

2637 Febres Cordero G., Julio. Historia del
periodismo y de la imprenta en Venezuela. Caracas: Academia Nacional de la
Historia, 1983. 640 p.: bibl., ill., indexes (Biblioteca de la Academia. Fuentes para la historia colonial en Venezuela; 158)

Invaluable reference for printing and
journalism in 1808–30, period of intense
publication. First press (1808) initiated flurry
of activity, mostly political pamphlets and
newspapers of patriots. Author provides complete list by year, region, and edition with
textual examples and brief synopsis. Samples
culled from long search of regional and metropolitan archives. Essential tool for early
19th-century historians. [KW]

Fernández, David W. El cabildo indígena de
las encomiendas de Guarenas. See item **1622.**

2638 García-Baquero González, Antonio. El
comercio de neutrales en Venezuela:

1796–1802, tópico y cambio en las actitudes
políticas de las élites venezolanas (IGFO/RI,
14:173, enero/junio 1984, p. 237–271)

After declaration of war with England
in 1796 and resulting interruption of trade
with Spain, Venezuelan economy nearly col-
lapsed as evidenced by statistics on commodity prices and levels of imports and
exports. To relieve situation, Intendent
sought to open up commerce to neutral nations, especially for exporting tobacco monopolized by Real Hacienda. Well-explored
topic but author's unique contribution is his
study of specific reactions of *hacendados*
and merchants, the Venezuelan elite. Argues
convincingly that merchants opposed competition from neutral countries while *hacendados* consistently pleaded for outlet to
markets. Intendent vascillated between opposing demands, while merchants proved inconsistent in their opinion of trade with
neutrals. [KW]

**2639 Hacienda y comercio de Venezuela en
el siglo XVI.** Caracas: Banco Central
de Venezuela, 1983. 236 p.: bibl., ill. (Serie
Proyecto hacienda pública colonial venezuela;
2. Col. histórico-económica venezolana; 19)

After a four year gap, Eduardo Arcila
Farías resumes publishing accounts of the
royal treasury, an ongoing project entitled
"Proyecto Hacienda Pública Colonial Venezolana" (for vol. 1, see *HLAS 44:2618*). This
monograph based on documents contained
in vols. 3–4 is a major contribution to 16th-
century economic history. Discovery of gold
and pearls spurred growth but economy suffered recession, price fluctuations and un-
favorable trade balance. By late century, trade
stabilized to permit accumulation of capital
sufficient for slave imports and consolidation
of land holdings. By 1600, Venezuela was
poised for cacao boom to follow. Study of
royal income, expenses, prices, taxes, and
commerce enhanced by informative charts
and tables. Best analysis of the early economy to date. [KW]

2640 Izard, Miquel. Sin domicilio fijo,
senda segura, ni destino conocido: los
llaneros del Apure a finales del período colonial (UB/BA, 33, 1983, p. 13–83, appendices)

Another example of Izard's fine work
on the *llaneros*. Violence which characterized Venezuelan independence wars was
already brewing in the *llanos* as *llaneros*

(aborigines, black cimarrones and white and mestizo/mulatto fugitives from justice) pitted themselves against their enemies, government officials and large *hacendados* who tried to eliminate banditry, rustling, and lawlessness. Confrontations between both groups intensified during 18th century as number of *llaneros* increased and Spanish authorities viewed problem as serious. Main issue became control of major resource (i.e., cattle herds) and implementation of royal authority throughout a region relatively unsettled. [KW]

2641 Izard, Miquel. "Ya era hora de empender la lucha para que en el ancho feudo de la violencia reinase algún día la justicia" (UB/BA, 26 : 34, 1984, p. 75–124, appendices)

Thoughtful analysis of conflict between *llaneros* and *caraqueño* elite during late colonial era. Small ranchers of *llanos* supplied cattle to Caracas and resented the capital's price controls. *Llanero* diversion of cattle to other areas and participation in contraband prompted creation of paramilitary patrols sent out by Caracas to control *llanos*. Patrols proved ineffective and costly. *Llanero* cabildos opposed interference of Caracas while small landowners resisted encroachment of large *hacendados*. Author believes resentments grew over decades and explain why *llaneros* first fought with royalist against Creole Caracas patriots during independence. [KW]

2642 Juicios de residencia en la provincia de Venezuela. v. 2, Juan Pérez de Tolosa y Juan de Villegas. Edición de Marianela Ponce de Behrens, Diana Rengifo y Letizia Vaccari de Venturini. Caracas: Academia Nacional de la Historia, 1980. 512 p.: indexes (Biblioteca de la Academia. Fuentes para la historia colonial de Venezuela; 145)

Vol. 2 in series of *juicios de residencias* of governors and other leaders of the province (for vol. 1 on Weslers, see *HLAS* 42 : 2741). Careful collection marred by shallow introduction that fails to provide biographical data on the two men under study or their significance for Venezuelan history. These judicial reviews were conducted (1553–54) by Alonso Arias de Villasinda against Juan Pérez de Tolosa and Juan de Villegas, under the much hated German Weslers. Both men died shortly after assum-

ing their positions (1547–48). Does not fully develop treatment of Indians under Pérez de Tolosa's rule and lack of compliance with New Laws of 1542. Useful information on mining and black slavery is difficult to extract from documents reproduced here. [KW]

2643 Juicios de residencia en la provincia de Venezuela. v. 3, Don Francisco Dávila Orejón Gastón, 1673–1677. Estudio introductorio de Letizia Vacarri. Caracas: Academia Nacional de la Historia, 1983. 1 v. in 3 pts. (523, 437, 484 p.): indexes (Biblioteca de la Academia. Fuentes para la historia colonial de Venezuela; 160–162)

Three additions to the Academia's series on *juicios de residencia* (see *HLAS* 42 : 2741 and item **2642**). Comprehensive introduction details most significant findings of the *residencia*. Orejón Gastón, who governed Venezuela for only two years (1673–74), was charged with nepotism, bribery, contraband, and favoritism. Author concludes that Orejón Gastón was not an exemplary governor, especially when compared to Bishop Antonio González de Acuña, an outstanding figure devoted to improving municipal services, building provincial fortifications against pirate attacks, and developing an educational system. Although the introduction makes these three volumes more useful than earlier ones, further editing is necessary. Includes too many repetitive documents of little historical value while lack of a topical index makes it difficult to extract very important data on encomiendas, piracy, contraband, and local government. [KW]

2644 Libros de la hacienda pública en Nueva Segovia, 1551–1577, y Caracas, 1581–1597. Caracas: Banco Central de Venezuela, 1983. 439 p.: bibl. (Serie Proyecto hacienda pública colonial venezolana; 3. Col. histórico-económica venezolana; 20)

Vol. 3 in series covers 1559–77 when provincial capital moved from Coro to Barquisimeto due to frequent pirate attacks on coast. Also includes account books of Real Hacienda (1581–97) when royal treasury again moved, this time finally finding a permanent location in Caracas. Aside from financial data, volume sheds light on French pirate Jacques de Sores who attacked Borburata, holding the town captive for several weeks. [KW]

2645 Libros de la Real Hacienda en la última década del siglo XVI. Caracas: Banco Central de Venezuela, 1983. 323 p.: bibl. (Serie Proyecto hacienda pública colonial venezolana; 4. Col. histórico-económica venezolana; 21)

More account books of the royal treasury conclude publication of 16th-century documents. Consolidation of provincial administration in Caracas resulted in better bookkeeping and increased revenues. During last decade of century, royal income doubled that of previous decade. Ancestors of Bolívar first appear here as functionaries of Real Hacienda. [KW]

2646 López Bohorquez, Ali Enrique. Los ministros de la Audiencia de Caracas, 1786–1810: caracterización de una élite burocrática del poder español en Venezuela. Caracas: Academia Nacional de la Historia, 1984. 242 p.: bibl., tables (Biblioteca de la Academia. Fuentes para la historia colonial de Venezuela; 174)

Prosopographic study that conforms with results of other audiencia histories which state that Creoles were denied access to high office during latter part of colonial period. Peninsulares accounted for 11 of 16 oidores appointed to the Audiencia of Caracas with no Venezuelan ever serving. Provides brief biographical data, all for judges. Concludes, but does not fully demonstrate, that Creole lawyers, trained in Consulado courts, gained preparation for independence there. First such study for Venezuela using collective biography, this work is helpful for understanding late colonial period. [KW]

2646a McKinley, P. Michael. Pre-revolutionary Caracas: politics, economy, and society, 1777–1811. Cambridge, England: Cambridge Univ. Press, 1985. 245 p.: indexes, maps.

Excellent monograph concludes that economic prosperity, political stability, and social cohesion characterized Caracas province during years studied. Analyzes over 800 wills of elite individuals to demonstrate shared economic interests of hacendados and merchants and close ties between Creoles and Spaniards. This "golden age" view presents problems for explaining bloody independence wars which author attributes to deliberately harsh tactics of Bolívar and Boves. [KB]

2647 Magallanes, Manuel Vicente. Luchas e insurrecciones en la Venezuela colonial. Caracas: Academia Nacional de la Historia, 1982. 240 p.: bibl. (El Libro menor; 28)

Relies on secondary sources to provide 45 succinct summaries of revolts and insurrections which occurred in Venezuela throughout the colonial period. Categorized into four types: Indian resistance to conquest; African slave uprisings; political intrigues of the cabildos; and pre-independence revolts. Lacks general interpretation of such movements, but is a good starting point. Particularly useful sections on the comunero movement in the Andes and revolts in the *llanos*, topics also studied by other scholars (see items **2636** and **2640**). [KW]

2648 Marcos, Jesús Varela. Las salinas de Araya y el origen de la Armada de Barlovento. Caracas: Academia Nacional de la Historia, 1980. 295 p.: ill., indexes, maps (Biblioteca de la Academia. Fuentes para la historia colonial de Venezuela; 146)

Well researched politico-military history of the 1605 expedition sent to the northeast coast of Venezuela to rid it of corsairs. Dutch pirates reduced royal tax collections, inhibited coastal communications and, more seriously, threatened Spain's access to the Caribbean. The armada completely surprised the Dutch interlopers who capitulated without a struggle. The victory aided the pro-military faction in the Spanish council of state which favored creating a separate Barlovento armada to patrol the south Caribbean. No analysis of lasting effect of this victory is given but mission did solidify Spanish control for some time. Useful maps enhance this well written monograph. [KW]

2649 Miranda, Francisco de. Colombeia. Sección 2, El viajero ilustrado. t. 3, 1783–1785. t. 4, 1785–1786. t. 5, 1787. t. 6, 1787–1788. Prefacio de J.L. Salcedo-Bastardo. Introducción, bibliografía, prólogo y notas de Josefina Rodríguez de Alonso. Caracas: Ediciones de la Presidencia de la República, 1978–1983. 4 v.: bibl.

Pt. 2 of new edition of documents contained in the Archivo del General Francisco de Miranda (for pt. 1, see *HLAS 42:2649*). Four volumes cover Miranda's 18-month sojourn in the US and four-year stay in Europe (1783–89). Miranda's famous diary is reproduced in a convenient form. [KW]

2650 Nectario María, Brother. Indice de documentos referentes a los obispos de Venezuela, 1532–1816, existentes en el Archivo General de Indias de Sevilla. Caracas: Univ. Católica Andrés Bello, Instituto de Investigaciones Históricas, 1975. 298 p.: bibl.

Although published in 1975, this is an important and impressive inventory of documentation relating to Venezuela's 28 colonial bishops. Lists over 3000 documents, each succinctly described with Archive's date and location. Brief summary of the life of every bishop is given with greater emphasis placed on the most important clerics (e.g., Rodrigo de Bastidas, Mauro de Tovar, Diego de Baños y Sotomayor, Mariano Martí, Francisco de Ibarra, Narciso Coll y Prat). [KW]

2651 Osorio C., F. Eduardo. Un "enclave" en la economía meridiana de mediados del siglo XVIII (UB/BA, 14:32, 1982, p. 315–381, appendices, bibl., graphs, maps, tables)

Detailed, well researched study of eight Jesuit haciendas which supported Jesuit college in Mérida. Following "golden" period in 17th century, Mérida declined because of falling commodity prices, external competition, deteriorating access to major trade routes, and outmoded technology. Concludes that Jesuit haciendas already experienced economic contraction before the Order's expulsion. New, secular owners were not responsible for later decline of the estates. Charts, graphs, and tables set out much statistical data. This represents only preliminary work expected from new Centro de Estudios Históricos of the Univ. de los Andes. [KW]

2652 Rey Fajardo, José del. La pedagogía jesuítica en la Venezuela hispánica. Caracas: Academia Nacional de la Historia, 1979. 781 p.: indexes (Biblioteca de la Academia. Fuentes para la historia colonial de Venezuela; 138)

Compendium of documents on Jesuit pedagogy and formation of Jesuit colleges in Mérida, Maracaibo, Coro, and Caracas. Rey's useful introduction summarizes difficulties Jesuits encountered in establishing schools. Competition from other orders, lack of funds, government apathy, and frequent reassignment of clerics interrupted individual efforts. Contains the Order's constitutions, formal instructions for professors, exercises for students, and official view on teaching

humanistic studies. Author claims this is first Spanish translation for many documents (published in Italy). Another valuable contribution by one of Venezuela's leading Church historians. [KW]

2653 Rodríguez Luis, José Angel. Clandestinidad, contrabando y consumo del aguardiente de caña en Venezuela en el siglo XVIII (VANH/B, 66:261, enero/marzo 1983, p. 145–165, tables)

Preliminary study of *aguardiente*. Author contends that despite royal prohibitions, Venezuelans produced and consumed great quantities of this alcoholic drink. Natural outgrowth of sugarcane agriculture, product was widespread throughout colony. Estimates existence of over 300 *trapiches* in 1775. Clandestine production and imports of contraband liquor prompted Intendent to suggest legalization of production (ca. 1783). Interesting topic requiring further study. [KW]

2654 Samudio de Chaves, Edda O. La mita en Mérida colonial (VANH/B, 66:261, enero/marzo 1983, p. 81–111, appendices, maps, tables)

Informative essay on origins of an urban *mita* for Mérida's regional capital. Santa Fé Audiencia promulgated ordenanzas in 1620 permitting city the use of men from surrounding 12 Indian villages for construction of city's public works. Number of *mitayos* per year (480 in 1620) represented 20 percent of local Indians subject to tribute. By 1657, quota dropped to 233 Indians, reflecting overall indigenous population decline. Reproduces 10 documents related to Mérida *mita*, including allocation of laborers and responsibility of cabildo for maintaining workers. [KW]

2655 Silva Montañes, Ismael. Hombres y mujeres del siglo XVI venezolano. Caracas: Academia Nacional de la Historia, 1983. 4 v.: bibl. (Biblioteca de la Academia. Fuentes para la historia colonial de Venezuela; 156, 159, 164, 166)

Curious four-volume catalog of 5250 individuals associated with Venezuela in the 16th century. Biographical data entirely drawn from 55 works published by other Venezuelan historians, a random selection with many notable gaps. Amount and quality of information varies from very brief to detailed, from obscure to renowned. Although in no way a systematic list of Venezuela's population, catalog might be useful as quick reference. Volumes are not indexed but arranged alphabetically. [KW]

2656 Suárez, Santiago Gerardo. Las milicias: instituciones militares hispanoamericanas. Caracas: Academia Nacional de la Historia, 1984. 301 p. (Biblioteca de la Academia. Fuentes para la historia colonial de Venezuela; 171)

Well documented and researched treatment of Spanish military presence in the Indies. Traces historic origins of institutional forces from ad hoc armies of explorer-conquistadors and military obligations of encomenderos to creation of the colonial militia in the 1760s. Describes formal establishment of militia units with emphasis on Venezuela. [D.E. Chipman]

2657 Tosta, Virgilio. Familias, cabildos y vecinos de la antigua Barinas. Caracas: Academia Nacional de la Historia, 1980. 130 p.: bibl. (El Libro menor; 10)

Popular history of Barinas during colonial era. More a series of short biographies of prominent *barineses* than regional history but still of some use for genealogists. [KW]

2658 Vásquez de Ferrer, Belín M. Tráfico comercial hispano-venezolano, 1765–1789 (UB/BA, 14:32, 1982, p. 409–439, tables)

Interesting summary of author's dissertation on economic relations between Spain and Venezuela based upon peninsular archival material. Trade increased during period 1765–89, especially as Crown removed restrictions. Critical analysis of ship registers provides data on value of cargos between six Venezuelan and nine Spanish ports. Between 1779–89, colonial exports were valued at more than 20 percent of imports (does not consider contraband). Commerce was concentrated in ports of La Guaira and Cadiz, colony exported cacao and hides in exchange for textiles and other manufactured goods. Conclusion that wealth from favorable trade balance remained with elite for consumptive rather than productive use is intriguing but not demonstrated. [KW]

COLOMBIA

2659 Agudelo Ramírez, Luis Eduardo. Génesis del pueblo caldense. Mani-

zales, Colombia: Imprenta Departamental, 1983. 141 p.: bibl., maps (Biblioteca de escritores caldenses)

Concise general history of 16th-century Caldas. Agudelo Ramírez and Ricardo de los Ríos Tobón (see item **2682**) both submitted works in response to a contest sponsored by the Dept. of Caldas's government to promote local history. Indians' resistance to Spaniards delayed colonization process until disease and war reduced native population. Competing conquistadors from Lima, Popayán, and Cartagena also contributed to creation of Spanish towns. Discovery of gold mines led to importation of African slaves and influx of Spanish settlers. Once mines were depleted and Indians disappeared, settlement could not be sustained. Useful summary despite absence of archival research. [KW]

2660 Amaya, José Antonio. Bibliografía de la Real Expedición Botánica del Nuevo Reyno de Granada. Bogotá: Instituto Colombiano de Cultura Hispánica, 1983. 184 p., 10 leaves of plates (some folded): ill., index.

Utilitarian bibliography of works by and on members of the Mutis expedition as well as on the findings of the expedition. Indexed. [MTH]

2661 Borrego Plá, María del Carmen. Cartagena de Indias en el siglo XVI. Prólogo de Luis Navarro García. Sevilla, Spain: Escuela de Estudios Hispano-Americanos, 1983. 556 p., 1 folded leaf of plates: bibl., ill., index, maps (Publicaciones; 288)

Thorough and original social history of Cartagena details foundation, distribution of encomiendas, and development of socially stratified urban society. Rapid growth in 16th century related to ideal port conditions and solid agricultural base. City soon emerged as important center of empire. Author painstakingly reconstructs holdings of 75 principal encomenderos who dominated municipal and military positions using them to promote urban growth. Elite prosperity spurred artisan, shopkeeper class which contributed to socially stratified urban society which included many slaves. Commendable study which successfully balances much detail with useful synthesis. Maps and charts are helpful. [KW]

2662 Caycedo, Bernardo J. Un obispo, un oidor y un alguacil de corte (ACH/

BHA, 70:740, enero/marzo 1983, p. 32−74, ill.)

Short article about three members of the Gil Martínez Malo family, all peninsulares who served Crown and Church in Colombia. José Joaquín was oidor (1721−41) while his two nephews Nicólas and Juan José served respectively as Bishop of Santa Marta and alcalde of the Bogotá cabildo and later as *alguacil de corte* during middle of 18th century. Author's major point is that Juan José integrated himself into colonial society by marrying and raising children in America. His uncle and brother could not or did not marry, thereby remaining more isolated from colonial, Creole elite. Concept is interesting but not proven by this one example. [KW]

2663 Colmenares, Germán. La Provincia de Tunja en el Nuevo Reino de Granada: ensayo de historia social, 1539−1800. Tunja, Colombia: Academia Boyacense de Historia, 1984. 254 p.: bibl., ill. (Biblioteca de la Academia. Serie Obras fundamentales; 1)

Reedition of major work by one of Colombia's most noted colonial historians. First published in 1970, monograph has been out of print. This edition is vol. 1 in new series sponsored by Academia Boyacense de Historia. [KW]

2664 Colmenares, Germán. Sociedad y economía en el Valle del Cauca. t. 1, Cali: terratenientes, mineros y comerciantes, siglo XVIII. Bogotá: Fondo de Promoción de la Cultura, Banco Popular; Cali, Colombia: Depto. de Publicaciones, Univ. del Valle, 1983. 1 v.: bibl., ill., indexes (Biblioteca Banco Popular. Textos universitarios)

Vol. 1 of five on society and economy of the Valley of Cauca. Sponsored by Univ. del Valle and Banco Popular, studies are designed as university texts but exceed that objective. Vol. 1: one of Colombia's leading scholars provides excellent history of 18th-century Cali, focusing on relationship among landowners, miners and merchants. Using notarial records, Colmenares reconstructs land tenure patterns to conclude that the formation of large estates did not occur until the end of the colonial period. [KW]

2665 Díaz de Zuluaga, Zamira. Sociedad y economía en el Valle del Cauca. t. 2, Guerra y economía en las haciendas: Popayán, 1780−1830. Bogotá: Fondo de Promoción de la Cultura, Banco Popular; Cali, Colombia: Depto. de Publicaciones, Univ. del Valle, 1983. 123 p.: bibl., index (Biblioteca Banco Popular. Textos universitarios)

Vol. 2 in excellent series of the Valley of Cauca. This study continues Germán Colmenares's careful research and broad synthesis in vol. 1 (item **2664**). Author adds to other studies of Popayán (see *HLAS 42:2777*) by focusing on rural economy during later period. Accumulation of land accelerated after 1767 when Creole hacendados annexed former Jesuit estates after Order's expulsion. Insightful chapter on effects of independence wars concludes that agricultural production declined when Creole landowners abandoned estates to assume leadership of armies with laborers as soldiers. Makes useful distinction between altiplano Popayán and valley estates. Former recovered more rapidly when local consumption resumed but latter did not reestablish markets with ruined mining communities. [KW]

2666 Documentos para la historia de la insurrección comunera en la Provincia de Antioquia, 1765−1798. Edición del Archivo Histórico de Antioquia. Medellín, Colombia: Univ. de Antioquia, Facultad de Ciencias Humanas, Depto. de Historia, 1982. 620 p. (Col. Huellas en la historia)

Useful, well selected collection of documents on Antioquia. Demonstrates that comunero movement was not confined to eastern provinces of Nueva Granada where most historians focus. Documents reveal that uprising occurred in response to new taxes imposed upon production and sale of tobacco and *aguardiente*. Participants were from all social groups, including slaves who revolted in hope of freedom. Selection includes viceregal instructions establishing taxes, testimonies of local officials, reports on slave uprisings, suspension of publication of *capitulaciones* of Socorro comuneros, and general pardon granted by Carlos III. Welcome addition. [KW]

2667 Echeverry E., Raúl. El discurrir de Mutis por el Departamento del Tolima, antigua Provincia de Mariquita. Bogotá: Colciencias, 1983. 30 p.: bibl., ill.

Brief review of early career of famous botanist José Celestino Mutis who served as mayordomo of Sapo gold mines, Tolima. Before leading renowned Botanical Expedition of New Granada in 1783, Mutis managed mines for six years where he developed his skills as a scientist (e.g., he recorded over 420 plant and 80 animal species). Mutis remained driving force behind introduction of natural sciences to Colombia and is known as the country's first minister of education. [KW]

2668 Fals Borda, Orlando. Historia doble de la costa. v. 1, Mompox y Loba. Bogotá: Carlos Valencia Editores, 1979. 167 p.: bibl., ill., indexes, photos.

Vol. 1 of three. Unique layout combines history and sociology of the Atlantic coastal area in a double arrangement of material which can be read as two books. Left side pages are social and anecdotal, while right side pages are historical and interpretative. Numerous photographs and sketches add to this delightful history which relies on archival sources and covers entire colonial period. Particularly interesting are sections on Chimila conquest, *palenques* led by slave "king" Domingo Bioho, and rise of Mier y la Torre family as major hacendados in Mompox. For vols. 2–3, see item **2941**. [KW]

2669 Filosofía de la pacificación en Colombia. Selección de textos e introducción de Roberto J. Salazar Ramos. Bogotá: Editorial El Buho, 1984. 298 p.: bibl. (Col. pensamiento Colombiano)

Part of series on Colombian thinking, vol. 2 attempts to define "philosophy of pacification" during immediate post-conquest period (1550–1600). Crucial issue was debate over treatment of Indians. Salazar Ramos's lengthy introduction places this well known debate within context of Colombian history, outlining conflict between cleric, encomendero, and royal official. Three opposing arguments are revealed through 22 documents. Although most appear elsewhere, editor's careful selection makes this an integrated and valuable addition to philosophy of Spanish colonization. [KW]

2670 Fonseca Truque, Marco Antonio. Historia del delito en Colombia: el veneno del arzobispo. Bogotá: Ediciones La Cara Oculta, 1983. 260 p.: bibl., ill., indexes.

Archbishop and Viceroy Caballero y Góngora continues to be a controversial figure. Author accuses him of many crimes (e.g., betraying the comuneros, introducing the "black hand" to Nueva Granada, organizing first secret police force, poisoning his political rivals). Author goes so far as to suggest that remains of one such victim, Juan de

Torrezar Díaz y Pimienta, be exhumed in Bogotá and examined for traces of arsenic. Despite scant historical evidence for such wild allegations, book is useful for revealing strong, emotional reaction still generated by historical figures involved with comunero revolt. [KW]

2671 Gredilla, A. Federico. Biografía de José Celestino Mutis y sus observaciones sobre las vigilias y sueños de algunas plantas. Prólogo de Guillermo Hernández de Alba. Bogotá: Plaza & Janés: Academia Colombiana de Historia, 1982. 381 p., 4 p. of plates: ill., index (Complemento a la Historia extensa de Colombia; 1)

Republication of 1911 edition in honor of the bicentennial of 1783 Botanical Expedition of New Granada. As Director of Madrid's Botanical Garden, author can appreciate Mutis's work on Colombia's flora and fauna. Mutis wrote on mathematics, astronomy, medicine, and metallurgy as well as botany, and led movement to reform colonial New Granada's educational system. Extensive inclusion of Mutis's letters (e.g., to Linneo, Humboldt) and scholarly investigations add to biography's value. [KW]

2672 Henao, Jesús María and **Gerardo Arrubla.** Historia de Colombia. Bogotá: Plaza & Janés: Academia Colombiana de Historia, 1984. 2 v.: bibl., ill., ports. (Complemento a la Historia extensa de Colombia; 11)

Another edition of standard text on Colombian history (first ed. 1910) by two Academia members. In 1984, the Academia decided to publish this two-volume version as vol. 11 in its ongoing series, *Complemento a la Historia extensa de Colombia*, despite dozens of other editions. The Academia notes that Henao and Arrubla wrote basic text used by high schools for over 50 years. Scholars are still wise to refer to this history for a narrative account. [KW]

2673 Julián, Antonio. La perla de la América, provincia de Santa Marta. Introducción de Luis Duque Gómez. Bogotá: Academia Colombiana de Historia, 1980. 303 p.: indexes, maps.

Facsimile of 1787 original edition written by Antonio Julián who arrived in Cartagena in 1749 to convert the Indians. The Jesuit wrote a lively account of the province describing flora, fauna, and Indians encountered during travels. Decried neglect of Santa Marta and warned against growing contraband trade. Introduction by Luis Duque Gómez. Welcome reedition of work long out of print. [KW]

2674 Lemaitre, Eduardo. Historia general de Cartagena. Con la asesoría y colaboración de Donald Bosso Herazo y Francisco Sebá Patrón. v. 1, Descubrimiento y conquista. v. 2, La colonia. v. 3, La independencia. v. 4, La república. Bogotá: Banco de la República, 1983. 4 v.: bibl., ill., indexes.

Masterful four-volume study of Cartagena from pre-conquest to the 1940s, which greatly extends author's previous *Breve historia de Cartagena, 1501–1901* (1980). Vol. 1 covers career of Pedro de Heredia, city's founder. Vol. 2 begins in 16th century with famous attacks of John Hawkins and Francis Drake which led to city's fortification. Also covers Dique Canal, political conflict between Church and State, and Vernon's 1741 siege. Most notable is vol. 3 on independence where Cartagena competed with Santa Marta. Pro-independence Cartagena suffered during Morillo siege and interruption of coastal trade, while rival Santa Marta gained during royalist ascendancy. Final volume is a lengthy chronological review (1820–1940) drawing heavily from author's *La bolsa o la vida* (1974). Essential work that goes beyond the history of one city. [KW]

2675 McFarlane, Anthony. Civil disorders and popular protests in late colonial New Granada (HAHR, 64:1, 1985, p. 17–54)

Provocative thesis that comunero rebellion "may be seen as another expression . . . of popular actions undertaken in defense of the customary arrangements and practices of local community life." Author investigates other popular protests in late colonial period to conclude that they reflected popular defiance of arbitrary government and excessive taxation. Shared traits include controlled violence, Creole elite participation, ritual behavior, urban setting, overlap with fiestas, and animosity toward government officials. Excellent beginning. [KW]

2676 Mantilla Ruiz, Luis Carlos. Los franciscanos en Colombia. t. 1, 1550–1600. Bogotá: Editorial Kelly, 1984. 1 v.: bibl., ill., index.

Voluminous and useful history based on dissertation of first 50 years of Franciscan influence in Colombia. Encomenderos, royal officials, and bishops all opposed Franciscan attempts to control Indian population. When friars' domination of Indian *doctrinas* passed to secular clergy in 1580, the Order lost its basic source of local financing (e.g., by 1600, only 72 friars in 17 monasteries). Author argues that Colombian Franciscans were impoverished (unlike their Peruvian counterparts) and suffered from attacks by hostile Indians. [KW]

2677 Marchena Fernández, Juan. La institución militar en Cartagena de Indias en el siglo XVIII. Sevilla, Spain: Escuela de Estudios Hispano-Americanos, 1982. 506 p.: bibl., ill., index (Publicaciones 0210–5802; 272)

Exhaustive military history of forts and garrison of Cartagena (1690–1810). Pt. 1 outlines major attacks and effects of Bourbon reforms to strengthen defenses. Pt. 2 focuses on economic costs of defense network. Pt. 3 lists officers, militias, and other details. Wealth of data overwhelms general conclusions of this vol. 1 of a proposed two. [KW]

2678 Meléndez Sánchez, Jorge. Ocaña colonial: el encuentro de las rutas coloniales de la Nueva Granada. Bogotá: Ecoe, 1984. 124 p.: ill, maps.

Vol. 1 of three on city and region of Ocaña is brief and based on scattered archival sources. Founded in 1570, the city became important as a crossroads along river routes linking coast to interior. City thrived as commercial and strategic center until the second half of 18th century when it was supplanted by Cúcuta. Indians fought growing Spanish influence until pacification or extermination. Several primitive maps indicate location of various tribes and region's geographic significance. Although research quality is uneven, major point about geographic importance is well made. [KW]

2679 Paz Rey, Felipe Santiago. El Palenque de Barbacoas: historia de un alzamiento de esclavos en el siglo XVIII (ICA/RCA, 23, 1980/1981, p. 415–462, bibl., map)

Excellent addition to slave history of Colombia. Uses *palenque* of Barbacoas near Remedios in Antioquia, to demonstrate how a runaway slave commuity survived (1741–51). Once nucleus formed, other slaves found refuge in Barbacoas which became a self-sufficient town. Cimarrons raided local haciendas and attacked merchants but withdrew from contact with Spanish society to preserve freedom. Based upon extensive archival sources, author notes that poor landowners lacked organization and resources to pursue fugitive slaves. Only when wealthier hacendados feared a general slave revolt and witnessed steady decline of trade did they form expedition. Captured blacks were resold after much debate among expedition leaders and local slave-owners. Concludes that slave insurrections were "pre-political" and more akin to social banditry à la Hobsbawm. [KW]

2680 Piedrahita Echeverri, Javier. Documentos y estudios para la historia de Medellín. Medellín, Colombia: Editorial Colina, 1984. 731 p.: bibl.

Lengthy history of Medellín which falls somewhere between a compilation of documents and anecdotes. Author attempts to cover development of city from its foundation to present but devotes most space to colonial period and ecclesiastic events (i.e., hodgepodge of facts, descriptions, lists of names, quotes). While volume includes useful information, lack of organization and indexes make it difficult to consult. [KW]

2681 Rausch, Jane M. A tropical plains frontier: the llanos of Colombia, 1531– 1831. Albuquerque: Univ. of New Mexico Press, 1984. 317 p.: bibl., ill., index, maps.

Excellent history of *llanos* from discovery through dissolution of Gran Colombia. Broad plains spreading out from the Andes were easternmost frontier of Nueva Granada, a region populated by Indians hostile to missionaries and colonizers. Severe climate and difficult communications prevented control of the region by royal officials who relied on missionaries to occupy frontiers and repel foreign aggressors. Rausch challenges view that missions failed after Jesuit expulsion in 1767, arguing that other religious orders kept missions flourishing as a source of textiles and cattle. Comunero revolt spread to *llanos* as opposition to taxes grew and Creoles resisted clergy's control of scarce resources. Author shows how *llaneros* joined forces with Venezuelan counterparts under Paéz to defeat royalists at Boyacá. An insightful comparison with other frontier regions adds to value of study for historians of all of Latin America. Concludes, however,

that Colombian *llanos* are distinct, with separate culture, economy, and people. [KW]

2682 Ríos Tobón, Ricardo de los. Historia del Gran Caldas. v. 1, Orígenes y colonización hasta 1850. Manizales, Colombia: Imprenta Departamental, 1983. 1 v.: bibl., ill. (some col.) (Biblioteca de escritores caldenses)

Vol. 1 of projected three on Gran Caldas, mountainous region in western Colombia comprising former parts of Antioquia, Chocó, Tolima, and Valle del Cauca. Very general type of regional history, descriptive more than analytical, impressionistic more than factual. Author uses artificial devise of three migratory waves to structure his work: 1) 1785–1810, characterized by a disorderly invasion of poor people seeking gold and settling for land; 2) 1820–60, more organized movement of workers induced to migrate by promises of land distribution; and 3) 1870 onwards, concerns intense coffee cultivation but not covered here. Much useful material, particularly on geography and early settlement but work is marred by poor organization and repetition. [KW]

2683 Silva, Renán. Saber, cultura y sociedad en el Nuevo Reino de Granada, siglos XVII y XVIII. Bogotá: Univ. Pedagógica Nacional, Centro de Investigaciones, 1984. 184 p.

Three succinct essays on the history of education in New Granada. One discusses importance of using original documents for historical research; another essay links state of the colonial economy to availability of educational resources; and the core essay, a general review of pedagogy (1600–1770), is fascinating. Author analyzes standard texts used by priests to teach logic, philosophy, and rhetoric throughout colonial period. Format and style were as significant as content and formal lectures, dictation and debate were emphasized. Subsidized education for poor, white males insured their socialization into elite mentality even when denied elite life style. Original study. [KW]

2684 Tisnés Jiménez, Roberto María. Caballero y Góngora y los comuneros. Bogotá: Instituto Colombiano de Cultura Hispánica, Ministerio de Educación Nacional, 1984. 624 p.: bibl. (Ediciones de la Segunda Expedición Botánica)

Excellent biography of Antonio Caballero y Góngora, Archbishop and Viceroy of Nueva Granada (1779–89). Author sets out to clear man often accused of undermining comunero revolt and betraying its leaders. Archbishop used religious persuasion, loyalty to Crown, and practical economic arguments to convince rebels to retire. Compassion and diplomacy account for cleric's success. Although relying heavily on John Phelan (see *HLAS 42:2779*) and other secondary sources, author's analysis provides new insights into methods used to resolve major colonial crisis. Following end of comuneros, Caballero y Góngora's intellectual curiosity and receptivity encouraged flow of ideas from Europe to Nueva Granada. Author claims this laid foundation for independence ideology as Creoles learned to question authority of Crown and Church. Thus, Caballero has indirect claim as precursor of independence. Concludes, perhaps too uncritically, that he was best viceroy of colonial period. [KW]

2685 Tovar Zambrano, Bernardo. La colonia en la historiografía colombiana. Bogotá: Carreta, 1984. 193 p.: bibl.

Excellent review of colonial historiography beginning with chronicles and ending with more recent publications. Author's intent is not to criticize specific works but to identify and analyze broad trends. Divided into three parts: 1) Joaquín Acosta's *Historia de la Nueva Granada* (1848) and José Manuel Restrepo's *Historia de la revolución de la República de Colombia* (1827); 2) history of liberal and conservative historians of 19th century, two groups are guilty of political interpretation based on their own perceptions of individual and State; and 3) some, but not all, 20th-century writings. Creation of Academia (1902) and professionalization of research is a central theme as is move toward regional history. Notes continuation of Liberal/Conservative views and spread of Marxist influence. Valuable contribution to understanding Colombian history. [KW]

2686 Zapatero, Juan Manuel. Historia de las fortalezas de Santa Marta y estudio asesor para su restauración. Bogotá: Academia Colombiana de Historia, 1980. 454 p.: ill., index, maps.

Zapatero continues studying military fortifications, this time of Santa Marta (see *HLAS 42:257* for earlier work). Neglect of defenses reflected city's secondary impor-

tance of Cartagena and difficulties of protecting an open bay. Gives plan for modern restoration of forts. Maps and plates of original plans enhance this exhaustive description of fortification strategy. [KW]

2687 Zarama, José Rafael. Reseña histórica. v. 2. 2a ed. Pasto, Colombia: Imprenta del Depto., 1980. 192 p.: bibl.

Reedition of 1942 history of Pasto. Concentrates on expeditions of Sebastián de Benalcázar north from Quito to Popayán, Cali, and Pasto. Includes capsule biographies of town notables over a 400-year span. Somewhat dated. [KW]

QUITO

2688 Achig Subia, Lucas. La estructura administrativa de la Gobernación de Cuenca (Revista del Archivo Nacional de Historia, Sección del Azuay [Casa de la Cultura Ecuatoriana, Cuenca, Ecuador] 2, 1980, p. 7–51, bibl.)

Well organized and researched essay on the institutional history of the late colonial governorship of Cuenca. [MTH]

2689 Anda Aguirre, Alfonso. El Adelantado Don Juan de Salinas Loyola y su Gobernación de Yaguarzongo y Pacamoros. Quito: Editorial Casa de la Cultura Ecuatoriana, 1980. 376 p.: bibl., ill.

Second hand notes (from the Archivo General de Indias via the Vacas Galindo collection) on 16th-century governors and ecclesiastics of Spanish towns and Indian pueblos in what is now the province of Jaén de Bracamoros in northern Peru. [MTH]

Benzoni, Girolamo. La historia del Mondo Nuovo: relatos de su viaje por el Ecuador, 1547–1550. See item **1594.**

2690 Caillavet, Chantal. Fuentes y problemática de la historia colonial de Loja y su provincia (BCE/C, 5:15, enero/abril 1983, p. 355–370)

Lists sources in archives of Ecuador, Peru, Colombia, and Spain for reconstruction of colonial history of the city and province of Loja, and suggests viable research topics.

2691 Caillavet, Chantal. Les rouages économiques d'une société minière: échanges et crédit, Loja, 1550–1630 (IFEA/B, 13:3/4, 1984, p. 31–63, ill.)

Case study of *censos* as a financial system. In the 16th century they bolstered a thriving economy; in the 17th—once the mines, especially those of Zaruma, had petered out—they hamstrung it. Significant contribution to the economic history of the southern highlands. [MTH]

2692 Carrasco Vintimilla, Manuel. Mito y realidad de Eugenio Espejo (Revista del Archivo Nacional de Historia, Sección del Azuay [Casa de la Cultura Ecuatoriana, Cuenca, Ecuador] 2, 1980, p. 52–74, bibl.)

Cogent reassessment of Espejo. Carrasco Vintimilla ably argues that the mestizo medic was first and foremost a quasi-philosophe, not necessarily a precursor of independence, and that he should be interpreted in terms of the 18th century rather than the 20th. [MTH]

2693 Chacón Zhapán, Juan. La república de los indios en la antigua Provincia de Cuenca (Revista del Archivo Nacional de Historia, Sección del Azuay [Casa de la Cultura Ecuatoriana, Cuenca, Ecuador] 3, 1981, p. 9–37)

Somewhat anachronistic overview of Spanish treatment of Indians in what are now the provinces of Cañar and Azuay. Redeemed by archival data on local *kurakas* or ethnic lords. [MTH]

Compilación de crónicas, relatos, y descripciones de Cuenca y su provincia. See item 1609.

2694 Descalzi, Ricardo. La Real Audiencia de Quito, claustro en los Andes. v. 1–2. Quito: s.n., 1978–1981. 2 v. (Historia de Quito colonial)

Only two volumes of this projected multi-volume "history" of the art of the former Audiencia of Quito have appeared thus far, both in the author's first series "Historia de Quito colonial" (the city—not the presidency—in this case). Vol. 1 comprises annals of the capital from its foundation through 1599, and vol. 2, those of 1600–44. [MTH]

2695 La Economía colonial: relaciones socio-económicas de la Real Audiencia de Quito. Introducción y selección, Manuel Miño Grijalva. Quito: Corporación Editora Nacional, 1984. 322 p.: bibl., ill. (Col. Ecuador, testimonios de autores extranjeros; 5)

Convenient anthology of four well known late colonial descriptions: Santi-

esteban's 1750 diary; Navarro's 1761 *Idea del Reino de Quito*; Caldas's accounts of his botanical excursions (early 1800s); and Baleato's 1820 *Monografía de Guayaquil*. Includes excellent essay by Manuel Miño Grijalvo on "La Economía de la Real Audiencia de Quito, Siglos XVII y XVIII," less an introduction than a monograph in its own right. [MTH]

2696 Fernández Martínez, Montserrat. La alcabala en la Audiencia de Quito, 1765–1810. Cuenca, Ecuador: Núcleo del Azuay, Casa de la Cultura Ecuatoriana Benjamín Carrión; Sevilla, Spain: Escuela de Estudios Hispano-Americanos, 1984. 185 p. (some folded): bibl., ill.

Original licentiate thesis on the administration and collection of the *alcabala* or sales tax in the Audiencia of Quito during the reigns of Charles III and IV, and on the socioeconomic impact of the Bourbon reforms on the urban elite as revealed by analysis of real property sales and other transactions. Altogether a novel and illuminating study. [MTH]

2697 García Regueiro, Ovidio. El quiteño Don Miguel de Gijón y León: contribución al estudio de la figura de un "ilustrado" criollo (CH, 400, oct. 1983, p. 91–118)

Archival notes on the Conde de Casa Jijón's first stay (1775–85) in Spain. [MTH]

2698 Jurado Noboa, Fernando. La árabe y lo judío en el tradicionalismo ecuatoriano (EANH/B, 21, 1982, p. 129–188, tables)

Genealogies of one Arab and 16 Jews who settled in Ecuador during the colonial period. [MTH]

2699 Jurado Noboa, Fernando. Los descendientes de Benalcázar en la formación social ecuatoriana, siglos XVI al XX. Quito: Amigos de la Genealogía 1984–1985. 5 v.: bibl., ill. (S.A.G.; 7–11)

Major genealogical study of descendants of the conquerer of Quito, mostly members of well known families. Will total nine or more volumes. Replete with biographical as well as biological data. Almost a who's who of past and present Ecuador. [MTH]

2700 Lafuente, Antonio. Una ciencia para el Estado: la expedición geodésica hispano-francesa al Virreinato del Perú, 1734–1743 (IGFO/RI, 43 : 172, julio/dic. 1983, p. 549–629)

Refreshingly objective study of the earth-measuring expedition of 1734–43. Lafuente contributes many new details on the organization of the expedition, diplomatic gestures required, conflicts with colonial authorities, particularly those of Quito and Lima, itineraries, explorations and discoveries of participants, tension and misunderstandings between the French and Spanish members and their repercussions. [MTH]

2701 Lavallé, Bernard. La rebelión de las alcabalas: Quito, julio de 1592 -abril de 1593: ensayo de interpretación (IGFO/RI, 14:173, enero/junio 1984, p. 141–201, appendix)

Laudable attempt to place the city of Quito's protest against the imposition of the sales tax in economic and social context. [MTH]

2702 Laviana Cuetos, María Luisa. Una descripción inédita de Guayaquil (Temas Americanistas [Univ. de Sevilla, Spain] 1, 1982, p. 25–28)

Comments upon and publishes an anonymous undated "Relación de Guayaquil." This previously unknown account appears to have been written by a visiting merchant in the early 1770s. [MTH]

2703 Laviana Cuetos, María Luisa. El estanco del tabaco en Guayaquil (Temas Americanistas [Univ. de Sevilla, Spain] 5, 1985, p. 21–32, ill., tables)

Most detailed study to date of the Royal Monopoly of Tobacco of Guayaquil. [MTH]

2704 Laviana Cuetos, María Luisa. La maestranza del astillero de Guayaquil en el siglo XVIII (Temas Americanistas [Univ. de Sevilla, Spain] 4, 1984, p. 26–32, tables)

Pioneering essay on salaries, numbers and ethnic composition of shipwrights and caulkers in 18th-century Guayaquil. Includes new data on the late colonial decline in shipbuilding. [MTH]

2705 Laviana Cuetos, María Luisa. Las ordenanzas municipales de Guayaquil (EEHA/AEA, 40, 1983, p. 39–69)

Publishes heretofore unknown municipal ordinances of 1593 of Guayaquil. Preceded by study of their differences from and similarities to ordinances of other colonial cities and towns. [MTH]

2706 Martín Cuesta, José. Jaén de Bracamoros. v. 1, Antecedentes históricos. v. 2, Historia siglo XVI. v. 3, Evangelización, siglo XVI. Lima: Librería Studium, 1984. 3 v.: bibl., ill., indexes.

Although part of Peru since independence, Jaén de Bracamoros was an integral part of the Audiencia and Presidency of Quito during the colonial period. Drawing on extensive research in the Archivo General de Indias, Martín Cuesta delineates the Spanish conquest and early history of Jaén and its province in vol. 2, and missionary activities of the regular and secular clergy in vol. 3. Vol. 1 is a rehash of the European discovery and conquest of Ecuador and Peru. [MTH]

2707 Minchom, Martin. Historia demográfica de Loja y su provincia desde 1700 hasta finales de la colonia (BCE/C, 5:15, enero/abril 1983, p. 149–169, appendices, graphs, tables)

Pioneering essay on the population history of the city and province of Loja (1700–1825). Based on parish registers—although only of the city—as well as on censuses and other coeval enumerations. [MTH]

Minchom, Martin. The making of a white province: demographic movement and ethnic transformation in the south of the Audiencia de Quito, 1670–1830. See item **1672.**

2709 Numeraciones del repartimiento de Otavalo. Compilación de Juan Freile Granizo. Transcripción paleográfica de María Mardorf de Larraín, Nadia Flores de Núñez y Juan Freile Granizo. Otavalo, Ecuador: Instituto Otavaleño de Antropología, 1981. 2 v. (Col. Pendoneros; 17–18. Serie Etno-historia)

Makes available two major sources for the reconstruction of the population history of the *corregimiento* of Otavalo: 1) the 1645–46 *visita* of Andrés de Sevilla; and 2) the 1685 *numeración* of Francisco de Sola y Ros. The latter constitutes part of the general census ordered by the Viceroy Duque de la Palata. [MTH]

2710 Ortiz de la Tabla Ducasse, Javier. Obrajes y obrajeros del Quito colonial (EEHA/AEA, 39, 1982, p. 341–365)

Authoritative review of what is known about textile sweat shops and their proprietors and the pivotal roles played by each in the economic and social history of the northern and central highlands. [MTH]

2711 Palomeque, Silvia. Historia económica de Cuenca y sus relaciones regionales: desde fines del siglo XVIII a principios del XIX (Revista del Archivo Nacional de Historia, Sección del Azuay [Casa de la Cultura Ecuatoriana, Cuenca, Ecuador] 1, 1979, p. 104–149, 247–259, tables)

Well documented quantitative study of the economy of the *corregimiento/ gobierno político y militar* of Cuenca during the late colonial period, especially of the region's agricultural base and patterns of trade. [MTH]

2712 Palomeque, Silvia. Loja en el mercado interno colonial (HISLA, 2, 1983, p. 33–45, bibl., tables)

Exploratory essay on the trade networks of Loja. [MTH]

2713 Petitjean, Martine and **Yves Saint-Geours.** La economía de la cascarilla en el Corregimiento de Loja (BCE/C, 5 : 15, enero/abril 1983, p. 171–207, bibl., graph, maps, tables)

Excellent study of a forgotten chapter in the economic history of Ecuador, the extraction of and trade in cinchona, the demand for which temporarily revived the flagging economy of the province of Loja in the third quarter of the 18th century. [MTH]

2714 Polémica universitaria en Quito colonial. Edición de José María Vargas. Quito: Pontificia Univ. Católica del Ecuador: Banco Central del Ecuador, 1983. 294 p.: bibl. (Biblioteca San Gregorio; 2)

Publishes late 17th-century exchange between Dominican Ignacio de Quesada and Jesuit Pedro Calderón regarding Quito's need for a second university, that which the Dominicans shortly thereafter founded. [MTH]

2715 Relaciones coloniales inéditas de la provincia de Loja (BCE/C, 5 : 15, enero/abril 1983, p. 441–479)

Publishes 11—heretofore mostly unknown—descriptions of the province of Loja, ranging in time from the 1570s through 1808. Transcribed and edited by Chantal Caillavet. See also "Mapas Coloniales de Haciendas Lojanas" published by her in the same issue (p. 513–531). [MTH]

2716 Relaciones geográficas de la Presidencia de Quito, 1776–1815. Transcripción de Nadia Flores de Núñez. Notas de explicación, Alfredo Costales y Juan Felipe Granizo. Ilustraciones de Tonino Clemente. Quito: Mundo Shuar, 1978. 155 p.: ill.

Reprints nine late colonial descriptions of the eastern provinces of the Audiencia of Quito. Originally published in *Boletín del Archivo Nacional de Historia* (No. 20; see *HLAS 40:3166*). The *relaciones* were transcribed by Nadia Flores de Núñez and explanatory notes added by Alfred Costales and Juan Freile Granizo. For ethnohistorian's comment, see *HLAS 46:1616*. [MTH]

Requena, Francisco. La descripción de Guayaquil por Francisco Requena, 1774. See item **1711**.

2717 Sínodos de Quito del siglo XVI (Revista del Instituto de Historia Eclesiástica Ecuatoriana [Pontificia Univ. Católica del Ecuador, Quito] 3 : 3/4, 1978, p. 1–200)

Texts of the first three councils of the Diocese of Quito. Includes introduction to the 1570 synod by José María Vargas and to the 1594 and 1596 synods by Jorge Villalba. [MTH]

2718 Vargas, José María. La economía política del Ecuador durante la colonia. Estudio introductorio, Carlos Marchán Romero. Quito: Banco Central de Ecuador: Corporación Editora Nacional, 1981 or 1982. 366 p.: bibl. (Biblioteca básica del pensamiento ecuatoriano; 15)

Reissue of pioneering account of economic history of the highlands during the colonial period. Proofed and slightly revised. [MTH]

2719 Velasco, Juan de. Historia del Reino de Quito en la América meridional. Edición, prólogo, notas y cronología, Alfredo Pareja Diezcanseco. Caracas: Biblioteca Ayacucho, 1981. 669 p. (Biblioteca Ayacucho; 82)

Yet another edition of this standard chronicle of colonial Quito, but only of pts. 2–3 (i.e., *Historia antigua* and *Historia moderna*). Nominally a blending of Espinosa Pólit's 1960 version and the more recent Casa de la Cultura Ecuatoriana's version (see *HLAS 44:2659*). This edition, however, is neither as satisfactory nor as useful as either of its immediate predecessors. For ethnohistorian's comment see item 1763. [MTH]

2720 Villalba, Jorge. Las haciendas de los jesuitas en Pimampiro en el siglo XVIII (Revista del Instituto de Historia Eclesiastica Ecuatoriana [Pontificia Univ. Católica del Ecuador, Quito] 7, 1983, p. 15–60, bibl., map)

Notwithstanding the title, a series of

notes on the Indian population of the parish of Pimampiro form the late 1500s through the 1700s, and on acquisition of land by Spaniards, particularly Jesuits, in said parish in the 1600s. [MTH]

2721 Zúñiga, Neptalí. Significación de Latacunga en la historia del Ecuador y de América. Quito: Instituto Geográfico Militar, 1982. 2 v. (647 p.): ill.

Detailed, textually well documented, eminently readable, quasi-integral history of Latacunga from its foundation as a Spanish town in 1573—previously it had been a tambo—through the 1820s. Thematically organized and remarkably free from native son bias. [MTH]

PERU

2722 Acosta Rodríguez, Antonio. Los clérigos doctrineros y la economía colonial: Lima, 1600–1630 (IPA/A, 16:19, 1982, p. 117–149)

Examines economic exploitation of Indians by *doctrineros clérigos* or members of diocesan clergy assigned to rural parishes. Exemplifies abuses from complaints found in the Archivo Arzobispal de Lima (see also Acosta's companion piece on *doctrineros religiosos* in *HLAS 46:2683*). [MTH]

2723 Acosta Rodríguez, Antonio. Los doctrineros y la extirpación de la religión indígena en el Arzobispado de Lima, 1600–1620 (JGSWGL, 19, 1982, p. 69–109, tables)

Reaffirms thesis that the campaign against idolatry was begun to divert attention from economic and other abuses of Indians by their pastors. Includes much more data than previous article (see *HLAS 44:2660*) and examines roles and motivations of clergy involved. [MTH]

2724 Alarco, Eugenio. El hombre peruano en su historia. v. 1–2, Los antepasados aborigenes. v. 3–4, Los antepasados hispánicos. v. 5–6, El encuentro de dos poderes: españoles contra incas. Lima: s.n., 1971–1983. 6 v.: bibl., ill.

Yet another monumental history of Peru that will run 10 volumes of which six have appeared to date. Unique features are detailed accounts of Indian and Spanish antecedents (vols. 1–4). Vols. 5–6 recount the Spanish conquest of the Tahuantinsuyu.

Alarco, apparently an armchair historian, has read widely and writes well. [MTH]

2725 Angles Vargas, Víctor. Historia del Cusco. Lima: Industrialgráfica, 1978–1983. 3 v.: bibl., ill. (some col.), index.

Popular history of Cuzco from pre-Inca times through the 1700s. Well illustrated. [MTH]

2726 Aramburú de Olivera, Clemencia and Pilar Remy S. La población del Cuzco colonial: siglos XVI–XVIII. Lima: Instituto Andino de Estudios en Población Desarrollo, 1983. 36 p.: bibl., ill.

Demographic study of colonial Cuzco, particularly of urban parishes of the Sagrario and San Pedro, whose populations were primarily Spanish and Indian, respectively, and of the rural parish of Yucay. Among other interesting findings is that the population of Yucay—in fact of the province of Urubamba at large—declined in the 18th century. [MTH]

2727 Arrequi Zamorano, Pilar. Poder de los virreyes del Perú: un manuscrito inédito del siglo XVII (EEHA/HBA, 29:2, 1985, p. 3–97)

Publishes with a brief introduction *Poder ordinario del virei del Perú . . .* a treatise written in the late 1620s by the otherwise unknown Matías de Caravantes. It is a detailed statement of the powers and responsibilities of the viceroy as of the early 17th century and hence a major source on the norms of early colonial administration. [MTH]

2728 Bradley, Peter T. The defenders of Lima and Callao in the seventeenth century (PAIGH/H, 97, enero/junio 1984, p. 87–113)

Novel account of groups who defended the City of Kings and its port from the Dutch and other interlopers in the 1600s, the militia of Lima and the garrison of Callao. [MTH]

2729 Brown, Kendall W. Bourbons and brandy: imperial reform in eighteenth-century Arequipa. Albuquerque: Univ. of New Mexico Press, 1986. 319 p.: bibl., index, maps, tables.

Takes up chronologically where *Landowners in colonial Peru* leaves off (see item **2737**), but thematically is more comprehensive. Furthermore Brown does not find that the Arequipans of the late colonial period were the elastic entrepreneurs Davies maintains their progenitors to have been. Be that as it may, *Bourbons and brandy* is an eminently readable account of virtually every aspect of the history of Arequipa and its district in the 1700s, and of the differential impact of the Bourbon reforms upon the region and its inhabitants. [MTH]

2730 Busto Duthurburu, José Antonio del. La pacificación del Perú. Lima: Librería Studium Editores, 1984. 402 p., 1 folded leaf of plates: ill.

Well researched and written account of the civil wars which began with Pizarro's assassination. Includes chapters on "La Soldadesca" and "Las Mujeres de los Conquistadores." [MTH]

2731 Cahill, David. *Curas* and social conflict in the *doctrinas* of Cuzco, 1780–1814 (JLAS, 16:2, Nov. 1984, p. 241–276)

Initial exploration of the socioeconomic dynamics of one of the components of the altiplano elite, the pastors and assistant pastors of Indian parishes in the diocese of Cuzco, and of their relationships with other groups. Fascinating piece which illuminates the social context of rebellions of 1780 and 1814. [MTH]

2732 Campbell, Leon G. Banditry and the Túpac Amaru rebellion in Cuzco, Peru: 1780–1784 (Bibliotheca Americana [Coral Gables, Fla.] 1:2, Nov. 1982, p. 131–162, ill., maps)

Cogent reassessment of the nature of the Túpac Amaru rebellion by leading student of the movement and the man. Although there were many incidents of brigandage and pillage during the uprising, banditry does not seem to have been an integral part of the movement, among other reasons because of Túpac's tactical, if not also ideological, opposition thereto. [MTH]

2733 Campbell, Leon G. Women and the great rebellion in Peru, 1780–1783 (AAFH/TAM, 32:2, Oct. 1985, p. 163–196, tables)

Thoughtful essay on the role played by Thomasa Titu Condemaita, better known as Micaela Bastida in the rebellion led by her spouse, Tupac Amarú. Also includes data on other women who loomed large in the rebellion. [MTH]

2734 Cárdenas Ayaipoma, Mario. El pueblo de Santiago: un ghetto en Lima virreinal (IFEA/B, 9:3/4, 1980, p. 19–48, bibl.)

Review of the history of the Indian "ghetto" of Lima. Among findings, perhaps the most important is that Santiago del Cercado was a center of native resistance and conspiracy. [MTH]

2735 Cieza de León, Pedro de. Descubrimiento y conquista del Perú. Introducción y notas de Mario A. Valotta. Madrid: Zero; Buenos Aires: Jamkana, 1984. 422 p.: bibl. (Las Culturas cronistas y viajeros; 1)

Critical edition of the *Tercera parte de la Crónica del Perú*, transcribed from the "definitive" text recently rediscovered in the Vatican Library by Francisca Cantú. Her edition (Rome, 1979), which I have not seen, was the first complete version of Cieza de León's *Descubrimiento y conquista del Perú*, previously known only in part. Basic source on the Spanish conquest of the Tahuantinsuyu. [MTH]

2736 Cuzco, Perú (*city*). Cabildo. El libro del Cabildo de la ciudad del Cuzco. Edición de Laura González Pujana. Introducción de Guillermo Lohmann Villena. Lima: Instituto Riva-Agüero, 1982. 188 p.: indexes (Publicaciones; 115)

Publishes actas of the Cabildo of Cuzco from 1559 and 1560. Well indexed. [MTH]

2737 Davies, Keith A. Landowners in colonial Peru. Austin: Univ. of Texas Press, 1984. 237 p.: bibl., ill., index, maps (Latin American monograph/ Institute of Latin American Studies; 61)

Impressively documented study of the economy and society of southwest Peru or Arequipa and its hinterland during the first half of the colonial period. Primarily concerned with Spanish landowners and their families, also treats Indians, blacks, and other members of the *castas*. Although almost all holdings were small or medium size at best— and perhaps because of it—Davies finds that early colonial Arequipans and their heirs were as profit oriented and efficient agriculturalists as the Jesuits. Major contribution to Peru's regional history and to the growing body of literature on the agrarian history of Spanish South America. [MTH]

2738 Deustua Pimentel, Carlos. El consulado Limeño y el Virrey Gil y Lemos: estudios de un informe (*in* Congreso Venezolano de la Historia, 4th, Caracas, 1980. Memoria [see *HLAS 46:2621*] v. 1, p. 435–453)

Analysis of Viceroy's Gil de Taboada y Lemos's heretofore unknown comments upon and glosses to the 1790 report of the Tribunal del Consulado de Comercio de Lima on the commerce of Peru. [MTH]

2739 Escobedo Mansilla, Ronald. Francisco López de Caravantes, tratadista de la hacienda virreinal peruana (JGSWGL, 21, 1984, p. 109–125)

Outlines the little that has been ascertained regarding the author of the soon to be published *Noticia general del Perú, Tierra Firme y Chile* and demonstrates that Solórzano plagiarized López de Caravantes. [MTH]

2740 Escobedo Mansilla, Ronald. El Tribunal de Cuentas de Lima: análisis de su eficacia (*in* Congreso Venezolano de la Historia, 4th, Caracas, 1980. Memoria [see *HLAS 46:2621*] v. 1, p. 457–500)

Detailed examination of the first three decades of the Tribunal Mayor de Cuentas de Lima. [MTH]

2741 Estabridis Cárdenas, Ricardo. El grabado colonial en Lima (EEHA/AEA, 41, 1984, p. 253–298, plates)

Interesting review of illustrations appearing in works printed in Lima during the colonial period and of known illustrators. [MTH]

2742 Fisher, John. Monarquismo, regionalismo y rebelión en el Perú colonial, 1808–1815 (PMNH/HC, 15, 1982, p. 117–139)

Spanish version of *HLAS 46:2702*. [MTH]

2743 Flores Galindo, Alberto and **Magdalena Chocano.** Las cargas del sacramento (CBC/RA, 2:2, dic. 1984, p. 403–434, tables)

Fascinating as well as novel study of the incidence and significance of marital disputes and divorces in late colonial Lima. Flores Galindo and Chocano demonstrate that the absolute and relative numbers of disputes and divorces increased appreciably in the 1790s and the first decade of the 19th century, and that the majority were initiated by women. Includes commentaries by Antonio Acosta, Bernard Lavallé, María Emma Mannarelli, Ward A. Stavig, Gonzalo Portocarrero, and a "rebuttal" by Flores Galindo. [MTH]

2744 Guerra, Arcadio. Testamento otorgado en 1592 por Luis Martínez de Salcedo en la Ciudad de Cuzco (DB/REE, 39:2, 1983, p. 343–362)

Publishes with a brief commentary the last will and testament of an early colonial merchant. [MTH]

Guillén Guillén, Edmundo. Tres documentos inéditos para la historia de la guerra de reconquista Inca: las declaraciones de Lorenzo Manko y Diego Yuqra Tikona, servidores de Manko Inka Yupanki y de Francisco Waman Rimaci, testigos presenciales de los sucesos de 1533 a 1558. See item **1632.**

2746 Gutierrez, Gustavo. Una teología política en el Perú del siglo XVI (IPA/A, 16:19, 1982, p. 7–29)

Recapitulation of the significance of the memorial of Yucay (1571). Its anonymous author refutes Las Casas and defends the encomienda system. [MTH]

2747 Hampe Martínez, Teodoro. En torno al levantamiento pizarrista: la intervención del Oidor Lisón de Tejada (IGFO/RI, 44:174, 1984, p. 385–414)

Well documented study of role played by Lisón de Tejada in deposition of Viceroy Núñez Vela. Concludes that the *oidor*'s behavior has to be understood in terms of a "funcionario . . . imbuido del propósito de extraer el mayor aprovechamiento económico y social posible, con el fin de disfrutar luego en la patria de una existencia cómoda, respetable." [MTH]

2748 Hampe Martínez, Teodoro. Los primeros libros en el Perú colonial (FENIX, 28/29, 1978/1979, p. 71–90, appendix)

Analyzes and publishes earliest sources found to date on imprints, including proscribed works, held by *vecinos* of Peru. [MTH]

2749 Huertas Vallejos, Lorenzo. Tierras, diezmos y tributos en el Obispado de Trujillo, colonia-república. Prólogo de Pablo Macera. Lima: Univ. Nacional Mayor de San Marcos, Seminario de Historia Rural Andina, 1984. 273 p.: bibl., ill.

Parish-by-parish analysis of the geography, population, and economy of the Diocese of Trujillo during the late 18th-century and first half of 19th. Largely based on tithe and tribute records. [MTH]

2750 Hunefeldt, Christine. Comunidad, curas y comuneros hacia fines del período colonial: ovejas y pastores indomados en el Perú (HISLA, 2, 1983, p. 3–31, appendices, bibl., tables)

Essay on revival of communalism during late colonial period. Contends that assumption of responsibility for payment of tithe by community at large rather than individual members thereof, was one of its manifestations. Also concerned with parish priests as agents of exploitation. [MTH]

Julien, Catherine J. Guano and resource control in sixteenth-century Arequipa. See item **1646.**

2751 Klaiber, Jeffrey. Religion y justicia en Tupac Amaru (IPA/A, 16:19, 1982, p. 173–186)

Somewhat tendentious review of Túpac Amaru's religious beliefs. That he saw himself as a savior of his people in Andean and/or Judeo-Christian terms is clear. That he was a "vínculo de continuidad entre el grito de Las Casas y la lucha moderna de muchos cristianos en América Latina en favor de la justicia y los derechos humanos" is debatable. [MTH]

2752 Lassegue, Juan Bautista. La fundación progresiva de un convento-hospital en Parinacochas, diócesis del Cusco: 1567–1586; apuntes de lectura e hipótesis de estudio (CBC/RA, 2:2, dic. 1984, p. 487–512)

Working paper on foundation of Dominican convent of San Cristóbal in the province of Parinacochas. [MTH]

2753 Lavallé, Bernard. Concepción, representación y papel del espacio en la reivindicación criolla en el Perú colonial. Prólogo de Germán Peralta R. Lima: Univ. Nacional Federico Villarreal, Depto. Académico de Ciencias Histórico-Sociales, 1982. 63 p.: bibl.

Cogent essay on Creole perceptions of their native land and ways in which they portrayed it. Also published in *Cuadernos Hispanoamericanos* (399, sept. 1983, p. 20–39). [MTH]

2753a Lavallé, Bernard. Divorcio y nulidad de matrimonio en Lima, 1651–1700: la desavenencia conyugal como revelador social. Talence, France: Univ. de Bordeaux III, Groupe interdisciplinaire de recherche et de documentation sur l'Amérique latine (G.I.R.D.A.L.), 1986. 51 p.: ill., tables.

An impressive research piece dealing with more than 1500 files kept in the Archdiocesis archives. Exploring the couple dynamics in a casta-society, Lavallé sheds new lights on the virreinal urban life. Illustrative of a new social history of colonial Latin America that links private and public spheres. [A. Pérotin-Dumon]

2754 Lohmann Villena, Guillermo. Algunas notas documentales sobre la presencia de alemanes en el Perú virreinal (JGSWGL, 19, 1982, p. 110–116)

Archival notes on Germans in colonial Peru, especially in Lima. [MTH]

2755 Lohmann Villena, Guillermo. La biblioteca de un peruano de la Ilustración: el Contador Miguel Feijóo de Sosa (IGFO/RI, 44:174, 1984, p. 367–384)

Describes library holdings of author of *Relación descriptiva de la ciudad y provincia de Trujillo del Perú* (1763) and *Nuevo gazofilacio real* (1771). [MTH]

2756 Lohmann Villena, Guillermo. El Contador Francisco López de Caravantes y sus obras (*in* Congreso Venezolano de la Historia, 4th, Caracas, 1980. Memoria [see *HLAS 46:2621*] v. 2, p. 157–172)

Outlines career and writings of López de Caravantes. See also item **2755.** [MTH]

MacCormack, Sabine. "The heart has its reasons:" predicaments of missionary Christianity in early colonial Peru. See item **1655.**

Mannarelli, María Emma. Inquisición y mujeres: las hechiceras en el Perú durante el siglo XVII. See item **1659.**

Martínez Compañón, Baltasar. Trujillo del Perú. See item **1663.**

Mayer, Enrique. Los atributos del hogar: economía doméstica y la encomienda en el Perú colonial. See item **1667.**

2757 Mazet, Claude. Mourir à Lima au XVIIIe siècle (IAA, 11:1, 1985, p. 83–126; 11:2, 1985, p. 127–170, bibl., facsims., ill., map, tables)

Two-part study: 1) "Les Tendances de la Mort" is a detailed analysis of mortality in Lima as a whole and its component parishes during the 18th century; and 2) "Les Ethnies et la Mort" is an analysis of mortality by ethnic groups. The most important contribution to date to the reconstruction of the population history of the City of Kings. [MTH]

2758 Millar Corbacho, René. La Inquisición de Lima y la circulación de libros prohibidos, 1700–1820 (IGFO/RI, 44 : 174, 1984, p. 415–444, appendix)

Extant records suggest that the Inquisition was lax in its vigilance over circulation of prohibited works, including those on the Index, and lenient in its treatment of those who read them without license during the late colonial period. [MTH]

Mörner, Magnus. The Andean past: land, societies, and conflicts. See item **1675.**

2759 Mogrovejo Rojas, Napoleón. Santo Toribio de Mogrovejo, defensor del indio americano. 2a ed. Caracas: Ediciones Trípode, 1985. 187 p.: bibl., ill. (Col. Evangelizadores de América; 1)

Popular biography of the second Archbishop of Lima, an advocate of Indian rights. [MTH]

2760 Mustapha, Monique. L'après lascasisme au Pérou chez les pères de la Compagnie de Jésus: Acosta (IAA, 11 : 3, 1985, p. 267–281, bibl.)

Quoting passages from original unpublished (i.e., uncensored) version of *De procuranda Indorum salute*, demonstrates that Acosta was far more in accord with Las Casas then has heretofore been thought. [MTH]

2761 Nieto Vélez, Armando. Una descripción del Perú en el siglo XVIII (IRA/B, 12, 1982/1983, p. 283–293)

Publishes brief but picturesque description of Lima, Pisco, Arica, and other towns of the coast of Peru. Written in 1755 by French Jesuit. [MTH]

2762 O'Phelan Godoy, Scarlett. Hacia una tipología y un enfoque alternativo de las revueltas y rebeliones del Perú colonial: siglo XVIII (JGSWGL, 21, 1984, p. 127–153)

Maintains that there were five types of native uprisings and rebellions in 18th-century Peru: 1) antifiscal; 2) anticlerical; 3) anti-ethnic lord; 4) anti-centers of production or exploitation such as *obrajes;* and 5) conflicts over land. Believes the Túpac Amaru rebellion was a cumulative movement, a generalized protest as it were against all abuses and exploiters. See also author's Ph.D. dissertation, *Rebellion and revolts in eighteenth century Peru and Upper Peru* (Cologne, FRG, 1985). [MTH]

2763 Pérez Cantó, Pilar. La población de Lima en el siglo XVIII (UB/BA, 14 : 32, 1982, p. 383–407, tables)

Competent but not necessarily valid analysis of the 1700 and 1790 censuses of Lima. Although Pérez Cantó takes into account the bills of mortality in the *Mercurio Peruano*, she ignores parish registers and *guías de forasteros*. [MTH]

2764 Ramírez, Susan E. Provincial patriarchs: land tenure and the economics of power in colonial Peru. Albuquerque: Univ. of New Mexico Press, 1986. 471 p.: bibl., ill., index.

Extraordinarily detailed study of "great estates," landowners and power in the Lambayeque region or the northwest coast of Peru throughout the entire colonial period. Superior monograph which not only details many aspects of the economic and social history of the region but also demonstrates that the history of haciendas in Spanish America is far more complex and variegated than some would have us believe. [MTH]

ALTO PERU

Abad Pérez, Antolín. Restauración de los colegios misioneros en Hispanoamérica: 1836–1905. See item **1797.**

2765 Arduz Eguía, Gastón. La minería de Potosí en la segunda mitad del siglo XVIII (SBH/HC, 5, abril 1985, p. 63–76, tables)

Discourse on the state of mining at Potosí in 1759. Includes data on yield, wages, and profitability. [MTH]

2766 Bakewell, Peter. Miners of the Red Mountain: Indian labor in Potosí, 1545–1650. Albuquerque: Univ. of New Mexico Press, 1984. 213 p.: bibl., ill., index, maps.

Well organized, researched, and written history of Indian labor and Indian-Spanish relations in early colonial Potosí. Bakewell demonstrates that voluntary as well as coerced labor were characteristic of the "silver-producing industry of Potosí from the outset" and maintains that *mingas* (i.e., voluntary workers) "were there because they chose to be." [MTH]

Barnadas, Josep M. Fuentes históricas sobre Mojos jesuítico. See item **1591.**

2767 Cole, Jeffrey A. The Potosí mita, 1573–1700: compulsory Indian labor in the Andes. Stanford, Calif.: Stanford Univ. Press, 1985. 206 p.: bibl., ill., index, maps.

Model monograph on Indian labor in 17th-century Potosí. Unlike Bakewell, Cole focuses primarily on forced labor, arguing that the *mita* was the lynch-pin of silver mining at the Red Mountain, not only because Indians were compelled to do work they would otherwise have refused, but also because the *mita* constituted a capital subsidy. [MTH]

2768 Cole, Jeffrey A. Viceregal persistence versus Indian mobility: the impact of the Duque de la Palata's reform program on Alto Perú, 1681–1692 (LARR, 19:1, 1984, p. 37–56)

Detailed, well documented study of Indian responses to the Duque de la Palata's attempt to reform the *mita* and tribute systems and to the census ordered by him. [MTH]

2769 García Recio, José María. La creación del Obispado de Santa Cruz de la Sierra (EEHA/AEA, 41, 1984, p. 55–92)

Detailed account of the problematic creation and establishment of the Diocese of Santa Cruz de la Sierra in the early 17th century. Major contribution to the poorly known ecclesiastical history of eastern Bolivia. [MTH]

2770 Helmer, Marie. Juli: un experimento misionero de los jesuitas en el altiplano andino, siglo XVI (IRA/B, 12, 1982/1983, p. 191–216)

Multifaceted monograph on the early years of the Jesuit mission of Juli. Sparkles with insights as well as data. [MTH]

Llanos, García de. Diccionario y maneras de hablar que se usan en las minas y sus labores en los ingenios y beneficios de los metales: 1609. See item **4574.**

2771 Minas e indios del Perú, siglos XVI–XVIII. Edición de Nadia Carnero Albarrán. Prólogo, Lorenzo Huertas Vallejo. Lima: Dirección Universitaria de Proyección Social San Marcos, 1981. 292 p., 1 leaf of plates: bibl., ill.

Major collection of early colonial sources, most of which date from the early 17th century and almost all of which are heretofore unknown, on mining and miners at Potosí (silver) and Huancavelica (mercury). Largely concerned with abuses of and attempts to regulate Indian labor. [MTH]

2772 Money de Alvarez, Mary. Los obrajes, el traje y el comercio de ropa en la Audiencia de Charcas. La Paz: Instituto de Estudios Bolivianos, Facultad de Humanidades, UMSA, 1983. 227 p., 24 p. of plates: bibl., ill., ports. (Col. Arzans y Vela)

Original licentiate thesis on textile manufacturing and trade, and costumes in the Audiencia of Charcas. Far from exhaustive, but novel for Bolivia and useful, given the lack of in-depth studies. [MTH]

2773 Parejas Moreno, Alcides J. Etnografía de la provincia de Chiquitos, siglo XVI (SBH/HC, 6, oct. 1984, p. 115–123, tables)

Analyzes data on ethnic groups in the Xaruyes region as contained in early colonial accounts, particularly that of Hernando de Loma Portocarrero. [MTH]

2774 Parejas Moreno, Alcides J. Historia del oriente boliviano: siglos XVI y XVII. Santa Cruz, Bolivia: Univ. Gabriel René Moreno, Depto. de Publicaciones, 1980. 150 p.: bibl., ill. (Col. Centenario)

Well documented study of Indian groups and of Spanish explorers, missionaries, and settlers in eastern Bolivia during the 16th and 17th centuries by leading authority on the area. See also Parejas Moreno's book on 18th-century Moxos (*HLAS 42:2802*). [MTH]

2775 Peñaloza Cordero, Luis. Nueva historia económica de Bolivia. t. 2, La colonia. La Paz: Editorial Los Amigos del Libro, 1981. 1 v.: maps (Enciclopedia boliviana)

Vol. 2 of projected nine on economic history of Bolivia. This work covers the established colony, and vol. 1—not available at press time—the prehispanic and conquest periods. Somewhat anachronistic. [MTH]

2776 Romano, Ruggiero and Geneviève Tranchand. Una encomienda coquera en los Yungas de La Paz: 1560–1566 (HISLA, 1, 1983, p. 57–88, bibl., map, tables)

Preliminary study of account records of an early colonial encomienda, the income from which was mostly generated by the sale of its principal tribute, coca leaves. [MTH]

Saignes, Thierry. Las etnías de Charcas frente al sistema colonial, siglo XVII: ausentismo y

fugas en el debate sobre la mano de obra indígena, 1595–1665. See item **1725.**

2777 Saignes, Thierry. Notas sobre la
contribución regional a la mita de
Potosí a comienzos del siglo XVII (EEHA/
HBA, 28, 1984, p. 47–63, tables)
Spanish version of item **1727.** [MTH]

Saignes, Thierry. Notes on the regional contribution to the *mita* in Potosí in the early
seventeenth century. See item **1727.**

2778 Tandeter, Enrique. Trabajo forzado y
trabajo libre en el Potosí colonial
tardío. Buenos Aires: Centro de Estudios de
Estado y Sociedad, 1980. 40 p.: bibl., ill.,
tables (Estudios CEDES; 3 : 6)
Spanish version of *HLAS 44 : 2723.*
[MTH]

2779 Tandeter, Enrique and **Nathan
Wachtel.** Conjonctures inverses: le
mouvement des prix à Potosí pendant le
XVIIIe siècle (AESC, 38 : 3, mai/juin 1983,
p. 549–613, bibl., graphs, tables)
Presents tabularly and graphically
fluctuations in prices of 40 Old and New
World products in Potosí (1696–1816). Analyzes and interprets price movements in
terms of European, intercolonial, regional,
and local events and trends. Extraordinarily
important piece, marred only by the lack of
stipulation of the actual prices. [MTH]

2780 Tandeter, Enrique and **Nathan Wachtel.**
Precios y producción agraria: Potosí y
Charcas en el siglo XVIII. Buenos Aires: Centro de Estudios de Estado y Sociedad, 1983.
91 p.: bibl., ill., tables (Estudios CEDES)
Spanish version of item **2779.** Also
published in *Desarrollo Económico* (29 : 90,
julio/sept. 1983, p. 197–230, graphs, no
tables). [MTH]

2781 Tepaske, John J. La estructura fiscal
del Imperio Español: Alto Perú, 1560–
1800 (*in* Congreso Venezolano de la Historia,
4th, Caracas, 1980. Memoria [see *HLAS
46 : 2621*] v. 3, p. 257–295, tables)
Spanish version of *HLAS 46 : 2743.*
[MTH]

2782 Valle de Siles, María Eugenia del.
Dinámica campesina, étnica y socio-
económica de la rebelión de Tupac Catari
(SBH/HC, 5, abril 1984, p. 77–115, tables)
Analyzes ethnic and socioeconomic
origins of prisoners taken at Peñas, their

motives, and the roles they played in the
rebellion. Concludes that the data demonstrate that it was truly a "peasant revolution
of popular elements." [MTH]

CHILE

2783 Eyzaguirre, Jaime. Historia de Chile.
t. l, Génesis de la nacionalidad. t. 2, La
definición del Estado y la integración de la
sociedad. 4a ed. de t. 1. 2a ed. de t. 2. Santiago: Zig-Zag, 1982. 2 v. in 1 (693 p.): bibl.,
ill., indexes.
Fourth edition of vol. 1 and second
edition of vol. 2 of the late Eyzaguirre's
useful account of colonial and early republican Chile. Vol. 2 truncated as author died before he could complete its revision. [MTH]

Flusche, Della M. and **Eugene H. Korth.** Forgotten females: women of African and Indian
descent in colonial Chile, 1535–1800. See
item **1624.**

**2784 Fuentes para la historia del trabajo en
el Reino de Chile: legislación, 1546–
1810.** Recopilación de Alvaro Jara y Sonia
Pinto. 2a ed. Santiago: Editorial Andrés Bello,
1982–1983. 2 v.: bibl., indexes.
Considerably augumented as well as
revised version of work first published as a
separate in 1965. This edition includes many
new sources and covers the entire colonial
period. Indispensable for analysis and interpretation of many aspects of colonial Chile,
not just of its labor history. [MTH]

Mamalakis, Markos. Historical statistics of
Chile. See *HLAS 47 : 3550.*

2785 Mellafe R., Rolando. La introducción
de la esclavitud negra en Chile: tráfico
y rutas. 2a ed. Santiago: Editorial Universitaria, 1984. 287 p.: appendices, bibl., index
(Col. Imagen de Chile)
Reprint rather than revised edition of
the standard work on the slave trade in colonial Chile. Nonetheless welcome as it has
long been out of print. [MTH]

2786 Mellafe R., Rolando. Latifundio y
poder rural en Chile de los siglos XVII
y XVIII (UC/CH, 1, dic. 1981, p. 87–108)
Seminal paper by a leading authority
on the great estate in the 17th and 18th centuries. Emphasizes variations in the characteristics of latifundia and in the type and

degree of power exercized by latifundistas. [MTH]

2787 Muñoz Correa, Juan Guillermo. San Antonio de Petrel: tenencia, producción y trabajo en una hacienda costera de Chile central, siglos XVII y XVIII (UCCIH/H, 18, 1983, p. 135–192)

Detailed history of a colonial estate. [MTH]

2788 Pinto Rodríguez, Jorge. Dos estudios de la población chilena en el siglo XVIII: distribución y crecimiento regional y tamaño de la familia. La Serena, Chile: Talleres Gráficos Imoffgrag, 1981. 65 p.: bibl., ill.

Two essays on the demography of late colonial Chile: 1) the most complete study to date of the growth and distribution of the population by regions (1700–1835); and 2) an analysis of regional variations in average family sizes, a first in historical population studies in Chile. For economist's comment, see *HLAS 47:3555*. [MTH]

2789 Pinto Rodríguez, Jorge. La población del Norte Chico en el siglo XVIII: crecimiento y distribución en una región minero-agrícola de Chile. La Serena, Chile: Sociedad de Explotación Minera El Sauce de Andacollo, 1980. 178 p.: bibl., ill.

Revised version of author's Ph.D. dissertation on the state and movement of the population of the Norte Chico in the 18th century. Based on parish registers as well as coeval censuses and other enumerations. [MTH]

2790 Sínodos de Santiago de Chile de 1688 y 1763. Presentación de Bernardo Carrasco Saavedra y Manuel de Alday y Aspee. Madrid: Instituto Francisco Suárez, Consejo Superior de Investigaciones Científicas; Salamanca, Spain: Instituto de Historia de la Teología Española, Univ. Pontificia de Salamanca, 1983. 424 p.: appendix (Tierra nueva e cielo nuevo; 9. Sínodos americanos; 2)

Photofacsimile reprint of 1858 edition of the fifth (1688) and sixth (1763) diocesan councils of Santiago. Includes pithy "Presentación" by Carrasco Saavedra and Alday y Aspee, and an extensive appendix of other ecclesiastical documents. [MTH]

2791 Suárez, Ursula. Relación autobiográfica. Prólogo y edición crítica de Mario Ferreccio Podestá. Estudio preliminar

de Armando de Ramón. Santiago: Biblioteca Nacional: Academia Chilena de la Historia, 1984. 275 p., 8 leaves of plates: bibl., ill., indexes, maps, 1 genealogy table (Biblioteca antigua chilena; 2)

Publishes autobiography of mid-colonial period Clarist. Treasure trove of data on life in the cloister as well as on Santiago society at large as Sister Ursula was quite worldly. Enriched by scholarly studies of her account as historical and lexographic source. [MTH]

2792 Urbina Burgos, Rodolfo. La periferia meridional indiana: Chiloé en el siglo XVIII. Valparaíso, Chile: Ediciones Universitarias de Valparaíso, Univ. Católica de Valparaíso, 1983. 246 p., 1 folded leaf of plates: bibl., ill. (Col. Universidad. Serie Investigación)

Multifaceted doctoral dissertation on 18th-century Chiloé. Covers territorial organization, administrative reorganization under the Bourbons, size and distribution of the population, Spanish cities and Indian towns, agriculture and commerce, social structure, the encomienda system, the Church, missionary activities, and problems of defense. [MTH]

2793 Valdés Bunster, Gustavo. El poder económico de los jesuitas en Chile, 1593–1767. Santiago: Imprenta Pucará, 1985. 141 p.: bibl., ill., index.

Original licentiate thesis on economic activities of the Jesuits in colonial Chile. Valuable for its model presentation of data. [MTH]

2794 Vergara Quiroz, Sergio. Edad y vida en el grupo conquistador (UC/CH, 1, dic. 1984, p. 65–86, graphs)

Novel analysis of average age of conquistadores and of coeval perceptions of life cycles. Finds that the majority of Europeans (51 percent) were between 21 and 30 years of age upon arrival in Chile and that people thought of themselves and were perceived as infants or adolescents (less than 20 years of age), young (between 20 and 40 years old), or old (40 or more). [MTH]

2795 Villalobos R., Sergio. Historia del pueblo chileno. v. 2, Investigación de Sol Serrano y Jorge Núñez. Santiago: Instituto Chileno de Estudios Humanísticos: Empresa Editora Zig-Zag, 1980–1983. 277 p.: bibl., facsim., maps, plates, tables.

Uses new approach to history of Chile, from prehistoric times through present. Vol. 2 treats economic, demographic, social, political, and cultural aspects—in that order—of the 16th century or conquest period (for vol. 1, see *HLAS 46:2751*). [MTH]

RIO DE LA PLATA

2796 Acevedo, Edberto Oscar. El gobernador Martínez de Tineo y el Chaco: aclaraciones y planteamientos (UNC/RHAA, 12:23/24, 1983/1984, p. 11–65)

Biography of a mid-18th century governor of Tucumán, concentrating on his attempts to control Chaco Indian groups. Describes him as able military administrator who first attempted to convert Indians by encouraging them to settle in *reducciones*, and later, when this strategy failed, made war on recalcitrant tribes. Based primarily on AGI materials, author includes excerpts from letters in which governor expressed his disdain for frontier residents who complained of Indians raids but were not willing to finance protecting the frontier. [SS]

2796a Anales del Instituto de la Patagonia. Vol. 12, 1981-. Magallanes, Chile.

This issue features two interesting articles: Oswald Dreyer-Eimbcke "Premio Mapa Impreso del Estrecho de Magallanes," and José Miguel Barros "Expedición al Estrecho de Magallanes en 1553: Gerónimo de Vivar y Hernando Gallego." Vol. 11 (1980) contained articles on the natural and social sciences. [J.T. Criscenti]

2797 Antequera y Castro, Joseph de. Cartas del Señor Doctor Don Joseph de Antequera y Castro . . . escritas al Ilmo. Sr. Maestro Don Fray Joseph de Palos . . . Asunción: Cabildo Editora, 1983. 374 p. (Col. Fundamentos y testimonios. Serie Comuneros; 1)

Fascimile of first edition (1768) of letters which José de Antequera, ex-governor of Paraguay wrote from his jail cell in Lima, to defend himself against the charges of treason leveled at him by the Bishop of Paraguay, for his role in the comunero rebellion (1721–35). Fascinating document, not only for the defense of his actions which Antequera presents, but also for the culture, education, and training which it reflects. [SS]

2798 Arteaga Zumarán, Juan José et al. Estudios sobre el Cabildo de Santiago del Estero, siglo XVIII. Montevideo: Instituto de Filosofía, Ciencias y Letras, Depto. de Investigación y Estudios Superiores de Historia Americana, 1982. 147 p.: bibl., ill.

Five studies based on published Cabildo proceedings which look at various aspects of the Town Council of Santiago del Estero during the first half of the 18th century. In addition to analyzing the functioning of the town council and its various officers, discusses open town council meetings (*cabildos abiertos*) and attempts of the body to respond to economic decline. Useful addition to the literature on town governance. [SS]

2799 Asdrúbal Silva, Hernán. Hamburgo y el Río de la Plata: vinculaciones económicas a fines de la época colonial (JGSWGL, 21, 1984, p. 189–209, tables)

Interesting article which concentrates on the 1797–1806 decade, setting growing trade with Hamburg within larger framework of "trade with neutrals." Asdrúdal Silva presents some scattered figures on hides exported via Hamburg or on ships from this city, documents the London-Hamburg-Río de la Plata trade axis, and underlines the continuation of this trade in spite of (or perhaps because of) inconsistent trade policies both in Spain and Buenos Aires. [SS]

2800 Avellá Cháfer, Francisco. Diccionario biográfico del clero secular de Buenos Aires. t. 1, 1580–1900. Buenos Aires: Instituto Salesiano de Artes Gráficas, 1983. 1 v.: bibl., index.

Important biographical tool for those interested in the history of the Church in Buenos Aires. Presents information on secular clergy who served in the diocesis using both published and archival sources; information is divided by century. While not a complete compendium, it should be of great value to researchers. [SS]

2801 Becker, Félix. La Guerra Guaranítica desde una nueva perspectiva: historia, ficción e historiografía (UB/BA, 14:32, 1982, p. 7–37)

Investigation into Guaraní opposition to the 1750 Spanish-Portuguese Boundary Treaty which turned over seven of the most important Jesuit missions from Spain to Portugal. Becker sees the Jesuits as behind this

Indian uprising and as responsible for the "King Nicolas I" myth (wrongly interpreted as an anti-Jesuit polemic). The Jesuits are also seen as having coopted Governor Cevallos so that his report absolved them of all blame for the Guaraní Wars. While claiming to be even-handed, Becker finds fault with just about every Jesuit author who has worked on the subject. [SS]

2802 Benítez, Luis G. Historia del Paraguay: época colonial. Asunción: Imprenta Comuneros, 1985. 263 p.: bibl.

Basic introduction to colonial history of Paraguay probably intended for local secondary school students. Covers major events from prehispanic period to Hernandarias, missions, comuneros, to beginnings of the independence movement pointing out major historical figures, dates and institutions. Of interest to the specialist only because it provides view of how young Paraguayans learn their own history. [SS]

2803 Betancur, Arturo Ariel. Contrabando y contrabandistas. v. 2, Don Cipriano de Melo, señor de fronteras. Montevideo: Arca, 1985. 132, 4 p.: bibl.

Biography of Portuguese-born Manuel Cipriano de Melo (1730?-1813). A soldier in the Guaraní Wars, he later moved on to commercial ventures along the Brazilian coast, returning to the Río de la Plata where he spent 20 years as second in command of Montevideo's Customs House. Author sees Melo as key figure in illegal commerce and corruption in late 18th-century Banda Oriental. Study is a sequel to author's vol. 1 study on contraband (see *HLAS 46: 2760*). Unfortunately, only a half-page bibliography and no footnotes. [SS]

2804 Canabrava, Alice Piffer. O comércio português no Rio da Prata, 1580–1640. Belo Horizonte: Editôra Itatiaia; São Paulo: Editôra da Univ. de São Paulo, 1984. 201 p.: bibl., maps (Col. Reconquista do Brasil; nova série, 82)

New edition of 1944 classic, documenting crucial role of the Portuguese in early trade of Río de la Plata area in general, and Buenos Aires in particular. Social and economic patterns that marked *porteño* society throughout the entire colonial period, linking city and hinterland to the Atlantic commercial world are attributed by Canabrava to Portuguese commercial penetra-

tion. Although marred by poor quality of maps, this is a fundamental study in Argentine colonial history. [SS]

2805 Chiaramonte, José Carlos. La crítica ilustrada de la realidad: economía y sociedad en el pensamiento argentino e iberoamericano del siglo XVIII. Buenos Aires: Centro Editor de América Latina, 1982. 178 p. (Capítulo. Biblioteca argentina fundamental; 162. Serie complementaria, sociedad y cultura; 14)

Collection of articles (all previously published) presents the best of Chiaramonte's work on the impact and transformation of Enlightenment ideas in the Río de la Plata. Among other interesting findings is the article on the importance of Italian economic thinkers in the writings of Manuel Belgrano and Mariano Moreno. Valuable work in a field frequently neglected, that of intellectual history. [SS]

2806 Coyer, Gabriel François. Sobre los gigantes patagones: carta del Abate François-Gabriel [i.e. Gabriel-François] Coyer al Doctor Matay. Traducción y prólogo de Alamiro de Avila Martel. Santiago: Univ. de Chile, Facultad de Filosofía, Humanidades y Educación, 1984. 152 p.: ill. (Serie Curiosa americana; 5)

Spanish translation of *Lettre au Docteur Maty secrétaire de la Sociéte Royale de Londres, sur les géants patagons* published anonymously (Brussels, 1767). Translator identifies author as Abbot Gabriel-François Coyer, French ex-Jesuit and man of letters who took advantage of the theme of the Patagonian giants to present his plan for an American utopia based on Rousseau's ideas. Wonderful example of French Enlightenment thinkers' ideas about the New World. Also an addition to published literature on Patagonian giants which so enthralled European audiences from the 16th century on and became a topic of serious debate during the Enlightenment. [SS]

2807 Díaz de Guerra, María Amelia. Documentación relativa a esclavos en el Departamento de Maldonado: siglos XVIII y XIX. Montevideo: Imprenta Cooperativa, 1983. 53 p.: bibl.

Survey of the types of documentation which author has located in various Maldonado (Uruguay) archives, including transcriptions of baptism and marriage records, *alcabala* receipts, sale of slaves and reports of fugitives. Sample of documents is unfortunately just that. Nowhere does the author offer any analysis of the material found. [SS]

2808 Documentación de Archivo: órdenes remitidas al Cabildo de San Luis en 1796 y 1797 (UNC/RHAA, 21/22, 1981/1982, p. 187–194)

Transcription of legal decision (10 p.) sent from the Real Audiencia of Buenos Aires to the Cabildo of San Luis, concerning lack of rural justices (Alcaldes de la Santa Hermandad) in the San Luis region. Minor document. [SS]

2809 Durán Estragó, Margarita. Los Dominicos en el Paraguay (UCNSA/EP, 11:2, dic. 1983, p. 171–253, appendices, bibl., ill.)

Traditional presentation of history of the Dominican Order in Paraguay from arrival of the first friar in 1582 to the Order's separation from Rome under Dr. Francia. Although author uses material from the Order's archives in Córdoba and Buenos Aires, much of this piece reads like a list of names and dates. [SS]

2810 Garavaglia, Juan Carlos. Economic growth and regional differentiations: the River Plate region at the end of the eighteenth century (HAHR, 65:1, 1985, p. 51–89, graphs, maps, tables)

Outstanding article by first-rate economic historian. Presents region-by-region analysis of economic growth mostly based on tithe collection. Garavaglia is well aware of limitations of his data but uses them and comparative findings from Mexico and Europe with sophistication and flair. Stresses importance of wheat production in the Buenos Aires-Montevideo area; growth of cattle raising in what he calls the "Nuevo Litoral" (Santa Fe and Entre Ríos); and re-emergence of cattle production in area surrounding city of Córdoba. Important article for all students of Latin American colonial economy. [SS]

2811 Garavaglia, Juan Carlos. Mercado interno y economía colonial. México: Editorial Grijalbo, 1983. 507 p., 10 p. of plates: ill., maps, tables.

Masterful study of the colonial Paraguayan economy, its geography, demography and society. Although modestly subtitled *Three centuries of the history of yerba mate,*

author ranges over a wonderful variety of topics, relating them always to the production of *yerba mate,* Paraguay's surrogate for sugar. This is a must for all scholars of colonial Latin America. [SS]

2812 Gelman, Jorge Daniel. Un "repartimiento de mercancías" en 1788: los sueldos "monetarios" de la milicias de Corrientes (Cuadernos de Historia Regional [Depto. de Ciencias Sociales, Univ. de Luján, Argentina] 3:1, 1985, p. 3–17, tables)

Interesting case study detailing way in which *porteño* merchants (in this case Domingo Belgrano Pérez) profited from the scarcity of specie to function extra-officially as paymasters to the interior's militia. Instead of shipping coin, merchants employed variation of *repartimiento de mercancía,* thereby earning handsome profits. Although Gelman's contention that Buenos Aires merchants dominated the hinterland is a bit too generalized, this is a fine study by a talented young historian. [SS]

2813 González de Santa Cruz, Roque. Pax Christi. Edición, presentación y notas, Francisco Pérez-Maricevich. Ensayo preliminar, Bartomeu Meliá. S.l.: Díaz de Bedoya y Gómez Rodas Editores, 1983. 196 p. (Seleccion cultural/Zenda; 3)

Letters of Paraguayan-born Jesuit Roque González de Santa Cruz, a missionary who spent three decades among the Guayacurúes and Guaraníes at the beginning of the 17th century. Valuable source for ethnohistorians and those interested in Church history as well as students of colonial Paraguay. [SS]

2814 Guaycochea de Onofri, Rosa T. Portugueses en Mendoza en el período colonial (UNC/RHAA, 12:23/24, 1983/1984, p. 67–93)

Weak article based entirely on secondary sources which attempts to explain "Luso-Brazilian" architectural influences in a colonial chapel located in Lagunas de Guanacache by citing vague references to possible Portuguese settlers in the Mendoza area. [SS]

2815 Laguarda Trías, Rolando A. Nave española descubre las Islas Malvinas en 1520. Montevideo: C. Casares, 1983. 69 p.: bibl., facsims., ill., maps.

After reviewing the historiography on the discovery of the Malvinas, author presents interesting evidence to support his view that the islands were first discovered by two ships sailing with Magellan's expedition which were sent to reconnoiter south of Colonia del Sacramento. Argument is based on careful reading of maps and written documents. Author also includes chapter on common misconceptions in reporting latitude, and a list of 37 Portuguese sailors who accompanied the two ships. Solid study. [SS]

2816 Libros registros-cedularios del Río de la Plata, 1534–1717: catálogo. Advertencia preliminar de Víctor Tau Anzoátegui. Buenos Aires: Instituto de Investigaciones de Historia del Derecho, 1984. 1 v.: bibl. (Edición de fuentes de derecho indiano, en conmemoración del V centenario del descubrimiento de América; 2)

Catalog of the royal *cédulas* relating to the Río de la Plata which can be found in the Archivo General de Indias, Audiencia de Buenos Aires (Legajos 1–4). We hope that another catalog of the more widely dispursed *cédulas* of the 18th century will follow. [SS]

2817 McNapsy, Clement J. Conquistador without sword: the life of Roque González, S.J. Illustrated by Ralph Creasman. Chicago: Loyola Univ. Press, 1984. 206 p., 1 leaf of plates: ill.

Hagiography of Roque González de Santa Cruz, Jesuit missionary who served in Paraguay at the beginning of the 17th century, and was killed while attempting to found a new mission in Caaró. [SS]

2818 Maeder, Ernesto J.A. Antonio Ruiz de Montoya, apóstol de los Guaraníes (CRIT, 58:1984, 13 junio 1985, p. 271–273)

Brief biography of early 17th-century Jesuit missionary, one of the first to work in the Guairá. [SS]

2819 Martínez, Beatriz. El paso de José Manuel Escalada por el Seminario de Nobles de Madrid, 1787–1793 (IHAAER/B, 17:27, 1982, p. 221–238, appendix, table)

Using six-year stay of *porteño* merchant's son in this Madrid school as an introduction, author presents interesting picture of the institution, its problems, its curriculum and student life [SS]

2820 Muñoz, María Rosa de. La Guerra de Sucesión en el Río de la Plata y las consecuencias del Tratado de Utrecht (LNB/L, 338/339, mayo/junio 1984, p. 114–129)

Overview of political and diplomatic relations between the Spanish and Portuguese Crowns over issue of Portuguese settlement in Colonia del Sacramento. Traces conflict from 1678 when the Portuguese established their outpost of 1777 when Pedro de Cevallos finally ousted them from the area. [SS]

2821 Musso Ambrosi, Luis Alberto. Los canarios en el Uruguay: 1724–1756 (*in* Coloquio de Historia Canario-Americana, 4th, Las Palmas, Spain, 1980. Cuarto Coloquio de Historia Canario-Americana. Coordinación y prólogo, Francisco Morales Padrón. Las Palmas, Spain: Ediciones de Excelentísimo Cabildo Insular, 1982. p. 391–485, bibl., tables)

Somewhat misleading title, this article combines a good general description of political and economic events leading up to the founding of the city of Montevideo with ample documents culled from early nominative lists reflecting the *canario* presence in the settlement. Unfortunately, documentation presented is never analyzed nor is there more than a passing mention of the question of cultural transference. Nonetheless, article should be of interest to students of colonial Río de la Plata both for the documents and bibliography. [SS]

2822 Olalla Mazón, Ricardo. El burgalés Juan de Garay, fundador de Buenos Aires. Burgos, Spain: Caja de Ahorros Municipal de Burgos, 1982. 182 p.: bibl., ill. (Biblioteca popular burgalesa)

Uncritical biography of founder of Buenos Aires (the second time around). Although there are no citations, author does provide limited bibliography. This is ethnocentric hero history; Garay pictured as a savior who brought civilization to a continent where only "darkness and savagery reigned." [SS]

2823 Plá, Josefina. Algunas mujeres de la conquista. Prólogo, Roberto Quevedo. Asunción: Asociación de la Mujer Española, 1985. 80 p.: bibl.

Weakly documented, romanticized vignettes about handful of Spanish and Indian women whose supposed valor helped make the conquest of Paraguay possible. Perhaps the book's most valuable contribution is names of women who took part in the conquest, a list garnered from Lafuente Machaín's work. Plá contends that more women than those listed were present in Asunción from early days of its founding. [SS]

2824 Porro, Nelly R. Conflictos sociales y tensiones familiares en la sociedad virreinal rioplatense a través de los juicios de disenso (IHAAER/B, 26, 1980, p. 361–392)

Based on cases of parental opposition to their children's marriage, Porro presents solid analysis of social conflicts which lay beneath more visible disagreements between parents and children. Factors leading to parental opposition are grouped under two categories: 1) moral issues, including criminal behavior, prostitution, and poverty; and 2) social prejudices such as race, occupation, foreign birth. In sum, Porro presents an intriguing glimpse of moral and social constraints which prevailed in late 18th-century *rioplatense* society. [SS]

2825 Porro, Nelly R. Extrañamientos y depósitos en los juicios de disenso (Revista de Historia del Derecho [Instituto de Investigaciones de Historia del Derecho, Buenos Aires] 7, 1980, p. 123–149)

Excellent discussion of the use of *depósito* (temporary physical guardianship) of both young men and women involved in marriage oppositions. Porro analyzes use of guardianship by examining different circumstances under which it was requested by parties to the legal case, or ordered by the court. Finds that ecclesiastical action in ordering *depósitos* gradually gave way to royal judges after 1786. Also discusses banishing of male children in order to dissuade them in marriage plans. In general, Porro believes that neither of these strategies were effective in changing the wedding plans of *porteño* couples. [SS]

2826 Porro, Nelly R. Los juicios de disenso en el Río de la Plata: nuevos aportes sobre la aplicación de la pragmática de hijos de familia (Anuario Histórico Jurídico Ecuatoriano [Corporación de Estudios y Publicaciones, Quito] 5, 1980, p. 193–228)

Structural analysis of 51 marriage opposition cases found in the Archivo General de la Nación in Buenos Aires. Porro looks at legislation coming from Spain and compares it to reality in the Río de la Plata. Considers question of who was legally empowered to give a couple permission to marry, who could

oppose a marriage, courts involved, legal proofs presented and local courts' knowledge of jurisprudence. Together with Porro's two other articles on the subject (items **2824** and **2825**), this piece is important for students of late 18th-century legal and social history. [SS]

2827 Quevedo, Roberto. Paraguay, años 1671 a 1681. Asunción: El Lector, 1983. 207 p.: bibl., ill., indexes (Col. histórica; 6)

Solid study based on report sent by the Cabildo of Asunción to the Crown detailing Indian uprisings in the area and analyzing commercial competition between the city and the Jesuit missions. In addition to reproducing the report, author provides readers with biographies of leading Cabildo members. [SS]

2828 Rosal, Miguel Angel. Artesanos de color en Buenos Aires, 1750–1810: política oficial y realidad rioplatense (CRIT, 17:27, 1982, p. 331–354, appendix)

After quick overview of Bourbon policy regarding use of black labor in agriculture, we are given a superficial discussion of attempt by black shoemakers to form a guild in Buenos Aires during the 1790s. Appendix, a résumé of different artisan lists drawn up (1748–1806) is the most valuable part. Piece is sad proof of isolation of Argentine historiography in that it was written without any reference to the path-breaking studies on *porteño* artisans by Lyman L. Johnson (see *HLAS 40:3280, HLAS 44:2762–2763,* and *HLAS 46:2779*). [SS]

Saeger, James Schofield. Another view of the mission as a frontier institution: the Guaycuruan reductions of Santa Fe, 1743–1810. See item **1720.**

2829 Saguier, Eduardo R. Church and State in Buenos Aires in the seventeenth century (BU/JCS, 26, Autumn, 1984, p. 491–514)

By far the strongest of Saguier's recent articles, this piece details interaction and conflict between the colonial Church and government. Examines relationship between the diocesan church, the cathedral chapter, regular and secular clergy, and the colonial State, underlining points of agreement and conflict between these institutions and mechanisms by which each institution balanced the others. Saguier finds that the Church was neither fully autonomous nor fully subjugated by the governors of the Río de la Plata, and sees the Church as gradually becoming more independent throughout the 17th century. [SS]

2830 Saguier, Eduardo R. The contradictory nature of the Spanish American colonial State and the origin of self-government in the Río de la Plata region: the case of Buenos Aires in the early seventeenth century (PAIGH/H, 97, enero/junio 1984, p. 23–44)

After an interesting historiographical review of various Argentine writers and their views of the function of the colonial *cabildo*, Saguier provides his interpretation of the town council during the early 17th century. Saguier sees a continual conflict between the council's *beneméritos* and *confederados*, the former were merchants linked to the city's internal commerce while the latter were tied to external markets. When the *beneméritos* held sway, they reduced merchandise entering the port and thereby lessening the commercial value of public office. The opposite effect was produced by *confederado* ascendancy. Interesting argument based on the premise of two conflicting commercial spheres, a division which is never proven. [SS]

2831 Saguier, Eduardo R. Economic impact on the emergence of a rural bourgeoisie in Buenos Aires during seventeenth century (History of Agriculture [International Assn. for the History of Agriculture, Kalyani, India] 2:3, p. 19–66, tables)

Saguier continues his analysis of 17th-century Buenos Aires, holding to the never-proved assumption (item **2830**) that the society was divided between the old founding families (*beneméritos*) and the newly arrived slave-traders. Finds this division reflected in how they acquired land, chose crops, used labor, and invested capital. Concludes that capitalist penetration transformed 17th-century rural Buenos Aires from petty commodity production combined with subsistence oriented, agrarian production. Although an interesting hypothesis, data presented fails to substantiate the theory. [SS]

2832 Saguier, Eduardo R. An "organic crisis" in the Spanish American colonial State: the case of Buenos Aires in the early seventeenth century (International Review of History and Political Science [Review Publications, Meerut, India] 21, May 1984, p. 48–59)

Traces eight occasions (1580–1640) when the Buenos Aires *cabildo* became embroiled in internal conflict or in a power struggle with the governor. Saguier sees all participants as representing either internal or external market forces, a somewhat simplistic dichotomy belied by the complexity of events described. Believes the fourth political crisis (1614) was the most important representing a first victory, albeit temporary of the external market people. Article would have benefitted from less jargon and clearer use of English, but author is right in underlying the complexity of the reaction to what he calls "the penetration of commercial capital." [SS]

2833 Saguier, Eduardo R. The social impact of a middleman minority in a divided host society: the case of the Portuguese in early seventeenth-century Buenos Aires (HAHR, 65, Aug. 1985, p. 467–491)

After reviewing the liberal, nationalist, and New Left historiography on the role of Portuguese immigrants, Saguier argues that they were neither an oppressed minority nor a dominant and innovative commercial element, but more of a middleman group operating between Spaniards and Creoles. Able to achieve assimilation into the prevailing society by joining merchant and artisan ranks, marrying local women, and purchasing property, the Portuguese rose from middlemen to elite. His model (inspired by the sociologist Bonacich) does not quite fit his historical evidence. [SS]

2834 San Luis, Argentina (*province*). Actas capitulares de San Luis. v. 2, Años 1751 a 1797. Introducción de José M. Mariluz Urquijo. Buenos Aires: Academia Nacional de la Historia, 1982–1983. 472 p.

Vol. 2 of the town council minutes of San Luis (for vol. 1, see *HLAS 46:2800*). Important primary source for historians interested in the development of northwest Argentina during the colonial period. [SS]

2835 San Martino de Dromi, María Laura. Gobierno y administración de las Islas Malvinas, 1776–1833. Tucumán, Argentina: Ediciones UNSTA, 1982. 37 p.: bibl.

Slight study based mainly on Argentine secondary sources. Outlines history of the Malvinas before 1776, and discusses administrative organization of the islands both before and after Independence. While lacking in analysis, this piece is nonetheless not a polemic, but rather a brief review of the island's governmental structure before 1833. [SS]

2836 Schmidel, Ulrich. Derrotero y viaje al Río de la Plata y Paraguay. Edición y prólogo de Roberto Quevedo. Asunción: Ediciones NAPA, 1983. 18, 263 p., 8 leaves of plates: bibl., facsims., port. (Biblioteca paraguaya)

New bilingual edition (modern Spanish and original German) of Schmidel's account of his 20-year sojourn in the Río de la Plata and Paraguay. Schmidel left Antwerp in 1534, joining Pedro de Mendoza's expedition to the River Plate. Abandoning the Buenos Aires settlement, Schmidel made his way north through areas controlled by Querandí and Cario Indians. Also participated in campaigns against the Guaraní, Mbayá, Macasis, and other Chaco tribes. Rousing story which is most welcome in an accessible edition. [SS]

2837 Speroni, José Luis. La real dimensión de una agresión: una visión político-estratégica de la intervención británica a América del Sur, 1805–1807. Buenos Aires: Círculo Militar, 1984. 140 p.: bibl., maps (Biblioteca del oficial; 715)

Another study of the English invasions of Buenos Aires, based in part on previously unused documentation, which argues that the invasions were part of an English plan to conquer Spanish America in retaliation for its loss of North America. By defeating the English, *porteños* supposedly handed Great Britain the "greatest defeat it has ever suffered," and protected all of Latin America from British exploitation. Nationalist-military interpretation of the 1805–07 incident. [SS]

2838 Tiscornia, Ruth. La política económica rioplatense de mediados del siglo XVII. Buenos Aires: Ediciones Culturales Argentinas, Secretaría de Cultura, Presidencia de la República, 1983. 485 p.: bibl.

Misleading title. Volume is concerned with politics and economy of Buenos Aires during first half of 17th century. Although lacking in coherent theme or interpretation, book presents wealth of detail drawn from *cabildo* proceedings and residencia of *gobernador* Jacinto de Lariz, as well as a wide selection of documents. Unfortunately, author is undecided about whether she is an historian or novelist. [SS]

2839 Villegas, Juan. La espiritualidad de la generación jesuítica fundadora de reducciones en el Paraguay (IFCL/E, 1, 1981, p. 61–82)

Based on personal letters and annual reports to the superior in Córdoba, article stresses deep spiritual commitment of the first generation of Jesuits to evangelize Paraguay. Author, himself a Jesuit, documents the devotion, obedience, hard work, physical poverty, spiritual exercises, and battles against the devil which motivated those who founded the early Jesuit missions. [SS]

2840 Zenarruza, Jorge G.C. General Juan Ramírez de Velasco: señor divisero de la Divisa Solar y Casa Real de la Piscina, gobernador del Tucumán, Paraguay y Río de la Plata, fundador de las ciudades de Todos los Santos de la Nueva Rioja, Nueva Billa de Madrid, San Salvador de Velasco, en el Valle de Jujuy: un estudio para su biografía. Buenos Aires: Instituto de Estudios Iberoamericanos, 1984. 467 p., 104 p. of plates: bibl., ill., tables (Publicaciones; 5. Serie histórica; 1)

History-cum-genealogy. Study of minor conquistador and governor of Tucumán during the late 16th century, full of minutiae, but also containing some interesting documents transcribed in their entirety. [SS]

INDEPENDENCE PERIOD

DAVID BUSHNELL, *Professor of History, University of Florida*

THE CONTENTS OF this section clearly reflect two developments: 1) the continuing decline in scholarly attention to independence as compared to other topics; and 2) the countercurrent represented by the Bolívar Bicentennial celebrations of 1983, whose by-products could not all be listed in *HLAS 46*. Most, of course, will never be listed at all. Particularly striking is the scarcity of Argentine publications, which no doubt is due in part to cutbacks in funding to those institutions (like the Academia Nacional de la Historia) that give greatest attention to independence studies. However, the article by Carlos S.A. Segreti (item **2894**) on economic history of Mendoza would win the prize for best entry in the independence section, if such a prize existed.

GENERAL

Heredia, Edmundo A. Los Estados Unidos de Buenos Aires y Chile en el Caribe. See item **3245.**

2841 Ibarguren, Carlos. La misión diplomática de Manuel Hermenegildo de Aguirre en los Estados Unidos de América (ANH/IE, 30, enero/junio 1981, p. 339–365)
On basis of private and other papers, gives account of Aguirre's 1817–18 mission to seek recognition for Río de la Plata, armament for Chile.

2842 Mörner, Magnus. Padrones de estratificación en los países bolivarianos durante la época del Libertador (CDAL, 29/30, jan./déc. 1984, p. 1–12)
Suggestive overview of principal social categories, possible changes in their positions during independence, and methodological problems in studying these.

BOLIVARIANA

2844 Aljure Chalela, Simón. Bibliografía bolivariana. Bogotá: Banco de la República, Biblioteca Luis-Angel Arango, 1983. 494 p. (Col. Banco de la République)
Strongest in coverage of newspapers and periodical publications of Gran Colombian countries, thus primarily useful for study of popular and academic image of Bolívar. Alphabetical listing under such headings as "Libros y Folletos" and "Cartas"

is not very helpful. But in lack of any truly comprehensive guide to literature about Bolívar, should not be wholly overlooked.

2845 Ayala Mora, Enrique. Tendencias del desarrollo del culto a Bolívar en el Ecuador (BNJM/R, 26:1, enero/marzo 1984, p. 53–79)
Excellent essay on image and "cult" of Bolívar in Ecuador, from his time to today. Emphasizes persistence and universality of admiration evoked by Bolívar, even though different groups may see quite different things in the legacy of his thought and action.

2846 Becco, Horacio Jorge. Simón Bolívar, el Libertador, 1783–1830: bibliografía selectiva. Washington: Secretaría General, OEA, 1983. 61 p., 1 leaf of plates: index, port.
Very incomplete, but then does not pretend to be more. Adequate as starting point.

2847 Bolívar, Simón. Bolívar agrarista. Caracas: Procuraduría Agraria Nacional, 1983. 303 p., 4 leaves of plates: bibl., facsims., ill. (some col.), index, maps, ports.
Quite useful compilation of previously pubished documents related in some way to agrarian matters, broadly interpreted. They refer to *secuestros*, Indian lands, ecology, etc.

2848 Bolívar, Simón. Simón Bolívar, la vigencia de su pensamiento. Selección y prólogo, Francisco Pividal. La Habana: Casa de las Américas, 1982. 290 p. (Col. Pensamiento de nuestra América)

Anthology which is better than most, with brief prologue expressing Cuban Revolutionary sympathy for Bolívar. Headings and notes to individual documents are brief but generally helpful.

2849 Bolívar día a día. Edición de Fabio Puyo Vasco y Eugenio Gutiérrez Cely. Bogotá: Procultura, 1983. 3 v.: bibl., map, ports. (Col. Colombia en su historia)

Not the first chronology of Bolívar, but certainly most detailed. Consists in considerable part of excerpts from his orders, decrees, letters, tracing his movements and activities. Useful reference material, not to be read straight through.

2850 Carrera Damas, Germán. Bolívar y el proyecto nacional venezolano (CDAL, 29/30, jan./déc. 1984, p. 163–189)

Lucid summation of main lines of Bolívar's political thought and action, emphasizing both his realistic critique of liberal democratic model and failure to offer effective alternative. Forms part of special issue devoted to Bolívar, whose contents tend to be somewhat narrow in focus or too general, but are of interest because they are mainly contributions of European authors. A few others are listed separately.

2851 Carrillo Batalla, Tomás Enrique. Bolívar en la historia del pensamiento económico y fiscal. Caracas: Academia Nacional de la Historia, 1984. 283 p.: bibl. (Biblioteca de la Academia. Estudios, monografías y ensayos; 43)

Catalogs concrete measures and policy statements of Bolívar concerning economic or fiscal matters, with much information on measures and policies of government of Gran Colombia even when Bolívar was absent. Based on printed sources, more descriptive than analytical—with numerous documentary excerpts included in text and interpretation sometimes of necessity superficial—but in all a useful work of reference.

2852 Castellanos, Rafael Ramón. Caracas 1883: centenario del natalicio del Libertador. Caracas: Academia Nacional de la Historia, 1983. 2 v.: bibl., ill., indexes, ports. (Biblioteca de la Academia. Estudios, monografías y ensayos; 33–34)

Another item bearing on Bolívar cult rather than Bolívar himself. Comprehensively examines observances of first centennial, held under auspices of Antonio Guzmán Blanco and exploited by him for political ends. Text includes many period documents and writings.

2853 Chassin, Joëlle and Martine Dauzier. L'image de l'indien dans l'oeuvre de Bolívar (CDAL, 29/30, jan./déc. 1984, p. 61–74)

Fresh look at familiar data, underscoring inability of Bolívar, as "enlightened creole," to think of or deal with Indians on their own terms.

2854 Ferrer Benimeli, José A. Bolívar y la masonería (IGFO/RI, 43:172, julio/dic. 1983, p. 631–687)

After briefly reviewing relationship between Masonry and Latin American independence generally (as in author's other work noted in *HLAS 46:1885*), he pinpoints Bolívar's joining of a French lodge in 1804–05, later establishment of Masonry in Gran Colombia, and abolition of Masonic and other lodges by Bolívar in 1828. Combines research and common sense in manner not always found in writings on these matters.

Figueroa, Loida. Puerto Rico y el sueño bolivariano respecto a la América Latina. See item **2514.**

2855 Filippi, Alberto. Las interpretaciones cesaristas y fascistas de Bolívar en la cultura europea (UNAM/L, 17, 1984, p. 165–204)

Covers use and abuse of figure of Bolívar by Italian fascist spokesmen, with perceptive prior discussion of European intellectual context and antecedents. Notes parallel developments in *gomecista* Venezuela and topic's importance for Italian-Latin American relations in fascist era.

González, Margarita. Bolívar y la independencia de Cuba. See item **1865a.**

2856 Mijares, Augusto. The Liberator. English version by John Fisher. Prologue by Pedro Grases. Caracas: North American Assn. of Venezuela, 1983. 594 p.: bibl., ill.

Biography in traditional style but well done. Originally published in 1964, often reissued in Spanish, now a welcome addition to English-language literature on Bolívar.

2857 Pabón Núñez, Lucio. Bolívar: alfarero de repúblicas. Ocaña, Colombia: Escuela de Bellas Artes, 1983. 175 p.: bibl., index (Biblioteca de autores ocañeros; 19)

Collected essays on Bolívar's thought and action by exponent of traditional Catholic conservatism: an interpretation of Bolívar which had of late been overshadowed by left-populist efforts to coopt him instead.

2858 Pastrana Rodríguez, Eduardo. Poética bolivariana (BNJM/R, 26:1, enero/marzo 1984, p. 81–115)

Despite what one might expect on a topic like this, Pastrana gives interesting and informative review of poetic tributes to Bolívar from his time to present. Inevitably selective, with some natural favoritism for leftist and Colombian writers, Pastrana being both. But he does cite poets he does not like.

2859 Pineda, Rafael. Simón Bolívar's monuments throughout the world. Foreword by Rafael Caldera. Translated by Jaime Tello. Caracas: Centro Simón Bolívar, 1983. 345 p.: bibl., ill. (some col.), indexes, ports.

Handsome commemorative volume. Deals with paintings and, to lesser extent, coins and medals as well as statues and other "monuments."

2859a Roca, José Luis. Bolívar y la Convención Preliminar de Paz de Buenos Aires de 1823 (SBH/HC, 5, abril 1985, p. 117–143, ill.)

On basis of published sources, examines repercussions in Peru of abortive peace mission sent by Spain to Río de la Plata in 1823. Mainly concerns intrigues that come to nothing, but indicative of interests and methods of parties involved, including both Bolívar and top royalist leaders.

2860 Shulgovski, Anatoli. Bolívar y la lucha ideológica en torno a las vías de desarrollo de los jóvenes estados latinoamericanos (URSS/AL, 12, dic. 1983, p. 4–17)

Sublimely ignoring contrary evidence, cogently expounds social revolutionary, "populist" interpretation of Bolívar's final dictatorship. Effective statement of viewpoint that is currently rather fashionable.

2861 Urdaneta Braschi, Ezequiel. Bolívar en la numismática conmemorativa y en las condecoraciones. Prólogo de J.L. Salcedo-Bastardo. Caracas: Comité Ejecutivo del Bicentenario de Simón Bolívar: Banco Central de Venezuela, 1983. 320 p.: bibl., ill. (some col.)

Another handsome volume covering exactly what title says, from Bolívar's own time to present, in Venezuela and other countries.

2862 Valencia-Villa, Hernando. La constitución de la quimera: Rousseau y la república jacobina en el pensamiento constitucional de Bolívar. Prólogo de Germán Arciniegas. Bogotá: Editorial La Caja de Herramientas, 1982. 158 p.: appendix, bibl.

Starting with discussion of Rousseau and French Revolution and culminating with dissection of Bolívar's "chimeric" constitution for Bolivia, gives provocative analysis of Liberator's political thought. It is seen as simultaneously liberal, constitutional, messianic, and authoritarian, and doomed to failure as out of tune with social reality of Latin America.

GRAN COLOMBIA

2863 Bache, Richard. La República de Colombia en los años 1822–23: notas de viaje con el itinerario de la ruta entre Caracas y Bogotá y un apéndice. Traducción de Angel Raúl Villasana. Caracas: Instituto Nacional de Hipódromos, 1982. 265 p.: appendix, bibl., facsims. (Col. Venezolanistas. Serie Viajeros; 4)

New edition of important set of contemporary observations. Translation of *Notes on Colombia taken in the years 1822–1823: with an itinerary of the route from Caracas to Bogotá, and an appendix, by an Officer of the United States Army* (Philadelphia: s.n., 1827).

2864 Brión, Luis. Documentos del Almirante Brión. Estudio introductorio de Manuel Díaz Ugueto. Caracas: Ediciones del Congreso de la República, 1982. 2 v.: bibl., facsims., ill., ports.

Valuable addition to sources on maritime war of independence, in Caribbean theater. Unremarkable introduction. Documents included are both previously published and inedited.

2865 Cacua Prada, Antonio. Custodio García Rovira, el estudiante mártir. Prólogo de Horacio Rodríguez Plata. Bogotá:

Plaza & Janés: Academia Colombiana de la Historia, 1983. 295 p., 4 leaves of plates: bibl., ill., indexes (Complemento a la Historia extensa de Colombia; 5)

History in traditional style, with numerous documents in text, on political and military figure of New Granada's Patria Boba.

2866 Cardozo, Lubio. La literatura venezolana durante la Guerra de Independencia (VANH/B, 67:266, abril/junio 1984, p. 317–344, bibl., facsims.)

Explicitly disclaiming any pretense of systematic treatment, consists of preliminary "notes" on writings of Bolívar, memoirs of participants, patriot and royalist poetry, etc. Useful as introduction to topic.

2867 Cubitt, David J. Economic nationalism in post independence Ecuador: the Guayaquil Commercial Code of 1821–1825 (IAA, 11:1, 1985, p. 65–82, bibl.)

Reconstruction and analysis of commercial code adopted by leaders of Guayaquil during brief period in which they maintained independence from both Quito and Bogotá (Oct. 1820-July 1822). Argues that the code promoted commercial needs and aspirations of local commercial elite, but that after annexation by Colombia, external pressures eroded the protectionist and proto-nationalistic position adopted through the code. Careful, scholarly work drawn from larger, on-going research. [J.M. Rausch]

2868 Destruge, Camilo. Historia de la Revolución de Octubre y Campaña Libertadora de 1820–22. 2a ed. Guayaquil: Banco Central del Ecuador, 1982. 480 p.: bibl., port.

Reprint of classic history of Guayaquil independence, first published in 1920 on centennial of same.

2869 La Gran Colombia. Compilación de José M. de Mier. v. 1, Decretos de la Secretaría de Estado y del Interior, 1821–1824. v. 2, Decretos . . ., 1824–1826. v. 3, Decretos . . ., 1826–1828. v. 4, Decretos . . ., 1828–1831. v. 5, Documentos de la Secretaría de Estado y de Relaciones Exteriores. v. 6, El Libertador y algunas misiones diplomáticas. v. 7, Indices. Bogotá: Presidencia de la República, 1983. 7 v.: ill., indexes.

Colombia's official Bolívar Bicentennial contribution, with prologue "Clarividencia y Generosidad" by Belisario Betancur

himself, as well as more lengthy introduction by José de Mier. Consists of documents both previously published and otherwise. Contains indexes.

2870 Los Héroes epónimos. Coordinación e introducción de Guillermo Morón. Caracas: Academia Nacional de la Historia: Univ. Centro Occidental Lisandro Alvarado, 1982. 241 p.: bibls., ill., ports (some col.)

Brief biographies of 26 prominent military leaders of Venezuelan independence, competently done and in most cases followed by short bibliography.

2871 Jaramillo, Juan Diego. Bolívar y Canning, 1822–1827: desde el Congreso de Verona hasta el Congreso de Panamá. Prefacio de Laureano Gómez. Bogotá: Banco de la República, Biblioteca Luis-Angel Arango, 1983. 357 p., 30 p. of plates: bibl., ill. (Col. Banco de la República)

This is really two monographs in one: detailed review of British policy on recognition of new Latin American nations, meticulously researched though tending to exaggerate importance of that recognition; and an analysis of Bolívar's foreign policy that rightly stresses his desire for close British connection but is more suggestive than solidly based. Ends with notable bibliographic essay, which anyone interested in international relations of independence period should consult.

2872 Leal, Ildefonso. La Universidad de Caracas en los años de Bolívar, 1783–1830. Caracas: Ediciones del Rectorado, Univ. Central de Venezuela, 1983. 2 v.: bibl., ill., indexes.

This volume offers long and comprehensive introductory study by Leal that covers subjects of instruction, finances, personnel, and ideological role in years leading up to independence movement and during struggle itself. Then come "Actas del Claustro Universitario," for period of Bolívar's lifetime, a rather artificial time span for this topic. Well indexed.

2873 Leyva Medina, Nelson. General Josef de Leyva: fundador de la primera escuela militar de la Nueva Granada, héroe y mártir de la patria. Bogotá: Imprenta y Publicaciones de las Fuerzas Militares, 1982. 454 p., ca. 400 leaves of plates: bibl., facsims., ill. (some col.), index.

Study of Spanish-born officer who joined New Granada patriots, headed their fledgling military school, and was executed in 1816 Reconquest. Numerous documents in text, much extraneous material, but withal a net contribution to military history of independence period.

2874 Littuma Arízaga, Alfonso. Presencia del General Antonio José de Sucre, Gran Mariscal de Ayacucho, en los territorios de la Real Audiencia de Quito. Quito: Editorial Voluntad, 1981. 197, 2 p., 10 leaves of plates: bibl., ill., maps.

Military history, by military author and in light of military principles. Numerous maps and diagrams add to reference value.

2875 Montilla, Mariano. General de División Mariano Montilla: homenaje en el bicentenario de su nacimiento, 1782– 1982. Caracas: Ediciones de la Presidencia de la República, 1982. 2 v. (1151 p.): bibl.

Major collection of writings and documents by and about a key second-rank figure who fought in both Venezuela and New Granada, served as pillar of Bolivarian cause in Gran Colombia as military commandant at Cartagena, and subsequently served Venezuela as diplomatic agent in Europe, where among other things he negotiated Spanish recognition.

2876 Moreno Egas, Jorge. Empréstito del Obispado de Quito al gobierno del Libertador, 1823 (EANH/B, 66:141/142, enero/dic. 1983, p. 32–42, charts)

Some unusual data on independence-era forced loan, showing how Ecuadorian clergy provided full quota asked of them and listing individual contributors.

Otero D'Costa, Enrique. El Dr. Juan Eloy Valenzuela, Subdirector de la Expedición Botánica. See item **1790a.**

2877 La Presidencia de Quito, 1822. Quito: Editorial Casa de la Cultura Ecuatoriana, 1983. 260 p.: index.

Contains chapters relating to Ecuador from Alexander Walker's *Colombia* (London: 1822) and index of materials of 1822 in Ecuador's Archivo Nacional relating to Audiencia of Quito and to Gran Colombia's Depto. del Sur.

2878 Rayfield, Jo Ann. Después del Santuario: la pacificación de Antioquia

por O'Leary, 1829 (ACH/BHA, 70:740, enero/marzo 1983, p. 291–320)

Skirting polemics over role of Daniel F. O'Leary in death of José María Córdova, gives really first authoritative account of his settlement of Antioquia after defeat of Córdova rebellion. Emphasizes conciliatory aspects.

2879 Romero Luengo, Adolfo. Presencia vital de Urdaneta en la emancipación y en el gobierno de Colombia La Grande: renovación estructural de la versión histórica del proceso de la independencia realizada por Bolívar, creador de Colombia La Grande. Caracas: Ediciones de la Presidencia de la República, 1981. 2 v.: bibl., port.

Massive history in traditional vein, devoted to key military figure, Rafael Urdaneta, who though Venezuelan by birth had close ties with New Granada and became strongman of Bolívar's final dictatorship. Supersedes earlier studies of Urdaneta.

2880 Tovar Pinzón, Hermes. Guerras de opinión y represión en Colombia durante la independencia, 1810–1820 (UNC/ACHSC, 11, 1983, p. 187–232, map)

Much new material on *secuestros* (including those decreed by one patriot faction against another) and efforts to mobilize popular support. Coverage somewhat uneven but an important contribution.

2881 Venezuela. Congreso de la República. Actas de los Congresos del Ciclo Bolivariano. Caracas: El Congreso, 1983. 4 v.: bibl., indexes.

In this one set: vols. 1–2, minutes of first Venezuelan constituent congress (1811–12); and vols. 3–4, Congreso de Angostura (1819).

2882 Verna, Paul. Bolívar y los emigrados patriotas en el Caribe: Trinidad, Curazao, San Thomas, Jamaica, Haití. Caracas: INCE, 1983. 200 p.: bibl., ill.

Studies dispersal of patriot refugees from royalist reconquest of Venezuela and New Granada, 1814–16, to different islands of non-Hispanic Caribbean, with some relative emphasis on Bolívar's stay in Haiti. Includes list of 336 émigrés and some biographical data on each.

2883 Verna, Paul. Pedro Antonio Leleux, el francés edecán, secretario y amigo de confianza de Bolívar y Miranda: homenaje de la Academia Nacional de la Historia y de la

Sociedad Bolivariana de Venezuela en los 200 años de Pedro Antonio Leleux, 1781–10 de noviembre-1981. Caracas: Comité Ejecutivo del Bicentenario de Simón Bolívar, 1982. 192 p.: bibl., ill., index (Col. Contorno bolivariano; 6)

Good short study of personage adequately described in title. Previously published in another volume (see *HLAS 38: 3245*), but here with documentary section added.

PERU AND ALTO PERU

2884 Abecia Baldivieso, Valentín. Bolívar y Sucre en la fundación de Bolivia (PAIGH/H, 96, julio/dic. 1983, p. 187–216)

Good synthesis, though nothing really new, by leading Bolivian historian on process whereby Bolivia emerged as independent republic.

2885 García Jordán, Pilar. Notas sobre la participación del clero en la independencia del Perú (UB/BA, 14:32, 1982, p. 139–147)

With introduction, presents seven documents from Archivo Arzobispal de Lima (1821–25), illustrating different attitudes of clergy and facets of their role in independence period.

2886 Hünefeldt, Christine. Lucha por la tierra y protesta indígena: las comunidades indígenas del Perú entre colonia y república, 1800–1830. Bonn: s.n., 1982. 258 p.: appendices, bibl. (Bonner amerikanische Studien; 9)

Valuable study of Peruvian Indians during independence period, touching relations among themselves, with State, and with *hacendados*, underscoring "las dimensiones étnicas del comportamiento campesino." With documentary and other appendices, deserves better than this rather low-grade reproduction.

CHILE

2887 Torres Marín, Manuel. Quintanilla y Chiloé: la epopeya de la constancia (SHM/RHM, 28:57, 1984, p. 71–93)

Favorable treatment of last Spanish commander of loyalist stronghold Chiloé,

Antonio de Quintanilla, who surrendered only in Jan. 1826. Also covers his subsequent career in Spain. Presented as "condensación" of larger forthcoming study.

RIO DE LA PLATA

2888 Bidondo, Emilio A. Los tenientes de gobernador de Jujuy. Buenos Aires: Ediciones Culturales Argentinas, Secretaría de Cultura, Presidencia de la Nación, 1983. 372 p.: bibl.

Competent local history, first explaining nature of office and then presenting brief sketches of incumbents (1810–34), when Jujuy became independent of Salta and "teniente" was deleted.

2889 Fernández López, Manuel and **Denaide Rosa del Valle Orellana.** Manuel Belgrano y las *Máximas* de Quesnay (UNC/REE, 25:1, junio 1984, p. 83–124, appendix)

Though no copies are known to exist, Manuel Belgrano definitely translated and published (in Madrid in 1794) the *Maximes* of Quesnay, whose physiocratic teachings formed one part of late colonial intellectual environment. Very good piece of research.

2890 Orsi, René. James Monroe contra la independencia argentina. Buenos Aires: Peña Lillo Editor, 1983. 190 p.: bibl., facsims.

Retells ambivalent US policy toward Spanish American independence, Argentina in particular. Polemical in tone, no important new data, but fully documented, mainly from US sources.

2891 Peña, Roberto I. La visita a la Universidad Mayor de San Carlos efectuada por el Doctor Don Manuel Antonio de Castro, gobernador-intendente de Córdoba (Revista del Instituto de Historia del Derecho Ricardo Levene [Buenos Aires] 26, 1980/1981, p. 120–143)

With extensive transcriptions of original documents, looks at 1818 survey of Univ. of Córdoba and resulting reforms. Few indications of revolution in progress.

2891a Piccinali, Héctor Juan. Vida de San Martín en Buenos Aires. Buenos Aires: s.n., 1984. 467 p., 32 p. of plates: ill.

Discusses in detail history, development, and training of the Regimiento de Granaderos a Caballo under the aegis of San

Martín (1812–13). Excellent unit history.
[J. T. Criscenti]

2892 Rato de Sambuccetti, Susana. La Revolución de Mayo: interpretaciones conflictivas. Buenos Aires: Ediciones Siglo Veinte, 1983. 254 p.: bibl. (La Nueva historia argentina)

Concerned not simply with facts of May Revolution but with conflicting and often confusing interpretations that have developed around them. Offers selection of original source materials organized in three broad groups: ideological foundations, economic implications, and political-institutional process. Each group preceded by introductory discussion that takes note of points under dispute. A good means of approach to a historiographical labyrinth.

2893 Sanz, Víctor. La conferencia de París sobre la Banda Oriental: 1817–1819 (UB/BA, 33, 1983, p. 119–142)

Summary of larger investigation, based on Spanish archives, concerning abortive attempt at mediation by European powers in dispute of Spain and Portugal over Uruguay.

2894 Segreti, Carlos S.A. La repercusión en Mendoza de la política comercial porteña en la primera década revolucionaria (JGSWGL, 19, 1982, p. 183–222, tables)

This article, a model of original research and analysis, delivers even more than title promises. Examines effects of revolutionary foreign trade policies on Mendoza wines and liquors, weighing gain from cutting off of Spanish competition against damage suffered from other directions. Also reviews impact of closings and openings of frontier with Chile, intra-Cuyo rivalries, and economic significance of San Martín's use of Mendoza as staging ground for Chilean campaign. Segreti cannot say last word on all these things in single article, but he points up complexity of economic developments in ways that very few have ever done.

2895 Uruguay. Comisión Nacional Archivo Artigas. Archivo Artigas. t. 18–20. Montevideo: Impresores A. Monteverde y Cía., 1981. 3 v. (449, 437, 490 p.)

Continuation of *HLAS 44:2843*. Vol. 18 offers documents mainly from Brazilian archives on repercussions in Brazil of *artiguista* activities, designs of Princess Carlota, and related matters. Vols. 19–20 concern "La Liga de los Pueblos Libres" and ramifications in the Litoral. Vols. 18–19 have useful "Advertencias" by Juan E. Pivel Devoto.

19th and 20th CENTURIES

VENEZUELA

WINTHROP R. WRIGHT, *Associate Professor of History, University of Maryland, College Park*

THE WORKS REVIEWED for this edition of the *Handbook* do not reveal any significant changes in the trends noted in recent years. Venezuelan historians of the modern era still pay a great deal of attention to political matters, particularly the lives and influence of the nation's two 20th-century "caudillos" Juan Vicente Gómez and Rómulo Betancourt.

Of those related to the Gómez era, few merit special notice. But one of them, *Actas y conclusiones: Primer Congreso de Municipalidades de Venezuela* (item 2904) makes available an important document from 1911 that shows the political thoughts of the positivists who supported Gómez's dictatorship. That book also demonstrates the high quality of the documentary collections produced under the sponsorship of the Congress of the Republic of Venezuela. Another interesting work on the Gómez period, written by Luis Cipriano Rodríguez (item **2921**), attacks the notion that Gómez created a nation-state, and claims that his administration actually accentuated Venezuela's neocolonial dependence.

Efforts to deal with questions related to the politics of Rómulo Betancourt and Marco Pérez Jiménez have led to mixed results. Journalists and other non-professional historians wrote the majority of these studies. Most bog down in polemical arguments that shed very little light on the topic of political change. Their overall lack of scholarship makes their importance difficult to judge. Nothing has come close to the quality of the efforts of the indefatigable Naúdy Suárez to publish solid documentary evidence of the political history of the period, although one of his collaborators, José Rodríguez Iturbe (item **2922**), has presented an interesting interpretation of the role played by the Christian Democrats (COPEI) during the dictatorship of Pérez Jiménez. Judy Ewell's book on 20th-century Venezuela (item **2911**) adds some fresh insights into the evolution of modern social, economic, and political institutions. It, along with John Lombardi's fine work on the 19th century (see *HLAS 46:2617*), provides general information about Venezuela in English.

Three other books deserve mention. All deal with regional rather than national themes. Although not destined to become classics, they do reflect a more innovative approach to history, and they all touch themes that have not received enough serious attention in the past. Lorenzo Vargas Mendoza's study of journalists during the Federal War (1859–63) leaves a firm impression of the partisan nature of the press during the past century. A more impressive book by Felipe S. Colmenter V. (item **2903**) traces the efforts of Antonio Guzmán Blanco to centralize his control over the state of Trujillo. In treating the theme of centralization, the author presents a useful survey of regional economic development. In a like manner, Alicia Ardao's study of coffee (item **2896**) and its influence upon Andean cities marks an important departure from traditional Venezuelan historiography in that it relies heavily on social and economic aspects of modernization between 1870 and 1930 in one part of a highly complex nation. Ardao has broken important ground, both methodologically and topically, in undertaking her project.

2896 Ardao, Alicia. El café y las ciudades en los Andes venezolanos, 1870–1930. Caracas: Academia Nacional de la Historia, 1984. 309 p.: bibl., ill., index (Biblioteca de la Academia. Fuentes para la historia republicana de Venezuela; 34)

Venezuela's Andean regions became important producers of coffee and part of an international trade network (1870–1930). Production and commercialization of coffee had profound effects upon urbanization. Author uses cities and small urban centers as means of observing modernization and change. Valuable addition to study of urban, regional, and economic history of Venezuela, based on models by Braudel, Morse, George, and others. Argues that nucleus of colonial urban centers formed base for growth and expansion of coffee in post-1870 period. Coffee production served as sole source of support of urban network, and ultimately the cause of its weakness. Despite modernization, no social changes in structure occurred; differences between urban and rural areas widened. At end of era, the Andes were less isolated, but not closely tied to the rest of Venezuela by road. Important study.

Arellano Moreno, Antonio. Orígenes de la economía venezolana. See *HLAS 47:3454*.

2897 Avendaño Lugo, José Ramón. El militarismo en Venezuela: la dictadura de Pérez Jiménez. Caracas: Ediciones Centauro, 1982. 393 p.: bibl., maps (Enero 23, 1958, XXV aniversario)

Depicts the period of the Pérez Jiménez dictatorship as decisive in determining the neocolonial direction Venezuela took.

Claims that foreign values replaced national ones, and that the "Nuevo Ideal Nacional" only rationalized the hegemonic tendencies of the armed forces under Pérez Jiménez.

2898 Betancourt, Rómulo. Rómulo Betancourt contra la dictadura de Juan Vicente Gómez, 1928–1935: *Repertorio Americano*, Costa Rica. Compilador, Alejandro Gómez. Caracas: Ediciones Centauro, 1982. 442 p.: bibl., ill.

Collection of various writings by Betancourt in exile (1929–35) in which he reveals evolution of his political ideology during the Gómez regime. Essays clearly reveal the influence of both communism and Peruvian Aprismo on his thinking. A large portion come from his contributions to the Costa Rican press, especially *Repertorio Americano*. Several documents appear elsewhere, but the majority appear for the first time. Useful for analyzing diverse sources of Betancourt's ideas, especially his position against the dictatorship. Among others are copies of the Plan of Barranquilla, and correspondence with José Rafael Pocaterra and Mariano Picón Salas.

2899 Betancourt, Rómulo. Rómulo Betancourt, 1948–1958: memoria del último destierro; *Revista Bomehia* [i.e. *Bohemia*], Habana, Cuba. Caracas: Ediciones Centauro, 1982. 360 p., 8 p. of plates: ports (Enero 23, 1958, XXV aniversario)

Selected writings from Cuban review *Bohemia* by Betancourt when he lived there in exile after 1948. Essays touch wide range of topics and subjects, from Betancourt's views of dictatorship, the Cold War, and other political issues, through immigration and democracy. Interesting source of information on the role of exiled Venezuelans in the resistance to Pérez Jiménez's dictatorship.

2900 Blanco, Andrés Eloy. Andrés Eloy Blanco, parlamentario. Compilación y selección de Luis Pastori. Prólogo de Luis B. Prieto F. 2a ed. Caracas: Ediciones Centauro, 1981. 3 v.: indexes.

Reedition of speeches, addresses, essays, and lectures of a founder of the Acción Democrática Party, with an introduction by fellow organizer Luis Beltrán Prieto Figueroa. Useful source of A.D. philosophy in its early stages.

2901 Blanco Muñoz, Agustín. La lucha armada. [v. 1], Hablan cinco jefes: Gustavo Machado, Pedro Ortega Díaz, Pompeyo Márquez, Teodoro Petkoff, Guillermo García Ponce. [v. 2], Hablan seis comandantes: Magoya, Luben Petkoff, Anselmo Natale, Luis Correa, Juan Vicente Cabezas, Alfredo Maneiro. [v. 3], La izquierda revolucionaria insurge: Domingo Alberto Rangel *et al*. [v. 4], Hablan tres comandantes de la izquierda revolucionaria: Lino Martínez, Moisés Moleiro, Américo Martín. Caracas: Univ. Central de Venezuela, Facultad de Ciencias Económicas y Sociales, División de Publicaciones, 1980–1982. 4 v. (411, 412, 384, 377): indexes, ports (Testimonios violentos; 2–3, 5–6. Serie Coediciones)

Four (unnumbered) volumes of interviews conducted by Blanco Muñoz with leaders of the post-1958 Venezuelan left: 1) discusses participation of leaders in guerrilla activities, Communist Party, and radical groups; 2) interviews three MIR organizers who explain reasons for their break from A.D.; 3) portrays sentiments of anti-Betancourt faction and their move away from A.D. after Pérez Jiménez's overthrow; and 4) describes activities as guerrillas and activists in Communist Party and radical groups. All four volumes are a good source of information on exiles, imprisonment, relations of the left with the Communist Party, guerrilla activities, and leftist politics in general.

2902 *Boletín del Archivo Histórico de Miraflores*. Año 25, No. 120, enero/junio 1985–. Caracas.

Issue entirely devoted to archival materials related to 1918–19, during dictator Juan Vicente Gómez's rule (e.g., Ministers' reports; consular and diplomatic reports; correspondence from Márquez Bustillos to Gómez; Colombian-Venezuelan relations in 1918; Arauca, Cúcuta, and Trinidad in 1918; strikes, conspiracies, and rumors of plots in 1919. [Ed.]

Braveboy-Wagner, Jacqueline Anne. The Venezuelan-Guyana border dispute: Britain's colonial legacy in Latin America. See *HLAS 48:7353*.

Briceño Monzillo, José Manuel. Nuestras fronteras con Colombia: reseña histórica. See *HLAS 47:5196*.

Cardozo, Lubio. Los repertorios bibliográficos venezolanos del siglo diecinueve. See *HLAS 47:78.*

2903 Colmenter V., Felipe S. Economía y política en Trujillo durante el guzmancismo, 1870–1887. Caracas: Fundación para el Rescate del Acervo Documental Venezolano, 1983. 121 p.: bibl. (Biblioteca de temas y autores trujillanos; 9)

Traces Guzmán Blanco's efforts to centralize his control over the state of Trujillo. Taxes from Trujillo's export of coffee benefited the national government and strengthened its fiscal position, while citizens of Trujillo got little. But revenue from sugar cane and sale of aguardiente produced funds for the State to undertake public building, education, sanitation, and militia. In general, Guzmán's central government tried to pacify and dominate it, but political instability in the province, which reflected economic tensions, led to conflicts. Gúzman ultimately controlled Trujillo through an alliance with Juan Bautista Araujo.

2904 Congreso de Municipalidades de Venezuela, *1st, Caracas, 1911.* Actas y conclusiones. Prólogo de Luis Salamanca. Caracas: Congreso de la República, 1983. 434 p.: forms (El Pensamiento político venezolano del siglo XX; 9. Ediciones conmemorativas del bicentenario del natalicio del Libertador Simón Bolívar)

Important document from early Gómez years. Congress was organized by Gómez's Minister of Internal Affairs Francisco Linares Alcántara, later a militant *antigomecista*, and César Zumeta, at the time a critic of militarism. Participants included Laureano Vallenilla Lanz, Pedro M. Arcaya, and José Gil Fortoul, all leading positivists. Acts show that this generation of Venezuelan elites placed order above all else, and show the political thoughts of positivists who supported the dictatorship, as well as some critics. In effect, the Congress did not want to produce a new social order by modernizing the municipalities, but rather sought criollo solutions to criollo problems by improving health, education, sanitation, and the like. Document not only contains useful inventory of Venezuela's municipalities, their public services, buildings, and their aspirations, but also chronicles inability of *gomecistas* to accomplish their own goals as set out in this congress.

2905 Cortina, Alfredo. Contribución a la historia de la radio en Venezuela. Presentación de Luis Pastori. Caracas: Instituto Nacional de Hipódromos, 1982. 157 p.: ill., plans, ports. (Col. venezolanista. Serie Testimonios; 4)

Well illustrated, technically interesting, and otherwise fascinating account of early radio days in Caracas by individual who took part in its growth. Not a detailed or complete study of the history of radio, but a useful start. For a history of Colombia's radio, see item **2976.**

Crist, Raymond E. Westward thrusts the pioneers zone in Venezuela: a half century of economic development along the Llanos-Andes border. See *HLAS 47:3470.*

D'Ascoli, Carlos Alberto. Del mito del Dorado a la economía del café: esquema histórico económico de Venezuela. See *HLAS 47:3471.*

2906 El Debate político en 1936. Prólogo de Arturo Sosa A. y Eloi Lengrand. Caracas: Congreso de la República, 1983. 3 v.: bibl., indexes (El Pensamiento político venezolano del siglo XX; 14–16. Ediciones conmemorativas del bicentenario del natalicio del Libertador Simón Bolívar)

Cross section of political debate that emerged in 1936, culled mostly from the partisan press. Touches broad selection of topics that captured public attention following Gómez's death. Represents right, left, and center views on matters such as workers' rights, economic reforms, foreign imperialism, petroleum, elections, López Contreras, and the Partido Democrático Nacional.

2907 Documentos del 23 de enero de 1958: recopilación de manifiestos del movimiento nacional que derrocó la dictadura. Caracas: Ediciones del Congreso de la República, 1983? 299 p., 1 leaf of plates: ill.

Useful collection of documents published to commemorate the 25th anniversary of Pérez Jiménez's overthrow. Includes anti-Pérez Jiménez statements selected from *La Religión, Tribuna Popular, Voz de Venezuela,* and *Frente a 1958.* Contributors: Luis Herrera Campins, Jovito Villalba, the Comité Central del Partido Comunista de Venezuela (PCU) as well as other *manifestos* against the dictatorship.

2908 Documentos para la historia de Acción Democrática. v. 1, 1936–1941. Compilación de José Agustín Catalá. Caracas: Ediciones Centauro, 1981. 1 v: bibl. (Los Partidos políticos en Venezuela)

Useful collection of documents taken from papers of Partido Democrático Nacional (PDN) through the first assembly of Acción Democrática (AD) at Nuevo Circo de Caracas (Sept. 13, 1941). Includes party's plans, speeches by A.D. members, and other important documents such as Supreme Court decisions that first banned the party and later legitimized it. Useful for a general understanding of A.D.'s positions on social justice, nationalism, and anti-communism.

Ellner, Steve. Los partidos políticos y su disputa por el control del movimiento sindical en Venezuela, 1936–1948. See *HLAS 47:6371.*

2909 Ernst, Adolfo. Obras completas. v. 3–4, La Exposición Nacional de Venezuela en 1883. Caracas: Fundación Venezolana para la Salud y la Educación, 1983. 2 v.: ill. (some col.)

Reprint of work published in 1883 by one of the founders of positivism in Venezuela. Worthy addition to any research library on modern Venezuela.

2910 Estrada, Pedro. La dictadura: Pedro Estrada habló. Entrevistas de Agustín Blanco Muñoz. Caracas: Consejo de Desarrollo Científico y Humanístico, Univ. Central de Venezuela, 1983. 344 p.: ill., index (Testimonios violentos; 7. Serie Coediciones).

Interview with Pedro Estrada who served as director of the Seguridad Nacional under Pérez Jiménez. After 25 years of silence, Estrada defended his actions and the basic policies of P.J. Though critical of Betancourt, he admired him. On terror, Estrada claimed that the State is justified in using force against those who use guns and bombs. In his mind, Acción Democrática initiated the violence. He denied having given orders to torture anyone, but did permit "severe interrogations." Moreover, he argued that he could not have had control over every uneducated policeman in the nation. Highly polemical account of the dictatorship, not so much oral history as an interview which exacerbated the political nature of Estrada's comments.

2911 Ewell, Judith. Venezuela, a century of change. Stanford, Calif.: Stanford Univ. Press, 1984. 258 p.: bibl., ill., index.

Largely a political history of modern Venezuela, from the era of Antonio Guzmán Blanco to the administration of Carlos Andrés Pérez. But Ewell also does a service by dealing with questions of social, economic, and cultural change during this very important period of national consolidation. Book not only updates that of her mentor Edwin Lieuwen, but replaces it as one of the best synthesis of modern Venezuela in English. Sensitive and common sense treatment of the role of petroleum in the modernization process.

Foro Los Socialcristianos y Venezuela, *Caracas, 1982.* Los copeyanos. See *HLAS 47:6376.*

2912 El Golpe contra el presidente Gallegos: documentos para la historia; gestores, animadores, autores, colaboradores, cómplices y opositores. Caracas: Ediciones Centauro, 1983. 400 p., 23 p. of plates: ports. (Enero 23, 1958, XXV aniversario)

Collected opinions from the press taken 30 days on either side of the golpe that overthrew Gallegos in 1948. Shows division in Venezuelan society at the end of the trieno.

Grases, Pedro. La imprenta en Venezuela. See *HLAS 47:121.*

2913 Guerrero, Ana Cecilia. Desierto para un *Oasis.* Caracas: Academia Nacional de la Historia, 1984. 155 p.: bibl., ill. (El Libro menor; 56)

Study of literary and cultural review published in Barcelona during 1856 by Nicanor Bolet Poleo and his sons Ramón and Nicanor. Although it folded up in troubled times, its appearance showed that not all culture in Venezuela emanated from Caracas. The rural "interior" shared a cultural view with urban Caracas. Like many newspapers of its time, *Oasis* suffered hard times economically, and during the Federal War gave way to political polemics of its owners and editors. Good examples of influence of French culture, whose works were tediously translated into Spanish for a minority to read.

2914 Historia de las finanzas públicas en Venezuela. Compilación, ordenación y análisis de Tomás Enrique Carrillo Batalla. Con la cooperación de un grupo de investigadores coordinado por Pedro Grases. Caracas: Cuatricentenario de la Ciudad de Caracas, 1982. 28 v.: bibl.

History of Venezuelan public finances which deals mostly with legislative, doctrinal, and statistical questions. For economist's comment, see *HLAS 47:3478.*

2915 Los Liberales amarillos en la caricatura venezolana. Caracas: Instituto Autónoma Biblioteca Nacional: Fundación para el Rescate del Acervo Documental Venezolano, 1982. 312 p.: ill.

Effective effort to demonstrate high calibre of political debate in Venezuela during late 19th century. Political ideas as revealed through pages of weekly humor magazine *Diablo* serve to illustrate Ramón J. Velásquez's contention that during 1890s an unprecedented free political debate of ideas took place in Venezuela before the tyranny of the Castro/Gómez era set in. Excellent quality of sketches, drawings, and cartoons shows coming of age of political caricature, which compensated for lack of photos in late 19th-century Venezuelan press.

2916 Misle, Carlos Eduardo. Venezuela, siglo XIX en fotografía. Caracas?: Gerencia de Actividades Culturales, Centro Nacional de Telecomunicaciones, 1981. 200 p.: bibl., ill., index, photos, plates.

Generally informative text accompanies selection of newspaper clippings and photographs (1850–1900). Collected and prepared by a journalist, book includes excellent views of Caracas valley, people, and scenes of the city. Useful index for the most part identifies plates. A great deal of the photography by Federico Carlos Lessman and Henrique Avril, two pioneers in the field of Venezuelan photography.

2917 Noticias de Venezuela: facsímil de órgano de los desterrados venezolanos del Partido Comunista en México. Caracas: Ediciones Centauro, 1983. 550 p.: ill.

Facsimile of a newspaper published in Mexico by exiled members of the Venezuelan Communist Party (1951–56). Gives PCV's positions on Betancourt/A.D., US influence in Venezuela, and the dictatorship. Good source of information on human rights abuses by Pérez Jiménez. Also chronicles part of the resistance in exile movement.

2918 Ojer, Pablo. Sumario histórico del Golfo de Venezuela. San Cristóbal,

Venezuela: Univ. Católica del Táchira, 1984. 147 p., 1 leaf of plates: maps (Col. Sumario; 5)

Short version of Ojer's well documented studies of the Venezuelan claim to own the Golfo de Venezuela, a subject of contention between Venezuela and Colombia for many years. Written for the general pubic, especially. After running through historical arguments and discussion of treaties, author concludes that gulf is Venezuelan in practice and theory.

Peña, Alfredo. Conversaciones con Carlos Andrés Pérez. See *HLAS 47:6383.*

Perna, Claudio. Evolución de la geografía urbana de Caracas. See *HLAS 47:5205.*

2919 El Pueblo y las fuerzas armadas de Venezuela en 1958. Edición de José Umaña Bernal. Caracas: Ediciones Centauro, 1980. 287 p.: ill.

Previously published as *Testimonio de la revolución en Venezuela* (see *HLAS 22:2719*). Collection of documents put together by the Colombian José Umaña Bernal, a witness to the overthrow of Marco Pérez Jiménez in 1958.

2920 Repertorio histórico-biográfico del General José Tadeo Monagas, 1784–1868. Estudio introductorio, recopilación y selección documental de Juan Bautista Querales D. Caracas: Academia Nacional de la Historia, 1983. 4 v.: bibl., ill., indexes (Biblioteca de la Academia. Fuentes para la historia republicana de Venezuela; 28–31)

Part of project headed by Ermila Tronconis de Veracoechea. Mostly a collection of documents—laws, decrees, letters, speeches—from the 1847–58 period of Monagas's career as president. Includes many biographical sketches by 19th- and 20th-century writers.

2921 Rodríguez, Luis Cipriano. Gómez: agricultura, petróleo y dependencia. Caracas: Fondo Editorial Tropykos, 1983. 157 p.: bibl. (Serie Estudios venezolanos)

Attacks argument that nation-state was formed under Juan Vicente Gómez, perceived as modernizer, road builder, and organizer of modern army. Rather, author sees period between 1920–35 as one that accentuated Venezuela's neocolonial dependence. As oil had an increasingly radical effect on Venezuela's economy and State, agriculture declined as its principal economic factor.

Gómez did not have a coherent agricultural program. His own land-holding expanded dramatically, but national production stagnated, as did technological aspects of agriculture. Labor left the land, and newly established Bank of Agriculture just served a small group of large landowners, and showed no interest in small producers. Throughout Gómez era the US gained influence in Venezuela, and controlled more and more of its economy.

Rodríguez Campos, Manuel. Venezuela, 1948–1958: el proceso económico y social de la dictadura. See *HLAS 47:3495.*

2922 Rodríguez Iturbe, José. Crónica de la década militar. Caracas: Ediciones Nueva Política, 1984. 576 p. (Historia contemporánea de Venezuela)

Work grew out of the editor's collaboration with Naudy Suárez on the documented history of the Christian Democratic Party of Venezuela (COPEI). Presents interpretative view of role and positions COPEI took during Pérez Jiménez's dictatorship. Invaluable source of information for students of the period, though somewhat disappointing in its lack of clear citations of specific documents. Includes excerpts from leading *perez-jimenistas*, such as Laureano Vallenilla Lanz (hijo), as well as from A.D. members and other opponents of the regime. Not an edited collection of documents as such, but rather, an extended essay with excerpted documental statements by major participants on both sides of the dictatorship.

Siwka, Colette. Historia, biografía y literatura: Venezuela, siglo XIX. See item **5160.**

2923 Vargas Mendoza, Lorenzo. La prensa en la Guerra Federal. Caracas: Petare, 1982. 94 p.

States that while journalists elsewhere in the world moved towards new techniques and used new technology to get the news to an increasingly broader mass of readers in an objective manner, Venezuelan newsmen remained partisan and were active in the nation's political fights. This was especially true during the Federal War (1859–63), when journalists knew that their editorials were expositions of doctrines, not news, but in the heat of the battle they ignored this fact. Author identifies the leading newspapers of the period and their political positions. In essence, the Venezuelan press did not work for the collective Venezuela, but rather for special interests.

2924 Velásquez, Ramón J. *et al.* Hombres y verdugos. Caracas: Ediciones Centauro, 1982. 519 p.: ill., ports.

Excellent sketches of leading figures of the resistance to the *dictadura* of Pérez Jiménez: Wilfrido Omaña, Leonardo Ruiz Pineda, Alberto Carnevali, Antonio Pinto Salinas, Luis Hurtado Higuera, and León Droz Blanco. Also a partial list of agents of the dictator's security forces who tortured opponents of the regime, as taken from testimonies of victims. Presents clear discussion of the strategic problems and ideological conflicts of the clandestine opposition to Pérez Jiménez. Book also includes brief treatments of two Pérez Jiménez supporters, Laureano Vallenilla Lanz (hijo) and Pedro Estrada.

2925 Venezuela, 1883. Edición de Ramón J. Velásquez. Caracas: Congreso de la República, 1983. 3 v.: bibl., ill.

Product of the bicentennial celebration of Bolívar's birth, directed by Ramón J. Velásquez. Includes essays by various historians, economists, and writers from the Univ. Central de Venezuela, about the Guzmán Blanco period. In general, provides good survey of the development of modern Venezuela during the Guzmán administration. Topics include urbanization, military problems, economic development, social change, demographic patterns, and regionalism. Well written and balanced analysis, with good essays by José Antonio de Armas Chitty, Jesús Rosas Marcano, Héctor Malave Mata, Irene Rodríguez, Tomás Pérez Tenreiro, and José Antonio Fernández.

2926 Zawisza, Leszek M. Alberto Lutowski, contribución al conocimiento de la ingeniería venezolana del siglo XIX. Caracas: Ministerio de la Defensa, 1980. 146 p., 24 p. of plates: bibl., ill.

Biography of Polish-born and French-trained engineer who worked on road, aquaduct, and municipal projects in Venezuela during the mid-19th century. Best known for his many inventions, especially in the area of locomotion. Well written and well researched.

COLOMBIA AND ECUADOR

JANE M. RAUSCH, *Professor of History, University of Massachusetts-Amherst*

A SURGE OF PUBLICATIONS on Colombian and Ecuadorian history in the last two years (more than twice the number of items recorded in *HLAS 42* and *HLAS 44*) has prompted the separation of these two countries from neighboring Venezuela in this volume of *HLAS*. The decision is justified for much of the Colombian output is of highest quality, and even the traditionally barren world of Ecuadorian historiography shows signs of life.

That a new group of professional Colombian historians—European-trained with ongoing research programs—has come of age is demonstrated by the papers which they presented at a seminar sponsored by the Fondo Cultural Cafetero in July 1981 (item **2933**). Their essays on the impact of La Regeneración, social conflicts and coffee production, the formation of political parties, and the development of regionalism and nationalism reflect the state of the art on these 19th-century issues and identify areas for further exploration.

These younger scholars, like their North American colleagues, continue to select economic and social topics as noted in *HLAS 42*. The growth of latifundia and concurrent peasant resistance after 1850 has attracted considerable interest. Le Grand's masterful survey (item **2958**) based on an exhaustive investigation of the Public Land Archives and her case study of rural protest against the United Fruit Co. between 1900–64 (item **2957**) demonstrate the potential of this line of research. In vol. 3 of his *Historia doble de la costa* (item **2941**), Fals Borda links the introduction of Zebu cattle, crop fumigation and barbed wire to the emergence of a new capitalistic class of landowners in San Jorge. In works of more limited scope, Arenas traces the Puyana family's accumulation of land and capital in Santander (item **2932**), Anrup surveys changing labor arrangements on an Andean estate (item **2928**), Negrete reviews agrarian conflicts in the Dept. of Córdoba between 1844–1970 (item **2972**), Arango Z. has compiled an oral history of the 1928 banana workers massacre (item **2930**), and Keremitsis compares women textile workers in Mexico and Colombia (item **2956**).

Personalities from the 19th century retain their fascination. The Academia Colombiana de Historia marked the 150th anniversary of Santander's return from exile in 1832 (items **2931, 2975,** and **2978**), the 100th anniversaries of José Manuel Restrepo's birth in 1781 (item **2946**) and Francisco Javier Zaldúa's death in 1882 (item **2940**). Inspiring somewhat pedestrian biographies were José Hilario López (item **2963**), José Manuel Lobo y Rivera (item **2966**), Mariano Vélez (item **2967**), and Florentino Vezga (item **2955**). More noteworthy is Tisnés Jiménez's fine study of María Martínez de Nisser (item **2985**), "La Dama Soldada" who led a counter-revolution in Antioquia against Salvador Córdova during the War of Los Supremos and published her diary of the events in 1843. A facsimile edition of Martínez de Nisser's diary (item **2965**) will enable others to plumb the attitudes and actions of this woman who has been called "the most authentic Colombian heroine of the nineteenth century." Both in scope and methodology, however, Fals Borda's biography of Juan José Nieto (item **2941**) transcends all the others. Like the companion volumes in his trilogy, *Historia doble de la costa*, *El Presidente Nieto* (item **2941**) is written from a Marxist viewpoint in two simultaneous narratives—one popular, the other scholarly. Based on newly discovered documents and oral tradition, the book promises to challenge historians for years to come and has already provoked a rejoinder from Eduardo Lemaitre (item **2959**).

Equally significant breakthroughs are appearing in Colombian history after 1910. The last two years has seen publication of writings by Laureano Gómez (items **2943** and **2944**), and the memoirs of Alberto Lleras Camargo (item **2961**) and Carlos Lleras Restrepo (item **2962**). A handsome volume edited by Germán Colmenares of political cartoons drawn by Ricardo Rendón in the 1920s (item **2937**) is complemented by Uribe Celis's innovative social history of that decade (item **2988**). Tirado Mejía's survey of the López Pumarejo regime (1934–38) (item **2984**) is a landmark study—a clear, objective analysis of López's political philosophy, the interactions of political factions, the impact of the Spanish Civil War, and Church-State relationships during his administration.

Innovative and well documented studies of La Violencia are beginning to take their places alongside the polemics and theoretical pieces of earlier decades. Gonzalo Sánchez has led the way with three fine volumes (items **2979, 2980,** and **2981**), the last written in collaboration with Meertens, while Henderson's regional history of La Violencia in Tolima stands as the best introduction in English to this tragic civil war (item **2949**). Two other essays published by the Centro Cultural Jorge Eliécer Gaitán measure the impact of the events of April 9, 1948, on Bogotá and outside Cundinamarca (items **2929** and **2954**). Finally, Urán Rojas's study of Rojas Pinilla's coup of 1953 (item **2987**) and critiques of the Colombian military by former officers (items **2934** and **2989**) underscore a nagging preoccupation with an increasingly powerful military in a civilian-dominated political system.

Ecuadorian historiography lags far behind Colombian, but even here there are encouraging developments. Former President Velasco Ibarra's admiration for Vicente Rocafuerte has resulted in the official publication of his writings—a four volume set that provides much insight into Ecuadorian, Mexican, Cuban, and Gran Colombian history during the early national period (item **3009**). For the later 19th century, Roig's survey of Ecuadorian philosophy (item **3011**), and the publication of the works of Juan León Mera (item **3004**) and Federico González Suárez (item **2999**) throw light on Conservative ideology of the era. Ayala's brilliant essay on the García Moreno regime refurbishes a tired subject (item **2992**). The most significant contributions, however, are two revised Ph.D. dissertations by North Americans that interpret economic developments in the critical years 1890–1925. In *El Ecuador en la época cacaotera* (item **2995**), Crawford de Roberts surveys the impact of the cacao boom on all aspects of society, while Rodríguez in *The search for public policy* argues that the Liberal reforms introduced after 1895 were firmly anchored in 19th-century traditions (item **3010**).

Hopefully, the efforts of Marxist scholars to record the personal accounts of workers involved in the strike of Nov. 15, 1922 (item **2997**) and the events of May 28, 1944 (item **3016**), to chart the evolution of the national labor movement from 1895 to the present (items **3005** and **3018**) and to utilize local archives to trace peasant resistance movements in Azuay and Cañar provinces (item **3017**) mark the dawning of a new age of professional scholarship long lacking in this country. For the contemporary period, Martz's essay on the rise and fall of the Concentración de Fuerzas Populares between 1962–81 enhances understanding of recent Ecuadorian politics and populism throughout Latin America (item **3003**).

COLOMBIA

2927 Alape, Arturo. El Bogotazo: memorias del olvido. 2a ed. La Habana: Casa de las Américas, 1983. 721 p.: bibl., ill.

Oral history of the Bogotazo compiled by a Colombian Marxist. Alape interviewed more than 45 individuals involved in the events of April 1948. Comments from their testimonies are arranged around the themes of "The Voice," "Years of Tension," "April 9, 1:05 P.M.," "The Other Days," "Epilogues." Includes unabridged interview with Fidel Castro about his activities during the Bogotazo. Extensive bibliography. Useful source book.

Alvarez Restrepo, Antonio. Los golpes de estado de Colombia. See *HLAS 47:6331.*

2928 Anrup, Roland. Changing forms of disposition on an Andean estate: an analytical case-study (Economy and Society [Routledge, Kegan & Paul, London] 14:1, 1985, p. 28–54, bibl.)

Swedish scholar proposes concept of "structure of disposition" as a theoretical alternative to the traditional Marxist concepts of relations of production, possession, and separation and then uses proposed conceptual framework to interpret changes of labor systems between 1905–44 on the Aurora coffee estate near Líbano, Tolima.

2929 Aprile Gniset, Jacques. El impacto del 9 de abril sobre el centro de Bogotá. Bogotá: Centro Cultural Jorge Eliécer Gaitán, 1983. 223 p., 7 leaves of plates (some folded): ill.

French architect draws on press accounts, maps, and other archival sources to document, from a Marxist perspective, the impact of the Bogotazo on Bogotá's urban development. Argues that the press exaggerated the extent of destruction at the time, but that damage was sufficient to end the "feudal" phase of urbanization and move into a modern "capitalist" phase dominated by North American influences. Makes some interesting comparisons with impact of the 1870 Comunero Revolt on Paris. Worth reading.

2930 Arango Z., Carlos. Sobrevivientes de las bananeras. Bogotá: Editorial Colombia Nueva, 1981. 120 p.: ports.

Interviews conducted in 1978 with 19 survivors of the Dec. 6, 1928 massacre of banana workers striking against the United Fruit Co. Respondents describe conditions before the strike, developments leading to it, actual massacre, and ensuing events. Fine investigative report which won the 1979 Premio Nacional de Periodismo "Simón Bolívar," and an essential source for scholars concerned with labor relations in the early 20th century.

2931 Arciniegas, Germán. Hace 150 años regresó Santander y la República quedó restaurada (ACH/BHA, 69:738, julio/sept. 1982, p. 605–613)

Commemorates the 150th anniversary of Santander's return to Colombia and restoration of the Republic. Announces that the Academia Colombiana de Historia will dedicate 1982 to these two events and that its first act was to inaugurate in Bogotá the Casa de Santander, a new museum-archive of Santander documents, and meeting place for the Sociedad Santanderista.

2932 Arenas, Emilio. La casa del diablo: los Puyana, tenencia de tierras y acumulación de capital en Santander. Bucaramanga, Colombia: Urbanas, 1982. 168 p., 16 leaves of plates: ill.

Social history of accumulation of land and capital in Santander by the Puyana family (1700–1909). Based on rigorous investigation of archives in Bogotá, Girón, and Bucaramanga. David Puyana Figueroa played a key role in the great initiatives of the late 19th century including the foundation of the first Banco de Santander in 1872 and the Compañía Santandereana de Vapores.

2933 Aspectos polémicos de la historia colombiana del siglo XIX: memoria de un seminario. Bogotá: Fondo Cultural Cafetero, 1983. 230 p.

Verbatim transcript of papers and commentaries presented at week-long seminar sponsored by Fondo Cultural Cafetero, July 1981. Participants were: Darío Bustamante, Germán Colmenares, Malcom Deas, José Escorcia, Jaime Jaramillo, Francisco Leal, Jorge Orlando Melo, José A. Ocampo, Marco Palacios, Frank Safford, Oreste Popescu, and Aída Martínez Carreño. Topics addressed included "Formation of Political Parties in the First Half of the Nineteenth Century," "La Regeneración and the War of a Thousand Days," "Social Conflicts and Coffee Production during the Second Half of the Nineteenth Century," "Economy and Social Classes in the Nineteenth Century," and "Regions and Nations in the Nineteenth Century." Papers provide incisive summaries of the state of historical thinking about each topic while commentaries reveal areas of lively debate and disagreement. Of vital interest to any scholar concerned with the 19th century.

2934 Bermúdez Rossi, Gonzalo. El poder militar en Colombia: de la colonia al Frente Nacional. Bogotá: Ediciones Expresión, 1982. 331 p.: bibl.

History and critique of the role of the armed forces in Colombia by retired major who became a sociology professor in 1975. Emphasizes 1944–80 period. Argues that the Bogotazo, Cuban Revolution, and recurrent guerrilla warfare has brought about increasing militarization of the country which under Julio César Turbay became a *fascistización* of the system. Documented, impassioned, and informative.

2935 Cabrera Ortiz, Wenceslao. San Andrés y Providencia: historia. Bogotá: Editorial Cosmos, 1980. 175 p.: bibl., ill., index.

Straightforward, narrative history of the islands (1510–1952) geared to high school students and tourists but useful as introductory survey. Includes excellent bibliography and index.

2936 Cacua Prada, Antonio. Historia del periodismo colombiano. 2a ed. Bogotá: Ediciones Sua, 1983? 513 p., 66 p. of plates: bibl., ill., indexes.

Encyclopedic survey of Colombian journalism from the 18th century to 1983. First published in 1968 and used as university textbook. In this second edition, author has abridged the colonial section and expanded chapters on the 20th century. Indexed and lavishly illustrated. Useful reference tool.

2937 Colmenares, Germán. Ricardo Rendón, una fuente para la historia de la opinión pública. Bogotá: Fondo Cultural Cafetero, 1984. 295 p.: ill.

Ricardo Rendón (1894–1931) was a distinguished political cartoonist whose work appeared in newspapers throughout the 1920s. Cartoons from *La República*, *El Espectador*, and *El Tiempo* are reproduced and

organized along 10 themes such as "The Treaty of 1914 and Its Consequences" and "The Petroleum Question." Accompanying narration explains context of each cartoon. Handsome edition but lacks a concise biographical sketch of Rendón. Unique and valuable source for understanding politics, society, and public opinion. Highly recommended.

2938 Díaz Piedrahíta, Santiago. Manifiesto de Don José Jerónimo Triana al Congreso de la Confederación Granadina, con comentarios (ACCEFN/R, 15:56, julio 1980, p. 99–107, bibl.)

Triana went to Europe in 1856 to prepare a treatise on Colombian flora under a contract celebrated with the New Granadan government. Learning that the government had cut off his subsidy in 1860, he published the manifesto transcribed here to urge the government to honor its agreement. Documents include Triana's defense of his project and letters of support from European scientists. Minor episode but one that reveals difficulties faced by 19th-century Colombian scientists.

2939 Discursos y mensajes de posesión presidencial. v. 2. Recopilación de Hernán Valencia Benavides. Bogotá: Imprenta Nacional, 1981–1983. 444 p.: bibl. (Col. Presidencia de la República. Administración Turbay Ayala; 7)

Collection of speeches made by 29 chief executives on their accession to the presidency (1904–82). Brief biographical sketch precedes each address. Handy reference tool. For political scientist's comment, see *HLAS 47:6342*.

2940 Durán Pombo, Jaime. Francisco Javier Zaldúa: "jurista y mártir" (ACH/BHA, 69:739, p. 1073–1084)

Undocumented biographical sketch of only Colombian chief executive to die in office. Author argues that Núñez made himself Primer Designado on Zaldúa's election in 1881 against the latter's expressed wishes, and thus succeeded on to the presidency on the old jurist's death on Dec. 21, 1882.

2941 Fals Borda, Orlando. Historia doble de la costa. v. 2, El Presidente Nieto. v. 3, Resistencia en El San Jorge. Fotos de Orlando Fals Borda. Acuarelas de Eduardo Mark. Dibujos de Iván Chalarca. Bogotá: C. Valencia

Editores, 1979–1984. 2 v.: bibl., ill., indexes, maps.

Three-volume history of Atlantic coast presented as two simultaneous approaches: "Canal A" on left-hand pages is anecdotal and atmospheric narrative history addressed to lay reader; "Canal B" on right-hand pages is author's erudite and complex Marxist interpretation of events drawing on vast knowledge of sociological/historical theories as well as primary documents and oral tradition. For vol. 1, see item **2668**. Vol. 2 examines career of Juan José Nieto (1804–66), caudillo of department of Bolívar. Contrasts Nieto with highland contemporaries as variant of the caudillo-anti-caudillo tradition. Compares his career with Adolfo Mier's who represents the popular masses. Provides insight into 19th-century role of Masonry and roots of La Violencia. Vol. 3 is social history of Mompox, Loba, and Jegua from precolumbian times to present. Pt. 1 focuses on colonial and 19th-century Indian, slave and peasant revolts. Pt. 2 deals with impact of capitalism, missionary movements, and liberation theology in the 19th and 20th centuries. Excellent maps and many beautiful illustrations. Ambitious, brilliant work but extremely difficult reading.

2942 Gast Galvis, Augusto. Historia de la fiebre amarilla en Colombia. Bogotá: Ministerio de Salud, Instituto Nacional de Salud, 1982. 95 p., 2 leaves of plates: bibl., ill.

Documents manifestations of yellow fever in Colombia from colonial times to present by region. Author is scientist who has worked for 40 years in eradication campaigns and is presently advisor to Instituto Nacional de Salud. Data is fragmentary but provides useful introduction to important topic.

2943 Gómez, Laureano. Obra selecta. v. 1. Compilación y presentación de Alberto Bermúdez. Bogotá: Cámara de Representantes, 1981. 836 p. (Col. Pensadores políticos colombianos; 15)

Selected writings by Conservative Party leader and President (1950–53). Contains editorials written between 1909–36, political speeches interpreting Conservative doctrine and parliamentary debates spanning 1912–42. Helpful introductory biographical sketch by Alberto Bermúdez. Editors plan a vol. 2 which will include editorials published in *El Siglo*, presidential papers, and letters and messages—especially those written in exile.

2944 Gómez, Laureano. Obra selecta: 1909–1956. Selección, prólogo y notas de Ricardo Ruiz Santos. Bogotá: Senado de la República, 1982. 469 p.

Editorials written between 1909–48, historical articles, critical reviews, funeral orations, public and parliamentary addresses judiciously selected from works by the most controversial Colombian of the 20th century. Enrique Gómez Hurtado's brief preface describes his father as a "lay Jesuit" whose appeal stemmed not from charisma but from his ability to explain his ideas to the people and to command their obedience through "authority."

2945 Gómez Aristizábal, Horacio. Diccionario de la historia de Colombia. Bogotá: Plaza & Janés, 1984. 269 p.: ill.

Hopelessly inadequate attempt to provide a quick reference tool on Colombian history. Geared to elementary school children. Entries appear to have been chosen at random and data is too meager to be helpful. Moreover, in order to foster a strong sense of nationalism, author has deliberately eliminated any information that might be destructive, negative or explosive because "Optimism creates optimists and motivates all initiatives." Best historical dictionary on Colombia is still the one prepared by Robert H. Davis in 1977 (see *HLAS 40:3423*).

2946 Gómez Hoyos, Rafael. Bicentenario del natalicio de Don José Manuel Restrepo, historiador de Colombia (ACH/BHA, 69:737, abril/junio 1982, p. 410–425)

Useful summary of career and writings of José Manuel Restrepo (1781–1863), "father of modern Colombian history," on the bicentennial of his birth. Notes that Bolívar read the *Historia de la Revolución* in five days, and, finding it an objective and brilliant work, criticized only Restrepo's negative portrayal of the role of José Fernández Madrid. Well written but lacking footnotes.

2947 Hartwig, Richard E. Roads to reason: transportation, administration, and rationality in Colombia. Pittsburgh, Pa.: Univ. of Pittsburgh Press, 1983. 276 p.: appendix, index (Pitt Latin American series)

Offers insight into the operation of Colombian politics and bureaucracy in the

20th century through analysis of transportation policies of successive administrations (1920s-1974). Uses case study of routine administrative operations of Ministry of Public Works based on field research and interviews. Difficult reading since author casts his data in a broad philosophical theory of rationality but stimulating nevertheless.

2948 Helg, Aline. Civiliser le peuple et former les élites: l'éducation en Colombia, 1918–1957. Paris: Editions L'Harmattan, 1984. 344 p.: bibl., index, maps, tables.

Revised doctoral dissertation. Analyzes development of all forms of public and private education except universities during first half of 20th century within broader context of Colombian history. Sees little difference between Conservative and Liberal school reforms arguing that they expanded opportunities but reinforced the caste nature of the system. Impressive research based on official documents, school archives, and 60 interviews with education ministers, priests, politicians, and teachers. Offers insight into the role of women in education and pervasive influence of the Catholic Church. Broad ranging social history worth reading.

Henderson, James D. Gaitán from without, or, no cheers for Liberalism. See *HLAS 47:6349.*

2949 Henderson, James D. When Colombia bled. University: Univ. of Alabama Press, 1985. 1 v.: bibl., index.

First regional history of La Violencia. Spurning structural paradigms, author relies on narrative history to trace development of dept. of Tolima from colonial times to 1970s and to chart growth and impact of the violence on this most representative Colombian region. Concludes that violence was a conservatizing force that caused Colombians to shy away from apocalyptic visions of social change. It also dealt a mortal blow to uncritical party allegiance. Highly readable. Excellent review of previous studies of La Violencia. Suitable for undergraduates as well as scholars. Major contribution to understanding Colombia in the 20th century.

2950 Hernández de Alba, Guillermo. Homenaje a la Compañía de María y al Colegio de la Enseñanza con ocasión del segundo centenario de su fundación (ACH/BHA, 70:741, abril/junio 1983, p. 539–546)

Homage by the Decano of the Academia Colombiana de Historia on the bicentennial of the first private female colegio in New Granada (founded 1783) by the French religious order, La Compañía de María. Much rhetorical flourish but little historical evidence.

2951 Hernández de Alba, Guillermo. Sesquicentenario del Colegio Departamental de La Merced (ACH/BHA, 69:737, abril/junio 1982, p. 447–460)

Homage by the Decano of the Academia Colombiana de Historia on the sesquicentennial of "first public female colegio founded on the American continent." The Colegio Departamental de La Merced was opened in Bogotá in 1832 and has been in continuous operation ever since. Lecture draws on primary sources but omits all references.

2952 Historia de la Cancillería de San Carlos. 2a ed. Bogotá: Imprenta Nacional, 1983. 1 v.: ill., index, ports.

Reprint of 1942 edition. Includes essay (88 p.) on evolution of Colombian foreign policy by Luis López de Mesa; a history of the Palacio de San Carlos and list of the 162 men who served as Minister of Foreign Relations (1821–1941) by Alberto Miramon; brief biographies and photographs of 100 of these individuals by Gustavo Otero Muñoz; essay on the definition and demarcation of frontiers by Daniel Ortega Ricaurte, and chronological list of 352 treaties signed by Colombia (1811–1942) with other countries. Cursory, dated, but still useful.

2953 Indalecio Liévano Aguirre: nota bibliográfica (ACH/BHA, 69:737, abril/junio 1982, p. 355–357)

By resolution of the Academia Colombiana de Historia, this issue of *Boletín de Historia y Antigüedades* was dedicated to the memory and historical writings of Indalecio Liévano Aguirre (1917–82). The "Nota Bibliográfica" lists Liévano's political offices, honors, societies to which he belonged, and his published books and articles.

2954 Jaramillo, Carlos Eduardo. Ibagué, conflictos políticos de 1930 al 9 de abril. Bogotá: Centro Cultural Jorge Eliécer Gaitán, 1983. 151 p., 3 p. of plates: bibl., ill.

Fascinating case study of impact of the Bogotazo on Ibagué between April 9–18, based on local archival material and interviews with inhabitants. Demonstrates that despite considerable property destruction, panic did not prevail in the city until after April 18 and that local Liberals in many instances made great efforts to protect Conservatives who were the first targets of mob animosity. Well researched and written. Puts the study of La Violencia on a new level.

2955 Jiménez Llaña-Vezga, Luis Enrique. Florentino Vezga, vida y obra (ACH/ BHA, 69:737, abril/junio 1982, p. 429–437)

Undocumented and uncritical biographical sketch of the Colombian botanist and Liberal politician. Argues that Vezga "was the most brilliant journalist which the country produced."

2956 Keremitsis, Dawn. Latin American women workers in transition: sexual division of the labor force in Mexico and Colombia in the textile industry (AAFH/TAM, 15:4, April 1984, p. 491–504, tables)

Comparison of role of women in the labor force of textile factories in Mexico and Colombia (1830–1975). Shows that women predominated in mills due to their willingness to accept low wages, but as the plants became more capital-intensive they were replaced by men. Promotion of welfare laws and union organization also contributed to the decline of women in the work force. Some discussion of working conditions in the mills and involvement of women in union organization.

2957 LeGrand, Catherine. Colombian transformations: peasants and wage-labourers in the Santa Marta banana zone (JPS, 11:4, July 1984, p. 178–200, bibl.)

Examination of various forms of rural protest directed against the United Fruit Co. (1900–64) based on comprehensive review of Colombian Public Land Archives. Elaborates on earlier studies by stressing role of peasant population and its relation to wage workers on banana plantations. Shows that just as peasants are often transformed into wage laborers through expansion of capitalist agriculture, wage laborers may purposely transform themselves back into peasants. Well written and important.

2958 LeGrand, Catherine. Labor acquisition and social conflict on the Colombian frontier, 1850–1936 (JLAS, 16:1, May 1984, p. 27–49, maps)

Argues that expansion of great estates (1850–1936) was a process by which private entrepreneurs seized large areas of public lands and coerced peasants into occupying those lands either as tenants or workers. Traces peasant resistance movements as response to illegal territorial dispossession. Seminal essay based on exhaustive review of documents held by the Colombian Public Land Archive and survey of earlier secondary works on Colombian economic history. Concludes that 19th- and 20th-century persistence of the Latin American hacienda is not necessarily a colonial heritage but the logical economic response to labor scarcity affecting most areas of export growth.

2959 Lemaitre, Eduardo. El General Juan José Nieto y su época. Bogotá: C. Valencia Editores, 1983. 96 p.: bibl.

Brief, straight-forward biography of Nieto (1804–66) by distinguished historian of Cartagena. Criticizes Fals Borda's interpretation of Nieto as a kind of Biblical patriarch (see item **2941**). Argues that he was a genuine caudillo but one whose human qualities defy the stereotype of tropical tyrants. First and foremost a man of the Liberal Party, Nieto was distinguished by his lofty ideas and ambitions. Good introduction to major protagonist in developments on the northern coast.

2960 El Libro de oro de Santander. Prólogo de Horacio Rodríguez Plata. Bogotá: Plaza & Janés, Editores-Colombia: Academia Colombiana de Historia, 1983. 324 p., 10 leaves of plates: ill., indexes, ports. (Complemento a la Historia extensa de Colombia; 4)

Select documents of and tributes to Santander; former relating primarily to his presidency of New Granada and latter exemplifying latter-day effort to promote "culto a Santander." [D. Bushnell]

2961 Lleras Camargo, Alberto. Memorias. v. 1, Mi gente. Bogotá: División de Publicaciones, Subdirección de Comunicaciones, Instituto Colombiano de Cultura, 1981. 1 v.: bibl. (Col. Autores nacionales; 52)

Vol. 1 of several projected volumes of autobiographical "memorias" of key Liberal leader who was President (1945–46 and 1958–62). Written in 1975 when author was 70 years old. Recounts lives of grandparents in 19th century. There is some insight into author's personality, but scholars looking for information on 20th century politics will have to wait for future volumes.

2962 Lleras Restrepo, Carlos. Crónica de mi propia vida. t. 1–4. Bogotá: Stamato Editores, 1983-. 4 v. (420, 496, 501, 439 p.): bibl., ill., ports.

Vols. 1–4 of planned multi-volume memoir of author's long and illustrious political career. Account begins abruptly without prefacing. Deals only cursorily with author's youth (1908–38) to focus mostly upon Santos Presidency and author's activities as Minister of Hacienda during World War II. Abundantly illustrated with photographs of prominent figures. Index.

2963 Llinás, Juan Pablo. José Hilario López. Bogotá: Ediciones Tercer Mundo, 1983. 257 p.: ill., maps.

Popularly written biography of key 19th-century figure. Based on secondary sources but uses some archival materials. Argues that López was motivated throughout his career by same spirit that animated knights in the tales of chivalry. Text includes helpful illustrations and maps of battle operations.

2964 Mantilla Ruiz, Luis Carlos. Fray Gregorio Arcila Robledo (ACH/BHA, 70:741, abril/junio 1983, p. 391–418)

Biography and assessment of writings of Arcila Robledo (1890–1958) who was pioneer of Franciscan historical studies in Colombia. Also discusses extinction and rebirth of the Order in second half of 19th century. Well written, objective, and incorporates material from Franciscan archives in Rome.

2965 Martínez de Nisser, María. Diario de los sucesos de la revolución en la provincia de Antioquia en los años de 1840–1841. Ed. facsimilar. Bogotá: Incunables, 1983. 82 p.

Facsimile edition of diary of María Martínez de Nisser (1812–72), "la dama soldado" who led a successful counter-revolution in Antioquia in support of the legitimate government of José Ignacio Márquez and against the revolt of Salvador Córdova. More authentic perhaps but also more difficult to read than the version edited by Tisnes (see item **2985**).

2966 Mejía Gutiérrez, Carlos. José Manuel Lobo y Rivera: biografía de un ex-canónigo. Medellín, Colombia: Academia Antioqueña de Historia, 1980. 224 p.: bibl., ill. (Col. Academia Antioqueña de Historia; 37)

Brief biography of controversial Antioquia priest (1813–73) that includes footnotes and draws on some archival sources. Provides insight into Church-State relations in the national period. Author regards Lobo y Rivera as "a flag ever present in the defense of the principles of the Catholic Church."

2967 Mejía Velilla, David. Marceliano Vélez, benemérito de la patria (ACH/BHA, 70:740, enero/marzo 1983, p. 76–108, ill.)

Biographical sketch of Marceliano Vélez (1832–1923), Conservative, five-time governor of Antioquia, member of congress (1860–1919) and twice candidate for president. Laudatory, uncritical but based on some original sources. Synopsis of larger work in progress which author presented to Academia Colombiana de Historia on becoming a corresponding member.

2968 Morales Benítez, Otto. Cátedra caldense. Bogotá: Banco Central Hipotecario, 1984. 124 p.: bibl., index, ports.

Lecture presented by distinguished lawyer-historian on taking possession of a newly created "Caldas Chair" at Univ. Autónoma de Manizales. Reviews historical development of greater Caldas and indicates questions, events and people deserving further investigation.

2969 Morales Benítez, Otto. Liberalismo: destino de la patria. Bogotá: Corporación Editorial Iberoamericana (CEIBA), 1983. 374 p.: bibl., index.

Speeches and essays (1948–82) by prominent Liberal lawyer, writer, politician, and pre-presidential candidate on several occasions. Topics include Uribe Uribe, Olaya Herrera, López Pumarejo, Eduardo Santo, Lleras Restrepo, Gaitán, Gabriel Turbay, and Dario Echandía.

2970 Moreno de Angel, Pilar. Panamá y la revolución de 1885 a través de las cartas del diplomático chileno José Antonio Soffia (ACH/BHA, 69:737, abril/junio 1982, p. 383–408)

Eight unedited dispatches transcribed from originals in Archivo Nacional de Chile that were sent by Soffia to Santiago (April-Dec. 1885). They concern the ongoing revolution in Colombia, burning of port of Colón,

US naval forces' intervention in Panama, imprisonment of Liberal leader Ricardo Gaitán Obeso, and the Constitutional Congress of 1885.

2971 Mount, Graeme S. The Colombian press and the Cold War: 1945–1968 (NS, 8:16, 1983, p. 21–41)

Two Canadian historians survey Colombian daily newspapers (1945–68) to ascertain positions expressed on seven Cold War issues including the 1954 Guatemalan crisis, 1959 Cuban Revolution, and 1965 Dominican crisis. Their data suggests that with the exception of relatively weak left wing publications, Liberal and Conservative newspapers have generally supported official US behavior affecting Colombia and Latin America. Number and identity of periodicals reviewed is not clear. Offers insight into role of the press in contemporary Colombia.

2972 Negrete B., Víctor. Origen de las luchas agrarias en Córdoba. Montería, Colombia: Fundación del Caribe, 1981. 129 p.: bibl., ill.

Former labor organizer traces development of agrarian conflicts in dept. of Córdoba (1844–1970s). Includes brief examination of slavery, impact of foreign investment, invasion of land by colonos at turn of century and development of labor organizations, struggle for land in 1920s and 1930s, disintegration of popular movements by 1950 and impact of La Violencia. Committed rather than scholarly, but still a useful survey of a little studied region.

2973 Obando, José María. Obras selectas: escritos civiles y militares. Prólogo de J. Aurelio Iragorri Hormaza. Compilación de Gerardo Andrade González. Bogotá: Cámara de Representantes, 1982. 385 p.: bibl. (Col. Fundadores. Col. Pensadores políticos colombianos; 1)

Collection of documents spanning the public life of controversial general and president (1825–61). Compiler Gerardo Andrade González argues that these materials reveal Obando as ardent defender of Colombian national territory and firm supporter of civilian rule. Table of contents but no index.

2974 Ocampo López, Javier. Liévano Aguirre y el revisionismo histórico (ACH/BHA, 69:737, abril/junio 1982, p. 358–366)

Incisive assessment of the historical works of Liévano Aguirre, whom author describes as "first Colombian revisionist historian" and dedicated "político historiador" (politician historian).

2975 Ocampo López, Javier. Santander y el civilismo colombiano (ACH/BHA, 69:738, julio/sept. 1982, p. 641–663, bibl.)

Brilliant, well documented essay that traces relationship between Santander's ideas and "civilismo colombiano"—the nationalist doctrine that embraces rule by law and rejects charismatic military force and armed intervention in domestic politics and international conflicts.

2976 Pareja, Reynaldo. Historia de la radio en Colombia, 1929–1980. Bogotá: Servicio Colombiano de Comunicación Social, 1984. 199 p.: bibl., ill.

Penetrating analysis of development of radio transmission in Colombia as faithful reproduction of imported US model tied to country's neocolonial dependency. Makes good use of fragmented sources to trace early history of radio, development of networks after World War II, and control of airways by economic monopolies. Important contribution written as doctoral dissertation for École des hautes études en sciences sociales de Paris. For a history of Venezuela's radio, see item **2905.**

Premo, Daniel L. The Colombian armed forces in search of a mission. See *HLAS 47:6360.*

2977 Restrepo Uribe, Jorge and **Luz Posada de Greiff.** Medellín: su origen, progreso y desarrollo. Medellín, Colombia: Servigráficas, 1981. 655 p.: bibl., ill. (some col.), maps, photos.

Encyclopedic source book generated by celebration of city's tricentennial in 1975. Focuses on 20th-century development of Medellín. Topics range from city's history to public and private enterprises, aviation, Ferrocarril de Antioquia, education, etc. One section contains over 40 city maps (1675–1972). Generous sampling of statistics and photographs. Good place to begin a search for information.

Ridings, Eugene W. Foreign predominance among overseas traders in nineteenth-century Latin America. See item **1868.**

2978 Rodríguez Plata, Horacio. Santander regresa del exilio (ACH/BHA, 69:738, julio/sept. 1982, p. 577–604, ill.)

Draws on Santander's letters to retrace his triumphant return to Bogotá from New York (May-Oct. 1832). Refutes notion that he was greedy because he demanded payment of his back salaries and argues that on his return, Santander was a representative figure of the Romantic Age.

2979 Sánchez G., Gonzalo. Los días de la revolución: gaitanismo y 9 de abril de provincia. Bogotá: Centro Cultural Jorge Eliécer Gaitán, 1983. 329 p.: appendices, bibl.

Studies spread of the Bogotazo to depts. of Cundinamarca, Tolima, Valle, Viejo Caldas, Antioquia, and Santander in 1948. Skillfully incorporates materials from local archives and interviews from participants. Author concludes that April 9, 1948 was for Bogotá "a great frustration" while in the provinces, it was an enormous "experience of struggle"—a double significance which reappears continually in national history. Appendices which comprise half the book, contain valuable documents related to La Violencia. Important contribution.

2980 Sánchez G., Gonzalo. Ensayos de historia social y política del siglo XX. Bogotá: El Ancora Editores, 1985. 275 p.

Collection of three essays dealing with violence in 20th-century Colombia. In "Los Bolcheviques del Líbano" (1976), Sánchez demonstrates that the 1929 revolt in the coffee zone of northwestern Tolima was the first armed insurrection in Latin America in which peasants in alliance with urban sectors tried to take power in the name of socialist ideas. In "Las Ligas Campesinas en Colombia" (1977), he traces rise and fall of peasant organizations in 1920s and 1930s. Finally, in "Raíces Históricas de la Amnistía o las Etapas de la Guerra en Colombia" published here for first time, he analyzes amnesties granted by Rojas Pinilla in 1953 and Lleras Camargo in 1958 within context of history of government-declared amnesties dating back to 1821. Clearly written and well documented, all three essays advance understanding of La Violencia, the agrarian movement, and formation of leftist parties in Colombia.

2981 Sánchez G., Gonzalo and Donny Meertens. Bandoleros, gamonales y campesinos: el caso de La Violencia en Colombia. 3a ed. Bogotá: El Ancora Editores, 1985. 255 p.: bibl., ill.

Uses indictments reposited in judicial archives, in addition to periodicals, oral testimony, and parliamentary debates to analyze stages of banditry spawned by La Violencia. Attention paid to regional differences between key bandit leaders and their ties with the central government, gamonales, hacendados, and campesinos. Incisive interpretation of this tragic era placed within context of theories of social banditry. Tightly written, well researched, and effectively illustrated. Indispensable for students of post-World War II Colombia.

Santa, Eduardo. ¿Qué pasó el 9 de abril?: itinerario de una revolución frustrada. See HLAS 47:6361.

2982 Santander, Francisco de Paula and Vicente Azuero. Antología política. Introducción, selección y bibliografías de Oscar Delgado. Bogotá: Instituto Colombiano de Cultura, División de Publicaciones, 1981. 590 p.: bibls., index (Biblioteca básica colombiana; 45)

Volume offers anthology of writings by Santander and his more doctrinaire Liberal collaborator Vicente Azuero plus a good bit more: various writings about Azuero, an introduction by Delgado setting forth plan of a larger "systematic anthology of liberal political thinking" in Colombia, and quite extensive bibliographies of 19th-century Liberal authors and writings on 19th-century politics. [D. Bushnell]

2983 Sierra García, Jaime. Cronología de Antioquia. S.l.: Depto. de Antioquia, 1982. 339 p.: bibl.

Chronological listing of major events in the history of Antioquia between 1492–1982. Also lists governors of Colombia, alcaldes of Medellín, dates of the founding of all towns in the department, rectors of the university, and periodicals which have been published in the department. Useful reference work.

2984 Tirado Mejía, Alvaro. Aspectos políticos del primer gobierno de Alfonso López Pumarejo, 1934–1938. Bogotá: Procultura: Instituto Colmobiana de Cultura, 1981. 1 v.: bibl.

First systematic analysis of the López regime based on a thorough review of archival materials and interviews with key personalities of the time. Reviews López's political philosophy, the political parties and factions and their ideologies, impact of the Spanish Civil War, relationship between Church and State. Objective, well written. Major contribution in every respect.

2985 Tisnés Jiménez, Roberto María. María Martínez de Nisser y la revolución de los supremos. Bogotá: Banco Popular, 1983. 383 p.: bibl., ill., indexes, ports. (Biblioteca Banco Popular; 111)

In 1841 Doña María Martínez de Nisser (1812–72) led a successful counterrevolution in Antioquia in support of the legitimate government of José Ignacio Márquez and against the revolt led by Salvador Córdova. Two years later she published her diary of the events, the first book written by a Colombian woman. Drawing on primary sources, Tisnés presents a detailed biography of Nisser, whom he regards as the most significant Colombian heroine of the 19th century. Pt. 2 reproduces the diary, introduced and annotated by Tisnés. Interesting, important volume which provides insight into the role of women in 19th-century Latin America as well as the Guerra de los Supremos.

2986 Udall, Alan. Urbanization and rural labor supply: a historical study of Bogotá, Colombia, since 1920 (GIT/SCID, 16:3, 1980, p. 70–83, bibl., graphs, tables)

Economist compares Bogotá's growth in the 1920s and 1930s with its growth after 1958. Concludes that changes in social and economic conditions in the Colombian countryside were more important than is generally believed and that artificially induced increases in urban wages may have played only a secondary role in accelerating urbanization. His thesis is weakened by a fragmentary data base and limited use of historical materials.

2987 Urán Rojas, Carlos H. Rojas y la manipulación del poder. Bogotá: C. Valencia Editores, 1983. 146 p.: bibl.

Political scientist analyzes the Rojas Pinilla regime as an example of a military coup under civilian tutelage. Emphasizes events leading to take over; little analysis of actual policies instituted by Rojas. Careful research which draws heavily on articles

published in *Revista Javeriana*. Probably the best study available on the Rojas regime up to now.

2988 Uribe Celis, Carlos. Los años veinte en Colombia: ideología y cultura. Bogotá: Ediciones Aurora, 1985. 206 p.: appendices, bibl., ill. (Col. Historia de Colombia)

Social history of the 1920s in Colombia which argues that this decade saw the beginning of the 20th century in that country. In concise, well written chapters, sociologist at the Univ. Nacional reviews developments in politics, intellectual thought, education, architecture, painting, science, technology, and popular culture. Places Colombian developments in a global context. Lavish use of illustrations. Narrative is free of jargon and immensely readable. Excellent introduction to all aspects of a Colombian society and culture in transition.

2989 Valencia Tovar, Alvaro. Contribución militar al afianzamiento del civismo constitucional en Colombia (ACH/BHA, 69:739, oct./dic. 1982, p. 893–921, bibl.)

Paper presented by author on becoming a member of the Academia Colombiana de Historia. Routine review of political history from 1810 to present. Chiefly interesting for the insight it offers into the historical viewpoint of a former highly-placed military officer.

ECUADOR

2990 Album didáctico de los sellos postales emitidos por el Estado ecuatoriano, 1865–1982. Quito: Banco Central del Ecuador, 1983. 414 p.: col. ill.

Handsome reproduction of postage stamps printed in Ecuador betewen 1865–1901, 1903–65, and 1965–82. Indexed and arranged in chronological, logical, and aesthetic order. Reproductions of many historical personages. Primarily for philatelists.

2991 Ayala, Enrique. Cacao, capitalismo y revolución liberal (BCE/C, 5:13, mayo/agosto 1982, p. 91–125, tables)

Argues that the Liberal Revolution was all that it could be. Changes that it brought were an enormous leap forward in the historical development of the country but these changes did not exceed limits of real condition and interest of the social class that brought them about. Fine work.

2992 Ayala, Enrique. Gabriel García Moreno
y la gestación del Estado nacional en
Ecuador (BCE/C, 4:10, mayo/agosto 1981,
p. 141–174)

Helpful, clear analysis of the García
Moreno regime based on earlier works by the
author and prepared for seminar on "Dictators and Dictatorships in Latin America"
(CLASCO/UNAM, México, 1980). Argues
that García Moreno tried to combine a
strong, modernizing impulse with a reactionary ideology of ultramontanism and that the
group that benefitted most directly from his
contractory policies was the commercial
bourgeoisie.

2993 Chiriboga, Manuel. Jornaleros y gran
propietarios en 135 años de exportación: cacaotera, 1790–1925. Quito: Centro
de Investigaciones y Estudios Socio-
Económicos, 1980. 435 p.: bibl.

Analysis of the cacao boom (1790–
1925) by French-trained Marxist sociologist.
States that the rise of cacao production
(1885–1912) resulted from internal as well as
external conditions and brought about the
expropriation of peasant lands and the subjugation of the workers. Includes description
of organization of cacao plantations at turn
of the century. Impressive research and extensive bibliography.

2994 Costales, Piedad and **Alfredo Costales.**
Historia de la Casa de Moneda de
Quito: 1534–1863 (EANH/B, 21, 1982,
p. 7–97, appendix)

Deals briefly with Casa de Fundación
y Rescate founded in Quito in 1535, but bulk
of essay concerns activities of the Casa de
Moneda (1831–63). Based on archival sources,
and a 1726 document is reprinted in appendix. Authors show that issues of providing
valid currency and controlling counterfeit
money faced every government and were especially critical in a country with scant gold
and silver mines to exploit.

2995 Crawford de Roberts, Lois. El Ecuador
en la época cacaotera: respuestas
locales al auge y colapso en el ciclo mono-
exportador. Quito: Editorial Universitaria,
1980. 276 p.: bibl.

Spanish translation of revised doctoral
thesis originally written in 1970. Comprehensive analysis of Ecuador during the cacao
boom (1890–1925) based on public and
private archival sources, and personal in-

terviews. Describes political and social developments between the Revolución Liberal
and the Revolución Juliana with emphasis
upon impact of cacao production on national
institutions, internal and external commerce, and coastal society. Reviews efforts of
local sectors to deal with post-World War I
"bust" in the export cycle. Avoids economic
jargon. Significant contribution.

2996 Destruge, Camilo. Historia de la
prensa de Guayaquil. Estudio introductorio, Abel Romeo Castillo. 2a ed. Quito:
Corporación Editora Nacional, 1982. 2 v.:
bibl., ill. (Biblioteca de historia ecuatoriana;
3–4)

New edition of classic work first published in 1924–25. Destruge, who directed
the Biblioteca Municipal de Guayaquil for 17
years, surveys history of printing in Guayaquil (1821–1920) and offers insight into the
city's and republic's political development. Introduction by Abel Romeo Castillo contains
biography of Destruge and assessment of the
value of his book.

2997 Donoso Armas, Manuel et al. El 15
[i.e. quince] de noviembre de 1922 y la
fundación del socialismo relatados por sus
protagonistas. Quito: Corporación Editorial
Nacional: INFOC, 1982. 2 v.: ill. (Col. popular 15 de noviembre; 1–2. Serie Testimonio)

An oral history of the strike of Novem-
ber 15, 1922, in Guayaquil that was brutally
repressed by the government of José Luis
Tamayo. The two volumes contain the transcript of testimonies made by eight former
labor leaders and participants of the strike
who attended a meeting held in December
1980 by the Instituto Nacional de Formación
Obrera y Campesina. In response to questions put to them by Jaime Durán Barba, the
respondents—six of whom are over 80 years
old—recall their role in the strike and comment on the industrial situation of Guayaquil
in 1922 and the development of the Socialist
and Communist Parties in 1926. An introductory essay traces the early history of the
Ecuadorian labor movement. The personal
accounts are vivid. A valuable source for
tracing the history of the workers.

2998 Estrada, Jenny. Personajes y circunstancias: entrevistas y reportajes.
Guayaquil, Ecuador: Casa de la Cultura Ecuatoriana Benjamín Carríon, Núcleo del
Guayas, 1982. 259 p.: ill., ports.

Interviews with 20 notable persons from Ecuador and other countries conducted 1974–80. Most were published originally in the daily, *El Universo* of Guayaquil. Includes interviews with five ex-presidents of Ecuador. Limited value but possible source for contemporary history.

2999 Federico González Suárez: la polémica sobre el Estado laico. Estudio introductorio y selección de Enrique Ayala Mora. Quito: Banco Central del Ecuador: Corporación Editora Nacional, 1980. 516 p.: bibl. (Biblioteca básica del pensamiento ecuatoriano; 4)

Federico González Suárez (1844–1917), Archbishop of Quito, was key Conservative *pensador* of his time and an energetic opponent of the Liberal regime that came to power in 1895. Ayala Mora's introductory essay analyzes conditions which contributed to the development of González Suárez's ideology and motives behind his political-religious writings. A selection of these writings follow including pastoral letters, manifestos and instructions to the clergy—for the most part well known documents but arranged here to make possible an analysis of the Conservative view of the relationship between Church and State which is still found in debates on contemporary Ecuador.

3000 García Velasco, Rafael. El territorio del Ecuador en el siglo XX. Quito: Ministerio de Relaciones Exteriores, 1981. p. 119–208, 2 folded leaves of plates: 2 maps.

Journalist reviews the history of the dispute between Ecuador and Peru over the provinces of Túmbez and Jaén which has dragged on since 1822. Clearly written, impassioned plea that the two countries resolve their differences. Undocumented.

3001 Guerra Bravo, Samuel. Introducción al documento sobre el arrastre de los Alfaro: pts. 1–2 (BCE/C, 4:11, sept./dic. 1981, p. 375–412, bibl.)

In long, philosophical introduction, author reviews 1895–1912 events and argues that Alfaro fell from grace because he was a victim of his own "historical errors" and especially because he was alienated from "the true and authentic course of the history of his people." He then reproduces the unpublished diary of Augusto Egás (1889–1961), an eyewitness to Alfaro's imprisonment and mob murder (Jan. 1912). Extensive bibliography of books dealing with events of 1912.

3002 Lara, Darío. Las cartas a Trinité y el asunto del Protectorado (BCE/C, 5:14, sept./dic. 1982, p. 161–181)

García Moreno wrote three letters in Dec. 1859 to the French chargé d'affaires Emile Trinité (d. April 1860) asking that Ecuador be made a French protectorate. Author reprints letters of his successor, Aime Fabré, to prove that Trinité never communicated García Moreno's request to the French Foreign Minister in Paris. Discussion of documents demonstrates potential value of researching French Foreign Ministry archives for material on Ecuador.

Macías, W. Problemas socioecónomicos del Ecuador. See *HLAS 47:3444.*

3003 Martz, John D. Populist leadership and the party caudillo: Ecuador and the CFP, 1962–81 (GIT/SCID, 18:3, Fall 1983, p. 22–49, bibl., table)

Examination of the rise and fall of the populist party, Concentración de Fuerzas Populares through careers of its three dynamic leaders: Carlos Guevara Moreno, Asaad Bucaram, and Jaime Roldós. In trading CFP's decline after its greatest electoral triumph in 1979, author concludes that Bucaram (d. 1981) may have been the last personification of the populist party caudillo in Ecuador typifying a traditionalist form that is now an artifact of simpler times in the past. Well written and carefully researched. Outstanding contribution to the literature on caudillism, populism, and the history of Ecuador since 1949.

3004 Mera, Juan León. La dictadura y la restauración en la República del Ecuador: ensayo histórico. 2a ed. Estudio introductorio, Rafael Quintero. Quito: Corp. Editorial Nacional, 1982. 278 p.: bibl., port. (Biblioteca de historia ecuatoriana; 2)

Second edition of work first published in 1931. Mera (1832–94) was leading 19th-century Conservative *pensador*. His book is a history of political and military events (1875–83) and civil war between the forces of Ignacio de Veintemilla and "Restauradoras." Excellent introductory essay by Rafael Quintero. Provides insight into 19th-century politics and society.

3005 Muñoz Vicuña, Elías and Leonardo Vicuña Izquierdo. Historia del movimiento obrero del Ecuador: resumen. 3a ed. Guayaquil, Ecuador: Depto. de Publicaciones, Univ. de Guayaquil, 1980. 135 p.: bibl., ill.

Brief outline of development of the workers' movement (1895–1979). Incorporates many statistics from the Ministry of Labor. Concludes that class struggle in Ecuador is intensifying and that in the last 13 years, the unions have made great progress, while throughout the world, imperialism and colonialism are on the defensive.

3006 Ordóñez Zamora, Aurelio V. Eloy Alfaro. Cuenca, Ecuador: Depto. de Difusión Cultural, Univ. de Cuenca, 1983. 363 p.: bibl.

Glowing praise of key Liberal president and general (1842–1912) in the form of an uncritical biography. Based on secondary sources.

3007 Quintero, Rafael and **Erika Silva.** La crisis nacional general de 1895 (BCE/C, 4:11, sept./dic. 1981, p. 93–107)

Paper presented at the 3rd National Congress of Schools and Faculties of Sociology (Machala, 1982). Draws on information presented in earlier work, *El mito de populismo en el Ecuador* (Quito: s.n., 1980). Argues that the revolutionary crisis of 1895 was a regional crisis that eventually divided the country into Coast and Sierra which would characterize the 20th century but had not been an important division before 1895.

3008 Rocafuerte, Vicente. A la nación. Prefacio y posdata de Robert Andrade. Guayaquil, Ecuador: Litografía e Imprenta de la Univ. de Guayaquil, 1983. 283 p. (Col. Univ. de Guayaquil; 3)

While in exile in Peru, Rocafuerte wrote a long protest against the third presidency of Gen. Flores calling on the people to overthrow him and restore national dignity. The work was published in 14 installments (1843–45) and contributed to the defeat of Flores by the national revolution on March 6, 1845. Excellent example of 19th-century polemic, it is reprinted here in its entirety with brief foreword and afterword by Robert Andrade to mark the bicentennial of Rocafuerte's birth.

3009 Rocafuerte, Vicente. Vicente Rocafuerte. Prólogo y notas de Neptalí Zúñiga. Quito: Corp. de Estudios y Publicaciones, 1983. 4 v.: bibl., ill., ports.

Collected works of Rocafuerte (1783–

1847), a major figure in the early national period. Vol. 1: "Rocafuerte Perfiles y Perennidad," "Rocafuerte y la Historia de México," "Rocafuerte y la Democracia de Estados Unidos de Norte América," "Rocafuerte y los Sistemas Políticos de América." Vol. 2: "Rocafuerte y las Ideas Liberales de América Independiente," "Rocafuerte y La Gran Colombia," "Rocafuerte y el Ideario Religioso del Mundo," "Rocafuerte y las Ideas Políticas de México." Vol. 3: "Rocafuerte y las Doctrinas Penales," "Rocafuerte y la República de Cuba," "Rocafuerte y el Periodismo en México," "Rocafuerte y el Periodismo en Inglaterra." Vol. 4: "Rocafuerte: Su Vida Pública en el Ecuador, Documentos," "Rocafuerte y Quince Años de Historia de la República del Ecuador," "Rocafuerte: Documentos Políticos," "Rocafuerte y Su Obra Diplomática en Europa." The breadth of Rocafuerte's writings nurtured by his residence at various times in Spain, France, and Mexico make these handsomely-printed volumes valuable for scholars of other parts of Latin America as well as Ecuador.

3010 Rodríguez, Linda Alexander. The search for public policy: regional politics and government finances in Ecuador, 1830–1940. Berkeley: Univ. of California Press, 1985. 281 p., 8 p. of plates: appendices, bibl., index, ports.

Revised doctoral dissertation that focuses on analysis of financial policies (1895–1925) but also offers excellent overview of Ecuadorian political economy (1830–1930) emphasizing role played by geographic fragmentation and limited natural resources. Argues that reforms introduced by Liberals after 1895 were firmly anchored in 19th-century traditions, differing only in the growth of the revenues. Sources include congressional debates, ministerial reports, laws, newspapers, private papers, and interviews. Impressive array of statistics presented in appendices support trends described in text. Free from jargon and well written. Valuable introduction to Ecuador in the national period.

3011 Roig, Arturo Andrés. Esquemas para una historia de la filosofía ecuatoriana. 2a ed. corr. y aum. Quito: Ediciones de la Univ. Católica, 1982. 195 p.: bibl.

Argentine scholar reviews trends and major figures in Ecuadorian philosophy in six concise, well written essays. Highlighted are key Liberal *pensador* José Peralta (1855–1935) and positivist Belisario Quevedo (1883–1921). Final essay cites growth of interests in Ecuador in this field in the 1970s and lists major recent publications dealing with the history of ideas. Useful introduction to little known topic.

3012 Saint-Geours, Yves. La provincia de Loja en el siglo XIX: desde la Audiencia de Quito al Ecuador independiente (BCE/C, 5 : 15, enero/abril 1983, p. 209–233, tables)

Sketches demographic and economic characteristics of the province of Loja in the 1800s. Preceded by an analysis of repositories and sources for the study of the 19th century in the southernmost province of highland Ecuador. Supplemented by a statistical appendix. [M.T. Hamerly]

3013 Saint-Geours, Yves. La Sierra du Nord et du Centre en Equateur: 1830–1875 (IFEA/B, 13 : 1/2, 1984, p. 1–15, tables)

Argues that after independence wars destroyed the Ecuadorian Andes population and economy, region recuperated slowly over next 45 years. Struggles to control land characterized north central region, but peasants and artisans lost out when successive governments supported the landlords. Agricultural industrialization began while traditional smallholder activities gave way to ranching. García Moreno's government tried (1859–75) to join the region to the national economy by way of organizing a national State. Uses French Foreign Ministry, commercial and consular reports, Ecuadorian Ministry of Finance, and executive branch sources. [V. Peloso]

3014 Santos Rodríguez, José. Eloy Alfaro: su personalidad multifacética y revolución liberal. Guayaquil, Ecuador: Litografía e Imprenta de la Univ. de Guayaquil, 1983. 99 p., 4 leaves of plates: ill.

Undocumented homage to Eloy Alfaro which describes him as the Ecuadorian equivalent of José Martí, Benito Juárez, Domingo F. Sarmiento, and Abraham Lincoln.

Uzcátegui, Emilio. La educación ecuatoriana en el siglo del liberalismo. See *HLAS 47 : 4428.*

Uzcátegui, Emilio. La educación en el Ecuador, 1830–1980. See *HLAS 47 : 4429.*

3015 Vargas, José María. Historia de la Provincia Dominicana del Ecuador en el siglo XIX. Quito: Editora Royal, 1982. 300 p., 8 leaves of plates: bibl., ports.

Pedestrian history (1804–1906) based on convent archives but largely undocumented. Author maintains that reforms instituted by Pope Pius IV in 1850 saved the Order from extinction in Ecuador and paved the way for a rennaisance. Primarily a review of dates and personalities. Forthcoming volumes will cover the colonial period and the 20th century.

3016 El 28 [i.e. Veintiocho] de mayo de 1944: testimonio. Guayaquil, Ecuador: Litografía e Imprenta de la Univ. de Guayaquil, 1984. 271 p.: ill. (Col. Univ. de Guayaquil; 8)

Accounts by 19 men and women who participated in the events of May 28, 1944, when popular protests unseated President Arroyo del Río and brought Velasco Ibarra into power. The Univ. de Guayaquil solicited statements to mark the 40th anniversary of the overthrow. Memoirs are short, varied and interesting, but it would be helpful to have some biographical information about each respondent.

3017 Vintimilla, María Augusta et al. Ensayos sobre historia regional: la región centro sur. Cuenca, Ecuador: Instituto de Investigaciones Sociales, Univ. de Cuenca: Casa de la Cultura Ecuatoriana, Núcleo del Azuay, 1982. 309 p.: bibl., ill.

Six thoughtful, well researched papers presented by scholars associated with the Instituto de Investigaciones Sociales, Univ. de Cuenca, at Tercer Encuentro de Historia y Realidad Económica y Social del Ecuador (Nov. 1980). Three deal with national era topics: María Augusta Vintimilla "Las Formas de Resistencia Campesina en la Sierra Sur del Ecuador," Iván González and Paciente Vázquez "Movilizaciones Campesinas en Azuay y Cañar durante el Siglo XIX," and Adrian Carrasco and Claudio Cordero "Testimonio de la Transición de una Sociedad Patriarcal a la Sociedad Burguesa en Cuenca: 'La Escoba'." All focus on developments in the "Sierra Sur," the modern provinces of Azuay and Cañar, use Marxist constructs, and draw on materials from archives in Cuenca.

3018 Ycaza, Patricio. Historia del movimiento obrero ecuatoriano: de su génesis al Frente Popular. 2a ed. rev. Quito: Centro de Documentación e Información de los Movimientos Sociales del Ecuador, 1984. 371 p.: bibl., ill. (Col. Análisis histórico; 1)

Well documented history of the labor movement by Marxist professor. Includes chapters on formation of workers' organiza-

tions at the turn of the 19th century, first workers' congresses, and development of the Socialist Party up to the 1920s. Extensive bibliography. Second edition but no date is mentioned for the original study.

PERU

VINCENT C. PELOSO, *Associate Professor of History, Howard University*

THE LIST OF RECENT WORKS on republican Peru contains a healthy mix of hoary themes and fresh ideas. There are no surprises in the standard elements of Peruvian historiography. No biennium has ever gone by without at least one study of the War of the Pacific, and this one is no different. The Mariátegui problem has taken on the seductive proportions of a legend and is well represented. APRA, the Church and indigenismo join these elements in the pantheon of time-worn subjects. At one time or another every historian of Peru will have written on these topics in the realms of military and intellectual history as a mark of entry into the guild. Less established—though no less important—are studies of the State, the regions, women, the economy, and democracy. The latter often are related to established subjects, but it is interesting to see that they are gaining independent attention in recent major studies.

Works on intellectual history combine the old and the new in Peruvian historiography. They usually take one of four forms. Some are biographical studies of José Carlos Mariátegui, others try to link a party's program to Mariátegui's ideas. A third genre studies Haya, and yet another focuses on the impact of Aprista ideas on politics. The article by Chang-Rodríguez (item **3029**) stands out among the studies that impute meaning to the essays of the persuasive, short-lived Mariátegui. Meanwhile, Frederick Pike (item **3070**) provides a brilliant explication of political ideas in Peru through an intellectual biography of Haya, a work that constitutes a genuine *tour de force* in Latin American history. Its special merit is that Pike gathers together within his purview so many bits of 20th-century Peruvian history and at the same time raises for our inspection a profound vision of recent Peruvian culture.

Within the realm of intellectual history falls also the work of José Tamayo Herrera, whose study of the indigenista movement in the Puno altiplano early in this century (item **3076**) provides further evidence of the social importance of this phenomenon for understanding the mainstream quality of Andean thought. Whether the most attractive refrain of indigenismo coincided with the success of APRA, the socialists, or the Communist Party is not yet clear. It may not have been any one of them alone. If, on the other hand, Andean nativism in its myriad forms turns out to be the strongest political force for creating a popular consensus in 20th-century Peru, then its strength may outdistance the promises made by all of the political tendencies together that currently vie for hegemony in the country.

Part of the confusion that hovers over the politics of indigenismo lies with the competing claims of varied interests. Two of them ignite much of the argument. One cluster of issues surrounds the relationship between Haya and Mariátegui in the 1920s, particularly between 1924 when Haya announced the formation of APRA from Mexico, and 1930 when Mariátegui died. A similar knot of problems criticizes the appropriateness of the APRA ideology for the creation of national solidarity. In this context, the publication of the memoirs of an aged peasant leader, Juan Pévez (item **3069**), whose commitment to the struggles of the rural and urban poor against their oppressors reaches back to his childhood days in the Parcona strikes before 1920. His testimony offers illuminating evidence of the usefulness of Marxist ideas in popular struggles. Most noteworthy among studies that explore popular movements is the effort of Deustua and Rénique (item **3035**) to trace the connection between intellectual elites in Cuzco and Arequipa and the rise of a popular, nativist political interest that acted as support for the Sánchez Cerro uprising in 1932.

Studies of Church activism bring in another important dimension of popular culture than links this ill-defined topic to intellectual history. Scholars like Klaiber (item **3050**) argue that the Church is the institution that mediates between the twin realms of culture and politics and gives radical thought and action in Peru their particular character. Indeed, Klaiber receives strong support for the argument that the Church long has had two faces from Jordan García (item **3049**), who views the Church as quite wary of the increasingly liberal state as the 19th century drew to a close, and from Jacobsen (item **3048**), who displays detailed evidence of Church economic activity that generated primitive capital accumulation in Puno. Jacobsen argues strongly against the standard view that the Church impeded economic progress in the Andes after the republic was founded.

The study of Peru's regions is attracting scholarly attention. Study of the Puno-Arequipa altiplano, perhaps the cradle of Andean culture, is difficult but the results can be powerful. Yet other regions are attracting local studies that signal caution to hasty efforts to capture the essence of Peru. Michael Gonzales (item **3042**) published an admirably detailed study of the social process of capital accumulation on the north coast, while Long and Roberts (item **3054**), with much less attention to documentary detail and a somewhat broader, sociological perspective, examine the dynamics of capitalism in the Mantaro region after the second world war. Gonzales's study suggests the value of the plantation documents in the Archivo del Fuero Agrario for revealing how labor mobilization on the large coastal export estates unleashed traditional forces before the turn of the 20th century. Long and Roberts combine archival materials with contemporary interviews to study the effects of internal migration after 1945. Perhaps the most impressive study of the formation of Peruvian society in the past century, in addition to those cited, is that of Jorge Grieve M. (item **3043**), where he argues that technological development in the 19th century was far more advanced in Peru before 1879 than heretofore has been understood.

It would not be fair to close this survey without mentioning the work of two historians whose impact on Peruvian studies is growing at a geometric rate. Magnus Mörner's sponsorship of an ongoing team study (item **3061**) of movements in land ownership in the Cuzco region is an enormous undertaking whose contribution is only beginning to be felt. The impact of the acerbic, brilliant Pablo Macera (item **3056**) upon the imaginations of Peruvians and Peruvianists alike serves as a healthy antidote to utopianism. The projection into the future that he exhorts Peruvianists to illuminate is one that will further reveal the unique character of Peruvian culture. On the less enthusiastic note, Mallon (item **3057**) reminds us that a number of areas continue to be ignored: women and family history have had far too few protagonists in Peruvian studies. Many economic themes remain unexplored, while the work of Lewis Taylor on capitalism in Cajamarca (item 3077) makes it worthwhile to repeat that important developments in numerous other regions continue to go unnoticed by students of history. Perhaps the new challenges regionalism brings to an understanding of the democratic movement itself, will stir the interest of this energetic group of fine historians.

3019 Angotti, Thomas. The contributions of José Carlos Mariátegui to revolutionary theory (LAP, 13:2[49], Spring 1986, p. 33–57)

Argues that recent studies of Mariátegui have taken his work and its meaning out of their historical context, a period in which an intense worldwide effort was underway to establish theoretical guidelines for building national independence and socialism, and during which there was a search for conscious leadership for achieving them. Careful consideration and evaluation of the thought of this leading Latin American thinker.

3020 Arce, Elmer. Comunidades campesinas y política del Estado: década del 70 (SP, 12, dic. 1980, p. 81–96, bibl., tables)

Examines the Peruvian government's legal perspective in the 1970s on rights and responsibilities of peasant communities. Refers to the 1969 Agrarian Reform Law and marshals evidence to show that the government consciously and aggressively prevented communities from participating effectively in the agrarian reform process even while it carried out reforms. Based on author's 1975 *licenciado* thesis at the Univ. Católica.

3021 Bonilla, Heraclio. La unidad y diversidad del área andina a través de su proceso de formación y segmentación (*in* Unité et diversité de l'Amérique latine. Bordeaux, France: Univ. de Bordeaux III, 1982, t. 1, p. 329–346)

Argues that a better understanding of the history of Andean countries can be achieved by looking at the historical dynamics of the region as a whole. Raises general questions about its economic and social structures within that framework, singling out the juncture of class, ethnic, and national consciousness as the axial problem for further research in the Andes.

3022 Brass, Tom. Permanent transition or permanent revolution: peasants, proletarians, and politics (JPS, 11:3, April 1984, p. 108–117, bibl., ill.)

Review article. Argues that lack of definition of concepts and theories, plus far too much generalizing of views presented in a study that evaluates Marxist debates on agrarian transition, does little to advance debate on the issue. Discussion ranges across Asia, Africa, and Latin America. Illustrated largely with reference to post-World War II conditions.

3023 Carlessi, Carolina. Mujeres en el origen del movimiento sindical: crónica de una lucha, Huacho, 1916–1917. Lima: Lilith: Tarea, 1984. 188 p., 8 leaves of plates: bibl., facsims., ill. (Col. Peruanicemos el Perú)

Study of massive strikes that paralyzed production and commerce in Huacho in 1916 and 1917, this work seeks to correct general ignorance of those events in standard histories. Based upon interviews with participants, local documentation, newspaper accounts and government records, it assesses activities of the region's women who dominated marketing and supported the plantation workers' demands, thus helping to spread strikes through other sectors of the population. Unfortunately, loose binding, poor printing, and low quality will make this work difficult to use and even to find. All too brief an account.

3024 Carlín Arce, Jorge. Historia general del Departamento de Tumbes: un compendio. Lima: Talleres de la Imprenta, Ministerio de Guerra, 1984. 170 p.: bibl., index.

One-volume synthesis of three-volume narrative local history of this northern department. Final two-thirds is devoted to survey of the impact of major national events on local affairs. Ends with brief discussion of government actions in the area after the torrential rains and floods of 1982.

3025 Carpio Muñoz, Juan Guillermo. Texao: Arequipa y Mostajo; la historia de un pueblo y de un hombre. Arequipa, Perú: El Autor, 1982?-1983. 4 v.: bibl., ill.

Account of Francisco Mostajo Miranda's life set in the context of political efforts to shift the basis of power in Arequipa (1868–1955). Mostajo (1874 -1953), a leading lawyer, journalist, and historian in early 20th-century Peru, wrote influential essays on agrarian labor and served in the national congress for years. These four volumes include myths, anecdotes, chronologies, photos, reprints of broadsides and manifestos, poetry, etc., reflecting Mostajo's life. Interesting compilation marred by whimsical organization. Arequipa and Arequipeños in the Chilean war receive much attention. Vol. 4 includes list of Mostajo's writings, bibliography, and list of photo titles.

3026 Castro de Mendoza, Mario. La Marina Mercante en la República, 1821–1968. Lima: Talleres de Arte Gráficas Martínez, 1980. 2 v.: ill., maps.

Takes chronological, government-by-government approach to rise of a State-sponsored, commercial fleet in Peru. Some attention to economic consequences: commercial regulations of 1852 and 1864, construction of docks at Callao and important commercial treaties. Despite detailed information, both volumes lack precise documentation and needed analysis. Vol. 1 runs to 1876. Vol. 2 surveys nearly 100 years of government activity in this field from War of the Pacific through the first Belaúnde administration. Numerous tables throughout on movement of Peru's coastal fleet.

3027 Cayo Córdoba, Percy *et al.* En torno a la Guerra del Pacífico. Lima: Pontificia Univ. Católica del Perú, Fondo Editorial: Pedidos, Oficina de Publicaciones, 1983. 168 p., 24 p. of plates: bibl., ill.

Compelling essays on social history of the country on the eve of war with Chile. Includes interpretative studies of military attitudes, generational content of population, architecture, social groups and social tensions, educational development, and the Church on the eve of the war. Largely based on newspapers and published accounts.

3028 Chambi, Martín. Martín Chambi: fotografía del Perú, 1920–1950. Textos de Sara Facio y José de Riva Agüero. Buenos Aires: La Azotea, 1985. 69 p.: chiefly ill., ports.

Perhaps the first Peruvian photographer to achieve international status for his work, Martín Chambi (b. Puno) became an English photographer's apprentice and later worked in Arequipa. Between 1920–50, from his Cuzco shop, he photographed Peru and Peruvians and participated in exhibitions. Thereafter his national and international reputation grew. This album, a representative collection of b/w photos from his work, provides excellent classroom illustrations of mid-20th-century Andean themes. Volume is part of monographic series on Latin American photographers.

3029 Chang-Rodríguez, Eugenio. El indigenismo peruano y Mariátegui (IILI/RI, 50:127, abril/junio 1984, p. 367–393)

Employs the writings of Mariátegui, contemporary essays and analyses, and recent studies to argue that Mariátegui's views on race in Andean society were informed by an indigenous brand of socialism. Argues that thus he rejected the Communist International Congress's view in 1929 that socialism should promote the formation of Quechua and Aymara states.

3030 Chang-Rodríguez, Eugenio. Opciones políticas peruanas, 1985. Lima: Centro de Documentación Andina, 1985. 466 p.: ill.

Volume of historical program notes for the 1986 presidential campaign. Chaps. 1–2 set out the republic's historical problems, and chap. 3 reminds readers of the protest tradition symbolized by Manuel González Prada and anarchism that arose against the oligarchy. Nine following chapters cover political perspectives and groups contending for power in the 1986 political process, including Sendero Luminoso. Chapters discuss historical growth of parties or movements, and well-known past and contemporary leaders. Most attention is devoted to APRA. Other chapters cover Mariátegui and the socialist content of his legacy, *velasquismo*, Communist parties, Trotskyist tendencies, Izquierda Unida, and Popular Action. Handy introduction to recent politics in historical perspective.

3031 Chirinos Soto, Enrique. Historia de la República: 1821-Perú-1982. 2a ed. Lima: Editorial Minerva, 1982. 671 p.: bibl.

New edition of well known patriotic survey. Entire chapter devoted to Nicolás de Piérola, none to Cáceres, hardly mentions Mariátegui and calls period 1956–68 "a democratic intermezzo." Brings coverage of events down through 1980–81 presidential and municipal elections and briefly discusses problem of inflation. Useful bibliography.

3032 Cotler, Julio. La formación del Estado
en los países andinos (*in* Unité et diversité de l'Amérique latine. Bordeaux,
France: Univ. de Bordeaux III, 1982, t. 1,
p. 347–366)

Surveys social dynamics of formation
of a republican state based on wide disparities between the law and activities of
popular sectors of society in the Andes.
Applies model to evolution of Andean
oligarchic liberal states and suggests how
they survived crises of economic growth. Attributes their survival, especially in the
1930s, not to a crisis of hegemony but to
lack of hegemonic leadership. Conceptual essay that addresses a growing debate over nature of 20th-century ruling class in the
Andean countries.

Cruz, Antonio and **Neptalí Carpio.** Movimiento universitario en el Perú: 1909–1980.
See *HLAS 47:4490.*

3033 Cuadros Silva-Santisteban, Gustavo.
Apuntes sobre Alfonso Ugarte. Arequipa, Perú: Librería Studium, 1982. 81 p.:
bibl., ill.

Brief but illuminating essay based on
research in the Lima's AGN and published
studies that speculates on mysteries obscuring activities of this Chilean war nitrate
baron/landlord who fought as an officer and
died at the Battle of El Moro in 1880.

3034 Cuche, Denys. Pérou negre: les descendants d'esclaves africains du
Pérou; des grandes domaines esclavagistes
aux plantations modernes. Paris: Editions
L'Harmattan, 1981. 192 p.: bibl. (Col. Alternatives paysannes)

French version of 1975 book (see
HLAS 38:3460). Impressionistic work largely
based on Roger Bastide's anthropological
theories. Most consistently used sources for
data on Peru's blacks are works by M.A.
Fuentes and other mid and late 19th-century
Peruvian intellectuals. Contains sections on
race mixture, discrimination, sexual conflict,
the family, rebellion, religion, and cultural resistance. This edition appends chapter on impact upon blacks of 1969 agrarian reform
processes.

3035 Deustua, José and **José Luis Rénique.**
Intelectuales, indigenismo y descentralismo en el Perú, 1897–1931. Cusco, Perú:
Centro de Estudios Rurales Andinos Bar-

tolomé de Las Casas, 1984. 134 p.: bibl., map,
tables (Debates andinos; 4)

Study of political and intellectual
combinations of early 20th century that
rested the political power of democracy on
the strengthening of regional educational and
cultural movements, particularly that of *indigenismo*, in the Andes. Highlights importance of Cusco intellectuals in the movement
and the relationship between the movement
and peasant uprisings around Cusco after
World War I. Concludes that regional, cultural, and political power was irreparably
damaged when the movement was abandoned
by Luis Sánchez Cerro in 1931. Important
contribution to history of democratic social
and political movements in Peru.

3036 Duarte, Luis Milón. Exposición que
dirije el Coronel Duarte a los hombres
de bien: con revelaciones importantísimas
sobre la ocupación enemiga, de 1879 a 1884.
Cajamarca, Perú: s.n., 1983. 64 p.

Mimeo publication of document from
War of the Pacific. Consists of explanation of
military actions conducted during the guerrilla campaign by Col. Luis Milón Duarte of
Cajamarca, assassinated the year after the
war ended.

3037 Fernández Llerena, Raúl. Arequipa, la
jornada de las 8 horas, la primera
huelga general. Arequipa, Perú: s.n., 1983. 2,
93 p.: bibl.

Based on documents from Arequipa's
municipal archive and library, plus the period's newspapers. Shows efforts among
Arequipa provincial artisans and workers to
form a united labor movement (1918–19) in
the face of a lengthened workday and reduced
pay for regional transport workers. The movement spread to include demands for cheaper
food and greater political liberty for the
working class, eventually turning into a general strike. The study is marred by failing to
indicate sources in a standard form and by
poor mimeographing.

3038 Fernández Llerena, Raúl. Los orígenes
del movimiento obrero en Arequipa: el
Partido Liberal y el 1° de mayo de 1906.
Arequipa, Perú: Amauta: Tarea, 1984. 271 p.,
7 leaves of plates: bibl., ill., ports. (Col.
Peruanicemos al Perú)

Study of electoral struggles of national, democratic, and socialist middle class
elites and their allies among workers in the

first half dozen years of this century in Arequipa. Suggests that the movement cast a wide net among artisans and intellectuals, women as well as men. Uses sociological rather than historical approach and is quick to theorize on the basis of scarce information. Devotes little attention to recent studies of the subject but includes documentation from important newspapers, municipal library, and departmental archives.

3039 Ferrari, Américo. El concepto de indio y la cuestión racial en el Perú en los *Siete ensayos* de José Carlos Mariátegui (IILI/RI, 50:127, abril/junio 1984, p. 395–409)

Sets Mariátegui's comments on the "Indian problem" in the context of rising race consciousness among early 20th-century Latin American thinkers and points out that the Peruvian thinker presented three different views of "the Indian." Views the problem from within the era's indigenista movement and compares Mariátegui to his contemporaries.

3040 Franco, Carlos. En relación con el ocaso del poder oligárquico (SP, 4, sept. 1978, p. 107–128)

Critically analyzes major work by Henry Pease on the "twilight of the oligarchs," discussing Pease's use of the concept of political space, his periodization of the Velasco era (1968–75), and his use of the term "tendencies." Pease's approach overemphasizes divisions between military "missionaries" and "progressives" within the regime as well as social sectors rotating around them. Discusses limitations of this perspective and suggests that Pease's sources of information during that period gave evidence contrary to his conclusions. Intended to reopen debate on the Velasco era.

3041 Gilbert, Dennis. The end of the Peruvian revolution: a class analysis (GIT/SCID, 15:1, 1980, p. 15–38, bibl., tables)

Despite the 1968–74 military, the degeneration of economic conditions resulted from contradictions inherent in the State's development program, particularly intensifying local capital's power. Even under Velasco domestic prices rose and public protest was suppressed by the military "populist" government. Gilbert faults the development model followed by Velasco and his successor, F. Morales Bermúdez, who favored local and international capital at the expense of domestic and working class needs. Though some privileged working-class and middle-class elements benefitted from expansion of the State's actions and import substitution industrial policy, the class orientation of the military was toward the metropolitan oligarchy. Peru's technological dependence increased in the 1970s, as did dependence on external financing of development.

3042 Gonzales, Michael J. Plantation agriculture and social control in northern Peru, 1875–1933. Austin: Univ. of Texas Press, 1985. 235 p.: index, maps, tables (Institute of Latin American Studies. Latin American monographs; 62)

Study of north coast plantation carefully examines problem of organization and control of agricultural labor by plantation owners in critical era of transition from old to new forms of plantation commerce. Divided into two sections: 1) studies problems faced by owners in use of capital, land and technological improvements without cost guidelines (1860–1933); and 2) discusses and evaluates impact of capitalization process on the labor force at Hacienda Cayaltí owned by the Aspíllaga family. Contains important insights into early attempts at hiring, rejection and manipulation of Chinese workers and their culture by owners, and especially useful examination of labor recruitment known as *enganche*. First major historical work published in English based upon voluminous documentation of Lima's Archivo del Fuero Agrario.

3043 Grieve M., Jorge. El desarrollo de las industrias mecánicas en el Perú entre 1800 y 1880 (PMNH/HC, 15, 1982, p. 23–68, graphs, tables)

Examines with care and clarity 18th-century origins and 19th-century development of industrial mechanization in Peru: application of steam engine to silver mining through independence wars, largely fostered by English engineers and merchants; railway development to the central Andes; steam engine spread to coastal plantations; etc. Discusses William Wheelwright's role in organizing Peruvian steam navigation, which lowered transport costs sufficiently to drive mining expansion. Challenging, convincing reexamination of major trends in the Peruvian economy before the War of the Pacific.

3044 Hampe M., Teodoro. José A. de la
Puente Candamo en la historiografía
peruana (IRA/B, 12, 1982/1983, p. 147–163)
Summary of data on the life of one of
Peru's best known historians. Shows his intellectual formation and influence in fostering historical studies of the republic. The
best of his work is to be found in his teachings at the Instituto Riva Agüero's Seminario
de Historia as well as through theses on the
origins of independence and the formation of
a Peruvian nation.

3045 Haya de la Torre, Víctor Raúl. Haya de
la Torre en 40 reportajes: prédica en el
desierto? Lima: Okura Editores, 1983. 444 p.:
ill., ports.
Series of interviews and newspaper articles that appeared largely outside Peru
(1922–78), only one of which is included in
the subject's "complete" works. Includes
some fascinating remarks made during the
1960s-70s on Cuba, Chile, and the military
regime of Peru, revealing Haya's conception of
democracy.

**3046 Haya de la Torre, Víctor Raúl and Luis
Alberto Sánchez.** Correspondencia. t.
1, 1924–1951. t. 2, 1952–1976. Lima: Mosca
Azul Editores, 1982. 2 v.: indexes.
Chronological arrangement of letters
includes final list of pseudonyms and other
necessary labels, a very valuable index of
names, and a general index. Vol. 1: correspondence from Haya to Luis Alberto Sánchez
(1924–51); vol. 2: Haya's travels, maturing
views, and inflexible anti-Soviet convictions
(1952–76). Sampling of original correspondence found in Pennsylvania State Univ. collection of the Luis Alberto Sánchez Archive.

3047 Holguín Callo, Oswaldo. Política y
literatura en un impreso limeño de
1876 (IRA/B, 12, 1982/1983, p. 217–250)
Discusses political poetry that emerged
in years preceding the Chilean war. Peruvian
intellectuals were encouraged to write such
works by Dionisio Derteano, wealthy landlord-merchant, banker and an associate of
Dreyfus Co., Banco Nacional de Perú, and national saltpeter monopoly. Analyzes the poetry's political content as it appeared in *La
Patria*. Footnotes include helpful biographical data on 19th-century figures.

3048 Jacobsen, Nils. Las propiedades rurales
de la Iglesia en Azángaro entre 1825 y
1920 (FENIX, 28/29, 1978/1979, p. 151–159,
tables)
Demonstrates that the Church was
major land and cattle holder in Azángaro in
1831 and, in contrast to other areas of Peru,
did not give its holdings up to the State. Nor
did it leave land unrented and fallow, but
rather stimulated the cattle industry, renting
mostly to locals. Concludes that as property
owner the Church in Azángaro was not an
impediment to economic progress as contemporary analysts charged. Effectively brings to
light important 19th-century provincial archive materials from Azángaro and Puno.

3049 Jordán García, Pilar. ¿Poder eclesiástico frente a poder civil?: algunas
reflexiones sobre la Iglesia peruana ante la
formación del Estado moderno, 1808–1860
(UB/BA, 26:34, 1984, p. 45–74)
Church's activities from late 18th century to mid-19th, especially the Church's
role in maintaining social and economic
equilibrium in Peru, a factor in the late onset
of capitalism after mid-19th century. Uses
documents from AGN, BN, and Archepiscopal Archives of Lima to illustrate high priority the Church placed on maintaining its
ecclesiastical independence and property in
the formation of republican legal codes. Only
when the State succumbed to pressures to
free land did the Church feel threatened by
socially powerful sectors of society. Presents
important angle on economic and social
change in first century of independence.

3050 Klaiber, Jeffrey L. The Catholic lay
movement in Peru: 1867–1959 (AAFH/
TAM, 40:2, Oct. 1983, p. 149–170)
Argues that changes in Peruvian
Church history since Vatican II can best be
understood in light of lay reformist impetus
with origins in the late 19th century and culminating in the 1930s Catholic Action movement. Surveys involvement of intellectuals
and students in various lay organizations in
early 20th century, and then focuses on organizational structure and activities of the
Catholic Action movement, suggesting that
upper-class dominance of lay Church can be
attributed to APRA's success among lower
classes.

3051 Kruijt, Dirk and Menno Vellinga. Estado, clase obrera y empresa transnacional: el caso de la minería peruana,
1900–1980. Traducción de Sandra Vallenas.

México: Siglo Veintiuno Editores, 1983.
287 p.: ill. (Sociología y política)

History of Cerro Corp. activities in
central Peru until 1974 when it was na-
tionalized, including analysis of the proletarianization of the miners. Also examines
internal structure of unions and brings all of
that to bear on a review of strikes of every
type over the course of the 20th century.
They note the State's intervention throughout and conclude that the labor movement
was hampered in its initiatives by late industrialization. Authors caution about translation (i.e., from Dutch to English to Spanish).

3052 Lausent, I. Constitution et processus
d'integration socioéconomique d'une
micro-colonie chinoise dans une commu-
nauté andine à la fin du XIXe siècle: Acos,
vallée de Chancay, Pérou (IFEA/B, 9:3/4,
1980, p. 85–106, bibl., tables)

Analyzes baptism and marriage rec-
ords of Huaral parish archive in search of patterns of integration of "second wave" of
Chinese immigrants to Peru. Mostly merchants attracted by petty capital opportunities, especially near large railway and mining
development projects. In Acos (ca. 350 inhabitants) in Andean sector of Chancay valley, Chinese settlers struck a bargain with
local powerful landholding villagers, trading
opportunities for marketing local products in
chinganas and restaurants in return for inter-
marriage. Illustrated effectively with genealogical analysis. Unusual and important
study.

3053 Lecaros Villavisencio, Fernando. El
joven Basadre. Lima: Ediciones Rikchay
Perú, 1983. 109 p.: bibl., ill., photos, ports.
(Rikchay Perú; 13)

Essay in homage to late dean of Peruvian history, consists of extended introductory essay outlining appearance of Basadre's
major book-length publications. Also includes brief discussion of shorter, youthful
works published before 1931, and bibliography of publications up to 1931. More a
study of historiography than biography. Interesting photos.

3054 Long, Norman and **Bryan R. Roberts.**
Miners, peasants, and entrepreneurs:
regional development in the central highlands of Peru. Cambridge, England: Cambridge Univ. Press, 1984. 288 p.: bibl., index,
maps, tables (Cambridge Latin American
studies; 48)

Focuses on economic activity in Mantaro region since 1945 and amplifies earlier
volume (see *HLAS 42:3105*). Discusses rise
of regional elite that fought centralizing authority of coastal bourgeoisie. In the wake of
the internationalization of the mines came
labor migration and village reliance upon
kinship and informal labor ties linking
villages to regional associations in Lima.
Asserts that regionalism in this form undermined classical dependency.

3055 López Martínez, Héctor. Piérola y la
defensa de Lima: con testimonios
sobre las jornadas del 13 y 15 de enero de
1881. Lima?: Editorial Ausonia Talleres
Gráficos, 1981. 202 p., 1 leaf of plates:
bibl., port.

Reviews President Piérola's efforts to
prepare defense of capital in 1880, reviews
his leadership and presents Piérola's "black
legend:" that he poorly planned city's defense
and fled under pressure. Eyewitness account
by writer-industrialist Alberto Ulloa, reserv-
ist in war against Chile, follows along with
reports on city's defense by foreign observers.
Ends with brief 1913 biography of Piérola.
Didactically engaging volume. Based on published sources, contemporary newspapers,
and Archivo Piérola in Lima.

3056 Macera, Pablo. Las furias y las penas:
entrevistas. Lima: Mosca Azul Editores, 1983. 410 p.

Interviews with Macera, Peru's most
respected historian and cultural commentator, published 1975–82. Also includes
essays and letters to the editor on many subjects. Comments range from war with Chile
to sources of his ideas for the history of Peruvian murals and the impact of Jorge Basadre
on Peruvian culture. Contemporary memoir
that is an essential document for students of
Peruvian affairs.

3057 Mallon, Florencia E. Gender and class
in the transition to capitalism: household and mode of production in central Peru
(LAP, 13:1[48], Winter 1986, p. 147–174)

Explores character of peasant household economy in Peru's central highlands
as national economy changed from pre-
capitalist to capitalist. Raises important
questions about long held views on precise
role of peasant household during that transition, questioning whether class analysis by
itself can effectively elucidate importance of

family relations, and calling for more gender-based analysis of the phenomenon to arrive at a better understanding of historical social relations.

3058 Masterson, Daniel M. Caudillismo and institutional change: Manuel Odría and the Peruvian armed forces, 1948–1956 (AAFH/TAM, 40:4, April 1984, p. 479–489)

Views the Odría dictatorship from the perspective of the growing professionalism of the Peruvian armed forces as represented by the establishment of the Center for Higher Military Studies in 1950, itself propelled by clashes with APRA (1932–48). Suggests that Odría-style personalism, though present, is increasingly rare.

3059 Mendoza Meléndez, Eduardo Néstor. Historia de la campaña de La Breña. 2a ed., rev., corr. y aum. Lima: Ital Perú, 1984. 451 p., 9 leaves of plates (1 folded): ill. (some col.), maps, ports.

Addition of biographical material and amplification of coverage of events reported in the period's newspapers constitute some of major revisions in latest edition of this one-volume narrative of the War of the Pacific by military historian. Work continues to err on the side of hagiography and patriotic enthusiasm as a gloss for events.

3060 Miller, Rory. The Grace Contract, the Peruvian Corporation, and Peruvian history (IAA, 9:3/4, 1983, p. 319–348, bibl., tables)

Questions conventional view that the Grace contract paved the way for late 19th-century foreign expansion into the Peruvian economy. Especially in the case of railways, strongest proof of British domination after Peruvian Corp. Argues bondholders extract considerably less from concession than claimed and supports Thorp/Bertram view that British investment expansion was short-lived. Uses Foreign Office and Peruvian Corp. records to argue that the company's pressures on government policy in Peru were weak and clumsy and that its accomplishments in transport were exaggerated. Company's greatest profits came after 1907 and reached apex with Leguía. Careful analysis.

Mörner, Magnus. The Andean past: land, societies, and conflicts. See item **2626.**

3061 Mörner, Magnus et al. Compraventa de tierras en el Cuzco: 1825–1869.

Stockholm: Institute de Estudios Latino-americanos, 1984. 66 p.: bibl., graphs, tables (Estudios históricos sobre estructuras agrarias andinas; 1)

Consists of *libros auxiliares de alcabalas de enagenaciones de fincas* for 1825–69. Describes materials, suggests most obvious uses, and provides illustrations of enormous value for examining socioeconomic structure of Andean society using the Pearson coefficient of correlation to arrive at land values per *topo.* Includes graphs of changes in value, prices, and analysis of credit. Very important project effectively discussed.

3062 Niezen Matos, Gabriel. El Diario: un proyecto de comunicación popular. Lima: Centro de Investigación de Comunicación, 1983. 88 p.: bibl.

Brief analysis of relationship between Peru's premier radical newspaper, *El Diario de Marka,* and issue of control of communications by the State in Peru after 1968. Emphasizes period since 1980 and provides basic information about the production of the periodical *Marka* and later the newspaper.

3063 Nueva visión histórica de Huanta: antología histórica siglo XIX. Recopilación, notas y comentarios de Simón Enrique Sánchez Torres. Lima: Instituto de Apoyo Agrario, 1984. 60 p.: bibl.

Brief, 19th-century essays, most of them culled from secondary sources and memoirs. They often tie this Ayacucho province—beset in the 1980s by unprecedented political and social upheaval—to national events. Helpful to researchers probing local notarial records. Compiler was Huanta's alcalde mayor.

3064 Ortiz de Zevallos Paz Soldán, Luis. Los urbanos mineros en la República (IRA/B, 12, 1982/1983, p. 295–312)

Stylized discussion of aspects of urban planning in Peru's history. Concentrates on idea of urban planning for mine-worker populations. Ideas based on author's personal observations in three Huancavelica towns. Distinguishes between planned communities and haphazard agglomerations like La Oroya. Preliminary findings.

3065 Pacheco Vélez, César. Jorge Basadre o la pasión por la historia (PMNH/HC, 15, 1982, p. 7–22, ill.)

Extensive necrology in homage to Basadre written in July 1980. Useful because it recalls the ever-widening vision of this prolific scholar of Peruvian culture and his profound influence on the country's historiography and history.

3066 Palma, Ricardo. Crónicas de la Guerra con Chile, 1881–1883. Compilación de C. Norman Guice y Oswaldo Holguín Callo. Prólogo de Héctor López Martínez. Lima: Mosca Azul Editores, 1984. 252 p.: bibl.

While Peru was occupied by Chilean forces (1881–82), author of this collection of newspaper articles, the famed poet and essayist, was supported in his efforts by Nicolás de Piérola as well as by the forces of Andrés Cáceres in Ayacucho. Includes 86 articles gathered by C.N. Guice who analyzes this episode elsewhere (see *HLAS 46:2977*), giving special attention to US mediation in the War of the Pacific.

3067 Peloso, Vincent C. Cotton planters, the State and rural labor policy: ideological origins of the Peruvian *república aristocrática*, 1895–1908 (AAFH/TAM, 40:2, Oct. 1983, p. 209–228)

Outlines political and social strategies adopted by progressive, commercial cotton planters of the south coastal region to guide national economic policy for their social sector. Argues that with peasant elements they were able to control and intellectuals they encouraged, these planters fostered narrow interests under the label of national modernization. Initiatives were timid because planters were suspicious of the one institution, the State, that could guarantee their success.

3068 Peloso, Vincent C. Succulence and sustenance: region, class, and diet in nineteenth-century Peru (*in* Food, politics, and society in Latin America. Edited by John C. Super and Thomas C. Wright. Lincoln: Univ. of Nebraska Press, 1984, p. 46–64)

Demonstrates that working-class and peasant access to food gradually diminished in the 19th century, due to the rise of Lima and a few other major cities and the decline of local marketing patterns. External causes (i.e., wars, shifting foreign demand, industrialization) also affected food availability. By early 20th century, food shortages were a major cause of popular riots and labor action. [M.L. Conniff]

3069 Pévez, Juan Hipólito. Memorias de un viejo luchador campesino: Juan H.

Pévez. Edición de Teresa Oré. Participación de Nelly Plaza, René Antezana y Jaime Luna. Lima: ILLA: Tarea, 1983. 368 p.: ill.

Extraordinary oral testimony details popular social actions in Parcona, near south coast Ica. Narrator describes involvement as indigenista leader and founder of Ica's peasant federation in 1920s and as founder of Peru's Communist Party. Relives struggle for eight-hour day, offers insights into Mariátegui and Leguía, recalls struggles against land grabs, links with national labor movement, confrontations with army, and 1929 Parcona massacre. Includes many early photos and documents of peasant movement. Valuable source for popular, labor, and party history.

3070 Pike, Frederick B. The politics of the miraculous in Peru: Haya de la Torre and the spiritualist tradition. Lincoln: Univ. of Nebraska Press, 1986. 1 v.: bibl., index.

Sumptuous intellectual biography places Haya within little known but significant tradition of spiritualism in Peru and Latin America. Pike views Haya and Aprismo as emerging from conflicting rationalist and traditionalist political visions, a "regeneration mythology" that rests upon "soft" Marxism. Examines Haya's ideas, especially the meaning of "historical space-time," fundamentals of (and US influence on) Aprismo, party politics, exile and final years (1963–79). Dispels many romantic and disparaging legends about the subject in a critical but not unsympathetic mode. Sources include prodigious readings on Haya and spiritualism. Stresses importance of spiritualism as a theme in Latin American intellectual history and political theory. Highly provocative and thoroughly stimulating work that is a masterpiece of Latin American intellectual history.

3071 Prado, Jorge del. En los años cumbres de Mariátegui. Lima: Ediciones Unidad, 1983. 271 p., 29 p. of plates: bibl.

Leading Communist party figure and national senator (1980–85) recalls his association with the party's founder during first two years of its life. Includes theoretical and organizational recollections and reaffirms view that Mariátegui's ideas placed him firmly within Comintern boundaries regarding relationship of working class and party. Memoir is accompanied by letters (1928–29) between Mariátegui and Communist leaders throughout Peru and Latin America.

3072 Requejo, Juan Vicente. El periodismo en Piura. Lima?: Colegio de Periodistas del Perú, 1983. 78 p.

Essay surveys "evolutionary cycles" of Piura's regional press from colonial period to present. Mostly devoted to chronology of 19th-century periodicals. Also includes similar list of 20th-century working-class and political journals. Useful catalogue of regional resources for historians.

3073 Rodríguez Beruff, Jorge. Los militares y el poder: un ensayo sobre la doctrina militar en el Perú, 1948–1968. Traducción del inglés, Patricia de Arregui. Lima: Mosca Azul Editores, 1983. 264 p.

Author views Peruvian military ideology as reformist and rooted in the post-World War II Center for Higher Military Studies. Like Davies and Villanueva's work (item **3075**), this book surveys the development of reformist ideology and its consequences for military action. Translation into Spanish of a York Univ. Ph.D. dissertation based on interviews with well known civilians, periodicals, and published accounts.

3074 Salisbury, Richard V. The Middle American exile of Víctor Raúl Haya de la Torre (AAFH/TAM, 40: 1, July 1983, p. 1–15)

Uses State Dept. documents and newspaper accounts to illustrate how Haya's 1928 Central American exile helped to develop his ideas about anti-imperialism, as well as his awareness of the irritation such ideas caused US officials. Study of little known episode in Haya's political life.

3075 Secretos electorales del APRA: correspondencia y documentos de 1939. Edición de Thomas M. Davies, Jr. and Víctor Villanueva. Lima: Editorial Horizonte, 1982. 156 p.

Continues collection of fascinating documents about Aprista electoral activities (1935–39, see also *HLAS 44:2995*). Concentrates on strategies and tactics that reveal Aprista party ambitions, personal relationships, duplicitous moves suggesting why the party failed to capture the presidency. Among the 94 documents are 24 letters exchanged with US officials found in State Dept. files.

3076 Tamayo Herrera, José. Historia social e indigenismo en el altiplano. Prólogo de Emilio Romero. Lima: Ediciones Trentaitrés, 1982. 389 p., 8 leaves of plates: bibl., ill.

Social history of Puno region organized in four sections: 1) effort to periodize the region's history; 2–3) discussion of *gamonalismo* and popular rebellion; and 4) characterization of Puno nativism through discussion of 20th-century groups, leaders, outlooks, arts, and medicine. Disagrees with Bourricaud (1967) and Hazen (Ph.D. 1974) that ideological change in the region began before the mid-1950s. Believes it came after 1956 with the advent of modern telecommunications.

3077 Taylor, Lewis. Cambios capitalistas en las haciendas cajamarquinas, 1900–1935. Cambridge, England: Centre of Latin American Studies, Univ. of Cambridge, 1983. 67 p.: bibl. (Working papers, 0306–6290; 39)

Extended essay on the rise of agrarian capitalism, outlines changes in Cajamarca's rural society from independence to 1930s, pointing out conflicts over land use, water, labor, and rents. Concludes that industrialization of sugar on Peru's north coast had marked impact on capitalization of rural society in Cajamarca. Makes effective use of plantation records from Lima's Archivo del Fuero Agrario and Cajamarca's Departmental Archive.

3078 Wachendorfer, Ute. Bauernbewegung in Peru: Handlungsspielräume und grenzen für Camposino-Organisationen unter Bedingungen abhängig-kapitalistischer Entwicklng, 1900–1983. Heidelburg, FRG: Verlag Heidelberg, 1984. 444 p.: bibl. (Heidelberg Dritte-Welt-Studien; 18)

Thorough overview of peasant movements in Peru throughout the 20th century with special emphasis on post-1960s period. Contains much information on land reform, organization of peasant cooperatives, and political groups. Marshals many facts in her presentation of these heterogeneous movements. Extensive bibliography. [G.M. Dorn]

3079 Wagner de Reyna, Alberto. Noticias y aventuras de Rattier (IRA/B, 12, 1982/1983, p. 391–406)

Member of a French mission to Peru (1823–25), Rattier wrote on public opinion, important personalities, government finances, and commerce. This study of his 1825 government report features his views on the independence wars, San Martín, Bolívar, and the 1824–25 peace negotiations. Concludes that Rattier performed well as a temporary diplomat in difficult circumstances.

3080 Wilson, Fiona. The conflict over Indian land in nineteenth century Peru (in State and region in Latin America: a workshop. Edited by G.A. Banck, R. Buve, and L. van Vroonhoven. Amsterdam: Centrum viir Studie en Documentatie van Latijns-Amerika, 1981, p. 77–112, bibl.)

Detailed analysis of the Tarma oligarchy's use of regional power to war off the encroachment of the central government. Examines how nine leading families tried to extend their control over local indigenous communities. Divisions within these families challenged their hegemony as merchants and the communities employed the law and the central government to help their case. Supports view that local landowners rejected the interference of the State in their drive to control local lands and labor. Based on archival sources.

Wilson, Fiona. Marriage, property, and the position of women in the Peruvian Central Andes. See *HLAS 47:1514.*

BOLIVIA AND CHILE

THOMAS C. WRIGHT, *Professor of History, University of Nevada, Las Vegas*

BOLIVIA

THE PAST BIENNIUM has brought forth relatively little noteworthy historical writing on Bolivia since 1825. One hopeful sign is the emergence of a new historical journal, *Historia y Cultura,* published in La Paz. A note of caution: New journals in Bolivia have a very short life expectancy.

With the passing of the centennial of the War of the Pacific and the golden anniversary of the Chaco War, military history has lost its vogue. Biography, politics, and local history have continued to attract Bolivian writers, while a few studies of economic and social analysis have appeared.

A few works deserve special mention. Early republican historiography has been enriched by Siles Guevara's article on the establishment of diplomatic relations with the US (item **3104**) and Parkerson's study of the Confederación Perú-Boliviana (item **3101**). Mitre's fine study of the silver barons and their operations (item **3099**) is a solid contribution. Demelas and Romero Pittari (items **3088** and **3102**) have reinterpreted 19th-century rebellions as social movements. Baptista Gumucio's study of the seat of national government, the Palacio Quemado, is a clever approach to political history (item **3084**). Finally, Dunkerley and Knudson have written solid studies of the National Revolution of 1952 (items **3090** and **3095**).

CHILE

Good work on Chile since independence has continued to appear in Chile, the US, and Europe. The Chilean journals, especially *Historia, Revista Chilena de Historia y Geografía,* and London-based *Nueva Historia,* are the primary sources of article literature. University presses in the US have continued to be a major source of quality work on Chilean history.

With the passing of the centennial of the War of the Pacific, a major theme of the past four years has faded. However, William Sater has contributed two important studies on the war: his award-winning article on financing the war (item **3174**) and the culmination of years of research, his fine, in-depth study of the war's impact on Chile (item **3173**). Ortega's and Ravest Mora's works on the causes of the war are also worthy of note (items **3154** and **3164**).

Several works have enhanced our understanding of specialized aspects of the period between independence and the War of the Pacific. Among these are Jocelyn-Holt's study of the generation of 1842 (item **3146**), Hernández Ponce's article on the Guardia Nacional (item **3142**), Garreaud's study of Valparaíso (item **3137**), and Tellez Lúgaro's account of the beginnings of Antofagasta (item **3179**). Documentary collections on O'Higgins (item **3152**) and the Egaña mission (item **3124**) further elucidate this period.

A few notable works have appeared on the society, economics, and politics of the nitrate era (1880–1930). Bermúdez Miral's posthumous work on nitrates in 1880s is a milestone (item **3113**). Remmer's study of party competition is a major addition (item **3165**). Romero's work on living conditions in Santiago (item **3169**), Salinas's study of popular religion (item **3171**), and Blancpain's article on French influence (item **3115**) are substantial contributions. The Campos Narducci study of a Santiago church is interesting for local history (item **3120**). Drake's review article covers studies of Chilean elites, primarily of the nitrate era (item **3127**).

Several other volumes deserve recognition. Zeitlin's provocative study of the civil wars of the 1850s and 1891 raises important questions (item **3184**). Ramírez Necochea's study of the armed forces (item **3162**) and Peri Fagerstrom's three volumes on police history are solid additions (item **3156**). The posthumous memoirs of Gen. Prats González and Cumplido and Frühling's study of transitions to democracy shed light on more contemporary problems (items **3159** and **3123**). Mamalakis's study of Chilean economic theory (item **3147**) and Ibáñez's article on the influence of engineers in government (item **3144**) are worthy of note.

BOLIVIA

Albó, Xavier and **Josep M. Barnabas.** La cara campesina de nuestra historia. See *HLAS* 47:*8300.*

3081 Alcázar, José Luis. Ñacahuasu, la guerrilla del Che en Bolivia. La Paz?: s.n., 1984? 296 p.: ill., ports.

Journalist's first-hand account of the military campaign against Che Guevara. Also contains material from interviews with former guerrillas and others in the war zone. Useful addition.

3082 Alcázar, Moisés. Abel Iturralde, el centinela del petróleo. 2a ed. La Paz: Librería Editorial Juventud, 1982. 235 p.: bibl.

Second edition (first 1944) of hagiographic biography of Abel Iturralde (1869–1935), conservative political leader who became prominent opposing Standard Oil concessions in 1920s, which later contributed to the outbreak of the Chaco War.

3083 Arze Aguirre, René. Historia escrita e historia oral: notas para un estudio de las fuentes de la historia de Bolivia (SBH/HC, 6, oct. 1984, p. 3–12)

After examining the lamentable state of conservation and organization of Bolivia's public and private historical records, author recommends the use of oral history techniques for contemporary history. The analysis of causes and results of the loss of written records is discouraging, to say the least.

3084 Baptista Gumucio, Mariano. Biografía del Palacio Quemado. La Paz: Empresa Editora Siglo, 1984. 411 p.: bibl.

Examines Bolivian political history to 1982 utilizing vignettes and episodes focusing on the edifice that started as the cabildo of La Paz and became the seat of republican government in the mid-19th century. Named for its destruction by fire during an 1875 coup, the Casa Quemada is "a symbol and synthesis of the country's history itself;" and the author does not exaggerate in pointing out that "few houses of government must exist in the world with such a dramatic and somber history . . ." (p. 6). This intimate chronicle is an engaging approach to Bolivia's tortured political history.

3085 Baptista Gumucio, Mariano. Otra historia de Bolivia. La Paz: Ediciones Los Amigos del Libro, 1983. 405 p.: bibl., maps.

Thematically organized series of essays on post-1810 Bolivian history emphasizes the independence period. Designed to probe new questions, it pursues topics such as European influences on independence, women's influence on politics, and the role of political secretaries. Useful complement to the usual narrative histories.

3086 Bowman, Charles H., Jr. Documents concerning a Bolivian diplomat: Vicente Pazos Kanki (PAIGH/H, 97, enero/junio 1984, p. 159–174)

Reproduces without commentary five documents written by or to Vicente Pazos Kanki, one of Bolivia's most influential early diplomats and intellectuals.

3087 Condarco Morales, Ramiro. Aniceto Arce: profeta de la primera fase de la revolución industrial en Bolivia (SBH/HC, 6, oct. 1984, p. 43–47)

Brief sketch, culled from forthcoming book, of the important role of Aniceto Arce in the revival of Bolivian mining in the second half of the 19th century.

3088 Demelas, Marie Danielle. Jacqueries indiennes, politique créole: la guerre civile de 1889 (UTIEH/C, 44, 1985, p. 91–111)

Examines the 1889 Bolivian civil war, focusing on the role of Indian communities. Mobilized by the attack on their land, the communities still had sufficient power to mount a general insurrection, which became the deciding factor in the struggle between elite factions.

3089 Demelas, Marie Danielle. Lo que está en juego en la lucha por el poder en los Andes: los casos de los departamentos del Cuzco y de La Paz entre 1880–1920 (SBH/HC, 6, oct. 1984, p. 63–74)

Preliminary study of contrasting developments shaping the power of local elites in Cuzco and La Paz during a 40-year period of modernization and changing relations with the outside world. Rather than offering answers, it raises questions for further research.

3090 Dunkerley, James. Rebellion in the veins: political struggle in Bolivia, 1952–82. London: Verso Editions, 1984. 385 p., 10 p. of plates: bibl., index, photos.

This essentially narrative account of Bolivian politics from the National Revolution forward is well researched and carefully documented. Incisive political analysis and

chronological coverage make it very useful reading for students of contemporary Bolivian and Latin American politics.

Flores, Gonzalo. Rebeliones campesinas en el período liberal: 1900–1920. See *HLAS* 47: 1428.

3091 Gómez de Aranda, Blanca. José Rosendo Gutiérrez: el político liberal (SBH/HC, 5, abril 1984, p. 181–188)

Brief sketch of the political activity of influential conciliatory Liberal (1880–83). Provides details of his views and activities during War of the Pacific and emergence of Bolivia's system of stable oligarchic civilian rule.

3092 Guevara, Ernesto. Diario del Che Guevara. Edición de Servando Serrano Torrico. 2a ed. Cochabamba, Bolivia: Editorial Serrano, 1984. 368, 3 p.: bibl., ill.

Second edition (first 1968) of this editor's version of the primary record of Che's Bolivian episode, with expanded notes.

3093 Hablemos de federalismo. Compilación de Carlos Valverde Barbery. Santa Cruz de la Sierra, Bolivia: s.n., 1983. 164 p.

Small book, compiled by politician and advocate of decentralization, contains a variety of historical and contemporary documents arguing the Bolivian federalist cause.

3094 Hillman, John. The emergence of the tin industry in Bolivia (JLAS, 16:2, Nov. 1984, p. 403–437)

Broad overview of the development of Bolivia's tin industry through 1900, with emphasis on the world market and its effects on production and export. Offers little new detail on operations in Bolivia. Good as introduction to the topic.

Ibarnegaray Ponce, Roxana. El desarrollo agrario en Santa Cruz: 1900–1952. See *HLAS* 47: 1431.

Kohl, James V. The Cliza and Ucureña war: syndical violence and national revolution in Bolivia. See *HLAS* 47: 6404.

3095 Knudson, Jerry W. Bolivia: press and revolution, 1932–1964. Lanham, Md.: Univ. Press of America, 1986. 488 p.: bibl., ill., index.

Carefully researched book examines role of the Bolivian press in the 1952 revolution, tracing press involvement from the

Chaco War to the overthrow of the MNR in 1964. Author knows his subject thoroughly and argues convincingly that despite the restricted reach of the press in a predominantly illiterate country, Bolivian newspapers were central to the onset of revolution and its demise.

Langer, Erick D. Labor strikes and reciprocity on Chuquisaca haciendas. See item **1649.**

3096 Lofstrom, William Lee. El Mariscal Sucre en Bolivia: la promesa y el problema de la reforma, el intento de cambio económico y social en los primeros años de la independencia boliviana. Prólogo y traducción de Mariano Baptista Gumucio. La Paz: Editorial e Imprenta Alenkar, 1983. 586 p.: bibl., ill.

First regularly printed version of important study that originally appeared in English in Cornell dissertation series (see *HLAS 36:2745*). [D. Bushnell]

3097 Lofstrom, William Lee. El puerto de Cobija en 1832 visto por un viajero norteamericano (SBH/HC, 5, abril 1984, p. 145–161, ill., map, table)

Annotated translation of chapter on Cobija from William S.W. Ruschenberger's anonymously published *Three years in the Pacific; including notices of Brazil, Chile, Bolivia and Peru* . . . (Philadelphia: 1834). A surgeon with the US Navy, author was a keen observer of natural and human phenomena.

3099 Mitre, Antonio. Los patriarcas de la plata: estructura socioeconómica de la minería boliviana en el siglo XIX. Lima: Instituto de Estudios Peruanos, 1981. 229 p.: appendices, bibl., ill., tables (Serie Estudios históricos; 8)

Well researched and thoroughly documented study of Bolivian silver mining in the 19th century. Includes detailed price data and sophisticated analyses of government policy, foreign penetration, labor recruitment, working conditions, and the social context of the mining enterprise. One chapter examines technology and production costs by focusing on a single large company. Includes very useful tables and appendices. This is a major contribution to 19th-century Bolivian historiography.

3100 Oblitas Fernández, Edgar. Historia secreta de la Guerra del Pacífico. 4a ed.

Sucre, Bolivia: Editorial Tupac Katari, 1983. 354 p.: ill.

Fourth edition (for first, 1978, see *HLAS 44:3046*) of popular xenophobic tract on the War of the Pacific.

3101 Parkerson, Phillip Taylor. Andrés de Santa Cruz y la Confederación Perú-Boliviana, 1835–1839. La Paz: Librería Editorial Juventud, 1984. 330 p.

Thoroughly researched study of the international relations aspects of the Confederación Perú-Boliviana uses Bolivian and Peruvian sources effectively to explore four basic questions about the background, functioning, and collapse of the union. Author is sympathetic to the Confederación and to Santa Cruz, whom he defends against charges of tyranny and overriding personal ambition. This work, a revision of a 1979 Univ. of Florida dissertation, offers useful new insights into this period of Andean history.

Platt, Tristan. Liberalism and ethnocide in the southern Andes. See *HLAS 47:1439.*

3102 Romero Pittari, Salvador. Copetudos y sin chaqueta: la revolución federal de Andrés Ibáñez (SBH/HC, 5, abril 1984, p. 163–180)

Provocative reinterpretation of the 1876–77 uprising in Santa Cruz de la Sierra. Known generally as a federalist movement, the uprising led by Andrés Ibáñez was more a social revolt by the local petit bourgeoisie against the aristocracy or "copetudos," according to author. Thesis is well developed and argued.

3103 Sanjinés, Jenaro. Adolfo Ballivián. Con textos de Nicolás Acosta, Mariano Baptista y Luis Subieta. La Paz: Ultima Hora, 1982. 76 p.: ill. (Col. juvenil de biografías breves; 23. Biblioteca popular boliviana)

Anthology of writings by Bolivian President (1873–74) Adolfo Ballivián. Useful for general information on this important political figure.

3104 Siles Guevara, Juan. La Misión Ladislao Cabrera en los Estados Unidos de América: 1880–1882 (SBH/HC, 6, oct. 1984, p. 49–62)

Well documented analysis of Bolivia's first diplomatic mission to the US. Born of wartime desperation, the mission failed, but contributed to the awakening in Bolivia of the desirability of establishing a permanent diplomatic presence in the US.

3105 Valencia Vega, Alipio. Historia política de Bolivia. v. 3. La Paz: Librería Editorial Juventud, 1984. 1 v.: bibl.

Vol. 3 of Valencia Vega's work covers end of the colonial period and early years of the republic, through end of the Peru-Bolivia Confederation. Narrative work with a geopolitical interpretative emphasis.

3106 Vázquez Machicado, Humberto; José de Mesa; and Teresa Gisbert. Manual de historia de Bolivia. Con 301 ilustraciones, 26 mapas y diagramas de José de Mesa y Teresa Gisbert. 2a ed. corr. y aum. La Paz: Gisbert, 1983. 568 p.: bibl., ill.

Second edition (first 1958), extended and expanded, of comprehensive narrative history of Bolivia from earliest civilization to present. Useful as a competent guide to major issues and themes.

CHILE

3107 Antología de Mostazal. Selección y prólogo de Carlos Ruiz-Tagle. San Francisco de Mostazal, Chile: Ilustre Municipalidad de San Francisco de Mostazal, 1983. 187 p.

This contribution to local history and lore of San Francisco de Mostazal, an agrarian village 60 km south of Santiago on main highway and rail line, consists of selected interviews, descriptions, reminiscences, and poetry.

3108 Arellano, José Pablo. Social policies in Chile: an historical review (JLAS, 17:2, Nov. 1985, p. 397–418)

Study attempts to assess evolution of State social expenditures in 20th-century Chile, a country which by 1970 had the highest level of State economic participation in Latin America excepting Cuba. Using an array of government statistics, author describes how the process of electoral expansion fostered the growth of State social expenditure, until the military reversed it after 1973. Good survey.

3109 Armas, Ramón de. El apoyo chileno a la revolución cubana de 1895: apuntes para la historia del internacionalismo revolucionario en América Latina (Araucaria de Chile [I. Peralta Ediciones, Pamplona, Spain] 25, 1984, p. 147–168)

This article surveys forms and degree of Chilean support for the Cuban independence movement of the 1890s, finding most of it in manifestations such as newspaper editorials, fund drives, and a small number of Chilean volunteers who fought in Cuba.

3110 Atria, Raúl. Tensiones políticas y crisis económica: el caso chileno, 1920–1938 (CPU/ES, 10:37, 1983, p. 177–218, graphs, tables)

This analysis, following a model developed by Dudley Seers, finds a close correlation between the economic changes of the 1920–38 period and the substantial degree of political change, culminating in the election of the Popular Front. Includes economic tables and graphs.

3111 Avila Martel, Alamiro de. La censura de libros y Andrés Bello (ACH/B, 49:93, 1982, p. 199–208)

Brief study of the role of Andrés Bello in a 1832 censorship case involving imported books. Bello's editorials in *El Araucano* are used to reveal his views on freedom of the press and the role of censorship.

Barrera, Manuel. Worker participation in company management in Chile: a historical experience. See *HLAS 47:3513*.

3112 Barros, Luis and Ximena Vergara. Los grandes rasgos de la evolución del Estado en Chile, 1820–1925 (CPU/ES, 10:37, 1983, p. 131–176)

Interpretative overview of the evolution of the Chilean State over a century offers few new insights and no surprises.

3113 Bermúdez Miral, Oscar. Historia del salitre desde la Guerra del Pacífico hasta la Revolución de 1891. Santiago: Ediciones Pampa Desnuda, 1984. 337 p., 14 p. of plates: bibl., ill., indexes.

Posthumous work by late historian of the Norte Grande is sequel to his acclaimed *Historia del salitre desde sus orígines hasta la Guerra del Pacífico* (1963, see *HLAS 28:1178*). Researched in company and state archives, this work covers the crucial period of the Chilean conquest of the nitrate zone and the subsequent alienation of ownership to largely foreign interests. Offering much detail on government policy, economic activity, etc., this book complements recent contributions of US scholars, especially O'Brien.

3114 Blanco, Guillermo and **Mónica Blanco.** Raúl Cardenal Silva Henríquez: aventura de una fe. Santiago: Academia de Humanismo Cristiano, 1984. 103 p., 4 p. of plates: ill. (some col.)

Picture book celebrating the life and deeds of Chile's Cardinal Silva Henríquez, a leading political activist over the past decade and a half.

3115 Blancpain, J.P. Francisation et francomanie en Amérique latine: le cas du Chile au XIXe siècle (PUF/RH, 544, oct./déc. 1982, p. 365–407)

Examines processes by which the Chilean elite became francophiles (not to the exclusion, of course, of their anglophilia). Traces influences of French thought, art, literature, social styles, and accesses impact of Chilean travel to France and French immigration to Chile. Solid piece.

3116 Bravo Elizondo, Pedro. *El Despertar de los Trabajadores,* 1912–1922: periódico, partido, cultura proletaria (Araucaria de Chile [I. Peralta Ediciones, Pamplona, Spain] 27, 1984, p. 15–28)

Analyzes early workers' newspaper established by Recabarren and its influence on the political development of Communist Party leader Elías Lafertte. Draws heavily on the paper itself.

3117 Campos Harriet, Fernando. Aníbal Pinto, Presidente de Chile, 1876–1881 (ACH/B, 51:95, 1984, p. 251–261)

Brief sketch offers primarily biographical and genealogical data on Chile's president during the War of the Pacific.

3118 Campos Harriet, Fernando. Breve semblanza de Doña Juana Ross de Edwards (ACH/B, 49:93, 1982, p. 337–356)

Biographical sketch of one of Chile's most powerful women of the 19th century (1830–1912). Includes her extensive will.

3119 Campos Harriet, Fernando. Jornadas de la historia de Chile. Santiago: Academia Superior de Ciencias Pedagógicas de Santiago, 1981. 191 p.: bibl.

Thin, witty history of Chile in the form of anecdotes, vignettes, and interpretative essays. Complements standard historical sources.

3120 Campos Narducci, Mariano. La Iglesia de la Preciosa Sangre: aproximación al centenario de su edificación (ACH/B, 51:95, 1984, p. 279–309, photos)

Interesting, well researched article on a church in the center of Santiago and its Italian-Chilean architect, Eusebio Chelli. Includes detailed description of the architectural plans and 10 photographs.

3121 Chaporro N., Patricio. Los actores sociales y políticos y el quiebre del sistema político democrático chileno (CPU/ES, 10:37, 1983, p. 277–296)

Examination of political participation and role of parties (1920–73) argues that the sustaining force in Chile's political system was a changing group of parties and movements of the center—a condition lost in 1973. Cites this as a lesson for the future.

3122 Collier, Simon. An interview with Mario Góngora (HAHR, 63:4, Nov. 1983, p. 663–675, bibl.)

One of the *Hispanic American Historical Review* series of interviews with distinguished historians of Latin America. Offers valuable insights into the late Mario Góngora's career, accomplishments, and contributions to historical literature.

3123 Cumplido, Francisco and **Hugo Frühling.** Problemas jurídico-políticos del tránsito hacia la democracia: Chile, 1924–1932 (CPU/ES, 10:37, 1983, p. 219–260)

Examines in depth the juridical and political problems of the two instances in this century of the restoration of elected governments after institutional breakdowns. Focusing on questions of the validity of decrees of de facto governments, authors argue that those two instances established the precedent that ratification by elected governments is necessary to sustain the validity of such decrees and decree-laws. Relevance to Chile's future is clear.

3124 Documentos de la Misión de Don Mariano Egaña en Londres, 1824–1829. Edición y estudio preliminar de Javier González Echenique. Santiago: Ministerio de Relaciones Exteriores de Chile, 1984. 655 p.: bibl., indexes, port.

Collection of 380 pieces of official correspondence between Egaña and the Chilean government during Egaña's important diplomatic mission in Great Britain. This valuable collection will facilitate research on international relations of the early republic.

3125 Donoso Vergara, Guillermo. Una victoria militar y una elección presidencial según periódicos talquinos (SCHG/R, 151, 1983, p. 31–64)

Attempts to shed light on local life in Talca during 1881 through newspaper accounts of the war and politics. Provides details of interest to local historians.

3126 Dooner, Patricio. La segunda administración Ibáñez: un mentís a la creencia sobre la tradición democrática chilena (CPU/ES, 43:1, 1985, p. 83–108)

Author uses second Ibáñez government (1952–58) to debunk the myth of the solidity of Chile's democracy, by emphasizing that the government's authoritarianism and the continuing suppression of the Communist Party provided a false impression of stability.

3127 Drake, Paul W. The buoyant bourgeoisie of Chile (LARR, 21:2, 1986, p. 166–177)

Review essay covers six recent studies of the 19th- and 20th-century Chilean intellectual, economic, and political elites published by US university presses (1981–85) by authors M. Monteón, K. Remmer, A. Woll, T. Wright, G. Yeager, and M. Zeitlin. Drake offers incisive critiques of each work, while emphasizing the common thread among those studies: the endurance of the elites through times of stress and change. Author believes these works collectively represent real progress in the study of Chile's elites.

3128 Escobar, Roberto. Vida intelectual de Chile en 1879 (UC/AT, 447, 1983, p. 111–128)

Superficial survey of Chilean intellectual life at the outbreak of the War of the Pacific, arguing that the lively cultivation of science, letters, and education in Chile helped prepare the country for success in war.

3129 Escudero, Alfonso M. Olegario Lazo Baeza: la vida en sus escritos. Santiago: Nascimento, 1983. 77 p.: bibl.

Brief overview of the personal and literary career of Lazo Baeza (1878–1964), a military man who wrote novels, stories, and essays primarily on military themes. Includes bibliography.

3130 Espinosa Moraga, Oscar. Los Andonaegui de Vizcaya, de Chile y de Argentina. Santiago: Editorial Nascimento, 1984. 231 p., 12 p. of plates: bibl., ill., ports.

Detailed history of a Basque family that settled in Argentina and Chile (Santiago, Quillota, and Rancagua). Citing contributions and tracing genealogy, this study by descendant is based on some archival research.

3131 Espinosa Moraga, Oscar. El destino de Chile, 1541–1984. Santiago: Esparza, 1984. 247 p.: bibl., ill. (some col.)

Jingoistic geopolitical survey of Chile's territorial history, this work argues that the Basque legacy of "pacifismo antimilitarista entreguista" (p. 16) condemned Chile to being a small powerless nation. Author argues that Chile could and should have integrated the transandine provinces of Argentina into the national territory.

3132 Ettmüller, Wolfgang. Germanisierte Heeresoffiziere in der Chilenischen Politik, 1920–1932 (IAA, 8:1/2, 1982, p. 85–160)

Survey of political role of the Chilean officer corps during the period of institutional disruption (1920–32). Analyzes motives of the "germanized" or professionalized officer corps in overthrowing civilian rule. Uncovers some new material.

3133 Eyzaguirre, Jaime. Historia de las instituciones políticas y sociales de Chile. 6a ed. Santiago: Editorial Universitaria, 1984. 213 p.: bibl. (Col. Imagen de Chile)

Sixth edition (first 1967) of late conservative historian's synthesis of Chilean history through 1938.

3134 Fernández, Gonzalo. Orden, libertad e igualdad: valores básicos de la evolución democrática en Chile hasta 1925 (CPU/ES, 10:36, 1983, p. 65–81)

Overview of the first century of the Chilean republic's political history, focusing on dominant values being debated and sought in three periods: social order from independence to mid-19th century; liberty to the turn of the century; and equality thereafter. Useful interpretative scheme.

3135 Fernández, Manuel A. Merchants and bankers: British direct and portfolio investment in Chile during the nineteenth century (IAA, 9:3/4, 1983, p. 349–379, bibl., ill.)

This analysis of British investment in 19th-century Chile distinguishes between direct and portfolio investment, arguing that the much smaller volume of direct investment had a significantly greater impact on the host country. Direct investment is found to be more influential in three ways: its greater degree of "insertion" and hence of control; its closer linkage with local economy; and its propulsion of British direct investors into the Chilean dominant class. Comparability is suggested with the rest of Latin America.

3136 Fernández Baeza, Mario. Presidencialismo, principio de gobierno de la mayoría y sistema electoral: relaciones conceptuales y aplicación al caso de Chile, 1932–73 (CPU/ES, 10:37, 1983, p. 261–275)

Brief examination of the Chilean form of presidential government. Concludes that lack of a required second round of balloting (when necessary) to produce a majority for the winning candidate was a serious weakness.

3137 Garreaud, Jacqueline. La formación de un mercado de tránsito: Valparaíso, 1817–1848 (Nueva Historia [Asociación de Historiadores Chilenos, London] 3:11, 1984, p. 157–194)

Co-winner of second prize in the Barros Arana competition on Chilean history, article argues for the importance of the first three decades of political independence in setting the conditions of Chile's economic dependence. Focusing on Valparaíso, this well researched piece demonstrates importance of trade and ways in which the fluctuation of this commerce impacted Valparaíso and the Chilean economy as a whole.

3138 Goldberg, Joyce S. Consent to ascent: the *Baltimore* Affair and the U.S. rise to world power status (AAFH/TAM, 41:1, July 1984, p. 21–35)

This piece reviews the *Baltimore* Affair of 1892 and the diplomacy surrounding it as an important step in the end-of-the-century rise of the US to major power status. The vigorous US response to the brawl in Valparaíso showed US resolve and convinced Chileans and Europeans of the emergence of a new world contender.

3139 Grant, Geraldine. The State and the formation of a middle class: a Chilean example (LAP, 10:2/3, Spring/Summer 1983, p. 151–170)

This interpretive piece argues that the Chilean State, primarily through its economic policies, was essentially responsible for the creation and sustenance of a middle class. Includes section of data on Cautín province. Overall, the article shows little understanding of historical processes at work prior to 1930.

Grenier, Philippe. Chiloé et les chilotes: marginalité et dépendance en Patagonie chilienne, étude de géographie humaine. See *HLAS 47:5154.*

3140 Guzmán Brito, Alejandro. Las ideas jurídicas de Don Diego Portales (ACH/B, 49:93, 1982, p. 12–41)

Overview of Portales's juridical thought relates his ideas to his policies and to the probable sources of his views.

3141 Hernández Ponce, Roberto. Los estudios históricos en la Universidad Católica de Chile: notas para una crónica (UCCIH/H, 18, 1983, p. 5–44, appendices, bibl.)

Useful sketch of the evolution of history as a discipline in Chile's Catholic Univ., with emphasis on the period since 1943, when history became a discreet discipline. Includes bibliography of three prominent professors, Mario Góngora, Carlos Grez Pérez, and Ricardo Krebs Wilckens.

3142 Hernández Ponce, Roberto. La Guardia Nacional de Chile: apuntes sobre su orígen y organización (UCCIH/H, 19, 1984, p. 53–113)

Substantial article offers detail on the background, development, and institutionalization of the National Guard in its formative period. Derived from the colonial militias, prominent in the independence wars, the National Guard was definitively subordinated to the regular army in 1848. This is solid institutional history.

3143 Hirsch-Weber, Wolfgang. Aufstandt der Massen?: Wahlkampf und Stimmenthaltung in Chile, 1915–1921 (IAA, 8:1/2, 1982, p. 5–83)

Analyzing the congressional elections of 1915, 1918, 1921, and the presidential election of 1920, author attempts to refute the common interpretation of Alessandri's election as the result of a revolt of the electorate or even as a mass mobilization. Citing lower voter participation in the presidential election than in the congressional elections studied, he suggests a disenchantment with parties is more apparent than an electoral revolt.

3144 Ibáñez Santa María, Adolfo. Los ingenieros, el Estado y la política en Chile: del Ministerio de Fomento a la Corporación de Fomento, 1927–1939 (UCCIH/H, 18, 1983, p. 45–102)

Well researched article traces background and emergence of the modern developmentalist State (1920s-39) arguing that the founding of CORFO in 1939 was less a political act of the Popular Front than a continuation of a trend toward a technocratic State first institutionalized by Ibáñez. Focuses on the growing role of engineers in public administration and, in particular, on the Instituto de Ingenieros de Chile. Substantiates Ibáñez's pivotal role.

3145 Illanes, María Angélica. Disciplinamiento de la mano de obra minera en una formación social en transición: Chile, 1840–1850 (Nueva Historia [Asociación de Historiadores Chilenos, London] 3:11, 1984, p. 195–226)

Co-winner of second prize in the Barros Arana international competition on Chilean history, this study analyzes mining labor in the Norte Chico during a period of chaos and change in labor supply and organization. Offers detailed information on wages, consumption, living conditions, and various approaches by mining companies to the problem of controlling the labor force.

3146 Jocelyn Holt Letelier, Alfredo. Tres aproximaciones a la generación de 1842: Lastarria, Bello y Monvoisin (SCHG/R, 151, 1983, p. 65–127)

Substantial article explores the phenomenon of the generation of 1842 by examining in depth three of its notable manifestations: Lastarria's speech founding the Sociedad Literaria; Bello's discourse inaugurating the Univ. of Chile; and visit of French painter Monvoisin (1843–45). From these analyses, author draws tentative conclusions about the generation of 1842 and poses questions for further research. Good piece of intellectual history.

Kay, Cristóbal. Political economy, class alliances and agrarian change in Chile. See *HLAS 47:3547*.

3147 Mamalakis, Markos. Explicaciones acerca del desarrollo económico chileno: una reseña y síntesis (UCCIH/H, 19, 1984, p. 115–158, tables)

Thoughtful essay covering the variety of theories of Chile's frustrated development is also an introduction to the history of Chilean economic thought of the past 100 years. After reviewing explanations from the geographic to neo-Marxist, author postulates his own explanations drawn in part from his respected earlier works. Useful contribution.

Mamalakis, Markos. Historical statistics of Chile. See *HLAS 47:3550*.

3148 Márquez-Bretón, Edmundo R. Luis Cruz a la luz de la verdad. Santiago: Adeza, 1983. 129 p.: bibl., facsims., ports.

Narrative of the role of the young hero from Curicó in the Battle of Concepción in 1882, where an entire Chilean contingent was wiped out in the Peruvian highlands.

3149 Méndez Beltrán, Luz María. La mujer y la historiografía chilena (SCHG/R, 152, 1984, p. 157–178, bibl.)

Article is billed as a first attempt to assess the contributions of women to the historical literature on Chile in the 19th century. Finds that women's role has been small, but has increased in recent years.

3150 Muñoz Gomá, María Angélica. La mujer de hogar en *Casa grande* de Orrego Luco y en documentos históricos de su época (UCCIH/H, 18, 1983, p. 103–133)

Article compares fundamental traits and domestic functions of upper-class housewife Gabriela Valdés in Orrego Luco's *Casa grande* (1908) with those of two contemporary aristocratic wives and mothers studied through memoirs and letters. Conclusion is that despite some differences, both the novel and documents portray faithful execution of domestic duty as common salient characteristic of aristocratic women.

3151 Nes-El, Moshé. Historia de la comunidad israelita sefardí de Chile. Prólogo de Enrique Testa A. Santiago: Editorial Nascimento, 1984. 385 p.: bibl., index.

Thorough study of immigration, settlement, activities, and organization of Sephardic Jews in Chile from 1890 to the present. Beginning with a small migration of Sephardics from a village in today's Yugoslavia to Temuco, the community has grown to approximately 4,000, constituting a maximum of 15 percent of Chile's Jewish population. Useful survey.

3152 O'Higgins, Bernardo. Archivo de Don Bernardo O'Higgins. v. 31. Santiago: Editorial Univ. Católica, 1981. 1 v.: facsims., ill.

Vol. 31 of valuable series launched in the 1940s. Contains 196 letters written by O'Higgins (1817–30) to wide variety of correspondants. Some letters have been pubished previously, while others appear here for the first time. Useful addition to the documentation on the early republic.

3153 Ojeda Ebert, Gerardo. El rol de la inmigración alemana en el proceso de formación de la nación chilena (PAN/EL, 7, 1980, p. 35–50)

Brief article offers schematic overview, with little detail, of how 19th-century German immigration, engineered by the Chilean State, affected the formation of the Chilean nationality. Potentially useful for raising questions for investigation.

3154 Ortega, Luis. Nitrates, Chilean entrepreneurs and the origins of the War of the Pacific (JLAS, 16:2, Nov. 1984, p. 337–380)

Close analysis of circumstances of the outbreak of the War of the Pacific, focusing on the Chilean domestic economic crisis and its sociopolitical ramifications. Cautiously but convincingly, author argues that a segment of the oligarchy ("politico-entrepreneurs") saw war as the solution to the crisis and pushed Chile into war, with the anticipated positive results. Urges further research on this thesis.

3155 Palomo, Juan Francisco. Problemas del desarrollo del capitalismo en Chile, 1865–1920 (Araucaria de Chile [I. Peralta Ediciones, Pamplona, Spain] 27, 1984, p. 31–45, tables)

Brief Marxist analysis of characteristics of the Chilean labor force (1865–1920) offers few statistical tables and little else.

3156 Peri Fagerstrom, René. Apuntes y transcripciones para una historia de la función policial en Chile. v. 1, Hasta 1830. v. 2, 1830–1900. v. 3, 1900–1927. Santiago: Carabineros de Chile, 1982–1983. 3 v.: bibl., ill. (some col.)

Three volumes carry the story of police function in Chile from indigenous peoples to Ibáñez's reorganization that established the modern Carabineros. Written by a criminologist, the work, as signalled in the title, is a rather disjointed collection of narratives and documents, such as regulatory laws, internal police codes, and crime statistics. Interesting in itself, this work will be valuable as a source for future studies of police history.

3157 Pinochet de la Barra, Oscar. Correspondencia del Japón de Carlos Morla Vicuña y de Luisa Lynch de Morla (SCHG/R, 151, 1983, p. 199–227)

Article reproduces 10 letters from the wife of Chile's first diplomatic representative to Japan, and one from the minister himself. Written shortly after arrival, the letters include interesting descriptions and chronicle reactions to a clash of cultures.

3158 Pinochet de la Barra, Oscar. El gran amor de Rugendas. Ilustraciones de Rugendas. Santiago: Editorial Universitaria, 1984. 275 p.: ill.

Romantic story of Carmen Arriagada García (1808–1900), a provincial writer, woman of letters, and observer of the Chilean scene. Based on her letters, the book focuses on her long, allegedly chaste love affair with the German painter J.M. Rugendas.

3159 Prats González, Carlos. Memorias: testimonio de un soldado. Santiago: Pehuén, 1985. 610 p., 26 p. of plates: ill., ports. (Col. Testimonio)

Memoirs of the commander of the Chilean army who served under Allende, written in exile and finished just prior to his assassination in 1974. Covering the length of his military career (1928–74), these memoirs provide important insights into the Frei and especially the Allende years, during which Gen. Prats was a tenacious opponent of military intervention. Important addition to the literature on the military's role in recent politics.

3160 Pregger-Román, Charles G. The origin and development of the bourgeoisie in nineteenth-century Chile (LAP, 10:2/3, Spring/Summer 1983, p. 39–59)

Reviews the transformation of the colonial aristocracy into a bourgeoisie during the course of the 19th century. Covers familiar ground and offers little new information.

3161 El Problema de límites con Argentina: pt. 2, Decisión de la corte de arbitraje (SCHG/R, 152, 1984, p. 179–187, map)

Two-part article. Pt. 2 reproduces the

1881 and 1977 decisions rendered by arbitration panels reviewing boundary disputes between Chile and Argentina.

3162 Ramírez Necochea, Hernán. Fuerzas armadas y política en Chile, 1810–1970: antecedentes para una historia. La Habana: Casa de las Américas, 1985. 195 p.: bibl. (Cuadernos Casa; 27)

Prolific Marxist historian examines evolution of the political role of the Chilean armed forces, to the election of Salvador Allende. Argues that following 50 years of military quiescence unique to Spanish America, the two decades following the War of the Pacific set the conditions for the military's new activist role in the 20th century. Constant international tensions, internal social upheaval, and new technology after 1880 created the modern armed forces, which despite the Chilean reputation for civilian supremacy, were increasingly politicized. Solid piece of interpretative writing.

3163 Ramírez Rivera, Hugo Rodolfo. La cuestión del Colegio San Jacinto y sus consecuencias políticas, sociales y religiosas, 1904–1905 (UCCIH/H, 18, 1983, p. 193–234)

Detailed chronicle narrates an episode, the temporary closing of the Colegio San Jacinto following a sexual scandal, that the anticlerical press blew up into a *cause célèbre*. Author offers incident as case study of the persistence of Church-State struggle into the 20th century.

3164 Ravest Mora, Manuel. La Compañía Salitrera y la ocupación de Antofagasta, 1878–1879. Santiago: Editorial Andrés Bello, 1983. 205 p., 2 leaves of plates: bibl., ill.

Researched in England and Chile, this work consists primarily of reprinted and translated correspondence of principals of Casa Gibbs regarding circumstances leading up to the Chilean occupation of Antofagasta (Feb. 1879). Author intends to exonerate Chile by proving Bolivian violations of the 1874 treaty with Chile. Useful as source of important correspondence and for providing a reasonable if not totally convincing new picture of origins of the War of the Pacific.

3165 Remmer, Karen L. Party competition in Argentina and Chile: political recruitment and public policy: 1890–1930. Lincoln: Univ. of Nebraska Press, 1984. 296 p.: bibl., index, tables.

In this well researched, comparative study of the Chilean Parliamentary Period (1891–1924) and the Argentine Radical Era (1912–30), Remmer examines how party development and electoral competition affected the struggle for power in both countries. For Chile, she demonstrates that despite its reputation for empty rhetoric and corruption, the Parliamentary Period laid the basis for party competition and individual liberties that sustained Chile's liberal democratic tradition to 1973, with the support of the elites. The Argentine elites' experience between 1912–30 was difficult, leading to a different pattern of political institutional development after 1930. Overall, a major contribution. For political scientist's comment, see *HLAS 47:6533.*

3166 Revista Geográfica. Instituto Panamericano de Geografía e Historia. No. 100, julio-dic. 1984-. Santiago.

Issue devoted to urbanization in Chile. Contains several articles of historical interest, especially those by authors Hernández (p. 9–17), González (p. 77–87), and Reyes (p. 151–161).

3167 Reyes Reyes, Rafael. El Premio Nacional de Moralidad (SCHG/R, 151, 1983, p. 7–30)

This article describes a historical curiosity, the National Prize for Morality, that was awarded five times (1849–53). Modeled on annual awards for academic and mechanical achievement, this award for civic virtue and charitable acts disappeared after a brief trial.

3168 Rodríguez Villegas, Hernán. La casa de los Velascos: evolución histórica de una propiedad urbana en Santiago (ACH/B, 49:93, 1982, p. 233–314, photos)

Detailed portrait of one of Santiago's most conspicuous colonial houses consists of genealogical and biographical sketches of its owners from 1556 to the present. Includes documents and photos. Of interest primarily to antiquarians and local historians.

3169 Romero, Luis Alberto. Condiciones de vida de los sectores populares en Santiago de Chile, 1840–1895: vivienda y salud (Nueva Historia [Asociación de Historiadores Chilenos, London] 3:9, 1984, p. 3–86)

Drawing on an impressive variety of sources, article examines two central features of the living conditions of Santiago's poor.

Romero first traces the geography of popular neighborhoods as they sprang up (1840–95), then analyzes construction and rental of popular housing as a business. Also examines sanitation, diseases common to the poor, and means of prevention and cure. Solid social history.

Ruiz, Carlos. Notes on authoritarian ideologies in Chile. See *HLAS 47:6489.*

3170 Saavedra, Abdón. Antecedentes acerca de la historia de la física en Chile (ACH/B, 49:93, 1982, p. 219–232)
Outlines history of instruction and research in physics from the founding of the Univ. of Chile in 1842 to present.

3171 Salinas, Maximiliano. Cristianismo popular en Chile, 1880–1920: un esquema sobre el factor religioso en las clases subalternas durante el capitalismo oligárquico (Nueva Historia [Asociación de Historiadores Chilenos, London] 3:12, oct./dic. 1984, p. 275–302, appendix)
Interesting article that explores working class and campesino popular religion as a form of sublimated class conflict and cultural resistance to oligarchic domination. Argues that popular religious poets of the nitrate era appropriated the figure of Christ while equating the country's leaders and their values with the anti-Christ. Includes several popular songs and poems in an appendix.

3172 Salvat Monguillot, Manuel. Tocqueville en Chile (ACH/B, 49:93, 1982, p. 209–217)
Superficial sketch of the influence of Alexis de Tocqueville's *Democracy in America* on Chilean intellectuals, including Lastarria, Marcial González, and Abdón Cifuentes.

3173 Sater, William F. Chile and the War of the Pacific. Lincoln: Univ. of Nebraska Press, 1986. 343 p.: bibl., index, tables.
Sater's thoroughly researched, well argued work is the story of the impact of the war on Chile, not a history of the war itself. Revising standard interpretations, author depicts a country ill-prepared for war and handicapped by inept military forces, political divisions, and financial crisis. Buttressed by 45 tables, this work offers a valuable in-depth look at a country during a crucial moment in its history. Essential for historians of Chile.

3174 Sater, William F. El financiamiento de la Guerra del Pacífico (Nueva Historia [Asociación de Historiadores Chilenos, London] 3:12, 1984, p. 237–273)
This article, which received first prize in the Barros Arana international competition on Chilean history, relies heavily on congressional debates and newspaper coverage to analyze government methods of financing the war. Having adopted new taxes in the late 1870s to counter a depression, the government relied on two new sources: export tax on nitrates, and issuance of paper money.

3175 Sínodo Chileno de la Epoca Republicana, 1st, Ancud, Chile, 1851. El Primer Sínodo Chileno de la Epoca Republicana. Santiago: Ediciones Univ. Católica de Chile, Facultad de Teología, 1983. 206 p.: bibl., ill.
Important chapter in Chilean Church history, book traces religious career of Justo Donoso (1800–68), first Bishop of Ancud, and examines setting of first Chilean synod after independence. Work consists mostly of the manuscript of the synod itself, discovered by author in archives of the Bishopric of Ancud.

3176 Somervell, Philip. Naval affairs in Chilean politics, 1910–1932 (JLAS, 16:2, Nov. 1984, p. 381–402)
Analyzes the navy's role in Chilean politics over two decades, suggesting a greater degree of involvement than is usually recognized (excepting the 1931 uprising). During this period, the navy also lost out in its rivalry with the army, ending the period in a clearly subordinate position.

3177 Sosa, Ignacio. Conciencia y proyecto nacional en Chile, 1891–1973. México: UNAM, Facultad de Filosofía y Letras, Centro de Estudios Latinoamericanos, 1981. 269 p.: bibl., ill. (Col. Seminarios)
Interpretative essay on Chile's political development from Balmaceda through Allende, analyzing varying approaches to achieving national economic independence and social justice. Based on sophisticated reading of secondary materials, this work considers three periods: 1) oligarchic epoch (1891–1938); 2) rise of modernizing bourgeoisie (1938–64); and 3) necessary revolution (1964–73). Sympathetic to the left, this is a useful addition to the literature on Chile's modern political development.

3178 Tagle D., Matías. Notas sobre el surgimiento y la configuración del Estado en Chile (CPU/ES, 10:37, 1983, p. 91–129)

Reviews early republican institutional history in search of the crystallization of a State capable of monopolizing force, regulating social relations, and controlling its territory. Author argues that such a State was in place by 1860, following the decade of civil wars.

3179 Téllez Lúgaro, Eduardo. Perfil histórico de Antofagasta: años de emergencia y fundación de una sociedad fronteriza, 1866–1869 (SCHG/R, 152, 1984, p. 36–64)

Detailed study of first three years of Antofagasta (originally La Chimba), focusing on its economic base, demography, and spatial evolution. Based largely on archival sources and newspapers, this work is a solid contribution to the history of the Norte Grande. Includes three documents on the founding of the city.

3180 Torres Marín, Manuel. Pedro Schumacher y su breve experiencia en Chile (ACH/B, 49:93, 1982, p. 315–327)

Sketch of German priest and his observations of Chile in the 1860s is derived from little known book by Schumacher (1839–1902) that centers on his extended residence in Ecuador. His observations of people and religion are useful.

3181 Tras la huella de Claudio Orrego. Edición de Patricio Dooner. Santiago: Instituto Chileno de Estudios Humanísticos, 1983. 181 p., 8 leaves of plates: bibl., ports.

Anthology celebrates and recounts life and accomplishments of Claudio Orrego (d. 1982). This respected and influential writer, historian, sociologist, journalist, and Christian Democratic leader is eulogized and re-membered in these pages by dozens of his colleagues from intellectual and political circles.

3182 Wright, Thomas C. The first Ibáñez administration in Chile, 1927–1931: a preliminary assessment (Proceedings of the Rocky Mountain Council on Latin American Studies Conference [Las Cruces, N.M.] 1984, p. 61–69)

Essay analyzes role of the first Ibáñez government in Chile's transition toward an activist, developmentalist State, focusing on the government's relationships with entrepreneurial and labor groups. Author also points out themes for further research. [V.C. Peloso]

3183 Wunder, Gerd. Hauptmann Körner und der Burgerkrieg in Chile, 1891 (IAA, 9:2, 1983, p. 225–240, bibl.)

Study of German Gen. Körner's role in the 1891 Civil War explores importance of his military reforms to the war's outcome. Offers interesting detail on Körner's mission in Chile.

3184 Zeitlin, Maurice. The civil wars in Chile, or, the bourgeois revolutions that never were. Princeton, N.J.: Princeton Univ. Press, 1984. 1 v.: bibl., index.

Provocative study of the civil wars (1851–59 and 1891) reinterprets Chilean history while challenging analysis of the world system school. Zeitlin sees the failure of Chile's 20th-century capitalist development as the result of the mining bourgeoisie's loss in both civil wars, and with it a failure of political will to resist foreign control of mineral resources. While historians will find this book lacking in several ways, including a solid base in research, it is essential reading for Chileanists and recommended for other Latin Americanists.

ARGENTINA, PARAGUAY AND URUGUAY

JOSEPH T. CRISCENTI, *Professor of History, Boston College*

ARGENTINA

HISTORICAL WRITINGS IN this biennium confirm a trend first noted in *HLAS* 46. Contemporary affairs, the post 1930-era in particular, now command more interest than the 19th century. Nearly two-thirds of the publications annotated below deal with the 20th century. This percentage would be even higher if the 1880s and 1890s were included as they often are in studies of the 20th century. The number of contributions by foreign authors has declined slightly, although they still predominate among those using the comparative approach. A number of bibliographical works have appeared. Unfortunately, many Argentine serial publications were unavailable for review, some scholarly journals having suspended publication for lack of funding, others being issued *cuando pueden*. There are encouraging signs that the situation may improve.

The pre-1880 era still lacks the monographic studies that will fill important gaps in our knowledge, but new approaches and documents are challenging many assumptions. Heredia's study (item **3245**) suggests a new interpretation of the corsairs that fought in the Wars of Independence. Szuchman's revealing essay (item **3315**) implies that the ordinary citizen was more responsive to *barrio* officials than to the weak provincial government. Nicolau's research (item **3273**) indicates that cattle interests did not attain immediate domination of policy making in the first Rosas administration. Bonura's work (item **3201**) clearly describes the mechanics of the Argentine financial and mercantile world to 1850. Both Hodge's excellent article (item **3250**) and the study directed by Pérez Guilhou (item **3252**) identify some of the forces working for national unification. McLynn succinctly describes the economy during the Mitre administration (item **3268**) and skillfully explains the consequences of the Paraguayan War for Argentina (item **3267**).

The political history of the period is a little clearer with the publication of Ruiz Moreno's *Elecciones y revolución: Oroño, Urquiza y Mitre* (item **3301**). His work gives new meaning to the crucial elections of 1867 in the province of Santa Fe.

The ideas of several men who influenced national policies have been reexamined. Botana (item **3203**) analyzes in detail Alberdi's and Sarmiento's thinking. Pérez Guilhou (item **3281**) examines the sources of Alberdi's conservatism. Gandía (item **3239**) focuses on Sarmiento's approach to inter-American relations, and as Ramírez de Rivera reveals (item **3291**), Sarmiento was not adverse to the use of force. Estanislao S. Zeballos also believed in a militant foreign policy, as a review of his publications reveals (item **3206a**). How Argentine jingoism affected Brazil is ably discussed by Bueno (item **3206**).

Military history as well as Indian history have benefited from several valuable contributions. Piccinali (item **2891a**) meticulously examines how San Martín built an elite unit, the source of future governors and generals. The well documented works of Piccinali (item **3286**) and Scunio (item **3307**) demonstrate the army's contribution to national unification and expansion, and the army's humane approach to the Indians during the Conquest of the Desert. Their conclusions clash with the views of novelist and essayist David Viñas (item **3323**), who believes that the aim of the army was to exterminate the Indians. Beretta Curi (item **3197**) traces the gradual adoption of an extermination policy by the government of Buenos Aires before 1852. Ortega (item **3276**) briefly defines the frontier woman.

In the field of foreign relations Parody Dorrego (item **3227**) has published documents which reveal the complex international and regional situation Governor Dorrego faced as he sought a peace treaty with Brazil in 1828. Pomer's controversial study (item **3288**) attempts to identify the domestic factors which influenced the foreign policies of the embryonic national governments in the region.

As it was indicated earlier, publications of the 20th century predominate. In labor history there are several notable contributions. Bilsky (item **3200**) presents new data in his detailed examination of the divisions within the labor movement during its first decade. Tamarin (item **3316**) studies the divisions that exited at a later date. Short sketches of some early union leaders appear in Troncoso's work (item **3319**). Coggiola's study (item **3217**) describes the schisms among the Trotsykites and their effects on the labor movement. Tosco (item **3317**) provides an insider's look at labor unions, labor leaders, and union bureaucracies. In an insightful essay Horowitz (item **3251**) explains why one group of laborers takes pride in their union. A well researched history of the Labor Party is found in Pont's study (item **3289**).

A number of socioeconomic studies seeks to explain Argentina's decline and failure to industrialize. The problem is approached from a variety of viewpoints. Botana and Gallo (item **3204**) see no evidence of an abrupt break between the pre- and post-1914 years. In two authoritative essays (items **3220** and **3278**) Panettieri maintains that prior experience led the early economic planners to endorse free trade and agricultural development rather than industrialization. Gravil's research (item **3242**) convinces him that economic policies were determined by the needs of Great Britain. Armstrong (item **3191**) suggests that the amount of industrialization was influenced by the internal social structure and the international trade system. Cortés-Conde (item **3218**) believes that economic rather than social factors guided the policy makers. This view receives some support from the experience of Mendoza (item **3270**).

The ability of Argentina to compete successfully in world agricultural markets is attributable to the fertility of its soil and to other factors. One reason, Solberg's careful study (item **3311**) shows, was the land tenure system. Another, Lafuente (item **3262**), was the availability of foreign capital and access to foreign markets. Argentina lost its relative preeminence in the world agricultural markets after 1929. Both Lascano (item **3263**) and Sidicaro (item **3310**) attribute the decline to the failure of national economic policies and to changes in the international agricultural markets. Alhadaff's investigations (item **3187**) reveal that Argentina's response to the Depression of the 1930s was basically similar to that of Canada and Australia.

Several noteworthy contributions have been made to the political history of the pre-Perón years. Ortega (item **3275**) has carefully examined the Argentine attitude toward electoral fraud and the caudillo, and his findings support Walter's (item **3324**) stress on the overriding importance of the rural caudillos and urban bosses in elections. Deutsch's study (item **3225**) is a significant work on the Argentine right. Del Mazo (item **3270a**) and Azaretto (item **3194**) do not settle the dispute over the reasons for the Revolution of 1930, but both provide new data. Etchepareborda's study (item **3270a**) effectively demonstrates that rivalry between two cabinet officers hoping to succeed Yrigoyen contributed to the revolution.

Luna has begun to fill the need for a comprehensive examination of the Perón administrations with the publication of the first of a multi-volume study of Argentina (1945–55, see item **3265**). Crawley's suggestive account (item **3219**) concentrates on Perón, peronism, and the politics of a fragmented Argentina after 1955. Ciria's thoughtful analysis (item **3215**) calls needed attention to the contradictory tendencies within peronism itself. Ceballos (item **3211**), a student leader, reports on the ideological disputes within the student groups. Both Alende (item **3186**) and Rodríguez Lamas (item **3297**) describe the disunity within the armed forces, the labor unions, and the political parties. Divisions within the Peronist Party itself, Itzcovitz (item **3257**) demonstrates, account for the fall of the peronist government in 1976. Troncoso (item **3320**) collected documents which help to explain what happened then. The party's poor performance in the elections of 1983 led to some soul-searching among peronists (item **3321**). It also inspired opposition leaders to publish party histories and documents in an effort to attract the young into their ranks (items **3186, 3194,** and **3312**).

The economic policies of the administrations that followed Perón await serious analysis. Buchanan's interpretative essay (item **3205**) documents in a unique manner the declining importance of the national labor office. Ceballos (item **3212**) is convinced all governments after 1976 have sought to weaken the labor movement. In a controversial essay Echagüe (item **3229**) explains why he objects to Argentina trading with the Soviet Union.

The Malvinas (Falklands) War of 1982 inspired a number of publications. The most authoritative review of Argentine claims to the islands are those of Destéfani (item *HLAS 47:7281*) and Santos Martínez (item **3304**). Sequeira (item **3309**) essentially has written a history of the Argentine Naval Air Force. Romero Briasco (item **3299**) analyzes the tactics and operations of the British and Argentine air force units involved in the war. Carballo's work (item **3208**) contains after-action interviews with Argentine Air Force pilots. González G. (item **3241**) evaluates the tactics and operations employed by both sides in the war. Townsend (item **3318**) discusses Conservative efforts to reestablish peace, while Christie (item **3214**) ably explains the reaction of the British Left to the war.

There are three new general histories worthy of note. The Menéndez volume (item **3271**) stresses the contributions of the military to the formation and expansion of the nation. The text by Rock (item **3296**) reflects both the author's interest in the 20th century and the best of current scholarship. Avni's study (item **3193**) of Jewish immigration to Argentina is very thorough.

Provincial histories are scarce. Castello (item **3210**) has incorporated the latest scholarship in the history of Corrientes. Segura (item **3308**) has done likewise for his history of Entre Ríos.

Among the biographies and memoirs worthy of note are Henault's *Alicia Moreau de Justo* (item **3244**), Pavón Pereyra's *Isabel* (item **3280**), Schallman's *Memorias documentadas* (item **3305**), Ripa's *Recuerdos de un abogado patagónico* (item **3295**), and the previously cited Piccinali's *Vida del Teniente General Nicolás Levalle* and Scunio's *Del Río IV al Lime Leuvú*. The previously mentioned works by Alende, Azaretto, and Ceballos are partly autobiographical, as is Sonego's *Las dos Argentinas . . .* (item **3312**).

The best way to conclude this overview of publications on Argentine history is to repeat what was noted in *HLAS 46*: ". . . contemporary topics and socioeconomic history command a great deal more attention among publications annotated below. Nevertheless, there are still regrettable gaps in our knowledge of Argentine history exemplified by the lack of rigorous scrutiny of the 1930s or of the 1958–66 civilian administrations."

PARAGUAY

This period is noteworthy for the appearance of four publications. Warren, author of a classic study on Paraguay, has contributed *Rebirth of the Paraguayan Republic: the first Colorado era, 1878–1904* (item **3345**). This is essential reading for those interested in Río de la Plata. Blinn Reber's significant study of the *yerba mate* trade (item **3333**) reinforces the trend to see pre-1870 governments in a more favorable light. Speratti (item **3343**), one of the organizers, explains the rationale for the Revolution of February 17, 1936, and the founding of the Partido Revolucionario Febrerista. In an insightful article Herken Krauer (item **3337**) emphasizes, as he did elsewhere (see *HLAS 46:3386*), that diplomatic pressure is not always successful.

Viola's lectures (item **3344**) summarize many recent revisionist interpretations of the Francia administration.

The military and diplomatic phases of the Chaco War receive considerable attention. Ayala (item **3331**) and Delgado (item **3334**), both former commanders, contribute to the ongoing evaluation of the campaign plans and tactics of military commanders and the search for heroes. An excellent unit history based on operation orders and after-action reports is Riart's *Senderos de gloria . . .* (item **3341**). *Album gráfico . . .* (item **3329**) contains a comprehensive pictorial history of the war from the perspective of the combatants, while Sosa Tenaillon's work (item **3342**) records the recollections of some veterans. Caballero reports the reminiscences of an elder Colorado statesman and veteran army commander in *Testimonios de un presidente . . .* (item **3339**).

URUGUAY

Barrán and Nohum (item **3349**) present the conclusions they reached upon completing their thorough-going reexamination of Uruguayan rural history. Sanz (item **3362**) carefully documents the efforts of Great Britain and France in 1817 to persuade Portugal and Spain to settle their differences over Brazil and Uruguay. Lista Viamonte's *Diario . . .* (item **3358**) reveals new aspects of the Guerra Grande. Medical history benefits from Buño's account (item **3352**) of the yellow fever epidemic of 1857. Finally, Fonseca (item **3356**) presents an informative and insightful description of Uruguayan leaders as seen from Brazil.

Cocchi *et al.* (item **3353**) examine the impact of three factors usually associated with the urbanization process and arrive at an unexpected conclusion. The Academia Nacional de Economía (item **3366**) has published a number of interpretative essays by economic historians, some of which should be read with Barrán and Nohum. Pereyra's biography of Barrios Amorín (item **3360**) serves as a good introduction to Uruguayan politics in the 20th century, while Aparicio's biography of Basilio Muñoz (item **3347**) fails to settle the controversy surrounding his political behavior.

Numerous contributions indicate that departmental history continues to attract attention. Gil Villamil (item **3357**) has written an enlightening history of Cerro Largo, the home of generals and presidents. How conditions in an interior city can shape the viewpoint of a metropolitan journalist is exemplified by Bacinno's study of Viana (item **3348**). In his essays Villegas (items **3364** and **3365**) documents the state of the Church and religious conditions in two frontier communities in the second half of the 19th century.

ARGENTINA

3185 Acevedo, Anacarsis L. Investigación a La Forestal: debate nacional. Buenos Aires: Centro Editor de América Latina, 1983. 166 p. (Biblioteca Política argentina; 34)

Decision of La Forestal to cease production of *tanino* in the northern section of the province of Santa Fe and to dismiss its employees led to an investigation by the provincial legislature. Acevedo reports findings of the Bicameral Commission he headed.

3186 Alende, Oscar Eduardo. ¿Qué es el Partido Intransigente? Buenos Aires: Editorial Sudamericana, 1983. 234 p., 16 p. of plates: bibl., ill., ports. (Col. de los partidos políticos nacionales)

Former governor of the province of Buenos Aires sees his party as the true heir of Alem and Yrigoyen, and describes its organization and development to 1983. Essentially the story of the struggle for leadership between and within the two ideological tendencies traditionally identified with the Unión Cívica Radical, and their relations with peronists and the military.

3187 Alhadeff, Peter. Public finance and the economy in Argentina, Australia and Canada during the Depression of the 1930s (*in* Argentina, Australia & Canada: studies in comparative development, 1870–1965. Edited by D.C.M. Platt and Guido Di Tella. New York: St. Martin's Press, 1985, p. 161–178)

Comparison of the Argentine, Australian, and Canadian response to the effects of the Depression of the 1930s shows that all three governments adopted conservative economic policies, relied more on the domestic economy than on foreign sources for public funds, and benefited especially from the savings accumulated during the prosperous 1920s.

3188 Alonso Piñeiro, Armando. La historia argentina que muchos argentinos no conocen. 5a ed., aum. Buenos Aires: Ediciones Depalma, 1984. 587 p.: bibl., index.

Consists of popular, well written short essays based on archival research. Originally published in *Siete Días Ilustrados* (1973–75). Contains seven more chapters than previous edition (see *HLAS 40:3682*).

3189 Arce, Facundo A. El primer gran historiador de Entre Ríos: Don Benigno Teijeiro Martínez (FNH/NH, 14:28, dic. 1981, p. 206–223)

Short but excellent biography of journalist, educator, publisher, and archivist who became the leading historian of the province of Entre Ríos. Teijeiro Martínez's historical works (1846–1925) constitute a valuable introduction to the history of Entre Ríos and its neighbors to 1853.

3190 Armagno Cosentino, José. Carolina Muzilli. Buenos Aires: Centro Editor de América Latina, 1984. 110 p. (Biblioteca Política argentina; 75)

Short biography of a Socialist woman who fought for women's rights, divorce, women's vote, abolition of child labor, and the economic emancipation of women. Based on press articles that appeared during her life.

3191 Armstrong, Warwick. The social origins of industrial growth: Canada, Argentina and Australia, 1870–1930 (*in* Argentina, Australia & Canada: studies in comparative development, 1870–1965. Edited by D.C.M. Platt and Guido Di Tella. New York: St. Martin's Press, 1984, p. 76–94)

Calls for national case studies which stress the relationship between internal social structure and the international trade system. Such studies are expected to contribute to a better understanding of development and underdevelopment.

3192 Arturo Frondizi: historia y problemática de un estadista. v. 1, El hombre. Directores de la obra, Roberto Gustavo Pisarello Virasoro y Emilia Edda Menotti. Prólogo de Enrique de Gandía. Buenos Aires: Ediciones Depalma, 1983–1984. 1 v.: bibl., ill.

Collection of essays by various authors who evaluate the intellectual formation of Frondizi and his approach to Argentine problems during a long political career. Vol. 1 of four projected on Frondizi's career.

3193 Avni, Haim. Argentina y la historia de la inmigración judía, 1810–1950. Traducción del hebreo, Etty E. de Hoter. Jerusalén: Editorial Universitaria Magnes, Univ. Hebrea de Jerusalén: AMIA Comunidad de Buenos Aires, 1983. 593 p., 8 p. of plates: bib., ill., index, map, ports.

Zionist interpretation of Jewish immigration to Argentina, primarily in the years after 1880. Extremely well researched.

3194 Azaretto, Roberto. Historia de las fuerzas conservadoras. Buenos Aires: Centro Editor de América Latina, 1983. 155 p. (Biblioteca Política argentina; 7)

Conservative forcefully reviews contributions made by the Partido Autonomista Nacional and its heirs to the formation of the Argentine State, its modernization and industrialization. Includes brief history of Partido Demócrata Nacional, a federation of provincial political parties, to 1983.

3195 Baigorria, Nélida *et al.* Testimonios sobre Ricardo Rojas. Buenos Aires: Univ. de Buenos Aires, Facultad de Filosofía y Letras, Instituto de Literatura Argentina Ricardo Rojas, 1984. 202 p.: bibl., ill.

Nélida Biagorria, Ronald Hilton, Dardo Cúneo, Bernardo González Arrili, Antonio Pagés Larraya, and Mariano Picón Salas recall their impressions of Ricardo Rojas. Interesting comments on his personality.

3196 Balzola, Eduardo B. Orígenes de La Cabaña argentina (SRA/A, 68:1/3, enero/marzo 1984, p. 10–14, bibl., table)

Maintains that the first Shorthorn (Durham) bull of English origins was introduced in 1836 by Juan Miller and was used for breeding at an *estancia* owned by Domingo Frías in Mercedes, province of Buenos Aires.

Barcala de Moyano, Graciela G. Bibliografía del Doctor Ricardo R. Caillet-Bois. See *HLAS 47:50.*

3197 Beretta Curi, Alcides. Hacendados, tierras y fronteras en la provincia de Buenos Aires: 1810–1852 (UB/BA, 14:32, 1982, p. 39–59, tables)

Examines the evolution of Indian policy from conciliation to extermination, and the provincial land policy that permitted some porteño merchants to survive British competition by becoming large landowners (1822–1839). Analysis based on land laws of the province of Buenos Aires.

3198 Bialet Massé, Juan. Informe sobre el estado de las clases obreras argentinas a comienzos del siglo: selección. v. 1. Buenos Aires: Centro Editor de América Latina, 1985. 1 v. (Biblioteca Política argentina; 111)

Selections from a basic work that first appeared in 1904 and was republished in 1968. This volume contains the author's observations and reflections on the Chaco and its Indians, foreign immigrants, agricultural labor conditions, and the sugar industry.

3199 Bilsky, Edgardo J. Contribution à l'histoire du mouvement ouvrier et social argentin: bibliographie et sources documentaires de la région parisienne. Nanterrre, France: Bibliothèque de documentation internationale contemporaine, 1983. 229 p.: ill., index.

Guide to collections on the Argentine working class available in 21 libraries and documentation centers in the Paris region. Works noted date from the late 19th century to 1982. There is a subject-author index, and the location of each work is given. Not an annotated bibliography.

3200 Bilsky, Edgardo J. La F.O.R.A. [i.e. Federación Obrera Regional Argentina] y el movimiento obrero, 1900–1910. Buenos Aires: Centro Editor de América Latina, 1985. 2 v. (243 p.): appendices, bibls. (Biblioteca Política argentina; 97–98)

Detailed and well documented exposition of the strife between and among anarchists, socialists, and syndicalists over control and direction of the labor movement. Maintains anarchists dominated in the

1900s. Carefully describes the membership in each labor union. Volume two contains the resolutions passed at the various F.O.R.A. congresses.

Borda, Gabriel S. Comercio internacional argentino. See *HLAS 47:3695.*

3201 Bonura, Elena. El crédito público bajo la administración de Juan Manuel de Rosas (FNH/NH, 14:28, dic. 1981, p. 195–205)

Important analysis of the meaning and origins of *crédito público* in Argentina and the failure of government efforts to eliminate its debt and to return to metallic currency.

3202 Bonura, Elena. El "sistema" económico de Rosas: introducción a su estudio. Buenos Aires: Imprenta Sellarés, 1982. 75 p.: bibls.

Contains two provocative essays, one maintaining that the purposes of the Tariff Law of 1835 was to protect provincial industries and to prepare the way for national organization, and the other claiming that Rosas wanted to eliminate all government debts so that metallic money could circulate. Needs more evidence to settle the dispute over the two issues.

3203 Botana, Natalio R. La tradición republicana: Alberdi, Sarmiento y las ideas políticas de su tiempo. Buenos Aires: Sudamericana, 1984. 493 p. (Col. Historia y sociedad)

Significant study shows how Alberdi and Sarmiento applied European political ideas to the Argentine environment and how their different approaches to civîl liberties and political rights influenced the development of modern Argentina.

3204 Botana, Natalio R. and Ezequiel Gallo. La política argentina entre las dos guerras mundiales (RO, 37, junio 1984, p. 45–58)

Excellent overview of fundamental features of Argentina (1916–43). Argues that there was no abrupt break with the pre-1914 era.

3205 Buchanan, Paul G. State corporatism in Argentina: labor administration under Perón and Onganía (LARR, 20:1, 1985, p. 61–95, graphs)

Detailed and insightful study of the internal organization and functioning of the national labor administration under two different regimes. Author concludes that a distinct type of corporatism has certain specific external and internal traits peculiar to it.

3206 Bueno, Clodoalo. O rearmamento naval brasileiro e a rivalidade Brasil-Argentina em 1906–08 (Historia [Univ. Estadual Paulista, São Paulo] 1, 1982, p. 21–35, bibl.)

Contemporary evidence suggests to author that Brazil embarked on naval rearmament because it sought prestige in the international world and feared possible aggression from Europe or a South American neighbor.

3206a Busala, Analía and **Analía Grosso.** La realidad histórica argentina desde 1880 hasta el centenario de la Revolución de Mayo: a través de la prensa; un sector de la opinión pública liberado por el Dr. Estanislao S. Zeballo y su posición frente a la comunidad de naciones, 1898–1909 (UNL/U, 95, enero/abril 1980, p. 61–104)

Zeballos, historian, diplomat, and economist, founded the important *Revista de Derecho, Historia y Letras.* He believed in a strong foreign policy, endorsed US intervention in the Caribbean, and favored arms build-up.

3207 Canclini, Arnoldo. Juan Lawrence, primer maestro de Tierra del Fuego. Buenos Aires: Marymar Ediciones, 1983. 103 p.: bibl., ports. (Col. Patagonia)

Biography of Protestant missionary who lived as a teacher among the disappearing Indians of Tierra del Fuego (1869–1932). Based on family archives, interviews with descendants, and the papers of Tomás Bridges. Very instructive.

3208 Carballo, Pablo Marcos. Dios y los halcones. Ilustraciones de Exequiel Martínez. Buenos Aires: Editorial Abril, 1983. 223 p., 32 p. of plates: col. ill. (Suplemento de *La Revista Siete Dias*; 9)

Group of Argentine Air Force pilots individually describe their experiences during the Falkland (Malvinas) War of 1982. Their accounts were collected during or shortly after the war.

3209 Castellan, Angel. Tiempo e historiografía. Buenos Aires: Editorial Biblos, 1984. 157 p. (Col. Historia. Serie mayor; 1)

Thoughtful epistemological study of historiography.

3210 Castello, Antonio Emilio. Historia de Corrientes. Buenos Aires: Plus Ultra, 1984. 629 p.: bibl., ill., ports. (Col. Historia de nuestras provincias; 12)

Essentially a provincial history with particular emphasis on the pre-1868 years. Excellent study updates older histories of the important province of Corrientes.

3211 Ceballos, Carlos A. Los estudiantes universitarios y la política, 1955–1970. Buenos Aires: Centro Editor de América Latina, 1985. 136 p. (Biblioteca Política argentina; 103)

Informed analysis of diverse tendencies and alliances within the university student body (1955–70), with particular emphasis on the 1963–66 period, by former president of the Federación Universitaria Argentina. Includes complete text of many congressional and regional junta resolutions.

3212 Ceballos, Ernesto S. Historia política del movimiento obrero argentino, 1944–1985. Buenos Aires: Ediciones del Mar Dulce, 1985. 155 p.

Interpretative essay on the role of the labor movement and laboring class in the political life of Argentina. Believes the aim of the national government since the Illia administration is to weaken the national labor federation.

3213 Chávez, Fermín. Historia del país de los argentinos. 6a ed., corr. y notablemente aum. Buenos Aires: Distribuidora y Editora Theoría, 1983. 345 p. (Biblioteca argentina de letras)

Prominent revisionist thoughtfully reviews Argentine political history to 1930. Emphasizes pre-1853 years. See *HLAS 40:3725* for comments on second edition.

3214 Christie, Clive. The British left and the Falklands War (PQ, 55:3, July/Sept. 1984, p. 288–307)

Stimulating analysis of how the Falklands (Malvinas) crisis forces the British left to reassess the relationship between nationalism and internationalism and between principles and realities in policy. Based on left-wing periodicals and newpapers.

3215 Ciria, Alberto. Política y cultura popular: la Argentina peronista, 1946–

1955. Buenos Aires: Ediciones de la Flor, 1983. 357 p.: bibl., ill.

Thoughtful analysis of peronist ideology, its implementation in the Chamber of Deputies and the Peronist Party, and its relation to popular culture. Significant work.

Clementi, Hebe. Juventud y política en la Argentina. See *HLAS 47:6512*.

Clementi, Hebe. El radicalismo, nudos gordianos de la economía. See *HLAS 47:6513*.

3216 Cócaro, Nicolás and **Emilio E. Cócaro.** Florida, la calle del país. Buenos Aires: Fundación Banco de Boston, 1984. 291 p., 12 p. of plates: bibl., ill.

Description of the social and economic activities that took place on Calle Florida from colonial times to 1944.

3217 Coggiola, Osvaldo. Historia del trotskismo argentino, 1929–1960. Buenos Aires: Centro Editor de América Latina, 1985. 159 p.: bibl. (Biblioteca Política argentina; 91)

Outlines political history of Argentine Trotskyism, paying special attention to the numerous schisms within the minority movement, failure of efforts to unify factions at the IV International, and its influence among union activities (1943–60). Extensive quotations from Trotskyite works.

Compilación cronológica de los Presidentes, Vice-Presidentes de la Nación Argentina, Ministros de Hacienda, de Economía, Secretarios de Estado de Hacienda y/o Finanzas, Secretarios de Estado de Programación y Coordinación Económica y sus respectivos Subsecretarios, 1854–1978. See *HLAS 47:6514*.

3218 Cortés Conde, Roberto. Some notes on the industrial development of Argentina and Canada in the 1920s (*in* Argentina, Australia & Canada: studies in comparative development, 1870–1965. Edited by D.C.M. Platt and Guido Di Tella. New York: St. Martin's Press, 1985, p. 149–160, tables)

Comparison with Canadian developments suggests that Argentina's feeble industrial growth may not have been due to the opposition of the landowners but to the shortage of imported raw materials, the concentration of new industries on the domestic market, and the absence of a large influx of foreign capital.

3219 Crawley, Eduardo. A house divided: Argentina, 1880–1980. New York: St. Martin's Press, 1984. 472 p.: bibl., index, map.

Argentine journalist's stimulating and suggestive account of Perón based on personal information. Brief treatment of Perón's opposition to Yrigoyen (1880–1943).

3220 La Crisis de 1890. Selección y prólogo de José Panettieri. Buenos Aires: Centro Editor de América Latina, 1984. 91 p.: bibl. (Historia testimonial argentina; 20)

Collection of contemporary articles describing and explaining the crisis of 1890. Editor provides a stimulating essay summarizing the decade.

3221 Cronología militar argentina, 1806–1980. Buenos Aires: Editorial CLIO, 1983. 334 p., 1 leaf of plates: bibl., ill., col. maps (folded in pocket)

Describes military activities year by year, day by day, to 1980. Based on documentary sources and the work of Luis Bertone des Balbes. Contains history of the military who died in the struggle against the subversives. Lacks an index to names and places.

3222 Cúneo, Dardo. Comportamiento y crisis de la clase empresaria. Buenos Aires: Centro Editor de América Latina, 1984. 2 v. (256 p.): bibl. (Biblioteca Política argentina; 68–69)

Reprint (see *HLAS 32:2527*).

3223 Demitrópulos, Libertad. Eva Perón. Buenos Aires: Centro Editor de América Latina, 1984. 156 p.: bibl. (Biblioteca Política argentina; 47)

Sympathetic biography of Eva Perón. Little documentation.

3224 Los Derechos humanos en la democracia: anexo, *Declaración universal de derechos humanos, Naciones Unidas, 1948.* Compilación de A. Bruno, M. Cavarozzi y V. Palermo. Buenos Aires: Centro Editor de América Latina, 1985. 108 p. (Biblioteca Política argentina; 92)

Collection of papers on human rights presented at conference organized by Centro de Estudios de Estado y Sociedad (March 1984). Participants included Vicente Palermo, Marcelo Cavarozzi, Jorge Vanossi, and Federico Storani.

Destéfani, Laurio Hedelvio. The Malvinas, the South Georgias, and the South Sandwich

Islands: the conflict with Britain. See *HLAS* 47:7281.

3225 Deutsch, Sandra McGee. Counter-revolution in Argentina, 1900–1932: the Argentine Patriotic League. Lincoln: Univ. of Nebraska Press, 1986. 1 v.: bibl., index.

Notable contribution to study of counterrevolutionary movements in Argentina. The influence of the Argentine Patriotic League is seen as continuing beyond 1932 and into the peronist years. Shows need for more studies of the Argentine right and a re-examination of peronismo.

3226 Di Tella, Torcuato S. Política y clase obrera. 2a ed., ampliada y rev. Buenos Aires: Centro Editor de América Latina, 1983. 128 p.: bibl. (Biblioteca Política argentina; 36)

Contains enlarged version of author's *El sistema político argentino y la clase obrera* (1964) and most of his *Socialismo en la Argentina* (1965). Additions emphasize his concern for Argentina's future.

3227 Dorrego, Manuel. Manuel Dorrego, el coronel del pueblo. Edición de César A. Parody Dorrego. Buenos Aires: Librería Editorial Palumbo, 1981. 175 p.: ill.

Contains unedited correspondence of Dorrego with his representative at the National Convention in Santa Fe in 1828. Shows his desire for peace with Brazil on the best possible terms.

3228 Dumrauf, Clemente I. Los salesianos y la historiografía patagónica (FNH/NH, 14:28, dic. 1981, p. 224–233)

Partial listing of memoirs and historical works written by Salesian missionaries in Patagonia. Briefly describes important contributions of later generation of Salesian fathers (e.g., Raúl Agustín Entraigas, Manuel Jesús Molina, Pascual R. Paesa).

3229 Echagüe, Carlos. El socialimperialismo ruso en la Argentina. Buenos Aires: Ediciones Agora, 1984. 367 p.: bibls., ill.

Writer criticizes the "Videla-Viola dictatorship" for replacing Argentine dependence on Great Britain with one on the USSR when it stressed cereal rather than meat and cereal exports, and warns that the USSR will use Argentina to control the South Atlantic. Interesting but not convincing.

3230 En tiempos de la república agropecuaria, 1930–1943. Compilación de Susana Pereira. Buenos Aires: Centro Editor de América Latina, 1983. 143 p. (Biblioteca Política argentina; 40)

Selections from newspapers, periodicals, and books which capture the spirit and feelings of the times.

Escude, Carlos. La Argentina: ¿paria internacional? See *HLAS* 47:7283.

Espinosa Moraga, Oscar. La cuestión de las Islas Falkland, 1492–1982. See *HLAS* 47:7284.

3231 Estampas informales de Buenos Ayres, 1865: relatos y dibujos de un viajero escocés que visita Buenos Aires y se radica en estancias del campo porteño, partido de Chascomús; descripción de costumbres, gauchos, carretas, diligencias, plantas y animales. Estudio preliminar y notas de Carlos Antonio Moncaut. La Plata, Argentina: Editorial El Aljibe, 1983. 116 p., 32 p. of plates: ill. (Col. Pampa virgen; 2)

Unknown author of this travel account arrived in Buenos Aires in 1865, and spent much of his time in the countryside, especially around Chascomús. Excellent descriptions of a *saladero, estancia* life, gauchos, and the use of the *carretas* in provincial trade. Original appeared in Edinburgh, 1868.

Estrada, Marcos de. Una verdad sobre las Malvinas. See *HLAS* 47:7285.

3232 Estudio socio-económico y cultural de Salta. t. 3, Area histórica. Salta, Argentina: Univ. Nacional de Salta, Consejo de Investigación, 1984. 1 v.: bibl., ill., ports.

Contains the results of research conducted at the Univ. Nacional de Salta (May 1, 1975-March 31, 1980). Vols. 1–2 were not available for review by press time. Vol. 3 consists of a section on the socioeconomic conditions that exist in the three geographical divisions of Salta, and another on the history of the Church in Salta. Outstanding contribution to provincial history.

3233 Etchepareborda, Roberto. La cuestión Malvinas en perspectiva histórica: historia de las controversias del siglo XVI hasta nuestros días (PAIGH/H, 96, julio/dic. 1983, p. 27–67)

Documented and tightly reasoned review of Falklands/Malvinas controversy, from time of discovery to eve of South Atlantic War. [D. Bushnell]

3234 Etchepareborda, Roberto. Historiografía militar argentina. Buenos Aires: Círculo Militar, 1984. 206 p.: bibls. (Biblioteca del oficial; 717)

Comprehensive guide to important body of literature. Titles are organized according to historical themes and periods down to 1980. Compiler contributes two important essays, one describing available source materials, another on Argentines who have written on military subjects. Indispensable. For bibliographer's comment, see *HLAS 47:28.*

3235 Ferrero, Roberto A. Sabattini y la decadencia del yrigoyenismo. Buenos Aires: Ediciones del Mar Dulce: Centro Editor de América Latina, 1981–1984. 2 v. (215 p.): bibl. (Biblioteca Política argentina; 82)

Political biography of Sabattini, a caudillo who hoped to succeed Yrigoyen, and his short-lived movement that emerged in the province of Córdoba.

3236 Galasso, Norberto. Scalabrini Ortiz y la lucha contra la dominación inglesa. Buenos Aires: Ediciones del Pensamiento Nacional, 1982. 121 p.: ill. (Col. Los Malditos; 3)

Sympathetic biography describing Scalabrini Ortiz's life-long battle against imperialism and especially against British dominance of the Argentine economy.

3237 Galmarini, Hugo Raúl. La situación de los comerciantes españoles en Buenos Aires después de 1810 (IGFO/RI, 14:173, enero/junio 1984, p. 273–290)

Ably demonstrates that many colonial Spanish merchants continued to function until they were replaced about 1818 by British merchants and a new group of native entrepreneurs, while others gradually found other uses for their financial resources. Significant study.

3238 Gandía, Enrique de. Nicolás Avellaneda: sus ideas y su tiempo. Buenos Aires: Comisión Permanente de Homenaje al Doctor Nicolás Avellaneda, 1984. 190 p.: bibl.

Useful digest of Avellaneda's ideas found in his *Escritos y discursos: crítica literaria e histórica.*

3239 Gandía, Enrique de. Sarmiento y los problemas internacionales americanos (JEHM/R, 10, agosto 1984, p. 201–216, ill.)

Impressive analysis of Sarmiento's views on the practicality of a continental American congress and on several inter-American conflicts, especially the Paraguayan War.

3240 Giudici, Ernesto. Imperialismo inglés y liberación nacional. Buenos Aires: Centro Editor de América Latina, 1984. 188 p. (Biblioteca Política argentina; 78)

Reprint of 1940 edition with minor additions (see *HLAS 6:3770* and *HLAS 38:3727*).

3241 González Guevara, Campo. La guerra de las Islas Malvinas o Falklands. Bogotá: Ediciones Tercer Mundo, 1984. 88 p.: bibl., maps.

Naval commander describes military and diplomatic events of 1982.

3242 Gravil, Roger. The Anglo-Argentine connection, 1900–1939. Boulder, Colo.: Westview Press, 1985. 267 p.: bibl., ill., index (Dellplain Latin American studies; 16)

Important analysis of Anglo-Argentine trade relations (1900–38) strongly based on archival research. Presents new data and insights into the Argentine grain and meat trades, Argentine tariff, and impact of World War I and the Great Depression on the Argentine manufacturing industry. Includes vast amount of statistics.

3243 Guerrero, César H. Semblanzas sanjuaninas. San Juan, Argentina: Academia Provincial de la Historia, 1983. 241 p.: bibl., ports.

Biographical sketches of individuals who have been prominent in provincial history. Most noteworthy are Pedro Pablo de Quiroga, Domingo de Oro, Juan Dolores Godoy, José Dolores Bustos, Rosauro Doncel, Santiago Albarracín, Lisandro Sánchez, and Cesáreo Domínguez.

3244 Henault, Mirta. Alicia Moreau de Justo: biografía. Buenos Aires: Centro Editor de América Latina, 1983. 154 p. (Biblioteca Política argentina; 31)

Biography of the first woman to join the Argentine Socialist Party. Fought for women's rights, women's vote, divorce, schools for immigrants, prohibition, and human rights. Based on speeches, writings, and interviews conducted by journalists.

3245 Heredia, Edmundo A. Los Estados Unidos de Buenos Aires y Chile en el Caribe. Buenos Aires: Ediciones Culturales Argentinas, Ministerio de Educación y Justicia, Secretaría de Cultura, 1984. 183 p.: bibl., index.

Impressive monographic study stressing the often overlooked side of the Wars for Independence, that is, the campaign on the sea. Author argues that the patriots wanted to establish republics that would dominate the Caribbean sea lanes and to seize the Isthmus of Panama. Execution of their plan was entrusted to corsairs like Luis A. Aury, who founded the Republic of Buenos Aires and Chile on three Caribbean islands about 400 km from Jamaica. Evidence is fragmentary, but author's thesis sounds plausible.

3246 Hernández Ruigómez, Manuel. El diferendo anglo-argentino en el Atlántico Sur: un acicate para la producción bibliográfia (IGFO/RI, 14:173, enero/junio 1984, p. 293–307)

Brief reviews of books on Argentina's claims to the Falklands (Malvinas) and on the consequences of the Falklands (Malvinas) War of 1982. Justifies the Argentine view on historical and legal grounds.

3247 Heyburn, Henry and Frances Heyburn. Postcards of the Falkland Islands: a catalogue, 1900–1950. Chippenham, England: Picton Publishers, 1985. 255 p.: bibl., ill., indexes.

Picture history of the Falklands (Malvinas) during 1900–50.

3248 La Historia de Eva Perón: un ejemplo de amor entre una mujer y un pueblo. v. 1. Buenos Aires: Gam Ediciones, 1983. 1 v.: bibl., ill. (some col.)

Well illustrated popular history of Eva.

3249 Historia de las Malvinas argentinas. S.l., Argentina: GAM Ediciones, 1983? 384 p.: bibls., ill. (some col.).

Popular history of the Malvinas (Falkland Islands). Bibliographical references are few and dated.

3250 Hodge, John E. The role of the telegraph in the consolidation and expansion of the Argentine Republic (AAFH/TAM, 41:1, July 1984, p. 59–80)

Succinct and well documented history of the origin, development, problems, and significance of the national telegraph system.

3251 Horowitz, Joel. Occupational community and the creation of a self-styled elite (AAFH/TAM, 42:1, July 1985, p. 55–81, tables)

In order to explain why members of the Unión Ferroviaria and La Fraternidad regarded themselves as an elite, author analyzes social services provided by their unions as well as importance of the railroad in the national economy and favorable working conditions.

3252 Hualde de Peréz Guilhou, Margarita and Yasmín G. de Perinetti. Consideraciones demográficas sobre los chilenos en Mendoza: 1855–1914 (UNC/RHAA, 12:23/24, 1983/1984, p. 219–248, graphs, tables)

Census data shows that the number of Chileans in Mendoza peaked in the 1870s, that they were a young group essentially employed in rural areas, and that they gradually were outnumbered by European immigrants, especially Italians.

3253 La Huelga de inquilinos de 1907. Selección y prólogo de Juan Suriano. Buenos Aires: Centro Editor de América Latina, 1983. 94 p. (Historia testimonial argentina; 2. Movimientos sociales)

Collection of documents describing conditions in the *casas de inquilinato* or *conventillos* which led to the strike of 1907. Primarily concerned with events in Buenos Aires (city).

3254 Las Huelgas azucareras de Tucumán, 1923. Selección y prólogo de Daniel J. Santamaría. Buenos Aires: Centro Editor de América Latina, 1984. 97 p.: bibl. (Historia testimonial argentina; 26. Movimientos sociales)

Contains eyewitness accounts of the strike given by government officials, journalists, industrialists, and legislators. No one presents the viewpoint of the worker. Informative introduction explains economic reasons for the strike and political developments that resulted in its suppression by the military.

3255 Ingenieros, José. Ensayos escogidos. Buenos Aires: Centro Editor de América Latina, 1980. 115 p.: bibl. (Capítulo; 40)

Selections from the writings of a founder of the Argentine Socialist Party.

3256 Iñigo Carrera, Nicolás. Violence as economic power: the role of the State in creating the conditions for a productive rural system (LAP, 10:4, Fall 1983, p. 97–113, bibl.)

Very sketchy description of campaign against the Chaco Indians in 1884 and their subsequent fate to 1936. Calls attention to a neglected area of Argentina.

3257 Itzcovitz, Victoria. Estilo de gobierno y crisis política, 1973–1976. Buenos Aires: Centro Editor de América Latina, 1985. 143 p.: bibl. (Bibioteca Política argentina; 93)

Close study of the 1973–76 years suggests that the peronist government fell because the governing party was divided and this divided party undermined the government.

3258 Jewish Colonization Association. Informe de la Jewish Colonization Association sobre la colonización judía en Argentina y Brasil, 1927. Compilación de Alberto Kleiner. Buenos Aires: Libreros y Editores del Polígono, 1983. 63 p.

Reprint of 1927 report of the Jewish Colonization Assn. Describes its activities in Argentina.

3259 Jones, Charles A. The fiscal motive for monetary and banking legislation in Argentina, Australia and Canada before 1914 (in Argentina, Australia & Canada: studies in comparative development, 1870–1965. Edited by D.C.M. Platt and Guido Di Tella. New York: St. Martin's Press, 1985, p. 123–138)

Important work successfully puts to rest many misconceptions concerning the role of commercial banks in "growing but impecunious states." Banking legislation, author demonstrates, was motivated by the need to finance public expenditures.

3260 Jones, Charles A. Personalism, indebtedness, and venality: the political environment of British firms in Santa Fe province, 1865–1900 (IAA, 9:3/4, 1983, p. 381–399)

Suggests that there is a connection between corruption and personalism and elite indebtedness, and that this connection helps to explain the poor image of British firms in Santa Fe. Based on records of British firms active in Rosario.

3261 Justo, Liborio. Argentina y Brasil en la integración continental. Buenos Aires: Centro Editor de América Latina, 1983. 183 p.: bibl. (Biblioteca Política argentina; 37)

Author, a Trotskyite, argues for Argentine and Brazilian cooperation to achieve the economic integration of Latin America by the application of socialist ideas. Consists essentially of quotations from a variety of works.

3262 Lafuente, Horacio Raúl. La región de los Césares: apuntes para una historia económica de Santa Cruz. Buenos Aires: Editorial de Belgrano, 1981. 199 p.: bibl. (Col. Ensayos)

Valuable introduction to the spread of the sheep-raising industry in the province of Santa Cruz (1880–1940), and its contribution to the settlement and development of the province, its dependence on foreign capital and markets, and its integration into the national economy.

Landaburu, Roberto E. Los campos del Venado Tuerto. See item **1648.**

3263 Lascano, Marcelo Ramón. Comercio exterior de carnes vacunas: la Argentina y Australia: dos experiencia históricas significativas, 1927–1979 (FNH/NH, 14:27, junio 1981, p. 139–146)

Examines statistical data on Argentine and Australian exports of chilled beef (1927–79). Concludes that Argentina started to lose its leadership position in 1929 and that the pace accelerated after 1973. Attributes Argentina's loss of preeminance to faulty state economic policies.

3264 Lukasz, Danuta. Las asociaciones polacas en Misiones, 1898–1938 (PAN/EL, 8, 1981, p. 169–185)

Brief but well documented description of the associations of a religious and national nature organized by Poles from Galicia region in Poland in southern Misiones and of unsuccessful efforts of the Polish government to create a "New Poland" in the region.

3265 Luna, Félix. Perón y su tiempo. v. 1, La Argentina era una fiesta, 1946–1949. Buenos Aires: Editorial Sudamericana, 1984. 1 v.: bibl.

Reflective political and social history

of the first years of the Perón administration (1946–49), replete with anecdotes and short biographies of leading political figures.

3266 Maceyra, Horacio. La segunda presidencia de Perón. Buenos Aires: Centro Editor de América Latina, 1984. 167 p.: bibls. (Biblioteca Política argentina; 51. Las Presidencias peronistas)

Perón's failure to rely more on the proletariat and less on the bourgeoisie, author maintains, accounts for obstacles he encountered during his second administration and for his overthrow in 1955. The "Revolución Libertadora" meant the return of the oligarchy and the workers' loss of a protector. Thesis needs more evidence.

3267 McLynn, Francis James. Consequences for Argentina of the War of Triple Alliance, 1865–1870 (AAFH/TAM, 41:1, July 1984, p. 81–98)

Excellent and insightful analysis of the military, political, economic, and international consequences for Argentina of its war with Paraguay.

3268 McLynn, Francis James. Economic trends and policies in Argentina during the Mitre presidency (JGSWGL, 19, 1982, p. 254–284)

Calls attention to developments often overlooked because of preoccupation with the outbreak of the Paraguayan War.

3269 McLynn, Francis James. The ideological basis of the Montonero risings in Argentina during the 1860s (PAT/TH, 46:2, Feb. 1984, p. 235–251)

Argues that the montoneros of the 1860s opposed "the absorption of Argentina into a world economy" and reflected a split between large and small landowners. Thesis lacks hard supporting evidence.

Mainwaring, Michael James. From the Falklands to Patagonia: the story of a pioneer family. See item **1657.**

3270 Masini, José Luis. Irrigación, economía, sociedad y gobierno en Mendoza a fines del siglo XIX (UNC/RHAA, 12:23/24, 1983/1984, p. 97–131)

Describes provincial water policy adopted on Dec. 16, 1884, and construction of an irrigation system. Summarizes provincial economic, social, and political developments during 1875–95.

3270a Mazo, Gabriel del and **Roberto Etchepareborda.** La segunda presidencia de Yrigoyen [by] Gabriel del Mazo. Antecedentes de la crisis de 1930 [by] Roberto Etchepareborda. Buenos Aires: Centro Editor de América Latina, 1984. 158 p.: bibls. (Biblioteca Política argentina; 52. Las Presidencias radicales)

Using available State Dept. papers, Etchepareborda reveals that cabinet officers, rivals for the presidency, plotted with the military for the overthrow of an aging Yrigoyen. Mazo finds other reasons for the overthrow of Yrigoyen.

3271 Menéndez, Rómulo Félix. Las conquistas territoriales argentinas. Buenos Aires: Círculo Militar, 1982. 359 p.: bibl., maps (Biblioteca oficial; 711; 1982)

Describes how force was used to form the Argentine Republic (1810–1978). This factor merits more attention, but it should be considered along with other influences.

3272 Mirelman, Victor A. The Jewish community versus crime: the case of white slavery in Buenos Aires (Jewish Social Studies [Conference on Jewish Social Studies, New York] 46:2, Spring 1984, p. 145–168, tables)

Surveys Jewish prostitution in Buenos Aires (1879–1934), stressing relations of traffickers with the Jewish community and successful efforts of that community to protect Jewish women and to destroy Jewish white slavery. Well documented.

Musso, Luis Alberto. Anotaciones de bibliografía uruguaya sobre historia argentina en el período 1831–1852: época de Rosas. See *HLAS 47:40.*

3273 Nicolau, Juan Carlos. Rosas y García: la economía bonaerense, 1829–35. Buenos Aires: Editorial Sadret, 1980. 229 p.: bibl.

Details economic policies unsuccessfully advanced by García to unite cattle interests and merchants engaged in foreign trade as well as gradual ascendancy of the former over the latter. García did provide Rosas with the financial resources he needed. Significant study.

3274 Oddone, Jacinto. Historia del socialismo argentino, 1896–1911. Buenos Aires: Centro Editor de América

Latina, 1983. 2 v. (298 p.) (Biblioteca Política argentina; 4, 13)

Reprint of classic study that first appeared in 1934.

3275 Ortega, Exequiel C. Belisario Roldán y la visión sobre el caudillo: a comienzos del siglo (UNLP/R, 26, 1979/1980, p. 29–38, ill.)

Opinions expressed by Belisario Roldán during the congressional debate over the electoral law of 1902 provide a contemporary view of caudillismo, the caudillo, and electoral fraud. The law of 1902 originally provided for a secret ballot.

3276 Ortega, Exequiel C. La mujer fortinera: ensayo para determinar un tipo histórico argentino (UNLP/R, 26, 1979/1980, p. 9–28, ill.)

Interesting introduction to the women who accompanied the settler or the soldier on frontier duty.

3277 Palacio, Ernesto. Historia de la Argentina, 1515–1976. Edición de Juan M. Palacio. 13a ed. Buenos Aires: Abeledo-Perrot, 1981. 732 p.

Juan M. Palacio has added to this 13th edition of his father's work a chronological summary of events (1955–76), and a chapter entitled "La Disidencia en el Poder: Ortiz y Castillo." Lacks index.

3278 Panettieri, José. Proteccionismo, liberalismo y desarrollo industrial: debate nacional. Buenos Aires: Centro Editor de América Latina, 1983. 158 p.: bibl. (Biblioteca Política argentina; 11)

In the 1870s three groups, the author convincingly argues, favored the adoption of protectionist policies to encourage industrialization: 1) wool exporters, adversely affected by the crisis of 1866; 2) industrialists, with limited objectives; and 3) young politicians. When wool prices increased, technological development made possible the export of chilled beef, and world demand for cereals grew, the clamor for industrialization subsided.

3279 Páramo de Isleño, Martha S. Primeros proyectos de coordinación de transportes de la Ciudad de Buenos Aires (UNC/RHAA, 12:23/24, 1983/1984, p. 133–174, bibl.)

Describes how the need to coordinate all transportation systems within the city and to end the rivalry between foreign-owned and locally-owned transportation firms led to the creation of the Corporación de Transportes for the city of Buenos Aires and a victory for the foreign investors.

3280 Pavón Pereyra, Enrique. Isabel: historia de una voluntad. Buenos Aires: Ediciones Mares del Sur, 1983. 156 p.: ports.

Laudatory biography of Isabel Perón by a member of Perón's entourage. Based on interviews with members of her family, people who know her, and Juan Perón. Sees her more as an extension of Perón than as his representative.

3281 Pérez Guihou, Dardo. El pensamiento conservador de Alberdi y la Constitución de 1853. Prólogo de Germán J. Bidart Campos. Buenos Aires: Ediciones Depalma, 1984. 177 p.: bibl.

Significant analysis of Alberdi's reaction to contemporary European and North American ideas, Spanish American reality, and the Chilean Constitution of 1833, and his influence on the Argentine Constitution of 1853.

3282 Perón, Juan Domingo. Mensajes del coronel: J.D. Perón al pueblo trabajador. Compilación y prólogo de Oraldo N. Britos. Avellaneda, Argentina: Pequén Ediciones, 1984. 213 p.

Selection of speeches (Dec. 2, 1943-Feb. 12, 1946) in which Perón encouraged labor to organize itself.

3283 Perón, Juan Domingo. Obras completas. v. 3, Apuntes de historia militar: parte teórica. v. 4, pt. 1, La Guerra Ruso-Japonesa de 1904–1905. v. 23, Latino América: ahora o nunca. Buenos Aires: Proyecto Hernandarias, 1984. 3 v.: ill. (some col.)

Each volume reproduces an important work of Perón. Vol. 3 contains *Apuntes de historia militar: parte teórica*; vol. 4, *La Guerra Ruso-Japonesa de 1904–05*; and vol. 23, *Latino América: ahora o nunca* (3rd ed., 1968).

3284 Perón, Juan Domingo. Perón y el justicialismo. Edición de Fermín Chávez. Buenos Aires: Centro Editor de América Latina, 1984. 161 p.: bibl. (Biblioteca Política argentina; 89)

Selection of Perón's speeches on the State and industrialization, the Third Position, the organized community, the Argentine Model, and national culture. Chávez provides an introductory essay describing the intellectual currents that influenced Perón.

3285 Perón, Juan Domingo. Tercera posición y unidad latinoamericana. Selección e introducción de Fermín Chávez. Buenos Aires: Editorial Biblos, 1985. 154 p.: bibl. (Col. Pensamiento político. Serie normal; 2)

Collection of documents illustrating Perón's anti-imperialist stand and his desire for a Latin American federation which would achieve the economic unity of the region.

3286 Piccinali, Héctor Juan. Vida del Teniente General Nicolás Levalle. Buenos Aires: Círculo Militar, 1982. 300 p., 16 p. of plates: bibl., ill. (some col.) (Biblioteca del oficial; 708)

Biography of Levalle, founder of the Círculo Militar, three times Minister of War and the Navy, and a participant in most military operations (1857–1907). Sought to improve military operations and customs, and to unify Argentina by encouraging the development of an esprit de corps among the military. Well documented.

3287 Platt, D.C.M. The financing of city expansion: Buenos Aires and Montreal compared, 1880–1914 (*in* Argentina, Australia & Canada: studies in comparative development, 1870–1965. Edited by D.C.M. Platt and Guido Di Tella. New York: St. Martin's Press, 1985, p. 139–148)

Briefly summarizes evidence that the modernization and expansion of Buenos Aires was made possible in part by its middle-income office workers and skilled workers who could borrow and repay their loans over a long period.

3288 Pomer, León. Conflictos en la Cuenca del Plata en el siglo XIX. Buenos Aires: Riesa, 1984. 310 p.: bibl., maps (Col. de ensayos)

Suggestive analysis of how intra-provincial, national, and international politics in the region intermingled and influenced one another (1810–92). Devotes special attention to impact of Rio Grande do Sul on imperial policies. Maintains the State appeared in the area before the emergence of any national spirit. Based essentially on secondary sources.

3289 Pont, Elena Susana. Partido Laborista: Estado y sindicatos. Buenos Aires:

Centro Editor de América Latina. 157 p.: appendix, bibl. (Biblioteca Política argentina; 44)

Discusses short history of the Labor Party. Argues that the Argentine populism that led to the rise of peronism owed its existence to the presence of a labor class in 1945–46 that was organized, politically independent, and restless. Partly based on the testimony of Luis Gay, ex-President of the Labor Party. Includes appendix of valuable documents.

Prieto, Adolfo. La literatura autobiográfica argentina. See item **5676.**

3291 Ramírez de Rivera, Hugo Rodolfo. El pensamiento político de Sarmiento y Alberdi a través de *Facundo o civilización y Barbarie en las pampas argentinas* y *Bases y puntos de partida para la organización política de la República Argentina*, dos obras escritas en Chile (VANH/B, 68:271, julio/sept. 1985, p. 757–785)

Brief comparison of Sarmiento's and Alberdi's political views during their exile in Chile. Contains two unedited letters of Sarmiento revealing his attitude toward Chile and the use of force in furthering Argentina's destiny.

3292 Ravenal, Eugenio A.L. Isles of discord: a file on the Falklands/Malvinas. Genève: Siboney and Ventura Books, 1983. 178 p.: bibl.

Journalistic history of the Falklands (Malvinas) to 1981.

Remmer, Karen L. Party competition in Argentina and Chile: political recruitment and public policy, 1890–1930. See item **3165.**

3293 Repetto, Roberto. Las Malvinas: nuestros títulos históricos y jurídicos (JEHM/R, 10, agosto 1984, p. 443–448)

Review of Argentine claims to the Malvinas (Falklands).

3294 Reyes, Cipriano. Yo hice el 17 de octubre: memorias. Buenos Aires: Centro Editor de América Latina, 1984. 2 v. (260 p.) (Biblioteca Política argentina; 87–88)

Reprint of 1973 edition (see *HLAS 36:3278*).

3295 Ripa, Julián I. Recuerdos de un abogado patagónico. Buenos Aires: Ediciones Marymar, 1984. 180 p. (Col. Patagonia)

Thought-provoking account of life

among the Indians in and about Esquel, province of Chubut, during the past 40 years.

3296 Rock, David. Argentina, 1516–1982: from Spanish colonization to the Falklands War. Berkeley: Univ. of California Press, 1985. 478 p., 32 p. of plates: bibl., ill., index.

Impressive interpretative history of Argentina which stresses 20th-century political and economic issues and developments. Based on a thorough knowledge of the historiographical literature.

3297 Rodríguez Lamas, Daniel. La presidencia de Frondizi. Buenos Aires: Centro Editor de América Latina, 1984. 191 p.: bibl. (Biblioteca Política argentina; 54)

Frondizi's weak constitutional government, author claims, began with segments of the military, labor unions, and peronismo, and the Unión Cívica Radical del Pueblo already determined to overthrow it. Frondizi's policies of concessions and economic development cost the regime whatever support it had. Clear and convincing analysis.

3298 Rojas Lagarde, Jorge Luis. El Malón de 1870 a Bahía Blanca y la Colonia de Sauce Grande. Buenos Aires: Ediciones Culturales Argentinas, Secretaría de Cultura, Ministerio de Educación y Justicia, 1984. 220 p., 3 p. of plates: bibls., ill.

History of the English colony at Sauce Grande from (1868–79). Based on articles by George Claraz in *The Standard*, military dispatches, and letters of settlers in the area.

3299 Romero Briasco, Jesús and **Salvador Mafe Huertas.** Malvinas: testigo de batallas. Valencia, Spain: F. Domenech, 1984. 253 p., 8 p. of plates: ill. (some col.), maps.

Essentially an after-action study analyzing the equipment and military tactics employed by contending air forces during the Malvinas (Falklands) War. Based on photographs, official documents, and the testimony of officers in both air forces. Argues that Argentina could have established adequate air defenses for the islands between April 2–30 and thus could have hindered the advance of the British naval forces.

3300 Ruiz, Hugo Alberto; Aníbal Mario Romano; and María del C. Mañas de Ruiz. La diversificación económica en Mendoza a través de la minería en el Primer Plan Quinquenal (UNC/RHAA, 12:23/24, 1983/1984, p. 175–217, bibl., tables)

Examination of the Primer Plan Quinquenal, census data, and mining laws of Mendoza convinces authors that no real effort was made to encourage economic diversification or the development of the mining industry in Mendoza. Necessary financial resources were simply lacking.

3301 Ruiz Moreno, Isidoro. Elecciones y revolución: Oroño, Urquiza y Mitre. Buenos Aires: Ediciones Culturales Argentinas, Secretaría de Cultura, Presidencia de la Nación, 1983. 271 p.: bibl.

Fundamental work on crucial elections of 1867 in the province of Santa Fe. The issue was not a proposed law authorizing civil marriage but control of the provincial electoral votes in the presidential elections of 1868. Based on the unedited correspondence of presidential candidates and their agents, particularly Urquiza, Mitre, Martín Ruiz Moreno, and Benjamín Victorica.

San Martino de Dromi, María Laura. Gobierno y administración de las Islas Malvinas, 1776–1833. See item **2835.**

3302 Santos, Estela dos. Las mujeres peronistas. Buenos Aires: Centro Editor de América Latina, 1983. 122 p.: bibl. (Biblioteca Política argentina; 23)

Sympathetic and solid account of women in national politics, starting with the law granting women the right to vote in 1947 and ending with the short-lived administration of Isabel Perón. Discusses Evita Perón and her foundation, women in Congress, and women in the resistance movement, but not women in the interior provinces.

3303 Santos Gómez, Susana. Bibliografía de viajeros a la Argentina. Buenos Aires: Fundación para la Educación, la Ciencia y la Cultura, 1983. 2 v. (650 p., 8 leaves of plates): bibl., facsims., index.

Most complete and accurate guide published to date to the travel literature of Argentina. Not all items are annotated. Indispensable.

3304 Santos Martínez, Pedro. Pasado y presente de las Malvinas e islas del Atlántico Sur (VANH/B, 66:261, enero/marzo 1983, p. 41–79, bibl., maps)

Prominent Argentine historian states his country's claims to the Falklands (Malvinas), Georgian Islands, Sandwich Islands, and the Antarctic. Summarizes post-1900 developments which bear on these Argentine claims.

3304a Scarzanella, Eugenia. Italiani d'Argentina: storie di contadini, industriali e missionari italiani in Argentina, 1850–1912. Venezia, Italy: Marsilio Editori, 1983. 175 p.: tables.

Based on thorough archival research and on aggregate data, this work analyzes Italian immigration to Argentina during its peak period, and the immigrants' contributions to economic, social, and cultural development in the host country. Includes excellent chapters on agricultural colonies, urban and rural intellectuals, and mutual aid societies. [G. M. Dorn]

3305 Schallman, Lázaro. Memorias documentadas. Buenos Aires: Editorial MOI, 1980. 305 p.: bibl., ill.

Biography of Jewish educator and journalist active in the province of Mendoza (1926–46), and in the city of Buenos Aires (1946–78). Wrote extensively on Jewish colonization in Argentina.

3306 Schamann, Mariel. Alejandro Bunge y la crisis del 30: reflexiones en torno a su pensamiento (Política, Economía y Sociedad [Fundación para el Estudio de los Problemas Argentinos, Buenos Aires] 2, julio/agosto 1982, p. 151–175, tables)

Scholarly examination of the ideas Bunge expressed in the *Revista de Economía Argentina*. Bunge believed in the need to develop a light industry, to increase internal consumer demand and agricultural diversification, and to draw closer to the US.

3307 Scunio, Alberto D.H. Del Río IV al Lime Leuvú. Buenos Aires: Círculo Militar, 1980. 460 p.: bibl., ill. (Biblioteca del oficial; 702)

Biography of Conrado E. Villegas, veteran commander of the Paraguayan War and the Conquista del Desierto. Extensive quotations from letters and documents in military and numerous family archives show that aim of the Conquista del Desierto was not the extermination of the Indians and that Villegas dealt with them in a very humanitarian way. Author calls attention to Argentina's debt to the army for defending the territorial integrity of the nation and for extending its boundaries.

3308 Segura, Juan José Antonio. Historia de Nogoyá. t. 1, Desde los orígenes hasta 1821. Paraná, Argentina: Editorial de la Mesopotamia, 1982. 496 p.: bibl., facsims., ill., plates, tables.

Vol. 1 of this important contribution to local history first noted in *HLAS 36:2469*.

3309 Sequeira, Sebastián; Carlos Cal; and Cecilia Calatayud. Aviación Naval Argentina. Buenos Aires: SS&CC Ediciones, 1984. 153, 3 p.: bibl., ill. (some col.)

History of the technical and operational capability of the Argentine Naval Air Force from 1910 to the recent Malvinas (Falklands) War. Well illustrated.

3310 Sidicaro, Ricardo. Poder y crisis de la gran burguesía agraria argentina (*in* Argentina hoy. Compilación de Alain Rouquié. México: Siglo Veintiuno Editores, 1982, p. 51–104)

Attributes Argentina's lost of its place in world agricultural markets to internal and international factors, and decline in political influence of the large landowners to their inability to form alliances with other sectors of society. Based largely on census figures.

3311 Solberg, Carl E. Land tenure and land settlement: policy and patterns in the Canadian prairies and the Argentine pampas, 1880–1930 (*in* Argentina, Australia & Canada: studies in comparative development, 1870–1965. Edited by D.C.M. Platt and Guido Di Tella. New York: St. Martin's Press, 1985, p. 53–75, tables)

Careful comparison of the evidence related to pampa and prairie development convinces author that "the pampa land-tenure system was [not] backward and inefficient," and that the tenancy system helps explain Argentina's ability to compete in world agricultural markets.

3312 Sonego, Víctor Mariano. Las dos Argentinas: pistas para una lectura crítica de nuestra historia. Prólogo de Enrique de Vedia. Buenos Aires: Ediciones Don Bosco Argentina, 1983. 430 p.: bibl. (Col. Comunión y participación)

Writer, a founder of the Christian Democratic Party, argues for a politically and economically independent Argentina.

3313 Stemplowski, Ryszard. Los eslavos en Misiones: consideraciones en torno al número y la distribución geográfica de los campesinos polacos y ucranianos, 1897–1938 (JGSWGL, 19, 1982, p. 320–390, maps, tables)

Examination of scanty and imprecise sources convinces writer that Slavic immigrants to Misiones were mostly Ukrainians and not Polish. Fails to settle the dispute.

3314 Strange, Ian J. The Falkland Islands. 3rd ed. rev. to include the impact of the Falklands War. Newton Abbot, England: David & Charles, 1983. 328 p.: bibl., ill., index.

Edition that contains two new chapters: 1) presents eyewitness account of events in Port Stanley during the Argentine occupation of the islands in 1982; and 2) discusses efforts at rehabilitation after the war. Informative.

3315 Szuchman, Mark D. Disorder and social control in Buenos Aires, 1810–1860 (JIH, 15:1, Summer 1984, p. 83–110, tables)

Concludes from an examination of Buenos Aires police records that the *juez de barrio* and barrio policeman had considerable autonomy in administering criminal justice. How they used this autonomy is discussed in detail. Significant study.

3316 Tamarin, David. The Argentine labor movement, 1930–1945: a study in the origins of peronism. Albuquerque: Univ. of New Mexico Press, 1985. 273 p.: bibl., ill., index.

Well researched analysis of ideological battles and schisms within the ranks of organized labor (1930–45). Unión Ferroviaria receives special attention.

3317 Tosco, Agustín. Agustín Tosco: conducta de un dirigente obrero. Compilación de Jorge O. Lannot, Adriana Amantea y Eduardo Sguiglia. Buenos Aires: Centro Editor de América Latina, 1984. 162 p.: bibls. (Biblioteca Política argentina; 80)

Collection of documents brings together thoughts of Agustín Tosco on the Cordobazo of 1969, the role of labor unions, imperialism, labor union bureaucracies, and conduct of labor leaders. Tosco was secretary-general of the Sindicato de Luz y Fuerza of Córdoba (1957–66).

3318 Townsend, C.D. The future of the Falkland Islands (Contemporary Review [London] 245:1427, Dec. 1984, p. 289–293)

Contains report on the results of a meeting held between a Conservative Party parliamentary delegation and representatives of various sectors of Argentine society to find a solution to the Falklands (Malvinas) issue.

3319 Tronsoco, Oscar. Fundadores del gremialismo obrero. Buenos Aires: Centro Editor de América Latina, 1983. 2 v. (264 p.): ill. (Biblioteca Política argentina; 27–28)

Short description of careers and thoughts of Diego Abad de Santillán (anarchist); Andrés Cabona (syndicalist); Federico J. García (anarchist); Sebastián Marotta (syndicalist); José Negri (socialist); Ruggiero Rúgilo (communist); and Alejandro J. Silvetti (socialist). All were active in a variety of labor organizations, were journalists, or held the office of secretary-general in a union. Based on interviews, unedited correspondence, and union newspapers.

3320 Troncoso, Oscar. El proceso de reorganización nacional: cronología y documentación. v. 1, De marzo de 1976 a marzo de 1977. Buenos Aires: Centro de Editor América Latina, 1984. 1 v. (Biblioteca Política argentina; 67)

Very useful historical chronicle and collection of documents for the March 1976-March 1977 period.

3321 Unamuno, Miguel et al. El peronismo de la derrota. Buenos Aires: Centro Editor de América Latina, 1984. 160 p. (Biblioteca Política argentina; 84)

In short essays Miguel Unamuno, Julio Bárbaro, Guido Di Tella, Hernán Benítez, Antonio Cafiero, and Adam Pedrini, representatives of various tendencies within the Peronist Party, seek to account for the party's failure to win a majority in the elections of Oct. 30, 1983, and suggest what the party should do now.

3322 Viajeros del siglo XX y la realidad nacional. Selección de Susana Pereira. Buenos Aires: Centro Editor de América Latina, 1984. 95 p. (Biblioteca Política argentina; 72)

Selections from the writings of Europeans, Latin Americans, and North Americans assembled with the aim of helping Argentines understand themselves.

3323 Viñas, David. Indios, ejército y frontera. México: Siglo Veintiuno Editores, 1982. 326 p.: bibl. (Historia)

Argentine novelist and essayist examines the Conquest of the Desert of 1879 and Indian-white relations in the province of Buenos Aires and Patagonia. Argues that the policy of the Argentine liberal positivist elite was to exterminate the Indian, and that the same policy existed wherever in Latin America liberal positivism and Social-Darwinism dominated. Validity of thesis not adequately demonstrated. For literary critic's comment, see *HLAS 46:5613*.

3324 Walter, Richard J. Politics, parties, and elections in Argentina's province of Buenos Aires, 1912–1942 (HAHR, 64:4, Nov. 1984, p. 707–735, graphs, tables)

Calls needed attention to greater importance of the rural caudillos and urban bosses rather than socioeconomic factors in determining party dominance in particular districts.

3325 Warren, Harris Gaylord. Roberto Adolfo Chodasiewicz: a Polish soldier of fortune in the Paraguayan War (AAFH/TAM, 41:3, Jan. 1985, p. 1–19)

Tells fascinating story of a Polish soldier of fortune who joined the Argentine army fighting Paraguay and contributed to the conduct of the war. Well documented.

3326 La Yerba mate y Misiones. Selección de prólogo de Leandro de Sagastizábal. Buenos Aires: Centro Editor de América Latina, 1984. 90 p.: bibl. (Historia testimonial argentina; 31. Regiones y sociedades)

Contains documents tracing revival of the yerba mate industry after 1876. Especially important are numerous extracts from the *informe* of José Elías Niklison, the national agent who investigated the industry in 1914.

3327 Zuberbühler, Ricardo F. Evocación de la estancia argentina. Buenos Aires: Grupo Editor Latinoamericano, 1984. 198 p. (Col. Memoria del país; MDP 401)

Professional administrator of estancias for over 30 years describes his experiences and observations. Very instructive.

3328 Zuccherino, Ricardo Miguel. Ensayos sobre la investigación historiográfica. La Plata, Argentina: Junta de Estudios Históricos, Provincia de Buenos Aires, 1984.

42 p.: bibls. (Col. Extensión histórica; 4)

Brief review of Argentine historiography by an Argentine historian who admires André Maurois.

PARAGUAY

3329 Album gráfico: cincuentenario de la Guerra del Chaco, 1932–1935. Dirección y textos de Alfredo M. Seiferheld. Compilación de María G. Monte de López Moreira. Asunción: El Lector, 1985. 271 p.: ill. (some col.)

Pictorial history of the war as seen by the soldier in the army, navy, and air force, and by the press.

3330 Anuario. Instituto de Investigaciones Históricas Dr. José Gaspar Rodríguez de Francia. Año 5, No. 6, Oct. 1984-. Asunción.

Contains the following documented articles: Roberto Romero "Proceso a los Defamadores del Dr. Francia;" Raúl Amaral "El Dr. Francia y los Tiranos;" Roberto Romero "Las Hijas del Dictador;" and Alfredo Viola "Usos, Costumbres y Aficiones en la Epoca Francista."

3331 Ayala, Juan B. Las batallas del Chaco a la luz de los principios de guerra. Asunción: El Lector, 1984. 156 p., 8 p. of plates: ports. (Col. histórica; 11)

Ayala, commander of the First Corps, gives his version of what happened during the Chaco War. Identifies authors of various campaign plans and describes their execution. He himself was responsible for the victory at Campovía. Does not settle dispute over conduct of the war.

3332 Benítez, Justo Pastor. Cuaderno de Peña Hermosa y otros escritos. Prólogo de Salvador Villagra Maffiodo. Asunción: Editorial Araverá, 1984. 193 p.: ill. (Serie Ensayos; 1)

Contains reflections of Peña Hermosa on national themes, written while he was in a concentration camp (Dec. 1, 1940-April 30, 1941). Very laudatory of José Felix Estigarribia, the victor in the Chaco War. Balance of books consists of journalistic articles published in Asunción (1925–37).

3333 Blinn Reber, Vera. Commerce and industry in nineteenth-century Paraguay: the example of *yerba mate* (AAFH/ TAM, 42:1, July 1985, p. 29–53, ill, tables)

Significant and scholarly examination of the economic underpinnings of *yerba mate* industry and of the government's revenue-oriented involvement in and regulation of domestic and foreign trade in *yerba mate*. Thesis is that prior to 1870 Paraguayan governments "were pragmatic and rational rather than dictatorial and monopolistic." Statistical tables show prices paid for *yerba mate* (1630–1869), and total production in *arrobas* and amount exported (1660–1906).

Cabonell de Masy, Rafael. El séctor agro-alimentario en Paraguay. See *HLAS 47:3650.*

Cooney, Jerry W. Repression to reform: education in the Republic of Paraguay, 1811–1815. See *HLAS 47:4482.*

3334 Delgado, Nicolás. Historia de la Guerra del Chaco, mis recuerdos personales . . . v. 1, Parte 27 de septiembre de 1932 a 14 de abril de 1933. v. 2, Parte 12 de junio de 1933 al 30 de septiembre de 1934. v. 3, Parte (no title). Asunción: Imprenta Militar, 193?-1985. 3 v.: maps (1 folded)

Delgado commanded the First Corps and participated in armistice negotiations. His account of his conduct during the Chaco War is based on operations orders and notes taken during battles.

3335 Duarte Barrios, Miguel Angel. Semblanza de un héroe: Contraalmirante S.R. Ramón E. Martino. Asunción: Escuela Técnica Salesiana. 122 p.: ill.

Biography of officer responsible for the defense of the Chaco Boreal during the Chaco War.

3336 Garay, Blas. Paraguay 1899. Prólogo y notas de Julia Velilla Laconich de Arréllaga. Asunción: Editorial Araverá, 1984. 349 p.: bibls., port. (Serie Ciencias sociales; 1)

Selection of articles written by militant Colorado journalist and intellectual for *La Prensa* of Asunción. Articles appeared the year (1898–99) in which Garay was assassinated and are grouped under three headings: national politics, history, and international relations.

3337 Herken Krauer, Juan Carlos. Ferrocarril, política y economía en el Paraguay: el acuerdo de 1907 entre Paraguay Central Railway Company y el gobierno para-guayo (IAA, 10:3, 1984, p. 291–316, bibl., maps)

The story of the Paraguay Central Railway Company involves competition between Argentina and Brazil for influence in Paraguay, the failure of Paraguay to free itself from dependence on the Río de la Plata and Buenos Aires for access to world markets, and the ineffectiveness of diplomatic pressure when personal interests are involved. Based on British consular records.

3338 Kaiser, Cathy. Carlos Antonio López and the birth of Paraguayan diplomacy (JGSWGL, 19, 1982, p. 238–253)

Close look at the origins and consequences of important Paraguayan-Correntine alliance of 1845. Would have benefited from the use of published Argentine primary sources.

Kharitonov, Vitali'i Aleksandrovich. Paraguay: dictadura militar-policial y lucha de clases. See *HLAS 47:6543.*

3339 Morínigo, Higinio. Testimonios de un presidente: entrevista al Gral. Higinio Morínigo. Compilación de Augusto Ocampos Caballero. Asunción: El Lector, 1983. 258 p.: ill.

Morínigo, Paraguay's Colorado President (1940–48), was interviewed when he was 85. Describes his youth, military career, organization of the revolution that ended Liberal rule in 1940, his opinion of the revolutions of 1904, 1908, and 1911, and his views on diplomatic relations with Argentina and the US. Especially noteworthy is his assessment of the accomplishments of the Revolución Paraguayo Nacionalista and of Paraguayan diplomacy during and after the Chaco War.

3340 La Paz del Chaco: documentos para el estudio de las tratativas que concluyeron en el Tratado de Paz, Amistad y Límites con Bolivia. Compilación de Félix Paiva Alcorta. Asunción: Instituto Paraguayo de Estudios Geopolíticos y de Relaciones Internacionales: El Lector, 1983. 289 p., 2 folded leaves of plates: ill. (Documentos para la historia. Col. histórica; 2)

Confidential correspondence between President Paiva of Paraguay and the Paraguayan delegation in Buenos Aires negotiating the peace treaty with Bolivia of July 21, 1938. Most of the documents deal with the Sept. 1937-July 1938 period, when the negotiations were in greatest danger of collapsing. Very revealing.

3341 Riart, Gustavo Adolfo. Senderos de gloria: historia del R.I. 14 Cerro Corá en la Guerra del Chaco. Asunción: Talleres Gráficos Asunción, 198? 2 v.: ill.

History of the Infantry Regiment 14 Cerro Corá during the Chaco War. Based on division and regimental operations orders, extensively reproduced, and on interviews with survivors and author's notes. Very revealing of Paraguayan perception of Bolivian activities. Excellent unit history.

Rivarola Paoli, Juan Bautista. Historia monetaria del Paraguay: monedas, bancos, crédito público. See *HLAS 47:3663.*

3342 Sosa Tenaillon, Horacio C. Cincuenta años después: recuerdos de la Guerra del Chaco. Asunción: Arte Nuevo Editores, 1985. 183 p. (Serie Literatura; 4)

Summarizes interviews with 22 survivors (e.g., combatants, women, priests, medics) of the war that ended on June 14, 1935. What they recall is told essentially in their own words. No editorial comments.

3343 Speratti, Juan. La revolución del 17 de febrero de 1936: gestación, desarrollo, ideología, obras. Asunción: Escuela Técnica Salesiana, 1984. 419 p.: bibls., ill. (some col.)

Member of original group that planned the revolution of Feb. 1936, describes their motives and objectives, their notable accomplishments during the Franco administration, and their reasons for forming the Febrerista Party.

3344 Viola, Alfredo. Doctrina, economía, obras públicas y la Iglesia durante la dictadura del Dr. Francia. Asunción: Editorial Clásicos Colorados, 1984. 97 p., 4 leaves of plates: bibl., ill., ports (some col.)

Contains four lectures Viola gave on the Francia government's political policies, economic policies, public works program, and relations with the Church. Presents revisionist views.

3345 Warren, Harris Gaylord and **Katherine F. Warren.** Rebirth of the Paraguayan Republic: the first Colorado era, 1878–1904. Pittsburgh, Pa.: Univ. of Pittsburgh Press, 1985. 379 p., 2 p. of plates: bibl., ill., index (Pitt Latin American series)

Scholarly account of the revival of the Republic of Paraguay and dominance of the

Colorado Party (1878–1904). Sympathetic and detailed description of political, economic, and social policies of the Colorados. Basic work.

3346 Zubizarreta, Carlos. Cien vidas paraguayas. Prólogo de Alfredo M. Seiferheld. Asunción: Editorial Araverá, 1985. 325 p.: bibls. (Serie Biografías; 1)

Short biographies of individuals prominent in Paraguayan history. Includes many not born in Paraguay. Reissue of older edition.

URUGUAY

3347 Aparicio, Fernando. Basilio Muñoz: caudillo blanco entre dos siglos. Montevideo: Arca, 1984. 250 p.: bibls.

Biography of a Blanco general who participated in the revolutions of 1897, 1904, 1910, and 1935. Relies on existing works and on interviews with descendants of Muñoz. Of questionable value.

3348 Bacinno, N. Javier de Viana en Treinta y Tres: pt. 1, La forja de un estilo (UBN/R, 12, 1983, p. 47–110, bibl.)

Argues convincingly that Viana, a criollista, was influenced primarily by his experience as a rural journalist in Treinta y Tres fighting for a local cacique. Extensive transcriptions from his articles and letters (1891–93).

3349 Barrán, José Pedro and **Benjamín Nahum.** Uruguayan rural history (HAHR, 64:4, Nov. 1984, p. 655–673)

Two leading Uruguayan economic historians summarize conclusions they reached in their important seven-volume study entitled *Historia rural del Uruguay moderno* (1967, see *HLAS 32:2718a*). Their thesis is that Uruguay had a "cattle-based civilization" (1700–1914), that sheep raising contributed to the growth of a rural middle class, and that little happened to affect the latifundium and "livestock mentality." Their work represents a comprehensive reexamination of Uruguayan rural history.

3350 Blinder, Samuel. Uruguay, las vísperas de la democracia. Prólogo de Rodolfo H. Terragno. Montevideo?: A.L.A. Agencia Latinoamericana, 1984. 57 p.: bibl., ill.

Blanco Party description of events leading up to the elections of 1984. Sympathetic to the candidacy of Wilson Ferreira of the Partido Nacionalista.

3351 Boronat, J. Yolanda and **Marta R. Risso.** Román Fresneda Siri: un arquitecto uruguayo. Montevideo: Univ. de la República, Facultad de Arquitectura, Instituto de Historia de la Arquitectura, 1984. 129 p.: bibl.

Life of the architect who designed the Organization of American States building in Washington, D.C. and the Organization of American States building in Brasília.

3352 Buño, Washington. Una crónica del Montevideo de 1857: la epidemia de fiebre amarilla. Montevideo: Ediciones de la Banda Oriental, 1983. 104 p., 1 leaf of plates: bibl., ill.

Excellent description of the medical profession and its response to the yellow fever epidemic of 1857.

Castellanos, Alfredo and **Romeo Pérez.** El pluralismo: examen de la experiencia uruguaya, 1830–1918. See *HLAS 47:6548.*

3353 Cocchi, Angel María; Jaime Klaczko; and **Juan Rial Roade.** La urbanización en Uruguay en la época de la inmigración europea (in L'Industrialisation des pays de La Plata: éveils et somnolences, 1890–1970. Paris: L'Institut des hautes études de l'Amérique latine, Univ. de Paris, 1980, p. 3–31, maps, tables)

Examination of pertinent statistical data convinces writers that immigration, industrialization, and railroad construction failed to create new urban centers of importance.

3354 Crawford, Leslie. La Provincia Uruguaya del Tape. Montevideo: Ediciones GEOSUR, 1983? 119 p.: bibl., maps.

Story of Indian community organized by the Jesuits. It was located in Uruguay, Brazil's province of Rio Grande, and Argentina's province of Corrientes and territory of Misiones.

3355 Díaz de Guerra, María Amelia. Historia del periodismo en Maldonado, 1873–1973. Montevideo: Imprenta Cooperativa, 1984. 82 p., 20 p. of plates: bibl., ill.

Report on Maldonado newspapers found in the Biblioteca Nacional, Montevideo. *El Departamento* appeared in 1873, and the first newspaper in 1880.

3356 Fonseca, Roberto Piragibe da. Uma introdução, metódica e crítica, à história da República Oriental do Uruguai (IHGB/R, 329, out./dez. 1980, p. 25–95, appendix)

Brazilian geopolitical historian summarizes his views on Brazilian and Uruguayan relations (1811–1972). Interesting assessment of Uruguayan leaders, militarism, and developments.

3357 Gil Villaamil, Germán. Ensayo para una historia de Cerro Largo hasta 1930. Melo, Uruguay: Intendencia Municipal de Cerro Largo, 1982. 187 p., 98 leaves of plates: bibl., ill.

Informative introduction to important Uruguayan department of Cerro Largo and its capital, Melo. Produced numerous generals and politicians. Discusses land ownership and racial mixtures.

Klaczko, Jaime and **Juan Rial Roade.** Uruguay, el país urbano. See *HLAS 47:5194.*

3358 Lista Viamonte, Ramón. Diario de los movimientos de la línea y de los que hacen los enemigos sitiadores, 10 de agosto de 1844–31 de octubre de 1851: con una selección de planos antiguos de Montevideo. Aportación histórica de Eduardo Martínez Rovira. Montevideo: Univ. de la República, Dirección General de Extensión Universitaria, División Publicaciones y Ediciones, 1983. 639 p.: ill., maps.

Diary of Unitarian army officer who recorded with few comments all he saw from his post on the Telégrafo de la Línea in Montevideo (Aug. 1, 1844-Oct. 31, 1851). Provides new information on the military conduct of the Guerra Grande.

Melitón Merino, Francisco. El negro en la sociedad montevideana. See *HLAS 47:8356.*

3359 Negro, Ramón Carlos. Pocitos era así. Montevideo: Arca, 1983. 186 p.

Fascinating description of how life in Pocitos has changed (1914–82). Touches upon social life, education, religion, sports, politics, and trade.

Perdomo, Indalecio. La política agraria uruguaya: una visión histórica. See *HLAS 47:3683.*

3360 Pereyra, Carlos Julio. Javier Barrios Amorín: pensamiento y acción en la democracia. Montevideo: Ediciones de la

Banda Oriental, 1983. 134 p., 4 p. of plates: bibl., ports.

Informative and insightful biography of Barrios Amorín based on years of close association in the political arena as members of the Partido Nacional. Barrios Amorín was the founder of *Vanguardia*.

Rodríguez Villamil, Silvia and **Graciela Sapriza.** La inmigración europea en el Uruguay: los italianos. See *HLAS 47:8360.*

3361 Rusiñol Sallúa, Gerardo Ariel. La Iglesia uruguaya: historia de su organización diocesana (IFCL/E, 2, 1982, p. 49–65, bibl., maps)

Describes origins and development of dioceses in Uruguay.

3362 Sanz, Víctor. La Conferencia de París sobre la Banda Oriental: 1817–1819 (UB/BA, 33, 1983, p. 119–142)

Impressive and revealing study of the diplomatic negotiations between Spain and Portugal over the future of Brazil, Uruguay, and Olivenza, and the mediating role of the Holy Alliance, and especially of Great Britain and France. Failure of the mediation effort contributed to the fall of the Spanish monarchy. Based on archival research in Paris, Madrid, and Lisbon, but there is little documentation.

3363 Torres Wilson, José de. Brevísima historia del Uruguay. Montevideo?: Ediciones de la Planta, 1984. 87 p.

Informative introduction to Uruguayan history as seen by a Blanco Party historian.

3364 Villegas, Juan. Los comienzos de la Parroquia San Fructuoso de Tacua-

rembó, 1832–1865 (IFCL/E, 5, 1983, p. 67–101)

Discusses religious conditions, clashes between pastors and curates, and conflicts between pastors and local government authorities in the border parish of Tacuarembó. Very enlightening.

3365 Villegas, Juan. Proceso fundacional de la Parroquia Inmaculada Concepción en Rivera (IFCL/E, 8, 1984, p. 7–39)

Informative on the state of religion in a border area, on struggle of pastors to support themselves, and on the conflicts between pastors. Reveals that parish records are deficient or missing.

3366 Williman, José Claudio h. et al. Contribución a la historia económica del Uruguay. Montevideo: Academia Nacional de Economía, 1984. 584 p.: bibls., ill.

Collection of papers read at several conferences (1982–83) on various aspects of Uruguayan economic history. Most writers are primarily concerned with the state of the Uruguayan economy in the 20th century. Of special interest are the following papers: José Claudio Williman (h.) "El Período del Modelo de 'Desarrollo Hacia Afuera,' 1830–1914;" Enrique Arocena Olivera "El Modelo del Desarrollo Hacia Adentro, 1931–1973;" Carlos Frick Davie "Bosquejo Histórico Económico de la Agropecuaria Uruguaya;" Lionel Osvaldo Rial "La Evolución de las Finanzas Públicas en el Uruguay, 1905–1981."

Zubillaga, Carlos. El reto financiero: deuda externa y desarrollo en Uruguay, 1903–1933. See *HLAS 47:3689.*

BRAZIL

RODERICK J. BARMAN, *Associate Professor of History, University of British Columbia, Vancouver, Canada*
JEAN A. BARMAN, *University of British Columbia, Vancouver, Canada*
MICHAEL L. CONNIFF, *Associate Professor of History, University of New Mexico, Albuquerque*

WITH RESPECT TO THE COLONIAL and Imperial eras of Brazilian history, the Portuguese language literature reviewed in this volume cannot be termed noteworthy either for its extent or its quality. The paucity of materials on the 19th century is particularly marked, with the exception of two regional studies on the late empire (items **3488** and **3517**). The themes which seem to arouse most interest in the colonial period are the roles played by race, class relations, and religion in the formation of Brazilian identity. Especially notable are studies on the interaction of Indians and missionaries, the impact of slavery, and the condition of the poor (items **3381, 3399, 3417,** and **3423**).

As was the case for *HLAS 44* and *HLAS 46*, a good part of the works being published are reeditions of source materials or classic studies, many of which originally appeared in the 1960s. One reason for this plethora of reprints, it would seem, is that Brazilian historians are not currently producing the quality of original studies needed by the book industry to fill its publication lists. Reprints, often subsidized by the government or businesses, are both easy and financially safe for publishers.

The lack of productivity among historians is, in a sense, paradoxical, because as Yeda Linhares notes in her introduction to Falcon (item **3398**), the past decades have seen the emergence of a professionalized historical community based primarily in a fully developed academic system with active post graduate programs. Linhares deplores the narrow and Brazil-centric focus of the scholarly works produced by graduates of these programs, and she lauds Falcon's study on the Pombaline era as exemplifying the type of European scholarship which Brazil should adopt. Linhares's complaint is directed against the practice of printing as books graduate theses which, in North America or Europe, would appear as one or two journal articles or book chapters.

The remedy she advocates is the adoption in Brazilian graduate studies of the French *grande thèse*, a massive treatise requiring years of work which exhausts both the research and theoretical dimensions of a topic. So long as Brazilian academe remains underfunded, however, such long-term projects seem unlikely. On the other hand, the continuing appearance of scholarly journals such as the *Revista Brasileira de História* and *DADOS* and the resuscitation of *História Brasileira* after a five-year hiatus offer hope that more short pieces will be published as articles.

A second, and far more controversial, explanation for the lack of works of substance is advanced by Silva (item **3521**), who deplores the current obsession with "scientific," that is general theoretical, explanations. In his opinion such discussion must spring from a strong empirical basis, and Silva advocates using specific case studies to elucidate our understanding of general problems. The historical approach thus attacked is well represented by Amaral Lapa (item **3380**) and by Mendes (item **3415**). The first, published in a series aimed at lay readers, is a historiographical discussion of the theoretical nature of the "old colonial system," while the second defends the theoretical basis of Gorender's study of slavery, claiming that Gorender's critics have misunderstood Marx's formulation of the capitalist mode of production in its formative period. Whatever the immediate merits and utility of Mendes's and Amaral Lapa's work, it must be granted that neither makes for easy reading and neither breaks new ground historiographically. With respect to the colonial and imperial periods, at least, historians in Brazil appear to be largely marking time.

Among the works in English on these two periods, Schwartz's new book (item **3422a**) stands preeminent, a massive study that increases our knowledge of both the sugar industry and social structures in the colonial era. The study by Kuznesof (item **3379**) on household economy and family organization in colonial São Paulo also warrants note. We should mention for possible classroom adoption an English translation of Kátia de Queiros Mattoso's book on slavery by Johns Hopkins (see item **3382** and *HLAS 46:3466*). Concerning the 19th century, both Seckinger's analysis of Brazilian foreign policy in the Rio de la Plata under Pedro I and Viotti da Costa's study of key aspects of the imperial regime (items **3519** and **3450**) are valuable works that add new dimensions to the English-language scholarship on the Empire.

It must be admitted that, these exceptions apart, works by established scholars on the two periods are in general incidental, while those by beginners are small in number and, if often interesting, not notable for their brilliance. Russell-Wood's historiographical study of writings on the colonial period (item **3388**), very much a cry from the heart, explains this lack of scholarship by the fact that, in the recent cutbacks on academia, Brazilian history has suffered most, being seen as an area of marginal importance when compared to Spanish America.

In sharp contrast to the foregoing comments, we can report on a boomlet in historical writings about the republican period. Boris Fausto edited the 11th and final volume of the *História geral* series, begun in 1960, and published a remarkable piece of social history as well (items **3467** and **3456**). Edgard Carone likewise concluded his multi-volume history of the republic and also gave us a study of the Communist Party (items **3445** and **3504**). The 50th anniversary of the 1930 revolution, celebrated with symposia in Rio and Pôrto Alegre, gave birth to proceedings containing papers by a great number of modern period specialists (items **3509** and **3525**). Finally, the Centro de Documentação em História Contemporânea (CPDOC) has produced a cornucopia of oral histories, the monumental *Dicionário histórico-biográfico brasileiro* (item **3453**), and some polished analyses of the Vargas era. Of special note among the latter are those by Hippolito and Brandi *et al.* (items **3466** and **3440**).

Biography is making a comeback, complemented by the usual number of memoirs and personal accounts. Many of the latter seem motivated by the redemocratization of 1985 and are written in the spirit, "only now can the story be told." Schwartzman *et al.*'s treatment of Capanema, Barros of Guinle, and Cony of Kubitschek warrant special note (item **3518, 3434,** and **3449**). And of course the aforementioned *Dicionário* is an inexhaustible source of biographical information.

Virtually the only important military histories were those by McCann (items **3480, 3481,** and **3482**), although they are complemented by PUC's administrative histories of the police and National Guard (items **3498** and **3512**). Economic history is represented by only three articles, those of Dean and Topik (items **3372, 3532,** and **3533**), and the book by Sallum Júnior (item **3513**).

Women and the family were the subjects of four new studies (items **3427, 3452, 3495** and **3529**), but labor history received little attention. Two books on the Old Republic appeared, those by Martins Filho and Nogueira (item **3485** and **3499**). Finally, two social histories (in addition to that by Fausto) merit note: those of Foot and Piletti (items **3460** and **3505**).

Just as heartening as the *volume* of publications on the modern period is news of continuing investigations in the universities and research centers of Rio de Janeiro and São Paulo. Not all are being conducted by historians, of course: political scientists, sociologists, economists, and anthropologists are active in republican era studies too. In most cases, collaboration occurs easily and yields good fruit. If scholars can avoid having to take two or three jobs due to salary pinches, we will undoubtedly see an increase in quality publications in coming years.

GENERAL

3367 Andrade, Paulo René de. Origens históricas da Polícia Militar de Minas Gerais. v. 1, 1706–1831. Belo Horizonte: Imprensa Oficial, 1981. 1 v.: appendix, bibl., port.

This laudatory, commemorative narrative, written by a member of the military police, has possibly some utility in discussing the role of police in colonial Minas Gerais and including a documentary appendix.

3368 Barbalho, Nelson. Cronologia pernambucana: subsídios para a história do agreste e do sertão. Recife: Centro de Estudos de História Municipal, Fundação de Desenvolvimento Municipal do Interior de Pernambuco, 1982–1984. 12 v.: bibls.

Comprising 2,236 entries in 12 volumes, this work is included only to note that its contents derive mainly from secondary sources and its approach is utterly antiquarian.

3369 Children of God's fire: a documentary history of black slavery in Brazil. Compiled by Robert Edgar Conrad. Princeton, N.J.: Princeton Univ. Press, 1983. 515 p.: bibl., ill., index.

Documentary overview of slavery in Brazil, emphasizing its harsh and exploitative nature. Certainly useful for students but suffers from serious weaknesses. Drawn almost entirely from printed materials, mainly official laws and reports and travellers' accounts; and thus disregards most unofficial records, including direct testimony of the slaves themselves which, despite the statement on p. xviii–xix, does exist.

3370 Cintra, Sebastião de Oliveira. Efemérides de São João del-Rei. 2a ed. rev. e aum. Belo Horizonte: Imprensa Oficial, 1982. 2 v. (622 p.): index.

Despite the absurdity of its organization and the arbitrariness of the entries, the work contains some good information for a social history of this *mineiro* town.

3371 Dean, Warren. Deforestation in southeastern Brazil (*in* Global deforestation and the nineteenth-century world economy. Edited by Richard P. Tucker and J.F. Richards. Durham, N.C.: Duke Press Policy Studies, 1983, p. 50–67)

Describes, primarily for a technical audience, the slow destruction of the tropical forests in present day Espírito Santo, Rio de Janeiro, São Paulo, and part of Minas Gerais. Initial cause was slash and burn, shifting farming by Tupi-Guarani and then by Portuguese. Deforestation was later accelerated by demand for wood and other products as export commodities. Also discusses role played by railroads and slow beginnings of conservationist sentiment. For geographer's comment, see *HLAS 47:5233.*

3372 Dean, Warren. Ecological and economic relationships in frontier history: São Paulo, Brazil (*in* Essays on frontiers in world history. College Station: Texas A&M Univ. Press *for the* Univ. of Texas at Arlington, 1983, p. 71–100, maps)

Overview of Portuguese occupation in western São Paulo, from colonial times to early 20th century. Farming methods destroyed the fertility of the land, so the frontier was hollow. For geographer's comment, see *HLAS 47:5234.*

Debret, Jean Baptiste. Viagem pitoresca e histórica ao Brasil. See *HLAS 47:5235.*

3373 Delson, Roberta M. and **John P. Dickenson.** Perspectives on landscape change in Brazil (JLAS, 16:1, May 1984, p. 101–125)

Argues that existing landscapes in Brazil were partly shaped by "deliberate strategies by central authorities." While the conceptual approach offers fresh insights, authors' grasp of historical reality is often shaky or incorrect (e.g., alleged legislative "discrediting" after independence of the colonial *sesmarias* "leaving landowners of enormous patrimonies without legal title"). Soundest on the contemporary period.

3374 Freitas, Décio. Escravidão de índios e negros no Brasil. Pôrto Alegre: Escola Superior de Teologia São Lourenço de Brindes: Instituto Cultural Português, 1980. 159 p.: bibl. (Col. Caravela; 6)

Reproduces laws, decrees, and other documents relating to indigenous and African slavery. Also includes chronology of major events in slavery and its abolition in Brazil and elsewhere (1570–1888). Possibly useful as a quick reference source.

3375 Freitas, Décio. Escravos e senhores de escravos. Pôrto Alegre: Mercado

Aberto, 1983. 176 p.: bibl. (Série Novas perspectivas; 4)

Consists of 13 essays on various aspects of slavery. Revised and expanded version of university lectures given in 1965. Author considers slavery to be of central importance in understanding the past, present, and future development of Brazil.

3376 Gurfield, Mitchell. Estrutura das classes e poder político no Brasil colonial. Tradução de Otávio Mendes Cajado. João Pessoa: Edições Univ. Federal do Paraíba, 1983. 205 p.: bibl.

Sociological reinterpretation of secondary scholarship, mainly in English, on colonial Brazil. Emphasizes peasant marginality and lack of alternatives in the formation of class and political structures. Translation of a New School of Social Research doctoral dissertation.

3377 História administrativa do Brasil. v. 2–3, 5, 7, 13. Brasília: Editôra Univ. de Brasília: Fundação Centro de Formação do Servidor Público, 1983. 5 v.: appendices, bibl.

Major governmental project, started in 1955 and resumed in 1981, to record Brazil's administrative history from colonial origins to present day. Forty volumes projected, each authored by a specialist in the field and concentrating on a specific time period and/or administrative body. Volumes so far produced combine detailed factual narratives, possibly statistics, with documentary appendices and bibliography.

3378 Karasch, Mary. Rio de Janeiro: from colonial town to imperial capital, 1808–1850 (in Colonial cities: essays on urbanism in a colonial context. Edited by Robert J. Ross and Gerard J. Telkamp. Dordrecht, The Netherlands: Martins Nijhoff, 1985, p. 123–151)

Short study argues that Rio de Janeiro retained the structure of a colonial city for a generation after independence in 1822. Provides not only a clear delineation of the physical and spatial aspects of the city but an original and incisive analysis of its social structure. Recommended reading and especially suitable for students.

Klein, Herbert S. and **Stanley L. Engerman.** Del trabajo esclavo al trabajo libre: notas en torno a un modelo económico comparativo. See item **2353.**

3379 Kuznesof, Elizabeth Anne. Household economy and urban development: São Paulo, 1765–1836. Boulder, Colo.: Westview Press, 1986. 216 p.: bibl., index, ill. (Dellplain Latin American studies; 18)

Traces transformation of household economy and family organization in São Paulo city from subsistence to exchange production, a change which author argues was engineered by a merchant and agricultural elite itself influenced by the Industrial Revolution in its move toward a sugar and coffee export economy. Well based in general historiography as well as in primary sources, including three household-level censuses, property inventories and genealogical data. Readable text buttressed by some 50 charts, figures, and maps. Highly recommended.

3380 Lapa, José Roberto do Amaral. O antiguo sistema colonial. São Paulo: Brasiliense, 1982. 110 p. (Primeiros vôos; 8)

Written for a general audience, this short work tries to elucidate and explain the ongoing theoretical debate concerning the nature and dynamics of the colonial system. Includes historiographical overview.

3381 Maestri Filho, Mário José. O escravo no Rio Grande do Sul: a charqueada e a gênese do escravismo gaúcho. Pôrto Alegre: Escola Superior de Teologia São Lourenço de Brindes; Caxias do Sul: Editôra da Univ. de Caxias do Sul, 1984. 203 p.: bibl., ill.

Study emphasizes crucial role played by slavery in the development of Rio Grande do Sul. Focuses on cattle economy and *charqueadas*, plants processing dried meat. Graduate thesis at Louvain in Belgium, based mainly on printed sources, but well organized and written in a direct, persuasive style. Includes interesting photographs of *charqueada* sites. Recommended.

3382 Mattoso, Kátia M. de Queirós. To be a slave in Brazil, 1550–1888. Translated by Arthur Goldhammer. Foreword by Stuart Schwartz. New Brunswick, N.J.: Rutgers Univ. Press, 1986. 250 p.: bibl., index, map.

Translation of *HLAS 46:3466.*

3383 Mendonça, Rubens de. Nos bastidores da história mato-grossense. Cuiabá: Univ. Federal do Mato Grosso, 1983. 236 p.: ill.

Ramshackle collection of short pieces on picturesque topics in Mato Grosso. Includes some biographical vignettes. Amateur.

3384 A Paraíba das origens à urbanização. Introdução e organização de José Octávio. João Pessoa: Fundação Casa de José Américo: UFPG, FUNAPE, Editôra Universitária, 1983. 119 p.

Introductory essays on aspects of Paraiban social history from 16th to 19th centuries, probably most useful for summaries of existing historiography.

3385 Reis, Arthur Cezar Ferreira. Aspectos da formação brasileira. Rio de Janeiro: Livraria J. Olympio Editôra; Brasília: Instituto Nacional do Livro, MEC, 1982. 273 p.: bibl. (Col. Documentos brasileiros; 191)

Leading establishment historian discusses in 21 essays aspects of Brazil's political formation and geographical expansion from a nationalist viewpoint. Includes appreciation of author.

3386 Ribeiro, Berta G. *et al.* A Itália e o Brasil indígena = L'Italia ed il Brasil indigeno. Rio de Janeiro: Index Editôra, 1983. 150 p.: bibl., ill., (some col.), plates.

Bilingual work containing three short studies on the Italian contribution to the colonization of Brazil and Brazilian ethnography. Also includes colored plates of Indian artifacts in the L. Pigorini Museum in Rome. More a public relations effort than a scholarly work.

3387 Rodrigues, Cláudio Oraindi. São Borja e sua história. S.l.: s.n., 1982. 156 p.: bibl. (Col. Tricentenário; 1)

Short, incomplete history of a garrison town on Rio Grande do Sul border compiled by devoted local librarian.

3388 Russell-Wood, A.J.R. United States scholarly contributions to the historiography of colonial Brazil (HAHR, 65:4, Nov. 1985, p. 657–682)

Author uses this bibliographical overview of principal US works on colonial Brazil to lament the persistent marginal status of Brazil as part of Latin American historical studies and proposes remedial steps. Useful source for students.

3389 Semana da História, 3rd, França, Brazil, 1981. Memória. São Paulo: Univ. Estadual Paulista, Instituto de História e Serviço Social, 198? 467 p.

Collection of over 50 historiographical papers on aspects of Brazilian history presented at a convention (França, São Paulo

state, 1981). The range of subjects and quality of some papers illustrates the rise of history as an academic profession in recent years.

3390 Skidmore, Thomas. Race and class in Brazil: historical perspectives (UW/LBR, 20:1, Summer 1983, p. 104–118)

Short overview, arguing that the traditional view of Brazil as a racial democracy is really a tactic for elite control and manipulation of the masses. Stresses the need to explain why independent mulatto and black movements have not emerged.

3391 A Vida religiosa no Brasil: enfoques históricos. Organização de Riolando Azzi. São Paulo: CEHILA: Edições Paulinas, 1983. 213 p.: bibl. (Estudos & debates latino-americanos; 5)

Collection of seven brief studies will interest the specialist. Heavy emphasis on the orders, from colonial times to present, including feminine ones. Part of larger research project conducted at CEHILA in São Paulo.

3392 Willeke, Venâncio. Os Franciscanos e a independência do Brasil. Brasília: Instituto Histórico e Geográfico Brasileiro, 1981. 190 p.: bibl.

Argues that members of the Franciscan order played critical role in achieving national independence by providing ideological support for the movement through sermons and journalistic activities. Includes biographical materials and numerous documents.

COLONIAL

3393 Abreu, Daisy Bizzocchi de Lacerda. A terra e a lei: estudo de comportamentos sócio-econômicos em São Paulo nos séculos XVI e XVII. São Paulo: R. Kempf, 1983. 108 p.

Close study of system of land grants in colonial São Paulo, showing that the legal acquisition of land occurred both by royal gift of *sesmarias* and by *datas de terra* granted by the town council. Legal provisions which in Portugal equated ownership with the effective occupation and exploitation of land could not function in the particular conditions of São Paulo. Land grants were manipulated to their own advantage by the dominant minority. Latifundism was therefore the product of a colonial regime. Originally M.A. thesis (Univ. of São Paulo).

Alves, Joaquim. História das secas: séculos XVII a XIX; homenagem ao primeiro centenário da abolição mossoroense. See *HLAS 47:5212.*

3394 Aula do Commercio. Compilação de Marcos Carneiro de Mendonça. Rio de Janeiro: Xerox, 1982. 643 p.: facsims. (Biblioteca reprográfica Xerox)

Compilation of laws, decrees, and official documents relating both to Aula do Comércio founded at Lisbon in 1759 and to commerce and education during the Pombaline period and thereafter. Curious assortment, intended to show that the Aula do Comércio was the font of economic development in the Portuguese world in the late 18th century.

3394a Bellotto, Heloísa Liberalli. O Presídio do Iguatemi: função e circunstâncias, 1767–1777 (USP/RIEB, 21, 1979, p. 33–56)

Overlong account, based on contemporary materials, of the fortified post of Iguatemi, founded in 1767 deep inside modern Paraguay. Intended to divert Spanish attention away from Portuguese posts on the Rio de la Plata, the settlement failed in this purpose and was taken by the Spanish in 1777. Claims that the post did prove the feasibility of settlements on the far western border.

3395 Cardoso, Ciro Flamarion Santana. Economia e sociedade em áreas coloniais periféricas, Guiana Francesa e Pará, 1750–1817. Rio de Janeiro: Graal, 1984. 201 p.: bibl., ill. (Biblioteca de história; 10)

Separate studies of two peripheral colonies geographically adjacent, followed by comparative analysis which concludes that their different patterns of development were due not to distinctive forms of colonization but to the availability of native labor, plentiful in Pará, absent in French Guiana. Portuguese occupation of the latter (1808–17) brought considerable economic benefits.

3396 Endres, José Lohr. A Ordem de São Bento no Brasil: quando Província: 1582–1827. S.l.: s.n., 198? 242 p., 8 leaves of plates: ill. (some col.)

Well researched, if rather pious, history of the Benedictine order in Brazil up to 1827. Most informative on the establishment of the Order and abortive attempt in late 17th century by the monasteries in Brazil to become independent of the mother congrega-

tion in Portugal. Includes several documents and some illustrations.

3397 Evolução física de Salvador. Centro de Estudos da Arquitetura na Bahia Salvador: Univ. Federal da Bahia, Núcleo de Publicações, Centro Editorial e Didático, 1980. 2 v.: bibl., ill. (Estudos baianos; 12–13)

These two volumes on the development of Brazil's first city contain a plethora of information, unfortunately diminished in value by inferior organization and poor reproductions.

3398 Falcon, Francisco José Calazans. A época pombalina: política econômica e monarquia ilustrada. São Paulo: Editôra Atica, 1982. 532 p.: bibl. (Ensaios; 83)

General analysis of the ideological conjuncture formed by mercantilism and the Enlightenment, and specifically of the literature about the economy produced in Portugal during the Pombaline period. Also studies the implementation of economic concepts. While not specifically concerned with Brazil, this Fluminense dissertation was written under the inspiration of Fernando A. Novais whose ideas the work largely follows.

3399 Fernandes, Francisco Assis Martins. A comunicação na pedagogia dos Jesuítas na era colonial. São Paulo: Edições Loyola, 1980. 131 p.: bibl., ill. (Série Comunicação; 10)

Interesting, if not definitive, study of processes by which early Jesuits communicated their doctrine and culture to indigenous population, including schools, theatre and music.

3400 Ferrez, Gilberto. Jean Barthélémy Havelle ou João Bartholomeu Houel ou Howell: espião à força (IHGB/R, 330, jan./março 1981, p. 49–106, ill.)

In 1762 a French military engineer, employed to work on Rio de Janeiro's fortifications for nine years, was taken prisoner at Colonia do Sacramento and persuaded by Buenos Aires's governor to enter the Spanish service. His manuscript (54 p.) detailing fortifications, military strength, and the economy of the city and captaincy of Rio is here translated with a long introduction.

3401 Flores, Moacyr. Colonialismo e missões jesuíticas. Pôrto Alegre: EST: Instituto de Cultura Hispánica do Rio Grande do Sul, 1983. 176 p.: bibl., ill.

Consists of 16 essays, usually summary and descriptive, on aspects of the Missões region in Rio Grande do Sul, during and after the Jesuit period.

3402 Freitas, Décio. O socialismo missioneiro. Pôrto Alegre: Movimento, 1982. 79 p.: bibl., ill. (Col. Documentos; 32)

Well written student text argues that not only were Guaraní active participants in Jesuit missions in the south but that the social organization which the Indians and missionaries jointly developed was in essence utopian socialist.

3403 French, John D. Riqueza, poder e mão-de-obra numa economia de subsistência: São Paulo, 1596–1625 (AM/R, 195, jan./dez. 1982, p. 79–107)

São Paulo in the early 17th century saw the emergence of an articulated community based on subsistence production. Some agriculture for the market was undertaken by a minority with greatest access to forced indigenous labor.

3404 Göldi, Emil August. Alexandre Rodrigues Ferreira. Brasília: Editôra Univ. de Brasília, 1982. 80 p.: bibl.

Short, pioneering biography written in 1895 by Brazilian naturalist emphasizing scholarly contribution of a fellow naturalist who was a major figure in the government expedition to the Amazon exploration in the late 18th century. The bibliography of works on Rodrigues Ferreira shows how scholarship on the subject has developed.

3405 Gudeman, Stephen and **Stuart B. Schwartz.** Cleansing original sin: Godparenthood and the baptism of slaves in eighteenth-century Bahia (*in* Kinship, ideology and practice in Latin America [see HLAS 47:259] p. 35–58, bibl., tables)

Given the important role played by godparenthood in providing a Church-sanctioned social bonding between individuals not necessarily related by blood or equal in rank, any study that examines the actual functioning of *compádrio* is welcome. Authors analyze data from four Bahian parishes, showing that godparents were likely superior in legal status and color to their godchildren but almost always came from the same occupational strata. Although the study is limited in both scope and the data it uses, it can be commended (particularly for students) as a succinct and revealing case study of a neglected social institution.

3406 Hall, John R. World-system holism and colonial Brazilian agriculture: a critical case analysis (LARR, 19:2, 1984, p. 43–69)

Critique by sociologist of Wallerstein's theory, using colonial Brazil as the field for study. Argues that Brazilian agriculture was shaped by pre-existing "patrimonial and trade capitalism" rather than by the emergent world capitalist economy. Based entirely on secondary sources.

3407 Higgs, David. Unbelief and politics in Rio de Janeiro during the 1790s (UW/LBR, 21:1, Summer 1984, p. 13–34)

Innovative article, using records of the Inquisition in Portugal, to explore the mind sets, religious and secular, of the petty professionals and artisans in late colonial Brazil. Shows that the *mentalité* of literacy had not yet taken root. Recommended.

3408 Kern, Arno Alvarez. Missões, uma utopia política. Pôrto Alegre: Mercado Aberto, 1982. 275 p.: bibl. (Série Documenta; 14. História)

Broad, interpretative treatment of 17th- and 18th-century Jesuit missions in Paraguay. Based on secondary works.

Linhares, Maria Yedda Leite and **Francisco Carlos Teixeira Silva.** História da agricultura brasileira: combates e controvérsias. See HLAS 47:5273.

3410 Luna, Francisco Vidal and **Iraci del Nero da Costa.** Minas colonial: economia & sociedade. São Paulo: Fundação Instituto de Pesquisas Econômicas: Livraria Pioneira Editôra, 1982. 85 p.: bibl., graphs, ill., tables (Biblioteca Pioneira de ciências sociais. Economia. Estudos econômicos/FIPE/Pioneira)

Useful summary essays, largely derived from author's earlier publications (see HLAS 42:3570; HLAS 44:3484; HLAS 44:3508; HLAS 44:3520–3523; HLAS 46:3488; and HLAS 46:3496). Analyzes structure of settlement and patterns of slaveholding in 18th- and early 19th-century Minas, with emphasis on Vila Rica. Good graphs and tables.

3411 Marcílio, Maria Luiza. População e força de trabalho em uma economia agrária em mudança: a província de São

Paulo, no final da época colonial (USP/RH, 114, jan./junho 1983, p. 21–30)

Demonstrates that the decline in the mining production and the Crown's desire to promote export agriculture led to a change in São Paulo's labor force. African slavery, commercial agriculture, and stratification increased, although on a small scale compared to other regions. Based largely on census rolls.

3412 Mattoso, Kátia M. de Queirós. Bahia opulenta: uma capital portuguesa no Novo Mundo, 1549–1763 (USP/RH, 114, jan./junho 1983, p. 5–20)

Review article summarizes dozen or so US Ph.D. dissertations that deal with colonial Bahia. Useful introduction, especially on social structure of the city. Little on slavery.

3413 Mauro, Frédéric. Recent works on the political economy of Brazil in the Portuguese empire (LARR, 19:1, 1984, p. 87–105)

General overview, descriptive rather than analytical, of relevant published sources, primarily from early 1970s. Most useful in that it covers the considerable French language literature which tends to be underconsulted by North American scholars.

3414 Maxwell, Kenneth R. The Atlantic empires in the eighteenth century: Portugal (International History Review [Univ. of Toronto, Canada] 6:4, Nov. 1984, p. 529–550)

Cast in the form of a critique of P.K. Liss's study (see *HLAS 46:2469*), this article contains a well written, intelligent overview both of the structure and dynamics of the Portuguese empire during the 18th and early 19th centuries and of the relevant historiography. Concludes that Liss's identification of entrepreneurs, intellectuals, and patriots as the prime movers in the Atlantic Revolution leading to independence does not apply for Brazil.

3415 Mendes, Claudinei Magno Magre. Considerações em torno da análise da escravidão colonial (Universidade Estadual Paulista [São Paulo] 1, 1982, p. 43–48, bibl.)

Contends that recent criticisms of the thesis characterizing colonial slavery as capitalist in nature are based on an inaccurate conception of Marxist theory, in particular Marx's perception of the formative stage of

capitalism, to which colonial slavery more correctly belongs.

3416 Mulvey, Patricia A. Slave confraternities in Brazil: their role in colonial society (AAFH/TAM, 39:1, July 1982, p. 39–68)

Based mainly on the statutes filed at Lisbon, surveys number and nature of lay brotherhoods for blacks and mulattoes, slave and free. Shows how they provided a means for preserving autonomous conduct and African culture. Interesting topic deserving more imaginative and extended treatment.

3417 Paiva, José Maria de. Colonização e catequese, 1549–1600. São Paulo: Autores Associados: Cortez, 1982. 108 p. (Col. Educação contemporânea. Série Memória da educação)

In the proselyzation of the Brazilian Indians by the Catholic Church an inherent element was the imposition of Portuguese culture, a process which strongly furthered, the author argues, mercantile interests and colonization itself.

3418 Rabello, David. A moeda luso-brasileiro numa época de crise: 1808–1821 (Universidade Estadual Paulista [São Paulo] 1, 1982, p. 49–60, bibl.)

Lack of specie endemic in Brazil before 1808 was aggravated thereafter due to adverse trade balances of both Brazil and Portugal, the external demand for bullion, and costs of financing the court at Rio de Janeiro and the government's ambitious foreign policies. Survey based on secondary sources.

3419 Regni, Vittorino. Frei Martinho de Nantes: apóstolo dos índios Cariris e fundador do Convento da Piedade, 1683–1983. Salvador: Centro de Estudos Baianos, 1983. 44 p.: bibl. (Publicação da Univ. Federal da Bahia; 102)

Slight, uninspired in-house biography of 17th-century Capuchin missionary.

3420 Rivero, Diego. The report prepared by Ambrosio de Siqueira on the receipts and expenditures of Brazil in 1605 (Bibliotheca Americana [Coral Gables, Fla.] 1:2, Nov. 1982, p. 165–321, tables)

Reproduces in its entirety, in original Portuguese, a 1605 financial report on the sources of income and payments in all the captaincies of Brazil, with detailed annotations in English. Introduction claims that the report shows incorrectness of the traditional view of Spanish rule as involving government neglect and lethargy and decline in the colony. While useful as a primary source, the document does not support this contention.

3421 Schwartz, Stuart B. Colonial Brazil: the role of the State in a slave social formation (*in* Essays in the political, economic, and social history of colonial Latin America. Edited by Karen Spalding. Newark: Univ. of Delaware, 1982, p. 1–23)

Assesses existing historiographical debate on nature of class relations during colonial period. Concludes that: a) "feudalism" was absent in both its legal and Marxist interpretations, but that b) to understand what was the dominant mode of production, given the reliance on slave labor, historians must analyze the evolving symbiosis between local socioeconomic groups and the Absolutist State pursuing its own policies.

3422 Schwartz, Stuart B. The plantations of St. Benedict: the Benedictine sugar mills of colonial Brazil (AAFH/TAM, 39:1, July 1982, p. 1–22)

Based on the triennial reports that Benedictine monasteries in Brazil submitted to the mother house in Portugal, this study concentrates on the Order's sugar estates (which provided its main source of income) and on slave labor used on them. Despite limitations in data used, concludes that the estates were run profitably and slaves well treated with a self-sustaining birth rate.

3422a Schwartz, Stuart. Sugar plantations in the formation of Brazilian society: Bahia, 1550–1835. Cambridge, England: Cambridge Univ. Press, 1985. 616 p.: bibl., ill., index, tables (Cambridge Latin American studies; 52)

Based on ten years of research and gathering of many materials previously published elsewhere, this blockbuster goes into every conceivable aspect of the sugar industry of Bahia, from its inception in the early 16th century until the 1830s. The thesis, which should prove controversial, holds that the mode of production was the single most important influence shaping the social structure of colonial Bahia. Contains many new and useful statistical tables. Largely for the specialist.

3423 Souza, Laura de Mello e. Desclassificados do ouro: a pobreza mineira no século XVIII. Rio de Janeiro: Graal, 1982. 237 p.: bibl. (Biblioteca de história; 8)

Graphic portrait of free poor who were shut out of the colonial mining economy due to its reliance on slave labor. Stresses process of "social declassification" (perception of free poor as rogues and vagabonds) and its consequences. Well based in primary sources and existing historiography, to which it is a welcome addition. Recommended.

3424 Tavares, Waldemar. Anchieta, patrono do Brasil. Belo Horizonte: Imprensa Oficial de Minas Gerais, 1982. 108 p.

Set of laudatory essays published to celebrate the beatification of the pioneer Jesuit missionary in Brazil. Of little historical utility.

3426 Vallejos, Julio Pinto. Slave control and slave resistance in colonial Minas Gerais, 1700–1750 (JLAS, 17:1, May 1985, p. 1–34)

Based on published materials. Provides a succinct overview of problems arising from the dominance of slave labor in the mining economy and the strong presence of free and freed blacks and mulattoes in local society. Recommended for students, to supplement Boxer's chapter in *Golden Age.*

NATIONAL

3427 Alvin, Zuleika M.F. A participação política da mulher no início da industrialização em São Paulo (USP/RH, 114, jan./junho 1983, p. 69–84)

Looks at Italian immigrant women in factory work (1880–1920) and especially their incipient political activity, using newspapers of the era.

3428 Amaral, Anselmo F. José Garibaldi: guerreiro da liberdade. Pôrto Alegre: Martins Livreiro, 1983. 175 p.: bibl.

Miscellaneous remarks designed to glorify one of the heroes of the Farropos rebellion who later played a central role in the unification of Italy. No scholarly apparatus and significant only as revealing the continued importance of mythologizing history.

Andrade, Gilberto Osório de and **Rachel Caldas Lins.** João Pais, do Cabo: o patriarca, seus filhos, seus engenhos. See *HLAS* 47:5213.

3429 Anuszweska, Ewa. A imigração alemã no Brasil à luz dos relatórios dos cônsules do Império Alemão no início do século XX (PAN/EL, 7, 1980, p. 51–65)

Undigested research notes from consular reports on German immigrants in Rio Grande and Paraná (1900–14).

3430 Arinos, Afonso et al. Um praticante da democracia, Otávio Mangabeira. Salvador: Conselho Estadual de Cultura da Bahia, 1980. 157 p.: bibl., port.

Essays which provide good biographical information although uneven in depth and quality. Not critical but to some extent based on archival research and personal acquaintance.

3431 Arruda, Antônio de. A Escola Superior de Guerra: história de sua doutrina. 2a ed., rev. e ampliada. São Paulo: Edições GRD: Instituto Nacional do Livro, Fundação Nacional Pró-Memória, 1983. 303 p.: bibls., ill., index (Col. Urca; 1)

Largely undigested materials from the Escola's curriculum and official publications. Important raw material for military ideology (1960s-70s). This edition includes curriculum changes introduced in 1980. For political scientist's comment, see *HLAS 45:6479.*

3432 Assis Brasil, Joaquim Francisco de. A democracia representativa na República: antología. Seleção e introdução de Vicente Barreto. Brasília: Câmara dos Deputados, Centro de Documentação e Informação, Coordenação de Publicações, 1983. 340 p.: bibl. (Biblioteca do pensamento político republicano; 17)

Assis Brasil might be termed the "ideologue of democracy" in Brazil for his writings and political stances in favor of popular representation. Excerpts included here span his career (1881–1934). He helped inspire the progressive electoral reforms of 1932. Important in view of current redemocratization in Brazil.

3433 Bak, Joan. Political centralization and the building of the interventionist State in Brazil: corporatism, regionalism and interest group politics in Rio Grande do Sul, 1930–1937 (UW/LBR, 21:1, 1985, p. 9–25)

Based on dissertation and following on article reported in *HLAS 46:3527,* this study focuses on continued reforms carried out by Vargas and conflict between federal and state goals. Efforts to promote producers' cooperatives generally failed as federal intervention grew.

3434 Barros, Geraldo Mendes. Guilherme Guinle, 1882–1960: ensaio biográfico. São Paulo: Livraria AGIR Editôra, 1982. 303 p., 7 leaves of plates: bibl., ill.

Professional biography of one of Brazil's great entrepreneurs, best known for building the Santos docks and for extensive public and private banking activities. His membership on many government boards gave him a role in shaping Brazil's economic destiny.

3435 Battistel, Arlindo Itacir and Rovílio Costa. Assim vivem os italianos. v. 1, Vida, história, cantos, comidas e estórias. v. 2, Religião, música, trabalho e lazer. v. 3, A vida italiana em fotografia. v. 4, Arquitetura da imigração italiana no Rio Grande do Sul. Pôrto Alegre: Escola Superior de Teologia São Lourenço de Brindes; Caxias do Sul: Editôra da Univ. de Caxias do Sul, 1982–1983. 4 v.: bibls., ill. (some col.), indexes, ports. (Col. Imigração italiana; 50–52, 60)

Fascinating contribution towards the study of popular culture of the Italian immigrant community in Rio Grande do Sul. Despite some interpretative articles, the work is mainly composed of raw evidence (e.g., oral interviews, written accounts, and photographs) obtained from the immigrants and their offspring. While the materials are not of equal scholarly value, the work is an innovative and absorbing undertaking. Recommended.

3436 Bellotto, Manoel Lelo. A imigração espanhola para o Brasil, a vertente canária: um estudo prévio (*in* Coloquio de Historia Canario-Americana, 4th, Las Palmas, Spain, 1980. Cuarto Coloquio de Historia Canario-Americana. Coordinación y prólogo de Francisco Morales Padrón. Las Palmas, Spain: Ediciones del Excelentísimo Cabildo Insular, 1982, p. 709–740, bibl., tables)

Some observations on immigration from the Canary Islands to São Paulo state (1935–61), but primarily an overview of immigration to that state from Spain and elsewhere during the 19th and 20th centuries. Includes useful tables on annual immigration by national origin to São Paulo (1936–51).

3437 Bibliografia histórica, 1930–45. Organização de Ana Lígia Medeiros e Mônica Hirst. Brasília: Editôra Univ. de Brasília, 1982. 226 p., 16 p.: index, ports. (Col. Temas brasileiros; 28)

Helpful listing of 1337 publications, divided into 13 general categories. No annotations or subject index.

3438 Bittencourt, Gabriel Augusto de Mello. Esforço industrial na república do café: o caso do Espírito Santo, 1889/1930. Vitória: Fundação Ceciliano Abel de Almeida, 1982. 155 p.: bibl., ill.

Study shows how industrialization failed when promoted by a state government without appropriate conditions for success. Based on M.A. thesis.

3439 Borges, Ricardo. O Pará republicano, 1824–1929: ensaios histórico. Belém: Conselho Estadual de Cultura, 1983. 391 p.: port. (Col. História do Pará. Série Arthur Vianna)

Lacking in scholarly apparatus, this study is only useful for establishing a basic chronology of Pará during the period chosen.

3440 Brandi, Paulo; Mauro Malin; and Plínio de Abreu Ramos. Vargas: da vida para a história. Revisão do texto de Dora Flaksman. Rio de Janeiro: Zahar Editores, 1983. 322 p., 16 p. of plates: bibl., index, ports.

Professional if not critical biography, written originally for CPDOC's *Diccionario histórico-biográfico brasileiro*. Based on a wide variety of sources, the book provides a narrative account of Vargas's entire life, with the emphasis on his political career. Virtually no interpretation.

Brazil. Congresso Nacional. Câmara dos Deputados. Comissão de Instrução Pública. Reforma de ensino primário e vários instituições complementares da instrução pública. See *HLAS 47:4531.*

3441 Camargo, Aspásia. Os usos da história oral e da história de vida: trabalhando com elites (IUP/D, 27:1, 1984, p. 5–28)

Leading practitioner of oral history writes a methodological piece, showing how essential the technique is for contemporary elite studies. Gives some examples from her experience as director of CPDOC's program in Rio de Janeiro. For the specialist.

3442 Campos, F. Itami. Coronelismo em Goiás. Goiânia: Univ. Federal de Goiás, 1983. 113 p., 1 folded leaf of plates: ill., map, tables.

Short, somewhat sketchy, this revised M.A. thesis shows that *coronelismo* in Goiás resembled its counterparts in other rural states. Limited to the Old Republic and heavily padded with statistical tables.

3443 Caneca, Joaquim do Amor Divino. O Typhis Pernambucano. Introdução de Vamireh Chacon. Apresentação de Moacyr Dalla. Brasília: Centro Gráfico do Senado Federal, 1984. 304 p.: ill.

First complete edition of *O Typhis Pernambucano*, a periodical voicing the liberal ideology which motivated the Confederation of the Equator rising in 1824. Author, a priest, was executed in early 1825 for his role in the revolt. Includes transcript of judicial proceedings and an introductory overview of Frei Caneca's thought by Vamireh Chacon.

3444 Carli, Gileno dé. Visão da crise. Brasília: Editôra Univ. de Brasília, 1981. 266 p. (Col. Temas brasileiros; 2)

Valuable insider's account of Quadro's resignation and subsequent events leading up to the 1964 coup. Includes many transcribed documents. Dispassionate narrative. Raw material more than analysis.

3445 Carone, Edgard. A República Liberal, 1945–1964. São Paulo: DIFEL, 1985. 2 v. (390, 257 p.): tables.

These volumes conclude a project launched in 1969, when author published *A Primeira República*. Format included anthologies of texts from the period, followed by narrative treatments that stayed close to the texts. Volumes were organized into sections, usually labeled institutions, economics, social classes, political systems, and political process. Bulk of material came from newspapers and memoirs. Somewhat leftist in interpretation, the books viewed Brazil's politics as shaped by economic forces and in particular by international capitalism. Second and third "sets" of volumes dealt with the periods 1930–37 and 1937–45. Their main utility has been to make available documents from each era and to provide a running narrative organized by themes. In fact, so obvious is the format that no index is provided nor required for access. Mostly useful as reference works. Like Hélio Silva's *O ciclo de Vargas* series, these books provide very little analysis.

3446 Cervo, Amado Luís. Intervenção e neutralidade: doutrinas brasileiras para a Prata nos meados do século XIX (IBRI/R, 26:101/104, 1983, p. 103–119)

Discussion of the underlying motivation of Brazilian policy towards the Rio de la Plata (1840–60) based on parliamentary debates, Council of State decisions and diplomatic records. Concludes that motivation was neutralist to mid-century, interventionist (1850–56), and then the two tendencies synthesized into a kind of "restricted neutrality." Useful for its presentation of data, the article underestimates the impact of such factors as internal politics and the policies of other governments.

3447 Chiavenato, Julio José. Os voluntários da pátria: e outros mitos. São Paulo: Global Editôra, 1983. 251 p.: ill.

Series of polemical essays attacking several myths in Brazilian history, most of them concerning the black and mulatto population. First and most substantial essay demonstrates that there was nothing voluntary about the enlistment of the Voluntários da Pátria in the Paraguayan War, which for the author was a sordid and mismanaged affair.

3448 Colson, R.F. European investment and the Brazilian "boom," 1886–1892: the roots of speculation (IAA, 9:3/4, 1983, p. 401–413, bibl.)

Argues that the 1886–92 boom was caused by an economic policy designed to attract foreign capital in order both to ease the transition from slave to free labor and to provide the Rio de Janeiro capital market with adequate funds. Contends that the Baring crisis in Argentina and the overthrow of the Empire reversed original enthusiasm in Europe for such investment and so undercut the boom which a government policy of easy credit could not prolong.

3449 Cony, Carlos Heitor. JK [i.e. Juscelino Kubitschek]: memorial do exílio. Rio de Janeiro: Edições Bloch, 1982. 188 p., 16 p. of plates: appendix, bibl., ill., ports.

Quasi-autobiography of Kubitschek, based on his notes, drafts, and dictation. Covers period 1961 until his death in 1976.

Good, somewhat bitter view of events in Brazil. Nice selection of documents in appendix.

3450 Costa, Emilia Viotti da. The Brazilian Empire: myths and histories. Chicago: Univ. of Chicago Press, 1985. 287 p.: bibl., ill., index.

Series of essays (some reworked from previous studies) relating to the theme that the ruling elites of planters, merchants, and allies in Imperial Brazil possessed a significant amount of independent power and that the social and economic policies they implemented were designed to maintain their dominance over the mass of the population rather than to promote the progress of the nation. Individual essays contain useful insights into several key subjects and should prove especially stimulating as student readings.

Costa, Francisco Augusto Pereira da. Arredores do Recife. See *HLAS 47:5232.*

Costa, Iraci del Nero da. Populações minerais: sobre a estrutura populacional de alguns núcleos mineiros no alvorecer do século XIX. See *HLAS 47:8378.*

3451 Decca, Edgar Salvadori de. A ciência da produção: fábrica despolitizada. (Revista Brasileira de História [Associação Nacional dos Professores Universitários de História (ANPUH), São Paulo] 6, set. 1983, p. 47–79)

Interesting discussion of changing definitions of industrial production in the 19th century and how Brazilian owners and workers conceived their roles. Concludes that great upheavals of the 1910s forced a radical shift that led industrialists to project their mode of production to the entire society, and laborers to take political action to defend their interests.

3452 Dias, Maria Odila Leite da Silva. Mulheres sem história (USP/RH, 114, jan./junho 1983, p. 31–45)

Fascinating look at women, mostly poor and illiterate, in São Paulo from late 18th to late 19th centuries. Based largely on census, judicial, and other archival sources; contains suggestive comparisons with other societies.

3453 Dicionário histórico-biográfico brasileiro: 1930–1983. Coordenação de Israel Beloch e Alzira Alves de Abreu. Rio de

Janeiro: Forense-Universitária: FINEP, 1984.
4 v. (3634 p.): bibls., ports.

Massive compilation of biographical materials on some 5,000 political figures (1930s-80s). Very professional and eminently useful, with bibliographic indications, plates, and cross-references. Will become a standard reference work for modern Brazilian history.

3453a Dulles, John W. F. The São Paulo Law School and the anti-Vargas resistance, 1938–1945. Austin: Univ. of Texas Press, 1986. 262 p., 12 p. of plates: bibl., ill., index.

Detailed account covers events during the Estado Novo, when students and faculty maintained their autonomy and nursed an opposition movement. Many later became important Paulista politicians. Sympathetic but honest treatment based on heavy documentation. Also in Portuguese translation, A Faculdade de Direito de São Paulo e a resistência anti-Vargas, 1938–1945.

3454 Eakin, Marshall C. Race and identity: Sílvio Romero, science, and social thought in late 19th century Brazil (UW/ LBR, 22:2, 1985, p. 151–174)

Overview of this literary critic's views on the racial makeup of Brazilian society, views based on European evolutionism and scientific racism. He emphasized the role of miscegenation and attached a positive value to it, foreshadowing Freyre and others in the 1930s. Still, he could not shake an underlying racism and hope for an ultimate whitening. Romero's views are seen as transnational between the racial pessimism of turn-of-the-century writers and the optimism of their 1930s successors.

3455 Fagundes, Morivalde Calvet. História da Revolução Farroupilha. Caxias do Sul: Editôra da Univ. de Caxias do Sul, 1984. 432 p.: bibl., ill., ports.

Prime example of mythologizing history, focusing on Bento Gonçalves as the ideal hero and on the Farroupilha revolt as a unifying struggle. Sees no contradiction in glorifying the revolt and extolling Brazil, perceiving the rebel republic as the model for the nation. Well produced but lacking scholarly apparatus. Author, an army bureaucrat, writer and fervent mason, epitomizes one stream of Brazilian historiography.

3456 Fausto, Boris. Crime e cotidiano: a criminalidade em São Paulo, 1880– 1924. São Paulo: Brasiliense, 1984. 293 p.: bibl., ill.

Absolutely brilliant piece of social history. By examining criminal court records over a period of time, Fausto manages to depict the coming of age of São Paulo and, by extension, of modern Brazil itself. Concludes that although changes of the era were dramatic, much remained constant (e.g., family, codes of honor, values). Does not endorse culture of poverty interpretation. Essential reading.

3457 Figueiredo, Euclides. De um observador militar: a 2a. Guerra Mundial vista de dentro de uma prisão do Estado Novo. Brasília: Câmara dos Deputados, Centro de Documentação e Informação, Coordenação de Publicações, 1983. 670 p.

More remarkable than the contents is the very existence of this collection of newspaper articles about World War II (1940–44). A commander in the São Paulo civil war and opponent of Vargas, the author spent the years 1938–41 in jail. Early articles were bootlegged out by his son for publication in the opposition O Jornal.

3458 Figueiredo, Euclides. Discursos parlamentares. Seleção e introdução de Vamireh Chacon. Brasília: Câmara dos Deputados, Centro de Documentação e Informação, Coordenação de Publicações, 1982. 306 p.: indexes, ports. (Perfis parlamentares; 23)

Selection of speeches and several documents of man who led 1932 revolt and later acted as political opponent of Vargas. Also father of President João Figueiredo. Continues series begun in HLAS 42:3681.

3459 Fonseca, Pedro Cezar Dutra. RS [i.e. Rio Grande do Sul]: economia & conflitos políticos na República Velha. Pôrto Alegre: Mercado Aberto, 1983. 143 p.: ill. (Série Documenta; 18)

This short overview of economic aspects of political dispute in Rio Grande began as a M.A. thesis and is based partly on published statistics, legislative debates, and official documents. Good introduction to subject.

3460 Foot, Francisco. Nem pátria, nem patrão!: vida operária e cultura anarquista no Brasil. São Paulo: Brasiliense, 1983. 199 p., 8 p. of plates: bibl., ill.

Excellent book interprets and reconstructs the culture of anarchism in the early 20th century as a means of recreating the *mentalité* of immigrants and their local working-class colleagues. Balanced, thoughtful, and timely, given the new approaches to labor history in Brazil.

Franco, Afonso Arinos de Melo and **Cláudio Pacheco.** História do Banco do Brasil. See *HLAS 47:3778.*

3461 Gambeta, Wilson Roberto. Ciência e indústria farmacêutica: São Paulo, Primeira República (IPE/EE, 21:3, dez. 1982, p. 87–98)

Examines the Instituto Pasteur and the Laboratório Paulista de Biologia as cases of frustrated technical/industrial development in São Paulo during the Old Republic. Concludes that the State did not protect or promote these enterprises, and they eventually lost out to multinational competition.

3462 Getúlio: uma história oral. Coordinação de Valentina da Rocha. Rio de Janeiro: Editôra Record, 1986. 321 p.: index.

Fascinating extract of commentary about Getúlio from CPDOC's huge collection of oral histories. Organized chronologically and by topic, as well as indexed by name, the volume is easy to consult. Based on depositions by 70 persons, including Kubitschek, Tancredo Neves, and Vargas family members, these comments view Vargas from many possible angles. Great raw material.

3463 Góes, Walder de and **Aspásia Alcântara de Camargo.** O drama da sucessão e a crise do regime. Rio de Janeiro: Editôra Nova Fronteira, 1984. 222 p.: bibl. (Col. Brasil século 20)

Two excellent essays pitched to mid-1980s themes: that by Camargo deals with succession crises in the past 50 years, and Góes's with the 1985 succession.

3464 Gouvêa, Fernando da Cruz. Uma conjuração fracassada e outros ensaios. Recife: Secretaria de Educação e Cultura, Fundação de Cultura Cidade do Recife, Prefeitura da Cidade do Recife, 1982. 184 p., 18 p. of plates: bibl., ill., ports. (Col. Recife; 26)

Three long essays by distinguished Pernambucan historian discuss: 1) frustrated revolt by civilian politicians against Governor Barbosa Lima (1892–96); 2) correspondence and contacts between Pedro II and the Recife Law School; and 3) debate between Joaquim Nabuco and José Joaquim Seabra over abolition that took place during the 1884 elections.

3465 Hilton, Stanley E. Brazil's international economic strategy, 1945–1960: revival of the German option (HAHR, 66:2, 1986, p. 287–318)

Argues that Brazil's 1970s emphasis on trade and investment with Europe, particularly West Germany, was not an innovation but rather the strengthening of long-standing economic ties with Germany. Article shows how both countries overcame postwar problems and reestablished those ties, usually with the blessing of the US, making Germany Brazil's second largest trade and investment partner. Explores mutual interests served by these developments.

3466 Hippolito, Lucia. Da raposas e reformistas: o PSD e a experiência democrática brasileira, 1945–1964. Rio de Janeiro: Paz e Terra, 1985. 328 p.: ill., tables.

Excellent study finds that the PSD served as majority party and ballast for the political system, as well as guarantor of its stability. It coordinated other parties' activities, through alliances and parliamentary bargains. In the late 1950s, however, it began to fragment internally, and it lost its ability to stabilize the rest of the system. The center evaporated, other parties became radicalized, and the military stepped in. Based in large part on oral histories in CPDOC.

3467 História geral da civilização brasileira. t. 3, O Brasil republicano: v. 4, Economia e cultura, 1930–1964. Edição de Boris Fausto. São Paulo: Difusão Européia do Livro, 1984. 1 v.

Volume completes the set begun by Sérgio Buarque de Hollanda in 1960. Maintaining the high standards of quality and synthesis with which the series began, editor Fausto has managed to bring in younger authors from the São Paulo area. Economic chapters lead off the volume, followed by strong chapters on the Catholic Church. Last five entries deal with education, poetry and prose, cinema, popular music, and theatre. All students of Brazil should own this fine, comprehensive collection.

3468 A História vivida. v. 2–3. Coordenação de Lourenço Dantas Mota. São Paulo: O Estado de São Paulo, 1981–1982. 2 v. (392, 397 p.) (Documentos abertos)

Transcriptions of oral history interviews, continues project annotated in *HLAS 46:3590*. Some prominent and not-so-prominent figures. Among the former, Ary Campista, Gouvéia de Bulhões, Roberto Campos, Barbosa Lima Sobrinho, Gen. Lott, Oscar Niemeyer, and Darcy Ribeiro.

3469 Hunsche, Carlos Henrique Trein. Protestantismo no sul do Brasil: nos 500 anos de [i.e. do] nascimento de Lutero, 1483–1983. Pôrto Alegre: Escola Superior de Teologia São Lourenço de Brindes; São Leopoldo: Editôra Sinodal, 1983. 77 p.: bibl., ill., ports.

Laudatory account of life and work of some two dozen Lutheran pastors who ministered to German immigrant community in Rio Grande do Sul during 19th and early 20th centuries. Well illustrated and based on primary sources.

3470 Impasse na democracia brasileira, 1951–1955: coletânea de documentos. Organização de Adelina Maria Alves Novaes e Cruz *et al.* Prefácio de Hélio Jaguaribe. Rio de Janeiro: Instituto de Documentação, Editôra da Fundação Getúlio Vargas, 1983. 477 p.: bibl., ill., index, ports.

This excellent collection of 147 letters and documents provides the specialist with a glimpse of the internal workings of the second Vargas presidency. Largely devoted to politics and economics.

3471 Ipanema, Marcello de and **Cybelle de Ipanema.** Súmula da atividade jornalística de Januário da Cunha Barbosa e crítica de atribuição (IHGB/R, 330, jan./março 1981, p. 115–120)

Brief overview of the journalistic career (1821–45) of a priest who, as co-editor of *O Reverbero Constitucional Fluminense*, played a critical role in the achievement of independence.

3472 Janotti, Aldo. Ato Adicional e unidade nacional (USP/RH, 114, jan./junho 1983, p. 47–60)

Uses parliamentary record to examine the constitutional reform of 1834 in the context of declining national unity during the Regency. Despite deep disagreements over the

Ato, virtually all members of parliament wanted to avoid fragmentation of the country.

3473 Janotti, Aldo. Monarquia, restauração monárquica e o problema da unidade nacional na época da Regência (USP/RIEB, 21, 1979, p. 19–32)

Argues that fears of Brazil's disintegration as a nation were an overriding concern in the 1830s. The monarchy had been essential in creating that unity and was seen as indispensable in its maintenance. It was for this reason that the ouster of Pedro I was not followed by the abolition of the monarchy. The inability of the Regency to maintain national unity was the main cause of the premature majority of Pedro II in 1840. Also notes that in 1833–34 the rulers of Brazil, rather than accept a restoration of Pedro I, were willing to split up Brazil.

3474 Lazzarotto, Danilo. Os capuchinhos na história e no desenvolvimento de Ijuí. Pôrto Alegre: Escola Superior de Teologia São Lourenço de Brindes, 1981. 120 p.: bibl. (Col. Religiosos no Brasil; 6)

Informative case study of the role of a Catholic order in a small town of Rio Grande do Sul (1948-ca. 1970). Critical assessment of Capuchins' activities in education and popular mobilization during a period of rapid modernization following their arrival to found a seminary.

3475 Levine, Robert M. Elite intervention in urban popular culture in modern Brazil (UW/LBR, 21:2, 1984, p. 9–22)

Argues that the Brazilian elite (1930s-40s), threatened with restive lower classes in the major cities, used a clever blend of repression and cooptation to assure that Carnival, samba music, and Afro-Brazilian religious cults contributed to a safe popular culture, one that reinforced elite hegemony.

3476 Lima, Haroldo and **Aldo Arantes.** História da Ação Popular: da JUC ao PC do B. São Paulo: Editôra Alfa-Omega, 1984. 176 p.: bibl. (Biblioteca Alfa-Omega de cultura universal. Série 2a, Col. Atualidade; 33)

Detailed and ideological account of how part of the Catholic student movement JUC was gradually radicalized and incorporated into Brazil's Communist Party (1960s-73). Written partly in prison by two of the movement's leaders. One of many "stories that can only be told now" books to appear in the 1980s.

3477 Lima, Valentina da Rocha and Plínio de Abreu Ramos. Tancredo fala de Getúlio: depoimento. Pôrto Alegre: L&PM; Rio de Janeiro: Fundação Getúlio Vargas, 1986. 127 p.: ill.

Extracts dealing with Vargas, from Tancredo's oral history file at CPDOC, are supplemented by a biographical note about Tancredo himself, the hero and perhaps martyr of the 1985 redemocratization movement. The deposition is at least as interesting for what it reveals about Tancredo, who may prove an enigma for biographers.

3478 Lisboa, João Francisco. Crônica política do Império. Introdução e seleção de Hildon Rocha. Rio de Janeiro: Francisco Alves, 1984. 322 p. (Col. Dimensões do Brasil; 15)

Selection from the political and historical writings of a Maranhão intellectual of the early Empire whose keen observation and mordant pen seems to have caught and held the attention of compilers. Provides a colorful view of the underside of provincial politics.

3479 Lorentz, Leônidas. Teófilo Otoni no tribunal da história. Rio de Janeiro: Editôra Luna, 1981. 261 p.

Refreshing diatribe against leading politician of the first and second empires. Seldom do we find a critical biography like this. Unfortunately lacking in the usual documentation, the book nonetheless is well researched.

3480 McCann, Frank D., Jr. The Brazilian general staff and Brazil's military situation: 1900–1945 (UM/JIAS, 25:3, Aug. 1983, p. 299–324)

Fine account of origins of Brazilian military gears of an Argentine invasion. Also summarizes major developments since 1945, when the balance of power shifted in Brazil's favor.

3481 McCann, Frank D., Jr. The formative period of twentieth-century Brazilian army thought: 1900–1922 (HAHR, 64:4, Nov. 1984, p. 737–765)

Essential reading for all students of modern Brazil, because it traces the formation of intellectual bases for multiple roles played by the army since the 1920s.

3482 McCann, Frank D., Jr. A nação armada: ensaios sobre a história do Exército Brasileiro. Tradução de Sílvio Rolim. Recife: Editôra Guararapes, 1982. 223 p.: bibl.

Fine collection makes available to Brazilian audiences and to specialists a number of separate articles on the military since 1889, some first published in English. Though the text is not comprehensive, it touches on key issues in military affairs in this century, such as the arms industry, professionalism, relations with the US, and the evolving definition of the military's mission.

3483 Madureira, Antônio de Sena. Guerra do Paraguai: resposta ao Sr. Jorge Thompson, autor da *Guerra del Paraguay* e aos anotadores argentinos D. Lewis e A. Estrada. Brasília: Editôra Univ. de Brasília, 1982. 168 p. (Col. Temas brasileiros; 22)

Reprint of a work written in 1870 by military engineer to rebut anti-Brazilian comments in Thompson's history of Paraguayan War.

3484 Magalhães Júnior, Raimundo. A maior mistificação da imprensa brasileira: a crônica escandalosa do Segundo Reinado nas falsas cartas de um diplomata. Com introdução e notas. Brasília: Editôra de Brasília, 1982? 227 p.: bibl., ill., ports.

Not a mistification but simply a journalistic trick practiced by a Rio de Janeiro newspaper in 1886, publishing a series of "letters" by a "foreign diplomat," full of innuendo against the Imperial family and the regime. Significant only in that it shows the type of information found credible by the reading public; also interesting since, shorn of their worst smears, the views presented in the letters are fairly similar to the current historical appreciation of the last years of the Empire.

Manfredi, Silvia Maria. As entidades sindicais e a educação dos trabalhadores. See *HLAS 47:4562*.

3485 Martins Filho, Amilcar Vianna. A economia política do café com leite, 1900–1930. Belo Horizonte: Univ. Federal de Minas Gerais, PROED, 1981. 145 p.: bibl., ill. (Série Dissertações e teses; 2)

Outstanding work on the political and economic alliance known as "café com leite," based on M.A. thesis. Frankly revisionist, it argues that coffee protection was not the principal aim of the alliance. Rather, each state oligarchy had different expectations from the federal government, including the presidential office.

3486 Martins Filho, Antônio. O outro lado da história. Fortaleza: Edições Univ. Federal do Ceará, 1983. 442 p.: bibl., index.

Memoirs of rector of the Univ. of Ceará (1955–67). More candid than most treatments, this might be of interest to historians of higher education in Brazil.

3487 Mattos, Carlos de Meira. O Marechal Mascarenhas de Moraes e sua época. Rio de Janeiro: Biblioteca do Exército Editôra, 1983. 2 v. (321 p.): bibl., ports. (Publicação; 527. Col. General Benício; 211–212)

Though not critical, this biography provides an introduction to the career of one of Brazil's leading military figures. Based partly on manuscript sources.

3488 Mello, Evaldo Cabral de. O Norte agrário e o Imperio, 1871–1889. Rio de Janeiro: Editôra Nova Fronteira, 1984. 298 p.

Series of linked essays studying impact of government policies on plantation economies of Northeast Brazil during last decades of the Empire. Firmly based in existing historiography and printed primary sources, the work shows a shrewd appreciation of the social and economic conjuncture which both discriminated against the Northeast and caused the fall of the Empire. Recommended.

3489 Mello, José Octávio de Arruda. A revolução estatizada: um estudo sobre a formação do centralismo em 30. Prefácio de Hélio Jaguaribe. Mossoró: Edições Escola Superior de Agricultura de Mossoró; Fundação Guimarães Duque, 1984. 436 p., 7 leaves of plates: bibls., ill. (Col. mossoroense; 274)

Dense, heavily documented account of the 1930 revolution in the Northeast, based on João Pessoa papers, newspapers, and many other local manuscript sources. Argues that the revolution was designed to eradicate *coronelismo* but it gained excessive momentum and extinguished regional participation in federal government. Mostly for specialists.

3490 Mello, Maria Regina Ciparrone. A industrialização do algodão em São Paulo. São Paulo: Editôra Perspectiva, 1983. 156 p.: bibl. (Col. Debates; 180. História)

Based on M.A. thesis, this useful monograph describes the small textile industry in São Paulo (1813–30), sponsored by João VI at first but killed off by financial difficulties.

3491 Mitchell, Michael. Cafundó: counterpoint on a Brazilian African survival (MSU/CR, 28:3, Summer 1984, p. 185–203)

Introduction to the 1978 discovery of an Afro-Brazilian rural community an hour's drive from São Paulo, and to the fascinating debates it has provoked.

3492 Monteiro, Tobias. O Presidente Campos Salles na Europa. Belo Horizonte: Editôra Itatiaia; São Paulo: Editôra da Univ. de São Paulo, 1983. 158 p.: bibl. (Col. Reconquista do Brasil; nova série, 76)

Reprint of contemporary press reports written during Campos Salles's visit to Europe to confirm the funding loan of 1898. Fairly standard travelogue with little inside information.

3493 Moraes, Maria Luiza de Paiva Melo. Francisco Schmidt: a formação de uma grande propriedade cafeeira (Universidade Estadual Paulista [São Paulo] 1, 1982, p. 77–90, bibl., tables)

Straightforward and well researched account of the rise of Schmidt—a German immigrant—to economic preeminence in São Paulo through coffee production and processing. Based on M.A. thesis.

3494 Moreira, Earle Diniz Macarthy. O reconhecimento da independência do Brasil pelo Espanha (PUC/V, 30:113, junho 1985, p. 217–239)

Superficial narrative, using some archival material, of the first decade of Brazilian independence from perspective of Spain and its priorities in Latin America. Diplomatic recognition of Brazil in 1834 flowed from a tardy realization of common political economic situation.

3495 Moura, Esmeralda Blanco Bolsonaro de. Mulheres e menores no trabalho industrial: os fatores sexo e idade na dinâmica do capital. Petrópolis: Vozes, 1982. 164 p.: bibl., ill.

Fine study of women and children in São Paulo's factory labor force between 1890 and 1920, the problems this created, and the attempts to solve them with legislation. Based on Univ. de São Paulo M.A. thesis.

Murtinho, Joaquim. Idéias econômicas de Joaquim Murtinho: cronologia, introdução, notas bibliográficas e textos selecionados. See *HLAS 47:3814.*

3496 Nascimento, Luiz do. Die zweite Kaiserzeit Brasiliens im Spiegelbild der deutsch-brasilianischen Handelsbeziehugen, 1840–1888. Bamberg, FRG: Aku-Fotodruck, 1983. 249 p.: bibl., ill.

Title of this dissertation, *The Second Reign as reflected in German-Brazilian commercial relations, 1840–1888,* accurately conveys the descriptive and superficial nature of this work which derives mainly from secondary sources. While containing useful statistics, it does not analyze the structure or nature of German-Brazilian trade.

3497 Navarro Swain, Tania. L'évolution des structures agraires et industrielles au Paraná de 1940 a 1970 (*in* L'Industrialisation des pays de La Plata: eveils et somnolences, 1890–1970. Paris: Univ. de Paris, 1980, p. 121–141, bibl., tables)

Upbeat, light treatment of recent economic growth in Paraná.

3498 Neder, Gizlene; Nancy Naro and José Luiz Werneck da Silva. A polícia na Corte e no Distrito Federal, 1831–1930. Rio de Janeiro: Centro de Ciências Sociais, Pontifícia Univ. Católica, 1981. 1 v.: tables (Série Estudos; 3)

Solid administrative treatment of police services in Rio de Janeiro during a century marked by much disorder. Generally sees police as instrument of social control.

3499 Nogueira, Arlinda Rocha. Imigração japonesa na história contemporânea do Brasil. São Paulo: Centro de Estudos Nipo-Brasileiros; Massao Ohno Editor, 1984. 190 p., 3 p. of plates: bibl., ill.

This updated and expanded version of her 1973 work on Japanese immigrants in the coffee regions is a good synthetic treatment. Though focused mostly on the 1900–20 period, it does briefly bring the story up to modern times. Well documented.

3500 Nonato, Raimundo. História social da abolição em Mossoró. Mossoró: s.n., 1983. 305 p.: ports. (Col. mossoroense; 285)

Poorly written, disorganized collection of facts about a town in Rio Grande do Norte, notable for its extinction of slavery in 1883.

Nunes, Clarice. A escola primária numa perspectiva histórica: 1922–1928. See *HLAS 47:4569.*

3501 Oberacker, Carlos H., Jr. *O Brasileiro em Coimbra* e ou seu redator (IHGB/R, 330, jan./março 1981, p. 107–113)

Brief account of the single issue of pro-Brazilian periodical published in 1823 at Portugal's Coimbra Univ. and of the subsequent career of its editor, then a law student.

3502 Oberacker, Carlos H., Jr. O Marechal-de-Campo Gustavo Henrique von Braun, Chefe do Primeiro Estado-Maior do Exército Brasileiro: com realce para os corpos alemães que participaram na Campanha da Cisplatina, 1826–1828 (JSGWGL, 21, 1984, p. 211–263)

Detailed vindication of the conduct in the Cisplatine War (1826–28) of German officer who served in the Peninsula War and was one of the foreign officers contracted for service by the government of Pedro I and dismissed in 1831.

3503 Oliveira, Lúcia Lippi; Mônica Pimenta Velloso; and Angela Maria Castro Gomes. Estado Novo: ideologia e poder. Rio de Janeiro: Zahar Editores, 1982. 166 p.: bibl., tables (Política e sociedade)

Set of essays, or seminar papers, on several themes from the late 1930s and early 1940s: authoritarianism, nationalism, political culture, and intellectuals and the State. The more focused deal with Almir de Andrade, Azevedo Amaral, and the journal, *Cultura Política.* Useful introduction to ideology in the Estado Novo.

3504 O P.C.B. [i.e. Partido Comunista do Brasil]. v. 3, 1964–1982. Compilação de Edgard Carone. São Paulo: Difel, 1982. 400 p.: bibl. (Corpo e alma do Brasil; 62)

Using the same format as his other publications, Carone transcribes documents from Brazil's Communist Party, with little comment and incomplete references to sources. Final volume is useful as a source for the military years. Fascinating raw data. For political scientist's comment on vols. 1–2, , see *HLAS 45:6512.*

Peláez, Carlos Manuel and **Wilson Suzigan.** História monetária do Brasil. See *HLAS 47:3821.*

Pessar, Patricia R. Unmasking the politics of religion: the case of Brazilian millenarianism. See *HLAS 47:8398*.

3505 Piletti, Nelson. A Reforma Fernando de Azevedo: Distrito Federal, 1927–1930. São Paulo: Faculdade de Educação, Univ. de São Paulo, 1982. 307 p.: bibl. (Publicação da Faculdade. Estudos e documentos; 20)

Solid, heavily documented, and professional account of the Rio de Janeiro educational reform undertaken by Azevedo (1927–30). Part of growing literature on educational history.

3506 Prado, João Fernando de Almeida. O século da República e seus antecedentes. São Paulo: IBREX, 1982. 220 p.

Last book by this distinguished historian of colonial Brazil is of uneven quality and pace. Argues that Brazilian leaders mistakenly adopted democratic liberalism from Europe in the 19th century and have yet been able to make it work. Some interesting interpretations of 20th-century presidents.

3507 Prado Júnior, Caio. Caio Prado Júnior: história. Organização de Francisco Iglésias. São Paulo: Editôra Atica, 1982. 207 p.: bibl., index (Col. Grandes cientistas sociais; 26)

Fine bio-bibliographical essay that opens this anthology is worth the purchase price of the book.

Reconstituição da memória estatística da Grande São Paulo. See *HLAS 47:5300*.

Reesink, E.B. The peasant in the sertão: a short exploration of his past and present. See *HLAS 47:8400*.

3508 Relatórios dos Presidentes da Província de São Paulo, 1836–1889: coleção microfilmada pelo Plano Nacional de Microfilmagem de Periódicos Brasileiros: pesquisa, descrição catalográfica, catálogo coletivo e notas informativas. Pesquisa de Rofran Fernandes. Descrição catalográfica de Rofran Fernandes e Ruth Werner. Revisão de Ruth Werner. Prefácio de Mário Chamie. Apresentação de João Carlos Martins. São Paulo: Imprensa Oficial, Estado de São Paulo: Divisão de Arquivo, Estado de São Paulo, 1982. 85 p. (Apoio; 1)

Well organized bibliography of one of the most important contemporary printed sources for the study of Imperial Brazil.

Needs to be done not just for São Paulo but for all the states.

3509 A Revolução de 30, seminário internacional. Seminário realizado pelo Centro de Pesquisa e Documentação de História Contemporânea do Brasil da Fundação Getúlia Vargas. Brasília: Editôra Univ. de Brasília, 1982. 722 p., 7 p. of plates: ill. (Col. Temas brasileiros; 54)

Papers and discussion transcript from very important conference held in Rio de Janeiro's CPDOC in 1980, to commemorate the 50th anniversary of the 1930 revolution. Panelists included specialists from throughout Brazil and the US. Essential for 20th-century historians and social scientists.

3510 Ribeiro, Francisco Moreira. A redemocratização no Ceará de 1945 a 1947. Fortaleza: Secretaria de Cultura e Desporto, 1982. 113 p.: bibl., ill.

Partially digested material from newspapers and official publications regarding the transition from dictatorship to democracy after Vargas's ouster.

3511 Rocha, Levy. Viagem de Pedro II ao Espírito Santo. 2a ed. Rio de Janeiro: Revista Continente Editorial, 1980. 221 p.: bibl., ill.

Using diary entries made by Pedro II during his visit to Espírito Santo in 1859 as a frame, describes physical and social conditions in the province in the mid-19th century.

3512 Rodrigues, Antônio Edmilson Martins; Francisco José Calazans Falcon; and Margarida de Souza Neves. A Guarda Nacional no Rio de Janeiro, 1831–1918. Rio de Janeiro: Centro de Ciências Sociais, Pontifícia Univ. Católica, 1981. 1 v.: ill., tables (Série Estudos; 5)

Administrative history gives much weight to the political role played by the Guarda in the state of Rio de Janeiro, emphasizing peace-keeping and unity of power. Based on decrees, laws, official reports, and archival sources. For companion studies, see item **3498** and *HLAS 44:3554*.

3513 Sallum Júnior, Brasilio. Capitalismo e cafeicultura oeste-paulista, 1888–1930. São Paulo: Livraria Duas Cidades, 1982. 258 p.: bibl. (Col. História e sociedade)

Originally a doctoral thesis, this study seeks to prove that the spread of coffee to São

Paulo's western district introduced capitalism as well. Though hardly original, the book synthesizes much that has been written and presents new information gleaned from archival and oral history sources.

3514 Sampaio, Fernando G. Bento Gonçalves: mito e história sobre o herói ladrão farroupilha. Pôrto Alegre: Martins Livreiro-Editor, 1984. 141 p.: bibl.

Vigorously defends the leader of the Farropos revolt against charges of contraband, cattle theft, and other accusations, primarily by placing facts within context of the times.

3515 Santos, Maria da Guia. Aussenhandel und industrielle Entwicklung Brasiliens unter besonderer Berücksichtigung der Beziehungen zu Deutschland: 1889–1914. Munchen, FRG: Wilhelm Fink Verlag, 1984. 363 p.: bibl., ill., tables (Lateinamerika-Studien; 15)

Study of the role of German immigration, trade, and investment in the external trade and industrial development of Brazil during the apogee of the Old Republic. Based solely on secondary sources, but intelligently organized with sound analysis. Contribution of the first to the second theme of the study does not appear to have been very significant, although German exports to Brazil switched increasingly from textiles to machinery and industrial products such as cement.

3516 Santos, Paulo de Tarso. 64 i.e. Sessenta e quatro] e outros anos: depoimentos a Oswaldo Coimbra. São Paulo: Cortez Editôra, 1984. 174 p., 5 p. of plates: ports.

Well written, moving oral history by a *mineiro*-turned-*paulista* who served as Minister of Education under Goulart in 1963. He was a leader of the Christian Democrats in the 1950s and part of the Catholic left in the early 1960s. Caught in the cross-fire and branded a communist, he spent nearly two decades in exile. A refreshingly personal look at the 1945–64 period.

3517 Santos, Ronaldo Marcos dos. Resistência e superação do escravismo na Província de São Paulo, 1885–1888. São Paulo: Instituto de Pesquisas Econômicas, Univ. de São Paulo, 1980. 142 p: bibl., ill., maps, tables (Ensaios econômicos; 5)

Well written, well organized study which argues that the effectiveness of slave protests were limited by narrow goals, that of

the abolitionist movement by its urban character. The latter gained strength through use of the former to reinforce its case. Univ. of São Paulo M.A. thesis based on contemporary press coverage and official records. Includes tables and maps detailing São Paulo slave population and abolition process at the local level. Recommended.

3518 Schwartzman, Simon; Helena Maria Bousquet Bomeny; and Vanda Maria Ribeiro Costa. Tempos de Capanema. São Paulo: EDUSP; Rio de Janeiro: Paz e Terra, 1984. 388 p., 13 leaves of plates: bibl., ill., ports. (Col. Estudos brasileiros; 81)

Excellent source for intellectual and cultural history (1930s-40s). Most material derives from Gustavo Capanema's term as Minister of Education (1934–45), a time of heightened political interaction in education. In addition to a well written and judicious text, the book contains over 100 selected letters from the Capanema papers.

3519 Seckinger, Ron. The Brazilian monarchy and the South American republics, 1822–1831: diplomacy and State building. Baton Rouge: Louisiana State Univ. Press, 1984. 187 p.: bibl., ill., index.

Clearly written study, set in a strong theoretical structure, of the relations between Brazil and the rest of South America in the era of independence, centering on the war between Brazil and Argentina for the control of Uruguay. Makes clear that an activist foreign policy, far from consolidating the newly independent states, served to dissipate their resources and undermine their internal credibility. Recommended to experts and students alike.

3520 Seitenfus, Ricardo Silva. Ideology and diplomacy: Italian fascism and Brazil, 1935–38 (HAHR, 64:3, Aug. 1984, p. 503–534)

Uneven account of Italo-Brazilian relations, based on Italian diplomatic archives. Concludes that little of importance occurred and that neither side accomplished much.

3521 Silva, Eduardo. Barões e escravidão: três gerações de fazendeiros e a crise da estrutura escravista. Rio de Janeiro: Editôra Nova Fronteira, 1984. 274 p.

Case study detailing how three generations of a major Paraíba Valley coffee family, the Lacerda Wernecks, reacted and adjusted to the changing labor economy of the 19th and early 20th centuries. Argues in theoretical terms for the necessity of such localized studies for refining and even redefining the dominant structuralist and ideological approach to the study of slavery and abolition, viewed as too abstract and sweeping in its generalizations. Originally a Fluminense M.A. thesis.

3522 Silva, Hélio and Maria Cecília Ribas Carneiro. Deodoro, proclamaçáo da República, 1889–1894. São Paulo: Grupo de Comunicação Três, 1983. 175 p.: ill., ports. (Os presidentes)

Authors of this series, *Os Presidentes*, provide competent and useful sketches of Brazilian presidents. Volumes have fewer than 200 p. and contain no footnotes or sources. They are pitched for high school audiences.

3523 Silva, Hélio and Maria Cecília Ribas Carneiro. O poder militar. Pôrto Alegre: L&M Editores, 1984. 565 p.

Light narrative treatment of the army's rise to power (1870s-1980s), with virtually no analysis and heavy transcription of documents. Scant footnotes suggest much was gleaned from author's earlier series *O ciclo de Vargas*.

3524 Silva, José Ariovaldo da. O movimento litúrgico no Brasil: estudo histórico. Petrópolis: Vozes, 1983. 399 p.: bibl.

Heavily documented and detailed study of liturgical practice in Brazil, from Cabral to the present. For the specialist only.

3525 Simpósio sobre a Revolução de 30, Pôrto Alegre, Brazil, 1980. Simpósio sobre a Revolução da 30. Pôrto Alegre: Univ. Federal do Rio Grande do Sul, Pró-Reitoria da Extensão, 1983. 719 p.: bibl., ill. (Estante Rio-grandense União de Seguros)

Contains papers, speeches, comments, and recollections by historians, social scientists, and historical figures, who gathered in Rio Grande in 1980 to commemorate the 50th anniversary of the 1930 revolution. Participants included some distinguished as well as unknown figures, and the level of scholarship was high. Specialists should plow through the difficult organization to sample the fine history within.

3526 Smith, Joseph. United States diplomacy toward political revolt in Brazil,

1889–1930 (IAMEA, 37 : 2, Autumn 1983, p. 3–21)

After analyzing attempted and successful coups, author concludes that US diplomats did not understand, much less control, Brazilian events.

3527 Smith, Peter Seaborn. Reaping the whirlwind: Brazil's energy crisis in historical perspective (IAMEA, 37 : 1, 1983, p. 3–20)

Sketches in three post-war decisions with regard to economic development that were to make the country heavily dependent on oil—and vulnerable to the 1970s oil crisis: nationalization of the oil industry; a shift from maritime and rail transport to highways; and choice of motor vehicles as the leading edge of the industrialization program. Good account of 1970s attempt to correct these problems.

3528 Soares, José Arlindo. A frente do Recife e o governor do Arraes: nacionalismo em crise: 1955–1964. Rio de Janeiro: Paz e Terra, 1982. 147 p.: bibl., ill., ports, tables (Série Estudos sobre o Nordeste; 13)

Superficial look at the leftist alliance that gathered momentum in Pernambuco in the late 1950s and elected Miguel Arraes in 1962. Originally a M.A. thesis, the study is based largely on newspaper accounts.

3529 Stolcke, Verena. The exploitation of family morality: labor systems and family structure on São Paulo coffee plantations, 1850–1979 (*in* Kinship, ideology and practice in Latin America [see *HLAS 47:259*] p. 264–296, bibl., table)

Examines transition from family sharecropping to wage labor on coffee plantations, and the mutual influences of family composition, productivity, morals, and general worker satisfaction.

Tannuri, Luiz Antônio. O encilhamento. See *HLAS 47:3845*.

Tavares, José Antônio Giusti. A estrutura do autoritarismo brasileiro. See *HLAS 47:6582*.

3531 Thön, Arlindo. Manoel Pereira Brodt, herói da Guerra do Paraguai. Pôrto Alegre: Escola Superior de Teologia São Lourenço de Brindes; São Leopoldo: Museu Histórico Visconde de São Leopoldo, 1982. 78 p.: ill.

Biography of a Dutch immigrant's son who, after serving in the Paraguayan War, became a very active mason in small town of Rio Grande do Sul. Most useful for documents on masonic movement both locally and nationally, including membership lists of Catholic priests and others.

3532 Topik, Steven. State autonomy in economic policy: Brazil's experience, 1822–1930 (UM/JIAS, 26:4, Nov. 1984, p. 449–476)

Argues that since about 1850, the "trajectory of state economic interference was a constantly rising one. The extent of state activity was independent of the will and ideology of state administrators" (p. 450). The stimuli for intervention was largely foreign and financial, and they overcame even the efforts of dedicated laissez-faire administrators in the 1890s.

3533 Topik, Steven. The State's contribution to the development of Brazil's internal economy, 1850–1930 (HAHR, 65:2, 1985, p. 203–228)

After examining monetary policy, taxation, and public expenditure, concludes that the often overlooked growth of the domestic economy in this period resulted to a considerable degree from government action, despite the prevailing ethic of laissez-faire. Moreover, argues that the State apparatus existed apart and to an extent independent from the planter-exporter elite, allowing bureaucrats to pursue policies that benefited less-privileged sectors.

3534 Trento, Angelo. Là dov'è la raccolta del caffè: l'emigrazione italiana in Brasile, 1875–1940. Padova, Italy: Editrice Antenore, 1984. 557 p.: appendix, bibl., tables (Univ. di Macerata. Publicazioni della Facoltà di Lettere e Filosofia; 21)

Analytical overview of Italian immigration, concentrating on the years 1880–1914. Based on printed materials of the period and recent scholarly research, does not break new ground. Best on working class immigrants in Brazil. Readable synthesis written from the immigrants' viewpoint.

Vargas e os anos cinqüenta: bibliografia. See HLAS 47:56.

3535 Wernet, Augustin. A cidade de São Paulo no início do período regencial: aspectos sociais e políticos, 1831–1836 (IRESI/RH, 2, 1981, p. 55–66)

Argues that activity of three major groups (i.e., professors and students in law academy, businessmen and public bureaucrats) combined during the 1830s to make Sao Paulo City not only the economic but also the political, social and cultural center of the province and so give it an identity separate from the rural aristocracy.

JOURNAL ABBREVIATIONS
HISTORY

AAA/AA American Anthropologist. American Anthropological Assn. Washington.

AAFH/TAM The Americas. Academy of American Franciscan History. Washington.

AATSP/H Hispania. American Assn. of Teachers of Spanish and Portuguese, Univ. of Cincinnati. Cincinnati, Ohio.

ACCEFN/R Revista de la Academia Colombiana de Ciencias Exactas, Físicas y Naturales. Bogotá.

ACH/B Boletín de la Academia Chilena de la Historia. Santiago.

ACH/BHA Boletín de Historia y Antigüedades. Academia Colombiana de Historia. Bogotá.

ACHA/CHR Catholic Historical Review. American Catholic Historical Assn., Catholic Univ. of America Press. Washington.

AES/AE American Ethnologist. American Ethnological Society. Washington.

AESC Annales: économies, sociétés, civilisations. Centre national de la recherche scientifique *avec le concours de la* VIᵉ Section de l'École pratique des hautes études. Paris.

AHA/R American Historical Review. American Historical Assn. Washington.

AJA American Jewish Archives. Cincinnati, Ohio.

AM/R Revista do Arquivo Municipal. Prefeitura do Município de São Paulo, Depto. Municipal de Cultura. São Paulo.

ANH/IE Investigaciones y Ensayos. Academia Nacional de la Historia. Buenos Aires.

ASE/E   Ethnohistory. Journal of the American Society for Ethnohistory. Buffalo, N.Y.

BCE/C   Cultura. Banco Central del Ecuador. Quito.

BISRA/BS   Belizean Studies. Belizean Institute of Social Research and Action [and] St. John's College. Belize City.

BNJM/R   Revista de la Biblioteca Nacional José Martí. La Habana.

BU/JCS   A Journal of Church and State. Baylor Univ., J.M. Dawson Studies in Church and State. Waco, Tex.

CBC/RA   Revista Andina. Centro Bartolomé de las Casas. Cusco, Perú.

CDAL   Cahiers des Amériques latines. Paris.

CH   Cuadernos Hispanoamericanos. Instituto de Cultura Hispánica. Madrid.

CIRMA/M   Mesoamérica. Centro de Investigaciones Regionales de Mesoamérica. Antigua, Guatemala.

CM/HM   Historia Mexicana. El Colegio de México. México.

CM/NRFH   Nueva Revista de Filología Hispánica. El Colegio de México [and] Univ. of Texas. México.

CM/RE   Relaciones. El Colegio de Michoacán. Zamora, México.

CPES/RPS   Revista Paraguaya de Sociología. Centro Paraguayo de Estudios Sociológicos. Asunción.

CPU/ES   Estudios Sociales. Corp. de Promoción Universitaria. Santiago.

CRI/CR   Caribbean Review. Caribbean Review, Inc. Miami, Fla.

CRIT   Criterio. Editorial Criterio. Buenos Aires.

CSSH   Comparative Studies in Society and History. Society for the Comparative Study of Society and History. The Hague.

CSUCA/ESC   Estudios Sociales Centroamericanos. Consejo Superior de Univs. Centroamericanas, Confederación Universitaria Centroamericana, Programa Centroamericano de Ciencias Sociales. San José.

DB/REE   Revista de Estudios Extremeños. Diputación de Badajoz, Institución de Servicios Culturales. Badajoz, Spain.

DGV/ZE   Zeitschrift für Ethnologie. Deutschen Gesellschaft für Völkerkunde. Braunschweig, FRG.

EANH/B   Boletín de la Academia Nacional de Historia. Quito.

EAZ   Ethnographisch-Archäologische Zeitschrift. Deutscher Verlag Wissenschaften. East Berlin.

EEHA/AEA   Anuario de Estudios Americanos. Consejo Superior de Investigaciones Científicas [and] Univ. de Sevilla, Escuela de Estudios Hispano-Americanos. Sevilla, Spain.

EEHA/HBA   Historiografía y Bibliografía Americanista. Escuela de Estudios Hispano-Americanos de Sevilla. Sevilla, Spain.

EHA/J   Journal of Economic History. New York Univ., Graduate School of Business Administration *for the* Economic History Assn. Rensselaer.

EPHE/H   L'Homme. La Sorbonne, l'École pratique des hautes études. Paris.

FENIX   Fénix. Biblioteca Nacional. Lima.

FHS/FHQ   The Florida Historical Quarterly. The Florida Historical Society. Jacksonville.

FIU/CR   *See* CRI/CR.

FNH/NH   Nuestra Historia. Fundación Nuestra Historia. Buenos Aires.

GIT/SCID   Studies in Comparative International Development. Georgia Institute of Technology. Atlanta.

HAHR   Hispanic American Historical Review. Duke Univ. Press *for the* Conference on Latin American History of the American Historical Assn. Durham, N.C.

HISLA   HISLA. Lima.

IAA   Ibero-Amerikanisches Archiv. Ibero-Amerikanisches Institut. Berlin, FRG.

IAI/I   Indiana. Beiträge zur Volker-und Sprachenkunde, Archäologie und Anthropologie des Indianischen Amerika. Ibero-Amerikanisches Institut. Berlin, FRG.

IAMEA   Inter-American Economic Affairs. Washington.

IAV/AIHM   Archivo Iberoamericano de Historia de la Medicina. Consejo Superior de Investigaciones Científicas, Instituto Arnaldo de Villanova. Madrid.

IBRI/R   Revista Brasileira de Política Internacional. Instituto Brasileiro de Relações Internacionais. Rio de Janeiro.

ICA/RCA   Revista Colombiana de Antropología. Ministerio de Educación Nacional, Instituto Colombiano de Antropología. Bogotá.

ICP/R   Revista del Instituto de Cultura Puertorriqueña. San Juan.

IFCL/E   Estudios de Ciencias y Letras. Instituto de Filosofía, Ciencias y Letras. Montevideo.

IFEA/B   Bulletin de l'Institut français d'études andines. Lima.

IFH/C   Conjonction. Institut français d'Haïti. Port-au-Prince.

IGFO/RI   Revista de Indias. Instituto Gonzalo Fernández de Oviedo [and] Consejo Superior de Investigaciones Científicas. Madrid.

IHAAER/B   Boletín del Instituto de Historia Argentina y Americana Emilio Ravignani. Univ. Nacional de Buenos Aires. Buenos Aires.

IHGB/R   Revista do Instituto Histórico e Geográfico Brasileiro. Rio de Janeiro.

III/AI   América Indígena. Instituto Indigenista Interamericano. México.

IILI/RI   Revista Iberoamericana. Instituto Internacional de Literatura Iberoamericana; *patrocinado por la* Univ. de Pittsburgh. Pittsburgh, Pa.

IJ/JJ   Jamaica Journal. Institute of Jamaica. Kingston.

IPA/A   Allpanchis. Instituto de Pastoral Andina. Cusco, Peru.

IPE/EE   Estudos Econômicos. Univ. de São Paulo, Instituto de Pesquisas Econômicas. São Paulo.

IRA/B   Boletín del Instituto Riva-Agüero. Pontificia Univ. Católica del Perú. Lima.

IRESI/RH   Relações Humanas. Instituto de Relações Sociais e Industrias. São Paulo.

IUP/D   Dados. Instituto Universitário de Pesquisas do Rio de Janeiro. Rio de Janeiro.

JDA   The Journal of Developing Areas. Western Illinois Univ. Press. Macomb.

JEHM/R   Revista de la Junta de Estudios Históricos de Mendoza. Mendoza, Argentina.

JGSWGL   Jahrbuch für Geschichte von Staat, Wirtschaft und Gesellschaft Lateinamerikas. Köln, FRG.

JHS/R   The Jamaican Historical Review. The Jamaican Historical Society. Kingston.

JIH   The Journal of Interdisciplinary History. Massachusetts Institute of Technology Press. Cambridge.

JLAS   Journal of Latin American Studies. Centers or institutes of Latin American studies at the univs. of Cambridge, Glasgow, Liverpool, London, and Oxford. Cambridge Univ. Press. Cambridge, England.

JPS   The Journal of Peasant Studies. Frank Cass & Co. London.

JW   Journal of the West. Manhattan, Kan.

LAP   Latin American Perspectives. Univ. of California. Riverside.

LARR   Latin American Research Review. Univ. of North Carolina Press *for the* Latin American Studies Assn. Chapel Hill.

LNB/L   Lotería. Lotería Nacional de Beneficencia. Panamá.

MHD/B   Boletín del Museo del Hombre Dominicano. Santo Domingo.

MSU/CR   The Centennial Review of Arts and Sciences. Michigan State Univ., College of Arts and Sciences. East Lansing.

NCFR/JFH   Journal of Family History. National Council on Family Relations. Minneapolis, Minn.

NS   NS NorthSouth NordSud NorteSur NorteSul. Canadian Assn. of Latin American Studies, Univ. of Ottawa. Ottawa.

NWIG   Nieuwe West-Indische Gids. Martinus Nijhoff. The Hague.

PAIGH/H   Revista de Historia de América. Instituto Panamericano de Geografía e Historia, Comisión de Historia. México.

PAN/EL Estudios Latinoamericanos. Polska Akademia Nauk (Academia de Ciencias de Polonia), Instytut Historii (Instituto de Historia). Warszawa.

PAN/ES *See* PAN/EL.

PAT/TH The Historian. Phi Alpha Theta, National Honor Society in History. Univ. of Pennsylvania. University Park.

PEMN/R Revista del Museo Nacional. Casa de la Cultura del Perú, Museo Nacional de la Cultura Peruana. Lima.

PF/AIA Archivo Ibero-Americano. Los Padres Franciscanos. Madrid.

PMNH/HC Historia y Cultura. Museo Nacional de Historia. Lima.

PP Past and Present. London.

PQ The Political Quarterly. London.

PUC/V Veritas. Pontifícia Univ. Católica do Rio Grande do Sul. Pôrto Alegre.

PUCP/H Histórica. Pontificia Univ. Católica del Perú, Depto. de Humanidades. Lima.

PUF/RH Revue historique. Presses universitaires de France. Paris.

PUJ/UH Universitas Humanistica. Pontificia Univ. Javeriana, Facultad de Filosofía y Letras. Bogotá.

RO Revista de Occidente. Madrid.

RU/SCID *See* GIT/SCID.

RUC Revista de la Universidad Complutense. Madrid.

SA/J Journal de la Société des américanistes. Paris.

SAA/AA American Antiquity. Society for American Archaeology. Menasha, Wis.

SAGE/JIAS *See* UM/JIAS.

SBH/HC Historia y Cultura. Sociedad Boliviana de Historia. Editorial Don Bosco. La Paz.

SCHG/R Revista Chilena de Historia y Geografía. Sociedad Chilena de Historia y Geografía. Santiago.

SHG/B Bulletin de la Société d'histoire de la Guadeloupe. Archives départamentales *avec le concours du* Conseil général de la Guadeloupe. Basse-Terre.

SHHG/R Revue de la Société haïtienne d'histoire et de géographie. Port-au-Prince.

SHM/RHM Revista de Historia Militar. Servicio Histórico Militar. Madrid.

SP Socialismo y Participación. Ediciones Socialismo y Participación. Lima.

SRA/A Anales de la Sociedad Rural Argentina. Buenos Aires.

SSG/RGI Rivista Geografica Italiana. Società di Studi Geografici e Coloniali. Firenze, Italy.

TM Les Temps modernes. Paris.

TSHA/SHQ Southwestern Historical Quarterly. Texas State Historical Assn. Austin.

TWF/TWQ Third World Quarterly. Third World Foundation, New Zealand House. London.

UB/BA Boletín Americanista. Univ. de Barcelona, Facultad de Geografía e Historia, Depto. de Historia de América. Barcelona, Spain.

UB/HC *See* SBH/HC.

UBAIA/R Runa. Univ. de Buenos Aires, Facultad de Filosofía y Letras, Instituto de Antropología. Buenos Aires.

UBN/R Revista de la Biblioteca Nacional. Ministerio de Educación y Cultura. Montevideo.

UC/AT Atenea. Univ. de Concepción. Concepción, Chile.

UC/CA Current Anthropology. Univ. of Chicago. Chicago, Ill.

UC/CH Cuadernos de Historia. Univ. de Chile, Facultad de Humanidades y Educación, Depto. de Ciencias Históricas. Santiago.

UC/S Signs. Univ. of Chicago Press. Chicago, Ill.

UCA/E Encuentro. Univ. Centroamericana, Instituto Histórico. Managua.

UCCIH/H Historia. Univ. Católica de Chile, Instituto de Historia. Santiago.

UCLA/JLAL Journal of Latin American Lore. Univ. of California, Latin American Center. Los Angeles.

UCLV/I Islas. Univ. Central de las Villas. Santa Clara, Cuba.

UCNSA/EP Estudios Paraguayos. Univ. Católica Nuestra Señora de la Asunción. Asunción.

UCNSA/SA Suplemento Antropológico. Univ. Católica de Nuestra Señora de la Asunción, Centro de Estudios Antropológicos. Asunción.

UCSB/NS New Scholar. Univ. of California, Committee on Hispanic Civilization [and] Center for Chicano Studies. Santa Barbara.

UEN/LS Lateinamerika Studien. Univ. Erlangen-Nürnberg, Sektion Lateinamerika. Nürnberg, FRG.

UM/JIAS Journal of Inter-American Studies and World Affairs. Institute of Interamerican Studies, Univ. of Miami. Coral Gables, Fla.

UN/C Chungará. Univ. del Norte, Depto. de Antropología. Arica, Chile.

UNAM/ECN Estudios de Cultura Náhuatl. Univ. Nacional Autónoma de México, Instituto de Historia, Seminario de Cultura Náhuatl. México.

UNAM/L Latinoamérica. Univ. Nacional Autónoma de México, Facultad de Filosofía y Letras, Centro de Estudios Latinoamericanos. México.

UNC/ACHSC Anuario Colombiano de Historia Social y de la Cultura. Univ. Nacional de Colombia, Facultad de Ciencias Humanas, Depto. de Historia. Bogotá.

UNC/REE Revista de Economía y Estadística. Univ. Nacional de Córdoba, Facultad de Ciencias Económicas. Córdoba, Argentina.

UNC/RHAA Revista de Historia Americana y Argentina. Univ. Nacional de Cuyo, Facultad de Filosofía y Letras, Instituto de Historia. Mendoza, Argentina.

UNCR/R Revista de Historia. Univ. Nacional de Costa Rica, Escuela de Historia. Heredia.

UNLP/R Revista de la Universidad Nacional de La Plata. La Plata, Argentina.

UNM/JAR Journal of Anthropological Research. Univ. of New Mexico, Dept. of Anthropology. Albuquerque.

UNM/NMHR New Mexico Historical Review. Univ. of New Mexico [and] Historical Society of New Mexico. Albuquerque.

UP/E Ethnology. Univ. of Pittsburgh. Pittsburgh, Pa.

UPR/RCS Revista de Ciencias Sociales. Univ. de Puerto Rico, Colegio de Ciencias Sociales. Río Piedras.

URSS/AL América Latina. Academia de Ciencias de la URSS (Unión de Repúblicas Soviéticas Socialistas). Moscú.

USP/RH Revista de História. Univ. de São Paulo, Faculdade de Filosofia, Letras e Ciências Humanas, Depto. de História. São Paulo.

USP/RIEB Revista do Instituto de Estudos Brasileiros. Univ. de São Paulo, Instituto de Estudos Brasileiros. São Paulo.

UTIEH/C Caravelle. Univ. de Toulouse, Institut d'Études hispaniques, hispano-américaines et luso-brésiliennes. Toulouse, France.

UW/LBR Luso-Brazilian Review. Univ. of Wisconsin Press. Madison.

UWI/JCH The Journal of Caribbean History. Univ. of the West Indies, Dept. of History [and] Caribbean Univs. Press. St. Lawrence, Barbados.

UWI/SES Social and Economic Studies. Univ. of the West Indies, Institute of Social and Economic Research. Mona, Jamaica.

UY/R Revista de la Universidad de Yucatán. Mérida, Mexico.

VANH/B Boletín de la Academia Nacional de la Historia. Caracas.

LANGUAGE

D. LINCOLN CANFIELD, *Professor Emeritus of Spanish, Southern Illinois University*

SINCE *HLAS 46*, several special studies of language and linguistic phenonena have appeared, an excellent depiction of Spanish gestures, with good photographs and indicators of motion, and strong evidence of their universality in the Spanish-speaking world (item **4507**); a very good analysis of mother-tongue claiming among our Hispanic population (item **4510**); a good computer vocabulary in Spanish (item **4583**) and an electronics vocabulary in Portuguese which includes computer and telecommunications terminology (item **4619**); a "model" book on the origins of a regional variety of Spanish, that of Puerto Rico in this case, diachronically oriented (item **4520**); studies that consider register (superior-inferior status, e.g., professor-student) as a social variable that is linguistically marked (item **4636**); and one of the best descriptions of the occurrence of *vos* in Spanish America, both in terms of geographical distribution and variation in verb forms (item **4596**). As far as field work is concerned, it would seem that the prize should go to John M. Lipski (item **4535**), who reports on on-the-spot analyses in all five republics of Central America, the north coast of Panama, and Equatorial Guinea.

Two groups of writers have contributed to the knowledge of the Spanish of the Dominican Republic (item **4518**), and for the first time in many years Honduras has been studied linguistically (item **4534**), and at least two articles have to do with language phenomena and language policy in bilingual Paraguay (item **4503**). Five more contributions to the *Proyecto de estudio coordinado de la norma lingüística culta de las principales ciudades de Iberamérica y de la Península Ibérica*, under the direction of Juan M. Lope Blanch, have been written (items **4519, 4539, 4547, 4550,** and **4558**), and the Seventh Colloquium on Hispanic Linguistics brought forth some 20 papers on sociolinguistic situations within populations of Spanish speakers and among people who speak Brazilian Portuguese.

Special Spanish glossaries and vocabularies (items **4562, 4568, 4577,** and **4579**) deal with the terminology of social work, foreign trade, agriculture and land reform, and petroleum production. Portuguese vocabularies (items **4610, 4613, 4614, 4621,** and **4622**) give us the lexicon of the stock market, foreign trade and commerce, journalism, the birds of Brazil, and sanitation and health.

As usual, there are several "regional" vocabularies (items **4517, 4520, 4525, 4528, 4544, 4551, 4604,** and **4606**) that tend to be more general than regional, probably because of the traditionally fragmented Hispanic cultural communication. Non-Hispanic Hispanists seem to notice this more than the writers of local word and phrase books.

The only two *polémicas* of note at this writing are the argument concerning Caribbean and Colombian "Spanish Creoles," notably Papiamentu and Palenquero. William Megenney (item **4650**) supports the monogenetic theory of a colonial Portuguese African origin during slave trade days: a *lingua franca* developed in Africa itself by those who did more slave trading than any. Megenney believes that this later became Hispanicized in a Spanish-speaking environment. Others think that Papiamentu and Palenquero developed from a Caribbean Spanish prototype or that they are dialectal manifestations of colonial Spanish. The second *polémica* of a sort is suggested by the articles of Poplack, Flórez, and Terrell (items **4548, 4529,** and **4511**) on cause and effect in the deletion of /s/ syllable-final in Puerto Rican Spanish. Terrell, the Hispanist, leans toward diachronic explanations.

SPANISH
GENERAL AND BIBLIOGRAPHY

4501 Alvar, Manuel. Proyecto de un atlas lingüístico de Hispanoamérica (CH, 409, julio 1984, p. 53–68)

Outlines proposal for gigantic undertaking, insisting first on uniformity of methods and materials, including questionnaire that would serve in all sections of the vast area. Alvar even indicates number of investigators per country: 75 for Argentina, five for Costa Rica, for instance, and recommends the project be based in Puerto Rico, probably for financial reasons! His plans might be taken more seriously had he brought his references up to date, especially the many years of work conducted by the Instituto Caro y Cuervo of Colombia, by Lope Blanch of Mexico, and by North Americans who have done considerable research in the general area. Indications are this article was written from old notes!

4502 Chávez Alfaro, Lizandro. Identidad y resistenca del "criollo" en Nicaragua (BNBD, 51, enero/feb. 1983, p. 17–27, ill.)

Reminder that three languages are spoken in Nicaragua: Spanish, Mískito, and English. Also plea for unity of English-speaking blacks of the Atlantic coast and the Hispanic interior and Pacific coast. Supporting the Sandinista revolution, the writer says that its benefits, including *alfabetización,* will be taken to those who speak only English in Bluefields and northward.

4503 Corvalán, Graziella. La política lingüística y su implementación en el Paraguay (UCNSA/SA, 18:1, junio 1983, p. 107–135)

Referring to Joan Rubin's *National bilingualism in Paraguay* (1968, see *HLAS 32:3146*), author proposes determining the role of different non-government social agencies, and to find relation between existing language policy and actual implementation in Paraguay's educational system. Examines differences among *official language, national language,* and *standard language* as understood by the public, and such problems as Guaraní orthography. There will always be complications because one language (Guaraní) is indigenous and the "home speech," not linked with outside world, and primary school years may not be enough to equip the child well in the use of other language—*castellano.*

4504 Guitarte, Guillermo L. Siete estudios sobre el español de América. México: Instituto de Investigaciones Filológicas, UNAM, 1983. 184 p.: bibl., ill. (Publicaciones del Centro de Lingüística Hispánica; 13)

Collection of varied articles which do not focus on the development of any theory with respect to the Spanish of America. Most references are to Cuervo, Henríquez Ureña, and Amado Alonso. Devotes little attention to more recent investigations, especially on *seseo* and regional differences, matters that have been written about by Colombians and North Americans, and referred to by Rafael Lapesa in his *Historia de la lengua española* (9th, ed. rev., Madrid: Gredos, 1981, 690 p.)

4505 Lavandera, Beatriz R. Variación y significado. Buenos Aires: Hachette, 1984. 267 p. (Col. Hachette universidad)

Valuable work on language variation by student of William Labov, one of many guided in recent times by his sociolinguistic concerns and approaches. Lavandera ably demonstrates that variation is not "free" but follows certain systematic patterns in terms of extra-linguistic factors and situations. Lavandera proposes to develop a "descriptive sociolinguistic semantics" that takes the text as a source beyond mere expression itself.

4506 Magariños de Morentín, Juan Angel. Del caos al lenguaje. Buenos Aires: Ediciones Tres Tiempos, 1983. 222 p.: ill. (Col. Ciencias del hombre; 7)

Calling man an *animal simbólico,* author says that from language comes the capacity to think, to reflect, even to philosophize. Without language there is chaos and man would be an insignificant organism. With language man roots himself in a universe of meaning, and with it he continues to generate ideas, beliefs, ideologies, and science. Language becomes, he says, the uterus of our existence.

4507 Meo Zilio, Giovanni and Silvia Mejía. Diccionario de gestos: España e Hispanoamérica. Bogotá: Instituto Caro y Cuervo, 1980–1983. 2 v.: ill., indexes.

Authors state that their dictionary is focused linguistically rather than psychologically or sociologically. It represents the gesture as means of communication, after several years of investigation. To this reviewer it is by far the most systematic and organized of all works that have appeared on Spanish gestures, and has, again by far, the most extensive treatment of the subject (2000 gestures). Gestures are arranged by topics (e.g., *asombro, atrás, callarse*) and have excellent facial and hand photographs with arrows to indicate motion. Entries show variations and countries where the gesture has been observed. Index with key words facilitates use of the dictionary. Includes list of *informantes* with city of origin. Beyond depicting gestures, book is one of the best indications of the common denominator of Hispanic culture.

4508 Morales Pettorino, Félix and Marina González Becker. Las encuestas lingüísticas. Valparaíso, Chile: Ediciones Universitarias de Valparaíso: Univ. Católica de Valparaíso, 1984. 368 p.

These *encuenstas* (polls, inquiries, surveys) were cleverly designed to be used in teaching the finer points of grammar and composition to native speakers of Spanish in Chile.

4509 Ravahi, Rafael. Hacia la formación de un "continente lingüístico" español (AHL/B, 24:26, junio 1982, p. 15–31)

Pointing out that Spanish is now one of the most important languages of the world, author says that some 231,000,000 speak it (actually more than 300,000,000). Proposes formation of a *continente lingüístico*: a tight and constant relationship among Spanish speakers in literary, scientific, technological, journalistic, and telecommunications production. Such a union would enrich Hispanic intellectual activity.

Creation of this *continente* would require intense interchange of students, which today hardly exists because of fear of accepting contributions of other nationalities or because of belonging to a "grupo de amigos" whose main intentions are political. Recommends formation of a Spanish Academy of the US. There has been one since 1974!

4510 Solé, Yolanda Russinovich. Spanish/English mother-tongue claiming: the 1980 census data, a sample, and their sociodemographic correlates (AATSP/H, 68:2, May 1985, p. 283–297)

Very important article, especially in its societal correlates. Of 14,608,000 people of Hispanic origin in the US (excluding ca. 4,000,000 illegals), 60 percent are of Mexican origin, 14 percent Puerto Rican, five percent Cuban, and 20 percent from other Spanish-speaking countries. Of all these, 86 percent claim to speak Spanish at home. Spanish is today the most widely used foreign language in the US. Statistics show that about 50 percent speak English well, and about eight percent not at all. Colorado, New Mexico, and Arizona show the best English-language proficiency among Spanish speakers. Hispanics, except for Cubans and peoples of Central and South Americas, have a lower than average educational profile; occupational profile is also low, Cubans at the top, Mexican-Americans at the bottom. One third of all the Hispanics is concentrated in Los Angeles, New York, and Miami.

4511 Spanish and Portuguese in social context. Edited by John J. Bergen and Garland D. Bills. Washington: Georgetown Univ. Press, 1983. 118 p.

Papers from the Seventh Colloquium of Hispanic Linguistics (Albuquerque, N.M., July 1980) devoted to the sociolinguistic study of Spanish and Portuguese. Elerick argues that Spanish itself was the product of a Latin influenced by Oscan and Umbrian. A.G. Lozano describes early lack of interest in the development of Spanish in the US, a development that is now a popular topic of study. A.M. Padilla examines problems in acquisition of Spanish and English in bilingual children, and M.B. Boyd explores variation of subjunctive use among Chicanos. Three pedagogical problems are addressed: 1) placement tests to determine initial level of study in a university (T. Pagán Hunnum and E.

Gonzales-Berry); 2) S. Burunat writes about attitudes of bilinguals toward their own Spanish; and 3) M. G. Goldin illustrates implications of sociolinguistics in teaching of Spanish to English-speaking people. B. Varela discusses mutual influences of English and Cuban Spanish on each other in Miami. T.D. Terrell studies effects of epenthesis in Caribbean Spanish. L. Wigdorsky's takes us to social and age stratifications in the Spanish of Santiago, Chile. There are three articles on the use of Portuguese in its social setting: J. Guitart's phonological study of English loanwords among Portuguese bilinguals in Buffalo, N.Y.; D. Koike's examination of variable use of inflected infinitives as markers of social dialects in Rio de Janeiro. I. Wherrit explains that variation in directives correlates with linguistic variables in Brazilian Portuguese.

4512 Spanish in the Western Hemisphere in contact with English, Portuguese, and the Amerindian languages. Edited by Eugenio Chang-Rodríguez and James Macris. New York: International Linguistic Assn., 1982. 198 p. (*Word*; 33:1/2)

Papers presented at two conferences: T.S. Beardsley, Jr., gives brief historical background on Spanish in the US and reviews dominant dialectal variations and their interaction with English; D.N. Cárdenas examines possible trend of historical displacement of synthetic language by new forces supported and hastened by language-in-contact factors; A.C. Zentella writes on the Puerto Rican experience, Spanglish, and code-switching; J.M. Guitart reports research among Miami Cubans, Venezuelan studies in an American university, and Mexican Americans of San Antonio, Tx.; R.C. Troike examines dialectal differences complicated by sociolinguistic factors and observes that in some sections of the country Spanish is becoming a language of public life; R. Nash studies employment advertisements in San Juan's major Spanish language newspapers and in sex discrimination; E. Alvarado de Ricord studies resistance that Panama's cultural institutions offer to widespread use of Anglicisms; D. Lincoln Canfield examines changes since the early 16th century resulting from contact of Spanish with Zapotec, Náhuatl and Quechua; F.G. Hensey writes on *castellanización* in Oaxaca, an area of five indigenous languages; P.V. Cassano reviews

misleading concepts of language "lending" and "borrowing" with regard to Quechua and Maya; M.J. Hardman-de-Bautista writes on mutual influence of Spanish and Andean languages, where the offcial language is *castellano*; J.C. Zamora studies distribution of Indianisms in Spanish and reasons for these borrowings; E. Chang-Rodríguez reviews different policies adopted by Peru until the legal designation of Quechua as one of the two languages in 1975, and discusses limitations of this policy.

4513 Travesset, Josep and Anna Roselló. No són 300 milons: estudi sobre les ètnies sotmeses a l'idioma espanyol. Barcelona, Spain: Pòrtic, 1983. 151 p.: facsim., maps (Pòrtic 71; 29)

Political diatribe dedicated to linguistic minorities "subjected" to Spanish language imperialism, denies claim that Spanish is spoken by more than 300,000,000. Authors use racial classifications ("mestizos, negros, indios," etc.) to show subjection by Spanish. Maps indicate distribution of languages other than Spanish in Latin America. Spanish-speaking world is still over 300,000,000, including millions racially not Hispanic but acculturated, a process authors avoid discussing.

4514 Wicki, Josef. The Castilian language in sixteenth century Portuguese India (*in* International Congress of Human Sciences in Asia and North Africa, 30th, Mexico, 1976. Asia and colonial Latin America. Edited by Ernesto de la Torre. México: El Colegio de México, 1981, p. 69–76)

Maintains that the Spanish language was well known in 16th-century India and that it served as the main language in Europe to make these countries known in wider circles. Based on numerous accounts of the period, especially from missionaries.

4515 Wood, Richard E. La sociolingüística actual en América Latina (CPES/RPS, 20:57, mayo/agosto 1983, p. 111–122, bibl.)

Brief survey of sociolinguistics in Latin America: Paraguay's national educational policy studied and discussed by G. Corvalán (see item **4503**); Portuguese incursions in Uruguay described by A. Elizaincín; A. Escobar's four monographs on Peruvian sociolinguistics; Köch's work on Rio Grande do Sul, Brazil; Perissinotto's description of segmental phonemes of Mexico City

Spanish; and V. Zúñiga de Tristán's efforts to stamp out Anglicisms in Costa Rica. Serious omissions are Argentines M.B. Fontanella de Weinberg and Donni de Mirande, and extensive data compiled by Colombia's Instituto Caro y Cuervo, now published in their ALEC (i.e., *Atlas lingüístico y etnográfico de Colombia*).

SPANISH DIALECTOLOGY

4516 Aguilar, Antonio. Refranero sanjuanino. San Juan, Argentina: Editorial Sanjuanina, 1982. 133 p.

Quite typically, this phrase book is more than anything a document of the Spanish language, and then secondarily, a regional vocabulary. On one single page, most of the expressions are common to virtually all Spanish-speaking people: *Estar calado hasta los huesos; estar como sardinas en lata; estar como pez en el agua; estar como unas castañuelas.* Among common phrases, one finds a few that depict that region (interior Argentina): *estar cargando; Tomando para la farra; fastidiando.* Such works say much about the lack of communication among Hispanic countries.

4517 Alario di Filippo, Mario. Lexicón de colombianismos. t. 1, A-LL. 2a ed. Bogotá: Banco de la República, Biblioteca Luis-Angel Arango, 1983. 439 p.: bibl. (Col. Banco de la República)

Carefully arranged vocabulary (A-LL) of terms heard in Colombia, with indications of what sections of the country they might be heard in. Author points out rightly that many words called *colombianismos* are actually common Spanish words of long standing and have the original Peninsular definition. Other terms from Spain have taken on a *criollo* definition in the New World. Especially valuable for its regional specificity.

4518 Alba, Orlando et al. El Español al día. Santiago, Dominican Republic: Univ. Católica Madre y Maestra, Depto. de Publicaciones, 1984. 253 p. (Col. Textos; 106)

Studies of Dominican Spanish by 14 writers (e.g., phonology in modern linguistic terminology, commercial correspondence forms and terminology, proverbs and common sayings, teaching reading to adults and composition to children). Most writers are *licenciados* in education.

4519 Alcalá Alba, Antonio. Oraciones condicionales introducidas por *cuando* en el español culto de la Ciudad de México (UNAM/AL, 21, 1983, p. 201–210)

Spin-off of *Proyecto de estudio coordinado . . .* directed by J.M. Lope Blanch of Mexico (see *HLAS 42:4537*). Often two values are present in subordinate clauses introduced by *cuando*: conditional and temporal with informants alternating between *si* and *cuando.* "Llovía cuando nos conocimos" is purely temporal, but "Cuando hayas hecho lo que te mandé, entonces hablamos," is both conditional and temporal or either. Material collected in Mexico City includes 248 cases of conditional-temporal structures. Also traces structure back to early Romance manifestations.

4520 Alvarez Nazario, Manuel. Orígenes y desarrollo del español en Puerto Rico: siglos XVI y XVII. Río Piedras: Editorial de la Univ. de Puerto Rico, 1982. 470 p.: bibl., ill., indexes.

Excellent book on a region's language and culture that may be losing certain elements of its original system of communication because of constant contacts with a very influential society, dominant in world affairs. Well researched and documented work with updated information on all aspects of Spanish of the period in Puerto Rico and in America. Topics: Hispanization of Borinquén; regional origins of Spanish settlers (information from studies of P. Boyd-Bowman); Spanish pronunciation in 16th and 17th centuries; syntax of period; lexicon of period, including American Indian and African contributions; works consulted. Information on levels of society and importation of slaves is interesting to others than linguists. One might take issue with Alvarez Nazario on chronology of sibilant development but not much else.

4521 Amaro Gamboa, Jesús. Hibridismos en el habla del yucateco: pts. 1–3 (UY/R, 147, julio/sept. 1983, p. 123–189; 148, oct./dic. 1983, p. 156–187; 149, enero/marzo 1984, p. 128–150)

Revealing vocabulary of common practice in Yucatan: combinations of Spanish and Maya in everyday speech. Focuses on "Uayeísmo en la cultura de Yucatán" (see item **4522**). Succeeds in building here convincing glossary of hybridization, extending into phonology (e.g., *hacer chul* is to scoop up last bit of gravy with tortilla; *x-tancia* shows phonological *mayización* of *estancia*). Includes index of words defined and lengthy explanations of usage.

4522 Amaro Gamboa, Jesús. Vocabulario del uayeísmo en la cultura de Yucatán (UY/R, 23 : 134, marzo/abril 1981, p. 103–153)

Having established justification for designations *uayé* and *uayeísmo* to refer to "this place" (i.e., Yucatán and what is typical of Yucatán), article is section *cachivache—cat* of what will be an extensive vocabulary. As with many regional vocabularies, entries are not only regional but Hispanic or at least characteristic of several areas. In this particular instance, however, combination of Spanish and Indian definitions and references is more marked than usual because Maya is still spoken by so many inhabitants.

4523 Barreto Peña, Samuel. Modismos y barbarismos trujillanos. Caracas: Santino Distribuidora Escolar, 1980? 160 p.: port.

Unrepresentative title. Although called *modismos y barbarismos*, book turns out to be a vocabulary of popular Venezuelan terms, which writer considers typical of his country. This is common among composers of regional Latin American glossaries, because their contacts are more often with Europe and the US than with other Spanish-speaking areas. Barreto's terms by the hundreds are used with same meanings in other parts of Latin America and Spain (e.g., *porra, pocillo, pucha*).

4524 Cahuazac, Philippe. La division dialectale de l'espagnol d'Amérique: une solution ethnolinguistique (*in* Unité et diversité en l'Amérique latine. Bordeaux, France: Univ. de Bordeaux III, 1982, t. 2, p. 289–301, bibl.)

Suggests that dialect zones for Spanish America could be drawn on the basis of regional terminology for *campesino* or "country type" of the vast area (e.g., a *charro* zone, *gaucho* zone, *guajiro*, *huaso*, and *llanero*). Unfortunately, author's references are at least 20 years out of date, and his terminology inaccurate (e.g., *charro* for Mexico suggests elite organization and in certain contexts today is insulting). His variant for this is *campesinaje*, which is a group, not an indi-

vidual. Map places US, Mexico, and all of Central America in one zone. Actually, parts of Central America dialectically resemble western Argentina more than Mexico!

4525 Caravedo, Rocío. Estudios sobre el español de Lima. Lima: Pontificia Univ. Católica del Perú, Fondo Editorial, 1983. 1 v.: bibl., ill. (Publicaciones del Instituto Riva-Agüero; 113)

Introduces study by reviewing articles of two North Americans: D.L. Canfield and Tracy Terrell, beginning in 1975, on aspiration and elision of /s/ in Caribbean Spanish, with special consideration of constraints on these tendencies. Caravedo considers dependable variables in manifestations of /s/ in different phonological contexts, and in sections of society and in different age groups. Book treats articulation of /s/ and sociolinguistic implications of its aspiration and deletion about as well as any.

4526 Cárdenas A., Renato and **Carlos Alberto Trujillo A.** Apuntes para un diccionario de Chiloé. Castro, Chile: Ediciones Aumen, 1978. 95 p.: bibl.

Language of island off coast of Chile is in its lexicon a mixture of Spanish and Mapuche (Araucano), with articulation favoring Spanish pattern. Authors say that their informants were their own parents, relatives and friends as well as bus riders and strangers in Puerto Castro and other areas. Interesting examples of influence of the radio, now common on the island, leading to certain changes perhaps but also revealing tendencies of hypercorrection: *milcados* for *milcaos* (a local type of bread). Here again, much of the vocabulary is also found as far away as Mexico: *corrido*, for example, has its same "Mexican" meaning.

4527 Carpi, Omar Georgi and **Gema Mestre Varela.** Algunas sustituciones y omisiones más frecuentes en las relaciones de subordinación del habla culta coloquial espirituana (UCLV/I, 74, enero/abril 1983, p. 201–234, tables)

Three-generational study undertaken in Sancti Spiritus, Cuba, among eight women and 11 men of the *culta* category. Purpose was to note irregularities in use of relative pronouns and accompanying prepositions in the community's colloquial speech. Among other cases, substitution of *que* for *donde*; *que* for *cuando*; *que* for *como*; *que* for a *quien;* etc. Writers found that women are more apt to make substitutions than men; young people tend to omit the preposition that is part of the relative.

4528 Diccionario fundamental del español de México. Comisión Nacional para la Defensa del Idioma Español. Dirección de Luis Fernando Lara. México: El Colegio de México: Fondo de Cultura Económica, 1982. 85, 480 p.

Introduced by section on orthography and proper terminology for tenses in Spanish, followed by list of verb paradigms and vocabulary itself. Latter seems almost encyclopedic, with multiple definitions and derived idioms and examples of usage. Even the preposition *a* has two examples: *voy a Oaxaca, voy al cine.* Two notable omissions are indigenous terms (one would expect much Náhuatl), and telecommunications vocabulary.

4529 Flórez, Luis; John Myhill; and Fernando Tarallo. Competing plural markers in Puerto Rican Spanish (LING, 21:6, 1983, p. 897–907, bibl., tables)

Investigates possible competing plural markers in Puerto Rican Spanish. Markers of plurality in NP's were concentrated in determiners; masculine plural determiners and nouns were found to be more likely than their feminine counterparts to lack plural /s/ inflection. Writers propose that /o/ in masculine determiners *los, estos, esos, unos,* and *aquellos* is beginning to take over as marker of plurality; this is why other plural markers are more likely to be deleted when there is a masculine determiner. Study was made from recordings of North Philadelphia Puerto Ricans (1978–79) and is a valuable case of interplay between phonological and grammatical processes.

4530 Fontanella de Weinberg, María Beatriz. Confusión de líquidas en el español rioplatense: siglos XVI a XVIII (UCP/RP, 37:4, May 1984, p. 432–445, bibl.)

Pointing to dialectologists interest in confusion or omission of liquids in syllable final position, Fontanella examines 16th-, 17th-, and 18th -century documents of Río de La Plata. Finds that there was considerable confusion among writers in matter of /l/ and /r/. Today this does not exist in that area. They may not indicate an articulatory phenomenon in most cases but rather many

cases of metathesis of the type: *catredal,* or omission where there is another liquid: *Getrudis.*

4531 Granda, Germán de. Origen y formación del leísmo en el español del Paraguay: ensayo de un método (CSIC/RFE, 57:3/4, 1982, p. 259–283)

Using concept of multiple causation, first defined and established by Y. Malkiel, Granda examines genetic processes that may have combined to bring about such common utterances as *le vi, le conocí* in Paraguay, while most of Spanish America says *lo vi* and *lo conocí.* Also uses where expected as indirect singular and as direct feminine as well as masculine and as direct object plural. In Paraguay *le* functions as only form of direct object, beyond its usual function as indirect object pronoun. Investigator attributes this to three causes: state of Spanish brought over from Spain to rather isolated region, *desmorfologización* of *les,* which happened elsewhere in Latin America, and influence of Guaraní structure.

4532 Hernando Cuadrado, Luis Alberto. Camilo José Cela y lenguaje popular venezolano. Prólogo de J. Fernández-Sevilla. Madrid: Castalia, 1983. 331 p.: bibl.

Study of interest to dialectologists and students of Spanish literature. Good examination of *venezolanismos* (hundreds) used by Spanish novelist in his work, *Catira.* Cuadrado and Alberto conclude that Cela, on his visit to Caracas, went to Instituto Andrés Bello of Univ. Central and carefully composed an extensive vocabulary of Venezuelan equivalents of terms wanted for his novel. They believe that he simply substituted these for Peninsular terms that he might have employed. One reason they think this is that of the 1050 words studied, 527 occur only once.

4533 Lipski, John M. Observations on the Spanish of Malabo, Equatorial Guinea: implications for Latin American Spanish (Hispanic Linguistics [Univ. of Pittsburgh, Pittsburgh, Pa.] 1:1, Spring 1984, p. 69–96, bibl.)

Reports on Spanish of Equatorial Guinea, only Spanish-speaking area in sub-Saharan Africa. Guinean Spanish is important to theories on the development of Latin American Spanish because it represents a stable bilingualism between Spanish and western African languages and permits separation of key sociolinguistic variables. Data show that Guinean Spanish is not creolized and that in terms of key consonantal variables most often associated with African influence on Latin American Spanish (/l/, /r/, /s/, /n/) Guinean Spanish does not represent major reduction of these consonants. Since Guinean Spanish was more strongly influenced by northern or central Castilian or by Catalan, it is suggested that data may be used to refine hypotheses on Andalusian and African phonetic influences on Latin American Spanish. Includes tables of percentages of occurrence of certain features and sample transcriptions, which aside from /r/ for /rr/ and final /t/ for /d/, read much like "normal" Spanish.

4534 Lipski, John M. Reducción de /s/ en el español de Honduras (CM/NRFH, 32:2, 1983, p. 272–288, map, table)

Excellent geolinguistic study based on realization of one phoneme in the Spanish dialect of Honduras, with data that also show sociolinguistic importance of educational experience in the allophonic manifestations of certain phonemes. Pointing out that there has been a dearth of information on Honduran speech and very little on other countries of Central America, Lipski describes results of 80 interviews conducted among subjects aged 15–70. Historical significance of this type of study lies in fact that although there is only one phoneme involved, the degree of accessibility to Andalusian changes in the colonial period is depicted, in this case a degree between Guatemala and Nicaragua or between Mexico and the Caribbean.

4535 Lipski, John M. /S/ in Central American Spanish (AATSP/H, 68:1, March 1985, p. 143–149)

Of all areas of Latin American Spanish, the Central American isthmus is the least studied in terms of dialectological investigation. Writer used 10 informants from each capital city. Realizations of /s/ were tabulated in terms of sC, s#C, s##, s#V́, s#V. Guatemala and Costa Rica are quite similar in retaining /s/, Honduras much less, El Salvador even less, and Nicaragua the least. Lipski has amassed a great deal of data on Central American sibilants (see items **4533** and **4534**).

4536 Lope Blanch, Juan M. Sobre la influencia del maya en el español de Yucatán (CM/NRFH, 31:1, 1982, p. 83–90, maps)

Based on data collected over 10 year-period by El Colegio de Mexico investigators. Part of project to designate Mexican dialect zones. Significant aspect of this particular phase is that in Yucatán the Indian language enjoys much more prestige than does Zapotec in Oaxaca or Náhuatl in Puebla. There is coexistence as well as hybridization (see item **4521**). Problem of *polimorfismo*, of which Lope Blanch often writes, is apparently intensified in an actually bilingual region, especially in articulation of final /r/.

4537 López Martín, Alfonso. Problemas idiomáticos del habla costarricense. Ciudad Universitaria Rodrigo Facio, San José: Univ. de Costa Rica, Vicerrectoría de Acción Social, 1982. 82 p.: bibl., index.

"Problems" discussed in this little book are not only those of Costa Rica: "¿Qué es un billón;" "Hispanos, no latinos;" "Uso incorrecto de hasta."

4538 López Morales, Humberto. Desdoblamiento fonológico de las vocales en el andaluz oriental: reexamen de la cuestión (Revista Española de Lingüística [Sociedad Española de Lingüística, Madrid] 14:1, enero/junio 1984, p. 85–97)

Aspiration and dropping of /s/ at end of syllable in Andalusia, the Caribbean, parts of Central and South America has caused these speakers of Spanish to form other markers in order to distinguish singular from plural and second person from third in verb forms. Present study tries to determine if nature of the vowel is the only mark of plurality or if it is only one sign. Research was done in five towns of Granada among 22 informants, corpus had 220 minutes of recording. Results show that in 97 percent of cases, vowel opening is a redundant mark of plurality or of the subject *tú* in the verb. Most other markers are either of phonological nature (aspiration, for instance) or semantic (numerals).

4539 Madero Knodrat, Maribel. La gradación del adjetivo en el habla culta de la Ciudad de México (UNAM/AL, 21, 1983, p. 71–118, tables)

Data obtained through 24 hours of recordings of 60 informants of Mexico City, representing three generations, and four types of interviews: single informant; a dialogue between two; formal talks; and secret recordings. *Gradación* is defined as the intensification or quantification of the quality or state indicated by the adjective. Adverb that Spanish calls *ponderativo* seems to be popular with these informants: *bastante, completamente, sumamente, totalmente, poco,* and in this level of society there is a marked tendency to form superlatives in *-ísimo,* and Mexicans of the capital tend to prefer *mejor, peor, mayor* to *más bueno, más malo, más grande.* Part of research project noted in *HLAS 42:4537.*

4540 Montes Giraldo, José Joaquín. Dialectología general e hispanoamericana: orientación teórica, metodológica y bibliográfica. Bogotá: Instituto Caro y Cuervo, 1982. 162 p.: bibl., ill. (Publicaciones; 63)

Updating of Montes's *Dialectología y geografía lingüística: notas de orientación,* published by the Instituto Caro y Cuervo in 1970. It would serve anywhere as a good introduction to the study of linguistic geography and dialectology, although it devotes special attention to problems of Spanish American dialectology (e.g., *andalucismo, yeísmo, las sibilantes, /r/ y /rr/*).

4541 Montes Giraldo, José Joaquín. El español bogotano en 1983: muestra fonética y gramatical (ICC/T, 40:2, mayo/agosto 1985, p. 293–307)

Based on a class exercise of the Instituto Caro y Cuervo's Seminario Andrés Bello in 1983. One group of students undertook the recording of /ll/ among age and class elements of the population of Bogotá. Most noticeable was the growth of *yeísmo* among the youth. Another group made *encuestas* of /rr/ which show that the famous assibilated allophone of the area is losing ground in favor of a strong multiple vibrant. In the forms of address, it would appear that *tú* is gaining ground in an area where, as Luis Flórez has said, "Todo el mundo ustedea."

4542 Montes Giraldo, José Joaquín. Etimología y ortografía de un colombianismo: *envolatar(se)* (ICC/T, 38:1, enero/abril 1983, p. 133–138, bibl.)

This *colombianismo,* which is often written *embolatar(se)* is apparently used only in the country of its origin and is found mostly in the written tradition, especially in the stories of Carrasquilla. It would seem to be a derivative of *volar* through *volate* and

has the meaning of being entertained or of being entangled or confused.

4543 Montes Giraldo, José Joaquín. Sobre estudios de fonética del español en Colombia (ICC/T, 40:2, mayo/agosto 1985, p. 396–400)

Handy once-over of Spanish pronunciation of Colombia, going back to the *Apuntaciones críticas* of Rufino José Cuervo (1868–72). Includes fairly long list of works such as Luis Flórez's, Montes Giraldo's, María Luis Rodríguez's, and many others, whose notes appeared serially in the Instituto Caro y Cuervo's *Noticias Culturales* and in vol. 6 of *Atlas lingüístico-etnográfico de Colombia* (ALEC). Spaniards Germán de Granda and Manuel Alvar have contributed much to knowledge of *fonética colombiana.*

4544 Morales Pettorino, Félix and **Oscar Quiroz Mejías.** Diccionario ejemplificado de chilenismos y otros usos diferenciales en el español de Chile: estudio preliminar. Santiago: Consejo de Rectores de las Univs. Chilenas, 1983. 150 p.: ill.

Product of 15 years of uninterrupted research and examination of over 1000 texts, author says that the people of Chile breathe in the pages of his book: *campesinos, mineros, pescadores.* Treating lexicon as the mainspring of functional language, the work deals in contrasts of meaning and temporal variations and includes variants among affixes, articles, and other parts of speech. Entry for *rebenque,* describes why it is this rather than *látigo* and refers to dictionaries of Santamaría, Morínigo, and others who write on *americanismos.*

4545 Muñoz Reyes, Jorge and **Isabel Muñoz Reyes Taborga.** Diccionario de bolivianismos y semántica boliviana. La Paz: Librería Editorial Juventud, 1982. 389 p.: bibl.

As is the case in so many regional vocabularies of Latin America, a majority of the terms defined are fairly common to all Spanish, and indications are that author may not be familiar with many "regional" dictionaries. This one does contain a number of quechuismos, as would be expected.

4546 Núñez Cedeño, Rafael R. Pérdida de trasposición de sujeto en interrogativas pronominales del español del Caribe (ICC/T, 38:1, enero/abril 1983, p. 35–58, bibl.)

Using approach of generative grammar,

article examines Caribbean tendency to fail to transpose the subject in certain interrogative utterances. Also tries to explain why *¿dónde los estudiantes están?* is not grammatical while *¿dónde ellos están?* is. Discarding previous phonological explanations (aspiration or loss of *s* in the *tú* form of the verb), points out that real difference between Standard Spanish and Caribbean is that Standard Spanish considers any question in which a subject, nominal or pronominal is placed before the verb as non-grammatical, where as Caribbean Spanish considers it only if the subject is nominal. The latter style is, therefore, more "inventive!"

4547 Palacios de Samano, Margarita. Sintaxis de los relativos en el habla culta de la Ciudad de México. México: UNAM, Instituto de Investigaciones Filológicas, Centro de Linguística Hispánica, 1983. 80 p. (Cuadernos de lingüística; 3)

Another contribution to *HLAS 42: 5537*. Examines frequency of occurrence and choice among possibilities of relatives *que, cual, quien, cuyo, cuanto, donde, cuando, como* in juxtaposition and coordination situations, in the speech of inhabitants of Mexico City. Finds that with choice of *que, quien, cual*, the Mexican uses *que* 95 percent of the time.

4548 Poplack, Shana. Variable concord and sentential plural marking in Puerto Rican Spanish (HR, 52:2, Spring 1984, p. 205–222, tables)

Based on 21 Puerto Rican residents of East Harlem, analyses of 2,426 sentences composed of a verb phrase and a preceding, following or deleted subject noun phrase. Principal historical development that has brought about the threat of ambiguity, not only in Puerto Rico, but in all of the Caribbean and much of coastal Spanish America is the tendency to aspirate or delete the /s/syllable-final, thus potentially destroying singular-plural distinction and distinction between second person and third in verb forms. Poplack shows that ambiguity rarely occurs because of several types of contextual disambiguation. Puts to rest the claim that English is to blame in the bilingual community.

4549 Rodríguez Demorizi, Emilio. Del vocabulario dominicano. Santo Domingo: Editora Taller, 1983. 297 p.: bibl. (Fundación Rodríguez Demorizi; 47)

As is the case in so many "regional" vocabularies, a majority of terms identified and defined are common to several other places in the Hispanic world, and in this collection there are so many that are *cubanismos, puertorriqueñismos,* and *venezolanismos.* After usual alphabetically arranged vocabulary, includes special section on archaic terms and on contrasts between urban and rural expressions (e.g., city words *ropa, llovizna, igualito, bíceps* become rural *remúa, jarina, taicualito, batata*).

4550 Rojas Nieto, Cecilia. Las construcciones coordinadas sintéticas en el español hablado culto de la Ciudad de México. México: UNAM, Instituto de Investigaciones Filológicas, 1982. 271 p. (Publicaciones del Centro de Lingüística Hispánica; 16)

Another contribution to *HLAS 42:4537.* Examines conjunctions *y, ni, o, pero, sino* in terms of parallel, "shared," and alternating situations. Very good bibliography.

4551 Rubio, J. Francisco. Diccionario de voces usadas en Guatemala. Guatemala: Editorial Piedra Santa, 1982. 392 p.: bibl.

Good depiction of rural existence of people of a country still largely rural. Definitions are expanded by examples to almost encyclopedic dimensions. Especially helpful on fauna and flora of the region. Most interesting is fact that many remedies are described for sicknesses common to area in terms of rural herb doctor practices, many of which would be suspect in Guatemala City (e.g., aguardiente to make mother's milk flow). Also contains fairly extensive section of *vegetales* with their scientific names, and list of government changes, also quite extensive, up to 1982.

4552 Santiesteban, Argelio. El habla popular cubana de hoy: una tonga de cubichismos que le oí a mi pueblo. La Habana: Editorial de Ciencias Sociales, 1982. 366 p.: bibl. (Lingüística)

Vocabulary of popular Spanish of present-day Cuba. Special attention has been given to *arcaísmos,* underworld slang, English influence, Indianisms and *afronegrismos* and a few post-Revolution items: *caballo* is a real go-getter; *trentitrestrentitres,* a traitor; *maumaus o maus* referred to soldiers of the Ejército Rebelde and the Russian automatic weapon is a *pepechá*. Even "O.K." has changed, is now *Ocá*!

4553 Simposio de Dialectología, 6th, Santiago, Dominican Republic, 1981. El español del Caribe: ponencias. Edición de Orlando Alba. Santiago: Univ. Católica Madre y Maestra, Depto. de Publicaciones, 1982. 318 p.: bibls., ill. (Col. Estudios)

Important collection of papers about area of great interest, principally because linguists have come to realize that phonological changes in Caribbean Spanish may effect the syntax and semantics of the language through elimination of markers of number and of person of the verb. Includes 17 papers. All but one or two on Dominican topics: O. Alba explains function of the accent in the process of the elision of /s/ in the Dominican Republic; S. Cabanes discovers that in written Spanish, examined by parts of speech, the adjective is gaining ground since 1975; F. d'Introno and H. Casalta advocate inculcation of linguistic attitudes in the teaching of reading; F. Fernández stresses importance of favorable attitudes in learning; C. González and C. Benavides question existence of Creole elements in the speech of Samaná; J. Guitart examines pronunciaton tendencies of the Caribbean in terms of velarization and glottalization; A. Hache de Yunen reports on /n/ of velar articulation, finding it much more common than had been thought; R. Hammond suggests theory of the optimum use of the articulatory space in quest for explanations of what seems to be an application of the principal of least effort; W. Megenney examines African elements in Dominican Spanish vocabulary; A. Morales looks into the *perspectiva dinámica* in the flow of Puerto Rican Spanish; R. Núñez Cedeño questions modern phonological theories in his "neutralization" of /d/ in favor of /r/ (Montes Giraldo and Granda have found this among the black population of western Colombia); and T. Terrell writes on need for "relexification" of Dominican Spanish because of ambiguity created by aspiration and loss of final consonants, especially /s/.

4554 Torreblanca, Máximo. La asibilación de 'r' y 'rr' en la lengua española (AATSP/H, 67:4, Dec. 1984, p. 614–616)

Once-over of occurrence of assibilation of both /r/ and /rr/ in Spanish-speaking world. Description of phenomena in terms of articulatory phonetics is worthwhile, but as far as linguistic geography is concerned, sources have not been brought up to date. Much has been done in recent years in Colombia, Mexico, and US with regard to the geographical and sociolinguistic distribution of the assibilation that the writer should have examined.

4555 Trujillo, Luis M. Diccionario del español del Valle de San Luis de Colorado y del Norte de Nuevo México. Alamoso, Colo.: O&V Printers, 1983. 203 p.: bibl.

Little vocabulary has authenticity of 20 years of effort by native of the region who also has the perspective of one who has lived in other Spanish-speaking areas. Spanish of northern New Mexico and Colorado's San Luis Valley represents only real continuum of the language since colonial times in the US. Lexicon here published shows that the speech is "real Spanish," but also that there are two major traits, combination of which makes it unique: a large number of *arcaísmos* and considerable English influence in phonology, morphology and syntax, and even more in lexicon. Such extremes as *wáchale* and *estopear* are two of hundreds of Anglicisms. Phonology section could have given more attention to the assibilation of /rr/ and /tr/.

4556 Valadez, Carmen Delia. Notas sobre variantes ortográficas en el español de México (CM/NRFH, 31:2, 1982, p. 276–281)

Discusses problem more common to Latin American speakers of Spanish than to Spaniards. Using *pretensioso* (*pretencioso*) as example, Valadez points out that Mexican current usage is *pretensión* and *pretencioso*. Example of hypercorrection is *exhuberante* for *exuberante* on the basis of *exhibir*, etc. It appears that *hojear* and *hojeada* are being preferred to *ojear* and *ojeada*, although either is conceivable. It is interesting to note that the whole matter of spelling is of less concern among those of Spanish speech than it is in the English-speaking world.

4557 Van Wijk, H.L. Algunos aspectos morfológicos y sintácticos del habla hondureña (AHL/B, 24:26, junio 1982, p. 111–126)

Observations based on reading of *obras costumbristas* and personal interviews (1961). Comments are made on adverbialization of adjectives, on the universal use of the *voseo* rather than the *tuteo: callate vos, si vos te vas, voy a ir con vos,* on addition of neuter *le* to various imperatives: *andale, echale, jalale.* Preposition *a* is preferred with *caer, entrar, meterse, ingresar* rather than *en; entre* is often used for *dentro de,* and there is very extensive nominal formation: *burrada, chanchada, basural, papayal, cipotero, culebrona, hombrón.* Present reviewer does not agree with author's conclusion: "... el castellano de Honduras ofrece una fisonomía propia, un estilo peculiar dentro del complejo dialectal hispánico." Actually practically every feature described is also found in El Salvador, and many in Nicaragua.

4558 Vigueras Avila, Alejandra. Sintaxis de los adverbios terminados en *-mente* en el habla culta de la Ciudad de México (UNAM/AL, 21, 1983, p. 119–145, tables)

Another study that forms part of *HLAS 42:4537* and item **4539**). Departing from a morphological point of view, classifies results of interviews with 42 Mexico City inhabitants, recording of 17 and a half hours, using questionnaire of Programa Interamericano de Lingüística y Enseñanza de Idiomas (PILEI). Syntactically, most common occurrence was function of modification of a whole clause, but adverbs that modify verbs were frequent, those that modify adjectives, less so. Semantically, adverbs that indicate gradation in assertions were much more numerous than those of emotional attitude. There were 50 cases of adverbs used that achieved absolutely no function. Evidently this class of society uses many more such modifiers than lower groups.

4559 Wojski, Zygmunt. El factor etnolingüístico como criterio de delimitación de la zona del Caribe (PAN/EL, 9, 1982/1984, p. 211–216)

Circumscribes a Caribbean ethnolinguistic Zone on bases of both the non-European origins of so much of the population and fairly common phonological traits of the Spanish today in Cuba, Puerto Rico, Dominican Republic, coasts and llanos of Venezuela and Colombia, and the Atlantic coast of Panama, Costa Rica, Nicaragua, Honduras, Guatemala, and Mexico. Suggests that non-European elements bring about common pronunciation features, such as aspirated /s/ syllable final, confusion of

implosive /l/ and /r/. Author not fully acquainted with recent investigations of a diachronic type that show rather convincingly that common phonological traits are due to common Andalusian origins of the *pobladores* and a common accessibility to changes from southern Spain during the later colonial period. Same changes occurred in other sections of Latin America where there were virtually no blacks or Indians.

SPANISH
LEXICON

4560 Acosta, Cecilio. Observaciones al *Diccionario de la Real Academia Española.* Transcripción de los manuscritos, notas y estudio preliminar de Pedro Grases. Caracas: s.n., 1981. 139 p., 80 p. of plates: facsims. (Biblioteca de autores y temas mirandinos. Col. Guaicaipuro; 1)

Recommendations made to Royal Spanish Academy by famous Venezuelan humanist (1874–76), most of which are corrections or additions. Also contains letters in his own handwriting.

4561 Alvar Ezquerra, Manuel and **Aurora Miró Domínguez.** Diccionario de siglas y abreviaturas. Madrid: Alhambra, 1983. 286 p.

Very extensive list of acronyms and abbreviations, many from non-Hispanic parts of the world. Quite useful except that it does not have any of the many acronyms that are now used in Computer Science and Telecommunications (e.g., CPU, LED, DOS, MBYTE, ROM).

4562 Ander-Egg, Ezequiel. Diccionario del trabajo social. Alicante, Spain: Caja de Ahorros de Alicante de Murcia, Obras Sociales, 1981. 392 p. (Publicaciones; 157)

Although this publication is from Spain, it undoubtedly has been very helpful to social workers in Latin America and US, where there are large populations of Spanish-speaking people and hundreds of "case workers."

4563 Araya, Guillermo. Le dictionnaire d'americanismes (*in* Unité et diversité en l'Amérique latine. Bordeaux, France: Univ. de Bordeaux III, 1982, t. 2, p. 271–287, bibl.)

Writer attempts a recipe for the composition of a future *Dictionary of Americanisms*. Lists those of Malaret, Santamaría, Morínigo as standard and cites the Haensch-Werner critique of them (1978) as well as certain special vocabularies of *indigenismos* or *lunfardo*. Notes three great sectors of Spanish lexicon as: 1) that which is common to all who speak Spanish; 2) that of Spain; and 3) American Spanish. After conceding that it is rather difficult to determine what is really American in origin, suggests that sources should be current oral usage, literature, periodicals, etc., and that there should be no limitations of frequency of occurrence. An insurmountable task because Spanish American lexicon is constantly "on the move."

4564 Arenas, Pedro de. Vocabulario manual de las lenguas castellana y mexicana. Edición fascimilar de la publicada por Henrico Martínez en la Ciudad de México, 1611. Con un estudio introductorio de Ascensión H. de León-Portilla. México: UNAM, 1982. 5, 160 p., 12 p. of plates: bibl., facsims. (Facsímiles de lingüística y filología nahuas; 1)

Facsimile edition of 1609 original, preceded by introduction and bibliography. As editor points out, these vocabularies and grammars written by Spanish priests during the 16th and 17th centuries, especially the works of Alonso de Molina, are valuable to historical linguistics in that they depict the application of the Spanish alphabet to the transcription of Indian languages that are still spoken, thus revealing the pronunciation of Spanish at that time, and also showing when changes took place in this pronunciation: ç was consistently used for /s/, s and ss were /ṡ/, not found in the Indian languages, and x was /ṡ/, j /ż/.

4565 Becerra, Marcos E. Rectificaciones i adiciones al *Diccionario de la Real Academia Española*. 3a ed. México: Consejo Editorial del Gobierno del Estado de Tabasco, 1980. 832 p.: indexes.

One of the many books written to criticize the famous *Dictionary of the Royal Spanish Academy*. Pt. 1 has "Voces de Origen Americano;" "Voces Comunes y Cultas Varias;" and "Rectificaciones." Pt. 2 takes up "Voces No Americanas."

4566 Boyd-Bowman, Peter. The *Léxico hispanoamericano* series: a progress report (Hispanic Linguistics [Univ. of Pittsburgh, Pittsburgh, Pa.] 1:1, Spring, 1984, p. 133–137)

Since 1967 Boyd-Bowman has been preparing reference works to illustrate evolution of the Spanish-American lexicon from the 16th century to present. Three volumes have appeared, corresponding to the 16th, 17th, and 18th centuries. Vol. 4, the largest, *Léxico hispanoamericano del siglo XIX*, is in preparation in a microfiche edition that will include vocabulary from several new sources, such as Molina's *Vocabulario en lengua castellana y mexicana* (Mexico: 1571) and Guamán Poma de Ayala's *Nueva Crónica*.

4567 Breve diccionario de ateísmo. Redactor principal, M.P. Novikov. Traducción de Félix de la Uz. La Habana: Editorial de Ciencias Sociales, 1981. 301 p.

Dictionary composed from the point of view of an atheist, but which defines what turns out to be mainly religious words and expressions. The original edition was in Russian, done under the direction of M.P. Noviko, "Doctor en ciencias filosóficas." The vocabulary defines *ateísmo marxista* as *forma superior del ateísmo*, and indicates that it is much better than *ateísmo burgués*. One notes that nearly every definition contains the word *propaganda*!

4568 Budić, Domingo Valentín. Diccionario del comercio exterior. Buenos Aires: Ediciones Depalma, 1983. 328 p.: bibl., indexes.

"Extended-definition" dictionary of terminology of economics, trade, customs activities, banking, jurisdiction and technology related to international commerce.

4569 Diccionario enciclopédico ilustrado tres columnas. Buenos Aires: Editorial Oriente, 1981. 2 v. (1218 p.), 29 p. of plates: ill. (some col.)

Beautifully printed two-volume work that advertises: "Láminas a todo color: arte, astronáutica, aviación, señales de circulación, color, cuerpo humano, indumentaria," found at end of vol. 1. Pictures are very attractive, but under entry *astronáutica*, information does not go beyond Shepard, Glenn, and Griswold. Dictionary is nowhere near up-to-date in matter of *informática* and *telecomunicaciones*, although Spanish terminology is now being used in Spain and some parts of Latin America. Good extra section on grammar, on the Beagle Canal dispute of

Argentina and Chile, and section called *actualización*, in which one finds, for instance, that information on developments in Nicaragua is vague and inaccurate.

4570 Diccionario temático de las cosas y de sus partes: facilita el hallazgo de la palabra precisa. Buenos Aires: Karten Editora, 1984. 417 p.: index.

What one might call in English a topical vocabulary of things and their parts, from *anatomía* to *transportes*, followed by vocabulary by way of index to *temas*. To find the meaning of *acollador*, the vocabulary refers you to topic *barcos*, where you learn more about the relation of one to the other. In light of recent developments in world societies, there is a section called *informática* (computer science), but is not up-to-date in actual computer terminology.

4571 Haensch, Günther. Apuntes de jerga escolar y estudiantil española e hispanoamericana (UEN/LS, 13:1, 1983, p. 279–287)

Interesting sampling of student slang from several Spanish American countries, presented as example of rather extreme variations that one finds at this level of lexicon. Besides *profe, viejo, míster, tícher* occur for *profesor;* to play hooky is *hacer novillos* in Spain, *hacerse la rabona* in Argentina, but *hacerse la sincola* in Mendoza of the same country. Mexicans *hacen la pinta* or *pintan venados*. To cheat on an exam is *usar el machete* in Argentina, while to be a book worm or burn the midnight oil is *quemarse el coco* in Mexico and *quemarse las pestañas* in Spain.

4572 Hutter, Harriett S. *El Milagrucho*: a linguistic comment on a Pachuco text (AATSP/H, 67:2, May 1984, p. 256–261)

Probably the first word-by-word commentary on the famous in-group *caló* known as Pachuco, which is no longer spoken but which represented a cry of pain among a small group of youths who felt alienated from the mainstream of the US in the 1940s. The text was written by Raquel Moreno and published in *El Grito* (Spring 1971, Quinto Sol Publications, Inc., Berkeley, Calif.). This private code language is based on distortions and skewings of border Spanish, with lots of English influence evident: *Orale, mi buen Tuercas. ¿Cómo te bailotea!* Hey there, Tuercas, good buddy. How's it goin'?

4573 Ianes Vera, Raúl and Juan A. Mariel Erostarbe. Diccionario de nombres. San Juan, Argentina: Univ. Nacional de San Juan, Facultad de Filosofía, Humanidades y Artes, Biblioteca Juan José Nissen, 1983. 162 p.: bibl.

Beginning in 1981, authors undertook research for the *Servicio de Información y Referencia* of the library of the Univ. Nacional de San Juan (Argentina), based on examination of the Civil Registry of the city, supplemented by months of search for origins and meanings of the *Bible*, books on mythology, etc. Works contain hundreds of given names and is quite informative on matter of regional selection (see item **4587**). In both cases, it may surprise many to see how many classical names have been chosen.

4574 Llanos, García de. Diccionario y maneras de hablar que se usan en las minas y sus labores en los ingenios y beneficios de los metales: 1609. Con un estudio de Gunnar Mendoza L. y un comentario de Thierry Saignes. La Paz: MUSEF Editores, 1983. 127 p.: bibl., index (Serie Fuentes primarias; 1)

Revelation of astounding technical and economic dimensions of mining projects of Spanish explorers and settlers in early 17th century, and in the heart of what turned out to be a world economic nerve center for *plata potosina*. García Llanos, who apparently wrote between 1598–1611, is also author of *Relación del Cerro de Potosí, el estado que tiene y desórdenes de él, con el remedio que en todo se podría dar*, in which he fought for social justice in the mines. Most of the 258 terms of the vocabulary are still used and to the modern reader constitute a trip to the heart of Cerro Rico and afford a diagnosis of colonial mining processes.

4575 Lope Blanch, Juan M. Antillanismos en la Nueva España (*in* International Congress of Hispanists, 4th, 1971, Salamanca, Spain. Actas. Dirección de Eugenio de Bustos Tovar. Salamanca, Spain: Univ. de Salamanca, 1982, v. 2, p. 147–156, bibl.)

Investigator refers to Boyd-Bowman's "Observaciones sobre el Español Hablado en México en el Siglo XVI" in *Actas del III Congreso de Hispanistas* (México: 1970) which lists 72 terms of Náhuatl origin extant at the time. Lope made a similar study of Caribbean Indian words that were already used in Mexico in the 16th century. *Antillismos* turned out to be as many as the *nahuatlismos*. Not only that but they have proven to have unusual vitality, due undoubtedly to the fact that they were the first indigenous designations learned by the Spaniards for the new and exotic things of the New World. Even in Quechua territory of the Andes, such things as *ají, cacique, maíz, guayaba, mangle, pita, sabana, tabaco*, and many other words, are commonplace.

4576 Megenney, William W. Sub-Saharan influences in the lexicon of Puerto Rico (CIDG/O, 30:1/2, 1981 [i.e., 1983] p. 214–260)

This recognized authority on African elements in Creoles, especially those of the Caribbean, indicates that the most comprehensive study done thus far on African influences in the Spanish language of Puerto Rico is M. Alvarez Nazario's *El elemento afronegroide en el español de Puerto Rico*, and that documents concerning slave trade provide no information on tribal origins, only on African ports from which slaves were shipped to America. Megenney circulated 108 words of supposed African origins from Alvarez Nazario's book among 150 Puerto Rican informants asking them to identify all words. Using dictionaries and native informants from Africa, he searched for sub-Saharan terms. His data includes 47 different languages from Sudanic and Bantu Africa, from both coasts and even interior regions, such as Zaire, Zimbabwe. Definitions as given by Puerto Ricans and writers number 89 (e.g., *conga, chango, chachachá, chévere, mandinga, ñame*).

4577 Martínez, Aníbal R. Diccionario del petróleo venezolano. Caracas: Editorial Ateneo de Caracas: Ediciones de Corpozulia, 1984. 156 p.: ill., indexes.

Vocabulary that incidentally presents a history of an industry that has been important to Venezuela since the 1920s. Author devoted much time to collection of data and technical definitions. From original file of 180 key terms, Martínez "branched out" into final refinements. The revision of 1982 had 852 items, and in such entries as *hidrocarburos* served a pedagogical function, and incidentally revealed English influence in term *hidrocraqueo* (English "cracking"). Many formulas and diagrams.

4578 Montes Giraldo, José Joaquín. Calcos recientes del inglés en español (ICC/T, 40:1, enero/abril 1985, p. 17–50)

Calcos may be phonetic, syntactic, semantic, structural (*políticas* from politics), and writer even finds some that are idiomatic: *olvídalo* for ¡no tengas cuidado! Of special interest are *aplicar, destacar, originar, asumir, esperar por, votar* (*vote lista bandera*). One of the principal origins of the correlative analogy would seem to be the wire services of the newspaper, where there is always a sense of haste in translating things that come in from AP, UPI, Reuters, etc., in English.

4579 Morais, Clodomir. Diccionario de reforma agraria: Latinoamérica. Prefacio de Josué de Castro. 2a ed. San José: Editorial Universitaria Centroamericana, 1983. 533, 19 p.: bibl. (Col. Seis)

Topical vocabulary of *términos* related to agricultural activities: *aspectos agrícolas, económicos, jurídicos, sociales*. Much space is dedicated to organizations of agricultural workers and to systems of tenancy.

4580 Morrison, Tirso M. Gran diccionario de sinónimos, antónimos e ideas afines. Nueva ed. rev. Buenos Aires: Ediciones Larousse Argentina; Santiago: Editorial Bibliográfica, 1983. 506 p.

Extensive listing of basic terms followed by words of similar meaning and in some cases by antonym: *agotar: gastar, acabar, consumir, apurar, cólmar*. Interesting study might be made of this vocabulary in terms of variables and circumstances of variation, which brings in many extra-linguistic factors. *Chile*, for example, would not even be understood in countries where the so-called synonym *ají* is used.

4581 Pérez Pinzón, Alvaro Orlando. Diccionario de criminología. Bogotá: Univ. Externado de Colombia, 1982. 245 p.: bibl., index.

Little book does not pretend to be beyond the basic vocabulary of criminology, determined by frequency of occurrence. Entries often have references to authors who have discussed cases that help define terms, many of these non-Hispanic.

4582 Rasico, Philip D. The Spanish lexical base of old St. Augustine *Mahonese*: a missing link in Florida Spanish (AATSP/H, 69:2, May 1986, p. 267–277)

Writer refers to L. Canfield's article on Tampa Spanish (*Modern Language Journal*, 35, 1951) which stated that there is no continuity in spoken Spanish of Florida from original settlements by Spain, and that today's Florida Spanish is a transplant, mainly from Cuba. Rasico maintains that although the British took over in 1763, there was a large group of Catalans and Corsicans who settled in 1768, and that there are vestiges of their language, mainly Catalan, today. Author tape-recorded many phrases of Minorcan or Spanish origin: *besa mi culo, compañero, ducha la cola* (at full speed), *loco bobo*. W. Cullen Bryant visited St. Augustine in 1843 and translated transcription of Mahonese song *Dexiem lo dol* (*Let us cease mourning*). Spanish and Catalan elements are referred to by Rasico.

4583 Rincón, Alexis and **Ned Davison.**
Glossary of English/Spanish computer terminology for the Spanish classroom (AATSP/H, 67:4, Dec. 1984, p. 701–706)

Very valuable vocabulary of terms that most dictionaries do not have. Writers used as sources trade journals from Madrid and Buenos Aires. Lexicon assumes that the reader know both languages, but gender of the Spanish terms is indicated by means of an article. Interesting entries: auto-boot, *autocarga*; beep, *pip, piip*; daisy wheel, *margarita*; computer science, *informática*; joystick, *palanca de juegos*; software, *logical*. The computer itself is *computadora* or *computador* in Spanish America but *ordenador* in Spain.

4584 Rivarola, José Luis. *Albaquía, baquía, baquiano*: notas sobre el origen de un americanismo (ZRP, 101:1/2, 1985, p. 45–51, bibl.)

Referring to data gleaned from P. Boyd-Bowman's *Léxico hispanoamericano del siglo XVI*, writer disputes suggested Arabic origin of terms *baquía* and *baquiano*, much used in gaucho literature and elsewhere for "practical knowledge of the countryside" and an "experienced guide with this knowledge." The words, he believes, are of Taíno origin and appear first in Cuba in 1521. *Albaquía*, an economic term of Arabic origin, is undoubtedly not related.

4585 Romagnoli, Jorge A. Diccionario teórico-práctico de la comunicación social interdisciplinada. Córdoba, Argentina: s.n., 1983. 849 p.: bibl.

Work starts with index of words to be defined ultimately. These are grouped by category of social communication: Información, Relaciones Humanas, Publicidad, Periodismo, Medios, etc. Entries of vocabulary itself refer to the *materias* of the index (*Ley de radiodifusión-medios; Letrista-publicidad*). Many references to practices in other countries. Bibliography has many works from other countries.

4586 Romero Gualda, María Victoria. Indo-americanismos léxicos en la crónica de Pedro Pizarro (ICC/T, 38:1, enero/abril 1983, p. 1–34, bibl.)

Useful vocabulary of mainly *quechu-ismos* from the *Relación del descubrimiento y conquista de los Reinos del Perú* (1571), ordered alphabetically, and with comments from reference works and dictionaries that are included in article's bibliography. Such widely-used terms as *cacique, coca, cóndor, palta, papa* from the language of the Inca are defined, along with words from Indian languages contacted previously, such as *camote* (náhuatl) and *maguey* (taíno).

4587 Tello, Jaime. Sobre onomástica venezolana (ICC/T, 38:3, sept./dec. 1983, p. 602–604)

Interesting note on unusual names that have been chosen by *venezolanos*. As he indicates there are certain national traditions in this respect. Juan Carlos is apt to be an Argentinian; Galo is apt to be from Ecuador; Jairo or Fabio are probably from Antioquia, Colombia; Nerio, Orángel, Teolindo are from Venezuela. Carpóforo, Esmelí, Nectario, Gualberto are men, and Yanet (Llaneth), Africa, Mildre, Yajaira, Morella, Zulay, Xiomara, Zaidah, are women.

4588 Varela, Beatriz. Argentinismos y cubanismos (UNC/RN, 24:2, Winter 1983, p. 123–131)

From a corpus of 400 lexical items gleaned while on a sabbatical in Argentina and from interviews with 50 Cubans now residing in the US, draws interesting comparisons in four concepts: negation, affirmation, bad coffee, and cuts of meat. To reinforce negation, the *argentino* says *Mongo Aurelio*, the Cuban *nananina* or *nanaína*, the first proably from *lunfardo*, the second fashioned after the first syllable of *nada*. In pre-Castro Cuba *sí, Cirilo Villaverde* was a form of affirmation, now it is *sí, Cirilo, verde olivo*. Bad coffee can be *jugo de paraguas* among *porteños* and *aguachirle*, pronounced *aguachirre* among Cubans. A meat cut from the hind quarter of the cow is *peceto* in Buenos Aires and *boliche* in Cuba, eye of the round in the US. She points out that the *boliche* in Argentina is a small store, and that *bacán* in Argentina is a Great Gatsby type and in Cuba a *tamal* made of banana.

4589 Vega, Julio César de la. Diccionario consultor político. S.l., Argentina: O.A. Aroz, 1983. 429 p.: index.

Extended definition dictionary of political terminology that would be useful in any part of Spanish-speaking world, but with limitations indicated by the author: Many entries are going to be defined and illustrated in terms of Argentina's history. Such is the case with *conservadores, radicalismo*, etc.

SPANISH
SEMANTICS

4590 Mayorga, Dora. Algunas observaciones a propósito de las voces españoles *emigrante, emigrado* y *exiliado* (UCLV/I, 76, sept./dic. 1983, p. 159–166)

Traces special meanings of *emigrado* and *exiliado* to intervention of France in life and politics of Spain in the 18th and 19th centuries and to the Spanish Civil War (1936–39). Believes that current popularity of *exiliado* in Hispanic America may correspond to the world vision that the Spanish Americans share with the Spanish *republicanos* of the Civil War.

4591 Scavnicky, Gary E. Nuevos gentilicios en el español colombiano (CM/NRFH, 31:2, 1982, p. 273–275)

Of special interest to this author is the suffix in Spanish (see *HLAS 46:4527*), and he cites the *gentilicio* as yet another testimony of the abundance of innovations in the realm of combinative analogy. Interesting examples from Colombia: *sumario*, a native of Santa Marta; *cundinamarqués* from Cundinamarca, and *vallecaucano* from Valle del Cauca.

SPANISH
SYNTAX

4592 Castillo Mathieu, Nicolás del. Testimonios del uso de "*vuestra merced*," "*vos*" y "*tú*" en América: 1500–1650 (ICC/T,

37:3, sept./dic. 1982, p. 602–644, bibl.)

Testimony from letters of Cortés, Pizarro, and *Historia de las Indias* of Fray Bartolomé de las Casas, as well as chronicle of Gonzalo Fernández de Oviedo would indicate that *vuestra merced* in place of *vos* was quite rare in America until well past the mid-16th century. One of first indications of the "devaluation" of *vos* comes in the *Comentarios Reales* of the Inca Garcilaso de la Vega, and during last years of 16th century and first half of 17th, *vos* really loses ground. Author relates interesting experience in Bogotá, having come from Cartagena, where the *tuteo* is rampant *entre familia*. He found *usted* prevailed there within the family and to inferiors. Even in 1982 if a boss used *tu* to a secretary, she may feel that she was in a difficult situation!

4593 García, Erica C. and **Ricardo L. Otheguy.** Being polite in Ecuador: strategy reversal under language contact (LINGUA, 61:2/3, Oct./Nov. 1983, p. 103–132, bibl., tables)

Semantic rather than syntactic analysis of case opposition between the Spanish clitics *le* and *lo/la* leads to a number of predictions concerning plausible correlations with extra-linguistic factors, and expected skewings in distribution. Predictions are tested by means of questionnaire administered to native speakers of six Latin American countries. Predicted skewings fail to be observed only in Ecuador. Local conditions of language contact (Quechua substratum) suggest a reevaluation of gender system as a potential sociolinguistic class marker, whereby gender, rather than case, becomes the relevant semantic dimension for politeness strategy. Authors reject traditional categorization of direct and indirect because of inability to define the test. They rank *le* as higher than *lo* in terms of activity of the referent compared to the most active referred to by the verb ending: *le compré el sombrero, lo compré de Pedro*. Seller is less active than the buyer but more active than the hat. Ecuador tends to categorize by gender in terms of activeness.

4594 Ledezma, Minelia de and **Luis Alvarez.** Dos ensayos de lingüística. Caracas: Centro de Investigaciones Lingüísticas y Literarias Andrés Bello, Depto. de Castellano, Literatura y Latín, Instituto Universitario Pedagógico de Caracas, 1981. 101 p.: bibls., ill.

Point of departure for first of these essays is *Gramática castellana* of Andrés Bello, and writer examines adverbs ending in *-mente* and confirms adjectival character of certain adverbs. Bibliography of this article should include Esteban Egea's work (see *HLAS 44:4513*). Alvarez's essay is a transformational explanation of adjective subordination: *El hombre, cuyo nombre es Luis.*

4595 Lope Blanch, Juan M. Análisis gramatical del discurso. México: UNAM, Instituto de Investigaciones Filológicas, Centro de Lingüística Hispánica, 1983. 181 p.: bibl. (Publicaciones; 17)

Articles published in various journals (1978–82) have something to do with Spanish syntactic structure, although they are not closely related to the sense of a common theme: "Notas sobre las Unidades Sintácticas del Discurso;" "La Estructura del Habla Culta en Puerto Rico y en México;" "La Estructura Sintáctica del Discurso en *Las cartas de Diego Ordaz*," and eight others.

4596 Páez Urdaneta, Iraset. Historia y geografía hispanoamericana del voseo. Caracas: Casa de Bello, 1981. 169 p.: bibl., index, maps (Col. hispanoamericana de lingüística)

Book is a genuine contribution to history and present manifestations of the use of *vos* and accompanying verb forms in Latin America, along with story of "competing" *directivas* (*tú, vuestra merced, su merced*). The instability of usage is indicated by author's analysis of *vos* with present tense: *comes, comés, coméis, comís,* depending on region or sub-region. Maps of general and of specific manifestations are well done, including rural-urban contrasts in Bolivia, for instance. One notes absence of work done by M.B. Fontanella de Weinberg in the bibliography.

4597 Silva-Corvalán, Carmen. Tense and aspect in oral Spanish narrative (LSA/L, 59:4, Dec. 1983, p. 760–780, bibl.)

Well wrought examination of historical present (HP) in 30 oral narratives, 27 Chilean and three Mexican. Shows that distribution of tense and aspect in oral Spanish narrative indicate that meaning of certain verb forms is in part delimited by the structural context in which they occur. Historical present/preterite alternation indicates that the present functions as an internal evaluation mechanism.

4598 Terker, Andrew. On Spanish adjective position (AATSP/H, 68:3, Sept. 1985, p. 502–509)

Study demonstrates that transformation of position of adjectives, based on Bello's original proposal, is untenable as explanation of the order of attributive adjectives in Spanish. Rather, D. Bolinger's excellent insights on Spanish word order serve to explain the position. His principle of linear modification says that each successive element to the right further narrows the reference of the concept at hand. Prenominal adjectives, therefore, indicate an essential, inherent characteristic because the noun is the more important datum in this case. Principle only works, it should be noted, in a language with fairly free word order. It would not work with English!

4599 Whitley, M. Stanley. "How:" the missing interrogative in Spanish (AATSP/H, 69:1, March 1986, p. 82–96)

In such cases as "How wide is the circle?," Spanish does not have a single form for *how*. Diachronically this was *cuán*, which is now obsolete. In some areas people say *¿Qué tan . . .?, ¿Qué tanto . . .?* Others ask a yes-no question to solve the problem. Native speakers (17) from several countries were interviewed on this matter. All were well educated. *Cuán* turned out to be almost non-occurrent, and the yes-no question was the usual way of answering, and *qué tan* was fairly common: How high is that jet? was, *¿A que altura vuela . . .?* or *¿Qué tan alto queda (vuela)?*

PORTUGUESE
GENERAL

4600 Estudos de filologia e lingüística: em homenagem a Isaac Nicolau Salum. Edição de T.A. Queiroz. São Paulo: Editôra da Univ. de São Paulo, 1981. 311 p., 2 leaves of plates: bibl., ill. (Biblioteca universitária de língua en lingüística; 2)

Book dedicated to Isaac Nicolau Salum, whose interesting career in both classical and Romance philology and Presbyterian theology was an inspiration to several contributors who write on classical philology, Portuguese philology, Romance philology, phonetics and phonology, lexicology, morphology, syntax and semantics, analysis of texts. One interesting article examines functions of the velum in creating the distinction between oral and nasal vowels but also in the shaping of the vowel sounds themselves.

4601 Orlandi, Eni Pulcinelli. A linguagem e seu funcionamento: as formas do discurso. São Paulo: Brasiliense, 1983. 237 p.: bibls.

The function of speech in different situations: pedagogy, science, literature, history, the typology of discourse itself. Lecturer and audience considerations that amount to a sociolinguistic analysis.

PORTUGUESE GRAMMAR

4602 Travaglia, Luiz Carlos. O aspecto verbal no português: a categoria e sua expressão. Uberlândia: Univ. Federal de Uberlândia, 1981. 332 p.: bibl., ill.

Book defines aspect as "the manner of being" of the action: indication of duration, indication of internal temporal structure, grade of development, indication of opposition between two notions. As writer suggests, this phase of syntactic analysis brings in psychological attitudes and semantics to an extent not realized before.

PORTUGUESE DIALECTOLOGY

4603 Bunse, Heinrich A.W. São José do Norte: aspectos lingüístico-etnográficos do antigo município. 2a ed. Pôrto Alegre: Mercado Aberto: Instituto Estadual do Livro, 1981. 134 p.: bibl., ill., ports.

Objective examination of habits, customs, trades, language of people of the south of Brazil between the Atlantic Ocean and Lagoa dos Patos. History of settlement of the area and typical *fazenda* life is followed by topical discussions of *A Agricultura, A Habitaçaõ, A Pesca,* etc., the language, and a glossary.

4604 Caruso, Pedro. A iotização do /-lh-/ segundo o atlas prévio dos falares baianos (FFCLM/A, 27, 1983, p. 47–52, map, tables)

Interesting case of apparent reconstruction of a phoneme that had suffered leveling to another. The *Atlas prévio dos*

Falares Baianos (1959) indicated extensive loss of the /lh/ in the interior of Bahia. More recent work by Nelson Rossi tends to show that words like *julho, mulher, orelha, coelho,* which had lost /lh/ in favor of /y/, are now recovering the original phoneme in some sections of the state. The tendency seems to be moving inland from the Atlantic coast.

4605 Major, Roy C. Stress and rhythm in Brazilian Portuguese (LSA/L, 61:2, June 1985, p. 259–282)

Writer argues that Brazilian Portuguese prosody is organized in a rhythmic hierarchy which governs the phonology of the language, and it has been demonstrated that it is present diachronically and synchronically in different styles of speech. Principles of stress apparently assign secondary stress to pretonic syllables and no stress to posttonic syllables. From this hierarchical relationship, vowel quality and syllable weight are predictable. Rhythmic hierarchy that governs the phonology of languages follows style changes from formal to normal to casual.

4606 Nonato, Raimundo. Calepino potiguar: gíria rio-grandense. Mossoró: Escola Superior de Agricultura de Mossoró, Fundação Guimarães Duque, 1980. 496 p. (Col. mossoroense; 119)

The Calepino title derived from name of Italian Augustianian monk Ambrosio Calepino (d. 1511). Term is often used in referring to a vocabulary, especially one of popular speech and expressions. This calepino is from Northeast Brazil, Rio Grande do Norte and is essentially a *Linguajar do Povo.* It enriches the collection of regional vocabularies from the general area: Pernambuco, Ceará, Paraíba, where Portuguese has received considerable attention in matters of Africanisms, dialectal variants, and slang. Definitions are rather extended, with examples in many cases.

4607 Nunes, Zeno Cardoso and Rui Cardoso Nunes. Dicionário de regionalismos do Rio Grande do Sul. Ed. rev. Pôrto Alegre: Martins Livreiro-Editor, 1982. 552 p.: index.

Excellent source of terms, expressions, and practices of Rio Grande do Sul. Many entries have long explanations of origins and related customs. *Assado,* for example, elicits two columns on country customs for preparation of the meat, and *jogo do osso* brings out detailed description of game involved.

Many definitions are illustrated by poetry. Vocabulary is followed by *índice onomástico*.

4608 Perrone, Charles A. and Linda Ledford-Miller. Variation in pretonic /e/ in Brazilian Portuguese: preliminary studies with popular music of the Northeast and Rio de Janeiro (AATSP/H, 68:1, March 1985, p. 154–159)

Explanations of vocalism in Brazilian Portuguese are frequently very sketchy. In particular elucidations of pretonic /e/ and /o/ to be found in the published work of Brazilian linguists are often minimal. Authors' data are from two major varieties of Brazilian Portuguese: Rio de Janeiro and the Northeast. They use popular songs for the analysis because of their naturalness and fact that both males and females participate. Totals confirm open variety of Northeast speech, while /e/ and /E/ are about evenly divided in Rio de Janeiro where /r/ follows an /e/ usually. They succeeded in showing that pretonic /e/ variation is more involved than had been thought.

PORTUGUESE LEXICON

4609 Abreu, Antônio Izaias da Costa. O linguajar do marginalizado. Petrópolis: Gráfica e Editôra Folha Serrana, 1983. 119 p.: bibl.

Vocabulary of words and expressions used habitually by the *toxicómanos* and *traficantes*, prepared especially for teachers, judges, and counselors who deal with such marginal elements of society. Since many of these terms are fly-by-night, it is good to have a written collection.

4610 Andrade, Gabriel Augusto de. Nomes populares das aves do Brasil. Belo Horizonte: Sociedade Ornitológica Mineira: Instituto Brasileiro de Desenvolvimento Florestal, 1982. 95 p.

Book lists 2000 birds that belong to about 200 species, some of African origin. Both the scientific and popular designations are given as well as place of first sighting and parts of Brazil where the bird is to be found.

4611 Becker, Idel. Grande dicionário latino-americano português-espanhol. São Paulo: Livraria Nobel, 1983. 499 p.

Book has good introductory section on pronunciation of Portuguese for Spanish-speaking people and one on Spanish for those who speak Portuguese, as well as information on the *seseo* and some on dialectal variants, accentuation, and spelling. Includes rather good vocabulary but lacks computer and tele-communications terminology.

4612 Caruso, Pedro. Amostra de um inquérito lingüístico prévio para o estado de São Paulo (FFCLM/A, 26, 1982, p. 69–77, bibl., maps)

Stated purpose is to present sample of what is already being done toward mapping linguistically the state of São Paulo and what is projected, in the hope that it will serve as a stimulus for similar efforts. One interesting lexical map is that for the term *terçol*, stye. Field work shows that four main words are used in the state, each with variants, and the word *terçol* has eight variants, the most common of which is *treiçor*.

4613 Carvalho, Benjamin de Araujo. Glossário de saneamento e ecologia. Rio de Janeiro: Associação Brasileira de Engenharia Sanitária e Ambiental, 1981. 203 p.

Glossary contains many entries rarely heard in conventions and seminars on sanitation and ecology. They are terms referring to interiors, that is terms that define, regulate, and promote good conditions in the interiors of buildings and residences with respect to the conservation of human hygiene. Each entry of the glossary may have several examples. There is quite a lot of pollution, including sound pollution.

4614 Carvalho, Nelly. Linguagem jornalística: aspectos inovadores. Recife: Governo do Estado, Secretaria de Educação: Associação de Imprensa de Pernambuco, 1983. 132 p.: bibl., ill.

Actually a treatise on neologisms, since journalistic composition tends to lean toward innovations of expression: loan words or phrases, correlative analogy, onomatopoeia, acronyms (now very popular). Author's three special interests: sociolinguistic aspects of terminology and its relevance as an index of change, purely linguistic aspects, and finally, permanency of new words and phrases.

4615 Costa, Eunice R. Ribeiro and Tatiana Douchkin. Thesaurus experimental de arquitetura. São Paulo: Fundação para e Pesquisa Ambiental, 1982. 142 p.: bibl.

Designed as instrument of control of terminology in the realm of architecture and urban development to bring to a common denominator for the country a vocabulary that would be accurate and "disciplined." *Esquema de Chaves* is an interesting device to represent in hierarchical form items to be considered under such general headings as Form, Function, Technique. Vocabulary entries are followed by definitions and then conceivable applications: *Cabina telefônica* is described as *compartimento reservado para comunicações telefônicas* and a long list of items such as *equipamento das vias, abrigo para pedestres,* etc.

4616 Cunha, Antônio Geraldo da *et al.* Vocabulário ortográfico Nova Fronteira da língua portuguesa. Rio de Janeiro: Editôra Nova Fronteira, 1983. 890 p.

Brings us up to Law No. 5765 (Dec. 18, 1971), with respect to the spelling of Portuguese in Brazil. Each entry is followed by indications of part of speech and gender. Irregular plural endings are spelled out in bold face, and all terms are syllabicated, with the stressed syllable in italics (in-for-*ma*-ti-ca, sf.)

4617 Ferreira, Francisco de Paula. Dicionário de bem-estar social. São Paulo: Cortez Editôra. 362 p.: bibl.

Author is very much concerned with defects in the structure of Brazilian society, and with what he terms the deterioration of well-being in the population, which is evident in statistics of all social indicators: diet, health education, housing, employment. Dictionary was written not with the idea of substantially improving conditions, but hoping to help mobilize the energy of the Brazilian people to an awareness of their problems. Under each entry the writer reviews developments signaled by the entry, and even philosophizes on unemployment, violence, poor communication.

4618 Fonseca Júnior, Eduardo. Dicionário yorubá (nagô)—português. Rio de Janeiro: Sociedade Yorubana Teológica de Cultura Afro-Brasileira, 1983. 436 p.: ill., photos.

Contribution to culture of both Nigeria and Brazil, and their relations. Introduction has explanation of phonological system of Yorubá (Nagó), in which diacritical marks are used to indicate vowel quality. Well

illustrated with photographs of Nigerian officials.

4619 Gardini, Giacomo and Norberto de Paula Lima. Dicionário de eletrônica inglês/português. São Paulo: Hemus, 1982. 480 p.: ill.

Up-to-date dictionary on computer and telecommunications terminology, with acronyms that go with new developments: RAM, LED, ROM, etc. Many helpful technical diagrams. Spanish computer terminology would seem to be more advanced, with words for software and computer science.

4620 Guérios, Rosario Farani Mansur. Dicionário etimológico de nomes e sobrenomes. 3a ed., rev. e aum. São Paulo: Editôra Ave Maria, 1981. 267 p.: bibl.

Study that might have been called *Antroponímia.* Writer shows that names come from so many different sources: moral qualities (Tranquillus), physical traits (Albinus), chronology of birth (Tertius), trades (Geógios), religious appellations (Carmen), etc. Vocabulary itself lists name, nickname, national origin, meaning.

4621 Luna, Eury Pereira. Terminglês: glossário de expressões inglesas de uso corrente no comércio exterior. 2a ed. Rio de Janeiro: Livros Técnicos e Científicos Editôra, 1983. 114 p.: bibl.

Very useful manual for those engaged in US-Brazilian trade and commerce.

4622 Mendonça, André Luiz Dumortout de and Alvaro Thomaz Gonçalves. Dicionário de sociedades comerciais e mercado de capitais. Rio de Janeiro: Forense, 1983. 823 p.: index.

Dictionary of very extended definitions of the terminology of the stock market, so thorough in its discussion of entries such as *acionista* that it recites regulations, laws, and practices related to each item.

4623 Schlesinger, Hugo and Humberto Pôrto. Crenças, seitas e símbolos religiosos. São Paulo: Edições Paulinas, 1983. 386 p.: bibl.

Result of great deal of investigation, this collection of extended definitions and asides goes into beliefs, sects, and symbols of many parts of the world. Of special interest is the attention given to religions and beliefs of African origin that are still extant in Brazil, including voodoo.

4624 Schwab, Artur. Novíssimas louçanias de linguagem. Rio de Janeiro: F. Alves, 1982. 116 p. (Loućanias de linguagem)

This is what might be called in English, a filigree of vivacious phrases. Author has selected 100 pithy phrases from famous authors, defined each and then adds eight-10 examples of use of the *frase*: Oh! Espetáculo, a todos as luzes, Admirável! *"A todas as luzes* é locução adverbial equivalente a *sob todos os aspectos,* . . . ." This would be followed by nine examples of the use of *todas as luzes.*

4625 Serpa, Oswaldo. Dicionário de expressões idiomáticas: inglês-português/ português-inglês. 4a ed. Rio de Janeiro: FENAME, 1982. 373 p.

Very good collection of idiomatic expressions in two languages, including even "Fly the coop" and "That's the way the cookie crumbles." It is to be noted that many of the English expressions are British rather than American, the latter being indicated by *US.* Regional and slang expressions have special indicators.

4626 Silva, Felisbelo da. Dicionário de gíria: gíria policial, gíria dos marginais, gíria humorística. São Paulo: Papelivros, 1982? 112 p.

Author claims that slang or jargon of the underworld, of the *antisociales,* the *caló* of the Spanish-speaking countries, has become so popular that it is almost impossible to carry on a conversation without one of these terms escaping. Author is a detective.

4627 Soares, Oswaldo. Pequeno dicionário burguês-proletário. Rio de Janeiro: Civilização Brasileira, 1983. 371 p.: bibl.

Fascinating vocabulary of political terminology, with two definitions for each entry, one bourgeois, the other proletarian. Thus two attitudes, two ideological reactions are described in detail for each term defined: *comunismo, parlamentarismo, família, ideologia, fascismo, estado, economia.* Difference turns out to be that one definition is traditional or Catholic, the other Marxist in most cases. Marx and Engels are often quoted.

4628 Taylor, James Lumpkin. Dicionário metalúrgico: inglês-português, português-inglês. São Paulo: Associação Brasileira de Metais, 1981. 619 p.

What would seem to be a rather complete vocabulary, notable for its sub-meanings and applications. Author was experienced translator and World War I veteran, private secretary of Gen. Pershing, and later recipient of Ordem do Cruzeiro do Sul do Governo Brasileiro.

4629 Terminologia da formação profissional. Brasília: Ministério do Trabalho, Secretaria de Mão-de-Obra, Formação de Mão-do-Obra, 1981. 53 p.: bibl.

Claimed to be first document that gives information on terminology used by the Sistema Nacional de Formação de Mão-de-Obra (SNFMO). Put out by Secretariat of Labor of Brazil, book deals with problems associated with training, qualifications, and acceptance of elements of the population going into the labor or professional working forces: information, technical schools, specialization, contracts, etc.

4630 Tito Filho, Arimatéia. Viagem ao dicionário. v. 2. Teresina: Companhia Editôra do Piauí, 1973–1983. 67 p.

Analysis of certain words that author believes are often misunderstood, misused, or not adequately defined in the dictionary.

PORTUGUESE SYNTAX

4631 Azevedo, Milton M. Loss of agreement in Caipira Portuguese (AATSP/H, 67:3, Sept. 1984, p. 403–409)

As in other Romance languages, there is number agreement between the head noun phrase and modifiers in Brazilian Portuguese, however, author finds much deviation among educated and semi-educated speakers, and frequency of deviant noun phrases seems to be in inverse proportion to formality of situation. Such sentences as these are heard: *Tem aí umas vaca gorda; essas semente velha não presta.* Since these are heard among the educated, they must constitute a feature beyond mere carelessness. Azevedo believes that it is a matter of code-switching, whose sociolinguistic import may eventually be known through more research.

4632 Em busca de uma "sintaxe" perdida: reflexões e depoimentos sobre o ensino da língua portuguesa, na escola de 10., 20. e 30. graus. Fortaleza: Imprensa Universitária,

Univ. Federal do Ceará, 1981. 86 p. (Col. Documentos universitáros; 9)

Series of recommendations designed to improve ultimately the teaching of Portuguese grammar in Brazil. Deals with training of teachers, advocacy of core of studies that might become general in the nation, studies that might improve methodology and make instructors aware of innovations. Indications are that present training and instruction are anything but satisfactory. Claims general ability to write compositions today is a disaster.

4634 Jensen, John B. Brazilian classroom address and multiple extra-linguistic factors (Hispanic Linguistics [Univ. of Pittsburgh, Pittsburgh, Pa] 1:2, 1984, p. 229–225)

Form of address used between teachers and students in Brazil is a sensitive measure of degree to which the semantics of "power" and "solidarity" function in modern Brazilian Portuguese, since the situation is by definition one of power difference. A written questionnaire was used in four areas of Brazil: Rio, São Paulo, Ceará, and Rio Grande do Sul. Informants indicated the address they would use toward and receive from four different teachers, and represented three social classes, three age groups, and two sexes for each of the four locations. Since Portuguese itself offers many address possibilities that do not exist in other languages, and since there is a sense of social class, and since there are several areas involved, a very complicated picture of power and solidarity emerges.

4635 Koike, Dale April. Differences and similarities in men's and women's directives in Carioca Brazilian Portuguese (AATSP/H, 69:2, May 1986, p. 387–394)

Departing from R. Lakoff's *Language and woman's place* (New York, 1975), author sets out to test Lakoff's claim that in English, men's language is more assertive than that of women, which is polite and non-assertive, especially in the use of tag questions (e.g., John is here, isn't he?). In Brazilian Portuguese the matter is complicated by the importance of speech register (i.e., the relation between speaker and hearer), men and women dealing with hierarchies of social power in ways causing them to be perceived as more or less assertive when they speak. More men are not comfortable with hierarchies of social power in addressing people of less or equal

power and use strategies to neutralize social distance. More women express directives more directly than men to those of higher power positions and somewhat less directly to a peer.

4636 Koike, Dale April. Register, social variables, and variation of the infinitive in Brazilian Portuguese (AATSP/H, 68:1, March 1985, p. 134–142)

Data collected here suggest that linguistic variation is correlated with social variables, speech register, and linguistic variables (sentence structure) in Carioca Portuguese. In tests of inflected infinitive, middle-middle and lower-middle economic groups tend to use it hypercorrectly, which may indicate a conscious monitoring of speech because one is using an unfamiliar structure, but one can exercise the use of grammatical rule that has been mastered.

4636a Melo, Lélia Erbolato. Caracterizações gerais das vozes em português (SBPL/RBL, 7:1, 1984, p. 127–134, bibl.)

Interesting attempt to present a semantic-syntactic model of type proposed by Bernard Pottier on the basis of "voices:" *existencial* (Eis um gato); *equativo* (O gato é um animal doméstico); *situativo* (O gato está no jardim); *descritivo* (O gato é negro); *possessivo* (O gato tem bigode); *subjetivo* (O gato olha o rato).

4637 Sabatini, R. Nicholas. The Portuguese personal infinitive vs. its absence in Spanish (AATSP/H, 67:2, May 1984, p. 245–248)

Points out to serious students of Portuguese something of the origin and use of the personal infinitive as a divergence from usage in other Romance languages, especially Spanish, and to appreciate its ability to dispense with, to a degree, subjunctive clauses and rigid requirements of sequence of tenses.

CREOLE

4638 Bilby, Kenneth M. How the "older heads" talk: a Jamaican Maroon spirit possession language and its relationship to the Creoles of Suriname and Sierra Leone (NWIG, 57:1/2, 1983, p. 37–87, appendices, bibl.)

In Jamaica's interior exist four major Maroon communities, inhabited by descendants of slaves who escaped from 17th- and 18th-century plantations and gained their freedom by treaty in 1739. Moore Town, Charles Town, and Scott's Hall are typical settlements and their inhabitants are distinguishable from their non-Maroon neighbors by a number of linguistic features, and have been described as centers of linguistic conservatism. One aspect is the Kromanti ceremony, studied by author in 1977–78 and centered around the possession of participants by ancestral spirits. Ancestors have their own form of speech, and it is this that must be used to communicate with them, however, it turns out to be a "middle" language between the living and the departed; an entrée into the past, as it were. Article has excellent notes, transcriptions of taped dialogue and good glossaries of each of the three towns. For ethnologist's comment, see *HLAS 47:1019.*

4639 Blanchard, Teódulo. Creole haitiano: vocabulario clasificado y avance gramatical. Santo Domingo: El Autor, 1983. 117 p.: bibl.

Rather unusual case of a text on Haitian Creole in Spanish! Writer insists that while in Haiti one calls the language simply Creole, it should be designated as Haitian Creole. Includes index of topically-ordered vocabulary: *Dias de la semana, el tiempo, artesanos, frutas, carnes,* etc. Vocabulary has Spanish on left, Creole on right.

4640 Brautigam-Beer, Donovan. La influencia de las lenguas africanas en Nicaragua (BNBD, 51, enero/feb. 1983, p. 15–16, table)

Writing with an anti-capitalist slant, author describes how the history of slavery finally brought to Nicaragua an English Creole, widely spoken along the Atlantic coast south of the region where Mísquito is spoken. He lists 20 words, giving the English, Mískito, Spanish, and African language and where it is spoken. Indications are that his source is in English.

4641 Carew, Joy Gleason. Language and survival: will Sranan Tongo, Surinam's *lingua franca*, become the official language? (UWI/CQ, 28:4, Dec. 1982, p. 1–15)

Arguments pro and con, a problem faced by other independent Caribbean societies—whether the languages of the European colonizer or that developed locally

should become the official vehicle of communication. Suggestions for rendering the local language capable of expressing new ideas and concepts are offered. [E.O. Davie]

4642 Carib. West Indian Assn. for Commonwealth Literature and Language Studies. No. 3, 1983-. Kingston.

Issue consists of articles by highly considered Creolists: R. Allsopp "The Lexicography of Creolized English as a Cultural Integrator in the Caribbean;" I.E. Robertson "The Dutch Linguistic Legacy in Guyana: Berbice and Skepi Dutch;" V. Pollard "Figurative Language in Jamaican Creole;" L.D. Carrington "Preparing a Creole for a Developmental Task: the Case of Antillean Creole French;" and several others.

4643 Castillo Mathieu, Nicolás del. El léxico negro-africano de San Basilo de Palenque (ICC/T, 39, 1984, p. 80–169, bibl.)

First notices of Palenquero date from about 1600. Community still has about 3000 inhabitants, all very black and of a distinct personality. They are well known in Barranquilla, Cartagena, and Venezuela as fruit vendors. Their vocabulary is especially well documented in matters of etymology and references and is ordered by African languages: *bantuismos, carabalismos.* Author has a separate section on "Afronegrismos o Indigenismos Usados en la Costa Atlántica, pero Desconocidos en Palenque," and others found in his book, *Esclavos negros en Cartagena y sus aportes léxicos* (Bogotá: 1982). One finds here such common terms as, *bemba, congo, marimba, cumbia.* Bibliography is excellent.

Devonish, Hubert. Creole languages and the process of socioeconomic domination in the Caribbean: a historical review. See *HLAS 47:1044.*

4644 Ferrol, Orlando. La cuestión del origen y de la formación del Papiamento. The Hague, The Netherlands: Smits Drukkers-Uitgevers BV, 1982. 93 p.: bibl. (Univ. van de Nederlandse Antillen; 4)

Book takes up various theories as to origin of Papiamentu: African Portuguese, Spanish origin, or Caribbean Spanish origin, and succeeds in presenting ample testimony of the fact that there are very few Portuguese terms as it is spoken today, and that the grammar may be more African than European. Ferrol finally concludes that it was and is a Spanish Creole, formed in the beginning, before Dutch occupation, on the three islands of Aruba, Bonaire, and Curaçao.

4645 Joly, Luz Graciela. Implicaciones sociolingûísticas del juego de congos en la Costa Abajo de Panamá (LNB/L, 338/339, mayo/junio 1984, p. 25–55, bibl., ill., map)

Intriguing study of ritualistic language of Afro-Hispanic population of the *Costa Abajo*, or northern coast of central Panama. Some features of speech are frequent use of proverbs, use of "colonial" words, tendency to stress antepenultimate syllable of such verb forms as trabájemos, allophonic occurrence of /l/ for /r/, the loss of /d/ between vowels. The Juego de Congos takes place in various places between the eve of San Sebastián and Martes de Carnaval. One of the participants' speech: *Cúchoso la purawa de lo que mi tene la chakere de mutene en la tarengo de masoto*, which is to say, *Escucha la palabra de lo que tiene la casa de ustedes en el terreno de nosotros.* Recordings were made on the spot in 1979 and 1980.

4646 Kremnitz, Georg. Français et créole: ce qu'en pensent les enseignants; le conflit linguistique à la Martinique. Hamburg, FRG: H. Buske, 1983. 343 p.: bibl., ill. (Kreolische Bibliothek, 0720–9983; 5)

Main concern is linguistic conflict on the island of Martinique and other parts of the Lesser Antilles, a situation that is described at times as even dangerous. Opposition to learning French is strong. On the other hand, it is recognized that French is essential for outside communication. Recommends that Creole be used up to a certain point and that plans be discussed objectively with all concerned.

4647 Lauriete, Gérard. Le créole de la Guadeloupe: l'enseignement du français à partir du créole. 2e éd. Pointe-à-Pitre: C.D.D.P., 1980. 127 leaves.

Recommendations for teaching French to children whose home language has been Creole: French, History of France, Geography of France, French songs, Natural Sciences.

4648 Lipski, John M. The speech of the *Negros Congos* of Panama: an Afro-Hispanic dialect (Hispanic Linguistics [Univ. of Pittsburgh, Pittsburgh, Pa.] 2:1, 1985, p. 23–47, appendices)

Afro-Colonial residents of Panama's Caribbean coast celebrate elaborate rituals during Carnival season, the *congo* games, which reenact aspects of life in colonial Panama. Part of the ceremony is the *hablar congo*, a special speech mode used principally during the games, and occasionally at other times. Author suggests that the speech is an indirect derivative of earlier Afro-Hispanic Creole Spanish, supplemented by elements of distortion and exaggeration. The *congo* structures do not coincide in many respects with other Afro-Iberian Creoles, and Lipski believes that there may have been a wide range of earlier Creole Spanish manifestations in the Spanish American colonies. Three appendices of conversation or monologue support the findings.

4649 Megenney, William W. La influencia portugués en el palenquero colombiano (ICC/T, 38:3, sept./dec. 1983, p. 548–563)

Based on the 1970 book of Derek Bickerton and Aquiles Escalante, *Palenquero: a Spanish-based Creole of Northern Colombia.* Author examines the language that was the speech of sub-Saharan African slaves brought by the Portuguese to America with a view to pointing out surviving Portuguese elements: nasal vowels, *nacer* as a passive, second person plural pronoun *bo*, *haber* for *tener*, *ter* for *hay*. Megenney believes, as do others, that this is a restructured original Portuguese Creole, now thought of as Spanish.

4650 Megenney, William W. Traces of Portuguese in three Caribbean creoles: evidence in support of the monogenetic theory (Hispanic Linguistics [Univ. of Pittsburgh, Pittsburgh, Pa.] 1:2, 1984, p. 177–189)

Author believes that evidence of Portuguese elements at all linguistic levels in three Caribbean Creoles—Papiamentu, Palenquero, and Afro-Cuban Creole—support a monogenetic theory of common Luso origin for Spanish-based Creole languages presently extant in the Caribbean basin. One finds more Portuguese elements in Papiamentu than in Palenquero and more in the latter than in Afro-Cuban. Megenney thinks that a Portuguese-based reconnaissance language of the 15th century was brought to America by sub-Saharan slaves.

4651 Mirville, Ernst. Kreyòl lessons for English speaking people. Port-au-Prince: Enstiti Lengistik Aplike Pòtoprens, 1982. 120 p.: ill., map, music (Siwolin; 1. Col. Coucouille)

French Creole lessons belong to a series, *Siwolin*, and are designed for English-speaking people, the first book of several on language and culture. One learns to pronounce, to converse, to sing folk songs, also that the donkey says *hi an*!

4652 Papiamentu: problems and possibilities: papers presented at the conference on Papiamentu, "Papiamentu: Problema i Posibilidat." Organized by the Univ. of the Netherlands Antilles and the Instituto pa Promoshon i Estudio di Papiamentu, 4–6 June 1981. Zutphen, The Netherlands: Walburg Pers, 1983. 96 p.: bibl., ill.

Collection of papers presented at Conference "Papiamentu: Problemi i Posibilidat" (Curaçao, June 4–6, 1981). This language is spoken by some 200,000 in Aruba, Bonaire, and Curaçao, three Leeward Islands of the Netherlands Antilles. Papers cover mostly educational problems such as fact that Papiamentu has not been granted any function in the educational system, although most teachers feel need to achieve real communication with the children and are inclined to use Papiamentu more and more. Prins-Winkel, Valeriano and Muller directly address problems associated with the present educational system and its failure to integrate the native language.

4653 Pollard, Velma. Frederic G. Cassidy: dictionary-maker; interview (IJ/JJ, 16:2, May 1983, p. 11–19, ill.)

Interview with author of *Jamaica Talk* (1961, 1971) reveals interesting techniques for collecting on-the-spot entries for a regional dictionary. Lexicographer explains how difficult it is to determine origins of African words, since many of them were quite general throughout West Africa in the slave trade before they were brought to America (e.g., *yam*).

4654 Pollard, Velma. Words sounds: the language of Rastafari in Barbados and St. Lucia (IJ/JJ, 17:1, Feb. 1984, p. 57–62, bibl., ill.)

Brief description of what has been called a "political cult," "escapist movement," and "curious ideational synthesis."

The Rastafari language or speech of those who share the vision of Rasta philosophically but who speak "stepped up" Jamaican Creole. The sound /l/ is important and there is a battery of l-words. Vocabulary items: *ital* (vital, pure, natural); *lotal* (unclean); *heights* (to understand); *sip* (to eat, drink); *dub* (to cook); *iration* (creation, time); *bashi* (calebash, gourd); *ombre* (to be aggressive; an aggressor). Pollard believes that Rastafari has been dynamic enough to move outside Jamaica and is more than a passing local slang.

4655 Poullet, Hector; Sylviane Telchid; and Danièle Montbrand. Dictionnaire des expressions du créole guadeloupéen. Fort-de-France: Hatier Antilles, 1984. 349 p.: ill.

Well ordered vocabulary preceded by section on pronunciation, another on grammar, and then the vocabulary itself, featured by the Creole term in bold face, the French translation, followed by examples of usage in both Creole and French, often several illustrations to show shades of meaning. Work has good list of proverbs with French equivalents as well as common idioms and what are called *Comparaisons courantes: Blan: Tout biten blan kon koton* (Tout est blanc comme du coton).

4656 Raymond, Roc J. Du créole au français: petit guide pratique, où certains mots, expressions et proverbes créoles trouvent leurs équivalences françaises. 2e éd. Port-au-Prince: Editions Fardin, 1983. 6, 333 p.: bibl.

Handy guide to words, expressions, proverbs of Haitian Creole with their French equivalents. Shades of meaning are given in many cases.

4657 Régulo Pérez, Juan. Afroamericanismos léxicos en el español de Canarias (*in* Coloquio de Historia Canario-Americana, 4th, Las Palmas, Spain, 1980. Cuarto Coloquio de Historia Canario-Americana. Coordinación y prólogo de Francisco Morales Padrón. Las Palmas, Spain: Ediciones del Excelentísimo Cabildo Insular, 1982, p. 763–782)

Stresses fact that the Canary Islands were a bridge between Sevilla and America during the colonial period, with traffic going both ways. Author examines several terms that may have gone back and forth between Africa and America by way of the Canarias during centuries of the slave trade and use of a rather extensive Portuguese *criollo* language: *bamba*, a coin or piece of metal; *funche*, a type of food; *pinga*, penis; *singar*, to fornicate. The last word may very well be the origin of Mexico's famous *chingar*.

4658 Rickford, John R. Standard and non-standard language attitudes in a Creole continuum. S.l.: Univ. of the West Indies, School of Education *for the* Society for Caribbean Linguistics, 1983. 27 p.: bibl., ill. (Occasional paper/The Society; 16)

Author insists that we must recognize language attitudes, which are multidimensional, and more complex and ambiguous than is normally assumed: "Creole is bad, standard is good," is a common attitude, and this attitude is extended to things designated by one or the other. A Creole dish is not as good as a standard one, and terms used by cane-cutters are automatically inferior to those used by office workers in the same society. One intervening variable is the *dimension* at which attitudes are tapped, such as occupational stratification or social class. This work is typical of a trend in sociolinguistics: examination of variables and bases for variation.

Studies in Caribbean languages. See *HLAS* 47:1134.

4659 Trouillot, Hénock. Les limites du créole dans notre enseignement. Port-au-Prince: Imprimerie des Antilles, 1980. 85 p.

Author makes plea for the study of French in an island that is almost universally Creole in speech: limits of Creole in communication with the outside; allocation of functions, so to speak, for both languages; review of certain writers who have contributed in Creole.

4660 Winford, Donald. The linguistic variable and syntactic variation in Creole continua (LINGUA, 62:4, April 1984, p. 267–288, bibl.)

An achievement of sociolinguistic research has been to show that fluctuation in language use traditionally referred to as free variation was in fact not free at all, but correlated with a variety of linguistic and extra-linguistic factors. Labov, *The social stratification of English in New York City* (1966), conceived of variants of a variable as socially and stylistically different alternative but linguistically equivalent ways of "saying the same thing." Originally this concept was applied only to phonological data, but it was soon extended to morphological and syntactic levels of structure. Winford shows difficulties of defining a syntactic variable in Creole continua: three Creole versions of the sentence, "I want (to be/turn a) nurse, teacher" and then raises the relationship among them. Concludes that although phonological variants are not hard to classify socially or stylistically, there is not yet any basis of equivalence between syntactic variants.

4661 Winford, Donald. The syntax of *Fi* complements in Caribbean English (LSA/L, 61:3, Sept. 1985, p. 588–624)

Describes a number of complement types in which the particle *fi* functions in Caribbean English Creole or CEC. Understanding syntax of the types lies in the variety and ambivalence of *fi*'s functions: Directional, *gaan fi riif* (going to the reef); Genetive, *dat a fi mi buk* (that's my book); Dative, *ai me fried fi i sniek* (I was afraid of the snake). Study provides evidence that CEC grammar is radically different from that of SE (Standard English), and poses a challenge for describing CEC speakers' linguistic competence.

JOURNAL ABBREVIATIONS
LANGUAGE

AATSP/H Hispania. American Assn. of Teachers of Spanish and Portuguese. Univ. of Cincinnati. Cincinnati, Ohio.

AHL/B Boletín de la Academia Hondureña de la Lengua. Tegucigalpa.

BNBD Boletín Nicaragüense de Bibliografía y Documentación. Banco Central de Nicaragua, Biblioteca. Managua.

CH Cuadernos Hispanoamericanos. Instituto de Cultura Hispánica. Madrid.

CIDG/O Orbis. Centre international de dialectologie générale. Louvain, Belgium.

CM/NRFH Nueva Revista de Filología Hispánica. El Colegio de México. México.

CPES/RPS Revista Paraguaya de Sociología. Centro Paraguayo de Estudios Sociológicos. Asunción.

CSIC/RFE   Revista de Filología Española. Consejo Superior de Investigaciones Científicas, Patronato Menéndez Pelayo, Instituto Miguel de Cervantes. Madrid.

FFCLM/A   Alfa. Univ. de São Paulo, Faculdade de Filosofia, Ciências e Letras. Marília, Brazil.

HR   Hispanic Review. Univ. of Pennsylvania, Dept. of Romance Languages. Philadelphia.

ICC/T   Thesaurus. Boletín del Instituto Caro y Cuervo. Bogotá.

IJ/JJ   Jamaica Journal. Institute of Jamaica. Kingston.

LING   Linguistics. Mouton. The Hague, The Netherlands.

LINGUA   Lingua. North-Holland Publishing Co. Amsterdam.

LNB/L   Lotería. Lotería Nacional de Beneficencia. Panamá.

LSA/L   Language. Journal of the Linguistic Society of America. Waverly Press, Inc. Baltimore, Md.

NWIG   Nieuwe West-Indische Gids. Martinus Nijhoff. The Hague, The Netherlands.

PAN/EL   Estudios Latinoamericanos. Polska Akademia Nauk (Academia de Ciencias de Polonia), Instytut Historii (Instituto de Historia). Warszawa.

SBPL/RBL   Revista Brasileira de Lingüística. Sociedade Brasileira para Professores de Lingüística. São Paulo.

UCLV/I   Islas. Univ. Central de las Villas. Santa Clara, Cuba.

UCNSA/SA   Suplemento Antropológico. Univ. Católica de Nuestra Señora de la Asunción, Centro de Estudios Antropológicos. Asunción.

UEN/LS   Lateinamerika Studien. Univ. Erlangen-Nürnberg, Sektion Lateinamerika. Nürnberg, FRG.

UNAM/AL   Anuario de Letras. Univ. Nacional Autónoma de México, Facultad de Filosofía y Letras. México.

UNC/RN   Romance Notes. Univ. of North Carolina, Dept. of Romance Languages. Chapel Hill.

UWI/CQ   Caribbean Quarterly. Univ. of the West Indies. Mona, Jamaica.

UY/R   Revista de la Universidad de Yucatán. Mérida, Mexico.

ZRP   Zeitschrift für Romanische Philologie. Tübingen, FRG.

LITERATURE

SPANISH AMERICA: General

SARA CASTRO-KLAREN, *Professor of Hispanic and Italian Studies, The Johns Hopkins University*

THIS BIENNIUM THE FIELD has seen the publication of several important studies that attempt to establish all encompassing structures for Latin American literature. Angel Rama's "La Literatura en su Marco Antropológico" (item **5038**) offers a sobering thesis on the transferral of European 19th-century pessimism and racism into the mind set of the Latin American *pensadores* of the last century. In his *Transculturación narrativa en América Latina* (item **5041**) as well as in his "Literatura y Cultura en América Latina" (item **5039**), Rama delves deeply into the will for originality that informs and shapes the history of the literary tradition in Brazil as well as that of the Spanish-speaking countries of this hemisphere.

In *Poetics of change: the new Spanish-American narrative* (item **5033**), as well as in "La Escritura Hispanoamericana: un Modelo Virtual" (item **5032**), Julio Ortega deals with the prevalence of aesthetic and cultural models that exist and determine the kinds of works produced in Latin America. According to his thesis there is a utopic model, a mythical model, etc. Some are themselves modeled on the works of key writers such as Inca Garcilaso, Borges, or Sarduy. Each essay, while offering an intriguing theoretical proposition, is also a penetrating reading of the work of the particular writer chosen as model. Ortega's approach is quite divorced from the more historical and broad social outlines used by Rama and also by Antonio Cornejo Polar in his *Sobre la literatura y crítica latinoamericana* (item **5009**).

A very new, suggestive, and useful essay is provided by Raúl Bueno Chávez who in "Sobre la Nueva Novela y la Nueva Crítica Latinoamericana" (item **5005**) demonstrates that Octavio Paz's assertion about the absence of criticism in Spanish America is no longer a viable statement. It is ironic that such an article should appear at this particular time, a period that witnessed the death of two of the most influential modern critics produced by Spanish America: Angel Rama and Emir Rodríguez Monegal.

More concise and more precisely focused are the readings by Paul Dixon on ambiguity in four Latin American novels (item **5012**) and the essays of González Echevarría in *Isla a su vuelo fugitivo* on questions of Cuban literature (item **5017**). One of the most important books published in this biennium, edited by Hans Bernhard Möeller, is *Latin America and the literature of exile* (item **5022**) and consists of a series of essays which place the issue at the crossroads of human history while offering important comparative cases.

Another notable development of these two years is the publication of anthologies and studies of women writers. At least two very important anthologies: *Las mujeres cuentan* (item **5018**) and *Mujeres en espejo* (item **5028**) have appeared in Argentina and Mexico, respectively. Along with these, a more disparate set of collections of studies on women writers has also been issued in this biennium. However, none of them treat the corpus of writings by women in a systematic way. Different questions and different approaches are used in each article, so that the collections of studies lack coherence as a body of knowledge. In spite of this common failing, *Women in Hispanic literature: icons and fallen idols*, edited by Beth Miller (see *HLAS 46: 5027*), includes some of the better individual contributions. Among critical essays on women's writings, those by Elena Poniatowska (item **5036**) and Cristina Peri Rossi (item **5035**) are of particular importance, because they address the place and the nature of such writing and discard persuasively the notion of a so-called "feminine" writing. Ironically, the broadly based attempts to reconceptualize Latin American literature described in the first paragraph of this essay, fail to take into consideration the contributions of women writers or critics who are studying such female texts.

I wish to thank Benigno Sánchez-Eppler for his assistance in preparing this contribution.

5001 Alfi, David et al. El comic es algo serio. Prólogo de Paco Ignacio Taibo II. México: Ediciones Eufesa, 1982. 198 p.: bibl., ill. (Col. Comunicación)

Collection of 17 essays that examine the comic strip as a cultural product. Some are reprints of previously published articles and/or parts of books (e.g., Mattelart) by well known students of the mass media. Some very thoughtful essays discuss the nature of the comic and its ideological content for mass consumption. Pt. 1 of the collection, "Apreciaciones Teóricas," is especially useful.

5002 Almarza, Sara. La frase "nuestra América:" historia y significado (UTIEH/C, 43, 1984, p. 5–22)

Documents uses of phrase "nuestra América." Explores its various meanings and ideological shades from the 17th century to Martí's own works. Very useful.

5003 Aponte, Barbara B. The initiation archetype in Arguedas, Roa Bastos and Ocampo (LALR, 11:21, Fall/Winter 1982, p. 45–55)

Departs from the notion that the short story, like poetry, "keeps its connections with myth." Seeks archetypal structures that may underlie the short story. Draws largely from Cortázar's views on the matter. Posits that modern "initiation" rituals are "destructive of the child."

5004 Block de Behar, Lisa. Una retórica del silencio: funciones del lector y procedimientos de la lectura literaria. México: Siglo Veintiuno Editores, 1984. 258 p.: bibl., index (Lingüística y teoría literaria)

Highly theoretical but accessible exploration of the function of the reader in Borges, Felisberto Hernández, and Cortázar. Doctoral thesis (École des hautes études, Paris) well acquainted with contemporary linguistic philosophy.

5005 Bueno Chávez, Raúl. Sobre la nueva novela y la nueva crítica latinoamericanas (RCLL, 9:18, 1983, p. 81–85)

Important survey on a topic that demands more attention. Proposes that Octavio Paz's statement regarding the absence of criticism in Spanish America is no longer valid after the 1970s. Addresses problem of "theoretical dependency" in the criticism of Latin American literature. Change is ascribed to the "new novel," which inaugurates the space of a great literature. Very suggestive and useful study.

5006 Burgos, Fernando. Modernidad y neovanguardia hispanoamericanas (UA/REH, 18:2, mayo 1984, p. 207–220)

Exploration of the difference between modernity and neo-avant garde in Nicanor Parra, A. Jodorowski, and Julio Cortázar. All three writers are considered post-modern. The basis for differentiating between the two terms used in the essay is not very clear.

5007 Cobo Borda, J.G.; María Julia de Ruschi Crespo; and Ricardo H. Herrera. Usos de la imaginación. Buenos Aires: El Imaginero, 1984. 164 p.: bibl. (El Imaginero; 8)

Earnest, well written collaboration by "three poets who like to talk about literature." They write on Vallejo, García Márquez, Gorostiza, Villaurrutia and others with sensitivity and elegance. Deliberate effort to avoid use of jargon.

5008 Contemporary women authors of Latin America. Edited by Doris Meyer and Margarite Fernández Olmos. Brooklyn, N.Y.: Brooklyn College Press, 1983. 2 v.: bibl. (Brooklyn College Humanities Institute series)

Collection of disparate essays and testimonies on and by women writers. Essays on Bombal and Ocampo, Castellanos, Bullrich, Poniatowska and Ferré cover a variety of topics and use many literary approaches. Essays on Castellanos and Poniatowska could be read with profit by students in search of introductory materials.

5009 Cornejo Polar, Antonio. Sobre literatura y crítica latinoamericanas. Caracas: Ediciones de la Facultad de Humanidades y Educación, Univ. Central de Venezuela, 1982. 141 p.

Collection of essays previously published in journals. Book is organized around four important theoretical problems of literary criticism in Spanish America, especially Peru. Also includes essays on *indigenismo,* José Donoso, and recent Peruvian narrative. Volume stands as a coherent whole because of Cornejo's consistent and lucid historical approach. Important contribution to problems in literary criticism, national literatures, historical fiction, and *indigenismo.*

5010 Daus, Ronald. La literatura novísima de América Latina (ECO, 44:3, enero 1984, p. 305–320)

Catalog of literary production of younger writers for whom Cabrera Infante would be the master. Interest in the aberrant, underground, marginal, drug-ridden population of Latin American cities. Selection includes work by José Agustín, João Antônio, Ruben Fonseca.

5011 Dehennin, Elsa. De lo fantástico y su estrategia narrativa (Iberoromania [Max Niemeyer Verlag, Tübingen, FRG] 19, 1984, p. 53–65)

Exploration of the fantastic. Takes into account the history of the term, as well as Sarduy's, Todorov's, and Bessierc's contributions to the debate on the subject.

5012 Dixon, Paul B. Reversible readings: ambiguity in four modern Latin American novels. University: Univ. of Alabama Press, 1985. 185 p.: bibl., ill., index.

Ambitious approach to *Dom Casmurro, Grande sertão, Pedro Páramo* and *Cien años de soledad.* Resorting to well known cases of representational ambiguity (e.g., "reversible goblet"), author attempts to describe and convey the complex nature of these novels. Useful account of the role of ambiguity in literature.

5013 Donahue, Francis. Feminists in Latin America (UA/AQ, 41:1, Spring 1985, p. 38–60)

Short, elementary vignettes of Sor Juana Inés de la Cruz, Amanda Labarca, Eva Perón, and Rosario Castellanos.

5014 Fernández, Ariel. Tres en la literatura de nuestra América: Borges, Vargas Llosa, Campos Menéndez. Santiago: Ediciones Tamarugal, 1984. 90 p.: ill.

Three elegant and very general essays on the work of the three writers mentioned in the title. Journalistic in style and approach.

Foster, David William. Alternate voices in the contemporary Latin American narrative. See item **5657.**

Foster, David William. Bibliografía literaria hispano-americana, 1980–1981. See *HLAS 47:30.*

5015 Glickman, Nora. Aproximaciones al tema del Holocausto en la literatura latinoamericana (ECO, 42:3, enero 1983, p. 287–297)

Useful catalog of works about the Holocaust. Points out areas that need further research.

5016 Goloboff, Gerardo. Hispanoamérica en su literatura: fenómenos de dependencia, resistencia y autonomía (SP, 17, marzo 1982, p. 107–114)

In journalistic fashion, proposes thesis that a great deal of Latin American literature could be regarded as documentation of cultural failure and sociopolitical ineptitudes. This awareness leads to efforts to achieve cultural autonomy.

5017 González Echevarría, Roberto. Isla a su vuelo fugitiva: ensayos críticos sobre literatura hispanoamericana. Madrid: J.P. Turanzas, 1983. 264 p.: bibl. (Ensayos)

Collected articles form coherent whole in the shared investigation of themes of origin, history, and myth. Includes work on Martí, Carpentier, Lezama Lima, Sarduy,

Arenas, also Borges and Ortega. Important contribution to the field.

5018 Guido, Beatriz *et al.* 12 [Doce] mujeres cuentan. Buenos Aires: Ediciones La Campana, 1983. 206 p.: bibl.

Selection of short stories by Argentine women. Prologue advances thesis that there is no such thing as "feminine" writing only women writing. Selection brings together very different writers interested in a wide variety of aesthetic and historical problems. Each writer excells because of her individual, indelible qualities as narrator. Includes works by Syria Poletti, Marta Lynch, Elvira Orphee, Alicia Dujovne Ortiz, Liliana Heker, and Alicia Absatz. Very useful though it could have included more biobibliographic information on each writer.

5019 Henríquez Ureña, Pedro and **Alfonso Reyes.** Epistolario íntimo, 1906–1946. Prólogo de Juan Jacobo de Lara. Santo Domingo: UNPHU, 1981–1983. 3 v.

From their respective exiles, Pedro Henríquez Ureña and Alfonso Reyes tell each other about their participation in Spanish and Argentine academic Hispanism. Essential record of how much the two *maestros* shared between the two wars despite obvious distances.

5020 Jitrik, Noé. La memoria compartida. Xalapa, Mexico: Editorial Univ. Veracruzana, 1982. 254 p.: bibl., ill. (Biblioteca Univ. Veracruzana. Humanidades)

Collection of previously published essays on Neruda, Arlt, Sarmiento, and García Márquez. Each essay is informed by a different question and method. Substantial contribution to the field.

Krauze, Ethel. Intermedio para mujeres. See item **5187.**

5021 Larrea, Juan. Apogeo del mito. Prólogo de Teresa Waisman. México: CEESTEM: Editorial Nueva Imagen, 1983. 313, 3 p., 28 p. of plates: bibl., ill. (Col. Cuadernos americanos; 4)

Published as part of the celebration of the 40th anniversary of *Cuadernos Americanos*, this is a reissue of Juan Larrea's contributions to the journal. Welcome collection of this surrealist writer's scant work.

5022 Latin America and the literature of exile: a comparative view of the 20th-century European refugee writers in the New World. Edited by Hans-Bernhard Moeller. Heidelberg, FRG: C. Winter, 1983. 473 p.: bibl. (Reihe Siegen; 47. Romanistische Abteilung)

Collection of 19 essays transforms random area of inquiry into a structured field of study. Spanish, German, East European, and French emigré lives illustrate effects of exile on writer's condition and problem of limited audiences for dislocated voices. Essential for students of exile and literature of exile.

5023 Lienhard, Martin. Las huellas de las culturas indígenas o mestizas-arcaicas en la literatura escrita de Hispanoamérica (HISPA, 13:37, abril 1984, p. 3–13)

Novel and productive approach to questions of colonialism, transculturation, *mestizaje,* and syncretism. Tries to determine whether texts such as the 16th-century *mestizo* chronicles of Mexico or the narrative of Asturias and Arguedas represent a process of fusion between two cultures or a "literatura culta con interferencias indígenas."

5023a La Literatura latinoamericana como proceso. Coordinación de Ana Pizarro. Buenos Aires: Centro Editor de América Latina, 1985. 147 p. (Bibliotecas universitarias)

Refleja la tarea realizada en la reunión llevada a cabo en la Univ. de Campinas, Brasil (Oct. 1983) con el co-patrocinio de la Univ. de Simón Bolívar (Caracas) y la Asociación Internacional de Literatura Comparada, y el apoyo de UNESCO. Participaron: Angel Rama, Antônio Cândido, Domingo Miliani, José Luis Martínez, Beatriz Sarlo, Roberto Schwartz, Jacques Leenhardt, Carlos Pacheco y Ana Pizarro. Consigna los trabajos y algunos pasajes de la discusión de esta segunda reunión del proyecto sobre historia de la literatura latinoamericana. Valioso por los interrogantes que postula y por los avances hacia una formulación comparada de las literaturas latinoamericanas, por las reflexiones sobre visiones fragmentadas de las literaturas nacionales y por los planteos sobre periodización. Util, además, como barómetro de un sector de la crítica que plantea el estudio de la producción literaria dentro del amplio encuadre social que le confiere uno de sus sentidos centrales. [S. Sosnowski]

5024 Losada, Alejandro. La internacionalización de la literatura latinoamericana (UTIEH/C, 42, 1984, p. 15–40, bibl.)

Attempts to develop a scientific approach to the study of Latin American literature by proposing a highly structured organization of the discipline centered on why, when, and how this literature became an international phenomenon.

5025 MacAdam, Alfred J. The boom: a retrospective; interview with Emir Rodríguez Monegal (REVIEW, 33, Sept./Dec. 1984, p. 30–36)

Probably one of the last interviews with the late Rodríguez-Monegal, himself an essential participant in the making of the "boom." Interview covers the "boom" as a publishing phenomena. Traces the economic transformation of the work of some Latin American writers from an artisanal object into a commodity traded in the international market. Very informative.

5026 Menton, Seymour. El realismo mágico y la narrativa del asalto inminente (Iberoromania [Max Niemeyer Verlag, Tübingen, FRG] 19, 1984, p. 45–52)

Examines Cortázar's "Casa Tomada" and three European novels as a literary group in which protagonists are beset by mysterious forces that threaten the stability of their precarious isolation. Author presents magic realism as a common approach used to create effect and develop a theme of non-reality.

5027 Merrim, Stephanie. Logos and the word: the novel of language and linguistic motivation in *Grande sertão: veredas* and *Tres tristes tigres*. Berne: P. Lang, 1983. 106 p.: bibl. (Utah studies in literature and linguistics; 23)

Centers Latin American writing around the problem of an "unnamed reality." Proposes that "many recent Latin American novels have come to be known as novels of language" which take Joyce as their model and deemphasize the mimetic aspects of the text. Author's subtle and revealing analysis is at its best when discussing *Grande sertão: veredas* and *Tres tristes tigres*, partly because these two novels are linguistically self-conscious on both the thematic and the stylistic planes. Very good example of a careful examination of an important aspect of the Latin American novel.

5028 Mujeres en espejo. Introducción y selección de Sara Sefchovich. México:

Folios Ediciones, 1983. 1 v.: bibl. (Col. Narrativa latinoamericana; NL3)

Vol. 1 of anthology of contemporary women writers. Mixes several generations, styles, and themes without apparent selection criteria. Prologue presents a sociology of writing and of women as writers in the Western tradition. Points out that "el error principal que han hecho [cometido] las feministas sobre la existencia de una literatura femenina [es pensar] que solo se refiere a una clase social; la mujer que escribe: la burguesía." Unfortunately lacks biobibliographic information on each author. Includes Teresa de la Pana, Syria Poletti, Elsa Mujica, Alicia Dujovne-Ortiz, María Luisa Puga, Carmen Lyra, Nélida Piñón and many others. Very useful.

Muñoz, Braulio. Sons of the wind: the search for identity in Spanish American Indian literature. See *HLAS 47:8025.*

5029 Narrativa hispanoamericana, 1816–1981: historia y antología. v. 7, La generación de 1939 en adelante: Bolivia, Chile, Perú. Selección y edición de Angel Flores. México: Siglo Veintiuno Editores, 1983. 1 v.: bibl. (La Creación literaria)

Vol. 7 of new history and anthology of Spanish American literature undertaken by Angel Flores. Devoted to writers born after 1939, this volume is particularly welcome and useful as it includes introductions about and selections from authors excluded from existing anthologies. Unfortunately, it includes only *one* woman writer.

5030 Natella, Arthur. Aspectos neomedievales de la nueva narrativa latinoamericana (CH, 411, sept. 1984, p. 166–174)

Discusses symbolic, mythic, millenarian, and irrational aspects of Latin American literature as manifestations of a medieval mentality. Old thesis about Latin American cultural contents revisited.

5031 Novísimos narradores hispanoamericanos en *Marcha*, 1964–1980. Selección de Angel Rama. México: Marcha Editores, 1981. 349 p. (Col. Letras)

Not inclusive but exclusive sample of writers now in their 40s. All are well known in their own countries, but few, with exception of Manuel Puig, are internationally recognized. Reader will find selections from the works of Ivan Egüiz, Rafael Humberto Moreno-Díaz, Juan José Saer, Luis Britto-García, etc. Introduction is of special interest. Rama attempts to outline the criteria for the characterization of a new period of "impetuosa reinvención realista."

5032 Ortega, Julio. La escritura hispanoamericana: un modelo virtual (SP, 3, mayo 1978, p. 83–92)
Examines the works of the Inca Garcilaso, the chroniclers, and the works of modern writers such as Mariátegui and Cabrera Infante as if they constituted a continuity in the projection of an American culture. Proposes thesis that this continuing discourse generates utopias in order to understand lived experience.

5033 Ortega, Julio. Poetics of change: the new Spanish-American narrative. Translated from the Spanish by Galen D. Greaser and the author. Austin: Univ. of Texas Press, 1984. 192 p.: index (The Texas Pan American series)
Collection of essays previously published in Spanish on separate occasions and in journals. Each essay deals with a particular writer: Borges, Rulfo, García Márquez, Sarduy, etc. Each study represents the best that the semiological approach can bring to literary analysis. With deceptively simple language, the author delves into the core of each work or writer, examining each as a "modeling" influence on Spanish American modern letters.

5034 Paz, Octavio. Literatura de convergencias (ECO, 42:5, marzo 1983, p. 455–461)
Brief overview of contemporary Latin American literature. Discusses the demise of ideological art, proposing that artistic endeavors are becoming more exploratory and less pragmatic.

5035 Peri Rossi, Cristina. Literatura y mujer (ECO, 42:5, marzo 1983, p. 498–506)
Argues forcefully that there is no such thing as "feminine" literature and that to seek what is "feminine" by comparing works signed by male names and works signed by female names is absurd. Differentiates between what, on the one hand, has traditionally been regarded as "feminine" and the ensuing pejorative view of "feminine" writing and, on the other, writing by specific

women whose works are not marked by so-called "feminine" characteristics. Basic to any discussion of the question of women's writing.

5036 Poniatowska, Elena. Mujer y literatura en América Latina (ECO, 42:5, marzo 1983, p. 462–472)
Contends that the place of origin of women's writing must be a place of solidarity with the oppressed, because women are the single most consistently oppressed class in the world.

5037 Por una labor de investigación colectiva: encuentro en la redacción de críticos literarios latinoamericanistas de los países socialistas (URSS/AL, 4, abril 1984, p. 66–73, ill.)
Identifies some of the institutions, individuals, and activities which in socialist countries are dedicated to the study of Latin American literature. Informative.

5038 Rama, Angel. La literature en su marco antropológico (CH, 407, mayo 1984, p. 95–101)
Shows how the pessimism and racism of European 19th-century anthropology deeply influenced the thought of eminent Latin American *pensadores* (e.g., Silvio Romero, Alcides Arguedas, Federico Bulnes, José E. Rodó, Juan Marinello), who at the time attempted to formulate concepts such as "national culture," "literature," "character," etc. Warns that their mistaken approach should serve to caution against undue influence of purely theoretical interpretations "con que nos abastecemos." Learned, thoughtful, and challenging.

5039 Rama, Angel. Literatura y cultura en América Latina (RCLL, 9:18, 1983, p. 7–35)
Holds thesis that though born of the opulent cultural tradition of Spain and Portugal, Latin American letters "nunca se resignaron a sus orígenes y nunca se reconciliaron a su pasado ibérico." Traces history of Latin America's many literary movements, which author regards as a search for an autonomous origin. Such quests eventually bore fruit in the resulting avant-garde of the first half of the 20th century and the narrative originality of the second half. Fundamental and innovative analysis of Latin American history and literature.

Rama, Angel. Las máscaras democráticas del modernismo. See item **5700**.

5040 Rama, Angel. La modernización literaria latinoamericana: 1870–1910 (HISPA, 36, 1983, p. 3–19)

Author, a cultural historian, traces in novel ways how modernism developed in conjunction with the growth of the cities in the late 19th century. Connects urban growth to an "amplísima e indiscriminada incorporación de literatura moderna." Proposes the "modernistas," once again, as the founders of an autonomous literature.

5041 Rama, Angel. Transculturación narrativa en América Latina. México: Siglo Veintiuno Editores, 1982. 305 p.: bibl. (Crítica literaria)

Excellent collection of essays. First essay reconceptualizes the history of Latin American literature. Clears up many problems heretofore noted but thus far insufficiently resolved. Last two essays, especially written for this collection, set forth a new and intriguing thesis of the novel as the opera of the poor. Illuminating historical approach to the quesiton and role of myth(s) in the Latin American novel. Entire book dwells on the historical need for and achievement of originality in Latin American letters. A must for anyone seeking a modern understanding of Latin American literature and its current preeminence in the world.

5042 Siebenmann, Gustav. Die neu Literatur Latinamerikas: eine neue Weltliteratur? (Iberoromania [Max Niemeyer Verlag, Tübingen, FRG] 18, 1983, p. 139–149)

Overview of Latin American literature uses Rodó's *Ariel* as a starting point. Author deliberates about the identity of New World writing and its impact on world literature. [G.M. Dorn]

5043 Viñas, David et al. Más allá del boom: literatura y mercado. México: Marcha Editores, 1981. 326 p.: bibl. (Col. Letras)

Collection of papers presented at the Woodrow Wilson Center (Washington, 1979) on: "Beyond the Boom." Useful papers outline the "boom" as a publishing phenomena. Some study individual authors, others emphasize general cultural structures that generated and ended the "boom" (e.g., chapter by Jorge Aguilar Mora "Sobre el Lado Moridor de la Nueva Narrativa Hispanoamericana").

5044 Voices from under: the black narrative in Latin America and the Caribbean. Edited by William Luis. Westport, Conn.: Greenwood Press, 1984. 263 p.: bibl., ill., index (Contributions in Afro-American and African studies; 0069–9624; 76)

Consists of 13 contributions that examine literature of and about blacks in Latin America and the Caribbean. Informative editor's introduction presents full spectrum of studies (e.g., direct African influences, single work, area analysis). Essential for those interested in black studies as well as for Hispanic-Lusophone scholars wishing to incorporate French, English, and Dutch-speaking areas into a more cohesive field of study.

5045 Zeitz, Eileen M. La alienación femenina en dos cuentos hispano-americanos (UH/RJ, 33, 1982, p. 355–366)

Demonstrates how women's portrayal as alienated creatures in short stories by Rosario Castellanos and Sylvia Lago, reflects their oppression and alienation as social beings. Author confuses fiction with referent. The Spanish could be improved.

5046 Zemskov. The modern Latin American novel (USSR/SS, 14:4, 1983, p. 51–67)

In the context of Western tradition, draws interesting historical parallel between the development of the 19th-century Russian novel and the 20th-century Latin American novel. Contrasts their vigor with the decadence of the European and North American novel. Worthwhile example of Soviet criticism of Latin American materials.

Colonial Period

DANIEL R. REEDY, *Professor of Spanish, University of Kentucky*

SCHOLARLY ACTIVITY DEVOTED to Spanish American literature of the colonial period continues to flourish as never before. Whereas three decades ago only a handful of scholars were working in this field, the number of persons who identify themselves today as colonial-literature specialists continues to grow. In particular, it is gratifying to note the proportional increase of doctoral dissertations being completed on topics related to colonial letters and culture. These young scholars demonstrate a zeal for archival research and bring imaginative approaches to their critical analysis and interpretation.

The appearance of accessible editions of known writers and of newly discovered or "rediscovered" authors continues to prompt a corresponding flurry of research among students and established scholars. Such was the case in 1977, for example, when the publication of Pedro de Solís y Valenzuela's *El desierto prodigioso y prodigio del desierto* (see *HLAS 42: 5120*) led to the present book-length study by Manuel Briceño Jáuregui (item **5050**) and a lengthy article by Héctor Orjuela (item **5080**), who declares Solís y Valenzuela's text to be the "first Spanish American novel."

In the current listing, several editions of works by other important authors appear. José Anadón provides a study and the edited text of a novelesque tale found in Barrenechea y Albis's 17th-century chronicle (item **5093**). And Caracas-based Biblioteca Ayacucho has published three important editions of colonial texts: Antonio Lorenta Medina's edition of Carrió de la Vandera's *El Lazarillo de ciegos caminantes* (item **5095**); *Letras de la Audiencia de Quito: período jesuítico*, edited by Hernán Rodríguez Castelo (item **5098**), which contains works by prose writers as well as lyric poetry by Juan Bautista Aguirre; and the *Obra completa* of Juan del Valle y Caviedes (item **5103**), edited by this contributing editor. This critical edition of Caviedes's works provides textual variants based on eight known manuscripts of the Peruvian's verse and dramatic pieces.

Persons interested in the Quechua theatre of the colonial period will be pleased to find the five major works contained in the *Teatro quechua colonial* (item **5102**) translated and edited by Quechua specialist Teodoro L. Meneses. Among other texts, of special interest to the English-speaking readership is the bilingual anthology of Sor Juana's *Poems* (item **5101**), translated and edited by Margaret Sayers Peden. Her accomplishments as a translator are abundantly evident in this splendid English recreation of a number of Sor Juana's verses.

Sor Juana continues to be the single figure, among writers of the colonial period, whose works draw the most critical attention. Noteworthy among these studies are Lee Daniel's article on the use of the echo device in Sor Juana's dramatic works (item **5055**); Paul Dixon's examination of the significance of geometric models in her poetry (item **5056**); Frederick Luciani's revealing comments on the epigraph (item **5074**); and the exegetical study of the language of the *Primero sueño* in the book by Rosa Perelmuter Pérez (item **5083**).

The article by Pedro Lasarte on Rosas de Oquendo's *Sátira de las cosas que pasan en el Pirú* (item **5072**) offers noteworthy insights into the significance of this writer. We are hopeful, as well, that Lasatre will soon provide a reliable edition of the works of Rosas de Oquendo—a primary figure in the early development of satire in Spanish America. The two articles on the *Llanto de Panamá* (items **5065** and **5075**) bring to our attention information on a little-known compendium of Panamanian prose and verse which was first published in 1638 and reedited in 1984.

Two comprehensive studies deserve to be highlighted: the book on narrative discourse in the conquest of America by Beatriz Pastor (item **5082**) and Hernán Vidal's provocative sociohistorical study of three stages of development of colonial letters and culture in the works of several major writers (item **5113**).

INDIVIDUAL STUDIES

5047 Anadón, José. En torno a Mogrovejo de la Cerda, autor del XVII peruano (CAM, 254:3, mayo/junio 1984, p. 133–142)

Surveys information which has come to light on Juan Mogrovejo de la Cerda (1600?–90?), whose known works include *La endiablada, Dama muda, Elogios, El predicador,* and *Memorias de la gran ciudad del Cuzco.* Valuable data and references.

5048 Bénassy-Berling, Marie-Cécile. Más sobre la conversión de Sor Juana (CM/NRFH, 32:2, 1983, p. 462–471)

Posits the argument that Sor Juana's conversion in 1693–94 may have been more the result of religious and moral fervor in Mexico at the time than the product of religious coercion and persecution by male superiors as others have explained. Of interest to Sor Juana's biographers.

5049 Bost, David H. From conflict to mediation: humanization of the Indian in *Cautiverio feliz* (SECOLAS/SELA, 29:2/3, Sept./Dec. 1985, p. 8–15)

Bascuñán's *Cautiverio feliz* is seen as a work which humanizes the Indian while countering stereotypes established by such historiographers as Oviedo and Las Casas. Worthy contribution.

5050 Briceño Jáuregui, Manuel. Estudio histórico-crítico de *El desierto prodigioso y prodigio del desierto* de Don Pedro de Solís y Valenzuela. Bogotá: Instituto Caro y Cuervo, 1983. 540 p., 36 leaves of plates (some folded): bibl., ill., index (Publicaciones; 65)

Comprehensive study of life, cultural environment, and works of Pedro de Solís y Valenzuela (1624–1711), whose *El desierto prodigioso y prodigio del desierto* is a hybrid text of narrative, history, *costumbrismo,* and novelesque tales (see *HLAS 42:5120*). Extensive documentation and bibliographical sources enhance the high quality of this study.

5051 Cacho Vázquez, Xavier. Sor Juana y la liturgia. México: Instituto de Estudios y Documentos Históricos, Claustro de Sor Juana, 1981. 17 p.: bibl. (Serie Cuadernos; 11)

Offers a personal reading of Sor Juana's *villancicos* and *letras sacras* with emphasis on liturgical aspects of selected works. Author points to San Juan's *Apocalipsis* as the primary source of Sor Juana's ideas relating to Christian liturgy. Brief but interesting study.

5052 Carrillo, Francisco. Tesis, historia y fábula en la crónica de Pedro Pizarro (RCLL, 10:20, 1984, p. 29–43, appendices)

Focuses on narrative aspects of Pedro Pizarro's *Relación del descubrimiento y conquista de Perú* relative to the chronicler's manipulation of historical fact through the interpolation of anecdotal materials, legends, and fables.

5053 Chang-Rodríguez, Raquel. A propósito de Sor Juana y sus admiradores novocastellanos (IILI/RI, 51:132/133, julio/dic. 1985, p. 605–619)

Compares Sor Juana's literary and intellectual stature to that of her contemporaries: Juan del Valle y Caviedes and Luis Antonio Oviedo Herrera y Rueda, Conde de la Granja, who addressed laudatory poems to the Monja. Of general interest.

5054 Cisneros, Luis Jaime. Sobre Espinosa Medrano: el "toro celeste" y Góngora (IRA/B, 12, 1982/1983, p. 61–66)

Traces the image of the "toro celeste," as metaphor for St. Thomas, from Góngora (*Soledad primera*) through several of Espinosa Medrano's works. Where did the image originate, in Góngora or some other source? Of interest to the specialist.

5055 Daniel, Lee A. The use of echo in the plays of Sor Juana (*in* Louisiana Conference on Hispanic Languages and Literatures, 4th, New Orleans, 1983. Selected proceedings. Edited by Gilbert Paolini. New Orleans, La.: Tulane Univ., 1983, p. 71–78)

Treats the technique of the echo, or recapitulation device, in Sor Juana's *loas* and the *auto*, *El divino Narciso*. Source of this technique was probably Ovid and the antiphonal choirs of Calderón. Valuable contribution.

5056 Dixon, Paul B. Balances, pyramids, crowns, and the geometry of Sor Juana Inés de la Cruz (AATSP/H, 67:4, Dec. 1984, p. 560–566)

Examines geometric models in representative poems by Sor Juana, in particular the *Primero sueño*, and finds in her utilization of balanced syntax, images, and geometric patterns evidence of her search for the abstract, universal patterns, and laws of existence. Perceptive article.

5057 Felker, William L. Las coplas y octavas de Antonio Lazcama (RPC, 38:181, oct./dic. 1983, p. 84–87, ill.)

Brief introduction describes discovery of poems by Antonio Lazcama in the Archivo Centro-América in Guatemala. Lazcama is known only by name; his poems appear to be from the 17th or 18th century and are of a popular nature.

5058 Friedman, Edward H. The paradox of the word in Sor Juana's "En Perseguirme, Mundo" (UT/RCEH, 9:2, invierno 1985, p. 215–219)

Analysis of various aspects of Sor Juana's sonnet "En Perseguirme, Mundo . . ." with emphasis on a system of paradoxes in this poem and two others described generally as philosophical/moral sonnets.

5059 González, Aníbal. *Los infortunios de Alonso Ramírez* (HR, 51:2, Spring 1983, p. 198–204)

Posits that Sigüenza y Góngora's novelette has antecedents in two 16th-century camps: 1) the chronicles of the conquest and the novelesque lives of writers such as Alvar Núñez, Bernal Díaz, Santa Teresa, Jerónimo de Pasamonte; and 2) the picaresque novel, *Guzmán de Alfarache*.

5060 Gostantas, Stasys. *La endiablada* de Don Juan Mogrovejo de la Cerda y *El diablo cojuelo* de Luis Vélez de Guevara (Bulletin of Hispanic Studies [Institute of Hispanic Studies, Liverpool, England] 85:1/2, Jan./June 1983, p. 137–159)

Enlarges knowledge and understanding of Mogrovejo de la Cerda and his tale *La endiablada* (ca. 1626) which shows influences of Cervantes, Lope, Quevedo, and especially the picaresque tradition of Vélez de Guevara. Excellent article on little-known topic.

5061 Guerra Bravo, Samuel. Eugenio Espejo y sus cartas desde el "exilio" (BCE/C, 4:10, mayo/agosto 1981, p. 225–239)

Well documented account of aspects of life and activities of Ecuadorian writer and political figure, Eugenio de Santa Cruz y Espejo (1740–96). Several letters by Espejo, written in exile, are appended. Provides significant data on Espejo.

5062 Guibovich P., Pedro. Documentos inéditos para la biografía de Espinosa Medrano (IRA/B, 12, 1982/1983, p. 137–145, appendix)

Previously unpublished documents (a letter, a legal declaration, and a census statement) reveal new biographical evidence about Espinosa Medrano. Introductory essay outlines their importance; transcribed documents form an appendix. Of importance to the Peruvianist.

5063 Hampe Martínez, Teodoro. Agustín de Zárate: precisiones en torno a la vida y obra de un cronista indiano (UTIEH/C, 45, 1985, p. 21–36)

Adds documentation to information on life and works of Peruvian chronicler Zárate (ca. 1514–85?), author of *Historia del descubrimiento y conquista del Perú* (1555). Reveals more about Zárate's personality.

5064 Hanisch, Walter. El barroco jesuita chileno: siglos XVI y XVII (AHSI, 1984, 53:105, p. 161–191)

Examination of Baroque aspects of works by Alonso de Ovalle (*Histórica relación del Reino de Chile*) and Diego de Rosales (*Historia general del Reino de Chile, Flandes Indiano*). Valuable to the literary historian.

5066 Herman, Susan. Conquista y descubrimiento del Nuevo Reino de Granada: "doncella huérfana" (CBR/BCB, 20:1, 1983, p. 77–85)

Finds that the tone of Rodríguez Freyle's *Conquista y descubrimiento* is both ironic and erotic. Opinions are based on the image of the "doncella huérfana" which appears early in the chronicle and becomes a repeated topic in subsequent sections. Worthwhile observations.

5067 Invernizzi, Lucía. La representación de la tierra de Chile en cinco textos de los siglos XVI y XVII (UC/RCL, 23, abril 1984, p. 5–37)

Details several modes in which five 16th- and 17th-century writers depicted Chilean reality. Authors include P. de Valdivia, G. de Vivar, A. de Góngora y Marmolejo, A. de Ercilla y Zúñiga, and A. de Ovalle.

5068 Jakfalvi-Leiva, Susana. Traducción, escritura y violencia colonizadora: un estudio de la obra del Inca Garcilaso. Syracuse, N.Y.: Maxwell School of Citizenship and Public Affairs, 1984. 130 p.: bibl. (Latin American series; 7)

Examines concepts of linguistic theory in the works of the Inca Garcilaso to reveal his counter-conquest views against the corruption and ambition of the Spaniards. Uses methodological approach of post-structuralism and semantics. Worthwhile addition to bibliography on the Inca.

5069 Jitrik, Noé. Los dos ejes de la cruz: la escritura de apropiación en el *Diario*, el *Memorial*, las *Cartas* y el *Testamento* del Enviado Real Cristóbal Colón. México: ICUAP, Centro de Ciencias del Lenguaje, Editorial Univ. Autónoma de Puebla, 1983. 133 p.: bibl. (Biblioteca Francisco Javier Clavijero. Serie mayor. Col. Signo y sociedad; 7)

Studies the "epistomological archeology" of Columbus's *Memorial, Cartas,* and *Testamento.* Author follows basic premises of Michel Foucault (*L'archéologie de savoir*) to approach certain concepts in these writings. Interesting ideas, obscured at times by theoretical concerns and methodological practice.

5070 Johnson, Julie Greer. Bernal Díaz and the women of the conquest (HISP, 82, Sept. 1984, p. 67–77)

Examination of the portrayal of women in the *Historia verdadera* with primary attention to Doña Marina as both flesh-and-blood person and literary figure. Comparison of Marina to figures from *Sergas de Esplandián,* sequel to *Amadís,* provides interesting hypothesis of how Bernal Díaz fictionalized women in his chronicle.

5071 Kasen, Nancy M. La influencia de la revolución norteamericana en la ideo-logía de Fray Servando Teresa de Mier (CAM, 262 : 5, sept./oct. 1985, p. 178–185)

Examines four important stages in the evolution of Padre Mier's political philosophy. Sees influence of Benjamin Franklin, Thomas Paine, John Adams and others in the writing of this pre-independence Mexican.

5072 Lasarte, Pedro. Mateo Rosas de Oquendo: *La Sátira* y el carnaval (HR, 53 : 4, Autumn 1985, p. 415–436)

Excellent comments on Rosas de Oquendo's *Sátira de las cosas que pasan en el Pirú* (1598). Casts doubt on value of poem as a mere historical, social, or biographical document; emphasizes the popular/learned aspects of the text. Mentions his own edition and study of the *Sátira* in a 1983 dissertation.

5073 Lastra, Pedro. Espacios de Alvar Núñez: las transformaciones de una escritura (UC/RCL, 23, abril 1984, p. 89–102)

Points out serious textual discrepancies among editions of *Naufragios* and *Comentarios* by Alvar Núñez. Textual omissions in González Barcia's edition (1749) have been corrected only in part; new reliable editions are vital. Important essay for specialists.

5074 Luciani, Frederick. Sor Juana Inés de la Cruz: epígrafe, epíteto, epígono (IILI/RI, 51 : 132/133, julio/dic. 1985, p. 777–783)

Revealing examination of epigraphs added by Sor Juana's editors to the editions of her poems. Finds they are occasionally useful, at times inoffensive, but often tending to pervert the sense of her verses and the manner in which the poems are read.

5075 Miró, Rodrigo. Sobre poesía panameña de la colonia: a propósito del *Llanto de Panamá* (LNB/L, 346/347, enero/feb. 1985, p. 5–15)

Brief overview of poets from Panama's colonial past with textual examples cited from various figures. Celebrates the 1984 publication of the *Llanto de Panamá,* texts of prose and verse by various authors, first published in 1638 on the death of Governor Enriquez Anriquez. Contributes to knowledge of Panama's colonial literary heritage (see item **5090a**).

5076 Mora Valcárcel, Carmen de. Naturaleza y barroco en Hernando Domíngues Camargo (ICC/T, 38 : 1, enero/abril 1983, p. 59–81)

Analysis of Domínguez Camargo's descriptive techniques and rhetorical skill in the *Poema heroico* with emphasis on his ability to envision nature in different fashions. Valuable insights on this important poet.

5077 Moreno-Durán, Rafael Humberto. Rodríguez Camargo: un "trozo de púrpura" en la poesía barroca de la colonia americana (ECO, 43:260[2] junio 1983, p. 113–127)

Reviews several divergent opinions on the place of Domínguez Camargo as a poet of the Spanish American Baroque. Relies chiefly on other sources, in particular Lezama Lima. Of limited value to scholars.

5078 Ocasio, Rafael. *El Lazarillo de ciegos caminantes*: una visión de la organización social en el mundo virreinal (CAM, 251:4, julio/agosto 1985, p. 170–183)

Notes that primary importance of Carrió de la Vandera's work is to be found in its vision of viceregal society, reflecting social prejudices of the time rather than in the book's supposedly literary or scientific values. Enlightening interpretation.

5079 Olsen de Serrano Redonnet, María Luisa. ¿Quién fue el poeta limeño satirizado por Lavardén?: enfrentamiento con el Parnaso de Buenos Aires (IHAAER/B, 17:27, 1982, p. 239–290, appendix)

Reveals that the object of Manuel José de Lavardén's *Sátira* (1786) was the Peruvian Juan Manuel Fernández de Agüero y Echave, whose "anonymous" *décimas* sparked Lavardén's barbed reply. Well documented study of interest to specialist.

5080 Orjuela, Héctor H. *El desierto prodigioso y prodigio del desierto* de Pedro de Solís y Valenzuela: primera novela hispanoamericana (ICC/T, 38:2, mayo/agosto 1983, p. 261–324)

Introductory sections deal with early manifestations of the novelesque narrative during the colonial period with the corpus of the article devoted to an analysis of Solís y Valenzuela's *El desierto prodigioso y prodigio del desierto*, declaring it to be a true Baroque novel and the first Spanish American novel (see item **5050**).

5081 Ortega, Julio. La corónica de Guamán Poma (SP, 10, mayo 1980, p. 111–115)

General introduction to major aspects of Guamán Poma's encyclopedic chronicle. Reviews editions of the *Primer nueva corónica* and comments on major writings about this topic.

5082 Pastor, Beatriz. Discurso narrativo de la conquista de América. La Habana: Casa de las Américas, 1983. 570 p. (Ensayo)

Valuable study which examines the transformation of the conquistador, his perception of America, and his vision of the world. Texts studied include works by Columbus, Cortés, Cabeza de Vaca, several chroniclers of the El Dorado myth, and Ercilla. Volume introduces numerous ideas worthy of thought and further consideration.

5083 Perelmuter Pérez, Rosa. Los cultismos no-gongorinos en el *Primero sueño* de Sor Juana Inés de la Cruz (CM/NRFH, 31:2, 1982, p. 235–256)

Presents a listing of the *cultismos* in Sor Juana's *Primero sueño* which do not have their origin in Góngora's works. Approximately two-thirds of these lexical elements are from other sources. Of interest to Sor Juana specialists and others.

5084 Perelmuter Pérez, Rosa. La estructura retórica de la *Respuesta a Sor Filotea* (HR, 51:2, Spring 1983, p. 147–158)

Studies function of precepts of rhetoric in the organization and context of the *Respuesta*, based on discussions of forensic discourse in manuals of rhetorical discourse (e.g., Cicero, Erasmus, Quintilian, Aristotle).

5085 Perelmuter Pérez, Rosa. Noche intelectual: la oscuridad idiomática en el *Primero sueño*. México: UNAM, Instituto de Investigaciones Filológicas, Centro de Estudios Literarios, 1982. 186 p.

Exegetical study of the language of the *Primero sueño* with attention to lexical and stylistic devices: the *cultismos* and hyperbaton. Introductory chapter deals with such precursors of Sor Juana as Jáuregui, López Pinciano, Carrillo y Sotomayor, and Espinosa Medrano. Subsequent sections list the poem's *cultismos* and analyze different manifestations of hyberbaton. Fundamental work on this aspect of Sor Juana's poetry.

5086 Pupo-Walker, Enrique. *La Florida* del Inca Garcilaso: notas sobre la problematización del discurso histórico en los siglos XVI y XVII (CAM, 139:417, marzo 1985, p. 91–111)

Important discussion of aspects of *La Florida* as a theoretical model of historical discourse—its relationship to the Inca Garcilaso's other works and to other writers of the 16th and 17th centuries.

5087 Ramos Escobar, José Luis. Viaje a la semilla: un análisis estructural de narraciones incaicas (IILI/RI, 50: 127, abril/junio 1984, p. 527–538)

Examination of Inca narrative tales incorporated into the works of Martín de Murúa (*Historia general del Perú*) and Miguel Cabello Valboa (*Miscelánea antártica*). Sees such colonial works as primary sources for the infusion of indigenous elements in modern fiction.

5088 Rojas, Ricardo; Enrique Martínez Paz; and Jorge M. Furt. Prólogos a Luis de Tejeda. Prólogo a los prólogos de Félix Gabriel Flores. Córdoba, Argentina: Dirección de Historia, Letras y Ciencias, 1980. 143 p.: ill.

Reproduces prologues to three editions of Luis de Tejeda's works by R. Rojas (1916), E. Martínez Paz (1917), and J.M. Furt (1947). Materials of interest primarily to the Tejeda specialist, or literary historian.

5089 Sabat de Rivers, Georgina. Sor Juana y sus retratos poéticos (UC/RCL, 23, abril 1984, p. 39–52)

Excellent contribution to Sor Juana studies examines the subject of poetic portraiture. Discussion of studies of this type in other literatures provides an appropriate framework for the analysis of this important aspect of Sor Juana's poetry.

5090 Sáenz de Santa María, Carmelo. Un manuscrito de Cieza localizado en la Biblioteca Apostólica Vaticana (IGFO/RI, 41: 163/164, enero/junio 1981, p. 31–42)

Describes the Vatican Library manuscript of pts. 1 and 3 of Pedro Cieza de León's *Crónica del Perú*. Publication of these parts will make available Cieza's complete works. Of interest to specialist. For ethnohistorian's comment, see *HLAS 46: 1708*.

5090a Serrano de Haro, Antonio. Mateo de Ribera (LNB/L, 346/347, enero/feb. 1985, p. 59–68)

Biographical information on Mateo de Ribera (1604–?), one of the authors of the *Llanto de Panamá* (see item **5075**). Includes general comments and value judgments about writings of a little-known poet of Panama's colonial period.

5091 Velasco, Mabel. La cosmología azteca en el *Primero sueño* de Sor Juana Inés de la Cruz (IILI/RI, 50: 127, abril/junio 1984, p. 539–548)

Provocative essay which finds parallels to elements in Aztec cosmology in classical Greco-Roman allusions and symbols of Sor Juana's *Primero sueño*. Influence of ideas of Sor Juana's contemporary, Sigüenza y Góngora, is suggested.

5092 Villoro, Luis. La figura del mundo: notas sobre *Sor Juana Inés de la Cruz* de Octavio Paz (VUELTA, 85: 8, p. 24–26, ill.)

Review article on Paz's monumental study of Sor Juana (see *HLAS 46: 5057*). Considers the accomplishment by Paz as having explained Sor Juana's works through a clear vision of her world.

TEXTS

5093 Anadón, José. La novela colonial de Barrenechea y Albis, siglo XVII: "Aventuras y Galanteos de Carilab y Rocamila." Santiago: Editorial Universitaria, 1983. 203 p.: bibl. (Col. Fuera de serie)

Preliminary study examines historical, literary, and utopian topics in an unpublished, novelesque tale found in Barrenechea y Albis's chronicle *La restauración de la Imperial y conversión de las almas infieles* (ca. 1698). Central theme of the work is based on Ercilla's *La araucana*. Text of the intercalated novel is reproduced. Important study and edition.

5094 Campoamor, Clara. Sor Juana Inés de la Cruz. Madrid: Júcar, 1984. 223 p.: bibl., ill. (Los Poetas; 53)

Anthology of selected texts of Sor Juana's poetry, including the *Primero sueño* and more than 50 other lyric poems. Introductory chapters provide biographical overview of the poet and her times.

5095 Carrió de la Vandera, Alonso. El Lazarillo de ciegos caminantes. Introducción, cronología y bibliografía de Antonio Lorente Medina. Caracas: Biblioteca Ayacucho, 1985. 316 p.: bibl., index (Biblioteca Ayacucho; 14)

Edition based on the *editio princeps* with modernized spelling. Introduction contains biographical account of Carrió, comments on the generic nature of the *Lazarillo*, and a brief analysis of the work.

5096 Fernández de Lizardi, José Joaquín.
Obras. v. 8, Novelas: *El periquillo sarniento*, t. 1–2. v. 9, Novelas: *El periquillo sarniento*, t. 3–5; *Noches tristes y día alegre*.
Presentación, edición y notas de Felipe Reyes
Palacios. México: UNAM, Centro de Estudios Literarios, 1982. 2 v. (439, 508 p.):
bibl., facsims., plates (Nueva biblioteca mexicana; 86–87)
Critical editions of two of Fernández
de Lizardi's major works based on their first
editions. Vol. 7, *El periquillo sarniento*
(t. 1–2); vol. 9, *El periquillo* (t. 3–5) and
Noches tristes y día alegre. Language of
original texts has been modernized without
significant textual changes. Notes contain
textual variants as well as explanatory information. Excellent edition.

5097 Juana Inés de la Cruz, Sor. Páginas escogidas. Selección de Fina García
Marruz. Prólogo de Loló de la Torriente. La
Habana: Casa de Las Américas, 1978. 292 p.
(Col. Literatura latinoamericana; 89)
Selected works by Sor Juana, including
two *autos*, a prose selection, and numerous
poems. Edition is without benefit of notes or
bibliography. Worthwhile primarily as a
school text.

5098 Letras de la Audiencia de Quito:
período jesuítico. Selección, prólogo y
cronología de Hernán Rodríguez Castelo. Caracas: Biblioteca Ayacucho, 1984. 312 p.:
bibl., index (Biblioteca Ayacucho; 112)
Edition of selected works by 14 writers
associated with the Audiencia de Quito: historians and chroniclers of the Marañón, religious writers, orators, and lyric poets. Of
particular importance are the lyric poems of
Juan Bautista Aguirre. Prologue provides
sound introduction to the society and literature of Quito during the Jesuit period.

5099 Núñez Cabeza de Vaca, Alvar. *Naufragios y Comentarios*. Edición de
Roberto Ferrando. Madrid: Historia 16, 1984.
318 p.: maps (Crónica de América; 3)
Excellent edition of Cabeza de Vaca's
Naufragios and *Comentarios*. Introduction,
explanatory notes, modernized spelling and
punctuation makes this a valuable classroom
text for students and general readership. Bibliography of critical sources would have improved this edition.

5100 Peden, Margaret Sayers. Sor Juana Inés
de la Cruz's: "Respuesta a Sor Filotea"

(REVIEW, 30, Sept./Dec. 1981, p. 7–9, facsim., plate)
Brief introduction serves as a preface
to an excerpt from Sor Juana's "Respuesta a
Sor Filotea" in English translation. Complete
translated text appears in Peden's *A woman
of genius* (see *HLAS 46 : 5048*).

5101 Sor Juana Inés de la Cruz: poems.
Translated from the Spanish by
Margaret Sayers Peden. Binghamton, N.Y.: Bilingual Press/Editorial Bilingüe, 1985. 136 p.
Translator's proven mastery captures
essence of the Baroque and maintains its vitality in these English recreations of Sor
Juana's verse. Anthology includes both Span-
ish/English texts of a good selection of
poems. Most welcome addition to Sor Juana's
bibliography and of great value for English-
speaking readership.

5102 Teatro quechua colonial: antología.
Selección, prólogo y traducción de
Teodoro L. Meneses. Lima: Ediciones Edubanco, 1983. 593 p., 21 p. of plates: bibl., ill.,
facsims.
Anthology of Quechua dramatic works
in Spanish translation: *El hijo pródigo, El
rapto de Prosérpina y Sueño de Endimidón,
Uscar Pancar, Apu Ollantay,* and *El pobre
más rico*. Volume contains brief introductions to each text and a bibliography of general and specialized sources.

5103 Valle y Caviedes, Juan del. Obra
completa. Edición, prólogo, notas y
cronología de Daniel R. Reedy. Caracas: Biblioteca Ayacucho, 1984. 553 p.: appendices
(Biblioteca Ayacucho; 107)
Edition of Caviedes's (1645–97?) complete works, verse and theater, based on eight
known manuscript sources. Textual variants
from all manuscripts are listed. Introduction
provides insights into Caviedes's life and
times, together with information on manuscript sources of his works. Includes texts of
poems attributed to Caviedes. Most complete edition of Peruvian poet's works to date.

MISCELLANEOUS

5104 Ainsa, Fernando. Presentimiento, descubrimiento e invención de América
(CH, 411, sept. 1984, p. 5–14, ill.)
Valuable article which reviews ideals
relating to the "finding" vs. "discovering" of

America, arguing that the search was to find Paradise. Sees the later process change from a search for Eden to the task of establishing the expected utopia. Source materials enhance this piece.

5105 Bronner, Fred. Advertencia privada de un Virrey peruano del siglo XVII a su presunto sucesor (IGFO/RI, 41:163/164, enero/junio 1981, p. 55–77)
Letter written in 1637 by Viceroy Conde de Chinchón is reproduced in article. Letter is a fascinating source for social, economic, and cultural aspects of Viceregal Lima. Of considerable value as an eyewitness account of daily life in early 17th-century Lima. For historian's comment, see *HLAS 46:2686.*

Castillo Mathieu, Nicolás del. Testimonios del uso de "vuestra merced," "vos" y "tú" en América: 1500–1650. See item **4592.**

5106 Irving, T.B. El alto barroco en Centroamérica (*in* International Congress of Hispanists, 4th, 1971, Salamanca, Spain. Actas. Dirección de Eugenio de Bustos Tovar. Salamanca, Spain: Univ. de Salamanca, 1982, v. 2, p. 9–18)
General, albeit informative overview of cultural aspects of the Baroque in Central America. Deals with literary, architectural, and other manifestations of period style.

5107 León-Portilla, Miguel. La palabra antigua y nueva del hombre de Mesoamérica (IILI/RI, 50:127, abril/junio 1984, p. 345–366)
Splendid article which compares examples of the ancient writings of Mesoamerica with contemporary literary texts in indigenous languages. Points of comparison are similar themes and motifs. Valuable documentation in notes.

Lohmann Villena, Guillermo. La biblioteca de un peruano de la Ilustración: el Contador Miguel Feijóo de Sosa. See item **2755.**

5108 Peñate, Julio. De la naturaleza del salvaje a la naturaleza de la conquista: la figura del indio entre los españoles en el siglo XVI (UTIEH/C, 43, 1984, p. 23–33)
Gives attention to several existing viewpoints about attitudes of Spaniards toward the Indian during the conquest. Debate over these views, according to author, divides along different socioeconomic and ideological choices as regards Spanish colonialism.

5109 Rela, Walter. Representaciones teatrales jesuíticas en la provincia del Paraguay (IFCL/E, I, 1981, p. 83–91, bibl.)
Historical account of Jesuit missionary activities in Paraguay and their use of theatrical representations in the process of catechizing the Indian population. Information gleaned from Jesuit accounts dating from late 16th and early 17th centuries.

5110 Reynolds, Winston A. El Corregidor Diego Díaz del Castillo, hijo del conquistador, ante la Santa Inquisición de México (*in* International Congress of Hispanists, 4th, 1971, Salamanca, Spain. Actas. Dirección de Eugenio de Bustos Tovar. Salamanca, Spain: Univ. de Salamanca, 1982, v. 2, p. 461–469)
Reveals heretofore unknown information on the mestizo son (Diego) of Bernal Díaz del Castillo, gleaned from documents found in the Archivo General de la Nación (Mexico), detailing charges brought against him by the Inquisition in 1568–71. Of historical and cultural interest.

5111 Saínz, Enrique. La literatura cubana de 1700 a 1790. La Habana: Editorial Letras Cubanas, 1983. 305 p.: bibl. (Col. Crítica)
Introduces several little-known Cuban writers of the 18th century. Four chapters discuss: 1) political-economic characteristics of the time; 2) drama; 3) lyric poetry; and 4) oratorical, historical, *costumbrista* prose. Of importance to literary historians. Primary and secondary bibliographical sources enhance this study.

5112 Schnelle, Kurt. El siglo XVIII e Hispanoamérica (*in* International Congress of Hispanists, 4th, 1971, Salamanca, Spain. Actas. Dirección de Eugenio de Bustos Tovar. Salamanca, Spain: Univ. de Salamanca, 1982, v. 2, p. 617–623)
Provides worthwhile insights into the interrelationships of cultural and literary activities with the political evolution of Spanish America during the Enlightenment.

5113 Vidal, Hernán. Socio-historia de la literatura colonial hispanoamericana: tres lecturas orgánicas. Minneapolis, Minn.: Institute for the Study of Ideologies and Literature, 1985. 255 p. (Series Toward a social history of Hispanic and Luso-Brazilian literature; 18.L)
Volume contains three lengthy essays

dealing with the organic and historical framework of texts by major colonial writers from Columbus to Olmedo. Primary ideological emphasis shows the relationship of social history to literary history. Treats literature of the conquest, literature of colonial stabilization, and pre-revolutionary and revolutionary literature. Provocative, yet fresh approach to colonial letters and culture.

19th Century: Spanish American Literature Before Modernism

NICOLAS SHUMWAY, *Associate Professor of Spanish, Yale University*

A NEW PREOCCUPATION WITH HISTORY marks the scholarly work of this biennium. The complex, theoretical works so common in the decade just past seem to have faded in popularity, giving way to historically based research as concerned with person and circumstance as with text. The call of history has also led to a reevaluation of writers nearly forgotten: Fray Mamerto Esquiú, Juan Cossío, Vicente Rocafuerte, Cecilio Acosta, José Milla, Félix Varela, José Batres Montúfar and Antonio Pereira Pacheco y Ruiz are just a few of the names research has reclaimed. Particularly interesting in this regard is the republication of Vicente Rocafuerte's *A la nación* (item **5166**) accompanied by a useful biography on this "tropical Sarmiento." Also worthwhile are the moving *episodios* Andriano M. Aguiar wrote showing a Paraguayan view of the tragic *Guerra de la Triple Alianza* (item **5163**).

Such dedication to less studied authors does not mean that the great and famous were neglected. Without question the publishing event of the decade is the 24-volume *Obras completas* of Andrés Bello (item **5125**) from La Casa de Bello in Caracas, dated 1981 to coincide with the bicentennial of Bello's birth. Not only does this splendid collection offer critical notes on Bello's staggering production, it also includes well selected essays by recognized critics, jurists, and linguists. Arturo Uslar Pietri, Amado Alonso, Samuel Gili Gaya, Mariano Picón-Salas, and Angel Rosenblat are just some of the authors who comment on Bello's variegated work. Also thanks to the bicentennial is a spate of essay collections and symposium proceedings devoted to Bello, all including material of varying quality (items **5121, 5122, 5126, 5126a, 5132a, 5141, 5141a, 5142,** and **5155**).

Also begun in this biennium is a new edition of José Martí's complete works, published this time by La Casa de las Américas in post-revolution Cuba (item **5149**). Except for a tediously doctrinaire introduction in vol. 1 (the only one I have seen), the notes and presentation promise to be of high scholarly quality.

Finally, this was a biennium of truly outstanding articles. First on the list should be Rubén Benítez's beautifully written discussion of Sarmiento's travels in Spain. Also deserving of high honors are Thomas R. Coates's rereading of *Facundo* (item **5134**) Oswaldo Holguín Callo's reconstruction of 1876 Lima (item **5140**) and Giaconda Mirún's discussion of Cambaceres's problematic relationship to naturalism (item **5150**).

PROSE FICTION AND POETRY

5114 Batres Montúfar, José. Obra poética de José Batres Montúfar. Prólogo de Virgilio Rodríguez Beteta. Notas de Adrián Recinos. 2a ed. San Salvador: Edición 15 de Septiembre, Instituto Salvadoreño de Cultura Hispánica, 1982. 147 p.: port. (Biblioteca del pensamiento centroamericano)

Reprint of a 1959 anthology of the black-humor poetry by Guatemalan poet, José Batres Montúfar. Includes intelligent foreword and worthwhile notes. Recommended.

5115 Bello, Andrés. Antología general. Selección y prólogo de Oscar Sambrano Urdaneta. Caracas: Ediciones Edime, 1981. 2 v. (1657 p.): bibl., ports. (Clásicos y modernos hispanoamericano)

Most valuable part of this anthology is vol. 1 which includes in its entirety Bello's Spanish grammar, free of the intrusive "modernizations" that mar most current editions. Vol. 2 consists of a good, representative selection of Bello's poetry and discursive writing.

5115a Carter, Boyd. El modernismo en las revistas literarias: 1894 (AHL/B, 24:26, junio 1982, p. 33–49)

Texto de una ponencia leida en 1978 por el autor, ya fallecido, uno de los grandes investigadores de las revistas literarias de Hispanoamérica. En esta ocasión analiza el contenido de siete de las revistas más señeras en el auge del modernismo: El Cojo Ilustrado, El Mundo, la Revista Gris, Cosmópolis, El Iris, la Revista Azul, y Revista de América, haciendo destacar su grado de adhesión a la nueva estética. [R. de Costa]

5116 Guanes, Alejandro. Antología poética. Edición, estudio preliminar, bibliografía y notas de Hugo Rodríguez-Alcalá. S.l.: Alcándara, 1984. 148 p.: ill. (Col. Poesía; 21)

Edición, estudio preliminar y notas de Hugo Rodríguez-Alcalá, constituyen dos tercios del volumen, seguidos de una selección de poemas de este poeta paraguayo que puede ubicarse generacionalmente entre las postrimerías del romanticismo y los comienzos del modernismo. Estudio importante para la historiografía de la poesía paraguaya de fines del siglo XIX. [M. García Pinto]

5116a La Lira argentina, o, Colección de las piezas poéticas dadas a luz en Buenos Aires durante la guerra de su independencia. Edición crítica, estudio y notas de Pedro Luis Barcia. Buenos Aires: Academia Argentina de Letras, 1982. 696 p., 2 leaves of plates: appendices, facsim., music (Biblioteca. Serie Clásicos argentinos; 15)

Excelente edición de la obra editada en Argentina e impresa en París en 1824, acompañada de una valiosa introducción y apéndices que incluyen un útil glosario de la época. [S. Sosnowski]

5117 Mejía Sánchez, Ernesto. Unos hexámetros latinos desconocidos de Andrés Bello (UNAM/AL, 21, 1983, p. 261–272, appendix)

The evidence by which Mejía Sánchez attributes to Bello Latin verses reproduced in this article is more circumstantial than concrete. His argument is nonetheless ingenious, and the verses themselves constitute an interesting example of neo-classicism so pure that even the language is imitated.

Pastrana Rodríguez, Eduardo. Poética bolivariana. See item **2858.**

5118 Plaza, Antonio. Poesías de Antonio Plaza. Selección de Armando Rodríguez. 2a ed. México: Libro-Mex, 1981. 158 p.

Caught in the intersection of neo-classicism and romanticism, Antonio Plaza's poetry, immensely popular in mid-19th century Mexico, is a good indication of the values of his times. Although accompanied by virtually no critical commentary, this short anthology brings attention to a forgotten and important poet. Also in the same series is an anthology of poetry by the better known Salvador Díaz Mirón.

LITERARY CRITICISM AND HISTORY

5119 Acerca de Cirilo Villaverde. Selección, prólogo y notas de Imeldo Alvarez. La Habana: Editorial Letras Cubanas, 1982. 430 p.: bibl. (Col. Crítica)

Important selection of published articles (1838–1980) about Cirilo Villaverde whose Cecilia Valdés is perhaps the most significant novel in 19th-century Spanish

American literature. Includes 22 contributors some as notable as Ramón de Palma, Martín Morúa Delgado, José Martí, Esteban Rodríguez Herrera, and Pedro Deschamps Chapeaux. Since some essays are based on earlier ones, information about Villaverde's life and writings is repeated throughout the collection. Includes chronology of his life and useful bibliography of and about his works. [W. Luis]

5120 Agoglia, Rodolfo Mario. Montalvo, Mera y el romanticismo (IPGH/RHI, 4, 1983, p. 63–71)

Agoglia convincingly argues that the alleged contradictions in Montalvo, attributed to a disjuncture between "romanticism" and "positivism," belies a method too enraptured with European movements to appreciate what was going on in America. Montalvo, he concludes, should be studied first as an Ecuadorian and a Latin American with only secondary reference to Europe.

5121 Alvarez O., Federico. El periodista Andrés Bello. 2a ed. Caracas: Casa de Bello, 1981. 178 p.: bibl.

Bello's work as a journalist reveals a special dimension of his remarkable life: not only was he a scholar of staggering breadth and originality, he was also a teacher, popularizer, and *divulgador*, as at home with wide-audience journalism as with any other intellectual genre. Alvarez's study (a reprint of the 1962 original) outlines Bello's work as a journalist and defends it as an intellectual task no less necessary than any other.

5122 Andrés Bello: homenaje de la UCV. Caracas: Ediciones de Rectorado, Univ. Central de Venezuela, 1982. 607 p.: bibl., facsims., ill., ports.

Odd collection includes a short anthology of the most obvious Bello writings ("Silva a la Agricultura," "Discurso de Inauguración de la Universidad en Chile," etc.) as well as grab-bag of essays mostly by established critics like Menéndez Pidal, Pedro Grases, and Alan Trueblood. Despite evident improvisation in the selection, it contains useful materials.

5123 Antología de ensayos y estudios sobre José Milla: homenaje en el I centenario de su muerte, 1882–1982. Guatemala: Univ. de San Carlos de Guatemala, 1982. 304 p.: bibl.

This collection includes both reprints of "prólogos" written by Milla's contemporaries and modern studies on the Guatemalan novelist and *costumbrista*. Of particular merit are the essays by Seymour Menton and Roberto Carrera Molina.

5123a Armas Chitty, José Antonio de et al. 16 [i.e. Dieciséis] estudios sobre Cecilio Acosta: en el centenario de su muerte. Prólogo de Manuel Alfredo Rodríguez. Los Teques, Venezuela: Ateneo de Los Teques, 1982. 285 p., 5 p. of plates: bibl., ill., indexes (Ateneo de Los Teques; 1. Biblioteca de autores y temas mirandinos)

Largely unknown outside of Venezuela, Cecilio Acosta (1818–81) was a major presence in Spanish American literary life of the last century. Member of the Real Academia, personal friend of Martí, poet, critic, and prolific letter writer, Acosta deserves wider attention. Despite some repetitions, this collection gives a good overview of his life and work; particularly useful are the bibliography and the index to the Acosta archives.

5124 Bastos, María Luisa. El naturalismo de Eugenio Cambaceres: falacias e indicios (ECO, 44[4]:268, feb. 1984, p. 391–406)

Careful, intelligent study of Cambaceres's much vaunted naturalism shows him to be both proponent and victim of a literary doctrine. Concentrates mostly on *Sin rumbo*, but with ample reference to other novels and criticism.

5125 Bello, Andrés. Obras completas de Andrés Bello. 2a ed. facsimilar. Caracas: Fundación La Casa de Bello, 1981. 23 v. (1–6, 8–24): bibl., ill.

This 23-volume edition of Bello's complete works is unquestionably among the most important publishing events of the decade. The edition is doubly important for its inclusion of significant critical essays by distinguished scholars and critics like Amado Alonso, Angel Rosenblat, Gili Gaya, Uslar Pietri and Picón-Salas. Highly recommended.

5126 Bello y la América Latina: Cuarto Congreso del Bicentenario. Caracas: Fundación La Casa de Bello, 1982. 585 p.: bibl., facsim., indexes.

Preceded in the same series by *Bello y Caracas*, *Bello y Londres* (see item **5126a**) and *Bello y Chile* (see *HLAS 46:5103*), this final collection of essays addresses areas in

Bello's work that are less linked to specific periods in Bello's life. Covers the gamut of Bello's subjects: jurisprudence, literature, grammar. Of varying quality, the essays range from perfunctory to exceptionally informative.

5126a Bello y Londres: Segundo Congreso del Bicentenario. Caracas: Fundación La Casa de Bello, 1980–1981. 2 v.: bibls., ill., indexes

Reunidos con ocasión del bicentenario del nacimiento de Bello, varios críticos y estudiosos de su obra examinan aspectos de su importante período londinense. Predominan los enfoques historicistas y los estudios sobre sus contactos con la filosofía inglesa. Una bibliografía sobre la obra inglesa de Bello completa el volumen. [J.M. Oviedo]

5127 Benítez, Rubén. El viaje de Sarmiento a España (CH, 407, mayo 1984, p. 5–34, ill.)

Unquestionably the best study yet to appear on Sarmiento's visit to Spain, this lengthy article not only documents in considerable detail Sarmiento's observations on Spanish culture, but also compares his observations with those of Alexandre Dumas, Théophile Gautier, and Alfred Cuvillier-Fleury, who visited Spain at the same time. This is first-class scholarship and one of the best articles of the biennium.

5128 Bermúdez, Manuel. Cecilio Acosto: un signo en el tiempo. Caracas: Academia Nacional de la Historia, 1983. 97 p. (El Libro menor; 47)

Short study provides a basic introduction to the life, works, and themes of Cecilio Acosta (see item **5123a**). Lucid and intelligent, it is also surprisingly thorough for its size.

5129 Bremer, Thomas. Buenos-Aires et Montevideo: sociologie de la "ville racontée" jusqu'à l'apparition du roman social urbain (UTIEH/C, 42, 1984, p. 123–140)

This tightly argued article traces the changing images of Buenos Aires and Montevideo (mostly of Buenos Aires), beginning with tourist manuals and travelogues of the 1850s and ending with the novels of Roberto Arlt and Manuel Gálvez. Useful and well documented.

5130 Caeiro, Oscar. Los milagros del Obispo: Esquiú y la literatura (CRIT, 57:1926, 12 julio 1984, p. 338–344)

Fray Mamerto Esquiú, like Carlos Guido y Spano and Olegario V. Andrade, is one of many 19th-century Argentine writers marginalized by the *porteño* cultural baronetage. Although Caeiro's article has more to do with those few critics who mention Esquiú than with Esquiú himself, it is at least an attempt to remember a significant but largely forgotten writer.

5131 Cardozo, Lubio. La literatura venezolana durante la Guerra de Independencia: escolios para componer un capítulo de la historia de la cultura literaria venezolana (VANH/B, 67:266, abril/junio 1984, p. 317–344, bibl.)

Spanish American independence was as much an enterprise of works as of military action. This article surveys the oratory, journalism, letters, diaries, and poetry that coincided with Venezuelan independence. Includes extensive quotations. For historian's comment, see item **2866.**

5132 Cardozo, Lubio. La poética de Andrés Bello y sus seguidores. Caracas: Academia Nacional de la Historia, 1981. 123 p.: bibl. (El Libro menor; 20)

El título es equívoco: sólo unas cuantas páginas tratan, con intención polémica pero sin consistencia, de Bello y su poesía. El autor se concentra más bien en sus seguidores, a los que llama "poetas bellistas," de los que presenta una breve antología. [J.M. Oviedo]

5132a Carrión Ordóñez, Enrique. De la campaña verbal durante la independencia: insurgente, patricio, sarraceno, tuitivo (IRA/B, 12, 1982/1983, p. 41-59, bibl.)

Carrión Ordóñez argues that the independence movement in Latin America was as much a campaign of words as of armies. Moreover, in that linguistic campaign he finds class conflicts, contradictions, and inconsistencies that affected rhetoric as much as similar social phenomena affected history.

5133 Carrión Ordóñez, Enrique. La lengua en un texto de la Ilustración: edición y estudio filológico de la *Noticia de Arequipa* de Antonio Pereira y Ruiz. Lima: Pontificia Univ. Católica del Perú, Fondo Editorial, 1983. 554 p.: bibl., ill., indexes.

Published for the first time in this volume is Antonio Pereira Pacheco y Ruiz's short *Noticia de Arequipa*, a late chronicle which in its manuscript version includes 49 drawings and maps. The present volume unfortunately does not reproduce the *láminas;* it does, however, include a bewilderingly thorough analysis of the author's language. Librarians should note that the book contains the original text as well as critical accoutrements.

5134 Coates, Thomas R. La lengua literal y la lengua expresiva en *Facundo* (Estudios de Literatura Argentina [Univ. de Buenos Aires, Facultad de Filosofía y Letras, Instituto de Literatura Argentina Ricardo Rojas] 2:7, 1982, p. 53–83)

Coates rereads *Facundo* on three linguistic planes: 1) referential, sociopolitical, and historical plane closest to Sarmiento's intentions: 2) a dramatic plane in which the book's figures assume archetypal dimensions as players in the emerging drama of Argentine nationhood: and 3) a mythopoetic plane in which the book assumes universal significance. Highly recommended.

5135 Congreso Cultural de Verano del CCP y la Universidad de Miami, 2nd, *Miami, 1982.* José Martí ante la crítica actual, en el centenario del Ismaelillo: memoria. Edición de Elio Alba-Buffill. Editores asociados, Alberto Gutiérrez de la Solana and Esther Sánchez-Grey Alba. Miami, Fla.: Círculo de Cultura Panamericano (CCP): Asociación de Estudios Internacionales, 1983. 199 p.: bibl.

Collection of papers given at a symposium on Martí at the Univ. of Miami (Aug. 1982). Subjects range from politics to literary theory to religion.

5136 Cordero de Espinosa, Susana. Panorama de los estudios críticos sobre la obra de Don Juan Montalvo (BCE/C, 5:12, enero/abril 1982, p. 15–93, bibl.)

This issue of *Cultura* (Quito) commemorates the 150th anniversary of Montalvo's birth with studies of varying quality. Cordero's lengthy annotated survey of critical works on Montalvo is particularly worthwhile. Also recommended in the same issue are Roberto Agramonte's "Montalvo y la Literatura Francesa," Noël Salomon's "Sobre la Imitación de *El Quijote* por Juan Montalvo" and Claude Dumas's "Montalvo y Echeverría: Problemas de Estética Literaria en la América Latina del siglo XIX."

5137 Díaz Sánchez, Ramón. Cecilio Acosta: 1818–1881. Caracas: Italgráfica, 1981.

83 p.: bibl. (Biblioteca de autores y temas mirandinos. Col. Cecilio Acosta; 2)

Short biography provides a good overview of Acosta's life, but unfortunately provides little in the way of documentation.

5138 Esquivel Pren, José. La soledad en la poesía yucateca del siglo XIX (UY/R, 23:134, marzo/abril 1981, p. 63–82)

With cause Esquivel complains that this article can hardly duplicate the 18 volumes of his *Historia de la literatura en Yucatán.* It nonetheless provides a good introduction to several virtually unknown 19th-century Mexican poets.

Guerrero, Ana Cecilia. Desierto para un *Oasis.* See item **2913.**

5139 Holguín Callo, Oswaldo. Palma y Torres Caicedo: una amistad literaria (FENIX, 30/31, 1984, p. 234–256)

Although largely forgotten as a poet, José María Torres Caicedo was a major influence in 19th-century Spanish American letters as editor of the widely read Paris literary magazine *El Correo de Ultramar.* This article documents Torres Caicedo's and Palma's correspondence as well as their public reactions to each other's work, thus providing an interesting glimpse of Palma as critic. Includes extensive quotations from each.

5140 Holguín Callo, Oswaldo. Política y literatura en un impreso limeño de 1876 (IRA/B, 12, 1982/1983, p. 217–251)

Holguín Callo does a splendid job of reconstructing the intellectual life of Lima just before the disastrous War of the Pacific. Draws on many texts, but concentrates principally on Juan Cossío's *Horas alegres.* Well documented and highly recommended. For historian's comment, see item **3047.**

5141 Homenaje a Andrés Bello. Edición de Juan M. Lope Blanch. México: UNAM, Instituto de Investigaciones Filológicas, Centro de Lingüística Hispánica, 1983. 199 p.: bibls. (Cuadernos de lingüística; 21)

Articles collected in this *homenaje* are exclusively dedicated to Bello's work as linguist and grammarian. Although varying in quality, all are competent and informative. Highly recommended.

5141a Homenaje a Andrés Bello en el bicentenario de su nacimiento, 1781–1981.

Amsterdam: Rodopi, 1982. 152 p.: bibl. (Diálogos hispánicos de Amsterdam; 3)

Fruto de un homenaje a Bello por el bicentenario de su nacimiento celebrado por las Universidades de Amsterdam y Utrecht, este volumen contiene siete ponencias que examinan su ideas filosóficas, el tema de América en su poesía, su obra de crítico y sobre todo sus ideas como gramático. [J.M. Oviedo]

5142 Homenaje a Don Andrés Bello: un motivo de la conmemoración del bicentenario de su nacimiento, 1781–1981. Santiago: Editorial Jurídica de Chile, 1982. 940 p., 5 leaves of plates: bibl., facsims.

One book that is actually three devoted respectively to humanistic studies, law, and international law. Well documented and well presented.

5143 Hoy sale *El Alacrán* (CBR/BCB, 20:1, 1983, p. 6–76)

El Alacrán was a Bogotá satirical weekly published in seven issues (Jan. 28-Feb. 22, 1849). Highly critical of the wealthy, pretentious, and corrupt, the newspaper landed its youthful publishers in jail where they prepared the final five issues. Also includes invaluable offprint reproduction of all seven issues. Highly recommended.

5144 Idrobo, Tarquino. Vicente Rocafuerte: el Sarmiento del trópico. Quito: Editorial Universitaria, 1984. 151, 2 p.: bibl.

Necessary companion volume to Rocafuerte's *A la nación* (see item **5166**). Although considerably weakened by minimal to non-existent documentation, this biography nonetheless provides a good overview of the man sometimes called "a tropical Sarmiento."

5145 Instituto de Literatura y Lingüística de la Academia de Ciencias de Cuba. Perfil histórico de las letras cubanas: desde los orígenes hasta 1898. La Habana: Editorial Letras Cubanas, 1983. 501 p.: bibl.

This could have been major study. Unfortunately, its usefulness is seriously compromised by the authors' stubborn refusal to use adequate documentation: quotations are attributed only to titles, usually without so much as a reference to edition used. Not only does such negligence fail to meet basic standards of modern scholarship, it also indicates a profound disregard for scholars who might

want to do additional research on the texts cited. This basic flaw is doubly tragic since the book in other regards is often intelligent and informative.

5146 Jaramillo Agudelo, Darío. Pombo y los románticos (ECO, 43:260[2] junio 1983, p. 128–159)

Fine overview of Romanticism in Colombia, this article also demonstrates (again) how poorly European terminology travels in Latin America. As Jaramillo Agudelo shows, Colombian Romanticism, like Romanticism throughout the continent, was its own movement, the nature of which can easily be lost if European terms are transferred too uncritically.

5147 Jiménez, José Olivio. José Martí: poesía y existencia. México: Editorial Oasis, 1983. 154 p.: bibls. (Col. Biblioteca de las decisiones; 4)

These four previously published essays with a new introduction demonstrate well what Jiménez does best: close, interpretative, largely subjective (in the best sense of that word) reading. Forms a nice counterpoint to the increasingly frequent focus on Martí's political thought.

5147a Jitrik, Noé. El mundo del ochenta. Buenos Aires: Centro Editor de América Latina, 1982. 104 p.: bibl. (Capítulo. Biblioteca argentina fundamental; 153. Serie complementaria, sociedad y cultura; 5)

Publicado originalmente en 1968 como introducción a *El 80 y su mundo: presentación de un época* (ver *HLAS 32:2558a*). Sigue siendo una de las mejores presentaciones de una de las épocas fundamentales en el desarrollo del liberalismo argentino. En una de sus mejores obras, Jitrik articula mas múltiples funciones del texto literario y de los niveles en que compone su sistema. Texto de referencia obligatoria. [S. Sosnowski]

5148 Larrazábal Henríquez, Osvaldo. Actitud de la novelística venezolana del siglo XIX hacia una idea de la integración nacional (*in* Unité et diversité en l'Amérique latine. Bordeaux, France: Univ. de Bordeaux III, 1982, t. 2, p. 207–216)

Creating national mythologies, building a sense of peoplehood and common purpose, explaining political failure—such is the stuff of the 19th-century Venezuelan novel according to Larrazábal Henríquez. Although too short to explore these premises in detail, this article nonetheless poses good questions for further study.

5149 Martí, José. Obras completas. La Habana: Casa de las Américas, 1983. 1 v.: bibl., ill., indexes (Col. Textos martianos)

This volume inaugurates a new critical edition of Martí's complete works, published by the Casa de las Américas. Despite insistence in the introduction that Martí must be studied to understand "la doctrina y la obra universales de la clase obrera y el socialismo" as well as to gain a "verdadera conciencia comunista," the critical notes are mostly textual and historical. Let us hope that the scholarly usefulness of this much needed critical edition remains uncompromised by the doctrinaire cant of the introduction.

5150 Marún, Giaconda. Relectura de *Sin rumbo*: floración de la novela moderna (ECO, 44[4]:268, feb. 1984, p. 415–431)

Holding that criticism on Cambaceres accepts too uncritically his avowed devotion to naturalism, Marún argues that *Sin rumbo*, rather than merely a naturalist text, is an excellent portrait of a society caught in a wrenching transition between tradition and modernity, with its attendant anxiety, nihilism, alienation, and disorientation. Provocative, well argued, and well documented.

5151 Morales, Salvador. Juan Marinello: esquema de una progresión interpretativa de su obra martiana (UCLV/I, 75, 1983, p. 101–127)

Juan Marinello decisively affected the course of Martí scholarship in two ways: first, he was in the 1920s a major figure in recovering and republishing many of Martí's works. Second, he played a major role in expropriating Martí for the Cuban Revolution. Despite its rhetorical bombast, this article illuminates Marinello's contribution in both areas.

5152 Olivera-Williams, María Rosa. Las *Graciosas y divertidas conversaciones* . . . de 1823 y 1825: valiosos aportes para el estudio de la poesía gauchesca (CH, 406, abril 1984, p. 108–116)

In 1968, two early gauchesque poems were discovered, written by an anonymous author but influenced by Bartolomé Hidalgo. This short article studies both poems in terms of subject and imagery.

5153 Pagés Larraya, Antonio. Unamuno y la valoración del *Martín Fierro* (*in* International Congress of Hispanists, 4th, 1971, Salamanca, Spain. Actas. Dirección de Eugenio de Bustos Tovar. Salamanca, Spain: Univ. de Salamanca, 1982, v. 2, p. 355–372)

Well documented study of Unamuno's contribution to criticism on Argentina's most controversial poem. One of the best articles of the biennium.

5154 Portuondo, José Antonio. Martí: escritor revolucionario. La Habana: Editora Política, 1982. 328 p.: bibl. (Col. de estudios martianos)

Fairly lengthy book covers a lot of ground, from Martí's explicitly political thought to his literary criticism to his poetry. Although Portuondo cites an impressive amount of evidence, he always returns to the same point: that Martí was an ideal prototype of the modern revolutionary intellectual. Constantly viewing Martí as an example for younger generations of Cuban revolutionaries inevitably leads to reductionist distortions that undermine the potential worth of the book.

Prieto, Adolfo. La literatura autobiográfica argentina. See item **5676.**

5155 Primer centenario del nacimiento de Bello, 1781–1881. Caracas: Ediciones de la Presidencia de la República, 1981. 247 p.: bibl., ill.

This book provides an interesting view of the first centennial anniversary of Bello's birth, just in time to compare our activities in this decade with those of a century ago. Beautifully bound and replete with reproductions of photos, newspaper clippings, and other realia.

5156 Rama, Angel. José Martí en el eje de la modernización poética: Whitman, Lautréamont, Rimbaud (CM/NRFH, 32:1, 1983, p. 96–135)

Lengthy article demonstrates that Martí's theories on poetry, rather than just reflecting the parnasian or symbolist dichotomy which often caricatures Modernism, run the entire gamut of literary debate of his time. Excellent article.

5157 Roig, Arturo Andrés. Andrés Bello y los orígenes de la semiótica en América Latina. Quito: Ediciones de la Univ. Católica, 1982. 90 p. (Serie Cuadernos universitarios; 4)

Short book is a careful reorganization of some of Bello's ideas on language according to premises taken from modern semiotics. Since semiotics is not a single field with a single doctrine, it is regrettable that Roig does not take specific ideas and their proponents more into account. The study is nonetheless helpful and indicative (again) of Bello's extraordinary modernity.

5158 Salcedo-Bastardo, José Luis. Andrés Bello americano: y otras luces sobre la independencia. Caracas: Academia Nacional de la Historia, 1982. 270 p.: bibl. (El Libro menor; 25)

Contains short biographies of five Venezuelan independence figures: Andrés Bello, Francisco de Miranda, Simón Bolívar, Antonio José de Sucre, and Simón Rodríguez. Despite a tediously panegyrical tone, the book is a useful guide to the lives and basic bibliography of all five figures.

5159 Santana, Joaquín G. Félix Varela: ¿quién fué? La Habana: Unión de Escritores y Artistas de Cuba, 1982. 122 p.

Useful little book illuminates the life of a 19th-century Cuban intellectual often overshadowed by Varona and Martí. Well documented and pleasantly written.

5160 Siwka, Colette. Historia, biografía y literatura: Venezuela, siglo XIX. Caracas: Dirección de Cultura, Univ. Central de Venezuela, 1983. 58, 6 p.: bibl. (Col. Humanismo y ciencia; 19)

Intelligent and concise, this short book effectively argues that positivist historians diminished their discipline by neglecting biography, just as literary critics impoverished literature by overlooking the literary nature of 19th-century biography. Very worthwhile for both historians and literary scholars.

5161 Zalazar, Daniel E. De *Facundo* a *Conflicto y armonías de las razas en América* (RIB, 35:2, 1985, p. 191–200)

Although too short for its subject, this article recommends a reevaluation of Sarmiento's last large work. Despite Sarmiento's own dictum that *Conflicto y armonías* was "un *Facundo* llegado a la vejez," Zalazar argues that the later work should be studied in its own right as both a reflection of Sarmiento's growing skepticism regarding democratic institutions in Latin America, and a response to racialist theories from Europe.

5162 Zalazar, Daniel E. Las posiciones de Sarmiento frente al indio (IILI/RI, 50:127, abril/junio 1984, p. 411–427)

Interesting and well documented article demonstrates that, while Sarmiento held many negative views towards Indians, he was also fascinated by their cultures, languages, history, and way of life.

MISCELLANEOUS
Essays, Memoirs, Correspondence

5163 Aguiar, Adriano M. Yatebó y otros relatos: episodios de la Guerra contra la Triple Alianza. Edición, compilación y noticia preliminar de Francisco Pérez-Maricevich. Asunción: Díaz de Bedoya & Goméz Rodas Editores: Zenda, 1983. 203 p.

Although the Paraguayan War (La Guerra de la Triple Alianza) is usually considered as unnecessary as it was bloody, our documentary histories of this tragic episode remain those of the victors: Mitre, Sarmiento and company. Aguiar's vivid, largely forgotten *episodios* tell the Paraguayan side of the story: the heroism, nobility, and patriotism of a people witnessing the massacre of nearly half their population. This is an essential collection, important for historians as for students of 19th-century Spanish American literature.

5164 Araujo Azarola, María Cristina. La democracia en el pensamiento de Juan Zorrilla de San Martín (IFCL/E, 2, 1982, p. 75–85)

Like virtually every other 19th-century *literato*, Zorrilla de San Martín was also a political commentator. According to this article, Zorrilla defended democracy but in terms that sound more Thomistic than Jacobian.

5165 Caro, Miguel Antonio. Epistolario de Miguel Antonio Caro y Rufino José Cuervo con Rafael Angel de la Peña y otros mexicanos. Edición, introducción y notas de Angelina Araújo Vélez. Bogotá: Instituto Caro y Cuervo, 1983. 473 p., 27 leaves of plates: bibl., facsims., index, ports. (Publicaciones. Archivo epistolar colombiano; 18)

The unusual conception of this book—as correspondence between two early Colombian linguists and their Mexican counterparts (1870–1900)—accounts for its interest. The 111 letters reproduced give not only a good account of the nature of philological studies in both countries, they also contain numerous examples of 19th-century spoken Spanish.

5166 Rocafuerte, Vicente. A la nación. Guayaquil, Ecuador: Litografía e Imprenta de la Univ. de Guayaquil, 1983. 283 p. (Col. Univ. de Guayaquil; 3)

Like the Argentines Sarmiento and Alberdi in their fight against Rosas, Vicente Rocafuerte was an Ecuadorian liberal who, exiled in Peru (1843–45), wrote a remarkable autobiographical essay that is also an acerbic attack on Gen. Juan José Flores and an impassioned defense of liberalism. Originally published in 14 installments, this essay later appeared as a book titled *A la nación*, now republished in this edition.

5167 Schwartz, Kessel. A source for three Martí letters: the art of translation and journalistic creation (UA/REH, 18 : 1, enero 1984, p. 133–153)

Compares Martí's translations to Spanish of several pieces that appeared in *The New York Herald* regarding President Garfield's assassination. This comparison is punctuated with interesting observations on Martí's knowledge of English, his prowess as a translator, and his philosophy of translation as more (or less) than a simple process of re-encoding.

20th Century: Prose Fiction: Mexico

FERNANDO GARCIA NUÑEZ, *Associate Professor of Spanish, The University of Texas at El Paso*

LA NARRATIVA DE ESTE BIENIO en México se desarrolla en medio de la crisis financiera más aguda del país, aneja al creciente descontento social, al cuestionamiento más abierto del sistema de gobierno y a la presencia de desastres naturales (el terremoto de sept. de 1985) cuyas consecuencias develaron con mayor claridad los diversos malestares nacionales; los cuales, directa o indirectamente, se filtran también a través de la narrativa casi siempre autorreferente, saturada de pesimismo e ironía, y situada en el marco de la Ciudad de México. Estas características destacan en *Calles como incendios*, de José Joaquín Blanco (item **5169**); *La vida no vale nada*, de Agustín Ramos (item **5203**); *Cangrejo*, de Octavio Reyes (item **5207**); e *Intramuros*, de Luis Arturo Ramos (item **5204**). Aunque a veces el malestar se concretiza vicaria y simbólicamente en uno sólo, como en el caso de *La gota de agua*, de Vicente Leñero (item **5189**), en torno a la escasez de agua en la capital. En otras la crítica intenta mostrar que a pesar de todo se sigue creando y leyendo con vigor e inventiva: tal es el propósito de los números de *Casa del Tiempo* (item **5219**) y de *La Palabra y el Hombre* (item **5237**) dedicados respectivamente a "Nuestra Hora Literaria" y "Novela Mexicana del Siglo XX," cuyo optimismo es avalado por la gran cantidad de novelas, cuentos y crítica publicados.

Algunos de los escritores consagrados publican obras sobresalientes: autobiográficas en el caso de Vicente Leñero, *Vivir del teatro* (item **5190**), Ricardo Garibay, *Fiera infancia y otros años* (item **5181**) y Salvador Elizondo, *Camera lucida* (item **5173**); o confrontadoras de la cultura mexicana y norteamericana como *Gringo viejo*, de Carlos Fuentes (item **5174**). Además continúa la producción ingeniosa e innovativa de Jesús Gardea, *Sóbol* (item **5179**), Luis Zapata, *En jirones* (item **5211**) y Margo Glantz, *El día de tu boda* (item **5185**). Se revelan como efectivos narradores Octavio Reyes en una novela de adolescentes: *Cangrejo* (item **5207**); Rafael Gaona al presentar evocativa y poéticamente la Revolución Mexicana desde la perspectiva de un niño en *Nadie diga que no es cierto* (item **5176**); Humberto Rivas con cuentos experimentales en *Falco* (item **5208**); Enrique López Aguilar en la composición del relato reflexivo, *Materia de sombras* (item **5191**), género no muy común en México; Alberto Dallal en la escritura de relatos eróticos, *El árbol de turquesa* (item **5172**) y, principalmente, Angeles Mastretta con una novela, *Arráncame la vida* (item **5193**) donde mezcla armoniosamente humorismo, ironía e historia. En la crítica persiste la variedad metodológica aplicada sobre todo a la obra de Juan Rulfo, recientemente fallecido, y de Carlos Fuentes. Acerca del primero se hizo una compilación interesante en *Para cuando yo me ausente* (item **5239**); un riguroso estudio semiótico en *Rulfo y Barthes, análisis de un cuento*, de Joaquín Sánchez MacGregor (item **5251**); un buen estudio general en *Juan Rulfo*, de Luis Leal (item **5232**) y uno particular: "Variantes en *Pedro Páramo*," de Humberto E. Robles (item **5248**). Este último apunta a una necesidad particular de la narrativa mexicana, extensiva también a la del resto de Hispanoamérica: la urgencia de ediciones críticas. A Fuentes le dedicó un número entero *World Literature Today* (item **5262**) y una gran cantidad de libros y artículos diversos estudiosos. El más innovador de ellos, por su cuestionamiento inteligente, apasionado y controversial, es José Joaquín Blanco en "Fuentes: de la Pasión por los Mitos al Polyforum de las Mitologías" (item **5213**).

Pero la crítica ahora cubre con mayor interés la obra de otros autores: a Agustín Yáñez, *Mester* (items **5218, 5235, and 5254**) le consagró un número entre cuyos colaboradores hay historiadores profesionales (John Skirius y José Luis Martínez) y un politólogo (Roderic Camp) que utilizan sus respectivas metodologías al análisis literario; se publicaron algunos artículos y libros sobre Salvador Elizondo, José Revueltas y Juan José Arreola; estudios sobre Mariano Azuela, Juan García Ponce, Carlos Monsiváis (un autor conocidísimo, pero muy poco estudiado), José Emilio Pacheco, Jorge Ibargüengoitia (muerto hace poco), Elena Poniatowska y Esther Seligson.

Por último, aparecieron dos libros panorámicos de la narrativa contemporánea, ambos la mejor fuente de información sobre ella hasta ahora: *La novela mexicana: 1967–1982*, de John S. Brushwood (item **5216**) y el magnífico estudio, más analítico que el primero, *Voices, vision, and a new reality: Mexican fiction since 1970*, de J. Ann Duncan (item **5225**).

PROSE FICTION

5168 Aguirre, Eugenio. Pájaros de fuego. México: Univ. Autónoma Metropolitana, 1984. 165 p. (Col. Molinos de viento; 26. Serie Narrativa)

Narración sobre la omnipresencia de la guerra en la historia humana. En tono apocalíptico proporciona una semblanza poética de Hiroshima, al principio de la novela. Después ésta se convierte en un diálogo informativo, casi inventariado, de las diversas contiendas, principalmente las contemporáneas, pero carente de fuerza fabuladora.

5169 Blanco, José Joaquín. Calles como incendios. México: Ediciones Océano, 1985. 162 p.

Lope de Vega, autor ficticio de la novela, emplea su ingenio para recrear una moderna comedia de enredo en la Ciudad de México actual. Blanco, como Lope, utiliza ese modelo para presentar en medio de risas y bufonerías un aspecto serio: la difícil situación social y económica por la que pasa el México contemporáneo; en el cual todo puede servir de paliativo provisional, inclusive una mística populachera basada en un boxeador en desgracia, inflada por la fiebre de un alcohólico y la ambición de unos cuantos. La novela se convierte así en una farsa dolorosa y divertida.

5170 Campbell, Federico. Todo lo de las focas. México: UNAM, Difusión Cultural, 1982. 135 p. (Cuadernos de humanidades. Serie Narrativa; 1)

Un narrador en primera persona y permanente monólogo, sin conciencia de la escritura, va presentándonos diversas imágenes de una mujer, real o ficticia, por quien siente obsesión compulsiva. Quizás el monólogo continuo responda a la exigencia de tenerla siempre presente aunque sea en la ausencia de las palabras, de las fotografías o de los lugares de Tijuana supuestamente recorridos por ambos en tiempos tan remotos como los años 30 de nuestro siglo y tan contemporáneos como los nuestros. Al final, después de innumerables intentos por verbalizarla, la mujer queda tan misteriosa como al principio.

5171 Cisneros Rivera, Icaro. Detrás del paraíso. México: Avelar Editores, 1983. 137 p.

Novela acerca de las inquietudes de un joven mexicano en el Barrio Latino de París durante el gobierno de De Gaulle. El narrador proporciona una imagen viva del ambiente de ese barrio, aunque esquematiza demasiado el actuar del protagonista.

5172 Dallal, Alberto. El árbol de turquesa. México: Editorial Katún, 1983. 160 p. (Col. Prosa contemporánea; 6)

Variaciones sobre el tema erótico en sus manifestaciones heterosexuales, bisexuales, homosexuales y lesbianas. Esta redundancia no aburre porque el autor manipula con destreza el momento erótico para que éste surja naturalmente del relato, puesto que su propósito no es la narración de lo erótico en sí mismo, sino de sus circunstancias generadoras. Cuando éstas brotan, Dallal les proporciona un ritmo basado en la descripción de los movimientos y sensaciones corporales.

5173 Elizondo, Salvador. Camera lucida. México: Joaquín Mortiz, 1983. 190 p. (Col. Confrontaciones. Los Relatores)

Este libro, como los anteriores de Elizondo, surge de una reflexión minuciosa e intensa sobre la escritura y su proceso; pero ahora se pone en el lente de la cámara al propio Elizondo y sus escritos para obtener de él, luego de filtrarse por los prismas, una imagen virtual de su biografía literaria. Allí se incluyen meditaciones, cuentos y crítica literaria sobre lo leído o publicado por el autor; éste, progresivamente va convirtiéndose a sí mismo en un personaje de ficción, envuelto en una prosa sutil y cuidadosísima.

5174 Fuentes, Carlos. Gringo viejo. México: Fondo de Cultura Económica, 1985. 189 p. (Col. Tierra firme)

Una voz narrativa omnisciente, en tercera persona, relata la rememoración interior de una estadounidense, ya anciana, de su corta estancia en el México revolucionario; cuya visión de la vida contrapuntea insistentemente con la del norteamericano de la época de las fronteras, tipificado por el periodista Ambrose Bierce. Esta oposición va delineando las semejanzas y diferencias de ambas culturas a principios del siglo, aunque indirectamente obliga a los lectores de hoy a verificar el mismo proceso en las circunstancias actuales.

5175 Gaona, Rafael. Cada quien para su santo. México: Ediciones Océano, 1983. 103 p.

En esta novela Gaona aborda un tema difícil: el lesbianismo. Lo hace recurriendo con éxito a la técnica de la entrevista implícita de la protagonista, lesbiana y asesina, y de las personas más cercanas a ella. Al no mostrarse visiblemente el entrevistador, Gaona permite que sus personajes utilicen exclusivamente un lenguaje directo, el coloquial. El lector nunca conoce los verdaderos motivos para la apertura de la protagonista con su interlocutor, aunque la justificación de sus crímenes puede vislumbrarse como el principal.

5176 Gaona, Rafael. Nadie diga que no es cierto. México: Martín Casillas Editores, 1982. 168 p. (Serie La Invención)

Gaona, un diplomático jubilado, recrea maravillosamente en un lenguaje poético y preciso la vida de una familia mexicana durante la Revolución, desde la perspectiva de un niño que se rememora a sí mismo y a los suyos siendo ya adulto. Los recuerdos inciden en acontecimientos tan íntimos como las relaciones de los padres, un desliz del papá, la iniciación sexual del niño y las tiernas intimidades con la madre y la abuela. Gaona todo lo presenta con sencillez y una distanciada e inmensa ternura, pero sin dejar a un lado la crítica ni la ironía, dado el caso. Esta primera novela de Gaona revela a un escritor maduro y original.

5177 Gardea, Jesús. De alba sombría. Hanover, N.H.: Ediciones del Norte, 1985. 151 p.

Colección de cuentos breves y poéticos, la mayoría orientados a presentar con detalle un objeto y, alrededor de él, las inquietudes de personajes solitarios, casi sin mundo que los acompañe, que se manifiestan avasalladoramente como únicas. Ellas pueden ser el amor tardío, el odio, el miedo, la esperanza, la muerte, etc. Destaca en todos los cuentos el cuidado, ya rutinario en Gardea, en la planeación y la escritura.

5178 Gardea, Jesús. Los músicos y el fuego. México: Ediciones Océano, 1985. 107 p.

En esta novela, donde la trama carece de importancia, se trabaja más en la creación de un ambiente detallado, saturado de imágenes metafóricas. Esta concentración hace que el relato tome un tiempo muy denso, aunque no necesariamente lento, sino lleno de espacios poéticos. Esto casi imposibilita el diálogo, el cual, en sus escasas instancias, se sitúa también en la línea metafórica. La densidad y extensión de las imágenes hacen que la lectura sea necesariamente cuidadosa, si en verdad se desea entrar al mundo de la novela. Pero una vez captado el sentido de las imágenes, el relato fluye con soltura. Gardea se adentra cada vez más en un cierto tipo de prosa neobarroca.

5179 Gardea, Jesús. Sóbol. México: Editorial Grijalbo, 1985. 120 p. (Col. Narrativa)

Hermosa novela donde se analiza y recrea en forma casi mítica la función del concepto de propiedad, acompañada de sus respectivas cargas de poder y sus consecuentes transgresiones. Todo ese ambicioso proyecto se lleva a cabo centrando el foco narrativo en el robo de una cuchara y redondeándolo con un ambiente metafórico fluído y denso donde los personajes resaltan por su elementalidad pasmosamente persuasiva.

5180 Gardea, Jesús. Soñar la guerra. México: Editorial Oasis, 1984. 104 p. (Col. Lecturas del milenio; 15)

La voz del protagonista, ya muerto, analiza y recrea los acontecimientos previos y posteriores al fallido ataque al cuartel de Placeres. Lo más importante no es lo que pasó, sino los motivos que propiciaron los ímpetus bélicos en hombres aparentemente tranquilos. De alguna forma la novela rastrea en la estructura elemental del acto bélico: éste no tiene un porqué definido; los desajustes sociales no lo ocasionan directamente, sino que le sirven de excusa.

5181 Garibay, Ricardo. Fiera infancia y otros años. México: Editorial Océano, 1982. 134 p.: ill.

Hermoso libro de memorias de la niñez de Garibay, escritor establecido, con la prosa medida, ágil y humorística que lo caracteriza. El narrador sabe que escribe lo vivido desde una perspectiva, la de los 60 años, transformadora de la propia biografía. En la imposibilidad de contarlo todo, selecciona pasajes clave organizados de tal forma que al mismo tiempo que le pertenecen a él, también pudieron ser de cada uno de los lectores en la infancia. De este modo el libro cobra universalidad e interés, reforzados por la vivacidad poética presente de principio a fin.

5182 Garrido, Felipe. La urna y otras historias de amor. Xalapa, Mexico: Univ. Veracruzana, 1984. 105 p. (Serie Ficción)

En estos cuentos Garrido aborda con ironía, aparentemente inocente, el tema del amor. Primero el del idealizado marido muerto, pero dejado a un lado por el amor sensual y furtivo del pariente adolescente en el cuento más extenso: "La Urna." Continúa en los cuentos restantes con el amor gastado de las parejas que siguen juntas por rutina e intercala uno otoñal y otro rechazado. El distanciamiento irónico del narrador y el cuidado de su prosa le permiten crear interesantes relatos sobre este eterno tema.

5183 Garro, Elena. Reencuentro de personajes. México: Editorial Grijalbo, 1982. 269 p. (Col. Autores mexicanos)

No es esta la primera vez que Garro utiliza como guía de su narración la huída, transformada después en reencuentro. Así sucedía en *Andamos huyendo Lola, Testimonios sobre Mariana* y *La casa junto al río.* (Ver *HLAS 46:5159* y *HLAS 46:5160*) Pero ahora son personajes creados por F. Scott Fitzgerald los que intentan salir del destino creado para ellos por el autor. También ahora conocemos desde un principio la trama, pero la autora nos va interesando obsesivamente en esta imposible e intermitente huída.

5184 Gasca, Argelio. Cuchillo. México: Editorial Oasis, 1983. 53 p. (Col. Lecturas del Milenio; 13)

Novela corta acerca de la iniciación sexual de un niño, prematura y dolorosa, a manos de la sirvienta. Esto crea en él exigencias a las que todavía no puede responder. El narrador presenta con rapidez y eficacia las sensaciones del niño, aunque a veces lo domina la conceptualización adulta.

5185 Glantz, Margo. El día de tu boda. México: Martín Casillas Editores, 1982. 57 p. (Col. Memoria y Olvido. Imágenes de México; 6)

Glantz crea un hermoso relato partiendo de su lectura perspicaz e imaginativa de las tarjetas postales amorosas (adjuntas al texto) que circularon por los años 20 entre la alta burguesía de la Ciudad de México, para caer después en manos del pueblo. Glantz hace ver que el universo idealizado con engañosa facilidad en el marco de la postal, sirvió de paliativo a sus consumidores para olvidar la violencia revolucionaria contemporánea a ellos.

5186 Glantz, Margo. Síndrome de naufragios. México: Joaquín Mortiz, 1984. 116 p. (Serie del volador)

En brevísimas composiciones sobre el incontenible afán humano de dominar las aguas de mares y ríos, Glantz aglutina a héroes de diversas mitologías: Noé, Ulises, Marco Polo y Hernán Cortés. Todos, en sus respectivas culturas, son fundadores. Glantz llega incluso a reunirlos en acción conjunta, autónoma de tiempos y espacios, mas cuidadosamente regenteada por la imaginación y la precisión discursiva de la autora.

5187 Krauze, Ethel. Intermedio para mujeres. México: Editorial Océano, 1982. 164 p.: ill.

Colección de cuentos eróticos y amorosos que dan principalmente el punto de vista de la mujer en las interrelaciones con el hombre. En este sentido se les podría calificar de lectura para mujeres, sobre todo por su intención de concientizarlas en los abusos masculinos por ellas sufridos. Pero como el libro no posee un tono moralizante, ni ataca lo masculino sólo por ser tal, puede despertar en el lector hombre inquietudes con respecto a su actitud sexual con las mujeres.

5188 Leñero, Vicente. Cajón de sastre. Puebla, Mexico: Editorial Univ. Autónoma de Puebla, 1981. 111 p. (Col. Ficciones)

Selección antológica de cuentos primerizos, incorporados posteriormente por Leñero en sus novelas, y de textos periodísticos. Los cuentos muestran interesante-

mente el camino recorrido desde ellos, principio ingenuo, imperfecto y obsesivo, hasta algunas de las novelas más logradas del autor. En esta perspectiva los llamados "Textos Periodísticos" poseen un desarrollo narrativo superior a los cuentos.

5189 Leñero, Vicente. La gota de agua. México: Plaza & Janés, 1984. 207 p. (Col. Narradores mexicanos)

Novela que plantea los diversos problemas del abastecimiento de agua en la Ciudad de México, vistos desde la perspectiva testimonial, casi personalizada, del autor que los sufre en carne propia y se inmiscuye también como personaje. En ella luce la habitual prosa ágil y clara de Leñero, pero detenida en demasía en explicaciones técnicas de plomería e ingeniería hidráulica, sobre todo después de la mitad de la novela.

5190 Leñero, Vicente. Vivir del teatro. México: Joaquín Mortiz, 1982. 255 p.: col. ill. (Col. Contrapuntos)

Memorias del autor en función, principalmente, de sus obras de teatro, pero abarcadoras también de sus novelas—casi siempre asociadas al teatro—, actividad periodística y demás circunstancias, privadas y públicas, que lo acompañan. Algo tienen de ficción en cuanto el escritor precisa de hablar o inventariar sobre sí mismo. Leñero las escribe con cariño, distanciamiento y humor. Además trazan en un contexto personalizado, el del autor y su obra, un panorama de la vida literaria del México contemporáneo.

5191 López Aguilar, Enrique. Materia de sombras. México: Univ. Autónoma Metropolitana, 1984. 198 p. (Col. Molinos de viento; 34. Serie Narrativa)

El autor muestra, en esta colección de cuentos, habilidades sorprendentes para crear una prosa fluida y reflexiva a la vez, cercana a la meditación filosófica casera, inteligente y humorística. Esta se orienta con frecuencia hacia temas religiosos, musicales, suburbanos e históricos. Entre estos últimos destacan los de la historia clásica y los relacionados con la masacre de Tlatelolco en 1968.

5192 Martín del Campo, David. Esta tierra del amor. México: Martín Casillas Editores, 1982. 433 p. (Serie La Invención)

Novela de una década de la Ciudad de México (1970–80) a través del encuentro progresivo de un provinciano con ella y sus diversos estratos sociales, tipificados panorámicamente: el mundo estudiantil (preparatorio y universitario), el periodístico, el cinematográfico, el sindical, el de la clase alta, etc. La visión es pesimista, aunque con una permanente alegría cínica y jovial que hace de la narración casi un reporte del adolescente provinciano recién llegado. Poco a poco éste se apropia de la malicia y vivacidad del "chilango," pero se convence también de que esas cualidades las traía ya consigo desde su familiar herencia cristera.

5193 Mastretta, Angeles. Arráncame la vida. 3a ed. México: Ediciones Océano, 1985. 226 p.

Magnífica novela que aborda al mismo tiempo un análisis del poder político machista en el México del Presidente Manuel Avila Camacho (1940–46) y el proceso de liberación de una mujer casada con un hombre del gobierno, pero dispuesta a tomar sus propias decisiones. Ella es precisamente la conductora de la voz narrativa en una primera persona un tanto parecida a la de la picaresca en el tono irónico, inquisitivo, confesional y juguetón. Estas características llevan a una prosa ágil, amena, incisiva y humorística que no descarta la aguda crítica social, principalmente en el ámbito de las ciudades de Puebla y México.

5194 Molina, Silvia. Lides de estaño. México: Univ. Autónoma Metropolitana, 1984. 109 p. (Col. Molinos de viento; 30)

Molina maneja bien todo lo referente a los asuntos domésticos diarios, propios de un ama de casa, como lo demuestra esta colección de cuentos breves, casi todos ellos relativos a la inquietud de una niña ante la escuela, las muñecas y la muerte; o al primer amor de la adolescente, así como al fracaso de la mujercita; o, simplemente, a las dificultades surgidas por el crecimiento de los hijos y la marcha inesperada de la sirvienta.

5195 Monsreal, Agustín. Sueños de segunda mano. México: Folios Ediciones, 1983. 124 p. (Col. Narrativa latinoamericana; 5)

En esta colección de cuentos amorosos Monsreal luce gran destreza en el manejo verbal: predomina el discurso inteligentemente juguetón, inquisitivo y libre. Estas características le proporcionan algo de prístino al principio de la narración amorosa, pero la ironía, manipulada por el narrador, se encarga de convertirla poco a poco en algo trivial y repetitivo; aunque esto no hace que decaiga el interés del lector.

5196 Ojeda, Jorge Arturo. Sabiduría. México: Univ. Autónoma Metropolitana, 1983. 76 p. (Col. Molinos de viento; 25. Serie Ensayo)

Colección de breves composiciones, escritas a modo de reflexiones personales hechas día a día. Una o dos se acercan a la verbalización esplendorosa de lo que ya conocíamos, pero la mayoría se quedan en balbuceos escuchados antes.

5197 Pacheco, Cristina. Sopita de fideo. 2a ed. México: Ediciones Océano, 1984. 115 p.

Libro de viñetas desarrolladas en la brevedad de dos o, a lo más, cuatro páginas. Pareciera continuación, en la temática y el estilo, de uno anterior: *Para vivir aquí* (ver *HLAS 46:5168*), aunque el presente muestra más ironía y pesimismo con respecto a algunos de los sempiternos problemas de la vida en la Ciudad de México: agresividad, miseria y violencia, certeramente ejemplificados en los relatos.

5198 Pettersson, Aline. Proyectos de muerte. México: Martín Casillas Editores, 1983. 191 p.

Un arquitecto enfermo, a través de la escritura de un diario en el hospital, va trazando los rasgos divisorios de un nueva vida de enfermo con la anterior. Lenta y detalladamente todo cobra una perspectiva distinta desde la posición horizontal de la cama de enfermo: los objetos, las personas, los ruidos son diferentes allí. El diario describe principalmente los cambios en el cuerpo y en su percepción, antes que adentrarse a un posible examen de conciencia casi inexistente. Al final el narrador ha terminado su proyecto: establecerse en la antesala de la muerte.

5199 Prieto, Raúl. Gracias, San Martín de Porres. México: Editorial Grijalbo, 1984. 226 p. (Col. Narrativa)

Colección de cuentos, en su mayoría urbanos, caracterizados por tratar los acontecimientos de la vida cotidiana con ironía, humor negro y hasta sarcasmo. En ellos el narrador comenta la situación política, económica y moral imperante en el México contemporáneo, cuya familiaridad proviene al autor del ejercicio periodístico por más de 35 años. Los más sobresalientes son los eróticos.

5200 Prieto, Raúl. Yoni Bich. México: Editorial Grijalbo, 1983. 169 p. (Col. Autores mexicanos)

Colección de cuentos breves, heterogéneos en sus logros. Los mejores son los eróticos: en ellos el narrador espía burlonamente a los amantes, a quienes describe en sus actos y motivaciones. El lector, un curioso más, participa del morbo del narrador y, junto con él, descubre la imposibilidad del amor en relaciones motivadas por el sadismo ("La Película"), el engaño piadoso o la remuneración pecuniaria ("La Virgen"); solapadas todas ellas por la hipocresía del clero, la gente decente y los magnates financieros.

5201 Puga, María Luisa. Pánico o peligro. México: Siglo Veintiuno Editores, 1983. 282 p. (Col. La Creación literaria)

Autobiografía ficticia de la narradora, quien intenta descubrirse a través de la escritura cotidiana de unos cuadernos acerca de sí misma y de los que la rodean. Al principio el destinatario es su amante, por quien ella desea ser conocida. Mas lentamente el ejercicio escritural la va concientizando en la naturaleza de la grafía que le permite dar presencialidad a lo pasado y encontrar un lenguaje personal para enfrentarse más adecuadamente al peligro de la Ciudad de México, en lugar de vivir sempiternamente en el pánico.

5202 Ramírez, Armando. Noche de Califas. 2a ed. México: Editorial Grijalbo, 1983. 103 p. (Col. Narrativa)

Ramírez, el escritor más sobresaliente de los arrabales de la Ciudad de México, poco a poco ha ido haciendo a un lado el estereotipo fácil y la frase manoseada. Ahora combina la problemática de la escritura de algo vivido en parte por el narrador y la necesidad de distanciarse de ello para poder recrearlo utilizando, entre otras cosas, el tú personal, dirigido a él mismo. Así va redactando y discutiendo su escritura en una narración trágica de Macho, un héroe arrabalero, quien al final es vencido y sacado fuera de razón por el amor de una mujer a la que no pudo someter.

5203 Ramos, Agustín. La vida no vale nada. México: Martín Casillas Editores, 1982. 189 p. (Col. 1982. Serie La Invención)

Novela juguetonamente experimental en lenguaje, estructura y tono: su modelo consciente es *Rayuela*, de la que toma la irracionalidad, lo lúdico, la extinción de la categoría del tiempo y el ajustar la narración en torno a un círculo de personajes aparentemente desequilibrados. La visible y reiterada intencionalidad paródica con la novela de Julio Cortázar, pero en el ámbito de la Ciudad de México, hace de la presente un texto original. En él importa más la creación verbal que el argumento repetitivo: un supuesto atentado a la vida de un senador y una supuesta fiesta, implicadores de un cuestionamiento casi total de los valores en el sistema de vida en la Capital.

5204 Ramos, Luis Arturo. Intramuros. Xalapa, México: Univ. Veracruzana, 1983. 277 p.

Interesante novela que explora el proceso de asimilación de un grupo de exilados españoles, de la Guerra Civil, al sistema de vida mexicano de Veracruz, en base al manejo que el narrador hace del supuesto diario de uno de ellos. Ninguno, en verdad, traspasa totalmente las barreras diferenciadoras de ambas culturas, omnipresentes en el texto que condicionan. Ramos utiliza un lenguaje preciso, con frecuencia cargado de ambigüedad poética.

5205 Ramos, Luis Arturo. Los viejos asesinos. México: Premiá Editora, 1981. 97 p. (La Red de Jonás)

Colección de seis cuentos breves y uno, "Cartas a Julia," casi novela corta. Ramos los ha construido de tal forma que el lector no puede dejar de interesarse progresivamente en el relato ni alarmarse con el sorpresivo final. Esto funciona sobre todo en "Médico y Medicinas," "El Visitante" y "Cartas a Julia." A la rigurosa planeación narrativa se añade una prosa ágil y libre.

5206 Reyes, Alfonso. Prosa y poesía. Edición de James Willis Robb. 3a ed. Madrid: Ediciones Cátedra, 1984. 203 p. (Letras hispánicas)

Amena e informativa antología de la inmensa obra de Reyes, hecha por uno de los estudiosos más conocedores de ella; quien proporciona una semblanza crítica y biográfica en unas cuantas páginas. La selección narrativa incluye dos cuentos autobiográficos ("El Testimonio de Juan Peña" y "Silueta del Indio Jesús") de tema indigenista y uno fantástico: "La Mano del Comandante Aranda." Algunos de los ensayos incluídos, sobre todo las divagaciones y los informales, funcionan también como breves y amenos relatos. Las numerosas y necesarias anotaciones del editor al pie de la página hacen más actual y asequible la prosa de Reyes al lector de hoy.

5207 Reyes, Octavio. Cangrejo. México: Editorial Katún, 1984. 174 p. (Col. Prosa contemporánea; 12)

Bien lograda novela acerca de la adolescencia de un grupo de jóvenes, rememorada años después por un uno de ellos, el narrador, cuando los sueños de libertad y originalidad han muerto ya en el ámbito caótico de la Ciudad de México de 1990. Allí los jóvenes pensaban encontrar la apertura negada a ellos en la tranquila ciudad de Orizaba, cuya gente es esclavizada por el rutinario trabajo de la cervecería. El lenguaje de la narración, fluído, libre y a veces coloquial, crea un elocuente discurso juvenil.

5208 Rivas, Humberto. Falco. México: Editorial Katún, 1984. 82 p. (Col. Prosa contemporánea; 9)

Una prosa alucinante caracteriza a esta colección de cuentos en los que se mezcla armoniosamente lo erótico, la sádico y lo terrible en secuencias casi de cine surrealista. Esto se manifiesta más acabadamente en los dos cuentos más extensos: "Falco" y "Función Continua," sin dejar de estar presente en los restantes, mucho más breves.

5209 Salazar, Severino. Donde deben estar las catedrales. México: Instituto Nacional de Bellas Artes y Editorial Katún, 1984. 128 p. (Col. Premio bellas artes)

En su primera novela Salazar proyecta al ficticio narrador adulto que desea explicarse acontecimientos acarreadores de decadencia en un pueblo zacatecano de su niñez. El narrador asume la escritura como exorcismo de sus propios fantasmas en la primera parte de la novela, supuestamente escrita por él con plena conciencia de su carácter ficticio. Pero la segunda parte, ajena a su inventiva, parece cobrar vida propia para explicar la decadencia desde génesis literarias. La novela posee madurez y planeación poco comunes en las primicias de cualquier autor.

5210 Vallarino, Roberto. Crónicas cotidianas. México: Editorial Katún, 1984. 171 p.: ill. (Prosa contemporánea; 7)

La Ciudad de México y sus alrededores constituyen el tema de este libro de crónicas, casi todas ellas publicadas antes en el periódico capitalino *Unomásuno*. En todas hay la perspicacia del observador profesional, aunada a la profunda reflexión sobre las minucias. Así hay las dedicadas a las ventanas, las puertas y los cinturones; además de las que recuerdan tiempos idos, lo rutinario y lo sórdido. En una prosa cuidadosa Vallarino inmiscuye, con aparente inocencia, una crítica persistente en el acontecer capitalino diario.

5211 Zapata, Luis. En jirones. México: Editorial Posada, 1985. 275 p.

Interesante novela cuyo texto va surgiendo simultáneamente de la utilización de las formas tradicionales de la narrativa amorosa y su cuestionamiento irónico que las destruye. Este contrapunto intermitente plantea la problemática de escribir algo original en el género amoroso; pero la solución del problema, aparentemente insoluble, como por el no olvidar nunca en el proceso de escritura la vaciedad repetitiva implicada en el discurso amoroso. Esta doble perspectiva proporciona un tono melodramático a la novela, con vigencia en amores homosexuales, los de la novela, o heterosexuales.

LITERARY CRITICISM AND HISTORY

5212 Alazraki, Jaime. *Terra Nostra*: coming to grips with history (WLT, 57:3, 1983, p. 551–558, ill.)

Terra Nostra, novela cuyo tema es la historia hispánica, tiene como función principal el recuperar el pasado de Hispanoamérica: el olvidado por los regenteadores del poder y el ocultado por los afanes parricidas de la Independencia. De este modo la novela intenta recuperar lo mejor de España para avivarlo (el afán libertario de los comuneros de Castilla, Don Quijote, Don Juan, Celestina) y lo peor de ella para destruirlo: la concepción de un sistema de gobierno despótico, trasplantado al Nuevo Mundo y asumido por dictadores, tiranos y caciques.

5213 Blanco, José Joaquín. La paja en el ojo: ensayos de crítica. Puebla, México: Univ. Autónoma de Puebla, Centro de Estudios Contemporáneos, 1980. 280 p. (Biblioteca Francisco Javier Clavijero. Serie mayor)

Recolección de ensayos varios, publicados antes en diversos periódicos y revistas de la capital. Entre ellos destacan los dedicados a *El vampiro de la Colonia Roma*, novela de Luis Zapata; *Los de abajo* y, sobre todo, el escrito sobre Fuentes: éste último es quizás uno de los estudios a la vez más críticos y apasionantes de su obra. Blanco le crítica a Fuentes el tener una visión de México semejante a la de los escritores norteamericanos y europeos; pero lo considera la influencia más poderosa en la narrativa mexicana contemporánea.

5214 Bruce-Novoa, Juan. Juan García Ponce y la ficción empírica (Iberoromania [Max Niemeyer Verlag, Tübingen, FRG] 20, 1984, p. 109–116)

En las novelas de García Ponce predomina lo analítico sobre lo imaginario; lo objetivo sobre lo subjetivo; y el ambiente sobre el acontecer porque el autor trata de presentarnos un mundo donde se intenta trascender el yo, origen de la enajenación, y encontrar así el bien de la impersonalidad. En eso se asemeja su obra a la novela empírica de Henry James, Robert Musil, Virginia Woolf y`otros.

5215 Bruce-Novoa, Juan. Julieta Campos' Sabina: in the labyrinth of intertextuality (Third Woman [Indiana Univ., Chicano-Riqueño Studies, Bloomington] 2:2, 1984, p. 43–63)

Informativo y riguroso rastreo de la gran cantidad de textos subyacentes en la novela *Tiene los cabellos rojizos y se llama Sabina*, cuyo título e intención habrían provenido de un modificación complementaria, hecha por la lectura de Campos, de unas novelas de Anais Nin, Virginia Woolf y Nathalie Sarraute, para hacer una deconstrucción feminista del logocentrismo masculino en un extenso monólogo interior de 168 p., el texto de la novela.

5216 Brushwood, John Stubbs. La novela mexicana, 1967–1982. México: Editorial Grijalbo, 1985. 130 p. (Col. Enlace)

Brushwood intenta aglutinar más de 200 novelas y continuar de alguna forma sus estudios del clásico *Mexico in its novel*. Para ello reitera la función temática y técnica de cinco características permanentes, alrededor de las cuales se comentan brevemente las novelas del período: 1) autorreferencia, presente en un 50 porciento de las novelas;

identidad inestable en un 25 porciento; la capital, como lugar natural de la narración en un 50 porciento; la tragedia de Tlatelolco (1968), en un 25 porciento; y, finalmente, la novela de nostalgia en menor porcentaje. De esta manera el estudio ofrece al lector, sobre todo al familiarizado con las novelas, una visión panorámica del período, acompañada de valiosas intuiciones críticas.

5217 Brushwood, John Stubbs. A place to belong to: Armando Ramírez and Mexico City (AATSP/H, 67:3, Sept. 1984, p. 341–345)

El ambiente y el lenguaje popular, casi arrabalero, de las novelas de Ramírez hacen que él parezca un autor ingenuo y primitivo; más el análisis de las novelas, con énfasis en las diversas y complejas funciones de las voces narrativas, hace ver que el autor conoce y maneja las técnicas más recientes de la narrativa contemporánea.

5218 Camp, Roderic. An intellectual in Mexican politics: the case of Agustín Yáñez (UCLA/M, 12:1/2, mayo 1983, p. 3–17)

Yáñez es presentado como modelo de estudio en las relaciones del gobierno mexicano con los intelectuales inmiscuidos en puestos políticos. Camp opina que a Yáñez le favoreció su prestigio y solidez intelectual en su carrera política. Esta es una faceta del novelista no estudiada antes con tanto rigor.

5219 *Casa del Tiempo*. Univ. Autónoma Metropolitana. Vol. 5, Nos. 49/50, feb./marzo 1985–. México.

Número doble intitulado *Nuestra hora literaria* y dedicado a la reflexión en torno a la literatura mexicana actual (poesía, cuento, novela y ensayo) en el contexto de la crisis económica de México. Los ensayos son cortos, panorámicos y—de ordinario—impresonistas. Quizás lo más destacado en crítica de la narrativa sea "La Muerte de la Literatura Política," de Christopher Domínguez y un interesantísimo ensayo de Luis Mario Schneider: "El Tema Homosexual en la Literatura Mexicana."

5220 Chevigny, Bell Gale. The transformation of privilege in the work of Elena Poniatowska (LALR, 13:26, July/Dec. 1985, p. 49–62)

El análisis de la obra narrativa de Poniatowska, enmarcado en su biografía de aristocracia europea, permite a Chevigny el ir descubriendo en su obra un constante abandono de sus privilegios de clase social para identificarse con las causas populares y dolorosas de sus personajes.

5221 Cossío, María Eugenia. El diálogo sin fin de Monsiváis (IUP/HJ, 5 : 2, Spring 1984, p. 137–143)

Días de guardar y Amor perdido son ejemplos del discurso constantemente inquisitivo de la cotidianeidad mexicana, hecho por Monsiváis. El la cuestiona humorísticamente utilizando inclusive los paradigmas del discurso oficial o autorizado y dejando, además, que se escuchen las otras diversas voces. De esta forma Monsiváis proporciona un mosaico crítico, pero no definitivo ni dogmático, del acontecer mexicano.

5222 Díaz, Nancy Gray. El mexicano naufragado y la literatura "pop:" "La Fiesta Brava" de José Emilio Pacheco (IUP/HJ, 6 : 1, 1984, p. 131–139)

La autora considera que el cuento de Pacheco polariza el arte "pop," caracterizado por sus clichés lingüísticos y la cosificación de denominación norteamericana, y la identidad verdadera, asociada aquí con la cultura azteca. La confrontación lleva consigo una invitación a reencontrar las raíces del mexicano.

5223 Domenella, Ana Rosa. La clase media no va al paraíso (CM/D, 114, nov./dic. 1983, p. 39–44, ill.)

En las novelas de Jorge Ibargüengoitia la ironía funciona como visión del mundo, cuyo fundamento son textos documentales y autobiográficos, engañosamente subordinados a esa visión. De este modo, sin enfrentamientos frontales ni solemnidad, sino con un tono ligero, el autor desmitifica la historia y los sentimentalismos dominantes de la clase media.

5224 Duncan, J. Ann. Nostalgia for the unknown in Ether Seligson (IAA, 10 : 1, 1984, p. 23–43)

La dificultad para clasificar los escritos de Seligson en un género determinado, la realidad y la fantasía en ellos, así como las voces narrativas y las identidades, no surgen de un afán gratuito; sino que responden a un intento nostálgico de reunificarlo todo en la pareja, la familia y la tradición cultural.

5225 Duncan, J. Ann. Voices, vision, and a new reality: Mexican fiction since 1970. Pittsburgh, Pa.: Univ. of Pittsburgh Press, 1986. 263 p.: bibl., index (Pitt Latin American series)

Excelente estudio de la narrativa publicada a partir de 1970 de José Emilio Pacheco, Carlos Montemayor, Humberto Guzmán, Esther Seligson, Antonio Delgado y Jesús Gardea. A todos ellos dedica capítulos individuales caracterizados por un riguroso y claro análisis textual de sus obras, unificado por la indagación de la forma en que cada uno ha utilizado con originalidad técnicas y tendencias de la Nueva Novela Hispanoamericana, así como la medida en que ellos las han enriquecido. Además Duncan extiende dicho análisis, aunque en forma más somera, a las obras principales de narradores que los precedieron o fueron contemporáneos a ellos y a las de los más jóvenes. Así el libro proporciona una visión global, la más incisiva y analítica hasta ahora, de la narrativa mexicana (1960–82).

5226 Elizondo, Salvador. Regreso a casa: discurso. Contestación de José Luis Martínez. México: UNAM, Coordinación de Humanidades, 1982. 42 p.

Informativo discurso del ingreso de Elizondo a la Academia Mexicana de la Lengua, en cuanto en él hace un resumen de los escritores mexicanos más influyentes en su obra. Martínez traza una semblanza biobibliográfica de Elizondo, con énfasis en Farabeuf, novela inaugural de la presencia de la perversión, el horror y la belleza en la literatura mexicana.

5227 Filer, Malva E. Los mitos indígenas en la obra de Carlos Fuentes (IILI/RI, 50 : 127, abril/junio 1984, p. 475–489)

Análisis del uso de los mitos indígenas por Fuentes en sus novelas, en cuanto generadores de conceptos e imágenes de la nacionalidad mexicana. Tal uso caería dentro de la perspectiva de Fuentes encaminada a reescribir críticamente el pasado, incluido el indígena, para asumirlo en una integración nacional necesariamente mestiza en lo cultural y lo biológico. En ese sentido Fuentes apoya la tesis de que el indigenismo es la ideología del mestizo.

5227a Francescato, Martha Paley. Distant relations: chronicle of various close readings (WLT, 57 : 3, 1983, p. 590–594, ill.)

Ingenioso ensayo donde la autora asume la responsabilidad de oír y contar la narración, según se prescribe en la novela de Fuentes *Una familia lejana*. Esto la obliga a buscar respuesta a las preguntas planteadas por la novela en *Cumpleaños* y *Aura*, narraciones contiguas a *Una familia lejana*, cuya temática común constituye le poética vigente en todas las novelas de Fuentes: el tiempo y la identidad.

5228 Fuentes, Carlos. On reading and writing myself: how I wrote *Aura* (WLT, 57:3, 1983, p. 531–539, ill.)

Fuentes comenta los acontecimientos anecdóticos y las lecturas que lo fueron motivando a escribir *Aura*. Sobresalen sus pláticas con Luis Buñuel acerca de Francisco de Quevedo y Villegas, mientras Buñuel planeaba sus películas *El ángel exterminador* y *La Vía Láctea*; su reencuentro con una amiga en quien vislumbra el cambio ocasionado por los años; y una plática con María Callas poco antes de su muerte. Los motivos textuales serían principalmente obras de Jules Michelet, Henry James, Charles Dickens y Pushkin.

5229 García Flores, Margarita. Aproximaciones y reintegros. México: UNAM, Difusión Cultural, Depto. de Humanidades, 1982. 164 p., 16 p. of plates: ports. (Textos de humanidades; 33)

Libro de entrevistas y ensayos de gente importante en la cultura mexicana, incluidos los novelistas Arturo Azuela, Agustín Yáñez y Vicente Leñero a quienes García Flores hace sagaces entrevistas. También escribe una entrevista imaginaria con Alfonso Reyes, quien expone sus ideas sobre el periodismo. Casi todos los textos aparecieron antes en publicaciones periódicas de la Ciudad de México. El libro sigue la tónica atrevida y juguetona de las entrevistas hechas por la autora en *Cartas marcadas* (México: UNAM, 1979).

5230 Gyurko, Lanin A. Fuentes' *Aura* and Wilder's *Sunset Boulevard*: a comparative analysis (IAA, 10:1, 1984, p. 46–86, bibl.)

Gyurko opina que el antecedente más fascinante de la novela de Fuentes es la película de Billy Wilder *Sunset Boulevard* (1950), ya que en ambas se encuentra la búsqueda de la identidad, su pérdida y los afanes por recobrarla. Esto se nota más destacadamente en Norma Desmond y Joe Gillis, personajes de la película, y en Doña Consuelo y Felipe Montero, de la novela.

5231 Knight, Thomas J. The setting of *Cambio de piel* (UNC/RN, 24:3, Spring 1984, p. 229–232)

La observación cuidadosa de la pirámide superpuesta de Cholula—en su interior indígena, su cúspide española y cristiana y sus alrededores pueblerinos, industrializados y alienantes—ayuda a la mejor comprensión de la novela; ya que en ésta las muertes y resurrecciones tienen como escenario la pirámide.

5232 Leal, Luis. Juan Rulfo. Boston: Twayne, 1983. 132 p.: bibl., index, port. (Twayne's world authors series; 692)

Leal, con su habitual diligencia y claridad, estudia la obra de Rulfo en su contexto sociológico e histórico dentro de México y la vida del autor, mas sin dejar de anotar críticamente la bibliografía más sobresaliente. Además de abordar la génesis, estructura e imaginería de *El llano en llamas* y *Pedro Páramo*, estudia también *El gallo de oro*, clasificada como novela corta por Leal, y algunos guiones cinematográficos.

5233 Lienhard, Martin. El sustrato arcaico en *Pedro Páramo*: Quetzalcoatl y Tlaloc (UEN/LS, 13:1, 1983, p. 473–490)

El autor considera que el sustrato mítico de la novela tiene más que ver con la cosmovisión tolteca-azteca que con la occidental: hay analogía entre el viaje de Quetzalcoatl al país de los muertos en busca de su padre y el de Juan Preciado; Comala y Mictlan (el país de los muertos); el pasado de Comala y el paraíso (Tlalocan); el tiempo mítico de la novela y el de las sociedades agrícolas arcaicas; y entre la identidad funcional de Pedro Páramo y Tlaloc.

5234 Martin, G. Mariano Azuela's point of view in *Los de abajo* (ATSP/VH, 32:2, Autumn 1983, p. 39–46, bibl.)

Azuela se identifica, a través de la novela, con el gusto por la libertad de los personajes, pero su conciencia de clase le impide asociarse verdaderamente con "los de abajo;" a quienes tiene dificultad para describir en su interior y, en consecuencia, nos los presenta como lo haría un extranjero. En cambio conoce muy bien el mundo interior de los personajes intelectuales, los de su misma clase.

5235 Martínez, José Luis. La formación literaria de Agustín Yáñez y *Al filo del agua* (UCLA/M, 12:1/2, mayo 1983, p. 26–40)

Informativa crónica biobibliográfica de Yáñez, enfocada hacia el estudio de *Al filo del agua*, una de las primeras novelas cuyo ambiente se sitúa en la provincia mexicana. En ella, alrededor del pueblo—el protagonista principal—se entrelazan varias acciones simultáneas en un estilo barroco, correspondiente a las exigencias interiores de expresión, para proporcionar una visión crítica del pueblo.

5236 Mata, Oscar. Apuntes sobre la novela *El hipogeo secreto*, de Salvador Elizondo. México: Univ. Autónoma Metropolitana, 1980. 50 p.

Mata considera *El hipogeo secreto* como una historia de una historia en la cual predominan los efectos del intelecto; mientras que en *Farabeuf* resaltan los sensoriales. El ensayista utiliza la comparación constante de ambas novelas para estudiar la primera. También alude a las coincidencias y diferencias de Elizondo con el *nouveau roman* y a las influencias de Poe, Kafka, Proust, Joyce y Borges.

5237 *La Palabra y el Hombre*. Univ. Veracruzana. Nos. 53/54, enero/junio 1985–. Xalapa, Mexico.

Número doble dedicado exclusivamente a la novela mexicana del siglo XX, con la inclusión de muchas de las interesantes ponencias presentadas en el Primer Encuentro de Novela Mexicana del Siglo XX (Jalapa, marzo 1984). Se escribe panorámicamente sobre novela joven, del 68, de "la onda," de la revolución, policiaca y feminina. Destacan los artículos individuales sobre Juan Rulfo, Rosario Castellanos, Luis Spota, Josefina Vicens, Fernando Del Paso y José Agustín.

5239 Para cuando yo me ausente. Compilación de Juan Rulfo. México: Editorial Grijalbo, 1983. 313 p., 8 p. of plates: bibl., ill., ports. (Col. Narrativa. Ensayo)

El libro tiene el mérito de recopilar algunos de los mejores ensayos (de Jorge Ruffinelli, Jean Franco, Emir Rodríguez Monegal, Luis Leal, Manuel Durán y Carlos Monsiváis, entre otros) sobre *Pedro Páramo* y *El llano en llamas*. Parece ser que Rulfo mismo no tuvo nada que ver con la selección ni con el título de la recopilación. El dijo haber dado sólo autorización para que se incluyeran sus fotografías; su nombre en la portada habría sido truco publicitario de los editores.

5240 Pérez, Laura Lee Crumley de. *Balún-Canán* y la construcción narrativa de una cosmovisión indígena (IILI/RI, 50:127, abril/julio 1984, p. 491–503, bibl.)

La novela de Castellanos lleva a cabo una cosmovisión indígena, aneja a una cosmogonía, a causa de que la niña narradora se siente más cercana a su nana india que a su madre blanca, quien la rechaza. Esto hace que la niña adopte lo indígena y rechace lo occidental.

5241 Pérez Huggins, Argenis. El mito como supra-realidad en la narrativa hispanoamericana: el ejemplo de *José Trigo* (*in* Unité et diversité en l'Amérique latine. Bordeaux, France: Univ. of Bordeaux III, 1982, t. 2, p. 217–225)

Opina que muchos novelistas hispanoamericanos, al reducir la función mítica a la vuelta primordial a los orígenes, excluyen el proceso histórico de la sociedad en América Latina. Con esto asimilan, en su visión de ella, la concepción europea. Así, por ejemplo, García Márquez considera la soledad como la responsable del proceso histórico latinoamericano; mientras que Del Paso resuelve las oposiciones, en la integración de *José Trigo*, en la madre. El ensayista propone el uso de una mitología que combine lo primordial con la promoción de los cambios sociales.

5242 Polgar, Mirko. Una análisis del misticismo revolucionario en *Los de abajo*, de Mariano Azuela (CH, 410, agosto 1984, p. 152–162)

Polgar hace ver que la primeras palabras de cada capítulo sugieren lo más importante del mismo en la novela, la cual capta admirablemente las pasiones en su afán de cambiar el orden establecido con la imposición de una fuerza a veces inocente, amoral e inmoral. Ante este movimiento de violencia Azuela asume la actitud profesional del médico que dictamina un diagnóstico poético y realista.

5243 Reeve, Richard M. Selected bibliography: 1949–1982 (WLT, 57:3, 1983, p. 541–546)

Reeve actualiza, aunque sin comentarla y seleccionándola, su "An Annotated Bibliography on Carlos Fuentes: 1946–1969," publicada en *Hispania* (53:4, oct. 1970). Incluye secciones sobre la narrativa, otros libros y ensayos, artículos críticos de Fuentes, entrevistas y traducciones al inglés. La sección dedicada al material crítico sobre el autor registra principalmente libros y artículos escritos (1970–82).

5244 Reeve, Richard M. The short stories of Agustín Yáñez (UCLA/M, 12:1/2, mayo 1983, p. 41–51)

Reeve analiza someramente una docena de cuentos de Yáñez para mostrar que éste también fue un destacado cuentista, aunque haya sobresalido más en la novela. Los cuentos le habrían servido a Yáñez de práctica para sus novelas, cuyos personajes y tesis anticipa en aquéllos.

5245 Revistas literarias mexicanas modernas: *Savia Moderna 1906, Nosotros 1912–1914.* México: Fondo de Cultura Económica, 1980. 679 p.

Savia Moderna acogió a los modernistas tardíos y a los nuevos escritores. En narrativa destacan las colaboraciones de Manuel Othón, Ricardo Gómez Robelo y Alfonso Reyes. Este continúa escribiendo narraciones en *Nosotros*, junto con Julio Torri, Martín Luis Guzmán, Luis González Obregón y Gregorio López y Fuentes, entre otros.

5246 Revistas literarias mexicanas modernas: *Vida Mexicana 1922–1923, Nuestro México 1932.* México: Fondo de Cultura Económica, 1981. 673 p.

En *Vida Mexicana* no se encuentra nada de narrativa mexicana; por el contrario, en *Nuestro México*, ésta abunda sobre todo con los "Cuentos Crueles" del Dr. Atl (Gerardo Murillo) y las "Notas de Provincia" de Salvador Novo. Pero además hay escritos de Mariano Azuela, Alfonso Reyes, Francisco Monterde, Gregorio López y Fuentes y Agustín Yáñez, entre otros.

5247 Robe, Stanley L. Yáñez y el regionalismo (UCLA/M, 12:1/2, mayo 1983, p. 53–77)

Yáñez, con la utilización de nuevas técnicas en sus novelas, desarrolla la psicología de los personajes en base a las costumbres e inclinaciones del lugar en donde viven. Es tan íntima la relación de los personajes con su tierra que ésta, sin perder su idiosincracia regional, sirve de escenario a situaciones de carácter universal.

5248 Robles, Humberto E. Variantes en *Pedro Páramo* (CM/NRFH, 31:1, 1982, p. 106–116)

Cotejo detallado e iluminador de los cambios de la quinta edición de *Pedro Páramo* (1964) con respecto a la primera (1955) y las consecuencias que ellos traen para la novela y su lectura. Estos pueden ser mecánicos (puntuación, montaje de las secciones, etc.), de añadidura u omisión de palabras, léxicos, sintácticos, de retoques metafóricos y de modificaciones sustantivas implicadoras de nuevos significados. Robles registra al menos 200 alteraciones. En conjunto ellas proponen una lectura más ambigua y sugestiva de la novela.

5249 Rosas, Patricia and Lourdes Madrid. Las torturas de la imaginación. México: Premiá Editora, 1982. 70 p.: ill. (Red de Jonás)

Riguroso análisis textual de dos difíciles novelas de Elizondo: *Farabeuf* y *El hipogeo secreto*, enmarcadas, respectivamente, en la concepción erótica de Georges Bataille y filosófica de Edmund Husserl. Ambas novelas surgen de una problemática existencial espacializada en un ambiente hipnótico donde impera el desdoblamiento del narrador y la imprecisión fluctuante de tiempo, espacio y significación.

5250 Ruy Sánchez, Alberto. Al filo de las hojas: voyeurismo y contemplación en *De Anima* (VUELTA, 8:92, julio 1984, p. 29–31, ill.)

La novela de Juan García Ponce implica una mística voyeurista y contemplativa, pero atea, cuyo objeto primordial es el cuerpo. Tal mística sigue un desarrollo paralelo a la de Miguel de Molinos, fundador del quietismo. En *De Anima* el éxtasis contemplativo para Gilberto y Paloma, su creación, se da cuando ella puede ser vista a la perfección en la lectura, la pintura y la filmación.

5251 Sánchez MacGregor, Joaquín. Rulfo y Barthes: análisis de un cuento. México: Editorial Domés, 1982. 126 p.: bibl., ill.

El autor formula un método didáctico, basado en los escritos de Barthes, para analizar textos narrativos. Después lo aplica concretamente al cuento de Rulfo "Nos Han

Dado la Tierra;" el cual es dividido en 47 lexias a las que se cuestiona individualmente para descubrir su código hermenéutico, de acciones, semántico, de referencias y estilístico.

5252 Schärer, Maya. Salvador Elizondo o el imperio de la palabra (UEN/LS, 13:2, 1983, p. 763–779)

Lúcido ensayo del porqué del inacabable cuestionamiento del texto en *Farabeuf*, de Elizondo. Según Schärer la novela propone la muerte como única posibilidad de asir la realidad; pero esa propuesta, al estar fuera de nosotros, es tan desrealizadora como las del espejo, el garabato y el ideograma chino, reiteradas en la novela.

5253 Sinnigen, John H. El desarrollo combinado y desigual en *La muerte de Artemio Cruz* (CH, 396, junio 1983, p. 697–707)

Aplica un concepto socioeconómico, el del subdesarrollo, con el objeto de mostrar cómo la situación socioeconómica, planteada en la novela de Fuentes, hace que los personajes se enmascaren para sobrevivir. La fragmentación de los personajes es consecuencia del enmascaramiento.

5254 Skirius, John. The cycles of history and memory: *Las vueltas de tiempo*, a novel by Agustín Yáñez (UCLA/M, 12:1/2, mayo 1983, p. 79–101)

La novela habría tomado sus lineamientos fundamentales de la nuevas técnicas narrativas combinadas con una concepción de la historia semejante a la de Giambattista Vico. De éste habría procedido la construcción de una estructura simbólica en la novela a través de los títulos de los capítulos, el concepto cíclico de la historia y el uso de arquetipos femeninos de la mitología y la religión para escribir una historia íntima de México. Todo ello lo aplica Yáñez al caso particular del Presidente Plutarco Elías Calles.

5255 Slick, Sam L. José Revueltas. Edited by Luis Dávila. Boston: Twayne, 1983. 226 p., 1 p. of plates: bibl., index, port. (Twayne's world authors series; 683)

Aproximación histórica, descriptiva e impresionista, más que analítica, a las novelas, principales cuentos, obras de teatro y ensayos de Revueltas. No se estudia su producción poética ni sus guiones fílmicos. Se incluye una bibliografía selecta y anotada.

5256 Stoopen, María. *La muerte de Artemio Cruz*: una novela de denuncia y traición. México: UNAM, 1982. 150 p.: bibl. (Seminarios-investigaciones)

Análisis mítico y semiótico de la novela de Fuentes con el objeto de, respectivamente, desenmascarar las superposiciones culturales constitutivas de la identidad mexicana y mostrar la asimilación de Artemio Cruz a un modelo de cultura privilegiado como una traición a la propia identidad. También se analizan las estructuras subyacentes en el montaje del narrador.

5257 Suplemento: Jorge Ibargüengoitia (VUELTA, 9:100, marzo 1985, p. 43–57, ill.)

Textos rememorativos de Ibargüengoitia, escritos por Joy Laville, José de la Colina, Manuel Felguerez, y Gabriel Zaid, con motivo de su muerte reciente. También se recopilan una entrevista y una hermosa nota autobiográfica, así como fragmentos de notas, artículos y una novela inconclusa del autor.

5258 Swietlicki, Catherine. Doubling, reincarnation, and cosmic order in *Terra Nostra* (HISP, 79, sept. 1983, p. 93–104)

Ensayo que analiza cuidadosamente los diversos tipos de doblaje encontrados en la novela de Fuentes, los cuales reencarnan sucesivamente para responder a la necesidad de continuar la función del cosmos: la conservación permanente del mismo universo con las mismas gentes y acontecimientos, a pesar de los cíclicos y aparentes cambios.

5259 Vallarino, Roberto. Textos paralelos. México: UNAM, 1982. 129 p. (Col. Poemas y ensayos)

Reagrupación de ensayos, previamente publicados en diarios y revistas de la Ciudad de México, principalmente sobre los poetas de la revista *Contemporáneos*. Uno de ellos, Salvador Novo, habría sido importantísimo para el desarrollo en México de la prosa periodística y la crónica urbana. La ironía, reflexión, musicalidad visual y verbal del poeta y cuentista Julio Torri, miembro del Ateneo de la juventud, son presentadas como influencias notables en la obra de Gilberto Owen (también de *Contemporáneos*), Juan José Arreola y Salvador Elizondo. Además hay un interesante análisis de los personajes de *El tañido de la flauta*, novela de Sergio Pitol, así como otro sobre Juan García Ponce como ensayista.

5260 Verdugo, Iber H. Un estudio de la narrativa de Juan Rulfo. México: UNAM, 1982. 380 p.: bibl. (Col. Letras del siglo XX)

Interesante aproximación semiótica a *Pedro Páramo* y *El llano en llamas* en base al análisis del argumento, las secuencias y los pesonajes de la novela y cada uno de los cuentos, con el objeto de establecer hipótesis de significado y sentido. La aplicación rigurosa y paulatina de esta metodología ofrece al final la siguiente perspectiva: la obra de Rulfo presenta el conflicto del hombre con el mundo y el dominio fatal de este último sobre el primero, el cual es destituido de su identidad. El discurso de Rulfo implica una posibilidad de reencontrar esa individualidad.

5261 Washburn, Yulan M. Juan José Arreola. Boston: Twayne, 1983. 143 p.: bibl., index (Twayne's world authors series; 693)

Estudio introductorio de la obra narrativa de Arreola, organizado alrededor de los temas de la situación existencial y artística, las relaciones hombre-mujer y las preocupaciones teológicas y nacionales. Proporciona, además, una biografía y bibliografía selecta y anotada. El autor se propone sugerir maneras de ver y leer a Arreola.

5262 *World Literature Today*. A literary quarterly of the Univ. of Oklahoma. Vol. 57, No. 4, Autumn 1983–. Norman.

Número colectivo dedicado al estudio de la obra de Carlos Fuentes. Reúne ensayos de Fuentes sobre sí mismo (item **5228**), Alazraki (item **5212**), Alfred J. Mac Adam ("Carlos Fuentes: the Burden of History"), Allen Josephs ("The End of *Terra Nostra*), Gustavo Sainz ("Carlos Fuentes: a Permanent Bedazzlement"), Margaret Sayers Peden ("Voice as a Function of Vision: the Voice of the Teller"), Wendy B. Faris ("The Return of the Past: Chiasmus in the Texts of Carlos Fuentes"), Jonathan Tittler ("*Cambio de zona/piel sagrada*: Transfigurations in Carlos Fuentes"), Gloria Durán ("*Orchids in the moonlight*: Fuentes as Feminist and Jungian Playwright") y Martha Paley Francescato (item **5227a**). También se incluye una bibliografía de Richard M. Reeve (item **5243**).

5263 Young, Dolly. Mexican reactions to Tlatelolco, 1968 (LARR, 20:2, 1985, p. 71–85, bibl.)

Bien desarrollada presentación panorámica de ensayos, textos documentales, crónicas, novelas y poesías generados en México por los trágicos acontecimientos de 1968, resaltando los considerados sobresalientes por la autora. Destaca su clasificación de "New Journalism" para los textos, generalmente clasificados como novelas, de *La noche de Tlatelolco* (de Elena Poniatowska), *Los días y los años* (de Luis González de Alba) y *Con él, conmigo, con nosotros tres* (de María Luisa Mendoza).

20th Century: Prose Fiction: Central America

RENE PRIETO, *Assistant Professor of Spanish, Southern Methodist University*

MORE THAN EVER BEFORE, Central American artists and writers are questioning the status quo, damning conventions and frequently (as in the case of testimonial literature) opting to record rather than ideate a society in turmoil. Their voices in fiction are carving original paths within three well defined tendencies: political indictment, eroticism, and indigenismo. Naturally, these three trends constitute in different—albeit related—ways, a formal rejection of repressive systems be they political, moral, or social. We know too well how such systems have institutionalized what Juan Goytisolo has aptly described as a veritable genocide of the American republics. But if we judge from the evidence at hand, much is being done to curtail such genocide, at least in one country. In Nicaragua, a veritable tide of publications has flooded the market since the Sandinista victory. The Editorial Nueva Nicaragua has been publishing a steady stream of testimonials which includes José Carlos Guadamuz's *Y . . . "Las casas quedaron llenas de humo"* (item **5979**) and Ricardo Morales Avilés's *No pararemos de andar jamás* (item **5985**), while Ediciones Primavera Popular of Managua recently printed Jorge Eduardo Arellano's thrilling account of the *agrarista* rebellion during the civil war, *Timbucos y calandracas* (item **5270**). Nevertheless, political indictment is not the only type of criticism brandished by men of letters nor is Nicaragua the only country crying out against repression. José León Sánchez's *Isla de hombres solos* (item **5292**), where the focus is life in prison, is not only a profoundly moving rebuke of man's cruelty to man, but also one of the most original works of fiction to be published in Latin America in the last few years. In a different vein, anti-clerical feeling is evident in some illuminating and varied works that challenge ecclesiastical narrow-mindedness and are exemplified by Arnoldo Castro Jenkins's ironic diatribes against the Church (item **5279**) and Francisco Albizúrez Palma's stirring indictment of religious orders in *Casa de curas y otras locuras* (item **5265**). In Central America, this relentless battle against repression is also evident in fiction that focuses on perceptions of and attitudes toward the human body in novels such as César Valverde's *La feliz indolencia* (item **5313**) and Enrique Chuez's *La casa de las sirenas pálidas* (item **5280a**), in which a lack of moral sensibility underlies more widespread social illnesses. The erotic and the bizarre are successfully combined in Carmen Naranjo's masterful short stories in *Ondina* (item **5296**) as well as in Rima de Vallbona's ground-breaking novel, *Las sombras que perseguimos* (item **5312**). In this work historical events (World War II and the deportation of German immigrants from Costa Rica) commingle with imaginary ones that exemplify man's ability to forge fictions. Finally, the third and certainly most enduring of the three thematic tendencies noted above, is one which only recently has led to a closer examination of its roots. Indigenista fiction thrives above all in Guatemala, an idiosyncracy which Francisco Albizúrez Palma examines in a very informative article (item **5317**). He believes the country's lack of industrialization and of major urban centers account for Guatemala's deep-seated rural traditions and thus the focusing of its fiction. Such emphasis notwithstanding, the fact remains that, until recently, works written about rural Guatemala were seldom if ever conceived by Indians. That this is no longer the case can be credited to the Centro de Estudios Folklóricos of the Univ. de San Carlos which began recording and publishing a fascinating body of folktales, *Cuentos populares de Guatemala* (item **5282**), thus preserving the rich material of the *cuenteros* or storytellers. The dissemination and understanding of indigenista fiction from Central America, as well as the interpretation of materials drawn from such classic stories, largely depends on access to periodicals such as *La Tradición Popular, Tradiciones de Guatemala* and *Latin American Indian Literatures Journal*. This is very much the case as we enter the much awaited era of Mayan literacy with the epoch-making hieroglyphic translations noted by Linda Schele and Mary Miller in *The blood of kings* (New York: George Braziller, 1986). Equally important in their own right although in a different field, are four works of literary and social criticism: Carlos Francisco Monge's fascinating essay on the relationship between historic reality and contemporary poetry in Costa Rica entitled *La imagen separada* (item **5955a**); Marielos Aguilar's monograph, *Carlos Luis Fallas: su época y sus luchas* (item **5316**); Manuel Picado Gómez's ambitious *Literatura/ideología/crítica: notas para un estudio de la literatura costarricense* (item **5339**); and last but not least, Pablo Antonio Cuadra's highly controversial article about Nicaragua's current repression against artists and writers, "Situación de la Cultura" in *Revista del Pensamiento Centroamericano* (item **5324**).

PROSE FICTION

5264 Aguilera, Fito. "Rosca, S.A.:" novela: prohibida para los mojigatos, los serviles y los hipócritas. 2a ed. Panamá: F. Aguilera, 1984. 348 p.

The "Rosca" is a Panamanian institution working ruthlessly for the enrichment of its members. The problem is that the members draw their wealth from the nation's coffers, membership depending strictly on blood ties. Engrossing novel portrays the political maneuverings of this blood brotherhood within the framework of a love triangle.

5265 Albizúrez Palma, Francisco. Casa de curas y otras locuras. Guatemala: Editorial Rin 78, 1982. 177 p. (Col. Literatura; 15)

Casa de curas y otras locuras is a lucid and truthful rebuke of religious orders and traditional ecclesiastical education in Guatemala. Sections composing the novel were first published as installments in the Guatemalan newspaper *El Imparcial* creating much commotion among Catholic readers.

5266 Albizúrez Palma, Francisco and Catalina Barrios y Barrios. Historia de la literatura guatemalteca. v. 2. Ciudad Universitaria, Guatemala: Editorial Universitaria de Guatemala, 1981. 338 p.: bibl. (Col. Historia nuestra; 2)

Vol. 2 of three-volume anthology focusing on 20th-century Guatemalan writers since *modernismo*. Most authors included were part of the so-called "generations of 1919 and 1920." Also includes chapters on journalism and women writers of Guatemala.

5267 Allwood Paredes, Juan. Osicala. San Salvador: Editorial Espacta, 1984. 279 p.

First-person narrative about the good old (and long gone) days in a peaceful village, Osicala, in eastern El Salvador. Progress and then the fury of violence and warfare transform the village into a sad, forlorn place.

5268 Alvarado Martínez, Enrique. Cuentos de calle y camino. Managua: Publicaciones UCA, 197? 45 p.: ill.

Two scripts for the radio and 13 short stories. "Pancho, Chico, Francisco, Frank," a tongue-in-cheek account of social mobility, rings most particularly with the stamp of truth.

5269 Alvarez, Oscar. El templo del jaguar. San José: Editorial Costa Rica, 1984. 151 p.: ill. (Ensayo poética; 4)

Polished collection of "poetic essays" on historic and philosophical concerns which reads like a non-fiction version of Borges's historical travesties. Terse to the point of being spartan and always with a disturbing element, these insightful essays—like Spanish versions of the haiku—are always food for thought. Some are a few sentences long, others, several pages. But all of them advertise the author's keen penchant for esotericism and the occult (be it the teachings of the cabala—"Historia de la Judería de Córdoba"—or of Mayan symbols—"La Biblioteca Maya de Mérida").

5270 Arellano, Jorge Eduardo. Timbucos y calandracas. Managua: Ediciones Primavera Popular, 1982. 140 p. (Ediciones Primavera popular; 3)

Action of this novel vividly recreates the 19th-century history of the Nicaraguan city of Granada. Action follows the *agrarista* rebellion which reached its apogee within the context of the civil war. Told in different terms, the novel describes the struggle between *timbucos* (future conservatives) and *calandracas* (later to be known as liberals).

5271 Asturias, Miguel Angel. Leyendas y poemas. Edición y prólogo de Francisco Albizúrez Palma. Guatemala: Editorial Piedra Santa, 1981. 51 p. (Lo mejor de Miguel Angel Asturias; 5)

Selection of five short stories (including the "Leyenda de la Tatuana" and the "Leyenda del Cadejo") and a handful of Asturias's best poems. The anthology is selected and prefaced by a good critical essay on Asturias written by Francisco Albizúrez Palma.

5272 Ayala, Alvaro Lagos de and Belén Lagos Oteiza. Nostalgias y migraciones. San José: SECASA, 1983. 78 p.: ill.

Collection of short stories rich in irony but poor on wit. In "La 'Beatificación' de Doña Mercedes Ferreira," two voices alternate. The priest reads a requiem for the soul of "saintly" Mercedes Ferreira, while the omniscient narrator points out how she was an ambitious madam who made her money exploiting girls from the orphanage.

5273 Balaguer, Carlos. Sentimientos. San Salvador: Editorial Hormiga, 1982. 168 p.: ill. (Palabras; 1)

Collection of 50 short and very personal essays on a variety of subjects including prisons, love, and the fleeting quality of life ("La Vida de Tres Días").

5274 Britton, Rosa María. El ataud de uso. Panamá: M. Arosemena, 1983. 303 p. (Col. Premio Ricardo Miró. Novela; 1982)

Recipient of the 1982 Ricardo Miró Prize, this imaginative novel relates the adventures of a poor man in the remote village of Chumico in southernmost Panama. Wealthy and powerful at the time of his death, he ends up (through a series of humorous mishaps) buried in a humble wrap like all the village poor. Pleasurable reading combining a daring handling of time with fleeting moments of Harlequin-type romance.

5275 Cañas, Alberto F. La soda y el F.C. San José: Editorial Costa Rica, 1983. 96 p. (Col. Colibrí)

Adventures of a green-fingered opportunist and politician in provincial Costa Rican town of San Luis. Novel narrated as if it were a football game by witty third party who brandishes a number of mimetic stratagems destined to add verisimilitude. *La soda y el F.C.* even has an "Intermission" during which narrator summarizes events of the first half.

5276 Candanedo, César A. Memorias de un caminante: relatos. Panamá: Impresora de la Nación, 1982. 111 p.

Consists of 15 short stories with a common theme: exploitation of Indians and workers of banana republics.

5277 Caso, Quino. Cuando la lechuza canta. San Salvador: Ministerio del Interior, 1983. 221 p.: port.

Collection of 15 portraits of the Salvadoran countryside and colorful characters who inhabit it ("La Abuela Josefa de los Angeles," "El Tío Tomás"). Written in vernacular style and liberally sprinkled with much local color.

5278 Castellanos Moya, Horacio. ¿Qué signo es usted, niña Berta? Tegucigalpa: Editorial Guaymuras, 1981. 167 p. (Col. Fragua)

Consists of 15 short stories with sociopolitical themes about El Salvador.

(Horacio Castellanos was born in Honduras but spent most of his life in El Salvador). Stories such as "¿Qué Signo Es Usted, Niña Berta?" give an insightful, ironic portrayal of social nuances.

5279 Castro Jenkins, Arnoldo. ¿Cuentos—? San José: Instituto del Libro, Ministerio de Cultura, Juventud y Deportes, 1984. 282 p.: ill.

Collection of short stories with strong anti-clerical penchant. Theme of homosexuality and the priesthood is broached in "La Mujer del Cura." In a tragically ironic story, "Aggiornamento," the archbishop replaces a self-sacrificing but leftist priest with a conventional, ambitious and self-serving one.

5280 Changmarín, Carlos F. El guerrillero transparente: Victoriano Lorenzo. Panamá: Ediciones del Instituto Nacional de Cultura, 1982. 101 p.

Awarded the Ricardo Miró Prize, this novel dramatizes the life and personality of Gen. Victoriano Lorenzo and vividly describes the period known as "war of a thousand days" (la guerra de los mil días).

5280a Chuez, Enrique. La casa de las sirenas pálidas: novela. Panamá: Editorial Signos, 1983. 104 p. (Col. Portobelo; 13. Serie Autores panameños)

Mixture of sex and politics in tawdry setting of small-town brothel named *Las Sirenas.* Novel develops as series of episodes in the form of character portraits of the prostitutes, their customers, and their shady pasts.

5281 Cuadra, Manolo. Solo en la compañía. Managua: Editorial Nueva Nicaragua, 1982. 173 p.: ill. (Biblioteca popular sandinista; 15)

Fascinating anthology of Cuadra's classics including selections from his masterful *Itinerario de Little Corn Island* (1937), *Contra Sandino en la montaña* (1942), his novel *Almidón* (1945), as well as two essays (on Darío and Rimbaud respectively) and a letter. This defiant jack of all trades (poet, writer, journalist, boxer, dockworker and soldier) never loses an opportunity to ridicule the institutions which prevent society from forging ahead.

5282 Cuentos populares de Guatemala. Primera serie. Edición de Celso A. Lara Figueroa. Ilustraciones de Roberto Cabrera.

Guatemala: Centro de Estudios Folklóricos, Univ. de San Carlos de Guatemala, 1982. 237 p., 15 leaves of plates: bibl., ill. (Col. Archivos de folklore literario; 2)

Fascinating collection of folktales compiled by the Centro de Estudios Folklóricos of the Univ. de San Carlos (Guatemala). Classified according to theme (stories about animals, the fantastic, religion, the devil, death, ogres, and witches) from a body of over 1400 tales recorded by field workers. Followed by brief, haunting biographies of the *cuenteros* or storytellers.

5283 Díaz Lozano, Argentina. Peregrinaje: novela. 7a ed. Guatemala: J. de Pineda Ibarra, 1981. 287 p.

Seventh edition of prize-winning novel in the Concurso Latinoamericano Farrar & Rinehart and Unión Panamericana of Washington. Argentina Díaz skillfully describes life in Honduras during early part of this century (1916–31). Events are seen through the eyes of a girl growing up and entering adolescence. *Peregrinaje* movingly portrays the relationship between a mother who is a self-sacrificing teacher, and her daughter.

5284 Dobles, Fabián. Cuentos de Fabián Dobles. San José: Editorial Universitaria Centroamericana, 1983. 141 p.

Collection of 15 acidly humorous short stories which vividly describe Costa Rican folkways. Includes tale of two brothers who exchange their lives and destinies with each other ("El Trueque"), of a rambunctious old lady who takes active part in her own funeral celebration ("Mamita Maura") and of murderous family rivalries "(La Mata de la Familia").

5285 Elizondo Arce, Hernán. La ventana. Ilustraciones de Hugo Díaz. San José: Editorial Costa Rica, 1983. 115 p.: ill. (Col. Colibrí)

Vivid chronicle of people of Costa Rica. Naturalistic, ironic ("La Vedette") and often painful portrayal (as in "Deforestación") of changes which transform this erstwhile bucolic Central American republic.

5286 Escobar Galindo, David. La estrella cautiva: novela. San Salvador: Editorial Ahora, 1985. 75 p.

Fascinating short novel on themes of jealousy, of unresolved mysteries which may or may not be a fiction within the fiction.

Winner of First Honorable Mention, Certamen Centroamericano de Quezaltenango, 1984.

5287 Fernández Hall Haroldo, Francisco. Letras chapinas. Guatemala: Editorial Fernández Hall, 1983. 2 v.: ill.

Reedition of selected writings (e.g., fiction, literary chronicles, poems, theater) commemorating centennial of author's birth. Originally published in newspapers (e.g., *Diario La República*) and magazines (e.g., *El Ideal, Juan Chapín*). Haroldo is a Christian author in whose work the presence of God plays a primordial role; his prose is decorative and markedly influenced by *modernismo*.

5288 Garache, Abel. Un agujero en la portada. Managua: Farach, 1977. 79 p.

Collection of short stories, some commonplace, crass, innovative or bizarre (e.g., "Antichrist!" concerns two fetuses who have intercourse in their mother's womb). Stories have element of surprise whether the theme is macabre ("Melgasbal"), social criticism ("El Pepenahierro") or science fiction ("Fetoprecoz").

5289 Gómez, Juan Antonio and **Digno Quintero Pérez.** El puente: prosas. Panamá: J.A. Gómez, 1983. 112 p.

Collection of short stories by two young Panamanians with widely differing styles. Gómez writes concise, often one-paragraph stories, while Quintero Pérez's prose is exuberant and frequently allegorical. Both share an interest in fantasy and the bizarre, as can be seen in the latter's "Cristina y su Universo" (about a woman and her prized doll) and in Gómez's "La Herencia" or the macabre "La Ultima Visita," much influenced by Poe.

5290 Gómez Estrada, Alvaro Rogelio; Calixto; and Jorge Gudiel Castellanos. Cuentos cortos. Guatemala: Editorial Universitaria de Guatemala, 1982. 44 p. (Col. Creación literaria; 14)

Anthology of short stories by three Guatemalan writers who share an interest in the supernatural. In Gómez's "Hacia la Noche" a prostitute describes her well-worn body with disgust before realizing she is dead. In "El Premio Novel" by Calixto, two writers (one of them being "Miguel Angel Aspuru") meet as children in a fateful dream which sets their destinies.

5291 Gutiérrez, Alejandra. María sin casa y sin amo. Santiago: Editorial Nascimiento, 1980. 67 p.

Very unusual book by Costa Rican author, long-time resident of Chile and Mexico. This elegiac prose poem tells the story of a folk heroine who is, in a sense, the embodiment of every suffering woman.

5292 León Sánchez, José. La isla de los hombres solos. San José: Editorial Costa Rica, 1984. 234 p.

Undoubtedly one of the most original and moving books written in Central America in the last few years, *La isla de los hombres solos* is a riveting *novela testimonio* about life and death in the island prison of San Lucas. José León Sánchez artistically reconstructs the hallucionatory world of the prison with its horror, cruelties and rare moments of human tenderness, but his novel is much more than a fascinating adventure; it is an impassioned homily against cruelty and a fervent exhortation in defense of human rights.

5293 Manjarrez, Héctor. No todos los hombres son románticos. México: Ediciones Era, 1983. 120 p. (Biblioteca Era)

Eight unusual and frequently morbid short stories in which death and self-hatred play prominent parts. Of particular note are "Historia" (an erotic liaison between a poor foreign artist and a British matron) and "Amor" (third person narrative in which all female characters are referred to by the clothes they wear). Manjarrez's style is always skillful but his endings are sometimes unresolved and disconcerting.

5294 Méndez, Francisco. Cuentos de Joyabaj. Guatemala: Tipografía Nacional, 1984. 403 p. (Col. Guatemala; 10. Serie Miguel Angel Asturias; 4)

Although not uniformly outstanding, Méndez's 17 short stories are, without exception, poignant examples of the criollista and indigenista traditions which continue to thrive in Guatemala. Author makes frequent reference to traditional Indian beliefs (in stories such as "El Nahual," "Cicimite," "El Omnipresente") and shows a profound understanding of his people in his masterpiece, "Mari'Antoña," the tale of a mother who dies of grief.

5295 Muñoz, Víctor. Lo que yo quiero es que se detenga el tren. Guatemala: Tipografía Nacional, 1983. 154 p. (Col. Literatura; 18)

Collection of short stories followed by literary fragment. In a straightforward, irreverent style, Víctor Muñoz relates the petty foibles and little vanities of his contemporaries. Concludes with a witty panegyric entitled "Oda al Huevo" in praise of man's favorite hard-shelled friend.

5296 Naranjo, Carmen. Ondina. San José: Editorial Universitaria Centroamericana, 1983. 123 p. (Col. Septimo día)

These wonderfully crafted short stories with a strong erotic cast were awarded the EDUCA prize (Editorial Universitaria Centroamericana) in 1982. Story that gives collection its title shows up—with a masterful sense of suspense—the shortcomings of erotic fantasies, while in "Las Peinetas del Elefante," Naranjo ironically relates the merits of learning.

5297 Narradores panameños. Compilación de Cipriano Fuentes. Caracas: Doble Fondo Editores, 1984. 164 p.: bibl. (Col. Narrativa)

Consists of 20th-century Panamanian short stories including works by Darío Herrera, Ricardo Miró and the more contemporary Dimas Lidio Pitty and Enrique Jaramillo Levi. Preface offers succinct and useful overview of Panama's literature.

5298 El Nuevo cuento hondureño. Selección e introducción de Jorge Luis Oviedo. Tegucigalpa: Ediciones AELUNAH, 1983. 91 p. (Letras hondureñas)

Collection of recent Honduran short stories. Of particular interest are Roberto Castillo's "Anita la Cazadora de Insectos," about a model student who goes suddenly mad and is thrown out of her house, and Horacio Castellanos Maya's "Como si lo Hubiéramos Jodido Todas," in which a maid kills a newborn baby to seek revenge against her mistress.

5299 Oqueli, Arturo. El gringo lenca. 3a ed. Tegucigalpa: Editorial Lypsa, 1983. 141 p. (Col. Cambal; 1)

Novela testimonio. Interviews with the son of a North American mine engineer and a Lenca Indian (autochthonous people whose culture flourished in the western section of modern Honduras). Colorful chronicle in which the country's mineral wealth takes the limelight.

5300 Peck Fernández, Federico. Renovación. Tegucigalpa: Univ. Nacional Autónoma de Honduras, Editorial Universitaria, 1982. 186 p. (Col. Letras hondureñas; 13)

Collection of short stories, conferences, and articles by the Honduran writer. Variety of themes include "The Lie of Panamericanism" as well as discussions of Nicaraguan politics between 1910–26 ("El Caso de Nicaragua") and of the class struggle in Honduras ("Problema Obrero").

5301 Pinto, Julieta. Abrir los ojos. San José: Mesen Editores, 1982. 66 p. (Col. 1856)

Sixteen stories with a common theme: the unfortunate lot of neglected and abandoned children. Drug involvement ("La Gente no Entiende") child abuse ("Lupita"), and rape ("Justicia") are portrayed with great poignancy.

5302 Pinto, Julieta. Los marginados. San José: Editorial Costa Rica, 1984. 136 p.

Sensitive, straightforward stories about the hardships of rural life in Costa Rica. All ring with the stamp of truth but particularly stirring are "Tierra Ajena," about a family stripped of their land by a foreign company, and "El Maestro Rural," the tale of a young teacher who chooses to return to a life of hardships in a god-forsaken town out of love for his fellow men.

5303 Ramírez, Sergio. ¿Te dió miedo la sangre? La Habana: Casa de las Américas, 1982. 308 p. (Col. La Honda Casa de las Américas Cuba)

Cuban edition of the lavish, well written and ironic portrayal of a dictator (patterned on Somoza) by Nicaragua's Vice-President and author of *Tiempo de fulgor* and *El pensamiento vivo de Sandino*.

5304 Rutilio Quezada, José. Dolor de patria: novela. El Salvador: Clásicos Roxsil, 1983. 307 p.

Costumbrista novel with strong emphasis on ecology. Author, a doctor in biology and entomology, is a tenacious critic of man's wastefulness and blind destruction of his biological patrimony. The role of women is also emphasized, and they are represented as foundations of the family and transmitters of transcendental values which make up the identity of Salvadorans. Author handles chronological shifts, epistolary form and a dialogue between the living and the dead with great skill.

5305 Salarrué. Cuentos de barro. 14a ed. San Salvador: UCA Editores, 1984. 122 p. (Col. Gavidia; 6. Cuento)

Reedition of classic collection of short stories about rural workers of El Salvador. Salarrué is a master in the portrayal of folkways; his insight and familiarity into the minds and hearts of his countrymen is nowhere more evident than in the poignant "La Honra" (about a girl's lost honor) and the humorous "La Botija" (about an Indian who learns to work without working while he searches for buried gold).

5306 Salarrué. Lo mejor de Salarrué: 11 cuentos. Guatemala: Piedra Santa, 1983. 64 p.

Selected short stories by one of the most inventive Salvadoran authors of the 20th century. Most of them are of folk origin and give ample evidence of Salarrué's masterful ability to reproduce the language of his people and portray their customs and beliefs.

5307 Sánchez Valladares, J. Wilfredo. Ticante. Edición de Ramiro Colindres O. Tegucigalpa: Corp. Editora Nacional, 1983. 221 p.: ill.

Novel conceived in the guise of a war journal and written by Honduran infantry colonel. Deals directly with action in the Ocotepeque front (the battlefield of "El Ticante") during the Soccer War between Honduras and El Salvador (June 1969).

5308 Sierra I., Oscar A. Verde Verapaz: cuentos. S.l.: Editorial José de Pineda Ibarra, 1982. 217 p.: ill.

Collected short stories. Hardships of the Guatemalan Indian unseated by the uncertainty of revolutions, historical events, and the greed and abuse of wealthy landowners.

5309 Solís Bolaños, Hernán. Sexto, no exterminar. San José: Editorial Costa Rica, 1984. 92 p.

Well written, mesmerizing plea in defense of freedom, justice and, above all, of peace. Student protagonist is sent to jail and tortured. Humanitarian author correlates the beginnings of a better age with dismissal of armies.

5310 Sorto, Manuel. Operación amor. San Salvador: Editorial Universitaria, 1980. 63 p. (Col. Literatura; 1)

Group of hippies takes over military camp with the help of its commander who has been turned on to drugs. Despite its seemingly farcical plot, *Operación amor* turns out to be a subversive appeal against oppression.

5311 Thorndike, Guillermo. El evangelio según Sandino. Lima: Editorial Labrusa, 1983. 261 p.: port.

Required reading for anyone interested in an insider's view of the activities of the Sandinista National Liberation Front up to 1979. Fascinating and terrifying account combines historical facts with reconstructed events such as the assassination of Pedro Joaquín Chamorro in 1978. Vivid chronicle culminating with Somoza's overthrow is prefaced by Sandino's gospel to the effect that the Final Judgement will take place in the 20th century with a "Proletarian Explosion" against the imperialists of the world.

5312 Vallbona, Rima de. Las sombras que perseguimos: novela. San José: Editorial Costa Rica, 1983. 183 p.

Historical events (World War II and the deportation of German immigrants from Costa Rica) commingle with the role of the imagination, of man's ability to forge a fiction which becomes a reason for being. Cristina's monologue, as she goes mad and imagines all the men in the city lusting for her, is a tour de force in this brilliant, original novel.

5313 Valverde, César. La feliz indolencia. San José: Editorial Costa Rica, 1982. 113 p.

Novel with widely contrasting settings. With artful irony, tells story of young Costa Rican, his student days in Europe and his return to San José. Explores problems of identity and cultural alienation.

5314 Zeceña Navas, Porfirio. La tierra no es de nayden: cuentos. Guatemala: Editorial José de Pineda Ibarra, 1982. 163 p.: port.

Author of poems (*Momentos líricos*) and romantic novels (*Primaveral*), Zeceña's short stories are set in the eastern region of Guatemala (around Santa Catarina Mita and the shores of Los Esclavos river). They usually convey a strong sociopolitical message and some (such as "La Tierra No Es de Nayden") advocate a peasant revolt.

5315 Zúñigo Díaz, Francisco. Todos los domingos: cuentos. San José: Editorial Costa Rica, 1983. 101 p.

Consists of 23 short stories, written in a straightforward manner, about daily experiences which are often painful ("La Carretica de Luis Angel") and elusive ("Todos los Domingos").

LITERARY CRITICISM AND HISTORY

5316 Aguilar, Marielos. Carlos Luis Fallas: su época y sus luchas. San José: Editorial Porvenir, 1983. 272 p.: bibl. (Col. Debate)

Valuable study of the celebrated author of *Mamita Yunai*. Unlike most previous monographs on Fallas, this original study sees his literary production in the light of sociopolitical events which were both the wick and the powder of his career. Aguilar highlights the role of both the Communist Party and of Fallas in the banana strike of 1934, as well as the militant author's participation in the workers' movement (1948–66).

5317 Albizúrez Palma, Francisco. Criollismo guatemalteco: 1930–1950 (Letras de Guatemala [Univ. de San Carlos, Guatemala] 2, dic. 1980, p. 13–27)

Criollista fiction is alive and well in Guatemala, undoubtedly because of the country's vigorous rural tradition. In this informative article critic glosses over life and works of key Guatemalan *criollistas* during the 1930s-50s: Carlos Samayoa Chinchilla, Francisco Méndez, Alfredo Balsells Rivera, Rosendo Santa Cruz, Mario Monteforte Toledo, Francisco Barnoya Gálvez, Rafael Zea Ruano, and Virgilio Rodríguez Macal.

5318 Albizúrez Palma, Francisco. Grandes momentos de la literatura guatemalteca: índice biobibliográfico de la literatura guatemalteca. Guatemala: Editorial J. de Pineda Ibarra, 1983. 123 p.: bibl.

Concise if somewhat brief overview of Guatemalan literature by the Director of the Institute for the Study of National Literature is divided into two parts: 1) focuses on roots, the colonial period, and 19th and 20th centuries, and 2) concentrates on cultural features of literary development as well as genres. Contains helpful and lengthy biobibliographical index of Guatemalan literature.

5319 Barahona Jiménez, Luis. Apuntes para una historia de las ideas estéticas en Costa Rica. San José: Ministerio de Cultura, Juventud y Deportes, Dirección de Publicaciones, 1982. 151 p.

Critical study of literary development in Costa Rica with chapters on realism, *modernismo*, the 20th-century novel, and the generation of post-modernist poets.

5320 Barrios y Barrios, Catalina. José Rodríguez Cerna (Letras de Guatemala [Univ. de San Carlos, Guatemala] 2, dic. 1980, p. 29–40, bibl.)

Biography and one-page bibliography on the esteemed, although today seldom mentioned Guatemalan chronicler and journalist.

5321 Brañas, César. Confines y problemas de la generación literaria del novecientos veinte (Letras de Guatemala [Univ. de San Carlos, Guatemala] 2, dic. 1980, p. 77–99)

Describes ideology and difficulties of generation which contributed to the fall of Estrada Cabrera in 1920 and founded the People's Univ. No one was ready to believe that a country with an agricultural economy could afford the luxury of recognizing the writer's profession as worthy. This attitude of the 1920s had a deleterious effect on today's generation of writers who have, for the most part, turned toward journalism. Other factors—uneven government support, illiteracy and the high cost of printing in Guatemala—hamper the production and interest of potential writers.

5322 Corral, Wilfrido H. Lector sociedad y género en Monterroso. Veracruz, Mexico: Centro de Investigaciones Lingüístico-Literarias, Instituto de Investigaciones Humanísticas, Univ. Veracruzana, 1985. 228 p.: appendix, bibl.

Based on doctoral dissertation. Examines the great Guatemalan writer's work with keen insight and impressive scholarship. Chap. 1 (on critical background) is written dissertation-style, but following ones contain very useful analysis of Monterroso's style (e.g., use of oxymoron, natural connectives, narration in *medias res*, use of colloquial language).

5323 Cuadra, Pablo Antonio. En el umbral de una nueva época: notas sobre el desarrollo de una literatura asediada (El Pez y la Serpiente [Editorial Unión, Managua] 24, verano 1981, p. 5–19)

Perceives Nicaragua as a bridge between cultures where North and South, Spanish and Indian commingle and transform each other. The autochthonous Indians (e.g., Chorotega and Nicaraguas) had no written literature. Indian culture is overwhelmed by outsiders who set back the essential process of expressing what is American. Since the 16th century and until Darío, literary expression took two forms: *literatura culta* and *literatura popular*. Both traditions are still preserved (as *interiorista* and *exteriorista*), although since the Sandinista revolution, it is clear that poetry has become one of the fundamental voices of Nicaraguan people.

5324 Cuadra, Pablo Antonio. Situación de la cultura (RCPC, 40:186, enero/marzo 1985, p. 91–100)

Written four years after item **5323**, this is a stirring outcry against an ideological takeover which forces Nicaragua back to where it was before the Sandinista victory: that is, full circle from one form of dictatorship (Somoza's) to another (Marxism-Leninism). Article is an eye-opening account of repressive means used by Nicaragua's revolutionary power structure to clip wings of artists and writers not aligned with the system. Cuadra claims that art and literature have been as betrayed as Sandino's own revolution.

5325 Domínguez de Rodríguez Pasqués, Petrona. El discurso indirecto libre en la narrativa de Miguel Angel Asturias (*in* International Congress of Hispanists, 4th, 1971, Salamanca, Spain. Actas. Dirección de Eugenio de Bustos Tovar. Salamanca, Spain: Univ. de Salamanca, 1982, v. 2, p. 479–486)

Purely descriptive itemization of the indirect style in two of Asturias's novels: *El Señor Presidente* and *El alhajadito*. In the latter, Asturias evinces an attraction for everything that is old and abandoned, a preoccupation that can be compared to that of García Márquez's in *One hundred years of solitude*.

5326 Escoto, Julio. Las instancias mágicas de *Hombres de maíz* de Miguel Angel Asturias (AHL/B, 24:26, junio 1982, p. 59–76)

Following discussion on magical realism, critic explains how Asturias turns to his

Mayan past in order to compose *Hombres de maíz*. Speaks knowledgeably about Maya beliefs but does little to elucidate Asturias's novel.

5327 García Monge, Joaquín. Cartas selectas de Joaquín García Monge. Selección e introducción de Eugenio García Carrillo. San José: Editorial Costa Rica, 1983. 154 p., 2 leaves of plates: ill. (Col. Colibrí)

Selected letters (some of only relative interest) written by the well known Costa Rican author of realist and costumbrista fiction (e.g., *El Mote, Las hijas del campo, La mala sombra y otros sucesos*).

5328 Guardia, Gloria. Aspectos de creación en la novelística centroamericana (El Pez y la Serpiente [Editorial Unión, Managua] 25, invierno 1981, p. 97–111)

Panamanian novelist (*Tiniebla blanca, Despertar sin raíces*) and critic ponders over the difficulties of writing in Central America where cultural traditions are limited and freedom of expression sorely lacking. Writers here produce either extremely local (rather than universal or "planetary") literature or frivolous escapist works. It is a collective responsibility to create channels for expression and creation in this part of the world.

5329 Guardia, Gloria. La búsqueda del rostro: temas literarios; ensayos. Panamá: Editorial Signos, 1983. 153 p. (Col. Portobelo; 14. Serie Autores panameños)

A fascinating collection of essays on a wide variety of literary themes such as the nature of criticism ("La Búsqueda del Rostro"), Unamuno's theatre ("Por Qué Fracasó el Teatro de Unamuno"), and the short stories of Panamanian author Rogelio Sinán ("Una Revisión de la Vanguardia en Panamá").

Hacia una política cultural de la Revolución Sandinista. See *HLAS 47:6192*.

5330 Horl, Sabine. Ironía y timidez: acerca de *Movimiento perpetuo* de Augusto Monterroso (Iberoromania [Max Niemeyer Verlag, Tübingen, FRG] 20, 1984, p. 101–108)

Monterroso is forever casting doubts on characters and events, in short, on everything that constitutes a story. In his *Movimiento perpetuo* generic boundaries disappear: essays read like fiction and fiction sounds like journalism (i.e., "El Informe 'Endymion'"). Furthermore, the reader becomes metamorphosed as author and vice-versa.

The result is that, in Monterroso's work, all narrative elements and categories turn out to be in perpetual motion.

5331 Jamieson Villiers, Martín E. Literatura panameña actual (CH, 407, mayo 1984, p. 108–117)

Useful overview of contemporary Panamanian literature focusing on poetry and criticism (e.g., Elsie Alvarado de Ricor, Victor Fernández Cañizález) and the novel and shorter narrative (e.g., Rafael Leónidas Pernett y Morales and Justo Arroyo).

5332 Jamieson Villiers, Martín E. La novela de Pernett y Morales. Panamá: Ediciones del Instituto Nacional de Cultura, 1982. 131 p.

Beginning with an intertextual reading, critic goes on to explore the linguistic innovation as well as social and psychological dimensions of Pernett y Morales's two skillful novels: *Loma ardiente y vestida de sol* and *Estas manos son para caminar*. Throughout, Jamieson Villiers highlights debt of young Panamanian author to the García Márquez of *One hundred years . . .* as well as to Cortázar and Cabrera Infante.

5333 Kalina de Piszk, Rosita. Escritores costarricenses: María Fernández de Tinoco (Káñina [Univ. de Costa Rica, San José] 5:2, julio/dic. 1981, p. 28–36, bibl., ill.)

First woman writer of Costa Rica. A look at María Fernández de Tinoco and at *Zulai y Yontá* (1909), her allegory of the origins of American Indians.

5334 Masoliver, Juan Antonio. Augusto Monterroso o la tradición subversiva (CH, 408, junio 1984, p. 146–154)

Critic aims to make the innovative work of Guatemalan Augusto Monterroso better known to the Spanish-speaking public. Includes insightful comments about his novel *Viaje al centro de la fábula* (1981) and about his transformations of classic genres such as fables (*La oveja negra y demás fábulas*, 1969) and memoirs (*Lo demás es silencio*, 1978). Concludes that in this author's work humor serves as a delicate way to reject dogmatic moralism and solemnity and argues that Monterroso is closer in spirit to South American authors such as Borges, Cortázar, and Sábato than to Central American literature.

5335 Monterroso, Augusto. Viaje al centro de la fábula. Entrevistas de Jorge Ruffinelli *et al.* 2a ed. aum. México: M. Casillas Editores, 1982. 155 p. (Serie Los Ensayos)

Series of insightful interviews with distinguished Guatemalan author conducted by many critics including Jorge Ruffinelli and José Miguel Oviedo. With great candor, Monterroso discusses a wide variety of subjects such as his fear of writing and the development of a badly needed generation of readers in Latin America. *Viaje al centro de la fábula* should be read as a pendant piece to *Monterroso* (see *HLAS 44:5284*).

5336 Monzón M. de Velásquez, Imelda. Biografía y bibliografía de y sobre Carlos Samayoa Chinchilla (Letras de Guatemala [Univ. de San Carlos, Guatemala] 2, dic 1980, p. 63–73)

Biography and detailed bibliography of the journalist, editor of the *Diario de Centro América*, and Director of the National Library of Guatemala (1947–48). For bibliographer's comment, see *HLAS 47:54*.

5337 Oviedo, José Miguel. La colección privada de Monterroso (ECO, 65[1]:271, mayo 1984, p. 45–50)

Beautifully written article which constitutes another attempt to take one of Central America's most outstanding and innovative authors out of undeserved obscurity. Oviedo ponders the reasons for Monterroso's lack of renown before focusing on his most recent work, *La palabra mágica*, a collection of essays that combine homage to favorite authors (such as Borges) with reflections on philology and translation ("La Autobiografía de Charles Lamb"). Typically, *La palabra mágica* is liberally sprinkled with Monterroso's unique brand of philosophy and humor.

5338 Pérez Valdés, Trinidad. Omar Cabezas en la nueva literatura nicaragüense (NMC/N, 4:9, abril 1983, p. 147–160)

In *Pasajes de la guerra revolucionaria*, Che Guevara argues in favor of a new type of documentary literature, belligerent even in the transmission of its message. Omar Cabezas's *La montaña es algo más que una inmensa estepa verde* (see *HLAS 46:5245*) is a prime example of this type of narrative, comparable to *El amanecer ya no es una tentación* by Tomás Borge, and *Haydée habla del Moncada* by Haydée Santamaría. Compa-

rable and yet unique, because in addition to outlining the sociological and aesthetic concerns of the Sandinista movement, Cabezas's original work represents the collective revolutionary process of Latin America.

5339 Picado Gómez, Manuel. Literatura, ideología, crítica: notas para un estudio de la literatura costarricense. San José: Editorial Costa Rica, 1983. 110 p.: bibl.

Penetrating critical study about broad theoretical concerns (e.g., verisimilitude and censorship, discursive method, the politics of literature) as well as, more specifically, about 20th-century Costa Rican authors (e.g. Adolfo Herrera García, José Marín Cañas, Carlos Luis Fallas).

5340 Pilolli, Mariapia. Sociología de la literatura panameña. Panamá: Univ. de Panamá, Centro de Investigaciones, Facultad de Humanidades, 1984. 131 p.: bibl. (Serie Ciencias sociales)

Critical study of José A. Cajar Escala's *El Cabecilla* and César A. Candanedo's *Los clandestinos* uses a sociological approach. First chapter sets forth author's methodology and discusses general concerns such as the function of literature and social origin of writers. Last two chapters adroitly examine the narrative development of two neorealist works paying special attention to their nationalistic and anti-imperialistic elements.

5341 Ruiloba, Rafael. Rogelio Sinán o la muerte de Don Juan (LNB/L, 320/321, nov./dic. 1982, p. 50–55)

Like Byron and Shaw, Rogelio Sinán chooses the Don Juan myth as an epic medium in order to transform society. His novel, *Isla mágica*, (1978) is a story made of repetition about a love which will never be fulfilled.

5342 Salgado, María A. America and Guatemala in the anti-Yankee novels of Miguel Angel Asturias: a love-hate relationship (HISP, 81, mayo 1984, p. 79–85)

Examines relations between the US and Guatemala in the love-hate relationships of several couples in Asturias novels (e.g., Geo. Maker Thompson and Mayarí). Concludes that Asturias wrote his anti-Yankee novels in hopes of accelerating his people's revolt.

5343 Thiercelin, Raquel. La estructura social en *Hombres de maíz* (*in* International Congress of Hispanists, 4th, 1971, Salamanca, Spain. Actas. Dirección de Eugenio de Bustos Tovar. Salamanca, Spain: Univ. de Salamanca, 1982, v. 2, p. 699–705)

The society which makes up the background to the drama portrayed in *Hombres de maíz* is hostile, even brutal to the poor. Peasants eke out an existence outside the

rich commercial circuits of the country. Most common feelings experienced by the characters are solitude and discontinuity; it is this lack of contact which engenders the myths, "those poetic beliefs of the collective unconscious."

Traba, Marta. Mirar en Nicaragua. See item **406.**

20th Century: Prose Fiction: Hispanic Caribbean

WILLIAM LUIS, *Associate Professor of Spanish, Dartmouth College*
CARLOS R. HORTAS, *Professor of Spanish, Hunter College*

THE OUTSTANDING DEVELOPMENT in the literature of the Hispanic Caribbean in the past few years has been research published inside as well as outside of Cuba. During this period, we witnessed the appearance of Araceli García-Carranza's *Bio-bibliografía de Alejo Carpentier* (item **5444**), the much awaited *Diccionario de la literatura cubana* (item **5434a**) compiled by the Instituto de Literatura y Lingüística of the Academia de Ciencias de Cuba, David William Foster's *Cuban literature: a research guide* (item **5440**), and José B. Fernández and Roberto G. Fernández's *Indice bibliográfico de autores cubanos: diáspora, 1959-1979/Bibliographical index of Cuban authors: diaspora, 1959–1979* (item **5437**). Of all these publications, the one by García-Carranza stands out for two reasons. First, her subject, Carpentier, continues to generate the most interest and the greater number of publications in Cuban literature. Second, García-Carranza's impressive research has produced the most complete bibliography of works by and about Carpentier, a total of 4,937 items.

Vol. 1 of the *Diccionario de la literatura cubana* was first published in 1980 (see *HLAS 44:5343*); vol. 2 from M to Z (item **5434a**) appeared four years later. This completes a set that will serve as the most thorough dictionary available, even though vol. 1, for political reasons, excluded writers such as Guillermo Cabrera Infante and Calvert Casey. Apparently, as of vol. 2 the editorial policy changed towards being more comprehensive of Cuban dissidents. Instead of making these writers "disappear," they are now included but with "clarifying" notations. The paragraph on José Triana ends with "He recently abandoned the country" and the one on Heberto Padilla with "After abandoning the country, he has maintained a hostile position towards the Revolution." However, Severo Sarduy was excluded and Armando Valladares continues to be unrecognized as a literary figure by the Cuban establishment.

Like research works published within Cuba, *Cuban literature: a research guide* is a most valuable bibliography of criticism up to 1982–83. With this work, Foster has made an important contribution to criticism about Cuban authors. But Foster omits entries on José A. Baragaño and *Lunes de Revolución* which is available in microfilm under the title of the newspaper *Revolución*. And although Calvert Casey appears as critic, he is absent as a writer.

The *Indice bibliográfico de autores cubanos* is a good companion to *Cuban literature: a research guide* to the extent that it contains many young writers of the diaspora not included in Foster's study. Unfortunately, the *Indice* is limited to the monographic literature and excludes numerous works published in periodicals. The fact that works by recent exiles such as Reinaldo Arenas, Antonio Benítez Rojo, and Heberto Padilla are not included, outdates the bibliography. These and other writers have been contributing in quantity and quality to the growing body of Cuban literature.

There have been few new works of fiction by established writers published inside and outside of Cuba. Except for Cabrera Infante (item **5382**) and Sarduy (item **5407**), writers such as Arenas and Benítez Rojo are publishing manuscripts in print some years before (e.g., Arenas's *El palacio de las blanquísimas mofetas*, item **5429**, and Benítez Rojo's *El mar de las lentejas*, item **5378**). Writers in Cuba are following a similar trend. Barring some committed writers such as Soler Puig (items **5408** and **5409**), authors such as Miguel Barnet (item **5416**) and older ones such as Onelio Jorge Cardoso (item **5383**) and Lisandro Otero (item **5401**), like their counterparts in exile, are republishing previous works. For the moment, some writers in exile are more concerned with earning a living than writing new fiction and others in Cuba are still experimenting with the boundaries of "acceptable" fiction.

"Committed" authors, especially younger ones, are adhering to the demands of some critics in Cuba that they document aspects of the Revolution. See for example Hugo Chinea's *De las raíces vive el árbol* (item **5388**) and Eduardo Heres León's *A fuego limpio* (item **5393**). Interestingly, writers exiled in recent times are also publishing works about the Revolution. But unlike their counterparts in Cuba, authors such as Belkis Cuza Malé (item **5431**) are revealing, also from an insider's point of view, not the Revolution's accomplishments but its injustices. As a result, Cuban literature continues to expand. US-based authors are writing about their lives in this country (see item **5398**), while those in Cuba are narrating their war experiences in Africa (item **5410**).

Of interest is *Del Caribe* (item **5432**), a new periodical published by the Casa del Caribe, in Santiago de Cuba, devoted exclusively to Caribbean literature. This is significant insofar as the Casa del Caribe and its magazine are physically and culturally closer to the other islands and will either duplicate or decentralize some of the activities carried out by the Havana-based Casa de las Américas and its magazine.

Editorial Letras Cubanas, under the direction of Imeldo Alvarez García, continues to do an outstanding and necessary job of publishing writers of the 19th century and first half of the 20th century (see item **5406**), some forgotten by critics. Many of these difficult to obtain books are distributed by Ediciones Vitral. The continued vitality of Puerto Rican prose fiction is particularly evident in the short stories of Juan Antonio Ramos (item **5401**), the journalistic fiction of Edgardo Rodríguez Juliá (see *HLAS 46:5299–5299a*) and the emergence of powerful feminist voices such as Lydia Vega's and Carmen Lugo Filippi's (see *HLAS 46:5289*).

The last few years have witnessed a spate of literary criticism aimed at producing the definitive book on Puerto Rican literature. So far, not one of these works has fully attained its objective; however, more closely focused works about a single author or theme which do not attempt to provide a master key to the interpretation of all of Puerto Rican literature seem more successful. A model of such a work is *Luis Rafael Sánchez: crítica y bibliografía* (item **5457**) edited by Nélida Hernández and Daisy Caraballo Abréu. This is but one volume of a series by the Univ. of Puerto Rico designed to provide collections of selected critical essays on important Puerto Rican writers. Also recommended is Luz María Umpierre's close readings of Enrique Laguerre and Pedro Juan Soto in *Ideología y novela en Puerto Rico* (item

5471). Rafael Falcón's study of the migration theme in Puerto Rican literature, though limited in its critical insights, is a useful research tool (item **5436**).

Of particular note is vol. 1 of a projected general anthology of Puerto Rican literature which is superbly edited and quite comprehensive (item **5370**). I look forward to future volumes.

The number of recent books devoted to criticism of the island's literature augur well for a continued improvement of the role accorded to Puerto Rico in the wider context of Latin American literature.

In 1984, Dominican scholars celebrated the centennial of Pedro Henríquez Ureña's birth with the publication of various works in honor of this great humanist and scholar (see item **5452**).

The Trujillo dictatorship and the US occupation continue as preeminent themes of contemporary Dominican literature (see items **5413** and **5443**). An important work is Lora Medrano's *Petán, la voz dominicana* (item **5456**) which attempts to recapture parts of the Trujillo era from a different point of view. Although Lora Medrano condemns the dictator's actions, he recognizes that his brother, José Arismendy Trujillo Molina, did make important contributions to the development and promotion of Dominican culture. Perhaps this work signals a more questioning trend for Dominican writers that may open new perspectives about the Trujillo era and other periods of the island's history. With some exceptions, Dominican literature and, in particular, criticism continue to lag behind Cuba and Puerto Rico.

PROSE FICTION

5369 Alonso, Dora. Agua pasada. La Habana: Unión de Escritores y Artistas de Cuba, 1981. 51 p. (Girón)

Consists of 37 vignettes in which Alonso recalls her childhood.

5370 Antología general de la literatura puertorriqueña: prosa, verso, teatro. t. 1, Desde los orígenes hasta el realismo y naturalismo. Edición de Josefina Rivera de Alvarez y Manuel Alvarez Nazario. Madrid: Partenón, 1982? 1 v.: index.

Very thorough and ambitious anthology which includes historical as well as literary works. Short but useful introductions and excellent footnotes throughout.

5371 Arenal, Humberto. Del agua mansa. La Habana: Editorial Letras Cubanas, 1982. 206 p. (Ocuje)

Arenal's first major work since 1967 consists of new stories except for one. They pertain to different human dramas before and during the Cuban Revolution.

5372 Arenas, Reinaldo. Arturo, la estrella más brillante. Barcelona, Spain: Montesinos, 1984. 94 p.

Captivating narration (written in 1971) about Cuban work camps for homosexuals in which Arturo is forced to create a fantasy world to escape persecution from militant homosexuals, the camp guards, and even his mother.

5373 Arenas, Reinaldo. Cantando en el pozo. Barcelona, Spain: Editorial Argos Vergara, 1982. 215 p.

Only authorized version of *Celestino antes del alba*, corrected and revised by the author. Published in 1967, it is the first of a series of five works and describes the narrator-protagonist's child fantasies in the Cuban countryside.

5374 Arenas, Reinaldo. El palacio de las blanquísimas mofetas. Barcelona, Spain: Argos Vergara, 1983. 292 p. (Col. En cuarto mayor; 137)

Another edition of Arenas's 1980 novel, written in 1972 and first published in French in 1975.

5375 Arrufat, Antón. La caja está cerrada. La Habana: Editorial Letras Cubanas, 1984. 701 p. (Ocuje)

In his first and at times humorous novel, Arrufat explores different facets, including sex, which adolescents experienced growing up in bourgeois families during the Republic. Written in 1970, it represents Arrufat's most important literary accomplishment since his problems resulting from *Los siete contra tebas* (1968).

5376 Balaguer, Joaquín. Los carpinteros. 2a ed. Santo Domingo: Editora Corripio, 1985. 431 p.

Historical novel by the incumbent President of the Dominican Republic (b. 1906) first written in 1984 documenting the bravery of young men known as the Carpinteros who fought for many years in civil wars for democracy. The novel develops between 1867–1911.

5377 Benítez Rojo, Antonio. Estatuas sepultadas y otros relatos. Edición de Roberto González Echevarría. Hanover, N.H.: Ediciones del Norte, 1984. 231 p.

Benítez Rojo's best published short stories include his acclaimed "La Tierra y el Cielo." González Echevarría's introduction highlights, within the context of the Cuban Revolution, Benítez Rojo's life and works and places him among such greats as Cortázar and Donoso.

5378 Benítez Rojo, Antonio. El mar de las lentejas. Barcelona, Spain: Plaza & Janés Editores, 1985. 301 p.

First published in 1979, this well documented novel narrates sixteenth-century Caribbean history.

5379 Blanco, Tomás. Los vates: embeleco fantástico para niños mayores de edad. Prólogo de Margot Arce de Vázquez. 2a ed. Río Piedras, P.R.: Ediciones Huracán, 1981. 96 p.: bibl. (Col. Obras completas de Tomás Blanco; 2)

New edition of Blanco's classic short novel, which includes a complete bibliography of his works and a chronology of his life.

5380 Bodallia, Emilio. A fuego lento. Prólogo de Salvador Bueno. La Habana: Editorial Letras Cubanas, 1982. 262 p. (Biblioteca básica de literatura cubana)

Reprint of Bodallia's first novel published in 1903. In this naturalist novel, the characters are consumed by a slow burning fire. Bueno's introduction discusses, within the context of the times, the author's life and works.

5381 Bosch, Juan. Cuentos. La Habana: Casa de las Américas, 1983. 259 p. (Col. Literatura latinoamericana; 111)

Good selection of tales by the most recognized short story writer of the Dominican Republic (also a leading political figure). This edition includes his well known story "Luis Pie" and his essay "Apuntes sobre el Arte de Escribir Cuentos." Also contains an outline of his life and works and related literary and historical events.

5382 Cabrera Infante, Guillermo. Holy smoke. New York: Harper and Row, 1985. 329 p.

Cabrera's latest novel is written in English. With his typical humor, he recounts the history of tobacco, from its inception to the present. Gathering information from many works, he makes references to real and fictitious smokers. Cabrera also appends comments about and quotes from literatures that make references to smoking.

5383 Cardoso, Onelio Jorge. Gente de pueblo. Fotografías de José Tabió. La Habana: Editorial Letras Cubanas, 1980. 140 p.: photos

Reprint of Cardoso's 1952 collection of articles describing his travels throughout Cuba. With photos by José Tabió, Cardoso captures effectively the simple life of country people. As separate pieces, they were published in *Bohemia* and *Carteles* (1954–57).

5384 Carpentier, Alejo. La ciudad de las columnas. La Habana: Editorial Letras Cubanas, 1982. 84 p.: photos.

Attractive 1970 reprint which combines Carpentier's *La ciudad de las columnas* with a photographic essay on the same subject.

5386 Carpentier, Alejo. Obras completas. v. 2, El reino de este mundo; Los pasos perdidos. v. 3, Guerra del tiempo; El acoso y otros relatos. v. 4, La aprendiz de bruja; Concierto barroco; El arpa y la sombra. Prólogo del cuarto volumen de Graziella Pogolotti. México: Siglo Veintiuno Editores, 1983. 3 v. (416, 237, 378 p.): bibl., facsims., port. (La Creación literaria)

These are vols. 2–4 of Siglo Veintiuno's projected 14-volume edition of Carpentier's complete works. The collection is organized in some chronological order though vols. 13–14 pertain to *La música en Cuba* (1946) and *Letra y Solfa* (1951–59), respectively. In vol. 2, *El reino de este mundo* (1949) contains Carpentier's essays on marvelous realism; and in vol. 3, *Guerra del tiempo* (1958), as in the original, includes "El Camino de Santiago," "Semejante a la Noche," and "Viaje a la Semilla," y "otros relatos" which are: "Los Fugitivos," "El Derecho de Asilo," and "Los Advertidos." Vol. 4 includes his play *La aprendiz de bruja*, previously unpublished in Spanish. Written in 1956, the present edition was translated from French and its theme pertains to the Mexican conquest. Unlike previous volumes, this one contains a prologue in which Graziella Pogolotti discusses the concept of theatre in some of Carpentier's works. She refers mainly to *La aprendiz de bruja* and mentions in passing the novels in this volume: *Concierto barroco* (1974) and *El arpa y la sombra* (1979). Alexis Márquez Rodríguez's *Lo barroco y lo real-maravilloso en la obra de Alejo Carpentier* (item **5458**) is a companion to the complete works.

5387 Carpentier, Alejo. Los pasos perdidos. Edición de Roberto González Echevarría. Madrid: Cátedra, 1985. 332 p.: bibl.

New edition of Carpentier's 1953 novel about the genesis of Hispanic America. Includes extensive and detailed introduction about Carpentier's life and works, González Echevarría's annotations open up the novel to the reader. Also includes useful bibliography of and about Carpentier and the novel.

5388 Chinea, Hugo. De las raíces vive el árbol. La Habana: Unión de Escritores y Artistas de Cuba, 1982. 84 p. (Contemporáneos)

Most of the stories in this collection describe the lives of those who are working to build a new Cuban society. Spanning a decade of writing, stories range from the 1970 sugar harvest to the 1980 Mariel boat lift.

5389 Cofiño López, Manuel. Andando por ahí, por esas calles. La Habana: Editorial Letras Cubanas, 1982. 279 p. (Ocuje)

Not a new work but a collection of all of Cofiño's published short stories under still another title. Consists of 32 stories culled from: *Tiempo de cambio* (1969); *Las viejitas de las sombrillas* (1972), which are children's stories; *Y un día el sol es juez* (1976), which originally included his first collection of stories; *Para leer mañana* (1976); and *Un pedazo de mar y una ventana* (1979), which included *Para leer mañana*.

5390 Correa, Miguel. Al norte del infierno. Miami, Fla.: Editorial SIBI, 1984. 121 p.

Correa's first publication is fascinating. Describes a particular Cuban reality in which people are pressured to behave in a certain manner. For them, exile represents a resurrection of sorts.

5391 Cossío Woodward, Miguel. Oasis. La Habana: Unión de Escritores y Artistas de Cuba, 1982. 70 p. (Contemporáneos)

In his latest novel, Cossío reconstructs 19th-century Europe to narrate a trip from Hamburg to London in which Karl Marx meets Elizabeth.

5392 González Maldonado, Edelmira. Alucinaciones. San Juan: Instituto de Cultura Puertorriqueña, 1981. 95 p.: ill. (Serie Literatura hoy; 1981)

Hallucinations in a "stream of consciousness" style but not much literary intelligence at work. The imprimatur of the Instituto de Cultura Puertorriqueña is misplaced here.

Habich, Edgardo de. Traspiés en el paraíso. See item **5547**.

5393 Heras León, Eduardo. A fuego limpio. La Habana: Editorial Letras Cubanas, 1980. 79 p. (Ocuje)

By highlighting the problems in contemporary Cuban society, Heras León narrates stories about the life of workers who consistently strive for a better society.

5394 Ibarzábal, Federico de. La isla de los muertos y otros relatos. Selección y prólogo de Enrique Sáinz. La Habana: Editorial Letras Cubanas, 1983. 402 p. (Biblioteca básica de literatura cubana)

Short stories in which the sea is a dominant theme. Taken from Ibarzábal's *Derelictos* (1937), *La charca* (1938), the magazines *Bohemia* and *Carteles*, and arranged chronologically (1932–52). Sáinz's introduction is redundant and undermines the author's style, except for those stories describing a social reality.

5395 Labrador Ruiz, Enrique. El laberinto de sí mismo. Prólogo de Elio Alba Buffill. New York: Senda Nueva de Ediciones, 1983. 179 p.: bibl., ill. (Senda narrativa)

Originally published in 1933, this first novel by one of Cuba's most innovative writers of his generation describes the life of a protagonist who recreates a reality into which he escapes. Alba Buffill's introduction provides a fair understanding of Labrador Ruiz's works. Unfortunately, the edition is poor and appears to be a photocopy of the original.

5396 Lima, Chely. Monólogo con lluvia. La Habana: Unión de Escritores y Artistas de Cuba, 1981. 95 p. (Col. David)

Within a contemporary revolutionary setting, Lima narrates with tenderness love stories about Cuba's youths.

5397 Morciego, Efraín. El crimen de Cortaderas. La Habana: Unión de Escritores y Artistas de Cuba, 1982. 214 p. (Girón)

Testimonial reconstructs the massacre of workers, including many Haitians, at Cortaderas in 1933. Based on historical information, it also makes use of numerous interviews by witnesses. Morciego uses the voices of those who participated to narrate events.

5398 Muñoz, Elías Miguel. Los viajes de Orlando Cachumbambé. Miami, Fla.: Ediciones Universal, 1984. 143 p. (Col. Caniquí)

In his first novel, Muñoz uses contemporary techniques to describe a Cuban exile narrator-protagonist who seesaws between two cultures as his mixture of Spanish and English suggests.

5399 Núñez Machín, Ana. Memoria amarga del azúcar. La Habana: Editorial de Ciencias Sociales, 1981. 213 p. (Historia de Cuba)

Testimony by individuals who dedicated their lives to cutting sugarcane. They narrate the 20th-century history of the sugar industry from an all encompassing viewpoint. Includes section about those who knew Jesús Menéndez, chronology of related events (1900–60), and brief but useful vocabulary pertaining to the sugar industry.

5400 Ortega, Gregorio. Una de cal y otra de arena. La Habana: Editorial Letras Cubanas, 1983. 149 p.

Reprint of Ortega's 1957 novel about gangsterism in the post-Machado period.

5401 Otero, Lisandro. La situación. La Habana: Editorial Letras Cubanas, 1982. 277 p.

Reprint of Otero's 1963 novel which describes bourgeois life in Cuba before the Revolution.

5402 Ramos, Juan Antonio. Hilando mortajas. Río Piedras, P.R.: Editorial Antillana, 1983. 91 p. (Cuadernos de Jacinto Colón; 2)

Excellent collection of short stories which reveal the nether side of contemporary Puerto Rican life. Highly recommended.

5403 Relatos de Girón. Selección, prólogo, apéndice y notas de Josué-Leonel Marrero. La Habana: Editorial Letras Cubanas, 1982. 367 p. (Col. Saeta)

Anthology of 45 testimonials and works of fiction whose themes pertain to the Bay of Pigs invasion. All but one have been published. Dora Alonso and Alejo Carpentier are among the contributors. Marrero's introduction is limited to plot summary.

5404 Rijo, José. Entre la realidad y el sueño. Santo Domingo: El Autor, 1983. 53 p.

This interesting long story about the Trujillo dictatorship intermingles different narrations.

5405 Robles, Mireya. Hagiografía de Narcisa La Bella. Hanover, N.H.: Ediciones del Norte, 1985. 155 p.

Feminist novel, with some lucid moments, about Narcisa's alienation and the decomposition of a bourgeois family before the Cuban Revolution. Robles makes no distinction between dialogue and narration and eliminates paragraphs and periods, even the last one.

5406 Rodríguez, Luis Felipe. Ciénaga y otros relatos. Compilación, prólogo y notas de Cira Romero. La Habana: Editorial Letras Cubanas, 1984. 558 p.: bibl. (Letras cubanas)

New edition of Luis Felipe Rodríguez's novels and short stories. Includes his La conjura de la ciénaga, Relatos de Marcos Antilla, and some forgotten stories published in magazines, but omits his El negro que se bebió la luna. Writing during the first half of the 20th century, his works reflect changing social realities. Romero's long but useful introduction discusses Rodríguez's life and works.

5407 Sarduy, Severo. Colibrí. Barcelona, Spain: Argos Vergara, 1984. 179 p.

In his latest novel, Sarduy continues to push back the boundaries of Spanish American literature. *Colibrí,* which suggests motion without movement or appearance and disappearance, includes characters who are anthropomorphic; simulation is a dominant part of the narration. The static description of nature is a reflection of language itself.

5408 Soler Puig, José. Un mundo de cosas. La Habana: Unión de Escritores y Artistas de Cuba, 1982. 301 p. (Contemporáneos)

In this novel, Soler Puig narrates the life of a family who earned a living by making rum. Shifting from first to second to third person, the novel unfolds from the end of the last century to the triumph of the Revolution to the year before Allende's downfall in Chile.

5409 Soler Puig, José. El nudo. La Habana: Editorial Letras Cubanas, 1983. 165 p. (Ocuje)

Another novel by Soler Puig which takes place in the country and in the city (Havana) and which narrates the protagonist's past and present. In spite of his medical education, the protagonist is tied to his past.

5410 Torres, Rodolfo. Mis hermanos en la guerra. La Habana: Letras Cubanas, 1982. 102 p.

Collection of some historical value in which Torres narrates his war experiences in Angola. Stories were written from 1976–78.

5411 Valdez, Diógenes. Todo puede suceder un día. Santo Domingo: Taller, 1984. 159 p.: ill. (Biblioteca Taller; 159)

Stories with a variety of themes, some better explored than others, ranging from a lost mailman to actors performing a guerrilla invasion.

5412 20 [i.e. Veinte] relatos cubanos. Selección de Juan Carlos Reloba. La Habana: Editorial Gente Nueva, 1980. 166 p.: bibl.

Anthology of 20 short stories by representative writers of the genre, written from the beginning of the century up to the Revolution. Each story is preceded by a biography and bibliographical note about the author. However, important writers such as Lino Novás Calvo and Enrique Labrador Ruiz are conspicuously absent.

5413 Veloz Maggiolo, Marcio. De abril en adelante. 2a ed. Santo Domingo: Taller, 1984. 286 p. (Biblioteca Taller; 53)

Second edition of 1975 novel in which narrator-protagonist reflects on the difficulty of writing fiction (perhaps this fiction) by narrating events during Trujillo's downfall and the US occupation.

LITERARY CRITICISM AND HISTORY

5414 Antología de oradores puertorriqueños del pasado. Compilación de Regino Cabassa Túa. Prólogo de Ernesto Juan Fonfrías. Palabras preliminares de Amador Ramírez Silva. Ordenación del material y notas de Vicente Géigel Polanco. San Juan: Instituto de Cultura Puertorriqueña, 1978. 547 p.: bibl., ill.

Very useful compendium of important addresses by Puerto Rican statesmen, public figures, and writers. The anthology ranges from an address on adequate parliamentary representation in Madrid for the American provinces of Spain, delivered by Ramón Power y Giral in 1811, to a graduation address on the theme of democracy and social justice given at the Inter-American Univ. by Ernesto Ramos Antonini in 1962.

5415 Augier, Angel I. Prosa varia. La Habana: Editorial Letras Cubanas, 1982. 499 p.: bibl. (Letras cubanas)

Collection of published journalistic articles (1943–78), some not dated, divided into "Motivos Literarios," "Arte y Artistas," "Notas de Viaje," "Tres Cubanos en París," "Crónicas de Ayer y de Hoy," and "Temas Históricos."

5416 Barnet, Miguel. La fuente viva. La Habana: Editorial Letras Cubanas, 1983. 241 p.: bibl. (Col. Crítica)

Collection of published articles (1964–81) are divided into "Testimonio" and "Raíces" and pertain to the testimonial novel and Cuban folklore respectively. Of interest is author's "La Novela Testimonio: Socio-Literatura" in which Barnet explains this important genre.

5417 Barradas, Efraín. Para leer en puertorriqueño: acercamiento a la obra de Luis Rafael Sánchez. Río Piedras, P.R.: Editorial Cultural, 1981. 151, 2 p.: bibl.

First full-length study of the works of Luis Rafael Sánchez. This critical volume contains a number of interesting essays about the use of language, sexuality, and myth and the presence of race and culture in Sánchez's works. The writer's prose is still maturing and his citations perhaps overdone, but his critical observations are often on target.

5418 Benítez Rojo, Antonio. La América "faraway" de Carpentier (CM/D, 21:6, junio 1985, p. 22–29, ill.)

Basing his analysis on Barthes's idea that travelers are "faraway" from knowing all, Benítez Rojo suggests that the same concept in Carpentier's life and works allows him to reinvent America. Carpentier, for example, incorporates writings of travelers in his narrations.

5419 Benítez Rojo, Antonio. La presencia de France en Carpentier (Linden Lane Magazine [Princeton, N.J.] 4:1, 1985, p. 22–23)

Anatole France was Carpentier's first influence and his *Les dieux ont soif* (1912) served as a model for "El Camino de Santiago" (1954). The repetition in the novel is transformed into a round in the story. Carpentier's use of music is a rebellion against the father which France, to some extent, represents.

5420 Benítez Rojo, Antonio. "Viaje a la Semilla," o el texto como espectáculo (Discurso Literario [Oklahoma State Univ., Stillwater] 3:1, 1985, p. 53–74)

Insightful and convincing article shows the presence of the *canon cancrizans* (crab canon) in "Viaje a la Semilla." Both works correspond to progressive and regressive moments.

5421 Bueno, Salvador. La imagen de la mujer en los cuentos de Onelio Jorge Cardoso (Santiago [Univ. de Oriente, Santiago, Cuba] 49, marzo 1983, p. 223–232)

Thematic analysis of exploited characters in Cardoso's stories, particularly women who suffer a double exploitation. All stories are set in the capitalist world, and Bueno selects those published up to 1973. Article also appeared in item **5428.**

5422 Cabrera Infante, Guillermo. Vidas de un héroe (VUELTA 9:97, dic. 1984, p. 5–11)

Moving recollection which dramatizes Gustavo Arcos's fall from grace. A revolutionary who served as Cuba's Ambassador to Brussels while Cabrera Infante was Cultural

Attaché, Arcos was later imprisoned. The essay publicizes his case and contains information about Cabrera's departure from Cuba.

5423 Carpentier, Alejo. Palabras en el tiempo de Alejo Carpentier. Compilación de Ramón Chao. Barcelona, Spain: Argos Vergara, 1984. 251 p. (Col. en línea)

Handy journalist compilation of selections of Carpentier's interviews, essays, and articles. They are divided into themes such as literature, music, politics, and residence abroad, but are arranged in no particular order. Book appears to be one continuous interview between Carpentier and Chao.

5424 Carpentier en *Letra y Solfa*. Edición de Araceli García-Carranza and Josefina García-Carranza. La Habana: Biblioteca Nacional José Martí, 1984. 159 p.: index.

Catalog of 1783 entries of Carpentier's pieces in the periodical *Letra y Solfa* (Nov. 21, 1951-April 17, 1959), some not dated. Includes useful thematic index. Serial collection donated by Carpentier is housed in the Biblioteca Nacional José Martí. Brief introduction underscores Carpentier the journalist, a profession he practiced throughout his life, and cites his contributions to numerous newspapers and magazines. Omits, however, Carpentier's contributions to the controversial *Lunes de Revolución*.

5425 Casaus, Víctor. Pablo, con el filo de la hoja. La Habana: Unión de Escritores y Artistas de Cuba, 1983. 235 p.: ill., facsims., ports. (Girón)

Montage of chronicles, photos, letters, and parts of an unfinished diary, arranged in dialogue form between Torriente Brau and figures such as his sisters, Raúl Roa, and José Zacarías Tallet. These conversations provide information from his childhood to his death in 1936.

5426 Cirules, Enrique. Los guarda fronteras. La Habana: Unión de Escritores y Artistas de Cuba, 1983. 250 p. (Girón)

Interesting testimonial of border guards who patrol Cuban waters and numerous islets. Stories vary in theme from combat against anti-revolutionary forces to rescue of Haitian boat people.

5427 Colón, Adolfo. Santa Olaya, estampas de un pasado: problemas de transición. Puerto Rico: El Autor, 1983. 97 p.

Don Tomás, an old storyteller, relates

a series of anecdotes and vignettes about rural life in Puerto Rico to a group of school children. These anecdotes come out of the 19th-century "cuadro de costumbres" tradition and are at times interesting, even if quite dated.

5428 Coloquio sobre la Cuentística de Onelio Jorge Cardoso, *La Habana*, 1981. Coloquio sobre la Cuentística de Onelio Jorge Cardoso. La Habana: Unión de Escritores y Artistas de Cuba, 1983. 76 p.: bibl. (Cuadernos Unión; 17)

Proceedings of colloquium on Cardoso's short stories meant to fill a vacuum of criticism on this important writer. Includes seven uneven studies that vary in methodology from thematic to structural analyses.

5429 Contín Aybar, Néstor. Historia de la literatura dominicana. v. 3. San Pedro de Macorís, Dominican Republic: Univ. Central del Este, 1984. 211 p.: bibl., indexes. (Univ. Central del Este; 53. Serie Literaria; 12)

Vol. 3 of history of Dominican literature (for previous volumes, see *HLAS 46: 5317*). This one covers the 1899–1924 period, is organized chronologically by author, and provides sketchy information about each writer and his works.

5430 Cuervo Hewitt, Julia. El mito de Ecué en la narrativa cubana (UNAM/RUM, 45, enero 1985, p. 34–39)

Sound study of African myth in 19th- and 20th-century Cuban narrative, and, in particular, in Guillermo Cabrera Infante's *Tres tristes tigres*.

5431 Cuza Malé, Belkis. La detención; Desde el balcón habanero; Retrato de una escritora con jardín (Linden Lane Magazine [Princeton, N.J.] 4:2, 1985, p. 6; 4:3, 1985, p. 3; 4:4, 1985, p. 9–11)

Selections from diary in progress in which author attempts to exorcise three stages of her painful past: 1) describes her husband Heberto Padilla's detention on April 30, 1971 and the salvaging of his manuscript; 2) covers 1975–77 and the daily lives of those who both prosper and suffer in the Revolution; and 3) returns to April 27, 1971 and events pertaining to Padilla's so-called "confession" and its consequences up to 1976.

5432 *Del Caribe.* Casa del Caribe. Vol. l, No. 2, 1983–. Santiago, Cuba.

New periodical dedicated to the study of the Caribbean. Directed by Joel James Figarola, it is published three times a year by Casa del Caribe which was founded in 1982 in Santiago de Cuba. Contains essays, poems, stories, research, and cultural notes and is divided into "Palabras Abierta," "Visión del Otro," "Hágase el Verso," "El Caribe que Nos Une," and "Entre Líneas." This issue includes Ladislao González Carbajal's "Recuerdos de Oriente," Arturo Arango Aria's "¿Ya la Novela?," Ambrosio Fornet's "Una Fiesta de Nuestra Narrativa," Josefa de la C. Hernández's "Caracterización y Lucha de Clases en *El derrumbe*," Roberto Fernández Retamar's "José Martí, Antillano," and Rafael Castro Mosqueda's "Verónica."

5433 Díaz Montero, Aníbal. Mirando el mundo: crónicas. San Juan: Editorial Díaz Mont, 1979. 101 p.

Collection of vignettes about the Puerto Rico of the first half of this century. Author recounts childhood memories and contrasts the Puerto Rico of his youth to that of today. Acute observations on contemporary Puerto Rican life.

5434 Díaz Quiñones, Arcadio. El almuerzo en la hierba: Lloréns Torres, Palés Matos, René Marqués. Río Piedras, P.R.: Ediciones Huracán, 1982. 168 p.: bibl. (Col. La nave y el puerto)

Three essays (on Lloréns Torres, Palés Matos, and René Marqués) originally published in literary periodicals and now reissued in this volume. Characterized by the author's close familiarity with Puerto Rican literature and criticism, and his ability to sort out literary influences and contexts, the essays tend toward literary history rather than interpretation.

5434a Diccionario de la literatura cubana. v. 2, M-Z. Compilación del Instituto de Literatura y Lingüística de la Academia de Ciencias de Cuba. La Habana: Editorial Letras Cubanas, 1984. p. 538-1132: bibl., ill., ports.

Vol. 2 of two-volume bibliography that covers all aspects of Cuban literature compiled by the Instituto de Literatura y Lingüística de la Academia de Ciencias de Cuba. Like vol. 1 (see *HLAS 44: 5343*), published four years earlier, vol. 2 embodies current cultural policy. Includes dissident writers who left Cuba in recent years (e.g., José

Triana, Heberto Padilla) but omits Severo Sarduy who lives in Paris and does not maintain a hostile position towards the Revolution. Highly recommended.

5435 Diego, Eliseo. Prosas escogidas. La Habana: Editorial Letras Cubanas, 1983. 489 p.: ill. (Letras cubanas)

Anthology of Diego's fiction and essays (1942–78). Some appear in print for the first time. His work on Faulkner, Hans Christian Andersen, and his prologue to Woolf's *Orlando* merit attention. Although Quintero's introduction discusses Diego's work, he rambles and tries to justify unnecessarily why a poet can write prose.

5436 Falcón, Rafael. La emigración a Nueva York en la novela puertorriqueña. Valencia, Spain: Ediciones Albatros Hispanófila, 1983. 37 p.: bibl. (Col. Monografías; 4)

Very useful and comprehensive guide to all Puerto Rican novels which touch upon or take as their central theme the Puerto Rican immigrant in New York. No bibliography provided, but extensive footnotes throughout.

5437 Fernández, José B. and **Roberto G. Fernández.** Indice bibliográfico de autores cubanos: diáspora 1959–1979 = Bibliographical index of Cuban authors: diaspora, 1959–1979. Miami, Fla.: Ediciones Universal, 1983. 106 p.: bibl., index.

Gathers literature of writers outside of Cuba and some non-Cuban born authors, independent of ideology. Prepared for both Spanish and English readers. Contains 971 entries divided into "Short Story," "Novel," "Poetry," "Theatre," "Folklore," "Literary Criticism and Culture," and "Linguistics," arranged in alphabetical order. Unfortunately, this study lacks biographical information on authors and is already outdated.

5438 Fernández Retamar, Roberto. Entrevisto. La Habana: Unión de Escritores y Artistas de Cuba, 1982. 217 p.: bibl. (Contemporáneos)

Informative selection and montage of published interviews and some articles (1963–76). Retamar talks about his life and works and expresses his ideas on literature and politics in Cuba, Latin America, and other parts of the world.

5439 Fernández Retamar, Roberto. Política y latinoamericanismo en Alejo Carpentier (CDLA, 149, 1985, p. 78–86)

Article designed to correct the record and show that since the 1920s, Carpentier had been a politically committed writer. For example, while in Venezuela, he made donations to the clandestine Communist Party. Uses mainly Carpentier's essays to support thesis.

5440 Foster, David William. Cuban literature: a research guide. New York: Garland Pub., 1985. 522 p.: index (Garland reference library of the humanities; 511)

Highly recommended bibliography of criticism divided into "General References" and "Authors." The latter includes secondary sources for 98 writers of different periods and genres. But studies on *Lunes de Revolución* and José A. Baragaño, for example, are omitted. A must for students of Cuban literature.

5441 Fuentes, Norberto. Hemingway en Cuba. Prólogo de Gabriel García Márquez. La Habana: Editorial Letras Cubanas, 1984. 712 p.: bibl., ill., maps, ports.

Important testimonial of the many who knew Hemingway in Cuba which includes corrections of assumptions about his life therein. The number of photographs make it a guided tour through his Cuban home, Finca Vigía (e.g., classification of different plants in the estate). Some information is drawn from what was left in the house (e.g., photographs, letters, documents). Also contains an introduction by García Márquez highlighting aspects of Hemingway's life in Havana, an inventory of each of the rooms, and a chronology of events up to 1970, the year *Islands in the stream* was published. No table of contents. See also *HLAS 46:5322.*

5442 Fuentes, Norberto. Posición uno. Introducción de Luis Pavón Tamayo. La Habana: Unión de Escritores y Artistas de Cuba, 1982. 175 p. (Girón)

Collection of journalistic articles (1963–78) written in the battlefield. Introduction by Luis Pavón Tamayo describes the people and events of the Revolution.

5443 Galván, William. Minerva Mirabal: historia de una heroína. Santo Domingo: Editora de la Univ. Autónoma de Santo Domingo, 1982. 357 p.: bibl., ill. (Publicaciones; 316. Col. Historia y sociedad; 56)

Reconstruction of the history of the Mirabal family and, in particular, of the heroine Minerva, whose political activities threatened the Trujillo dictatorship. After her fourth imprisonment, she and her two sisters were assassinated. Galván gathers some information from interviews and testaments; his narration is at times unimaginative and monotonous.

5444 García-Carranza, Araceli. Biobibliografía de Alejo Carpentier. La Habana: Editorial Letras Cubanas, 1984. 644 p.: indexes.

The most complete bibliography of and about Carpentier. Divided into primary and secondary sources and three indexes, it contains more than 4937 entries, including posters, records, and films. Items are part of collections housed at Biblioteca Nacional José Martí and Casa de las Américas. Also provides a useful chronology of Carpentier's life and works. Impressive research.

5445 González Echevarría, Roberto. Socrates among the weeds: blacks and history in Carpentier's *Explosion in a cathedral* (in Voices from under: black narrative in Latin America and the Caribbean. [see item **5044**], p. 35–53, ill.)

Goes beyond the analysis of *Explosion in a cathedral* contained in author's *Alejo Carpentier: the pilgrim at home* and demonstrates convincingly how neo-African culture in the Caribbean shapes history. Constitutes one of the best articles written on this important novel.

5446 González Echevarría, Roberto. Son de la loma (Enlace [New York] 1, sept. 1984, p. 12–17, ill.)

González Echevarría proposes that *De donde son los cantantes* marks a new stage in Sarduy's writings and in Spanish and Spanish American narrative. By analyzing the novel's title and its reference to Matamoros's song, the critic discusses the question of origin and the relationship between the novel and society.

5447 González Echevarría, Roberto. The voice of the masters: writing and authority in modern Latin American literature. Austin: Univ. of Texas Press, 1985. 195 p.: bibl., index (Latin American monographs. Institute of Latin American Studies; 64)

Ambitious and rigorous work in which the discourse of authority is discussed independently of political or textual affiliations. Some articles have been previously published and "Cuban Master Voices" make up half of the book and include: Miguel Barnet, Alejo

Carpentier, and Guillermo Cabrera Infante. With this work, González Echevarría has established a convincing methodology for Latin American criticism.

5448 Hart Dávalos, Armando. Cambiar las reglas del juego. Entrevista de Luis Báez. La Habana: Editorial Letras Cubanas, 1983. 124 p., 8 p. of plates: ports.

Long interview clarifies the Revolutionary government's position regarding writers, artists, and cultural policies in Cuba. Báez's questions reflect concerns reporters expressed while Hart traveled in Europe in 1983.

5449 Henríquez Ureña, Camila. Estudios y conferencias. La Habana: Editorial Letras Cubanas, 1982. 644 p.: bibl. (Letras cubanas)

Posthumous homage to Henríquez Ureña consists of compilation of her writings housed in the Instituto de Literatura y Lingüística of the Academia de Ciencias de Cuba. Divided into "General Literature," "Women in Literature," and "Interviews," it includes her recognized essays on Goethe and Shakespeare. Aguirre's brief introduction praises her not as a Dominican but as a Cuban scholar and highlights her accomplishments.

5450 Hernández Azaret, Josefa de la C. Algunos aspectos de la cuentística de Onelio Jorge Cardoso. Santiago, Cuba: Editorial Oriente, 1982.

Fair overview of Cardoso and his realistic rural short stories within the context of Cuban history and Hispanic American literature. Hernández Azaret analyzes stories according to dominant social themes.

5451 Historia y ficción en la narrativa hispanoamericana: coloquio de Yale. Compilación y prólogo de Roberto González Echevarría. Caracas: Monte Avila Editores, 1984. 408 p. (Col. Estudios)

Collection commemorating Carpentier's visit to Yale in 1979. Includes his "La Novela Latinoamericana en Víspera de un Nuevo Siglo," which is significantly different from a previously published essay of the same title. Although essays vary in theme, some pertain to Carpentier's work and others to the novel in the Cuban Revolution.

5452 La Integridad humanística de Pedro Henríquez Ureña: antología. Compilación de José Rafael Vargas. Santo Domingo:

Editora de la Univ. Autónoma de Santo Domingo, 1984. 371 p.: bibl., ports.

Montage of comments and quotations by foreign critics about Henríquez Ureña, with some correspondence of and about him. Though of little critical value, it contains a useful bibliography. Errors include identifying Jean Franco as a man.

5453 Lara, Juan Jacobo de. Sobre Pedro Henríquez Ureña y otros ensayos. Santo Domingo: Univ. Nacional Pedro Henríquez Ureña, 1982. 368 p.

Consists of 21 essays, some previously unpublished, about Pedro Henríquez Ureña, Spanish America, and Spain. Those pertaining to the great Dominican humanist discuss aspects of his life and works.

5454 Leante, César. ¿Existe una novela revolucionaria cubana? (CH, 428, 1986, p. 137–143)

In response to the title's question, Leante shows convincingly that the novel of the Cuban Revolution, one that would express objectively the transformation towards socialism, is yet to be written.

5455 El Libro jubilar de Pedro Henríquez Ureña. Edición de Julio Jaime Juliá. Santo Domingo: Univ. Nacional Pedro Henríquez Ureña, 1984. 2 v.: bibl., port. (Publicaciones de la Univ.)

Two-volume homage to a notable critic of Spanish-American literature on the 30th anniversary of his death. Gathers essays by critics of many Spanish-speaking countries, Argentina being over-represented. Vol. 1 pertains to unpublished articles about Henríquez Ureña's work; vol. 2 to brief testimonies by those who knew him and includes letters. Vol. 3, announced but not received, will include published articles about his works.

5456 Lora Medrano, Luis Eduardo. Petán, La Voz Dominicana: su gente, sus cosas y sus cuentos. Santo Domingo?: Editora Tele-3, 1984. 305 p.: ill., photos.

Recollection of cultural promotions sponsored by the Palacio Radio Televisor La Voz Dominicana, Channel 4, founded and owned by José Arismendy Trujillo Molina, the dictator's brother. Lora Medrano includes photos of and comments about actors and programs thus allowing Trujillo Molina and his deeds to assume a place in history. Useful for a study of Dominican popular and mass culture.

5457 Luis Rafael Sánchez: crítica y bibliografía. Edición de Nélida Hernández Vargas y Daisy Caraballo Abréu. Río Piedras: Editorial de la Univ. de Puerto Rico: Seminario de Estudios Hispánicos Federico de Onís, 1985. 292 p.: bibl. (Literatura puertorriqueña; 1a serie)

Excellent compendium of critical articles with extensive bibliography and complete list of works to date. Very useful and important reference tool.

5458 Márquez Rodríguez, Alexis. Lo barroco y lo real-maravilloso en la obra de Alejo Carpentier. México: Siglo Veintiuno Editores, 1983. 587 p.: bibl. (La Creación literaria)

Exhaustive and unnecessarily long thematic introduction to Carpentier's work, rightfully situating him as the initiator of contemporary Latin American literature. Márquez Rodríguez uses the Baroque and marvelous realism to discuss Carpentier's essays and fiction. Although at times insightful, it contributes little to the study of Carpentier. The bibliography is selective and has serious omissions.

5459 Méndez, José Luis. Para una sociología de la literatura puertorriqueña. La Habana: Casa de las Américas, 1982. 141 p.: bibl. (Cuadernos Casa; 26)

Author's theory is that literary works in Puerto Rico cannot be explained away by literary schools and movements alone, without also taking into account social conditions in Puerto Rico. Attempt at a sociological analysis of Puerto Rican literature.

5460 Meyn, Marianne. Lenguaje e identidad cultural: un acercamiento teórico al caso de Puerto Rico. Río Piedras, P.R.: Editorial Edil, 1983. 122 p.: bibl.

Much of book's discussion centers on the broad relations among language, culture, colonialism, and dependence; within this discussion reference is made to the case of Puerto Rico. In the last few chapters, some findings related to Puerto Rico seem to be "grafted" onto the more theoretical discussion that constitute the real focus of this work. Author's observations are somewhat interesting but offer no new insights into the case of Puerto Rico.

5461 New England Review and Bread Loaf Quarterly. Kenyon Hill Publications. Vol. 7, No. 4, 1985-. Hanover, N.H.

Special issue devoted to the Spanish, English, and French Caribbean. Includes trialogue defining Caribbean literature and culture by William Luis, Antonio Benítez Rojo, and Edward Kamau Brathwaite. Also contains stories and poems, some translated into English for the first time, by Cuban, Puerto Rican, and Dominican writers, including Guillén, Sarduy, Luis Rafael Sánchez, and René del Risco Bermúdez. Important issue.

5462 Padilla, Heberto. El Carpentier que conocí (Linden Lane Magazine [Princeton, N.J.] 4:1, 1985, p. 20–21)

Padilla's recollections add to Carpentier's biography. Describes Carpentier as an opportunist with no real political convictions.

5463 Pérez Firmat, Gustavo. El lenguaje secreto de Los pasos perdidos (MLN, 99:2, March 1984, p. 342–357)

Explores language and in particular the narrator-protagonist's writing of Spanish from an English perspective. Combining his infant language, Spanish, with his adult language, English, results in a work written in neither one language nor the other, but a third which is fiction.

5464 Por la novela policial. Selección y prólogo de Luis Rogelio Nogueras. La Habana: Editorial Arte y Literatura, 1982. 314 p.

Essays pertaining to the detective genre, from its inception to the Revolution. Contributors vary from Poe and Chesterton to Carpentier and Cristóbal Pérez. Nogueras's introduction attempts to define the genre and underscore its popularity. However, his argument is biased when stating that under capitalism the genre alienates people whereas under socialism it educates them.

5465 Revista de Estudios Hispánicos. Univ. de Puerto Rico. Año 10, 1983–. Río Piedras.

Issue devoted to Carpentier gathers essays read during a conference sponsored by the Univ. of Puerto Rico (Nov. 1981). Nine essayists include Alexis Márquez Rodríguez, Irlemar Chiampi, and Rubén Ríos.

5466 Rosario Candelier, Bruno. La imaginación insular: mitos, leyendas, utopías y fantasmas en la narrativa dominicana. Santo Domingo: Taller, 1984. 190 p.: bibl., ill. (Col. Ensayo; 6)

Good study using "realismo mágico," "lo real maravilloso," and "realismo maravilloso," to analyze Juan Bosch's "El Difunto Estaba Vivo," Sócrates Nolasco's Cuentos cimarrones, Virgilio Díaz Grullón's "De Niños, Hombres y Fantasmas," and Manuel Mora Serrano's Goeíza. Although references appear in the text, it lacks a bibliography.

5467 Sarduy, Severo. La serpiente en la sinagoga: entrevistas de Julia Kushigian (VUELTA, 8:89, abril 1984, p. 14–20, ill.)

Interview which explores Orientalism mainly in Sarduy's novels. His responses include personal anecdotes and reflect Sarduy's Buddhist experiences and beliefs.

5468 Shaw, Donald L. Alejo Carpentier. Boston: Twayne Publishers, 1985. 150 p.: bibl., index, port. (Twayne's world authors series; 756. Latin American literature)

In Twayne's recognition of Carpentier, Shaw provides an overview of the writer's fiction, textual analyses, plot summaries, and insights. Omits some information on Carpentier, including an English translation of "Histoire de Lunes."

5469 Silén, Juan Angel. Literatura, ideología y sociedad en Puerto Rico. San Juan: Editorial Edil, 1979? 155 p.: bibl.

Essays that are more ideological than literary include interesting observations on class and racial bias in Puerto Rican literature. Heavy dose of polemics and politics is somewhat tiring.

5470 Tardieu, Jean-Pierre. Religions et croyances populaires dans Biografía de un cimarrón de M. Barnet: du refus à la tolérance (UTIEH/C, 43, 1984, p. 43–67)

Tardieu highlights and questions religion in Biografía de un cimarrón. According to him, Montejo mixes Judeo-Christian and Greek and Roman myths with African ones.

5471 Umpierre-Herrera, Luz María. Ideología y novela en Puerto Rico: un estudio de la narrativa de Zeno, Laguerre y Soto. Madrid: Playor, 1983. 151 p.: bibl. (Col. Novo scholar)

Excellent close reading of some of the novels of Manuel Zeno Gandía, Enrique Laguerre, and Pedro Juan Soto. Includes biographical sketches of writers and bibliography.

5472 Umpierre-Herrera, Luz María. Nuevas aproximaciones críticas a la literatura puertorriqueña contemporánea. Río Piedras, P.R.: Editorial Cultural, 1983. 132 p.

Author makes use of recent critical theories in her analysis of a number of contemporary works of Puerto Rican literature. Of particular interest are her analyses of the novels of Pedro Juan Soto.

5473 Valdez Moses, Michael. *The lost steps*: the Faustian artist in the New World (LALR, 12:24, Spring/Summer 1984, p. 7–21)

This interesting study analyses Carpentier's narrator-protagonist as a Romantic figure and compares him to Mann's Adrian Leverkühn insofar as both are composers concerned with the birth of music.

5474 Valladares, Armando. Contra toda esperanza. Barcelona, Spain: Plaza y Janés Editores, 1985. 447 p., 8 p. of plates: ports. (Biografías y memorias)

Shocking and detailed testimony of Valladares's 22 years of political imprisonment in Cuban jails. Book describes a reality which some may find difficult to believe but which few know as well as Valladares.

5475 Vargas, José Rafael. El nacionalismo de Pedro Henríquez Ureña. Santo Domingo: Editora de la Univ. Autónoma de Santo Domingo, 1984. 311 p.: bibl., ill., ports.

Substantial full-length study of and about Henríquez Ureña's works, stressing his nationalism.

Voices from under: black narrative in Latin America and the Caribbean. See item **5044.**

5477 Zayas Micheli, Luis O. Mito y política en la literatura puertorriqueña. Madrid: Partenón, D.L., 1981. 192 p.: bibl.

Although author offers some useful comments on a number of well known Puerto Rican literary works, he makes too obvious an effort to relate literature to myth, and in so doing, skews what could otherwise be a more balanced reading of these works.

20th Century: Prose Fiction: Andean Countries (Bolivia, Colombia, Ecuador, Peru and Venezuela)

JOSE MIGUEL OVIEDO, *Professor of Spanish, University of California, Los Angeles*
DJELAL KADIR, *Professor of Spanish and Comparative Literature, Purdue University*

EN LA PRODUCCION CRITICA de este período se ha mantenido la primacía, en cuanto a calidad y volumen, de los trabajos provenientes de (o relativos a) Perú y Colombia, con un marcado incremento en el número de ensayos venezolanos; en cambio, ha habido un casi vertical descenso en la producción de la crítica originada en Ecuador y Bolivia, países que tradicionalmente han ido a la zaga en esta región.

La crítica sobre temas peruanos ha seguido privilegiando a José María Arguedas y Mario Vargas Llosa como los novelistas nacionales de mayor importancia continental. El trabajo más abarcador sobre Arguedas debe ser el que le dedica Alberto Escobar (item **5498**), y la contribución más original la de Jean-Paul Borel (item **5493**). Como de costumbre, la crítica arguediana atiende a la cuestión del "indigenismo," y eso ayuda a explicar el interés que este tema sigue despertando, según se aprecia por los items **5496, 5504, 5508,** y **5511**). La atención crítica por Vargas Llosa se renovó con ocasión de haber aparecido *La guerra del fin del mundo* (ver *HLAS 46:5473*) por entonces la última novela del autor y, sin duda, uno de sus más grandes esfuerzos narrativos. Pero sus libros anteriores fueron sometidos también a nuevas revisiones y exámenes, como lo demuestran los items **5499** y **5507**. Otros autores que han atraído a los críticos son: Ricardo Palma, específicamente por el influjo de los clásicos españoles (Quevedo, Cervantes) en sus *Tradiciones peruanas* (items **5509** y **5510**); Julio Ramón Ribeyro (items **5500** y **5501**), que sigue siendo un autor semidesconocido fuera del ámbito peruano; y Ciro Alegría (items **5492** y **5512**), quien parece ser el objeto de una revaloración. Asimismo, cabe mencionar el trabajo bibliográfico de D.W. Foster (item **5505**), uno de los aportes más valiosos de su tipo.

Más rica en calidad es la contribución crítica sobre literatura colombiana que, esta vez, se ha centrado de modo casi excluyente en la gran figura de García Márquez. Aparte de un nuevo libro en inglés sobre el autor (item **5489**), destacan las tres recopilaciones de su cuantiosa obra periodística realizadas por Jacques Gilard (items **5481** y **5482**), contribuciones que echan luz sobre la etapa formativa del colombiano; las revisiones críticas globales de su obra y persona hechas por Angel Rama (item **5488**) y Juan Gustavo Cobo Borda (item **5480**); el trabajo de Roberto González Echevarría sobre *Cien años de soledad* y sus resonancias antropológicas (item **5485**); y los de Martha L. Canfield y Michael Palencia-Roth sobre *El otoño del patriarca* (items **5479** y **5487**). Completando esta abrumadora concentración en la obra de García Márquez, la *Latin American Literary Review* publicó un número especial dedicado al autor, con 12 textos críticos (item **5486**).

La crítica de tema venezolano no ofrece tanta calidad, pero sí ha mostrado una actividad más intensa que en años anteriores. Esto quizá haya sido estimulado por la colección de ensayos y trabajos críticos publicados por la Academia Nacional de Historia, que ha significado una conveniente vía de difusión para muchos estudios. Dos libros (items **5126** y **5126a**) dan testimonio de distintas reuniones celebradas con ocasión del bicentenario del nacimiento de Bello. Rómulo Gallegos es el autor contemporáneo que sigue siendo central en la literatura venezolana; de los trabajos que se le dedican, hay que destacar el de Maya Schärer-Nussberger (item **5521**), que ofrece una versión diferente y moderna de textos que han sido apreciados más por sus valores tradicionales y realistas. De otro de los grandes escritores venezolanos, Mariano Picón-Salas, se ha publicado la mejor y más amplia recopilación de su prosa crítica y ensayística (item **5520**), aparte de una reedición de su clásico texto de historia literaria nacional (item **5519**). Dos recopilaciones críticas sobre autores del primer tercio del siglo como Teresa de la Parra (item **5522**) y Julio Garmendia (item **5517**), comparten el mismo carácter antológico: son selecciones de la crítica sobre esos autores, que cubren desde su época hasta el presente, lo que tiene bastante utilidad. Igualmente útil es la bibliografía de casi 100 años de crítica venezolana preparada por R.J. Lovera De-Sola (item **5518**).

Hay poco que decir sobre el deprimido aporte de la crítica ecuatoriana y boliviana. Quizá lo único digno de mención sea el trabajo de Clementina Christos Rabassa sobre la obra narrativa y teatral de Demetrio Aguilera Malta (item **5490**).

Cabría agregar que la dispersión metodológica que estos libros y trabajos revelan, es tan amplia como siempre, pero que, si quisiese señalarse tendencias dominantes, habría que reconocer que en el área peruana ha predominado el enfoque sociohistórico y cultural sobre el formalista, mientras que en el área colombiana y venezolana ha habido una inclinación por las interpretaciones antropológicas y simbólicas. [JMO]

The biennium sees a considerable shift in the production of prose fiction from Venezuela to Peru as the center of activity that rivals Colombia's perennially strong publishing industry. The bleak situation in Peru, as reported in *HLAS 44*, seems to have been reversed in convincing fashion. Mario Vargas Llosa has given us another important novel (item **5556**), even if in literary terms it may not come up to his previous accomplishment. Even more significant, however, is the emergence of the biannual COPE literary prize for short fiction. The prize has been sponsored by Petroperú since 1981. The two volumes of short stories selected from the hundreds

submitted for the 1981 and 1983 competitions (items **5544** and **5552** respectively)
are a good indication of the interest and output generated by the prize. The fact that
nearly a thousand submissions were entered for the two competitions combined
gives us an indication about the level of intensity with which short fiction is
produced in Peru in the first five years of the present decade. Other publication out-
lets exist for this production as the high quality anthology edited by Cornejo Polar
and L.F. Vidal indicates (item **5551**). In addition, collections by Huaraga Alvarez
(item **5548**), Ledezma Izquieta (item **5549**), Mora (item **5550**), Ribeyro (item **5553**),
and Villanes Cairo (item **5557**) are a fairly accurate index to the salutary state of
short prose fiction in the Peruvian literary scene. A historically significant compilation of this regard is Vidal's edition of selections from a 30-year period by a
number of important authors—*Cuentos limeños, 1950–1980* (item **5546**). There
is some interesting longer prose as well, in addition to Vargas Llosa's, that emerges
from Peru during this biennium (e.g., Corzano in item **5545** and Sánchez in item
5554). Most significant in this category is Edgardo de Habich's historical novel
(item **5547**) that fictionalizes the historic events at the Peruvian embassy in Havana
in 1980.

By contrast, the publication of prose fiction in Venezuela seems to have fallen
on hard times. Nonetheless, there are some notable achievements. The outstanding
Venezuelan narrator, Salvador Garmendia, has given us another collection of short
stories (item **5560**) and a younger writer, Humberto Mata, has published his third
book of stories and it is as delightful as his previous two collections. A significant
experimental novel by Alberto Guaura (item **5561**) is the most exciting new work
out of Venezuela. There is, too, an important reissue of a key work form the 1920s:
Teresa de la Parra's *Ifigenia* (item **5563**) makes a timely reappearance to address the
issue of woman's rights, or lack of same, in Latin society.

The Bolivian scene continues to be rather predictable (*costumbrismo*, violence, exploitation, death). Notable in this context is Cáceres Romero's tightly
linked short stories in a collection that chronicles Bolivia's 1980 and 1982 military
coups (item **5523**).

The same thematic preoccupation takes on a wry twist in the context of Ecuadorian prose, where the publication industry seems to have lost the impetus it
had received in previous years from government subsidies. Gustavo Alfredo Jácome
(item **5541**) gives the perennial problem of militarism and political instability a
new twist by interjecting a note of satire and acrid irony in the Swiftian vein. Equally
noteworthy in Ecuador is the publication of a first novel by the already well established author of short fictions, Jorge Velasco Mackenzie (item **5543**).

The most varied and most prodigious output of prose fiction in the region
continues to come from Colombia. Perhaps the impetus of García Márquez's 1982
Nobel Prize may be instrumental in this regard. At any rate, a good number of novelists and short-story writers are in hot pursuit of Colombia's premier narrator.
They range from the more traditional to the highly experimental and innovative.

In the case of the first, the black novelist, Zapata Olivella, has added another
title to his incisive corpus (item **5540**). On the other hand, younger authors such as
David Sánchez Juliao (item **5536**) and Roberto Burgos Cantor (item **5529**) engage the
unmistakable García-Márquezian style with direct challenge and parodic verve.
Sánchez Juliao has produced a masterful and hilarious parody that targets not only
García Márquez's narrative trade mark but takes on, as well, Mexico's sacred cow,
Juan Rulfo. Burgos Cantor, for his part, in a more serious and non-parodic work,
synthesizes the resounding voice of García Márquez with the playful reverberations
of the Cuban Guillermo Cabrera Infante's narrative intensities.

Colombia's first lady of narrative prose delivers a devastating demystification of male-centered femininity in her iconoclastic novel, *Los amores de Afrodita* (item **5528**). Fanny Buitrago may well have found her male counterpart in Rafael Humberto Moreno-Durán, however. This highly talented novelist culminates his trilogy with his *Finale capriccioso con madonna* (item **5534**). Moreno-Durán is a profound, artful and, at times, overwhelming writer with great narrative range.

Two collections of short stories by younger writers who form part of the group gathered around the literary journal, *El Papagayo de Cristal* of Bogotá, are noteworthy. The publication has engendered an innovative constellation of young talent. From among them, two are represented here by a collection of short stories each—Henry Canizales (item **5530**) and José Cardona López (item **5531**).

The most exciting young talent to emerge in this area, however, is that of Sergio Vieira (item **5539**). His award-winnning collection of short stories is by far the most promising first book to have come out of Colombia during this biennium. [DjK]

LITERARY CRITICISM AND HISTORY
BOLIVIA

5478 Quiroga, Giancarla de. Los mundos de *Los deshabitados*: estudio de la novela de Marcelo Quiroga Santa Cruz. Cochabamba, Bolivia: Offset Casema, 1980. 125 p.: bibl.

Examen de la psicología y relaciones de los personajes en el relato del escritor boliviano. Aunque detallado, el trabajo se resiente por su método y presentación convencionales. [JMO]

COLOMBIA

5479 Canfield, Martha L. El patriarca de García Márquez: padre, poeta y tirano (IILI/RI, 50:128/129, julio/dic. 1984, p. 1017–1056)

Inspirada en unas ideas de Barthes (la distinción entre "textos de placer" y "textos de goce"), la autora hace una valiosa revisión crítica de algunos aspectos claves de la novela: el tema del caudillo bárbaro, el zoomorfismo, la presunción divina del héroe, el motivo excremental, la polivalencia, etc. [JMO]

5480 Cobo Borda, J.G. Vueltas en redondo en torno a Gabriel García Márquez (*in* Usos de la imaginación. Edición de J.G. Cobo Borda *et al.* Buenos Aires: El Imaginero, 1984, p. 13–54)

Trata principalmente dos cuestiones: los influjos universales y nacionales (de Joyce a la música popular colombiana) en la forma-

ción estética de García Márquez, y su activismo político en nombre de la izquierda revolucionaria. El ensayo es inteligente, provocador y amenísimo. [JMO]

5481 García Márquez, Gabriel. Obra periodística. v. 1–2, Textos costeños. v. 3–4, Entre cachacos. Recopilación y prólogo de Jacques Gilard. Bogotá: Editorial La Oveja Negra, 1983. 4 v. (v. 1–2, 711 p.; v. 3–4, 799 p.): bibl.

Los vols. 1–2 contienen los artículos periodísticos y los primeros textos narrativos que el autor publicó en *El Universal* de Cartagena (1948–49) y *El Heraldo* de Barranquilla (1950–52). Los vol. 3–4 contienen crónicas periodísticas escritas para *El Espectador* de Bogotá (1954–55) e incluyen la que luego se haría famosa como *Relato de un naúfrago*. Traen con dos informativos estudios de Jacques Gilard sobre los períodos respectivos. [JMO]

5482 García Márquez, Gabriel. Obra periodística. v. 4, De Europa y América, 1955–1960. Recopilación y prólogo de Jacques Gilard. Barcelona, Spain: Bruguera, 1983. 860 p.: bibl. (Narradores de hoy; 76)

Cubre el período más activo y largo de García Márquez como periodista: sus años (1955–60) de corresponsal de *El Espectador* de Bogotá y otros periódicos de Colombia y Venezuela (ver item **5481**). [JMO]

5483 García Márquez, Gabriel. El olor de la guayaba: conversaciones con Plinio Apuleyo Mendoza. Barcelona, Spain: Bruguera, 1982. 186 p., 16 p. of plates: ill. (Cinco estrellas; 83)

Revisión general de la personalidad, la obra y la actitud intelectual y política del novelista colombiano. Más anecdótico que crítico, el libro ofrece datos interesantes sobre el último aspecto, desgraciadamente sin citar sus fuentes. [JMO]

5484 Gilard, Jacques. El grupo de Barranquilla (IILI/RI, 50:128/129, julio/dic. 1984, p. 905–935)

Estudio sobre el grupo de escritores, periodistas y amigos intelectuales del joven García Márquez, que luego él inmortalizaría en sus novelas. Muy útil para conocer la etapa formativa del autor. [JMO]

5485 González Echevarría, Roberto. *Cien años de soledad*: the novel as myth and archive (MLN, 99:2, March 1984, p. 358–380)

Aunque centrado en un ejemplo concreto, este importante trabajo trata una cuestión de mayor alcance: las relaciones que la novela y la historia de América Latina han tenido a lo largo del tiempo, y cómo han evolucionado según su modelo de "verdad," fuese ésta la ley, la ciencia o la antropología. [JMO]

5486 *Latin American Literary Review.* Univ. of Pittsburgh. Vol. 13, No. 25, Jan./June 1985-. Pittsburgh, Pa.

Número especial dedicado a García Márquez. Contiene 12 textos críticos de otros tantos autores (aparte de breves notas y comentarios) que se concentran en los más diversos aspectos de su obra. Los enfoques son también variados: desde el histórico hasta el desconstructivo. [JMO]

5487 Palencia-Roth, Michael. El círculo hermenéutico en *El otoño del patriarca* (IILI/RI, 50:128/129, julio/dic. 1984, p. 999–1016)

El autor estudia, capítulo por capítulo y apoyado en las teorías del conocimiento, la forma como García Márquez presenta los hechos al mismo tiempo que insinúa la dificultad para conocer todo el proceso que está detrás de ellos. Todo conocimiento de la verdad es parcial y relativo; detrás de la verdad, hay otra. En el círculo infinito de interpretaciones se incluyen el propio autor y los lectores. [JMO]

5488 Rama, Angel. El puesto de Gabriel García Márquez (ECO, 42:3, enero 1983, p. 225–237)

Recuento crítico de la obra creadora de García Márquez escrito con ocasión del Premio Nobel de Literatura que ganó en 1982. Usando un enfoque sociológico, Rama analiza las relaciones del autor con su público y las de su mundo ficticio con el proceso histórico de Colombia y América Latina. [JMO]

5489 Williams, Raymond L. Gabriel García Márquez. Boston: Twayne Publishers, 1984. 176 p.: bibl., index, port. (Twayne's world authors series; TWAS 749. Latin American literature)

Este es el tercer libro dedicado a García Márquez que aparece en inglés. Dirigido al público en general, ofrece una visión coherente y comprehensiva (abarca hasta *Crónica de una muerte anunciada* y cubre su obra periodística) del autor. Incluye estudios específicos sobre sus libros más importantes, aparte de cronología y bibliografía. [JMO]

ECUADOR

5490 Rabassa, Clementine Christos. En torno a Aguilera Malta: temas épicos y negros. Guayaquil, Ecuador: Casa de la Cultura Ecuatoriana, Núcleo del Guayas, 1981. 269 p.: bibl. (Col. Nuestramérica; 5)

Usando un método básicamente comparatista, con algunos toques antropológicos, la autora estudia los elementos épicos en la narrativa del autor ecuatoriano, y los "temas negros" en su teatro. Thomas Mann, García Márquez, el teatro caribeño de la *négritude* y O'Neill, son los modelos invocados. [JMO]

5491 Seminario-Simposio de la Literatura Ecuatoriana en los Ultimos 30 Años, *1st, Quito, 1983.* La literatura ecuatoriana en los últimos 30 años, 1950–1980. Hernán Rodríguez Castelo *et al.* Quito: Editorial El Conejo, 1983. 132 p.: bibl. (Col. Ecuador/ letras)

El principal mérito de este volumen es el de ofrecer breves y prácticos resúmenes de lo producido en la literatura ecuatoriana durante los últimos 30 años de tres géneros: poesía, cuento y novela. Se agrega un trabajo sobre el escritor, la sociedad y el poder. [JMO]

PERU

5492 Arriola Grande, Maurilio. Diccionario literario del Perú: nomenclatura por autores. 2a ed., corr. y aum. Lima: Editorial Universo, 1983. 2 v.: ill.

Reedición ampliada del trabajo publicado en 1968. La ampliación es desmesurada: dos volúmenes y casi mil páginas no se justifican del todo. El material es indiscriminado, porque el autor incluye a pintores y otros artistas, en un diccionario que se titula *literario*. [JMO]

5493 Borel, Jean-Paul. Arguedas o la literatura imposible (UTIEH/C, 42, 1984, p. 77−91)

Enfoca principalmente las cuestiones socioculturales que plantea la obra arguediana: desde el uso de la literatura como un modo de establecer una relación con un mundo escindido, hasta su visión de un país desgarrado por tensiones sociales extremas, lo que hace de su novelística un "proyecto imposible." [JMO]

5494 Compton, Merlin D. Las *Tradiciones peruanas* de Ricardo Palma: bibliografía y lista cronológica tentativas (FENIX, 28/29, 1978/1979, p. 99−129, tables)

Aunque publicado hace nueve años, este trabajo sigue siendo el mejor aporte para establecer la cronología de la publicación de las tradiciones. Fuente de consulta indispensable. [JMO]

5495 Cornejo Polar, Antonio. La literatura peruana: totalidad contradictoria (RCLL, 9:18, 1983, p. 37−50)

Planteamiento teórico que discute las distintas interpretaciones críticas del concepto "literatura peruana," y que propone, para entenderlo mejor, las categorías de "pluralidad" y "totalidad." El trabajo hace una defensa algo dogmática del enfoque sociohistórico, aparte de incurrir en expresiones tan poco felices como "inactual," "descondicionamiento" y "conductual." [JMO]

5496 Cornejo Polar, Antonio et al. Vigencia y universalidad de José María Arguedas. Lima: Editorial Horizonte, 1984. 61 p.: ports.

Transcripciones de las intervenciones de cuatro estudios de la obra de Arguedas, durante una mesa redonda realizada en Lima en 1982. Los descuidos de la edición limitan el valor del conjunto. [JMO]

5497 Escajadillo, Tomás G. Alegría y *El mundo es ancho y ajeno*. Lima: Instituto de Investigaciones Humanísticas, Univ. Nacional Mayor de San Marcos, 1983. 197 p.: bibls., ill. (Literatura. Serie mayor; 1)

Revisión crítica de los aspectos esenciales de la novela de Ciro Alegría: estructura, personajes, símbolos, técnicas, etc. Lamentablemente, el estilo trabajoso del estudio, el tono vindicativo de su argumentación (véase la "Introducción") y las notas abrumadoramente largas, hacen penosa a la lectura. [JMO]

5498 Escobar, Alberto. Arguedas, o, La utopía de la lengua. Lima: Instituto de Estudios Peruanos, 1984. 250 p.: bibl., ill. (Serie Lengua y sociedad; 6)

Resumen de seis años de constante estudio, este libro observa la obra de Arguedas desde distintos ángulos y con diversos enfoques: sus relaciones con el pensamiento social de los años 30, su ideal de lengua literaria, las variantes de *Agua* y *Warma Kuyay*, los espacios en su novela póstuma. Cada capítulo tiene sus méritos, aunque la estructuración del libro es laxa. [JMO]

5499 Kerr, Roy A. The secret self: Boa in Vargas Llosa's *La ciudad y los perros* (UNC/RN, 24:2, Winter 1983, p. 111−115)

Breve análisis de la psiquis del indicado personaje, cuya apariencia brutal esconde un "second self," dominado por temores, supersticiones y hasta un sentido de compasión. [JMO]

5500 Kristal, Efraín. El narrador en la obra de Julio Ramón Ribeyro (RCLL, 10:20, 1984, p. 155−169)

Estudia el modelo típico del narrador ribeyriano: el de "una consciencia reflexiva . . . del mundo que observa," lo que permite un cruce entre lo objetivo y lo subjetivo. Las técnicas narrativas del autor (relato *in medias res*, personajes-testigos, contrapunto y cambios de punto de enfoque) guardan relación con el tono escéptico de sus relatos. [JMO]

5501 Luchting, Wolfgang A. Los mecanismos de la ambigüedad: *La juventud en la otra ribera* de Julio Ramón Ribeyro (UV/PH, 49, enero/marzo 1984, p. 53−64)

Detallado análisis (a veces, un tanto forzado) de los *leitmotiven* como un mecanismo para crear un efecto de simbólica ambigüedad. La conclusión del crítico es que en el relato predomina un "intrínseco determinismo existencial." La alusión a Henry James a propósito de la ambigüedad, no parece aquí muy justificada. [JMO]

5502 Miller, Beth. Peruvian women writers: directions for future research (RRI, 12:1, Spring 1982, p. 36–48)
Reseña de la situación de las mujeres escritoras en el Perú y su situación social. Con un sesgo marcadamente feminista, la autora hace una crónica del problema, cuyo valor es más informativo que crítico. [JMO]

5503 O'Hara, Edgar and Guillermo Niño de Guzmán. La guerra victoriosa de Vargas Llosa (CNC/RPC, 1, julio 1982, p. 9–36)
Extenso reportaje sobre diversos aspectos (contexto, contenido histórico, enfoque estético) de *La guerra del fin del mundo.* [JMO]

5504 Pantigoso, Edgardo J. José María Arguedas y la nueva concepción del indigenismo (Káñina [Univ. de Costa Rica, San José] 5:2, julio/dic. 1981, p. 59–68, bibl.)
El autor comienza discutiendo el uso de los términos "indianismo" e "indigenismo" por imprecisos, por lo que propone la expresión abarcadora "literatura de la indianidad." Pero luego sigue usando "indigenismo" cuando trata de situar la obra de Arguedas dentro de ese movimiento. [JMO]

5505 Peruvian literature: a bibliography of secondary sources. Compiled by D.W. Foster. Westport, Conn.: Greenwood Press, 1981. 324 p.
Importante contribución al estudio de la literatura peruana, posiblemente la más completa de su tipo. Dividida en dos grandes secciones: una recoge trabajos críticos generales, desde bibliografías hasta estudios sobre géneros y períodos históricos; la otra reúne entradas sobre 38 autores individuales. El aporte es considerable, a pesar de los inevitables errores y omisiones. [JMO]

5506 Pinto Gamboa, Willy F. Sobre fascismo y literatura: la Guerra Civil española en *La Prensa, El Comercio* y *La Crónica,* 1936–1939. Lima: Editorial Cibeles, 1983. 125 p.: bibl.
El interés de este trabajo reside en el hecho de que toca un tema poco estudiado: el pensamiento y las letras de orientación fascista, tal como quedan registrados en el periodismo peruano durante los años de la Guerra Civil española. Incluye una valiosa sección documental. [JMO]

5507 Prieto, René. The two narrative voices in Mario Vargas Llosa's *Aunt Julia and the scriptwriter* (LALR, 11:22, Spring/Summer 1983, p. 15–25)
Nuevo examen de un tema ya estudiado por otros: la doble perspectiva narrativa (Camacho/Marito) de la novela del peruano. Se apuntan algunas ideas nuevas, inspiradas en la crítica francesa. El trabajo presenta 64 notas; en un texto de apenas ocho páginas, eso parece algo excesivo. [JMO]

5508 Sánchez, Luis Alberto. Indianismo e indigenismo en la literatura peruana. Lima: Mosca Azul Editores, 1982. 66 p.
Leído como discurso de orden al ser incorporado a la Academia Peruana de la Lengua, este texto de Sánchez es una rápida reseña sobre el tema, en la que el autor recicla ideas y afirmaciones expuestas en obras anteriores. [JMO]

5509 Tanner, Roy L. Ricardo Palma and Francisco de Quevedo: a case of rhetorical affinity and debt (UK/KRQ, 31:4, 1984, p. 425–435)
Breve trabajo, análogo en alcance y método al item **5510** del mismo autor, que señala las significativas coincidencias estilísticas entre los dos escritores. Los recursos de exageración, juegos de palabras y formas sintéticas de caracterización, son los más destacados. [JMO]

5510 Tanner, Roy L. Ricardo Palma's rhetorical debt to Miguel de Cervantes (UA/REH, 17:3, Oct. 1983, p. 345–361)
Interesante y documentado estudio de los ecos cervantinos en el lenguaje de las *Tradiciones peruanas.* El autor trata especialmente el uso de antítesis, sinónimos, acumulaciones verbales, reiteraciones y frases en aposición (ver item **5509**). [JMO]

5511 Wise, David O. *La Sierra,* 1927–1930: the voice of the men of the Andes (RIB, 35:2, 1985, p. 166–190)
Tiene el mérito de llamar la atención sobre una publicación, prácticamente olvidada, que defendió y exaltó los valores de la cultura andina en el Perú de la época del Presidente Leguía. El trabajo incluye una cronología de la revista. [JMO]

5512 Zavaleta, Carlos Eduardo. Retrato de Ciro Alegría. Lima: Lluvia Editores, 1984. 31 p.

Semblanza del autor de *El mundo es ancho y ajeno*, leída en un homenaje realizado en 1984, en la que hay referencias a la novela póstuma *Lázaro* y a sus semejanzas literarias con José María Arguedas. [JMO]

VENEZUELA

5513 Barroeta, José. La hoguera de otra edad. Mérida, Venezuela: Univ. de Los Andes, Consejo de Publicaciones, 1982. 92 p. (Col. Actual. Serie Ensayo)

Esta crónica sobre dos grupos literarios venezolanos ("El Techo de la Ballena" y "Tabla Redonda") contiene algunos datos interesantes, pero en general es demasiado anecdótica y superficial. [JMO]

5514 Caldera, Rafael Tomás. La respuesta de Gallegos: ensayos sobre nuestra situación cultural. Caracas: Academia Nacional de la Historia, 1980. 177 p.: bibl., index (El Libro menor; 12)

El pensamiento y la narrativa de Gallegos son aquí un pretexto para reflexionar sobre el tema de la identidad cultural hispanoamericana y examinar la contribución del novelista a esa cuestión. En términos relativos, el trabajo de mayor interés es el primero, dedicado al cuento "Pataruco." [JMO]

5515 Garmendia, Salvador. Memorias de Altagracia. Edición de Oscar Rodríguez Ortiz. Madrid: Cátedra, 1982. 232 p.: bibl. (Letras hispánicas; 156)

Esta edición anotada del libro narrativo que el autor publicó en 1979, facilita al lector no venezolano el conocimiento de una obra singular. Le brinda además un útil estudio introductorio a la narrativa del autor y una bibliografía. [JMO]

5516 Georgescu, Paul Alexandru. Rómulo Gallegos. Caracas: Academia Nacional de la Historia, 1984. 119 p. (El Libro menor; 52)

El origen de este libro es una serie de cuatro conferencias sobre: ontología y deontología en Rómulo Gallegos, sus modelos narrativos, la tipología de sus personajes, y su significación histórica como novelista. El autor usa un enfoque básicamente académico, que sería más valioso si no fuese tan rígido. [JMO]

Izaguirre, Rodolfo. Rómulo Gallegos y el cine. See item **1104.**

5517 Julio Garmendia ante la crítica. Selección y nota preliminar de Juan Carlos Santaella. Caracas: Monte Avila Editores, 1980. 325 p.: bibl., index (Col. Ante la crítica)

Este volumen tiene un interesante carácter antológico, pues recoge 16 comentarios y trabajos críticos dedicados al autor, desde 1927 al presente. El valor individual de cada uno es, por cierto, muy variado. El volumen incluye una bibliografía de y sobre el autor, y un índice temático. [JMO]

5518 Lovera De-Sola, Roberto J. Bibliografía de la crítica literaria venezolana, 1847–1977. Caracas: Instituto Autónomo Biblioteca Nacional: Servicios de Bibliotecas, 1982. 489 p.: indexes.

Más de un siglo de obras y colecciones críticas publicadas en forma de libro, se recopilan aquí, con una sección especial para la crítica teatral (1891–1981). Las casi 1,800 fichas habrían sido más fáciles de consultar si estuviesen agrupadas cronológicamente, no en orden alfabético. [JMO]

5519 Picón-Salas, Mariano. Formación y proceso de la literatura venezolana. Presentación de María Fernanda Palacios. Bibliografía de Rafael Angel Rivas. Caracas: Monte Avila Editores, 1984. 348 p.: bibl.

Este clásica historia literaria fue publicada originalmente en 1940 y reeditada y ampliada, en 1961, con otro título. Ahora se la reedita otra vez, añadiéndole páginas sueltas del ensayista dedicadas a nuevos autores venezolanos. Pionera en su tiempo, la obra luce ahora bastante envejecida y anecdótica. [JMO]

5520 Picón-Salas, Mariano. Viejos y nuevos mundos. Selección, prólogo y cronología de Guillermo Sucre. Caracas: Biblioteca Ayacucho, 1983. 685 p.: bibl. (Biblioteca Ayacucho; 101)

Esta debe ser la más amplia y abarcadora de la prosa crítica y ensayística del autor: contiene tres de sus libros clásicos y recopila páginas sueltas sobre temas hispanoamericanos, la civilización actual y el arte de escribir. Lo precede un comprensivo estudio del antólogo. [JMO]

5521 Schärer-Nussberger, Maya. Rómulo Gallegos: el mundo inconcluso. Caracas: Monte Avila Editores, 1979. 246 p.: bibl. (Col. Estudios)

Inspirada en ideas de Bachelard y Eliade, la autora hace una lectura simbólico-cultural de los mitos y alegorías encerrados en las tres obras mayores de Gallegos: *Doña Bárbara, Cantaclaro* y *Canaima*. El enfoque, aunque no siempre compartible, es al menos una mirada nueva y original, que deja de lado las más obvias interpretaciones historicistas. [JMO]

5522 Teresa de la Parra ante la crítica. Selección, prólogo, cronología, hemerografía y foro imaginario de Velia Bosch. Caracas: Monte Avila Editores, 1982. 255 p. (Col. Ante la crítica)

Semejante al volumen dedicado a Julio Garmendia (ver item **5517**), ésta es una antología crítica de lo publicado sobre la autora entre 1925–81. Entre otros, figuran textos de Zaldumbide, Vasconcelos y Juan Ramón Jiménez. Se incluyen una cronología y una recopilación hemerográfica sobre la escritora. [JMO]

PROSE FICTION
BOLIVIA

5523 Cáceres Romero, Adolfo. Los golpes: cuentos. La Paz: Editorial Los Amigos del Libro, 1983. 101 p.

Perspectivist narration of Bolivia's 1980 military coup refracted through the varied circumstances of its innocent victims and of the Bolivian people in general. Consists of seven perspectives on the 1980 coup with an eighth focusing on the 1982 coup that displaced the military ruler of the previous takeover. An intense narrative and desperate indictment of militarism and political instability. [DjK]

5524 Ludueña Isasmendi, Hernán. La muerte no envejece: cuentos. La Paz: Editorial Roalva, 1982. 90 p.

Half dozen short stories thematically linked by death and violence although temporally dispersed over Bolivia's violent history and hostile geography. The setting for these stories ranges from the altiplano and its Indian superstitions to the Chaco War, political violence in the 1970s and in the current decade. Title story by far the most accomplished as narrative. [DjK]

5525 Rodrigo, Saturnino. La espera inútil. La Paz: Biblioteca Popular Boliviana de Ultima Hora, 1982. 283 p. (Biblioteca popular boliviana de Ultima Hora)

Novela costumbrista set in Sucre in the second decade of the present century. Interesting documentary of what used to be the Bolivian capital and of its privileged social class at the turn of the century. Students of social history might find it of interest. [DjK]

5526 Vargas, Manuel et al. Cuatro narradores bolivianos contemporáneos. La Paz: Palabra Encendida, 1982. 109 p.

Collection of 14 contemporary short stories from Bolivia. Represented are Manuel Vargas (four stories), Felix Salazar González and Jaime Nisttahuz (three stories each), and René Bascopé Aspiazú (four stories). A thumbnail bio-bibliography precedes the stories of each writer. The more convincing of the four are Manuel Vargas and René Bascopé Aspiazú. Valuable collection. [DjK]

COLOMBIA

5527 Arciniegas, Triunfo et al. La mujer cometa y otros relatos. Pasto, Colombia: Ediciones Testimonio, 1984. 96 p.

Consists of the winner and seven other short stories from the third annual "La Fundación para la Cultura 'Testimonio'" competition of Pasto, Colombia. Entries are generally of high quality. As in previous two competitions, a good number of young talented writers are emerging from Colombia's new generation. [DjK]

5528 Buitrago, Fanny. Los amores de Afrodita. Bogotá: Plaza & Janés, 1983. 276 p. (Novelista del dia. Narrativa colombiana)

Fanny Buitrago delivers a devastating demystification of eros and human frailty. Focused through a series of women, or "Afroditas," the novel functions as an exposure of human ambition, hypocricy, self-indulgence and cruelty. Aphrodite's vocation seems to be irremediably flawed or hopelessly undermined. As social commentary, particularly from a feminist perspective on Latin American social structures, Buitrago's novel packs an indictment hard to dispute. Author has emerged as Colombia's most convincing female voice in prose fiction with a deserved international reputation. [DjK]

5529 Burgos Cantor, Roberto. El patio de los vientos perdidos. Bogotá: Planeta, 1984. 275 p. (Autores colombianos)

Accomplished piece of fiction that combines some of the best narrative techniques of Guillermo Cabrera Infante and Gabriel García Márquez. This is the author's first novel and it is an exciting achievement. Burgos Cantor is a master of run-on monologue with an uncanny ear for the language of the character types he portrays—a failed boxer, lonely prostitutes, a would-be jazz musician. Author manages to infuse the realistic ravings of these characters with a magical quality that is captivating. [DjK]

5530 Canizales, Henry. Cambalache. Bogotá: *Papagayo de Cristal*, 1983. 124 p. (Narrativa)

Collection of 12 stories with a mordant, ironic twist that carnivalizes language, including the author's own, and human illusions. Canizales has a penchant for black humor and the cold, mathematical presentation of the most distressing human circumstances. The stories are tinged with a dramatic absurdity that is frequently hilarious. [DjK]

5531 Cardona López, José. La puerta del espejo. Bogotá: *Papagayo de Cristal*, 1983. 156 p. (Narrativa)

This is the author's first book and consists of 10 short stories. He has a commanding narrative style that is masterfully exasperating. His stories verge on the absurd and the grotesque. He is an accessible narrator who plays with agility on the commonplace fantasies and self-serving delusions of ordinary people. He is a member of the group of writers gathered around the literary magazine El *Papagayo de Cristal*. [DjK]

5532 Garcés González, José Luis. Los extraños traen mala suerte. Montería, Colombia: Gráficas Corsa, 1984. 131 p.

Garcés González's novel, a finalist in the 1982 Concurso Latinoamericano de Novela "Jorge Isaacs" in Colombia, is a long interior monologue and stream of consciousness narration. Its central character and narrating voice is that of an alienated and skeptical newspaper-man whose dispassionate confessions of his own inadequacies provoke genuine compassion. Effective technical accomplishment. [DjK]

5533 Molinares Sarmiento, Ramón. Exiliados en Lille. Barranquilla, Colombia: Editorial El Gallo Capón, 1982. 183 p.

Thematically this is an interesting novel that belongs to what may become a literary genre in itself: the novel of the Latin American political exile. Molinares Sarmiento narrates the plight of a group of Chilean refugees in northern France, focusing on the psychological demoralization wrought by displacement, the family conflicts brought about by adverse economic circumstances, and the generational problem between exiled parents whose French-born children cannot share the shock of uprooting and political defeat. A significant sociological and political statement. [DjK]

5534 Moreno-Durán, Rafael Humberto. Finale capriccioso con madonna. Barcelona, Spain: Montesinos Editor S.A., 1983? 322 p.

Dense but rewarding novel that culminates a triology. The previous two novels (*Juego de damas*, 1977 and *El toque de Diana*, 1981), like the present work, explore the female psyche and the manifold faces and phases of the female gender. The Colombian Moreno-Durán is an able narrator with a unique voice and great narrative range. His manipulation of language, his weaving of theme and mythos, the exploration of congruity and differentiations in subject and linguistic expression make his work a mine field for the uninitiated but a rich and textured world for the strong reader. Moreno-Durán is a superb novelist and sensibility. [DjK]

5535 Pardo, Carlos Orlando. Los lugares comunes. Bogotá: Ediciones Pijao, 1982. 133 p.

As the title indicates, this is a collection of 19 short pieces depicting the ordinary, the hackneyed, the commonplace in an exasperatingly effective, ordinary tone. Pardo aims his darts at everyone: petty bureaucrats, political demogogues, guerrillas, bored middle-class women. Snippets of a *comedia humana* in modern society. [DjK]

5536 Sánchez Juliao, David. Pero sigo siendo el rey: Sinfonía para Lector y Mariachi, Opus 1. Bogotá: Plaza & Janés, Editores Colombia, 1983. 269 p. (Novelistas del día. Narrativa colombiana)

Hilarious spoof by one of Colombia's

most talented writers. As the title and subtitle of the work indicate, Sánchez Juliao uses an old mexican *ranchera* as the frame for his novel/soap opera/radio novel. For the initiated reader, there is a more serious side to the author's game. The novel is in large measure a playful satire of Juan Rulfo's and Gabriel García Márquez's narrative styles. Sánchez Juliao has demonstrated, as he has done in earlier works, his astonishing mimetic capability and uncanny ear for narrative voices. [DjK]

5537 Tejada, Juan Manuel. La segunda muerte de la tía Milita: cuentos. Medellín, Colombia: Lealon, 1982. 239 p.

Collection of 14 stark and moving short stories that dramatize life in the Colombian countryside. Violence and a profound lyricism dominate Tejada's narrations. The stories are anecdotal, seemingly simple, and powerfully evocative. A peculiar mystery haunts the countryside and the lives and deaths of laconic characters. A uniform and consistent collection. [DjK]

5538 El Tolima cuenta. Prólogo de Fernando Ayala Poveda. Bogotá: Pijao Editores, 1984. 196 p. (Biblioteca de autores tolimenses; 16)

Collection of 14 regional writers from Colombia's Tolima province, each represented with one story. The theme of La Violencia is still a primary occupation of these writers who compete favorably with other literary centers of Colombia (Antioquia, the Caribbean coast). A brief introduction by Fernando Ayala Poveda places the region of Tolima and its writers in the broader context of Colombian letters. Valuable collection of uniformly good quality fiction. [DjK]

5539 Vieira, Sergio. Historias de vecinos. Medellín, Colombia: J.J.W.J., 1984. 164 p.

Intense, lyrical, evocative, insightful. Vieira (b. 1959) is perhaps the most exciting young writer to emerge in the last two years. His collection of masterful short stories won the national prize "Jorge Gaitán Durán" for 1983. Vieira has a wonderful mastery of terseness and implied dialogue. His stories are charged with human emotion and poetic evocation. His first book and hopefully the first of many. [DjK]

5540 Zapata Olivella, Juan. Pisando el camino de ébano. Bogotá: Ediciones Lerner, 1984. 190 p.

Latest novel by one of Colombia's most established black writers. It is in the same vein as the author's earlier works: a dramatization of race relations in the Americas and the role of the black in Latin American society. [DjK]

ECUADOR

5541 Jácome, Gustavo Alfredo. Los pucho-Remaches. Quito: El Autor, 1984. 335 p.

We could call this novel "a modest proposal" in the manner of Jonathan Swift. The author subjects social and historical conditions of the Indians, the ignorant military, the privileged class, and the clergy to such dire hyperbole that the results of his narrative almost come off as real documentary portrayal. Jácome attempts a drastic satire and, like most satire, his target is sociopolitical. Ridiculously hilarious book with a deadly serious undertow. [DjK]

5542 Ubidia, Abdon. Ciudad de invierno y otros relatos. Quito: Ediciones Nueva, 1982. 126 p.

Collection of five stories of varying length, the first of which is long enough to be a *novella*. Follows interesting thread of psychological narration in an urban (Quito) setting. Ubidia's characters are portrayed as typical phenomena of the Ecuadorian middle class and its modern neuroses. Of particular interest is the penultimate piece, "La Gilette," that deals with the predicament of the writer in front of a mute typewriter and the resolution of that impasse as writing. [DjK]

5543 Velasco Mackenzie, Jorge. El rincón de los justos. Quito: Editorial El Conejo, 1983. 176 p. (Col. Ecuador/letras)

Depressing novel about the shadowy night-life of contemporary Guayaquil and its human fauna. A devastating portrayal of social outcasts and disowned social elements in the chiaroscuros of a "modern" Latin American city. Jorge Velasco Mackenzie is one of the more talented contemporary writers of Ecuador. This is his first novel. [DjK]

PERU

Arguedas, José María. Yawar fiesta. See item **6549.**

5544 Avenida Oeste y los cuentos ganadores del Premio Copé, 1981. Lima: Ediciones COPE: Depto. de Relaciones Públicas, Petroperú, 1982. 268 p.

Consists of 17 of the 568 entries for the 1981 COPE Short Story Prize of Peru. A clear indication of the intensity and breadth of narrative production. Volume's title story by Julio Ortega is the most accomplished and is characteristic of the poignancy that marks a number of the stories in the collection. For the most part, these are stories of introspection and search for native authenticity. Significant collection. See also item **5552.** [DjK]

5545 Corzano, Néstor. El ordenanza. Lima: El Autor, 1984. 207 p.

Fascinating novel thematically, quite predictable otherwise. Corzano dramatizes the theme and perspective of the underling, the predicament and psychology of the individual fated to assume the role of deputy, adjunct, or assistant. Interesting exploration of human relationships and the exercise of power. [DjK]

5546 Cuentos limeños, 1950–1980: antología y estudio preliminar. Edición de Luis Fernando Vidal. Lima: Ediciones PEISA, 1982. 226 p.: bibl. (Biblioteca peruana; 64)

Very valuable and diverse collection of Peruvian short stories spanning 30 years. Anthologizes 18 of Peru's most notable literary figures (e.g., Vargas Llosa, Bryce Echenique, Ribeyro, Zavaleta, Salazar Bondy). Includes brief bio -bibiographical sketch of each author and a useful, albeit schematic, study of the genre in modern Peru. [DjK]

5547 Habich, Edgardo de. Traspiés en el paraíso. Lima: Editora y Distribuidora Triunfaremos, 1984. 354 p.: ill. (Col. El Hombre y su mundo)

Fictionalized chronicle of the 1980 invasion of the Peruvian Embassy in Havana, Cuba, by first 12 and subsequently 10,800 Cubans seeking political asylum. Those events are interwoven with the Mariel exodus of hundreds of refugees headed for Florida and the diplomatic crisis those events precipitated. A compelling historical novel from a privileged vantage point since the author was the Peruvian Ambassador to Cuba at the time of these historical events. This work should be of interest to historians and political scientists as much as to students of literature. Author is no novice as a writer, having published an earlier novel and poetry. [DjK]

5548 Huarag Alvarez, Eduardo. Una partida sin retorno. Lima: El Autor, 1982. 93 p.

Collection of six short stories in a neo-realist vein. Author's subjects are the socially marginal elements that occupy an increasing role in contemporary life, the failed and frustrated members of the middle class, and those who dream more than their social realities can ever allow them to attain. Some of the stories are more accomplished than others, with the title story the more convincing of the six. [DjK]

5549 Ledesma Izquieta, Genaro. Cuentos de carne y hueso. Lima: Editora Siglo Veintiuno, 1982. 220 p.: ill.

Collection of 12 stories by one of Peru's most colorful and incorrigible political figures. The book reads like a chronicle of Peru's political life spanning a 20-year period (1963–82). The narratives are intense, lyrical, at times sardonic. While a valuable socio-political document, they are not without literary merit. Insightful portrayal of modern Peru's political oscillations. [DjK]

5550 Mora, Ernesto. Hola, soledad: cuentos. Lima: Punto y Trama, 1983. 94 p.

Collection of six stories thematically focused on adolescence and rites of passage. The most accomplished are the title story and "Tentaciones." Ernesto Mora is a master of dialogue and narrative efficiency. His characters tend to be middle class adolescents who mirror their social surroundings with devastating understatement. [DjK]

5551 Nuevo cuento peruano: antología. Edición de Antonio Cornejo Polar y Luis Fernando Vidal. Lima: Mosca Azul Editores, 1984. 145 p.: bibl.

Very useful anthology consisting of 10 contemporary Peruvian writers each represented by one story. Editors offer introductory study of the contemporary short story in Peru, surveying major trends and thematic tendencies. Also includes brief bibliography of primary works by each writer, bibliography of secondary sources for the study of the genre, and an annual bibliography of prose fiction publications in Peru (1968–83). [DjK]

5552 Premio Copé de Cuento, 1983. Lima: Depto. de Relaciones Públicas, Petroperú: Ediciones COPE, 1984. 205 p.

Collection of 13 finalist short stories from among 366 submitted for the 1983 COPE Prize of Peru. Collection is uneven but it does reveal the vitality of the genre in the Peruvian literary scene and the success of this biannual competition in encouraging younger writers. Of the 13 included here none figure among the coterie of "canonized" authors. See also item **5544.** [DjK]

5553 Ribeyro, Julio Ramón. La juventud en la otra ribera. Barcelona, Spain: Argos Vergara, 1983. 309 p. (Bibliotheca del fenice; 15)

Valuable anthology of 22 short stories selected, arranged by the author according to thematic criteria and drawn from the more than 100 written by this versatile Peruvian. Ribeyro's attempt to give an editorial coherence to a cross section of his short story production is revelatory of the author's self-apprehension as a practitioner of the genre. [DjK]

5554 Sánchez, Luis Alberto. Los burgueses: relato esperpento. Lima: Mosca Azul Editores, 1983. 166 p.

Interesting (and useful) historical novel by one of Peru's venerable man of letters. It fictionalizes, as chronicle, the life of the elegant ruling class under Leguía at the turn of the present century. Revealing glance at the sociopolitical realities of the epoch through an easily accessible anecdotal narrative. [DjK]

5555 Tola Mendoza, María Teresa. El tiempo que vuelve. Lima: Librería Studium, 1984. 123 p.

Collection of five short stories set in the Peruvian capital and environs. The common thread is the problem of time and recurrence, the inability of human nature to transcend certain entanglements and to learn from experience of the past. There is a lyrical quality to Tola Mendoza's language that evokes a nostalgia free of sentimentalism. [DjK]

5556 Vargas Llosa, Mario. Historia de Mayta. Barcelona, Spain: Seix Barral, 1984. 346 p. (Biblioteca breve; 658)

Roman à clef takes as its subject the Trotskyite revolutionary Alejandro Mayta who, in 1958, led a revolutionary uprising against the Peruvian government. Vargas Llosa reconstructs and fictionalizes the life of this Peruvian revolutionary, framing his tale in the context of contemporary Peru and its social deterioration. Symbolically enough, the novel opens and closes with the garbage dumps of Lima that threaten to choke the life of the city. [DjK]

5557 Villanes Cairo, Carlos. La lluvia de cielo ajeno. Lima: Univ. Nacional del Centro del Perú, 1984. 137 p.

Collection of eight, uniformly well-executed short stories by an able and convincing narrator. Villanes Cairo has a natural style that exacerbates the naturally awkward circumstances of his characters. A socially committed narrator, the author does not sacrifice literary merit to ideological facility. The people in his stories have a penchant for the compromising, at times exasperating predicaments that human beings and their social circumstances naturally attract. [DjK]

VENEZUELA

5558 Angarita, Ana Rosa. Hormiguero de concreto. Caracas: Alfadil Ediciones, 1983. 101 p. (Col. Orinoco; 3)

Period piece from the late 1960s and early 1970s. Stream-of-consciousness narration of a woman's self-search and her reflections on human interaction in the context of a modern metropolis—the "hormiguero de concreto." Interesting reflection on the cultural and counter-cultural scene from a feminist perspective. [DjK]

5559 Crema, Antonio. El punto de Belgrades. Introito de Otrova von Gomás. Caracas: Editorial Arte, 1984. 174 p.

Collection of 27 short narratives by a philosophically sophisticated writer who spares no sacred cows in literature or social hierarchy. The narrative tone is sardonic, the irony is acerbic, the satire devastatingly parodic. If one accepts the author's point of departure—a zero point below which nothing can go wrong—his punto de Belgrades—the short pieces and their hilarious dialogues may even prove entertaining. [DjK]

5560 Garmendia, Salvador. Difuntos, extraños y volátiles: novela. Caracas: Monte

Avila Editores, 1983. 141 p. (Col. Continente)
This collection of 22 short "takes" shows, once more, why Garmendia is one of the masters of contemporary Venezuelan narrative. These are for the most part brief and effective sketches of urban life in Caracas. Garmendia is a master of first-person narrative and characterization. His stories could be read as parables of alienation and existential *ennui*. [DjK]

5561 Guaura, Alberto. S que no se llama. Caracas: Monte Avila, 1983. 197 p. (Col. Continentes)
Guaura's is an experimental novel that foregrounds the problem of narrative language and the acts of reading. The reader habituated to the anecdotal storyline will have difficulty since the strategy is deliberately aimed at undermining anecdote and privileging the problem of linguistic representation. Author is partially successful in his narrative experiment and the initiated reader is bound to experience a sense of recognition in the artistic and musical allusions woven into the text. [DjK]

5562 Mata, Humberto. Luces: 1978–1981. Caracas: Monte Avila Editores, 1983. 102 p. (Col. Donaire)

Delightful collection of nine short stories by one of Venezuela's most talented young writers. As in his previous two volumes, Humberto Mata displays his mastery of narrative technique and entertaining humor. Mata is a decidedly intrusive narrator who operates self-consciously giving his narration a texture and literariness that enhance the enjoyment of reading. [DjK]

5563 Parra, Teresa de la. Ifigenia. La Habana: Editorial Arte y Literatura, 1983. 544 p. (Col. Huracán)
Timely reissue of one of Latin America's first feminist novels by one of the earliest advocates of women's rights in this century. Ana Teresa Parra Santojo (her real name) was a Paris-born Venezuelan woman who used the myth of Ifigenia's sacrifice as a frame for the condition of women as she perceived it in the early 1920s. The novel initially appeared in 1924. The author published a second novel in 1929 (*Memorias de la Mamá Blanca*) as well as a number of articles addressing the issue of women's rights. Valuable social document with a good deal of literary merit. [DjK]

20th Century: Prose Fiction: Chile

CEDOMIL GOIC, *Domingo F. Sarmiento Professor of Spanish American Literature, The University of Michigan, Ann Arbor*

LA PRODUCCION LITERARIA de los dos últimos años muestra un considerable incremento que se extiende por igual a la publicación y reedición de importantes obras de la literatura consagrada, como a la producción de nuevos autores. De los consagrados ya desaparecidos, hay reediciones nacionales y extranjeras de Manuel Rojas (items **5578** and **5592**), J.S. González Vera (item **5573**) y M.L. Bombal (item **5570**). Entre los activos, E. Lafourcade ha publicado una novela de la dictadura (item **5574**) y han sido reeditados Braulio Arenas (item **5568**) y Antonio Skármeta (item **5579**). Arenas a los 73 años de edad continúa su extensa producción de poeta y narrador, a pesar de lo cual el Premio Nacional de Literatura le ha sido esquivo. Entre los nuevos y novísimos, nacidos después de 1935 ha publicado, con notable vigor Isabel Allende (n. Lima, 1942), cuya primera novela (item **5565**) ha tenido una traducción al inglés (item **6543**). Otros jóvenes autores destacados de la novísima generación, nacidos a partir de 1950, son Jorge Marchant Lazcano (n. Santiago, 1950) con su segunda obra (item **5575**) y Juan Mihovilovich (n. Punta Arenas, 1951) con su primera novela (item **5577**). Los estudios literarios se concentran en algunos valores constantes. Luis Orrego Luco, Manuel Rojas, J.S. González Vera, María Luisa Bombal, José Donoso, Enrique Lihn y Antonio Skármeta despiertan el interés dominante. Aunque debe destacarse la atención especial prestada a la obra de Bombal y Donoso. Jaime Giordano aborda en un artículo las formas narrativas de alusión y elusión en las referencias al contexto político (item **5585**). Varias biografías de escritores han venido a llenar vacíos importantes. Debe mencionarse entre ellas especialmente las dedicadas a los narradores González Vera (item **5583**), y Bombal (item **5586**), dos contribuciones de importancia.

Estudios de conjuntos ambiciosos se agregan con los libros sobre Carlos Droguett (item **5589a**), M.L. Bombal (item **5586**) y Donoso (item **5587**). Sobre Skármeta puede hallarse un estudio de conjunto más breve (item **5593**). El profesor, poeta y crítico Roque Esteban Scarpa recibió el Premio Nacional de Literatura. El Premio Andrés Bello de Novela fue otorgado en 1984 al escritor Hernán Poblete Varas por su obra *El voltiche de la revolpita*. Un número considerable de antologías del cuento acredita por un lado el propósito de decantar la producción cuentística contemporánea y, por otro, sirve de puerta de entrada a los cuentistas inéditos de talleres colectivos o concursos literarios. Los talleres literarios deben ser apreciados en su función extraordinariamente significativa para la formación y para la publicación de los autores. En parte, representan la solución para la actividad creadora, mientras su forma exigua de publicación es el resultado de la magra situación económica que vive el país. Abundan los libros en octavo menor y de delgada factura. Matías Rafide contribuye con entusiasmo a una vasta tarea irrealizada aún con su *Diccionario de autores de la Región del Maule* (item **5590**). Entre los escritores fallecidos figura el crítico Hernán Díaz Arieta, pseudonimo Alone (1899–1984), de extensa actividad periodística. Sus publicaciones semanales marcaron una época inconfundible en la crítica literaria chilena, en la que fue el mantenedor de una tradición que lamentablemente se ha perdido. También se lamentó la temprana muerte del novelista Cristián Hunneus (1939–85).

PROSE FICTION

5564 Allamand, Maité *et al.* Tres veces siete. Santiago: Ediciones Andrómeda, 1984. 194 p.

Antología de cuentos del Grupo Andrómeda de 21 escritores de los cuales dos tercios son mujeres. La mayor parte de ellos escritores de experiencia y anteriormente publicados. Algunos jóvenes muestran inquietud por formas nuevas, por encima de la anécdota y la nota sensible.

5565 Allende, Isabel. La casa de los espíritus. Madrid: Plaza y Janés, 1982. 380 p.

Novela que más allá de sus méritos intrínsecos ha merecido la traducción y comentarios de *Time* y de la televisión norteamericana. Dos componentes se reiteran: el influjo de García Márquez y las resonancias del golpe militar y el proceso chileno. Traducción al inglés, item **6543**.

5566 Allende, Isabel. De amor y de sombra. Buenos Aires: Sudamericana, 1985. 314 p.

Segunda novela de la autora.

5567 Anguita, Ruby *et al.* Cuentos. Santiago: Taller Soffia, 1984. 158 p.

Colección de cuentos del Taller Soffia. Grupo que se reune para escribir cuentos y provee el marco para la recepción y la discusión de las narraciones de sus miembros. Entre ellas hay modalidades diversas y calidad dispar.

5568 Arenas, Braulio. La promesa en blanco. La vida ordinaria y extraordinaria de Sanson. Edición definitiva. Santiago: Editorial Universitaria, 1984. 223 p.

Segunda edición, definitiva, de la novela.

5569 Arenas, Braulio. Visiones del país de las maravillas. Santiago: Editorial Andrés Bello, 1983. 82 p. (Biblioteca Andrés Bello; 61)

Notable lectura de la obra de Lewis Carroll como partida de ajedrez. Lectura a la que atrae además la historia, terminología, dichos, héroes nacionales e internacionales del juego. Postula el juego de ajedrez como metáfora de la realidad, del tiempo y el espacio y como símbolo de un misterioso legado de otro mundo. La paranoia crítica conduce el relato con los resabios del antiguo surrealismo del autor.

5570 Bombal, María Luisa. La última niebla; La amortajada. Barcelona, Spain: Seix Barral, 1984. 1 v. (Biblioteca breve)

Primera edición española de estas importantes obras. Les valdrá una difusión de la que acaso carecieron hasta ahora en España.

5571 Edwards Bello, Joaquín. Memorias. Ordenación y prólogo de Alfonso Calderón. Santiago: Leo Ediciones, 1983. 179 p.

Recolección de las páginas autobiográficas del gran *croniqueur* del periodismo y la literatura chilena. Cubre 70 años de historia literaria y social con estilo ligero, fino e irónico, que lo hizo único e inimitable en el periodismo chileno.

5572 Encuentro: narradores chilenos de hoy. Santiago: Bruguera, 1984. 211 p.

Buena colección de cuentos que reune 21 narradores, principalmente de las nuevas generaciones. Las alusiones al contexto son múltiples, el tono entero, descontento, no sin angustia. Destaca la calidad del lenguaje y la habilidad narrativa. Infortunadamente no se provee información sobre los autores incluidos. La más ambiciosa y legítima de las antologías de estos años. Entre los más destacados Carlos Olivares, José L. Rosasco.

5573 González Vera, José Santos. Alhué. Santiago: Editorial Andrés Bello, 1982. 114 p. (Biblioteca Andrés Bello; 53)

Publicada por primera vez en 1928 en Santiago, con segunda edición en 1946 (Editorial Cruz del Sur, 1946, 146 p., Col. de autores chilenos). Estas "estampas de una aldea" conservan el encanto y la sencillez de una autobiografía sensible, finamente humorística e irónica y de una visión de objetos, circunstancias y personas evocados con precisión descriptiva.

5574 Lafourcade, Enrique. El gran taimado. Santiago: Bruguera, 1984. 207 p. (Narradores chilenos de hoy)

Novela que se suma a las llamadas novelas de dictadores, especie a la que el autor había contribuido antes con *El festín delrey Acab*. Se trata de una *roman à clef* que se desarrolla con base en la crónica externa del régimen e imagina las circunstancias secretas. El interés de la lectura reside en el placer que despierta en el lector el adivinar, en la coherencia de los personajes y de los hechos, las personalidades y las circunstancias aludidos por la ficción. La visión del mundo es satírica y postula la autodestrucción de la dictadura.

5575 Marchant Lazcano, Jorge. La noche que nunca ha gestado el día. Santiago: Ediciones Santa Lucía, 1982. 70 p.

Esta es la segunda novela del autor. Se trata más bien de una novela corta con dos personajes en contrapunto. Pretexto para proponer la experiencia de la persecución y el holocausto, y del crimen y la culpa. Sin descontar la irracionalidad del resentimiento criollo.

5576 Los Mejores cuentos de mi país. Santiago: Biblioteca Nacional, Depto. de Extensión, 1982. 183 p.

Colección de cuentos premiados en el Concurso Bata cuyo carácter nacional *Cuentos de mi país* es la fuente engañosa del título. Estimables por sus virtudes narrativas, pero verbosos, sin economía de recursos. Abarcan desde el asunto anecdótico y citadino hasta el de lengua y temas rurales. Todos son autores nuevos.

5577 Mihovilovich, Juan. La última condena. Santiago: Pehuén, 1983. 127 p.

Juan Mihovilovic (n. Punta Arenas, 1951) es uno de los jóvenes narradores de la nueva generación más premiados. Esta es su primera novela. Su relato se mueve entre la biografía y la saga familiar en provincias sureñas y en el área rural. Hay en la narración indudable talento narrativo, y también imaginación, humor y talante satírico. La voz narrativa vierte la narración con dominio total de los hechos: define, representa lo interno o lo externo, diversifica las voces e imaginaciones de los personajes, recorta el tiempo, sin más índices que los verbales. Todo ello presentado con desprecio absoluto de los signos gráficos convencionales y en favor de la corriente de la consciencia. La modalidad narrativa se distingue por el carácter fluyente y la coordinación ilativa de su prosa. Sólo está cortada por la división en 19 segmentos o capítulos de la novela.

Molinares Sarmiento, Ramón. Exiliados en Lille. See item **5533.**

5578 Rojas, Manuel. La oscura vida radiante. La Habana: Casa de las Américas, 1982. 554 p. (Col. Literatura latinoamericana; 104)

Segunda edición de la última novela publicada de Rojas. La primera edición (Buenos Aires: Editorial Sudamericana, 1970, 445 p., Col. El Espejo) se publicó 12 años antes. Dividida en nueve partes la novela tiene dos factores de unidad dentro de un contenido disperso y constantemente variado. Por una parte, la figura de Aniceto Hevia que presta unidad fundamental al ciclo de cuatro novelas que se completa con esta obra con su énfasis biográfico. Por otra, los acontecimientos político-sociales de 1920 vistos desde el plano de los grupos marginados y de los intelectuales anarquistas de la clase trabajadora. Como en ninguna otra obra de Rojas, el narrador elabora con agresividad desacostumbrada y considerable extensión los antecedentes ideológicos del pensamiento socialista y anarquista, y, también, el enjuiciamiento de la represión brutal del orden establecido en el año 1920. Más que la capacidad organizativa de sus obras más notables, predomina en ésta la facultad del narrador de ensartar series de historias y anécdotas relacionadas con la experiencia de Aniceto Hevia y con los antecedentes ideológicos, políticos y sociales de su formación.

5579 Skármeta, Antonio. Soñé que le nieve ardía. Introducción de Soledad Bianchi. Madrid: Literatura Americana Reunida, 1984. 242 p.

Segunda edición de la novela con introducción de Soledad Bianchi. Novela del proceso chileno que muestra dos series narrativas diversas en las que las tensiones entre lo individual—aspiración de gloria futbolística—y lo colectivo de un grupo juvenil cotidiano y vulgar; entre el compromiso político y la indiferencia; y, por otra parte, de esa vulgaridad con la extrañeza de la pareja del Señor Pequeño y de la Bestia, pícaros que rompen el excesivamente cargado enfoque de la narración. Otra edición fué publicada en Cuba (La Habana: Casa de las Américas, 1983).

LITERARY CRITICISM AND HISTORY

5580 Bente, Thomas O. María Luisa Bombal's heroines: poetic neuroses and artistic symbolism (HISP, 82, Sept. 1984, p. 103–113)

Caracterización incomprensiva de las heroínas en la obra de M.L. Bombal.

5581 Bianco, José. Sobre María Luisa Bombal (VUELTA, 8:93, agosto 1984, p. 26–27)

Excelente artículo de interés biográfico sobre la estancia de M.L. Bombal en Buenos Aires en los años 30. Provee un animado retrato de la personalidad de la escritora chilena, desde el ángulo del conocimiento personal y la amistad. Incluye alguna información importante en relación a Borges.

5582 Boschetto, Sandra M. La inversión como aproximación al modo femenino en algunos relatos de José Donoso (AATSP/H, 66:4, dic. 1983, p. 532–541)

Extenso artículo que analiza la figura de inversión en la caracterización ambigua de los personajes y en otros planos narrativos en los cuentos de Donoso. Con referencia especial a "El Güero," "Dinamarquero" y *El lugar sin límites.*

5583 Espinoza, Enrique. José Santos González Vera: clásico del humor. Santiago: Editorial Andrés Bello, 1982. 120 p.

Estudio de la vida y obra del escritor por uno de sus amigos inseparables. Está escrito con gran honestidad intelectual y *ex abundantia cordis.* Es justo y comprensivo en el reconocimiento del humor y otros valores de la obra y de la personalidad de González Vera.

5584 Fraysse, Maurice. Aristocracie et révolution au Chili: *A través de la tempestad* de Luis Orrego Luco (UTIEH/C, 42, 1984, p. 107–122)

Excelente y pormenorizado análisis de la novela de Luis Orrego Luco. Analiza los conflicto de la sociedad chilena representada y las peculiaridades interpretativas del narrador, alusivos ambos a la revolución del 91.

5585 Giordano, Jaime. Transformaciones formales en la literatura chilena después de 1973 (AR, 9:35, 1983, p. 29–32)

Excelente ensayo que describe diversas formas de aludir y eludir referencias directas al contexto político de los últimos años en Chile. Estas consisten en "alegorías vindicativas," metáforas de la realidad activadas por la situación del lector, "objetividades distanciadas" mediante la elipsis, figura de detracción y "crueles parodias." Las considera tanto en poesía, como en narrativa y teatro.

5586 Gligo, Agata. María Luisa: sobre la vida de María Luisa Bombal. Santiago: Editorial Andrés Bello, 1984. 180 p.

Documentado estudio biográfico de la gran escritora chilena. Atrae un importante material informativo a la investigación biográfica y debate con objetividad y esclarece las cuestiones más delicadas de la vida de María Luisa Bombal. El enfoque es dominantemente psicológico, acompañado de una medida y firme apología de los méritos de la gran escritora frente a la indiferencia oficial.

5587 Gutiérrez Mouat, Ricardo. José Donoso: impostura e impostación, la modelización lúdica y carnavalesca de una producción literaria. Gaithersburg, Md.: Hispamérica, 1983. 283 p.: bibl.

Obra ambiciosa y de no escaso mérito. La interpretación de la obra del novelista chileno aparece sujeta a dos modelos teóricos principales, pero no los únicos: los del juego y del carnaval. Su principal limitación es que sirve más a la teoría que a la obra. Si bien afecta a ésta parcialmente, en múltiples casos resulta inadecuada y acaba por dar una visión parcial y enfadosamente teorética de su objeto. Las numerosas consideraciones intertextuales que se hacen no resultan siempre bien informadas.

5588 Hahn, Oscar. Los efectos de irrealidad en un cuento de Enrique Lihn (UC/RCL, 22, nov. 1983, p. 93–104)

Análisis de los procedimientos narrativos en el cuento "Huacho y Pochocha" de Enrique Lihn. Alterando la conocida noción de R. Barthes de "efectos de realidad," ve en la construcción múltiple de los caracteres a partir de un *grafitto* y en la configuración del narrador los que llama "efectos de irrealidad."

5589 Levine, Suzanne Jill. El espejo de agua: hacia una lectura de La última niebla de María Luisa Bombal (ECO, 44:3, enero 1984, p. 326–336)

Interesante aunque excesiva elaboración de un aspecto reducido de la obra de M.L. Bombal. La múltiple intertextualidad propuesta está igualmente marcada por el exceso.

5589a Noriega, Teobaldo A. La novelística de Carlos Droguett. Madrid: Pliegos, 1983. 166 p.: bibl. (Pliegos de ensayo)

Estudio ambicioso sobre este narrador.

5590 Rafide, Matías. Diccionario de autores de la Región del Maule: biobibliográfico crítico. Talca, Chile: Imprenta Delta-Talca, 1984. 572 p.: bibl., index.

Util contribución al estudio regional de la literatura chilena.

5591 Robles, Mercedes M. Thomas Mann's *The Magic Mountain* and Manuel Rojas' *Born guilty* (LALR, 11:23, Fall/Winter 1983, p. 15–24)

Retoma la afirmación de F. Alegría sobre las "reminiscencias" de La Montaña Mágica en Hijo de ladrón, intentando establecer las relaciones intertextuales. Reconoce las semejanzas, pero ignora las diferencias. Saca finalmente las conclusiones equivocadas.

5592 Rojas, Manuel. Imágenes de infancia y adolescencia. Santiago: Zig-Zag, 1983. 171 p. (Col. universal Zig-Zag)

Primera edición póstuma que recoge páginas inéditas junto con la reedición de las conocidas Imágenes de infancia (Santiago: Babel, 1955). Las nuevas adiciones comprenden de la p. 122 a la 171. El autor planeaba denominarlas originalmente Desde el principio como la continuación que leemos ahora. El textos prolonga en dos años (1910–12) la información autobiográfica. Importante para la precisión de los datos y el contexto biográfico de la obra del autor.

5593 Rojo, Grínor. Explicación de Antonio Skármeta (HISPA, 13:37, abril 1984, p. 65–72)

Completa presentación de vida y obra del narrador chileno (n. 1940). Incluye bibliografía de las primeras ediciones en español de su obra.

5594 Swanson, Philip. Concerning criticism of the work of José Donoso (RIB, 33:3, 1983, p. 355–365)

Excelente artículo que clasifica y evalúa buena parte de la crítica de la obra novelística de Donoso atendiendo al punto de vista del análisis y su adecuación de las obras. Vale la pena extender su alcance a las interpretaciones más recientes.

20th Century: Prose Fiction: River Plate Countries (Argentina, Paraguay and Uruguay)

MARIA LUISA BASTOS, *Professor of Spanish, Lehman College and the Graduate School, City University of New York*

SAUL SOSNOWSKI, *Professor and Chairman of the Department of Spanish and Portuguese, University of Maryland*

ARGENTINA

EL LAPSO ANALIZADO—1981–84—abarca las etapas finales del régimen militar (en que se aflojó el control de la letra escrita) y el comienzo del gobierno constitucional (1983), que, con la consiguiente liquidación del sistema represivo oficial, favoreció la publicación de obras de ficción y las ediciones locales de textos editados originariamente en el exilio. Tanto en cuentos como en novelas, el espectro de argumentos y, sobre todo, de estructuras y sintaxis narrativas es amplio; en gran número de obras examinadas, la violencia institucionalizada y su corolario, la hipertrofia de la arbitrariedad hasta extremos apocalípticos, son tema explícito o marco más o menos implícito. Son reveladores muchos títulos, aunque sean metafóricos: *Cambio de armas, Cuarteles de invierno, Ejércitos imaginarios, En defensa propia, Primera línea* ejemplifican la tónica dominante en la Argentina del llamado Proceso. Es notable que esa tónica se advierta aun en los autores de *best sellers*; muchos de ellos, simpatizantes profesos o vergonzantes del régimen militar, acabaron por dar cabida en sus textos a un reconocimiento, siquiera anecdótico y superficial, de la violencia oficializada, como rindiéndose a una realidad que habrían preferido obliterar pero que terminó por imponérseles.

Dentro del grupo numeroso de relatos que recogen de maneras múltiples las experiencias que padecieron (y, a veces, quisieron negar) los argentinos inmersos en el terrorismo de Estado, sobresalen *Los pichy-cyegos* de Rodolfo Fogwill (item **5603**) y *Primera línea* de Carlos Gardini (item **5604**). Fogwill ensambla un episodio documentado de la aventura lamentable de las Malvinas de manera que lo real y lo fantasmagórico se funden. Gardini da cuenta del caos creado por el aparato represivo en narraciones que retratan el horror desde ángulos inusitados, y su discurso narrativo, simultáneamente onírico y realista, es de una extraña tersura. Tres relatos de *Cambio de armas* de Luisa Valenzuela (item **5624**) anecdotizan con vigor los extremos de sadismo del régimen, mostrando cómo el sistema represivo desencadena y reactiva un mecanismo de tensiones, socializadas en las relaciones sexuales entre hombre y mujer. *Luna caliente* y *Vidas ejemplares* de Mempo Giardinelli (items **5606** y **5607**) y *Cuarteles de invierno* de Osvaldo Soriano (item **5618**), aunque tienden a exagerar los trazos de humor negro, son obra de escritores con sentido de la puesta en escena y de la funcionalidad de la lengua oral.

Entre las novelas centradas en experiencias subjetivas, incluso solipsistas, se destacan *En el corazón de junio* de Luis Gusmán (item **5609**), *Ampolla* de Fernando Sánchez Sorondo (item **5616**) y *Su espíritu inocente* de Alicia Steimberg (item **5621**); por caminos distintos, muestran los tres libros cómo es posible hacer de la lengua hablada instrumento artístico. *En breve cárcel* de Sylvia Molloy (Barcelona: Seix Barral, 1981)—que no ha llegado a la Biblioteca del Congreso al preparar esta entrega del *Handbook*—es el recuento de obsesiones: la seducción, el abandono, el despecho, la venganza en las relaciones amorosas entre mujeres se entremezclan y se equilibran con reconstrucciones de recuerdos de infancia. Una escritura rigurosa y matizada consigue el efecto de movilidad, esencial para una novela, en un texto cuyo tema central es el encierro.

Tampoco ha llegado a la Biblioteca *Respiración artificial* de Ricardo Piglia (Buenos Aires: Pomaire, 1981), exploración de los entrecruzamientos, posibles o inevitables, entre historia y ficción, y de los alcances y debilidades del discurso referido. Entre los pliegues del relato denso y complejo—en que se inserta una teoría sobre la literatura argentina—se oculta la historia de un personaje desaparecido. *Ema, la cautiva* de César Aira (item **5596**), *Libro de navíos y borrascas* de Daniel Moyano (item **5597**) y *Cola de lagartija* de Luisa Valenzuela (item **5625**) son otros ejemplos del predicamento creciente del tema histórico, que se manifiesta en muchas otras novelas de mérito dispar, y en la que acaso sea la mejor del período: *El entenado* de Juan José Saer (item **5615**), texto en el que se exploran los dinamismos de la memoria y en el que se alude con sutileza a la fuerza y la arbitrariedad de las ideas recibidas.

Si carecemos todavía de perspectiva para determinar cuáles narradores de este período se verán en el futuro como los más significativos de nuestro fin de siglo, la tenemos en cambio para anotar que el último libro de cuentos de Cortázar, *Deshoras* (item **5600**), que antecedió brevemente a la muerte de su autor, cierra el capítulo que *Bestiario* abrió en la literatura argentina en 1951.

Las abundantes reediciones y las antologías de autores individuales, seleccionadas por ellos mismos o por compiladores, fueron un recurso para eludir la censura pero el efecto más importante de ciertas reediciones es que al actualizar textos agotados se ayuda a crear el sentido de continuidad de la producción literaria. Unos pocos nombres de entre los muchos de autores reeditados son los de José Bianco (item **5598**), Isidoro Blastein, Miguel Briante (item **5599**), Abelardo Castillo, Marco Denevi (item **5601**), Juan José Hernández, y Noemí Ulla (item **5623**). [MLB]

En cuanto a la crítica literaria, cualquier informe sobre la Argentina debe cumplir la ineludible tarea de registrar las últimas novedades sobre Borges. Entre las muchas entrevistas dedicadas a conservar cada uno de sus pronunciamientos alguna merece atenció (item **5644**). Diversos libros han ampliado el territorio ya explorado y han inaugurado áreas adicionales para expandir la investigación. Los especialistas en Cortázar insisten en sus aventuras literarias; sus propios trabajos— compilaciones de ensayos breves y artículos periodísticos sobre la rápidamente cambiante historia de América Latina (items **5649** y **5667**)—acentúan su figura monumental, uno de los ejemplos más puros del intelectual comprometido: su escritura y su conducta siguen siendo un "Cuaderno de Bitácora" tanto para la literatura como para las realidades que ella transforma a través del lenguaje. En términos generales se puede describir la producción de este bienio mencionando un número especial de *Cuadernos Hispanoamericanos* (item **5669**) dedicado a Sábato; libros sobre Martínez Estrada, Marechal, Arlt (items **5647, 5674** y **5661**); entrevistas con Silvina Ocampo (item **5686**) y testimonios de Manuel Mujica Láinez (items **5671** y

5672); un estudio que compara las ideologías y propuestas de Borges y Viñas (item 5685); artículos sobre una diversidad de temas relacionados con esos autores y Bioy Casares, Güiraldes, Macedonio, entre otros. Una mención especial corresponde al tono reflexivo de varios argentinos al sopesar asuntos literarios y políticos (items 5663, 5664 y 5681); la mayor atención que se presta a las literaturas regionales; la atención creciente dedicada a autores con prácticas tan dispares como Saer y Kordon y el interés más amplio por la escritura judeo-argentina (items 5636 y 5682) y por asuntos referentes a la definición de lo nacional y de la identidad. [SS]

PARAGUAY Y URUGUAY

El panorama de la ficción se presenta estático en los dos países. Abundan entre los libros paraguayos las reediciones de autores considerados clásicos de este siglo, Augusto Roa Bastos entre ellos. La producción uruguaya se enriqueció con una edición, impresa en México, de las *Obras completas* de Felisberto Hernández (item 5634). *Primavera con una esquina rota*, de Mario Benedetti (item 5633), trata el problema del exilio exterior, que junto con el interior, es sin duda responsable de la aparente postración de las letras de los países pequeños y oprimidos. [MLB]

La investigación sobre Roa Bastos sigue siendo importante e invita exploraciones adicionales de las muchas facetas del ya clásico *Yo, El Supremo* (recientemente—por fin—traducido al inglés), mientras que los trabajos sobre Bareiro Saguier, Casaccia y el exilio ofrecen lecturas serias y pertinentes de la producción contemporánea. El número especial de *Escritura* (item 5697) sobre Felisberto Hernández y los estudios sobre Quiroga, Amorim y Onetti (items 5696, 5670 y 5701) subrayan el interés por las figuras establecidas. Con el retorno al gobierno civil, se han iniciado proyectos sobre las voces más recientes. La muerte de Angel Rama determinó un número especial de *Texto Crítico* (item 5702) que incluye serias evaluaciones de su impacto en la investigación sobre la literatura latinoamericana. Su fuerza—y su trágica ausencia—es particularmente notable en el volumen que resultó de un taller sobre el proceso de la producción cultural (item 5023a) que tuvo lugar, significativamente, en Brasil. Otra lamentable muerte, la de Emir Rodríguez Monegal seguramente será registrada en círculos estadounidenses, donde ejerció mayor influencia, en estudios futuros.

Como se informara en volúmenes anteriores del *Handbook*, se continuá prestando gran atención a los escritores establecidos y, maś especialmente en los Estados Unidos, se sigue apostando enfoques a "seguros." Dados varios trabajos en curso, es de esperar que en los años venideros se advierta mayor énfasis en la generación de escritores más recientes, en las direcciones multidisciplinarias que dan cuenta de la producción literaria y en una expansión del canon literario. [SS]

PROSE FICTION
Argentina

5595 Aguinis, Marcos. Importancia por contacto: cuentos. Buenos Aires: Editorial Planeta Argentina, 1983. 148 p. (Biblioteca universal Planeta)

Una escritura que suele forzarse en busca del efecto no desmerece la calidad narrativa—suspenso, lucidez irónica—de estos siete cuentos. En ellos, Aguinis ficcionaliza con imaginación epígrafes del libro de Jonás, suerte de hilo conductor subterráneo de anécdotas dispares. [MLB]

5596 Aira, César. Ema, la cautiva. Buenos Aires: Editorial de Belgrano, 1981. 234 p. (Col. Narradores argentinos contemporáneos)

La acción se desarrolla en la frontera entre "civilización y barbarie" en el siglo XIX. La novela es una anti "historia oficial," implacable, sagaz y convincente, cuyos niveles de significado—el literal, el histórico, el alegórico—se alternan en secuencias algo morosas pero concebidas con riqueza imaginativa. [MLB]

5597 Aira, César. La luz argentina. Buenos Aires: Centro Editor de América Latina, 1983. 130 p. (Capítulo; 815. Las Nuevas propuestas; 17)

Las situaciones, simultáneamente insólitas y triviales, recuerdan los textos de Felisberto Hernández, o la incongruente objetividad de las películas alemanas de la década del 70, pero Aira se presenta como más deliberado, y lo prueban las páginas finales, en que no se da conclusión a la novela sino se reflexiona sobre la ficción. Cortes de electricidad cada vez más frecuentes son los marcos de escenas in-significantes de la vida de un matrimonio que espera un hijo. *La luz argentina*, parece decir el texto, ilumina las parcelas absurdas que constituyen la realidad. [MLB]

5598 Bianco, José. La pérdida del reino. Buenos Aires: Centro Editor de América Latina, 1983. 2 v. (399 p.) (Capítulo. Las Nuevas propuestas; 19–20)

Reedición de la novela publicada en 1972, en la que Bianco había trabajado muchos años, y que contribuyó a que se revaloraran sus dos obras previas, *Sombras suele vestir* (1941) y *Las ratas* (1943), que se cuentan entre las mejores novelas de la literatura argentina de esos años. [MLB]

5599 Briante, Miguel. Ley de juego, 1962–1982. Buenos Aires: Folios Ediciones, 1983. 231 p. (Col. Los Mundos posibles; MP1)

Doce relatos, escritos entre 1962–82, arquitecturados con un rigor que matiza ironía, patetismo, sorpresa sin caer en frivolidades o efectismos. [MLB]

5600 Cortázar, Julio. Deshoras. México: Editorial Nueva Imagen, 1983. 168 p. (Serie Literatura)

Ultimo libro de Cortázar, que recoge ocho cuentos. El relato final, "Diario para un Cuento," especie de testamento literario, es un homenaje explícito a Bioy Casares, cuya capacidad para mostrar personajes desde adentro y manteniendo distancia declara añorar Cortázar, a la vez que su mismo relato despliega la misma destreza, que ha hecho de él un cuentista memorable. [MLB]

5601 Denevi, Marco. Obras completas. t. 2, Cuentos: v. 1. t. 3, Cuentos: v. 2.

Compilación de Haydée M. Joffre Barroso. Buenos Aires: Ediciones Corregidor, 1980–1984. 2 v.

Estos dos volúmenes son una antología, aparentemente seleccionada por Haydée M. Joffre Barroso, cuya presentación—así como los breves textos que la siguen, firmados respectivamente por María Angélica Bosco, Delfín L. Garasa y Syria Poletti—es mera tautología encomiástica de la que la obra de Denevi puede prescindir. [MLB]

5602 Fogwill, Rodolfo Enrique. Ejércitos imaginarios. Buenos Aires: Centro Editor de América Latina, 1983. 141 p. (Capítulo. Las Nuevas propuestas; 36)

Ocho relatos cargados de alusiones y datos de órdenes diversos, que integran lo trivial, lo excéntrico y lo excesivo. El discurso es denso pero sin acumulaciones preciosistas porque la auto-conciencia crítica y la tensión narrativa se dosifican con lucidez y eficacia. [MLB]

5603 Fogwill, Rodolfo Enrique. Los pichy-cyegos: visiones de una batalla subterránea. Buenos Aires: Ediciones de la Flor, 1983. 135 p.

Relato basado en la experiencia de un grupo de desertores del ejército de las Malvinas. Gracias a su oído de narrador y a su sentido del montaje y de los espacios entre episodios, Fogwill ha logrado, con un material estremecedor, una novela notable. [MLB]

5604 Gardini, Carlos. Primera línea. Buenos Aires: Editorial Sudamericana, 1983. 172 p. (Col. El Espejo)

Estos 15 documentos de experiencias límite—trasmutaciones narrativas notables de la represión, la tortura, el asesinato institucionalizados en el país durante el llamado Proceso—son a la vez admonitorios y catárticos. Llama la atención que una escritura extraordinariamente tersa (donde se advierten reelaboraciones felices del Expresionismo, Kafka, Borges) logre con tanta eficacia atmósferas de pesadilla, de fantasmagoría gótica, de alucinación. [MLB]

5605 Giardinelli, Mempo. El cielo con las manos. Hanover, N.H.: Ediciones del Norte, 1981. 173 p.

En esta novela—cuya trama tiene lugar en la provincia durante los años previos a la violencia; en el exilio después—se plantea un tema que informa muchos textos del autor: la relación hombre/mujer es un conflicto insoluble porque "El cielo se toca con las manos una sola vez: en el mundo de las fantasías." [MLB]

5606 Giardinelli, Mempo. Luna caliente. Buenos Aires: Bruguera, 1984. 175 p. (Narradores argentinos de hoy; 227)

Nouvelle cuyo discurso acusa el autoritarismo en los dos sentidos del término: por una parte, inculpándolo de maneras diversas; por otra, haciéndolo parte de la sintaxis de la narración. El resultado es un texto que en la superficie se inscribe en la tradición del humor negro y en lo profundo se quiere imponer al lector con la fuerza de una convicción apasionada: mediante un final de efecto, que reactiva, en el Chaco argentino, en los años de la represión institucionalizada, el cliché de la hembra destructora del hombre. [MLB]

5607 Giardinelli, Mempo. Vidas ejemplares. Hanover, N.H.: Ediciones del Norte, 1982. 141 p.

Clave de la ironía lacónica que pervade los cuentos es el interjuego entre el título y las "vidas" que ejemplifican. En 14 narraciones muy bien construidas, Giardinelli mantiene un control que logra plantear con sobriedad y resolver con soltura situaciones invariablemente atroces o sórdidas. [MLB]

5608 Gorodischer, Angélica. Mala noche y parir hembra. Buenos Aires: Ediciones La Campana, 1983. 131 p.

Estos 12 cuentos exponen en registros diferentes las formas que asumen las convenciones. La autora ilumina muy bien la idiocia de ciertas socializaciones cuando se vale de tics coloquiales, es decir cuando se apoya sobre todo en el discurso. Menos felices resultan las puestas en escena como de cuento de hadas o de literatura popular, porque la narración parece tomarse en serio y se pierde la distancia imprescindible para que la anécdota no sea unidimensional. [MLB]

5609 Gusmán, Luis. En el corazón de junio. Buenos Aires: Editorial Sudamericana, 1983. 296 p. (Col. El Espejo)

Novela de logros parciales, sin una coherencia detectable. Mediante presentaciones divergentes—yuxtaposiciones de escenas, imaginaciones, relecturas—se procura mostrar lo inexplicable de una experiencia;

pero la acumulación no consigue crear del todo la atmósfera mágica, o misteriosa, que parece perseguirse. [MLB]

5610 Laiseca, Alberto. Matando enanos a garrotazos. Buenos Aires: Editorial de Belgrano, 1982. 134 p. (Col. Narradores argentinos contemporáneos)

Con personajes de nombres imposibles, impronunciables o francamente grotescos, ha construido Laiseca 13 cuentos que son como variaciones de una gran parábola del caos generado por el abuso del poder y la violencia. El cúmulo de referencias y datos distorsionados y sintetizados como *collages*; las alusiones caricaturizadas hasta lo grotesco; las situaciones urdidas farsescamente; los recursos de humor negro dan como resultado unos textos laboriosos que, paradójicamente, se debilitan y acaban proponiendo sobre todo un desafío intelectual solipsista y no un discurso narrativo eficaz. [MLB]

5611 Marcucci, Carlos. Enemigos de todo lo bueno: cuentos. Buenos Aires: Ediciones de la Pluma, 1983. 120 p.

Son 14 relatos, perfectamente articulados, con notable sentido del humor que conjuga empatía e inteligencia. [MLB]

5612 Medina, Enrique. Con el trapo en la boca. Buenos Aires: Editorial Galerna, 1983. 272 p.

Novela presentada por los editores como "una cruda indagación en las incertidumbres, conflictos y esperanzas de la juventud de hoy," es sobre todo una crónica que documenta el discurso de los jóvenes en la década de 1970; comete errores notables en la caracterización de cierto sector de la burguesía alta e insiste en las obsesiones sexuales—sobre todo de la protagonista mujer—hasta lindar con lo pornográfico. [MLB]

5613 Moyano, Daniel. Libro de navíos y borrascas. Buenos Aires: Editorial Legasa, 1983. 316 p.

Novela densamente alegórica, cuyo *setting*, cargado de elementos de órdenes dispares, trae a la memoria las incongruencias, significativas o crípticas, de alguna película de Fellini aun antes de que se la mencione explícitamente. Parten al exilio, 700 habitantes del Cono Sur, y algunos de ellos recuerdan, distorsionan, reactúan sus experiencias. Las anticipaciones de la fantasía, las teatralizaciones que reinterpretan la historia argentina, las reactivaciones de vivencias de los personajes se suceden sin dejar resquicios, con un exceso acumulativo que suele ser fatigoso. [MLB]

5614 Rodríguez, Guillermo. Encerrar la dama. Buenos Aires: Editorial Pomaire, 1981. 246 p.

Historia (1936–76) de las familias de dos hermanos españoles: uno, republicano que hace dinero en Buenos Aires; franquista el otro, que permanece en España. Se yuxtaponen, con agilidad teatral y buen oído para los tics lingüísticos, diálogos porteños y peninsulares. Contribuye a mantener el interés la intervención de personajes históricos (Eva Perón, sutilmente reivindicada a través de una aparente desmitificación). Pero el hilo narrativo es lineal y las interpretaciones históricas que se intercalan carecen de solvencia documental. El resultado recuerda las series televisivas, por el dinamismo de los diálogos y por su carácter híbrido, que lo acerca a un relato testimonial sin elementos convincentes y a una novela sin solución narrativa. [MLB]

5615 Saer, Juan José. El entenado. Buenos Aires: Folios Ediciones, 1983. 155 p. (Col. Los Mundos posibles; 2)

Relato, notable por la libertad de su discurso narrativo, cuyo narrador—un sobreviviente de la expedición de Solís—escribe para rememorar sus experiencias con los indígenas en el más ceñido, expresivo e inconfundible español contemporáno. La anécdota histórica es pura experiencia individual, cuya evocación genera una constelación de presentes. Saer articula los dinamismos de la memoria de su personaje con una visión poética, unificadora, segura de sí. [MLB]

5616 Sánchez Sorondo, Fernando. Ampolla. Buenos Aires: Editorial Sudamericana, 1984. 336 p. (Col. El Espejo)

Sánchez Sorondo, que es un muy buen narrador, logra con el improbable tema de la adicción a las drogas una trama que trasciende la historia clínica. La novela se sostiene gracias al contrapunto del protagonista/narrador consigo mismo—la alternancia de primera y segunda persona para el yo enunciador—, que elimina la monotonía del tono confesional y consigue un texto con validez narrativa. [MLB]

5617 Soriano, Osvaldo. Artistas, locos y criminales. Buenos Aires: Bruguera, 1983. 255 p. (Narradores argentinos de hoy; 157)

Recopilación de artículos aparecidos en La Opinión (1972–74), de factura endeble, que proporcionan elementos importantes para reconstruir la realidad argentina de esos años. [MLB]

5618 Soriano, Osvaldo. Cuarteles de invierno. Barcelona, Spain: Bruguera, 1983. 190 p. (Narradores de hoy; 69)

Relato bien articulado que tiene lugar en un medio provinciano donde se ha instalado implacablemente la violencia institucionalizada. Un cantor popular y un boxeador llegados de Buenos Aires se pierden en el laberinto de variaciones del absurdo, manejados por "poderosos" arbitrarios y crueles. [MLB]

5619 Soriano, Osvaldo. No habrá mas penas ni olvido. Buenos Aires: Bruguera, 1982. 158 p. (Narradores de hoy; 32)

Novela encomiada por Italo Calvino, en la que se tematizan el absurdo, la arbitrariedad y la violencia que irrumpieron en los años del segundo peronismo. A partir de un núcleo de rivalidades y ambiciones mezquinas de politiqueros de pueblo, Soriano elabora una trama que es el crescendo incontrolable de situaciones grotescamente violentas debidas a la irracionalidad patética de los personajes. [MLB]

5620 Sorrentino, Fernando. En defensa propia. Buenos Aires: Editorial de Belgrano, 1982. 125 p. (Col. Narradores argentinos contemporáneos)

Son 13 relatos, en general muy bien contruidos y de sostenido interés narrativo, cuyo sentido del humor recuerda el tono de Augusto Monterroso, escritos entre 1976–81. Las fábulas de Sorrentino, que se podrían llamar antiapólogos, son desarrollos hiperbólicos en lenguaje claro y mesurado de situaciones puramente imaginarias. Lo notable es que esas arquitecturas de ficción ejemplifican, sin apoyos documentales aparentes, las circunstancias aberrantes de la realidad en que fueron producidas. [MLB]

5621 Steimberg, Alicia. Su espíritu inocente. Buenos Aires: Editorial Pomaire, 1981. 255 p.

Incapaz de hacer pie en el presente, la

protagonista—que anuda y desanuda sus recuerdos en monólogos suscitados por interlocutores diversos o por asociaciones—superpone, entrecruza, reacomoda épocas diferentes de su vida. Telón de fondo de esas percepciones es un Buenos Aires—entre 1940–60—donde las clases sociales ya no son compartimientos estancos. Pero la introspección no consigue vencer la alienación producida por las aun vigentes convenciones disociadoras. El oído de narradora de Steimberg trasmite fielmente el registro oral, porque mantiene la necesaria distancia entre lo hablado y lo escrito. [MLB]

5622 Tizón, Héctor. El cantar del profeta y el bandido. Buenos Aires: Centro Editor de América Latina, 1982. 156 p. (Capítulo; 172. Las Nuevas propuestas; 4)

Reedición de un relato publicado en 1972, de tono nostálgico y escritura morosa. [MLB]

5623 Ulla, Noemí. Ciudades. Buenos Aires: Centro Editor de América Latina, 1983. 160 p. (Capítulo. Las Nuevas propuestas; 25)

Antología de cuentos publicados previamente. La capacidad introspectiva de los personajes—víctimas de desencuentros irreparables—genera narraciones cavilosas y melancólicas en una de las mejores tradiciones rioplatenses. [MLB]

5624 Valenzuela, Luisa. Cambio de armas. Hanover, N.H.: Ediciones del Norte, 1982. 146 p.

Cinco cuentos, que son variaciones de lo atroz y que tienen un elemento común, el exponer un antagonismo insoluble entre hombre y mujer. Aunque la tensión a veces se debilita, porque Valenzuela cede a juegos de palabras, tics y aun modismos que rompen al equilibrio del discurso, no se pierden sus cualidades: la imaginación narrativa con que están concebidos y la visión, de testigo crítico de un mundo, con que están realizados. [MLB]

5625 Valenzuela, Luisa. Cola de lagartija. 2a ed. Buenos Aires: Bruguera, 1983. 302 p. (Cinco estrellas; 163)

Novela centrada en uno de los adláteres de Isabel Perón, José López Rega, "El Brujo." Las características y la mitología del personaje—elusivo y caricaturesco en la vida real—dan pie para las tiradas delirantes del

protagonista. Hay también parodias de los *non sequitur* del discurso autoritario y sátiras contra las interpretaciones intelectuales de la realidad. La voz narrativa unifica de alguna manera los elementos dispares de esta metáfora de una de las muchas etapas incongruentes de la historia argentina. [MLB]

5626 Valenzuela, Luisa. Donde viven las águilas. Buenos Aires: Editorial Celtia, 1983. 92 p.: ill. (Col. ProCuento)

Narraciones muy breves, de anécdotas diversas, irónicas algunas, predominantemente lúdicas otras, condensan y resumen las mejores cualidades de Valenzuela: sentido del humor e imaginación crítica. [MLB]

Paraguay

5627 Casaccia, Gabriel. Los exiliados. Asunción: El Lector, 1983. 232 p. (Col. Literatura; 7)

Reedición de la novela premiada en 1966 por la revista *Primera Plana*, con un prólogo de factura escolar de autor anónimo que provee datos para situar a uno de los narradores paraguayos más renombrados. [MLB]

5628 Casaccia, Gabriel. La llaga. Asunción: Ediciones NAPA, 1981. 188 p., 8 p. of plates: ill. (Libro paraguayo del mes; 1:4)

Reedición de la novela premiada en 1964 por la Editorial Kraft. [MLB]

5629 Casola, Augusto. La catedral sumergida. Prólogo de Francisco Pérez-Maricevich. Asunción: Editorial La República, 1984. 135 p. (Ediciones La República; 6)

Son 11 relatos, precedidos de un breve prólogo de F. Pérez-Maricevich y una presentación del presidente del PEN Club paraguayo. [MLB]

5630 Ficción breve paraguaya: de Barrett a Roa Bastos. Compilación e introducción de Francisco Pérez-Maricevich. 2a ed., Zenda. Asunción: Díaz de Bedoya & Gómez Rodas, 1983. 215 p. (Selección cultural; 1)

Reedición de una antología aparecida originariamente en 1969. Cuentos publicados entre 1911–67, el primero de Rafael Barrett, de Augusto Roa Bastos el último; se incluyen además relatos de Gabriel Casaccia, Julio Correa, Eloy Núñez Fariña, Natalicio González, Vicente Lamas, Josefina Plá, Hugo

Rodríguez-Alcalá, José Villarejo, Carlos Zubizarreta. La breve introducción de Francisco Pérez-Maricevich, a pesar de sus flaquezas retóricas es útil para conectar a los autores entre sí y para ayudar a ponderar un material que hace patentes las posibilidades y las limitaciones de un realismo documental que no excluye toques de humor negro. [MLB]

5631 Roa Bastos, Augusto Antonio. Madera quemada. Asunción: El Lector, 1983. 196 p. (Col. Literatura; 2)

Selección de 11 relatos, de los cuales el primero es el único fechado (1959), precedidos por una nota preliminar "del antologador," identificado solamente por las iniciales L.P. [MLB]

Uruguay

5632 Benedetti, Mario. Cuentos. Madrid: Alianza, 1982. 288 p. (Sección Literatura. El Libro de bolsillo; 899)

Antología que incluye cuentos de cinco libros, publicados entre 1949–77. [MLB]

5633 Benedetti, Mario. Primavera con una esquina rota. México: Editorial Nueva Imagen, 1982. 239 p.

Novela que se desarrolla en el período 1974–80, cuya trama está dibujada por las voces yuxtapuestas de los personajes: un uruguayo encarcelado en su país y su familia, exilada en España—el padre, la mujer, la hija preadolescente, el amigo íntimo que inicia una relación sentimental con la mujer. De la cuotidianeidad chata y gris representada en la novela no están ausentes ni los problemas de conciencia de órdenes diversos ni cierta desaprensión en la que los personajes se solazan y con la que pretenden obliterar los conflictos. Sin embargo, de los textos obviamente documentales intercalados entre los que van tejiendo la trama, se desprende la esperanza de una solidaridad inédita, generada por las situaciones límite, a la que los personajes—acaso por su carga burguesa—se resisten. [MLB]

5634 Hernández, Felisberto. Obras completas. v. 1, Primeras invenciones; Por los tiempos de Clemente Colling. v. 2, El caballo perdido; Nadie encendía las lámparas; Las hortensias. v. 3, Tierras de la memoria;

Diario del sinvergüenza; Ultimas invenciones. Edición de David Huerta. México: Siglo Veintiuno Editores, 1983. 3 v. (Creación literaria)

Recopilación de las ficciones del gran narrador uruguayo, precedidas por unas pocas páginas con datos biográficos y bibliográficos escritas por David Huerta. [MLB]

5635 Medeiros, Paulina. Resplandor sobre el abismo. Buenos Aires: Plus Ultra, 1983. 147 p.

Novela localizada en la frontera entre Brasil y Uruguay, en donde se entretejen intrigas familiares y locales con luchas políticas internas. [MLB]

LITERARY CRITICISM AND HISTORY
Argentina

5636 Aizenberg, Edna. The aleph weaver: biblical, kabbalistic and judaic elements in Borges. Ann Arbor, Mich.: Scripta Humanistica, 1984. 1 v. (Scripta humanista)

Elabora un retrato de Borges como admirador de "lo hebreo." Luego pasa a un muestreo de las fuentes hebreas que Borges asimila y transforma en sus textos, fundando así su propia versión de sus precursores. Con un diestro manejo de las fuentes y de la bibliografía sobre el tema, la autora identifica correcta y muy útilmente "la diversa entonación de algunas metáforas judías." Sólida lectura y eficaz repertorio de motivos centrales en la obra de Borges. [SS]

5637 Alazraki, Jaime. En busca del unicornio: los cuentos de Julio Cortázar: elementos para una poética de lo neofantástico. Madrid: Gredos, 1983. 248 p.: bibl., index (Biblioteca románica hispánica. II, Estudios y ensayos; 324)

Deslinda lo maravilloso, lo fantástico propiamente dicho, la ciencia ficción y lo que denomina "neofantástico" para posibilitar en este último caso "un acceso más inteligente a su semántica y establecer su sintaxis narrativa." Se apoya en los relatos de Cortázar para formular una posible "poética del género" y una "gramática de sus significantes." La lectura de los cuentos de *Bestiario* es particularmente reveladora de los alcances de esta categoría que sin lugar a dudas inaugura diversos espacios de reflexión teórica en torno a las propuestas últimas de Cortázar. [SS]

5638 Altamirano, Carlos and **Beatriz Sarlo.**
Literatura/sociedad. Buenos Aires:
Hachette, 1983. 279 p.: bibl.

El punto de partida es la *relación* lite-
ratura/sociedad que están "mutuamente
implicadas" y que "varía según los períodos y
las culturas." Sin plantear esquemas doctri-
narios, muestra una de las vertientes más
fructíferas que se deslizan desde y hacia la
sociología de la literatura subrayando el análisis del texto como eje central de toda lectura crítica para luego pasar a su relación con
lo social. Bajtín, Lotman, Bourdieu, Jauss,
entre otros, sirven de base para su planteos.
En los apéndices ("Las Estéticas Socio-
lógicas") hay textos de Lukács, Goldmann,
Adorno y della Volpe, seguidos de la práctica
que aportan textos de Sarlo y Altamirano
leyendo *Recuerdos de Provincia*, de Rama in-
dagando los *Versos sencillos* de Martí, y de
Antonio Candido sobre estructura literaria y
función histórica. Rica información y un
planteo riguroso que se presta *didáctica-
mente* como texto imprescindible para esta
zona de la crítica literaria. [SS]

5640 Balderston, Daniel. El precursor
velado: R.L. Stevenson en la obra de
Borges. Traducción de Eduardo Paz Leston.
Buenos Aires: Editorial Sudamericana, 1985.
181 p.

Fruto de un trabajo exhaustivo, este
libro entreteje minuciosamente y con solidez
las correspondencias y divergencias entre
Stevenson y Borges. Constituye, además, una
contribución valiosa para el estudio de la ficción de Borges, y abre caminos para abordar
con una concepción dinámica el problema de
las "fuentes" en la literatura contemporánea.
[MLB]

5641 Barcia, Pedro Luis. En torno a algunos
textos desconocidos de Güiraldes
(UNLP/R, 26, 1979/1980, p. 51–71)

Rescate de páginas que no fueron
incluidas en las *Obras completas* (1962, con
prólogo de Francisco Luis Bernárdez y un
"Apéndice Documental" y bibliografía de
Horacio Jorge Becco). Recoge dos cartas abier-
tas publicadas en *Martín Fierro*: la primera
reacciona ante una reseña de *Xaimaca* hecha
por Horacio Rega Molina; la segunda comenta
La musa de la mala pata, de Nicolás Olivari.
La tercera es una carta que le dirige a Borges
con motivo de la publicación de *Luna de
enfrente* (1925). Incluye también textos pu-

blicados en la revista *Plus Ultra*, perteneciente a la empresa que editaba *Caras y
Caretas*: "La Maja Negra" y "Andando."
Excelente documentación en un texto cele-
bratorio. [SS]

5642 Barrenechea, Ana María. La expresión
de la irrealidad en la obra de Borges.
Ed. aum. Buenos Aires: Bibliotecas Universitarias, Centro Editor de América Latina,
1984. 153 p.: bibl., index (Lengua y literatura)

Reedición de uno de los textos básicos
de crítica borgiana (1a ed.: 1957, El Colegio
de México; 2a ed.: 1967, Paidós) al que incorpora "Borges y la Narración que se Auto-
analiza" (1975) y "Borges y los Símbolos"
(1977). Sigue siendo una de las mejores introducciones a los motivos que "organizan" y
"desmontan" sus propuestas literarias. [SS]

5643 Barrera López, Trinidad. La estructura
de *Abaddón, El Exterminador*. Sevilla, Spain: Escuela de Estudios Hispano-
Americanos, Consejo Superior de Investigaciones Científicas, 1982. 255 p.: bibl.
(Publicaciones de la Escuela, 0210–5802; 277
[no. general])

Abaddón—"la 'expresión autobiográfica' más desgarrada que de sí ha
ofrecido Ernesto Sábato"—, que se basa en
los aportes de Todorov, Bremond, Greimas y
Genette con incursiones ocasionales en otras
líneas de trabajo. Particularmente útil para
los interesados en los aspectos "formales" de
su tercera novela. [MLB]

5644 Borges, Jorge Luis. Borges en diálogo:
conversaciones de Jorge Luis Borges
con Osvaldo Ferrari. Ilustraciones de Raúl
Perrone. Barcelona, Spain: Ediciones Grijalbo, 1985. 298 p.: ill. (Grijalbo paperback)

Son 30 diálogos sostenidos inicialmente por Radio Municipal de Buenos Aires
en 1984. Renovada prueba de que el arte de la
conversación que tanto admirara en Macedonio Fernández sostiene una veta crucial
que atraviesa las tradiciones literarias y las
formalidades de las esquinas porteñas; las revisiones de textos propios y las evocaciones
de los heredados; las insistencias en los
motivos que lo marcaron para siempre y los
resquicios de la novedad ante un viaje el
Japón un cruce por las mitologías escan-
dinavas. [SS]

5645 Borges, Jorge Luis. Twenty-four conversations with Borges: including a se-

lection of poems: interviews, 1981–1983.
Compiled by Roberto Alifano. Conversations
translated by Nicomedes Suárez Araúz,
Willis Barnstone, and Noemí Escandell.
Poems translated by Willis Barnstone, Jorge
Luis Borges, and Nicomedes Suárez Araúz.
Photographs by Willis Barnstone. Housa-
tonic, Mass.: Lascaux Publishers, 1984. 157
p.: ill., photos (Altamira inter-American
series)

Innumerables entrevistas continúan
fatigando los anaqueles borgianos. En este
caso, frente a las inevitables (y aún bien-
venidas) reiteraciones, merecen atención las
páginas sobre Capdevila y Xul Solar quizá por
ser menos frecuentes que temas como la traducción y Cervantes, el tiempo y el insom-
nio. Para los devotos que se regocijan en los
múltiples reencuentros con lo conocido. [SS]

5646 Cattarossi Arana, Nelly. Literatura de
Mendoza: historia documentada desde
sus orígenes a la actualidad, 1820–1980.
Mendoza, Argentina: Inca Editorial, 1982.
2 v. (796 p.): bibls., indexes.

Loable y fiel "obra de rescate y recopilación" de diversos materiales sobre
autores y obras mendocinas. Entre las figuras
más conocidas se destacan Antonio Di Benedetto, Abelardo Arias, Iverna Codina, y Armando Tejeda Gómez. Es particularmente útil
el relevamiento final con índices que facili-
tan la consulta de apretadas páginas. [SS]

5647 Cavallari, Héctor Mario. Leopoldo
Marechal: el espacio de los signos.
Xalapa, Mexico: Centro de Investigaciones
Lingüístico-Literarias, Instituto de Investigaciones Humanísticas, Univ. Veracruzana,
1981. 164, 3 p.: bibl. (Cuadernos del Centro;
11)

El sentido de los núcleos semánticos,
el valor de los símbolos, la intervención de
factores colaterales a cada etapa de la obra de
Marechal, las variantes en cada uno de los
géneros que practicara, son vistos mediante
una amplia bibliografía que va de Cirlot y
Eliade a Barthes y Foucault—con el obligado
reconocimiento a la crítica sobre Marechal.
"Las Figuras del Espacio Ideológico" y "Vicisi-
tudes del Discurso Narrativo" son las dos
partes de este estudio tras las que se llega a la
suscinta y clara definición final de "El Contorno de la Obra Marechaliana" sin aban-
donar un apego singular a las propuestas del
analizado. [SS]

**5648 Confluencia: literatura argentina por
brasileños, literatura brasileña por argentinos.** Edición organizada y traducida por
Raúl Antelo. Buenos Aires: Centro de Estudios Brasileños, 1982. 206 p.: bibl., ill. (Col.
Iracema; 7)

Paisajes, procesos, poéticas, personas:
argentinos y brasileños reconociénose en
mundos que en muchos círculos siguen defi-
niéndose por su "ajenidad." Fructífera meta
que—como la ilustración de la tapa—
muestra las raíces al desnudo de un único
tronco. Páginas que merecen especial memoria son las que rastrean el cruce de fronteras
del siglo XIX, las escritas por Jorge Amado,
Carlos Drummond de Andrade, y las proximi-
dades del modernismo/vanguardia. [SS]

5649 Cortázar, Julio. Argentina: años de
alambradas culturales. Edición de Saúl
Yurkievich. Buenos Aires: Muchnik Editores,
1984. 149 p.

Artículos periodísticos, conferencias,
testimonios, un fructífero diálogo entre
Polanco y Calac, reunidos en dos secciones—
"Del Exilio con los Ojos Abiertos" y "Del Escritor de Dentro y de Fuera"—dan cuenta en
este libro póstumo de uno de los grandes
legados de Cortázar: la comprensión y la
práctica del intelectual comprometido con su
literatura y su tiempo histórico. Si bien algunas páginas son producto de la urgencia del
momento, la mayoría es el resultado de una
larga y productiva reflexión sobre América
Latina. Ninguna de sus directrices podrá ser
omitida de la lectura total de la obra de
Cortázar. [SS]

5650 Cortázar, Julio. Cuaderno de bitácora
de *Rayuela*. Estudio preliminar de Ana
María Barrenechea. Buenos Aires: Editorial
Sudamericana, 1983. 289 p.: ill.

Leyendo el proceso de construcción
que llevaría a *Rayuela* e hilando sus *pre-
textos*, Barrenechea aporta uno de los estudios más significativos sobre esta novela,
siendo de especial utilidad sus puntualiza-
ciones teóricas sobre "crítica genética." Al
facilitarle el *Cuaderno de bitácora*, Cortázar
ha dado la más amplia cabida a sus reiteradas
invitaciones al taller del escritor. [SS]

5651 Cúneo, Dardo. Cultura, país y época.
Buenos Aires: Editorial Pleamar, 1983.
247 p. (Col. Itinerario americano)

Retomando el mismo título de su obra
de 1973, éstas son, en efecto, páginas para

documentar una visión de los años 70 y comienzos de los 80 desde la formalidad de la Sociedad Argentina de Escritores, que presidiera al publicar este libro, a través de una miscelánea de entrevistas, notas periodísticas, ensayos y breves esquelas. Aboga por la defensa del patrimonio nacional y por "una revolución" estructurada sobre el Estado de Derecho como elemento de progreso. [SS]

5652 En torno a Borges. Recopilación de Justo R. Molachino y Jorge Mejía Prieto. Buenos Aires: Hachette, 1984. 191 p.: port.

Montaje de citas de Borges (poemas, declaraciones hechas en entrevistas . . .) y de sus lectores y críticos para perfilar un "entorno" biográfico y literario. Ciertas perspectivas están dadas por expresiones como las siguientes (siempre sin indicar fecha ni procedencia): "No bebo, no fumo, como poco. Mis únicos vicios son la Enciclopedia Británica y no leer a Enrique Larreta;" y "Mi fama basta para condenar a esta época," entre otras reflexiones mitigadas por la seriedad risueña del saber. [SS]

5653 En torno al criollismo: Ernesto Quesada, *El criollismo en la literatura argentina* y otros textos. Estudio crítico y compilación de Alfredo V.E. Rubione. Buenos Aires: Centro Editor de América Latina, 1983. 286 p. (Capítulo. Biblioteca argentina fundamental; 190. Serie complementaria, Sociedad y cultura. Las Nuevas propuestas; 22)

Excelente presentación de una vasta polémica iniciada por Ernesto Quesada en 1902 y que excede los límites literarios del "criollismo" para entrar a precisiones sobre "lo nacional" y sus consiguientes presupuestos ideológicos y ramificaciones políticas. Incluye textos de Unamuno, Olivera, Wilde, Quesada, Cané, Estrada, del Solar, Abeille, Pellegrini, Linares, Correa Luna, y Soto y Calvo. Es particularmente útil—dados los cruces posteriores y la obstinación de algunos por definir "el idioma nacional"—la incorporación de Unamuno a ambos polos de la muestra. [SS]

5654 Feinmann, José Pablo. El mito del eterno fracaso. Buenos Aires: Editorial Legasa, 1985. 252 p. (Omnibus)

Recopilación de notas publicadas en su mayoría entre 1981–83 (algunas en 1984), en *Medios y Comunicación, Superhumor, Feriado Nacional, Argumento Político,*

Clarín, y *Humor.* La postulación ideológica del peronismo, el maridaje de pilares de la filosofía con figuras centrales de la cinematografía, análisis perspicaces de la literatura (notables páginas sobre Soriano), y reflexiones centrales sobre el impacto de la dictadura militar, agregan este libro a la exigente nómina de la páginas que pueden dar cuenta del pensamiento lúcido y urgente en la época de la ignominia. Textos que acompañan a sus novelas *Ultimas días de la víctima* y *Ni el tiro del final* y a sus ensayos en *Filosofía y Nación.* [SS]

5655 Ferrari, Américo. Macedonio Fernández: belarte contra realismo y las perspectivas de la narrativa hispanoamericana contemporánea (UEN/LS, 13:1, 1983, p. 221–238)

Analiza los "tres conatos novelísticos" de Macedonio marcando que su asunto es el amor y la pasión; revisando sus propuestas teóricas, acota que "propiamente el asunto es la ausencia o vacío que llenan los libros." Señala la importancia de Macedonio dentro del "desconcertante proceso de construcción/descontrucción" en *Museo de la novela de la Eterna,* primer libro abierto de la literatura hispanoamericana moderna. Desarrolla también los interrogantes que Macedonio suscita sobre la relación realidad-ficción y sus ramificaciones en torno a criterios de verosimilitud que apuntan a una "realidad-otra" que otros escritores mayores han intentado formular en proyectos posteriores (e.g., Borges, Bioy, Cortázar, Lezama). [SS]

5656 Fleming, Leonor. Una literatura del interior: el noroeste argentino (CH, 408, junio 1984, p. 132–145)

Esbozos informativos sobre algunas caracterizaciones propias de las obras de Héctor Tizón, Juan José Hernández y Carlos Hugo Aparicio que abogan por la identidad autónoma de esta literatura regional. [SS]

5657 Foster, David William. Alternate voices in the contemporary Latin American narrative. Columbia: Univ. of Missouri Press, 1985. 163 p.

Habiéndose reconocido ya excesivamente el caudal de la crítica sobre ciertas figuras dominantes de las últimas décadas, este libro propone la lectura de otras vertientes no menos merecedoras de un escrutinio atento a sus propuestas. Entre otros, estudia textos de Asís, Barnet, Ibargüengoitia, Louzeiro, Medina, Poniatowska, Puig, Roffé y Valdés. No deja de sorprender en este contexto el capítulo "Narrative Persona in Eva Perón's *La razón de mi vida*." Es particularmente útil el balance de lo que requiere mayor atención (Cap. 4). [SS]

5658 Gai, Mijal. Metonimia y censura: claves para un relato de Augusto Mario Delfino (HISP, 14:42, dic. 1985, p. 3–27) Estudia el cuento "El confidente" (*Fin de siglo*, 1944) observando "los procedimientos de figuración metonímica presentes en el texto y de sus correspondencias con el desplazamiento y la censura." Sigue inicialmente la amplia acepción de Jakobson sobre la metonimia, luego pasa a la "índole figural de la metonimia" (Metz) para interpretar movimientos de desvío y los trayectos de desplazamiento en la construcción del discurso apoyándose en las correspondencias señaladas por Lacan. [SS]

5659 Gimelfarb, Norberto. Buenos Aires en las novelas de Sábato (UEN/LS, 13:1, 1983, p. 263–277) Tránsito (analítico, por cierto, en sus sugerencias) por las calles de Buenos Aires recorridas en las obras de Sábato hecho con la seriedad del juego de un patafísico que también ha compuesto la banda sonora de *Rayuela*. [SS]

5660 Giordano, Carlos. La literatura social en la Argentina: 1920–1930. Cosenza, Italy: Editrice MIT, 1983. 90 p. Reúne dos ensayos, "Boedo y el Tema Social," que re-elabora lo escrito para Capítulo (CEDAL) en 1966, y "La Literatura Social en la Argentina, El Grupo de Boedo: Nueva Propuesta Crítica." Con una útil contextualización que señala el desconcierto de las izquierdas frente al acceso del radicalismo, indica que "la literatura del grupo de Boedo estuvo más cerca del reformismo que de la revolución, fue más la expresión de un inconformismo antiburgués que la expresión de la lucha del proletariado en sentido histórico; su finalidad pareciera orientarse, sobre todo, a producir un impacto transformador en lo que prodríamos llamar el universo de los sentimientos." También mide su importancia por las polémicas que inaugurara frente a la "realidad nacional." [SS]

5661 Gnutzman, Rita. Roberto Arlt o el arte del calidoscopio. Bilbao, Spain: Ser-

vicio Editorial Univ. de País Vasco, 1984. 240 p.: bibl. Frente al énfasis que otros críticos le han otorgado a la obra de Arlt—hay una revisión suscinta de la crítica y de la recepción más reciente de Arlt—, se propone "someter técnicas y recursos estilísticos a un examen detallado, analizándolo sobre el fondo de las técnicas empleadas en la nueva narrativa hispanoamericana desde los años cincuenta, derivados de modelos introducidos por Joyce, Proust, etc." luego de estudiar las influencias literarias y la simbología. También aporta una clasificación de los personajes arltianos e importantes páginas sobre el "lector" desde la teoría alemana de la recepción. Entre los múltiples méritos de este estudio está la atención que le presta a las *Aguafuertes porteñas* y, en menor grado, a los cuentos. [SS]

5662 Guibourg, Edmundo. El último bohemio: conversaciones. Entrevistas de Mona Moncalvillo. Buenos Aires: Editorial Celtia, 1983. 213 p., 8 p. of plates: ill., ports. A los 90 años de edad Guibourg recorre memoriosamente—gracias a la eficacia de Mona Moncalvillo—más de medio siglo de la vida cultural argentina; los días y las noches de Buenos Aires (también de París); su relevante actuación como periodista, crítico, dramaturgo. Comentarios incisivos, agudos, perspicaces; líneas que alumbran con inteligencia la amplia "bohemia" que se recrea en esta singular "historia de vida." [SS]

5663 Jitrik, Noé. Las armas y las razones: ensayos sobre el peronismo, el exilio, la literatura, 1975–1980. Buenos Aires: Editorial Sudamericana, 1984. 311 p. A pesar del supuesto distanciamiento que propone el ensayo en cuanto género, el tono apasionado que caracteriza todo aquello que se refiere al presente de la violencia— frente a la reflexión mesurada sobre el barroco, por ejemplo—muestra las instancias de un intelectual marcado por el exilio. Conjunto que debe incorporarse al balance general de lo desencadenado por el colapso de la razón y de la ética. La introducción está fechada en México en 1982. [SS]

5664 Kovadloff, Santiago. Argentina, oscuro país: ensayos sobre un tiempo de quebranto. Buenos Aires: Torres Agüero Editor, 1983. 131 p. (Memoria del tiempo) "Los efectos del totalitarismo sobre la conducta ciudadana" es el eje que organiza

estos breves ensayos publicados originalmente en *Clarín* y *Humor* (1981–82). Poeta y
traductor de las mejores páginas de la literatura luso-brasileña, Kovadloff se muestra
aquí como profundo conocedor de argucias
políticas que se devanean ante argumentos
éticos. Páginas perdurables en su testimonio
de tiempos en vías de superación. [SS]

5665 Liberman, Arnoldo. Grietas como
templos: biografía de una identidad.
Prólogos de Abelardo Castillo y Félix Grande.
Madrid: Altalena Editores, 1984. 253 p.:
photos.

Entrañable búsqueda de los resquicios que iluminan el impacto del vivir en
los límites. Ser judío-argentino-poeta-
psicoanalista-exiliado que adopta a España
(es adoptado) como nueva patria recuperada a
través de la lengua son algunos de los componentes que conjugan múltiples pertenencias.
Se insiste, sobre todo, en el legítimo "derecho a ser," ser uno y múltiple, nacional y
universal. Tránsito obligatorio por las mi-
radas de Kafka, Mahler, Antonio Machado,
Freud, Marx y Sartre (también Chaplin, siempre), y por las innumerables (no infinitas)
vidas y lecturas a partir del exilio y de la in-
serción en un nuevo territorio. [SS]

5666 Lindstrom, Naomi. David Viñas: the
novelistics of cultural contradiction
(IAA, 10:1, 1984, p. 87–102, bibl.)
Estudio de *Dar la cara* (1962) centrán-
dose en lo judío como factor étnico, y en la
asociación con problemas de clase como uno
de los ejes medulares de la producción de
Viñas. El sentido de responsabilidad hacia
la comunidad y frente a la historia están
intregados como definiciones propias del
judaísmo, si bien desde la hetorodoxia que
caracteriza a Viñas, lo cual emerge de las
caracterizaciones del personaje Bernardo
Carman. [SS]

5667 Manjarrez, Héctor. La revolución y
el escritor según Cortázar (CP, 41,
julio/dic. 1984, p. 84–109)
Meritorio y singular entre tantos esca-
moteos, devaneos y alusiones al tema. Lee
las actitudes vitales y los textos de Cortázar
inscribiéndolos—justa y obligadamente—en
una revisión crítica de ciertos momentos cruciales: la "Carta" a Fernández Retamar (1967)
y su toma de posición ante la Revolución
Cubana; el "caso Padilla;" en menor grado
las dictaduras del Cono Sur luego de una

acertada mirada al peronismo y la guerrilla a
través de *Libro de Manuel*; Nicaragua. Pero
sobre todo Cuba, desde las promesas iniciales
y las rupturas de ciertos intelectuales, a las
críticas internas que Cortázar hiciera desde
su lealtad al socialismo y manteniéndose res-
petuoso, siempre, de las exigencias que le im-
ponía la independencia de su literatura.
Texto testimonial, además, del excelente narrador y crítico mexicano que arroja (casi)
una crítica generacional al legado, las frustra-
ciones, el romanticismo fallido y el lenguaje
de los 60 y de algunos de sus epígonos. [SS]

5668 Masiello, Francine. Argentine literary
journalism: the production of a critical
discourse (LARR, 20:1, 1985, p. 27–60)
Excelente revisión del lugar que han
ocupado las revistas literarias dentro de la
producción cultural argentina y que mediante referencias explícitas a textos sin-
gulares también aporta un repertorio
sistemático de diversas corrientes teóricas,
a partir de la noción de "autoría." Cubre
*Nosotros, Sur, Martín Fierro, Proa, Centro,
Ciudad, Contorno, Hoy en la Cultura, El Es-
carabajo de Oro, Nuevos Aires* y *Los Libros*,
entre otras, para articular el debate que sus-
citan en torno a lo social y a las manifestaciones de la ideología en toda producción
cultural. [SS]

5669 Matamoro, Blas. En la tumba de los
héroes (CH, 391/393, enero/marzo
1983, p. 485–497)
Lúcida lectura del "Sábato histórico"
de *Sobre héroes y tumbas* al "Sábato apocalíptico" de *Abaddón, El Exterminador*; de la
"gran catábasis"—"viaje al mundo inferior de
los muertos"—al espacio que sólo pueden ver
el loco, el iluminado, el inocente, cuando ya
ningún cambio es factible. Señala el "reflujo
espiritualista de sesgo neorromántico" de
los personajes de Sábato y el dominio de
Kierkegaard y Unamuno en su pensamiento.
La red que teje el aprendiz, el tramo que
atraviesa la ideología nacionalista y sexista
del patriciado, son algunas de las pautas de
este texto. [SS]

5670 Morales T., Leónidas. Historia de una
ruptura: el tema de la naturaleza en
Quiroga (UC/RCL, 22, nov. 1983, p. 73–92)
Postula que Quiroga porta consigo su
pertenencia al mundo industrial aún al
adentrarse en la selva misionera. Al igual
que otros escritores de la época que focalizan

las dimensiones de la naturaleza en una centralidad protagónica, Quiroga también representa un mundo que fracturándose ante el ímpetu de la industrialización y la modernización urbana comienza su lento desfasaje hacia la desaparición. De allí, también, que la naturaleza obtenga un carácter ominoso y amenazador para el hombre que deberá hallar su salvación refugiándose en restos de dignidad y ternura. [SS]

5671 Mujica Láinez, Manuel. Cartas. Recopilación de Oscar Monesterolo. Buenos Aires: Editorial Sudamericana, 1984. 169 p.

La carta que "Manucho" firma el 12 de junio 1983 acepta que el poeta cordobés publique este libro para que "los escritores jóvenes recojan la sola enseñanza que mi experiencia puede facilitarles, o sea que sin trabajar (y sin trabajar mucho, a menudo desesperándose) es vano proponerse la tentativa de una obra seria." Quizá la moraleja también radique en las otras zonas de lo dicho y actuado (o no) en esa vertiginosa década argentina. [SS]

5672 Mujica Láinez, Manuel. Placeres y fatigas de los viajes: crónicas andariegas. Buenos Aires: Editorial Sudamericana, 1983–1984. 2 v.

Las escalas de un dandy (1959–77). Crónicas de la curiosidad y el asombro de un viajero que reitera itinerarios vastamente superados en los mundos literarios que ideara, y que justifican estos placeres y fatigas a partir de ese mismo reconocimiento. ¿Será inevitable el recuerdo de algunos gentlemen de la generación del 80 y de su sana complacencia ante la imagen que se asomaba del espejo? [SS]

5673 Ocampo, Victoria. Autobiografía. v. 6, Sur y Cia. 2a ed. Buenos Aires: SUR, 1984. 122 p.: indexes, plates.

"Juez y parte" en la continuación de memorias autobiográficas redactadas a partir de enero de 1953. La correspondencia con Keyserling, Eisenstein y algunas cartas de Waldo Frank desarrollan la saga de Sur y Cia. y siguen definiendo el estilo singular de una época. [SS]

5674 Orgambide, Pedro G. Genio y figura de Ezequiel Martínez Estrada. Buenos Aires: Editorial Universitaria de Buenos Aires, 1985. 165 p., 16 p. of plates: bibl., ill. (Col. Genio y figura)

La generación de Orgambide acusó el impacto de un escritor liberal que reflexionaba agudamente sobre los presupuestos de una línea histórica tergiversada en su desarrollo primario. En *Radiografía de la pampa, La cabeza de Goliat*, sus ensayos sobre Martí, en poemas y cuentos, Martínez Estrada mostró una Argentina y una América ajenas al pensamiento convencional que se prestaba a la indagación en torno a sus múltiples identidades y futuros potenciales. Con un tono que incorpora los ribetes de la extrañeza melancólica, Orgambide incita a las (re)lecturas de la obra del ciudadano americano de Bahía Blanca. [SS]

Osán de Pérez Sáez, Fanny and **Iris Rossi.** Contribución a la bibliografía de la literatura salteña. See *HLAS 47:43*.

Peri Rossi, Cristina. Julio Cortázar: bibliografía. See *HLAS 47:55*.

5675 Prada Oropeza, Renato. Texto, contexto e intertexto de *Abaddón, El Exterminador* (CH, 391/393, enero/marzo 1983, p. 517–525)

Continuación de un ensayo previo sobre *El túnel*. Estudia la "expansión narrativa y las clases que se presentan en el sistema narrativo de Sábato." De la oposición sémica entre *comunicación/no-comunicación* en la primera novela, pasa a *maldad-no maldad* en *Sobre héroes y tumbas* y analiza los niveles intertextuales marcados en *Abaddón* como avances de un corpus único que a la vez sostiene la "independencia" de sus partes. [SS]

5676 Prieto, Adolfo. La literatura autobiográfica argentina. Buenos Aires: Centro Editor de América Latina, 1982. 219 p. (Capítulo. Biblioteca argentina fundamental; 154. Serie complementaria. Sociedad y cultura; 6)

La literatura autobiográfica argentina "condensa, en un plano insospechado, la historia de la *élite* del poder en la Argentina." Estudiarla es comprender vastos segmentos (¿la totalidad acaso?) de la historia argentina desde el régimen amplio y rigurosamente preciso de este lenguaje literario. Hablar de uno mismo es significativo en estos casos pues se hace desde el afianzamiento en el poder. En este sentido, las páginas de Prieto son imprescindibles cuando deja hablar a Sarmiento, cuando Mansilla contempla su estampa, cuando Miguel Cané o Joaquín V.

González fijan la imagen de una época. Ensayo ineludible, reiterada y justificadamente citado desde su primera edición en 1966. [SS]

5677 Rivera, Jorge B. Bernardo Kordon: escorzo de un narrador argentino (CH, 398, agosto 1983, p. 372–385)

Fundamentada presentación de un escritor poco conocido fuera de su región, autor de entre otros, *Vagabundo de Tombuctú* (1956), *Hacele bien a la gente* (1961), *A punto de reventar* (1971) y *Bairestop* (1975). Arraigado en los mejores legados del realismo, Kordon es un excelente cronista del detalle cotidiano y del mundo de los marginados. [SS]

5678 Romano, Eduardo. *Sobre héroes y tumbas* en sus contextos (CH, 391/393, enero/marzo 1983, p. 361–392)

Puntualiza el contexto político-cultural dentro del cual se inscribe la obra de Sábato, haciendo hincapié en la narrativa de los años 1955–65 y en su "marcado sesgo sociológico." Subraya las referencias al peronismo y a la marcada oposición (e incomprensión) de sus características entre los autores derivados del grupo *Sur* tanto como la de aquellos que provenían de la izquierda (e.g., revista *Contorno*). Ve en *Sobre héroes y tumbas* "un reencuentro de segmentos sociales y variantes ideológicas opuyestas" y "una reconciliación de los dos escritores más influyentes en la literatura argentina de este siglo (Roberto Arlt y Jorge Luis Borges)." [SS]

5679 Sábato, Ernesto R. Páginas seleccionadas por el autor. Estudio preliminar de Carlos Catania. Buenos Aires: Celtia, 1983. 265 p. (Col. Escritores argentinos de hoy)

Advierte Sábato: "Ahora que empiezo a contemplar mi vida retrospectivamente, observo que no he hecho más que rumiar algunas pocas obsesiones que a veces se manifestaron en tentativas racionales, en ensayos sobre el drama del hombre en esta catástrofe universal de nuestra época; y a veces en ambiguas, oscuras y contradictorias fantasías del inconsciente." A partir de lo cual las páginas seleccionadas—entrevistas, bocetos, críticas, reflexiones—por Sábato comienzan a perfilarse como una autobiografía literaria. [SS]

5680 Sarlo, Beatriz. El imperio de los sentimientos: ficciones de circulación

periódica en la Argentina, 1917–1925 (HISPA, 13:39, dic. 1984, p. 3–17)

La Novela Semanal, La Novela de Día, La Novela de Hoy, El Cuento Ilustrado ponían semanalmente en circulación un texto de ficción. Con gran éxito para suplir la necesidad de ensoñación, también "contribuyeron a producir esa particular densidad cultural del campo medio y popular argentino, afianzaron las disposiciones y el hábito de lectura, prepararon sectores de público para el pasaje hacia otras zonas de la literatura." Define la "teoría del obstáculo," a partir de textos de José Ingenieros sobre el amor, y el modelo de felicidad y desgracia que rige el imperio de los sentimientos. Propone la lectura de algunos códigos narrativos y discursivos, en especial del lenguaje del cuerpo y la mirada, tan marcados por la ideología y las costumbres de la época y por el repertorio estilístico que elaboraron. [SS]

Schwartz, Jorge. Vanguarda e cosmopolitismo na década de 20: Oliverio Girondo e Oswald de Andrade. See item **6379**.

5681 Sebreli, Juan José. El riesgo del pensar: ensayos, 1950–1984. Buenos Aires: Editorial Sudamericana, 1984. 222, 10 p.: bibl.

Miscelánea antológica de artículos, notas, respuestas, del autor de *Buenos Aires, vida cotidiana y alienación* y del reciente *Los deseos imaginarios del peronismo*. Título apto para toda una carrera caracterizada por el riesgo del pensamiento, por la negativa a la palabra fácil y claudicante. Eliseo Verón y Victoria Ocampo; Dashiel Hammett y Pavese; Kordon y Medina; Massota, Sartre y Hegel pueblan páginas en las que alternan los tonos y la familiaridad manteniendo el rigor de una lectura informada. [SS]

5682 Senkman, Leonardo. La identidad judía en la literatura argentina. Buenos Aires: Ediciones Pardes, 1983. 493 p. (Col. Ensayos y estudios)

El libro más significativo y completo sobre una zona de creciente interés crítico. Dado el criterio temático del ensayo, organizado en torno a la polifacética definición de "identidad," son comprensibles ciertas reiteraciones. De los amplios registros que detecta Senkman, desde los textos de los recién llegados hasta los nietos de los inmigrantes, cabe destacar las lúcidas páginas que le dedica a Alberto Gerchunoff, barómetro, además, del fracaso del liberalismo argentino. Material de consulta ineludible por el análisis general y por su riqueza bibliográfica. [SS]

5683 Stern, Mirta E. Juan José Saer: construcción y teoría de la ficción narrativa (HISPA, 13 : 37, abril 1984, p. 15–30)

La minuciosa corrección de la obra de Saer (1937) promueve el análisis de los mecanismos constructivos del texto que busca concientemente "una reorganización o reformulación interna del campo del discurso literario." A partir de referencias a otras obras, se centra en *El limonero real* (1974) que pone en escena "en un plano estrictamente funcional, la génesis de una determinada relación con la escritura." [SS]

5684 Tamargo, María Isabel. La narrativa de Bioy Casares: el texto como escritura-lectura. Madrid: Playor, 1983. 140 p.: bibl. (Col. Nova scholar)

Una presentación superior de las rupturas que efectúa el discurso de Bioy Casares a partir de *La invención de Morel.* Utilísimo para considerar la problematización del carácter referencial del lenguaje y la desconstrucción de convenciones literarias. [SS]

5685 Tealdi, Juan Carlos. Borges y Viñas: literatura e ideología. Madrid: Orígenes, 1983. 168 p.: bibl. (Col. Tratados de crítica literaria)

Ensayo nutrido que enfrenta en y a través de textos de Borges y de Viñas las proyecciones literarias de dos ideologías opuestas. "Disolver la realidad," en Borges, y "Materializar lo espiritual," en Viñas, son acápites que definen la tesis del libro generosamente demostrada a través de textos medulares. Si bien tiende a ceñirse a cierto lenguaje formulaico que dista, sin embargo, de todo fácil reduccionismo, la oposición de las propuestas literarias resulta esclarecedora para una lectura que es, fundamentalmente, ideológica. [SS]

5686 Ulla, Noemí. Encuentros con Silvina Ocampo. Buenos Aires: Editorial de Belgrano, 1982. 154 p. (Col. Diálogos)

Excelente acceso a la obra, al pensamiento, a los artificios de una singular escritora que merece una mayor difusión. Frente a tantas entrevistas guiadas por la charla fácil, la tarea de Ulla revela un serio conocimiento de Silvina Ocampo y de sus

precisiones literarias. Afortunadamente distante de las manipulaciones de la vida privada. [SS]

5687 Veiravé, Alfredo. Juan L. Ortiz: la experiencia poética. Buenos Aires: C. Lohlé, 1984. 239 p.: bibls.

El mejor estudio hasta la fecha sobre el autor de *En el aura del sauce.* Conecta reflexiones en torno a la poesía y la vida de Juanele para dar cuenta de una búsqueda interior que le creara "una aparente marginalidad temporal." Aun en la formalidad de los análisis predomina la muy adecuada voz poética de quien alcanzó el goce de una amistad privilegiada. [SS]

5688 Yurkievich, Saúl. Julio Cortázar: al calor de su sombra (IILI/RI, 130/131, enero/junio 1985, p. 7–20)

En rápidos trazos, concitando imágenes y figuras entrañables, dibuja el impacto de la obra de Cortázar: "el explorador del ser, el buscador de absolutos, el estremecedor de los trasfondos;" "precursor inserto en un proceso que se llama vanguardia," también es quien "consuma la modernización de nuestra narrativa." El conocimiento claro de su producción y la cercanía amistosa a un transformador de vidas y visiones de mundo se conjugan en uno de los mejores textos elaborados sobre el aura que deja Cortázar al clausurarse su ciclo biográfico. [SS]

5689 Zuleta, Emilia de. Relaciones literarias entre España y la Argentina. Madrid: Ediciones Cultura Hispánica, Instituto de Cooperación Iberoamericana, 1983. 278 p.: bibl., index.

El título pudo ser *Presencia de las letras españolas en algunas revistas literarias argentinas.* Estudia dicha presencia entre 1907, lanzamiento de *Nosotros,* y 1949, cierre de *Realidad* , y en las revistas *Síntesis, Criterio, Sur, Sol y Luna, De Mar a Mar, Correo Literario, Cabalgata* y *Los Anales de Buenos Aires.* Deja para otro estudio la fundamental *Caras y Caretas.* Sólido rastreo e inventario de funciones protagónicas y de su impacto sobre estas publicaciones. [SS]

Paraguay

5690 Bareiro Saguier, Rubén. Estructura autoritaria y producción literaria en Paraguay (UTIEH/C, 42, 1984, p. 93–106)

A partir de la "represión-persecución sistemática" que han sufrido los escritores paraguayos, propone tres franjas en la producción literaria: 1) literatura oficialista; 2) literatura crítica, especialmente narrativa, producida en el exilio; y 3) "una ambigua zona de claroscuro que dentro del país—con predominancia de la poesía—intenta afirmar una palabra de amenazada libertad." Natalicio González (1897–1966) sigue nutriendo la vena nacionalista; Angel Peralta Arellano es el "más acabado ejemplo al servicio de la dictadura;" en la segunda franja se destacan Gabriel Casaccia, Roa Bastos, y el propio Bareiro Saguier, entre otros; Ruiz Nestosa es una figura de transición hacia la tercera franja que, lamentablemente, no se desarrolló en este trabajo. [SS]

5691 Casaccia, Gabriel. Cartas a mi hermano. Asunción: Ediciones NAPA, 1982. 131 p., 4 leaves of plates: ill. (Libro paraguayo del mes; 18, abril 1982)

Texto de valor autobiográfico ya que son las cartas que el autor, que vivía en la Argentina, intercambió entre 1937–48 con su hermano que vivía en el Paraguay. [SS]

5692 Lienhard, Martin. Una intertextualidad "indoamericana" y *Moriencia* de Augusto Roa Bastos (IILI/RI, 50:127, abril/junio 1984, p. 505–523)

Utiliza el concepto "intertextualidad" en su acepción más amplia para precisar las condiciones que rigen la producción literaria latinoamericana desde sus inicios, y así documentar la presencia del sustrato indoamericano, también de la culturas orales, en textos contemporáneos. Demuestra la "conflictiva heterogeneidad" de los códigos que atraviesan el relato *Moriencia* (1969) marcando la presencia de la cultura y del lenguaje guaraní y, de este modo, su apropiación a configuraciones autóctonas. [SS]

5693 Madrid, Antonieta. Lo bello/lo feo. Caracas: Academia Nacional de la Historia, 1983. 187 p.: bibls., ill. (El Libro menor; 43)

Demasiado heterogéneo y algo confuso en su estructuración, este conjunto de ensayos y notas se ocupa de temas tan distintos como Roa Bastos, Avilés Fabila, el cuento modernista y Jean Rhys. Lo más valioso es el estudio sobre *Yo El Supremo* de Roa Bastos, curiosamente fragmentado en dos textos distintos. [J.M. Oviedo]

5694 Méndez-Faith, Teresa. Paraguay: novela y exilio. Prólogo de Rubén Bareiro-Saguier. Sommerville, N.J.: SLUSA, 1985. 201 p.: bibl.

Estudia con particular atención las obras de Casaccia y de Roa Bastos e identifica tres motivos recurrentes: "el tema del exilio, la obsesión por el pasado, y los tópicos relacionados con el presente nacional hoy dominado por la realidad de la tiranía," luego de una detenida contextualización. Propone tres "contenidos formantes" de la literatura paraguaya del exilio: 1) "espacios-cárceles;" 2) "aquí vs. allí;" y 3) la presencia de un "narrador intelectual, 'doble' o 'vocero' ideológico de su autor," y afirma que esta literatura debe ser vista como categoría literaria propia. [SS]

5695 Plá, Josefina. La cultura paraguaya y el libro. Asunción: Univ. Católica Nuestra Señora de la Asunción, 1983. 224 p.: bibl. (Biblioteca de estudios paraguayos; 4)

Rastrea el destino del libro en el Paraguay desde la colonia hasta la Guerra de la Triple Alianza. La interpretación de las ramificaciones de ciertos libros se enriquece notablemente con el inventario de algunas bibliotecas, entre ellas la del Dr. Francia, El Supremo, según el inventario de los bienes de Patiño. Importante veta para los estudiosos de Roa Bastos. [SS]

Uruguay

5696 Amorim, Enrique. El Quiroga que yo conocí. Montevideo: Arca/Calicanto, 1983. 76 p.

Nacidos ambos en Salto Oriental, a 20 años de distancia, Amorim y Quiroga establecen un diálogo a través de estos testimonios que aportan más a cierta versión viva de la literatura que a una comprensión crítica de su narrativa y de sus respectivos aportes a la tradición cultural uruguaya y latinoamericana. [SS]

Bremer, Thomas. Buenos-Aires et Montevideo: sociologie de la "ville racontée" jusqu'à l'apparition du roman social urbain. See item **5129.**

5697 *Escritura.* Teoría y crítica literaria. Univ. Central de Venezuela, Escuela de Letras. Nos. 13/14, enero/dic. 1982–. Caracas.

Número monográfico dedicado a Felisberto Hernández con textos de José Pedro Díaz, Alazraki, Barrenechea, Molloy, Echavarren, Ludmer, Lockhart, Panesi, Mora, Ferré, Pezzoni, Mercier, Rama, Morillas, Pallares Cárdenas, Antúnez, Giraldi, y un apéndice que contiene un manuscrito inédito de Felisberto, "Almacén;" "Mis Recuerdos" de Ana María Hernández; y una nota de Penco sobre sus *Obras completas*. El conjunto constituye uno de los mayores aportes hechos hasta la fecha sobre este autor. [SS]

5698 Hernández, Felisberto. ¿Otro Felisberto?: cartas a Reina Reyes. Edición de Ricardo Pallares. Montevideo: Editorial Imago, 1983. 92 p.: bibl., ill. (Ensayo. Casa del Autor Nacional)

A medida que aumenta la justificada atención crítica a la obra de Felisberto, se renuevan las búsquedas de inéditos. En este caso, las cartas que le enviara a Reina Reyes, quien fuera su cuarta esposa: cuatro fechadas en agosto de 1954 en Treinta y Tres, y cuatro en agosto y septiembre de 1954 en Montevideo. La divulgación de los desatinos del amor se salva por unas líneas que se refieren al Premio Nobel. Curiosidad inevitable para los que completan bibliografías. [SS]

5699 Larre Borges, Ana Inés. Felisberto Hernández: una conciencia filosófica (UBN/R, 12, 1983, p. 5–40, ill.)

Estudia la incidencia de Vaz Ferreira en la obra de Felisberto para demostrar filiaciones que apocarían la descripción de "raro" y que promuevan una lectura coherente de sus propuestas literarias desde la (auto)percepción de la marginalidad cultural. Valiosa confrontación de textos. [SS]

5700 Rama, Angel. Las máscaras democráticas del modernismo. Montevideo: Fundación Angel Rama, 1985. 195 p.

Libro póstumo e inconcluso que logra, sin embargo, conjugar algunas de las preocupaciones fundamentales que ocuparan en

sus últimos años al eximio crítico uruguayo. La democratización de la modernidad; la modernización en los ensayos democráticos nacionales y en la práctica de una literatura singularmente propia aun ante las ilaciones internacionales que conjuraba; el afianzamiento de la identidad a través del lenguaje y su práctica literaria; son algunos de los temas que conducen a los apuntes que esboza en torno a la "interpretación americana del texto universal." [SS]

5701 Ruffinelli, Jorge. Palabras en orden. Xalapa, Mexico: Univ. Veracruzana, 1985. 300 p.

Reedición de la obra publicada en 1974 por Ediciones de Crisis en Buenos Aires. Excelentes entrevistas con 10 escritores realizadas por un vasto conocedor de la literatura uruguaya (e.g., Zum Felde, Espínola, Juan Carlos Onetti, Martínez Moreno, Arregui, Da Rosa, Benedetti, J.P. Díaz, Jorge Onetti, Eduardo Galeano). Incluye una nueva entrevista a Onetti y agregados a los encuentros con Martínez Moreno y Galeano. [SS]

5702 *Texto Crítico*. Univ. Veracruzana, Centro de Investigaciones Lingüístico -Literarias. Nos. 31/32, enero/agosto 1985–. Xalapa, Mexico.

Número monográfico dedicado a Angel Rama (1926–83) que contiene análisis de su obra, semblanzas, valoraciones, enfoques de sus múltiples actividades intelectuales a cargo de Ruffinelli, Osorio, Leenhardt, Prieto, Pacheco, Alegría, Benedetti, Oviedo, Gutiérrez Girardot, Jitrik, Alazraki, Arthur Miller, J.P. Díaz, Martínez Moreno, Shavelzon, Migdal, Lavín Cerda, Verani, Losada, Corral, Cosse, y Cobo Borda sobre Marta Traba. Otro homenaje singular al maestro constituye el rescate de su cursillo sobre García Márquez dictado en la Univ. Veracruzana en 1972 y que se publica como "La Narrativa de Gabriel García Márquez: Edificación de un Arte Nacional y Popular: (p. 147–245). [SS]

Poetry

RENE DE COSTA, *Professor of Spanish, University of Chicago*
MAGDALENA GARCIA PINTO, *Associate Professor of Spanish, University of Missouri*
JAIME GIORDANO, *Associate Professor of Spanish, State University of New York at Stony Brook*
OSCAR HAHN, *Professor of Spanish, University of Iowa*
NORMA KLAHN, *Assistant Professor of Spanish, Columbia University*
PEDRO LASTRA, *Professor of Spanish, State University of New York at Stony Brook*
JULIO ORTEGA, *Professor of Latin American Literature, Brandeis University*
RUBEN RIOS AVILA, *Assistant Professor of Spanish, University of Puerto Rico, Río Piedras*
GEORGE YUDICE, *Assistant Professor of Spanish, Hunter College*

A PESAR DE LAS CRISIS políticas y económicas que aquejan a una gran parte del continente, la poesía sigue logrando hacer la difícil transición de un discurso privado y solitario al discurso público y solidario en la forma de nuevos libros, nuevas ediciones, nuevas revistas, nuevas colecciones, y nuevas empresas editoriales. Aunque algunos países, de larga y pujante tradición lírica como Perú y Chile están algo callados y marginados del fenómeno general en este bienio, otras regiones, como por ejemplo, Centroamérica y el Caribe parecen haber entrado en una nueva edad literaria—una suerte de "boom" lírico.

Entre las tendencias poéticas en Centroamérica, destacan: 1) La *metafísico-existencialista* con una poesía que se ancla en la tradición, en las búsquedas personalistas, y que en algunos casos registra una vaga crítica social. 2) La *revolucionaria-social-popular,* tendencia que predomina, como es lógico, en los países más afectados por las insurrecciones populares. En El Salvador, Roque Dalton (items **5795** y **5796**) constituye el punto de partida para la poesía que se compromete con las luchas sociales. Los poetas más jóvenes siguen sus pasos al cultivar una poesía compleja e irónica que rebasa la inmediatez del momento. Habría que mencionar aquí el trabajo de CODICES o Centro de Documentación e Investigación Cultural de El Salvador (item **5974**) que recoge el trabajo de los escritores comprometidos con la insurrección en las zonas de control así como en el exilio. Cabe añadir que algunos de los poetas más destacados como Argueta (item **5761**) y Alegría (item **5885**) han optado por formas narrativas para mejor ahondar en las motivaciones de la cultura popular desde donde surge la insurección. La poesía comprometida nicaragüense, en cambio, está muy influenciada por la línea "exteriorista" propagada por Cardenal. La producción de los Talleres de Poesía (item **5751**) y la de varias figuras más establecidas como Bosco Centeno (item **5715**) poetizan sobre el anecdotismo en que se basa esta nueva modalidad. Todas las vertientes de esta poesía comprometida se encuentran en el excelente "collage"-análisis preparado por Zimmerman (item **5986**). 3) La *cristiana* cuyo autor más destacado es Pablo Antonio Cuadra (item **5793**). No se trata, como en el caso de Cardenal (item **5781**), del uso directo de textos sagrados, sino de la plasmación poética de una visión profundamente cristiana de la naturaleza y del hombre. Esta diferencia de visión entre los dos poetas-nacional se traduce además, en diferencia ideológica. 4) La *feminista,* quizás la tendencia más interesante y fresca en la poesía centroamericana actual. Frente a las abstracciones metafísicas o las concreciones prosaicas de muchos de los comprometidos, esta vertiente aporta nuevos temas y sensibilidades. La erótica-gráfica es blandida con especial ímpetu por la costarricense Ana Istaru (item **5821**). Las guatemaltecas Alaida Foppa (item **5713**), Margarita Carrera (item **5783**) y Luz Méndez de la Vega (item **5713**) han establecido una tradición femenina si bien no feminista en su país, con Ana María Rodas y otras jóvenes tomando la antorcha en lo que se ha llamada una "nouvelle vague" feminista. En Nicaragua esta tendencia está representada por Gioconda Belli y Rosario Murillo (item **5730**), quienes logran integrar la experiencia insurreccional y la reconstrucción socialista del país sin acudir al "exteriorismo" cardenalista o al cristianismo metafísico de Cuadra. Es significativo que de los 35 escritores incluídos en *Poetas jóvenes de Panamá* (item **5745**) sólo las mujeres van más allá de los temas estereotípicos de la metafísica maldita y el compromiso prosaico.

En el Caribe los elementos más notables son la aparición de la obra completa de Luis Palés Matos (item **5855**), cuya edición ha estado a cargo de Margot Arce de Vázquez y el libro de Raymond Sousa (item **5965**) que introduce la obra de Lezama Lima en el sector amplio de la academia angloparlante. Tres cubanas, una residente en Madrid, Edith Llerena (item **5828**), otra en Florida, Juana Rosa Pita (item **5858**) y Marilyn Bobes León, cuya obra está revelada en un magistral estudio de Eliana Rivero (item **5919**), dan testimonio de la importante actividad poética realizada dentro y fuera de la isla.

En México la poesía sigue siendo la gran literatura. El Fondo de Cultura organizó ciclos de lecturas y publicó algunos de los libros más comentados de 1985: *Lotes baldíos* de Fabio Morávito (item **5848**), *El circo silencioso* de Luis Cortés Bargalló (item **5790a**) y *Heridas que se alternan* de Francisco Cervantes (item **5716**). Y en la serie "Lecturas Mexicanas" del Fondo de Cultura (que divulga en grandes tiradas y a precio reducido) se han reeditado la obra de los "Contemporáneos" (Novo, Gorostiza, Pellicer, Cuesta). El homenaje nacional rendido a este grupo en 1982 ha generado además una serie de estudios, antologías y homenajes en revistas (ver items **5707, 5711, 5917, 5923, 5932, 5941, 5942, 5956, y 5960**). Joaquín Mortiz sigue publicando a los ganadores del Premio Nacional de Poesía: en 1981, Coral Bracho; 1982, Francisco Hernández; 1984: *Música solar* de Hernán Efraín Bartolomé. *Canciones para los que se han separado* de Manjarrez (item **5831**) fue uno de los libros más comentados por su elaboración de un hablante nuevo que dice el amor de una manera original. Las voces de las provincias se hicieron notar a través de importantes antologías (items **5722, 5723, 5752 y 5753**) mientras la ciudad capital sigue siendo el punto de partida de la mayoría de los poemarios, ciudad en estado de desintegración: *Zona de derrumbe* de Aguilera Díaz (item **5755**), *Lotes baldíos* de Morávito (item **5848**), *El circo silencioso* de Cortés Bargalló (item **5790a**), *Saldo ardiente* de M.A. Flores (item **5809**), *Trabajo ilegal* de Olivar (item **5732**). En este contexto dijo Arreola (tras la explosión de San Juanico y el terremoto) que entre mayor es la pobreza material más definitiva ha de ser la riqueza cultural.

Este parece ser el caso en el México de hoy cuya última producción editorial ha aumentado tanto en cantidad como en calidad.

Colombia en 1983 celebró el centenario de Porfirio Barba Jacob con diversas publicaciones, siendo la más destacada la edición de su poesía completa bajo el título de *Antorchas contra el viento* (item **5765**) y un número de *Lingüística y Literatura* (item **5949**) de Medellín dedicado a la revaloración de su obra. Otro hecho importante para la crítica fue la publicación de una entrega doble de la *Revista Iberoamericana*, No. 129, julio-dic. 1984 dedicada integramente a la literatura colombiana.

En Venezuela, aparecieron libros importantes de Rafael Cadenas (item **5776**), Juan Calzadilla (item **5778**) y Eugenio Montejo (item **5847**) cuya obra, cada vez más madura, es de una extraordinaria tensión lírica.

En cuanto al Perú la noticia más prometedora es la que la nueva administración del Instituto Nacional de Cultura inició con el libro de Cisneros (item **5789**) una serie poética que debe seguir con otros poetas bajo la dirección de Carlos Orellana. Cabe destacar también la labor de COPE (item **5803**) que sigue promoviendo nuevos valores poéticos y la aparición de un nuevo libro del "amanuense," Carlos Germán Belli (item **5769**), uno de los valores más sólidos en la poesía del continente.

Entre los libros más interesantes que circularon en Chile durante el bienio 1984–85 cabe destacar *La Tirana* de Diego Maquieira (item **5832**), *Luis XIV* de Paulo de Jolly (item **5823**), *El alumbrado* de Gonzalo Rojas (item **5869**) y en especial la segunda edición de *La nueva novela*, que a pesar del título es altamente poética (item **5835**). Este último es de Juan Luis Martínez, representante destacado de la neovanguardia chilena. Hasta 1984 la dictadura militar había inhibido considerablemente la actividad editorial en este país, obligando a muchos poetas a callarse o a publicar en el exterior. En años recientes un número significativo de escritores exiliados han iniciado su retorno, en particular los de llamada generación "emergente" (los que empezaron a publicar en los años 60). Estos poetas y otros residentes de Chile sacaron en dic. de 1985 el primer número de una revista prometedora, titulada *El Espíritu del Valle* y dirigida por Gonzalo Millán. La empresa de pronto ha asumido un cierto liderazgo al proponer una reordenación de las promociones vigentes, y al cuestionar tácita pero decididamente la idea promovida por el crítico sacrosanto de *El Mercurio* para quien sólo merecen atención las cuatro o cinco figuras mayores de la poesía chilena, eclipsando así cualquier otro valor "emergente." Obviamente es éste un momento de reagrupación de fuerzas poéticas influido por las luchas para el retorno a la democracia.

Uno de los hechos más notorios en la Argentina es lo que parece ser un intento global de rescatar el pasado cultural y poético después de terminada la dictadura. Abundan las ediciones de obras completas, antologías y el rescate de los clásicos olvidados. El impacto sobre las generaciones jóvenes del exilio personal así como la lucha de las Madres de la Plaza de Mayo se registra en la poesía de muchos de los jóvenes. Está surgiendo además, una especie de nueva escena poética, que tiende a partir de cero y a elaborar sus propios códigos poéticos independientemente de un enfrentamiento con las generaciones anteriores, por ejemplo: Rafael Felipe Oteriño, Néstor Perlongher, Vicente Zito Lema (item **5883**), Jorge Brega (item **5774**), y Carlos Roca (item **5866**) entre otros.

En el Uruguay, la labor editorial ya ha cobrado bastante dinamismo, haciendo posible la publicación de una serie de poemarios que representan a varias generaciones, especialmente a los nacidos a partir de 1940. La forma poética más generalizada parece ser el poema breve, con lenguaje muy trabajado, extremadamente depurado, con tendencia a la experimentación textual. En cuanto a referente, la dirección más extendida es el desarrollo de estrategias poéticas que accedan críticamente al contexto político que sirve de telón de fondo para muchos de los escritos. Es también importante señalar que la reciente apertura política en este país ha facilitado el retorno de numerosos exiliados cuya presencia ha empezado a marcar una nueva etapa cultural en Montevideo. Ejemplo de ello es el suplemento cultural del periódico *Jaque*, que cuenta entre sus redactores con el poeta Hugo Achúgar.

La Editorial Alcandara de Asunción del Paraguay continua su programa de rescate de las voces poéticas anteriores y el estreno de las más recientes. Además, en este bienio se editaron varias recopilaciones realizadas por sus autores, junto con nuevas ediciones de poemarios de escritores exiliados, como es el caso de Elvio Romero (item **5870**) y Augusto Roa Bastos (item **5865**). Las direcciones actuales del discurso poético en el Paraguay tanto como en el Uruguay parecen indicar: 1) el alejamiento del tono intimista; 2) la conjunción de experiencia personal junto a una postura crítica de la realidad histórica problematizada; y 3) formalmente, el poema breve, cuyo lenguaje propone un nuevo orden sintáctico y una nueva concepción del texto como espacio contestatario.

No se pueden concluir estas notas sin dejar constancia de la aparición de un nuevo tipo de poesía "sin autor:" poesía de la necesidad, escrita en las cárceles, (item **5780**) y publicada bajo seudónimo o en el anonimato, poesía cuyo distintivo es no haber sido engendrada desde dentro de la tradición literaria sino al margen de ella. Se entronca, por su frescura, su fuerza y su orginalidad con la poesía de los Talleres de Nicaragua—y en cierto sentido también con la nueva poesía femenina, todas ellas impactantes por lo diferentes para un lector habitual de poesía. [RdC]

ANTHOLOGIES

5703 Adán, Martín. Poemas escogidos. Selección de Mirko Lauer y Abelardo Oquendo. Lima: Mosca Azul Editores, 1983. 134 p.

Aunque todavía ignorado por la crítica académica, Martín Adán es uno de los mayores poetas latinoamericanos; esta antología, que coincide con su muerte pero también con la reciente publicación de su obra completa por Edubanco, debe ayudar a divulgar las calidades de esa obra. La selección de Lauer y Oquendo, editores de *Hueso Húmero*, la mejor revista literaria peruana, y directores de Mosca Azul, la más interesante editorial en Perú, se propone hacer accesible al lector promedio una poesía dispersa en ediciones ya agotadas o en tomos poco manuables. De allí que resulte una edición muy útil para manejar en clases de poesía moderna. La de Martín Adán (seudónimo de Rafael de la Fuente Benavides) parte de ejercicios vanguardistas, se desarrolla como una rama fecunda y preciosista del barroco, se desdobla como reflexión metafísica, y culmina en un desgarramiento confesional. Su propia voz es distintiva, compleja, única. [JO]

5704 Alonso de las Heras, César et al. Ortiz Guerrero en el cincuentenario de su muerte, 1933–1983: ensayos, artículos, antología. Asunción: Lector, 1983. 162 p.: bibl., port. (Col. de homenaje; 1)

Este volumen contiene una colección de 12 ensayos sobre el poeta paraguayo junto a una breve selección de su poesía, extraída de *Surgente* (1922), *Nubes del este* (1928), *Pepitas* (1930), *Arenillas de mi tierra* (1969) y *Poema*, aunque su obra es más extensa. Interesa a los investigadores de la poesía para-

guaya del primer tercio del siglo XX. [MGP]

5705 Alvarez, Mario Rubén et al. Poesía taller. Asunción: Taller de Poesía Manuel Ortiz Guerrero, 1982. 84 p.

Este volumen ofrece una muestra representativa del taller de poesía "Manuel Ortiz Guerrero" que ha llevado a cabo una labor importante en Asunción del Paraguay. Entre los textos que forman este libro, son de particular interés los poemas escritos en guaraní de Sabino Giménez Ortega, Miguel Angel Meza y Ramón R. Silva de valor para los interesados en la poesía paraguaya actual y para los estudiosos del guaraní. [MGP]

5706 Antología de la poesía hispanoamericana moderna. v. 1. Caracas: Equinoccio, 1982. 1 v.: bibl.

Panorama de la poesía hispanoamericana desde el modernismo hasta las últimas décadas. Este vol. 1 (se proyectan dos) ofrece una acertada y generosa selección de textos de las grandes figuras (de Martí a Mistral . . . de Huidobro a Pellicer) con el propósito de hacer más evidente el "sistema poético" de cada autor. El aparato erudito es igualmente acertado (breves ensayos de orientación complementados por una bibliografía básica). [RdC]

5707 Antología de la poesía mexicana moderna: 1928. Edición facsimilar de Jorge Cuesta. Presentación de Guillermo Sheridan. México: Cultura SEP, 1985. 247 p. (Lecturas mexicanas)

Reedición de la polémica antología que bajo la rúbrica de Jorge Cuesta apareció en 1928 y en cuyo prólogo se filtraron las ideas de los que un mes después integraron la revista que les dio nombre: *Contemporáneos*. El estudio iluminador de Guillermo Sheridan y la inclusión de reseñas y cartas críticas que aparecieron después de la publicación hacen de éste un texto indispensable para el mexicanista. [NK]

5708 Antología de la poesía venezolana contemporánea. Edición de Pedro Pablo Paredes. Caracas: Asociación de Escritores de Venezuela, Fondo Editorial, 1981. 398 p.: bibl., indexes, port.

Incluye 82 poetas, desde Leoncio Martínez (1888–1941) a Enrique Hernández D'Jesús (1947). Paredes reconoce cuatro "tiempos estéticos" o promociones en este proceso: 1) Generación actual (p. 13–164, C. Ovalles, R. Palomares, G. Sucre, J. Sánchez Peláez); 2) Generación del 40 (p. 165–260, Ida Gramcko, J.R. Medina, J. Tello); 3) "Grupo Viernes" (p. 261–305, V. Gerbasi, O. De Sola); 4) Generación del 18 (p. 307–378, A. Eloy Blanco, F. Paz Castillo *et al.*). Aunque algo cruzado, el orden propuesto es aceptable; en general, también lo es la selección de textos. Carece de información bibliográfica sobre los autores, lo que reduce considerablemente su utilidad. Omisiones notorias: Eugenio Montejo y Rafael Cadenas. [PL]

5709 Antología de poesías populares. Selección de Manuel Ibáñez G. México: Editorial Universo, 1980–1981. 2 v.

Un abecedario de poesías españolas e hispanoamericanas del canon de los ya antologizados cuya única gracia es su fácil manejo puesto que los textos van ordenados por título. [RdC]

5710 Antología general de la poesía nicaragüense. Edición de Jorge Eduardo Arellano. Managua: Ediciones Distribuidora Cultural, 1984. 523 p.: ill.

Antología que se remonta al período precolombino y llega hasta los poetas de los 50. Según el prefacio procura ser una "representación colectiva." Lamentablemente, faltan fechas y otros datos; tampoco hay justificación del criterio de selección. No obstante, es un libro útil por los textos que reúne. [GY]

5711 Antología poética: homenaje a los Contemporáneos. Introducción, selección y notas de Luis Mario Schneider. México: Instituto Nacional de Bellas Artes, Cultura SEP, 1982. 167 p.: photos.

Excelente y útil antología, con un estudio preliminar que sirve de introducción al grupo Contemporáneos. Incluye poemas de Pellicer, Ortiz de Montellano, González Rojo, Gorostiza, Torres Bodet, Villaurrutia, Nandino, Cuesta, Owen y Novo. [NK]

5712 Cardoza y Aragón, Luis. Guatemala con una piedra adentro. México: CEESTEM: Editorial Nueva Imagen, 1983. 317 p., 30 p. of plates: bibl., ill. (Col. Cuadernos americanos; 5)

Cronista y crítico de arte, la visión poética forma el centro de la obra cardoziana. Aparece aquí sólo una breve selección poética de *Entonces, sólo entonces . . .* que recuerda *Residencia en la tierra* de Neruda por su plasmación de lo metafísico en lo material: "El tiempo: una posición en tu cuerpo." [GY]

5713 Carrera, Mario Alberto. Panorama de la poesía femenina guatemalteca del siglo XX. Guatemala: Editorial Universitaria de Guatemala, 1983. 264 p.: ports. (Col. Creación literaria; 16)

Sin duda el libro más inteligente sobre poesía de los últimos años, consiste en crónicas-retratos de 14 poetas que, por su estilo y temática, se pueden ubicar en tres grupos: postmodernistas, posjuanramonianas, *nouvelle vague* feminista. Cabe destacar a Alaíde Foppa, Margarita Carrera y Luz Méndez de la Vega entre las del segundo grupo y a Ana María Rodas dentro del tercero. [GY]

5714 Casaldáliga, Pedro. Cantares de la entera libertad: antología para la nueva Nicaragua. Prólogo de José Coronel Urtecho. Managua: Instituto Histórico Centro Americano, 1984. 81 p.: ill.

En el prólogo, Coronel Urtecho identifica pueblo, poesía, catolicismo y revolución como un frente unido en contra de la vida burguesa. Así contribuye a la función ideológica de la poesía—como la que desempeña en los Talleres de Poesía—en la Nicaragua actual. [GY]

5715 Centeno, Bosco. Puyonearon los granos. Managua: Ministerio de Cultura, 1983. 69 p.

De lo mejor que hayan producido los talleres de Solentiname dentro de una línea exteriorista. Breves epigramas al estilo clásico o impresiones tipo hai-kai, tratan del amor, de la naturaleza, de las experiencias en la campaña, la vida cotidiana. Todo con una serenidad que parece manar naturalmente. Premio Nacional de Poesía Joven de 1982. [GY]

5716 Cervantes, Francisco. Heridas que se alternan. México: Fondo de Cultura Económica, 1985. 305 p.

Texto que reúne seis libros de poesía (*Los varones señalados, La materia del tributo, Esa sustancia amarga, Cantado para nadie, Aulaga en la Maralta* y *Heridas que se alternan*), y representa más de 25 años de quehacer poético. Admirador y crítico de la poesía en lengua portuguesa, su poesía intenta seguir u originar otra tradición. El hablante poético se sitúa en los lindes de la Edad Media y el Renacimiento buscando recuperar un pasado más heroico. Los poemas que cantan esas acciones pasadas, a partir de formas populares antiguas, se instalan, a menudo, en el recuerdo y en los sueños. [NK]

5717 Cortés, Alfonso. 30 [Treinta] poemas de Alfonso. Managua: Editorial Nueva Nicaragua, 1981. 133 leaves, 6 of plates: ill. (some col.) (Biblioteca popular sandinista; 4)

Rescate de una poesía anormal, paradójica, contradictoria, absurda, de un poeta que se volvió loco. Extrema la veta metafísica del modernismo, no a la manera de un Herrera y Reissig, sino en busca de la "palabra absoluta." [GY]

5718 Diego, Eliseo. Poesía. Compilación e introducción de Enrique Saínz. La Habana: Editorial Letras Cubanas, 1983. 428 p.

Esta recopilación de la obra del distinguido miembro de la generación de *Orígenes* constituye un hermoso homenaje a la obra fecunda de este poeta dedicado al desentrañamiento de la transparencia lúcida de las cosas. Diego cumple con esa adánica misión del poeta de nombrarlo todo como si se nombrara por primera vez. De los poetas de *Orígenes* es el menos hermético y quizás el más candorosamente espiritual. El lector cuenta ahora con una estupenda recopilación de sus poemarios, desde *En la calzada de Jesús del Monte* hasta *Los días de tu vida.* En todos sobresale la maestría extraordinaria de este gran poeta. [RRA]

5719 Escobar Velado, Oswaldo. Patria exacta y otros poemas. Selección, prólogo y notas de Italo López Vallecillos. San Salvador: UCA Editores, 1978. 196 p. (Col. Gavidia; 14)

Destaca Escobar Velado (1918–61) entre los del *Grupo Seis* por la honda nota emocional con que critica la realidad social enajenante y con que articula la protesta contra los regímenes opresores. Se encuentra en su poesía, además, el tema del amor, ya a la patria, ya a la mujer, ya a un amor universal: "Amo los exilios/ por la alta luz dorada que recogí con ellos,/ por esta voz universal y simple/ que aprendí a repartir/ entre todos los hombres." Su voz tiene gran vigencia en la actualidad. [GY]

5720 Fernández, Guillermo. El asidero en la zozobra. Selección y prólogo de Sandro Cohen. Jalisco, México: Depto. de Bellas Artes, Gobierno de Jalisco, 1983. 141 p.

Selección de la poesía de un importante poeta mexicano cuya poesía de tono nostálgico y escéptico se encuentra entre la mejor de las últimas décadas. El estudio preliminar de Cohen sirve de excelente introducción a la poesía escogida de *Visitaciones* (1964), *La palabra a solas* (1965), *La hora y el sitio* (1973) y *Bajo llave* (1984). [NK]

5721 Fernández Moreno, Baldomero. Antología de antologías. Selección y prólogo de César Fernández Moreno. La Habana: Casa de las Américas, 1984. 263 p. (Col. Literatura latinoamericana; 113)

César Fernández Moreno nos regala con un trabajo completo, limpio, contenidamente admirativo en esta "antología de antologías" de su padre Baldomero. En un solo volumen, podemos apreciar el mito Baldomero en toda su extensión, más allá del publicitado "sencillismo." La división de la parte lírica en tres épocas: "sencillista," "formal," "sustancial," puede ser discutible y hasta ingenua, pero el resultado final, en cuanto ordenación eficaz del material, es excelente. También incluye prosa y amplio material informativo. [JG]

5722 Festival Internacional de Poesía, 2nd, Morelia, Mexico, 1983. Antología. Edición y selección de Evodio Escalante. México: Joaquín Mortiz, 1984. 306 p. (Confrontaciones. Los Poetas)

Recopilación de poemas de los autores que participaron en el Segundo Festival Internacional de Poesía (Morelia, oct. 1983). Entre ellos, E. Cardenal, A. Cisneros, A. González, E. Mejía Sánchez, S. Ibargoyen y J. Teillier, de fuera, E. Bartolomé, R. Castillo, K. Galván, C. Illesca, Montemayor, T. Nava y O. Oliva, de México. No tan concurrido como el primer festival del 81. [NK]

5723 La Flor de la palabra. Edición de Víctor de la Cruz. 2a ed. México: Premiá, 1983. 148 p.: bibl., ill. (La Red de Jonás. Cultura popular)

Antología bilingüe de la poesía zapoteca desde la época prehispánica hasta la contemporánea, con excelente introducción del editor. [NK]

5724 Girri, Alberto. Páginas. Seleccionadas por el autor. Estudio preliminar de Horacio Castillo. Buenos Aires: Editorial Celtia, 1983. 221 p. (Col. Escritores argentinos de hoy)

Uno de los raros poetas hispanoamericanos que no sólo no se espanta de desarrollar un lenguaje lírico inteligente, ricamente abstracto, conceptual y frecuentemente ingenioso e irónico, sino que trabaja las estructuras lógicas del discurso hasta el punto de obtener de ellas toda su elocuencia trágica. Este libro será un hallazgo para quienes todavía no hayan leído a Girri. Hay un muy buen prólogo de Horacio Castillo. [JG]

5725 González Tuñón, Raúl. Poemas de Buenos Aires. Antología y notas de Luis Osvaldo Tedesco. Buenos Aires: Torres Agüero Editor, 1983. 125 p. (Memoria del tiempo)

Elaboración culta de motivos y discursos populares que suele convencer como lenguaje original e incluso como poesía. Está González Tuñón entre quienes con más éxito han querido enfrentar los discursos del poder en Argentina y elaborar textos que se disfrutan en cuanto subversivos y contestatarios. Esta antología de Luis Osvaldo Tedesco es hábil y representativa. [JG]

5726 Hernández, Francisco. Cuerpo disperso. México: UNAM, 1982. 146 p. (Col. Cuadernos de poesía)

Texto que reúne cuatro poemarios breves: *Gritar es cosa de mudos* (1974), *Portarretratos* (1976), *Cuerpo disperso* (1978) y *Textos criminales* (1980). "Poeta maldito" que desconstruye con irónica sabiduría y humor negro el mundo y la imaginación conocidos para elaborar su original poética del cuerpo y del crimen. [NK]

5727 Lezama Lima, José. Imagen y posibilidad. Selección, prólogo y notas de Ciro Bianchi Ross. La Habana: Editorial Letras Cubanas, 1981. 203 p. (Col. Crítica)

Colección de ensayos, algunos inéditos, de Lezama Lima que no aparecen en sus *Obras completas* publicadas por Aguilar. La edición es de Virgilio López Lemus con la colaboración de Cintio Vitier. Sobresalen, entre otros, los artículos escritos para *Grafos* antes de la publicación de *Muerte de Narciso* en 1937. El volumen es valioso porque recoge ensayos dispersos que de otra manera hubiera sido muy difícil localizar, y también porque nos ofrece una cara nueva de Lezama, con pequeños ensayos sobre Che Guevara, el 26 de julio, Alicia Alonso y hasta la radio y la televisión. Se nota también en la edición un esfuerzo por hacer a Lezama más accesible y paladeable a un público cubano más general. [RRA]

5728 Mieses Burgos, Franklin. Antología. Edición de Freddy Gatón Arce. Santo Domingo: Biblioteca Nacional, 1985. 1 v. (Col. Orfeo)

Esta reimpresión de la antología publicada originalmente en 1953 vuelve a poner en circulación la modesta pero importante obra de uno de los fundadores de La Poesía Sorprendida. De un lirismo sencillo y sosegado, es poesía de tono declamatorio y de un sobrio romanticismo. [RRA]

5729 Molina, Enrique et al. Alta marea y otros poemas. Estudio preliminar, notas y selección de Daniel Freidemberg. Buenos Aires: Centro Editor de América Latina, 1983. 136 p. (Poesía hispanoamericana del siglo XX; 3. Biblioteca básica universal; 267)

Escueta antología de los poetas más destacados del llamado "posvanguardismo" con un informativo estudio preliminar y datos bio-bibliográficos esenciales sobre cada uno de los seleccionados. [RdC]

5730 Murillo, Rosario. Amar es combatir: selección de *Gualtayan* y *Sube a nacer conmigo*. Managua: Editorial Nueva Nicaragua, 1982. 150 p.: ill. (Letras de Nicaragua; 1)

Selección de dos libros previos (*Gualtayan* y *Sube a nacer conmigo*). Los primeros poemas son demasiado prosaicos y obvios. Los de amor (la mayoría) están entre los más exuberantes escritos en Nicaragua (como un Aleixandre filtrado a través de Joaquín Pasos). Nada de exteriorismos, aquí fluye la fantasía, la invitación a inventar, a nacer en un nuevo mundo signado por el amor y la sorpresa. [GY]

5731 Nuevos poetas costarricenses, 1982: antología. San José: Editorial Costa Rica, 1982. 64 p. (Libros de poesía; 13)

Sorprende que los poetas jóvenes (nacidos en los 50) no vayan más allá de la impugnación de los "abismos insoportables" (José Antonio Cabrera), lo que "orina la gracia del cuerpo" de la patria (Luis Enrique Arce Navarro), o la asesinación de la poesía (Leonel Sanabria Varela). En esto, siguen los pasos de las generaciones previas y manifiestan estados de ánimo y emociones de modo abstracto. [GY]

5732 Oliva, Oscar. Trabajo ilegal: poesía, 1960–1982. México: Katún, 1984. 333 p.

Texto que reúne la poesía de este miembro de "La espiga amotinada" cuyo poemario *Estado de sitio* mereció el Premio Nacional de Poesía en 1971. Su compromiso con la realidad que vive no ha cambiado. *Trabajo ilegal*, dice, en una entrevista reciente, "es el proceso del derrumbe de una realidad como la nuestra, en medio de la lucha de clases, del amor, de la esperanza y la desesperanza." Destrucción que implica reconstrucción en estos poemas cuya hechura formal confirma también su compromiso con el arte poético. [NK]

5733 Pacheco, José Emilio. Alta traición. Selección y prólogo de José María Guelbenzu. Madrid: Alianza Editorial, 1985. 116 p.

Util antología de la poesía seleccionada de este reconocido poeta. Incluye un estudio introductorio y muestras representativas de los poemarios, *Los elementos de la noche* (1963), *El reposo del fuego* (1966), *No me preguntes cómo pasa el tiempo* (1969), *Irás y no volverás* (1973), *Islas a la deriva* (1976), *Desde entonces* (1980), *Los trabajos del mar* (1983). [NK]

5734 Paz, Octavio. Instante y revelación. Fotos de Manuel Alvarez Bravo. México: A. Muñoz para el Fondo Nacional para Actividades Sociales, 1982. 100 leaves: chiefly ill.

Bella edición que va alternando poemas de Paz con fotografías de Alvarez Bravo. En el excelente prólogo sobre el arte de la fotografía, Paz nos advierte: "Ni los poemas son comentarios a las fotos ni las fotos son ilustraciones de los poemas: son obras independientes. Las relaciones . . . se deberán sobre

todo al libre juego de la imaginación, la sensibilidad y la simpatía del lector-espectador." [NK]

5735 Poesía compartida: quince poetas latinoamericanos de hoy. Diagramación y coordinación de Rubinstein Moreira. Montevideo: Ediciones La Urpila, 1983. 60 p.

Antología breve y curiosa que pone juntos a una serie de jóvenes (en su gran mayoría desconocidos) con un gran poeta de ayer algo olvidado hoy: Alberto Baeza Flores. No se nota ninguna línea estética ni tendencia poética que justifique la selección de autores, salvo la alta calidad lírica de algunos de los textos recogidos. [RdC]

5736 Poesía de El Salvador. Selección, notas y prólogo de Manlio Argueta. San José: Editorial Universitaria Centroamericana, 1983. 359 p. (Col. Séptimo día)

Acompañada de un importante prólogo, notas y acotaciones de Manlio Argueta, esta antología presenta un panorama de los poetas salvadoreños más destacados, desde principios del siglo hasta la actualidad. Destaca esta obra por su criterio de selección (más de poemas que de poetas), procurando "descubrir la fuerza oculta de nuestro antepasado cultural." Se trata de una reescritura de la historia de la poesía salvadoreña desde la perspectiva del compromiso cultural (y no meramente ideológico) con el pueblo. Rematan esta sucesión de poetas, los más jóvenes y prometedores de la actualidad: Mario Castrillo, Rigoberto Góngora, Miguel Huezo Mixzco, David Hernández, Roger Lindo, Horacio Castellanos Moya. [GY]

5737 Poesía feminista del mundo hispánico: desde la Edad Media hasta la actualidad; antología crítica. Selección de Angel Flores y Kate Flores. México: Siglo Veintiuno Editores, 1984. 285 p. (La Creación literaria)

Excelente y revelante selección de poesía feminista desde los comienzos de la lírica en lengua castellana hasta la época actual (siendo la más joven Gioconda Belli, n. 1948). Las notas de presentación, aunque brevísimas, se destacan por su nutrida y siempre orientadora documentación. [RdC]

5738 Poesía guerrillera de El Salvador. S.l.: Las Fuerzas Populares de Liberación Farabundo Martí, 1982. 68 p.: photos.

Como muestra de la que Mario Benedetti llamara "poesía de emergencia," esta antología incluye 15 poemas anónimos de "compañeros militantes de las F[uerzas] P[opulares de] L[iberación], un poema de Delfy Góchez Fernández, caída en acción, y dos de Roque Dalton." Aqueja a la mayoría de estos poemas un retoricismo un tanto torpe. No obstante, los mejores poemas convierten la visión revolucionaria en un auténtico vehículo de la cultura popular. [GY]

5739 Poesía hispanoamericana. Selección de Francisco Montes de Oca. México: Editorial Porrúa, 1982. 427 p. (Sepan cuantos; 381)

Exponiendo más de 140 poetas de cuatro siglos en unas 400 p. de texto, sin bibliografía ni notas de orientación este libro escolar sólo logra dar una vaga idea de la continuidad del quehacer poético en el continente. [RdC]

5740 El Poeta y la muerte: antología de poemas a la muerte. Selección de J. Boccanera. México: Editores Mexicanos Unidos, 1981. 314 p.: ill. (Col. Poesía)

Antología (organizada por países latinoamericanos) de excelentes poemas cuyo tema principal es la muerte. Los datos bio-bibliográficos esenciales sobre los autores antologizados están complementados por un ambicioso ensayo de presentación sobre la presencia de la muerte en la poesía del continente desde la época precolombina hasta hoy. [RdC]

5741 Los Poetas a Bolívar. Selección de Jaime Tello. Caracas: Instituto Venezolano de los Seguros Sociales, 1983. 180 p.

Esta antología—producto típico del bicentenario de Bolívar—recopila poemas de variada calidad inspirados en la gloria del Libertador en orden cronológico invertido (desde los poetas actuales a Olmedo) y así logra impresionar por la vigencia del tema tanto entre los escritores jóvenes como entre los consagrados, verbigracia, Neruda, Huidobro, Cardenal . . . [RdC]

5742 Poetas de hoy en España y América. Madrid: Taller Prometeo de Poesía Nueva, 1983. 2 v.: bibls., ill. (Col. Poesía nueva; 21–22)

Segunda entrega sobre poesía contemporánea que incluye poemas relativamente nuevos de más de 40 poetas hispanoamericanos y otros tantos españoles (ancianos y jóvenes, buenos y malos) de una meritoria

publicación periódica con intención más publicitaria que crítica: mostrar su obra, sea buena o mala. [RdC]

5743 Poetas de una generación, 1940–1949. Selección y notas de Jorge González de León. Prólogo de Vicente Quirarte. México: Difusión Cultural, Depto. de Humanidades, 1981. 167 p. (Textos de humanidades; 25)

Antología que reúne a 22 poetas nacidos entre 1940–49 que empiezan a escribir en los años 60. Según Quirarte se trata de una poesía conceptual en la que "los poetas le exigen cuentas a la palabra y la obligan a vincularse con la vida." Excelente introducción a un grupo de poetas que hoy se encuentra en plena madurez, entre otros, M.A. Campos, E. Cross, M.A. Flores, F. Hernández, D. Huerta, C. Montemayor, O. Quillen, J. Reyes, R. Yáñez. [NK]

5744 Poetas en abril. v. 2. Recopilación y presentación de Luz Eugenia Sierra. Medellín, Colombia: Fundación Talleres, 1984. 1 v.: ports.

Muestra de una poesía que "ha encontrado una mayor fuerza en la imagen logrando trascender la rima y la métrica en persecución de una sensación . . ." (p. 15). Recoge textos de 30 poetas, desde escritores nadaístas (Jotamario, n. 1940; D. Lemos, n. 1941; E. Escobar, n. 1943) hasta autores nacidos en la década del 60 (Liana Mejía, n. 1960; C.E. Ortiz, n. 1961; A. Ospina, n. 1963). Un sector de la literatura colombiana actual seriamente amenazado por la monotonía. [PL]

5745 Poetas jóvenes de Panamá. Selección y prólogo de Jaime García Saucedo. México: Editorial Signos, 1982. 95 p.

Da a conocer 35 poetas "nuevos" (nacido el más viejo en 1947). Según el antólogo, todos tienen "los mismos intereses estéticos y morales." Pero quizás ello se deba a su selección. La gran mayoría de poemas incurren en la misma retórica de desaliento y abstracta angustia metafísica. Las verdaderas voces nuevas son las de las poetas: Julia del Carmen Regales, sencilla y barroca a la vez; Virginia Fábrega, sonora y erótica; Ernestina Rojas, lírica hasta la profundidad; Merici Morales, exenta de retóricas; Consuelo Tomás, cantora de la felicidad. [GY]

5746 Poets of Chile: a bilingual anthology, 1965–1985. Edited by Steven F. White.

Introduction by Juan Armando Epple. Greensboro, N.C.: Unicorn Press, 1986. 283 p.: bibl., ports.

Sin duda alguna, la antología de poesía chilena más responsable de que tenemos noticia. Porque White, en vez de limitarse a la zona central de Chile, como ha ocurrido en otros casos, se dio el trabajo de viajar pueblo por pueblo, de Arica a Punta Arenas, recopilando el corpus de poemas del cual extraería los textos para su libro. Excepto la introducción, que está a cargo de Juan Epple, tanto la selección de poemas como las excelentes notas preliminares, las utilísimas bibliografías de y sobre los poetas, y las traducciones al inglés, corresponden a White. En suma, una obra indispensable para el conocimiento cabal de la poesía chilena del período 1965–85. Los poetas incluidos son los siguientes: Teresa Calderón, Juan Camerón, Mauricio Electorat, Aristóteles España, Oscar Hahn, Walter Hoefler, Omar Lara, Rodrigo Lira, Sergio Mansilla, Diego Maqueira, Juan Luis Martínez, Gonzalo Millán, Paz Molina, Gonzalo Muñoz, Jaime Quezada, Clemente Riedemann, Waldo Rojas, Armando Rubio, Manuel Silva Acevedo, y Raúl Zurita. [OH]

5747 Post-coup Chilean poetry: a bilingual anthology; Gonzalo Millán, Edgardo Jiménez, Enrique Valdés, Jaime Quezada, Jorge Narváez, Omar Lara. Selection, edition, bibliography and notes by Silverio Muñoz. Translated by Mary Ellen Acevedo. Collegeville, Minn.: Ediciones Arauco, 1986. 1 v.: bibl., ill.

Muestra bilingüe escueta pero importante que recoge poemas (casi todos inéditos) de seis jóvenes de los grupos *Arúspice* (Millán, Jiménez, Quezada, Narváez) y *Trilce* (Valdés, Lara). [RdC]

5748 La Protesta a través de la poesía comprometida. Selección y presentación de Pedro Condo. La Paz: Ediciones Ruphay, 1983. 151 p.: bibl., ill.

Antología y ensayo de presentación que rescata una parte de la llamada "nueva poesía política" boliviana. Hay poemas de calidad, aparecidos originalmente en revistas y volantes, bajo seudónimo o en el anonimato. [RdC]

5749 Salvador: en sufrimiento armado. Selección e introducción de Juvenal Herrera Torres. Medellín, Colombia: Editorial Aurora, 1981. 1 v. (Antología universal de poesía revolucionaria; 6)

Antología de poetas de toda América Latina (e.g., Neruda, Cardenal, Cuadra, Sosa, Alegría, Dalton) que suscriben la concepción de que la poesía debe cambiar la realidad. Dicha idea se concretiza en estos poemas que pretenden contribuir a la lucha por el cambio como si fuesen otras tantas armas. [GY]

5750 Segovia, Tomás. Poesía, 1943–1976. México: Fondo de Cultura Económica, 1982. 441 p. (Letras mexicanas)

Doce colecciones de poemas (*País del cielo, Fidelidad, La voz turbada, La triste primavera, En el aire claro, Luz de aquí, El sol y su eco, Historias y poemas, Anagnórisis, Terceto, Figura y secuencias, Cuaderno del nómada*) integran este volumen que constata la admirable trayectoria poética de Segovia y el lugar indiscutible que ocupa en la poesía mexicana de este siglo. [NK]

5751 Talleres de poesía: antología. Introducción de Ernesto Cardenal. Selección y prólogo de Mayra Jiménez. Managua: Ministerio de Cultura, 1983. 318 p.

La participación más heterogénea—obreros, indios, campesinos, empleadas domésticas, soldados, policías, etc.—demuestra que la revolución ha "socializado los medios de producción poética" (Joaquín Marta Sosa). En la introducción Cardenal puntualiza que esta socialización ha introducido elementos jamás registrados en la poesía nicaragüense: "lo que se siente cuando se deja una novia para marchar al combate y a una posible muerte." Casi todos los poemas encarnan un mismo estilo cotidiano, humilde y colectivamente épico. El que sigan las "reglas" de Cardenal para la "buena poesía" (exteriorista) es un problema. [GY]

5752 20 [i.e. Veinte] años de poesía en Monterrey, 1962–1982. Selección y prólogo de Margarito Cuéllar y Humberto Salazar. Monterrey, México: Stuanl, 1983. 189 p.

Selección de poesía de 19 poetas que pertenecen a dos generaciones importantes (del 60 y del 80) en el desarrollo de la poesía regiomontana. El prólogo detalla la vida literaria y cultural en Monterrey desde los 50 hasta principios de los 80. [NK]

5753 Wong, Oscar. Nueva poesía de Chiapas: antología. México: Editorial Katún, 1983. 150 p. (Antologías literarias; 1)

Esta antología se presenta como continuadora de *12 poetas chiapanecos* de José Casahonda Castillo, y reconoce una tradición poética chiapaneca en la que se inscriben Sabines, Castellanos, Bañuelos, Oliva, Zepeda. Una excelente introducción al mundo de Chiapas y su cultura literaria precede los textos poéticos de, entre otros, Javier Molina, Elva Macía, Raúl Garduño, Joaquín Vásquez, Oscar Wong, y Hernán Efraín Bartolomé. [NK]

5754 Zepeda, Eraclio. Relación de travesía. México: Editorial Villicaña, 1985. 127 p.: ill. (Col. Caballo verde de la poesía; 2)

Libro valioso para quien estudie la poesía de los 60 en México. Reúne la obra poética entre 1960–65 (ediciones en su mayoría agotadas) de este miembro de "La Espiga Amotinada" que actualmente es mejor conocido por su cuentística, merecedora de varios premios nacionales. [NK]

BOOKS OF VERSE

5755 Aguilera Díaz, Gaspar. Zona de derrumbe. México: Katún, 1985. 87 p. (Serie Arte-poesía; 7)

Poeta desmitificador que capta con su mirada aguda y sensible las zonas marginadas de la existencia; lugares citadinos concretos, estados mentales en que la soledad, la tristeza y la nostalgia se imponen. Versos libres cuyo ritmo y sonoridad cristalina anuncian una voz nueva en la poesía mexicana que merece ser escuchada. [NK]

5756 Albán, Laureano. Geografía invisible de América. San José: Editorial Costa Rica, 1983. 152 p.

Son 20 cantos que evocan la fundación, origen y raíz de los tiempos de los dioses, de las cosas en su elementaridad. Cada canto elabora un aspecto tomado de *El libro de Chilam Balam*, el *Popol Vuh*, las *Crónicas de los antiguos mexicanos*, o *Los anales de los Chakchiqueles*. Albán parece tener una voluntad de convertir su poesía en la sagrada Poética Escritura de lo subyacente. [GY]

5757 Albán, Laureano. El viaje interminable. San José: Editorial Costa Rica, 1983. 200 p.

A partir de sucesivos viajes entre América y España, del 78 al 81, surgen estas

visiones del descubrimiento de América, hipóstasis de la "aventura hacia lo desconocido." Característicamente, Albán se inspira en los escritos de los cronistas de Indias y antiguos textos indígenas para su indagación del *ontos* americano. "Piedra," "espejo" y "ceniza" son los elementos fundantes de esta recreación del "alba." [GY]

5758 Alonso, Rodolfo. Alrededores. Buenos Aires: Centro Editor de América Latina, 1983. 119 p. (Capítulo. Las Nuevas propuestas; 35)

Alonso ha realizado una amplia labor poética desde los años 50: numerosos libros, además de traducciones desde el italiano y el portugués. Su poesía representa las últimas floraciones de la estética de vanguardia, con un gran talento para la expresión poética de las zonas irreales de la imaginación. Este libro, por ser una recolección de poemas sueltos del autor no incluidos en libro, proporciona un amplio panorama de todos sus registros. [JG]

5759 Arbeleche, Jorge. La casa de la piedra negra. Prólogo de Martha Canfield. Montevideo: Arca, 1983. 56 p.: bibl.

Uno de los poetas que se destaca en la poesía uruguaya de la década de los 60, contemporáneo de Enrique Estrázulas, Enrique Fierro, Eduardo Milán y Hugo Achúgar, entre otros, ha publicado cinco poemarios: *Sangre de la luz* (1968), *Los instantes* (1970), *Las vísperas* (1974), *Los ángeles oscuros* (1976) y *Alta noche* (1979). Los poemas de este volumen van precedidos de un prólogo de Martha Canfield que ubica a este poeta en la línea que trabaja "la emoción dicha sin artificio, poesía más vivida que creada." Utilizando como centro semántico el equivalente español de "arbeleche:" la casa de la piedra negra, el yo lírico persigue su propia identidad, la que se oculta en su propio nombre, el otro yo. [MGP]

5760 Arenas, Reinaldo. El central. Barcelona, Spain: Seix Barral, 1981. 105 p. (Poesía. Biblioteca breve; 475)

Estremecedor poema en prosa y en verso libre escrito en 1970 sobre una plantación cañera de trabajo forzoso en Cuba. El poema es un canto en contra de la esclavitud y de los sistemas totalitarios ubicado en tres estratos de la vida cubana: la esclavitud de los indios, la de los negros y la del presente de la redacción en el campo de trabajo forzado. La indignación de Arenas asume el tono de su imponente poderío verbal para producir un texto importante en la distinguida carrera de este joven narrador. [RRA]

5761 Argueta, Manlio. En el costado de la luz: poemas. San Salvador: Editorial Universitaria de El Salvador, 1968. 68 p. (Col. Contemporáneos; 5)

Transposiciones de recuerdos, amores y auto-observaciones que hacen vibrar la sensibilidad y la percepción poéticas: "ventanas nuevas," "flauta mágica," "sangre [que] hacia una red de poemas." [GY]

5762 Arráiz, Antonio. De la facilidad del canto. Caracas: Ediciones Con Textos, 1983. 43 p.: ill. (Plural: col. de poesía del PEN Club de Venezuela; 3)

Multiplicación de variaciones sobre el tema poético, referidas a diversas instancias de la escritura, sentida como problema por un hablante que reflexiona acerca del acto de producirla: la fragilidad o elusividad del poema, su sentido, las oscuridades o posibilidades de la palabra, etc. Interesante proyecto realizado con eficacia y rigor expresivos. [PL]

5763 Arroyo, Jorge. Para aprisionar nostalgias. San José: Editorial Costa Rica, 1984. 97 p.: ill.

En un lenguaje sencillo mas grávido de nostalgia, Arroyo procura inscribir la poesía en el cuerpo (su "piel de horas/ soledades de valle en tu pelo"), en el "abrir gavetas olvidadas," en las campanadas y otras instancias de la memoria involuntaria. [GY]

5764 Avilés Blonda, Máximo. Vía crucis. Santo Domingo: Ediciones Tolle Lege, 1983. 1 v.

Poesía religiosa, de sentido tono piadoso, pero sin grandes rasgos distintivos. Sobresale el estilo sobrio y clasicista que caracteriza la obra de este veterano poeta dominicano. [RRA]

5765 Barba Jacob, Porfirio. Antorchas contra el viento: poesía completa y prosa selecta. Compilación, prólogo y notas de Eduardo Santa. S.l.: Imprenta Departamental de Antioquia, 1983. 362 p.: ill.

Con apreciable criterio abarcador, dispone la poesía en seis partes. Tal división puede parecer insólita y desarticulada, pero se advierte en notas que responde a características de la obra y personalidad del autor:

sus poemas predilectos; juveniles; de madurez; sin fecha; rechazados, y prosas líricas. Una séptima parte recoge textos autobiográficos y autocríticos, más una exégesis polémica de *El hombre que parecía un caballo,* de R. Arévalo Martínez (ver item **5949**). [PL]

5767 Barnet, Miguel. Carta de noche. La Habana: Unión de Escritores y Artistas de Cuba, 1982. 102 p. (Manjuarí/poesía)

Se trata mayormente de un recorrido por la conciencia americana del poeta "de paseo" por Europa; una Europa fría y decadente ante los ojos nuevos del poeta-testigo. El resto son poemas de los más diversos temas y modos: dedicados, de ocasión, narrativos o vanguardistas. El talento de Barnet es indiscutible, pero todavía el poeta en él no compite favorablemente con el audaz narrador de sus novelas testimonio. Faltan aquí la fuerza y la coherencia de un universo poético. [RRA]

5768 Bartolomé, Hernán Efraín. Música solar. México: Joaquín Mortiz, 1984. 79 p.

El título de este poemario, ganador del Premio Nacional de Poesía, 1984, anticipa el uso de la sinestesia como recurso organizativo del texto para situar el amor, el tiempo, la soledad, la muerte. Versos libres cuya original disposición tipográfica marca un ritmo de alta tensión poética. [NK]

5769 Belli, Carlos Germán. Canciones y otros poemas. México: Premiá, 1982. 52 p. (Libros del bicho; 41)

Carlos Germán Belli es uno de los poetas más inquietantes en el actual escenario de la poesía hispanoamericana. Su obra no conoce retrocesos ni tentaciones temáticas de la actualidad: prosigue impertérrita, igual a sí misma, sin avanzar ni repetirse, en la variación permanente de sus grandes temas: la retórica de las vanidades humanas, el lugar marginal del poeta en el teatro de la modernidad, y las lecciones de vida sabia que la tradición clásica dicta para gozo de la existencia fugaz. Sobre esos ejes semánticos, este libro añade variaciones formales, que Belli explora con la paciencia artesanal de un clásico que, involuntariamente, ha hecho de su discurso una máscara (una persona discursiva) que es el espejo de la conciencia crítica y la reducción paródica. El eros y la muerte dialogan en la trama de una ceremonia de develamiento arqueológico, mortuoria y solemne; y a la vez desgarrada por su propia voluntad de vida, por su demanda de un diálogo más pleno. De esas tensiones íntimas de discreción clásica y desmedida barroca, de rebelión anti-burguesa y consolación artesanal, está hecha esta poesía, una de las voces que mejor encarna la crisis latinoamericana—el desastre de los discursos de Occidente frente a la vida deshumanizada, desposeída. [JO]

5770 Blanco, Alberto. Tras el rayo. Guadalajara, México: Cuarto Menguante, 1985. 76 p.

Poeta cuyos libros anteriores *Pequeñas historias del misterio ilustradas* (1978), *Giros de faros* (1979), *El largo camino hacia ti* (1980), y *Antes de nacer* (1983), le han dado un sitio destacado en la poesía mexicana de la última promoción. En este poemario vuelve a las formas tradicionales. Sigue la línea del rayo, símbolo de energía e iluminación en esta búsqueda de orígenes que conduce al equilibrio del cual surge un optimismo vital. [NK]

5771 Borges, Jorge Luis. Los conjurados. Buenos Aires: Alianza Editorial, 1985. 97 p.

Obra que enriquece la obra poética de este genio argentino. El material, en verso y prosa, está a la altura de las intenciones del autor: "Escribir un poema es ensayar una magia menor." [JG]

5772 Bracho, Coral. El ser que va a morir. México: Joaquín Mortiz, 1982. 61 p.

Segundo poemario, ganador del Premio Nacional de Poesía, 1981, de la joven poeta. La persona poética, desde una distancia intelectualizada, en diálogo con Sor Juana y Gorostiza, configura, a través de una imaginería barroca y sensual, los espacios del amor, el sitio del erotismo y del "ser que va a morir." [NK]

5773 Brandi, Alberto. En el fondo del bolsillo. Buenos Aires: Ediciones Carra, 1982. 92 p.

Un nuevo libro de un poeta interesante, de vena narrativa y sarcástica, y que combina efectos líricos sugerentes con desfachatez antipoética que impacta por su verosimilitud. El volumen es generoso en textos y proporciona un material que se presta para el placer de la lectura. [JG]

5774 Brega, Jorge. Poemas de ausencia. Buenos Aires: Nudos en la cultura argentina, 1984. 58 p.

Trabajo de extraordinario valor, donde se combina la maestría del poema breve con la intensidad sostenida del poema largo. Las fotografías y dibujos de Manuel Amigo amplían el horizonte significativo de un lenguaje que aparece bien logrado a la vez que novedoso. [JG]

5775 Cabañas, Esteban. Los cuatro lindes. S.l.: Ediciones NAPA, 1981. 74 p. (Serie Poesía; 1:3)

Poemario en cuatro partes, con poemas fechados en distintos períodos (1964–81). Poeta de la generación del 60, concibe la poesía como imprecación. El intenso tono lacerado, pero contenido, de un violento pesimismo, de una búsqueda de escapar la hipérbole de estar vivo, representa una voz diferente en la poesía paraguaya contemporánea: "Pongo en cruz estas manos/ para indicar caminos olvidados/ donde cuelgan los antiguos cadáveres/ de todos mis amigos." Otro título de este poema es *El tiempo, ese círculo* (1980). Importante voz lírica en la poesía contemporánea del Paraguay. [MGP]

5776 Cadenas, Rafael. Anotaciones. Caracas: Fundarte, 1983. 116 p. (Col. Delta; 13)

Cadenas ha hecho del poema en prosa y del fragmento una práctica que en este libro alcanza una gran eficacia. Su escritura crítica y reflexiva despliega una intensa vivencia del texto como asombro y problema. El autor señala que se trata no tanto de "poemas" como de "momentos, anotaciones" (ver item 5964). [PL]

5777 Cadícamo, Enrique D. Viento que lleva y trae. Ilustraciones de tapa e interiores de Arístides Rechain. 3a ed., nueva versión. Buenos Aires: Editorial Fraterna, 1983. 140 p.: ill.

Tercera edición de un libro publicado por primera vez en 1945, y que nos sumerge plenamente en lo mejor del tango. Los tonos oscilan entre la amargura del marginado hasta la bravuconada del matón o el sarcasmo del pícaro. Debe quedar como un clásico en su género. [JG]

5778 Calzadilla, Juan. Tácticas del vigía. Mérida, Venezuela: Ediciones Oxígeno, 1982. 62 p.

Lecciones bien asumidas del superrealismo, más una atenta recepción de la teoría contemporánea, hacen de este libro una variada y brillante aventura poética. Algunos textos atraen resonancias de escritores como Jean Tardieu, que invocan a un "lector cómplice:" son situaciones, teoremas o reflexiones de insólitos desarrollos. El despliegue imaginativo de Calzadilla (n. 1931) es tan notable como su exigente control del poema. [PL]

5779 Campos Cervera, Herib. Ceniza redimida. Edición e introducción de Miguel Angel Fernández. S.l.: Alcándara, 1982. 119 p.: ill. (Col. Poesía; 1)

Este poeta pertenecía al grupo Vy'a Raity, junto con Augusto Roa Bastos y Roque Molinari Laurin. Fue uno de los que participaron en la guerra civil de 1947 y tuvo que salir de su país, donde murió en 1953. Se lo considera precursor de una línea poética que incluye a Elvio Romero y Roa Bastos. Los textos de esta colección de poemas forman el vol. 1 de la colección Alcándara y datan de fines de la década del 30 y principios de la del 40. Los poemas están agrupados en siete secciones cuyos temas abarcan tres líneas temáticas predominantes: una visión agónica relacionada con la experiencia vital; poemas dedicados a exaltar el valor humano de un grupo de compañeros y precursores literarios; poemas políticos de liberación. Voz precursora de una línea poética que debe tenerse en cuenta para una historiografía de la poesía paraguaya contemporánea. [MGP]

5780 La Canción de los presos: poemas anónimos penal de libertad, Uruguay. Prólogo de Eduardo Galeano. Ilustraciones de José Luis Liard. Montevideo?: Grupo de Madres y Familiares de Procesados por la Justicia Militar, 1984? 71 p.: ill.

Este volumen de poemas anónimos que fueron escritos por los presos políticos del Penal de "Libertad" del Uruguay lleva un prólogo de Eduardo Galeano que encuadra la colección. Interesa este volumen particularmente a los que estudien la poesía política latinoamericana que cobra vigor durante la década de los 70. Fueron recopilados bajo condiciones extremas, en "hojillas de papel de fumar y a través de los barrotes" de las prisiones. Aunque varían en calidad poética, la colección es un aporte a la poesía política testimonial. [MGP]

5781 Cardenal, Ernesto. Tocar el cielo: poesías. Managua: Editorial Nueva Nicaragua, Ediciones Monimbó, 198? 60 p.: col. ill.

Poemas escritos alrededor de la libera-ción de Nicaragua que tocan todos los aspectos de la vida: lucha, ecología, amor, religión, etc. El lector no puede sino reconocer el *pathos* de esta visión ingenua—transposición del idealismo pitagórico-cristiano a una revolución cósmica—a la luz de las atrocidades de que se acusa a los contras en la actualidad. [GY]

5782 Carranza, Eduardo. Hablar soñando. Antología y estudio preliminar de Fernando Charry Lara. México: Fondo de Cultura Económica, 1983. 261 p. (Col. Tierra firme)

Selección de 10 libros de Carranza (1913–85), dispuesta cronológicamente y presentada por F. Charry Lara (ver item **5936**). La antología muestra la fidelidad a una poética de la armonía y de la claridad, desde *Canciones para iniciar una fiesta* (1936) hasta *Epístola mortal y otras soledades* (1975) (ver *HLAS 40:7055, HLAS 42:5701* y *HLAS 42:5913*). [PL]

5783 Carrera, Margarita. Toda la poesía de Margarita Carrera. Guatemala: Tipografía Nacional, 1984. 359 p. (Col. Guatemala; 17. Serie José Batres Montúfar; 3)

Su extensa obra poética se divide, *grosso modo*, en dos épocas. Si en la primera, marcada por la sencillez de raigambre juanramoniana, es capaz de decir: "Hermano/ yo tomo tu sangre/ y la incorporo a mi historia," en la segunda, de poesía barroca, maldita, hermética, declara que "Escribir es retorcerse los cabellos absolutos de deseo/ es hablar al pueblo que no escucha/ o escupe en tu palabra." [GY]

5784 Carreto, Héctor. La espada de San Jorge. México: Premiá, 1982. 90 p. (Libros del bicho; 49)

Carreto, poeta iconoclasta, trastoca los mitos clásicos y cristianos, los contemporiza y humaniza en este singular poemario de tono irónico y humorístico, ganador del Premio Carlos Pellicer, 1983. [NK]

5785 Castillo, Otto René. Informe de una injusticia. S.l.: Taller de Gráfica Popular, 1982. 89 p.: ill.

Precursor de la actual poesía revolucionaria, Castillo se destaca por la sencillez (todo lo contrario de Roque Dalton, su compañero durante su estadía en El Salvador) y la falta de retórica. Procura el rescate de lo popular, protesta contra los regímenes opresores y canta el amor a la patria. Su "arte

poética" es "la lucha por la construcción/
hermosa de nuestro planeta." [GY]

5786 Cea, José Roberto. Los pies sobre la
tierra de Preseas. San José: Editorial
Universitaria Centroamericana, 1985. 68 p.
(Col. Séptimo día. Premio Poesía)

Puesta en poesía (a menudo de manera
irónica) de la insurrección salvadoreña—
lucha, muerte, guerrilla, diáspora, vida cotidiana, etc.—por medio de confesiones, conversaciones, monólogos, sueños, testimonios,
y hasta parodias de anuncios publicitarios. La
obra de Cea es paradigma de la nueva poesía
salvadoreña que se vale de todos los géneros
posibles en su afán de registrar íntegramente
la realidad. [GY]

5787 Cedrón, José Antonio. De este lado y
del otro. 2a ed. México: Editorial
Univ. Autónoma de Puebla, 1983. 86 p. (Col.
Ficciones; 5)

Otro de los jóvenes poetas argentinos
de interés continental. Dividido en cuatro
partes, el volumen manifiesta unidad de tono,
"ritmo sostenido, vasta cultura" y clara conciencia de la disciplina poética. [JG]

5788 Charpentier, Jorge. Tú tan llena de mar
y yo con un velero. San José: Editorial
Costa Rica, 1985. 58 p.: ill.

El mar es metáfora de extensión in-
abarcable que suscita la conciencia de pe-
queñez y soledad y, a la vez, el ansia de
comunicación. Se apela al amor, pero en un
lenguaje que es "carencia [. . .] destino/ que
bifurca la tierra/ en [las] dos esquinas de esta
contradicción irresoluble." La poesía, viaje
marítimo, es la única opción: "Quita el
ancla/ Haz barca de mí." [GY]

5789 Cisneros, Antonio. Monólogo de la
casta Susana. Lima: Instituto Nacional
de Cultura, 1986. 1 v.

Cisneros demuestra en este nuevo
libro su extraordinaria destreza formal: con
un lenguaje vivo, hecho de coloquialismos
pero también de un ritmo agudo, controlado,
recobra al personaje de la Casta Susana para
levantar una sátira a los prejuicios de la clase
media, a los tabús eróticos, a las imágenes
convencionales de lo femenino. Cisneros está
muy cómodo, más lleno de recursos, cuando
escribe desde dentro de las mitologías bur-
guesas y modernas, erosionando el edificio de
lo establecido, lo ideológico, las ideas recibidas. A la vez, nunca abusa de su destreza y,

concluye el poema sin quizá haber explotado
todas sus posibilidades narrativas. Se comp-
lace no en la expansión sino en la concentración, y así lo prueban los otros textos de este
libro: sátiras de la vida moderna, escritas en
Alemania; poemas amorosos de sesgo contemplativo; homenajes a voces paralelas. Un
libro importante, maduro y lectura vivifi-
cante e imaginativa. [JO]

5790 Cisneros, Mina. Ego: poemas. Tegucigalpa: Cettna, 1980. 94 p.

Collection of poems of varying degrees
of interest with emphasis on love and the
family ("A Él," "Fiera"). Also includes reflections on a wide variety of subjects such as
disease and death ("Miedo") and social injustice ("Cosmos-Caos"). [R. Prieto]

5790a Cortés Bargalló, Luis. El circo silencioso. México: Fondo de Cultura Económica, 1985. 74 p.

Impulsador de la poesía en la ciudad
fronteriza de Tijuana, Cortés Bargalló ofrece
en éste su segundo libro una excelente
muestra de su quehacer poético. Variedad
temática y formal en una poesía cuyas imágenes derivadas ya de la naturaleza o de la
ciudad captan las inquietudes que surgen del
diario vivir. [NK]

5791 Coselino, Luis Alberto. Desde las
postrimerías de la razón. S.l.: Front,
1982. 53 p. (Col. Poesía; 4. Hispano-América)

Este poemario lleva una introducción
del ensayista peruano Xavier Abril que expresa: "Coselino renueva la poesía del Uruguay y de América. Su poesía es un signo
nuevo y fecundo." Poemas y textos en prosa
que trabajan el tema central de la alienación
junto a los pasos de la muerte y sus presagios
iluminados, "los sueños de la razón" trágica.
[MGP]

5792 Costantini, Humberto. Cuestiones con
la vida: antología poética. S.l.: Editorial Katún, 1982. 183 p. (Poesía centro y
suramericana; 3)

Se puede definir a este autor como un
escritor de competente y honesta antipoesía,
la que se advierte muy deudora de su voca-
ción narrativa. Esto hace esta antología un
libro de lectura agradable, que se repasa con
un interés que rara vez decae, y que permite
asimilar placenteramente un aspecto bastante logrado de una trayectoria literaria importante. [JG]

5793 Cuadra, Pablo Antonio. Canciones de pájaro y señora: poemas de Nicaragua. San José: Libro Libre, 1983. 166 p. (Obra poética completa; 1. Serie literaria)

El vol. 1 recrea lo vernáculo con la sencillez de las tradicionales canciones castellanas, ya lúdicamente ya narrativamente (como en el *Romancero gitano* de García Lorca). En vol. 2 plasma la identidad nicaragüense en un lenguaje que es todo amor a la naturaleza. [GY]

5794 Cuadra Mejía, Alberto. Lo que muy pocos escribirían. 2a ed., aum. con nuevos poemas. Granada, Nicaragua: Editorial Magys, 1982. 76 leaves (Col. Los Subterráneos)

Poesía apocalíptica inspirada en la Biblia que busca definir los límites temporales de lo metafísico. Además del derrumbe metafísico, Cuadra se fija en la miseria y el hambre en la "estrecha calle del estómago." [GY]

5795 Dalton, Roque. Poesía escogida. San José: Editorial Universitaria Centroamericana, 1983. 538 p. (Col. Sétimo día)

Se recogen en esta obra todos los volúmenes del primer poeta salvadoreño. Esta poesía parte de la experiencia y desemboca en la política ("Yo llegué a la política a través de la poesía") y vuelve a la experiencia renovada y recreada como arma crítica de todos los imperialismos, tanto los de la "nación ajena" como los de la "enajenación," aún en los países socialistas (ver "Taberna"). Así, se pretende ir más allá de las palabras a la acción. [GY]

5796 Dalton, Roque. Taberna y otros lugares. Santo Domingo: Ediciones de Taller, 1983. 214 p. (Biblioteca Taller; 146)

Quizás la más profunda expresión irónica de la poesía contemporánea, ironía que rescata de la angustia. El enunciante polemiza consigo mismo, cuestiona, duda de sus propios cimientos onto-ideológicos: "ironizar sobre el socialismo/ parece ser aquí un buen digestivo . . ." El ensayo de introducción, "Oficio de Poeta," por Pedro Conde Sturia, es de los mejores sobre Dalton. [GY]

5797 Delgado, Francisco. Canciones de exterminio. Heredia, Costa Rica: Editorial de la Univ. Nacional, 1984. 88 p.: ill. (Col. Barva. Serie Creación. Subserie Poesía)

"Canto a la Amargura" que proviene de los "sueños rotos" de este poeta "maldito"

que "blasfem[a] sin esperanza," y "grita en soledad." Rechaza solidaridades y entona una condena existencial radicalmente individualista que si bien parece caricatura, no obstante, entona con las corrientes poéticas actuales en Costa Rica. [GY]

5798 Dorio G., Jorge. Huésped de sí mismo. Buenos Aires: Editores Cuatro, 1982. 67 leaves. (Col. Ambigua selva)

Libro primero de un escritor joven que se muestra con voz propia, y que inicia su camino por los espacios de la "nueva escena" poética. [JG]

5799 Duverrán, Carlos Rafael. Tiempo grabajo. Heredia, Costa Rica: Editorial de la Univ. Nacional, 1980. 165 p. (Col. Barva. Serie Creación. Subserie Poesía)

Flujo fenoménico del tiempo y del espacio que invita al "infinito desierto del No/ que es la eternidad," a la indagación del Enigma con mayúscula. Lucha contra filisteos, esta poesía proclama una "insurrección personal," una abstracta "negación absoluta de la dictadura." Destacan los poemas epigramáticos al estilo clásico. [GY]

5800 Echavarren Welker, Roberto. La planicie mojada. Caracas: Monte Avila Editores, 1981. 76 p. (Col. Altazor)

Segundo poemario del talentoso poeta y crítico uruguayo (el primero: *El mar detrás del nombre*, 1966). Los 26 poemas que conforman este volumen configuran un universo poético de textos diversos y a veces dispares, que se han estructurado en campos semánticos que integran estas discrepancias. Un ejemplo es la presencia de lo cotidiano que se ve enriquecida por contextualizarse en ámbitos puramente creados, como bien es el caso del poema en nueve partes que da título a toda la colección ("La Planicie Mojada"): "Yo soy el hombre de mi destino . . . aquí en una casa/ sola, la técnica del bebé o la viudita/ . . ." [MGP]

5801 Escobar Galindo, David. Canciones para el álbum de Perséfone. Prólogo de Eugenio Florit. San Salvador: Ministerio de Educación, Subsecretaría de Cultura, Juventud y Deportes, Dirección General de Cultura, 1982. 74 leaves (Col. Poesía; 33)

Escobar Galindo escribe una poesía que se basta a sí misma. Su realidad se construye dentro del poema: "Mundo, te llevo/ preso en lo oscuro/ de mí mismo." Su poesía,

pues, es la revelación del *ontos*: "Y os-
curidad/ ardiendo en vilo." [GY]

5802 Escobar Galindo, David. Sonetos de la
sal y la ceniza: enero de 1979. San Salvador: El Autor, 1980. 1 v.

Poemas de amor al estilo clásico donde
el poeta comprueba su existencia en la búsqueda de una amante-palabra poética que
revele la "sitiada verdad del sentimiento."
Como en casi toda la producción de Escobar
Galindo, se esquiva aquí la sitiada verdad *sufrimiento* del pueblo. Le atrae más poetizar
abstracciones cuasi filosóficas: "Toda tu miel
pervive en la segura/ respiración del párrafo
absoluto." [GY]

5803 Eslava, Jorge. Ithaca. Lima?: Petroperú:
Ediciones Copé, 1983. 48 p., 4 leaves
of plates: ill.

El concurso literario Copé, auspiciado
por la empresa pública Petróleos del Perú,
sigue promoviendo nuevos valores poéticos,
y este tomo es uno de sus mejores hallazgos.
La última poesía peruana ha pasado del uso y
abuso del coloquio inmediatista y el repertorio existencial básico, a una dicción más
elaborada, aunque siempre vivificada por la
huella del habla temporal. Eslava maneja con
soltura ese coloquio testimonial, cálido, juvenil, pero al mismo tiempo preciso, formalmente ajustado y con una pulsión rítmica
fluida. No es aún libro suficientemente sistemático y de propuestas innovativas, pero sí
uno que anuncia a un poeta interesante, que
se mueve, con las voces de su generación,
lejos de sus cultistas maestros y más lejos de
sus vitalistas ejemplos inmediatos. [JO]

5804 Espina, Eduardo. Valores personales.
México: Ediciones La Máquina de
Escribir, 1983. 115 p.

Ha publicado dos libros de poemas:
Niebla de pianos (1975) y *Dadas las circunstancias* (1977). Este volumen incluye
textos escritos entre 1976–78. La sección 1a,
"Valores Personales," consiste en fragmentos
en prosa que fijan una poética y una ética del
acto de escribir. Hay una marcada orientación lúdica y hermética en el lenguaje poético de este volumen en el que la palabra se
define como "oscuro márgenes del blanco."
Se diferencian estos poemas en su forma de
los de la generación nacida en la década de
los 40, en que son tiradas que llegan a veces a
más de 100 versos. Los temas del poemario
son reflexiones líricas en diálogo con ele-

mentos de la cultura occidental: "Los ori-
ficios de la razón (podría pensar en Emily
Dickinson)," "Canto a ti mismo (A ti, Walt
Whitman)," "Una sustancia organiza en las
vestiduras," "(Conde de Lotremon, de viejo
océano, capa no usaba)," etc. Importante
poeta de la nueva generación nacida en los
años 50. [MGP]

5805 Espinosa B., Félix Pedro. Ideal frus-
trado. Estelí, Nicaragua: Editorial
Unión Cardoza, 1982. 87 p.

Interesa este libro no por la calidad de
la poesía sino por la lucha ideológica que se
libra en él. Predomina la típica retórica de la
poesía revolucionaria: abajo yanquis, amor a
la patria, admiración a Sandino y al Che, solidaridad con el pueblo, etc. Los últimos tres
poemas, empero, son una impugnación del
gobierno sandinista por la imposición de
los C[omités] de D[efensa] S[andinista] y el
desplazamiento de los indios miskitos. [GY]

5806 Fierro, Enrique. Fuera de lugar. México: Premiá Editora, 1982. 111 p.
(Libros del bicho; 36)

Poemario en cuatro secciones que
incluye textos escritos entre 1973–75. Continúa la experimentación con los límites del
lenguaje poético, como en su poesía anterior,
junto a la insistencia de nombrar poéticamente la realidad concreta. Continúa la
cuidadosa reconstrucción sintáctica como
procedimiento para enfatizar la autonomía
de la palabra que es equivalente a los juegos
espaciales de la página en blanco donde se
elabora el poema. En Fierro se ve no rupturas
entre poemario y poemario, sino más bien un
programa poético coherente que se persigue
con notable disciplina. [MGP]

5807 Figueroa, José Angel. Noo Jork. Traducción de Víctor Fernández Fragoso.
San Juan: Instituto de Cultura Puertorriqueña, 1981. 81 p.: ill. (Serie literatura hoy;
1981)

Estos poemas, traducidos, o más bien
interpretados por el malogrado poeta Víctor
Fernández Fragoso establecen un sentido
puente de correspondencias con la versión en
inglés. No es poesía depurada, pero su fuerza
y frescura le confieren un interés especial a
esta memoria lírica de la emigración. [RRA]

5808 Fijman, Jacobo. Obra poética. Buenos
Aires: La Torre Abolida, 1983. 165 p.:
ill.

Emocionante recopilación de los poemas, desde *Molino rojo* a *Estrella de la mañana*, de un mito literario argentino. Recluido la mayor parte de su vida en un hospicio, su poesía respira inspiración y fanatismo que pueden llegar a ser contagiosos. Contiene varios prólogos de interés y una útil cronología. [JG]

5809 Flores, Miguel Angel. Saldo ardiente. México: Editorial Villicaña, 1985. 95 p. (Col. verde de poesía)

Más reciente poemario de uno de los mejores poetas de la última promoción en México. Concisa y cuidadosa construcción verbal de tono reflexivo. Indagación sobre la desintegración actual que sufre el hombre y el espacio que habita. [NK]

5810 Gaitán Durán, Jorge. Si mañana despierto. Cúcuta, Colombia: Lotería de Cúcuta, Instituto Colombiano de Cultura, 1983. 93 p. (Col. Regionales Norte de Santander)

Se reedita el libro de 1961, incluido en 1975 en la recopilación *Obra literaria* (ver *HLAS 40:7071*). El amor y la muerte son motivos centrales en la poesía de Gaitán Durán (1924–62), y el segundo insinúa en algunos textos inquietantes intuiciones premonitorias (ver item **5982**). El volumen reactualiza la presencia poética del animador de tareas culturales tan significativas como *Mito* (1955–62; ver item **5922**). [PL]

5811 Garduño, Raúl. Los danzantes espacios estatuarios. San Andrés Tuxtla, México: Publicaciones del Gobierno del Estado de Chiapas, 1982. 108 p., 1 leaf of plates (Col. Libros de Chiapas)

Edición póstuma de este reconocido poeta chiapaneco que muere prematuramente en 1980. Comprende: 1) una selección de poemas basados en manuscritos proporcionados por la familia; y 2) una recopilación de poemas sueltos. Poesía de desahogo cuyas imágenes de desintegración y caos nos sitúan en un mundo de desamparo "que cifra el colapso y la rosa de los destiempos." [NK]

5812 Gelman, Juan. La junta luz: Oratorio a las Madres de Plaza y Mayo. Buenos Aires: Libros de Tierra Firme, 1985. 62 p.: ill. (Col. de poesía Todos bailan; 6)

Bello canto lírico donde se combinan los efectos líricos con severos golpes dramáticos, alrededor de un asunto que ha conmovido a la patria del autor en los últimos años. Es poesía de la más alta calidad, muy gelmaniana y alejada de todo panfletarismo. [JG]

5813 Gerbasi, Vicente. Edades perdidas. Caracas: Monte Avila Editores, 1981. 61 p. (Col. Altazor)

El hablante de estos poemas recorre un vasto escenario inventado que lo lleva hacia los orígenes, hacia "una era sudorosa del mundo" (p. 7). Las diversas instancias de su errar configuran una aventura poética novedosa: se sugieren los recuerdos de una "memoria ancestral," ordenados y transformados por el trabajo de la imaginación (ver *HLAS 42:5749* y *HLAS 44:5686*). [PL]

5814 Girri, Alberto. Lírica de percepciones. Buenos Aires: Editorial Sudamericana, 1983. 122 p.

Continuación de la vasta y rica obra poética del autor. Libro escrito con maestría, es probablemente uno de sus más intensos textos líricos. Además de la sección que da título al libro, están "Asediar en lo Escrito" y "G.M. Hopkins: Cuatro Poemas." [JG]

5815 Girri, Alberto. Monodías. Buenos Aires: Editorial Sudamericana, 1985. 123 p.

El lenguaje de Girri ha ido asumiendo cada vez más una tonalidad irónica que no se contamina en ningún momento de escepticismo, que hubiera sido la salida fácil. Así es este sorprendente libro que impresiona como la palabra de un gran maestro de la disciplina poética. No hay nada de sencillo en estos textos hechos con toda la riqueza del idioma y toda la audacia del pensamiento. [JG]

5816 González Real, Osvaldo. Memoria del exilio. Asunción: Alcándara, 1984. 100 p. (Col. Poesía; 22)

Una muestra interesante de una línea poética diferente en el marco de la poesía paraguaya, este volumen ofrece seis secciones que trabajan temas y formas varias: los mitos de América indígena: "Génesis I," "Génesis II," "Elegía de Chilam Balam," entre otros; Una serie de "haikai;" otra serie titulada "Esotérica: Poemas de Amor, el Exilio y el Viaje a Itaca." La última sección ofrece traducciones de poemas de T.S. Eliot, Dylan Thomas, Ezra Pound. [MGP]

5817 Güiraldes, Ricardo. Poemas últimos. Ilustraciones de Nani Capurro. Buenos Aires: La Torre Abolida, 1984. 113 p.: ill.

Más conocido como novelista, fue también un poeta adelantado a su tiempo, antecesor del vanguardismo en algunos de sus aspectos más líricos como la desenvoltura irónica de la imagen. Aunque no todo en esta selección es propiamente poesía, el material incluído es rico y, desde luego, valioso para completar la imagen de Güiraldes. Contiene tres conjuntos: "Poemas Solitarios," "Poemas Místicos" y "El Sendero." [JG]

5818 Hernández, Francisco A. Mar de fondo. México: Joaquín Mortiz, 1983. 82 p.

Excelente poemario, ganador del Premio Nacional de Poesía, 1982. Dividido en tres partes: "Postales," poemas cortos, algunos hai-kai, que captan el pulso de lugares recorridos; "Imposibilidad de Cornejas," sonetos de derrumbe y desencanto; y "Mar de Fondo," poemas en prosa desde el delirio. [NK]

5819 Hernández, Luis. Obra poética completa. Prólogo de Javier Sologuren. Edición y notas de Ernesto Mora. Recopilación de Nicolas Yerovi. 2a ed., ampliada con nuevos textos. Lima: Punto y Trama, 1983. 586 p.: col. ill.

Junto a Antonio Cisneros y Rodolfo Hinostroza, Luis Hernández es una de las voces poéticas de la generación peruana del 60 más vivas e interesantes. Como Javier Heraud, Hernández murió muy joven (en 1977) y dejó casi toda su obra dispersa, manuscrita en cuadernos que regalaba a sus amigos. Médico de profesión, educado en la Univ. Católica, becado en Alemania, Hernández fue un poeta anti-profesional, muy poco académico, y más bien iconoclasta y radicalmente autoirónico. La poesía fue para él un ritual perpetuador del juego, el humor y la juventud. Su estilo parte del acto poético integrador: palabra, dibujo, música y acción son una trama sin forma final, una anotación dispersa, instantánea, fugaz. Hernández podría haber elaborado una teoría del juego como acción ética y estética, pero aunque era un crítico y satírico de los estilos, no le interesaba justificar o fundamentar su obra. Se consideraba un poeta casual, inspirado y seguramente irresponsable. No obstante, su obra demuestra la pasión y la inteligencia de su constante indagación poética. A partir de Juan Ramón Jiménez, y luego de José María Eguren y Martín Adán, Luis Hernández fue un purista de lo cotidiano, un poeta que llevó la poesía a su barrio; y que prolongó los

juegos adolescentes en un culto dionisíaco de la inocencia extraviada. [JO]

5820 Herrera Velado, Francisco. Mentiras y verdades: leyendas. 2a ed. San Salvador: Ministerio de Educación, Dirección de Publicaciones, 1977. 261 p.

Paradigmática muestra de la literatura costumbrista de El Salvador, estas 15 "leyendas" o historias versificadas (editadas por primera vez en 1923) hacen burla de los afanes aristocráticos en boga entre las clases pudientes a principios de siglo. [GY]

5821 Istaru, Ana. La estación de fiebre. San José: Editorial Universitaria Centroamericana, 1983. 52 p. (Col. Séptimo día)

Sin duda, la voz más fresca de la actual poesía costarricense, Istaru elabora unos poemas eróticos que erizan la piel del lector. Late aquí un feminismo que rehace el mundo a la medida del cuerpo femenino y se lo ofrece al hombre como defensa y como seducción para un nuevo ser: "Porque tomo la punta de mis senos, / . . ./ este himen puntual/ . . ./ lo mato y lo remato/ con mi sexo abierto y rojo . . ." [GY]

5822 Jaramillo Levi, Enrique. Cuerpos amándose en el espejo, 1978–1980. Dibujos de Gustavo Aceves. México: Editorial Katún, 1982. 62 p.: ill. (Col. Libro de bolsillo. Serie Arte-poesía; 15)

Hablante voyeur y partícipe se instala en el deseo para elaborar una poética de la mirada y del cuerpo. Poesía del erotismo y erotismo de la palabra en este poemario del recopilador de *Poesía erótica de México, 1889–1979* (1982). [NK]

5823 Jolly, Paulo de. Louis XIV. Río Piedras, P.R.: Ediciones Mairena 1983. 69 [i.e. 36] leaves.

Durante el modernismo, los reyes de Francia solían poblar la poesía hispanoamericana del período. Muchas décadas después, Luis XIV reaparece como protagonista de este curiosímo libro de Paulo de Jolly, para dialogar con sus amantes, consigo mismo y con otros personajes ligados a la corte. Pero el lenguaje de Jolly nada tiene de modernista. El poeta se dedica a una minuciosa y progresiva desarticulación del lenguaje, mediante la ampliación de los blancos que separan a las palabras en la página, la eliminación de las tildes y de la puntuación, el entrecruce de vocablos extranjeros, y algunas dislocaciones sintácticas y morfológicas, en un proceso análogo al de Huidobro en los últimos cantos de *Altazor*. Este homenaje al Rey Sol es sin duda uno de los textos más interesantes y novedosos de la joven poesía chilena. [OH]

5824 Juárez, Salvador Antonio. Puro guanaco. 2a ed. San Salvador: Abril Uno, 1983. 52 p.: ill. (Col. Los de acá; 1)

En este poemario desigual se destacan los poemas satíricos en que, en lenguaje coloquial y de referencias costumbristas, se burla de los lugares comunes de la vida cotidiana. El poema homónimo del título es una respuesta satírica a la acusación de que en El Salvador no exista poesía ni cultura. [GY]

5825 Kozer, José. Bajo este cien. México: Fondo de Cultura Económica, 1983. 140 p. (Col. Tierra firme)

La poesía epigramática de este poeta cubano de origen checo y polaco es un intento de traducir el pasado, sobre todo el de una niñez exuberantemente multiétnica, a un activo y vigente presente del indicativo. Es poesía abrupta, obstinadamente descriptiva y anti-lírica. Las reiteradas frases parentéticas intentan poner al descubierto todos los intersticios de la experiencia que la accidentada percepción pudo recoger. En el fondo subyace la imagen ancestral de la familia, que el poeta rescata sin caer nunca en la nostalgia ni en la melancolía. [RRA]

5826 Kupchik, Christian. Jonás y los sueños diurnos. Dibujos de Ignaci Morató. Buenos Aires: Corregidor, 1983. 70 p.: ill.

Este es uno de los textos importantes de la nueva poesía en Hispanoamérica. Va por el camino de una escena poética abierta a las experiencias inéditas creadas por la explosión política y cultural de los últimos años. Contiene excelentes ilustraciones de Ignaci Morató y Sánchez. Los títulos de las cuatro partes que forman el libro son sugerentes: "Jonás y Aquellos Lejanos Puertos del Otoño," "Islas," "Las Revelaciones del Vampiro" y "Jonás y las Entrañas de Europa tras los Cristales." [JG]

5827 Langagne, Eduardo. Donde habita el cangrejo. México: Premiá, 1982. 104 p. (Libros del bicho; 30)

La nota distintiva de este poemario, ganador del Premio Casa de las Américas, 1980, es la diversidad. Distintos temas y estilos integran esta poesía singular cuya elaboración de una realidad vital y dinámica

no esconde sus lazos con aquella de Sabines, D. Tomás, Gelman, y Dalton. [NK]

5828 Llerena, Edith. Canciones para la muerte. Madrid: Cuadernos Playor, 1982. 1 v. (Nueva poesía)

Este poemario de esta escritora cubana que reside en España asume un tono urgente y desgarrado. El tremendismo infernal de su visión de la muerte recuerda las Danzas de la Muerte medievales, como lo nota el prologuista Armando Alvarez Bravo, pero falta aquí el fondo metafísico o escatológico que caracteriza esa poesía. Es un libro visceral, donde cada texto está tejido alrededor de un sentimiento recogido en una palabra que da inicio al poema (ira, envidia, nostalgia, amor, dolor, discordia, celos, rencor, etc.), y en cada poema ese sentimiento se convierte en un poderoso y persistente rival. La dramatización de cada una de estas "luchas" es tan visual que las tangencias inmediatas vienen del arte gráfico: Goya, El Bosco y Gustavo Doré vienen a la imaginación durante la lectura de este intenso texto. [RRA]

5829 Lombardi, Lyda C. Las flores de Lyda: reflexiones. Buenos Aires: Celtia, 1983. 157 p.: ill.

Curiosidad poética de gran ingenio e ironía. Se trata de una colección de fragmentos líricos, agudezas y pensamientos en un nivel superior a lo acostumbrado en el género. Hay aquí ingenuidad a la vez que desfachatez de pueblo inteligente. [JG]

5830 López, Nila. El brocal amarillo. Asunción: Asedio, 1984? 132 p. (Col. La Garza; 12)

Este poemario de una joven poeta paraguaya va introducido por Josefina Plá, quien marca como acontecimiento importante la emergencia de voces femeninas en el discurso lírico actual del Paraguay. El tema central es el amor como experiencia que transcurre entre lo trivial de lo cotidiano y el proyecto inalcanzable de lo perfecto: ". . . Este vacío/ termina/ allí donde te habitas/ y donde yo me miro/ para encontrar mi espejo . . ." Aunque es su primer libro, es ilustrativo de la joven poesía del Paraguay. [MGP]

5831 Manjarrez, Héctor. Canciones para los que se han separado. México: Era, 1985. 83 p.

Poesía de tono coloquial del ganador del Premio Villaurrutia por su libro de cuen-

tos *No todos los hombres son románticos*
(1984). En este muy comentado poemario insiste en reconstruir la experiencia del amor y
la sexualidad de su generación. Voz anti-
sentimental que revive el dolor y el placer de
esa experiencia desde el sitio solitario de la
separación. [NK]

5832 Maquieira, Diego. La Tirana. Santiago:
Edición Tempus Tacendi, 1983. 57 p.
Serie de poemas dispuestos en secuencias cinematográficas, cuyo trasfondo es una
leyenda nortina del siglo XVI. La Tirana era
una princesa inca que viajó con Diego de
Almagro al Desierto de Atacama y que después se estableció por su cuenta en un
pequeño poblado de la zona y lo gobernó
en forma cruel y despótica. En ese pueblo,
bautizado con el apodo de la princesa, se realiza todos los años una celebración pagano-
religiosa muy popular en Chile: la Fiesta de
la Tirana. Pero por una curiosa forma de desplazamiento, la Virgen que es celebrada allí
por los fieles se llama Virgen de la Tirana,
provocándose con ello ciertos extraños en-
trecruces. En el texto de Maquieira se escucha una voz, que tanto puede ser la de la
Tirana primitiva como la de la Virgen, ape-
lando a sus amantes españoles en un lenguaje
desfachatado, semejante al que emplean los
adolescentes chilenos, y mezclando, sin
ningún temor al anacronismo, personajes y
situaciones del siglo XVI con personajes y situaciones del siglo XX. Uno de los libros más
complejos e inquietantes de la nueva poesía
chilena. [OH]

5833 Marechal, Leopoldo. Poesía: 1924–
1950. Edición y prólogo de Pedro Luis
Barcia. Buenos Aires: Ediciones del 80, 1984.
309 p.
Marechal elabora un proyecto lírico
ambicioso que a veces se realiza en sus textos. Este libro permite al lector constituir su
propia antología. Tras un prólogo útil, crítico,
informativo, siguen los libros poéticos de
Marechal, desde *Días como flechas* (1926),
pasando por sus *Poemas australes* (1937),
hasta llegar a *Canto de San Martín* (1950).
Se agregan poemas no incluidos en libro,
muchos de los cuales son meras curiosidades.
[JG]

5834 Martín, Carlos. Epitafio de piedra y
cielo:—y otros poemas. Presentación
de Eduardo Carranza. Bogotá: Instituto Caro
y Cuervo, 1984. 139 p., 1 leaf of plates: port.
(Serie La Granada entreabierta; 35)

E. Carranza define el temple de ánimo
de este poesía al presentarla como "palabra
funeral." La modalidad expresiva piedracie-
lista se manifiesta con plenitud en el espacio
abierto por la evocación, y en el cual el epitafio cambia de signo: no es la concentración
lapidaria sino el desarrollo del retrato de poetas del conocido grupo literario. [PL]

5835 Martínez, Juan Luis. La nueva novela.
2a ed. Santiago: Ediciones Archivo,
1985. 147 p.: ill. (some col.)
Segunda edición (la primera es de
1977) de este libro capital de la neovanguardia chilena, cuyo autor, J.L. Martínez, es
indiscutiblemente el fundador de dicha tendencia. A pesar de su título, el libro no tiene
nada que ver con el género novelesco tal
como lo conocemos. Más bien sobrepasa la
barrera de los géneros, al operar con audaces
intertextualidades, trasgresiones tipográficas,
imágenes visuales y discursos no literarios,
en una verdadera fiesta de la imaginación y
de la inteligencia. ¿Poesía? Por supuesto.
Y quizás en el sentido más originario del
término. [OH]

5836 Martínez Maldonado, Manuel. Palm
Beach blues. Río Piedras, P.R.: Editorial Antillana, 1985. 40 p.
Disección agridulce del culto al poder
adquisitivo. Desde el espacio central de una
exclusiva zona turística del sur de los Estados Unidos, el autor, un médico y poeta
puertorriqueño, reconstruye ese tejido de su-
perficialidades en el que la vulgaridad y la ex-
quisitez se disuelven para convertirse en la
versión elitista de la cultura del "mainstream." El ojo poético transita entre la fas-
cinación y el desengaño, y un melancólico
sentido del humor es el hilo conductor entre
uno y otro poema. [RRA]

5837 Martínez Rivas, Carlos. La insurrección solitaria. 3a ed. Managua: Editorial Nueva Nicaragua, 1982. 172 p.
(Biblioteca popular sandinista; 7)
A pesar de sus dejos un tanto existen-
cialista-vanguardistas ("Hacer un poema era
planear un crimen perfecto"), este libro sigue
teniendo vigencia. Poesía rebelde y persona-
lista, no a la manera actual en Nicaragua (ver
Talleres de Poesía, items **5714** y **5751**), sino
con un profundo conocimiento de la cultura.
Esmerado trabajador de la palabra exacta.
[GY]

5838 Mayorga, Jesús. Historias de amor:

poesía y narrativa. San Salvador: Ediciones Nosotros, 1983. 62 p.

Mayorga inscribe los casi inefables momentos cotidianos del amor y la "perplej[idad] de la existencia" según una poética que equipara realidad y poesía. Alienta este breve volumen una voz sencilla que por momentos se exalta y encuentra en el destinatario (que ella misma se construye) fulgurantes intuiciones que ahuyentan las "sombras" que pesan sobre el existir. [GY]

5839 Melendes, Joseramón. La casa de la forma. Prólogo de Cintio Vitier. Río Piedras, P.R.: Ediciones qeAse, 1986. 1 v.

En este libro, confeccionado meticulosamente en edición limitada por el mismo autor, Melendes explora las posibilidades del soneto, que se convierte aquí en emblema de la forma y sus proliferaciones. Escritos en ese estilo tan peculiar del autor, donde se intenta inscribir el habla popular en los moldes tradicionales del clasicismo, y redactados con la a veces exasperante escritura fonética que Melendes ha convertido en fuente de su poética de la naturalización del artificio, la colección de sonetos conforma un espacio poético delirante. Cintio Vitier es el autor del brillante prólogo, que Melendes coloca como epílogo. Se trata de un texto inusitado y ambicioso, probablemente destinado a ocupar un lugar prominente en la nueva poesía hispanoamericana. [RRA]

5840 Meneghetti, Cristina. Estación al norte. Puebla, México: Premiá Editora, 1982. 92 p. (Libros del bicho; 47)

Es el quinto poemario (*Intento*, 1968; *Juego abierto*, 1972; *Tiempo fiero*, 1976; *Gestos y maneras*, 1978) de este poeta de la generación uruguaya de los 70. Este volumen contiene poemas breves que oscilan entre los cinco versos hasta los ocho o nueve, sin título, sin mayúsculas, en desafío del blanco de la página que textualizan la experiencia amorosa y la idea del amor. Este poemario tiene dos partes: "Estación al Norte" y "Signos Irreverencias." Su poesía difiere de la de los poetas de su generación que muestran una preocupación particular por la textualización de la experiencia humana que supere las limitaciones del miedo y del terror, y recupere la realidad histórica del Uruguay. [MGP]

5841 Meneses, Vidaluz. El aire que me llama. Managua: Edición conjunta de la Unión de Escritores de Nicaragua:

IMELSA, 1982. 83 p. (Edición Primavera popular; 2)

Aquejan a los poemas "revolucionarios" los clisés archiconocidos. No obstante, la mayoría de los poemas—recuerdos familiares, discursos íntimos dirigidos a familiares y amigos, otros poemas de viajes—logran una auténtica nota lírica si bien matizada por un lenguaje sencillo y conversacional. [GY]

5842 Mieses, Juan Carlos. Urbi et orbi. Santiago: Taller, 1984. 74 p.: ill. (Col. Poesía; 5)

Ganador de uno de los premios de poesía más prestigiosos de la República Dominicana, este poemario de un joven poeta se destaca por la elaboración de un verso limpio y sereno, que tiende hacia lo abstracto, hacia lo diluido y lo cósmico. Hay aquí visiones de la ciudad colonial, versos de amor y otros más metafísicos, pero en todos resalta cierta frialdad marmórea. Le falta a esta poesía más latido, más vitalidad. Premio Siboney 1983. [RRA]

5843 Mistral, Gabriela. Reino: poesía dispersa e inédita, en verso y prosa. Recopilación y prólogo de Gastón von dem Bussche. Valparaíso, Chile: Ediciones Universitarias de Valparaíso, Univ. Católica de Valparaíso, 1983. 223 p., 8 leaves of plates: bibl., facsim., ports.

El compilador rescata textos en prosa y en verso de Gabriela Mistral, que no habían sido incluidos en sus libros fundamentales, y los reintegra a los siguientes ciclos poéticos: 1) Ciclo 1915–25, de *Desolación*; 2) Ciclo 1925–40, de *Tala*; y 3) Ciclo 1941–57, del *Poema de Chile*. Interesante trabajo que permite visualizar los textos de la Mistral en sus contextos naturales. [OH]

5844 Molinari, Ricardo E. El desierto viento delante. Buenos Aires: Emecé Editores, 1982. 89 p.

Emocionante libro de un clásico argentino que tiene toda la fuerza de un réquiem. El tono queda marcado desde el primer verso: "Oh, muerte!, te veo descender con tu ropa obscura . . ." El propio poeta define su libro en una nota: "Estos trabajos, con los demás, son las últimas paciencias que suelta mi mano." Esta atmósfera de últimas palabras traspasa todos estos textos, incluso los dolorosamente sencillos como "La Cucaña." [JG]

5845 Mondragón, Sergio. Pasión por el oxígeno y la luna. Dibujos de Felipe

Ehremberg. Puebla, México: Premiá, 1982. 72 p.: ill. (Libros del bicho; 33)

El hablante rehusa ver el mundo circundante desde el hábito que opaca la mirada. Enamorado de la belleza, la busca, y en ese recorrido transforma y renueva la percepción del lector-cómplice. Mondragón, fundador de la revista *El Corno Emplumado*, continúa su experimentación formal en este poemario de metáforas e imágenes insólitas que dan constancia de su virtuosidad poética. [NK]

5846 Monge, Carlos Francisco. Los fértiles horarios. San José: Editorial Costa Rica, 1983. 107 p. (Libros de poesía; 15)

Indagación lírica de la historia, colectiva y personal, grabada en las cosas, oculta en las sombras, dable en la desnudez del cuerpo herido: "Para llegar a ti/ mi cuerpo es la memoria de tus pasos." Si bien a veces la herida tomó la forma de guerra, ésta sólo tiene valor trascendental y poco se refiere a la actual condición centroamericana. [BY]

5847 Montejo, Eugenio. Trópico absoluto. Caracas: Cromptip: Fundarte, 1982. 68 p. (Col. Delta; 10)

Libro de rigor ejemplar, en el que Montejo (n. 1938) continúa el tratamiento de una temática de dimensiones míticas. Su poesía se propone como rescate de otro tiempo y como refundación de otros espacios en el lenguaje, mediante un trabajo escritural extremadamente cuidadoso de los procedimientos intensificadores de la tensión lírica: por ejemplo, la fluencia rítmica del texto, lograda con singular sabiduría constructiva (ver *HLAS 44:5708* y *HLAS 46:5851*). [PL]

5848 Morávito, Fabio. Lotes baldíos. México: Fondo de Cultura Económica, 1984. 69 p.

Nacido en Egipto de padres italianos, Morávito radica en México desde 1976, y con este su primer libro, merecedor del Premio Carlos Pellicer 1985, ha conquistado el territorio de la poesía. A través de versos cuya regularidad métrica de arte menor proviene de las canciones populares y los romances, busca recuperar un yo poético comunal. Encuentra la voz del nómada que somos todos en nuestro tránsito por la tierra, y nos lleva a los simbólicos "lotes baldíos," áreas de despojos o fronteras por explorar. [NK]

5849 Moreno Jimeno, Manuel. Centellas de la luz: poesía, 1934–1980. Barcelona,

Spain: Ediciones Rondas, 1981. 258 p., 1 leaf of plates: ill.

Moreno Jimeno es uno de los grandes paradigmas de la fidelidad poética en América Latina. Desde los años 30, en que formó parte de la vanguardia activista junto a César Moro y José María Arguedas, Moreno Jimeno ha dedicado a la poesía un afán de perfección poco común; y ha explorado la experiencia poética con precisión, economía y lucidez. La suya es una poesía esencialista sobre una experiencia tangible y diaria (no es un poeta intelectual sino uno vital); de modo que si la precisión y lucidez del poema evocan a Valery, la energía existencial convoca a Claudel. Poesía severa pero resonante, que gira en torno a un repertorio simbolista de imágenes (la sangre, el fuego), está emparentada con la poética visionaria, con la palabra simbolizadora de San Juan de la Cruz y la palabra sustantiva de René Char. En esa filiación, Moreno Jimeno ha levantado su obra solitaria y solidaria, hecha de convicciones y emociones sustentadas en la pasión del diálogo poético. Este tomo de su poesía completa merece ser mejor conocido y estudiado. [JO]

5850 Muñoz, Rafael José. Obra poética: selección del Círculo de los 3 soles. Prólogo de J. Liscano. Caracas: Ediciones Centauro/81, 1981. 388 p., 1 leaf of plates: ill.

Textos de una personalidad singular, a la que conviene la definición de "visionario," por la extrañeza de su mundo y por su paroxismo expresivo. La escritura compleja y fascinante de Muñoz (1928–81)—"cábalas," "entrañables ejercicios de visión," p. 231— es acertadamente descrita y situada por J. Liscano en un prólogo indispensable (p. VII–LXVI; ver item **5982**). [PL]

5851 Naranjo, Carmen. Mi guerrilla. Notas de José Coronel Urtecho. San José: Editorial Universitaria Centroamericana, 1984. 103 p. (Col. Séptimo día)

Largo poema profético a lo Apollinaire o Huidobro que impugna la existencia pequeña burguesa, especialmente la comodidad y conveniencia que se escudan en los símbolos. En contraste, solidariza con los héroes que han cambiado el mundo: Gandhi, Ho Chi Minh, el Che, Mao, Fidel. La poesía, pues, es una guerrilla paralela. [GY]

5852 Orozco, Olga. La noche a la deriva. México: Fondo de Cultura Económica, 1983. 55 p. (Col. Tierra firme)

Una voz poética existencial, que se extiende en respiraciones hondas, ritmos de pie amplio y métrica versicular. Este es uno de sus últimos libros. Olga Orozco está considerada entre los mejores poetas hispanoamericanos actuales. [JG]

5853 Orozco, Olga. Poemas. Medellín, Colombia: Depto. de Bibliotecas, Univ. de Antioquia, 1984. 104 p.: ill.

Aunque Olga Orozco debe ser conocida en la integridad de su obra poética, este libro puede ser una forma práctica de acercarse a esta gran poeta argentina. La selección es aceptable y la cantidad de textos, generosa. [JG]

5854 Oviedo, Jorge Luis. La muerte más aplaudida; Aproximaciones. Tegucigalpa: Itzam na, 1983. 92 p.

Aproximaciones contiene poemas prometedores por la frescura de la voz que indaga cosas y vida cotidiana directamente, sin retóricas. En los mejores Oviedo logra ritmos rápidos y nerviosos que, si bien son refractarios al lujo de la palabra, no obstante impelen al lector a enfrentarse a los hechos y a solidarizar con el hombre sencillo. [GY]

5855 Palés Matos, Luis. Obras: 1914–1959. t. 1, Poesía. t. 2, Prosa. Edición, prólogo, cronología, notas y variantes de Margot Arce de Vásquez. Introducción de Federico de Onís. Río Piedras: Editorial de la Univ. de Puerto Rico, 1984. 2 v.: bibls., indexes.

La esperada edición de la obra completa de Palés, a cargo de una de las más distinguidas estudiosas de su obras, es una ampliación de la edición de *Poesía y prosa escogidas* que preparara anteriormente para la Biblioteca Ayacucho Margot Arce de Vásquez. El criterio editorial ha sido el de la mayor inclusividad posible, a riesgo de darle cabida a algunos poemas que el autor probablemente hubiese rechazado por ser obviamente poemas de juventud o de principiante. La editora ha preferido ofrecerle al lector el corpus más completo posible de la poesía y la prosa palesianas, organizado con una cuidadosa cronología de la redacción y de la revisión de cada texto. [RRA]

5856 Parra, Nicanor. Hojas de Parra. Edición y notas de David Turkeltaub. Santiago: Ediciones Ganymedes, 1985. 141 p.: ill. (Col. de poesía Ganymedes; 11–12)

Compilación de textos del antipoeta chileno escritos a partir de 1969 y que previa-

mente sólo habían aparecido en revistas y en hojas sueltas. Incluye una serie de antipoemas, algunos poemas que siguen el modelo de la poesía popular chilena y unos pocos ejercicios experimentales poco convincentes. Entre los antipoemas destacan dos: "Los Profesores" y "El Antilázaro;" el resto poco o nada agrega a lo ya realizado por Parra. Irónicamente, el mejor texto del libro y verdadera pieza de antología, "El Hombre Imaginario," está mucho más cerca de la poesía que de la antipoesía. [OH]

5857 Pedroni, José. Obra poética. Buenos Aires?: Ediciones del 80, 1982. 2 v.: bibl., ill.

Dos tomos suculentos de poesía fácil (en el buen sentido de la palabra) que frecuentemente se lee con gusto y que se va encontrando con felices hallazgos de expresión. Este es otro meritorio esfuerzo de preservar lo más rescatable del acervo lírico argentino. [JG]

5858 Pita, Juana Rosa. Viajes de Penélope. Introducción de Reinaldo Arenas. Ilustraciones de César Bermúdez. Miami, Fla.: SOLAR, 1980. 89 p.: ill. (Ediciones de poesía. Segunda serie; 17)

La imagen arquetípica del viaje, que en la conciencia occidental adquiere su forma ejemplar en *La Odisea*, es vista aquí, no desde el punto de vista del Ulises errante, sino desde el de la inmóvil Penélope, que teje y desteje el texto profundo y estacionario del dolor ante el pasar del tiempo. Como nos dice Reinaldo Arenas en su sugestivo ensayo introductorio: ". . . este libro nos muestra que la verdadera Odisea es la espera de Penélope en tanto transcurre imperturbable el tiempo, acosan los jóvenes pretendientes y se acerca insoslayable la vejez." El aliento mitopoético de estos versos, y su búsqueda de las raíces ancestrales de la voz femenina está en consonancia con lo mejor de la nueva poesía femenina del Caribe, por ejemplo, con la poesía de la cubana Nancy Morejón (ver *HLAS 44:5711*) y de la puertorriqueña Rosario Ferré (ver *HLAS 46:5705*). [RRA]

5859 Pozzi, Edna. La madre. Ilustraciones de Angel Períes Correño. Buenos Aires: Ediciones La Rosa de Oro, 1983. 118 p.: ill.

Este libro no sólo impacta, sino que agrada por la competencia lírica de la autora. La coherencia del tono y la perseverancia del ritmo son la base de un lenguaje rico y cuidado. Es un bello libro que crea su propio espacio poético, muy atractivo para el lector de buena poesía. [JG]

5860 Puig, Salvador. Lugar a dudas. Montevideo: Arca, 1984. 68 p.

Tercer poemario (*La luz entre nosotros*, 1963 y *Apalabrar*, 1980) que desarrolla en sostenido tono lírico una postulación de la realidad que se inscribe en los intersticios del deseo y del dolor de un mundo que se derrumba por circunstancias externas, entre ellas el contexto del Uruguay de los años 70. Son poemas que reflexionan sobre la realidad política mediatizadas por las vivencias del yo lírico: "Y de mañana mi país estaba viejo/ Y de ayer mi país estaba triste/ Que parecía un triángulo isósceles." [MGP]

5861 Quezada, Jaime. Huerfanías. Santiago: Pehuén, 1985. 115 p.: ill.

Nuevo libro de poemas de una de las figuras más interesantes de la joven poesía chilena. Versos de gran pujanza lírica inspirados en lo cotidiano, amalgamando la experiencia literaria con la triste realidad política. [RdC]

5862 Ramos Otero, Manuel. El libro de la muerte. Maplewood, N.J.: Waterfront Press; Río Piedras, P.R.: Editorial Cultural, 1985. 67 leaves.

Poesía oblicua, enigmática, excéntrica. Ramos Otero instaura una voz camaleónica que asume las varias modalidades de esa tangencia oscura entre el sexo y la muerte. La primera parte, "Fuegos Fúnebres," es el carnaval de la muerte: la pompa, el ritual, la tumba. La segunda es una cadena de elegías, "Epitafios," donde se canta y se llora la muerte de los poetas del amor oscuro. La tercera, "Epílogo," es sentida y personal: la muerte en carne propia del amado ausente. Exhibiendo una maestría en el exotismo verbal infrecuente en nuestra lengua, salvo en ilustres excepciones, como en el caso de Julián del Casal y Lezama Lima, Ramos Otero funda un espacio poético donde el equívoco posee una violencia ancestral y seductora. [RRA]

Reyes, Alfonso. Prosa y poesía. See item **5206.**

5863 Reyes, Jaime. La oración del ogro. México: Ediciones Era, 1984. 82 p.

Texto híbrido compuesto de poemas largos, fragmentos poéticos, poemas epistolares, y transcripciones de entrevistas a miembros de los sectores marginados de la sociedad mexicana. Poesía testimonial, que intenta reemplazar la voz individual del poeta por una voz comunitaria. Interesante experimento por este poeta inserto en la vertiente de la poesía social. No supera su libro anterior, *Isla de raíz amarga, insomne raíz*, Premio Villaurrutia, 1977. [NK]

5864 Riedemann, Clemente. Karra Maw'n. Valdivia, Chile: Ediciones Alborada, 1984. 84 p.: col. ill.

Karra Maw'n quiere decir "ciudad de la lluvia," en mapundungu, que es la lengua de los indios mapuches del sur de Chile. Apartándose a propósito de las corrientes neovanguardistas, antipoéticas y "láricas" (de Teillier y compañía), este extenso poema quiere ser una crónica de la llamada Frontera Sur de Chile en tiempos de la colonia, mediante el relato de la instalación de los primeros indígenas en Valdivia (la ciudad de la lluvia) y la narración y descripción de los viajes de los colonizadores alemanes, la destrucción de Valdivia por un maremoto y de la ecología por los exportadores. Para su empresa el poeta elige los procedimientos característicos de Ernesto Cardenal y del "exteriorismo." En suma, un respetable intento por poetizar la formación cultural de la Frontera, apartándose del canon nerudiano, tan gravitante en la poesía del Sur lluvioso. [OH]

5865 Roa Bastos, Augusto. El naranjal ardiente: nocturno paraguayo, 1947–1949. Asunción: Alcándara, 1983. 111 p. (Col. Poesía; 11)

Cinco conjuntos de poemas y un poema largo en tres partes, "Nocturno Paraguayo," constituyen este volumen que reúne la obra poética breve del novelista paraguayo. En la nota introductoria, el autor señala que estos textos pertenecen a una etapa de su evolución literaria que quedó desgajada de su obra posterior. Los poemas se relacionan con el levantamiento del año 1947 y se conservaron por contener "las cenizas de un tiempo de sangre y de muerte" para la sociedad paraguaya en lucha por su libertad. Al investigador de la obra de Roa Bastos le interesará consultar el poemario que incluye una sección de textos en guaraní "Ñañe ne'Eme." [MGP]

5866 Roca, Carlos. La voz de Edith Piaf y el fonógrafo del loco. Buenos Aires: Editorial Boedo, 1983. 105 p.: ill.

Poesía lingüísticamente atrevida, rica en audacia poética, lograda en versos duros y fuertes. El autor es joven y su lenguaje tiene la riqueza expresiva y la novedad que sólo se encuentran en otros poetas de las nuevas generaciones, como Pizarnik, Perlongher, Oteriño. [JG]

5867 Roca, Juan Manuel. Antología poética. Bogotá?: F. Burgos, 1983. 190 p.

Selección de una obra abundante, desde *Memoria del agua* (1972) hasta *Umbrales* (1982). El despliegue libre de lo imaginario caracteriza el trabajo de Roca (n. 1946), cuya "euforia verbal" algo debe, y no en sus mejores momentos, a las preferencias nadaístas. Es más interesante su cercanía a la estética superrealista, registrada en varios epígrafes indicadores de procesos intertextuales productivos (ver *HLAS 44:5736* e item 5892). [PL]

5868 Rodas, Ana María. El fin de los mitos y los sueños. Guatemala: Editorial Rin-78, 1984. 100 p.: ill. (Col. Literatura; 21)

Fundadora de la *nouvelle vague* feminista, ahonda aquí en la frustrante condición de la mujer. Si en su obra previa dominaba la pasión, la beligerancia erótica, ahora dice: "Yo, que montaba en pelo la pasión/ que soñaba bajo el sol/ mis sueños./ No queda nada. Nada." [GY]

5869 Rojas, Gonzalo. El alumbrado. Santiago: Ediciones Ganymedes, 1986. 57 p.

Gonzalo Rojas, desde Chicago, desde California, desde Utah y desde su refugio del "renegado" en un pico de los Andes cerca de su querido Chillán sigue escribiendo y escribiendo con una asombrosa vitalidad lírica. Este libro, recogiendo una treintena de sus últimos poemas, aparece en Santiago de Chile bajo el sello de Ganymedes, serie poética dirigida por el poeta David Turkeltaub, y trae una hermosa portada de Roberto Matta, "Las Parlarinas de Medianoche." [C. Grau]

5870 Romero, Elvio. El sol bajo las raíces, 1952–1955. Presentación de Miguel Angel Asturias. Epílogo de Gonzalo Zubizarreta-Ugarte. 2a ed., versión corr. Asunción: Alcándara, 1984. 118 p. (Col. Poesía; 23)

Es el primer volumen de este poeta publicado en el Paraguay. Lo precede un breve texto de Miguel Angel Asturias que caracteriza esta poesía como "poesía invadida por la vida, por el juego y el fuego de la vida." Concluye el poemario con un pequeño estudio por el poeta paraguayo Gonzalo Zubizarreta-Ugarte. La poesía de Elvio Romero representa una voz profundamente arraigada en los valores de su tierra, una voz poética que incorpora el pueblo, la naturaleza y el destino de América, dentro de la línea poética de *Canto general* de Pablo Neruda. [MGP]

5871 Rueda, Manuel. Las edades del viento: poesía inédita, 1947–1979. Santo Domingo: Alfa y Omega, 1979. 254 p.

Colección de poemas escritos entre 1949–79 que recogen los modos diversos, desde sonetos clásicos hasta poemas "pluralistas" (nombre con que el poeta denomina su particular práctica de la poesía concreta) que han caracterizado su producción poética. Hombre de variados intereses, (dramaturgo, narrador, pianista, compositor, periodista) Rueda es, quizás, el intelectual más completo de la República Dominicana. Este libro es testimonio de que es también un poeta experimentado y original. [RRA]

5872 Ruiz Dueñas, Jorge. Tornaviajes. México: Premiá, 1984. 116 p.

Versos libres, recordativos de Coleridge, que nos remiten de manera encantatoria, a veces mítica, al mar y al viaje como símbolos arquetípicos desde los cuales el hombre busca definir su estadía en la tierra. [NK]

5873 Sáenz, Felipe. Epigramas de guerra. Managua: Ediciones Primavera Popular, 1982. 64 p.

Recuerdos, experiencias, comunicaciones, meditaciones concernientes a la guerra de liberación. Testimonios de muertes, triunfos y muestras de solidaridad. Prosa coloquial que, conforme a su "Arte turbapoética," reproduce una "poesía viviente,/ atónita/ asombrosamente real . . ." [GY]

5874 Sampietro, Fernando. Marilyn Monroe y yo. México: Martín Casillas Editores, 1983. 91 p.: ill. (Serie La Poesía)

Ecos de la antipoesía de Parra y de la poesía exteriorista de Cardenal en este poemario hiperrealista cuyo hablante critica y rechaza la realidad circundante para ubicarse en un mundo de ensoñación. [NK]

5875 Sánchez, Enriquillo. Pájaro dentro de la lluvia. Santo Domingo: Secretaría de Estado de Educación, Bellas Artes y Cultos, 1985. 163 p. (Col. Premios nacionales)

Este libro ganó el Premio Nacional de Poesía de 1983. Es una colección de breves poemarios, la mayoría de inspiración amatoria y de un depurado lirismo. Aunque es poesía sensual y altamente sensorial, se trata de un tropicalismo refrenado y refinado, pleno de anáforas y eufonías. [RRA]

5876 Sánchez León, Abelardo. Buen lugar para morir. Lima: Haraui, 1984. 84 p.

Escenarios y hablantes de la vida cotidiana de la urbe latinoamericana encuentran una voz inmediata y urgida en Abelardo Sánchez León, uno de los poetas peruanos de la promoción del año 70 que mejor ha sabido comunicar la perspectiva crítica y testimonial de esa promoción. Aquí la urbe ya no es la promesa de la modernización sino, más bien, la anti-utopía de la desurbanización; el lugar de la sobrevivencia, la crisis y el nihilismo. De allí la calidad dramática de estos poemas, que analizan situaciones vitales características, limítrofes y sin resolución. La perspectiva descarnada e hiperrealista es también irónica y hasta truculenta. Sánchez León es uno de los pocos poetas jóvenes que ha intentado darle una voz a la experiencia común de la crisis. Su coloquio, narrativo y escueto, es casi informativo y transparente: no requiere de mayor elaboración para dar su testimonio, y es típico de este poeta influido con provecho por el periodismo y la sociología, sus dos ocupaciones, y también dos de sus fuentes para la poética factual y verosímil que se propone. [JO]

5877 Sánchez Peláez, Juan. Por cuál causa o nostalgia. Caracas: Fundarte, 1981. 69 p. (Col. Delta; 9)

Fiel al dictado superrealista, esta poesía se desarrolla según un dinamismo asociativo que manifiesta o sugiere ciertas vivencias en su estado originario: ". . . me dirijo a ti/ con palabras anteriores/ a cualquier reflexión" (p. 19). Ese fragmento resume una poética, corroborada por la disposición textual abierta. Una obra bien descrita como "discurso contra el método" (ver *HLAS 40:7179*). [PL]

5878 Urquiza, Concha. El corazón preso. México: UNAM, 1985. 228 p. (Col. Renacimiento; 8)

Excelente poesía mística que dialoga con aquella del siglo XVI español. Queda implícita la revaloración de la obra de Urquiza (n. 1910), hasta hoy inasequible, en este texto

que reúne toda su poesía y va precedida por dos estudios comprensivos de Gabriel Méndez Plancarte y José Vicente Anaya. [NK]

5879 Vega, José Luis. La naranja entera. Río Piedras, P.R.: Editorial Antillana, 1983. 101 p. (El Sapo concho, col. de poesía; 1)

La mujer precisada (bailarina, madre, cocinera, bañista o amante), no en la idea, sino en el gesto, atisbada por los ojos deseantes del poeta, que la multiplica en versos de sabrosa austeridad. Es poesía erótica agradablemente exenta de angustias metafísicas, casi conversada, y escrita en un tono elocuentemente modesto. [RRA]

5880 Vega, José Luis. Tiempo de Bolero. Río Piedras, P.R.: Editorial Antillana, 1986. 1 v. (Col. El Sapo concho)

En un lenguaje llano, a la vez clásico y coloquial, Vega logra conferirle al ritmo caribeño del bolero el prestigio neoplatónico de la música de las esferas, convirtiéndolo en el vaso apto de todas las depuradas revelaciones de este bello libro. Es sin duda el texto más perfecto y armonioso de este joven autor, que se une, junto a Luis Rafael Sánchez, Ana Lydia Vega y otros a la celebración de la cultura popular que tanto auge ha tenido en la nueva literatura puertorriqueña. [RRA]

5881 Vélez, Jaime Alberto. Biografías. Antioquia, Colombia: Univ. de Antioquia Ediciones, 1982. 103 p.

Cerca de la modalidad epigramática ensayada en *Reflejos* (1980; ver *HLAS 46: 5780*), Vélez inicia una práctica que podría denominarse como "instantánea poética:" imagina o recrea situaciones y personajes distanciados por un hablante-observador cuya escritura es un canje de tiempos y espacios, un "ajuste de cuentas/ entre la realidad y la memoria" (p. 51). [PL]

5882 Walsh, María Elena. Los poemas. Buenos Aires: Editorial Sudamericana, 1984. 203 p.

Util recorrido por toda la poesía de una autora de notable presencia en el panorama lírico argentino. Se nota el progreso de este discurso lírico, desde las vacilaciones de *Otoño imperdonable* (1947) hasta al atrevimiento de su última producción, sobre todo "Sección Bronca." [JG]

5883 Zito Lema, Vicente. Mater. Dibujos de Carlos Alonso. Buenos Aires: Ediciones Libros de Tierra Firme, 1984. 77 p.: ill. (Col. de poesía Todos bailan; 4)

Severa e intensa colección de excelente poesía, por un autor representativo de las nuevas direcciones líricas argentinas. [JG]

5884 Zurita, Raúl. Canto a su amor desaparecido. Santiago: Editorial Universitaria, 1985. 27 p.

Extenso poema que sobrepasa el concepto tradicional de poesía al emplear de preferencia estructuras narrativas y dialógicas, y al disponer tipográficamente los "versos" a la manera de la novela o dibujando nichos de palabras. El propósito del texto es elevar un canto a los desaparecidos políticos y a los países del Tercer Mundo, canto que es también un epitafio. Poema ambicioso, neovanguardista, que delata la obsesión del poeta por cantarlo todo a escala mundial. [OH]

GENERAL STUDIES

5885 Alegría, Fernando. Aporte de la mujer al nuevo lenguaje poético de Latinoamérica (RRI, 12:1, Spring 1982, p. 27–35)

Ensayo más lírico que crítico. Mediante unas consideraciones sobre Virginia Woolf propone una relectura de las figuras cumbres de la poesía no "feminista," sino de *mujeres*, estas mujeres (Agustini, Storni *et al.*) que al margen del modernismo y la vanguardia lograron en su obra una renovación poética basada en su liberación personal del machismo latinoamericano reinante. [RdC]

5886 Araújo, Helena. Algunas postnadaístas (IILI/RI, 50:128/129 julio/dic. 1984, p. 821–837)

Comenta la producción de un grupo de poetas posteriores al movimiento nadaísta, que desconoció a las escritoras. Señala las distintas modalidades de búsqueda y expresión de la identidad femenina en la poesía, recogida o no en libros, de María Mercedes Carranza, Anabel Torres, Renata Durán, Mónica Gontovnik, Amparo Villamizar y Orietta Lozano. [PL]

5887 Baciu, Stefan. Mis experiencias con escritores nicaragüenses (RPC, 39:182, enero/marzo 1984, p. 54–86)

Traductor de la literatura latinoamericana a varios idiomas, Baciu ha conocido a fondo obras y autores nicaragüenses. Entre las anécdotas recogidas en este artículo destacan las concernientes a Ernesto Cardenal: su "malquerencia" con Salomón de la Selva. [GY]

5888 Bajeux, Jean-Claude. Antilia retrouvée: Claude McKay, Luis Palés Matos, Aimé Césaire; poètes noirs antillais. Paris: Editions caribéenes, 1983. 427, 4 p.: bibl. (Col. Arc et littérature)

Estudio de las filiaciones entre estos tres grandes poetas de Jamaica, Puerto Rico y Martinica. El elemento unificador según Bajeux es la conciencia negra afro-antillana, y el propósito del estudio es perseguir las modulaciones de esa conciencia en las tres lenguas principales del Caribe. Desgraciadamente el último capítulo, que es el que el autor dedica a establecer conexiones claras entre los tres poetas, es demasiado breve y aproximativo. El texto es mayormente una interpretación de la obra de cada poeta independientemente. El capítulo sobre Palés sintetiza mucho de lo ya dicho sobre su poesía por Federico de Onís, Margot Arce y Arcadio Díaz Quiñones, y la idea de negritud se aplica sin las debidas matizaciones, muy importantes sobre todo en el caso de un poeta como Palés, que escribió, entre otras cosas, poesía afro-antillana, pero que nunca se autodefinió como "poeta negro." Además, con este tipo de lectura que tiende hacia un rígido molde positivista se pierde mucho de la dimensión irónica y elusiva de Palés. No obstante, la escasez de este tipo de lectura comparativa y la amplia documentación de su autor hacen de este libro una contribución valiosa a los estudios del Caribe. [RRA]

5889 Bejel, Emilio. Literatura de nuestra América: estudios de literatura cubana e hispanoamericana. Xalapa, México: Centro de Investigaciones Lingüístico-Literarias, Univ. Veracruzana, 1985. 1 v.

Bejel se ocupa de la poesía de Lezama Lima en cinco de los artículos recopilados en esta colección. En ellos analiza, principalmente por vía del acercamiento estructuralista, *Muerte de Narciso, Aventuras sigilosas, Enemigo rumor* y la poética lezamiana en general. Los ensayos abundan en aciertos interpretativos y son contribuciones para la todavía exigua bibliografía sobre la poesía de Lezama Lima. [RRA]

5890 Beverly, John. Sandinista poetics (The Minnesota Review [New York] 20, Spring 1983, p. 127–134)

Para Beverly, la poesía centroamericana examina la laguna entre la esperanza y la inmediatez, la posibilidad de revolución y los parcos logros de la militancia. Todo ello hace de la poesía un arma de lucha y no un antídoto. La poesía revolucionaria actual se estudia a la luz del más amplio marco de la historia nicaragüense. [GY]

5891 Bianchi, Soledad. Un mapa por completar: la joven poesía chilena. Santiago: CENECA, 1983. 45 p.: bibl. (Documento de trabajo; 44)

Loable intento por caracterizar la llamada "joven poesía chilena," pero que se topa con dos problemas: uno práctico y otro metodológico. El problema práctico tiene que ver con las dificultades de la autora para reunir libros publicados en Chile (Bianchi reside en París) y textos dispersos por el mundo a raíz del exilio. Resultado: un corpus incompleto. El problema metodológico proviene de que la autora, al parecer, carece de las herramientas teóricas indispensables para abocarse a este tipo de estudio. Lo anterior redunda en un trabajo impresionista, realizado como al tanteo, y cuyo único aporte es dar cuenta de algunos nombres y de algunos títulos publicados en el período 1973–83. [OH]

5892 Carranza, María Mercedes. Poesía post-nadaísta (IILI/RI, 50:128/129, julio 1984, p. 799–819)

Panorama esquemático de la actividad coetánea y posterior al auge nadaísta, de poetas distanciados de "gestos publicitarios" y del "irracionalismo ingenuo" de ese movimiento. Vale como aproximación informativa, aunque ligera, al trabajo de G. Quessep, J. García Maffla, E. Restrepo, J.M. Roca, D. Jaramillo Agudelo, J.G. Cobo Borda y otros autores aparecidos desde la década del 60 (ver item **5896**). [PL]

5893 Céspedes, Diógenes. Lenguaje y poesía en Santo Domingo en el siglo XX. Santo Domingo: Editora Universitaria UASD, 1985. 450 p. (Publicaciones; 374. Col. Arte y sociedad; 19)

Exhaustivo estudio de los movimientos poéticos determinantes en el siglo XX en la República Dominicana: vedrinismo, postumismo, la poesía sorprendida, el Grupo del 48, y la poesía actual. Se trata de un gran esfuerzo de recopilación e investigación, pero muchas veces está obstruído por el estilo oblicuo e innecesariamente técnico del crítico. No obstante es una muestra significativa del interés creciente en la creación de una crítica seria y académica de la litera-

tura dominicana, y una alternativa a los estudios de corte más sociológico del joven crítico Alcántara Almánzar. [RRA]

5894 Céspedes, Diógenes. Seis ensayos sobre poética latinoamericana. Santo Domingo: Taller, 1983. 218 p.: bibl. (Biblioteca Taller; 148)

Ensayos sugerentes y a veces incitantes sobre el concepto de la poesía y la práctica poética de Darío, Henríquez Ureña, Reyes, Borges, Neruda y Paz. Polemiza algo energuménicamente con todos, pero siempre con estallidos iluminadores. [RdC]

5895 Charry Lara, Fernando. Los poetas de Los Nuevos (IILI/RI, 50:128/129, julio/dic. 1984, p. 633–681)

Examen muy iluminador del proceso de la poesía colombiana, a partir de la circunstancia estimulante que fue la revista Los Nuevos (junio-agosto 1925). De gran interés las observaciones críticas sobre la asunción de la vanguardia en Colombia, que Charry Lara relaciona adecuadamente con el acontecer hispanoamericano. Notable lectura de los poetas del grupo, y en especial de León de Greiff (p. 659–668; ver item **5945**). [PL]

5896 Cobo Borda, J.G. Dos décadas de poesía colombiana (ECO, 42:6, abril 1983, p. 617–639)

Caracterización histórico-sociológica del proceso, cercana al "recuento periodístico" (p. 623). Las valoraciones de la poesía nadaísta oscilan entre la reserva y la aprobación; pero resulta más significativa—por estar mejor fundada en los textos—la presencia de individualidades como Darío Jaramillo, Giovanni Quessep, Jaime García Maffla y Elkin Restrepo. Trabajo interesante, aunque el tono enfático de la exposición puede restarle eficacia (ver items **5892, 5904, y 5921**). [PL]

5897 Cuadra, Pablo Antonio. El Dios de Darío, el Dios de Vallejo, el Dios de Neruda (RCPC, 38:179, abril/junio 1983, p. 7–15)

Lúcida y sentida exploración del tema de Dios a través del "pensamiento poético" de tres grandes poetas de América—por otro grande: Pablo Antonio Cuadra. [RdC]

5898 Cuchí Coll, Isabel. Grandes poetisas de América: Clara Lair, Alfonsina Storni, Julia de Burgos, Gabriela Mistral. San Juan: s.n; Santo Domingo: Editora Corripio, 1982. 93 p.: ports.

Antología básica de cuatro grandes figuras (Lair, Storni, Burgos, Mistral) con sendos ensayos de enfoque tradicional (vida y obras) enriquecidos por reminiscencias de la autora que tuvo un trato personal con todas. [RdC]

5899 El Estridentismo: memoria y valoración. México: Fondo de Cultura Económica, 1983. 322 p.: bibl. (SEP/80; 50)

Importante recopilación que recoge los testimonios y trabajos críticos del simposio que organizó el Centro de Investigaciones Lingüístico-Literarias de la Univ. Veracruzana sobre el movimiento de vanguardia en México conocido como "El Estridentismo." Aunque se originó en la ciudad de México, Maples Arce, su fundador, fue Secretario de Gobierno en Xalapa y logró que se radicaran allí la mayor parte de sus miembros. Desde allí publicaron su revista principal, *Horizonte*, y fundaron su propia editorial. Esta antología incluye los testimonios de Ramón Alva de la Canal, Germán List Arzubide, Leobardo Chávez Zenteno y Gerardo García, una entrevista con Arzubide, y las ponencias de, entre otros, Stefan Baciu, Nelson Osorio, Luis Leal, Jorge Ruffinelli, Renato Prada Oropeza, Luis Mario Schneider. Valiosa bibliografía al final. [NK]

5900 Fernández Morera, Darío. The term "modernism" in literary history (*in* Congress of the International Comparative Literature Association, 10th, New York, 1982. Proceedings. New York: Garland, 1985, v. 2, p. 271–279)

Ensayo exploratorio de un comparatista que quisiera coordinar el modernismo hispánico con otros "modernismos" (el alemán, brasileño, anglo-americano . . .) tomando en cuenta sus divergencias así como sus convergencias. Para tal fin propone una nueva terminología de periodización que reconozca la "modernidad" como un fenómeno "pos-romántico" para facilitar su análisis desde el punto de vista de la literatura comparada. [RdC]

5901 Gelman, Juan. Citas y comentarios. Madrid: Visor, 1982. 143 p. (Col. Visor de poesía; 144)

Excelente libro donde la maestría poética del autor dialoga con otros poetas, entre ellos Santa Teresa de Jesús y San Juan de la Cruz. El efecto de este juego intertextual es de trágica sublimidad en cuanto se entrelaza

el verbo religioso con el verbo de un escritor que ha vivido los momentos más dolorosos de su lucha política. [JG]

5902 Girri, Alberto. Notas sobre la experiencia poética. Buenos Aires: Editorial Losada, 1983. 196 p. (Col. Prisma)

Si hay que leer textos de poética contemporánea, este es uno de ellos. Repartido en notas fragmentarias, puede leerse con reposada rapidez. Es una ventana a veces extremadamente lúcida a las intenciones del autor. [JG]

5903 Gutiérrez Girardot, Rafael. Los problemas del modernismo (ECO, 43:6, abril 1983, p. 604–616)

Incitante despojamiento de varios equívocos latentes en los acercamientos tradicionales al modernismo como fenómeno generacional, epocal, espiritual, estetizante . . . El autor aboga por una revalorización del fenómeno desde un punto de vista social y comparatista. Es de suponer que el ensayo forma parte de un libro que eventualmente profundizará las ideas aquí esbozadas. [RdC]

5904 Jaramillo Agudelo, Darío. La poesía nadaísta (IILI/RI, 50:128/129, julio/dic. 1984, p. 757–798)

Propuesto como testimonio y análisis de la artesanía poética nadaísta, este notable texto sobrepasa ese designio y resulta una detenida exposición crítica de las actitudes vitales y de sus consecuencias en las obras de ese movimiento. Adelanta valoraciones sobre el alcance y los límites del trabajo de Gonzalo Arango, Jaime Jaramillo Escobar, Amílcar Osorio, Darío Lemos, Jotamario y Eduardo Escobar (ver item **5896** y **5921**). [PL]

5905 Jiménez, José Olivio. Hacia la modernidad: la poesía modernista hispanoamericana (ECO, 45:272, junio 1984, p. 207–216)

Sin insistir en identificar (ni pretender oponer) *modernismo* y *modernidad* el autor hace destacar la relación entre la poesía más atrevida de autores de la generación de Martí y Darío y la plenamente moderna y desacralizadora de Luis Carlos López, Lugones, López Velarde y Herrera y Reissig. [RdC]

5906 Kamenszain, Tamara. El texto silencioso: tradición y vanguardia en la poesía sudamericana. México: UNAM, Coordinación de Humanidades, 1983. 92 p.

Con el bordado agudo de dos apéndices

fundamentales y una brevísima introducción a "las provincias de la lengua," estas lecturas de Girondo, Juan L. Ortiz, Lihn, Macedonio y Francisco Madariaga establecen la tradición de una vanguardia propia haciendo de una fallida marginalidad el punto de partida para comprender la centralidad de las transformaciones poéticas del siglo. [S. Sosnowski]

5907 Laurenza, Roque Javier. Los poetas de la generación republicana (LNB/L, 348/349, marzo/abril 1985, p. 139–152)

Crítica de la "inflación" poética desde la instauración de la república panameña (1903) hasta el presente. Tras una historia de las sucesivas generaciones poéticas, delinea las influencias literarias (Darío, Valencia, Chocano, Lugones, Martí), la casi ausencia de un concepto de la poesía, y el uso del verso "para escalar las alturas gratas de la burocracia." Severa condena de la poesía panameña. [GY]

5908 Masiello, Francine. Tradición y resistencia: la poesía uruguaya de los años setenta (ECO, 42:4, feb. 1983, p. 340–355)

Este trabajo señala los desplazamientos textuales del discurso poético uruguayo durante una década de censura cultural. Se destaca el cambio de la modalidad intimista de la lírica anterior por un lenguaje poético de resistencias que busca integrar la experiencia personal con aspectos de la realidad histórica contemporánea. Se proponen ciertos rasgos claves de esta poesía joven utilizando textos de Eduardo Milán, Jorge Arbeleche, Enrique Fierro, Cristina Peri Rossi, Hugo Achúgar, Enrique Estrázulas, Alberto Mediza, entre otros. [MGP]

5909 Medio siglo de poesía dominicana. Coordinación y edición de José Alcántara Almánzar. Santo Domingo: Instituto Tecnológico de Santo Domingo, 1983. 47 p.: bibl. (Monografía; 19)

Resumen breve pero abarcador de los diferentes movimientos y generaciones de la poesía dominicana moderna y contemporánea, desde la poesía sorprendida hasta el pluralismo. La antología de ensayos es un esfuerzo de los estudiantes del Círculo de Literatura del Instituto Tecnológico de Santo Domingo. El volumen está editado por José Alcántara Almánzar y los ensayos son: "Medio Siglo de Poesía Dominicana" de Alcántara Almánzar; "Los Poetas Independientes" de José Ademes Chapman; "La Poesía Sorpren-

dida" de Augusto C. Ogando; "¿Generación del 48?" de Andrea Paz; "Generación del 60: Poesía Comprometida o del Testimonio" de Gerardo Antonio Méndez; "La Joven Poesía" y "El Pluralismo" de Pablo Jorge Mustonen; "¿Y Ahora Qué?" de Lucía Bayona. [RRA]

5910 Monge, Carlos Francisco. La imagen separada: modelos ideológicos de la poesía costarricense, 1950–1980. San José: Instituto del Libro, Ministerio de Cultura, Juventud y Deportes, 1984. 204 p.: bibl., index.

Very important essay on the relationship between history and poetry in contemporary Costa Rica. From a successful poet's dual perspective as artist and critic, Monge examines with great lucidity the relationship between art and ideology as well as the aesthetics of poetic realism, language fetishism, and nostalgia for the past. [R. Prieto]

5911 Moraña, Mabel. Autoritarismo y discurso lírico en el Uruguay (in Fascismo y experiencia literaria: reflexiones para una recanonización. Edited by Hernán Vidal. Minneapolis, Minn.: Society for the Study of Contemporary Hispanic and Lusophone Revolutionary Literatures, 1985, p. 407–468)

Valioso estudio panorámico de la producción poética más reciente con enfoque especial en el panorama cultural de los años 1973–78, a partir de postulados teóricos extraídos de Adorno, Althusser, Todorov y Culler. Se analiza la problemática cultural creada por un sistema político totalitario, sus efectos en el desarrollo de la literatura, y se propone luego un conjunto de rasgos que se postulan como paradigmáticos del discurso lírico bajo condiciones de censura en todas sus formas. Estos rasgos son importantes para el esclarecimiento de las estrategias desarrolladas en la práctica poética reciente. [MGP]

5912 Orihuela, Augusto Germán. *Las Tres Américas* y el modernismo. Caracas: Centro de Estudios Latinoamericanos Rómulo Gallegos: Consejo Nacional de la Cultura, 1983. 372 p., 1 leaf of plates: facsims., ill. (Col. Manuel Landaeta Rosales)

Indice, selección antológica y análisis del contenido de esta importante revista ilustrada publicada en Nueva York por Nicanor Bolet Peraza (el promotor también de *La Revista Ilustrada de Nueva York*), en cuyas páginas se registra el desarrollo del modernismo. [RdC]

5913 Osorio T., Nelson. El futurismo y la vanguardia literaria en América Latina. Caracas: Centro de Estudios Latinoamericanos Rómulo Gallegos, 1982. 76 p.: bibl. (Cuadernos)

Seis capítulos críticos a manera de reflexión sobre la literatura contemporánea y sus distintos vínculos a Marinetti y al futurismo en América Latina, especialmente Venezuela, constituyen la primera parte de este libro. La segunda es muy valiosa por reproducir documentos esenciales provenientes de revistas literarias vanguardistas (desde Buenos Aires a Maracaibo). El breve estudio de Osorio es un aporte significativo para descifrar el vasto y complejo problema literario concerniente al génesis de las vanguardias. [K. Müller-Bergh]

5914 Pearsall, Priscilla. An art alienated from itself: studies in Spanish American modernism. University, Miss.: Romance Monographs, 1984. 103 p.: bibl. (Romance Monographs; 43)

Estudios concretos (sobre Casal, Nájera y Darío), basados en una cuidadosa lectura de textos tocantes al tema de la enajenación—especialmente en cuanto a la mujer—con el fin de interpretar el fenómeno como una característica singular del modernismo literario. [RdC]

5915 Percas de Ponseti, Helena. Reflexiones sobre la poesía femenina hispanoamericana (RRI, 12:1, Spring 1982, p. 49–55)

Análisis de "Lo Inefable" de Delmira Agustini, "La Flor del Aire" de Gabriela Mistral, y "A Madame Poesía" de Alfonsina Storni, y "A Madame Poesía" de Alfonsina Storni como poemas sobre la poesía con el fin de destacar la representativa singularidad del destino poético de estas tres poetas así como el dolor de su creación artística "femenina." [RdC]

5916 Plural. UNAM. Vol. 15, No. 171, dic. 1985–. México.

Número dedicado a "La Espiga Amotinada," celebra los 25 años de la publicación del libro que dio su nombre al grupo. Ese libro que incluye a Juan Bañuelos, Jaime Labastida, Oscar Oliva, Jaime Augusto Shelley, y Eraclio Zepeda, y el siguiente Ocupación de la palabra (1965), marcaron un cambio en la poesía mexicana de los 60. Este homenaje incluye poemas de Oliva y Shelley, entrevistas con Bañuelos, Oliva, Shelley y Zepeda, un ensayo de conjunto de Françoise

Perús, y varios ensayos sobre sus obras en particular. [NK]

5917 Revista de Bellas Artes. Instituto Nacional de Bellas Artes y Literatura. No. 8, nov. 1982–. México.

Este número está dedicado al grupo de Contemporáneos con motivo del Homenaje Nacional que el INBA (Instituto Nacional de Bellas Artes) les rinde en 1982. Incluye testimonios y artículos de, entre otros, Luis Cardoza y Aragón, Rubén Salazar Mallén, Carlos Monsiváis, John S. Brushwood, Inés Arredondo y David Huerta; poemas seleccionados por Luis Mario Schneider, representativos de sus poéticas; y una encuesta de Ethel Krauze sobre la actualidad del "grupo sin grupo." Reproducción de fotografías, dibujos y cartas. [NK]

5918 Risking a somersault in the air: conversations with Nicaraguan writers. Interviews by Margaret Randall. Edited by Floyce Alexander. San Francisco, Calif.: Solidarity Publications, 1984. 215 p., 2 leaves of plates: ill.

Informative conversations with Nicaraguan writers such as Cardenal, Ramírez, Belli, Chávez Alfaro but especially with Sandinista writer-poets better known as political and military leaders (e.g., Tomás Borge, Omar Cabezas, Carlos Guadamuz, Francisco de Asís Fernández). Engrossing attempt to explain the relationship between poetry and creativity in today's Nicaragua. [R. Prieto]

5919 Rivero, Eliana. Hacia una definición de la lírica femenina en Hispanoamérica (RRI, 12:1, Spring 1982, p. 11–26)

Tras unas reflexiones teóricas y una crítica tajante sobre los enfoques tradicionales a la llamada "literatura femenina," Eliana Rivero nos revela dos poemarios actuales de extraordinaria calidad: Alguien está escribiendo su ternura de Marilyn Bobes León (cubana) y Circuito amores y anexas de Elena Milán (mexicana). [RdC]

5920 Roggiano, Alfredo A. Modernismo: origen de la palabra y evolución de un concepto (ECO, 42[2]:254, dic. 1982, p. 210–223)

Examen de los distintos conceptos de "moderno," "modernidad" y "modernismo," desde la primera aparición de los vocablos en el medioevo y el Renacimiento hasta su consagración por Darío. [RdC]

5921 Romero, Armando. El nadaísmo y la literatura (ECO, 43[2]:260, junio 1983, p. 175–192)

Anota algunos aspectos que ligan el trabajo de los poetas nadaístas con manifestaciones de la vanguardia: surrealismo, poesía de los Beatniks, existencialismo. Util contextualización del controvertido movimiento colombiano de la década del 60 (ver items 5896 y 5904). [PL]

5922 Romero, Armando. Los poetas de *Mito* (IILI/RI, 50:128/129, julio/dic. 1984, p. 689–755)

Extenso e ilustrativo trabajo de situación y balance de una empresa fundamental en la literatura colombiana. La primera parte (p. 689–704) comenta la trayectoria ideológica de la revista y su función en un momento crítico de la cultura nacional (1955–62); la segunda (p. 704–755) evalúa con estimable precisión la tarea poética del grupo "Mito:" F. Charry Lara (n. 1920), A. Mutis (n. 1923), J. Gaitán Durán (1924–62), F. Arbeláez (n. 1924), R. Echavarría (n. 1926), E. Cote Lamus (1928–64), H. Rojas Herazo (n. 1921). [PL]

Seminario-Simposio de la Literatura Ecuatoriana en los Ultimos 30 Años, *1st, Quito, 1983.* La literatura ecuatoriana en los últimos 30 años, 1950–1980. See item **5491.**

5923 Sheridan, Guillermo. Los Contemporáneos ayer. México: Fondo de Cultura Económica, 1985. 411 p.

Excelente estudio de los Contemporáneos que toma en cuenta no sólo sus escritos, sino testimonios, anotaciones personales y notas periodísticas del momento, en un intento logrado de reconstrucción epocal. Incluye en un primer grupo, a Jaime Torres Bodet, Bernardo Ortiz de Montellano, Enrique González Rojo, y en un segundo, a Xavier Villaurrutia y Salvador Novo, Jorge Cuesta y Gilberto Owen. Indagación valiosa para la comprensión de este grupo y su postura intelectual, actitud que renovó y marcó toda la literatura mexicana posterior. [NK]

5924 Sierra, José Luis. Poesía actual de Guatemala (CH, 397, julio 1983, p. 81–100)

Muestra de poetas de los 60 en adelante. Se hace hincapié en las circunstancias violentas en que surgen estas promociones. Destaca el grupo denominado de Nuevo

Signo, que lanzó un libro colectivo, *Las plumas de la serpiente*, en 1970. Predominan temáticas referentes a la muerte, lo popular, y el compromiso. [GY]

5925 Vallbona, Rima de. Trayectoria actual de la poesía femenina en Costa Rica (Kañina [Univ. de Costa Rica, San José] 5:2, julio/dic. 1981, p. 18–27)

La poesía femenina arranca con el vanguardismo, que se caracteriza por su subjetividad en las poetas: Eunice Odio, Carmen Naranjo, Victoria Urbano y Julieta Dobles. También se destacan Esmeralda Jiménez por su tradicionalismo folklórico y Virginia Grütter, la única que aboga por la liberación artística de la antipoesía. Estas poetas tienen en común el rechazo de la realidad social, la elaboración de la temática existencial angustiada, la indiferencia al feminismo. [GY]

5926 Yudice, George. Poemas de un joven que quiso ser otro (Inti [Providence] 18/19, otoño 1983/primavera 1984, p. 1–10)

La "juventud" en Joaquín Pasos no es sino una visión poética dirigida hacia el otro, con quien busca fundirse. Cardenal y Cuadra observan que supo hacerse indio; es decir, recrear la cosmovisión del otro por excelencia. Conocer, para Pasos, es hacer brotar en forma de poema la falla irremediable que nos separa y aúna al otro. [RdC]

5927 Yurkievich, Saúl. Fundadores de la nueva poesía latinoamericana: Vallejo, Huidobro, Borges, Girondo, Neruda, Paz, Lezama Lima. Barcelona, Spain: Ariel, 1984. 309 p.: bibls. (Letras e ideas. Studia)

Reedición, aumentada con capítulos nuevos sobre Huidobro y Lezama Lima, de un libro ya fundamental sobre los "fundadores"—los grandes poetas latinoamericanos del primer medio siglo. El libro sigue vigente y más actual que nunca por sus acertados juicios y bien fundamentadas explicaciones sobre el por qué de la importancia de cada "fundador:" Vallejo, Huidobro, Borges, Girondo, Neruda, Paz—y ahora Lezama Lima. [RdC]

5928 Zurita, Raúl. Chile: literatura, lenguaje y sociedad, 1973–1983 (*in* Fascismo y experiencia literaria: reflexiones para una recanonización. Edited by Hernán Vidal. Minneapolis, Minn.: Society for the Study of Contemporary Hispanic and Lusophone Revolutionary Literatures, 1985, p. 299–331)

Este trabajo se caracteriza por el desarrollo confuso de ciertas nociones extraídas de la crítica sociológica, y mal digeridas por el autor, para referirse a la literatura chilena del período 1973–83 y muy en particular a la poesía. Como resultado de lo anterior, se observa un divorcio casi total entre la extensa parte teórica y la descripción de los tópicos literarios y la situación del hablante, fenómenos que podrían haber sido apuntados y descritos exactamente igual sin el aparataje teórico. [OH]

SPECIAL STUDIES

5929 Aguirre, Mirta. Un poeta y un continente. La Habana: Editorial Letras Cubanas, 1982. 139 p. (Col. Crítica. Cumpleaños de Nicolás Guillén; 8)

Guillén visto a través del ojo inteligente y afectivo de la conocida poeta y ensayista. Son casi todos ensayos de ocasión, escritos desde 1948 hasta 1979, y en todos ellos resalta su estilo incisivo y directo. Guillén es el texto y el pretexto donde una importante intelectual marxista inscribe el desarrollo de su pensamiento en torno a Cuba y la revolución cubana. [RRA]

5930 Albizúrez Palma, Francisco. Luis Cardoza y Aragón (Letras de Guatemala [Univ. de San Carlos de Guatemala, Facultad de Humanidades, Instituto de Estudios de la Literatura Nacional, Guatemala] 1, junio 1980, p. 9–30, bibl.)

Tras ubicar al poeta en su época, se trazan los elementos de su ideología estética: libre creación, no compromiso, universalidad, subjetivismo, antimimetismo, fusión de prosa y poesía. [GY]

5931 Andrés Eloy Blanco, humanista. Prólogo de Jesús Sanoja Hernández. 2a ed. Caracas: Ediciones Centauro, 1981. 2 v.

Recopilación de escritos sobre A.E. Blanco (1897–1955). El vol. 1 contiene poemas, prólogos a la primera edición de este libro (1981), crónicas y notas de duelo de la prensa mexicana, el último discurso de Blanco y textos de los homenajes realizados en 1955 en México, Costa Rica, Chile y Colombia. El vol. II recoge los trabajos leídos y publicados en Venezuela en 1980, al conmemorarse el XXV aniversario de su muerte, y en 1981, con ocasión del traslado de los restos del poeta al Panteón Nacional. Material interesante para fijar el perfil bio-bibliográfico de Blanco y las proyecciones de su figura en la vida política nacional y continental (ver *HLAS 40:7045–7046* y *7224; HLAS 44:5807,* y *HLAS 46:5846*). [PL]

5932 Arredondo, Inés. Acercamiento a Jorge Cuesta. México: SEP Diana, 1982. 139 p.: bibl. (SepSetentas Diana; 137)

El análisis de un ensayo de Cuesta sobre Salvador Díaz Mirón es el punto de partida de este estudio que sistematiza las ideas estéticas de este "Contemporáneo maldito," en vías de una mejor lectura de su poesía. [NK]

5933 Balladares, José Emilio. El jeroglífico descifrado (El Pez y la Serpiente [Editorial Unión, Managua] 25, invierno 1981, p. 191–205)

Según este análisis "hermenéutico," "Jeroglífico en la pared de un templo Maya," de *El jaguar y la luna* de Pablo Antonio Cuadra, es un "ars poética" que propone trascender la ironía de la historia y dar voz a la (inefable) naturaleza/ tierra prometida. [GY]

5934 Balseiro, José Agustín. Rubén Darío, o la agonía ambivalente (UPR/LT, 25:95/98, enero/dic. 1977, p. 123–142)

Balseiro apoya la interpretación de la obra dariana como manifestación de una ambivalencia irresoluble entre un ancestral catolicismo y su pasión erótica que lo hacía "eterno prisionero del deseo," como el vate dijera de Verlaine. [GY]

5935 Bihler, Heinrich. Los "salmos" de Ernesto Cardenal en su relación con los salmos bíblicos (UEN/LS, 13:1, 1983, p. 77–104, bibl.)

Bihler estudia la selección y transposición que lleva a cabo Cardenal en sus *Salmos:* se limita a los de lamentación, los de sapiencia y los hímnicos, con clara intención de denunciar injusticias y abusos contra la humanidad. [GY]

5936 Charry Lara, Fernando. Eduardo Carranza en la poesía colombiana (ECO, 42:6, abril 1983, p. 561–578)

Es el prólogo a la antología *Hablar soñando* (1983; ver item **5782**). Sitúa a Carranza en el contexto de la poesía colombiana, destacando su gestión fundadora en el grupo "Piedra y Cielo." Bien caracterizadas las diversas líneas de influencia que operaron sobre Carranza y sus compañeros, y especialmente sus relaciones con la tradición hispánica (ver *HLAS 40:7055* y *HLAS 42:5701* y *5913*). [PL]

5937 Costa, René de. Huidobro: los oficios de un poeta. México: Fondo de Cultura Económica, 1984. 215 p. (Col. Tierra firme)

Sustentado en novedosos materiales investigados por el autor en los archivos de la familia Huidobro, de Juan Larrea, de Gerardo Diego, y de la Biblioteca Jacques Doucet, el libro revela aspectos inéditos de la vida y obra de Vicente Huidobro. Es de particular interés el capítulo dedicado al cubismo. Otro valioso aporte de René de Costa a la bibliografía huidobriana, que lo cuenta entre sus más acuciosos especialistas. [OH]

5938 Darío, Rubén. Rubén Darío y su tiempo. Pórtico de Carlos Tunnermann Bernheim. Presentación y cronología de Edelberto Torres Espinosa. Selección y notas de José Santos Rivera. 2a ed. Managua: Editorial Nueva Nicaragua, 1981. 135 p.

Importante documento para entender cómo se viene rehaciendo la imagen de Darío en el nuevo clima ideológico. Se presentan poesías y prosas que, según el antólogo, Edelberto Torres, aúnan a Darío con Sandino. Pero ¿y qué de todo lo que escribió Darío que desentona con la ideología sandinista? [GY]

5939 Escoto, Julio. El equilibrio de las dimensiones espaciales en *Crepusculario* de Pablo Neruda (UPR/LT, 25:95/98, enero/dic. 1977, p. 45–67, tables)

Basado en conceptos semánticos de Greimas, este trabajo muestra que *Crepusculario* de Neruda se funda en la valoración de los niveles espaciales de Verticalidad (de grado positivo) y Horizontalidad (de grado negativo), lo que en obras posteriores conduce a una estratificación ética: presencia del bien y del mal. Artículo lúcido, pero que puede ser irritante para los lectores no familiarizados con la semiología. [OH]

5940 Fernández Retamar, Roberto. Entrevisto. La Habana: Unión de Escritores y Artistas de Cuba, 1982. 217 p.: bibl. (Contemporáneos)

Recopilación y montaje de diversas entrevistas hechas al poeta a lo largo de su carrera de poeta, crítico, profesor y editor. Es una estupenda oportunidad de conocer de cerca las opiniones, los prejuicios y las

teorías del director de Casa de las Américas en torno a la poesía, la literatura en general, así como su visión de la realidad cubana y de la cultura hispanoamericana. [RRA]

5941 García Terrés, Jaime. Los tres mundos de Gilberto Owen. México: Era, 1980. 177 p.

García Terrés, poeta y crítico, busca en la tradición hermética, la cábala, la alquimia y el esoterismo las fuentes para una lectura novedosa y detallada de la obra de Gilberto Owen, uno de los miembros menos estudiados de los Contemporáneos, y cuyo *Perseo vencido* (1948), según Manuel Durán, resiste comparación con Eliot. [NK]

5942 Gelpí, Juan. Enunciación y dependencia en José Gorostiza: estudio de una máscara poética. México: UNAM, Coordinación de Humanidades, 1984. 223 p.

Estudio valioso de la obra de uno de los grandes poetas de México del grupo Contemporáneos. Gelpí analiza las diferentes posturas de enunciación que asume la voz poética desde *Canciones para cantar en las barcas* hasta *Muerte sin fin*. [NK]

5943 González, José Emilio. Apuntes sobre la poesía de José Luis Vega (ICP/R, 22:83, abril/junio 1979, p. 1–5)

González provee un recuento del proceso de formación poética de este joven poeta puertorriqueño muy útil para los que sólo lo conocen por sus últimos libros: *La naranja entera* y *Tiempo de bolero*. Su trayectoria se marca desde un inicial período neo-romántico que se mueve hacia un período de poesía cortante, urbana, escrita bajo el signo de Vallejo, y una última poesía fuertemente anclada en el lenguaje cotidiano. [RRA]

5944 Güilmil de Usher, Elena. El concepto de Dios en los *Sonetos de las agonías y los éxtasis* de Carlos Sabat Ercasty (IFCL/E, 3/4, 1982, p. 53–73, bibl.)

Estudio que propone el símbolo de la Trinidad como tres pautas para la interpretación de los sonetos de Sabat Ercasty: la fuente y la rosa (símbolo de afirmación); el "quizás," el "habrá" (lo contingente, lo dudoso y lo negativo); la misión del poeta (intérprete de la palabra divina). Incluye una cronografía de la obra de este poeta uruguayo. [MGP]

5945 Gutiérrez Girardot, Rafael. Poesía y "crítica" literaria en Fernando Charry

Lara (IILI/RI, 50:128/129, julio/dic. 1984, p. 839–852)

Examina las condiciones socioculturales negativas que los poetas de "Piedra y Cielo" y de los siguientes grupos coetáneos intentaron cambiar, a partir de un cambio en el lenguaje y en el concepto poéticos. Destaca el papel relevante cumplido por Charry Lara en ese empeño que aproxima filosofía y poesía en una dimensión crítica y productiva. [PL]

5946 Jirón Terán, José and Jorge Eduardo Arellano. Rubén Darío, primigenio: nuevas investigaciones de sus inicios literarios. Managua: Ediciones Convivio, 1984. 66 p.

Breves artículos sobre el reciente hallazgo de las primeras obras del Darío adolescente. Destaca el de Arellano donde caracteriza "de caza" como el primer poema nicaragüense que "nombra la geografía, flora y fauna de su país" y como un precursor del exteriorismo, de la antipoesía, coloquialismo y la vanguardia. [GY]

5947 Jrade, Cathy Login. Rubén Darío and the romantic search for unity: the modernist recourse to esoteric tradition. Austin: Univ. of Texas Press, 1983. 182 p.: bibl., index (The Texas Pan American series)

Según Jrade, el tradición esotérica aporta la unidad central de la visión dariana. El estudio de esta tradición y su indagación en la obra de Darío son excelentes, si bien a veces se extrema su influencia, v.gr., cuando se interpreta la "luz" de la espiga, en la que "duerme la espiga," como "the golden light of the sun, which Darío, under the influence of the occult religions, associates with the Supreme Deity." ¿No es obvio que se trata aquí de religión cristiana? [GY]

5948 Larrazábal Henríquez, Osvaldo et al. 4 [i.e. Cuatro] ensayos sobre José Antonio Ramos Sucre. Cumaná, Venezuela: Biblioteca de Temas y Autores Sucrenses, 1980. 58 p. (Col. La Torre de timón; 4)

Breves trabajos presentados en el "III Simposio de Docentes e Investigadores de la Literatura Venezolana" (Mérida, 1977). Sobresalen el texto de Argenis Pérez sobre los códigos románticos de raíz alemana y francesa en la escritura de Ramos Sucre, y las observaciones sobre la función del símbolo que Gustavo L. Carrera desarrolla en la línea analítica de T. Todorov (ver *HLAS 44:5466* y *HLAS 46:5849* y *5881a*). [PL]

5949 Lingüística y Literatura. Univ. de Antioquia, Depto. de Lingüística y Literatura. No. 6, enero/junio 1983–. Medellín, Colombia.

Homenaje a Porfirio Barba Jacob (1883–1942) en el centenario de su nacimiento. Contiene trabajos de Oskar Püigróss, "Notas para una Biografía Analítica acerca de la Vida y Obra de P.B.J." (p. 9–33); Saúl Sánchez, "La Imagen de un Poeta" (p. 35–48); Germán Posada, "P.B.J., Poeta de la Muerte" (p. 49–69); Alvaro Legretti, "A propósito de 'Acuarimántima'" (p. 83–116); dos muestras de la labor periodística de Barba Jacob (p. 117–128); y una sección documental a cargo de Alberto Lebrún: "Barba Jacob No Nació en Hoyorrico," que incluye partida de bautismo del escritor (p. 129–135). Mérito irregular del conjunto: sólo destaca la lectura de G. Posada (ver item **5765**). [PL]

5950 Lozada, Alfredo. Migas de Nietzsche: el subtexto de *El hondero entusiasta* (IILI/RI, 123/124, abril/sept. 1983, p. 389–402)

Convincente trabajo intertextual en el que Lozada conecta *El hondero entusiasta* de Neruda y *Así hablaba Zaratustra* de Nietzsche. El libro juvenil del poeta chileno reflejaría la doctrina extramoral del filósofo alemán, que afirma con entusiasmo la voluntad de poder del individuo, mediante la liberación de su vitalidad instintiva. [OH]

5951 Lutz, Robyn R. The inseparability of opposites in José Lezama Lima's *Muerte de Narciso* (UK/KRQ, 31:3, 1984, p. 329–339)

Robyn Lutz describe eficazmente la imagen de Narciso como una exploración de la idea de la identidad de los contrarios, según ésta se funde en la doble función de Narciso como víctima y cazador simultáneamente. También alude con acierto a la serie de oxímoros que proveen un paralelo retórico al fondo ideológico del poema. [RR]

5952 Maggi, María Elena. La poesía de Ramón Palomares y la imaginación americana. Caracas: Centro de Estudios Latinoamericanos Rómulo Gallegos, 1982. 133 p.

Examina la obra de Palomares (1935) desde *El reino* (1958) hasta *Adiós Escuque* (1974). Considera los componentes del mundo imaginario—fábula, magia, mitos—y las particularidades expresivas—lenguaje

coloquial, versolibrismo, función del ritmo—
en seis libros del período acotado. Estimables
aproximaciones en esos aspectos, pero el
enunciado del título resulta excesivo. [PL]

5953 Méndez de Penedo, Lucrecia. Visión de
la soledad en un poemario de Luis Cardoza y Aragón (Letras de Guatemala [Univ.
de San Carlos de Guatemala, Facultad de Humanidades, Instituto de la Literatura Nacional, Guatemala] 1, junio 1980, p. 31–57)

En las primeras 10 de las 14 composiciones de *Soledad* (1936), Cardoza sienta la
dialéctica básica entre vida y soledad, de
manera que ésta, al apuntar hacia la muerte
que acecha al hombre, suscita el impulso
creador—amatorio que propone a la poesía
como resolución. En los poemas restantes se
ahonda esta dialéctica: el mismo viaje a la
muerte engendra la trascendencia de amor,
vida y poesía. [GY]

5954 Miller, Beth. Rosario Castellanos, una
conciencia feminista en México. México: Univ. Autónoma de Chiapas, Depto. de
Literatura, 1983. 109 p. (Col. Maciel)

Util estudio desde una crítica feminista de la obra poética, novelística y ensayística de la reconocida escritora chiapaneca. [NK]

5955 Miró, Rodrigo. Cuatro ensayos sobre la
poesía de Ricardo Miró. Panamá: Editorial Universitaria, 1983. 97 p.

Los primeros dos ensayos reseñan la
obra de Miró, ubicándola en el contexto histórico de la constitución de la república
(1903). Debido a una general falta de cultura,
según Miró Grimaldo, ni Miró ni los otros
poetas de la época forman auténticos modernistas, con toda la panoplia cultural que
ello implica. Miró fue "romántico de la más
pura estirpe," cuyos temas dilectos fueron
mujer, luna, mar, gaviotas, garzas y noche.
Apolítico, escribió con sentimiento patrió-
tico. [GY]

5955a Monge, Carlos Francisco. La imagen
separada: modelos ideológicos de la
poesía costarricense. San José: Instituto del
Libro, Ministerio de Cultura, Juventud y
Deportes, 1984. 1 v.

Very important essay on relationship
between historic reality and contemporary
poetry of Costa Rica. From his dual perspective as artist and critic, this successful poet
examines with great lucidity the relationship

between art and ideology, aesthetics of poetic
realism, fetishism of language and nostalgic
posture of the poet. [R. Prieto]

5956 Montemayor, Carlos. Tres Contemporáneos. México: UNAM, 1981. 134 p.

Tres ensayos lúcidos y penetrantes
sobre la obra de tres Contemporáneos: Jorge
Cuesta, José Gorostiza y Gilberto Owen.
[NK]

5957 Ormes, María Celia G. de. David
Escobar Galindo: su contenido social a
través del proceso de reducción metafórica
en "Duelo Ceremonial por la Violencia"
(ESME/C, 63, enero/dic. 1978, p. 113–159)

Lengthy study about Salvadorean poet
presented in tightly didactic format and including: biography, bibliography, general
features of Escobar Galindo's poetry, and
structural analysis of his poem, "Duelo Ceremonial por la Violencia." [R. Prieto]

5958 Ortega, Julio. Entrevista con Antonio
Cisneros (HISPA, 13:37, abril 1984,
p. 31–44)

Aunque un tanto verbosa, esta entrevista tiene valor para los lectores interesados
en la obra poética del autor peruano. [J.M.
Oviedo]

5959 Ortiz, Juan L. Juan L. Ortiz: antología
poética. Selección y estudios de Edelweis Serra. Rosario, Argentina: Coquena Ediciones, 1982. 184 p.

Un gran poeta de la naturaleza (1897–
1978) formado en la tradición de Páscoli y
Perse, en que los objetos se valoran en su des-
lumbramiento y gesto ontológico, evitándose
la mayor parte de los lugares comunes de este
tipo de poesía. El prólogo de Edelweis Serra,
quizás demasiado entusiasta, informa bien
acerca de las preferencias temáticas y algunas
particularidades formales del autor. [JG]

5960 Panabière, Louis. Itinerario de una
disidencia, Jorge Cuesta, 1903–1942.
Traducción de Adolfo Castañón. México:
Fondo de Cultura Económica, 1983. 404 p.:
bibl., index (Vida y pensamiento de México)

Panabière analiza el itinerario poético
de Cuesta trazando vínculos entre este Contemporáneo disidente, su obra, y su tiempo.
Le interesa, además una mejor comprensión
del conflicto entre el intelectual y el Estado.
Sitúa el paradigma del conflicto en el México
de 1920–40, época clave en la que se lleva a
cabo la institucionalización de la Revolución,

y ve en el caso concreto de Cuesta una expresión ejemplar y de "asombrosa actualidad." Presenta a Cuesta como "la voz auténtica del intelectual" y su obra como "creadora de sentido, de Saber y de Poder no instituido, ante una situación política." Extensa bibliografía al final. [NK]

5961 Paoletti, Mario. Poemas con Arlt. Madrid: Ediciones del Monte Negro, 1983. 133 p.

Astuto esfuerzo poético construido sobre la base de hablantes líricos ficticios recogidos de la narrativa de Arlt. Aunque es preferible haber leído a Arlt, muchos poemas respiran un aire personal, independientemente del diálogo intertextual. [JG]

5962 *Revista del Pensamiento Centroamericano.* Centro de Investigaciones y Actividades Culturales. No. 177, oct./dic. 1982–. Managua.

Este indispensable número recoge el inédito *Cuadernos del sur* (poemarios de viajes) y la más destacada crítica sobre la obra de Cuadra. Dignos de mención: Stefan Baciu, "Pablo Antonio Cuadra, Poeta de lo Hispánico," hace hincapié en el cristianismo como visión de centro que abarca la solidaridad con el pueblo; Gloria Guardia de Alfaro, "Visión del Mundo o Centro Espiritual de Pablo Antonio Cuadra a través de Su Evolución Temática," entiende la visión de la naturaleza como resolución del problema ontológico, y el cristianismo y el mito como subtemas que vienen a encajar dentro de la primera visión; Franco Cerutti, "Introducción a la Poética de Pablo Antonio Cuadra," prefiere ver en Cuadra una religiosidad amorosa que se identifica con todo lo marginal y con la cotidianidad, más que con el cristianismo tradicional (Cuadra ha defendido su ortodoxia católica). Sus dos grandes temas son la antihistoria (rechazo de las grandes figuras y solidaridad con los humildes) y la naturaleza, que define el ámbito nacional; Carlos Tünnermann Bernheim, "La Poesía Nicaragüense y Universal de Pablo Antonio Cuadra," asocia el Jesús de Cuadra con la teología de la liberación; Jean Louis Felz ve en *Cantos de Cifar* y *El jaguar y la luna* la expresión de una cultura mestiza que, a la vez, trasciende la dicotomía americano/universal. Cierra el volumen una nutrida bibliografía preparado por Jorge Eduardo Arellano. [GY]

5963 Seluja, Antonio. Julio Herrera y Reissig: vida y obra. Montevideo: Ministerio de Educación y Cultura, 1984. 328 p., 16 p. of plates: bibl., ill., ports.

Otro aporte al estudio de Herrera y Reissig. Este volumen incluye un capítulo sobre la vida del poeta. Le sigue un largo estudio de la obra poética y una última sección dedicada a su obra en prosa. Este estudio recibió el premio de la Academia Nacional de Letras del Uruguay. [MGP]

5964 Serra, Jesús. Rafael Cadenas: poesía y vida. Maracaibo, Venezuela: Univ. del Zulia, Facultad de Humanidades y Educación, 1983. 67 p.

Esquemático acercamiento a la poesía de Cadenas (ver item **5776**), limitado a sus tres primeros libros: *Cantos iniciales* (1946), *Los cuadernos del destierro* (1960), y *Falsas maniobras* (1966). Comentario superficial (p. 9–46) que deja prácticamente intocada la interesante obra del autor. Cierra el volumen una breve antología (p. 47–66). [PL]

5965 Souza, Raymond D. The poetic fiction of José Lezama Lima. Columbia: Univ. of Missouri Press, 1983. 149 p.: bibl., index.

El primer libro en inglés dedicado por completo a la obra de Lezama. Es un estudio conciso y abarcador, que tiene la virtud de hacer accesible al lector anglo-parlante un poeta voluntariamente difícil. Es un compendio ponderado de las constantes del universo poético lezamiano, y aunque no posee un fuerte argumento central o una lectura renovadora de la obra del autor, ofrece en cambio una descripción articulada y sobria de la poética de Lezama, incluyendo su poesía, sus novelas y su ensayística, sin caer en la tentación en que han caído tantos de imitar el estilo hermético del poeta al tratar de explicarlo. [RRA]

5966 Teitelboim, Volodia. Neruda. Madrid: Michay, 1984. 425 p., 16 p. of plates: facsims., ill., index, ports. (Meridion)

Biografía de Pablo Neruda relatada por el novelista y dirigente del Partido Comunista de Chile, Volodia Teitelboim, quien fuera amigo inseparable de Neruda durante muchos años. El libro desilusiona, porque cuando se refiere a hechos de la vida del poeta en los que Teitelboim no estuvo presente, repite informaciones ya muy manidas, y cuando habla de sucesos que él conoció de primera mano, deja gusto a poco. [OH]

5967 Valdés, Jorge H. The evolution of Cardenal's prophetic poetry (LALR, 11:23, Fall/Winter 1983, p. 25–40)

Por "profético" no se quiere decir predicción sino guía hacia un nuevo mundo basada en una sapiencia derivada de la fe en Dios y en un conocimiento de la historia derivada, en parte, del marxismo. Tal profetismo arranca con los *Salmos* y llega a su plenitud en "Oráculo sobre Managua." [GY]

5968 Zavala, Iris M. Genética de *Los cisnes IV* de Rubén Darío: alegoría de la escritura (CM/NRFH, 32:2, 1983, p. 472–490)

Riguroso análisis, asistido por instrumentos de la crítica estructuralista, de la relación entre este poema y su "pre-texto manuscrito." Darío se desdobla en emisor y receptor que diáloga y polemiza consigo mismo sobre los materiales de la escritura. Esta alegoría narcisista de la escritura es figurada en el coito del cisne, vehículo del poema que se autoarrebata. [GY]

MISCELLANEOUS

5969 Aguirre, Raúl Gustavo. Las poéticas del siglo XX. Buenos Aires: Ediciones Culturales Argentinas, Secretaría de Cultura, Presidencia de la Nación, 1983. 223 p.

Breviario que ofrece un resumen de las ideas estéticas informando los grandes "ismos" de la poética moderna, desde el simbolismo al surrealismo. Aunque europeizante, derivativo, y harto elemental, es útil por sus consideraciones sobre el ultraismo, el creacionismo, y otras vertientes hispánicas insertándolo todo en un marco más amplio que el habitual. [RdC]

5970 Amighetti, Francisco. Poesía. San José: Editorial Costa Rica, 1983. 173 p.: ill.

Recopilación selectiva de la obra poética de uno de los más destacados pintores costarricenses. Paradójicamente, en sus poemas escasea la imagen visual, predominando una prosaica voz autoconfesional. Sus mejores poemas indagan la elementaridad de la naturaleza; la insipidez anecdótica estropea los otros. [GY]

5971 Chacón, Alfredo. Ensayos de crítica cultural, 1964–1981. Caracas: Ediciones Galería de Arte Nacional (GAN), 1982. 279 p.: bibl. (Col. Galería. Serie Crítica cultural)

De todos los ensayos y artículos periodísticos sobre literatura, cultura y política recogidos en este volumen, sólo el primero ("Experiencia de la Poesía," de 1964) puede tener interés como testimonio de Chacón sobre su obra poética. [J.M. Oviedo]

5972 Chase, Alfonso. El tigre luminoso. San José: Editorial Costa Rica, 1983. 140 p.

Más que poemas se trata de aforismos sobre la poesía y el papel del poeta, pronunciados en una rabiosa voz Lautréamontina-Rimbaldiana-Huidobresca. Interesa más su valor de "arte poética:" Martí como la auténtica voz americana; impugnación del aburguesamiento de voces alguna vez rebeldes (Dengo, Sáenz, Zeledón, Sancho, García Monge); valorización de las poetas (Gallegos, Naranjo, Oreamuno, Odio). [GY]

5973 Cobo Borda, J.G. Dos poetas colombianos (CM/D, 120, nov./dic. 1984, p. 24–31, ill.)

Caracteriza con claridad y agudeza la poesía de Alvaro Mutis y de Fernando Charry Lara. Una recomendable introducción a los espacios poéticos creados por dos de los escritores más significativos surgidos en torno a la revista *Mito* (ver item **5922**). [PL]

5974 CODICES. Centro de Documentación e Investigación Cultural de El Salvador, Frente Cultural de El Salvador. No. 1, 1985–. Managua.

Fuente indispensable para conocer la producción poética y cultural de la gran mayoría de escritores que se han integrado a la insurrección. CODICES (Centro de Documentación e Investigación Cultural de El Salvador) hace hincapié en la expresión de la identidad salvadoreña. No se esquiva el tradicional lirismo, pues la poética por la cual se aboga lo funde con la inscripción de la realidad social. [GY]

5975 Coronel Urtecho, José. Conversando con José Coronel Urtecho. Relatado por Manlio Tirado. Managua: Editorial Nueva Nicaragua, 1983. 143 p., 4 leaves of plates: ports. (Col. Letras de Nicaragua; 5)

Coronel Urtecho evoca pasajes memorables de su vida; lee y comenta algunos de sus poemas, explica su pasado político y suscribe la causa sandinista. De especial interés son sus recuerdos de EE.UU. y las influencias que los norteamericanos tuvieron en su obra. [GY]

5976 Cuadra, Pablo Antonio. Entre poesía y política: entrevista por Steven F. White (VUELTA, 9:102, mayo 1985, p. 29–33)

Entrevista clave donde Cuadra rememora: el inicio de Vanguardia y sus proyectos políticos (nacionalismo cuasi fascista, antiyanquismo, hispanismo, la adhesión a Sandino). Explica su oposición al actual gobierno nicaragüense por: imposición de modelos foráneos (estatismo soviético-cubano) con repercusiones en la poesía y en la revolución. No obstante, Cuadra opina que la originalidad nicaragüense prevalecerá sobre toda imposición. [GY]

5977 Cuadra, Pablo Antonio. Situación de la cultura en Nicaragua (VUELTA, 9:105, agosto 1985, p. 50–53)

Además de lo dicho en la entrevista con Steven White (ver item **5976**), se hace hincapié en la censura a que es sometida *La Prensa* y que los sandinistas o niegan o justifican (por la guerra). Cuadra impugna la hipocresía, según él, de un poder que se arroga la absolutez bajo la máscara ideológica de la democracia, y que tiene repercusiones en la cultura. Aboga por la autonomía de la poesía. Pero, ¿no es esta posición también ideológica? El mismo artículo apareció en *Revista del Pensamiento Centroamericano* (Managua, 40:106, enero/mayo 1985, p. 191–197). [GY]

5978 Edwards, Jorge. Homenaje a Nicanor Parra (VUELTA, 8:87, feb. 1984, p. 16–19, ill.)

Este homenaje a Nicanor Parra es el único poema que se conoce del novelista y cuentista Jorge Edwards. Escrito a la manera de los antipoemas, el hablante pasa revista a distintos momentos de su amistad con el homenajeado, y al igual que éste, se vale de la narratividad, del lenguaje coloquial y del humor como arma para embestir contra los enemigos del antipoeta. Queda en claro que la antipoesía es el vehículo apropiado para los narradores que desean incursionar en otro género. [OH]

5979 Guadamuz, Carlos José. Y—"las casas quedaron llenas de humo." Managua: Editorial Nueva Nicaragua, 1982. 109 p.: ill. (Biblioteca popular sandinista; 12)

Written in 1970, this unusual journal written by Guadamuz in the prison of Tipitapa covers years between the FSLN founda-tion in 1961 and the Sandinista patriarch Julio Buitrago's death on July 15, 1969. Contains poems and illustrations by Sandinista Commander Lenín Cerna as well as information on Buitrago's student activities by his cellmates. Most of the characters mentioned under pseudonyms are living and dead Sandinista heroes (e.g., Carlos Fonseca Amador, Oscar Turcios). [R. Prieto]

Hacia una política cultural de la Revolución Popular Sandinista. See *HLAS* 47:6192.

5980 *Inti.* Dept. of Modern Languages, Providence College. No. 18/19, Autumn 1983/Spring 1984–. Providence.

Número especial (entrega doble) de una importante revista norteamericana dedicada a la literatura de América Latina. Intitulado "Catorce Poetas Hispanoamericanos de Hoy," este número se destaca por ser una "muestra" de los poetas más actuales y otros tantos 14 ensayos de presentación preparados por los críticos más autorizados sobre cada uno de los antologizados. [RdC]

5981 Larrea, Juan. Apogeo del mito. Prólogo de Teresa Waisman. México: CEESTEM: Editorial Nueva Imagen, 1983. 313, 3 p., 28 p. of plates: bibl., ill. (Col. Cuadernos americanos; 4)

Recopilación de los ensayos de Larrea aparecidos originalmente entre 1944–48 en *Cuadernos Americanos*, revista de la que fue fundador. [RdC]

5982 Liscano, Juan. Descripciones. Prólogo de Alberto Girri. Buenos Aires: Ediciones de la Flor; Caracas: Monte Avila Editores, 1983. 257 p.: bibl.

Reúne nueve ensayos, principalmente referidos a poetas hispanoamericanos: C. Vallejo, O. Paz, O. Orozco, A. Girri, R.J. Muñoz, y J. Gaitán Durán, entre otros. Estas sugestivas indagaciones logran transmitir con inmediatez una reflexión crítica fundada en la atención "a la vida concreta de los poemas." Son notables los estudios "Dentro del Círculo de los Tres Soles" (p. 129–198), sobre la poesía de Rafael José Muñoz (ver item **5850**), y "Gaitán Durán: Erotismo y Pulsión de Muerte" (p. 103–128; ver item **5810**). [PL]

5983 *Literature and Contemporary Revolutionary Culture.* Society for the Study of Contemporary Hispanic and Lusophone Revolutionary Literature. No. 1, 1984/1985–. Minneapolis, Minn.

Imprescindible primer número de esta nueva revista—entre otros—una sección sobre la teoría de la producción literaria revolucionaria que aporta mucho a la comprensión de la poesía popular y el género testimonial en los países centroamericanos. Destacan los ensayos de James Iffland, "Hacia una Teoría de la Función del Humor en la Poesía Revolucionaria (a propósito de Roque Dalton)," Santiago Daydi-Tolson, "Formas de Oralidad en la Poesía Revolucionaria Hispanoamericana," y Eliana Rivero, "Testimonios y Conversaciones como Discurso Literario: Cuba y Nicaragua." Otra sección trata específicamente de Centroamérica: Marc Zimmerman y Ellen Banberger, "Poetry and Politics in Nicaragua: the Uprising of 1978," John Beverly, "Poetry in the Central American Revolution: Ernesto Cardenal and Roque Dalton," Hugo Achúgar, "Poesía Política e Interpelación Populista: el Caso de la Poesía Salvadoreña," Monique J. Lemaître, "Apuntes sobre Estructura e Ideología en Algunos Textos de Roque Dalton," John M. Kirk, "Revolutionary Music, Salvadoran Style: Yolocamba Ita." [GY]

5984 Lizalde, Eduardo. Autobiografía de un fracaso: el poeticismo. México: Martín Casilla, 1981. 118 p.

Importante autobiografía para el conocimiento de este excelente poeta inconforme, donde hace memoria de sus años adolescentes de formación estética. Historia y antología que presenta poemas inéditos y poemas publicados en 1949–50, no recogidos en volúmenes posteriores, "para impedir que otros consuman más tarde esta misma antología para victimar, por cuenta ajena, al autor." [NK]

5985 Morales Avilés, Ricardo. No pararemos de andar jamás. Recopilación de textos del Instituto de Estudio del Sandinismo. Prólogo de Jaime Wheelock Román y Bayardo Arce Castaño. 2a ed. Managua: Editorial Nueva Imagen, 1983. 172 p. (Col. Pensamiento vivo)

Political prose poems and letters by theoretician and military leader of the Sandinista National Liberation Front. Compiled by the Institute of Sandinista Studies and prefaced by Jaime Wheelock Román and Bayardo Arce Castaño, Commanders of the Revolution. [R. Prieto]

5986 Nicaragua in reconstruction & at war: the people speak; a collage of chronology, analysis, poetry, etc. portraying insurrection, reconstruction, cultural revolution & U.S. intervention. Edited and translated by Marc Zimmerman. Minneapolis, Minn.: MEP Publications, 1985. 314 p.: bibl., ill. (Studies in Marxism; 17)

No existe mejor fuente para comprender la actual producción poética de la revolución nicaragüense en su contexto histórico y político. Zimmerman inventa un nuevo género entre el ensayo analítico y el collage—que incluye poesía, eslogans, discursos, grafitti, canciones, etc.—para presentarnos, casi hacernos presenciar, el proceso multidimensional en que se produce la cultura. [GY]

5987 Rugama, Leonel. The earth is a satellite of the moon. Translated by Sara Miles, Richard Schaff, and Nancy Weisberg. Willimantic, Conn.: Curbstone Press, 1985. 1 v.

Su poesía combina la ironía sofisticada de un Roque Dalton (a quien se parece) y el relajo de un adolescente (cayó en la lucha a los 20 años), pero en solidaridad con el pueblo. Este volumen incluye algunos testimonios sobre él y varios de sus ensayos. [GY]

5988 Silva, Ludovico. Ensayos temporales: poesía y teoría social. Caracas: Academia Nacional de la Historia, 1983. 247 p. (El Libro menor; 45)

Colección de breves ensayos y notas periodísticas escritas en la última década por un ensayista quizá más conocido como investigador social y marxista heterodoxo. Los textos son dispares en valor, contenido y enfoque. Quizá merezca destacarse el polémico "Octavio Paz y el Marxismo." [J.M. Oviedo]

Drama

GEORGE WOODYARD, *Professor of Spanish, University of Kansas*

THE RATE OF GROWTH IN LATIN AMERICAN THEATRE in recent years has been exponential. In the course of preparing this section of *HLAS*, the number of plays exceeded 200. A great number of anthologies, both with individual and multiple authors, supplement the single editions. Spanish American theatre continues to be highly political, emphasizing the close relationship between life and art in the hemisphere. The overwhelming reality of socioeconomic and political issues in everyday life easily transposes to the stage and finds an enthusiastic and receptive audience. A new trend of psychological, family-oriented theatre is promising. Argentina, Chile, Cuba, and Mexico continue to be the major publishers of theatre, although nearly every country is represented. The well established writers continue to appear (e.g., Carballido, Chocrón, Dragún, Gambaro, Garro, Leñero) at the same time that other newer writers of importance are emerging. Pacho O'Donnell (item **6032**) and Hebe Serebrisky (item **6046**) are new lights in Argentina, on a level with de la Parra (item **6033**) in Chile, Navajas (item **6031**) in Colombia, Ramos-Perea (item **6040**) in Puerto Rico, and Villegas (item **6056**) in Mexico. Fuentes (item **6011**) and Vargas Llosa (item **6055**), masters of narrative, are both represented with new plays. Cuban theatre continues to be published in great quantities, although the experimentation has peaked and both thematic and technical redundancy has become problematical.

New bibliographical studies are of particular value in enhancing the efforts of research scholars, and several new ones are available: the monumental two-volume work by Fernando de Toro and Peter Roster (item **6060**), Luzuriaga's work on Ecuador (item **6091**), and Duane Rhoades's compilation of the monologue (item **6110**). As better bibliographical control becomes available in the field, the direction clearly points toward more intensive, monographic studies of particular playwrights whose work remains relatively untouched, as well as broader treatments, well-founded in theory, that look at major trends and developments. Semiotics has become the accepted methodological approach in dealing with theatre, and a book such as David William Foster's study on the independent theatre in Argentina (item **6079**) is a good model, as is, in microcosm, Østergaard's article on *Relevo 1923* (item **6106**). Fernández's book on Chilean theatre (item **6076**) is more traditional in approach but no less useful for its comprehensive overview of a particular period. A symbiotic relationship between creative texts and insightful criticism is, in the long run, exactly what is needed.

PLAYS

5989 Acosta, Iván. *El super*: tragi-comedia. Miami, Fla.: Ediciones Universal, 1982. 72 p.: ill. (Col. Teatro)
Cuban immigrant theatre in New York that depicts problems of working-class exiles despondent over poor living conditions, nostalgic for Cuba, betrayed by the Revolution, unable to speak English, and with bilingual/bicultural children without historic memory, who are unsympathetic. A sad and cynical view of Cubans in exile.

5990 Babot, Jarl Ricardo. *La fiera en el jardín*: obra que bien podría llamarse *El gato está herido* (LNB/L, 334/335, enero/feb. 1984, p. 72–87)
Strange two-character play of tormented individuals searching for love and meaning in life and death.

5991 Babot, Jarl Ricardo. *Historias verdaderas*: obra en dos actos (LNB/L, 348/349, marzo/abril 1985, p. 93–120)

Strange story of lies and fictions, of presumptions and false identities, of suicides, murders, solitude and anguish—in a context of absurd love.

5992 Baksht Segovia, Pablo. *Hacia el futuro* (UNAM/PP, 81, 1984, p. 61–71, ill.)

Solution provided by a time machine for a couple escaping wartime misery and persecution. Enigmatic and sketchy one-act play that needs more development.

5993 Bravo-Elizondo, Pedro. Teatro documental latinoamericano. México: UNAM, Coordinación de Humanidades, 1982. 2 v. (399 p.) (Serie Teatro)

Two-volume anthology that chronicles the development of documentary theatre in Latin America, following the models of Peter Weiss and Rolf Hochhuth. Vol. 1 contains Buenaventura's *La denuncia* and Sergio Arrau's *Manuel viene galopando por las alamedas*.

5994 Brene, José R. Teatro. Prólogo de Manuel Galich. La Habana: Editorial Letras Cubanas, 1982. 351 p. (Repertorio teatral cubano)

Four representative plays of a Cuban Revolutionary writer best known for his *Santa Camila de La Habana*. The popular language, humor, lower-class settings, and weak dramatic structures also characterize the other three plays: *El gallo de San Isidro*, *Miss Candonga*, and *El corsario y la abadesa*.

5995 Britto García, Luis. *La misa del esclavo*. Caracas: Centro Latinoamericano de Creación e Investigación Teatral: Ateneo de Caracas, 1983. 62 p. (Col. Concurso Andrés Bello. Dramaturgia latinoamericana. Dramaturgo venezolano; 1)

First Prize in the first Andrés Bello competition sponsored by CELCIT, this play posits conflicts by social class and race during the period of the war of independence to suggest universal and eternal issues of individual liberty and equality. Elaborate musical directions give the play the structure of a mass.

5996 Carballido, Emilio. *Tiempo de ladrones*: la historia de Chucho El Roto. México: Grijalbo, 1983. 256 p. (Col. Narrativa)

Carballido's epic version of Jesús Arriaga, alias Chuco El Roto, the Mexican Robin Hood who undermines traditional law and justice with his daring escapades. Written in two *tandas*, packed with 19th-century adventure, the play is an excellent example of total theatre. Carballido suggests various scenic selections, almost by lottery.

Carpentier, Alejo. La aprendiz de bruja; Concierto barroco; El arpa y la sombra. See item **5384.**

5997 Chocrón, Isaac E. *Okey; La revolución; El acompañante*. Caracas: Monte Avila Editores, 1981. 219 p. (Teatro/Isaac Chocrón; 1. Col. Teatro)

Three of Chocrón's best plays, collected into a new anthology, dealing with important themes in Venezuela: consumerism, homosexuality, and power.

5998 Crespo Paniagua, Renato. *Dar posada al peregrino*: comedia en 3 actos. Cochabamba, Bolivia: s.n., 1981. 107 p.

Drawing-room comedy about a political activist who seeks refuge in a five-star hotel after a street demonstration. Neither funny nor polemical.

5999 Crespo Paniagua, Renato. *Morir un poco*: teatro. Cochabamba, Bolivia: Editorial Serrano, 1977. 109 p.

Passable comedy in which the "whodunit" of a theater company gets confused with reality. Light and entertaining.

6000 Cuadra, Pablo Antonio. *Por los caminos van los campesinos*. 5a ed. Managua: Ediciones El Pez y la Serpiente, 1982. 108 p.

Reprint of classic 1937 Nicaraguan protest play previously anthologized by Solórzano. Takes on new meaning as politics shift from Somocistas to Sandinistas.

6001 Cuvi, Pablo. *El hermano menor de Marlon Brando*. Quito: El Autor, 1983. 163 p.

Collection of four plays, a monologue, and a short story for which the title play establishes the tone of modern-day youth dealing with crime, leftist politics, and various social ills and issues. Engaging material.

6002 Dalton, Roque and Peperuiz. *Los helicópteros*: pieza teatral en varias escenas. San Salvador: Editorial Universitaria de El Salvador, 1980. 82 p. (Col. Literatura)

This play, finished by Peperuiz after Roque Dalton's death, uses the helicopter as a central image and vehicle in the ongoing struggle between oppressors and oppressed. Lightened by the intervention of the *máscaras*, it is nonetheless disjointed and naive, suffering structural deficiencies.

6003 Dávila Vázquez, Jorge. *Con gusto a muerte.* 3a ed. Cuenca, Ecuador: Impreso Offset Monsalve Moreno, 1981. 78 p.: ill.

Brief play about three sisters, consumed by hatred, jealousy, and frustration, isolated with the phantoms of their crime of passion. Possibly effective with strong actresses.

6004 Díaz, Gabriel; Mauricio Kartun; Eduardo Pogoriles; and Víctor Winer. *Teatro.* Prólogo de Ricardo Monti. Buenos Aires: D. Kartun, 1982. 138 p.

Four plays, mostly first attempts, of uneven quality, by young writers of the 1970s. The common denominator is the disillusion, the desperate search for values and meaning. Includes: Gabriel Díaz, *Con el otro*; Mauricio Kartun, *Chau Misterix*; Eduardo Pogoriles, *Agonía para soñadores*; Víctor Winer, *Buena presencia*. Only Kartun's is full length, others are brief.

6005 Díaz Mora, Margarita. *La mariposa incorruptible*: comedia de carácter en 2 actos, el último dividido en 3 cuadros. México: Dirección de Difusión Cultural, Depto. Editorial, Univ. Autónoma Metropolitana, 1980. 86 p. (Molinos de viento; 3)

When a young man's best friend kidnaps him to force skeletons out of the closet, the victim's family comes to grips with honor and ethics. Worthwhile effort by young Mexican writer with only one other play to her credit.

6006 Dragún, Osvaldo. *Historias para ser contadas al perdedor.* Rosario, Argentina: Ediciones Paralelo 32, 1982. 95 p., 1 leaf of plates: ill. (Col. Teatro del hombre; 1)

Reprint of Dragún's three classic one-act *Historias* plus *Al perdedor* (companion piece of *Al vencedor*), which uses the metaphor of a boxer programmed to win who finds his own identity and happiness when he loses the match, thus cutting through pretenses and false illusions of religion, politics, and family.

6007 Enríquez Gamón, Efraín. *La guerra inconclusa*: esquema para una ideología nacional. Asunción: Editora Litocolor, 1982. 114 p.: ill.

Essayistic play eulogizes the ideology of Natalicio González in Paraguayan politics. Interesting as history, but not as theatre. Includes author's 1978 lecture on the subject.

6008 Esayag, Abraham. *El hombre que hacía click.* S.l.: Dirección General de Cultura, Gobernación del Distrito Federal, 1980. 83 p. (Cuadernos de difusión. Serie Breves)

Photographer turned blackmailer sees his plan to court the country's lead actress turn sour when his standards of morality differ from society's norm. Light comedy.

6009 Estorino, Abelardo. *Teatro.* Prólogo de Salvador Arias. La Habana: Editorial Letras Cubanas, 1984. 394 p.

Four plays by Cuba's senior playwright: *El robo del cochino* (1961), *La casa vieja* (1964), *La dolorosa historia del amor secreto de Don José Jacinto Milanés* (1974), and *Ni un sí ni un no* (1980). Different styles over the years reveal Estorino's penchant for innovation while expressing the psychological and political realities of contemporary Cuba.

6010 Ferrari, Juan Carlos. *Las nueve tías de Apolo.* Buenos Aires: Ediciones Colihue, 1983. 123 p.: ill. (Col. Literatura LYC [leer y crear])

A mythology of Apollo's nine "aunts" on Parnassus as transposed to rural Argentina where Apollo searches for a life project. Issues transcend to other generations (Apollo's son) who returns after the war. A time span of 40 plus years offers a good, diachronic vision of Argentine problems.

6011 Fuentes, Carlos. *Orquídeas a la luz de la luna*: comedia mexicana. Barcelona, Spain: Seix Barral, 1982. 111 p. (Teatro. Biblioteca breve; 494)

Fuentes wrote simultaneously the Spanish and English version of this play in which he examines the Mexican national image and popular conceptions of stars of stage and screen incarnate in María Félix and Dolores del Río. Captivating material, rich in myth and legend, and very playable as theatre.

6012 Galotto, Roque M. *Papá Arbol*: drama en dos actos. Concepción, Uruguay: El Autor, 1982. 34 p.

Brief two-act psychological play explores a 19-year-old boy's relationship with a father who does not love him. Deserving of Argentores' promotional plan.

6013 García Velloso, Enrique. *Gabino El Mayoral*; *Fuego fatuo*. Prólogo de Roberto A. Tálice. Buenos Aires: Ediciones Culturales Argentinas, Secretaría de Cultura, Presidencia de la Nación, 1983. 124 p. (Col. de teatro breve argentino; 2)

New edition of two *sainetes* by García Velloso: *Gabino El Mayoral*, written at age 18 (in 1898), has a credible dialogue but melodramatic development in a typical Buenos Aires ambiance. *Fuego fatuo* (1906) presents a more complex and enigmatic structure in a similar setting.

6014 Garro, Elena. *Un hogar sólido*, y otras piezas. Ilustraciones de Juan Soriano. Xalapa, México: Univ. Veracruzana, 1983. 332 p.: ill. (Ficción)

Expanded version of the 1958 edition which included only the first six plays. The second six echo themes and techniques that reveal Garro's preoccupation with the bizarre and mysterious. *Los perros, El árbol* and *El rastro* are emotionally charged personal experiences abut rape, torture, and death. *La dama boba* is a delightful comedy with the intertextuality of a play by Lope de Vega.

6015 González de Cascorro, Raúl. *Traición en Villa Feliz*. La Habana: Editorial Letras Cubanas, 1978. 295 p. (Repertorio teatral cubano)

Four plays by this Cuban novelist and short story writer, written and set both before and after the Revolution, all reveal concern for human values within oppressive situations. The best and most complex technically is the title play, although *Una paloma para Graciela* (1956) is a tender portrayal of disillusioned love against excessive machismo and exploitation.

6016 González Dueñas, Daniel. *El espacio discreto*: monólogo para dos actores en un acto (UNAM/PP, 81, 1984, p. 23–59, ill.)

Long one-act two-character play dependent on metatheatrical principles to explore concepts of therapy and analysis along with aspects of political theory. Ambitious perhaps, but interesting.

6017 Gregorio, Jesús. *¡Chocolate campeón!* La Habana: Unión de Escritores y Artistas de Cuba, 1982. 153 p.

This second play by Gregorio (b. 1939) won the 1981 UNEAC Prize. Based on historical boxers from the period 1918–35, Eligio Sardiñas as Kid Chocolate is the protagonist whose strong discipline enables him to defeat his decadent opponents. A musical play, open to any spectator. Political references (to the fall of Machado) are minimal.

6018 Gutiérrez, Ignacio et al. Teatro y revolución. La Habana: Editorial Letras Cubanas, 1980. 390 p. (Letras cubanas)

From Cuba, six plays that reflect Revolutionary principles and values, by six excellent writers who look at both rural and urban issues from different perspectives. Useful introduction by Graziella Pogolotti.

6019 Heiremans, Luis Alberto; Fernando Debesa; and Egon Wolff. Teatro chileno contemporáneo. Santiago: Editorial A. Bello, 1982. 185 p.

In *El tony chico* Heiremans uses the universally popular figure of the circus clown to express fundamental meanings; Debesa's *El árbol Pepe* presents a 14-year-old polio victim whose illusions about life are shattered by those closest to him; Wolff's *Alamos en la azotea*, his only comedy, is not his best effort.

6020 Herrera, Larry; Mariela Romero; and Aulio Urdaneta. Textos teatrales. Caracas: Centro de Estudios Latinoamericanos Rómulo Gallegos: Monte Avila Editores, 1982. 139 p. (Col. Voces nuevas)

Three new plays by young Venezuelans with a common thread of death in various guises: 1) in mythical and allegorical contexts; 2) in the poverty and counterculture of contemporary life; and 3) in abstract and ritualistic terms. With language appropriate to each.

6021 Hiriart, Hugo; Héctor Azar; and Ignacio Arriola Haro. *Diálogos del alma y el cuerpo* [de] Hugo Hiriart; *Los diálogos de la clase medium* [de] Héctor Azar; *Diálogo de espejos* [de] Ignacio Arriola Haro (CM/D, 118, julio/agosto 1984, p. 1–40, ill.)

Three "dialogues" by three Mexican writers with different perspectives: Hiriart's Greek setting is mythical and mysterious; Azar's middle-class farce is precious, clever, multilingual and part of a trilogy; Arriola's two-character piece is limpid and naked. If not representative, the three are at least playable and interesting.

6022 Jaramillo, Juan. *La falla;* y *El día de los gallinazos*: teatro. Bogotá: Ediciones Puesto de Combate, 1981. 99 p. (Col. La Cuerda floja)

Two plays with common thread of oppressive power. *La falla*, dedicated to Gênet, deals symbolically with brutal encounters in a fascist mode, using games to convey a ritual process. *El día de los gallinazos* is more direct theatre of protest.

6023 Leñero, Estela. *Casa llena* (UNAM/PP, 81, 1984, p. 73–90)

With resonances of *Flores de papel*, this two-character play deals with a man's invasion of a woman's space, with a more definitive resolution in this case.

6024 Leñero, Vicente. *Las noches blancas*: obra en cuatro noches. México: Difusión Cultural, UNAM, Depto. de Teatro, Depto. de Humanidades, 1980. 47 p., 8 p. of plates: ill. (Textos de teatro; 14)

Play set in 19th-century St. Petersburg, Russia, which gives it an exotic and romantic air. Consists of four parts with a Villaurrutian-quality in which a young girl vacillates between two suitors. Poignant.

6025 Leñero, Vicente. Teatro completo. v. 1. Edición y prólogo de Bruce Swansey. México: Extensión Universitaria/UNAM, Dirección de Actividades Teatrales, Unidad Editorial, 1982. 1 v.: bibl. (Textos de teatro)

Vol. 1 contains four documentary plays: 1) *Pueblo rechazado* (1967–68) about Father Lemercier's episode in the Cuernavaca Monastery; *Compañero* (1967–68) about Che Guevara; *El juicio* (1971) about José de León Toral's and Madre Conchita's trial for the assassination of President-elect Obregón; and *Martirio de Morelos* (1980–81) about a Mexican independence hero. Invaluable edition that includes copious reviews, documentation and bibliography, and an excellent introduction by Bruce Swansey.

6026 Martínez Vizcarrondo, Antonio. *Teorema, alfa y omega.* Hato Rey, P.R.: Master Graphics, 1982. 148 p.

Two conjoined plays steeped in philosophy and allegory that use Yahweh and Jesus, Aristotle and Plato to reflect on meanings in life, especially from the perspective of a young Puerto Rican trying to adapt to the vicissitudes of life in New York. Interesting first attempt, but a long way to go.

6027 Minera, Otto. *Siete pecados en la capital*: teatro; a partir de *Los siete pecados capitales de la pequeña burguesía*, texto para ballet de Bertolt Brecht. México: M. Casillas Editores, 1983. 100 p. (Serie El Teatro)

Fashioned on Brecht's homonymous ballet, this lyrical play, much of it in verse, is structured around two sisters named Ana tempted through various settings by the seven capital sins. Placards and techniques point to the overriding social message for the bourgeoisie. Premio Casa de las Américas, 1983.

6028 Montes Huidobro, Matías. *La navaja de Olofé* (CM/D, 114, nov./dic. 1983, p. 68–73, ill.)

An intensely sexual—and emasculating—play about male/female roles in an early 20th-century Afro-Cuban environment filled with superstition, myth, and magic.

6029 Morales, Jacobo. *Aquélla, la otra, éste y aquél*: pieza en nueve cuadros. San Juan: Instituto de Cultura Puertorriqueña, 1981. 153 p. (Serie Literatura hoy)

Two-character full-length play that achieves the dislocations associated with Pirandellian metatheatre through the use of a "mentalist" who transports a woman to other times, places, and personalities, finally killing her to retain her in his enigmatic "other" world.

6030 Morales, José Ricardo. *Fantasmagorías*: cuatro apariciones escénicas. Santiago: Editorial Universitaria, 1981. 151 p. (Cormorán. Col. Teatro; 9)

Metatheatrical monologue, a one-act mystery and two full-length plays, one that threatens nuclear destruction and the other that describes 8th-century Spanish politics in 20th-century terms, comprise this collection in which the common denominators are the fantastic and the inevitability of human gullibility and self-destruction.

6031 Navajas, Esteban. *Canto triste a una sombra de boxeo.* Antioquia, Colombia: Ediciones Literatura, Arte y Ciencia, Univ. de Antioquia, 1983. 69 p.

By the author of *Agonía del difunto*, this play portrays a pathetic boxer who never made "champ" and who now serves as trainer for his granddaughter in a dance marathon. Failure is the common denominator of this emotional setting.

6032 O'Donnell, Pacho. Teatro. Buenos Aires: Editorial Gelerna, 1982. 212 p.
Four plays by one of Argentina's most promising young playwrights. Of the four, *Vincent y los cuervos*, based on Van Gogh à-la-Antonin Artaud, is a stunning representation of relationships between life and art.

6033 Parra, Marco Antonio de la. Teatro: *Lo crudo, lo cocido, lo podrido; Matatangos: disparen sobre el zorzal*. Prólogo de Juan Andrés Piña. Santiago: Editorial Nascimiento, 1983. 159 p. (Biblioteca popular nascimiento)
Two plays by Chile's best young psychiatrist/playwright: *Lo crudo, lo cocido, lo podrido* invoked the wrath of the military regime the night before the plays opened at Teatro de la Univ. Católica; and 2) *Matatangos: disparen sobre el zorzal*, also set in 1978, demythifies Gardel with an engaging ritual technique. Innovative plays that reveal a linguistic talent worthy of Jorge Díaz.

6034 Paz Hernández, Albio. Teatro. La Habana: Editorial Letras Cubanas, 1982. 360 p. (Repertorio teatral cubano)
Of the 11 plays in the collection, three deserve special attention: 1) *La vitrina*, of an early collaborative work of Teatro Escambray; 2) *Antón, Antón Pirulero*, an intimate portrayal of individual and collective responsibility; and 3) *Huelga*, a confrontation with the American Steel Co. in 1936–38. Paz is redundant at times, but there are flashes of talent.

6035 Perozzo, Carlos and Alberto Dow. *La Cueva del infiernillo* [de] Carlos Perozzo. *El pequeño dictador* [de] Alberto Dow. Bogotá: Editora Cinco, 1982. 191 p.
Two prize-winning plays in a 1982 Colombian competition; both have an engaging freshness and humor in realistic situations. Perozzo intertwines characters and themes from *Hamlet* in ingenious ways into a play with political overtones. Dow's *El pequeño dictador* depicts a dictatorship in Latin American but with refreshing dialogue and characters.

6036 Prado, Horacio del; Germán González Arquati; Diego Mileo; and Roberto Perinelli. Teatro. Buenos Aires: Los Autores, 1983. 143 p.

Continuation of previous volume designed to make known members of Argentina's new generation. Includes: Horacio del Prado, *El descenso*; Germán González Arquati, *El fondo*; Diego Mileo, *Benemérita institución*; and Roberto Perinelli, *Los pies en remojo*. Plays are less political, more attuned to farce, fable, and family.

6037 Radrigán, Juan. *Hechos consumados*. Santiago: Ediciones Minga, 1982. 142 p.: ill. (Col. Hombre y sociedad)
One of the best plays by this new Chilean playwright who exploded on the scene in 1979, *Hechos consumados* focuses on hunger in the lower class. Also includes a monologue, *Isabel desterrada en Isabel*, plus *El invitado*, also about hunger.

6038 Radrigán, Juan. Teatro: 11 obras. Santiago: CENECA; Minneapolis: Univ. de Minnesota, 1984. 418 p.: bibl.
Nine (not 11) plays in five years by Chile's new playwright who focuses on the marginal class. *Hechos consumados* (1981) and *El toro por las astas* (1982) are particularly good portrayals of the suffering, anguish, and misery of the poor. Excellent introductions by María de la Luz Hurtado, Juan Andrés Piña, and Hernán Vidal analyze techniques of language and structure.

6039 Ramos, José Antonio. Teatro cubano: tres obras dramáticas. Recopilación de Esther Sánchez-Grey Alba. New York: Senda Nueva de Ediciones, 1983. 153 p.: bibl. (Senda antológica)
Consists of three plays, each preceded by critical analysis, one of which ably traces influences of Ibsen, O'Neill, and others on Ramos, the father of modern Cuban theatre. *Calibán Rex*, *El traidor*, and *La recurva* all reveal Ramos's preoccupations with values and social justice as well as his attention to classical and experimental techniques of theatre.

6040 Ramos-Perea, Roberto. *Revolución en el infierno*: drama histórico basado en la Masacre de Ponce del 21 de marzo de 1937, Domingo de Ramos. Río Piedras, P.R.: Editorial Edil, 1983. 79 p.
Based on the Puerto Rican massacre (Ponce, 1937), this play by one of the island's best young playwrights brings dramatic life and intensity to a dark historical episode.

6041 Rascón Banda, Víctor Hugo. *Voces en el umbral*: nueva dramaturgia mexicana. México: Dirección de Difusión Cultural, Depto. Editorial, 1983. 45 p. (Molinos de viento; 19)

Death-bed reminiscences of an old lady, daughter of a German immigrant miner, set against the Indian background of her life-long companion. New and Old World cultures and values in conflict.

6042 Rivarola Matto, José María. Tres obras y una promesa. Asunción: Ediciones NAPA, 1983. 195 p., 7 leaves of plates: ill. (Libro paraguayo del mes; 23)

In addition to the well known *Chipi González* with its voice for personal freedom in spiritual and economic matters, this anthology includes two other plays that examine different aspects of good and evil, mortality and justice.

6043 Rossell, Levy. Ocho piezas de teatro venezolano. Caracas: El Autor, 1983. 344 p.

Of Rossell's eight plays, five are experimental pieces in one act, ranging through humor, farce, self-referentiality, and audience participation. *Vimazoluleka* has many quick scenes with songs and humor à la *Hair*. *La Atlántida* uses a chorus to mix mythology and evolution with a documentary flavor at the end.

6044 Rovinski, Samuel. *El martirio del pastor.* San José: Editorial Universitaria Centroamericana, 1983. 155 p. (Col. Séptimo día)

Well developed picture of conflict between Church and State, between democracy and communism, between rich and poor, as seen in the events leading up to the March 1980 assassination of Monseñor Oscar Arnulfo Romero, Archbishop of San Salvador, during the celebration of mass.

6045 Sánchez, Herminia. Teatro. Prólogo de Carlos Espinosa y Francisco Garzón. La Habana: Editorial Letras Cubanas, 1982. 276 p.: ill. (Repertorio teatral cubano)

The Teatro de Participación Popular, with direction and collaboration of Herminia Sánchez, created the three Revolutionary plays of this collection during the 1970s. *Cacha Basilia de Cabarnao* highlights three women in useful new roles; *Amante y penol* deals with life in the wharf area of Havana; *Audiencia en la Jacoba* studies the CDR (Comités de Defensa de la Revolución). Some good scenes of human interest.

6046 Serebrisky, Hebe. Teatro. Prólogos de Graciela M. Peyrú y Ernesto Schóo. Buenos Aires: Ediciones Teatrales Scena, 1982. 166 p.: ill.

Six short plays written 1979–82 by one of Argentina's brightest new (although not young) playwrights. Typical of the emotional intensity, play with symbol and image, and character doubling is *Don Elías, campeón*, a portrait of conflict and resolution after an identity crisis in provincial Argentina.

6047 Serulle, Haffe. *Bianto y su señor.* Santo Domingo: Ediciones Gramil, 1984. 141 p.

In a master-servant relationship, two characters use literary pretexts to search for metaphysical meaning and social justice. Well structured.

6048 Somigliana, Carlos. *Amarillo; Historia de una estatua.* Rosario, Argentina: Paralelo 32, 1983. 104 p.: ill. (Col. Teatro del hombre; 4)

Somigliana's first play and a recent one. *Amarillo* (written 1959) uses pre-Christian Rome as a metaphorical setting for land reform. *Historia de una estatua* (1983) dramatizes Gen. Lavalle's suicidal opposition during the Rosas era, again with metaphorical intent.

6049 Teatro breve contemporáneo argentino: antología. v. 2. Introducción, selección, notas y propuestas de trabajo de Elvira Burlando de Meyer y Patricio Esteve. Buenos Aires: Ediciones Colihue, 1983. 1 v.: appendix, bibl., ill. (Col. literaria LYC; 065)

Didactic edition with good introductions and biographical data. Adellach and Esteve deal with game-playing, the latter dependent on palindromes for communication, which reflects the absurdist dialogue of Pavlovsky's play as well. *Decir sí* is an intense study of dominant and submissive relationships marked by cruelty. An unannounced appendix contains Alberdi's *El gigante Amapolas*, a warning against excessive military control.

6050 El Teatro independiente. v. 2–3. Selección, prólogo y notas de Luis Ordaz. Buenos Aires: Centro Editor de América Latina, 1981. 2 v. (El Teatro argentino; 14–15. Capítulo. Biblioteca argentina fundamental; 94, 101)

Reprint with introductions, of four

classic Argentine plays that reflect different themes and styles, ranging through vituperative economic sanctions (*Una libra de carne*) to existentialist value systems (*El pan de la locura*), the melodramatic sainete (*Narcisa Garay*) and absurdist political repression (*El campo*).

6051 Teatro peruano. v. 6, *Requiem para siete plagas* [de] Grégor Díaz. *Ascenso y declive de una maroca* [de] J. Rivera Saavedra. *Los aprendices de brujo* [de] J. Schul. *Por la patria* [de] C. Vega Herrera. v. 7, Mimo. v. 8, El teatro universitario. Lima: Ediciones Homero Teatro de Grillos, 1982. 3 v.

Three volumes: vol. 6 consists of Grégor Díaz's play, an interesting expressionistic piece about marginal folk in an urban setting; Vega Herrera's and Schul's works are promising but ultimately too predictable; and Rivera Saavedra's play crosses parodies of bureaucracies and contemporary paranoia with an effective reversal at the end. Vol. 7 is a very short treatise that defines and illustrates the basics of mime, with notes on performances given. Vol. 8 reproduces results of survey sent to all universities about their theatre programs. Valuable reference for information on some ephemeral groups.

6052 Teatro venezolano. v. 1, *Caín adolescente* [de] Román Chalbaud. *Vida con mamá* [de] Elisa Lerner. *Madame Pompinette* [de] José Gabriel Núñez. Caracas: Monte Avila Editores, 1982. 1 v. (Antología fundamental de la literatura venezolana. Teatro)

Three plays with far-reaching repercussions in the political and artistic spectrum of Venezuela. *Madame Pompinette*, for example, is a brilliant monologue of human foibles intertwined with the political reality of Venezuela.

6053 Ugarte Elespuru, Juan Manuel. Teatro para leer. Ilustraciones y diagramación del autor. Lima: El Autor, 1982. 217 p.: ill.

Two plays the author values for their literary quality. *La rebelión de Atusparia* (1975) combines history and fiction to commemorate the Huaylas 1885 uprising of an Inca chief; *El Pedro eterno* (1978) is an equally long disquisitionary effort to denounce injustice in social class oppositions.

6054 Usigli, Rodolfo. *El gesticulador* y otras obras de teatro. México: Secretaría de Educación Pública, Cultura SEP, 1983. 263 p. (Lecturas mexicanas; 5)

Reprint of three of Usigli's best plays: 1) the classic *El gesticulador*; 2) the pathological *El niño y la niebla*; and 3) the sexual *Jano es una muchacha*. Also includes Usigli's autobiographical commentaries on all three plays.

6055 Vargas Llosa, Mario. *La chunga*. Barcelona, Spain: Seix Barral, 1986. 117 p. (Biblioteca breve. Teatro)

Third play by this major novelist relies on proved techniques of story-telling, of creating images of truth and fiction to expose the phantoms we carry inside.

6056 Villegas, Oscar. *La Atlántida; Santa Catarina*. México: Univ. Autónoma del Estado de México, 1982. 142 p. (Col. La Abeja en la colmena; 10)

Two full-length plays by one of Mexico's best young writers. *Atlántida* (1976) unmasks the mythical elements of a contemporary lower-class community plagued by false values; *Santa Catarina* (1969) looks at the superchanged emotional states that develop within the monosexual school for boys aged seven to 20.

6057 Villegas, Oscar. *Mucho gusto en conocerlo* y otras obras. México: Editores Mexicanos Unidos, 1985. 251 p.

Three of Villegas's best plays, *La paz de la buena gente*, *Santa Catarina*, and *Atlántida*, join his most recent and the title play in this volume that reveals his talent for experimental theatre where basic human experiences (love, sex, death) are manipulated with symbolic language, often to the accompaniment of rock music.

6058 Zavala Cataño, Víctor. Teatro campesino. Carátula y dibujos de Francisco Izquierdo López. 2a ed. Lima: Ediciones Escena Contemporánea, 1983. 194 p.: ill.

Seven short plays dedicated to revolutionary concepts, focusing on poverty and exploitation of the rural poor. Realistic dialogue and techniques are countered by occasional poetic interludes. Worthy of consideration.

THEATRE CRITICISM AND HISTORY

6059 Arcila, Gonzalo. Nuevo teatro en Colombia: actividad creadora, política cultural. Bogotá: Ediciones CEIS, 1983. 208 p.: bibl. (Col. CEIS; 11)

Intensive study of the theatre in Colombia since 1957, with separate chapters on the TEC, La Candelaria, various festivals, and other events and productions of importance. The ideological bias is consistent with the formation and development of the "new theatre" groups.

6060 Bibliografía del teatro hispanoamericano contemporáneo, 1900–1980. v. 1–2. Compilación de Fernando de Toro and Peter Roster. Frankfurt, FRG: Verlag Klaus Dieter Vervuert, 1985. 2 v. (473, 226 p.)

Vast and enormously useful bibliographic compilation that builds on all previous work to enhance information available on 20th-century Spanish American theatre. Vol. 1 lists alphabetically by author all known published plays, and includes section on anthologies and translations. Vol. 2 documents, again by author, critical studies—books, articles, theses, etc.—available on Spanish American theatre. Impressive reference.

6061 Bixler, Jacqueline Eyring. Games and reality on the Latin American stage (LALR, 12:24, Spring/Summer 1984, p. 22–35)

Three contemporary plays (*El juego, Extraño juguete,* and *Juegos a la hora de la siesta*) are studied in the light of game theory; Bixler concludes that all three share important fundamental attributes but more importantly, they serve as metaphors to heighten the consciousness of the reader/ spectator about the real world.

6062 Bixler, Jacqueline Eyring. Myth and romance in Emilio Carballido's *Conversación entre las ruinas* (IUP/HJ, 6:1, Fall 1984, p. 21–35)

Myth theories developed by Northrop Frye and Mircea Eliade inform this insightful reading of a Carballido play which transcends modern Mexico to dramatize recurrent and universal patterns of heroes and romance.

6063 Brenes, René. El Teatro Nacional (LNB/L, 334/335, enero/feb. 1984, p. 28–59)

Informative history of the construction, management, and recent renovation of Panama's National Theatre.

6064 Bryan, Susan E. Teatro popular y sociedad durante el Porfiriato (CM/HM,

33:1, julio/sept. 1983, p. 130–169, bibl., graphs, table)

Bryan argues convincingly that Mexican theatre after 1911 can only be understood in terms of the introduction of the *tanda* in 1880 with forms of popular theatre that constituted an escape valve and contributed to a myth of social mobility.

6065 Carrera, Mario Alberto. Las ideas políticas en el teatro de Manuel Galich. Guatemala: Impresos Industriales, 1982. 98 p.: bibl.

With the premise that Galich's theatre is basically political, Carrera gives thumbnail sketches of each of his edited plays within a context of Guatemalan theatre and against a backdrop of Marxism. Lightweight study of this recently deceased editor of *Conjunto* in Cuba.

6066 Castagnino, Raúl H. Proposición metodológica para un estudio sobre el teatro porteño del ochenta (Estudios de Literatura Argentina [Instituto de Literatura Argentina Ricardo Rojas, Buenos Aires] 2:7, 1982, p. 17–26)

Castagnino proposes an approach to Argentine theatre in the key years of the 1880s that includes a study of: 1) plays isolated from performance; 2) plays performed; 3) circus/gaucho plays; and 4) testimonial theatre. These four features, he indicates, provide clues to the development of theatre into the 1920s.

6067 Castagnino, Raúl H. Sobre historia del teatro argentino (UNL/U, 96, enero/ junio 1984, p. 123–129)

Bird's-eye view of those critics who have made serious efforts to record Argentine theatre history in this century, by one of the central participants. Brief but interesting.

6068 Conjunto. Casa de las Américas. No. 57, julio/sept. 1983 [through] No. 65, julio/sept. 1985-. La Habana.

Cuba's long-established theatre journal provides coverage on socialist theatre throughout the Americas (e.g., articles, interviews, performance reviews, book summaries, photographs). Each issue contains an unpublished play: No. 57, Claus Hammel, *Humboldt y Bolívar;* No. 58, El Galpón, *Artigas, general del pueblo;* No. 59, Creación Colectiva, *Sebastián Guzmán: principal de principales;* No. 60, Oscar Castro, *La noche suspendida;* No. 61–62, Nelson Mezquida,

Terror y miserias de Montevideo and Virgilio Piñera, *El álbum*; No. 64, César Vega Herrera, *El secreto de la papa* and Creación Colectiva del Libre Teatro Libre, *¡Glup, Zas, Pum, Crash! o La verdadera historia de Tarzán*; No. 65, Jorge Galván, *Clase e medias*.

6069 Cypess, Sandra Messinger. I, too, speak: "female" discourse in Carballido's plays (UK/LATR, 18:1, Fall 1984, p. 45–52)

With the help of Michel Foucault's theories, author studies discourse patterns in two Carballido plays to point out the relationship between assumed roles in the society and accompanying linguistic features.

6070 Dauster, Frank. Carlos Solórzano o la tragedia como subversión (CM/D, 21:6, junio 1985, p. 36–39, ill.)

Convincing analysis of the correlation between form and content in Solórzano's theatre (i.e., thematic liberty is matched by the subversive structures of the play themselves).

6071 La Dramaturgia de Egon Wolff: interpretaciones críticas, 1971–1981. Selección, introducción y notas de Pedro Bravo-Elizondo. Santiago: Editorial Nascimento, 1985. 134 p.

Useful compilation of mostly previously published articles on Wolff's dramaturgy that indicate his stature as a major Latin American playwright.

6072 Durán, Gloria. *Orchids in the moonlight*: Fuentes as feminist and Jungian playwright (WLT, 57:3, 1983, p. 595–598)

Sensitive reading of the Fuentes play that defines its feminist attributes and Jungian characteristics, including the Great Mother and the Trickster figures, and follows with social and psychic interpretations. Study that posits several intriguing possibilities about this play.

6073 Elías, Eduardo F. Carlos Fuentes and movie stars: intertextuality in Mexican drama (UK/LATR, 19:2, Spring 1986, p. 67–77)

Insightful reading of Fuentes's *Orchids in the moonlight*, using semiotic theory to study the complex identities of the two major characters, and the relationships of reality, fiction, life, and death.

6074 Esquina Latina: diez años de teatro. Cali, Colombia: Univ. del Valle, 1982. 44 p.: ill. (Serie Pliegos; 16)

Brief history (1972–82) of student theatre group from Univ. del Valle (Cali, Colombia). Includes short play, *El enmaletado*, mounted as a collective effort in their 1981–82 season.

6075 Falcón, Rafael. El tema de la emigración a Nueva York en el teatro puertorriqueño (RCLL, 9:18, 1983, p. 97–106)

Rapid overview of Puerto Rican theatre in/about New York with special attention to plays by Méndez Ballester, Marqués, Arriví, Carrero and others who have dealt effectively with the massive problems of alienation, cultural adjustment, discrimination, and sundry other issues.

6076 Fernández, Teodosio. El teatro chileno contemporáneo, 1941–1973. Madrid: Playor, 1982. 213 p. (Col. Nova scholar)

Comprehensive treatment of Chilean theatre from the inception of the professional university theatre to the fall of the Allende regime. Includes names, titles, and analyses but, more importantly, imparts a sense of a dynamic movement in all its multiple facets. Highly recommended.

6077 Festival Internacional de Teatro, 5th, Caracas, 1981. Quinto Festival Internacional de Teatro. Auspiciado por la Presidencia de la República. Caracas: Gobernación del Distrito Federal, 1983. 248 p.: ill.

Handsome program book, fully illustrated, with documentation and commentary on each of the plays and groups participating in this fifth important world theatre festival, in which the highlights were Brazil's *Macunaíma* and Venezuela's *El viejo grupo*.

6078 Festival Internacional de Teatro, 6th, Caracas, 1983. Sexto Festival Internacional de Teatro. Auspiciado por la Presidencia de la República. Caracas: La Presidencia, 1983. 314 p.: ill.

Bigger and better organized than the 1981 Fifth Festival (see item **6077**), this encounter brought groups from most countries in Central and South America, the Caribbean, Mexico, Eastern and Western Europe, and even Japan. Concurrent events included seminars for playwrights, directors, and critics. Magnificent, handsomely funded volume provides superb photo-documentary of the festival.

6079 Foster, David William. The Argentine teatro independiente, 1930–1955.

York, S.C.: Spanish Literature Publishing Co., 1986. 143 p.: ill.

Intensive semiotic study based primarily on six plays spanning from Arlt to Dragún, with detailed references to the larger Argentine theatre milieu, that asserts that function and importance of the independent theatre movement in Argentina during a 25-year period. Invaluable work.

6080 Gesualdo, Vicente. Teatros del Buenos Aires antiguo. Buenos Aires: Librería Platero, 1983. 55 p.: bibl., ill.

Historical account of the principal theatres built in Buenos Aires from 1757 (Teatro de Operas y Comedias) to 1879 (Teatro Politeama), plus the various theatres of the *género chico*. Story of the original Teatro Colón's construction (built 1857, razed 1944) is particularly interesting.

6081 Golluscio de Montoya, Eva. Los cuentos de *La señorita de Tacna* (UK/LATR, 18:1, Fall 1984, p. 35–43)

Using speech act theory, author studies the relationships between the *historia* of Belisario and the *cuentos* of Mamaé in order to determine the function and effect of the discrepancies as well as the shared narrative processes in Vargas Llosa's play.

6082 Golluscio de Montoya, Eva. Del circo colonial a los teatros ciudadanos: proceso de urbanización de la actividad dramática rioplatense (UTIEH/C, 1984, p. 141–149)

Self-explanatory title of article that traces the importance of the circus, especially throughout the 19th century, in the development of a theatre movement in the River Plate area.

6083 Guerrero del Río, Eduardo. Historia generacional del teatro chileno en el siglo XIX, a partir del discurso de Lastarria: 1842 (CH, 409, julio 1984, p. 117–128)

Succinct yet enlightening look at the development of 19th-century Chilean theatre through three periods: 1) *pre-costumbrista* (generation of 1852); 2) *costumbrista* (generation of 1867); and 3) *naturalista* (generation of 1882). Includes analysis of one play per period.

6084 Hopkins R., Eduardo. El teatro de Julio Ramón Ribeyro (RCLL, 10:20, 1984, p. 129–153)

Good overview of Ribeyro's entire dramatic output which is useful but would have been even better with a critical methodology and an acknowledgement of existing criticism.

6085 Hurtado, María de la Luz. Sujeto social y proyecto histórico en la dramaturgia chilena actual. v. 1, pt. 1, Constantes y variaciones entre 1960 y 1973. Santiago: CENECA, 1983. 1 v.: bibl.

Valuable and perceptive analysis by one of Chile's best critics of social theatre. Monograph delimits years 1960–73, and gives special attention to Sieveking, Aguirre, Vodanović, Wolff, Díaz, and other playwrights who responded to changing political and social climates with a great variety of technical approaches.

6086 Hurtado, María de la Luz; Carlos Ochsenius; and Hernán Vidal. Teatro chileno de la crisis institucional, 1973–1980: antología crítica. Minneapolis: Minnesota Latin American Series, Univ. of Minnesota; Santiago: Centro de Indagación y Expresión Cultural y Artística, 1982. 339 p.: bibl.

Two excellent essays that provide in-depth analysis of the times, the theatre, styles, and groups that performed during the fateful years 1978–80 are followed by six plays of the 1978–79 seasons. Three are designated anti-naturalist (*El último tren*, *¡Cuántos años tiene un día?*, *Tres Marías y una Rosa*), two anti-grotesque (*Lo crudo . . .*, *Baño a baño*), and one affirmative (*Una pena y un cariño*).

6087 Hurtado, María de la Luz and **María Elena Moreno.** El público del teatro independiente. Santiago: CENECA, 1982. 89, 10 p.: bibl. (Documento de trabajo; 25)

Valid data base derived from questionnaires facilitated this interpretative assessment of the composition, interests and habits of the public audience for independent theatre in Chile.

6088 Kaluzhénina, Larisa. Aleph y otros (URSS/AL, 7:67, julio 1983, p. 33–38, plates)

A brief visit with Aleph, the Chilean theatre group exiled in France, during a visit to Cuba. Interesting historical perspective on the basis of their production of *Mateluna*.

6089 *Latin American Theatre Review.* Univ. of Kansas, Center for Latin American Studies. Vol. 18, No. 1, Fall 1984 [through] Vol. 19, No. 2, Spring 1986–. Lawrence.

In addition to articles annotated elsewhere in this section, these volumes contain reports of festivals in Manizales, Buenos Aires, New York, and other major capitals, as well as theatre season reports throughout Latin America. Also includes major articles on plays by Aguirre, Gorostiza, Arlt, Orihuela, and various others. Vol. 18, No. 2, Spring 1985, is a special issue devoted to Mexican theatre in its various manifestations.

6090 Leal, Rine. Hacia una dramaturgia del socialismo (*in* La Cultura en Cuba socialista. La Habana: Editorial Letras Cubanas, 1982, p. 230–253)

Analysis by Cuba's senior theatre critic of the process of change from a pre-revolutionary bourgeois theatre to the politically-oriented and open-ended Cuban theatre of recent years, with explanations and justifications.

Leñero, Vicente. Vivir del teatro. See item **5190.**

Lovera De-Sola, Roberto J. Bibliografía de la crítica literaria venezolana, 1847–1977. See item **5518.**

6091 Luzuriaga, Gerardo. Bibliografía del teatro ecuatoriano, 1900–1982. Quito: Editorial Casa de la Cultura Ecuatoriana, 1984. 131 p.

Invaluable bibliography of Ecuadorian theatre organized in three sections: 1) important reference works; 2) plays published and/or performed 1902–82; and 3) critical studies. Useful extension of Descalzi's work in theatre history (see *HLAS 46:5976*).

6092 Magnarelli, Sharon. Art and the audience in O'Donnell's *Vincent y los cuervos* (UK/LATR, 19:2, Spring 1986, p. 45–55)

Studies the inherent relationships between art and life in the 1984 production of Pacho O'Donnell's play which is based on scenes from the life of Vincent van Gogh as interpreted by Antonin Artaud. The production was masterful, as is the analysis.

6093 Marga, Iris. El teatro, mi verdad. Buenos Aires: Ediciones Tres Tiempos, 1983. 386 p., 24 p. of plates: ill., ports. (Col. Memorias y autobiografías; 2)

Sentimental journey through 60 years

of theatre history with one of Argentina's first ladies of the stage.

6094 Mego, Alberto. El teatro popular y de aficionadas en Lima, 1970–1980: características y perspectivas. S.l.: s.n., 198? 75 p.: ill. (Cuadernos de teatro; 7)

Mimeographed on poor quality paper, this little volume nevertheless contains good information about the popular and amateur theatre in Lima during the 1970s, with a focus on method, groups, authors, plays, and locations.

6095 Molinaza, José. Historia crítica del teatro dominicano. v. 1, 1492–1844. v. 2, 1844–1930. Santo Domingo: Editora de la Univ. Autónoma de Santo Domingo, 1984. 2 v. (385, 647 p.): bibl., index (Publicaciones; 332. Col. Arte y sociedad; 12, 14)

Enormously valuable two-volume contribution on Dominican theatre includes compilation of titles, reviews, dates, and impressions, but is somewhat short on critical interpretation.

6096 Montes Huidobro, Matías. Teatro dentro del teatro: técnica preferencial del teatro cubano contemporáneo (*in* International Congress of Hispanists, 1971, Salamanca, Spain. Actas. Dirección de Eugenio de Bustos Tovar. Salamanca, Spain: Univ. de Salamanca, 1982, v. 2, p. 289–310)

Using plays primarily by Carlos Felipe Triana and Virgilio Piñera, author contends that three elements lie behind the 20th-century Cuban preference for metatheatrical effects: José Martí, Afro-Cuban magic, and a fundamental schizophrenia.

6097 Morfi, Angelina. El teatro puertorriqueño: afirmación de nuestro ser (ICP/R, 22:84, julio/sept. 1979, p. 8–14, ill.)

Easy synthesis of Puerto Rican theatre from its beginnings through René Marqués. Nothing new.

6098 Morris, Robert J. The theatre of Julio Ortega since his *Peruvian hell* (UK/LATR, 19:2, Spring 1986, p. 31–37)

Examines Ortega's theatre since 1980 to show the shift from individual concerns to larger social and political issues in Peru.

6099 Naios Najchaus, Teresa. Conversaciones con el teatro Argentino de hoy, 1981–1984. Buenos Aires: Ediciones AGON, 1984. 223 p.

Collection of interviews and reports with some 50 Argentine theatre personalities (actors, directors, writers, etc.) that reveals aspects of creation and production during 10 difficult years of Argentine theatre history. Unfortunately, sketchy entries limit work's value.

6100 Neglia, Erminio G. El hecho teatral en Hispanoamérica. Roma: Bulzoni Editore, 1985. 216 p.: ill. (Letterature iberiche e latino-americane)

Collection of separate essays, some reprinted, that signal the variety and richness of themes and techniques in Latin American theatre, ranging from vanguardism and Pirandello's influence to aspects of torture, oppression, and tyranny. Eclectic choice.

6101 Neglia, Erminio G. El tema de la tortura en el teatro hispánico (NS, 8:16, 1983, p. 91–102)

Neglia points out that Benedetti's *Pedro y el capitán*, Pavlovsky's *El señor Galíndez* and a play by the Spaniard Buero Vallejo share a message that torture cannot be tolerated in a civilized society.

6102 Ochsenius, Carlos. Expresión teatral poblacional. Santiago: CENECA, 1983. 58 p.: bibl. (Documento de trabajo; 43)

Mimeographed document that focuses on three periods of organization (1975–76), proliferation (1977–79), and crisis (1980–82) of popular theatre groups during the post-Allende years. Light on analysis.

6103 Ochsenius, Carlos. Teatros universitarios de Santiago, 1940–1973: el estado en la escena. Santiago: CENECA, 1982. 145, 3 p.: bibl. (Documento de trabajo; 24)

Another account that concerns the development of the university theatre movement in Chile, starting in 1900 and extending through 1973. Promising but occasionally shallow overview.

6104 Ordaz, Luis et al. Historia del teatro argentino. Buenos Aires: Centro Editor de América Latina, 1982. 408 p. in various pagings: bibls., ill., index.

Oversized and richly illustrated history of the Argentine theatre from its origins to the Teatro Abierto (1981), designed and prepared almost totally by the inexhaustible Argentine theatre historian, Luis Ordaz. Valuable item.

6105 Østergaard, Ane-Grethe. Dinámica de la ficción en *El beso de la mujer araña* (UK/LATR, 19:1, Fall 1985, p. 5–12)

Semiotic approach to Puig's play reveals the function of fiction in the development of the close relationship between the two characters.

6106 Østergaard, Ane-Grethe. *Relevo 1923*: discurso metateatral; análisis de la enunciación (UTIEH/C, 41, 1983, p. 63–80, bibl.)

Goldenberg's documentary play functions on different levels of external and internal reality. Using semiotic principles of analysis, Østergaard studies character/actor/spectator roles in a theoretical staging of this work to illuminate new facets of perceived relationships.

6107 Panorama del teatro dominicano. t. 1. Coordinación de Danilo Ginebra. Santo Domingo: Editora Corripio, 1984. 237 p.: bibl., plates.

Prepared by Teatro Gratey, one of the most active Dominican theatre groups, vol. 1 is a history and compilation of reprinted materials, taken from more than 50 sources, that recount Dominican theatre from the precolumbian period through the 19th century. Useful though not evaluative. Vol. 2 is planned.

6108 Podestá, Guido. César Vallejo, su estética teatral. Prólogo de Antonio Cornejo Polar. Minneapolis: Univ. of Minnesota, Institute for the Study of Ideologies & Literature, 1985. 313 p. (Series Toward a social history of Hispanic and Luso-Brazilian literature)

Handsome volume dedicated to correcting misconceptions and documenting the record of Vallejo's theatre, largely ignored, forgotten, or distorted. Carefully edited text is followed by dramatic selections.

6109 Podol, Peter L. Dramatizations of the conquest of Peru: Peter Shaffer's *The royal hunt of the sun* and Claude Demarigny's *Cajamarca* (IUP/HJ, 6:1, Fall 1984, p. 121–129)

Solid interpretation of Artaudian influence on these two plays about the conquest that share distancing techniques, incantatory language and symbolism in achieving theatrical success.

6110 Rhoades, Duane. The independent monologue in Latin American theatre: a primary bibliography with selective secondary sources. Westport, Conn.: Greenwood Press, 1986. 242 p.: indexes (Bibliographies and indexes in world literature, 0742–6801; 5)

Preceded by informative introduction, this is an extraordinary bibliography of the often undervalued monologue form in Latin America; organized alphabetically by entry and country in three major time periods of development: 1) 1550–1840; 2) 1840–1940; and 3) 1940-present.

6111 Rivera-Rodas, Oscar. El código temporal en *La señorita de Tacna* (UK/LATR, 19:2, Spring 1986, p. 5–16)

Complex interpretation of the complex relationship of five temporal levels in the Vargas Llosa play, showing their intrinsic patterns and the projections to other levels. Valuable study.

6112 Salgado, María A. La visión grotesca de la sociedad en el teatro de Miguel Angel Asturias (*in* International Congress of Hispanists, 4th, 1971, Salamanca, Spain. Actas. Dirección de Eugenio de Bustos Tovar. Salamanca, Spain: Univ. de Salamanca, 1982, v. 2, p. 575–585)

Salgado examines Asturias's largely ignored theatre (nine plays) and concludes that he effectively manipulated stylized, grotesque techniques to unmask the aristocracy, the army, and the Church as institutions responsible for physical and spiritual oppression.

6113 San Félix, Alvaro. Teatro de intención política en el Ecuador (BCE/C, 5:13, mayo/agosto 1982, p. 209–225)

Thorough review of political theatre in Ecuador from colonial times to the present, with an intensive look at efforts of Boal, Saad, Pachioni, and others to develop a *teatro coyuntural* in recent years, a theatre that incorporates revolutionary tendencies. Useful article, in that little is available on Ecuador.

6114 Seibel, Beatriz. Los artistas trashumantes. Buenos Aires: Ediciones de la Pluma, 1985. 322 p., 8 p. of plates: ill. (Teatro popular; 2)

Continuation of the study of the itinerant actors with textual fragments and testimonies that indicate the "interior" life of popular theatre forms amply distributed throughout the country.

6115 Seibel, Beatriz. El teatro "bárbaro" del interior. Buenos Aires: Ediciones de la Pluma, 1985. 230 p., 8 p. of plates: ill. (Teatro popular; 1)

Fascinating compendium of popular theatre in Latin America, mostly in Argentina, far from the urban elite, that chronicles the circus and radio theatre forms in interviews, scripts, texts, photos, and commentaries that infuse them with life, meaning, and character. A heroic effort.

6116 Smith, Paul Christopher. Theatre and political criteria in Cuba: Casa de las Américas awards, 1960–1983 (UP/CSEC, 14:1, Winter 1984, p. 43–47, table)

Brief, cogent analysis of relationships between two major events in Cuba (the purge of homosexuals, the Padilla affair) and the sociopolitical character of subsequent Casa de las Américas prize-winning plays.

6117 *Tablas.* Centro de Investigación y Desarrollo de las Artes Escénicas. Vol. 1, No. 1, 1982–. La Habana.

Cuba's second theatre journal (after *Conjunto*), published quarterly. Each issue contains a play as well as several articles that deal with staging, promotion, criticism, or ideology.

6118 Taylor, Diana. Art and anti-art in Egon Wolff's *Flores de papel* (UK/LATR, 18:1, Fall 1984, p. 65–68)

Brief article that focuses on the creative vs. the destructive characteristics of Merluza and his art, as they relate to Eva and the larger society.

6119 Teoría y praxis del teatro en México: especulaciones—en busca de escuela. Compilación de Sergio Jiménez y Edgar Ceballos. S.l.: Grupo Editorial Gaceta, 1982. 396 p.: ill.

Excellent collection of essays by Mexican theatre artists and critics ranging from Usigli, Novo, and Seki Sano to Azar, Mendoza, Gurrola, and others. Includes "Documents," "Testimonies," and "Theatre Practice." Although unedited, the essays give a valuable look at theory and performance in Mexican theatre.

6120 Vallejo, César. Piezas y escritos sobre teatro con una nota preliminar y traducción de Carlos Garayar (CNC/RPC, 1, julio 1982, p. 107–161)

Consists of four plays by Vallejo, published in 1979, as well as fragments of other plays, some translated from the French, scenes, sketches of scenes, and some of Vallejo's musings about drama and theory. Of historical importance even if not functional as stageable theatre.

6121 Villegas, Juan. El discurso dramático-teatral latinoamericano y el discurso crítico: algunas reflexiones estratégicas (UK/LATR, 18:1, Fall 1984, p. 5–12)
Studies the relationship of dramatic discourse and critical discourse, and suggests the importance of decoding the ideological content of critical discourse at the time of its application to theatrical discourse during performance.

6122 Woodyard, George. Estorino's theater: customs and conscience in Cuba

(LALR, 11:22, Spring/Summer 1983, p. 57–63)
Using Arnold Kettle's theories on realistic literature, author examines Estorino's early plays, especially *El robo del cochino*, and compares them with *Ni un sí ni un no* (1981), a play that also adheres to revolutionary principles of male/female equality while entertaining with metatheatrical techniques.

6123 Zayas de Lima, Perla. Relevamiento del teatro argentino, 1943–1975. Buenos Aires: Editorial R. Alonso, 1983. 222 p.: bibl.
Overview of recent Argentine theatre, organized primarily by author, with special emphasis on Ferretti, Cuzzani, Dragún, Gorostiza, Monti, Adellach, Casali, Gentile, Pavlovsky, and Gambaro. Brief but useful observations.

BRAZIL: Novels

REGINA IGEL, *Associate Professor, Department of Spanish and Portuguese, University of Maryland, College Park*

AMONG THE NUMEROUS THEMES addressed by Brazilian novelists in the last biennium, two appear to command the most attention: the search for a national identity and the need to reawaken political awareness. Other popular topics were sports, foreign politics, science fiction and self-analysis.

The quest for a national identity can be traced back to the romantic movement of the 19th century and its culmination in the 1922 Week of Modern Art in São Paulo. That same quest reemerged in the 1980s in works that fictionalized the history of European immigrants and their contribution to the agricultural and industrial development of 20th-century Brazil. Since the vast majority of immigrants were Italians, they dominate most novels on the subject. Among the more notable examples of the genre are Fiorani's *A herança de Lundstrom* (item **6134**), based on "documents" and "interviews" with descendants of immigrants, and Chiavenato's *Coronéis e carcamanos* (item **6131**), a denunciation of the humiliating treatment endured by the first Italians who arrived in Brazil as well as an account of their eventual contributions to the country. Other immigrants who also contributed to the cultural and social development of modern Brazil were the Galicians whose saga is narrated by one of their descendants, the renowned Nélida Piñon, in *A república dos sonhos* (item **6148**), and the Azoreans whose spokesman is Caldeira in *Arca açoriana* (item **6186**).

Like the novels about immigrants, historical novels also serve as quests to determine what is Brazil's national identity. These works seek to reinterpret Brazilian history, to set the record straight about the nation's past, and to redefine heroism and patriotism in ways that diverge from traditional textbooks. Thus, reinterpretations of epic events can be dense as Marques Rebelo's *O espelho partido* (item 6152) or as slight as Castelo's *Senhores e escravos* (item 6129). These works are either sharply focused on a specific episode as in the case of Martins's *Gaúchos no obelisco* (item 6142), or else they offer a panoramic view as in the depiction of the two centuries of relentless struggle for freedom on the part of African slaves in Ribeiro's well deserved success of a best-seller, *Viva o povo brasileiro* (item 6154).

The need to reawaken political awareness among Brazilians is a theme that underlies many works dealing with the consequences and repercussions of the military's dominance of the country. Sinval Medina's *Memorial de Santa Cruz* (item 6143) incorporates much of Mário de Andrade's *Macunaíma* by attempting to portray the social illnesses that plague the nation because of the long-lasting political repression; Lessa's invisible tenants in his *O edifício fantasma* (item 6138) call attention to the existence of an American-Brazilian combination of forces that rules the country. Some novelists convey the impression that the repression experienced during military rule continues today. The police corps is depicted as embodying such continuity in detective stories in which the boundaries between "the law" (i.e., the police) and those outside the law are not clear. Examples of such works are Silva's *A história de Lili Carabina* (item 6158) and Adonias Filho's *Noite sem madrugada* (item 6124). An exception to such a portrayal is Ledo Ivo's *A morte do Brasil* (item 6137), in which a reasonable sheriff treats his prisoners humanely. In 1986, on his eighth attempt, Ivo was elected to the Brazilian Academy of Letters where he occupies the chair vacated by the late Orígenes Lessa.

Sports themes, new to Brazilian novels, are emerging in works such as Ortiz Porto's portrayal of soccer in *O sol e o verde* (item 6149) and Marcos Rey's story about jockeys in *Ferradura dá sorte!* (item 6153). The theme of international politics and its impact on the living conditions of factory workers throughout the world is the subject of Sirkis's *Corredor polones* (item 6169).

Very new but very promising is Brazilian science fiction and it is likely that these works will attain more international recognition for Brazilian authors than other genres. Written with much verve and imagination, these novels about spatial wars, related paraphernalia, and attempts to improve human life via unprecedented and still unknown technologies are exemplified by Calife's trilogy *Padrões de contato* (item 6127). Self-analysis is a recurrent topic in Brazilian literature, as conveyed in Bin's *Jogo de fiar* (item 6125), and Hilst's *A obscena Senhora D.* (item 6135).

6124 Aguiar, Adonias. Noite sem madrugada. São Paulo: DIFEL, 1983. 158 p.

Author of the emblematic *Memories of Lazarus* (1969), among other novels in a similar vein, this one is a policy story. A murder is solved because of the persistence of a woman whose husband is accused of a murder and who does not rest until she finds the real perpetrator. Discloses the perversions and subhuman conditions pervading the labyrinthine prison system of Rio de Janeiro.

6125 Bins, Patricia Jogo de fiar. Rio de Janeiro: Editora Nova Fronteira, 1983. 138 p.

Fictional autobiography that, in con-cise and lyrical language, discloses two dimensions in the narrator's personal evolution: her tangible heritage as a descendant of German immigrants in southern Brazil, and her intangible experience as an individual who questions her own feelings, passions, and renunciations. A spiritual novel that leads the reader into the unutterable by means of innuendo and suggested images. First novel of author known for her weekly column in a Porto Alegre newspaper.

6126 Caldeira, Almiro. Arca açoriana. Florianópolis: Editora da Univ. Federal de Santa Catarina, 1984. 154 p. (Rocamaranha; 2)

Historical novel about the settlement

of Azorean families in the state of Santa Catarina towards the end of the 18th century. Focuses on Spanish incursions and how the settlers' daily tribulations turned some into heroes. Published last, this is pt. 2 of a trilogy composed of *Rocamaranha* (1961), a story of the Azoreans' Atlantic crossing, and *Ao encontro da manhã* (1966), an account of the lives of descendants towards the end of the 19th century. Interesting fusion of history and fiction.

6127 Calife, Jorge Luiz. Padrões de contato: romance. Rio de Janeiro: Editora Nova Fronteira, 1985. 254 p.

Four interlocked stories make up a novel about life on earth as of the year 2426 and of life in space up to 3002. Everything will be simpler than at present, from pills replacing meals to orbital homes and floating industries. Earth will be left undisturbed to nature and wildlife. Stresses the prolonged youth of a female character who lives as a 25-year-old through five centuries. She becomes a key force in promoting technology geared towards developing better living conditions for humans. Work that successfully combines utopian dreams and science fiction.

6128 Cardoso, Lúcio. Inácio. Rio de Janeiro: Salamandra, 1984. 136 p.

Second edition of introspective novel published 40 years ago. Reveals embryonic phase of *Cronica da casa assassinada*, a book that became the author's best known fictional work.

6129 Castelo Branco, Renato. Senhores e escravos, a balada: romance histórico. São Paulo: LR Editores, 1983. 135 p.

Historical narrative of social revolution that took place in northern Brazil (1838–41). A group of slaves, cattle ranchers, and free peasants defied the local oligarchy. Successful transmutation of historical events into fiction through the description of battles, lootings, and acts of repression perpetrated by landowners and the rural power structure.

6130 Celso, Antônio. A porta de Jerusalém: romance. Rio de Janeiro: Livraria J. Olympio Editora: Instituto Nacional do Livro, Fundação Nacional Pró-Memória, 1982. 113 p.

Novel that presents a vast canvass of 200 years of history and mythology in Minas Gerais. Depicts landowners, slaves, priests,

and tyrannical provincial ladies of the colonial period as well as their contemporary counterparts, the unscrupulous oppressors of today. Atmosphere that alternates between mysticism and violence.

6131 Chiavenato, Julio José. Coronéis e carcamanos. São Paulo: Global, 1982. 267 p.: ill.

Novel that exposes the underside of Italian immigration to Brazil. The country, depicted as a "golden opportunity," was in fact a harsh land of immense virgin forests that the immigrants had to master on their own. Government help evaporated after the immigrants' arrival. In 10 chapters covering 40 years (1890–1930), the author denounces the exploitation of Italians (*carcamanos*), in coffee plantations owned and run by Brazilians (*coronéis*).

6132 De Luca, Olindo. Eles voltaram para ficar. São Paulo: Editora do Escritor, 1982. 188 p.: ill. (Col. do escritor; 60)

Another novel about the immigrants' saga of turn-of-the-century Brazil. Describes their adjustment to the new land and Brazilian reaction to this new working force. These particular settlers went back to Italy but then decided to return to Brazil. Author is the son of immigrants.

6133 Facchin, Emyr Carlos. Aldeia colonial. Caxias do Sul: O Autor, 1983. 145 p. (Col. Imigração italiana; 59)

Another fictional account of Italian immigration to Brazil told from the viewpoint of a member of the first Brazilian-born generation. A simple novel that exemplifies the ongoing trend of narratives on the subject.

6134 Fiorani, Silvio. A herança de Lundstrom. São Paulo: Global Editora, 1984. 175 p.: ill. (Col. Múltipla)

One more novel about Italian immigrants in Brazil's coffee region. Author describes his novel as non-fictional and based on "documents," "interviews," and people's "recollections." Author's intention is realized in a well constructed novel about the beginnings of the Rovelli family, pioneers of the city of Ibipiu.

6135 Hilst, Hilda. A obscena Senhora D. São Paulo: Masso Onho/Roswitha Kempf Editores, 1982. 64 p.

Author, better known as a poet, writes a deeply introspective experimental text that constitutes a search for identity. Her writings recreate the innovative language of Clarice Lispector and recall her masterful portrayals of intimate feelings in a literary context.

6136 Inda, Ieda. Baguala: romance de rédeas e rendas. Porto Alegre: Movimento, 1982. 92 p. (Col. Rio Grande; 55)

This novel, set in the Brazilian and Argentine *pampas*, transcends the traditional genre of gauchos, mate, and cattle. Although the conventional plot about a love affair between an Argentine military officer/polo player and a frustrated Brazilian wife is shallow and commonplace, the novel reproduces with unusual accuracy the speech patterns found among the sophisticated elite that live along Brazil's southern frontier. The novel also portrays colloquialisms characteristic of *portunhol*, the pidgin of Spanish/Portuguese also typical of the region.

6137 Ivo, Lêdo. A morte do Brasil: romance. Rio de Janeiro: Record, 1984. 173 p.

Nihilistic atmosphere is exemplified by the novel's title. A narrator's desire to seek the truth behind misleading façades leads to his present job as sheriff. Empowered to ask questions and to interpret answers, he applies these prerogatives to Brazilian history. His indagations lead to intriguing interpretations of historical events ranging from President Getúlio Vargas's suicide to mass immigration to ceremonies honoring Brazil's unknown soldier. Author combines his knowledge of the Portuguese language and abilities as a narrator to create a sympathetic portrayal of a police officer.

6138 Lessa, Orígenes. O edifício fantasma. Rio de Janeiro: Editora Nova Fronteira, 1984. 107 p.

Fantastic story told with much humor about how the inhabitants of a building in Copacabana become invisible overnight. Local authorities request help from foreign countries in order to solve the mystery. This lighthearted novel's intentional irony is apparent in the building's name "Alvorada," same as that of Brazil's presidential palace in Brasília. Moreover, most of the building's condominium owners are of American origin. A message for international peace underlies the story.

6139 Lins, Ronaldo Lima. A lâmina do espelho. Rio de Janeiro: F. Alves: Ins-

tituto Nacional do Livro, Fundação Nacional Pró-Memória, 1983. 291 p.

A hospitalized teacher reviews his own life while observing other patients. Their personal stories are told through vivid conversations which eventually reveal the underlying significance of the novel. Characters alternate moving thoughts about the meaning of life, sickness, and death with petty feelings about their individual destinies. Despite the grim setting and subject matter, the novel succeeds as a literary endeavor.

6140 Marques, Aracyldo. O tempo, cavalo doido: romance. São Paulo: Editora do Escritor, 1982. 192 p. (Col. do escritor; 65)

Despite the large number of novels written about the Northeast, its droughts, and related social problems, little fiction has appeared on northeastern migration to southern Brazil. This *Bildungsroman* type novel about the lives of two young migrant peasants turned construction workers in São Paulo fills the void. The novel develops in a linear fashion and presents a faithful portrait of the combination of aloofness and comraderie of blue-collar workers towards newcomers.

6141 Mársico, Gladstone Osório. Gatos à paisana. 2a ed., rev. Porto Alegre: Movimento, 1982. 133 p. (Col. Rio Grande; 51)

Second edition of humorous novel (1st ed., 1961; reprinted 1975 and 1982) which probably owes its popularity to its puns, verbal tricks, and other word play. Plot concerns small town notables on a business trip: mayor, judge, notary public, their wives, a priest, and the narrator. Conflict of interest arises when they face an offer made by the bidding company which financed their trip.

6142 Martins, Cyro. Gaúchos no obelisco: romance. Porto Alegre: Movimento, 1984. 242 p. (Col. Ensaios; 29)

Rio de Janeiro and Rio Grande do Sul in 1929–37 serve as the geographic and historical setting for this novel about military actions for and against President Getúlio Vargas. The novel's title refers to the daring gesture of *gaúcho* soldiers who tied their horses to the obelisk, a Rio historical monument facing the Senate. Vivid dialogue, author's sense of humor, and well paced love scenes enhance an otherwise overly descriptive narrative.

6143 Medina, Sinval. Memorial de Santa Cruz. Porto Alegre: Mercado Aberto, 1983. 299 p. (Série Novo romance; 1)

Lengthy, uninterrupted narrative without paragraphs or chapters about "Brazil de Santa Cruz," a not-so-subtle allusion to the original name given by the Portuguese to the country. Born incognito, in an unidentified place, and unconcerned about these facts, Mr. Santa Cruz is a picaresque, chameleon-like individual who travels across the country, rediscovering its folklore, habits, food, accents, etc. His wanderings come to an abrupt halt when he is arrested and taken prisoner as No. 1964, a figure which coincides with the year the military took over Brazil.

6144 Montello, Josué. Labirinto de espelhos: romance. 7a ed. rev. Rio de Janeiro: Nova Fronteira, 1983. 210 p.

Seventh edition of 1952 novel centered on a lonely, rich woman whose relatives hopefully and anxiously await her will. Reflects the way of life and peculiar atmosphere of São Luís do Maranhão at a certain time in history.

6145 Montello, Josué. Pedra viva: romance. Rio de Janeiro: Editora Nova Fronteira, 1983. 474 p.

Another novel set in the author's birthplace, São Luís do Maranhão. A *Bildungsroman* that evolves into a *roman á clef* including President José Sarney (1975)— also from Maranhão—as a character in his roles as state senator and later, governor. Covers the development of three generations in one family (end of 19th century to 1970s). Novel strongly influenced by Machado de Assis about the dreams, infidelities, and religious obsessions of middle-class entrepreneurs. It should be commended for the clarity of its language, the skillful psychological delineation of characters, and careful plotting.

6146 Montello, Josué. Uma varanda sobre o silêncio: romance. Rio de Janeiro: Editora Nova Fronteira, 1984. 350 p.

Most accounts concerning people missing during Brazil's military dictatorship are painfully similar. This novel describes the search undertaken by a mother and other relatives of a young man 16 years after he vanished from Rio's streets. The novel is simply written and apparently devoid of further literary ambitions.

6147 Nassar, Raduan. Lavoura arcaica. 2a ed., rev. Rio de Janeiro: Nova Fronteira, 1982. 173 p.

First published in 1975, this novel received great critical acclaim because of its powerful language and reflections. Narrative about time and the independence of the mind, the story reverses the Biblical tale of the prodigal son and imbues it with a contemplative mood inspired by the Koran. Revised second edition omits "Author's Note" which provided sources for the book's quotations.

6148 Piñon, Nélida. A república dos sonhos: romance. Rio de Janeiro: Francisco Alves, 1984. 761 p.

Lengthy novel about Galician immigrants to Brazil, "the Republic of Dreams." Two narrative voices interpret the newcomers pioneering efforts at the turn of the century. A grandfather describes their adjustment to the new land, a lifetime of work and hard earned wealth; his granddaughter visits the old country one day and retells the stories of her ancestors. Richly detailed, historically accurate account of Brazil for almost two centuries. Includes many autobiographical elements confirmed by the author in interviews. Archetypical psychological portraits drawn in word prose style.

6149 Porto, Sérgio Ortiz. O sol e o verde: romance. Porto Alegre: Editora Movimento, 1982. 258 p. (Col. Rio Grande; 56)

Ortiz Pôrto shares Mario Vargas Llosa's fondness for soccer as is exemplified in this portrayal of the game and its socioeconomic, political, and psychological implications. Unliterary, modest, linear narrative. One of the few fictional treatments of Brazilian soccer.

6150 Prado, Adélia. Os componentes da banda. Rio de Janeiro: Editora Nova Fronteira, 1984. 149 p.

Novel's title refers to musical bands which stroll through small towns in the Brazilian backlands. Author draws comparison between the life of Violeta, schoolteacher and housewife, whose works are elevated by Prado to the level of mystical sacrifices and the monotonous but intriguing rhythm of a musical band. Humor and lyricism alternate in a narrative that discusses poetry, religion, and a trivial philosophy.

6151 Rainho, Cleonice. Uma sombra nas ruas. Rio de Janeiro: Livraria J. Olympio Editora, 1984. 173 p.

First person narrative in chapters named after the days of the week about seven days in the life of a man whose mother just died. Innovative transcription of dialogue without dashes or conventional paragraphing. Author is better known as a writer of short stories and children's fiction. Promising first novel.

6152 Rebelo, Marques. O espelho partido. t. 1, O trapicheiro. t. 2, A mudança. 2a ed. Rio de Janeiro: Editora Nova Fronteira, 1984. 2v.

Three-volume large historical novel. Vols. 1–2—published between 1959–68 and reissued after author's death in 1973—describe Brazilian and world events in 1936–39 and 1939–41. More than a realistic portrayal of the period, author projects his view of those times in a fictional prose that oscillates between diary and *roman à clef*.

6153 Rey, Marcos. A última corrida: Ferradura dá sorte?: romance. 2a ed. São Paulo: Editora Atica, 1982. 157 p.: ill., port. (Col. de autores brasileiros; 80)

New edition of 1963 novel acknowledged as an original first in Brazilian prose fiction because of its portrayal of the world of horse-racing including betting, stables, jockeys, etc. Plot involves a stubborn trainer and teen-age boy who believe in an aging horse, a former turf winner.

6154 Ribeiro, João Ubaldo. Viva o povo brasileiro: romance. Rio de Janeiro: Editora Nova Fronteira, 1984. 673 p.

Highly accomplished narrative in terms of language, internal coherence, and literary excellence. Describes almost 200 years of Brazilian history, emphasizing the experience of black slavery and its important repercussions in the social makeup of modern Brazil. Author's search for an independent and genuine Brazilian identity leads him to emphasize language as the principal means towards decolonization and self-determination.

6155 Saboya, Ligia and **Maria Helena Nóvoa.** A noiva do super-homem: teorema do espelho: romance. São Paulo: LR Editores, 1983. 203 p.

Two narrators are fused into the one narrative voice of this novel. Two female friends unfold their personal traits in a quasi-autobiographical way. Superficial plot is enhanced by a literary context, lyrical language, and good psychoanalytic descriptions and perceptions of oneself and others.

6156 Santiago, Silviano. O olhar. 2a ed. São Paulo: Global Editora, 1983. 199 p. (Col. Múltipla)

Innovative and intriguing narrative describes author's intellectual attempt to control the writing process in the creation of fiction. The result is experimental.

6157 Scliar, Moacyr. A festa no castelo. Porto Alegre: L&PM Editores, 1982. 101 p.

Reminiscences of middle-aged lawyer who attempts social reforms in Brazil. His recollections alternate with descriptions of a fancy meal served in a medieval castle. The Brazilian political scenario of the mid 1960s underlies both narratives.

6158 Silva, Aguinaldo. A história de Lili Carabina: um romance da Baixada Fluminense. Rio de Janeiro: Editora Codecri, 1983. 99 p. (Col. Edições do Pasquim; 173)

Factual and fictional elements combine in a novel written somewhat in the style of a film script. Rio de Janeiro policemen are denounced as legalized thugs who murdered an innocent man without trial, Lili Carabina's husband. Her murders were motivated by revenge for her husband's death. Author is an accomplished journalist who writes educational documentaries for Brazilian television and is well known for his sympathy for victims of Brazil's unjust social system.

6159 Sirkis, Alfredo. Corredor polonês. Rio de Janeiro: Editora Record, 1983. 227 p.: ill.

Fictional documentary about political life in Poland that starts in 1981 but goes back to World War II. Novel opens with an encounter among young international photographers in a Polish plaza where a strike is attracting world attention. Configuration of stories that combine to examine two unusual subjects in Brazilian literature: the Solidarity uprising led by Lech Walesa and the Holocaust.

6160 Souza, Márcio. A condolência: romance. Rio de Janeiro: Editora Marco Zero, 1984. 321 p.

Struggle between a group of Brazilian political exiles and their police oppressors is trivialized in a novel that uses the framework of a Western movie in an urban setting. Narrative that is thin in real content and loaded with meaningless details (e.g., flights, disguises, threats, attempted murders). Author of a great novel, *The Emperor of the Amazon*, he has not lived up to its promise.

6161 Steen, Edla van. Corações mordidos. São Paulo: Global Editora, 1983. 254 p. (Col. Múltipla)

Small urban residential development serves as author's metaphor for mankind. Daily, trivial aggravations of its inhabitants with a real estate company generate feelings of frustration and helplessness. Well known as an accomplished short story writer, this is the author's second novel.

6162 Véras, Everaldo Moreira. O canto de sal. Rio de Janeiro: J. Olympio Editora:

Instituto Nacional do Livro, Fundação Nacional Pró-Memória, 1984. 113 p.

Self-analytical writing imbued with far-reaching associations exposes the narrator's personal quest and discloses suffering undergone in the process of literary creation. Precise and terse language is used to challenge and ridicule author's surrounding world where he pursues an anguished search to know more than human limitations will allow. Awarded the 1983 Brasília Prize of Fiction.

6163 Vilela, Luiz. Entre amigos: romance. São Paulo: Editora Atica, 1983. 111 p. (Col. de autores brasileiros; 82)

Couple plays host to another couple and a writer, somewhere in a big Brazilian city during an afternoon of talking, laughing, eating, and drinking. Characters reveal personal reactions to important topics, and constitute an interesting cross section of the Brazilian bourgeoisie and their way of thinking. Vivid dialogue is transcribed without interruption as if it had been tape-recorded. The novel could be the author's least imaginative yet most humourous.

Short Stories

MARIA ANGELICA GUIMARÃES LOPES, *Assistant Professor, Department of Foreign Languages and Literatures, University of South Carolina, Columbia*

GENERAL TRENDS NOTED for the Brazilian short story in the late 1970s and early 1980s continue through this biennium with few surprises. There are no extraordinary newcomers such as those that emerged in the late 1960s and early 1970s. The geographic origin, however, has shifted from Minas Gerais to Rio Grande do Sul where the best short stories by well established writers (e.g., Lobato, Menezes) are also being published.

Such a development attests to the fact that mature authors are not repeating themselves, that they are addressing new themes and adopting new techniques to suit their style. Another sign of the stabilization without stagnation of the short story is exemplified by the reissue of many celebrated collections long out of print. These new editions make accessible to younger generations two masters of *modernismo*: Alcântara Machado and Marques Rebelo. Important collections by more recent authors such as Dourado (item **6174**), Ivo (item **6183**), Scliar, and Pedrosa were also reprinted. Anthologies compiled for didactic purposes include works by individual authors such as Lispector, João Antônio, G. Figueiredo, Caio P. Carneiro, and Perez. Anthologies of lesser-known writers also attest to the importance of the story for Brazilian publishers and readers. Story collections with a regional emphasis have also been published for different states such as Mato Grosso, Minas Gerais, São Paulo; various city literary contests; and others.

Among the most notable collections of this biennium are those awarded literary prizes such as the Nestlé and F. Chinaglia. The winners of the 1982 Nestlé Prize are two well known authors, Pólvora and Perez, and a newcomer, Schlee. A scrupulous writer, Schlee is a lawyer who has researched the history of his state, Rio Grande do Sul, in order to use it as the background for his admirably developed stories. His second collection, *Uma terra só* (São Paulo: Melhoramentos, 1984, 152 p.) won the First Nestlé Prize in 1984. With F. Borges (item **6166**) and R. Modernell (item **6191**), Schlee restores Rio Grande do Sul to its former preeminence in Brazilian literature. These three *gaúchos* are *superregionalists*, to employ A. Cândido's expression: they transcend regionalism to reach the universal.

Another newcomer of note is R. Castro Neves, whose *Baleia branca* (item **6193**) has a unifying theme (the aging male) as well as an unusual coda in which the reader is told what happened to the story's major characters after the tale ends. A wry, bawdy, and intensively vivid writer, Castro Neves wields a magnificent punch. M. Lobato, also concerned with problems of the aging male (see *HLAS 46: 6053*), has produced some exemplary stories that subtly incorporate the burlesque (item **6186**). Another celebrated author, E. Coutinho, also combines new and old stories in *O jogo terminado* (item **6170**). Like his previous writings, these tales perceive and present life as a game played according to different categories. It is unfortunate that two outstanding collections annotated below are posthumous: Costa Filho's (item **6196**) and H. Trevisan's (item **6203**). One regrets the death of these authors who would have continued to produce valuable fiction, especially in the latter's case, a relatively young man.

The relationship beteen the short story and Brazilian publishing houses has changed. Possibly because of the Guimarães Rosa/Lispector "boom" and the so-called Brazilian "economic miracle," short story publishing flourished in the late 1960s and early 1970s. Atica brought forth a great number of fine, lavishly illustrated collections by both new and established writers. However, by the 1970s, this publisher began issuing scholarly monographs and concentrating on didactic material. In addition, the publisher, José Olympio, also changed course by focusing more on "popular" than "literary" fiction. One hopes that these new trends do not imply that two such important houses will no longer publish short fiction at the rate they were until a few years ago.

6164 Barbosa, Alaor. Os rios da coragem: contos. Goiânia: Imery Publicações, 1983. 128 p. (Obras de Alaor Barbosa)
Regional fictional by Goiás writer that is earthy and sensitive. Not all stories attain the high level of the ones consisting of monologues by illiterate characters.

6165 Barbosa, Cacilda Soares. Alma barranca: contos. Amazonas: União Brasileira de Escritores, 1982. 130 p.: ill.
Stories written in a rough, almost careless style but with narrative strength attest to author's passion for her region. Leg-

ends of the Amazon convey love of place as well as concern for social justice. The jungle stands for the *caboclo espoliado* (the Indian/European mestizo raped by white society).

6166 Borges, Fernando. Milonga porteña: contos. Porto Alegre: Movimento, 1983. 86 p. (Col. Rio Grande; 61)
Regional fiction by compassionate and daring author whose stories focus on varied aspects of southern Brazil (e.g., long-time lovers' ranchhands who go hungry, a dying calf). Written in the *gaúcho* language of

estancias of southern Brazil, a Portuguese strongly influenced by Spanish.

6167 Brill, Zina. O joelho de Eva. Campinas, Unigrag, 1981. 167 p.

Competent stories by Goiás writer that focus on woman and her vulnerability (i.e., Eve's knee). Carefully examines the female psyche and looks at love as if through the lenses of death—something irretrievably lost as if in the past. Stories deal with emotions akin to love: envy, compassion, humility, anger.

6168 Buarque, Cristovam. Astrícia. Rio de Janeiro: Civilização Brasileira, 1984. 159 p.

Unusual work which, according to author, defies classification. A literate and literary exercise in the fantastic influenced by Borges who is quoted in a text sprinked with epigraphs (eg., Picasso, Eco, Barthes). The mysterious, ambivalent protagonist Astor/Astricia lives in a distant land where he changes sexes periodically. Abstruse but interesting "book on writing."

6169 Costa Filho, Odylo. Histórias da beira do rio. Introdução de Rubem Fonseca. Prefácio de J. Amado. Ilustrações de Nazareth Costa. Rio de Janeiro: Record, 1983. 189 p.: ill.

Posthumously published *histórias* by poet, journalist, novelist, and essayist, which charm as plainly told family tales. Their overt simplicity, however, is deceptive as Costa Filho is a deft narrator and creator of character. As if by magic, he conjures for the reader a varied cast of 1920s Maranhão. Includes exquisite illustrations by Nazareth Costa, enthusiastic foreword by J. Amado, and introduction by Rubem Fonseca.

6170 Coutinho, Edilberto. O jogo terminado: uma seleta de ficções curtas, a seu modo exemplares, sobre estes jogos da vida: o jogo do amor e do sexo, o jogo grotesco e carnavalesco, o jogo das máscaras, o jogo da política, o jogo esportivo, o jogo da infância e da adolescência, o jogo da solidão e da morte. Rio de Janeiro: Livraria J. Olympio Editora, 1983. 121 p.

Collection by distinguished author, critic, and journalist consists of both new and published stories that are poetic and elliptic. They deal with the poor and disadvantaged (i.e., sailors, prostitutes) and are

divided into several "game categories" (e.g., love, sex, politics, sports).

6172 Daunt Neto, Ricardo. Endereços úteis. Rio de Janeiro: Codecri, 1984. 172 p.: ill. (Col. Edições do Pasquim; 165)

Fine collection of eclectic stories includes some that are meditations on the past (e.g., "Quadro Familiar," "No Waldorf Astoria") and others which are fantastic (e.g., "Ciao," "Bete Dumbo").

6173 Denser, Márcia M. Exercícios para o pecado: duas novelas. Rio de Janeiro: Philobiblion, 1984. 106 p. (Col. Prosa brasileira; 4)

Author deals with her usual concerns in two novellas (e.g., metaphysical questions, the world of journalists, effects of alcohol and other drugs, beautiful women who sleep with repulsive men, the equivalence of religion and sex). The grotesque is meticulously embodied in the characters of a sadistic editor and photographer. A fine but grim writer whose stories grow increasingly more somber and convoluted.

6174 Dourado, Autran. Solidão solitude. 3a ed. Rio de Janeiro: Record, 1983. 139 p.

Reprint of author's critical and popular success written in his impeccable style and marvelous language—a blend of colloquial and erudite Portuguese. The stories tell us about loneliness, suffering, and daily living. A major collection of Brazilian short stories which owes much to Mário de Andrade—more than its title and epigraph.

6175 Elis, Bernardo. Apenas um violão: novela e contos. Rio de Janeiro: Editora Nova Fronteira, 1984. 230 p.

Limpid, flowing narratives by master story-teller who began writing in the 1940s. They recount childhood memoirs about various relatives in a small town, the major figure being the grandfather, a still young but aging patriarch who regrets the onset of old age. Excellent.

6176 Emerenciano, Nilo Sérgio A. Aconteceu na quinta delegacia. Natal: Fundação José Augusto, 1982. 96 p.

Stories by young Rio Grande do Norte author are couched in easy, colloquial tone and deal primarily with the *nego moderno* ("modern guy") in city and country. Some tales consist of jokes; one is told by a *cafifa* (shoemaker); others are more developed and psychological. Auspicious start.

6177 Engrácio, Arthur. Restinga: contos. 2a ed. rev. Manaus?: União Brasileira de Escritores, 1982. 79 p.

Second edition proves the success of this regional collection about Amazonia. Engrácio captures the quality of his region well, noting its fantastic legends ("Boto") and brutality ("Pagode, Sanfona e Morte na Madrugada"). A superior collection to the author's previous one (see *HLAS 46: 6094*), *Restinga* has equal documentary value but more literary sophistication.

6178 França Júnior, Oswaldo. As laranjas iguais: contos. Rio de Janeiro: Nova Fronteira, 1985. 134 p.

Very short fables told as if from a great distance by narrator who, like an Oriental sage, contemplates the world from high. Elegant stories that break new ground but also remind one of the writer's novels. Themes are cowardice and laziness told in a static tone; others are fantasies about prodigies. All are moral fables.

6179 Garcia, José Ribamar. Os cavaleiros da noite. Rio de Janeiro: Shogun Arte, 1984. 63 p.

Crônicas or short stories? These are hybrid pieces that deal with the northern states of Maranhão and Piauí. Precise, incisive, and dramatic, they are well worth reading.

6180 Godoy, Heleno. Relações: narrativas. Goiânia: CERNE, 1981. 89 p.

Difficult but exciting narratives that are syntactically idiosyncratic, each consisting of an uninterrupted long sentence. A tour de force, the collection conveys portraits that are highly metaphorical.

6181 Gomes, Dias. Odorico na cabeça: contos. Rio de Janeiro: Civilização Brasileira, 1983. 183 p. (Col. Vera Cruz: literatura brasileira; 345)

Stories by competent playwright which are actually extensions of his famous television soap opera, *O bem-amado* (*The beloved*). Stories also draw on the soap's sequel, *Sucupira: ame-a ou deixe-a* (*Sucupira: love it or leave it*). A mythical city and the soap's setting, Sucupira has become part of Brazilian consciousness.

6182 Guerra, Guido. Ela se chama Joana Felicidade. Rio de Janeiro: Editora Record, 1984. 114 p.

Book consists of two novellas: 1) pre- and post-suicide events involving a cancer victim, including funeral arrangements; and 2) ironic and witty tale that pits João Bispo's illness and suicide against similar fate of two relatives, his grandfather and great-grandfather. Macabre but well done narratives.

6183 Ivo, Lêdo. Use a passagem subterrânea e outras histórias. 2a ed. Rio de Janeiro: Editora Record, 1984. 125 p.

Important new edition of stories by Ivo who, like C. Drummond de Andrade, is a poet-cum-story teller. The immediacy of daily life is splendidly conveyed in stories that border on the *crônica* genre. Versatile in theme and technique, these narratives are well structured, their style limpid, superb. Some (e.g., "O Flautim" and "A Mulher Gorda") remind one of Machado de Assis.

6184 Ladeira, Julieta de Godoy. Era sempre feriado nacional: contos. São Paulo: Summus Editorial, 1984. 175 p.

Well wrought fictions emphasize stream-of-consciousness techniques, fantasy, and social consciousness. Often lucid, these tales explore fantasies of modern day São Paulo, including autobiographical touches. Some stories pay homage to literature and cinema making allusions to techniques and characters out of Osman Lins, Faulkner, and Eisenstein.

6185 Leitão, José Maria. A estranha estória de Bebeto Areião e outros contos: contos. Brasília: Thesaurus, 1983. 142 p.: ill.

Stories tell about country and village life from anonymous viewpoint. Skilful creation of sensitive and humorous narrator who describes family ties, animals, and the rural community—from the fantastic to the realistic. First published fiction by physician author.

6186 Lobato, Manoel. O cântico do galo. São Paulo: Global Editora, 1985. 208 p. (Col. Múltipla)

Collection consists of two parts: 1) longer section comprising new stories, mostly erotic according to author; and 2) older, previously published tales. As is usual with Lobato, his fiction is superb combining insight, compassion, and sly humor. A world of diverse characters is incisively portrayed. Many stories focus on the aging male's fears of losing sexual powers.

6187 Machado, Aníbal. Aníbal Machado. Seleção e prefácio de Antônio Dimas. 1a ed. São Paulo: Global Editora, 1984. 228 p. (Os Melhores contos; 1)

Important edition reprints 11 of 13 stories already published in Machado's definitive edition. "One of four strongest Modernist short story writers," and a "classical author," Machado combines keen humor, imagination, and compassion with an admirable writing style. It is paradoxical that the editor's short preface ignores existing scholarship on Machado while accusing critics of this neglect.

6188 Machado, Antônio de Alcântara. Brás, Bexiga e Barra Funda: notícias de São Paulo. Comentários e notas de Cecília de Lara. Ed. fac-similar. São Paulo: Imprensa Oficial do Estado de São Paulo: Divisão de Arquivo do Estado de São Paulo, 1982. 141 p.; supplement (126 p.): ill

Welcome once again to a landmark book by Brazil's most celebrated Modernist short story writer. His tales focus on the Italian immigrant experience in early 20th-century São Paulo. The children of these strangers from the Old World, "the new *mamalucos*," to whom the collection is dedicated, have become an integral part of the new country. The situations and characters depicted are lively and witty. Alcântara's extraordinarily fluid language continues to delight 50 years later.

6189 Maranhão, Haroldo. As peles frias: contos. Rio de Janeiro: F. Alves, 1983. 172 p.

Author of *Voo de galinha* (see *HLAS 42:6144*) presents here longer, more sustained stories which received the 1981 Short Fiction Prize of the prestigious Instituto Nacional do Livro. These are powerful and dramatic tales whether realistic ("O Leite em pó da Bondade") or surrealistic ("O Batizado"). They strongly convey the author's social concerns, his humor, and outstanding craftsmanship.

6190 Menezes, Holdemar Oliveira de. Os eleitos para o sacrifício: contos. Porto Alegre: Editora Movimento, 1983. 111 p.: port. (Col. Santa Catarina; 22)

Powerful fiction by acclaimed author of *A coleira de Peggy* (see *HLAS 38:7385*), his stories deal with picaresque, sometimes grotesque subjects (e.g., underground world, corruption, castration, catastrophes such as floods and avalanches). Brutality is an overriding theme. Settings are varied (e.g., circus bullfight arena, brothel, belfry, Salvation Army). Well worth reading.

6191 Modernell, Renato. O homemo do carro-motor: contos. São Paulo: Melhoramentos, 1984. 270 p.

Another admirable *gaúcho* author who is able to create living characters in specific circumstances (e.g., woman physician threatened by stranger, professional but self-appointed comedian, mad scientist, smugglers). Peculiarities of characters do not detract from their verisimilitude. Written with magnificent, classic syntax in a style that combines wry irony with gentleness. A book that should be read.

6192 Neves, Amilcar. Dança de fantasmas: contos de amor. Florianópolis: FCC Edições; Porto Alegre: L&PM Editores, 1984. 103 p.

Stories by prize-winning author told by serious, gentle, humorous narrator. Imbued with philosophical inquiries into love, politics, life. The atmosphere is ethereal, evanescent but the author very much in control. Fine collection.

6193 Neves, Roberto de Castro. Baleia branca. Rio de Janeiro: Livraria Taurus Editora, 1983. 166 p.

Winner of Chinaglia Prize. Stories consist of long monologues (e.g., end of telephone conversation) that are admirably controlled. Written in a picaresque vein, stories deal with males approaching 40 in Rio (e.g., dentist, doorman, sniper, bank teller gone mad). Quick dialogue and acid wit are conveyed through slang and four-letter words. Eminently readable and imaginative examination of the male menopause.

6194 Peregrino, Umberto. Pedro Cobra e outros acontecidos: contos. Rio de Janeiro: J. Olympio Editora, 1984. 80 p., 1 p. of plates: port.

Distinguished and well established author is also statesman and public official. His collection consists of regional tales as well as philosophical fables. The author's classic, unpretentious style and his scrutiny of feelings and events lend the stories a Machadian quality. His philosophical disquisitions also remind one of Guimarães Rosa.

6195 Perez, Renard. Trio: contos. São Paulo: LR Editores, 1983. 96 p.

Critically acclaimed author and critic presents trio of *carioca* stories about simple folks (e.g., children's nanny, night watchman, shy man on Carnival night). Perez's smooth and discerning narrative is outstanding: in particular his use of everyday Portuguese has the simplicity of elegance. Collection was awarded Second Prize in the 1982 Bienel Nestlé de Literatura Brasileira (together with Aldyr Garcia Schlee, see item **6200**).

6196 Pólvora, Hélio. O grito da perdiz: contos. São Paulo: Difel, 1983. 153 p.

Magnificent collection of four novellas reveal the author's skill and eclecticism as well as his compassion. "Além do Mundo Azul" is a horror story in the form of a childhood memoir; "O Arrenegado" concerns a witch-hunt complete with *auto-da-fé*; "Bicuíba" is everyman as hero. As powerful as author's previous collection. The focus on brutality, however, is not as harsh as each tale unfolds a memory softened by the passing of time.

6197 Rainho, Cleonice. João Mineral. Rio de Janeiro: Livraria J. Olympio, 1983. 98 p.

Skilful stories by poet are clearly designed to convey the lives of country people by using their language in various monologue-type narrations. Rainho's style is so poetical as to be almost elliptical.

6198 Reis, Marcos Konder. A bola encantada: cinco novelas: de-repente. Rio de Janeiro: Livraria Editora Cátedra, 1983. 174 p.

Dense, textured stories by another poet. In them, an oneiric atmosphere permeates each tale where the boundaries shift between reality and imagination, inner monologue and outward talk. In some a cryptic style combines with eccentric lists ("7 de Outubro"). Konder Reis is a more successful poet than short story writer (see also *HLAS 44:6222*).

6199 Samuel, Heli. Chão dos puris: contos. Rio de Janeiro: Livraria Editora Cátedra, 1984. 73 p.

Abrupt, sometimes cryptic, but vivid stories set in a town in Rio state where a variety of characters speak on many distinct voices.

6200 Schlee, Aldyr Garcia. Contos de sempre. São Paulo: LR Editora, 1983. 149 p.

Most distinguished collection by newcomer. Powerful, forceful, and poetical stories based on Rio Grande do Sul's history. Brazil's *gaúcho*, past and present, are recreated in tales that are true works of art. Winner of the Second Nestlé Bienal Prize (with Perez, see item **6195**).

6201 Silveira, Joel. Milagre em Florença: contos e novelas. Rio de Janeiro: Livraria Editora Cátedra, 1983. 145 p.

Traditional type stories with themes such as the Brazilian army in Italy during World War II. Best ones are "Ismael" and "Moças."

6202 Távola, Artur da. Do amor, da vida e da morte. Ilustrações de Augusto Rodrigues *et al.* Rio de Janeiro: Movimento Cultural, Internacional de Seguros, 1983. 1 portfolio (92 p., 1 leaf of plates): ill.

Beautifully printed and illustrated volume of stories that are unfortunately inferior to author's previous collection (see *HLAS 46:6139*). Could this be one of those coffeetable books now produced in Brazil for Christmas shoppers?

6203 Trevisan, Hamilton. O bonde da filosofia. São Paulo: Global Editora, 1984. 111 p. (Col. Múltipla)

Posthumous, excellent collection by author of *Brinquedo* (see *HLAS 38:7414*). The stories, about urban São Paulo, have a varied cast of characters (e.g., young students, political revolutionaries, intellectuals, aging beauties). The narrator is a melancholic, middle-class intellectual worried about aging. Distinguished tales that also make for entertaining reading.

6204 Vieira, Iara. Interiores. Aracaju: Subsecretaria de Cultura, Estado de Sergipe, 1982. 71 p.: ill. (Col. Ofenisia freire)

Skilful, quiet stories that are brief meditations drawn from epigraphs and which focus on ordinary aspects of daily life.

Crônicas

RICHARD A. PRETO-RODAS, *Director, Division of Language, University of South Florida*

OVER THE PAST TWO YEARS there has been no reduction in the popularity of the *crônica* in Brazil. Anthologies of contemporary masters like *Quatro vozes* (item **6206**) have appeared along with other collections by newcomers such as those included in *De quatro, ou, Como fazer sucesso . . .* (item **6207**) and *As melhores crônicas do 6.o Concurso Sérgio Porto* (item **6213**). Once considered a minor craft akin to gossip columns and other lesser forms of journalism, the *crônica* is now re-garded as a truly Brazilian literary genre. Proof of the recognition accorded are re-cent editions of collected *crônicas* by eminent authors such as Clarice Lispector, Carlos de Laet, and Raul Pompéia. Indeed, the dean of Brazilian critics, Afrânio Coutinho, devotes more than 30 pages to an analysis of the genre, from mid-19th century to the present, in his preface to the first four volumes of Pompéia's *crô-nicas* (item **6230**). It is most likely that, given the genre's remarkable capacity to please by combining variety with lyrical sensitivity and literary charm, similar edi-tions of well known writers from the past will be published in the future.

Although a *crônica* is easily recognizable, the definition of its precise charac-teristics is not easy. Some *crônicas*, for example, constitute such perfect narrations that they become virtually indistinguishable from short stories. Thus, we have the case of Carlos Drummond de Andrade's pieces in *Boca do luar* (item **6205**) which are described as *historinhas*. A similar blurring distinction between *crônica* and *conto* is apparent in Darcy Penteado's *crônicas* which are subtitled: *Uma narrativa fragmentada em contos e crônicas*. Other writers such as Laet and Pompéia strike a decidedly philosophical tone in their *crônicas* by emphasizing the transcendental over the ephemeral. Other authors have such a defined approach and focused point of view that their *crônicas* could be regarded as disquisitions in politics, history, or sociology. Affonso Romano de Sant'Anna's fascinating *Política e paixão* (item **6232**) exemplifies such a trend.

Notwithstanding the genre's several manifestations, the essense of any good *crônica* remains its ability to capture a moment in all its complexity and to convey it in language that is simultaneously literary and colloquial. Conversely, *crônicas* that are purposely didactic and imbued with a sense of the author's importance vio-late the close writer-reader rapport that is basic to the genre. Therefore, pieces marked by pomposity or trivialty have been purposely excluded from the very se-lective sample of annotated items that follows, samples culled from scores of titles published over the past two or three years.

Once an urban genre mostly confined to two or three cities, the *crônica* now encompasses all of Brazil and is exemplified by pieces that range from São Luís do Maranhão in Nonnato Masson's *Ines é morta* (item **6223**) and Alagoas in Valter Pedrosa's *O fenomeno Hítler* (item **6226**) to southern regions such as Dante Martorano's Florianópolis in *Temas catarinenses* (item **6222**). Another recent de-velopment has been a trend away from a traditionally sunny outlook towards a more somber perspective. This tendency is exemplified in *crônicas* that discuss the depredations that "development" inflicts on the environment, the rise of random violence, the average citizen's mistrust of social institutions, the threat of inflation, the impact of national insolvency, and the role of the International Monetary Fund in contemporary life. Indeed, that such grave problems can be presented with such literary skill and individual style attests to the vitality of the genre and bodes well for its future success.

6205 Andrade, Carlos Drummond de. Boca de luar. Rio de Janeiro: Editora Record, 1984. 217 p.

Another collection by a master whose *crônicas* depicting our era and all its polarities are a delight. Includes observations that are invariably accurate and marked by a bitter-sweet, tragicomic tone. Many of the lively dialogues could serve as one-act plays and ingenious situation comedies.

6206 Andrade, Carlos Drummond de; Rachel de Queiroz; Manuel Bandeira; and **Cecília Meireles.** Quatro vozes. Rio de Janeiro: Editora Record, 1984. 128 p.

The title's four voices belong to masters of the genre such as Rachel de Queiroz, Cecília Meireles, Manuel Bandeira, and Carlos Drummond de Andrade. Well chosen samples from their best work include Bandeira's memories of João Guimarães Rosa's induction into the Academy, Rachel de Queiroz's sociological insights about domestic employees of middle-class households, and Drummond's memories of his first glimpse of the sea. The tone of each case is unique yet familiar. Who else but Cecília Meireles could comment on a stray dog— a subject of no fewer than three of her *crônicas*—with such gentle melancholy and wisdom?

6207 Caetano, Michele *et al.* De quatro, ou, Como fazer sucesso à sombra de Luís Fernando Verisimo. Porto Alegre: Globo, 1983. 126 p.

Four young public-relations executives from Rio Grande do Sul write painfully contemporary *crônicas* about divorce, John Lennon, Freudian analysis, the virtues of mineral water, and (again and again) Hollywood. The tone is irreverent and the humor zany.

6208 Campos, Renato Carneiro. Sempre aos domingos: crônicas. Seleção e organização de Jaci Bezerra. Apresentação de Maximiano Campos. Recife: Fundação Joaquim Nabuco, Editora Massangana, 1984. 231 p.

With a title reminiscent of Zorba the Greek, this collection was compiled posthumously by the *cronista*'s friends from his daily column in *Diário de Pernambuco*. Topics range from the weather to popular culture, the viewpoint being decidedly democratic and anti-authoritarian. A major theme is the author's love-hate relationship with Pernambuco, a place as central to his work as Dublin was to Joyce's and Lisbon to Pessoa's. The compiler's preface provides an excellent introduction to the genre as well as to the works of a gifted writer.

6209 Cardoso, José Muriel. Estórias de um Tio Juca. Belo Horizonte: UNAGRAPHOS, 1983. 119 p.

As indicated by the title, these *crônicas* approximate short stories. Reminiscent of the proverbial "tall tales" of fishermen or country yarns, these episodes were indeed first published in *Revista de Pesca* (1963–80). Topics are vindictive fathers, docile women, and submissive blacks. Author deftly captures the tone and diction of shrewd country folk in dialogues basic to the structure of these *crônicas*.

6210 Carneiro, Manoel de Castro. O menino e o velho. São Paulo: Editora Pannartz, 1982. 96 p.: ill.

Child and old man of title represent the social polarities of poverty-ridden Ceará. One is a bright 13 year-old boy stunted by chronic malnutrition, the other, a rancher in his 60s much given to meditation and analysis. Around them stands a harsh world where conventional morality is rarely observed. Especially insightful portrayal of individuals who suceed in maintaining their sense of worth against formidable odds.

6211 Chagas, Mário. Na chapada: crônicas de uma região diamantina. Juiz de Fora: Esdeva Empresa Gráfica, 1979. 91 p.

Another collection set in a rural area, specifically a deserted mining town in Bahia's hill country. Notwithstanding a somewhat stuffy, dated style (e.g., "crystalline waters," "pure air"), the pieces combine the *crônica* and memoir genres in an effective homage "to my land and my people." Fascinating array of human types and events that involve all superstitions, bizarre scandals, and odd personalities that made for an unforgettable life in Campos de São José.

6212 Chiesa, Dirceu Antônio. As vantagens do Coronel Mindeco. Porto Alegre: Siluna, 1984. 165 p.: ill.

Crônicas culled from business trips and vacations (i.e., Rio Grande do Sul, Venice, New York). Describe daring indicents, names and peccadillos, and casts a farcical light on Portuguese, Argentines, gay people, senior citizens, and women. In somewhat dubious taste but for that reason, a representative example of a particularly raffish strain of Brazilian humor.

6213 Concurso Sérgio Porto, 6th, Goiânia, Brazil, 1983. As melhores crônicas. Brazil: FENAB, 1983. 77 p.

Award-wining selections that concern humorous bureaucratic foibles, urbanization, childhood reveries. Unfortunately, the judges' aversion to controversy and criticism has resulted in a rather trivial collection.

6214 Cunha, Liberato Vieira da. Miss Falklands: contos e crônicas. Porto Alegre: Martins, 1983. 126 p.

Escapist, charming accounts written in sophisticated but accessible language (e.g., lovely woman on passing train as symbol of lost opportunities, ugly stranger redeemed by beautiful, mysterious voice).

6215 Diaféria, Lourenço. A morte sem colete. São Paulo: Editora Moderna, 1983. 118 p.: ill.

Representative example of traditional urban *crônicas* of the 1960s-70s culled from author's writing in *Folha de São Paulo* and *Journal da Tarde.* They describe life in Brazil's largest city (e.g., pervasive random violence, often instigated by ill-trained policemen, grim struggle of the working poor attempting to survive despite inflation, pollution, and an indifferent bureaucracy).

6216 Dirceu. Edipo é a mãe! Rio de Janeiro: Nova Fronteira, 1985. 135 p.

Nephew of Stanislaw Ponte Preta shares his uncle's satirical outlook. Mocks contemporary foibles ranging from absurd aspects of child psychology to superficial bromides and facile answers to the human condition. Dirceu's incisive wit is devastating on, for example, the Brazilian obsession with plastic surgery, urban violence, superpatriots, and national bogeymen such as the IMF.

6217 Fidelis, Guido. O homem fatal. São Paulo: Soma, 1982. 95 p. (Grandes temas do jornalismo: a crônica)

Contemporary, pessimistic views of political institutions, whether right or left

(e.g., the past as repression, the future as chaos, violence as part of the human condition). To be aware or informed is to be alienated or deviant, bourgeois tolerance being a sham. Author's grim perspective rings true in taut, impeccable language.

6218 Gomes, Roberto. O demolidor de miragens. Curitiba: Criar Edições, 1983. 93 p.

Lively pieces about deceptively ordinary situations which point to instances of "metaphysics gone awry." Touches of magical realism are apparent in the case of a computer that feels but is undercut only by the know-it-all realist of the title, destroyer of illusions.

6219 Grein Filho, Lauro. Hora de lembrar: crônicas. Curitiba: Editora Lítero-Técnica, 1983. 320 p.: ill.

Pieces that portray a fast changing Curitiba where fast food joints and bars are displacing the more leisurely haunts of the past. Constants that endure include wily gypsies in the parks and the Brazilian knack for problem solving (*o jeitinho*).

6220 Laet, Carlos de. Obras seletas. v. 1, Crônicas. Ed. anotada. Rio de Janeiro: Fundação Casa de Rui Barbosa: Livraria AGIR Editora: Instituto Nacional do Livro, Fundação Nacional Pró-Memória, 1984. 377 p.: ill., index.

Enduring *crônicas* by profound, turn-of-the-century Brazilian thinker provide rich panorama of social and cultural history. A monarchist who lamented the rise of republicanism, Laet was a progressive forerunner of Gilberto Freyre in his defense of miscegenation and inclusion of women in the Academy (66 years before such acceptance). Includes excellent pieces on the abolition of slavery, Machado de Assis's death, and his countrymen's indifference to the past. Includes author index.

6221 Lispector, Clarice. A descoberta do mundo. Rio de Janeiro: Editora Nova Fronteira, 1984. 781 p.

Delightful selections from *Jornal do Brasil* column (1967–73). Extraordinarily varied in length, theme, and tone, these *crônicas* reflect the author's novels and short stories in progress. They include many insights on language, writing, the art of the *crônica*, and human beings (e.g., from domestic servants and childhood friends to prominent Brazilian writers and musicians).

6222 Martorano, Dante. Temas catarinenses. Florianópolis: Editora da UFSC: Lunardelli, 1982. 193 p.

Culled from author's newspaper columns in Florianópolis, these selections focus on contemporary Santa Catarina, its gauchos and disappearing forests and the ravages of urban renewal in the cities. Especially noteworthy are the vignettes dedicated to the mountain town of São Joaquim whose snow-covered landscape attracts thousands of Brazilians every July.

6223 Masson, Nonnato. Inês é morta. São Luís: Serviço de Imprensa e Obras Gráficas do Estado, 1984. 109 p.

Title of collection and final *crônica* refers to the devastation of São Luís de Maranhão by the wrecker's ball. Culled from author's apt contributions to the state's major newspaper. Reflections on drought, flood, and poverty by a libertarian who rails against restrictions on such individual freedoms as smoking in public or being gay.

6224 Menezes, Holdemar. A vida vivida: crônicas. Florianópolis: Editora da UFSC: Editora Lundardelli, 1983. 163 p.

Self-confessed skeptic offers his jaundiced, ironic impressions of Brazil ranging from his native Ceará to his adopted Santa Catarina where he practices medicine. Well wrought *crônicas* discuss death, illness, popular culture, and contemporary moral confusion. Author's social conscience is apparent in his references to Camus, Pessoa, the effect of conspicuous consumption amidst poverty, and the arrogance of the few who relegate all others to the subaltern status of "Third World."

6225 Novaes, Carlos Eduardo. Crônica de uma brisa eleitoral. Charges de Chico Caruso. Rio de Janeiro: Nórdica 1983. 160 p.: ill.

Unusual collection about politics in a society newly restored to the democratic process after a long eclipse. Deft pieces provide a sometimes uproarious view of elections, ambitious candidates, dirty politics, television packaging, and campaign strains on a candidate's family life.

6226 Pedrosa, Valter. O fenômeno Hitler: crônicas/ensaios. Brasília: Roteiro Editorial, 1982. 168 p. (Col. Momento literário)

Unusually well written anthology by Alagoan with an *engagé* point of view. He is as repelled by the poverty of his state and its environmental problems as he is enamored of its people and threatened scenery. Other *crônicas* show real insight about literary matters (e.g., Vargas Llosa, García Márquez).

6227 Penalva, Gastão. Patescas e marambaias: episódios de terra e mar. 2a ed. rev. e atualizada. Rio de Janeiro: Serviço de Documentação Geral da Marinha, 1981. 103 p. (Col. Jacequay; 2)

Unusual anthology of *crônicas* about the world of professional seafarers (e.g., *patecas* or dedicated salts who have abjured landlubbers; *marambaias*, sailors with a girl in every port). A love for the sea is the common trait of assorted personalities (e.g., religious fundamentalists, con-men, reconteurs). Somewhat affected style and ponderous grammar but interesting material.

6228 Penteado, Darcy. Menino insone: uma narrativa fragmentada em contos e crônicas, 1964–1982. São Paulo: Editora Soma, 1983. 94 p.: ill.

Accounts that straddle the short story and crônica and structured as a diary in the form of a dialogue between the present-day author and his boyhood-self. Childhood memories of plantation life in the 1930s are filtered through an ironic, iconoclastic consciousness. Effective evocations of a handicapped uncle, the death of a grandmother, and early childhood stirrings of homosexuality.

6229 Pinto, Antisthenes. Quelonios do Carabinani: crônicas. Manaus: Casa Editora Madrugada, 1984. 187 p.

Title refers to turtle species of an Amazonian river. *Crônicas* depict life in the region over the past 30 years and recount the gradual destruction of the ecology (e.g., illegal fishing, industrial pollution, poor urban planning, foreign investment). Author's harshest comments are directed at the establishment of a duty-free zone in Manaus, "an act of madness that has constricted our heart and soul." Well written, informative collection.

6230 Pompéia, Raul. Obras. v. 6, 8–9, Crônicas. Organização de Afrânio Coutinho e Eduardo de Faria Coutinho. Rio de Janeiro: MEC, FENAME, Oficina Literária Afrânio Coutinho: Editora Civilização Bra-

sileira, 1982–1983. 3 v. (321, 370, 581 p.):
plates (Col. Vera Cruz; 324)

Major compilation of Pompéia's *crô-nicas* for a 10-volume edition of his complete works prepared by Afrânio Coutinho who provides an exhaustive introduction to the genre in vol. 4, *Crônicas I.* Culled from a variety of newspapers and magazines, these pieces offer a comprehensive view of Brazilian society (1888–92) in a conversational, informal tone with topics ranging from the whimsical to the grave. The perspective is conservative/nationalist as the author deplores the Latin spirit that has stifled the development of his nation in contrast to the US and Australia. In a caustic tone, he also registers his opposition to universal suffrage, especially that of women who turn into viragos when allowed to vote.

6231 Rangel, Flávio. Diário do Brasil:
crônicas. Rio de Janeiro: Paz e Terra,
1982. 210 p.

Pieces by popular journalist discuss current social and political events with insight and style.

6232 Sant'Anna, Affonso Romano de. Política e paixão. Rio de Janeiro: Rocco,
1984. 187 p.

More essays than *crônicas*, the pieces were culled from the author's *crônicas* published in *Jornal do Brasil*, *Folha de São Paulo*, and other periodicals. In a critical, often angry tone, the writer confronts contemporary Brazil, its left/right polarities, dour authoritarianism vs. ribald levity, notions of unique civilization vis-à-vis a derivative culture, poverty, academic writing, and in one famous *crônica*, President Figueiredo's sloth and negligence.

6233 Sant'Anna, Affonso Romano de; Fernando Sabino; Carlos Drummond de Andrade; and Henrique Souza Filho. Crônicas mineiras. São Paulo: Editora Atica,
1984. 112 p.: bibl., ports. (Minas de livros)

Curious collection by and about writers of Minas Gerais, the country's most traditional as well as its most literary state.

Includes genial caricatures of the region's laconic inhabitants (Fernando Sabino), their propensity for censorship (Carlos Drummond de Andrade), biting satire about US cultural influences (Henrique Souza Filho), and the perennial conflict between government oppression and individual rights (Affonso Romano de Sant'Anna). *Crônicas* that succeed in combining literary skill with sociological and historical insights.

6234 Silvestre, François. Dormentes: a serra da festa encantada. Natal: s.n., 1983.
85 p.

Another unusual collection of *crô-nicas* about a utopian setting reminiscent of the rural Northeast. In an ideal society similar to Manuel Bandeira's Passárgada, the inhabitants are equally kind and rational with a "marvelous capacity for living happily." Narrator candidly acknowledges fanciful character of his episodes (*lorotas*) while making a strong case against injustice, violence, vindictive penal codes, and dehumanizing technology.

6235 Sousa, Paula E. Rosa reencontrada: crô-nicas. Manaus: UBE/AM, 1981. 104 p.

Somewhat precious and whimsical but sincere, lyrical pieces about freedom and happiness in an artificial world. An intimate of writers such as Jorge Amado, Rubem Braga, and Carybe, author derives inspiration from a closely knit family.

6236 Wainberg, Paulo. O homem de papel:
crônicas. Porto Alegre: Movimento,
1982. 90 p. (Col. Rio Grande; 57)

Crônicas interspersed by a serialized parody of a gothic novel (*Misterio da mansão*). Exemplifies a growing trend toward black humor where cops are indistinguishable from robbers, spies, and transvestites compete with alienated spirits, all in the shadow of nuclear war. Written in an irreverent tone, decidedly macho (i.e., philandering is admirable), the pieces are humorous and insightful as well as exasperating if not infuriating. Book is so poorly bound it could not survive a second reading.

Poetry

RALPH E. DIMMICK, *General Secretariat, Organization of American States*

THE REMARKABLE CAREER of Carlos Drummond de Andrade, one of the longest and most fruitful in the history of Brazilian literature, now extends into his ninth decade: *Corpo* (item **6239**) ranks with the best he has written to date. Honored on his 80th birthday with an exhibit at the National Library (item **6428**), he also received the novel tribute of publication of a selection of his poems in Latin translation (item **6238**). Continuing public interest in his *oeuvre* is attested by a reissue of his socially oriented *A rosa do povo* (item **6241**) and a new, augmented edition of his collected verse (item **6240**).

In what must be the most belated "debut" on record, Drummond's near-contemporary, the distinguished educator Abgar Renault, finally yielded to the pressures of literary friends who had long admired his privately circulated verse, bringing out under the title *A outra face da lua* (item **6293**), one of the most rewarding volumes of recent years. Other first appearances worthy of note are those of Maria Abadia Silva (item **6303**) and Olívia Villaça (item **6309**).

Carlos Drummond is not the only poet of established reputation to continue productive. João Cabral de Melo Neto brought out a "poem for voices" (item **6276**) which might serve as the libretto for an opera on the death of the 19th-century revolutionary Frei Caneca. João de Jesus Paes Loureiro brought his Amazonian trilogy to a splendid conclusion with publication of *Altar em chamas* (item **6272**). Walmir Ayala (item **6245**), Homero Homem (item **6267**), and Nauro Machado (item **6273**) maintain, or in Ayala's case surpass, the standards they have previously set.

Voices of protest are less numerous than in past years. The black presence is evidenced in the verse of Abdias do Nascimento (item **6282**), much of which is written in the US, and in the anthology organized by Hamilton de Jesus Vieira (item **6290**), but the interest is sociological rather than literary. The feminist poets Glória Perez and Leila Míccolis (item **6287**) take a disabused, but by no means one-sided, view of relations between the sexes.

Useful to students of literary history are the reissue of Felipe d'Oliveira's *Lanterna verde* (item **6284**), the anthology of poets of the "mimeograph generation" of the 1970s organized by Heloisa Buarque de Hollanda and Carlos Alberto Messeder Pereira (item **6289**), and a study of Concrete poetry made by Iumna Maria Simon and Vinicius Dantas (item **6288**).

6237 Alves, Audálio. Canto por enquanto: poesia. Rio de Janeiro: Livraria J. Olympio Editora, 1982. 201 p., 1 leaf of plates: port.

"Morrer é meta—a liberdade, o permanente fim," says Alves, reflecting human solidarity, particularly with the rural poor, in the new section, "Espaço Migrante," here added to previously published work.

6238 Andrade, Carlos Drummond de. Carmina Drummondiana. Tradução de Silvia Bélkior. Rio de Janeiro: Salamandra, 1982. 143 p.: ill., ports.

Surely the most unusual of tributes to the greatest of living Brazilian poets is this handsomely printed translation into Latin of 52 of his compositions.

6239 Andrade, Carlos Drummond de. Corpo. Rio de Janeiro: Record, 1984. 124 p.: ill.

Ever himself yet ever new ("O problema . . . é . . . nunca ficar pronta nossa edição convincente"), Drummond voices consciousness of age and his approaching end but remains passionately concerned for the welfare of the great underclass.

6240 Andrade, Carlos Drummond de. Nova reunião: 19 livros de poesia. Rio de Janeiro: Livraria J. Olympio Editora: Instituto Nacional do Livro, Fundação Nacional Pró-Memória, 1983. 2 v. (969 p.): bibl., ill., index.

While maintaining high quality in abundant production, in his later years a nostalgic Drummond has turned increasingly to the past for poetic inspiration.

6241 Andrade, Carlos Drummond de. A rosa do povo. Rio de Janeiro: Editora Record, 1984. 205 p.

Written during the last years of World War II and the Vargas dictatorship, these poems more than any others reflect Drummond's concern for social causes.

6242 Andrade, Mário de. Poesias completas. v. 1, Paulicea desvairada; Losango cáqui; Clan do jaboti; Remate de males. v. 2, O carro da miséria; A costela do Grão Cão; Livro azul; O café. v. 1, 6a ed.; v. 2, 5a ed. São Paulo: Livraria Martins; Belo Horizonte: Editora Itatiaia, 1980. 2 v. (375 p.) (Obras completas de Mário de Andrade; 2–2A)

In themes and techniques the "Pope of Modernism" is viewed by many Brazilian critics as "nosso mais completo poeta." Reprints all save verse disowned by Andrade; respects his spelling.

6243 Ascher, Nelson. Ponto da língua: poemas 1978/1983. São Paulo: O Autor, 1983. 46 p.

Ingenious word-play lends zest to these humorously satiric compositions in Concretist style.

6244 Assumpção, Lucy. Canto de plantonista: poesias. Apresentação de Ivan Cavalcanti Proença. Rio de Janeiro: Nórdica, 1983. 87 p.

Capsule-like, imagistic verse ("Pedras registram/ histórias/ do rumo de gente/ às pressas/ No seco bater/ dos pés/ quebrando e polindo/ arestas").

6245 Ayala, Walmir. Aguas como espadas: poesia. São Paulo: LR Editores, 1983. 72 p.

The power of Ayala's imagery and the intensity of the emotion it conveys are admirably exemplified by "A Baleia," a masterpiece of contemporary Brazilian poetry.

6246 Azevedo Filho, Leodegário Amarante de and **Sílvio Elia.** As poesias de Anchieta em português: estabelecimento do texto e apreciação literária. Rio de Janeiro: Antares: Instituto Nacional do Livro, Fundação Nacional Pró-Memória, 1983. 170 p. (Antares universitária)

Thoroughgoing linguistic and literary study of the earliest Portuguese-language poetry composed in Brazil.

6247 Barros, Manoel de. Arranjos para assobio. Rio de Janeiro: Civilização Brasileira, 1982. 61 p. (Col. Poesia hoje; 62)

"Escrevo com o corpo/ Poesia não é para compreender mas para incorporar/ Entender é parede," declares Barros, saying it takes sensitivity rather than intelligence to understand him.

6248 Bell, Lindolf. As Annamárias: poesia. 2a ed. São Paulo: Massao Ohno Editor, 1979. 63 p.: col. ill.

Stress on sound and on imagery evoked through play on words mark this cycle of impassioned but unerotic love poems. Handsome graphic presentation.

6249 Bernis, Yeda Prates. Pêndula. São Paulo: Massao Ohno & M. Lydia Pires e Albuquerque Editores, 1983. 69 p.

"Vou cortando, recompondo/ todo o esgarçado da vida . . . Teço a trama . . . do que não foi nem será," says Bernis, likening her work to that of Penelope.

6250 Bezerra, Jaci. Livro de Olinda. Recife: Edições Pirata, 1982. 53 leaves: ill.

Quatrains in the Renaissance manner, emotionally inspired in figures associated with the dead city of Olinda.

6251 Bomfim, Paulo. Sonetos do caminho. São Paulo: Roswitha Kempf/Editores, 1983. 131 p.

Selections dating from the years 1956–81, showing Bomfim as the most skilled practitioner of the art of the sonnet in contemporary Brazil.

6252 Cancioneiro da revolução de 1835. Coligido e comentado por Apolinário Porto Alegre. Apresentação e notas por Lothar Hessel. Porto Alegre: Cia. União de Seguros Gerais, 1981. 141 p.: bibl., ill. (Estante rio-grandense União de Seguros-ERUS)

Folk poetry inspired by the Revolution of the Ragamuffins, of more historical than literary interest.

6253 Carvalho, Francisco. Quadrante solar: poesia. São Paulo: LR Editores, 1983. 91 p.

Conservative in language but fresh in vision, this carefully crafted, death-infused verse well merited the 1982 Nestlé Prize.

6254 Castro, Antônio Fernando Ribeiro. Material de exposição. Porto Alegre: Movimento, 1983. 110 p.: ill. (Col. Poesiasul; 35)

Inspired in sexual love, abundant in imagery drawn from the Guaíba River, Castro's verse is notable for rhythmic effects, often accented by the typographical arrangement of the page.

6255 Cirne, Moacy. Cinema pax. Rio de Janeiro: Achiamé, 1983. 47 p.: ill., ports.

"O poeta, fingidor de sonhos," recalls in metaphoric language, from the viewpoint of maturity, the emotions aroused by movies seen in his youth.

6256 Costa, Eduardo Alves da. Salamargo. Ilustrações de Guilherme de Faria. São Paulo: Massao Ohno & M. Lydia Pires e Albuquerque Editores, 1982. 90 p.: ill.

Attacking injustice and inhumanity, Costa adopts a variety of satiric stances (e.g., speaking of "amantes do proletariado,/ ocultos sob o manto da opulência,/ . . . a passar fome/ com o ventre alheio").

6257 Cotrim, Lupe. Encontro. São Paulo: Brasiliense, 1984. 142 p.: port. (Cantadas literárias; 19)

While love is the principal theme, the poet's gift for capturing in metaphor the magic of the commonplace is most strikingly evidenced in treatment of animals, birds, fish, and insects.

6258 Duncan, Sílvio Gomes Wallace. Profetas do cimento. Porto Alegre: Movimento: Instituto Estadual do Livro, 1983. 103 p.: ill. (Col. Poesiasul; 37)

Duncan captures the essence of a personality, scene, or event in concise, incisive, often satiric verse.

6259 Elias, Zêqui. O passageiro: poemas. São Paulo: Edições Excelsior, Divisão de Produção, T.A. Queiroz, 1983. 119 p.

Writing in a style reminiscent of early Modernism, Elias alternates between banalities and refreshingly personal reactions to existence.

6260 Faria, Alvaro Alves de. Motivos alheios. Ensaio de Carlos Felipe Moisés. São Paulo: Massao Ohno, 1983. 71 p.

Less subjectively concerned with death than in the past, more involved in daily existence, Faria treats the commonplace in a highly imaginative, lyric manner.

6261 Farias, Elson. Palavra natural: poemas. Brasília: Clube de Poesia e Crítica, 1980. 67 p.

"Não forces a mão com a palavra . . . deixa que a imagem floresça . . . que a canção nasça sem tanto" writes Farias in calm, nature-inspired verse.

6262 Fernandes, Millôr. Poemas. Porto Alegre: L&PM, 1984. 194 p.

Ingeniously witty light verse satirizing the failings of individuals and society in present-day Brazil.

6263 Ferreira, Sônia Maria Fernandes. Sonância. Natal: CLIMA, 1983. 46 p.: ill. (Col. Edições CLIMA; 19)

Simplicity, conciseness, sonority, and emotional restraint characterize Ferreira's evocations of aspects of her native Northeast and moments of love.

6264 Fonseca, Lucia. Rede fluvial. Rio de Janeiro: Livraria J. Olympio, 1983. 87 p.

The elusiveness of human experience—and of life itself—is a constant motif in Fonseca's musical verse. Winner of 1980 Emílio Moura Prize.

6265 Gama, Mauro. Expresso na noite, 1968–1976. Introdução de Ivan Junqueira. Rio de Janeiro: Nova Fronteira, 1982. 143 p. (Col. Poiesis)

Gama uses words much as an abstract painter employs colors, more for sensuous effect than for the transmission of a message. Lengthy introductory essay by Ivan Junqueira.

6266 Guarnieri, Rossine Camargo. Porto inseguro: poemas. Prefácio de Mário de Andrade. Apreciação crítica de Jorge Amado et al. 2a ed. São Paulo: SEL Editora, 1981. 111 p.

Poems of social protest and human solidarity, first published in 1938. Includes comments of Jorge Amado, Pablo Neruda, and other writers.

6267 Homem, Homero. O luar potiguar: poema. Rio de Janeiro: Presença; Fundação José Augusto, 1983. 89 p.: ill.

Inspired by moonlight, Homem recalls in metaphoric language, in a manner now lyric, now ironic, scenes of his native Rio Grande do Norte.

6268 Horta, Anderson Braga. Cronoscópio: poemas. Rio de Janeiro: Civilização Brasileira: Instituto Nacional do Livro, Fundação Nacional Pró-Memória, 1983. 95 p. (Col. Poesia hoje; 71)

Poems of the late 1960s, ranging from Camonean imitations to Concretist verse, indicative of technical skill and facility, but as yet no clearly defined literary personality.

6269 Jordão, Yolanda. Autologia. Rio de Janeiro: Antares: Instituto Nacional do Livro, Fundação Nacional Pró-Memória, 1983. 173 p.: ill.

"O aqui, o agora sempre estiveram/ Sempre estão./ Mudadas, sim, foram as palavras," says Jordão, who views composition as a re-creation of self (hence the neologism "autologia").

6270 Leal, Cláudio Murilo. A velhice de Ezra Pound. Rio de Janeiro: Antares, 1983. 190 p.

Rich in cultural references, felicitous in expression, so musical as to beg for notation, these lyrics are curiously lacking in personal feeling.

6271 Lima, Batista de. Os viventes da Serra Negra: poesia. Fortaleza: Secretaria de Cultura e Desporto, 1981. 99 p.

Lines such as "a noite penteou-se de lua" and "poço de histórias verticais/ vertiginoso espelho/ onde mora meu medo" reveal a poet of lyric imagination and grace.

6272 Loureiro, João de Jesus Paes. Altar em chamas: poesia. Rio de Janeiro: Civilização Brasileira, 1983. 170 p. (Col. Poesia hoje; 66)

In a brilliant conclusion to his "Trilogia Amazônica" (see *Porantim* in *HLAS* 42:6279 and *Deslendário*, following item **6272a**), Loureiro evokes suggestively the spirit of a multifaceted Belém do Pará.

6272a Loureiro, João de Jesus Paes. Deslendário. Rio de Janeiro: Civilização Brasileira, 1981. 141 p. (Col. Poesia hoje; 43)

In these dithyrambic compositions, corporate greed and the destruction forces of development replace traditional jungle perils, real and mythological, in the Amazon region.

6273 Machado, Nauro. O cavalo de Tróia. Rio de Janeiro: Edições Antares, 1982. 126 p.

Agonized by consciousness of universal mortality, Machado is awed rather than comforted by the "fim descomunal da eternidade" in a "Deus que, de ausente, presença se faz."

6274 Marçal, Ayrton Carlos Pereira. Fundação de novembro. Porto Alegre: Secretaria Municipal de Educação e Cultura, Divisão de Cultura, 1982. 70 p.

A preference for the sonnet as form and the sea as motif characterizes the verse of this poet who is Symbolist in spirit but post-Modernist in language.

6275 Meirelles Filho, João Carlos. Licença poética. Ilustrações de Arcângelo Ianelli. São Paulo: Massao Ohno & M. Lydia Pires e Albuquerque, 1982. 69 p.: col. ill.

Intimist, markedly musical verse, rural in inspiration, reminiscent of the *Província* phase of Ribeiro Couto.

6276 Melo Neto, João Cabral de. Auto do frade: poema para vozes. Rio de Janeiro: Livraria J. Olympio Editora, 1984. 89 p. (Obras de João Cabral de Melo Neto)

Impressive ballad-like treatment of the defrocking and execution of Frei Caneca, leader of the abortive 1825 republican revolution in Recife, told in the voices of principals and spectators.

6277 Mendes, Luís Antônio Martins. O acrobata. Florianópolis: FCC, 1982. 75 p. (Col. Cultura catarinense. Série Literatura: poesia)

Nostalgia, loves, social protest, and word-play provide the substance of these "post-Concretist" poems.

6278 Monegal, Carmen. Duração ordinária da vida. São Paulo: Massao Ohno & M. Lydia Pires e Albuquerque, 1982. 22 leaves: col. ill.

Veiled but intense sensuality characterizes these lyrics of a girl's awakening to womanhood.

6279 Monteiro, Fernando. Ecométrica. São Paulo: Massao Ohno & M. Lydia Pires e Albuquerque, 198? 33 leaves: ill.

Experimental verse: fixed-form, 19-line compositions in which an accumulation of evocative phrases leads up to the title.

6280 Monteiro, Fernando. A interrogação dos dias. Recife: Edições Encontro: Gabinete Português de Leitura, 1984. 63 p.

With ironic humor, and not without a sense of tragedy, Monteiro faces life in all its grandeur . . . and monotony.

6281 Morais, João Francisco Regis de. O caminho dos ventos: poemas. Campinas: Papirus, 1983. 72 p.

"Faço comungarem o novo e o remoto. O canto que me encanta é . . . a nudez dos sentimentos nos lençois do intemporal," writes Morais, who finds a soul-mate in Emily Dickinson.

6282 Nascimento, Abdias do. Axés do sangue e da esperança: orikis. Rio de Janeiro: Achiamé: RIOARTE, 1983. 109 p.: ill.

Poems of black protest and exaltation of Africa, especially aspects of Yoruba religion.

6283 Nogueira, Zé Luiz. Migrantes do tempo. S.l.: Durazno, 1980. 46 p.: ill.

"A curva do agora/ no limite dos olhos,/ inventa o tempo,/ intercalando imagens,/ mas/ o tempo esconde/ realidades paralelas,/ dançando nas/ entre/ linhas do agora."

6284 Oliveira, Felippe Daudt Alves de. Homenageando Felippe d'Oliveira. Edição e estudos de Zosymo Lopes dos Santos e Ernesto Wayne. Santa Maria: Univ. Federal de Santa Maria: Prefeitura Municipal de Santa Maria, 1980. 95 p.: ill.

Long out of print, *Lanterna verde*, the principal work of this short-lived Modernist, reappears accompanied by studies (biobibliographic and stylistic) by Zosymo Lopes dos Santos and Ernesto Wayne.

6285 Oliveira, Sylvio de. O caos e o cosmo: poemas. Prefácio de Fernando Py. Rio de Janeiro: Livraria J. Olympio Editora, 1983. 69 p.

Light, agile verse exemplified by "A esquiadora" and "Poema à mulata" is preferable to excursions into more profound subjects.

6286 Pena Filho, Carlos. Os melhores poemas de Carlos Pena Filho. Seleção de Edilberto Coutinho. São Paulo: Global, 1983. 128 p. (Os Melhores poemas; 5)

Manuel Bandeira called attention to this short-lived poet's "oralidade, fluência

narrativa e força lírica." Noteworthy also is Pena's preference for the sonnet and themes of his native Northeast.

6287 Perez, Glória and Leila Míccolis. Mercado de escravas. Rio de Janeiro: Achiamé: Trote, 1984. 95 p.

Though feminists, the poets find no winners in the war of the sexes: "Nosso caso de amor/ acabou em perícia:/ eu condenada aos filhos/ e tu, à pensão alimentícia."

6288 Poesia concreta. Seleção de textos, notas, estudos biográfico, histórico e crítico e exercícios por Iumna Maria Simon e Vinicius Dantas. São Paulo: Abril Educação, 1982. 109, 3 p.: bibl., ill. (Literatura comentada)

Drawing on material difficult to access, reproducing in all their graphic peculiarities poems of the principal Concretists plus their statements of aesthetic position, this anthology provides an excellent introduction to the movement.

6289 Poesia jovem—anos 70. Seleção de textos, notas, estudos biográfico, histórico e crítico e exercícios por Heloísa Buarque de Hollanda, Carlos Alberto Messeder Pereira e Lula Buarque de Hollanda. São Paulo: Abril Educação, 1982. 112 p.: ill., ports. (Literatura comentada)

Illuminating sampling of the variety of wild directions taken by the "mimeograph generation" of poets of the 1970s.

6290 Poetas baianos da negritude. Organização de Hamilton de Jesus Vieira. Salvador: Univ. Federal da Bahia, Centro de Estudos Afro-Orientais, 1982. 66 p. (Série Arte: literatura; 2)

Little intrinsic value but reflects interest of Brazilian blacks and whites in Afro-American themes.

6291 Pozenato, José Clemente. Carta de viagem. Caxias do Sul: Editora da Univ. de Caxias do Sul, 1981. 63 p.

Whether the subject be early Christian martyrdom or present-day foibles, Pozenato recognizes that "O simples é o difícil/ o moderno é a palavra."

6292 Ramadan, Ebrahim. Vida comprometida. São Paulo: Massao Ohno, 1982. 56 p.: ill.

"Suporto a vida,/ Só por causa dos meus sonhos/ De primavera falida" declares the poet in verse poignant with disillusion.

6293 Renault, Abgar de Castro Araújo.
A outra face da lua. Rio de Janeiro:
J. Olympio: Instituto Nacional do Livro, Fundação Nacional Pró-Memória, 1983. 154 p.:
port.

Acute awareness of "o fugir das coisas
frágeis . . . que morrem sem acabar" pervades
Renault's product of six decades, in which he
shows himself an artist of rare sensitivity,
whose skill with words borders on magic.

6294 Ribeiro, Marcos. Vagas obscenidades.
Salvador: Fundação Cultural do Estado
da Bahia, 1982. 29 leaves (Col. dos novos.
Série Poesia; 12)

Sense of solitude and awareness of the
mortality of the flesh are recurring motifs in
the disturbing compositions of this promising beginner.

6295 Rodrigues, Sérgio Leopoldo. Tal hoje.
São Paulo: T.A. Queiroz, 1982. 76 p.

Tumult of daily existence in the modern metropolis is reflected in the constant
disquietude that affects dwellers therein.

6296 Savary, Olga. Magma. São Paulo:
Massao Ohno & Roswitha Kempf,
1982. 51 p.

Carnal love passionately evoked in unaccustomed imagery, frequently drawn from
water. In Savary's words, "as línguas, festivas
e mais sábias, inventam outra linguagem."

6297 Secchin, Antônio Carlos. Elementos:
poesia. Rio de Janeiro: Civilização
Brasileira, 1983. 78 p. (Col. Poesia hoje; 73)

For Secchin, reality is "miragem" and
"excesso," to which he gives succinct expression in the "língua iludida da linguagem."
Contains his earlier *Aria de estação* in "2a
ed., revisitada e diminuída" (see *HLAS
38:7512*).

6298 Sepúlveda, Carlos. Agua rara. Rio de
Janeiro: Edições Tempo Brasileiro,
1983. 106 p. (Col. Tempoesia; 26)

Summing up consciousness of his gift
and its limitations, the poet exclaims: "Na
palavra eternizada, a certeza do fim."

6299 Silva, Antônio Francisco da Costa e.
Antologia. 2a ed., rev. e ampliada.
Teresina: Livraria e Editora Corisco, 1982.
164 p.

Reproduces (with three additions) the
selection of Symbolist and Neo-Parnassian
compositions published by the poet in 1934.
Biographical and critical note by his son;

short bibliography of criticism relative to
his work.

6300 Silva, Ayrton Pereira da. Corpo de
delito & prosipoemas. Rio de Janeiro:
Livraria J. Olympio Editora, 1982. 81 p.

Describing poetry as an "arte marginal," Silva writes precise, concise, harmonious verse suggestive of far more than the
words literally express.

6301 Silva, Dora Ferreira da. Talhamar. São
Paulo: Massao Ohno & Roswitha
Kempf Editores, 198? 79 p.

In mood pieces set in classic Greece,
Egypt of the Pharaohs, and Brazil of today,
the poet strives to capture the essence of
ephemeral emotion.

6302 Silva, Francisco Ivan da. Persona: uma
face perversa. Natal: Univ. Federal do
Rio Grande do Norte: Fundação José Augusto, 1981. 88 p.: ill.

Swept away by the power of words
("Poetar sobre poesia: . . . ser das palavras!"),
Silva carries the reader with him in his rhapsodic rush.

6303 Silva, Maria Abadia. Espaços: poemas.
Goiânia: Cerne, 1980. 77 p.: ill.

"Só o pensamento é meu,/ . . . é o espaço em que me abrigo,/ é a liberdade que eu
persigo." Feminine verse at its best. Excellent debut.

6304 Sousa, Afonso Félix de. Antologia poética. Seleção do autor. Organização de
Domingos Félix. Introdução de Gilberto
Mendonça Teles. 2a ed., rev. e ampliada.
Goiânia: Oriente, 1979. 172 p.: port. (Publicação; 292)

Regarding Sousa, Luís Felipe Ribeiro
acutely observes: "Toda a sua linguagem se
volta para a captação de experiências passadas." Anthology enhanced by extensive excerpts from criticism of his writing.

6305 Sousândrade. Revisão de Sousândrade.
Textos críticos, antologia, glossário
biobibliografia de Augusto e Haroldo de
Campos, Erthos A. de Souza, e Luiz Costa
Lima. 2a ed., rev. e aum. Rio de Janeiro: Editora Nova Fronteira, 1982. 477 p., 1 leaf of
plates: bibl., port. (Col. Poiesis)

Updated, enlarged edition of work
first published in 1964 (see *HLAS 28:2641a*).
Author's real name was Joaquim de Sousa
Andrade.

6306 Souto, Esdras. Miramante: poesia. Rio
de Janeiro: Livraria J. Olympio Editora,
1982. 60 p.

"Louco, libertino, impulsivo" of heart,
"meticuloso, comedido, racional" of mind,
Souto vacillates between lyric outbursts and
sober reflections on the ambient world. A
poet of promise.

6307 Trentin, Ary Nicodemos. Barcas e
arcas. Caxias do Sul: Editora da Univ.
de Caxias do Sul, 1981. 66 p.

Avoiding banalities of local color,
Trentin's compositions breathe the spirit of
Rio Grande do Sul and the immigrants
whose descendants work its soil.

6308 Veiga, Cláudio. Sete tons de uma
poesia maior. Rio de Janeiro: Editora
Record: Fundação Emílio Odebrecht, 1984.
138 p.: bibl.

Systematic study of a relatively unknown Bahian poet, Artur de Sales (b. 1879),
here viewed as a Symbolist evolving toward
Parnassianism, plus a selection of his works.

6309 Villaça, Olívia. Poesia de cada dia.
Rio de Janeiro: Editora Artenova, 1982.
74 p.

Clarity, harmony, and spontaneity
characterize Villaça's remembrances of
things past and expressions of anxiety as to
what the future may hold. Outstanding
debut.

Drama

JUDITH ISHMAEL BISSETT, *Associate Professor of Spanish and Portuguese, Miami University, Oxford, Ohio*

ALTHOUGH SEVERAL EXCELLENT CRITICAL works are included in this review, two of the most intersting are: *Teatro, o seu demonio é beato: o nacional e o
popular na cultura brasileira* by José Arrabal and Mariângela Alves de Lima (item
6332) and *Monografias, 1980* (item **6343**), a collection of award-winning essays.
Both volumes offer detailed studies, often including alternative versions of accepted
views, of the playwrights and movements examined focusing on theme and structure, strengths, and weaknesses. Among the plays available for examination, the
best representatives of at least two of the trends evident in Brazilian theatre of the
past and the present are: *Bella ciao* by Alberto de Abreu (item **6310**), *Calabar* by
Chico Buarque de Hollanda and Ruy Guerra (item **6314**), and *No Natal a gente vem
te buscar* by Naum Alves de Souza (item **6329**).

   Bella ciao and *Calabar* are examples of the use of history to examine political problems or national development. An historical approach, particularly in political protest drama, has often been a necessary tool for committed dramatists.
Although censorship in Brazil is not the problem it has been in the past, playwrights like Boal still use this technique. In the autumn of 1985, Boal along with
Chico Buarque and Edu Lobo produced *O Coarsario do Rei* in Rio de Janeiro using
two historical time periods to comment on present-day injustice. *Bella ciao* does
not use history only to frame its examination of a moment in Brazil's progress but
also to document the lives of a politically active group, Italian immigrants.

   No Natal a gente vem te buscar depicts the disintegration of a family. A study
of the effect of indifference on the part of family members, the play does incorporate the theme of political involvement. The only successful member of the family
is a cousin who becomes politically active and is subsequently killed. Another play
by Consuelo de Castro (item **6316**), annotated below, portrays a family in distress

because of poverty. Here political comment is made through music which contrasts the family's circumstances with the official version of Brazilian society.

Two trends in political and social protest theater not evident in the above-mentioned works are: plays concerning the plight of the worker (peasant and urban) and drama combining a political theme with explicit sexual scenes. *Galindo* (item **6318**) and *Pesadelo* (item **6327**) use documentary techniques and Brechtian structures to illustrate the struggle workers must face in order to survive. *O Edipo da Vila Nova* (item **6324**) shows a working-class family as it succumbs to both internal and external pressures.

Crime e impunidade (item **6311**), *As Tres moças do sabonete* (item **6319**), and Dias Gomes's *Amor em campo minado* (item **6322**), all concentrate on political violence as it is committed against either innocent victims or those who attempt to transform society. Here, however, instead of pitting a weaker oppressed against a strong oppressor, middle- or upper-class characters fight existing political structures. Their efforts to escape or eliminate injustice are framed by graphic homosexual or heterosexual relationships.

Not all the critical and historical works and plays described in the following bibliography are political in nature. However, this does continue to be a significant part of Brazilian drama.

ORIGINAL PLAYS

6310 Abreu, Alberto de. *Bella ciao*
(SBAT/RT, 450, abril/junho 1984, p. 27–64, ill.)
Play won awards for text and production. Tells story of immigrant family from Italy to Brazil. Flashback format: Interviewer questions family members, answers dramatized. Documents political activity of workers before World War II. Begins in Italian, moves gradually into Portuguese as generations progress.

6311 Athayde, Roberto Austregésilo de.
Crime e impunidade e outras peças. Rio de Janeiro: Record, 1983. 264 p.
Three plays by author of *Apareceu a Margarida*. *Crime e impunidade*: Woman anthropology student is held hostage and raped by terrorist. In later scenes tries to discover reasons for his actions. Now supported by theater critic, terrorist reveals nothing but aggression. Other plays concern psychiatrists and characters' search for past.

6312 Azevedo, Arthur. Teatro. t. 1. Rio de Janeiro: Instituto Nacional de Artes Cênicas, 1983. 1 v.: bibl., ill., ports. (Clássicos do teatro brasileiro; 7)
Contains 14 plays. Some annotations, introduction, and bibliography of works by playwright including translations and list of manuscripts.

6313 Bajur, Aziz. *Velório a brasileira*
(SBAT/RT, 451, julho/set. 1984, p. 36–64, ill.)
Comedy: While at wake, family and friends of dead man discover he purchased winning ticket in partnership with three others. Search for lost ticket reveals man had homosexual lover. Lover and one partner deceive family and escape with money.

6314 Buarque de Hollanda, Chico and **Ruy Guerra.** *Calabar*: o elogio da traiçao. Música de Chico Buarque. 14a ed. com texto revisto e modificado pelos autores. Rio de Janeiro: Civilização Brasileira; s.l.: Difel, 1983. 120 p. (Col. Teatro hoje; 24)
Using historical frame: the conflict between Dutch and Portuguese in Brazil, play portrays "traitor" Calabar, in effort to re-examine concept of treason as Brecht did with hero. Same actor plays both Portuguese and Dutch leaders to emphasize superimposition of foreign structures on Brazil. Music underscores action.

6315 Callado, Antônio. *A revolta da cachaça*: teatro negro. Rio de Janeiro: Editora Nova Fronteira, 1983. 220 p.
Four plays for black theater. First, *A revolta da cachaça* concerns black actor's de-

sire for good part. He attempts to force writer to finish a play for him. In a violent struggle he is killed while writer lives. Others treat problems of blacks in society at present and in history.

6316 Castro, Conseulo de. *O grande amor de nossas vidas.* São Paulo: Promoção do Depto. de Artes e Ciências Humanas, Secretaria Estadual de Cultura, Comissão Teatro São Paulo, 1981. 78 p.

A poor family turns on each other in hate and despair as result of misery they live in. Only escape for daughters is loveless marriage for money or prostitution. Male members are failures in society and in family. All seek relief through fantasy. Song about Brazil's beauty contrasts with reality.

6317 Concurso Estadual de Dramaturgia, 2nd, Florianópolis, Brazil, 1982. Dramaturgia. Florianópolis: FCC Edições, 1983. 164 p.

Four award-winning plays from Santa Catarina. For adults and children. First prize, adult: Fragmented scenes protest violence and war. Character paralyzed writer/revolutionary. First prize, children: Uses detective motif and Brechtian distancing to present social theme. Second prize, adult: Interesting portrayal of peasant leaving land for city.

6318 Cunha, Marlei. *Galindo, o profeta das águas.* S.l.: Gráfica do Lira, 1982. 97 p.: ill. (Teatro)

Introduction relates real-life story of character, Galindo, placed in insane asylum for fighting hydroelectric plants. Story dramatized with Brechtian techniques: Actors break down audience/stage barrier eliciting comments on local problems and soliciting participation of spectators.

6319 Daniel, Herbert. *As tres moças do sabonete: um apólogo sobre os Anos Médici*: peça em dois atos. Rio de Janeiro: Rocco, 1984. 134 p.

Takes place in Minas Gerais during Médici dictatorship. Subversive hiding from authorities seeks help from his cousin. Reveals to cousin he is homosexual. Makes contact with local homosexuals thereby placing everyone in danger. All suffer as subversive places personal desire above safety of friends. Explicit sexual scenes and language.

6320 Dramaturgia. Instituto Nacional de Artes Cênicas. Vol. 12, 1980–. Rio de Janeiro.

Three award-winning plays. First prize: Portrays family caught up in son's political involvement. Second prize: Satirical view of world of commercial advertising. Third prize: Strongest of group due to dramatic structure which effectively supports theme. A man's life is reviewed in flashbacks framed by events in lives of famous people.

6321 Flores, Moacyr. *Os fósseis* (Revista da Academia Rio-Grandense de Letras [Porto Alegre] 1, 1980, p. 32–46, ill.)

First prize for student production. Explores theme of freedom. A young man visits a commune to challenge values of inhabitants. He is killed in the name of liberty—theirs. Dialogue emphasizes language of non-communication the author thought characteristic of youth in 1970s.

6322 Gomes, Dias. *Amor em campo minado.* Rio de Janeiro: Civilização Brasileira, 1984. 125 p. (Teatro de Dias Gomes; 8)

Published in 1972 as *Vamos soltar os demonios.* Concerns subversive intellectual hiding from police in love nest. Confrontations with his wife and another couple concentrate on political and personal commitment. Finally, subversive and wife are killed by police who watch obscene movie already on. Weaker than author's other protest drama.

6323 Gomes, Dias and **Ferreira Gullar.** *Vargas, ou, Dr. Getúlio, sua vida e su glória.* Música de Chico Buarque e Edu Lobo. Prefácio de Antônio Callado. Posfácio de Helio Silva. Rio de Janeiro: Civilização Brasileira, 1983. 124 p. (Col. Teatro de Dias Gomes; 7)

Formerly titled *Dr. Getúlio, sua vida e sua glória.* Contains same theme and format as previous play but is updated to emphasize present-day reality. Music by Chico Buarque and Edu Lobo along with new choreography and set design improve the production. Presented in 1983 in Rio de Janeiro.

6324 Marques, José Expedito. Teatro premiado. São Paulo: Fundação Educacional de Ituverava; Nova Granada: Editora Horizonte, 1982. 86 p.: ill.

Two award-winning plays. First, *Os olhos verdes da neurose* deals with woman underdoing medical treatment for mental illness. Monologue reveals possibility of rape or torture and instability seeking security and peace. Second, *O Edipo da Vila Nova* about working-class, abusive husband who sells son. Son returns to marry mother.

6325 Pedroso, Bráulio. *Uma trilogia fálica.* Rio de Janeiro: Paz e Terra, 1984. 206 p. (Col. Teatro; 7)

All three plays explore sexual relationships. *Dor de amor*, for example, treats love triangle among a man, his wife who seeks personal freedom, the mistress (their maid), and the man's mother. When mother arranges for wife's poisoning, nothing happens. Husband points out that all are in reality, dead.

6326 Sá, Lenita de. *Ana do Maranhão*: teatro. Rio de Janeiro: Livraria Editora Cátedra, 1982. 93 p.: ill.

Story based on historical figure. A woman begins as a dressmaker and through marriage acquires fortune. Through own efforts becomes powerful. Passage of time from youth to old age done through use of fast-paced scenes and division of stage into four areas.

6327 Sindicato dos Metalúrgicos de São Bernardo do Campo e Diadema. Grupo de Teatro Forja. Pesadelo. Prefácios de Octavio Ianni e Tin Urbinatti. São Paulo: Editora HUCITEC, 1982. 81 p., 5 p. of plates: ill.

Collective work written as sequel to *Pensão liberdade.* Documentary in that research included interviews with unemployed. Concerns factory worker who sides with management in period of layoffs, is ostracized, and commits suicide. Fragmented scenes depict problems of workers. Flaw: Character's personal dilemma not well drawn.

6328 Siqueira, João et al. Teatro de bonecos, 1979. Rio de Janeiro: MEC, Secretaria de Cultura, Instituto Nacional de Artes Cênicas, 1983. 178 p. (Col. Prémios)

Puppet plays for adults. For example, *Honório dos anjos e dos diabos* is story of boy given away to farmers. Through loss of parents, he is forced to move from place to place. Finally, in city becomes involved in union activities. When he betrays workers,

he destroys past and self. Explicit sexual scenes.

6329 Souza, Naum Alves de. *No Natal a gente vem te buscar.* São Paulo: MG Editores, 1983. 143 p.

Story of family unable to communicate or support each other. Focuses on old-maid sister who must live in nursing home ignored by other relatives. Flashbacks examine breakdown of family relationships. Reveals that only adopted cousin, killed for political beliefs, is successful in family or society. Includes critical comments.

HISTORY AND CRITICISM

6330 Aguiar, Flávio. A comédia nacional no teatro de José de Alencar. São Paulo: Editora Atica, 1984. 204 p.: bibl. (Ensaios; 103. Linguagens)

Author discusses completed plays only. Begins with examination of national theater focusing on theme: national "I" in contrast with "other" or Portugal, Europe, and national "other." Asserts Alencar's work examines national "I" in conflict with Brazilian "other" (e.g., slavery, injustice, mediocrity). Examines influences, theme, structure, and productions of comedy and drama.

6331 Albuquerque, Severino João. Verbal violence and the pursuit of power in *Apareceu a Margarida* (UK/LATR, 19:2, Spring 1986, p. 23–29)

Using Sherman Stanage's theories, author examines this popular monologue to show how Dona Margarida manipulates language in order to maintain power and control. [G. Woodyard]

6332 Arrabal, José and **Mariângela Alves de Lima.** Teatro, o seu demônio é beato. São Paulo: Brasiliense, 1983. 220 p.: bibl. (O Nacional e o popular na cultura brasileira)

Study of consciousness-raising theater from Anchieta to Teatro Oficina. Examines theatrical reception concluding that theatre which seeks social change is itself altered by the public. Focuses on moments in national/popular theater which have characteristics in common. Studies Brazilian playwrights as well as Brecht. Proposes new relationship between people and stage.

Festival Internacional de Teatro, 5th, Caracas, 1981. Quinto Festival Internacional de Teatro. See item **6077.**

6333 Guimarães, Carmelinda. Um ato de resistência: o teatro de Oduvaldo Vianna Filho. São Paulo: MG Editores Associados, 1984. 162 p.: bibl.
Life and work of Vianna Filho. Biography includes extensive quotes from friends and relatives. Chronicles all aspects of playwright's work in theater. Studies plays from biographical viewpoint with some attention to structure and theme—includes philosophy behind productions, critical reactions. Bibliography of works by and about dramatist.

6334 Hermilo vivo: vida e obra de Hermilo Borba Filho. Organização de Marcos Cirano, Ricardo Almeida, e Ivan Maurício. Recife: Editora Comunicarte Produções Jornalísticas, 1981. 107 p.: bibl., ports. (Col. Documento Nordeste; 01)
Work designed to document artistic contributions of the Northeast. Focuses on life and work of Borba Filho. Although contains portrait of writer as a whole, also valuable to those interested in regional theater. Of particular interest: description of *Sobrados e mocambos*, dramatic adaptation of book by Gilberto Freyre.

6335 Lima, Mariângela Alves et al. Nelson 2 Rodrigues, de Nelson Rodrigues. São Paulo: Serviço Social do Comércio (SESC), Administração Regional do São Paulo, 1984? 48 p.: ill.
Program printed in French and somewhat flawed English as well as Portuguese. Explains purpose of SESC and recounts founding of research center (Centro de Pesquisa Teatral) under Antunes Filho. Contains reviews from London and Berlin of presentations of Grupo de Teatro Macunaíma's adaptation of Rodrigues's plays. Articles on playwright's work include discussions of mythical quality of plays.

6336 Monografias, 1979. Rio de Janeiro: MEC, Secretaria da Cultura, Instituto Nacional de Artes Cênicas, 1983. 151 p.: ill. (Col. Prêmios)
Three award-winning essays: 1) treats Teatro Oficina according to cultural significance of group within a cultural process; sees Rei da vela as turning point—end of innovative productions; 2) describes theater

project in prison system—organization, problems, successes; and 3) examines integration of theater, literature, and audiovisual techniques as educational tool.

6337 Peixoto, Fernando. Teatro oficina, 1958–1982: trajetória de uma rebeldia cultural. São Paulo: Brasiliense, 1982. 124 p.: bibl., ill. (Tudo é história; 60)
Abbreviated version of report for Instituto Nacional de Artes Cênicas published in *Dionysos*. Chronicles founding of Oficina, its problems with financing, censorship. Traces development from amateur to professional theater. Year-by-year account details relationship with Teatro de Arena, plays presented, artists involved. Covers thematic approaches, successes, and failures. Bibliography.

6338 Pinto, Paul A.M. Jorge Andrade's three enigmas (AATSP/H, 67:3, Sept. 1984, p. 364–376)
Good analysis of the psychological coherence and underlying themes of Jorge Andrade's theater. One of the best articles about this author published in the US. [W. Martins]

6339 Prado, Décio de Almeida. João Caetano e a arte do ator: estudo de fontes. São Paulo: Editora Atica, 1984. 192 p.: bibl. (Ensaios; 108)
Analysis of writings of influential 19th-century actor. Studies European influences on Caetano, contradictions between his ideal of classical actor and the reality of romanticism which dominated his work. Searches for true character of actor and for evidence of Brazilian characteristics in his publications. Finds little evidence of either.

6340 O Rei da vela. Direção geral da opera de Zé Celso. Edição de Noílton et al. São Paulo: Escrita, 1984. 80 p.:ill.
Interesting presentation of Teatro Oficina's O rei da vela through pictures, national and international reviews, and related commentaries. Includes copy of official censorship document.

6341 Rela, Walter. Noticia sobre el teatro jesuítico en el Brasil: siglo XVI (IFCL/E, 2, 1982, p. 99–104, bibl., table)
Description of Jesuit theater including conflicts surrounding "obras profanas." Emphasis on Anchieta. Lists Jesuit productions

(1567–94) giving place presented. Short bibliography on Anchieta and Jesuit theater.

6342 Rosenfeld, Anatol. O mito e o herói no moderno teatro brasileiro. São Paulo: Perspectiva, 1982. 122 p. (Debates. Teatro; 179)

Analysis of function of hero and mythical hero in contemporary theater. First defines hero according to universal dramatic tradition. Then examines use of hero in plays by Boal, Jorge Andrade, and Dias Gomes. Also studies mysticism in Dias Gomes and cyclic vision of Andrade's work as reflections of Brazilian reality.

6343 Soares, Lúcia Maria MacDowell et al. Monografias, 1980. Rio de Janeiro: MEC, Secretaria da Cultura, Instituto Nacional de Artes Cênicas, 1983. 213 p. (Col. Prêmios)

Three award-winning essays. First concerns Teatro de Arena and its contributions to national theater. Examines revolutionary work and points out flaws in Boal's description of Arena's history. Studies political plays by Guarnieri. Second discusses Nelson Rodrigues's work as production. Third traces and analyzes history of Centros Populares de Cultura.

6344 Souza, Márcio. O palco verde. Rio de Janeiro: Editora Marco Zero, 1984. 120 p., 18 p. of plates: ports. (Teatro Experimental do SESC)

About Teatro Experimental do SESC in Manaus. Includes pictures of productions and programs. Entertaining description of all facets of group—artists, failures, successes, philosophical arguments. Traces historical development, discusses themes used, describes tours including audiences in various areas.

6345 Teatro operário na cidade de São Paulo. São Paulo: Prefeitura do Município de São Paulo, Secretaria Municipal de Cultura, Depto. de Informação e Documentação Artísticas, Centro de Documentação e Informação sobre Arte Brasileira Contemporânea, 1980. 218 p.: bibl., ill. (Pesquisa; 7)

Publication is result of research conducted by IDART and designed to make information on theater available to public. Describes research projects. Of particular interest: bibliography from Jesuits to 1976. Discusses Italian workers' theater in contrast with commercial stage in São Paulo. Due to political nature, workers' theater often lost.

Literary Criticism and History

WILSON MARTINS, *Professor of Portuguese, New York University*

THE PERIOD COVERED in this volume of *HLAS* was marked by a clear decline of interest in theory—one exception being Luiz Costa Lima's anthology (item **6383**)—and the predominance of literary history, be it in the form of conventional textbooks such as Massaud Moisés's (item **6367**) or as regional literary histories. Unfortunately, the majority of such histories are not concerned with scholarship as much as with indiscriminate praise of local celebrities. One notable exception to this trend is the brilliant study by Gemy Cândido (item **6354**) as well as a number of good biographies, in particular Pedro Calmon's about Franklin Dória, Barão de Loreto (item **6353**).

Another fashionable but declining trend concerns the "rediscovery" of writers supposedly "suppressed" or "repressed" because of the prejudices or indifference of their contemporaries (item **6424**). Concomitant with this trend are efforts to recover writers recognized in their time but unjustly forgotten such as the above mentioned Franklin Dória, Bastos Tigre (item **6407**), and Júlia da Costa (item **6421**). Machado de Assis, of course, continues to inspire different exegeses, some more imaginative than others (items **6351** and **6400**).

To conclude, there is no major work issued in this biennium that deserves to be singled out. However, many competent studies continue to be published, and they attest to the fact that Brazilian literary criticism and history are alive and well. [WM]

MISCELLANEOUS

Vol. 6 of Pedro Nava's monumental memoirs, devoted like the major part of vol. 5 to the career of his cousin José Egon Barros da Cunha, breaks off in as intriguing a fashion as did the author's life (item **6435**). Whether a posthumous vol. 7 resolves the literary mystery remains to be seen.

Josué Montello initiated publication of a literary journal of unusual interest (item **6432**); like the Montello volume, Helena Silveira's *Paisagem e memória* (item **6439**) tells us more about others than about the author. Zélia Gattai's delightful memoir, *Um chapéu para viagem* (item **6429**), throws interesting light on the character and writing processes of her husband, Jorge Amado.

Mário de Andrade's voluminous correspondence continues to appear in book form, the exchange with Oneyda Alvarenga (item **6427**) being of unusual significance. Of interest to biographers of João Guimarães Rosa are the letters to family and friends published by his daughter (item **6438**). [R.E. Dimmick]

GENERAL

6346 Academia Mineira de Letras. Efemérides da Academia Mineira de Letras. Edição de Martins de Oliveira e Oiliam José. Belo Horizonte: A Academia, 1980. 273 p.
Good reference work.

6347 Alves, Luiz Roberto. Confissão, poesia e Inquisição. São Paulo: Editora Ática, 1983. 213 p.: bibl., ill. (Ensaios; 93)
A *cristão novo* who was suspected of practicing Judaism, Bento Teixeira (1561–1600), author of *Prosopopéia* (1601), was arrested and condemned by the Inquisition. This is the first complete account as well as competent analysis of both his trial and its implications for the religious, intellectual, and social life of the time.

6348 Andrade, Mário de. Entrevistas e depoimentos. Edição organizada por Telê Porto Ancona Lopez. São Paulo: O Editor, 1983. 114 p.: ill. (Biblioteca de letras e ciências humanas. Série 1a: Estudios brasileiros; 5)
Useful compilation of texts culled from old periodicals, prepared by one of Brazil's most authoritative *andradistas* (see also item **6349**).

6349 Andrade, Mário de. A lição do amigo: cartas de Mário de Andrade a Carlos Drummond de Andrade, anotadas pelo destinatário. Rio de Janeiro: Livraria José Olympio Editora, 1982. 301 p., 1 leaf of plates: bibl., port.
Another important compilation of Andrade's letters, with clarifying comments by the recipient. Of interest to biographers of both writers as well as to literary historians (see also item **6348**).

6350 Brazil. Biblioteca Nacional. Seção de Promoções Culturais. Lima Barreto: 1881–1922; catálogo da exposição comemorativa do centenário de nascimento. Apresentação de Plinio Doyle. Prefácio de Francisco de Assis Barbosa. Rio de Janeiro: A Biblioteca, 1981. 70 p., 8 p. of plates: ill.
Useful reference.

6351 Broca, Brito. Machado de Assis e a política mais outros estudos. Prefácio de Silviano Santiago. São Paulo: Polis: Instituto Nacional do Livro, Fundação Nacional Pró-Memória, 1983. 326 p.: bibl., index (Obras reunidas; 14. Col. Estética)
Most of the volume consists of *Outros estudos*, chiefly articles of passing interest. An insatiable reader, author was fascinated by literary curios.

6352 Brookshaw, David. Raça & cor na literatura brasileira. Tradução de Marta Kirst. Porto Alegre: Mercado Aberto, 1983. 266 p.: bibl. (Série Novas perspectivas; 7)
Author never could make up his mind

about racial relations in Brazil: he proposed miscegenation as a desirable end result but also saw it as "racial suicide." His ideas are badly served by an incompetent translation, full of misreadings, false cognates, and plain ignorance of Portuguese.

6353 Calmon, Pedro. Franklin Dória, Barão de Loreto. Rio de Janeiro: Biblioteca do Exército Editora, 1981. 233 p.: bibl., ill. (Publicação; 515. Col. General Benício; 194)

Definitive biography of 19th-century intellectual who became famous because of the biography he wrote about Junqueira Freire. A well deserved tribute and an important addition to the fashionable trend of *memória nacional*.

6354 Cândido, Gemy. História crítica da literatura paraibana. João Pessoa: Governo do Estado da Paraíba, Secretaria da Educação e Cultura, Diretoria Geral de Cultura, 1983. 126 p.: bibl.

Author means this to be a *critical* literary history of Paraíba, perhaps *too* critical, but still brilliant, challenging, and a refreshing change from the usual ones (see items **6369, 6374, 6378, 6385**, and **6390** as well as *HLAS 38:7612, HLAS 38:7634, HLAS 38:7640, HLAS 38:7646, HLAS 40:7695, HLAS 42:6416, HLAS 42:6429*, and *HLAS 44:6179*).

6355 Cavalcanti, Paulo. Eça de Queiroz, agitador no Brasil. 3a ed., rev. e aum. Recife: Editora Guararapes, 1983. 364 p., 24 p. of plates: bibl., ill.

Reprint of important book first published in 1959 and the only one on the subject.

6356 Coelho, Odette Penha. A expressão do sentimento nacional na *Revista* da Sociedade Filomática (Revista de Letras [Univ. Estadual Paulista, São Paulo] 20, 1980, p. 21–31)

Useful for those interested in the subject.

Confluencia: literatura argentina por brasileños, literatura brasileña por argentinos. See item **5648.**

6357 Coutinho, Afrânio. O processo da descolonização literária. Rio de Janeiro: Civilização Brasileira, 1983. 267 p. (Col. Vera Cruz: literatura brasileira; 335)

Afrânio Coutinho makes a 180-degree turn and finds the key for literary explanation in political factors.

6358 Faury, Mára Lúcia. Uma flor para os malditos: a homossexualidade na literatura. Campinas: Papirus Livraria Editora, 1984. 115 p.: bibl. (Col. Krisis)

Shallow and hasty study clearly intended to take advantage of the subject's topicality. Should be taken merely as a pop introduction to the theme.

6359 Goldstein, Norma. Do penumbrismo ao modernismo: o primeiro Bandeira e outros poetas significativos. São Paulo: Editora Atica, 1983. 193 p.: bibl., ill. (Ensaios; 95)

Excellent survey of a generally neglected period, overlooked by critics and literary historians: the no-man's land between the turn of the century and 1922 Modernismo. It challenges us to reconsider our accepted commonplaces about books, authors, and trends.

6360 Lima, Alceu Amoroso. Diálogo. Entrevistas por Lourenço Dantas Mota. São Paulo: Brasiliense, 1983. 90 p.

An addition to the dozens of Lima's interviews (see also item **6361**).

6361 Lima, Alceu Amoroso. Memorando dos 90. Entrevistas e depoimentos coligidos e apresentados por Francisco de Assis Barbosa. Rio de Janeiro: Nova Fronteira, 1984. 439 p.

Compilation of interviews given by Lima during his lifetime and published posthumously. They concern literary, social, political, and personal topics (see also item **6360**).

6362 MacAdam, Alfred. Euclides da Cunha y Mario Vargas Llosa: meditaciones intertextuales (IILI/RI, 50:126, enero/marzo 1984, p. 157–164)

Discusses Vargas Llosa's novel, *The war of the end of the world* (see *HLAS 46: 5473*) as a model of intertextuality. Also examines influences of Sarmiento and Euclides da Cunha through Cunninghame Graham's *pastiche* and the question of *plagiarism* from *Os sertões*.

6363 Martins, Heitor. Do Barroco a Guimarães Rosa. Belo Horizonte: Editora Itatiaia: Instituto Nacional do Livro, Fundação Nacional Pró-Memória, 1983. 247 p.: bibl. (Col. Ensaios; 12)

Collected articles by competent scholar and fine critic.

6364 Martins, Luís. Um bom sujeito. São Paulo: Secretaria Municipal de Cultura, Prefeitura do Município de São Paulo; Rio de Janeiro: Paz e Terra, 1983. 261 p. (Col. Depoimento/A Secretaria; 3)

Memoirs of famous *cronista*, poet, and novelist offers good insights into Brazilian literary, social, and political life since the 1930s.

6365 Merquior, José Guilherme. O elixir do apocalipse. Rio de Janeiro: Editora Nova Fronteira, 1983. 210 p.: bibl. (Col. Logos)

Another compilation of sundry articles (e.g., Goethe, Eliot, Zweig, Canetti, Machado de Assis, Euclides da Cunha) by the child prodigy of Brazilian letters.

6366 Milliet, Sérgio. Diário crítico de Sérgio Milliet. v. 2–4. 2a ed. São Paulo: Livraria Martins Editora: Editora da Univ. de São Paulo, 1981–1982. 3 v. (334, 210, 287 p.): indexes.

Reprint of work first published in the 1940s by leading Brazilian literary critic (see also *HLAS 11:3383, HLAS 15:1949, HLAS 15:2503, HLAS 17:1951, HLAS 17:2590,* and *HLAS 20:4333*).

6367 Moisés, Massaud. História da literatura brasileira. v. 1, Origens, barroco, arcadismo. v. 2, Romantismo, realismo. São Paulo: Editora Cultrix: Editora da Univ. de São Paulo, 1983–1984. 2 v.: bibls., index.

Another history of Brazilian literature? Yes, but in this case written by a well informed professor, and clearly intended as a college textbook. Up-to-date, competent attempt at reevaluation that may be somewhat controversial.

6368 Moog, Clodomir Vianna. Uma interpretação da literatura brasileira: um arquipélago cultural. 2a ed. Rio de Janeiro: Antares: Instituto Nacional do Livro, Fundação Nacional Pró-Memória, 1983. 53 p. (Antares universitária)

Reprint of controversial interpretation of Brazilian literature that divides it geographically according to regions.

6369 Moraes, Herculano. Visão histórica da literatura piauiense. 2a ed. rev. e aum, incluindo a nova literatura piauiense. Tere-

sina: Academia Piauiense de Letras, 1982. 196 p.: bibls., ports.

Another contribution to the growing number of regional literary histories (see also items **6354, 6374, 6378, 6385,** and **6390** as well as *HLAS 38:7612, HLAS 38:7634, HLAS 38:7640, HLAS 38:7646, HLAS 40:7695, HLAS 42:6416, HLAS 42:6429,* and *HLAS 44:6179*).

6370 Nejar, Carlos et al. Eduardo Portella: ação e argumentação; trinta anos de vida intelectual. Rio de Janeiro: Edições Antares, 1985. 181 p.

Compilation of articles in homage of Portella on the 30th anniversary of his debut as a writer. More laudatory than informative or evaluative.

6371 Nunes, Cassiano. A felicidade pela literatura. Rio de Janeiro: Civilização Brasileira: Instituto Nacional do Livro, Fundação Nacional Pró-Memória, 1983. 249 p. (Col. Vera Cruz; 332)

Compilation of articles and lectures. Of particular interest is the one on Oswald de Andrade.

6372 Oliveira, Américo Lopes de. Escritoras brasileiras, galegas e portuguesas. Braga, Portugal: Tipografia S. Pereira, 1983? 215 p.

Invaluable reference work.

6373 Oliveira Lima, Manuel de. Aspectos da literatura colonial brasileira. Rio de Janeiro: F. Alves: Instituto Nacional do Livro, Fundação Nacional Pró-Memória, 1984. 290 p.: bibl. (Col. Dimensões do Brasil; 16)

Long out-of-print classic that should be read as a classic (i.e., for scholarly purposes only).

6374 Onofre Júnior, Manoel. Salvados: ensaios e notas. Natal: Fundação José Augusto, 1982. 137 p.

Unscholarly but useful compilation of data on the literary history of Rio Grande do Norte (see also items **6354, 6369, 6378, 6385,** and **6390** as well as *HLAS 38:7612, HLAS 38:7634, HLAS 38:7640, HLAS 38:7646, HLAS 40:7695, HLAS 42:6416, HLAS 42:6429,* and *HLAS 44:6179*).

6375 Prado, Antônio Arnoni. 1922 [i.e. Mil novecentos e vinte e dois] Itinerário de uma falsa vanguarda: os dissidentes, a Semana e o Integralismo. São Paulo: Brasiliense, 1983. 111 p.: bibl. (Primeiros vôos; 19)

Clearly influenced by the assumption that the only "real" avant-garde was that of the São Paulo *modernistas*, author sees Rio de Janeiro's avant-garde as "false." Why "false?" The Rio program was as revolutionary as any, a fact Arnoni's own study makes evident despite his intention to prove otherwise.

6376 Pragana, Maria Elisa Collier. Literatura do Nordeste: em torno de sua expressão social. Posfácio de Gilberto Freyre. Nota introdutória de Ivan Cavalcanti Proença. Rio de Janeiro: Livraria José Olympio: Instituto Nacional do Livro, Fundação Nacional Pró-Memória, 1983. 166 p.: bibl.

Does not live up to the title's promise. Another unscholarly, self -congratulatory book about the region's writers, mainly Gilberto Freyre, author's mentor. Includes data for regional literary history (see also items **6354, 6369, 6374, 6378, 6385,** and **6390** as well as *HLAS 38:7612, HLAS 38:7634, HLAS 38:7640, HLAS 38:7646, HLAS 40:7695, HLAS 42:6416, HLAS 42:6429,* and *HLAS 44:6179*).

6377 Preti, Dino. A linguagem proibida: um estudo sobre a linguagem erótica; baseado no *Dicionário moderno* de Bock, de 1903. São Paulo: T.A. Queiroz, 1984. 280 p.: appendix, bibls., ill. (Biblioteca de letras e ciências humanas. Série 1a: Estudos brasileiros; 6)

Very interesting work about a forgotten dictionary of slang which includes four-letter words and unconventional Portuguese.

6378 Sant'Ana, Moacir Medeiros de. História do modernismo em Alagoas, 1922–1932. Maceió: Univ. Federal de Alagoas, 1980. 228, 16 p., 24 leaves of plates: bibl., ill., ports.

Excellent critical study which includes very valuable documentation and constitutes an addition to the bibliography of regional literary histories (see also items **6354, 6369, 6374, 6385,** and **6390** as well as *HLAS 38:7612, HLAS 38:7634, HLAS 38:7640, HLAS 38:7646, HLAS 40:7695, HLAS 42:6416, HLAS 42:6429,* and *HLAS 44:6179*).

6379 Schwartz, Jorge. Vanguarda e cosmopolitismo na década de 20: Oliverio Girondo e Oswald de Andrade. Tradução de Mary Amazonas Leite de Barros e Jorge

Schwartz. Revisão de Jorge Schwartz e Plínio Martins Filho. São Paulo: Editora Perspectiva, 1983. 253 p.: bibl., ill. (Col. Estudos; 82. Literatura)

Good study about Latin American avant-gardes in Brazil and Argentina, which developed independently of each other. There was no intellectual or artistic relationship between these authors as suggested by the title.

6380 Silva, Maximiano de Carvalho e. Sousa da Silveira, o homem e a obra: sua contribuição à crítica textual no Brasil. Prefácio de Pedro Nava. Rio de Janeiro: Presença: Instituto Nacional do Livro, Fundação Nacional Pró-Memória, 1984. 364 p., 1 leaf of plates: bibl., facsims., index, port. (Col. Linguagem; 24)

First comprehensive biography of prestigious linguist. Meticulous and thorough if somewhat uncritical, this study should serve as a model for future biographers.

6381 Teles, Gilberto Mendonça. Estudos goianos. 2a ed. rev. Goiânia: Editora UFG, 1983. 1 v.: bibl., index (Col. Documentos goianos; 13. Publicação; 54)

Good reference work and the only comprehensive study of the subject.

6382 Teles, José Mendonça. Gente & literatura. Goiânia: Univ. Católica de Goiás, 1983. 185 p.: bibl., port.

Neither systematic nor scholarly work that offers useful information about the literary history of Goiás (see also items **6354, 6369, 6374, 6378, 6385,** and **6390** as well as *HLAS 38:7612, HLAS 38:7634, HLAS 38:7640, HLAS 38:7646, HLAS 40:7695, HLAS 42:6416, HLAS 42:6429,* and *HLAS 44:6179*).

6383 Teoria da literatura em suas fontes. Seleção, introdução e revisão técnica de Luiz Costa Lima. 2a ed., rev. e ampliada. Rio de Janeiro: F. Alves, 1983. 1 v.: bibl., index.

Anthology of theoretical texts that range from Paul Valéry to Roman Jakobson. Divided into three sections: 1) Questões Preliminares; 2) A Estilística; and 3) O Formalismo Russo.

6384 Teyssier, Paul. La *brasilidade* du Rio Grande do Sul vue par les intellectuels modernistes, ou le Brésil de la frontière (*in* Unité et diversité en l'Amérique latine.

Bordeaux, France: Univ. de Bordeaux III, 1982, t. 2, p. 183–205)

Excellent introduction to controversial question influenced by the fashionable "history-of-mentalities" school.

6385 Tufic, Jorge. Existe uma literatura amazonense?: ensaios. Amazonas: União Brasileira de Escritores (UBE), 1983? 104 p. (Col. Norte/nordeste de literatura; 7)

Unsatisfactory answer to good question but useful addition to the bibliography on the subject (see also items **6354, 6369, 6374, 6378,** and **6390** as well as *HLAS 38:7612, HLAS 38:7634, HLAS 38:7640, HLAS 38:7646, HLAS 40:7695, HLAS 42:6416, HLAS 42:6429, HLAS 44:6179*).

6386 Zagury, Eliane. A escrita do eu. Rio de Janeiro: Civilização Brasileira, 1982. 169 p.: bibl., index (Col. Vera Cruz; 337)

Hateful as the "I" may be according to Pascal, it is nonetheless the leading preoccupation of writers, including those who pretend otherwise. Zagury points to the wealth of such close self-analysis in Brazilian literature (e.g., Graciliano Ramos, Augusto Meyer, Joaquim Nabuco, Thiers Martins Moreira).

PROSE FICTION

6387 Aguiar, Vera Teixeira de et al. Atualidade de Monteiro Lobato: uma revisão crítica. Porto Alegre: Mercado Aberto, 1983. 156 p.: bibls. (Série Novas perspectivas; 8)

Papers presented at Encontro Nacional de Literatura Brasileira (Porto Alegre, Oct. 1982). Interesting reevaluations by young professors of literature.

6388 Appel, Carlos Jorge et al. O romance de 30. Porto Alegre: Movimento: Prefeitura Municipal de Porto Alegre, 1983. 78 p.: bibl. (Col. Ensaios; 25)

More revealing about literary criticism of 1980s (i.e., its set patterns, commonplaces, ideologies) than about the novel of the 1930s which is misread (see also item **6401**).

6389 Arroyo, Leonardo. A cultura popular em *Grande sertão: veredas*: filiações e sobrevivências tradicionais, algumas vezes eruditas. Rio de Janeiro: Livraria José Olympio Editora: Instituto Nacional do Livro, Fundação Nacional Pró-Memória, 1984. 315 p.,

1 leaf of plates: bibl., ill., indexes, port. (Col. Documentos brasileiros; 195)

Complete survey of traditional folkloric themes in Guimarães Rosa's novel, specifically the theme of the *donzela guerreira*.

6390 Cardoso, Zélia Ladeira Veras de Almeida. O romance paulista no século XX. São Paulo: Academia Paulista de Letras, 1983. 157 .: bibl. (Biblioteca Academia Paulista de Letras; 12)

Somewhat superficial but informative addition to regional literary histories (see also items **6354, 6369, 6374, 6378,** and **6385** as well as *HLAS 38:7612, HLAS 38:7634, HLAS 38:7640, HLAS 38:7646, HLAS 40:7695, HLAS 42:6416, HLAS 42:6429,* and *HLAS 44:6179*).

6391 Coutinho, Edilberto. A imaginação do real: uma leitura da ficção de Gilberto Freyre. Prefácio do Antônio Carlos Villaça. Rio de Janeiro: Livraria J. Olympio Editora: Instituto Nacional do Livro, Fundação Nacional Pró-Memória, 1983. 207 p., 1 leaf of plates: bibl., port.

Although lacking in critical insight and somewhat hagiographic, this is an informative work.

Espejo Beshers, Olga. Clarice Lispector: a bibliography. See *HLAS 47:53.*

6392 Fitz, Earl E. Clarice Lispector's *Um sopro de vida*: the novel as confession (AATSP/H, 68:2, May 1985, p. 260–266)

Sensitive analysis of Lispector's posthumous book perceived as unintentionally confessional.

6393 Franco, Georgenor. Ferreira de Castro e a Amazônia. Belém: Imprensa Oficial, 1983. 125 p.

An unscholarly work that contains interesting biographical data.

6394 Igel, Regina. A planta topográfica de *Avalovara* (UTIEH/C, 43, 1984, p. 97–108)

Useful and first cryptographic study of this novel.

6395 Lara, Cecília de. *Memórias de um sargento de milícias*: memórias de um repórter do Correio Mercantil (USP/RIEB, 21, 1979, p. 59–84)

Interesting survey of "Pacotilha," perceived as the factual background of Manuel Antônio de Almeida's novel, first published in installments in *Correio Mercantil*'s "Pacotilha" section.

6396 Leite, A. Roberto de Paula. O terceiro instante: um ensaio sobre a ficção de Ibiapaba Martins. São Paulo: Livraria Pioneira Editora, 1983. 242 p.: bibl.

Only comprehensive biography of this minor novelist but written in a naive, hagiographic tone.

6397 Leite, Ligia Chiappini Moraes. Quando a pátria viaja: uma leitura dos romances de Antônio Callado. La Habana: Casa de las Américas, 1984. 222 p. (Ensaio)

First major study of Callado's work and a brilliant analysis of his novels, chiefly *Quarup* and *Sempreviva*.

6398 Nunes, Maria Luísa. Time and allegory in Machado de Assis's *Esau and Jacob* (LALR, 11 : 21, Fall/Winter 1982, p. 27–38)

Sophisticated analysis of Machado's most enigmatic novel (see also item **6400** and **6402**).

6399 Sant'ana, Moacir Medeiros de. Hildebrando de Lima e o romance policial brasileiro. Maceió: Arquivo Público de Alagoas, 1984. 69 p., 19 p. of plates: ill.

Only study of Hildebrando de Lima as author and pioneer of mystery novels in Brazil (under English pen names). Marginal but interesting.

6400 Schüller, Donaldo. A prosa fraturada. Porto Alegre: Editora da Univ. Federal do Rio Grande do Sul, 1983. 133 p.: bibl.

New reading of Machado de Assis: his novels reflect the agony of the leisure class (see also items **6398** and **6402**).

6401 Seminário sobre o Romance de 30 no Nordeste, Fortaleza, Brazil, 1981. O Romance de 30 no Nordeste. Fortaleza: Edições Univ. Federal do Ceará: PROED, 1983. 209 p.: bibl.

Somewhat disappointing conference, given the renown of its participants (e.g., Eduardo Portella, Josué Montello, Luiz Costa Lima). Worth reading is Gilberto Mendonça Teles's excellent survey "A Crítica e o Romance de 30 no Nordeste" (see also item **6388**).

6402 Stein, Ingrid. Figuras femininas em Machado de Assis. Rio de Janeiro: Paz e Terra, 1984. 146 p.: bibl. (Col. Literatura e teoria literária; 54)

Systematic study that is also the only comprehensive one on its subject (see also items **6398** and **6400**).

6403 Süssekind, Maria Flora. Tal Brasil, qual romance?: uma ideologia estética e sua história; o naturalismo. Rio de Janeiro: Achiamé, 1984. 203 p.: bibl.

Interesting but flawed interpretation in which author misreads a number of novels failing to distinguish between realism and naturalism.

6404 Waldman, Berta. Do vampiro ao cafajeste: uma leitura da obra de Dalton Trevisan. São Paulo: Editora HUCITEC-Ponto Editorial; Curitiba: Secretaria da Cultura e do Esporte do Governo do Estado de Paraná, 1982. 135 p. (Linguagem e cultura)

It is ironic that Dalton Trevisan, essentially a satirist, is invariably perceived as tragic by literary critics. Waldman takes "o vampiro de Curitiba" to refer to the Transylvanian variety rather than recognizing it as a mockery of the vocabulary of yellow journalism.

6405 Wasserman, Renata R. Mautner. The red and the white: the "Indian" novels of José de Alencar (PMLA, 98 : 5, Oct. 1983, p. 815–827, bibl.)

Good if somewhat debatable re-examination of Alencar's so-called *indianista* novels.

POETRY

6406 Araujo, Jorge de Souza. Jorge de Lima e o idioma poético afro-nordestino. Maceió: EDUFAL, 1983. 219 p.: bibl.

Upon his death, Jorge de Lima sank into the so-called "purgatory" of oblivion reserved for writers overestimated in their lifetime. This is among the best "rescue" efforts, certainly worth reading (see also item **6408**).

Azevedo Filho, Leodegário Amarante de and **Sílvio Elia.** As poesias de Anchieta em português: estabelecimento do texto e apreciação literária. See item **6246**.

6407 Bastos Tigre: notas biográficas. Coordenação de Sylvia Bastos Tigre. Brasília: s.n., 1982. 64, 3 leaves: bibl., port.

Useful and possibly indispensable work that will serve as the single most complete source on a poet that was much celebrated at one time.

6408 Brayner, Sônia. Jorge de Lima e a *Invenção de Orfeu* (IILI/RI, 50:126, enero/marzo 1984, p. 175–187)

The poem that this critic regards as lengthy and uneven can also be considered challenging and erudite. In brief, another analysis that is useful if not conclusive (see also item **6406**).

6409 Cara, Salete de Almeida. A recepção crítica: o momento parnasiano-simbolista no Brasil. São Paulo: Editora Atica, 1983. 112 p.: bibl. (Ensaios; 98)

Good survey of the reception accorded Symbolism by Brazilian literary critics. Based on author's Ph.D. dissertation.

6410 Carlos Nejar, poeta e pensador. Organização de Giovanni Pontiero. Porto Alegre: Edições Porto Alegre: Prefeitura Municipal de Porto Alegre, Secretaria Municipal de Educação e Cultura, Divisão de Cultura, 1983. 376 p.: bibl.

Comprehensive analysis of one of Brazil's most renowned poets.

6411 Coutinho, Edilberto. O livro de Carlos: Carlos Pena Filho, poesia e vida. Rio de Janeiro: Livraria J. Olympio, 1983. 152 p., 16 p. of plates: ill.

To date, the best and most comprehensive study of a poet who died tragically at a young age. Somewhat hagiographic and sentimental in parts.

6412 Denófrio, Darcy França. O poema do poema em Gilberto Mendonça Teles. Rio de Janeiro: Presença, 1984. 214 p. (Col. Atualidade crítica; 5)

Comprehensive study.

6413 Feliciano Mendoza, Ester. De viaje con Cecília Meireles (UPR/LT, 25:95/98, enero/dic. 1977, p. 11–43, bibl.)

Good introduction to a poet insufficiently well known outside Brazil.

6414 Junqueira, Ivan. A sombra de Orfeu: ensaios. Rio de Janeiro: Nórdica, 1984. 286 p.

Anthology of literary reviews of the poetry of young writers.

6415 Knoll, Victor. Paciente arlequinada: uma leitura da obra poética de Mário de Andrade. São Paulo: Editora HUCITEC: Secretaria de Estado da Cultura, 1983. 261 p.: bibl., ill. (Linguagem)

Dense prose that combines philosophi-cal jargon with literary theory. Still, a comprehensive reading of the imagery in Mário de Andrade's poetry (see also item **6417**).

6416 Londres, Maria José F. Cordel: do encantamento às histórias de luta. São Paulo: Livraria Duas Cidades, 1983. 318 p.

Presumably written at the same time but independent of Candace Slater's study of the subject. Although more limited in scope, it may complement Slater's work on *cordel* literature (see *HLAS 46:1031* and *HLAS 46:6346*).

6417 Lopez, Telê Porto Ancona. Arlequim e modernidade (USP/RIEB, 21, 1979, p. 85–100, bibl.)

Examination of Mário de Andrade's *Paulicéia desvairada* as a reflection of the period's European avant-gardes. Critic may attribute more to the book than the writer intended (see also item **6415**).

6418 Mendonça, Antônio Sérgio Lima and **Alvaro de Sá.** Poesia de vanguarda no Brasil: de Oswald de Andrade ao poema visual. Rio de Janeiro: Antares, 1983. 283 p.: bibl., ill.

Somewhat weak in scholarship and critical acumen and more partisan than comprehensive, but nevertheless a useful survey of recent trends.

6419 Olinto, Antônio. A invenção da verdade: crítica de poesia. Rio de Janeiro: Nórdica, 1983. 231 p.

Major survey of modernist poetry in Brazil, followed by compilation of reviews originally published in *O Globo* (Rio de Janeiro). Interesting reading that includes perceptive interpretations of older and younger poets.

6420 Peixoto, Marta. Poesia com coisas: uma leitura de João Cabral de Melo Neto. São Paulo: Editora Perspectiva, 1983. 215 p.: bibl. (Col. Debates; 181)

Another paraphrastic analysis of João Cabral's work.

6421 Pereira, Carlos da Costa. Traços da vida da poetisa Júlia da Costa. Florianópolis: FCC: IOESC, 1982. 125 p.: ill. (Col. Cultura catarinense. Série Literatura: biografia)

Important contribution to the biography of the almost forgotten poet Júlia da Costa.

6422 Sant'Anna, Affonso Romano de. O canibalismo amoroso: o desejo e a interdição em nossa cultura através da poesia. São Paulo: Brasiliense, 1984. 318 p.: bibl.

Survey of all important instances in which desire (i.e., sexual) found its "repressive" expression in literature, in the sense of images, periphrases, metaphors, etc. Since literature has always expressed desire through such images, one wonders what the study proves.

6423 Silva, Elanir Gomes da. O africanismo em Batuque de Bruno de Menezes. Belém: Governo do Estado do Pará, Secretaria de Estado de Cultura, Desportos e Turismo: Falangola Editora, 1984. 101 p.: bibl.

Good introduction to an important Modernist poet of Pará that has been neglected by critics and literary historians.

6424 Süssekind, Maria Flora and Rachel Teixeira Valença. O sapateiro Silva. Poemas de Joaquim José da Silva. Rio de Janeiro: Fundação Casa de Rui Barbosa, 1983. 179 p. (Literatura popular em verso; 5)

If Joaquim José da Silva was a "renowned" poet in his lifetime, and if all historians of Brazilian literature, from Varnhagen to Romero to Antônio Cândido, recognized his few works, it is difficult to believe that the poet has been "suppressed," as the authors contend. Still, their study is the best and the most one can say on the subject.

Veiga, Cláudio. Sete tons de uma poesia maior. See item **6308.**

MISCELLANEOUS (Essays, Memoirs, Correspondence, etc.)

6425 Albuquerque, José Joaquim de Campos da Costa Medeiros e. Quando eu era vivo: memórias, 1867 a 1934. Rio de Janeiro: Editora Record, 1982. 443 p.

These highly readable anecdotes—literary, political, amatory—of a founder of the Brazilian Academy of Letters were long out of print. [R.E. Dimmick]

6426 Andrade, Mário de. Cartas de Mário de Andrade a Alvaro Lins. Estudos de Alvaro Lins. Apresentação de Ivan Cavalcanti Proença. Comentários de José César Borba e Marco Morel. Rio de Janeiro: Livraria J. Olympio Editora, 1983. 129 p.: bibl., facsims.

Letter of May 22, 1943, contains significant statements of critical views; others are of a routine nature. [R.E. Dimmick]

6427 Andrade, Mário de and Oneyda Alvarenga. Cartas. São Paulo: Livraria Duas Cidades, 1983. 308 p.: bibl.

Largely concerned with musical and literary matters. Mário's lengthy letter of Sept. 14, 1940, constitutes an important statement of his aesthetic position and source of information on his intellectual and spiritual formation. [R.E. Dimmick]

6428 Carlos Drummond de Andrade: exposição comemorativa dos 80 anos. Catálogo organizado pela Seção de Promoções Culturais, Biblioteca Nacional. Apresentação de Célia Ribeiro Zaher. Rio de Janeiro: A Biblioteca, 1982. 53 p.: ill.

Catalog of exhibit honoring Drummond's 80th birthday; contains useful bibliographic information. R.E. Dimmick]

6429 Gattai, Zélia. Um chapéu para viagem. 2a ed. Rio de Janeiro: Editora Record, 1982. 251 p.

Covering the first years of Gattai's conjugal life with Jorge Amado, these eminently readable memoirs throw interesting light on the character and writing processes of the celebrated novelist. [R.E. Dimmick]

6430 Konder, Leandro. Barão de Itararé. São Paulo: Brasiliense, 1983. 70 p.: ill. (Col. Encanto radical; 37)

Less a biography than a collection of quotes from the most ingenious and characteristically Brazilian humorist of the first half of the century, Aparício Torelly, "Barão de Itararé." [R.E. Dimmick]

6431 Leite, Ascendino. Jornal literário. v. 2, Passado indefinido. v. 10, Os dias esquecidos. Rio de Janeiro: Livraria Editora Cátedra, 1983. 2 v. (391, 396 p.): index.

Extending from the 1930s-80s, Leite's well indexed literary journal is rich in sensitive reflections on readings and other writers. [R.E. Dimmick]

6432 Montello, Josué. Diário da Manhã. Rio de Janeiro: Editora Nova Fronteira, 1984. 684 p.: port.

Rich in anecdote concerning other Brazilian writers, this literary journal for the years 1952–57 makes fascinating reading but tells remarkably little about the author himself. [R.E. Dimmick]

6433 Mota, Mauro. Antologia em verso e prosa. Organização de Ivan Cavalcanti Proença. Rio de Janeiro: Livraria J. Olympio Editora; Recife: Fundação do Patrimônio Histórico e Artístico de Pernambuco, 1982. 154 p.: bibl., port.

Critical note by Cavalcanti Proença and extensive bibliography of works by and about Mota are useful for study of a leading poet of the post-Modernist period. [R.E. Dimmick]

6434 Motta Filho, Nelson. Sobras completas. Rio de Janeiro: Editora Nova Fronteira, 1984. 227 p.

Intelligence, humor, feeling, and critical perception make the poems, narratives, and maxims of this jack of all literary trades lively reading. [R.E. Dimmick]

6435 Nava, Pedro da Silva. Memórias. v. 6, O círio perfeito. 2a ed. Rio de Janeiro: Editora Nova Fronteira, 1983. 586 p.

Brilliant portrait gallery of the medical profession on the western frontier of São Paulo and in Rio during the 1930s, embellished by poetic reflection and enlivened by incidents ranging from the comic to the profoundly tragic. [R.E. Dimmick]

6436 Nava, Pedro da Silva. Pedro Nava. Seleção de textos, notas, estudo biográfico, histórico e crítico e exercícios de Maria Aparecida Santilli. São Paulo: Abril Educação, 1983. 108 p.: ports. (Literatura comentada)

This well organized school text, based on a work still in progress, illustrates that a decade suffices for a writer to become a "classic." [R.E. Dimmick]

6437 O Partenon Literário: poesia e prosa; antologia. Compilação de Regina Zilberman, Carmen Consuelo Silveira e Carlos Alexandre Baumgarten. Porto Alegre: Escola Superior de Teologia São Lourenço de Brindes: Instituto Cultural Português, 1980. 206 p.: bibl. (Col. Caravela; 5)

Selections from authors associated in the 1870s with the Sociedade Partenon Literário, providing a "panorama da criação literária [no] momento inicial da literatura sul-rio-grandense." [R.E. Dimmick]

6438 Rosa, Vilma Guimarães. Relembramentos: João Guimarães Rosa, meu pai. Rio de Janeiro: Nova Fronteira, 1983. 457 p.: ill.

Correspondence of Guimarães Rosa addressed to family and friends and texts of two addresses, accompanied by interviews and statements in his regard by his daughter. [R.E. Dimmick]

6439 Silveira, Helena. Paisagem e memória. Rio de Janeiro: Paz e Terra; São Paulo: Secretaria Municipal de Cultura, Prefeitura do Municipio de São Paulo, 1983. 240 p. (Col. Depoimento; 2)

This "relato costurado à minha vida" provides fascinating glimpses of writers, artists, and actors of mid-century São Paulo but gives a confusingly fragmented account of Silveira's life and literary development. [R.E. Dimmick]

FRENCH AND ENGLISH WEST INDIES AND THE GUIANAS

ETHEL O. DAVIE, *Chair and Professor, Department of Modern Foreign Languages, West Virginia State College*
NAOMI M. GARRETT, *Professor Emeritus, West Virginia State College*

A GREATER VOLUME OF LITERATURE is currently being published in the French and English West Indies with many works by promising young writers. On the other hand, there is a noticeable lack of production on the part of established English-speaking writers. Most of the prose in this area is commentary.

French language works are still preponderant in this section of *HLAS* with an almost even division between poetry and prose fiction. There has been great interest in older out-of-print works. This section includes five reprints of novels by well known Haitian writers, among them Jacques Roumain's classic, *Gouverneurs de la rosée* (item **6456**). The rest of the francophone fiction, some of which is outstanding, is by authors most of whom are newcomers. Similarly, the majority of French language poets are appearing here for the first time.

The local milieu serves as inspiration for the English language fiction which consists mainly of tales, short stories, and folklore. Several of the former British islands supply verse with St. Lucia, one of the smaller isles, predominating. Most important is an anthology of St. Lucian Derek Walcott's poetry which is intended for school use (item **6512**).

There is very little activity in drama although a history of the theatre in the anglophone islands is worthy of mention (item **6517**).

Women writers are active in all genres with particular emphasis on literary criticism. Karen Smyley Wallace's article (item **6491**) treats the prize winning novel, *Pluie et vent sur Télumée Miracle,* by Guadeloupean Simone Schwarz-Bart who is featured on the cover of the Feb. 1986 issue of *French Review.*

FRENCH WEST INDIES
PROSE FICTION

6440 Cham, Philippe Sotie—un amour tragique. Port-au-Prince: Imprimerie Le Natal, 1983. 59 p., 1 leaf of plates: ill.

Volume contains brief recollections from the author's career as a military officer and a complicated short story of jealousy.

6441 Cinéas, Jean-Baptiste. Le drame de la terre: roman. Port-au-Prince: Editions Fardin, 1981. 168 p.

Reprint of earlier regional novel of family rivalry and feuds. Sought in marriage by sons of two influential, antagonistic families, a young woman refuses her father's choice and elopes with the one she loves. Feuding intensifies.

6442 Cinéas, Jean-Baptiste. L'héritage sacré: roman paysan. Port-au-Prince: Fardin, 1981. 198? 214 p.

New edition of earlier novel depicting peasant life in the northern part of Haiti. A young man chosen by the gods to succeed his deceased grandfather as *houngan* rebels against the idea. He finally accepts and becomes the region's greatest vodun priest.

6443 Dambreville, Claude. Un goût de fiel: récit. Port-au-Prince: Imprimerie H. Deschamps, 1983? 141 p.

Very industrious father for whom things have taken a bad turn joins a group leaving Haiti to seek work in the US. They are arrested as soon as they arrive. Author describes terrible experiences of this group of

"boat people." Winner of the 1983 Prix Deschamps.

6444 Delsham, Tony. Lapo Farine: roman antillais. Fort-de-France: Editions M.G.G., 1984. 266 p.

Clever story of social outcast inspired to achieve wealth and position through his love for an abandoned baby girl. Gifted author comments on unequal distribution of wealth, misery, and ostracism of the impoverished.

6445 Delsham, Tony. Ma justice. Fort-de-France: Editions M.G.G., 1982. 250 p.

Roman-engagé narrates story of friendship between a *béké*, scion of a dominant wealthy family, and the son of a poor, black fisherman. Intrigue provides background for commentary on racism, politics, social and economic problems.

6446 Depestre, Louis Jacques. La femme, cette inconnue, ou, Une tranche de la vie haïtienne. Pétion-Ville, Haïti: Editions Alix Damour, s.d. 58 p.: ill.

Curious recital of the unfortunate love and marriage of a Haitian couple. Frequently interrupted by author's discourse on sanctity and preservation of matrimony.

6447 Labetan, Richard. Sainvillias, sainvilliens: roman-récit. Ilustration de Isabelle Osenat. Fort-de-France?: Imprimerie Désormeaux, 1982. 111 p.: ill.

Amusing description of games and escapades engaged in by a group of young boys growing up in a small Martinican community. Author nostalgically depicts village life during the middle of the present century.

6448 Mathon, Alix. La relève de Charlemagne: les cacos de la plume: chronique romancée. Port-au-Prince: Editions Fardin, 1984. 279 p.

Chronicle of unfortunate political events during the American occupation of Haiti interwoven with a light tale of love and jealousy. Rivalry between governmental factions is mirrored in the social life of the youth.

6449 Métellus, Jean. Jacmel au crépuscule. Paris: Gallimard, 1981. 353 p.

Through the story of an illiterate but enterprising hero, author gives an insightful characterization of Jacmelian society during the Magloire presidency. Constant struggle for position and power is highlighted. Introduction of historical events lends authenticity to this intriguing first novel by an established poet.

6450 Novastar, Charles. Omega noir: récit. Port-au-Prince: Editions Choucoune, 1982. 129 p. (Série Récit: roman; 2)

Sophisticated science fiction tale warning against concentrated urban development at the expense of an open society. Well written story presents chilling plot in a fictional locale bearing resemblance to a certain island. Its inhabitants live in a state of apprehension as their perverted religion serves an evil god. Love and human feelings are scorned but sexual license and veniality are rampant. Final cataclysm inflicts appropriate punishment.

6451 Papillon, Pierre. L'âme qui meurt: roman. Port-au-Prince: Imprimerie des Antilles, 1984. 144 p. (Col. du tricinquantenaire de l'indépendance d'Haïti)

Reprint of 1950 novel in strong condemnation of social injustice.

6452 Perfey, Liza.—guère froides et poings chauds. Fort-de-France?: Imprimerie Berger-Bellepage, 198? 204 p. (Col. L.A.O.)

During school vacation a group of young people organize for fun and games as well as for community service in small Martinican coastal town. Their activities involve all levels of the population resulting in broad delineation of characters and good depiction of community life. Intriguing story.

6453 Raymond, Yvonne. L'enfant abandonné: roman. Port-au-Prince?: s.n., 1985? 213 p.

Story of foundling who suffered greatly in his youth. Adopted by one of the three women who influenced his life, he becomes a successful pediatrician. Prevented by his uncertain background from marrying the woman he loves, the problem is resolved when his real father, member of a very important family, acknowledges the young doctor as his son. Well told though rather melodramatic story.

6454 Raymond, Yvonne. Une raison d'esperer: roman. Port-au-Prince: Les Editions Fardin, 1985. 222 p.

Young girl of mixed Haitian-Dominican parentage has been sent back to her village from Port-au-Prince by her foster mother because the latter's sons have both fallen in love with the intelligent, attractive peasant. Local community is inspired by her educational accomplishments to make their region a desirable center, even drawing people from the capital including the girl's admirers.

6455 Robinel, André. Silhouettes martiniquaises. v. 1. Schoelcher, Martinique: Imprimerie Absalon, 1983. 1 v.

Amusing tales and poems from folk custom and the ancestral past. Collection written in Creole and in French and intended to recall the melange of cultures which form the originality of Martinican identity.

6456 Roumain, Jacques. Gouverneurs de la rosée: roman. Fort-de-France: Désormeaux, 1979. 269 p. (Col. Les Grands récits antillais)

New edition of Jacques Roumain's excellent novel of suffering, love, and hope in Haiti.

6457 Rouzier, Arthur. La vengeance de loas: histoire d'une famille jérémienne: roman. Port-au-Prince: Imprimerie La Phalange, 1984. 223 p. (Col. Racines)

Fictional history of prosperous, successful family from Jérémie. Adversity overtakes the descendants when they break their link with ancestral African gods. Refusal to placate the loas leads to misfortune and death. New perspective on a popular belief.

6458 Tauriac, Michel. La catastrophe: roman. Paris: La Table ronde, 1982. 485 p.

Historical novel of romantic intrigue, political and scientific rivalries prior to the catastrophic eruption of Mt. Pelée. History and fiction are skillfully blended offering insights into daily life and social tensions in the French Antilles during the period.

6459 Verne, Marc. Marie Villarceaux: un roman d'amour. 2e éd. Port-au-Prince: Fardin, 1985. 255 p.

Tragic story of innocent woman persecuted by unwanted attentions of her hated former husband and the insane jealousy of her adored spouse. Reprint of 1945 novel.

POETRY

Bajeaux, Jean-Claude. Antilia retrouvée: Claude McKay, Luis Palés Matos, Aimé Césaire; poètes noirs antillais. See item **5888.**

6460 Burton, Robert. Au commencement, le mensonge. Fort-de-France: L'Auteur, 1980. 67 p.

Bitter indictment of masters, priests, and corrupt world for the betrayal of the black race.

6461 Chanlot, Jean. Les chants de mon âme: poèmes. Basse Terre?: L'Auteur, 1984? 76 p.: ill.

Calm, optimistic poetry celebrating nature's joys, harmonious love, pleading for universal peace. Conventional versification with often banal expression, rhymes not always felicitous.

6462 Doret, Michel R. Poèmes en marge. Port-au-Prince: Imprimerie La Phalange, 1982. 28 p.

International poetry by experienced, capable poet. A poem in Spanish pleading for peace; others in French praising France and America, land of liberty.

6463 Egouy, José. La passion des misérables: poèmes. Paris?: Editions du vent, 198? 89 leaves.

Poems expressing sympathy and encouragement for the underprivileged of the poet's island. Creole is used to address compatriots directly.

6464 François, Jean Avin. Mes ciels volants: poésies. Port-au-Prince?: Editions Choucoune, 1983. 94 p. (Série Poésie; 22)

Works of a talented poet who finds a refreshing variety of ideas "from everywhere on everything."

6465 Gowoe, Nick Simbral. Etoile poignardée: poèmes. Port-au-Prince: Editions Choucoune, 1983. 72 p.: ill. (Poésie; 20)

Variety of poems appealing for peace and redress of injustice. Miscellaneous verse is erotic at times but favors virginal love. Often talented, expression is sometimes inept and not well sustained in long poems.

6466 Guichard, Marie-Claude. Le sang de nos larmes: poèmes. Préface de Margareth Lizaire. Port-au-Prince: Editions Choucoune, 1982. 40 p. (Série Poésie)

Poems aptly described in preface as realistic, brutal, and violent; their unusually forceful expression demands relief for the suffering of others.

6467 Jean, Yanick. Recommencer Paule. Port-au-Prince: Editions Fardin, 1982. 85 p.

Long poem characterized by singular images and a surprising juxtaposition of ideas.

6468 Jérôme, Ludmilla Joseph. Epitaphe pour un printemps. Illustration de Philippe Dodard. Port-au-Prince: Imprimerie H. Deschamps, 1983. 63 p.:ill.

First volume of verse by talented granddaughter of late 19th-century Haitian poet, Charles Moravia. These 33 well written poems tinged with melancholy, long nostalgically for childhood, grieve over unrequited love, and express concern for Haiti's suffering masses. There is an occasional glimmer of hope for the future.

6469 Malivert, Mario. Arène noire: poèmes. Port-au-Prince: Editions Choucoune, 1982. 59 p.: ill. (Série Poésie; 15)

First work of poet who feels that he speaks in general for the disinherited of the earth, but particularly for his deprived Haitian compatriots. Verse is often bitter and violent.

6470 Michel, Bayard. L'aurore d'une petit coeur. Port-au-Prince: Imprimerie La Phalange, 1980. 44 p.: ill.

Plaquette of 19 poems, first efforts of promising young poet who can benefit from maturing inspiration and artistic mastery.

6471 Rosemain, Antonius; Claude Rosemain; and Marceau Elisée-Désir. Tête de morne et bord de canal. Fort-de-France: Script, 1980. 147 p.: ill.

Noteworthy poems by Claude Rose-main whose earlier work was included in the "Nouvelle Somme de Poésie du Monde Noir" in (*Présence africaine*, 1966). The poet decries Martinican intellectual stagnation, lack of indigenous music and painting, and disinterest in folklore. "Ballades Antillaises," by his father, Antonius Rosemain, is a poetic evocation of island scenes. Also includes "Recherches Créolophoniques," treating problems of Creole orthography.

6472 St-Philippe, Louis. Evangile pour les miens: poèmes. Port-au-Prince: Editions Choucoune, 1982. 53 p. (Poésie Choucoune; 17)

Revolutionary cry of despair in face of human misery. Dedicated to Third World peoples.

6473 Samuel, Marc. Méditations poétiques. Port-au-Prince: Ateliers Fardin, 1984. 59 p.

Verse expressing personal reflections of love, life, and the poet's native city, Jacmel, all highly tinged with deep religious sentiment.

6474 Simon, Marc Antoine. Le drame de l'existence. Port-au-Prince: Imprimerie M. Rodríguez, s.d. 79 p., 1 leaf of plates: ill.

Pessimistic poems reflecting on life's disappointments and insecurities and the absence of social concern. In strong alexandrine verse, the poet sees the coming of Christ's reign on earth as the only solution.

6475 Thélemaque, Louis Edmond. Miscellanées: poèmes. Préface de Jean-Baptiste Cinéas. 2e éd. Port-au-Prince: Editions Fardin, 1984. 139 p.

New edition of 1949 volume of mainly patriotic poems which are as relevant today as at their earlier appearance.

6476 Valentin, Frankel. Vague alarme: poème. Port-au-Prince?: Imprimerie La Phalange, 1984. 41 p. (Col. Racines; 4)

First verse of young "Jérémien" who believes that the solution to Haiti's present problems can be found by studying her past.

6477 Vingt poèmes pour Saint-Domingue. Illustrations hors texte de Jean-Claude Leboucher. Pointe-à-Pitre, Guadeloupe: Assn. guadeloupéenne des amis de la poésie, 1980. 91 p.: ill.

Well composed poems on a variety of subjects including some unusual thoughts on cement, pollution, and tropical storms. Dedicated to the Dominican Republic in sympathy for destruction by Hurricane David.

6478 Vipart, Serge de. Poèmes de mon Ajoupa. Pointe-à-Pitre, Guadeloupe: L'Auteur, 1983 or 1984. 86 leaves: port.

Collection of poems representing many aspects of daily life, traditions, and culture in Guadeloupe. The sensitive poet who draws his inspiration from his native island has won several national awards for his verse.

DRAMA

6479 Alpha, José. 1902 [i.e. Mil neuf cents deux]: la catastrophe de Saint-Pierre. Fort-de-France: Hatier-Martinique, 1983. 51 p.: ill.

Dramatic presentation of life in Saint-Pierre in 1902 and the events taking place immediately before and during the devastating eruption of the volcano, Pélée. Underlines social, economic, and political effects of the catastrophe.

6480 Stephenson, Elie. Les Délinters: théâtre. Cayenne: Imprimerie Municipale de Cayenne, 1978. 74 p. (Théâtre populaire guyanais)

Two plays of revolutionary inspiration for popular audiences. In French and Creole.

SPECIAL STUDIES

6481 Daniel, Neptune. Dissertations de littérature haïtienne. 3e éd. augm. Port-au-Prince?: L'Auteur, 1984. 277 p.

Recommended by Dept. of National Education, guide designed for the appreciation of literary works at the secondary level of instruction. Furnishes examples of critical study and original compositions. Third edition includes 25 additional dissertations.

6482 Dolcé, Jacquelin; Gérald Dorval; and Jean Miotel Casthely. Le romantisme en Haïti: la vie intellectuelle, 1804–1915. Port-au-Prince: Editions Fardin, 1983. 269 p.: index (Col. Pensée haïtienne)

Links the history of Haitian literature to preservation of supremacy of "Ancien Libres." Choice of French language by an educated elite was responsible for stylistic resemblance to French literary movements. Conversely, effect of local milieu and environment renders Haitian writing distinctive. Separate essays by each of the authors creates some repetition.

6483 Gardiner, Madeleine. Sonate pour Ida. Port-au-Prince: Imprimerie H. Deschamps, 1984. 124 p.: ill.

Examination of the life and works of Ida Faubert, daughter of exiled Haitian President Salamon. Twice married Ida was hostess of Parisian literary salon and associate of Colette, Anna de Noailles, and other *literati*. Her poetic themes include tropical scenes, obsession with death, maternal and passionate love. Later volume contains folk tales and legends.

6484 Gardiner, Madeleine. Visages de femmes, portraits d'écrivains: étude. Port-au-Prince: Imprimerie H. Deschamps, 198? 199 p.

Scholarly study (1981 Prix Deschamps), of novels by accomplished female authors: Marie Chauvet, Marie-Thérèse Coliman-Hall, Adeline Moravia, Lilliane Devrieux -Déhoux. Offers convincing evidence that their novels are equal to any by contemporary male writers and that their works have been unfairly neglected in Haitian literary history.

6485 Glissant, Edouard. Le discours antillais. Paris: Seuil, 1981. 503 p.: bibl.

Selections from lectures and publications by important author on a variety of Martinican topics: history, colonialism, Creole language, literature, cultural identity, political and economic conditions.

6486 Gouraige, Ghislain. Histoire de la littérature haïtienne: de l'indépendance à nos jours. Port-au-Prince: Editions de l'action social, 1982. 507 p.: bibls., index.

Much needed reprint of Gouraige's thorough study of his country's literature.

6487 Price-Mars, Louis. Les maîtres de l'aube. Port-au-Prince: Le Natal, 1982. 117 p.

Lectures and essays reflecting on Haitian arts and popular culture, treating the country's fundamental intellectual problems. A tribute to the author's father, Jean Price-Mars. Praises his foresight in the classic, *Ainsi parla l'oncle.*

6488 Racine, Daniel. Léon-Gontran Damas: l'homme et l'oeuvre. Préface de L.-S. Senghor. Paris: Présence africaine, 1983. 236 p.: bibl.

An impressive study of the life and works of Léon-Gontran Damas, one of the founders of Négritude. The critic discusses the French Guyanese writer as poet, raconteur, and essayist and analyzes his style, philosophy, and ideology. Stresses Damas's humor, rhythm, and creative imagination as stemming from his deep love for his people and traditions. Selected bibliography.

6489 Rémy, Raoul P. Le négrigénisme: nous, les nègres! v. 1. Port-au-Prince: Editions Fardin, 1982. 149 p.: ill. (Classique haïtiano-africain)

Author sketches the history of blacks in their African homeland, during the diaspora and through their settling in the New World. Praises the liberators and founders of Haiti, naming Toussaint Louverture the father of Négritude. Tribute is paid to the three apostles of that movement: Léopold Senghor, Aimé Césaire, Léon Damas, and to others who have made significant contributions to it. Odes to black heroes are distributed throughout the volume.

6490 Walker, Keith L. Aimé Césaire and the problem of language: in quest of the long song of self (UCSB/NS, 8, 1982, p. 223–234)

Césaire's poetry epitomizes the black man's search for his original self from which colonialism and slavery have alienated him. The poet's hermetic imagery and unusual use of words which renders them more powerful are necessary tools in this search.

6491 Wallace, Karen Smyley. The female and self in Schwarz-Bart's *Pluie et vent sur Télumée Miracle* (French Review [American Assn. of Teachers of French, Champaign, Ill.] 59:3, Feb. 1986, p. 428–436)

Perspective study of Simone Schwarz-Bart's fictional autobiography of an old Guadeloupean woman. Focusing on two central themes, the novel pays tribute to a generation of black Caribbean women, treating attitudes, behavior and self-concepts. Offers valuable insights into the novel's imagery and symbolism.

6492 Zimra, Clarisse. Négritude in the feminine mode: the case of Martinique and Guadeloupe (Journal of Ethnic Studies [Western Washington Univ., Bellingham] 12:1, Spring 1984, p. 53–77)

Establishes Négritude as sociopolitical term in response to a given time and situation and distinguishes between its African and Caribbean forms. Suggests that women writers speaking out against the double burden of racist and feminist inequalities imply a particular version of Négritude.

ENGLISH WEST INDIES
PROSE FICTION

6493 Focus 1983: an anthology of contemporary Jamaican writing. Edited by Mervyn Morris. Kingston: Caribbean Authors Publishing Co., 1983. 294 p.

Collection of stories and poems not previously published. Includes 56 authors who are either Jamaican or write about that culture; they range from students to well established writers. A representative number of selections can be expected to appear in later publications.

6494 Folklore from contemporary Jamaicans. Compiled by Daryl C. Dance. Drawings by Murry N. DePillars. Knoxville: Univ. of Tennessee Press, 1985. 229 p., 16 p. of plates: bibl., ill., indexes, maps.

Collection of nearly 300 rhymes, songs, games, riddles, myths, and legendary tales representing popular, contemporary Jamaican folkore. The volume provides an index of motifs, tale types, and a useful glossary.

6495 Is town say so!: dialect poetry and short stories. Compiled by Paul Keens-Douglas. Port of Spain: Keensdee Productions, 1981. 94 p.: ill.

Collection of stories and poems written in folk language and presenting daily problems and experiences of the common people. The pervasive humorous tone reflects the ability of the inhabitants to cope with life's difficulties.

6496 Jonson, L.W. The rocking chair murders and other stories. St. Johns, Antigua: The Author, 1983. 60 p.

Brief selection of fairly predictable mysteries with themes of greed, violence,

and revolution. The scathing political satire of a prime minister who was formerly a nightsoil collector crowns the stories.

POETRY

6497 Allison, Judy and C.L.G. Harris. White is apartof [i.e. apart of] Maroon. Kingston: Kingston Publishers Ltd., 1982. 62 p., 1 leaf of plates: ill.

Poems in praise of island homeland and customary virtues by Maroon leader, Col. Harris, contrast with Allison's emotional verse appreciating tropical vistas and people of another race.

6498 Augier, Adrian. Of tears and triumph: poems. Canada: s.n., 1982. 43 p.

Consists of 31 moody, reflective poems, the majority from previously published collections. The St. Lucian prize-winning poet successfully combines metaphor and music.

Bajeux, Jean-Claude. Antilia retrouvée: Claude McKay, Luis Palés Matos, Aimé Césaire; poètes noirs antillais. See item **5888.**

6499 Brathwaite, Edward Kamau. National language poetry. Mona, Jamaica: The Author, 1982. 53 leaves (Savacou working paper; 5)

Important study in spirited defense of nation language as an authentic linguistic medium, comparing the thrust for recognition to Dante's defense of Tuscan vernacular as an *appropriate literary vehicle*. Stylistically relates the language's characteristic orality to native musical structures and links its vocabulary to environmental and cultural experience. Local speech rhythm is reflected in verse form. Author traces early poetic uses of nation language through present-day examples by popular performers and major writers.

6500 Cummings, Joseph. Uphill downhill. St. James, Trinidad: Village Publications, 1981. 66 p.

Poems of nostalgia for people and the islands counsel hope and endurance. Imaginative figures of speech.

6501 Daway, Dawen. We are fighting. Roseau: Ites, Green & Gold, 1983. 31 p.: ill.

Consists of 15 poems stressing Rastafarian doctrine, demanding black liberation, and arguing for the preservation of moral standards by the black woman.

6502 Gidroncodycadogan and **St. C. Jimmy Prince.** I'll have an island: a book of poems. Kingston: Printed by Model Printers & Publishers, 198? 42 p.

Verse by two writers on themes of poverty, social justice, and respect for troubled humanity. Growing talent in need of technical development.

6503 John, Giftus R. Words in the quiet moments. Illustrated by Ronald Deschamps. Roseau: Tropical Printers, 1981. 21 p.: ill.

Young poet's first promising work accompanied by handsome illustrations.

6504 Manley, Rachel. Poems 2. S.l.: Coles, 1978. 62 p.

Sensitive poet's perceptions of life's passing episodes. Notable for interesting metaphors and comparisons.

6505 Martial, Portia. Second time around. Castries?: Advance, 1984? 23 p., 1 p. of plates: ill.

Some of the 26 poems are reprinted from a previous plaquette. Thought shows signs of originality, but poetic expression is occasionally trite.

6506 Miguel, Brother. Rastaman chant. Castries: African Children Unltd., 1983. 151 p.: ill.

Poems and musings on Rastafarian philosophy and social protest. Language of the lawyer author varies from literate standard to Rasta idiom.

6507 Rabess, Gregory. Eruptions: poems. Illustrations by Ronald Deschamps. Roseau?: Movement of Cultural Awareness, 1983. 32 p.: ill.

Consists of 16 selections of revolutionary but lyrical and rhythmic verse. Occasional felicitous images.

6508 St. Clair, Gandolph. Reaching out: a first collection of poems. Castries: Abbeystone Productions, 1982. 17 p.

First poetic efforts, largely rooted in traditions of the St. Lucian poet's homeland. Skillfully chosen words enhance the artistic value.

6509 Speech anthology '80: supplement. Kingston: Jamaica Festival Commission, 1980. 66 p.

West Indian poems written in 1980 and classified according to the age of the writers. Some are noteworthy in imagery, ideology, and expression. The majority are in standard English while a few are in nation language. Includes several prose extracts.

6510 Thoughts of a poet. Compiled by Portia Martial. Castries?: s.n., 1982? 19 p., 1 p. of plates: port.

Consists of 22 poems by a number of young writers expressing hopes, ambitions, and memories.

6511 A Treasury of Guyanese poetry. Edited by Arthur J. Seymour. Georgetown: Guyana National Lithographic, 1980. 233 p.: ill.

Compiled by Guyana's premier literary critic and author, the historical anthology concentrates on poetry portraying the people and the landscape of the country. Includes several national classics (1830–1950). Illustrated.

6512 Walcott, Derek. Selected poetry. Selected, annotated, and introduced by Wayne Brown. London: Heinemann, 1980. 142 p. (Caribbean writers series; 15)

Anthology of well chosen poems for the use of teachers and students with selections organized according to original publications. Includes extensive explanatory notes and study questions demonstrating critical understanding of an admired poet.

SPECIAL STUDIES

6513 Conference of the Association of Caribbean Studies, 4th, *Havana, 1982*. Tradition, change, and revolution in the Caribbean: abstracts of selected papers. Edited by Marian B. McLeod. Coral Gables, Fla.: The Assn., 1982. 1 v.

Abstracts of conference papers covering a wide range of disciplines. Conference purpose was to encourage research and develop understanding of the Caribbean as a common entity despite divergent heritages and social systems. Includes 17 literary papers.

6514 Conference on Critical Approaches to West Indian Literature, *Saint Thomas,*

V.I., 1981. Critical approaches to West Indian literature. Edited by Roberta Knowles and Erika Smilowitz. Sponsored by the College of the Virgin Islands and the Univ. of the West Indies. Charlotte Amalie: Humanities Division, The College, 1981. 281 p.: bibl.

Position papers of literary criticism by faculty scholars. Reports contain original ideas, extensive notes, and bibliography. Of interest to researchers.

6515 Critical issues in West Indian literature: selected papers from West Indian literature conferences, 1981–1983. Edited by Erika Sollish Smilowitz and Roberta Quarles Knowles. Introduction by Lloyd Brown. Parkersburg, Iowa: Caribbean Books, 1984. 136 p.

Essays of traditional criticism plus an introduction by Lloyd Brown culled from proceedings of colloquia sponsored by university English departments in the Caribbean. Articles stress importance of regional criticism and concern aesthetic appreciation, stylistic and linguistic analyses, and thematic studies.

6516 Crusader vignettes. Compiled by George Odlum. Castries: Offset Printers, 1984? 64 p.: ill.

Collection of articles on social issues, people, and events, published in the 50-year-old journal, *Crusader*. Wide range of styles reflect editorial personality and give a broad picture of St. Lucian life. Includes knowledgeable criticism of works by Derek Walcott, native son, from local perspective.

6517 Omotoso, Kole. The theatrical into theatre: a study of the drama and theatre of the English-speaking Caribbean. London: New Beacon, 1982. 173 p., 8 p. of plates: bibl., ill., index.

Comprehensive study of the development of the theatre in the anglophone Caribbean from its early roots in carnival, Eu-

ropean importation, and African cultural manifestations to the present. While a common official language has been an advantage, each island's dramatic production has varied according to cultural influences. Excerpts, notes, and bibliography are very useful.

6518 Pyne-Timothy, Helen. V.S. Naipaul and politics: his view of Third World societies in Africa and the Caribbean (CLA/J, 28:3, March 1985, p. 247–262)

Views Naipaul's negative and pessimistic vision of independent post-colonial societies as an anomaly even though he is currently perceived as "the foremost expositor of Third World political philosphy."

6519 Rohlehr, Gordon. Pathfinder: black awakening in *The arrivants* of Edward Kamau Brathwaite. Tunapuna, Trinidad: The Author, 1981. 344 p.: appendices, bibl.

Important learned explication of Brathwaite's major poem by an authoritative critic who demonstrates empathy with the poet's creative processes, and benefits from personal communication. Mastery of the style and experiences which shape the background of Brathwaite's complex accomplishment inform the criticism. Appendices include perceptive studies of music central to the poetry, a list of Brathwaite's essays and articles by diverse critics. Extensive chapter notes.

Sandall, Roger. "Colonia" according to Naipaul. See *HLAS 47:7091.*

6520 Seymour, Arthur J. The making of Guyanese literature. Georgetown: Guyana National Lithographic Co., 1980. 108 p.: bibl., index.

Former editor of *Kykoveral*, outstanding literary figure, A.J. Seymour, shares extensive knowledge of Guyanese literature. Important historical compendium of major creative forms and writers.

Translations into English from the Spanish and Portuguese

SUZANNE JILL LEVINE, *Associate Professor of Romance Languages and Comparative Literature, University of Washington, Seattle*

THE LAST FEW YEARS HAVE BEEN an important period for consciousness-raising: Latin American literature in English translations was the main focus of the New Latin American Poetry Conference (Oct. 1985) sponsored by the Colorado Endowment for the Arts; distinguished poets, translators, and scholars from at least three continents attended. Indeed, literary translation has been the key topic of several international gatherings, among them the International PEN Congress in New York (Jan. 1986) and the First North American Congress of Translators in Mexico City (Feb. 1986).

Fiction, poetry, and documentary works of varying quality but dealing with urgent political issues in South and Central America continue to appear in English editions. One novel to receive much media attention last year was Isabel Allende's *The house of the spirits* (item **6543**), a *One hundred years of solitude*-type family saga presenting the history of patriarchy (and matriarchy) in Chile—and the brutal Pinochet coup—from one woman's point of view. On a more documentary note, Carlos Franqui's *Family portrait with Fidel: a memoir* (item **6568**) gives us a privileged view of the Cuban leader, his inner circle and his adoption of pro-Soviet policy which led to the alienation of leftist intellectuals in the late 1960s, and to the repressive measures of the 1970s culminating in the Mariel exodus of 1980. Out of that exodus emerged Reinaldo Arenas, perhaps the most brilliant of the "post-boom" writers whose ambitious poetic novel, *Farewell to the sea* (item **6548**) tells a "collective history" of Cuba through the imagined story of a man and a woman. But more than the written word, the cinema has hopefully helped open US eyes to Latin American politics, notably *Kiss of the spider woman* based on Manuel Puig's novel (see *HLAS 44:6315*) which investigates political and sexual repression in Argentina; *Official story*, a film dealing with the painful issue of the "disappeared;" and *Improper conduct*, a documentary exposing the persecution of homosexuals and other "marginals" (mainly intellectuals) in Cuba.

Some neglected classics and avant-garde works, such as the Brazilian Mário de Andrade's *Macunaíma* (1928, item **6547**) and Argentinian Adolfo Bioy Casares's "The Invention of Morel" (1940, item **6533**) have been published this year but more strenuous efforts should be made to rescue from oblivion other great writers of Latin America (e.g., Juan Carlos Onetti). *Macunaíma*, a parody and celebration of the rich northern Brazilian folklore and language, is certainly a forerunner of the most innovative contemporary works of fiction and language play such as José Lezama Lima's *Paradiso* and Guillermo Cabrera Infante's *Three trapped tigers*. And Bioy Casares's subtle fantasy and detective fictions have been cast out as works don't fit the "sure-fire narrative recipe known as magical realism . . . popularized by the Colombian Gabriel García Márquez," wrote recently Spanish author Juan Goytisolo (*The New York Times*, May 26, 1985). In his essay, "Captives of Our 'Classics'," Goytisolo criticizes the "ready-made images" North American and European readers have of Iberian and Ibero-American literature. He concludes that "the battle against what is 'typically' Spanish will be a hard-fought one, but I am convinced that sooner or later new literary realities will carry the day."

584 / Handbook of Latin American Studies

A final note: Latin American literature suffered a great loss in 1985 with the death of Emir Rodríguez Monegal, the distinguished Uruguayan literary critic who discovered and helped promote many of the finest writers who we read today, among them Jorge Luis Borges, Gabriel García Márquez, Guillermo Cabrera Infante, and Manuel Puig. In a recent issue of *Review*—the major US journal on Latin American literature in English—the editors observe that the demise of this great scholar has left us with "a void, both in our lives and in the life of Hispanic letters."

Postscript: In June 1986, Jorge Luis Borges, the Argentine master of the short story, died. Readers and writers not only in Latin America but throughout the world mourned his passing (items **6551, 6566,** and **6567**).

ANTHOLOGIES

6521 Borges, Jorge Luis. Dreamtigers. Translated by Mildred Boyer and Harold Morland. Austin: Univ. of Texas Press, 1985. 1 v.

Reissued paperback of Borges's most personal book (originally titled *El hacedor* [The maker]), an anthology of short prose pieces and poems which first came out in English in 1964.

6522 Brazilian poetry: 1950–1980. Edited, with an introduction, by Emanuel Brasil and William Jay Smith. Middletown, Conn.: Wesleyan Univ. Press, 1983. 187 p.: bibl., ill. (Wesleyan poetry)

Of the seven poets represented (i.e., Jorge Mautner, Ferreira Gullar, Haroldo de Campos, Mario Faustino, Augusto de Campos—Haroldo's brother—, Decio Pignatari, and Lindolf Bell), Augusto de Campos's concrete poems are probably the most striking, but many of the poems chosen are noteworthy. One can only wish that the translations—particularly those of the Concrete poets—were more creative, and that women poets had not been excluded (except in the volume's dedication to Elizabeth Bishop, the distinguished North American poet who lived many years in Brazil). Useful introduction.

6523 Fernández, Macedonio. Macedonio: selected writings in translation. Edited by Jo Anne Engelbert. Fort Worth, Tex.: Latitudes Press, 1984. 124 p.: appendix.

Macedonio Fernández (1874–1952) was the Argentine Socrates to Borges's Plato. A self-made philosopher and man of letters, Macedonio was a pre-Dadaist whose metaphysical games with time, space, narrative form, and language were to inspire the creations of Borges, Cortázar, and other "River plate" writers. Macedonio remained in relative obscurity until after his death when his most important work, *Museum of the Novel of the Eterna*, was published in Spanish in 1967. Borges's pioneer anthology of Macedonio's work published in 1961, is the source for this present volume in English which also includes as an appendix two revealing portraits, written by Borges and by Macedonio's son, Adolfo de Obieta. The translations by a team reflect the indelible fact that Macedonio's ideas outdistanced his style, and that Borges fulfilled in language what Macedonio generated in thought. Nonetheless, the publication of this anthology is an important event; readers of Latin American literature must acquaint themselves with this occult master.

6524 *Fiction*. CUNY. Vol. 6, No. 3, 1981–. New York.

Anthology of translations of works by: Alejo Carpentier, Lydia Cabrera, Lino Novás Calvo, Virgilio Piñera, Calvert Casey, G. Cabrera Infante, Severo Sarduy, Reinaldo Arenas, Heberto Padilla, and José Lezama Lima.

Poets of Chile: a bilingual anthology, 1965–1985. See item 5746.

6525 Woman who has sprouted wings: poems by contemporary Latin American women poets. Edited by Mary Crow. Pittsburgh, Pa.: Latin American Literary Review Press, 1984. 168 p. (Discoveries)

Offers a bird's-eye view (14 poets) of the vast panorama of Ibero-American women poets as yet unexplored. The quality of translations and poems varies.

POETRY

6526 Arenas, Reinaldo. El central: a cuban sugar mill. Translated by Anthony Kerrigan. New York: Avon Books, 1984. 93 p.

Prose epic poem portraying the disturbing continuity between Cuba's history of slavery and enforced labor in Cuba today. Tony Kerrigan's translation is appropriately Baroque.

Figueroa, José Angel. Noo Jork. See item **5807.**

6527 Hispanic feminist poems from the Middle Ages to the present. Edited by Angel Flores and Kate Flores. New York: Feminist Press at CUNY, 1986. 1 v. (The Defiant muse)

Provocative selection of women's poetry—the *most interesting* bilingual Hispanic feminist anthology to date—from anonymous 13th-century ballads, Sor Juana Inés de la Cruz and Rosalia de Castro, but also from lesser known pre-modern poets, through to the 20th-century major women poets, and to more obscure but brilliant figures such as the fiercely nonconformist (and ill-fated) Julia de Burgos (Puerto Rico, 1914–58), and from the younger generation, talented figures such as Cristina Peri Rossi who explores woman's need and capability to break out of her mediated roles under patriarchy. Translations are for the most part adequate but poetry should be translated by poets.

6528 Neruda, Pablo. Art of birds. Translated by Jack Schmitt. Illustrations by Jack Unruh. Austin: Univ. of Texas Press, 1985. 87 p.: bibl., ill. (Texas Pan American series)

Art of birds (50 poems to 50 birds) is a delightful addition to the repertory of Neruda's works in English translation. Though a minor work compared to *Residence on earth, Art of birds* celebrates Neruda's Whitmanesque love of the elements, of Chile's lush and infinitely diverse nature. The Chilean Pigeon and the Gray Gull become supernatural presences, just as certain invented, fanciful creatures like the "beardtrick" and "mooncracker" invade the realm of real. English version is often colorless and languid in comparison with the colloquial verve and staccato playfulness of Neruda's original, but then again, Neruda has never been easy on his translators.

6529 Neruda, Pablo. Still another day. Translated by William O'Daly. Port Townsend, Wash.: Copper Canyon Press, 1984. 69 p.

Long poem divided into 28 sections, or poems, composed by Neruda toward the end of his life as a farewell to the Chilean people. A minor work within the context of Neruda's opus but certainly a very personal, painful document. Translations sometimes achieve subtle alliterative effects.

6530 Parra, Nicanor. Sermons and homilies of the Christ of Elqui. Translation by Sandra Reyes. Foreword by Miller Williams. Columbia: Univ. of Missouri Press, 1984. 105 p.: bibl. (ATLA Richard Wilbur prize for poetry; 1)

As the introduction says, "Guilelessly illogical, flagrantly contradictory, Parra's Christ of Elqui takes on an almost Groucho Marx personality, in the guise of a soapbox preacher who presents his own ideas of how the world ought to be, assuming the language of the Bible and ascending to the heights of poetry just long enough to snare the reader, only to bring him down to earth again with absurdity." Important as political satire, attacking authoritarians and totalitarians alike, this collection does not quite smack of the brilliance of Parra's earlier volume, *Poems and antipoems* (1967), a more inventive incursion into the sacred shrine of poetry. Translations are adequate, though somewhat literal.

6531 Paz, Octavio. Selected poems. Edited by Eliot Weinberger. Translations from the Spanish by G. Aroul *et al.* New York: New Directions, 1984. 147 p.: appendix.

Though many of these poems have appeared in previous volumes published by New Directions, this is a handy and discriminating selection of works of Mexico's most distinguished poet (1935–80). Translations are excellent. Includes useful notes by author in the appendix.

Rugama, Leonel. The earth is a satellite of the moon. See item **5987.**

Sor Juana Inés de la Cruz: poems. See item **5101.**

BRIEF FICTION AND
THEATER

6532 Bianco, José. Shadow play; The rats: two novels. Translated by Daniel Balderston. Pittsburgh, Pa.: Latin American Literary Review Press, 1983. 99 p. (Discoveries)

Talented Argentine writer, José Bianco, has finally been translated. Bianco was editor of the important literary journal, *Sur,* founded by Victoria Ocampo, and aside from these two novellas has written a "roman à clef," *La pérdida del reino (The loss of the kingdom).* Bianco's "unreliable" narrators weave tales of love and madness, revealing the infinite ambiguities of human behavior through elaborate Jamesian narrative strategies. Translation is at times awkward, though an admirable attempt to be "faithful."

6533 Bioy Casares, Adolfo. "The Invention of Morel" and other stories: from *La trama celeste.* Translated by Ruth L.C. Simm. Illustrated by Norah Borges de Torre. Prologue by Jorge Luis Borges. Austin: Univ. of Texas Press, 1985. 237 p.: ill. (Texas Pan American series)

A hybrid literary genre was invented by Jorge Luis Borges and his young friend, Adolfo Bioy Casares, in Argentina in the late 1930s. The "Invention of Morel," Bioy Casares's first novella, accompanied by Borges's key prologue, constituted a manifesto of "la literatura fantástica" when it first appeared in 1940. Borges wrote in the preface: "In Spanish, works of reasoned imagination are infrequent and even very rare . . . 'The Invention of Morel' . . . brings a new genre to our land and our language . . ." Science fiction, the detective novel, metaphysics, and irony are some of the ingredients which make "The Invention of Morel" and the six stories from *La trama celeste (The celestial plot,* 1948) profound and richly entertaining works of art. This English volume, illustrated by the "naif" drawings of Borges's sister, Norah, and originally published in 1964, has *finally* been reissued in paperback. Translations reveal curious omissions. These masterpieces deserve a new translation.

6533a Carballido, Emilio. *¡Orinoco!*: a play in two acts. Translated by Margaret S. Peden (LALR, 11:23, Fall/Winter 1983, p. 51–83)

Superb English rendition of one of Carballido's most entertaining plays, about two women—degenerate and slightly decrepit—wandering aimlessly and enigmatically along the Orinoco River. All the usual Carballido humor, tension, and theatricality. [G. Woodyard]

6534 Cortázar, Julio. A certain Lucas. Translated from the Spanish by Gregory Rabassa. New York: Knopf, 1984. 160 p.

Playful miscellany of anecdotes, commentaries, fantasies, *A certain Lucas* can be read as a novel-in-fragments revolving around Cortázar's alter ego, Lucas. In the spirit of *We love Glenda so much* and other recent volumes by the late Argentine fabulator, *A certain Lucas* repeats the games and artifices of earlier stories but without their novelty. Fluent translation by Rabassa who is an old hand at translating Cortázar.

6535 García Márquez, Gabriel. Collected stories. New York: Harper & Row, 1984. 311 p.

Collection of García Márquez's stories from age 19 to present. Two of the three volumes included had already been published in English (*Big Mama's funeral,* published with *No one writes to the Colonel* in 1972, translated by S.J. Bernstein; and *The incredible and sad tale of innocent Eréndira and her heartless grandmother,* basis of the movie Eréndira, translated by Gregory Rabassa). The "new" material is a volume of 11 stories titled *Eyes of a blue dog,* also translated by Rabassa. Perhaps the most masterful of these early stories is the Faulknerian "Monologue of Isabel Watching It Rain in Macondo," where we can already observe García Márquez's uncanny ability to manipulate time and create a startling sensation of simultaneity, of a deathly eternity. Rabassa's translations are smoother than Bernstein's.

6536 Lispector, Clarice. Family ties. Translated from Portuguese by Giovanni Pontiero. Austin: Univ. of Texas Press, 1985. 1 v. (Texas Pan American series)

Paperback reissue of stories published in 1972. Clarice Lispector (d. 1983) is perhaps the most original and powerful female voice in not only Brazilian but Latin American narrative.

6537 Machado de Assis, Joaquim Maria. "The Devil's Church" and other stories. Translated by Jack Schmitt and Lorie Ishimatsu. Austin: Univ. of Texas Press, 1985. 1 v. (Texas Pan American series)

Paperback reissue of lively, satiric stories from the classic Brazilian pen of Machado de Assis. Adequate translations.

6538 Marqués, René. The look—La mirada. Translated by Charles Pilditch. New York: Senda Nueva de Ediciones, 1983. 91 p. (Senda narrativa)

René Márquez (d. 1979) is one of Puerto Rico's most distinguished writers. His works (plays, stories, novels) are characterized by a mixture of stark realism, Christian and mythological symbolism, and existential and political angst. *The look*, his second novel, is no exception: he exposes a world of sex, drugs, and violence, haunted by the presence of a mysterious Christ figure. The translation—particularly the dialogue—reads like a dubbed foreign film.

6539 Quiroga, Horacio. "The Decapitated Chicken" and other stories. Translated by Margaret Sayers Peden. Austin: Univ. of Texas Press, 1985. 1 v. (Texas Pan American series)

Reissue in paperback of a selection of jungle stories and horror tales by the classic Argentine story-teller, Horacio Quiroga. Good translations.

6540 Sarduy, Severo. For voice. Translated by Philip Barnard. Pittsburgh, Pa.: Latin American Literary Review Press, 1985. 136 p.

Anthology of radio-plays (in an adequate translation) by one of Cuba's most innovative writers. Sarduy, living in Paris since 1960, is the author of *From Cuba with a song* and *Cobra*.

NOVELS

6542 Aguilera Malta, Demetrio. Babelandia. Translated by Peter Earle. Illustrated by George Bartko. Clifton, N.J.: Humana Press, 1985. 375 p.: ill. (Contemporary literature)

Babelandia is a good title for this book in more than one sense: it babbles on, spouting forth now fatigued clichés, at least in translation. Mixture of political satire and allegorical fable by the late Ecuadorian Ambassador to Mexico.

6543 Allende, Isabel. The house of the spirits. Translated from the Spanish by Magda Bogin. New York: A.A. Knopf, 1985. 368 p.

Though modeled after García Márquez's *One hundred years of solitude* in its "magical real" vision of a family's (and Chile's) history, this first novel by Isabel Allende, Salvador Allende's niece, views *machista* violence from a feminine perspective. It ends by exploding the clichés of magical realism in an epilogue which recreated in documentary fashion the brutality of recent Chilean events.

6544 Amado, Jorge. Jubiabá. Translated by Margaret A. Neves. New York: Avon Books, 1984. 294 p.

Jubiabá, Jorge Amado's fourth novel (1935), focuses on Bahia's slum, Capa-Negra, and on the "marginalized" life of the black, lower classes. The protagonist, Antônio Balduíno, begins as a young street waif and, gaining a political consciousness through his contact with a *candomblé* priest, Jubiabá, ends up as leader of a labor strike. Political didacticism coupled with a romantic portrayal of slum life. The language is stitled at times.

6545 Amado, Jorge. Pen, sword, camisole: a fable to kindle a hope. Translated by Helen R. Lane. Boston: D.R. Godine; New York: Avon Books, 1985. 274 p.

Described battle between poetry and the military in pro-Nazi Brazil of the 1940s. *The New Yorker* qualified the translation as "verbose," but this may very well be the original's problem. Minor work.

6546 Amado, Jorge. Sea of death. Translated from the Portuguese by Gregory Rabassa. New York: Avon Books, 1984. 273 p.

Sea of death, Jorge Amado's fifth novel (1936), is a lyrical love story about a young sailor, his women, his involvement in a smuggling ring, and his obsession with the sea, ruled by the *candomblé* goddess Iemanjá. Amado shares with singer-composer Dorival Caymmi a dedication to Bahia, Brazil's most African capital city (Caymmi wrote a song inspired in Amado's book titled "It's Sweet to Die in the Sea"). Amado's novels offer pleasurable reading experiences, with a definite commercial appeal; *Sea of death* is no exception. Gregory Rabassa's translation matches Amado's brand of lyricism.

6547 Andrade, Mário de. Macunaíma.
Translated from the Portuguese by
E.A. Goodland. New York: Random House,
1984. 168 p.

Macunaíma (its subtitle, *the hero
without character* has not been translated in
this edition), written by Mario de Andrade,
a leading poet and essayist of Brazilian *modernismo*, was first published in 1928. An
exuberant parody of northern Brazilian folk
tales, *Macunaíma* introduced the literary notion of *antropofagia*—cannibalism—central
to the avant-garde Brazilian Modernist movement and, indeed, to a theoretical understanding of Latin American culture. This
mock epic recounts the travels and adventures of the metamorphic jungle spirit,
Macunaíma, who is nearly swallowed by a
giant urban "cannibal" Venceslau Pietro
Pietra. Brazil is really the hero, born of its
eclectic cannibalization of Old and New
Worlds, of European, Africa, and indigenous
influences. Playful language, textured by
slang and regionalisms, loses some of its
richness—perhaps inevitably—in translation. E.A. Goodland, a chemical engineer
from England, did extensive research in order
to recreate this challenging work.

6548 Arenas, Reinaldo. Farewell to the sea:
a novel of Cuba. Translated by Andrew
Hurley. New York: Viking Press, 1985. 413 p.

Arenas (b. 1943) is probably the most
powerful and original of Latin America's
"post-boom" writers. After *Hallucinations*
(see *HLAS 46: 5270*), his imaginary "biography" of a revolutionary Mexican priest, came
out in 1970 in English, nothing was heard of
him for 10 years. Imprisoned for "improper
conduct" (a bureaucratic catchword in Fidel's
Cuba), his manuscripts censored and confis-
cated, Arenas finally left his native country
in the 1980 exodus. *Farewell to the sea*, the
third novel in a five-volume series called
"Pentagonía," is a poetic statement, a symphony of monologues in which the story of a
man and a woman and Cuba's collective history are intimately intertwined. Admirable
translation effort by Andrew Hurley.

6549 Arguedas, José María. Yawar fiesta.
Translated by Frances Horning Bar-
raclough. Austin: Univ. of Texas Press, 1985.
200 p. (Texas Pan American series)

Indigenist novel about racial, social,
and cultural conflicts in Puquio, a small

town in Peru. Includes essay by Arguedas,
"Puquio: A Culture in Process of Change,"
and the translator's glossary of both Quechua
and Spanish terms. In this "scholarly" translation, the novel has greater value as anthropological treatise than as literary work.

6550 Azuela, Arturo. Shadows of silence: a
novel. Translated by Elena C. Murray.
Notre Dame, Ind.: Univ. of Notre Dame
Press, 1985. 278 p.

Study of the lives of a group of intellectuals in Mexico City during the 1960s-
70s, focusing on the often frustrating interaction between public, political, and private
issues. Azuela is the grandson of Mariano
Azuela, author of *The underdogs*, a classic
novel of the Mexican Revolution. It is interesting that both Azuelas came to political fiction writing via other occupations: Mariano
Azuela, a doctor, and his grandson, a UNAM
professor of mathematics and the history of
science. The late 1960s turmoil, particularly
the violent repression of student upheavals
in 1968, motivated Arturo Azuela just as the
Mexican Revolution had urged his grandfather to write.

6551 Borges, Jorge Luis and **María Kodama.**
Atlas. Translated and annotated by
Anthony Kerrigan. New York: Dutton, 1985.
95 p.: bibl., ill.

The last of Borges's books to appear in
English before his death—and our great
loss—recalls the Argentine fabulist's favorite, most heterogenous genre. Like *Dreamtigers* and *A personal anthology*, Atlas
(translated lovingly by Borges's first English
translator, Tony Kerrigan) is a *miscellany*, a
"personal geography" created out of dreams,
meditations, verse, and prose poems written
in or about places recently visited, or fondly
re-visited, haunted by the phantom of
Buenos Aires. Such personal texts as "Geneva"—the city where Borges died on Friday,
June 13, 1986—may strike us now as the
final words of a sage who has left us for another universe whose dimensions he mapped
out in his *ficciones* and poems. (The photographs, recording Borges's and collaborator
Maria Kodama's trajectory around the Old
and New Worlds, are mysteriously
uncredited).

6552 Brandão, Ignácio de Loyola. Zero.
Translated by Ellen Watson. New
York: Avon Books, 1983. 317 p.: ill.

The hero is Zero: Loyola Brandão replays the parodical devices of the pop novel to portray the grotesque, nighmarish world of political persecution in Brazil. The book's ferocious denunciation of repression—the terrifying Death Squads—does not encompass the treatment of women: *machismo* as usual, even among the "good guys." Good parodies should transcend their objects of ridicule; *Zero* seems to repeat the clichés of the alienated commercial media which it criticizes, at least in translation.

6553 Cabrera Infante, Guillermo. Three trapped tigers. Translated from the Spanish by Donald Gardner, Suzanne Jill Levine, and the author. New York: Avon Books, 1985. 473 p.

Paperback reissue of 1971 translation of Cabrera Infante's classic celebration of Havana and the Cuban language. At the time, reviewer David Gallagher wrote: "a remarkable book . . . one of the most inventive novels that has come out of Latin America."

6554 Costantini, Humberto. The long night of Francisco Sanctis. Translated from the Spanish by Norman Thomas di Giovanni. New York: Harper & Row, 1985. 184 p.

Humorous novel about Argentina's "dirty war" of the 1970s, centered around the "Everyman" figure of middle-class Francisco Sanctis. The translation reflects the stylistic difficulties—an unsuccessful juggling act between satire and solemnity—of the original.

6555 Fuentes, Carlos. The old gringo. Translated by Margaret Sayers Peden and the author. New York: Farrar, Straus & Giroux, 1985. 199 p.

Intriguing tale: the imagined conclusion of the life of Ambrose Bierce, the North American journalist and sentimental story writer who disappeared in Mexico in search of Pancho Villa in 1914. Fuentes's play narrative artifice (i.e., juxtaposing symbolic and "real life" characters, dream sequences with "documentary" narration) strikes a self-conscious note, but his profound understanding of the history and myths of Mexico, particularly in its conflictive relations with the "Colossus to the North," is convincingly crystallized in his compassionate portrayal of the "old gringo." Fuentes's intellectual projects often outweigh his artistic achievements: *The old gringo* is no exception: the translation, by Margaret Sayers Peden in

close collaboration with the author who is fluent in English, reflects his often labored style.

6556 Machado de Assis, Joaquim Maria. Helena: a novel. Translated, with an introduction, by Helen Caldwell. Berkeley: Univ. of California Press, 1984. 197 p.

Machado de Assis's incisive, ironic treatment of social and religious conventions, and his witty but compassionate insights into the paradoxes of human behavior have gained him the reputation as not only Brazil's but Latin America's greatest 19th-century realist. Though one of his minor works, *Helena*, an ironic yet romantic meditation of the imperfections of love and marriage (with an underlying tale of incest) is a captivating novel. Translation is uneven—sometimes ungrammatical—but Machado's subtlety is discernible.

6557 Padilla, Heberto. Heroes are grazing in my garden. Translated from the Spanish by Andrew Hurley and the author. Afterword by the author. Rev.ed. New York: Straus & Giroux, 1984. 249 p.

Cuban poet Padilla was imprisoned by Castro as a dissident in 1971, and allowed to leave Cuba in 1980. *Heroes are grazing in my garden*, his only novel to date, is about "disappointment and creeping fear, of hardening of revolutionary fervor into dogma, and of the pollution of private lives by politics" (Michael Wood). Afterword, relating Padilla's experiences in prison, is a valuable document. Translated and revised in collaboration with the author.

6558 Puig, Manuel. Blood of requited love. Translated from the Spanish by Jan L. Grayson. New York: Vintage Books, 1984. 202 p. (Aventura: the Vintage library of contemporary world literature)

Puig is finally receiving the recognition he merits thanks to the movie version of his *Kiss of the spider woman*, directed by Héctor Babenco. Puig has gone beyond more "mainstream" writers (like García Márquez, Fuentes, and Vargas Llosa) in exploring the repressive underpinnings of fascism through his original and insightful novelistic dissections of sexual politics and of the ways in which popular culture manipulates the "collective unconscious." In *Blood of requited love*, Puig once again radically de-centers the authorial voice, letting the characters speak for themselves. Josemar, a young Brazilian bricklayer (Puig now lives in Brazil) and the teen-aged María are the protagonists of a love affair that may or may not have occurred. *Machismo* and the stultified sex roles of men and women in Latin America are again examined but the spoken language which Puig so vividly recreated in his first three novels (*Betrayed by Rita Hayworth, Heartbreak tango,* and *The Buenos Aires affair*) seems to have been neutralized by exile. As most critics agree, the translation of *Blood of requited love* is inept.

6559 Queiroz, Rachel de. The Three Marías. Translated by Fred P. Ellison. Illustrated by Aldemir Martins. Austin: Univ. of Texas Press, 1985. 178 p.: ill. (Texas Pan American series)

Classic "novel of the Northeast" by one of the first women writers to receive national recognition in Brazil. The story of the lives of three young women from different social backgrounds who first meet in a convent, *The three Marías* (the name of a constellation in the Southern Hemisphere) is narrated in a simple, almost pastoral style. The introduction is informative.

6560 Serrano, Miguel. Nos, book of the Resurrection. Translated by Gela Jacobson and the author. London: Routledge & Kegan Paul, 1984. 190 p.: ill.

Symbolic tale of relevation based on Jungian mythology. Despite (or perhaps because of) the sincerity of Miguel Serrano—former Ambassador of Chile to India—*Nos* smacks of Hessian mumbo-jumbo.

6561 Skármeta, Antonio. I dreamt the snow was burning. Translated by Malcolm Coad. New York: Readers International, 1985. 1 v.

There are big novels on small themes, and small novels on big themes: *I dreamt the snow was burning* belongs to the latter category. Skármeta writes about the last days of the Allende era in a style that attempts to approximate Puig's or Cabrera Infante's virtuosity with spoken language.

6562 Soriano, Osvaldo. A funny dirty little war. Translated by Nick Caistor. London: English Readers International, Inc., 1986. 108 p.

Story of a political confrontation in a small village in Argentina. Obscure differences between peronist supporters and leaders escalate in a crescendo of violence culminating in the final massacre . . . "Black humor, dizzying action, crisp, sparking dialogue, rapid unemotional style . . . make this novel gripping reading" (Italo Calvino). Made into an excellent movie, directed by Héctor Olivera, won award at 1984 Berlin Film Festival.

6563 Traba, Marta. Mothers and shadows. Translated from the Spanish by Jo Labanyi. New York: Readers International, 1985. 1 v.

Argentine writer, Marta Traba, died in a plane crash in Madrid in 1983, along with her husband Angel Rama and other Latin American writers. *Mothers and shadows*, focuses on the struggle of two women against military repression in Chile, Argentina, and Uruguay. A drawing-room sensibility pervades this political novel.

6564 Urbanyi, Pablo. The nowhere idea. Translated by Nigel Dennis. Toronto, Canada: Williams-Wallace, 1982. 169 p.

Spoof of (North American) academia by Argentine (b. Czechoslovakia), now an expatriate teaching Spanish at Ottawa Univ. Crisp translation.

6565 Vargas Llosa, Mario. The war of the end of the world. Translated by Helen Lane. New York: Farrar, Straus & Giroux, 1984. 568 p.

Based on Euclides da Cunha's *Os sertões* or *Rebellion in the backlands* (1902), Vargas Llosa's ambitious novel tells a powerful tale of revolution and religious fanaticism—a fictional recounting of events which did occur in northern Brazil in the 19th century, centered around the controversial figure of Antonio Conselheiro. Good translation.

ESSAYS, INTERVIEWS, AND REPORTAGE

6566 Borges, Jorge Luis. Evaristo Carriego: a book about old-time Buenos Aires. Translated, with an introduction and notes, by Norman Thomas di Giovanni with the assistance of Susan Ashe. New York: Dutton, 1984. 173 p.: bibl.

Introduction explains that *Evaristo Carriego*, first published in 1930, is the earliest volume of Jorge Luis Borges's prose that we have in English and the earliest that he allowed to remain in print in Spanish. Borges's "biography of Carriego," a minor Argentine poet who died young (1883–1912) is really "about Borges himself and about old-time Buenos Aires." Translation too prosaic to capture Borges's colloquial elegance but his charm still shines through.

6567 Borges, Jorge Luis. Seven nights. Translated by Eliot Weinberger. Introduction by Alastair Reid. New York: New Directions, 1984. 121 p.: photo.

Collection of public lectures, originally given by the Argentine *maestro* in Buenos Aires in 1977, covering his ecletic range of literary pets and philosophical obsessions (e.g., *The divine comedy*, *The thousand and one nights*, Buddhism, *The Kabbalah*). Two personal pieces are perhaps the most moving, "Blindness" and "Nightmares." Well translated by Eliot Weinberger. Includes fine photograph of Borges by Lydia Rubio.

6568 Franqui, Carlos. Family portrait with Fidel: a memoir. Translated by Alfred MacAdam. New York: Random House, 1984. 262 p.

Franqui, a journalist and a close confidant of Fidel Castro for many years, gives a unique and valuable "portrait" of the Cuban leader and his inner circle. Franqui, who struggled for autonomous, non-aligned socialism in Cuba, broke with the regime in 1968 when it was clear that Fidel had chosen to "link his fate with Moscow" and to adopt the "Soviet model of political control" (Robert S. Leiken). Franqui lives in exile in Italy.

6569 Paz, Octavio. One earth, four or five worlds: reflections on contemporary history. Translated by Helen Lane. New York: Harcourt Brace Jovanovich, 1985. 213 p.: bibl.

Well translated collection of recent essays by the Mexican poet and thinker on world politics today and the historical origins of current conflicts. "The most fascinating passages," writes Naomi Bliven, "show his insight into another foreign culture: our own," but his deep understanding of Latin America's political needs make this book an essential contribution to the field of Latin American studies.

BIBLIOGRAPHY, THEORY, AND PRACTICE

6570 *Descant*. Univ. of Toronto, Graduate English Assn. Vol. 51, Winter 1985–. Toronto, Canada.

Issue includes essays by Borges on "Sherlock Holmes" and "The Detective Story," and translations of stories by the Argentines Adolfo Bioy Casares and Marco Denevi.

6571 Difference in translation. Edited by Joseph F. Graham. Ithaca, N.Y.: Cornell Univ. Press, 1985. 253 p.

Essays focusing on a deconstructive view of translation by Jacques Derrida, Barbara Johnson, Alan Bass *et al.* While difference wrought by the act of translation is traditionally viewed as defeat, these writers posit the function of differences in language as the basis of all communication, and therefore, of all translations.

6572 Honig, Edwin. The poet's other voice: conversations on literary translation. Amherst: Univ. of Massachusetts Press, 1985. 218 p.: bibl.

Interesting collection of interviews of poet-translators by poet-translator Edwin Honig. Interviewees include Octavio Paz, Richard Wilbur, Edmund Keeley, Christopher Middleton *et al.*

Schwartz, Kessel. A source for three Martí letters: the art of translation and journalistic creation. See item **5167.**

6573 Silveira Júnior, Potiguara Mendes da. A tradução: dados para uma abordagem psianalítica. Rio de Janeiro: Aoutra: Colégio Freudiano do Rio de Janeiro, 1983. 79 p.: bibl., index.

Useful overview of Brazilian research on the possible relations between linguistics, psychoanalysis, and theories of (or toward) translation. Linguistics posits that translation is theoretically impossible because of the irreplaceable relationship between signified and signifier; psychoanalysis posits the tenuousness of the signifier's connection to the signified, thus suggesting that all communication is (must be) translation. This volume includes statements by Georges Mounin and J.C. Catford which contextualize the theoretical investigations of Haroldo de Campos, Decio Pignatari *et al.*

Also includes invaluable documents (e.g., Guimarães Rosa's correspondence with his Italian translator) which confirm that translation is (and must be) a creative act.

6574 Territorio de tradução. Organização de Iumna Maria Simon. Campinas: Univ. Estadual de Campinas, Instituto de Estudos da Linguagem, Depto. de Teoria Literária, 1984. 247 p.: bibl., ill., plates (*Remate de Males*; 4)

Versatile collection of translations and of essays on translation. Reveals that Brazilian poets and scholars obviously have a healthy respect for translation as a creative art. Translators include great poets such as Mario de Andrade and João Cabral de Melo Neto as well as fine younger poets such as Augusto and Haroldo de Campos, Decio Pignatari, and Cecília Meireles. Translatees include Sappho, Horace, Shakespeare, Donne, Baudelaire, Dylan Thomas, Allen Ginsberg, Mayakovsky, Akhmatova, Borges, Sarduy, Cavafy, Celen, Stevens, and "transcreator" Pound. Particular emphasis on the Modernist tradition, its origins and legacy. Includes "Translation, Ideology and History" by Haroldo de Campos, perhaps Brazil's foremost theoretician of translation.

6575 Translation. Journal of literary translation. Columbia Univ. Vol. 12, Spring 1984–. New York.

Essays on translation by Anthony Burgess, Kurt Vonnegut, Graham Greene, William Weaver, Gregory Rabassa, Suzanne Jill Levine, Richard Wilbur *et al.* Anthology of translations includes short prose and poetry by Marcel Proust, Paul Morand (translated by Ezra Pound), Cabrera Infante, Peter Handke, Antônio Machado, Simone de Beauvoir, Clarice Lispector *et al.*

6576 Translation Review. Univ. of Texas at Dallas. No. 18, 1985–. Richardson.

Features interview with Anthony Kerrigan who emphasizes that a translator should be an *homme de lettres* (which he also extends to *femmes*), that a good translator *is* a writer, that theory is inevitably subordinate to practice ("the translator makes his own theory as he works"), and that translation has an essential place in the academic world.

JOURNAL ABBREVIATIONS
LITERATURE

AATSP/H Hispania. American Assn. of Teachers of Spanish and Portuguese. Univ. of Cincinnati. Cincinnati, Ohio.

AHL/B Boletín de la Academia Hondureña de la Lengua. Tegucigalpa.

AHSI Archivum Historicum Societatis Iesu. Rome.

AR Areíto. Areíto, Inc. New York.

ATSP/VH Vida Hispánica. Assn. of the Teachers of Spanish and Portuguese. Wolverhampton, U.K.

BCE/C Cultura. Banco Central del Ecuador. Quito.

CAM Cuadernos Americanos. México.

CBR/BCB Boletín Cultural y Bibliográfico. Banco de la República, Biblioteca Luis-Angel Arango. Bogotá.

CDLA Casa de las Américas. Instituto Cubano del Libro. La Habana.

CH Cuadernos Hispanoamericanos. Instituto de Cultura Hispánica. Madrid.

CLA/J CLA Journal. College Language Assn. Morgan State College. Baltimore, Md.

CM/D Diálogos. El Colegio de México. México.

CM/HM Historia Mexicana. El Colegio de México. México.

CM/NRFH Nueva Revista de Filología Hispánica. El Colegio de México. México.

CNC/RPC Revista Peruana de Cultura. Comisión Nacional de Cultura. Lima.

CRIT Criterio. Editorial Criterio. Buenos Aires.

ECO Eco. Librería Bucholz. Bogotá.

ESME/C Cultura. Ministerio de Educación. San Salvador.

FENIX Fénix. Biblioteca Nacional. Lima.

HISP Hispanófila. Univ. of North Carolina. Chapel Hill.

HISPA Hispamérica. Revista de literatura. Takoma Park, Md.

HR Hispanic Review. Univ. of Pennsylvania, Dept. of Romance Languages. Philadelphia, Pa.

IAA Ibero-Amerikanisches Archiv. Ibero-Amerikanisches Institut. Berlin, FRG.

ICC/T Thesaurus. Instituto Caro y Cuervo. Bogotá.

ICP/R Revista del Instituto de Cultura Puertorriqueña. San Juan.

IFCL/E Estudios de Ciencias y Letras. Instituto de Filosofía, Ciencias y Letras. Montevideo.

IGFO/RI Revista de Indias. Instituto Gonzalo Fernández de Oviedo [and] Consejo Superior de Investigaciones Científicas. Madrid.

IHAAER/B Boletín del Instituto de Historia Argentina y Americana Emilio Ravignani. Univ. Nacional de Buenos Aires. Buenos Aires.

IILI/RI Revista Iberoamericana. Instituto Internacional de Literatura Iberoamericana *patrocinada por la* Univ. de Pittsburgh. Pittsburgh, Pa.

IPGH/RHI Revista de Historia de las Ideas. Instituto Panamericano de Geografía e Historia [and] Editorial Casa de la Cultura Ecuatoriana. Quito.

IRA/B Boletín del Instituto Riva-Agüero. Pontificia Univ. Católica del Perú. Lima.

IUP/HJ Hispanic Journal. Indiana Univ. of Pennsylvania, Dept. of Foreign Languages. Indiana.

LALR Latin American Literary Review. Carnegie-Mellon Univ., Dept. of Modern Languages. Pittsburgh, Pa.

LARR Latin American Research Review. Univ. of North Carolina Press *for the* Latin American Studies Assn. Chapel Hill.

LNB/L Lotería. Lotería Nacional de Beneficencia. Panamá.

MLN Modern Language Notes. Johns Hopkins Univ. Press. Baltimore, Md.

NMC/N Nicaráuac. Ministerio de Cultura. Managua.

NS NS NorthSouth NordSud NorteSur NorteSul. Canadian Assn. of Latin American Studies. Univ. of Ottawa. Ottawa.

PMLA Publications of the Modern Language Assn. of America. New York.

RCLL Revista de Crítica Literaria Latinoamericana. Latinoamericana Editores. Lima.

REVIEW Review. Center for Inter-American Relations. New York.

RIB Revista Interamericana de Bibliografía (Inter-American Review of Bibliography). Organization of American States. Washington.

RPC Revista del Pensamiento Centroamericano. Consejo Superior de la Empresa Privida (COSEP). Managua.

RRI Revista/Review Interamericana. Univ. Interamericana. San Germán, Puerto Rico.

SBAT/RT Revista de Teatro. Sociedade Brasileira de Autores Teatrais. Rio de Janeiro.

SECOLAS/SELA South Eastern Latin Americanist. Southeastern Conference on Latin American Studies. Clemson Univ. Clemson, S.C.

SP Socialismo y Participación. Ediciones Socialismo y Participación. Lima.

UA/AQ Arizona Quarterly. Univ. of Arizona. Tucson.

UA/REH Revista de Estudios Hispánicos. Univ. of Alabama, Dept. of Romance Languages, Office of International Studies and Programs. University.

UC/RCL Revista Chilena de Literatura. Univ. de Chile, Depto. de Literatura. Santiago.

UCLA/M Mester. Univ. of California, Dept. of Spanish and Portuguese. Los Angeles.

UCLV/I Islas. Univ. Central de las Villas. Santa Clara, Cuba.

UCSB/NS New Scholar. Univ. of California, Committee on Hispanic Civilization [and] Center for Chicano Studies. Santa Barbara.

UEN/LS Lateinamerika Studien. Univ. Erlangen-Nürnberg, Sektion Lateinamerika. Nürnberg, FRG.

UH/RJ Romanistishes Jahrbuch. Univ. Hamburg, Romanisches Seminar, Ibero-

Amerikanisches Forschungsinstitut. Hamburg, FRG.

UK/KRQ   Kentucky Romance Quarterly. Univ. of Kentucky. Lexington.

UK/LATR   Latin American Theatre Review. Univ. of Kansas, Center for Latin American Studies. Lawrence.

UNAM/AL   Anuario de Letras. Univ. Nacional Autónoma de México, Facultad de Filosofía y Letras. México.

UNAM/PP   Punto de Partida. Univ. Nacional Autónoma de México, Dirección General de Difusión Cultural. México.

UNAM/RUM   Revista de la Universidad de México. México.

UNC/RN   Romance Notes. Univ. of North Carolina, Dept. of Romance Languages. Chapel Hill.

UNL/U   Universidad. Univ. Nacional del Litoral. Santa Fe, Argentina.

UP/CSEC   Cuban Studies/Estudios Cubanos. Univ. of Pittsburgh, Univ. Center for International Studies, Center for Latin American Studies. Pittsburgh, Pa.

UPR/LT   La Torre. Univ. de Puerto Rico. Río Piedras.

URSS/AL   América Latina. Academia de Ciencias de la URSS. Moscú.

USP/RIEB   Revista do Instituto de Estudos Brasileiros. Univ. de São Paulo, Instituto de Estudos Brasileiros. São Paulo.

USSR/SS   Social Sciences. USSR Academy of Sciences, Section of the Social Sciences. Moscow.

UT/RCEH   Revista Canadiense de Estudios Hispánicos. Asociación Canadiense de Hispanistas, Univ. de Toronto. Toronto.

UTIEH   Caravelle. Univ. of Toulouse, Institut d'Etudes hispaniques, hispano-americaines et luso-brésiliennes. Toulouse, France.

UV/PH   La Palabra y el Hombre. Univ. Veracruzana. Xalapa, Mexico.

VANH/B   Boletín de la Academia Nacional de la Historia. Caracas.

VUELTA   Vuelta. México.

WLT   World Literature Today. Univ. of Oklahoma. Norman.

MUSIC

ROBERT STEVENSON, *Professor of Music, University of California, Los Angeles*

DESPITE ECONOMIC DIFFICULTIES, Argentina, Brazil, Chile, Mexico, and Venezuela have continued to publish excellent music periodicals throughout the biennium. In 1985, the *Revista del Instituto de Investigación Musicológica Carlos Vega*, published by the Catholic Univ. of Buenos Aires, issued vol. 6, ably edited by former Guggenheim fellow, Carmen García Muñoz. In Sept. and Dec. 1986 and April 1987, the Asociación Argentina de Musicología (AAM) published valuable issues of its *Boletín* (Nos. 2–4), each highly informative concerning present-day musical research activities in Argentina. The second issue of *Temas de Etno-musicología* (97 p., 8 p. of plates) was published in March 1986 for the Instituto Nacional de Musicología (not related to the Instituto de Investigación Musicológica Carlos Vega of Catholic Univ.). Finely directed by Irma Ruiz (printed by Tipnic, A. del Valle 1338, Buenos Aires), this handsome second issue contained impressive contributions by the current president of the AAM, Gerardo V. Huseby (Stanford Univ., Ph.D.), Héctor Luis Goyena, and María Mendizábal (all three *licenciados* in music of the Univ. Católica Argentina). The Sociedade Brasileira de Musicologia, with headquarters in São Paulo, put out in 1985 a voluminous double issue of its *Boletim* covering the years 1984–85, and *Art*, the organ of the Fine Arts Faculty of the Univ. Federal da Bahia, published issue No. 13 in April 1985.

Chile continues to lead by publishing the senior scholarly periodical in Latin America: *Revista Musical Chilena* (now sponsored by the Facultad de Artes of the Univ. de Chile, and no longer by the Instituto de Extensión Musical). The editor, Luis Merino Montero, ranks among the world's preeminent music scholars. He is also the author of several excellent articles on subjects such as Claudio Arrau's relationship with his native country and Acario Cotapos's creative career. In addition, Merino Montero has trained a coterie of able younger scholars who are making their mark with articles on important subjects such as the trajectory of *Marsyas* (item **7113**) and José Bernardo Alzedo's style (item **7153**). Not only are articles published in *Revista Musical Chilena* uniformly of highest quality, but its reviews are invariably objective and informative.

Mexico can continue taking pride in Esperanza Pulido's splendid periodical, *Heterofonía* (founded in 1968). This journal has been faithful to its declared mission of serving Mexican interests. Each issue strikes a happy medium between the erudite and the *popular*. Always concerned with accuracy and amenity, *Heterofonía* has also avoided catering to the interests of a clique and becoming a partisan organ. *Pauta*, directed by the important avant-garde composer and 1987 Guggenheim fellow Mario Lavista (1982–87), specializes in articles reprinted from publications now out-of-print or of difficult access. *Pauta*'s articles to 1986 would indicate that its readers lack any strong nationalistic urge and are more interested in foreign music. Now in recess, Venezuela's *Revista INIDEF* reflected the ethnomusicological priorities of the founders and editors, Isabel Aretz and her husband, Luis Felipe Ramón y Rivera—both of whom have been leading figures in their disciplines for more than a generation. The more recent *Revista Musical de Venezuela*, edited with consummate tact since 1980 by José Vicente Torres, enlists among its frequent and illustrious contributors Walter Guido and Mario Milanca Guzmán.

All the above mentioned music periodicals published in Latin America include only articles in Portuguese or Spanish (English summaries appear in *Heterofonía*). Nonetheless, they all deserve the encouragement that subscriptions north of the Rio Grande provide. In the US, *Latin American Music Review*, admirably edited by Gerard Béhague at the Univ. of Texas, Austin, publishes two issues per year. It differs from Latin American journals in that it anticipates a readership fluent in the three languages, Spanish, Portuguese, and English. Known for his farsightedness and acumen, the editor has surrounded himself with a corps of editorial assistants who handle publication details with great professionalism.

Striking out on its individual path, *Inter-American Music Review* (founded in 1978 at Los Angeles) chose to focus on historic developments prior to 1900. Despite an occasional necrology and/or tribute in Spanish, its articles have thus far been published in English. *Inter-American Music Review* has concentrated on remedying the regrettable lack of historic music scores, and therefore, much space has been devoted to publishing ready-to-perform Latin American high-art works. Thus, issues published in 1985 consisted entirely of engraved music scores by 24 composers ranging from 16th-century Gutierre Fernández Hidalgo, active at Bogotá, Quito, Cuzco, and Sucre (La Plata), to mid-18th-century Manuel Thadeo de Ochoa, active at Puebla, Mexico.

Recognizing that the great weakness in Latin America's historic patrimony is the lack of published music, Brazilian FUNARTE (Fundação Nacional de Arte) sponsored the most lavish music publication series of the decade. In 1980, Cleofe Person de Mattos initiated a 150th-anniversary series of substantial works by José Maurício Nunes Garcia (1767–1830), the Afro-Brazilian father of the nation's music. Each volume exhibits the highest standards of scholarly accuracy and finesse as well as bilingual introductions (Portuguese and English) and learned comment by the eminent choral conductor and present president of the Brazilian Musicological Society (who published a landmark catalog of Garcia's works in 1970). Future plans call for a series of digitally recorded disks (begun in 1985) to advertise the beauties of Brazil's classic repertory.

A much welcomed recent trend that deserves special mention is the publication of local music histories (e.g., Loja, Ecuador; Belém and Porto Alegre, Brazil). Only by reaching out beyond the capitals of Latin America will the nations' infrastructure be revealed. At present, the musical life of nations such as Bolivia, Chile, Colombia, Ecuador, Mexico, and Peru is concentrated in La Paz, Santiago, Bogotá, Quito, Mexico City, and Lima. In past centuries, however, such monopoly was not always the rule. Cochabamba and Sucre (La Paz), Valparaíso, Cartagena, Guayaquil, Guadalajara, Morelia (Valladolid), Oaxaca, Puebla, Arequipa, Ayacucho (Guamanga), Cuzco, and Trujillo experienced important local music developments that challenge the best researchers of their nations.

GENERAL

7001 Béhague, Gerard. La música en Latinoamérica: una introducción. Traducción de Miguel Castillo Didier. Caracas: Monte Avila, 1983. 502 p.: music (Serie Estudios)

Translation of *Music in Latin America: an introduction* (Englewood Cliffs, N.J.: Prentice-Hall, 1979), but minus an index.

7002 Bergman, Billy *et al.* Hot sauces: Latin and Caribbean pop. New York: Quill, 1985. 144 p.: discs., ill., index (Series Planet rock; 1)

Four of the five contributors to this intriguing volume are publicists living in New York City: Billy Bergman (contributor of chapters on Reggae, Soca, Rara); Andy Schwartz (Reggae after Marley, New Orleans Rhythm and Blues); Tony Sabournin (Latin International); and Rob Baker (Tropicalista). The fifth contributor, Isabelle Leymarie (Salsa and Latin Jazz), the only academician in the group, teaches Afro-American subjects at Yale Univ. Designed for English speakers who buy Latin American (mostly Caribbean island and Brazilian) records, this guide includes extremely useful discographies and "mail-order sources for hard-to-find records." The unifying factor in nearly all the diverse musics discussed in this guide is the African impulse. Latin American pop of the languorous type as composed by Agustín Lara is not considered.

7003 Bispo, Antônio Alexandre. Francisco Curt Lange: 80 anos (SBM/B, 2, 1984/1985, p. 47–67, bibl., photo)

A musicological genius in his time, Lange rescued the Brazilian Baroque, edited the most important musicological periodicals in Latin America (until the founding of *Revista Musical Chilena*) made unexcelled contributions to the music history of Argentina before 1900, and provided a model of dedication and idealism to all younger musicologists.

7004 Bonniers Musik Lexikon. Stockholm: Bonnier Fakta, 1983. 528 p.: ill., music facsim.

All Latin American country entries merely refer the reader to the 39-line "latinamerikansk musik" article that names 19 composers; for Chile only the unrepresentative [Leni] Alexander and Asuar enter the list of 19. For the Iberian world as a whole, this luxurious dictionary represents a step backward.

7005 Cobham, Bill. Drum machine techniques: Latin-rock rhythms; pts. 1–2 (Keyboard [GPI Publications, Cupertino, Calif.] 11:3, March 1985, p. 87; 11:4, April 1985, p. 75, rhythm notations)

Black recording artist who has worked with drum machines since 1974 and used

them in albums since *Total eclipse* (Atlantic 18121) diagrams Latin-rock rhythmic patterns, using among other effects congas, timbales, shakers, claps.

7006 Congreso Interamericano de Etnomusicología y Folklore, 1st, Caracas, 1983. Memorias (INIDEF, 6, dic. 1983, p. 1–132, ill.)

Proceedings of the First Inter-American Congress include 17 papers by such well known ethnomusicologists and/or folklorists as María Ester Grebe Vicuña (ethnomusicology as science), J.H. Kwabena Nketia (joining objectivity to experience), Terry Agerkop (role of *Revista Inidef*), Luis Felipe Ramón y Rivera (appreciation of ethnic music), and José Jorge de Carvalho (ethnomusicology in Latin America). Also includes papers by recognized authorities such as Martha E. Davis, Manuel Dannemann, Arturo Chamorro, Max H. Brandt, Igor Colima Castillo, Ronny Velásquez, María Teresa Melfi, and Clara Passafari. Papers emphasized theory and methodology. Isabel Aretz chaired the Congress.

7007 Ensayos de música latinoamericana: selección del *Boletín de Música* **de la Casa de las Américas.** La Habana: Casa de las Américas, 1982. 481 p.: bibl, ill., music (Col. Nuestros países. Serie Música)

Consists of 48 essays divided into five sections: 1) four on music and society; 2) 18 on panorama of music in Latin America and the Caribbean; 3) eight on Cuban musical panorama; 4) eight on musical thought; and 5) nine on music and the people. None of the essays carries either an original date or source. Authors are vaguely identified as "writer and essayist," "musicologist," or "anthropologist and folklorist." Such authors as Lauro Ayestarán, José Antonio Calcaño, and Antonoi González Bravo are long dead and their conclusions compromised by new findings. Essays with current value include Fernando García's on the music of Lima's nuns and on classification of Andean panpipes. His essay on the Chilean music is much outdated (p. 16–21). The tendentious political character of essays in Secs. 3–4 vitiates their scholarly value.

7008 Hill, Jonathan D. Myth, spirit-naming and the art of microtonal rising: childbirth rituals of the Arawakan Wakuénai (LAMR, 6:1, Spring/Summer 1985, p. 1–30, bibl., chart, ill., music)

The Wakuénai living along the Isana and Guainía rivers in Venezuela, Colombia, and Brazil number ca. 3,500 northern Arawakan stock indigenes. At childbirth rituals "the chant owner begins his search for the tobacco spirits of the newborn infant" with low humming. By his fourth phrase, the pitch begins rising from A flat (lowest space on bass clef). During the next five minutes the pitch ascends microtonally a major third to C. Meantime volume increases. Author who completed Indiana Univ. dissertation on Wakuénai society in 1983, now professor of anthropology at the Univ. of Georgia, used digital pitch analyser to measure and graph the slow rise.

7009 Hispanic American music treasury: pts. 1–2 (IAMR, 6:2, Spring 1985, p. 1–105; 7:1, Fall/Winter 1985; p. 1–127, music)

Pt. 1 (6:2) consists of 14 compositions by seven South Americans: Juan de Araujo, Cristóbal de Belsayaga, Manuel Blasco, José Cascante, Roque Ceruti, Roque Jacinto de Chavarría, Antonio Durán de la Mota. Pt. 2 (7:1) consists of 41 compositions by seven South Americans and 10 Central Americans and Mexicans: Gaspar Fernandes, Gutierre Fernández Hidalgo, Juan García de Zéspedes, Juan Gutiérrez de Padilla, Juan de Herrera, Tomás de Herrera, Francisco López Capillas, Manuel Thadeo de Ochoa, Juan Mathías, José de Orejón y Aparicio, Tomás Pascual, Juan Pérez Bocanegra, Antonio de Salazar, Duyn Sjntujjguy, Tomás de Torrejón y Velasco, Pedro Ximénez, and Manuel de Zumaya.

7010 Kennedy, Michael. The Oxford dictionary of music. Oxford, England: Oxford Univ. Press, 1985. 810 p.

Includes short biographical notices of Julián Carrillo, Carlos Chávez, Alberto Ginastera, Juan Orrego-Salas, Manuel Ponce, Silvestre Revueltas, Domingo Santa Cruz, Heitor Villa-Lobos, Alberto Williams. Mauricio Kagel rates 33 lines, Mario Davidovsky eight. Brazilian Antônio Carlos Gomes gets 10 lines, Camargo Guarnieri nine, Francisco Mignone five, but Marlos Nobre is omitted. Popular figures such as Roberto Carlos, Carlos Gardel, and Agustín Lara do not appear. A popular piece such as *Salut d'amour* (Love's greeting) 1888, rates an entry but not the equally popular *Sobre las olas* (Over the waves) published four years

later. Martha Argerich, Jaime Laredo, and Jesús Sanromá are profiled but not Guiomar Novaës. William Billings has an entry but not any Latin American Renaissance or Baroque composer.

7011 Larousse encyclopedia of music based on *La musique: les hommes, les instruments, les oeuvres.* Edited by Norbert Dufourcq. New York: Excalibur Books, 1981–1984. 576 p.: ill., index.

Edited by Geoffrey Hindley, this Larousse offshoot contains a chapter on "The Music of South America" (p. 475–482) that includes Mexico. Appalling geographical mistakes are compounded by the outdated information.

7012 Lima, Paula Costa. Articulando o nagô (Art [Univ. Federal da Bahia, Escola de Música e Artes Cênicas, Salvador] 013, abril 1985, p. 85–93)

Using Béhague's remarks concerning Rodolfo Halffter as test case, author questions a value system that equates obedience to international vogues as signalling growth toward "a truly contemporary maturity."

7013 Marco, Guy A. Opera: a research and information guide. New York: Garland Publishing, Inc., 1984. 373 p.: bibls., indexes.

In contrast with all other currently available opera guides, this splendid volume goes outside the narrow circle of central European countries to give "peripheral" nations their due. Spain, Portugal, and Latin America (e.g., Argentina, Brazil, Chile, Colombia, Cuba, Mexico, Peru, Uruguay, and Venezuela) are well covered.

7014 Paesky, Efraín. Prólogo to Hispanic music treasury: 1580–1765 (IAMR, 7:1, Fall/Winter 1985, p. 1)

Two issues of *Inter-American Music Review* (6:2 and 7:1; see item **7009**) contain works by the same composers included in *Latin American colonial music anthology* (see *HLAS 38:9022*), except that Flores, José Maurício Nunes Garcia, Lucas Ruiz de Ribayaz, and Domenico Zipoli are now omitted, and Tomás Pascual of Huehuetenango, Guatemala, and Manuel Thadeo de Ochoa of Puebla, Mexico, are included.

7015 Palmer, Richard. Stan Getz: an appraisal: pt. 2 (Jazz Journal International [Billboard Ltd., London] 37:1, Jan. 1984, p. 14–15, disc.)

Informed assessment of the influential Verve albums *Jazz samba* (SVLP 9013), *Jazz samba encore* (SVLP 9038), *Big band bossa nova* (SVLP 9024), *Getz-Gilberto* (SVLP 9065 and 9132), and *Stan Getz with Laurindo Almeida* (SVLP 9150).

7016 Paraskevaidis, Graciela. El dodecafonismo y el serialismo en América Latina (Pauta [Univ. Autónoma Metropolitana, México] 4 : 14, abril/junio 1985, p. 73–87, ill.)

Spanish version of following article (item **7017**), but with nine more notes, two music excerpts (Paz and Santoro), and a picture of Isamitt (1935).

7017 Paraskevaidis, Graciela. An introduction to twelve-tone music and serialism in Latin America (Interface Journal of New Music Research [The Hague?] 13 : 3, 1984 [i.e. 1985] p. 133–147, bibl., ports.)

Author (b. Buenos Aires 1940) settled as a teacher at Montevideo in 1975. Juan Carlos Paz in 1934 and Hans-Joachim Koellreutter in 1937, introduced twelve-tone concepts in Argentina and Brazil. Serialism gained ground after World War II in other countries as an alternative to worn-out nationalism. Its introducers were in almost all cases foreign-born immigrants (e.g., Focke and Eitler in Chile, Rodolfo Halffter in Mexico, Holzmann in Peru).

7018 Slonimsky, Nicolas. Supplement to music since 1900. New York: Charles Scribner's Sons, 1986. 39 p.: index.

Felipe Boero's *Raquela* produced at Buenos Aires, 25 June 1923; Sergio Cervetti's *Cocktail party* performed at Malmö, Sweden, 9 Nov. 1970; Carlos Chávez's symphonic ode, *Clio*, conducted by him at Houston, 23 March 1970 and trombone concerto at Washington, D.C., 9 May 1978, *Initium* performed by the Akron Symphony, 9 Oct. 1983, and *Prometheus bound* for chorus, solo voices, and orchestra premiered under his baton at the Cabrillo Festival in Aptos, Calif., 27 Aug. 1972; Roque Cordero's *Six mobiles for orchestra* conducted by the composer at Normal, Ill., 8 May 1975; Constantino Gaito's operas, *Lázaro* and *Shafras*, mounted at Buenos Aires, 19 Nov. 1932 and 20 Oct. 1907; Alberto Ginastera's *Beatrix Cenci* mounted at Washington, D.C., 10 Sept. 1971, *Second cello concerto* played by his second wife at Buenos Aires, 6 July 1981, *Concerto*

for strings performed at Moscow, 21 May 1984, *Jubilum*, orchestra work, composed for the 400th anniversary of the city of Buenos Aires, premiered at the Teatro Cólon, 12 April 1980, *Milena*, cantata for soprano and orchestra setting texts from Kafka's letters, premiered at Denver, 16 April 1973, *Turba ad Passionem Gregorianum* for three soloists, treble choir, mixed chorus, and orchestra, commissioned by Mendelssohn Club of Philadelphia, premiered 20 March 1975 on the club's centennial; Jocy de Oliveira's *Polinteracões*, a multimedia noise event programmed at St. Louis, 7 April 1970; Mario Perusso's one-act opera, *La voz del silencio*, mounted at the Buenos Aires Teatro Colón, 23 Nov. 1969; Silvestre Revueltas's *Sensemayá* premiered at Mexico City, 15 Dec. 1938; Aurelio de la Vega's orchestral *Intrata* played at Los Angeles, 12 May 1972; Heitor Villa-Lobos's opera, *Yerma* to a libretto after Federico García Lorca mounted at Santa Fe, N.M., 12 Aug. 1971.

7019 Southern, Eileen. Biographical dictionary of Afro-American and African musicians. Westport, Conn.: Greenwood Press, 1982. 478 p.: bibl., indexes (Greenwood encyclopedia of black music)

Although including José Maurício Nunes Garcia (alphabetized as a Spanish name, with wrong biographical data, and an incorrect tilde over the second "n" in Nunes), Southern omits all other Brazilians—among them José Joaquim Emerico Lôbo de Mesquita and the rest of the Minas Gerais group advertised by Lange. Nor do Felippe Nery da Trinidade, Manuel de Almeida Botelho, Luiz Alvares Pinto, Jerónimo de Sousa Pereira, Antônio Alves, Nuno da Cunha, and Antônio Manso da Mota enter Southern's dictionary (all of them 17th- and 18th-century blacks profiled in *Yearbook*, Inter-American Institute for Musical Research, 4, 1968, p. 12–26). Southern does include a smattering of Cubans but no South Americans from Spanish-speaking countries. Lacking are the composers of the Peruvian and Venezuelan national anthems. In 1961, Vicente Gesualdo published names, dates, and portraits of five prominent Argentinian Black composers: Zenón Rolón (b. Buenos Aires, 23 June 1856; d. Morón, 13 May 1902), Cayetano Silva (b. San Carlos, Uruguay, 1868; d. Rosario, 12 Jan. 1920), Casildo Thompson (b. Buenos Aires, 9 April 1826; d. 12 Nov. 1873), Alfredo

Quiroga (b. Buenos Aires, 1846; d. 1874), and Manuel Posadas (b. Buenos Aires ca. 1860; d. 1916).

7020 Stevenson, Robert. The music of colonial Spanish America (*in* The Cambridge history of Latin America. v. 2, Colonial Latin America [see item **1808**] p. 771–798, 891–892, bibl., disc.)

Spanish American music during the Renaissance and Baroque periods.

7021 Stevenson, Robert. Wagner's Latin American outreach to 1900 (IAMR, 5:2, Spring/Summer 1983, p. 63–88)

Wagner toyed with the idea of premiering *Tristan und Isolde* at Rio de Janeiro. History of his Brazilian contacts, followed by record of première performances in Argentina, Brazil, Chile, Colombia, and Mexico.

7022 Stover, Richard. Guitarra americana (Soundboard [Guitar Foundation of America, Riverside, Calif.] 12:1, Spring 1985, p. 86–89, ill., music)

Plea for more attention to the Latin American repertory, with Atahualpa Yupanqui's Cricket Zamba (*Zamba del grillo*) as a musical appendix. Félix Luna's *Atahualpa Yupanqui* (Madrid: Ediciones Jucar, 1974), identifying the Argentine guitarist-singer-composer as Héctor Bohento Chavero, dates his first recording of the *Zamba del grillo* as a danza, 18 July 1945, as a zamba, 19 Aug. 1954.

7023 Uribe Echevarría y Uruarte, Juan and **Juan Guillermo Prado Ocaranza.** La Virgen de Andacollo en Chile y en la Argentina (IPGH/FA, 36, julio/dic. 1983, p. 6–52, music, photos)

Andacollo is a village 55 km SE of Coquimbo. Its name is a corruption of Quechua *Anta-Coya* (copper queen). Dances there 24–26 Dec. have for centuries been a focus of popular devotion. Authors cite scholarly studies mounting to 1874. Eight music examples (p. 13–14) derive from Pereira Salas's *Los orígenes del arte musical en Chile* (see HLAS 7:5566). Authors who since 1933 have been present five times for the fiestas at Andacollo and Sotaquí see no great differences between the parent festivities in Chile and their offshoot in Argentina. Some small distinctions are listed at p. 51.

7024 Woolley, Stan. The Spanish tinge: from Cuba through Mexico to New Orleans and New York, Stan Wooley follows the Afro-

Cuban jazz (Jazz Journal International [Billboard Ltd., London] 38:7, July 1985, p. 8–10, disc., ill., ports.)

The Cuban Mario Bauza became musical director of the band of Frank Grillo = Machito (d. London, 1984) shortly after its founding. Machito used René Hernández as pianist and arranger, and at various times Carlos Vidal, José Mangual, and Tito Puente (who later established their own bands) as percussionists.

7025 Zavadiker, Ricardo A. La guitarra y la vihuela en Hispanoamérica (INIDEF, 5, 1981/1982, p. 44–49, bibl., ill.)

In the Americas, Felipe Guamán Poma de Ayala's *Nueva corónica* (written ca. 1587–1615) was the first to picture a guitar. Although somewhat equivocal, the drawing (p. 856) seems to document a guitar with double strings in only one course of the four courses. Poma de Ayala mentions the guitar in this context: "dansas y fiestas y bayles [de los indios] con tanbores y guitaras" (p. 890). Earlier writers mention vihuelas—Las Casas in 1503 and 1509 in *Historia de las Indias* (Mexico: 1965, v. 2, p. 236, 374), Fernández de Oviedo in 1526 in *Historia* (Madrid: 1851–55, v. 1, p. 281–282), and Díaz del Castillo referring to the year 1538 and an imprecise date in *Historia* (Mexico: 1969, p. 506, 537).

ARGENTINA

7026 Aguirre, Laura Inés. Cantiga castellana. Buenos Aires: Artes Gráficas Maisalún. 109 p.: ill., music.

First 70 p. contain 54 poems by the author (b. Valencia, Spain), the rest (p. 74–109) contains attractive musical settings by María Milans del Bosch (piano or guitar and voice) of 20 of her poems (in six instances words are not fitted to the music). Identified at p. 110 as Spanish, the composer must be the poet's cousin (at p. 24). Aguirre dedicates her poem *Valencia* to her grandmother, Angeles Guerrero Milans del Bosch). The poet's father was a *marino petrolero* (p. 36).

7027 Arroyuelo, Javier and **Rafael López-Sánchez.** Tango-mania (Vanity Fair [Condé Nast Publications, New York] 48:10, Oct. 1985, p. 94-101, ill.)

Tango argentino, a show with six

dancing couples and a soloist, visited New York City in summer and Oct. of 1985, reviving interest in the history of the tango. Although designed for the general public, the article conforms with received scholarship.

Cadícamo, Enrique D. Viento que lleva y trae. See item **5777**.

7028 Chase, Gilbert. Remembering Alberto Ginastera (LAMR, 6 : 1, Spring/Summer 1985, p. 80–84)

After first meeting the composer during his Dec. 1945-March 1947 trip to the US subsidized by the Guggenheim Foundation, Chase renewed his friendship while stationed at Buenos Aires as Cultural Affairs Officer (1953–55). Ginastera took exception to Chase's mentioning various early works in his landmark article "Alberto Ginastera: Argentine Composer" (*Musical Quarterly*, 43 : 4, Oct. 1957, p. 439–460) such as his first symphony, "Porteña," and *Concierto argentino* for piano and orchestra. Chase, therefore, heeded Ginastera's wishes, omitting mention of these in both the *Quarterly* and his Ginastera article in *The New Grove* (1980). On the other hand, Slonimsky, as recently as *Baker's* (1984) continues itemizing Ginastera's "withdrawn" works—even giving place and date of the première of the *Concierto argentino* (p. 834).

7029 García Muñoz, Carmen. Florio Ugarte, 1884–1975: catálogo (Revista del Instituto de Investigación Musicológica Carlos Vega [Univ. Católica, Buenos Aires] 6, 1985, p. 79–88)

Catalog expands and improves the catalog published in *Compositores de América* (l, 1954, p. 85–88). Author gives exact dates and places of première, cites opus numbers, and carries Ugarte's works beyond 1954 (*Sonatina porteña* for bandoneón, 1956; *Concierto para violín y orquesta*, 1963).

7030 Gravano, Ariel. La música de proyección folklórica argentina (IPGH/FA, 35, enero/junio 1983, p. 5–71)

A Salta group calling themselves Los Fronterizos had its debut in Buenos Aires in 1958. Composed of three guitars and a bombo player, they differed from Los Chalchaleros in their vocal arrangements—the tenor singing straight melody supported by bass, while the two other voices sang mostly in thirds but with some ornamentation in the second

voice. "This is not folkloric" complained traditionalists. But in time, their novel style became accepted as folkloric. Analyzes style and practice of Los Abalos, Atahualpa, Los Chalchaleros, Los Cantores de Quilla Huasi, and various individuals whose careers were promoted by Ariel Ramírez during the folklore "boom" years that ended ca. 1964.

7031 Lange, Francisco Curt. La música culta en el período hispano. Buenos Aires: Academia Nacional de Bellas Artes, s.d. 1 v.: ill. (Historia general del arte en la Argentina)

This synthesis (14 chaps.) effectively brings together information from widely diverse sources on music in colonial Argentina. The review in *Revista Musical Chilena* (38 : 161, 1984, p. 85–86) pays tribute to Lange's outstanding contribution.

7032 Meierovich, Clara. El bandoneón: retrato de un instrumento unilateralmente conocido (HET, 89, abril/junio 1985, p. 5–38, bibl., ill., music)

Exhaustive history and description of a River Plate concertina-type instrument favored since the early 1900s as solo or member of the tango ensemble ("invented in the 1840s by Heinrich Band of Krefeld," according to the superficial ten-line article in the 1984 *New Grove dictionary of musical instruments*). Includes catalog of works for bandoneón.

7033 Pope, W. Stuart. The composer-publisher relationship: chronicle of a friendship (LAMR, 6 : 1, Spring/Summer 1985, p. 97–107)

History of Ginastera's relationships with his publishers, especially with Boosey and Hawkes beginning in 1964.

7034 Poulin, Jean Claude. Homenaje a Alberto Ginastera: rigor e integridad, 1916–1983 (UC/RMC, 37 : 159, enero/junio 1983, p. 111–112)

Obituary translated from *Journal de Genève* (2 July 1983) pays tribute to the composer who died in Geneva (25 June 1983) where he resided for more than a decade. Although Ginastera's output was relatively low (54 opuses), it will long outlast the composer.

7035 Ruiz, Irma. Los instrumentos musicales de los indígenas del Chaco central (Revista del Instituto de Investigación

Musicológica Carlos Vega [Univ. Católica, Buenos Aires] 6, 1985, p. 35–78, bibl.)

The region covered in this useful study includes all of Formosa province and the northeast portion of Salta province. The taped data (1966–72) was deposited by author and Jorge Novati (d. 1980) in the Archivo Científico del Instituto Nacional de Musicología Carlos Vega. None of the following names is registered in the *New Grove dictionary of musical instruments* (1984): *heligday, ikjús, pimpim, poketá, porongo, tahús.*

7036 Smith, Carleton Sprague. Alberto Ginastera's *Duo for flute and oboe* (LAMR, 6:1, Spring/Summer 1985, p. 85–93, music)

Background of the first performance of the duo by the author (flute) and Lois Wann, 23 Feb. 1947, at a concert in the New York Public Library sponsored by the League of Composers.

7037 Stevenson, Robert. Ginastera's arrangement of an organ toccata by Domenico Zipoli: some recollections about the career of a master composer (LAMR, 6:1, Spring/Summer 1985, p. 94–96)

Analysis of Ginastera's transcription of the first in Zipoli's *Sonate d'intavolatura* (Rome, 1716) followed by memories of personal contacts with Argentina's foremost composer.

7038 Stevenson, Robert. Williams conducts Wagner (IAMR, 5:2, Spring/Summer 1983, p. 95)

Alberto Williams (1862–1952), who conducted an all-Wagner program at Buenos Aires on 22 Oct. 1984, pioneered in breaking down Argentine resistance to Wagner.

7039 Suárez Urtubey, Pola. La musicografía después de Caseros: pt. 1 (Revista del Instituto de Investigación Musicológica Carlos Vega [Univ. Católica, Buenos Aires] 6, 1985, p. 89–108)

Alberto Williams pioneered in publishing biographies of Argentine composers. He later gathered in his *Antología de compositores argentinos* (Buenos Aires: Academia Nacional de Bellas Artes, 1941), *Cuaderno 1: Los precursores,* his various biographies originally published in the Argentine National Library periodical, *La Biblioteca.* These articles profiled Salustiano Zavalía, Juan Pedro Esnaola, Juan Bautista

Alberdi, Amancio Alcorta *et al.* José André (1881–1944) published biographies of seven Argentine composers in the magazine *Música* (13–14, 17–24, 1906), Julián Aguirre, Arturo Berutti, Constantino Gaito, Eduardo García Mansilla, Héctor Panizza, Antonio Restano, Alberto Williams. However, most early Argentine musicography consisted of rehashes of European music histories.

BOLIVIA

7040 Baumann, Max Peter. Music of the Indios in Bolivia's highlands: survey (The World of Music [Bärenreiter. Kassal, Basel, Switzerland] 15:2, 1982, p. 80–98, bibl., ill.)

This valuable survey of the music of peasant Andeans living in rural areas of Bolivia includes instruments (varied types of notched, vessel, and duct flutes, panpipes, a few trumpets and clarinets, small and large drums, bronze llama bells, animal hoof rattles) and the occasions for their use. Rural ensembles bring several players of identical family instruments together; city *conjuntos* do not present different types of music instruments playing together—"that is, sikus, quenas, pinkillos, and charangos will not be mixed in an ensemble."

7041 Céspedes, Gilka Wara. New currents in música folklórica in La Paz, Bolivia (LAMR, 5:2, Fall/Winter 1984, p. 217–242, bibl., music)

Written by a Bolivian who heads the Dept. of Ethnomusicology and Folklore at the Instituto Boliviano de Cultura at La Paz, this survey of approved performing groups from 1965 onward includes Los Jairas, Los de Canata, Aymara, Wara, Los Takipayas, Los Koriwayras, Savia Andina, and Los Yuras.

7042 Holzmann, Rodolfo. Musical activity in 1983 at Santa Cruz de la Sierra, Cochabamba, and La Paz, Bolivia (IAMR, 5:2, Spring/Summer 1983, p. 96–98)

Record of a Bolivian tour, including teaching activities in three urban centers.

7043 Plant, Sarah and Dino Papalardi. Grupo Aymara: living Bolivian tradition (Sing Out! [New York] 30:4, Oct./Dec. 1984, p. 22–26, music, photos)

The five-to-seven member Grupo Aymara playing *sikus* and *kenas* with drum accompaniment was founded in 1971 and toured the US for a third time in summer of 1984. Plant transcribed the melody line (natural E minor) of *Alturas de Huallapacayu* (p. 26). *Charangos* play chordal accompaniment outlined with letters (Em, C, G, B⁷).

BRAZIL

7044 Andrade, Mário de. Obras completas. v. 18, Danças dramáticas do Brasil. 2a ed. Belo Horizonte: Editora Itatiata; Brasília: Instituto Nacional do Livro, Fundação Nacional Pró-Memória, 1982. 3 v. (383, 205, 322 p.): bibl., music.

Vol. 18 of Andrade's *Obras completas* consists of three vols. (its first edition was annotated by Bruno Nettl in 1961; see *HLAS 23 : 5712*). In the present second edition, copious music examples have been corrected by Juvenal Fernandes and redrawn by Miguel Poligicchio. Vol. 3 includes a 337-item bibliography (p. 309–322) covering all three volumes. It must be constantly referred to because Andrade's text makes a habit of including (within parentheses) bibliographical item number followed by page-number. Part of vol. 1 (p. 23–84) of the second edition originally appeared in *Boletín Latino-Americano de Música* (6, 1947, p. 49–97), there enriched with 17 valuable photographs. Endnotes in this edition were there printed as footnotes which greatly enhanced their usefulness. In *Yearbook Inter-American Institute for Musical Research* (1, 1965, p. 49), Gilbert Chase rightly drew attention to vol. 18 (1959) of Andrade's complete works as a "contribution of immense value to Brazilian ethnomusicology" which could not have been assembled from the *disjecta membra* left at Andrade's death (São Paulo, 25—not 15—Feb. 1945) without a decade of intense labor by his devoted pupil Oneyda Alvarenga.

7045 Azevedo, Luiz Corrêa de. Henriqueta Rosa Fernandes Braga (SBM/B, 2, 1984/1985, p. 31–32)

Author of *Musica sacra evangélica no Brasil* (1961) and numerous other valuable historical studies, Braga (b. Rio de Janeiro, 12 March 1909; d. 21 June 1983) began teaching musical pedagogy in 1936 at the Instituto Nacional de Música (after Nov. 1965, Escola de Música da Univ. Federal do Rio de Janeiro). She added musical theory in 1939,

folk music, 1948–58, and history of music in 1957.

7046 Béhague, Gerard. Patterns of *candomblé* music performance: an Afro-Brazilian religious setting (*in* Performance practice: ethnomusicological perspectives. Edited by Gerard Béhague. Westport, Conn.: Greenwood Press, 1984, p. 222–254, bibl., music)

Béhague's "factual data concerning drum 'baptism' are based on about fifteen such ceremonies observed between 1967 and 1979 among the Gêge-Nagô and other cult groups." Many of Herskovits's supposed 671 songs that were analyzed by Alan P. Merriam in his Northwestern 1951 Ph.D. dissertation were not recorded in the "context of the ceremonies, but in a laboratory installed in the State Museum." Therefore, comparison of what songs Herskovits collected with later contextually recorded songs does not yield secure data on changes in the Afro-Bahian ritual repertory and performance practice between 1941–42 and 1967–79. As second among his eight musical examples, Béhague offers a sacrificial song (*Ogum choro*) sung "at the moment the head of the animal [chicken or rooster] begins to be severed;" after this song "two more songs (*E eje ofere bará laje* and *Omie kilo pao*) presenting the same pentatonic or hexatonic melodic structure, are performed as a further offering of the blood to the *ilus*. All the songs are accompanied by the *agogo* [cow-bell type musical instrument, including one or two bells stuck with a metal stick] (occasionally the *adjá* or *xeré*, a shaken double-coned bell, is also used to call the spirit of the deity), the 'baptism' being one of the few musical occasions of *candomblé* in which singing is not accompanied by drums."

7047 Bispo, Antônio Alexandre. Die *Missa Solemnis sub titulo Sancti Francisci* von Sigismund Ritter von Neukomm, 1820 (Leichlinger Musikforum, [Leichlingen, FRG], 3, 1984, p. 21–78, ill., music)

Completed at Rio de Janeiro, 8 Nov. 1820, Neukomm's *St. Francis Mass* was dedicated to Emperor Franz I. Written on request of Franz's daughter Leopoldina, wife of Neukomm's royal pupil at Rio de Janeiro, this *Missa Solemnis sub titulo Sᵘ Francisci, Sac. Caes. Regiaeque Cath. Majestatis Francisco II Imperatori et Regi D.D.D.* survives as 296-pages MS SM9863 at the Austrian National

Library. Neukomm himself testified to having heard "an ideal performance of it by the imperial choir at Vienna in 1842." Thanks to Bispo, Mass was revived 13 Dec. 1984, by choir and orchestra of his music school at St. John Baptist Church in Leichlingen during week devoted to Austrian composers. Bispo's article contains a wealth of not easily accessible data on Neukomm's career at Rio de Janeiro, where he arrived in May 1816, for a five-year stay at the court of D. João VI. *Baker's Biographical Dictionary* (6th ed., 1978, p. 1117) wrongly states that Neukomm was ennobled by Louis XVII (should be Louis XVIII), and among many errors claims that he was appointed court music director at Rio de Janeiro by "Emperor Dom Pedro, whom he accompanied to Lisbon on the outbreak of the revolution in 1821."

7047a Bricando da roda. Coleção de Iris Costa Novaes. Rio de Janeiro: Agir Editora, 1983. 258 p.: music.

Consists of 93 young children's game songs (melodies only) used in elementary classes at Rio (city), with instructions for their use, followed by 107 of wider provenience. The informants (most of them elementary teachers) gave the collector (a professor of physical education) the songs in this anthology (1952–60).

7048 Camargo, Oswaldo de. Alberto Nepomuceno, precursor da moderna música brasileira (Clave [Revista ilustrada de música, São Paulo] 1:1, nov. 1984, p. 13–14, ill.

Homage to composer (b. Fortaleza, 6 July 1864), who in 1902 became director of the Instituto Nacional de Música at Rio and died there 16 Oct. 1920.

Dasilva, Fabio B. and **Evandro Camara.** Music and society in Brazil: the recent experience. See *HLAS 47:8379.*

7049 Franceschi, Humberto Moraes. Registro sonoro por meios mecânicas no Brasil. Rio de Janeiro: Studio HMF, 1984. 136 p.: ill. (some col.)

Lavish history of Brazil's recording industry opens with prefácio by Darcy Ribeiro, Minister of Education and Culture (1962–63), highly lauding the meticulousness and completeness of his epochmaking book. Author takes into account every aspect of the industry, from wax cylinders, disks, and piano rolls (with their means

of reproduction) to 1922. Fred Figner, Czechborn US citizen who travelled extensively in South America, reached Belém in Aug. 1891, bringing with him a Pacific Phonograph. His first Brazilian recording included a few works by the owners of the Hotel Central on João Alfredo street and a political utterance by Belém attorney Joaquim Cabral. Many precise details (e.g., facsimiles of advertisements, catalogs, letters, bills, diagrams, labels) make the history in itself a museum piece. For the music historian the 1902 catalog of Fred Figner's Casa Edison, listing 573 cylinders (e.g., 59 *modinhas*, 81 *cançonetas* and *lundús*, and *marchas*, polkas, *valsas*, tangos, *maxixes*), tells where the Brazilian buying public's interest lay at the turn of the century. Popular recording groups ranged from Banda do Corpo de Bombeiros led by Anacleto de Medeiros to Os Oito Batutas. The Dec. 1904 issue of monthly *Echo Phonográphico*, published at São Paulo, rated the singer calling himself Bahiano the most popular singer of the epoch, Cadete a close runner-up. Flautist Pattapio Silva who recorded for Odeon was best-seller instrumentalist before World War II.

7050 Garcia, José Maurício Nunes. Aberturas: *Zemira; Abertura em ré.* Pesquisas e texto de Cleofe Person de Mattos. Rio de Janeiro: FUNARTE, 1982. 26, 89 p. (PM 1004)

Of Garcia's four single-movement orchestral works, only the 1790 *Sinfonia funebre* is extant in composer's autograph. The so-called *Zemira* overture survives only in late 19th-century arrangement by Leopoldo Miguez, who dated the now lost original parts 1803. The *Overture in D* exists only in 12 orchestral parts at Carlos Gomes Museum in Campinas, and *Sinfonia tempestade* at Rio Escola de Música in a partial score arranged by Alberto Nepomuceno. Original parts used by Miguez to prepare the *Zemira* score, Garcia's most substantial independent orchestral work, carried the legend (in Portuguese), "Overture or introduction expressing light and thunder (*relampagos e trovoadas*) for violins, viola, cello, horns, *trombe lunghe*, flutes, bassoon, and bass."

7051 Garcia, José Maurício Nunes. *Justus cum ceciderit*: gradual de São Sebastião para coro, soprano solo, orquestra e orgão. Pesquisa e texto de Cleofe Person de

Mattos. Rio de Janeiro: FUNARTE, 1982?.
51 p.: facsims.

Composed for the annual celebration
of St. Sebastian's feast day (20 Jan. 1799), this
charming D Major 3/4 gradual (score at
p. 33–51 of the present volume) is the only
one that survives among many that Garcia
wrote honoring Rio de Janeiro's patron saint.

7052 Garcia, José Maurício Nunes. *Missa de
Santa Cecília*, 1826, para solistas, coro
e grande orquestra. Pesquisa e texto de Cleofe
Person de Mattos. Rio de Janeiro: FUNARTE,
1984. 371 p.: facsims., music, table.

In bilingual (Portuguese and English)
introduction, the distinguished editor gives
appropriate reasons for considering this work
the apex of Garcia's creative achievement. He
composed 19 still extant Masses (not count-
ing four Requiem Masses and two belonging
to Palm Sunday *Oficios*). Among characteristics of this St. Cecília Mass common to his
other Masses: 1) *Kyrie* and *Gloria* (234 p.) are
much longer than *Credo, Sanctus,* and
Agnus together (102 p.); and 2) *Kyrie* starts in
his favorite key, E flat Major (10 of his 19
Masses start in E flat). The solo movements
in the present Mass (*Laudamus, Qui tollis,*
and *Quoniam*) call for operatic stars. Very
evidently, the tenor singer, Cândido Inácio da
Silva, who was responsible for commission-
ing the St. Cecília Mass premiered 22 Nov.
1826 and who was his former pupil and himself a celebrated composer of *modinhas,*
wanted a number of virtuosic display numbers. After quickly composing the first version of this Mass (30 days), Garcia spent his
last four years revising the orchestration. Because of its monumental proportions, this
Mass has defied frequent performances, but,
becoming better known through adequate interpretations, it would confirm his renown as
a great master.

7053 Garcia, José Maurício Nunes. *Missa
pastoril para noite de Natal,* 1811,
para solistas, coro e orquestra. Pesquisa e
texto de Cleofe Person de Mattos. Rio de Janeiro: FUNARTE, 1982. 119 p.: facsims.

Originally composed in 1808 for SATB
soloists and SATB chorus with organ accompaniment, this Christmas Mass was rewritten with orchestra minus violins three years
later. The 1811 score includes paired clarinets, bassoons, French horns, trumpets in
B flat, first and second violas, first and second

cellos, organ, and timpany. The 6/8 C Major
music for the *Kyrie, Gratias, Cum Sancto
Spiritu,* and *Agnus* movements is substantially the same. Solos demand virtuoso
operatic singers. *Qui sedes* pits a solo soprano against three harmonizing basses.

7054 Garcia, José Maurício Nunes. *Oficios
dos defuntos,* 1816, para solistas, coro
e orquestra. Pesquisa e texto de Cleofe Person
de Mattos. Rio de Janeiro: FUNARTE, 1982.
196 p.: facsims., table.

Composer's mother was Victoria Maria
da Cruz, a black (b. Cachoeira do Campo,
Minas Gerais; d. Rio, 20 March 1816, same
day as Queen Maria I). Present *Officium de-
functorum* consisting of nine responsories
belongs with Garcia's most famous composition, his Requiem Mass, *Catalógo temático
185,* sung "in the Chapel Royal with extraordinary pomp" during a ceremony sponsored
by the Third Carmelite Order in memory of
Maria I. Musical quality of the responsories
matches that of the Requiem. Orchestral
forces include paired clarinets and French
horns, plus strings (first and second violins,
first and second violas, cello, and bass).

7055 Garcia, José Maurício Nunes. *Salmos
Laudate pueri Dominum Laudate
Dominum omnes gentes* para flautas, trom-
pas, coro, solos, violinos, violoncelo, con-
trabaixo. Pesquisa e texto de Cleofe Person
de Mattos. Rio de Janeiro: FUNARTE, 1981.
131 p.: facsims., table.

Total number of psalms composed by
Garcia (1797–1820) may reach as high as 89.
Those antedating 1809 call for organ accompaniment; thereafter orchestral accompaniment is the rule. Most heavily orchestrated is
Laudate pueri for Holy Ghost vespers (1820).
Present volume includes scores for two Latin
Psalms 112 and 116, both in D Major, and
both composed in 1813 for his friend, João
dos Reis (p. 25–31). The *rondo* structure of
both is the same: an opening choral ritornello which is repeated after each vocal solo
in a related key. *Laudate pueri,* the longer
(291 bars), has the shorter ritornello (13 measures). Each solo is assigned a different voice
(or pair, in Psalm 116). Joviality is the intended hallmark of these two psalms (no
Gregorian verses).

7056 Garcia, José Maurício Nunes. *Dies
sanctificatus:* gradual para o dia de
Natal para coro, orquestra e orgão. Pesquisa e

texto de Cleofe Person de Mattos. Rio de Janeiro: FUNARTE, 1981. 48 p.: facsims.

In introduction, editor lists 17 graduals for masses dated 1793–1800, and 10 for undated Masses. In addition, Garcia wrote graduals for three Requiem Masses dated 1799, 1809, and 1816, and a half-dozen undated graduals for Holy Week and Easter observances. The 1793 Christmas gradual published at p. 33–47 in the present volume is a D Major 3/4 work of 96 bars, scored for SATB, two French horns, first and second violins, viola, cello and string bass, and figured organ. Notable among characteristics of this early work for Rio de Janeiro cathedral are the dynamic markings (calling for sharp contrasts between loud and soft).

7057 Gilberto Gil: Expresso 2222. Edição de Antônio Risério. Prefácio de Caetano Veloso. Salvador: Corrupio, 1982. 287 p.

Prefaced by Caetano Veloso, this collection of 38 reprinted articles by and about the popular recording artist (b. Salvador, 29 June 1942) covers topics ranging from religion and politics to philosophy, but has little on music.

7058 Graham, Laura. Semanticity and melody: parameters of contrast in Shavante vocal expression (LAMR, 5:2, Fall/Winter 1984, p. 161–185, bibl., music)

The Shavante (Xavante) living on six indigenous reserves in Mato Grosso state belong to the central branch of the Gê linguistic family. Author, doctoral student in anthropology at Univ. of Texas, Austin, spent Oct. 1981-May 1982 in two Shavante villages. Transcriptions include *Dawanta* (ritual wailing, p. 175–178) and *Daño're* (collective singing, p. 179).

7059 Lange, Francisco Curt. História da música na Capitania Geral das Minas Gerais. v. 8, Vila do Príncipe do Sêrro do Frio e Arraial do Tejuco. Belo Horizonte: Conselho Estadual de Cultura de Minas Gerais, 1983. 470 p.

Vol. 8 of Lange's monumental series investigates late 18th-century musical life in two foci of Minas Gerais creative activity. As would be expected because of his transcendence, José Joaquim Emerico Lôbo de Mesquita (d. Rio, 1805) figures largest among composers discussed. Approximately two-thirds of this volume consists of documentation collected from account and entry books, contracts, and other financial records.

7060 Lange, Francisco Curt. Sobre o ensino da musicologia no Brasil (SBM/B, 2, 1985, p. 122–129)

Among the most serious problems confronting musicology in Brazil is the absence of adequate research libraries. With his usual acuity and comprehensiveness, Lange surveys what is happening in other South American countries. In Chile musicology flourishes best, in Argentina second best.

7061 As Mais belas modinhas. Compilação de Milene Antonieta Coutinho Maurício. Ilustrações de Delza Fratezzi. 3a ed., rev. e ampliada. Belo Horizonte: Editora São Vicente, 1982. 292 leaves: bibl., ill., music.

First edition of this anthology of one-line melodies transcribed by Antônio Antero de Almeida, appeared in 1976. The collector begins with 17 *modinhas* sung in her hometown, followed by 10 sung in Diamantina, eight in Ouro Preto, eight in Mariana, six in Santa Luzia, nine in Sabará, five in São João del Rei, and so forth through Congonhas, Sêrro, Itabira, Tiradentes, and Caeté. In each section, she prefaces the *modinhas* with a brief history of the place where they were collected and an attractive b/w woodcut by Delza Fratezzi. Composers to whom the melodies (without accompaniment) are credited range from national figures such as Carlos Gomes, Chiquinha Gonzaga, Marcelo Tupynambá, Miguel Emídio Pestana, Protásio Guerra, and Sátiro Bilhar to many local figures not profiled in the *Enciclopédia da música brasileira*. Any later edition would profit from indexing and biographical profiles of such composers as João Chaves, Elipídio César, João Marcelo Andrade, Modesto Antônio Ferreira, etc. Texts should underlay the melodies, which in most instances are sentimental salon music—not anonymous folk music.

7062 Mariz, Vasco. Brasílio Itiberê da Cunha (SBM/B, 2, 1985, p. 129–131)

According to Bruno Kiefer, not Cunha's *A sertaneja* (1869) but rather Carlos Gomes's *A cayumba* (1857) should take pride of place as the first nationalistic piece composed in Brazil. Mariz reveals many new and fascinating details about Cunha's diplomatic career.

7063 Mattos, Cleofe Person de. João de Deus de Castro Lobo, *Missa e Credo a oito vozes e grande orquestra* [liner notes]. Rio de

Janeiro: Clio, 1985. 1 v. (Unpaged) (Clio; 100.050-AB)

Composer (b. Villa Rica, now Ouro Preto, 16 March 1794; d. Mariana, 1832) studied at Mariana, was organist of the Mariana Church of the Third Penitential Order of St. Francis (1817–24), and thereafter *mestre de capela* of Mariana Cathedral. His splendid eight-voice orchestral Mass probably dates from 1825. Petrobrás sponsored present recording (made 27–29 Jan. 1985 by the Associação de Canto Coral and the Carmerata Rio de Janeiro directed by Henrique Morelenbaum).

7064 Mattos, Cleofe Person de. José Maurício Nunes Garcia, *As matinas do natal*; Manoel Dias de Oliveira, *Magnificat* [liner notes]. Rio de Janeiro: Clio, 1985. 1 v. (Unpaged) (Clio; ACC 100–002)

Liner notes for both works. Composed for Christmas matins of 1799, Garcia's original score for the eight responsories called for only organ accompaniment. But he expanded this by 1801 to include first and second violins, flute, paired clarinets and French horns, with separate parts for trumpets and bassoons. Oliveira (b. São José d'el Rei, now Tiradentes; d. 1813) created a brilliant orchestral *Magnificat* that attests the high plane to which church concert music had risen in the interior of Minas Gerais by 1800.

7065 Miranda Netto, Antônio Garcia de. Andrade Muricy, 1895–1984 (SBM/B, 2, 1984/1985, p. 32–35, photo)

José Cândido de Andrade Muricy (b. Curitiba, 4 Feb. 1895) excelled as musicologist, journalist, and music critic and professor. This biographical summary fails to give exact date and place of death.

7066 Muricy, Andrade. O Teatro Guaíra (SBM/B, 2, 1984/1985, p. 87–90)

Muricy (b. Curitiba) reviews chief musical events in his hometown's Teatro Guaíra. Leo Kessler (b. Switzerland, 12 Sept. 1882; d. Blumenau, Santa Catarina, 29 Sept. 1924) settled at Curitiba in 1911 and strongly impelled local music. He orchestrated *Sidérea*, the three-act opera of his pupil Augusto Stresser (b. Curitiba, 18 July 1872; d. 18 Nov. 1918) and premiered it 3 May 1912 in Teatro Guaíra with an orchestra and singers brought from Rio de Janeiro.

7067 Nobre, Marlos. Cantata do Chimborazo (UC/RMC, 38:162, julio/dic. 1984, p. 154–158)

Analysis of author's work (Op. 56) for tenor, baritone, chorus and orchestra, on text taken from Simón Bolívar's *Mi delirio sobre el Chimborazo*. Divided into three connected movements, *El manto de Iris, El tiempo,* and *El delirio,* this cantata was commissioned for the Bolívar bicentennial and premiered 24 Oct. 1983, at Maracaibo in the Teatro de Bellas Artes by the Orquesta Sinfónica and its Coro Estable with Otto Soto and Ramón Iriarte as soloists, and Eduardo Rahr as conductor. It received its Brazilian première 26 Nov. 1983, in the Sala Cecília Meireles at Rio de Janeiro, the composer conducting.

7069 Oliveira, Jamary. Black key versus white key: a Villa-Lobos device (LAMR, 5:1, Spring/Summer 1984, p. 33–47, music)

Analysis of *A baratinha de papel, O Lobozinho de vidro, Uma camponesa cantadeira, Fui no Tóróró,* and other works to show how Villa-Lobos combined figures on black and white keys. Author combats the idea that Villa-Lobos lacked any system of composition.

7070 Oliven, Ruben George. A malandragem na música popular brasileira (LAMR, 5:1, Spring/Summer 1984, p. 66–96)

According to author, a Porto Alegre university anthropologist, what was once considered ferociousness and misbehavior, has been progressively domesticated in the lyrics of Brazilian popular songs.

7071 Penalva, José de Almeida. Roberto Schorrenberg, 1929–1982 (SBM/B, 2, 1984/1985, p. 9–31, photo)

Excellent chronological summary of the life of the distinguished conductor, composer, and music educator (b. São Paulo, 25 June 1929; d. 12 Oct. 1983). In 1982, he was elected first president of the Sociedade Brasileira de Musicologia.

7072 Pereira, Niomar de Souza. Cavalhadas do Brasil: de cortejo a cavalo e lutas de mouros e cristãos. São Paulo: Escola de Folclore, 1984. 214 p.: bibl., ill., map, music, ports. (Col. Pesquisa; 6)

In 1973, author began collecting data at Pirenópolis, Goiás, concerning jousts on horseback. Fascinated by usages in Goiás, she widened investigations to include França, São Paulo. History of horseback tournaments in Pernambuco is documented as early as 1584 (Cardim) and 1609 (Bahia). Combats between

Moors and Christians were theme of most historic horseback tournaments throughout Brazil (as in other parts of Latin America, still today). Music notations in present survey include those for the first and second gallops at França, and for 13 major-mode melodies (harmonized in thirds) sung at Pirenópolis (p. 140–149). Director of Banda Phoenix refused author access to instrumental music but she took field recordings, which she then transcribed. Antônio da Costa Nascimento, *mestre de capela* at Nossa Senhora do Rosário Church there, probably composed most of the seven band numbers (p. 173–175). Either he or Padre Amancio da Luz in 1826 composed the *Hino do Divino* (p. 176) sung with great emotion all three days of the spectacle.

7073 Perrone, Charles A. From Noigandres to "Milagre de Alegria:" the concrete poets and contemporary Brazilian popular music (LAMR, 6:1, Spring/Summer 1985, p. 58–79, ill.)

Author, recipient in 1985 of Ph.D. in Brazilian literature, "assumes a basic familiarity with Brazilian concrete poetry." *Noigandres*, the name of a group of São Paulo writers headed by Augusto and Haroldo de Campos, is a Provençal word used in Pound's *Cantos* and in the lyrics of Caetano Veloso's song, *Talismã* (Philips Recording No. 6328 302, 1979). "In the Tropicália repertory, the only song that clearly pursues a concretist concept of composition is the *macumba-rock, Batma-cumba* (Gilberto Gil-Caetano Veloso on *Tropicália ou Panis et Circenses*, Philips Recording No. 765.040L, 1968).

7074 Real, Antônio Tavares Corte. Subsídios para a história da música no Rio Grande do Sul. 2a ed., rev. Porto Alegre: Editora Movimento, 1984. 351 p.: bibl., ill., music.

Second edition of valuable history contains chapter on ballet in Brazil's southernmost state not found in first edition. In both editions, author who played first violin in Porto Alegre chamber groups and orchestras since 1935, groups his chapters within larger sections dealing with orchestral, operatic, and music educational life in the state; Porto Alegre is always the focus. Last chapter in both editions deals exhaustively with the *Hino Rio Grandense* composed by Joaquim José Mendanha in May 1838. Apart from a short reference to Men-

danha's sacred compositions written while he was *mestre-de-capela* of Porto Alegre Cathedral (p. 312), author omits any facts concerning church music in Porto Alegre. Even the short section on the Depto. Artístico da Pontifícia Univ. Católica do Rio Grande do Sul (p. 90–98) treats exclusively of secular concerts given in the 1949–51 seasons. For all secular aspects of music in Porto Alegre, this local history is very informative. Photographs in the 1984 edition and all other physical aspects are a decided improvement over the 1980 edition. Reviewed in *Inter-American Music Review* (7:2, Spring/Summer 1986, p. 116–118).

7075 Ribeiro, Agnaldo; Ernst Widmer; Lindembergue Cardoso; and Paulo Lima. Obras para piano. Salvador: Univ. Federal da Bahia: FUNARTE, 1985. 46 p.: music (Série Compositores da Bahia; 9)

Four composers' works enter this collection: Agnaldo Ribeiro (*Momentus.* 2, Op. 13, No. 2); Ernst Widmer (*Sonata para piano solo*, Op. 122, and *Monte Pascoal — Paisagem bahiana*, No. 2); Lindembergue Cardoso (*Relatividade* III, Op. 82, para piano e triángulo); and Paulo Lima (*Cuncti-Serenata*, Op.19). Although each is individualized, all four are high-art composers whose music stays abreast of latest European vogues. Their university does well to sponsor this publication of their works.

7076 Salles, Vicente. A música e o tempo no Grão-Pará. Belém: Conselho Estadual de Cultura, 1980. 424 p.: bibl., ill., music.

Compendious local history, dealing chiefly with events at Belém before 1900, amply fulfills promise made by *Música e músicos do Pará* (Belém: Conselho Estadual de Cultura, 1970, 297 p.). Author (b. Pará, 27 Nov. 1931) began his publishing career with a *Resenha histórica da música sacra no Pará* and (in contrast with Corte Real) deals amply with all aspects of religious music. As he correctly emphasizes, Henrique Eulálio Gurjão (b. Belém, 15 Nov. 1834; d. Belém, 27 July 1885) who in his century was Pará's most famous native-born composer, has been misrepresented by all Brazilian music historians to date as primarily an opera composer (*Idália*, three acts, Teatro da Paz, 3 Nov. 1881), whereas his Brazilian production consisted chiefly of sacred works. Reviewed in Inter-American Music Review (7:2, Spring/Summer 1986, p. 104–116).

7077 Squeff, Enio. A música contemporânea brasileira e o Brasil (Art [Univ. Federal da Bahia, Escola de Música e Artes Cênicas, Salvador] 13, abril 1985, p. 73–83)

Marlos Nobre's commemorative salute to Bolívar reminded Squeff of radio novels of the 1950s—with its bombastic choral interjections lacing spoken declamation and recitatives accompanied by "clusters." Raul do Valle (b. São Paulo, 27 March 1936) returned to kitsch in a misbegotten work premiered by the Campinas symphony orchestra in 1984. But these works were but symptoms of the difficult times through which the nation itself was passing, according to the author. Exact dates, places, and titles would benefit this provocative article.

7078 Stevenson, Robert. A note on the music of Brazil (in The Cambridge history of Latin America. v. 2, Colonial Latin America [see item **1808**] p. 799–803, disc.)

Covers Bahia, Minas Gerais, Rio de Janeiro areas (1759–1830).

7079 Timóteo, Agnaldo. Alo, mamâe . . . Agnaldo Timóteo, o garoto de Caratínga. Brasília: Don Quixote Editora e Distribuidora, 1983. 93 p.: photos.

The Horatio Alger story of a black turner-mechanic (b. Minas Gerais, 16 Nov. 1936) who emigrated to Rio de Janeiro in 1960 and five years later made his first LP for Odeon, Surge um astro. After its success he began making one every year. The singer was elected to the Brazilian Congress in 1982. Pretending to call his mother long distance from the congressional floor, he used the incident to call attention to the misery from which he had risen. Seven newspaper articles on the incident preface Timóteo's own reflections, which range widely on drug abuse, homosexuality, and suicide, but never come to grips with music as such.

7080 Veiga, Manuel Vicente Ribeiro. Lançamento: modinha e lundú; Bahia musical, século XVIII e XIX (Art [Univ. Federal da Bahia, Escola de Música e Artes Cênicas, Salvador] 12, dez. 1984, p. 87–105, bibl., ill.)

The outcome of a seminar sponsored by the Centro de Estudos Baianos of the Univ. Federal da Bahia in 1982, was an album of 16 lundús and modinhas by the Conjunto Anticália (four instrumentalists and the soprano, Renata Becker), with the cooperation of singer-instrumentalist, Helder Parent. Liner notes (p. 91–105) provide a gold mine

of documented information, together with lyrics. Every phase of the project reflects highest credit on Veiga and his collaborators.

7081 Veiga, Manuel Vicente Ribeiro. Portuguese chroniclers: Caminha's letter as an ethnomusicological document (Art [Univ. Federal da Bahia, Escola de Música e Artes Cênicas, Salvador] Dec. 1983, p. 3–61, bibl.)

Pedro Vaz de Caminha's letter to King Manuel I dated 1 May 1500 mentions Brazilian Indians playing corno ou vozina ("horn or buzina") during the preaching that followed the first Mass on Brazilian soil. Possibly buzina meant a "shell trumpet" to Caminha (p. 21). Diogo Dias crossed to the other side of the river parallelling the beach, taking with him a bagpipe player from the fleet. To the sound of the bagpipe, he danced with the Indians "who followed its sound very well." On April 30, Indians danced with the Portuguese, to the sound of the tamboril (double membranophone with snares attached to both membranes, p. 33). Among the eight Franciscan friars sent in Cabral's fleet were Frei Maffeu, an organist priest, and Frei Pedro Neto, a chorister. Veiga continues with a superbly documented study of missionary impact on 16th-century Brazil—stressing constantly the role of music. A 1583 festivity at Espírito Santo, described in detail by Fernão Cardim, included the singing and dancing of Indians "in their own way" (p. 49). Sixteenth-century missionary endeavor by no means vanquished all indigenous cultural expressions.

7082 Villaça, Magaly França. Oneyda Alvarenga: apontamentos para uma cronologia e bio-bibliografia (SBM/B, 2, 1984/ 1985, p. 35–46, bibl.)

Very complete chronological overview of the life and publications of musicologist, folklorist, and poet Oneyda Paoliello de Alvarenga (b. Verginhas, Minas Gerais, 6 Dec. 1911; d. São Paulo, 23 Feb. 1984). Fully establishes her as one of the best of her time.

7083 Wanke, Eno Teodoro. Vida e luta do trovador Rodolfo Coelho Cavalcante: biografia. Rio de Janeiro: Folha Carioca Editora, 1983. 322 p.: bibl.

Written by petroleum engineer (b. Paraná, 23 June 1919), this biography of a balladeer (b. 12 March 1919) from a poor family (13 children) in Rio Largo in Alagoas reads like a novel. Mark J. Curran's article in Pro-

ceedings of the Pacific Coast Council of Latin American Studies (5, 1975) identifies him chiefly as "propagandist of the *Literatura de Cordel*." Martine Kunz did a Sorbonne thesis on him in 1982. In 1955, Cavalcante presided at the First National Congress of Balladeers and Guitarists (Primeiro Congresso Nacional de Trovadores e Violeiros) held at Salvador, Bahia. Nothing in Wanke, Curran, or Kunz deals directly with musical aspects of Cavalcante's career.

7084 Widmer, Ernst. Travos e favos (Art [Univ. Federal da Bahia, Escola de Música e Artes Cênicas, Salvador] 13, abril, 1985, p. 63–71)

The Grupo de Compositores da Bahia organized in 1966 took for its motto: "no preconceived principles, no musical dogmas, no avowed systems." In 1979, at the Bienal de Música Brasileira Contemporânea (Sala Cecília Meireles, Rio), Widmer (b. Aarau, Switzerland, 25 April 1927; emigrated to Bahia in 1956) heard his Opus 100, *RELAX: requiem em forma de variações sobre um choral de J.S. Bach*, called "music for a massage parlor." Widmer closes with a call for more controversy, for festivals, editions, recordings, symposia.

THE CARIBBEAN
(except Cuba)

Clarke, Sebastian. Jah music: the evolution of the popular Jamaican song. See *HLAS 47:1030*.

Davis, Martha Ellen. Voces del purgatorio: estudio de la salva dominicana. See *HLAS 47:1041*.

7085 Dower, Catherine. Puerto Rican music following the Spanish American War, 1898: the aftermath of the Spanish American War and its influence on the musical culture of Puerto Rico. Lanham, Md.: Univ. Press of America, 1983. 203 p.: bibl., ill., index.

This book is devoted to disproving Fernando Callejo Ferrer's contention that Puerto Rican music culture suffered a decline during the years 1898–1915. Donald Thompson contests the author's acquaintance with musical life in the island prior to 1898 in his review (see *Latin American Music Review*, 6:1, Spring/Summer 1985, p. 112–117).

7086 Duany, Jorge. Popular music in Puerto Rico: toward an anthropology of *salsa* (LAMR, 5:2, Fall/Winter 1984, p. 186–216)

According to the author, *salsa* "represents a new phase in the evolution of Afro-Hispanic culture: that is the urban-industrial working class; the backbone of *salsa* music is the Puerto Rican proletariat . . . The messages range from Rubén Blades's spirited indictments of inequality and injustice, to the humorous depiction of these issues by El Gran Combo, to the alienated tropical babble of many *salsa* songs."

7087 Gilbault, Jocelyne. A St. Lucian *kwadril* evening (LAMR, 6:1, Spring/Summer 1985, p. 31–57, appendix, bibl., music, photos)

The quadrille (five dances) entered St. Lucia with English colonials in the first half of the 19th century. Quadrille evenings still persist among blacks despite independence in 1979. Instruments include percussion along with strings and winds. Plucked banjo, cuatro, and mandolin strum the harmony. Guitar supplies the bass. Sole complete *kwadril* = quadrille dance tune supplied by the author (p. 52–54) contains no note outside the diatonic scale of F Major. Never hinting at modulation, the brisk 12/8 tune played by violin is accompanied by alternating F and C Major chords (mandolin and banjo) and a guitar bass line outlining those chords. Syncopating *chakchak* imparts its rhythmic urgency to the ensembles.

7088 Jorge, Bernarda. La música dominicana: siglos XIX–XX. Santo Domingo: Univ. Autónoma de Santo Domingo, 1982. 207 p.: bibl., music, photos (Publicaciones de la Univ.; 306. Col. Arte y sociedad; 10)

Designed as a textbook for classroom use, this compilation rests on already published data, not the author's own archival or fieldwork. Martha Ellen Davis's review noted defects as well as strengths of this book (see *Latin American Music Review*, 6:1, Spring/Summer 1985, p. 108–112)

Nagashima, Yoshiko S. Rastafarian music in contemporary Jamaica: a study of socioreligious music of the Ratafarian movement in Jamaica. See *HLAS 47:1094*.

7089 Nolasco, Flérida de. Vibraciones en el tiempo; Días de la colonia. 3a ed. Santo Domingo: Editora de Santo Domingo, 1982. 412 p.: music.

Posthumous publication by prolific doctor of philosophy and letters of the Univ. of Santo Domingo (b. 27 Feb. 1891; d. 12 Feb. 1976) combines two disparate volumes first issued in 1948 (see *HLAS 14:3381*) and 1952 (see *HLAS 18:1795*), and again reissued separately in 1974 by Editora del Caribe. Pt. 1 contains 22 essays of which "Música Indígena," "Instrumentos Tradicionales," "La Expresión Culta en la Música Dominicana," "Las Canciones," "Ritmos Vernáculos," and "En Busca del Origen de los Ritmos Tradicionales" relate most closely to music, so far as titles go. At p. 88, she gives the names of musicians who comprised the cathedral capilla on 11 Aug. 1811 (maestro de capilla: José Tabares; organist: Antonio de Quezada). At p. 135, she names the nine members of the cathedral orchestra on 11 March 1862 (José Agüero, Sebastián Morcelo, José Zoilo del Castillo, violins; Emeterio Arredondo, flute; Juan B. Alfonseca, clarinet; León Polanco, José Mena, horns; Pablo Morcelo, cellist; José Reyes, bass; gives the names that year of the cathedral singers (four adults, four choirboys) and name of the maestro de capilla and organist brought from Puerto Rico, Miguel Herrera. Pt. 2, "Colonial Days," consists of 20 brief articles that rarely touch on music—even when the professed subject is a compendious history of the cathedral of Santo Domingo built between the laying of the cornerstone, 26 March 1521 and 1540. At p. 304, author does list by name seven 16th-century cathedral musicians, but omits their dates and forgoes any citation of authority. Still lacking either analytic or name index, bibliographic footnotes or a bibliography in this third edition, these well-intentioned essays forfeit their potential usefulness. Even the diligent reader finds only relative value in a bald recital of unvalidated names and events. The *Son de Ma Teodora* at p. 37 is a 19th-century forgery exposed as such in 1971 by Mugercia Mugercia (see *HLAS 38:9126*).

Pérez, Nancy *et al.* El Cabildo Carabalí Isuama. See item **2372.**

Reckford, Verena. Reggae, Rastafarianism and cultural identity. See *HLAS 47:1117.*

7090 Saint-Cyr, Jean. Le méringue haïtienne (INIDEF, 5, 1981/1982, p. 62–74, bibl., music)

Antalcidas O. Murat's composed méringue shown as culminating music example

(p. 72) is a verse-and-refrain 2/4 F Major song with vocal range of major 9th. Measures of four eighth-notes are interspersed now and then with bars consisting of two dotted-eighths followed by an eighth.

7091 Stevenson, Robert. Música secular en Jamaica: 1688–1822 (RMV, 4:9–11, enero-dic. 1983, p. 143–151, music)

Article surveys secular aspects of Jamaican musical history up to the time of Simón Bolívar's residence on the island.

Tanna, Laura. African retentions: Yoruba and Kikongo songs in Jamaica. See *HLAS 47:1137.*

7092 Thompson, Donald. La música contemporánea en Puerto Rico (UC/RMC, 38:162, julio/dic. 1984, p. 110–118)

Authoritative review of recent developments by the head of the Univ. of Puerto Rico Music Dept. Devotes special attention to such composers as Héctor Campos Parsi (b. 1922), Amaury Veray (b. 1922), Luis Antonio Ramírez (b. 1923), Rafael Aponte-Ledée (b. 1938), Francis Schwartz (b. 1940), Ernesto Cordero (b. 1946), William Ortiz (b. 1947), Roberto Sierra (b. 1953), and Carlos Vásquez (b. 1952). Esther Alejandro (b. 1947) is the only noted female composer presently active on the island.

7093 Warner, Keith Q. Kaiso!, the Trinidad calypso: a study of the calypso as oral literature. Washington: Three Continents Press, 1982. 155 p.: bibl., disc., ill., music.

Trinidadian author (b. 1943), chaired the Dept. of Romance Languages, Howard Univ., when this book was published (previously Senior Lecturer in French Literature at Univ. of West Indies, St. Augustine, Trinidad). Two music examples—each complete calypsos—are Sparrow's *Welcome to Trinidad* and Shadow's *Sugar plum*, both elegantly arranged by Tony Prospect. The many difficult and controversial aspects of calypso history (e.g., language, political relevance, male and female interplay, humor and fantasy in the lyrics) are treated with rare discernment and in an irenic spirit too often absent from writings on this subject.

CENTRAL AMERICA

7094 Lemmon, Alfred E. Antropología y música (HET, 80, enero/marzo 1983, p. 50–55)

Carroll Edward Mace, professor of Spanish at Xavier Univ. in New Orleans, comments on Guatemalan dance-dramas, of which there are at least 70 types. His 221-page *Two Spanish-Quiché dance-dramas of Rabinal* (see *HLAS 36:899*) provided not only texts in Spanish and Quiché of the dance-comedies *Patzcá* and *Charimex*, but also included music, photos, and detailed information concerning Corpus Christi rituals and dances that have been overlooked by ethnomusicologists.

7095 Melfi, María Teresa. Investigación en Nicaragua (INIDEF, 5, 1981/1982, p. 128–133, ill.)

During Fall of 1980, various field recordings made for INIDEF archive began with 16 songs (marimba, guitar, guitarilla) played 29 Sept. by the Conjunto de Manuel Palacios of Barrio Monimbó in Depto. Masaya. During 8 Dec. celebrations, the most popular songs included *Toda hermosa, Pues concebida, Tú gloria,* and others. At this season the lyrics are hawked about and Nicaraguan recordings are sold and played day and night in many households.

7096 Música en la época colonial en Guatemala: primera antología. Transcripción y comentarios de Dieter Leinhoff. Antigua, Guatemala: Centro de Investigaciones Regionales Mesoamericanas, 1984. 34 p.: bibl., music.

Three short Latin works: Fernando Franco's *Lumen ad revelationem, a 5;* Pedro Bermudes's *Christus natus est nobis, a 4;* and Gaspar Fernandes's Tone 7 *Benedicamus Domino,* are included (p. 9–32). Two vernacular works follow: Manuel Joseph de Quirós's duo of 1747, *Jesús y lo que subes,* and Raphael Antonio Castellanos's villancico, *Pastoras alegres.* This anthology is a brave attempt to do something valid with the extraordinarily rich and diverse Guatemalan musical heritage. See Robert J. Snow's review in *Latin American Music Review* (7:1, Spring/Summer 1986, p. 108–113).

7097 Sider, Ronald R. Contemporary composers in Costa Rica (LAMR, 5:2, Fall/Winter 1984,p. 263–276, music)

Updated study and catalogs of the works of Bernal Flores and Benjamín Gutiérrez, by author whose Univ. of Rochester 1967 dissertation on "The Art Music of Central America" was followed by later exten-

sive research (including four weeks in Costa Rica, summer of 1982).

CHILE

7098 Amenábar Ruiz, Juan. Algunas claves para acercarse al conocimiento del músico: Juan Lémann (UC/RMC, 38:161, enero/junio 1984, p. 47–52)

Trajectory of Lémann's studies (mathematics, architecture, piano, theory, composition), teaching career (Univ. de Chile in the 1960s, Vice-Dean of the Faculty of Arts in 1981), and compositional activities.

7099 Barrientos Pacheco, Lina. "La Cruz de Mayo:" un ritual aymara en el interior de Arica (UC/RMC, 38:162, julio/dic. 1984, p. 119–124, bibl., music)

In the Valley of Azapa, the Cross of May celebration lasts either from the evening of 2 May to the end of the next week, or only a week. The *Adoremos al Señor* (22 strophes), *Gracias a Dios,* and *Alabado sea el Santísimo* consist of verse-and-chorus Spanish music in major keys (many feminine endings). But the indigenes in the valley march to a melody (in 6/8) played by *lichiguayos* (notched flutes) accompanied by *bombo* (doubled-headed frame drum) during the bringing of the cross from the hillside and its return after the week of festival. The intervals in the transcribed melody more or less suggest a reiterated dominant-7th chord over D.

7100 Benson, Andrew. Carta a Don Domingo Santa Cruz (UC/RMC, 37:160, julio/dic. 1983, p. 97–99)

Stimulated by far-seeing Efraín Paesky, the OAS issued the disk OEA-011 ("Tres Compositores Chilenos") containing Domingo Santa Cruz's *Preludios dramáticos* (composed in 1956). Youthful US Navy Officer, Benson's letter to him dated 25 Dec. 1983 documents not only his enthusiasm for the work but also the nonpareil value of Paesky's recording project.

7101 Boswell, Stephen. A visit to Chile (Soundboard [The Guitar Foundation of America, Riverside, Calif.] 12:1, Spring 1985, p. 66–70, ill.)

Report on a paid-expenses trip to Viña del Mar, where the Canadian author competed in an international guitar contest. Contestants were sent by 16 nations. The three

finalists were from Germany, Argentina, The
Netherlands (Germany won).

7102 Bustos Valderrama, Raquel. Carmela
Mackenna Subercaseaux (UC/RMC,
37:159, enero/junio 1983, p. 50–75, music,
port.)

Wife of the diplomat Enrique Cuevas,
from whom she separated in midlife, the
composer (1879–1962) thereafter led a
wanderer's life, finally returning to her natal
city (Santiago) to die there, age 83. Bulk of article contains music analysis. Her official
opus 1 is dated 1929 at Berlin; during the next
five years she produced a stream of privately
published works including *Klavierkonzert*
premiered at Berlin, 21 May 1934, and an unaccompanied *Missa a 4* that in 1936 won second prize in a German composition context.
Includes catalog of works.

7103 Dannemann, Manuel. Autochthonous
musical culture in Chile (World of Music [Bärenreiter Kassel, Basel, Switzerland]
24[i.e. 26]:1, 1984, p. 68–77, bibl., photo)

With his usual authority, Dannemann
surveys what is happening among the 8,500
Aymara and Quechua speakers, 3,000 Atacameños, 430,000 Mapuches, 50 Fuegians,
and 1,700 Polynesians on Easter Island. The
loss of indigenous culture to commercial in-
roads is only delayed by what remaining
tribal pride remains and the continued speaking of aboriginal tongues.

**7104 Exposición: la música en el arte pre-
colombino: 30 de septiembre al 30 de
diciembre, 1982.** Ilustraciones de José Pérez
de Arce. Santiago: Museo Chileno de Arte
Precolombino, Fundación Familia Larraín
Echenique, 1982. 32 p.: bibl., ill.

Some 24 Chilean museums and private
collectors made available ca. 100 precolumbian instruments exhibited at the Chilean
museum. Present catalog includes detailed
drawings of each of these by the excellent
artist José Pérez de Arce, who provided
equally impressive illustrations for Samuel
Claro Valdés's *Oyendo a Chile* (see *HLAS*
42:7100). Whatever pitches can be extracted
from each instrument are usually shown on
a five-line staff with plus- or minus-signs
indicating variants from tempered scale
pitches. Spanish-speaking nations from
Guatemala to Chile were represented with
archaeological specimens.

7105 González Rodríguez, Juan Pablo. Cronología epistolar de Pablo Garrido
(UC/RMC, 37:160, julio/dic. 1983, p. 4–46,
bibl., facsims., ill., ports.)

Important article contains facsimiles
of letters to Pablo Garrido Vargas (b. Valparaíso, 20 March 1905; d. Santiago, 24 Sept.
1982) written by Arnold Schoenberg (27 Feb.
1948), Charles Seeger (2 Sept. 1948), Virgil
Thomsom (20 Sept. 1955), Aaron Copland
(22 April 1975), and various South American
celebrities. Concludes with useful chronology of Garrido's life.

7106 González Rodríguez, Juan Pablo.
Roberto Puelma y la identidad cultural
del músico chileno (UC/RMC, 38:162,
julio/dic. 1984, p. 46–68, bibl., photos)

Roberto Puelma Francini (b. Santiago,
24 March 1893) composed erudite as well
as popular music published by Ricordi in
Buenos Aires (1946) and by Casa Amarilla in
Santiago. Between 1931 and 1956, he directed
10 standard-repertory operas in the Teatro
Municipal. He died at age 83 (in 1976) but
had withdrawn from musical life after retirement at age 70. Includes catalog of works.

7107 Lémann Cazabón, Juan. Consideraciones sobre el medio artístico-musical
y la composición en Chile (UC/RMC,
38:161, enero/junio 1984, p. 35–46)

In this speech delivered at his incorporation as member of the Chilean Academy
of Fine Arts of the Institute of Chile (29 Nov.
1983), Lémann reflects on the influence of a
Chilean composer's ambience on his production and productivity.

7108 Lorenz Abreu, Ricardo. El *Concierto
para violín y orquesta*, Opus 86, de
Juan Orrego-Salas (UC/RMC, 38:162, julio/
dic. 1984, p. 147–153, music)

Premiered 3 Oct. 1984 at the Musical
Arts Center of Indiana Univ., Bloomington,
by the Indiana Univ. Symphony Orchestra directed by Thomas Baldner with the Italian vi-
olinist, Franco Gulli as soloist, this concerto
in three movements (*Allegro gentile, Adagio
espressivo, Allegro rutilante*) has been
described by its eminent composer as an "intimate work, filled with expressions of tenderness, happiness, contemplation, and
drama," and as an opportunity for both virtuoso display and lyrical intensity against an
orchestral background that explores such
novelties as xylophone prominently dis-

played (along with other percussion in the last movement). Frangipani Press, Bloomington, authorized reproduction of the music excerpts.

7109 Merino Montero, Luis. Claudio Arrau en la historia de la música chilena (UC/RMC, 38:161, enero/junio 1984, p. 5–34, bibl., photo)

Authoritative analysis of the favors extended the famous Chilean pianist by his homeland government and other official entities, buttressed by 98 documentary footnotes.

7110 Merino Montero, Luis. Elvira Savi: talento y tenacidad (UC/RMC, 37: 160, julio/dic. 1983, p. 76–78)

Reception speech (Academia Chilena de Bellas Artes, Instituto de Chile, 28 July 1983) delivered for Elvira Savi Federici—pianist who has performed in concert more than 80 works by Chilean composers (piano solo or accompanied by piano) and participated in first Chilean performance of large works by Bartók, Brahms, Ginastera, Mendelssohn, Messiaen, Stravinsky, and Villa-Lobos.

7111 Merino Montero, Luis. En torno al centenario de tres compositores chilenos (UC/RMC, 38:162, julio/dic. 1984, p. 3)

Although all three composers were born in 1884—Alfonso Lang (Santiago, 11 Feb.), Javier Rengifo (Santiago, 17 March), and Enrique Soro (Concepción, 15 July)—Rengifo (whose extensive biographical article in Otto Mayer-Serra's *Música y músicos,* 1947, p. 825–827, contains wrong birth year) inspired no centennial observances. Chilean musicology can tackle no more worthwhile task than rescuing the deeds of such valuable artists as Carmela Mackenna (1879–1962), Próspero Bisquertt (1881–1959), and Carlos Lavín (1883–1962).

7112 Merino Montero, Luis. Nuevas luces sobre Acario Cotapos (UC/RMC, 37:159, enero/junio 1983, p. 3–49, bibl., music)

This superb monographic article on Cotapos (b. Valdivia, 30 April 1889; d. Santiago, 22 Nov. 1969) by a paramount researcher sheds new light on the composer's New York years. Arriving there at the end of 1916, he soon mixed on equal terms with leading musical vanguardists. Supported by

his father, he remained there composing (and having some of his music performed and criticized) until 1924 when he returned to Chile, obtained a diplomatic appointment (Vice-Cónsul de Profesión, worth an annual US $2,000), and then returned to New York for a few months before transferring to Paris (before 10 Oct. 1925). This study corrects the article on Cotapos in *The New Grove* (v. 4, p. 827). As source material, Merino used manuscripts deposited in the Chilean Biblioteca Nacional. Includes catalog of works.

7113 Peña Fuenzalida, Carmen. Aporte de la revista *Marsyas,* 1927–1928, al medio musical chileno (UC/RMC, 37:160, julio/ dic. 1983, p. 47–75, bibl., indexes)

This splendid history of the periodical, *Marsyas,* and analysis of its contents derives from the author's 1982 thesis for the *licenciatura* in musicology. Organ of the Sociedad Bach, *Marsyas* began publication in March 1927 and continued through issue No. 12 (marzo/abril 1928). Seven of the 12 issues contained a musical supplement with pieces by Europeans and in five issues by Chileans (Pedro Humberto Allende, Alfonso Leng, Jorge Urrutia). Although not able to continue for lack of financial support, *Marsyas* was a worthy forerunner of the best musical periodical yet seen in Latin America—*Revista Musical Chilena.*

7114 Peña Fuenzalida, Carmen. Concurso anual de composición del Instituto de Música de la Universidad Católica de Chile, IMUC (UC/RMC, 38:162, julio/dic. 1984, p. 132–138)

The first annual competition for Chilean composers sponsored by IMUC (presided over by Juana Subercaseaux L.) took place in 1978. Usually the terms of the competition are announced in Jan. with a month between July and Sept. of the same year designated for reception of works. Chamber music has predominated in the seven competitions to 1984. The winners have included Wilfried Junge (*Divertimento R.F. 78* for strings and piano, 1978; *Cantata del pan y sangre,* 1980, text by Miguel Arteche); Hermán Ramírez (*Quinteto No. 1,* Op. 61, second prize, 1979; *Concierto* for percussion and chamber orchestra, first prize, 1981); Eduardo Cáceres (*Variaciones: siete velos de un prisma,* chamber orchestra, second prize, 1982); Gabriel Matthey Correa (*Las oca-*

siones de Ema, violin, flute, clarinet, cello, piano, theme with 12 variations, first prize, 1983); Andrés Alcalde (*Mon cher Lit*, clarinet and piano, second prize, 1984).

7115 Peña Fuenzalida, Carmen. Gabriel Matthey Correa, un joven compositor chileno (UC/RMC, 38:162, julio/dic. 1984, p. 69–85, music, photo)

Matthey (b. Santiago, 31 March 1955) won first prize in 1983 in the Sixth Composition Competition sponsored by the Univ. Católica of Chile. Author traces his life, summarizes his esthetics, and analyzes his compositions (1981–84). Includes catalog of works.

7116 Silva Solís, Mario. Alejandro Guarello Finlay (UC/RMC, 37:159, enero/junio 1983, p. 76–105, music, port.)

The subject of the article (b. 21 Aug. 1951) obtained his *licenciatura* in composition from the Arts Faculty of the Univ. of Chile in 1982. A consistent prizewinner, he has already had three-fourths of his oeuvre premiered. In 1975, he began teaching at the Univ. Católica in Valparaíso and from 1980 conducted the composition workshop there and taught harmony at the Pontificia Univ. Católica in the capital. Includes catalog of works.

7117 Silva Solís, Mario. La Facultad de Artes y los compositores chilenos en 1983 (UC/RMC, 37:160, julio/dic. 1983, p. 79–96, music)

In 1983, the Facultad de Artes sponsored 52 performances of works by 32 Chilean composers. Author analyzes works by Eduadro Cáceres, Rolando Cori, Pablo Délano, Jaime González, Sergio Cornejo, and Sergio Díaz.

7118 Van Kessel, Juan. Danzas y estructuras sociales de los Andes. Cuzco, Peru: Instituto de Pastoral Andina, 1982. 315 p.: bibl., ill., music.

Dutch missionary author—who took his doctorate at the Katholieke Hogeschool Tilburg in 1980 with the thesis *Holocausto al progreso: los Aymarás de Tarapacá* (Chile) published that year at Amsterdam—views the "72 religious dances at the great shrines in northern Chile, La Tirana, Las Peñas, and Ayquina" as evidences of a profound Andean cosmic vision. Most of the present volume is taken up with dance diagrams and their in-

terpretation. However, at p. 44–54, the author inserts the music (vocal, instrumental [zampoñas]) for the Baile Moreno sung and danced at Arica. "The music of the zampoñas is of special interest because of its age," according to Van Kessel.

7119 Vásquez de Acuña, Isidoro. Evocación de Don Carlos Lavín (UC/RMC, 38:162, julio/dic. 1984, p. 125–131)

Memories of the composer-ethnomusicologist Lavín (1883–1962) evoked by letters from him (18 Dec. 1956, 12 March 1957, 12 Feb. 1959, 22 Aug. 1960, 1 July 1962) to the author, whose *Costumbres religiosas de Chiloé y su raigambre hispana* (1956), begins with a prologue by Lavín.

COLOMBIA

7120 Friedmann, Susana. Las fiestas de junio en el Nuevo Reino. Prólogo de Joaquín Piñeros Corpas. Bogotá: Editorial Kelley, 1982. 208 p.: bibl., ill., indexes, music.

In addition to Corpus Christi, the saints' feasts celebrated during June in the Real Audiencia de Santa Fé included those of Barnabas, Anthony of Padua, John the Baptist, Peter and Paul (11, 13, 24, 29). With great felicity, the author traces European antecedents for the Corpus Christi and San Juan Bautista observances in Nueva Granada. The three years that she spent gathering material resulted in a fundamental study, excellent throughout, that reaches its climax in the fourth section, *La música de las fiestas de junio*. Here she cites nine polyphonic music examples, 10 incomplete from Europe, one complete (p. 163–171). Written by a Baroque composer presumably based at Bogotá, Miguel Ossorio, the latter is a villancico in Tone VI, *Deseos bien nacidos*, for three trables and continuo, the text honoring San Juan Bautista. Author rightly laments the commercialization of celebrations in present-day Colombia ("El deterioro de las fiestas de junio," p. 144).

7121 List, George. Music and poetry in a Colombian village: a tri-cultural heritage. Bloomington: Indiana Univ. Press, 1983. 601 p.: bibl., disc., ill., music, ports.

Exhaustive report based on the author's ethnomusicological investigations at the village of Evitar, Corregimiento de

Makkates, Depto. de Bolívar. Reviewd in *Revista Musical Chilena* (37:160, julio/dic. 1983, p. 105); *Notes* (41:2, 1984, p. 285–286); *Latin American Music Review* (5:2, 1984, p. 286–289); *Journal of American Folklore* (98:387, 1985, p. 109); and *Western Folklore* (44:1, 1985, p. 62–64).

CUBA

7122 Erin, Ronald. Cuban elements in the music of Aurelio de la Vega (LAMR, 5:1, Spring/Summer 1984, p. 1–32, music)

Following sentences summarize author's argument: "De la Vega's music demonstrates that unique stylistic elements of Cuban music, beyond folk melodies and harmonies, can be successfully utilized in creating a modernist compositional language. Rhythm is primary in his music; his 'vigorous rhythmic cells' that pervade his music are built from the same basic *clave* patterns that give Cuban music its rhythmic essence . . . Polyrhythmic counterpoint and the call-and-response technique are devices of Cuban music that he has translated to contemporary syntax."

7123 Fuentes Matons, Laureano. Las artes en Santiago de Cuba: Laureano Fuentes Matons. Prefacio de Abelardo Estrada. La Habana: Editorial Letras Cubanas, 1981. 464 p.: bibl., ill., indexes, music, ports.

Abelardo Estrada prefaces the republication of Fuentes Matons's 1891 book with a learned study of the author's predecessors, life, and ambience ("Estudio de un Libro, Su Autor y la Orbita de Ambos, p. 113–287). "Apéndices" beginning at p. 349 include Enrique Trujillo's open letter to Fuentes Matons published at New York in *El Porvenir* (20–26 Dec. 1893), a serialized "In Memoriam" published in *El Cubano Libre* (July/Aug. 1915) by fellow townsman Rafael Salcedo, a hitherto unpublished speech given sometime between 1925–29 by Guillermo Tomás in Laureano Fuentes Matons's honor, and a chronological catalog of Fuentes Matons's musical compositions. The indexes range from persons and titles to subjects (p. 429–459). This critical edition deserves highest praise. Henceforth what Estrada has done will rank as a grand monument of Cuban musicology. Serafín Ramírez now awaits a similar revindication.

7124 Martí, José. La música: verdad porque no cesa (Pauta [Univ. Autónoma Metropolitana, México] 4:14, abril/junio 1985, p. 30–43, photos)

Cuban patriot's review of José White's concerts at Mexico City published in *La Revista Universal* (Mexico, 25 May, 1 June, and 12 June 1875), followed by a reprinted *Patria* (New York, 10 April 1892) article concerning Emilio Agramonte.

7125 Ortiz, Fernando. Los bailes y el teatro de los negros en el folklore de Cuba. Prólogo de la 1a ed. de Alfonso Reyes. Prólogo de la 2a ed. de Argeliers León. 2a ed. La Habana: Editorial Letras Cubanas; New York: Ediciones Vital, 1981. 602 p.: bibl., ill., music.

In addition to the prologue of the 1951 first edition by Alfonso Reyes (see *HLAS 17:2861*), this second edition contains a new *prólogo* by Argeliers León that assesses and summarizes what follows (p. 7–24).

7126 Vega, Aurelio de la. Alejo Carpentier's musical phases (IAMR, 5:2, Spring/Summer 1983, p. 17–19)

Biographical information correcting popular legends.

ECUADOR

7127 Correa Bustamante, Francisco José. Cantares inolvidables del Ecuador. Guayaquil, Ecuador: Editorial Arquidiocesana Justicia y Paz, 1982. 402 p.: bibl., ill., music.

Exceptionally fine anthology by attorney who became professor in the Institute of Diplomacy and International Sciences at the Univ. of Guayaquil. Concludes with 12 piano-accompanied songs (lyrics and music). All but one begin with a *pasacalle* (2/4) or *pasillo* (3/4). Composer of each song (except E-flat minor *Reina y señora* by Leonardo Páez and A minor *Chulla Quiteño* by Alfredo Carpio F.) is profiled with exact dates and a picture in the section on "Intérpretes y Compositores." Ages of the composers range downward from Francisco Paredes Herrera (b. Cuenca, 8 Nov. 1891; d. 1 Jan. 1952) whose *passillo Manabí* apostrophizes his native heath and Carlos Brito Benavides (b. Uyumbicho, Pichincha, 12 Nov. 1891; d. Quito, 1943) whose *passillo Sombras* with lyrics by Rosario Sansores ranks as the "best known Ecuadorian song, worldwide." Most recent *cantar* of the 12 is the author's own charming *pasacalle Huigra tierra linda* composed at Guayaquil, 8 Nov. 1982. At p. 15–27, Correa Bustamante summarizes Ecuadorian music history, at p. 32–33 illustrates and defines popular national instruments, and next gives an aperçu of Ecuadorian folk music. Section on the national anthem is precise and accurate, without however going into the details of Neumane's life outside Ecuador. Lyrics that form the bulk of this book often carry fascinating author's notes (p. 66, 97, 112, 134, 155, 159, 209, 273).

7128 Jaramillo Ruiz, Rogelio. Loja: cuna de artistas; monografía sobre la música de la provincia de Loja. Quito: Banco Central del Ecuador, 1983. 470 p.: bibl., music, photos.

Model history of music in Loja province mentions 506 names of composers, performers, and teachers. The musical compositions bear such generic subtitles as *danzante, habanera, jota, pasacalle, pasillo, pasodoble, sanjuanito,* and *vals,* with *pasillos* greatly outnumbering every other type. Author's diligence in gathering precise data can scarcely be overpraised. Carlos Manuel Espinosa's introduction (p. 19–24) dated at Loja, Nov. 1977, presupposed a six-year interval in getting so vast and detailed a history into print. Footnotes locate the author's authorities, but his list of names at p. 465–470 lacks page-references. Reviewed in *Inter-American Music Review* (7:2, Spring/Summer 1986, p. 118–119).

MEXICO

7129 Alberti, Rafael. Retrospectiva crítica en torno a Silvestre Revueltas (HET, 85[17:2] abril/junio 1984, p. 53–54)

Reprint of article from *La Voz* (24 Sept. 1937) welcoming Revueltas to Madrid.

7130 Bellinghausen, Karl. *Verdadera historia* of the *Tesoro, volume II* (IAMR, 5:2, Spring/Summer 1983, p. 99–103)

Fradulent transcription credits and misinformed introductory notes prevented *Tesoro de la música polifónica en México,* t. 2, *13 obras de la Colección J. Sánchez Garza* (México: Centro Nacional de Investigación, Documentación e Información Musical, 1981) from gaining recognition.

7131 Bernal Jiménez, Miguel. He hablado a Stravinski (Pauta [Univ. Autónoma Metropolitana, México] 4:16, oct./dic. 1985, p. 61–67, photos)

Stravinsky's first visit to Mexico; two-part article reprinted from *Schola Cantorum* (Morelia, Mexico, 2:8, 1940, p. 12–14; 2:9, 1940, p. 10–12).

7132 Boilès, Charles Lafayette. A paradigmatic test of acculturation (*in* Cross-cultural perspectives in music. Edited by Robert Falck and Timothy Rice. Toronto, Canada: Toronto Univ. Press, 1982, p. 53–78)

Effort by statistical means to prove the "Indianness" of a Cora melody used in the exposition of Carlos Chávez's *Sinfonía India.*

7133 Carmona, Gloria. En los ochenta años de Luis Sandi (Pauta [Univ. Autónoma Metropolitana, México] 4:16, oct./dic. 1985, p. 48–54, music, photo)

Eightieth birthday tribute to Sandi.

7134 Carrizosa, Selvio. La artesanía de la guitarra en México (HET, 81[16:2] abril/junio 1983, p. 4–9)

Valuable essay on guitar construction in Mexico by professor of guitar playing at the National Conservatory.

7135 Cetrangolo, Aníbal E. Aplicación de su texto nahuátl a un himno de Franco (HET, 80 [16:1] enero/marzo 1983, p. 30–36)

In an unnumbered four-page musical insert after p. 40, Argentine author who teaches at Padua Univ., Italy, adjusts text in a manner that differs from that shown in *Music in Aztec & Inca territory* (1976, p. 211–219).

7136 Chávez, Carlos. El dodecafonismo en México (Pauta [Univ. Autónoma Metropolitana, México] 4:16, oct./dic. 1985, p. 39–43, ill.)

Reprint of article published 5 Nov. 1954. Not himself a serialist, Chávez voiced no arguments in favor of rigid systems.

7137 Cosmos, Angel. Semblanza de Lan Adomián: entrevista a María Teresa Toral Adomián (HET, 83, oct./dic. 1983, p. 20–25, ill., music)

Adomián joined the Lincoln Brigade fighting in Spain during the last days of the Republic. In question-and-answer form, his widow supplies details concerning his musical education, his US experiences, and his creative life in Mexico.

7138 Dallal, Alberto. La danza contra la muerte. 2a ed., corr. y aum. México: UNAM, Instituto de Investigaciones Estéticas, 1983. 322 p.: ill., index (Monografías de arte; 2)

Pt. 2 of three large sections treats modern dance in Mexico; first deals with dance theory, last with distinguished visitors. Although dance music scarcely enters the author's thinking, he does mention in passing Chávez's music having been used for *Tozcatl* and *Mural*, José Pablo Moncayo's for *Zapata*, Silvestre Revueltas's for *Planos* and *Grito*.

7139 Escorza, Juan José and José Antonio Robles-Cahero. Trayectoria de la música en México: lecciones de una grabación universitaria de música novohispana (HET, 89, abril/mayo 1985, p. 39–64, facsims., ill.)

Epoca colonial (vol. 1, discs 1–4), a record collection reproduced by UNAM in 1984 and marked as *Voz viva, Serie música nueva (MN-23)*, was a project coordinated by Uwe Frisch Guajardo (who died before emission of the four discs) and three others. The quality of sound was throughout compromised by mostly mediocre, unidentified live performances. Liner notes wrongly identify transcribers of the music. Disc No. 4 includes badly played works by Corelli and Samuel Trent, not Mexicans. The accompanying booklet is a mine of misinformation.

7140 Escorza, Juan José and José Antonio Robles-Cahero. Two eighteenth-century treatises, at Mexico City, on instrumental music (IAMR, 6:1, Fall 1984, p. 1–28, music)

Both treatises—Joseph de Torres Martínez Bravo's printed *Reglas* (1702) and Juan Antonio Vargas y Guzmán's manuscript, *Explicación* (1776)—exist elsewhere (but not the appendix of 13 guitar and continuo sonatas appended to the latter and published here in facsimile of the manuscript).

7141 Frisch, Uwe. Las siete hojas de Ternari (HET, 83, oct./dic. 1983, p. 17–19, ill.)

Analysis of "Seven Pages of Ternari" [María Teresa] by Lan Adomián (1905–79). This series of album leaves exists in two versions, the first dating from 1967–68 for piano solo, the second (1971) for two pianos.

7142 Huehuetl (*in* The New Grove dictionary of musical instruments. Edited by Stanley Sadie. London: Macmillan Press, 1984, v. 2, p. 258, ill.)

Lacking bibliography, this article is too fragmentary to serve the reader.

7143 Johnson, Tom. El maestro del canon a los 70 (HET, 81[16:2] abril/junio 1983, p. 24–26)

Naturalized Mexican citizen, Conlon Nancarrow's pianola compositions abound in vertiginous canons. In *Estudio No. 24*, by way of example, one voice moves at 80 measures per minute, its answering voice at 110 per minute. The answerer ends sooner than the begetter.

7144 Meierovich, Clara. Génesis y evolución de la Orquesta Sinfónica de México bajo la dirección de Carlos Chávez (HET, 80[16:1] enero/marzo 1983, p. 4–24)

Invaluable synthesis of documents in the Chávez archive at the AGN having to do with the founding in 1928 of the orchestra—after Chávez's return from New York City (where he resided Sept. 1926-June 1928). She concludes with his letter of resignation dated 23 June 1945.

7145 Meierovich, Clara. Jacobo Kostakowsky: apuntes para conocer a un músico olvidado (HET, 82, julio/sept. 1983, p. 4–61, bibl., ill., music)

Definitive study of the composer-violinist (b. Odessa, Russia, 24 Jan. 1893; d. Mexico, 16 Aug. 1953) who arrived at Veracruz, 7 Sept. 1925, and became a Mexican citizen in 1930. Includes catalog of works.

7146 Parker, Robert L. Carlos Chávez, Mexico's modern-day Orpheus. Boston: Twayne Publishers, 1983. 166 p.: bibl., disc., ill., index, music.

Chap. 1 (p. 1–31) recounts Chávez's life, chap. 8 (p. 121–135) contains Parker's summary and conclusion. The rest deals with Chávez's works (solo instrumental, chamber, solo vocal and unaccompanied choral, symphonies and concertos, late orchestral and band, dramatic). Eminent author—holder of his Ph.D. from the Univ. of Texas, Austin—was Assistant Dean of the School of Music at the Univ. of Miami, Coral Gables, Florida, when this sympathetic account appeared. Clara Meierovich favorably reviewed it in *Heterofonía* (83, Fall 1983, p. 51–52). Includes catalog of works.

7147 Velazco, Jorge. La fiesta del fuego de Antonio Gómezanda, 1894–1961 (HET, 84, enero/marzo 1984, p. 40–44, ill.)

Before Carlos Chávez, only Ricardo Castro and Gómezanda among 20th-century Mexicans had any of their orchestral works published in Europe. On 9 Feb. 1928, Gómezanda's Aztec ballet, *Xiuhtzitzquilo* (Fire Feast) premiered at Berlin, and that same year Maurice Senart brought out a piano reduction at Paris. In 1980, Velazco conducted the world première of an orchestral suite from the ballet at Kennedy Center, Washington, D.C. (opening concert of the 22nd Inter-American Music Festival).

7148 Wagar, Jeaninne. La *Sonatina* de Enríquez (Pauta [Univ. Autónoma Metropolitana, México] 4 : 14, abril/junio 1985, p. 60–64, music)

Analysis of insufficiently identified orchestral work in three sections, translated by Leonora Saavedra. A paramount Mexican composer deserves better from this author.

PERU

7149 Bolaños, César et al. La música en el Perú. Prólogo de Edgar Valcárcel. Presentación de Alvaro Llona Bernal. Lima: Patronato Popular y Porvenir Pro-Música Clásica, 1985. 270 p.: bibls., charts, facsims., ill., maps.

César Bolaños, José Quezada Macchiavello, Enrique Iturriaga and Juan Carlos Estenssoro, Enrique Pinilla, and Raúl Romero—authors of the five chief sections (music in ancient Peru, the Viceroyalty, 19th century, 20th century, traditional and popular music)—were all born in Lima (1931, 1951, 1918 and 1964, 1927, 1953) and all agree that any true history of Peruvian music must be written from a Peruvian perspective by Peruvians. According to one contributor (p. 67), a history of Peruvian music remains to be written. However, most readers will accept the present book as a first step towards such a history. Any future edition will profit from an analytic index, bibliography appended to each section ("Viceroyalty" lacks bibliography), overall editing to bring sections into harmony with one another (spelling of names), and especially footnote citations that do not betray the reader. Dates giving only year of birth and death, year of performance, and year of other events, need to be expanded. Edgar Valcárcel wrote the prologue, Alvaro Llona Bernal the *presentación*.

7150 Cuentas Ormachea, Enrique. La Wiphala danza del Departamento de Puno (Boletín de Lima [Editorial Los Pinos] 5 : 9, sept. 1983, p. 45–53, ill.)

Wiphala dance ritual, belonging to carnival season in provinces of Azángaro, Melgar, and Lampa, is both a propitiation of the animals to be killed in chase and a symbol of youthful love. Music accompanying the ritual is of two types: languorous alternating with fast outbursts, played on five-hole *pinkillos* and small drums called *unucaja* ("watered drums"); or fast 6/8 played by a *qasa-qena* sextet or quintet and side drums.

7151 Kike Pinto, Arturo. Instrumentos musicales nativos y mestizos (Boletín de Lima [Editorial Los Pinos] 7 : 40, julio 1985, p. 41–48, bibl., ill., photos)

In this splendid study by renowned collector of instruments, he explains such names as *andara* or *antara, aru, chipli, chisga* or *chioco, cashtaina, choq'ela, erq'e, esquila, huishaco, llungur, mamaq, ndmutá, pampa corneta, phala, phalawita* or *phalawata, pijún* or *pijuq, pinkullo, pinkuyllo, potamentotsi ivotamento, puli, pusi ppia, pututu, qena-qena, quena través, quena wari, rayán, richuvu, roncadora, sanka, siku, tampún, tarawilla* or *jashua, tayka, tinya, turka, waqra puku* or *waka-waqra*, and *wankara*. Also describes how and where these instruments are played and how, when, and why European-derived harps, violins, guitars, woodwinds, and percussion instruments entered both indigenous and mestizo repertories. Last of several photos shows dorse and front of a *charango de kirikincho* from Puno.

7152 Meza, Luis Antonio. Semblanza de un maestro (EC, 27 nov. 1985, p. 2)

Tribute on the 75th birthday of leading immigrant composer, music historian, pedagogue, cataloger, and ethnomusicologist.

7153 Sargent, Denise. Nuevos aportes sobre José Bernardo Alzedo (UC/RMC, 38 : 162, julio/dic. 1984, p. 5–45, bibl., facsims., music)

Cut-down version of the author's *licenciatura* in musicology thesis (1984) goes far beyond previous studies, because for the first time Alzedo's musical production is thoroughly analyzed. Composer's baptismal record of 31 Jan. 1790 certifies his birth at Lima, 19 Aug. 1788, of a free mulatto mother and an unknown father. Illustrated with an abundance of music examples drawn from Alzedo's Good Friday passion and *Miserere mei Deus*, both of 1848, and from his *Gloria laus* and *Christus factus est* of 1849. Splendid essay does the composer of the Peruvian national anthem highest honor and imposes upon Peruvians the duty of publishing integrally some of his masterpieces in the Santiago Cathedral archive.

7154 Schechter, John M. Kena (*in* The New Grove dictionary of musical instruments. Edited by Stanley Sadie. London: Macmillan Press, 1984, v. 2, p. 373–374, bibl., ill.)

Conforming with modern spelling, author discusses present-day notched flute rather than the *quena* or *quena quena* known to the lexicographer Diego González Holguín (1552–1618).

7155 Stevenson, Robert. Perú en las enciclopedias internacionales de música (HET, 83, oct./dic. 1983, p. 4–11)

Coverage of Peru in *The New Grove* compared with Peruvian data in the Spanish translation of *The Oxford companion* and in other international lexicons.

7156 Stevenson, Robert. La primera ópera compuesta en el Nuevo Mundo (HET, 80, enero/marzo 1983, p. 25–29)

Yale College was founded in the same year as the earliest extant New World opera was composed and mounted at the viceroyal palace in Lima.

7157 Turino, Thomas. The urban-mestizo charango tradition in southern Peru: a statement of shifting identity (SE/E, 28:2, May 1984, p. 253–270, bibl., music)

During the post-World War I period, caste distinctions governed mestizos' way of playing the *charango*—a hybrid "created in the Andean region in the colonial period." "The mestizo charango style is fundamentally distinguished by the use of *t'ipi* (a Quechua term meaning to pinch, which refers to a plucked melodic mode of performance)." The older *campesino charanguistas* "played only in the strumming style."

7158 Valencia Chacón, Américo. Análisis musical de la Wifala de Asillo (Boletín de Lima [Editorial Los Pinos] 5:29, sept. 1983, p. 53–56, bibl., music)

The music of the Wifala ceremony

danced in Asillo district, Puno, breaks down into three segments: Pandilla, Guerra Tupay, and Carnaval. *Pinkillos* accompanied by drummers reiterating 16th-notes execute the music in all three segments. What they play is shown in transcriptions that are extremely precise within the limits of staff notation.

7159 Valencia Chacón, Américo. *Jjaktasiña Irampi Arcampi*: el diálogo musical (Boletín de Lima [Editorial Los Pinos] 4:22, julio 1982, p. 8–21, ill., music)

Aymara title of this article means "receiving and taking back between both" and refers to the hocketing that is characteristic of panpipe playing in the high Andes today, and that was its characteristic in Incaic times. The *siku bipolar*, as author calls the two panpipes making a masculine and feminine pair, constantly answer each other back and forth to make a one-line melody (five transcribed examples from the Dept. of Puno illustrate author's point).

7160 Valencia Chacón, Américo. El *siku* bipolar antiplánico: estudio, método y proyección del *siku* o *zampoña* altiplánica; recopilación y aspectos de la música del Altiplano. v. 1, Los *sikuris* y *pusamorenos*. Lima: Editorial Artex E.I.R.L., 1983. 151 p.: bibl., ill., music, photos.

Research for this study centered in the Dept. of Puno (where the author was born). Former studies of Aymara panpipes music neglected present-day practice. Author compares and contrasts indigenous musical style of rural *sikuris* ensembles with urban mestizo style of the *pusamorenos* (present century offshoot of the *sikuris*). Hocket-like panpipes performance-practice is graphically illustrated in the music examples annexed to the fourth section of this study (p. 97–146). Author, an "ingeniero mecánico electricista, especialidad electrónico," is a graduate of the Univ. Nacional de Ingeniería (1963–70) and of Escuela Nacional de Música (1975–82). Book was reviewed by Fernando Villiger in *Boletín de Lima* (5:30, nov. 1983, p. 6) and by Thomas Turino in *Latin American Music Review* (5:1, Fall/Winter 1984, p. 289–293).

7161 Valencia Chacón, Américo. El *siku* bipolar en el antiguo Perú (Boletín de Lima [Editorial Los Pinos] 4:23, sept. 1982, p. 29–48, bibl., ill.)

Continuing the thesis advanced in the July issue, author traces the hocketing technique back to the Moche, illustrating with Vaso Moche No. 1/1331 in the Peruvian National Museum of Anthropology and Archaeology (MNAA) and other Moche *vasos* in it and at the Ethnological Museum in Berlin. Author also offers MNAA *antaras* Nos, 1/1130–1135 (and other museum *antaras*) as evidence that Nazca panpipers formed "orchestral" ensembles playing collectively. Dancers kept strict time to their playing, contends the author.

7162 Villiger, Fernando. Primer mes del folklore peruano (Boletín de Lima [Editorial Los Pinos] 7:40, julio 1985, p. 4)

During June 1985, Banco Continental sponsored six highly acclaimed events held in its auditorium: 1) "Folklore Andino;" 2) "Elementos Autóctonos y Elementos Hispánicos" (Josafat Roel Pineda); 3) "Folklore de la Sierra Central" (Agripina Castro); "El Proceso Socio-Cultural Peruano en la Coreografía Tradicional" (Mildred Merino); 5) "Recitales de Charango y Violín" (Jaime Guardia and Máximo Damián); 6) "Del Folklore Puneño" (Enrique Cuentos Ormachea); 7) "Recital de Guitarra" (Raúl García Zárate).

URUGUAY

7163 Salgado, Susana. Cluzeau-Mortet: tesis de musicología. Montevideo: A. Monteverde y Cía., 1983. 541 p.: bibl., indexes, photos.

Published 18 years after the author defended her thesis at Montevideo in 1965, this extended study of the life and works of Luis Cluzeau-Mortet (1889–1957) was noticed favorably by Gerard Béhague in *Latin American Music Review* (6:1, Spring/Summer 1985, p. 117–119). Book includes none of the composer's music, thus making judgment of his creative merits a matter of faith in Uruguayan critics' opinions.

VENEZUELA

7164 Calzavara, Alberto. Noticias acerca de Cayetano de Castro, primer violoncellista venezolano (RMV, 4:9/11, enero/dic. 1983, p. 285–288)

Cayetano de Castro (b. Caracas, 7 Aug. 1722) became *bajonista* of the cathedral there 2 July 1748 (as successor to Miguel

Cervantes y Román who was probably his teacher). On 12 June 1757, the cathedral *majordomo* reimbursed him for a violoncello bow to replace a defective one. At his death in Caracas, 22 Oct. 1771, he bequeathed a cello and bow to his brother, Fray Juan José de Castro. Throughout his life, Caracas cathedral employed on fixed salaries a *maestro de capilla*, organist, assistant organist, *bajonista*, and three adult singers.

7165 Castillo Didier, Miguel. El instrumento que resonó en el centenario del Libertador: un documento inédito para la historia del órgano dorado (RMV, 4:9/11, enero/dic. 1983, p. 153–171, ill.)

Juan Bautista Plaza discovered the contract of the archbishop of Caracas with the *maitre de chapelle*, Félix Chevreux, dated 6 Jan. 1881, for a two-manual 22-rank cathedral organ (56 keys, each manual) with two-octave pedal, to be built in France. Here reproduced in French original and Spanish translation, the contract called for a total payment of 25,000 francs. Only in 1883 did it function well. Already in 1884 it needed costly repairs, and by 1897 a new smaller Cavaillé-Coll had replaced it in most cathedral services.

7166 Díaz, Alirio. Música en la vida y lucha del pueblo venezolano: ensayos. Caracas: Presidencia de la República, 1980. 214 p., 24 p. of plates: appendices, ill,. music (Consejo Nacional de la Cultura, Instituto Latinoamericano de Investigaciones y Estudios Musicales Vicente Emilio Sojo. Serie Investigaciones; 2)

Collection of essays by the leading Venezuelan guitarist (b. La Calendaria, Carora, 12 Nov. 1923) may attract less attention than it deserves because most articles are reprinted from Caracas newspapers and magazines, and because book lacks an analytic index and even a table of contents. Personages treated include Heraclio Fernández (b. Maracaibo, 1851; d. Caracas, 12 Aug. 1899), Antonio Lauro (b. Bolívar, 3 Aug. 1917), Pedro Montesinos (b. El Tocuyo, 20 Oct. 1864), and Laudelino Mejias (b. Estado Trujillo, Aug. 1893). Appendices contain *inter alia* facsimiles of Heraclio Fernández's *El diablo suelto* and Sebastián Díaz Peña's *Marcela*, both for piano solo.

7167 Guido, Walter. Contribución a la biobibliografía y catálogo de obras musicales de Eduardo Plaza Alfonso (RMV, 4:9/11, enero/dic. 1983, p. 291–327)

Eduardo (b. Caracas, 9 Nov. 1911) was the youngest brother of Juan Bautista Plaza. The famous elder brother conducted the orchestra at Eduardo's wedding ceremony, 12 Oct. 1936. After a distinguished diplomatic and university teaching career, Eduardo died at Caracas, 2 July 1980. Throughout life he composed sacred and secular vocal works, songs, piano, chamber, and orchestral works—many of them performed, recorded, and published (as revealed in Guido's valuable catalog).

7168 Guido, Walter. Ficha biográfica y catálogo de la obra musical de Juan Vicente Lecuna (RMV, 2:3, enero/abril 1981, p. 12–25, port.)

Lecuna's birth date, erroneously given as 20 Nov. 1899 in UTET (Unione Tipográfico Editrice Torinese, 1971) *Riemann Erganzungsband: L-Z* (1975), and *The New Grove* (1980), was actually 20 Nov. 1891 at Valencia, Carabobo State. He was the second in a family of 12 children. On 2 Aug. 1906, he graduated from the Escuela Normal No. 2 de Varones in his hometown with the title Maestro Elemental de Segunda Enseñanza. This article and catalog correct many other dictionary errors.

7169 Milanca Guzmán, Mario. La música en el centenario del Libertador (RMV, 4:9/11, enero/dic. 1983, p. 13–141, bibl., ill.)

Magnificent monograph records musical events of 1883. Preceded by President Antonio Guzmán Blanco's decree of 3 Sept. 1881, the 1883 centennial celebrations for Bolívar's birth were the "grandest, costliest, and most unforgettable in the history of Caracas." On 1 Aug. 1883, the Santa Capilla (presidential chapel) was inaugurated. At its consecration 27 Sept. 1883, the two best women soloists in Caracas sang to the accompaniment a newly installed (Cavaillé-Coll) organ brought from Le Havre on the steamship Ferdinand de Lesseps. The 1883 opera season beginning 1 July with Verdi's *Ernani* was chronicled minutely, not only in the Caracas daily *La Opinión Nacional* by Manuel Revenga, but also in the first solidly music periodical published at Caracas—*La Lira Venezolana* (20 issues by 1883) founded 28 oct. 1882 by Salvador Narciso Llamozas (b. Cumaná, 29 Oct. 1854; d. Caracas, 13 Jan.

1940). After *La traviata, La favorita, Il trovatore, Linda di Chamounix, Il barbiere di Siviglia, Ruy Blas* (1869, by Filippo Marchetti, 1831–1902), *Rigoletto, Lucrezia Borgia, Un ballo in maschera, Aida,* and *Faust,* the season closed 3 Oct. with a benefit for Venezuelan tenor-impresario Fernando Michelena. Crowning contribution by native-born Venezuelan composer to the bicentennial was narrative cantata by Federico S. Villena (1835–99) for voices, orchestra, and military band, *El centenario del Libertador,* performed the night of 24 July in Teatro Guzmán Blanco.

7170 Milanca Guzmán, Mario. Ramón de la Plaza Manrique, 1831?–1886: autor de la primera historia musical publicada en el continente latinoamericana (UC/RMC, 38:162, julio/dic. 1984, p. 86–109, bibl., ill.)

In this exhaustively researched article, the brilliant author confirms the date for Ramón de la Plaza's death at Caracas, 15 Dec. 1886, given in *The New Grove* (vol. 15, p. 5) but documents a birth year of 1831 or 1832 in Aug. The youngest of nine children, he was descended from a family line that as early as 1716 included an alcalde of Caracas. Other hitherto neglected biographical data include de la Plaza's having spent two years in New York City (ca. 1861–63) where he settled with the intention of studying "artes y comercio." On 12 March 1869, six years after returning to Caracas, he married rich Mercedes Ponce Valdés, who after his death erected a sumptuous monument to his memory carved at Genoa by the famous Federico Fabiani (Ulrich Thieme, *Allgemeines Lexikon,* Leipzig, 1915, v. 11, p. 160). Plaza began writing his *Ensayos* in 1879.

7171 Peñín, José. Elementos de canto llano y figurado: un documento para la historia (RMV, 4:9/11, enero/dic. 1983, p. 249–267, facsims., music)

In 1844 while chapelmaster at Mérida, Venezuela, Cathedral, José María Osorio (1803–51) issued a 48-page lithographed plainsong instructor, *Elementos de canto llano y figurado,* dedicated to the Bishop of Mérida, Juan Hilario Boset. Peñín's article contains reductions of it—four pages to a single page.

7172 Ramón y Rivera, Luis Felipe. Del villancico al aguinaldo (INIDEF, 5, 1981/1982, p. 34–42, bibl., music)

After discussing structure of *villancicos* in the *Cancionero musical de Palacio*, the *Cancionero de Upsala*, and orally transmitted *villancicos*, author contrasts it with the structure of the Christmas songs in Vicente Emilio Sojo's *Aguinaldos venezolanos, No. 1*.

JOURNAL ABBREVIATIONS
MUSIC

EC   El Comercio. Lima.

HET   Heterofonía. México.

IAMR   Inter-American Music Review. Published by Robert Stevenson. Los Angeles, Calif.

INIDEF   Revista Inidef. Instituto Interamericano de Etnomusicología y Folclor. Caracas.

IPGH/FA   Folklore Americano. Instituto Panamericano de Geografía e Historia, Comisión de Historia, Comité de Folklore. México.

LAMR   Latin American Music Review. Univ. of Texas. Austin.

RMV   Revista Musical de Venezuela. Instituto Latinoamericano de Investigaciones y Estudios Musicales Vicente Emilio Sojo, Consejo Nacional de la Cultura (CONAC). Caracas.

SBM/B   Boletim. Sociedade Brasileira de Musicologia. São Paulo.

SE/E   Ethnomusicology. Wesleyan Univ. Press *for the* Society for Ethnomusicology. Middletown, Conn.

UC/RMC   Revista Musical Chilena. Univ. de Chile, Facultad de Artes. Santiago.

PHILOSOPHY: LATIN AMERICAN THOUGHT

JUAN CARLOS TORCHIA ESTRADA, *General Secretariat, Organization of American States*

ESTUDIOS SOBRE EL PENSAMIENTO LATINOAMERICANO

LA HISTORIOGRAFIA SOBRE EL pensamiento latinoamericano no presenta mayores cambios con respecto al pasado inmediato, a la vez que sigue siendo un campo cultivado con asiduidad.

En esta entrega, el permanente problema de la filosofía latinoamericana está presente en trabajos de varios autores, como Marcondes César (item **7508**), Dettoni (item **7514**), Montiel (item **7525**), Ossandón (item **7527**), y Zea (item **7540**). Por extensión, dentro del mismo tema podría incluirse el buen artículo de Rodolfo Agoglia sobre historia de las ideas (item **7503**). Con mayor amplitud, el asunto es tratado en el libro de Fornet Betancourt, *Problemas actuales de la filosofía en Hispanoamérica* (item **7518a**). Por último, han contribuido también a este tema algunas de las ponencias presentadas a dos Congresos Internacionales de Filosofía Latinoamericana, celebrados en la Univ. Santo Tomás, de Bogotá (items **7512a** y **7512b**).

Abunda la literatura sobre la posición teológico-política actual de la Iglesia latinoamericana. Teología de la liberación, relación con el marxismo, discusiones sobre las conclusiones de Medellín y Puebla son asuntos que se reiteran. Un panorama muy útil para quien quiera internarse en el tema es *Crisis and change: the Church in Latin America today*, de Edward L. Cleary (item **7511**). En la posición más moderada de Puebla se encuentran, entre los materiales aquí recogidos, *Conflictos y no-creencia en América Latina* (item **7512**), la obra de G.T. Farrell sobre la doctrina social de la Iglesia (item **7517**) y el libro de Alberto Methol Ferré, *Il risorgimento cattolico latinoamericano* (item **7524**). El de Silva Gotay, prologado por Dussel (item **7533**), está de lleno en el cristianismo revolucionario. De naturaleza más general y más vinculada a la historia de las ideas es la obra *Iglesia y cultura latinoamericana* (item **7532**). Los trabajos incluidos en esta sección son sólo algunos de los que pudimos ver, lo que muestra que la literatura no es escasa.

La filosofía de la liberación está representada en esta entrega principalmente por dos autores contrapuestos dentro de la misma tendencia: Horacio Cerutti Guldberg, con su libro *Filosofía de la liberación latinoamericana* (item **7506**) enfoque polémico de conjunto, y Enrique Dussel, especialmente con el vol. 5 de su *Filosofía ética latinoamericana* (item **7515**). Dussel es Coordinador General del *Boletín* que publica la Asociación de Filosofía y Liberación (AFYL), con sede en México. El *Boletín* ilustra sobre la difusión del movimiento y el tipo de adhesión que despierta en ciertos sectores.

Las obras críticas de conjunto más importantes en esta entrega son la de Leopoldo Zea sobre el positivismo latinoamericano (item **7530**), valiosa antología de cuyo primer volumen dimos noticia en *HLAS 44:7558*; y la de Marta Pena (item **7529**) sobre el romanticismo político hispanoamericano, obra de particular interés. También debe destacarse el artículo de Javier Ocampo López sobre la idea de americanidad (item **7526**), el cual se emparenta, por su temática, con el libro de Arturo Ardao sobre la idea y el nombre de América Latina (ver *HLAS 44:7501*).

En el caso de México encontramos dos obras de especial valor: *Cultura mexicana moderna en el siglo XVIII* (item **7551**) de Bernabé Navarro, y *México en el horizonte liberal* (item **7557**) de Abelardo Villegas. Ambas son buenas contribuciones a la historia de las ideas en México. Hernández Luna, por su parte, contribuye a dibujar el perfil intelectual de Samuel Ramos en *Samuel Ramos: etapas de su formación intelectual* (item **7547**).

En el área del Caribe encontramos dos valiosos artículos sobre Pedro Henríquez Ureña por Anderson Imbert (item **7564**) y Zuleta Alvarez (item **7578**). En Cuba y con reiterado enfoque marxista, continúa sus estudios sobre el positivismo cubano Pablo Guadarrama González (items **7571, 7572** y **7573**), en tanto en ese mismo país se ha publicado en español la obra del autor soviético O.C. Ternevoi, *La filosofía en Cuba, 1790–1878* (item **7577**). En lo que respecta a Venezuela continúa el interés por Andrés Bello. Los trabajos de Arturo Ardao (item **7580**) y Javier Sasso (items **7592** y **7593**) son particularmente dignos de mención. Obra documental de gran volumen y utilidad es *El pensamiento político venezolano del siglo XX* (item **7586**), compañera de una edición semejante para el caso del siglo XIX (ver *HLAS 25:3767*). Se destacan también el artículo de Arturo A. Roig sobre Simón Rodríguez (item **7589**) y el libro de Pedro Grases, *La tradición humanística* (item **7583**).

Dos antologías del pensamiento político son lo más importante de lo recogido en relación con Colombia: items **7595** y **7596**.

Dentro de una valiosa colección, y continuando una labor de méritos bien reconocidos, Arturo A. Roig hace una nueva y excelente contribución historiográfica al pensamiento ecuatoriano con *El humanismo ecuatoriano de la segunda mitad del siglo XVIII* (item **7609**).

Prácticamente todo lo que se recoge en esta sección respecto de Perú trata—confirmando una marcada tendencia anterior—sobre Mariátegui. Mencionamos especialmente dos artículos de Carlos Franco (items **7613** y **7614**) y otro de Hugo Neira (item **7619**).

En el caso de Chile merece destacarse el artículo de Iván Jaksic, "Philosophy and University Reform at the University of Chile: 1842–1973" (item **7623**) que es parte de una excelente labor que sobre el tema viene desarrollando este autor.

Dentro de la bibliografía sobre Brasil encontramos buenas obras monográficas sobre Arthur Orlando por Rosa Mendonça de Brito (item **7626**), Alberto Salles por João Ribeiro Júnior (item **7636**), Alcides Bezerra por Francisco Martins de Souza (item **7637**), y Mont'Alverne por Miguel Spinelli (item **7638**). También apareció la tercera edición (ampliada) de la importante obra de Antônio Paim, *História das idéias filosóficas no Brasil* (item **7634**), a la cual nos hemos referido en volúmenes anteriores de este *Handbook*.

Una contribución sin duda significativa en el caso de Argentina es *El movimiento positivista argentino*, compilada y presentada por Hugo Biagini (item **7661**). Este autor es responsable también por un breve pero útil panorama del pensamiento filosófico argentino (item **7648**). En el orden bibliográfico son importantes la obra de Lértora Mendoza (item **7659**) y los índices de la *Revista de Filosofía*, que dirigiera José Ingenieros (item **7663**). Por su parte, Daniel Zalazar continúa su perspicaz revisión de Sarmiento desde el punto de vista de la historia de las ideas (items **7666** y **7667**).

En la literatura sobre el pensamiento en Uruguay satisface notar la atención concedida a Carlos Vaz Ferreira, en una publicación colectiva del Centro de Estudios Latinoamericanos Rómulo Gallegos (item **7643**) y en una reedición de su *Lógica viva* (item **7645**).

BIBLIOGRAFIA FILOSOFICA RECIENTE

Debe considerarse un acontecimiento la aparición del volumen *El análisis filosófico en América Latina* (México: Fondo de Cultura, 1985). La obra es una combinación de antología y estudio crítico, con la particularidad de que prácticamente crea u organiza el campo estudiado, porque no existía nada anterior con esa magnitud y su tema es un fenómeno filosófico reciente, históricamente no decantado. Son sus autores (y las correspondientes áreas geográficas de que se ocupan) los siguientes: Jorge J.E. Gracia (introducción; países andinos; América Central; Caribe; autores latinoamericanos en Estados Unidos y Canadá); Eduardo Rabbossi (Argentina); Enrique Villanueva (México); y Marcelo Dascal (Brasil). Cada parte antológica tiene una introducción, escrita por el autor del caso entre los que mencionamos. En conjunto, estas introducciones conforman la breve historia del movimiento analítico en la región. Los autores incluidos en la parte antológica son: Argentina: C.E. Alchourrón, E. Bulygin, G. Carrió, G. Klimovsky, C.S. Nino, R. Orayen, E.A. Rabbossi, Th.M. Simpson; México: J. Esquivel, H. Margán, C.U. Moulines, M.H. Ortero, A. Rossi, F. Salmerón, R.J. Vernengo, E. Villanueva, L. Villoro; Brasil: B. Barbosa Filho, M. Dascal, L.H. Lopes dos Santos, Z. Loparić, J.P. Monteiro; Otros países: R. Burgos, P. Lluberes, F. Miró Quesada, J.A. Nuño, A. Salazar Bondy, R. Torretti; Estados Unidos y Canadá: I. Angelelli, M. Bunge, H.N. Castañeda, J.A. Coffa, J.J.E. Gracia, E. Sosa. El volumen es una clara muestra de la expansión adquirida por el movimiento analítico (tomando esta expresión en un sentido muy amplio) en América Latina en los últimos 20 o 25 años. No deja de ser interesante señalar el paralelo crecimiento de esta corriente (o más bien modalidad) filosófica y el de otra de signo tan distinto como la filosofía de la liberación. Podríamos decir que ambas constituyen las antípodas de la filosofía latinoamericana actual.

Con la filosofía analítica ingresó a América Latina la influencia del mundo filosófico de habla inglesa, anteriormente mucho menos actuante que el pensamiento francés o el alemán. El grupo analítico presenta una intensa cohesión interna y actualmente se encuentra bien representado en el plano académico-institucional, especialmente en México y Argentina.

La filosofía hoy, en Alemania y en América Latina es una publicación del Círculo de Amigos del Instituto Goethe, de Córdoba, Argentina, resultado de unas Jornadas realizadas en 1983 y cuyo contenido se publicó en 1984. Ernildo Stein, de Brasil, escribe allí sobre Gadamer y Habermas. Ricardo Maliandi se ocupa de la ética en la filosofía alemana actual y, en un segundo artículo, de la polémica entre el "racionalismo crítico" (Hans Albert) y la "pragmática trascendental del lenguaje" (Karl-Otto Apel). Concluye la parte dedicada a Alemania un trabajo de Mario A. Presas, "Investigaciones Actuales sobre Fenomenología y Hermenéutica en la República Federal de Alemania."

La parte correspondiente a la filosofía latinoamericana contiene tres trabajos de Jorge J.E. Gracia: "Panorama General de la Filosofía Latinoamericana Actual," síntesis muy útil, cuyos juicios de valoración responden a la orientación analítica; "El Problema de la Identidad Filosófica Latinoamericana: Perspectiva e Historia," análisis crítico de las posiciones que se han sustentado en relación con este debatido tema; y "El Análisis Filosófico en América Latina," que es parte de la introducción que el autor escribiera para *El análisis filosófico en América Latina*, antes mencionado. Ernildo Stein traza un sintético panorama de la filosofía brasileña en "A Filosofía no Brasil." El volumen concluye con sendos trabajos sobre la investigación filosófica en Buenos Aires, de Mario A. Presas, y sobre la filosofía en Tucumán, de Lucía Piossek Prebisch. En conjunto es un volumen valioso.

Con *Cultura y conflicto: investigaciones éticas y antropológicas* (Buenos Aires: Editorial Biblos, 1984), Ricardo Maliandi ofrece el resultado de una meditación sostenida sobre el tema. Se compone de ocho trabajos, algunos publicados previamente y otros inéditos, producidos en 1974–83. Más allá de eso, la obra quiere ser un primer paso hacia el análisis sistemático de la conflictividad y, sin pretender hacer de este fenómeno "el fundamento último de toda la realidad," el autor considera que la conflictividad puede ser "un lícito recurso metodológico para enfocar o afrontar algunas importantes cuestiones de la filosofía." Se trata de una obra de auténtica calidad filosófica, aun moviéndose entre lo crítico y lo sistemático.

Como vol. 12 de las *Obras completas* de José Gaos apareció *De la filosofía*, una de las contribuciones más importantes de dicho autor (México: UNAM, 1982). Corresponde a un curso dictado en 1960. Se publicó por primera vez en 1962. El excelente prólogo de Luis Villoro aclara el significado de la obra y destaca su valor, a la vez que la sitúa dentro del pensamiento de habla española. Gaos estaría, según Villoro, en el deslinde de dos épocas: la de su formación como filósofo—durante su etapa española y los primeros años de su estancia en México, coincidente con la influencia de la filosofía alemana de las primeras décadas del siglo—, y la actual, de gustos filosóficos diferentes. Uno de los rasgos de la "modernidad" de Gaos sería su preocupación por el problema del lenguaje.

Claudio Gutiérrez, de Costa Rica, señalado por Jorge J.E. Gracia como el representante centroamericano más destacado de la corriente analítica, ha publicado *Nueve ensayos epistemológicos* (San José: Editorial Costa Rica, 1982). Los trabajos fueron escritos entre 1966 y 1979. Los más importantes se refieren a filosofía de la lógica y, en general, casi todos tienen un sesgo epistemológico. Por su parte, Julia Barragán señala que *Hipótesis metodológicas* (Prólogo de Ernesto Garzón Valdés. Caracas: Editorial Jurídica Venezolana, 1983), es "un trabajo de Metodología de la Investigación Empírica en el área de las Ciencias Humanas."

Filosofía y vida se titula el vol. 6 de las *Obras* de Ismael Quiles (Buenos Aires: Depalma, 1983). Contiene los siguientes trabajos: *Filosofar y vivir*, publicado originalmente en 1948 y reeditado en 1962; *¿Qué es la filosofía?* (1955, 1966, y 1972 en edición ampliada); "Ciencia, Filosofía y Religión" (1982); y "Clasificación y Coordinación de las Ciencias" (1954).

En *Cuestiones de estética* (Buenos Aires: Correo de Arte, 1979), Rosa María Ravera manifiesta que su intento es reunir lo filosófico con lo científico. Así, las dos principales partes de la obra se denominan "Estética y Ontología" y "Estética y Semiótica," respectivamente. La primera contiene sendos ensayos sobre Bergson y Heidegger. Algunos de los estudios de la segunda parte son: "La Especificidad del Signo Pictórico," "El Arte como Lenguaje," y "¿Más Acá de los Códigos?," todos de alguna manera vinculados a la temática semiológica, en tanto el ensayo "Interrelación de las Disciplinas Científicas y Filosóficas" es expresivo de la idea básica del volumen.

Discusión sobre ideología, de Ipola, Abouhamad y Lanz (Caracas: Ediciones Faces, 1981) contiene tres trabajos: Emilio de Ipola, "Crítica a la Teoría de Althusser sobre la Ideología," cuya conclusión es que para fundar la teoría de las ideologías deben buscarse otras bases que las althusserianas; Jeannette Abouhamad, "Incursiones Teóricas para Fundar, Teoréticamente una Teoría Crítica de la Ideología," con base en Lacan y Habermas; y Rigoberto Lanz, "Ideología y Marxismo," continuación de un libro anterior: *Dialéctica de la ideología* (1975).

La UNAM publicó, 1981–82, la *Memoria del X Congreso Mundial Ordinario de Filosofía del Derecho y Filosofía Social* (1981), en varios volúmenes. Los temas especiales fueron, entre otros, "Filosofía del Derecho y Filosofía de la Cultura," "Filosofía del Derecho y Problemas de Filosofía Social," "Filosofía del Derecho y Filosofía Económica y Política."

El tema de la teoría de la filosofía es retomado por Bento Prado Jr., Oswald Porchat Pereira y Tercio Sampaio Ferraz Jr. en *A filosofia e a visão comum do mundo* (São Paulo: Editora Brasiliense, 1981).

En *La ideología anarquista* (Caracas; Barcelona: Alfadil Ediciones, 1985), Angel J. Cappelletti da una visión global de esta doctrina, con intención didáctica. Especialista en temas de filosofía griega, una vertiente de su producción ha sido, sin embargo, la difusión del pensamiento anarquista. Obras anteriores en la misma línea son: *Etapas del pensamiento socialista* (Madrid: La Piqueta, 1978); *Francisco Ferrer y la pedagogía libertaria* (Madrid: La Piqueta; México: Editores Mexicanos Unidos, 1980); *La teoría de la propiedad en Proudhon y otros momentos del pensamiento anarquista* (Madrid: La Piqueta; México: Editores Mexicanos Unidos, 1980); y *Prehistoria del anarquismo* (Madrid: Queimada Editores, 1983). Dentro de su principal línea de investigación ha publicado recientemente *La filosofía de Anaxágoras* (Caracas: Sociedad Venezolana de Filosofía, 1984), volumen que contiene, con un amplio aparato de notas, una traducción de los testimonios y los fragmentos, y una exposición de la filosofía de dicho filósofo.

Como vol. 5 de la Biblioteca do Pensamento Brasileiro, Miguel Reale reunió y prologó escritos de Leonardo Van Acker, con el título: *O tomismo e o pensamento contemporâneo* (São Paulo: Editora Convivio: Editora da Univ. de São Paulo, 1983). Dividido en dos partes, la primera contiene estudios sobre el tomismo. La segunda se define por su título: "El Diálogo del Tomismo con la Filosofía Contemporánea," y en ella se confronta la doctrina tomista con Bergson, Blondel y Dewey, entre otros. Reale señala precisamente que Van Acker no se quedó en un tomismo inalterado, sino que más bien lo utilizó para apreciar otras corrientes contemporáneas.

Se comprende que como natural extensión de la revaloración de la lógica medieval, ocurrida en años recientes, exista también interés en la filosofía del lenguaje vinculada a aquella lógica, y en general a la filosofía escolástica. Mauricio Beauchot, en *La filosofía del lenguaje en la Edad Media* (México: UNAM, 1981), presenta un oportuno panorama, abarcando desde el siglo XII hasta el XVI, con útil bibliografía.

Guillermo Malavassi presenta, en traducción suya al castellano, *El libre albedrío*, de San Agustín (San José: Cooperativa Universitaria de Libros, Univ. de Costa Rica, 1983). Contiene una introducción del propio Malavassi y un cuadro cronológico de las obras de San Agustín.

En *Entre la ontología y la antropología filosófica* (Mendoza, Argentina: Univ. Nacional de Cuyo, 1981), Diego F. Pro recoge varios trabajos, de franca inspiración aristotélica y en su mayoría dedicados al tema de la metafísica.

Pessoa e existência: iniciação ao personalismo de Emmanuel Mounier (São Paulo: Editora Autores Asociados: Cortez Editora, 1983), de Antônio Joaquim Severino, es una monografía panorámica sobre la obra de Mounier, con indicaciones biográficas y una útil bibliografía. Resulta una buena introducción al asunto.

Por último, Alfonso Florez Florez, en *La ética de Meister Eckart* (Bogotá: Facultad de Filosofía, Pontificia Univ. Javeriana, 1983), presenta una buena monografía basada en la obra alemana de Eckart, especialmente las *Reden der Unter-schriding* y el *Liber "Benedictus."*

A todo lo anterior hay que sumar una copiosa producción en revistas, que mantiene las características que hemos señalado en otras oportunidades y que sería muy difícil de abarcar en esta sintética introducción.

GENERAL

7501 Abello, Ignacio. Condiciones para un pensamiento latinoamericano (in Unité et diversité de l'Amérique latine. Bordeaux, France: Univ. de Bordeaux III, 1982, t. 2, p. 77–91)

La preocupación del autor se refiere a "las posibilidades de una reflexión sobre nuestra práctica social." Propone aplicar el principio de diferencia y no el de identidad, pues este último fue aplicado por los dominadores para imponer sus modelos y sus valores, sirviéndose, paradójicamente, de la doctrina de la igualdad de todos los hombres.

7502 Acosta Rodríguez, Antonio. Religión, ideología y colonización española en América: siglo XVI y XVII (in Unité et diversité de l'Amérique latine. Bordeaux, France: Univ. de Bordeaux III, 1982, t. 2, p. 3–19, bibl.)

En la medida en que la religión fue parte esencial de la cosmovisión de los conquistadores—religiosos y laicos—se utilizó en el andamiaje de ideas y justificaciones para la conducta que se adoptaba; o , en palabras del autor, funcionó como una ideología. En señalarlo así consiste el sentido del presente trabajo.

7503 Agoglia, Rodolfo M. El estudio histórico de las ideas (PAIGH/H, 98, julio/dic. 1984, p. 99–104)

A pesar de su brevedad, es uno de los mejores artículos que se han escrito recientemente sobre la frecuentada cuestión de la Historia de las Ideas en América Latina. Destaca especialmente la transformación que las ideas sufren al convertirse en instrumentos de la praxis histórica.

7504 Arciniegas, Germán. Los pinos nuevos: diario de un sonámbulo enamorado. Tunja, Colombia: Editorial Bolivariana Internacional: Instituto de Estudios para el Desarrollo y la Integración de América Latina, 1982. 515 p. (Serie Fundamentos y doctrina; 3. Publicaciones del Instituto)

Conjunto muy numeroso de artículos periodísticos, todos sobre temas americanos. Mezcla la información histórica, el comentario y la habitual simpatía del autor por todo lo que pertenece a América Latina.

Bolívar, Simón. Simón Bolívar, la vigencia de su pensamiento. See item **2848.**

Cardoso, Fernando H. *et al.* Medina Echavarría y la sociología latinoamericana. See *HLAS 47:8007.*

7505 Castillo Velasco, Jaime. Dialéctica entre democracia y dictadura en el pensamiento político latinoamericano. Santiago: Editorial Aconcagua, 1984. 67 p.

Contiene dos trabajos: 1) el que da título al libro, una fundamentación general de la doctrina democrática, y 2) un discurso de homenaje al líder de la democracia cristiana chilena, Eduardo Frei.

7506 Cerutti-Guldberg, Horacio V. Filosofía de la liberación latinoamericana. México: Fondo de Cultura Económica, 1983. 326 p.: bibl., ill. (Col. Tierra firme)

Probablemente la obra de más amplio contenido sobre la filosofía de la liberación. Tiene, sin embargo, un intenso tono polémico. El principal blanco de esa polémica actitud es el llamado sector "populista" de la filosofía de la liberación, algunos de cuyos autores son J.C. Scannone, O. Ardiles, M. Casalla, R. Kusch, y muy especialmente E. Dussel, sin agotar la lista. Hay también capítulos sobre la teoría de la dependencia, la teología de la liberación y los antecedentes de la filosofía de la liberación. Es previsible la crítica de otros sectores de la misma corriente al enfoque del autor. La obra es presentada, con simpatía, por Leopoldo Zea.

7507 Cerutti-Guldberg, Horacio V. La manifestación más reciente del pensamiento latinoamericano (CH, 379, enero 1982, p. 61–85)

Con la salvedad de que el autor es parte del proceso (y de las polémicas) que describe, y que esto, naturalmente, puede influir en sus juicios, el panorama que traza es aprovechable. Distingue cuatro corrientes principales de la filosofía de la liberación.

7508 Cesar, Constança Marcondes. Filosofia na América Latina: polémicas (Reflexão [Pontificia Univ. Católica de Campinas, Instituto de Filosofia e Teologia] 9 : 30, set./dez 1984, p. 51–61, bibl.)

Ilustra, seleccionando algunos autores, sobre las dos principales modalidades del pensamiento latinoamericano actual: la "universalista" y la "filosofía de lo americano." En esta última incluye la filosofía de la liberación.

7509 Chavarri, Raúl. Ortega y América (CH, 403/405, enero/marzo 1984, p. 361–374)

Datos sobre el asunto, divididos en dos partes: testimonios de la repercusión de Ortega en sus viajes a América, y escritos de Ortega sobre la realidad hispanoamericana.

7510 Chevalier, François. Un positivisme specifique comme modèle d'integration culturelle en Amérique latine, XIX–XX siècles (in Unité et diversité de l'Amérique latine. Bordeaux, France: Univ. de Bordeaux III, 1982, t. 2, p. 53–75)

Destaca la magnitud y la peculiaridad del positivismo latinoamericano. Tomando unos cuantos ejemplos, contribuye a aclarar ciertas cuestiones, como la orientación positivista de la enseñanza secundaria, el aspecto político, el religioso, etc. Señala temas que requerirían mayor estudio. Trabajo de lectura recomendable.

Chilcote, Ronald H. Theories of development and underdevelopment. See *HLAS 47 : 2804.*

7511 Cleary, Edward L. Crisis and change: the Church in Latin America today. Maryknoll, N.Y.: Orbis Books, 1985. 202 p.: bibl., index.

Claro y, en general, equilibrado resumen del pensamiento religioso latinoamericano desde Medellín hasta Puebla (y sus antecedentes) incluyendo un capítulo central sobre la teología de la liberación. También se refiere a las relaciones de la Iglesia latinoamericana con sus adherentes laicos y las masas. Util por la cantidad de información contenida en un solo volumen.

7512 Conflictos y no-creencia en América Latina: hacia una superación a la luz de Puebla. Bogotá: CELAM, 1983. 244 p.: bibl., ill. (CELAM; 63)

El libro es una síntesis—clara, sistemática y un tanto didáctica—de trabajos individuales presentados previamente a un seminario. La posición es la de la Iglesia comprometida, pero en la dirección de Puebla, no en la de Medellín o la teología de la liberación. Los conflictos a que se refiere el título son los que la Iglesia puede tener con otras doctrinas (especialmente económicas, políticas y sociales), y aun dentro de la misma Iglesia.

7512a Congreso Internacional de Filosofía Latinoamericana, 1st, Bogotá, 1980. Ponencias. Bogotá: Univ. Santo Tomás, Centro de Enseñanza Desescolarizada, 1981. 388 p.: bibl., ill.

Algunas de las ponencias de mayor interés para el estudio del pensamiento latinoamericano son las siguientes: Leopoldo Zea, "La Historia de la Filosofía Latinoamericana;" María Luisa Rivara, "Filosofía e Ideología en Latinoamérica;" Hilton Japiassu, "¿Para Dónde Va la Filosofía en América Latina?;" Samuel Guerra Bravo, "El Pensamiento Ecuatoriana en los Siglos XVI, XVII y XVIII" (ver *HLAS 44 : 7545*); Constanza Marcondes César, "Vicente Ferreira da Silva y el Pensamiento Suramericano" (ver *HLAS 44 : 7532*); Gabriel Vargas Lozano, "La Función Actual de la Filosofía en México: la Década del Setenta;" Juan Mora Rubio, "Proyecto y Perspectivas de la Filosofía en México;" Jaime Rubio Angulo, "Hermenéutica y Crítica en el Filosofar Latinoamericano Actual;" Enrique Hernández, "Concepto y Método en la Filosofía Latinoamericana Actual;" Francisco Beltrán Peña, "Perspectivas de una Antropología Filosófica Latinoamericana;" Germán Marquínez Argote, "Horizontes Históricos de la Metafísica: hacia una Metafísica desde Latinoamérica;" Luis J. González Alvarez, "José Ingenieros: un Idealismo Etico en Función de la Experiencia Social;" Mario Sambarino Silva, "Sobre la Imposibilidad de Fundamentar Filosóficamente una Ética Latinoamericana" (ver *HLAS 46 : 7532*); Juan Carlos Socamanno, "Del Vino y los Odres o Destrucción y Novedad en la Etica de Dussel;" Roberto J. Salazar Ramos, "Perspectivas de la Filosofía Política en América Latina."

7512b Congreso Internacional de Filosofía Latinoamericana, 2nd, Bogotá, 1982. Ponencias. Bogotá: Univ. Santo Tomás, Facultad de Filosofía, Centro de Enseñanza Desescolarizada, 1983. 455 p.: bibl., ill.

Destacamos algunas ponencias vinculadas más directamente al estudio del

pensamiento filosófico latinoamericano:
Arturo A. Roig, "Momentos y Corrientes del
Pensamiento Humanista durante la Colonia
Hispanoamericana: Renacimiento, Barroco e
Ilustración;" Walter Redmond, "Filosofía Tra-
dicional y Pensamiento Latinoamericano: Su-
peración y Vigencia;" Germán Marquínez
Argote, "La Ilustración en Colombia;"
Samuel Guerra Bravo, "Las Ideas Positivistas
en el Ecuador;" Miguel da Costa Leiva, "Las
Ideas Filosóficas en Chile en el Siglo XIX;"
Roberto J. Salazar Ramos, "Características de
la Reacción Antiutilitarista y Antipositivista
en Colombia;" Enrique Rocha Franz, "El Des-
tino de Nuestra Esencia en Cuanto Latino-
americana;" Alberto Cárdenas Patiño, "Hans
Kelson y su Influjo en el Pensamiento Jurí-
dico Colombiano;" Enrique Dussel, "Hipó-
tesis para una Historia de la Filosofía en
América Latina, 1492–1982;" Víctor R.
Martín, "Criterios sobre la Historia de las
Ideas Filosóficas en América Latina y su
Aplicación a la Investigación Regional."

7513 Cornejo, José. La identidad latinoamericana de la teología de la liberación: ¿autenticidad u organicidad? (SP, 27,
set. 1984, p. 103–112)
Lo propio latinoamericano de la teología de la liberación es establecer "una
relación de organicidad con la praxis de
liberación del pueblo latinoamericano."
Señala diferencias con la teología populista y
la filosofía de la liberación de autores argentinos recientes.

7514 Dettoni, José. Filosofia latinoamericana: imitação e autenticidade
(Reflexão [Pontifícia Univ. Católica de
Campinas, Instituto de Filosofia e Teologia]
8:26, maio/agôsto 1983, p. 25–31)
Responde a la concepción "universalista" de la filosofía latinoamericana. Esta
será propia no por negación del pasado europeo, sino por realizar un aporte al pensamiento mundial.

**The Discourse of power: culture, hegemony,
and the authoritarian State.** See HLAS
47:8344.

7515 Dussel, Enrique D. Filosofía ética
latinoamericana. v. 5, Arqueológica
latinoamericana: una filosofía de la religión
antifetichista. México: Editorial Edicol,
1980. 175 p.: bibl. (Col. Filosofía y liberación
latinoamericana; 6)

"Arqueológica" se entiende como el
logos de la arjé (principio, comienzo). El trabajo principal del volumen fue escrito en
1970. Se agregan dos apéndices: "Religión
como Supraestructura y como Infraestructura" (1976) y "El Ateísmo de los Profetas y
de Marx" (1971).

7516 Dussel, Enrique D. Respondiendo algunas preguntas y objeciones sobre
filosofía de la liberación (Reflexão [Pontifícia
Univ. Católica de Campinas, Instituto de
Filosofia e Teologia] 8:26, maio/agôsto 1983,
p. 15–24, bibl.)
Las respuestas que ofrece contribuyen
a clarificar la posición del autor dentro de la
filosofía de la liberación.

**El Ensayo político latinoamericano en la for-
mación nacional.** See HLAS 47:6010.

7517 Farrell, Gerardo T. Doctrina social de
la Iglesia: introducción e historia de
los documentos sociales pontificios y del
episcopado latinoamericano y argentino.
Buenos Aires: Editorial Guadalupe, 1983. 221
p.: bibl. (Col. Comunión y participación)
Resume, aclara y ofrece el contexto
histórico de los documentos recogidos, incluyendo los de Medellín y Puebla. Dentro de la
polarización actual de la Iglesia, la posición
corresponde al ala no radicalizada.

Filippi, Alberto. Las interpretaciones cesaristas y fascistas de Bolívar en la cultura
europea. See item **2855.**

7518 Filippi, Alberto. La relación Hegel-
Marx y las interpretaciones de la historia latinoamericana (Historias [Dirección de
Estudios Históricos, Instituto de Antropología e Historia, México] 2, oct./dic. 1982,
p. 102–112)
Se refiere principalmente a los escritos
de José Aricó que estudian las opiniones de
Marx sobre América Latina. La obra de Aricó
es Marx y América Latina (México: Alianza,
1982).

7518a Fornet Betancourt, Raúl. Problemas
actuales de la filosofía en Hispanoamérica. Buenos Aires: Fundación el Estudio
del Pensamiento Argentino e Iberoamericano
(FEPAI), 1985. 173 p.: appendix.
Se compone de cinco capítulos, sobre
los siguientes temas: 1) la existencia de una
filosofía hispanoamericana; 2) la autenticidad
de esta filosofía; 3) América como problema;

4) el problema de los valores (en la filosofía hispanoamericana); y 5) la filosofía de la liberación. El método, que se reitera en cada capítulo, consiste en exponer con amplitud las opiniones de los principales autores y, al final y brevemente, extraer una conclusión propia. El autor participa de la posición "universalista" en la concepción de la filosofía latinoamericana. El apéndice bibliográfico es útil.

7519 Guardia, Roberto de la. El estado de la cuestión hispanoamericana después de Bolívar (LNB/L, 348/349, marzo/abril 1985, p. 5-51, bibl.)

Sobre el tema de la realidad hispanoamericana y su interpretación. Las referencias no son siempre de primera mano. Puede ser útil como inventario, pues abraza varios aspectos del asunto.

Kaplan, Marcos. La teoría del Estado en la América Latina contemporánea: el caso del marxismo. See *HLAS 47:8018.*

7520 Lancha, Charles. El ideal unionista latinoamericano en Bolívar y Martí (*in* Cuba: les étapes d'une libération. Hommage à Juan Marinello et Noël Salomon: actes du Colloque international des 22, 23 et 24 novembre 1978. Toulouse, France: Centre d'études cubaines, Univ. de Toulouse-Le Mirail, 1979, v. 1, p. 197-219)

Puede utilizarse como guía del tema unionista en los dos personajes elegidos. En el caso de Martí, su anti-imperialismo se interpreta con resonancias modernas y procubanas.

7521 Leenhardt, Jacques. Le mythe de la France libérale en Amérique latine (UTIEH/C, 42, 1984, p. 7-14)

La idea de la "Francia liberal" es compleja, y algunos de sus componentes son contradictorios entre sí. Sin embargo, este "mito," según el autor, ha influído en el pensamiento latinoamericano, aunque a la hora de construir modelos constitucionales lo más influyente en América Latina ha sido la tradición británica.

7522 Martinière, Guy. L'invention de la "latinité" de l'Amérique (*in* Unité et diversité de l'Amérique latine. Bordeaux, France: Univ. de Bordeaux III, 1982, t. 2, p. 21-27)

El tema es tratado brevemente, y no tanto desde el punto de vista de la historia de la cultura o de las ideas como desde el ángulo de las relaciones internacionales de poder.

7523 Marzal, Manuel. El problema indígena en Lombardo Toledano y Mariátegui (SP, 11, sept. 1980, p. 209-216)

Aunque solamente descriptivo de la posición indigenista de Lombardo Toledano en México y de Mariátegui en Perú, el artículo es de utilidad.

7524 Methol Ferré, Alberto. Il risorgimento cattolico latinoamericano. Bologna, Italy: Centro studi Europa Orientale, 1983. 266 p. (CSEO incontri. CSEO biblioteca)

Nueve trabajos sobre problemas actuales de la Iglesia latinoamericana, durante el lapso que media entre Medellín (1968) y Puebla (1979). El autor evidentemente adhiere al espíritu de Puebla. Los artículos fueron publicados originalmente en español. Según el interés de esta sección del *HLAS*, destacamos los artículos "Scienza e Filosofia in América Latina" y "Sviluppi della Sociologia Latinoamericana."

Montaner, Carlos Alberto. América Latina y USA. See *HLAS 47:7073.*

7525 Montiel, Edgar. Three decisive battles for Latin American philosophy (UNESCO/CU, 8:2, 1982, p. 131-147)

Una filosofía latinoamericana debe hacer de la historia de América Latina la principal fuente de su reflexión. Las tres "batallas" aludidas en el título son: creación contra imitación, actitud crítica contra receptividad e identidad contra "aculturación." Aunque es una posición más cercana al "americanismo" filosófico que al "universalismo," tiene características peculiares.

7526 Ocampo López, Javier. Historia de la idea de la americanidad en los pensadores colombianos (ACH/BHA, 70:740, enero/marzo 1983, p. 130-151)

Provee abundante información sobre el tema, desde el siglo XVIII hasta la obra de Germán Arciniegas. Interesa no sólo para la idea de América, sino también para la historia de sus nombres.

7527 Ossandón B., Carlos. Hacia una filosofía latinoamericana. Santiago: Nuestra América Ediciones, 1984. 96 p.: bibl.

Contiene cuatro trabajos previamente publicados: "¿Qué Entender por una 'Filosofía Americana'?;" "Acerca del Sentido de la Filosofía Latinoamericana;" "Alejandro Venegas y las Posibilidades de un Pensamiento Nacional;" "El Concepto de 'Normalidad Filosófica' en Francisco Romero." De orientación americanista y cercano a la filosofía de la liberación.

Pabón Núñez, Lucio. Bolívar: alfarero de repúblicas. See item **2857.**

Paladines, Carlos. Notas sobre "modelos" de conocimiento de la cultura latinoamericana en la tradición universitaria alemana. See *HLAS 47 : 125.*

7528 Peña, Horacio. *La raza cósmica* y *Pueblo enfermo:* ser y porvenir de Hispanoamérica en el ensayo de sus escritores (Káñina [Univ. de Costa Rica, San José] 5 : 2, julio/dic. 1981, p. 79–89)

De naturaleza descriptiva, sobre *Pueblo enfermo,* de Arguedas, y *La raza cósmica,* de Vasconcelos.

7529 Pena de Matsushita, Marta E. El romanticismo político hispanoamericano. Buenos Aires: Academia Nacional de Ciencias, Centro de Estudios Filosóficos, 1985. 528 p.

Trabajo monográfico, muy completo, de buena calidad. Persigue la peculiaridad del romanticismo latinoamericano y destaca su importancia para la historia de las ideas políticas. Además de tratar asuntos que ofrecen el contorno del tema central, analiza en detalle los casos de Argentina, Uruguay y Chile, representándolos en Alberdi, Andrés Lamas y José V. Lastarria, respectivamente.

El Pensamiento comunista, 1917–1945. See *HLAS 47 : 6442.*

7530 Pensamiento positivista latinoamericano. v. 2. Compilación, prólogo, y cronología de Leopoldo Zea. Traducciones de Marta de la Vega, Margara Russotto, y Carlos Jacques. Caracas: Biblioteca Ayacucho, 1980. 774 p.: bibl. (Biblioteca Ayacucho; 72)

El vol. 1 de esta obra fue registrado en *HLAS 44 : 7558.* Este vol. 2 está dedicado a la educación, la política, la historia, y las relaciones USA-América Latina. No podría encomiarse bastante la utilidad de esta obra para investigadores y estudiosos del pensamiento latinoamericano.

Pinto Gamboa, Willy F. Sobre fascismo y literatura: la Guerra Civil española en *La Prensa, El Comercio,* y *La Crónica,* 1936–1939. See item **5506.**

Rodríguez, Atahualpa. Los científicos sociales latinoamericanos como nuevo grupo de intelectuales. See *HLAS 47 : 8030.*

7531 Sauerwald, Gregor. ¿Es América el eco del viejo mundo y el reflejo de vida ajena? (BCE/C, 5 : 14, sept./dic. 1982, p. 33–66)

El título alude a la famosa afirmación de Hegel sobre América en sus *Lecciones sobre la filosofía de la historia universal.* Ese tema se pone en relación con opiniones de autores como Salazar Bondy, Leopoldo Zea, Enrique Dussel, y Arturo A. Roig.

7532 Semana Latinoamericana de Intelectuales Católicos, 1st, Bogotá, 1982. Iglesia y cultura latinoamericana: [memorias]. Bogotá: CELAM, 1984. 498 p.: bibl. (CELAM; 60)

De este volumen interesan para esta sección los siguientes artículos: J.M. Batista, "Octavio Paz: Nuestras Raíces Culturales" (especialmente sobre *El laberinto de la soledad, Postdata,* y *El ogro filantrópico);* Aníbal Fornari, "La Filosofía en la Formación de América Latina" (ensayo histórico, pero basado en propuestas doctrinarias personales); Alberto Methol Ferré, "La Ruptura de la Cristiandad Indiana: Siglo XIX" (sigue el proceso de esa "ruptura," "hasta su consumación, al abrirse el siglo XX"); Pedro Morandé, "Del Romanticismo Católico Hispanoamericanista al Socialcristianismo Desarrollista;" Carlos Alberto Floria y Marcelo Montserrat, "El Pensamiento de Gustavo J. Franceschi y la Revista *Criterio* en la Política de la Argentina Contemporánea: 1928–1978;" y Ana María Moog Rodrigues, "Esbozo de un Panorama del Pensamiento Católico en el Brasil."

7533 Silva Gotay, Samuel. El pensamiento cristiano revolucionario en América Latina y el Caribe: implicaciones de la teología de la liberación para la sociología de la religión. Salamanca, Spain: Sígueme, 1981. 393 p.: bibl. (Agora)

Desde una posición militante en favor del cristianismo revolucionario, la obra es un análisis detallado de la teología de la liberación en América Latina. También entiende que el fenómeno estudiado debiera modificar la sociología de la religión de los marxistas. Lleva una breve presentación de Enrique Dussel, quien señala que el autor ha incorporado materiales del sector protestante de la religión cristiana.

7534 Temas de filosofía de la cultura latino-
americana. Bogotá: Editorial El Búho,
1982. 216 p.: bibl. (Col. Antología; 5)
Obra antológica y de divulgación. Los
textos corresponden a Juan Bautista Alberdi,
Sarmiento, J.E. Rodó, Alcides Arguedas,
González Prada, P. Henríquez Ureña, Alfonso
Reyes, Haya de la Torre, Fernández Retamar,
Rodolfo Kusch, Darcy Ribeiro, Abelardo
Villegas y Leopoldo Zea.

7535 Temas de filosofía política latino-
americana. v. 1, La nacionalidad
latinoamericana. Edición preparada por Luis
José González Alvarez. Bogotá: Editorial El
Búho, 1983. 167 p.: bibl., ill.
Breve antología de escritos sobre la
unidad hispanoamericana. Además de textos
clásicos de Bolívar, Alberdi y Bilbao, hay
otros de Justo Arosemena, José María Samper,
Hostos, Martí, Ingenieros, Mariátegui,
Augusto César Sandino, y Ricaurte Soler.

7536 Terán, Oscar. Latinoamérica: naciones y marxismos (SP, 11, sept. 1980,
p. 169–190)
Interesante comparación entre José
Carlos Mariátegui y Aníbal Ponce sobre la relación entre el marxismo y el problema de la
nacionalidad. Por ser el segundo autor menos
difundido, lo expuesto sobre él resulta
más útil. (Sobre el problema nacional y el
marxismo, ver también *HLAS 46:7533*.

7537 Terán Dutari, Julio César. Fundamentos filosóficos de un nuevo orden político: aportes desde América Latina (BCE/C,
4:11, sept./dic. 1981, p. 13–32)
Según el autor, ocuparían el campo del
pensamiento político latinoamericano tres
corrientes: la tradicional, la "hegeliano-
marxista," y la cristiana. Simplificando, los
conceptos capitales de las tres serían, respectivamente, el derecho, la justicia y el amor.
El artículo es un análisis comparado de esas
tendencias.

7538 Torchia Estrada, Juan Carlos. El problema de América en Pedro Henríquez
Ureña (SUR, 355, julio/dic. 1984, p. 133–
148)
Sobre la visión que Henríquez Ureña
tuvo de los rasgos particulares de la cultura
hispanoamericana, de su "expresión" propia y
de la "utopía" como ideal de acción de esa
cultura.

Valencia-Villa, Hernando. La constitución de
la quimera: Rousseau y la república jacobina

en el pensamiento constitucional de Bolívar.
See item **2861**.

7539 Ycaza Tigerino, Julio César. La cultura
hispánica y la crisis de Occidente. Madrid: Ministerio de Cultura, Secretaría General Técnica, 1981? 176 p.: bibl.
Reflexiones sobre la historia hispanoamericana—especialmente de la Independencia—de franco sabor hispanista. Es opinión
del autor que la Independencia americana
nació como un intento—desnaturalizado
posteriormente—de salvar "las bases del Imperio Cristiano" que se había perdido en
España.

7540 Zea, Leopoldo. La filosofía en América
Latina (Reflexão [Pontifícia Univ.
Católica de Campinas, Instituto de Filosofia
e Teologia] 8:26, maio/agôsto 1983, p. 5–14)
1983, p. 5–14)
Resume tesis suyas ya expuestas en
otras ocasiones, y mediante las cuales tiende
a justificar la autenticidad de un pensamiento filosófico latinoamericano.

7541 Zea, Leopoldo. Latinoamérica y el
Tercer Mundo (UEN/LS, 6, 1980,
p. 17–46)
De tono reivindicatorio para América
Latina y el Tercer Mundo en general. Ninguna forma de salida dentro del marco capi-
talista dará resultado o evitará la dependencia. Ejemplos que para el autor son
encomiables: la revolución cubana, China, y
Vietnam.

Zea, Leopoldo. Sentido de la difusión cultural
latinoamericana, 1980. See *HLAS 47:4373*.

MEXICO

Adame Goddard, Jorge. El pensamiento político y social de los católicos mexicanos,
1867–1914. See item **2037**.

7542 Bar-Lewaw, I. La revista *Timón* y la
colaboración nazi de José Vasconcelos
(*in* International Congress of Hispanists, 4th,
Salamanca, Spain, 1971. Actas. Dirección de
Eugenio de Bustos Tovar. Salamanca, Spain:
Asociación Internacional de Hispanistas,
1982, v. 1, p. 151–156)
De acuerdo con las búsquedas del autor, en 1940 apareció en México la revista
Timón, financiada por la Embajada de Alemania, de la que habría sido Director Vasconcelos y en la cual éste habría publicado
artículos de orientación pro-nazi.

Camp, Roderic A. The influence of European and North American ideas on students at Mexico's National School of Law and Economics. See *HLAS 47:8055.*

7543 Castillo Vales, Víctor M. Reflexiones en torno a un nuevo tratado de metafísica: pts. 1 and 3 (UY/R, 25 : 147, julio/sept. 1983, p. 95–115; 26:149, enero/marzo 1984, p. 97–118, bibl.)

Crítica muy minuciosa a la obra del filósofo mexicano Agustín Basave, *Tratado de metafísica.*

7544 Dumas, Claude. L'utopie positiviste au Mexique face à la critique contemporaine (*in* Unité et diversité de l'Amérique latine. Bordeaux, France: Univ. de Bordeaux III, 1982, t. 2, p. 29–51)

Cuestiona interpretaciones generalmente aceptadas sobre el positivismo en México, especialmente juicios que se han emitido sobre el grupo de los llamados "científicos," que tuvo destacada actuación durante el Porfiriato. Desde luego, hay frecuentes referencias a la obra de Zea.

7545 González-Caminero, Nemesio. La filosofía mexicana de la liberación según Leopoldo Zea (Revista Portuguesa de Filosofía [Braga] 41 : 2/ 3, abril/set. 1985, p. 161–180)

Formula una crítica, de índole muy general y desde el punto de vista de "un intérprete filósofo y cristiano," a la obra de Zea, pero más especialmente al tipo de filosofía que dicho autor practica.

7546 González Navarro, Moisés. Tipología del liberalismo mexicano (CM/HM, 32:2, oct./dic. 1982, p. 198–225, bibl.)

Afirma que se han dado en México dos tipos de liberalismo: el individualista y el social. Señala las principales ideas sobre la organización de la sociedad en Ignacio Ramírez, Guillermo Prieto, Justo Sierra, José López Portillo y Rojas, Francisco Madero y Ricardo Flores Magón.

7547 Hernández Luna, Juan. Samuel Ramos: etapas de su formación espiritual. Morelia, Mexico: Univ. Michoacana de San Nicolás de Hidalgo, 1982. 224 p.: bibl., ill. (Biblioteca de nicolaitas notables; 16)

Biografía intelectual del autor de *El perfil del hombre y la cultura en México,* escrita con gran simpatía.

7548 Hoy, Terry. Octavio Paz: the search for Mexican identity (UND/RP, 44 : 3,July 1982, p. 370–385)

Buena exposición de la visión de Paz sobre la realidad mexicana. Al final, sin disminuir los méritos del autor mexicano, expresa reservas frente a algunas de sus interpretaciones por falta de comprobación empírica.

Kasen, Nancy M. La influencia de la revolución norteamericana en la ideología de Fray Servando Teresa de Mier. See item **5071.**

7549 Maciel, David R. An interview with Leopoldo Zea (HAHR, 65 : 1, 1985, p. 1–20)

Util para conocer la evolución intelectual de Zea, su pensamiento y su posición ante algunas críticas que se le han dirigido.

7550 Mallo, Tomás. El antipositivismo en México (CH, 390, dic. 1982, p. 624–637)

Datos y observaciones sobre la Revolución mexicana y el antipositivismo de los jóvenes que compusieron el Ateneo de la Juventud a comienzos del siglo XX (ver item **7556**).

7551 Navarro B., Bernabé. Cultura mexicana moderna en el siglo XVIII. México: UNAM, Facultad de Filosofía y Letras, Seminario de Historia de la Filosofía en México, 1982. 230 p.: bibl., index.

Navarro es autor de una obra clásica sobre este mismo tema: *La introducción de la filosofía moderna en México* (1948). La presente, también indispensable, es una reimpresión. Reúne artículos sobre figuras como Gamarra, Clavigero y Alzate, y sobre otros aspectos de la filosofía en México en el siglo XVIII.

7552 Redmond, Walter. La lógica formal en la Nueva España: aspectos de la obra de Fray Alonso (UNAM/L, 12, 1979, p. 225–253)

Junto con los estudios de Muñoz Delgado, es uno de los pocos trabajos que enfocan la Lógica de Fray Alonso de la Veracuz desde un punto de vista moderno. El trabajo se había publicado antes en *International Philosophical Quarterly* (1979).

7553 Reunión Hispano-Mexicana de Historia, 1st, La Rábida, Spain, 1980. Memorias. Edición de Emilio Azcárraga Milmo y Valentín Molina Piñeiro. México: Instituto de Estudios y Documentos Históricos, 1981. 137 p. (Coloquios; 1)

Interesa para la historia del pensamiento filosófico hispanoamericano el artículo de Agustín Basabe, "Pensamientos Filosóficos en la Nueva España," que es un panorama de la filosofía en México desde el siglo XVI al XVIII. Dicho artículo, sin embargo, concluye con una exposición del pensamiento personal del autor.

7554 Suárez-Iñiguez, Enrique. Los intelectuales en México: los grupos generacionales (UNAM/RMCPS, 25:95/96, enero/junio 1979, p. 185–201)

Panorámico y general, pero útil. Se refiere a varios grupos, nucleados en torno a una revista o a ciertas ideas, y a su grado de influencia.

7555 Torchia Estrada, Juan Carlos. Fray Alonso de la Veracruz: guía temático-bibliográfica (UNAM/L, 17, 1984, p. 287–319)

Examina la bibliografía sobre Veracruz en función del "estado de la cuestión" de cada uno de los aspectos de su pensamiento.

7556 Torchia Estrada, Juan Carlos. Pedro Henríquez Ureña y el desplazamiento del positivismo en México (RIB, 35:2, 1985, p. 143–165)

Analiza la actuación cultural de Pedro Henríquez Ureña dentro del grupo del Ateneo de la Juventud en México, a principios del siglo, y en especial sus escritos filosóficos de esa época.

7557 Villegas, Abelardo. México en el horizonte liberal. México: UNAM, Coordinación de Humanidades, Centro Coordinador y Difusor de Estudios Latinoamericanos, 1981. 156 p.: bibl. (Nuestra América; 3)

Muy buena contribución a la historia de las ideas. Contiene trabajos sobre Juárez, Justo Sierra, Andrés Molina Henríquez y su libro *Los grandes problemas nacionales*. En lo que se refiere al siglo XX, hay sendos ensayos sobre Alfonso Reyes y Octavio Paz (una crítica equilibrada y serena). Aunque las simpatías políticas del autor tienen otra orientación, esto no le impide apreciar el peso histórico del liberalismo mexicano y la necesidad de estudiarlo a fondo.

7558 Zavala, Silvio. En el camino del pensamiento y las lecturas de Vasco de Quiroga (UY/R, 23:134, marzo/abril 1981, p. 52–62)

Artículo de síntesis de uno de los mejores conocedores de Vasco de Quiroga.

AMERICA CENTRAL

Berryman, Phillip. The religious roots of rebellion: Christians in Central American revolutions. See *HLAS 47:6103.*

7559 Capasso, Caterina. La filosofía cívico-social de Carlos Alberto Siri (ESME/C, 66/67, julio/dic. 1979, p. 151–244, ill.)

Monografía sobre el pensador salvadoreño Carlos Alberto Siri, autor, entre otras obras, de *La preeminencia de la Civitas y la insuficiencia de la Polis.*

Nolan, David. The ideology of the Sandinistas and the Nicaraguan revolution. See *HLAS 47:6193.*

Partido Liberación Nacional. Volvamos a la tierra: programa de gobierno: 1982–1986. See *HLAS 47:6133.*

7560 El Pensamiento liberal: antología. Prólogo, selección y bibliografía de Eugenio Rodríguez. San José: Editorial Costa Rica 1979. 431 p. (Biblioteca patria; 14)

Antología de textos de figuras políticas de Costa Rica. El liberalismo costarricense, se aclara en el prólogo, "más que una doctrina es un estilo de vida," y su presencia se extiende desde los comienzos de la Independencia hasta la actualidad. Señala como rasgos comunes a los liberales, en medio de otras diferencias: "civilidad, tolerancia, fe profunda en las posibilidades de la educación y del derecho, laicismo, defensa general de 'las libertades', creencia arraigada en el progreso inevitable." Todos los autores incluidos nacieron antes de comenzar el siglo XX.

El Sandinismo: documentos básicos. See item 2310.

7561 Sandino, Augusto César. El pensamiento vivo de Sandino. Introducción de Sergio Ramírez. Caracas: Ediciones Centauro, 1981. 560 p.: bibl.

Conjunto de documentos (cartas, manifiestos, declaraciones, etc.) de Augusto César Sandino. Tiene una introducción de Sergio Ramírez, miembro del movimiento sandinista, titulada "El Muchacho de Ni-

quinohomo" (ver *HLAS 42:2475*). El texto
tiene una nutrida historia editorial, desde la
primera edición (San José: EDUCA, 1974)
hasta la presente (1981). (Para la edición de
1978, ver *HLAS 44:2454*). La presente es "la
primera que se realiza en Nicaragua" y "está
enriquecida con una treintena de nuevos
documentos."

CARIBE INSULAR

7562 Achugar Ferrari, Hugo. Presencia
krausista en las ideas de Martí entre
1875 y 1877 (Fragmentos [Centro de Estudios
Latinoamericanos Rómulo Gallegos, Depto.
de Investigaciones, Caracas] 12, enero/abril
1982, p. 1 -19)
Analiza escritos de Martí, de su época
de México, especialmente los aspectos filosóficos que tienen vinculación con el krau-
sismo, llegados a través de Tiberghien y los
krausistas españoles.

7563 Alfonseca, Iván. Pedro Henríquez
Ureña: su arraigao como pensador dominicano (UNPHU/A, 45, abril/junio 1983,
p. 71–90, bibl.)
Destaca el interés de Henríquez Ureña
por los temas dominicanos.

7564 Anderson Imbert, Enrique. La filosofía
de Pedro Henríquez Ureña (SUR, 355,
julio/dic. 1984, p. 5–19)
Uno de los pocos artículos dedicados
a explorar los aspectos propiamente filosóficos en el pensamiento y la obra de Pedro
Henríquez Ureña.

7565 Bellegarde-Smith, Patrick. International relations/social theory in a
small state: an analysis of the thought of
Dantès Bellegarde (AAFH/TAM, 49:2, Oct.
1982, p. 167–184)
Sobre las ideas internacionalistas—en
general y en relación con Haití—del diplomático y pensador haitiano. Trabajo oportuno
por su contenido y lo poco conocido del
tema. Ver la reseña del politólogo en *HLAS
47:7213.*

7566 Bustamante y Montoro, A.S. de. La polémica filosófica de 1838–1840 en
Cuba (BNJM/R, 72[23]:1, enero/abril 1981,
p. 17–33)
En la oposición de José de la Luz y
Caballero al espiritualismo de Cousin ve el
autor "la contradicción metrópolis-colonia,"
y en general, opina que lo que se ha llamado
"la polémica filosófica" fue "una fase victoriosa de la lucha ideológica entre Cuba y
España."

7567 Céspedes, Diógenes. Ideas filosóficas,
discurso sindical y mitos cotidianos en
Santo Domingo. Santo Domingo: Taller,
1984. 177 p.: bibl., ill. (Biblioteca Taller; 166)
De este libro interesará al historiador
de las ideas el ensayo "Filosofía e Ideas Socialistas en República Dominicana," que
trata autores prácticamente desconocidos
como Ricardo Sánchez Lustrino y Adalberto
Chapuseaux."

7568 Cuban and North American Marxism.
Papers presented at the Cuban-North
American Marxist Philosophers Conference,
May 1982, Havana. Edited by Edward D'Angelo. Amsterdam: B.R. Grüner, 1984. 214 p.:
bibl.
Resultado de una conferencia de filó-
sofos marxistas de Estados Unidos y de
Cuba. El punto de vista es marxista-leninista
estricto. En la parte correspondiente a Cuba
hay artículos sobre la situación económica,
social, educativa y cultural, entre otros. Un
artículo se refiere a las ideas filosóficas de
Martí.

Estrade, Paul. Sur les perspectives d'union
des Antilles au XIX siècle. See item **2511.**

7569 Fernández Retamar, Roberto. Algunos
problemas de una biografía ideológica
de José Martí (*in* Cuba: les étapes d'une libération. Hommage à Juan Marinello et Noël
Salomon: actes du Colloque international
des 22, 23 et 24 novembre 1978. Toulouse,
France: Centre d'études cubaines, Univ. de
Toulouse-Le Mirail, 1979, v. 1, 89–111 bibl.)
El autor reconoce una especie de "radi-
calización" en la evolución de Martí, lo que
se ilustra con textos de las épocas en que éste
vivió en México y Estados Unidos. Cierta
bibliografía y la identificación del autor con
la actual situación cubana caracterizan el
enfoque.

7570 George, Omar and **Pablo Guadarrama
González.** La influencia del positivismo en Emilio Bobadilla (UCLV/I, 66,
enero/abril 1981, p. 119–135)
Tratándose de un tema poco conocido
(Bobadilla, 1862–1921, expuso ideas filosóficas pero su campo era el de la literatura y
el periodismo), la información es oportuna.

En cuanto a la parte crítica, lo bueno y lo malo se juzgan con criterio marxista clásico (Engels es una fuente citada con frecuencia).

7571 Guadarrama González, Pablo. Algunas particularidades del positivismo en Cuba (UCLV/I, 76, sept./dic. 1983, p. 103–124)

Util en los aspectos descriptivos, la interpretación marxista es muy marcada en este trabajo. En general, los positivistas son vistos con cierta simpatía histórica, por el carácter "progresista" de algunas de sus ideas. Debe destacarse que este autor tiene ya una obra de cierto volumen sobre el positivismo en Cuba.

7572 Guadarrama González, Pablo. La huella del positivismo en la obra de Fernando Ortiz (UCLV/I, 70, sept./dic. 1981, p. 39–70)

Con formato y críticas semejantes a los de otros trabajos suyos sobre el tema, el autor continúa su análisis del positivismo cubano. En este caso se trata de Fernando Ortiz (1881–1969) proveniente del campo criminológico y adherido a la Escuela positiva de Lombroso.

7573 Guadarrama González, Pablo. Significación de la obra de Enrique José Varona en la filosofía cubana (Siglo XIX [Univ. Autónoma de Nuevo León, Facultad de Filosofía y Letras, Monterrey, México] 1 : 2, julio/dic. 1986, p. 39–68)

Es de destacar en este artículo la detallada atención que se presta al tema religioso en Varona.

7574 Jimenes Grullón, Juan Isidro. La ideología revolucionaria de Juan Pablo Duarte. 2a ed. Santo Domingo: Gobierno de Concentración Nacional, 1983. 37 p.: bibl.

Desde el punto de vista de la historia de las ideas interesan las afirmaciones sobre la influencia del romanticismo en Duarte. Muy crítico de las obras de Troncoso Sánchez y Joaquín Balaguer sobre el personaje estudiado.

Judson, Fred. Anti-imperialism in the Cuban rebel army: the sum of precedents and experiences of armed struggle. See item **2585**.

Montaner, Carlos Alberto. The roots of anti-Americanism in Cuba: sovereignty in an age of world cultural homogeneity. See item **2364** and *HLAS* 47:7243.

7575 Morales, Salvador. El bolivarismo de José Martí (UB/BA, 26 : 34, 1984, p. 161–177)

Sobre cómo Martí interpretó a Bolívar. Es opinión del autor que Martí no hizo mera exégesis, sino que adecuó "los postulados revolucionarios de Bolívar a un cuerpo doctrinal nuevo." Ver la reseña del historiador en item **2529**.

7576 Pimentel, Miguel A. Hostos y el positivismo en Santo Domingo: filosofía y política. Santo Domingo: Depto. de Filosofía, Univ. Autonóma de Santo Domingo, 1981. 99 p.: bibl. (Cuadernos de apoyo a la docencia)

El capítulo más aprovechable es el dedicado a a ética de Hostos. De estructura monográfica, pero con escasos elementos bibliográficos de apoyo. En el examen de Hostos expresa algunas opiniones marxistas muy generales, pero no es una crítica sistemática desde ese punto de vista.

7577 Ternevoi, O.C. La filosofía en Cuba, 1790–1878. La Habana: Editorial de Ciencias Sociales, 1981. 350 p.: bibl. (Filosofía)

Quizá sea la primera historia del pensamiento filosófico de un país latinoamericano escrita en la Unión Soviética. Trata principalmente de José Agustín Caballero, Félix Varela y José de la Luz y Caballero, es decir, del período anterior al positivismo. La orientación declarada de la obra es la marxista-leninista, con particular apego a las tesis de Lenin que se adaptan al asunto estudiado. El período analizado es considerado como "progresista."

Vega, Bernardo. La migración española de 1939 y los inicios del marxismo-leninismo en la República Dominicana. See item **2391**.

Vitier, Cintio. Temas martianos. See item **2553**.

7578 Zuleta Alvarez, Enrique. Humanismo y ética en Pedro Henríquez Ureña (SUR, 355, julio-dic. 1984, p. 177–191)

Trata con acierto el perfil ético de Pedro Henríquez Ureña.

VENEZUELA

7579 Acedo, Clemy Machado de. La incidencia del positivismo en las ideas políticas de Rómulo Gallegos. Baruta, Venezuela: Equinoccio, 1982. 172 p.

Investigación interesante, que se refiere a escritos de Rómulo Gallegos publicados hacia principios de siglo en la revista *La Alborada*. Difiere en algunas de sus tesis de la historiografía sobre el tema.

Andrés Bello: homenaje de la UCV. See item 1863a.

7580 Ardao, Arturo. La relación de Bello con Stuart Mill (USB/RVF, 14/15, 1981, p. 7–38)

Excelente trabajo. Cuestiona, en la obra filosófica de Bello, la influencia de Hamilton, la de Stuart Mill y la del positivismo. De una forma u otra esas influencias han sido mencionadas por expositores o intérpretes anteriores.

7581 Bello, Andrés. Pensamientos de Andrés Bello, libertador espiritual. Selección y prólogo de R.J. Lovera De-Sola. Caracas: Alfadil, 1983. 95 p.: bibl. (Col. AmeriTextos; 6)

Volumen de utilidad escolar. Es una antología de pasajes de Bello, aunque sin indicación de procedencia. La introducción y la bibliografía son útiles en consonancia con el propósito del libro.

Betancourt, Rómulo. Rómulo Betancourt contra la dictadura de Juan Vicente Gómez, 1928–1935: *Repertorio Americano*, Costa Rica. See item **2898.**

Caldera, Rafael Tomás. La respuesta de Gallegos: ensayos sobre nuestra situación cultural. See item **5514.**

Carrera Demas, Germán. Bolívar y el proyecto nacional venezolano. See item **2850.**

Congreso de Municipalidades de Venezuela, 1st, Caracas, 1911. Actas y conclusiones. See item **2904.**

7582 Cussen, Anthony. Bello y la Ilustración inglesa (Estudios Públicos [Centro de Estudios Públicos, Santiago] 8, 1982, p. 5–22)

Util a pesar de que la relación anunciada en el título no llega a concretarse en una tesis definida.

7583 Grases, Pedro. Obras. v. 5, La tradición humanística. Barcelona, Spain: Seix Barral, 1981. 726 p.: bibl., facsims., ill., index, ports.

Parte de la valiosa obra bibliográfica y erudita de Pedro Grases. Los autores considerados son todos venezolanos. Los tratados con mayor extensión son: Francisco de Miranda (1750–1816), Juan Germán Roscio (1763–1821), Simón Rodríguez (1771–1854), Andrés Bello (1781–1865), Juan Vicente González (1810–66), Rafael María Baralt (1810–60), y Cecilio Acosta (1818–81).

7584 López Martín, Alfonso. Los orígenes filosóficos del pensamiento de Andrés Bello (UCR/RF, 21:53, 1983, p. 63–82)

Persigue minuciosamente las citas que hace Bello de otros autores filosóficos, en busca de las influencias que obraron sobre él. Util aunque un tanto escolar. Véase especialmente el resumen (p. 79–80).

7585 Pensamiento político venezolano del siglo XIX: textos para su estudio. Caracas: Congreso de la República, 1983. 15 v.: bibl., indexes.

Reedición de una valiosa obra documental publicada por primera vez en 1961 (ver *HLAS* 25:3767) donde esta obra fue considerada "of major significance for the study of Venezuelan national period history."

7586 El Pensamiento político venezolano del siglo XX: documentos para su estudio. Ofrecimiento de Godofredo González. Presentación de Ramón J. Velázquez. Caracas: Congreso de la República, 1983. 15 v.: bibl. (Ediciones conmemorativas del bicentenario del natalicio del Libertador Simón Bolivar)

Como la serie correspondiente al pensamiento político del siglo XIX (ver item 7585), la presente es una valiosa y extensa colección documental. El plan de la obra comprende 26 volúmenes. He aquí el contenido de los disponibles al preparar esta entrega del *Handbook*: t. 1, vol. 1) *El pensamiento político de la restauración liberal*: después de un extenso prólogo de Eleonora Gabaldón y Judith Gamus de Wiesel sobre "La Ideología Política de Cipriano Castro y el Problema del Poder," se reproducen en facsímil tres volúmenes de *Documentos del General Cipriano Castro*, publicados en 1903, 1904 y 1905, respectivamente; t. 1, vol. 2) Reproducción de otros tres volúmenes de documentos del General Castro (1906?, 1906, 1908); t. 1, vol. 3) *La oposición a la dictadura de Cipriano Castro*: prólogo de Ramón J. Velázquez (p. xi–lix); documentos de Antonio Paredes (m. 1907), tomados de sus libros *Cómo llegó Cipriano Castro al poder* y *Diario de mi prisión de San Carlos*; papeles del Gen. M.A. Matos y otros autores (1899–1907); "Ante la Reelección Presidencial de Cipriano Castro" (1905); "La Oposición de César Zumeta" (1906–08); documentos relativos a la muerte del Gen. Antonio Paredes; t. 3, vol. 1) *Los pensadores positivistas y el gomecismo*: va precedido de dos estudios preliminares: "El Pensamiento Político Positivista y el Gomecismo," de Arturo Sosa A., e "Introducción Histórica al Pensamiento Político del Positivismo Venezolano," de Luis Salamanca; el contenido documental corresponde al período 1908–18, y está representado por autores como Pedro Manuel Arcaya, José Gil Fortoul, Laureano Vallenilla Lanz y César Zumeta, entre otros; t. 3, vol. 2) Continúa la misma documentación entre los años 1919–25; t. 3, vol. 3) *id.*, Período 1926–35; t. 6, vol. 1) *El comienzo del debate socialista*: contiene un prólogo de Arturo Sosa A., "Las Ideas Socialistas bajo Juan Vicente Gómez," y luego documentos (cartas, conferencias, manifiestos, etc.) de diversos autores y correspondientes al período 1924–31; t. 6, vol. 2) Continuación del anterior, con documentos del período 1932–35; t. 7, vol. 1) *El debate político en 1936*: después de un prólogo que firman Arturo Sosa A. y Eloi Lengrand, y una cronología de los hechos políticos de 1936 (en realidad, a partir de dic. 17, 1935, fecha del fallecimiento del Gen. Juan Vicente Gómez), se presentan documentos de naturaleza similar a los anteriores, mes por mes, desde dic. 1935 hasta junio (parcial) 1936; y t. 7, vol. 2) Continuación del anterior, junio-nov. 1936. En todos los casos hay índices de nombres y de autores, además del índice general.

7587 Pescador Sarget, Augusto. La lógica de Andrés Bello (UC/AT, 443/444, 1981, p. 281–290)
Presentación básica del tema.

7588 Riu, Federico. El tema de la alienación en la filosofía venezolana: la polémica Mayz-Vázquez sobre el concepto marxista de alienación (USB/RVF, 14/15, 1981, p. 139–155)
Mayz Vallenilla publicó, en 1968, *Del hombre y su alienación*, examen de la alienación en Marx, desde una perspectiva heideggeriana. Eduardo Vázquez contestó (1969), desde una posición marxista, con *En torno al concepto de alienación en Marx y Heidegger*. El presente artículo es una exposición de esa polémica.

7589 Roig, Arturo Andrés. Educación para la integración y utopía en el pensamiento de Simón Rodríguez (BCE/C, 4:11, sept./dic. 1981, p. 33–59)
Trabajo importante para la interpretación del pensamiento de Simón Rodríguez. No son de menor interés otros aspectos de este estudio, y que constituyen el contexto en que Rodríguez es situado, tales como el romanticismo hispanoamericano, la función del ensayo como género literario y como "praxis social," el pensamiento utópico, etc.

7590 Rojas, Clara Marina. El positivismo de Laureano Vallenilla y la tesis del gendarme necesario (Argos [Univ. Simón Bolívar, División de Ciencias Sociales y Humanidades, Caracas] 2, 1981, p. 39–53, bibl.)
Trabajo aprovechable. Los positivistas se habrían dividido en "democráticos" y "autoritarios" (Vallenilla Lanz entra en la segunda categoría). Ambas soluciones habrían respondido al mismo problema: la desorganización social posterior a la Independencia. Vallenilla es expuesto y discutido, y también se tratan otros autores.

7591 Romero, Matías. Andrés Bello, Cid Campeador de la filosofía hispanoamericana (ESME/C, 71, 1981, p. 145–188, bibl.)
Respetable como esfuerzo de divulgación. No es un trabajo académico.

7592 Sasso, Javier. Andrés Bello y la teoría nominalista de la abstracción (UNAM/L, 12, 1979, p. 209–223)
Sitúa la teoría de la abstracción de Bello (expuesta en su *Filosofía del entendimiento*) dentro de la filosofía moderna—especialmente en sus semejanzas con Berkeley y su rechazo de Destutt de Tracy—y prolonga el tema en relación con algunas visiones contemporáneas sobre el problema de los universales.

7593 Sasso, Javier. Inmaterialismo y verificacionismo en *Filosofía del entendimiento* (CNC/A, 6, 1980/1982, p. 21–28)
Se refiere, con cierto grado de detalle, al tratamiento que Andrés Bello da, en su *Filosofía del entendimiento*, a la tesis inmaterialista de Berkeley.

7594 Squella Narducci, Agustín. Ideas de Bello sobre educación y su vigencia (OAS/LE, 27:89, 1982, p. 2–28)
Artículo extenso e informativo sobre la

educación dentro de la obra y la acción de Bello.

COLOMBIA

7595 Antología del pensamiento conservador en Colombia. v. 1. Introducción, selección, y bibliografía de Roberto Herrera Soto. Bogotá: Instituto Colombiano de Cultura, División de Publicaciones, 1982. 1 v.: bibl. (Biblioteca básica colombiana; 49)

Este vol. 1 está compuesto por una antología de 27 autores, agrupados según generaciones desde el siglo XVIII al XX. Es importante que para cada uno, además de la selección de textos, se ofrece una bibliografía. Entre los autores representados se encuentran: Antonio Nariño (1765–1823), Simón Bolívar (1783–1830), José Eusebio Caro (1817–53), Miguel Antonio Caro (1843–1909), Rafael M. Carrasquilla (1857–1930) (1857–1930), y Gonzalo Restrepo Jaramillo (1895–1966).

7596 Filosofía de la emancipación en Colombia. Selección de textos e introducción de Germán Marquínez Argote. Bogotá: Editorial El Buho, 1983. 216 p.: bibl., ports. (Col. Pensamiento colombiano)

Textos de Nariño, Fernández de Sotomayor, Antonio de León, Miguel de Pombo, Bolívar, y F.A. Zea. Los temas son: Legitimidad de la Independencia; Formas de Estado y Gobierno (que podrían adoptarse después de la Independencia); e Integración de los Estados Americanos (ideas de unidad de las antiguas colonias). Introducción breve pero clara y útil.

Filosofía de la pacificación en Colombia. See item **2669.**

7597 Herrera Restrepo, Daniel. La filosofía en la Colonia (UN/IV, 55/56, agosto 1979, p. 59–81)

El título no permite conocer el objeto del artículo, que es contestar a la pregunta de cómo explicar "la pobreza y mediocridad de la reflexión [filosófica] durante el período colonial." Propone varios factores. El análisis muestra muy escasa estima por la filosofía en el período estudiado, en Colombia, pero por implicación en el resto de Hispanoamérica.

Ocampo López, Javier. Historia de la idea de la americanidad en los pensadores colombianos. See item **7526.**

7598 Ordenes, Jorge. El ser moral en las obras de Fernando González. Medellín, Colombia: Univ. de Antioquia, 1983. 459 p.

Fernando González (1895–1964), de Colombia, fue el tipo de pensador que expresa su pensamiento en forma libre o ensayística. El autor de este libro ha realizado un cuidadoso trabajo al organizar en forma sistemática ideas y opiniones sobre "el ser moral" que se encuentran esparcidas en varios libros de Fernando González.

Santander, Francisco de Paula and **Vicente Azuero.** Antología política. See item **2982.**

7599 Sierra Mejía, Rubén. Cayetano Betancur: 1910–1982 (UN/IV, 62, agosto 1983, p. 5–9)

Nota breve pero justiciera sobre una figura que fue pionera del actual desarrollo filosófico en Colombia. Destaca la proximidad de Betancur a la filosofía de Ortega y Gasset y su pensamiento en filosofía del derecho.

Silva, Renán. Saber, cultura y sociedad en el Nuevo Reino de Granada, siglos XVII y XVIII. See item **2683.**

ECUADOR

Agoglia, Rodolfo Mario. Montalvo, Mera y el romanticismo. See item **5120.**

7600 Agramonte, Roberto. Montalvo como filósofo (BCE/C, 5:12, enero/abril 1982, p. 195–233)

Tiene la virtud de reunir opiniones e ideas de Montalvo que se encuentran dispersas en sus escritos, y que constituyen su *Weltanschauung.* De tono entusiasta y, por momentos, laudatorio.

Carrasco Vintimilla, Manuel. Mito y realidad de Eugenio Espejo. See item **2692.**

7601 Cerutti-Guldberg, Horacio V. Aproximación a la historiografía del pensamiento ecuatoriano (UNAM/L, 11, 1978, p. 215–244)

Combina el examen crítico de producciones historiográficas con observaciones generales sobre metodología de historia de las ideas.

7602 Cerutti-Guldberg, Horacio V. Situación de los estudios filosóficos y sociales en el Ecuador en la actualidad (UEN/LS, 7, 1980, p. 503–511)

De acuerdo con el título, da indicaciones en tres campos: historia económicosocial, historia de las ideas y literatura.

7603 Chacón, Jorge. Juan Montalvo, bosquejo. Guayaquil: s.n., 1982. 83 p.: bibl.

En tono de ensayo, resulta una síntesis de la vida y la obra de Montalvo. Crítico de varios aspectos de este autor clásico, la nota más alta del elogio es reservada para el prosista de *Capítulos que se le olvidaron a Cervantes.*

Federico González Suárez: la polémica sobre el Estado laico. See item **2999.**

7604 Guerra Bravo, Samuel. Eugenio Espejo, pensador filosófico (UNAM/L, 11, 1978, p. 245–267)

Breve pero útil biografía intelectual de Eugenio de Santa Cruz y Espejo, pensador ecuatoriano del siglo XVIII.

7605 Martz, John D. El marxismo en el Ecuador (UNCR/R, 4:8, enero/julio 1979, p. 31–57)

Circunscrito a la acción política directa o de partidos, y al siglo actual. Síntesis muy útil.

7606 Morales Benítez, Otto. Cercanías a un tema: Don Juan Montalvo y sus diversas expresiones indoamericanas (ACH/BHA, 70:740, enero/marzo 1983, p. 153–190, bibl.)

Ensayo apreciativo, de índole general.

7607 Paladines E., Carlos. Filosofía e historia de las ideas en la década de los 70: el caso de Ecuador (BCE/C, 4:11, sept./dic. 1981, p. 247–264)

Contiene muy útiles datos sobre el reciente progreso de los estudios de la historia de las ideas en el Ecuador, pero expresa también opiniones sobre la relación que el cultivo de la filosofía debe guardar con la realidad nacional (ver también *HLAS 46:7583*).

7608 Paladines E., Carlos. Notas sobre metodología de investigación del pensamiento ecuatoriano (UNAM/L, 11, 1978, p. 179–213)

No se refiere sólo a Ecuador. Trata además el tema de la metodología de la historia de las ideas en América Latina.

Rocafuerte, Vicente. A la nación. See item **5166.**

Rocafuerte, Vicente. Vicente Rocafuerte. See item **3009.**

Roig, Arturo Andrés. Esquemas para una historia de la filosofía ecuatoriana. See item **3011.**

7609 Roig, Arturo Andrés. El humanismo ecuatoriano de la segunda mitad del siglo XVIII. Quito: Banco Central del Ecuador: Corp. Editora Nacional, 1984. 2 v.: bibl. (Biblioteca básica del pensamiento ecuatoriano; 18–19)

Los temas principales son la *Historia del Reino de Quito*, de Juan de Velasco (1727–92), obra concluida a fines del siglo XVIII pero no publicada hasta el XIX, y el pensamiento de Eugenio Santa Cruz y Espejo (1747–95). Esta de Roig es una obra de gran envergadura, y una contribución de la mayor importancia a la historia de las ideas en Ecuador, a la cual el mismo autor había hecho aportes de magnitud anteriormente. Continúa una muy oportuna colección del Banco Central del Ecuador.

PERU

Angotti, Thomas. The contributions of José Carlos Mariátegui to revolutionary theory. See item **3019.**

7610 Cassetta, Giovanni. La Revolución mexicana en el pensamiento de José Carlos Mariátegui (Historias [Dirección de Estudios Históricos, Instituto de Antropología e Historia, México] 2, julio/sept. 1982, p. 23–41 bibl.)

Mariátegui escribió varios artículos sobre la Revolución mexicana entre 1924 y 1930. El presente trabajo los analiza, mostrando que hubo, en el autor peruano, un entusiasmo cada vez más limitado por dicha Revolución, hasta calificarla como "democrático-burguesa." El cambio en la apreciación coincide con su separación del APRA. El artículo es útil, de clara exposición y basado en buena bibliografía.

Chang-Rodríguez, Eugenio. El indigenismo peruano y Mariátegui. See item **3029.**

7611 Cometta Manzoni, Aída. Vigencia de José Carlos Mariátegui (CONAC/RNC, 41:247, abril/nov. 1981, p. 79–89)

Breve y ajustada visión de conjunto

de la vida y la obra de Mariátegui. Asombra, sin embargo, que la autora considere que Mariátegui es una figura olvidada y desconocida.

Deusta, José and José Luis Rénique. Intelectuales, indigenismo y descentralismo en el Perú, 1897–1931. See item **3035.**

7612 Falcón, Jorge. Mariátegui, Marxmarxismo: el productor y su productor. Lima: Empresa Editora Amauta, 1983. 103 p.: bibl.

Lo que más interesa de este volumen son las transcripciones de textos de Mariátegui (presentados en orden cronológico) sobre Marx y el marxismo.

Ferrari, Américo. El concepto de indio y la cuestión racial en el Perú en los *Siete ensayos* de José Carlos Mariátegui. See item **3039.**

Flores Galindo, Alberto. Un viejo debate: el poder. See *HLAS 47:6423.*

7613 Franco, Carlos. Sobre la idea de nación en Mariátegui (SP, 11, Sept. 1980, p. 191–208)

Extensa exégesis sobre el desarrollo de las ideas de Mariátegui respecto de la nacionalidad peruana. Algunos aspectos (valor de lo europeo, lo indígena, lo mestizo, etc.) serán de interés para el mismo tema en otros países y para América Latina en su conjunto.

7614 Franco, Carlos. El surgimiento del marxismo latinoamericano: Haya de la Torre y Mariátegui (Historias [Dirección de Estudios Históricos, Instituto de Antropología e Historia, México] 2, julio/sept. 1982, p. 3–22)

La tesis principal es que Mariátegui y Haya distinguieron, frente al marxismo clásico, el carácter original de la realidad latinoamericana, y vieron el marxismo más como un instrumento que como una teoría. El artículo es de lectura muy aprovechable.

7615 Gaete Avaria, Jorge. La unidad entre pensamiento y vida: implicaciones epistemológicas y praxiológicas de una retórica (Fragmentos [Centro de Estudios Latinoamericanos Rómulo Gallegos, Caracas] 10, mayo/agosto 1981, p. 61–91)

Capítulo de un libro en preparación sobre Mariátegui. Se analiza su "retórica" (en el sentido de Perelman), o la relación que un tipo o estilo de lenguaje tiene con una toma de posición teórica.

7616 Gutiérrez, Marco. Vanguardia del teatro: Mariátegui y Pirandello. S.l.: Ediciones Quilca, 1982. 71 p.: ill. (Col. Testimonio del hombre)

Tras exponer la influencia de las letras italianas en Perú y el sentido de la obra de Pirandello, trata las relaciones de Mariátegui con el autor italiano. Es conclusión del autor que, a pesar de las diferencias ideológicas, los dos autores "coinciden en más de una instancia en la demolición del orden tradicional y en el establecimiento de un nuevo programa."

Hampe M., Teodoro. José A. de la Puente Candamo en la historiografía peruana. See item **3044.**

7617 Ibáñez, Alfonso. La utopía realista de Mariátegui (SP, 19, 1982, p. 87–95)

Sobre la combinación de lo utópico (o imaginativo, o anticipatorio) y lo realista (o crítico y racional) en Mariátegui, aludiendo a una supuesta semejanza con Ernst Bloch, salvando las diferencias.

7618 Mires, Fernando. Los indios y la tierra: o como concibió Mariátegui la revolución en el Perú (NOSALF/IA, 8/9:2[1/2] 1980, p. 68–99)

Pone el asunto en el contexto de la conquista española, la Independencia, la burguesía peruana, la contradicción costa-sierra, etc., según vió Mariátegui estos temas. Defiende a Mariátegui de las acusaciones resultantes de la posición de la Tercera Internacional. Trabajo detallado.

7619 Neira, Hugo. El pensamiento de José Carlos Mariátegui: los "mariateguismos" (SP, 23, sept. 1983, p. 55–76, bibl.)

Interesan en este trabajo, de lectura recomendable, las consideraciones sobre el Mariátegui ensayista (que no son meramente de naturaleza literaria); el repaso histórico de los diferentes enfoques utilizados para interpretar al autor peruano; y el carácter abierto de la crítica que realiza y de la interpretación que propone. La bibliografía, al final, sin ser exhaustiva, es amplia.

Pike, Frederick B. The politics of the miraculous in Peru: Haya de la Torre and the spiritualist tradition. See item **3070.**

Prado, Jorge del. En los años de Mariátegui. See item **3071.**

7620 Rivera de Tuesta, María Luisa. Las ideas en el Perú: Ilustración y romanticismo, 1780–1826 (Siglo XIX [Univ. Autónoma de Nuevo León, Facultad de Filosofía y Letras, Monterrey, Mexico] 1:2, julio/dic. 1986, p. 119 -174)

Extensa exposición (desde el fin de la época colonial hasta la consumación de la Independencia) en la cual las ideas se presentan en el marco de los acontecimientos políticos.

CHILE

Avila Martel, Alamiro. La censura de libros y Andrés Bello. See item **3111.**

7621 Bio-bibliografía de la filosofía en Chile desde el siglo XVI hasta 1980. Dirigida por Fernando Astorquiza Pizarro. Santiago: Univ. de Chile, Facultad de Filosofía, Humanidades y Educación: Instituto Profesional de Santiago, Depto. de Bibliotecología, 1982. 295 p.: bibl., index.

El material bibliográfico está dividido en períodos históricos, y cada uno de éstos es precedido por una introducción, que es en realidad un trabajo crítico sobre esa etapa. Consta de 3.085 entradas bibliográficas, la mayoría de ellas correspondientes al siglo XX.

Guzmán Brito, Alejandro. Las ideas jurídicas de Don Diego Portales. See item **3140.**

7622 Hallet, Charles. *El congregante perfecto* del Padre Ignacio García Gómez, S.J.: manuscrito chileno del siglo XVIII. Estudio y edición de Charles Hallet. Santiago: Pontificia Univ. Católica de Chile, 1982. 271 p.: bibl., index (Anales de la Facultad de Teología, 0069–3596; 32:1)

La obra que aquí se presenta es un típico manual de orientación práctica para la vida cristiana. Estudio, aparato crítico, fuentes y bibliografía utilizada muestran el cuidado de una excelente labor académica.

7623 Jaksić, Iván. Philosophy and university reform at the University of Chile: 1842–1973 (LARR, 19:1, 1984, p. 57–86)

Excelente capítulo de historia de las ideas, que concluye con el examen de la reforma universitaria chilena de 1968, donde el modo de concebir la filosofía tuvo un importante papel, por lo menos en las discusiones teóricas. Imprescindible para el tema.

7624 Pensamiento teológico en Chile: contribución a su estudio. v. 2, Epoca de la reorganización y consolidación eclesiásticas, 1840–1880. Edición de Juan A. Noemi Callejas. Santiago: Pontificia Univ.

Católica de Chile, 1982. 219 p.: bibl., index (Anales de la Facultad de Teología, 0069–3596; 31:1)

Resume y expone la obra de cinco autores, precedido de una presentación general. Además de ser contribución a la historia del pensamiento teológico sirve al propósito de la historia de las ideas en Chile en el siglo XIX.

7625 La Presencia de la filosofía en la Universidad Católica, 1888–1973. Coordinación de Luis Celis M. Santiago: Pontificia Univ. Católica de Chile, 1982. 215 p.: bibl. (Anales de la Escuela de Educación; 3:5)

Aunque la exposición se organiza en función de lo institucional (*pensum*, profesores, publicaciones, etc.), también se ofrece el contexto de la historia de la Universidad y la del país. Puede considerarse material para la historia de la filosofía en Chile.

Ruiz, Carlos. Notes on authoritarian ideologies in Chile. See *HLAS 47:6489.*

Salvat Monguillot, Manuel. Tocqueville en Chile. See item **3172.**

BRASIL

Assis Brasil, Joaquim Francisco de. A democracia representativa na República: antología. See item **3432.**

7626 Brito, Rosa Mendonça de. Filosofia, educação, sociedade e direito na obra de Arthur Orlando da Silva, 1858–1916. Recife: Fundação Joaquim Nabuco, 1980. 116 p.: bibl. (Série Estudos e pesquisas; 18)

Con la estructura y el estilo de una tesis de post-grado, esta obra es una buena presentación del pensamiento de Arthur Orlando en sus diversos aspectos (filosofía, derecho, educación, teoría social), colocándolo en el contexto de su vida y de la Escuela de Recife. Util bibliografía. Presenta la obra Antonio Paim.

7627 Cesar, Constança Marcondes. A filosofia como saber interdisciplinar na epistemologia de Hilton Japiassu (Reflexão [Pontifícia Univ. Católica de Campinas, Instituto de Filosofia e Teologia] 21, set./dez 1981, p. 5–18, bibl.)

Expone las líneas esenciales de la epistemología defendida por Japiassu, de carácter no positivista y más bien inspirada en Bachelard, Popper y Piaget, entre otros.

Eakin, Marshall C. Race and identity: Sílvio Romero, science, and social thought in late 19th century Brazil. See item **3454.**

7629 Lazzaro, Luis Aaron. O conceito de cultura e sociedade de Tobias Barreto (Reflexão [Pontifícia Univ. Católica de Campinas, Instituto de Filosofia e Teologia] 7:22, jan./abril 1982, p. 27–37, bibl.)

Exposición de los conceptos de cultura y de sociedad y de la crítica a la sociología en Tobias Barreto, tomando como base su *Introdução ao estudo do direito* (1887?).

7630 Machado, Geraldo Pinheiro. Filosofia brasileira do direito (Reflexão [Pontifícia Univ. Católica de Campinas, Instituto de Filosofia e Teologia] 8:26, maio/agôsto 1983, p. 38–42)

Fundamenta la necesidad de sistematizar el estudio de la filosofía del derecho tal como se ha cultivado en Brasil.

7631 Mendes, Evelyse Maria Freire. Bibliografia do pensamento político republicano, 1870–1970. Revisão de Edson Nery da Fonseca. Brasília: Câmara dos Deputados: Editora Univ. de Brasília, 1980. 210 p.: bibl., index (Biblioteca do pensamento político republicano; 1)

Se trata del vol. 1 de una "Biblioteca del Pensamiento Político de la Epoca Republicana de Brasil," que al parecer cuenta o contará con volúmenes sobre *O apostolado positivista e a República, O socialismo brasileiro, A Igreja na República*, etc. La colección ha sido coordinada por Vicente Barreto y Antônio Paim. La presente *Bibliografía* abarca el siglo que va de 1870 a 1970 y se organiza en dos principales partes: 1) la bibliografía sistemática de títulos relacionados con la política y el pensamiento político; y 2) una sección que abarca casi dos tercios de la obra y que se destina a sumarios de obras significativas y a bibliografías de autores sobresalientes (Rui Barbosa, Euclides da Cunha, Alberto Sales, Getulio Vargas, etc.). Obra de evidente utilidad.

7632 1.000 [i.e. Mil] títulos de autores brasileiros de filosofia. v. 1, Livros e capítulos de livros. v. 2, Artigos de periódicos. Organização de Geraldo Pinheiro Machado. São Paulo: Pontifícia Univ. Católica de São Paulo, Unidade Central de Documentação e Informação Científica Profesor Casemiro dos Reis Filho, 1984. 2 v. (139,

143 p.): indexes (Col. 1.000 títulos. Série Filosofia)

Proyecto de naturaleza muy particular, pues se continuará, acumulativamente, en nuevos volúmenes realizándose la ordenación definitiva al final. Entre los dos presentes volúmenes suman 2.000 títulos, 1.000 libros (o capítulos de libros), y 1.000 artículos de periódicos. La obra, según se anuncia, se ha pensado para uso universitario. Sobre bibliografía filosófica brasileña, ver *HLAS 42:7591.*

7633 Oliveira, Beneval de. A fenomenologia no Brasil. Rio de Janeiro: Pallas Editora e Distribuidora, 1983. 84 p.: bibl.

Compuesto de cinco trabajos, estudia algunos aspectos de la influencia fenomenológica en Brasil. El artículo más importante, creemos, es el dedicado a Ernildo Stein y la cuestión del método en la filosofía heideggeriana.

Oliveira, Lúcia Lippi; Mônica Pimenta Velloso; and **Angela Maria Castro Gomes.** Estado Novo: ideologia e poder. See item **3503.**

7634 Paim, Antônio. Historia das idéias filosóficas no Brasil. 3a ed., rev. e aum. São Paulo: Editora Convívio; Brasília: Instituto Nacional do Livro, Fundação Nacional Pro-Memória, 1984. 615 p.

Edición modificada y ampliada de una obra clásica e imprescindible sobre el tema.

7635 Pombal e a cultura brasileira. Organização de Antônio Paim. Rio de Janeiro: Fundação Cultural Brasil-Portugal: Tempo Brasileiro, 1982. 137 p.

Examen de algunos aspectos de la obra modernizadora del Marqués de Pombal y sus consecuencias en Brasil.

7636 Ribeiro Júnior, João. Alberto Salles: trajetória intelectual e pensamento político. São Paulo: Editora Convívio, 1983. 241 p.: bibl., port. (Biblioteca do pensamento brasileiro. Ensaios; 5)

De buena calidad monográfica, es una detallada biografía intelectual y un examen del pensamiento político del autor estudiado. Alberto Salles (1857 -1904) fue defensor de las ideas republicanas. Anteriormente sólo se había publicado sobre él la obra de Luis Washington Vita, *Alberto Salles: ideólogo da República* (1965), otro volumen de A.R. de Paulo Leite, y algunos artículos.

7637 Sousa, Francisco Martins de. O culturalismo sociológico de Alcides Bezerra. Apresentação de Antônio Paim. São Paulo: Editora Convívio, 1981. 86 p.: bibl. (Biblioteca do pensamento brasileiro. Ensaios; 3)

Buena monografía sobre Alcides Bezerra (1891–1938), que el autor considera (al igual que Antônio Paim, que presenta el libro) como parte del movimiento culturalista que comienza con Tobias Barreto. Al final se incluye el texto de una conferencia de Bezerra sobre "A Filosofia no Brasil do Século XIX," de 1937.

7638 Spinelli, Miguel. O empenho filosófico de Mont'Alverne na época do Brasil imperial: seu valor histórico e interesse filosófico (Reflexão [Pontifícia Univ. Católica de Campinas, Instituto de Filosofia e Teologia] 8;26, maio/agôsto 1983, p. 43–73)

Trabajo extenso y detallado, a pesar de considerar limitada la importancia filosófica de Mont'Alverne.

7639 Tavares, José Nilo. Marx, o socialismo e o Brasil. Rio de Janeiro: Civilização Brasileira, 1983. 157 p.: bibl., ill., plates (Col. Documentos da história contemporânea; 79)

Interesante a pesar de no ser obra de investigación o de historia sistemática, sino más bien de comentario sobre aspectos del tema. Contiene anexos sobre obras de Marx y Engels publicadas en Brasil y sobre revistas obreras brasileñas del siglo XIX.

Teixeira, Luiz Gonzaga. Utopia: manual do militante. See *HLAS 47:6583.*

7639a Vélez Rodríguez, Ricardo et al. Filosofia luso-brasileira. Rio de Janeiro: Univ. Gama Filho, Depto. de Filosofia, 1983. 49 p.: bibl.

Contiene trabajos de Antônio Paim, R. Vélez Rodríguez, E. Abranches de Soveral, G. Pinheiro Machado, V. Borges de Macedo y Nelson Saldanha, entre otros, dedicados al análisis comparado de las filosofías portuguesa y brasileña. Volumen de interés, no obstante su brevedad.

PARAGUAY

7640 Benítez, Justo Pastor. Influencias del positivismo en la cultura nacional: para una historia de las ideas. Asunción: NAPA, 1983. 176 p. (Col. Prisma)

Paraguay ha estado muy poco represen-

tado en el desarrollo de la filosofía latinoamericana, y consiguientemente en el de su historiografía. De ahí la importancia relativa de esta contribución, que además de ser obra de crítica reproduce algunos textos. Realizada con ciertas limitaciones de información general, lo más importante de esta obra es la exposición de autores vinculados al positivismo en varios campos, destacándose la figura de Cecilio Báez. El autor señala la necesidad de prestar mayor atención al estudio de la cultura y las ideas en el Paraguay.

URUGUAY

7641 Araujo Azarola, María Cristina. La democracia en el pensamiento de Juan Zorrilla de San Martín (IFCL/E, 2, 1982, p. 75–85)

Exposición de algunas ideas del gran poeta uruguayo, Zorrilla de San Martín, sobre la democracia, y la raíz cristiana de las mismas. Ver la reseña del crítico literario en item **5164.**

7642 Araújo Azarola, María Cristina. Dr. Enrique Grauen Iribarren (IFCL/E, 1, 1981, p. 33–51, bibl.)

Utilizable como aporte de datos sobre Grauen Iribarren (1916–72), figura filosófica uruguaya poco conocida, perteneciente al pensamiento católico, y autor de *Conocimiento y existencia* (1952).

7643 Fragmentos. Centro de Estudios Latinoamericanos Rómulo Gallegos. Depto. de Investigaciones. No. 7, mayo/agosto 1980–. Caracas.

Esta entrega está dedicada a Carlos Vaz Ferreira. Más que exégesis, resulta ser una revaloración del filósofo uruguayo desde perspectivas filosóficas actuales. Contiene una introducción ("¿Por qué Vaz Ferreira Hoy?") de Mario Sambarino, y los siguientes trabajos: "Lógica Viva y Psico-Lógica" de Goiz-Eder Calvo Albizu; "La Originalidad de la Ética de Vaz Ferreira" de Miguel Márquez; "Vaz Ferreira y la Tradición Positivista: el Caso de las Falacias Verbo-Ideológicas," de Javier Sasso. Contribución importante.

7644 Larre Borges, Ana Inés. Felisberto Hernández: una conciencia filosófica (UBN/R, 12, 1983, p. 5–40, ill.)

Con abundante detalle muestra la influencia del filósofo uruguayo Carlos Vaz

Ferreira sobre la literatura de su compatriota, Felisberto Hernández.

7645 Vaz Ferreira, Carlos. Lógica viva: adaptación práctica y didáctica. Estudio preliminar, índice analítico y notas de Jorge Liberati. Texto al cuidado de Sara Vaz Ferreira. Montevideo: Editorial Técnica, 1983. 250 p.

La importancia de la reedición de esta obra (que apareció en 1910) es el extenso estudio preliminar de Jorge Liberati, que examina la obra de Vaz Ferreira a la luz de la filosofía lingüística contemporánea. El autor había interpretado a Vaz Ferreira desde esa orientación en un libro previo: *Vaz Ferreira, filósofo del lenguaje* (ver *HLAS 44:7549*).

ARGENTINA

7646 Biagini, Hugo E. Macedonio Fernández y su ideario filosófico (Estudios de Literatura Argentina [Univ. de Buenos Aires, Facultad de Filosofía y Letras, Instituto de Literatura Argentina Ricardo Rojas, Sec. Crítica] 2:7, 1982, p. 7–16 bibl.)

Resume las no fácilmente resumibles ideas filosóficas del escritor argentino Macedonio Fernández. Interesan los datos que proporciona sobre la bibliografía que se ocupó de dicho autor.

7647 Biagini, Hugo E. Ortega en la Argentina (Todo es Historia [Buenos Aires] 220, agosto 1985, p. 38–49)

Aunque panorámicamente, las tres visitas de Ortega quedan bien caracterizadas, tanto en lo que respecta a la repercusión en el ambiente filosófico como en la relación del filósofo español con el público argentino y viceversa.

7648 Biagini, Hugo E. Panorama filosófico argentino. Prólogo de Arturo Andrés Roig. Buenos Aires: Editorial Universitaria de Buenos Aires, 1985. 135 p. (Col. Lectores)

Este breve volumen consta de dos partes: un sintético panorama apreciativo del pensamiento filosófico argentino en su historia, y una parte instrumental (bibliografía, reuniones, instituciones, etc.). Además de las opiniones que expresa, cumple una función introductoria.

7649 Botana, Natalio R. El problema del orden político según Sarmiento y Alberdi: notas acerca de una polémica (*in* Cien-

cias sociales: palabras y conjeturas [ver *HLAS 45:8309*] p. 120–141, bibl.)

Ilumina con acierto una polémica clásica sobre la ordenación política de la Argentina en el momento de constituirse como nación moderna, es decir, después de la caída de Rosas en 1852.

7650 Castillo Arráez, Alberto. Comentarios a las ideas éticas de Alejandro Korn. Caracas: Ediciones MRI, 1982. 87 p.: bibl.

Contiene tres ensayos: uno sobre la axiología de Korn; otro sobre la idea de libertad como creación; y el último en el cual se comparan opiniones de Korn con otros autores. La designación del conjunto como "comentarios" es acertada. Escrito con simpatía hacia el filósofo argentino.

7651 Caturelli, Alberto. La restauración del tomismo en Fray José María Liqueno (UCA/S, 37:143, enero/marzo 1982, p. 36–60?)

Franciscano de orden y tomista de orientación filosófica, el Padre Liqueno murió en 1926. Escribió una *Historia de la filosofía* y un tratado de psicología. El presente es un trabajo casi único y muy detallado sobre el aspecto filosófico de su obra, poco conocida, aun en Argentina.

Chiaramonte, José Carlos. La crítica ilustrada de la realidad: economía y sociedad en el pensamiento argentino e iberoamericano del siglo XVIII. See item **2805.**

7652 De Ipola, Emilio. Ideología y discurso populista. México: Folios Ediciones, 1982. 225 p.: bibl. (Col. Alternativas; AT3)

Lo que para esta sección interesa de este libro—cuyo principal trabajo es un examen de la ideología en Althusser—es el análisis del "discurso populista peronista."

7653 Etchecopar, Máximo. Crónica sucinta de una apasionada amistad: la de Ortega con Argentina y los argentinos (CH, 403/405, enero/marzo 1984, p. 375–390)

Como lo señala el título, es una crónica, centrada en las tres visitas de Ortega a la Argentina (1916, 1928, 1939–42), con mayor énfasis en las dos primeras.

Fernández López, Manuel and **Denaide Rosa del Valle Orellana.** Manuel Belgrano y las *Máximas* de Quesnay. See item **2889.**

Gandía, Enrique de. Nicolás Avellaneda: sus ideas y su tiempo. See item **3238.**

7655 Guy, Alain *et al.* Estudios en homenaje a Luis Farré. Introducción de Celina A. Lértora Mendoza. Buenos Aires: Fundación para el Estudio del Pensamiento Argentino e Iberoamericano (FEPAI), 1985. 133 p.

Presenta el volumen Celina A. Lértora Mendoza. Hay seis trabajos—breves, en general—sobre Farré (entre otros, de Alain Guy y Zdenek Kourim) y 12 dedicados a temas que fueron caros a Farré.

Ingenieros, José. Ensayos escogidos. See item 3255.

7656 Jornadas del Pensamiento Filosófico Argentino, 1st, Buenos Aires, 1983. Primeras Jornadas del Pensamiento Filosófico Argentino. Buenos Aires: Fundación para el Estudio del Pensamiento Argentino e Iberoamericano (FEPAI), 1983. 99 p.

Contribuciones de valor desigual, con algunos descuidos de presentación. Los trabajos de Hugo E. Biagini sobre la identidad argentina, de Clara A. Jalif de Bertranou sobre Jorge F. Nicolai, de Diego Pro sobre Juan Dalma, y de Arturo García Astrada sobre el hombre argentino y la crisis de la filosofía pueden destacarse en el conjunto.

7657 Kudriavtsev, Alexei. La concepción del hombre de Francisco Romero (URSS/AL, 4, abril 1983, p. 30–41)

Hay afirmaciones como: "las búsquedas teóricas de Romero eran . . . una respuesta a la crisis general del capitalismo." Las críticas son las previsibles desde el marxismo oficial soviético. No debe desconocerse sin embargo el interés por el pensamiento latinoamericano que el artículo significa.

7658 Lértora Mendoza, Celina Ana. Tres figuras para la historia de las ideas en la Argentina decimonónica (Siglo XIX [Univ. Autónoma de Nuevo León, Facultad de Filosofía y Letras, Monterrey, Mexico] 1:2, julio/dic. 1986, p. 13–26)

Las tres figuras aludidas son: Manuel Moreno, Juan María Gutiérrez y Carlos Octavio Bunge.

7659 Lértora Mendoza, Celina Ana and Matilde Isabel García Losada. Bibliografía filosófica argentina, 1900–1975. Buenos Aires: Fundación para la Educación, la Ciencia y la Cultura, 1983. 359 p.: appendices, bibl., indexes.

Primera bibliografía filosófica argentina del siglo XX. Contiene 5.182 entradas, divididas por disciplinas filosóficas, además de un índice de autores y otro de materias. Se anuncian apéndices que ampliarán la obra. Esfuerzo altamente meritorio.

7660 Mayer, Jorge M. El espíritu religioso en Alberdi (CRIT, 54:1863, 9 julio 1981, p. 385–389)

Datos extraídos de la vida y de algunos textos de Alberdi que mostrarían su espíritu religioso.

7661 El Movimiento positivista argentino. Compilación de Hugo E. Biagini. Buenos Aires: Editorial de Belgrano, 1985. 590 p.

Por su extensión y la naturaleza de su contenido, se trata de un volumen único sobre el positivismo argentino. Esta dividido en dos partes ("Asuntos" y "Figuras") y su contenido es el siguiente: Hugo E. Biagini, "Acerca del Carácter Nacional;" Hebe Campanella, "La Atmósfera Literaria;" Angel Castellán, "Accesos Historiográficos;" María C. Galati, "El Problema Estético;" Alfredo Galetti, "Ideas Políticas y Sociales;" Alfredo G. Kohn Loncarica y Abel L. Agüero, "El Contexto Médico;" Enrique E. Marí, "El Marco Jurídico;" Marcelo Montserrat, "La Presencia del Evolucionismo;" Dina V. Picotti C.,"La Cuestión Religiosa;" María Lucrecia Rovaletti, "Panorama Psicológico;" Félix Gustavo Schuster, "El Concepto de Ciencia;" Juan Carlos Tedesco, "La Instancia Educativa;" Hugo Vezzetti, "El Discurso Psiquiátrico;" Marcos Victoria, "Pedro Scalabrini, 1848–1916;" Hebe Clementi, "José María Ramos Mejía, 1849–1914;" Margarita Oriola Rojas, "Florentino Ameghino;" Juan Carlos Saccomanno, "Agustín Alvarez, 1857–1914;" Juan Carlos Torchia Estrada, "Alejandro Korn ante el Positivismo;" Aldo J. Pérez, "Juan Agustín García, 1862–1923;" Diego F. Pro, "Joaquín V. González, 1863–1923;" Luis A. Dozo, "Alfredo Ferreira, 1863–1938;" Emilio J. Corbiere, "Juan B. Justo y el Positivismo;" Raúl O. Sassi, "Rodolfo Senet, 1872–1938;" Clara A. Jalif de Bertranou, "Jorge Federico Nicolai, 1874–1964;" Eduardo J. Cárdenas y Carlos M. Payá, "Carlos Octavio Bunge, 1875–1918;" José Luis Damis, "José Ingenieros, 1877–1925;" Celina A. Lértora Mendoza, "Ciencia y Filosofía en José Ingenieros;" Luis Farré, "La Etica de Ingenieros;" Carlos Alemián, "Aníbal Ponce, 1898–1938;" José G. Vazeilles, "Irradiaciones: Rojas, Gálvez, Lugones."

Pérez Guihou, Dardo. El pensamiento conservador de Alberdi y la Constitución de 1853. See item **3281.**

7662 Quintanilla, Miguel A. Conceptos y cosas: acerca del *Tratado de filosofía* de Mario Bunge (CIF/RLF, 7:2, julio 1981, p. 165–175)

Como lo afirma el autor, la filosofía de Mario Bunge es demasiado compleja y, en algunos aspectos, original, como para dar cuenta de ella en moderado espacio. Pero aunque sólo destaca algunas líneas del pensamiento de Bunge, el artículo es de gran utilidad.

Ramírez de Rivera, Hugo Rodolfo. El pensamiento político de Sarmiento y Alberdi a través de *Facundo o civilización y Barbarie en las pampas argentinas* y *Bases y puntos de partida para la organización política de la República Argentina*, dos obras escritas en Chile. See item **3291.**

7663 La *Revista de Filosofía, Cultura, Ciencias y Educación*: 1915–1929. Estudio e índices analíticos de Hugo E. Biagini, Elena Ardissone, y Raúl Sassi. Buenos Aires: Academia Nacional de Ciencias, Centro de Estudios Filosóficos, s.d. 229 p.: ill.

Indices de la revista que dirigió José Ingenieros hasta su muerte en 1925. Obra de gran utilidad. Contiene más de 1.700 asientos, un "Indice Alfabético de Materias," un "Indice de Nombres," y una "Guía Conceptual."

7664 Terán, Oscar. El pensamiento de Aníbal Ponce en el marxismo latinoamericano (IPGH/RHI, 5/6, 1984/1985, p. 203–218)

Sobre Aníbal Ponce y la cuestión argentina y latinoamericana, en relación con su ingreso al marxismo durante la década de los años 30. Señala los resabios de pensamiento liberal-positivista en el autor estudiado.

Viñas, David. Indios, ejército y frontera. See item **3323.**

7665 Weinberg, Gregorio. El descontento y la promesa: sobre educación y cultura. Buenos Aires: Editorial de Belgrano, 1982. 199 p. (Col. Testimonios contemporáneos)

Los artículos, como lo indica el subtítulo, versan sobre educación y cultura. Los de materia educativa hacen constante referencia a problemas y casos de América Latina, y los de materia cultural se refieren principal-

mente a la situación argentina. Todos tienen el valor de ser proyectivos, de advertir problemas con preocupación de solucionarlos.

7666 Zalazar, Daniel E. Las posiciones de Sarmiento frente al indio (IILI/RI, 50:127, abril/junio 1984, p. 411–427)

La importancia de este trabajo, de buena calidad, consiste en que presenta y analiza numerosos pasajes de Sarmiento, yendo más allá de generalidades o de las manifestaciones sarmientinas más altisonantes. Matiza así ideas generalizadas sobre la opinión de Sarmiento respecto de los indios.

7667 Zalazar, Daniel E. Utopismo y antiutopismo en Domingo F. Sarmiento (IUP/HJ, 6:1, Fall 1984, p. 143–156)

A lo largo del desarrollo de su pensamiento, Sarmiento tuvo rasgos utópicos y a la vez criticó utopías. El autor lo señala con diversos y acertados ejemplos.

7668 Zuleta Alvarez, Enrique. Una autocrítica del 80: la visión histórica de Korn (*in* Congreso Internacional de Historia de América, 6th, Buenos Aires, 1980. Sexto Congreso Internacional de Historia de América [ver *HLAS 46:3214*] v. 6, p. 499–514)

El tema general es una apreciación de la obra de Korn, *Influencias filosóficas en la evolución nacional*, y el más específico, la crítica de Korn a los hombres de la generación del 80. Considera que *Influencias*, a pesar de ser una visión desde la perspectiva de la filosofía, es una aportación al enfoque histórico-político, lo que condice con la preocupación ético-política que había en Korn. Se trata de un trabajo agudo y claramente escrito.

JOURNAL ABBREVIATIONS
PHILOSOPHY

AAFH/TAM The Americas. Academy of American Franciscan History. Washington.

ACH/BHA Boletín de Historia y Antigüedades. Academia Colombiana de Historia. Bogotá.

BCE/C Cultura. Banco Central del Ecuador. Quito.

BNJM/R Revista de la Biblioteca Nacional José Martí. La Habana.

CH Cuadernos Hispanoamericanos. Instituto de Cultura Hispánica. Madrid.

CIF/RLF Revista Latinoamericana de Filosofía. Centro de Investigaciones Filosóficas. Buenos Aires.

CM/HM Historia Mexicana. El Colegio de México. México.

CNC/A Actualidades. Consejo Nacional de Cultura, Centro de Estudios Latinoamericanos Rómulo Gallegos. Caracas.

CONAC/RNC Revista Nacional de Cultura. Consejo Nacional de Cultura. Caracas.

CRIT Criterio. Editorial Criterio. Buenos Aires.

ESME/C Cultura. Ministerio de Educación. San Salvador.

HAHR Hispanic American Historical Review. Duke Univ. Press *for the* Conference on Latin American History, American Historical Assn. Durham, N.C.

IFCL/E Estudios de Ciencias y Letras. Instituto de Filosofía, Ciencias y Letras. Montevideo.

IILI/RI Revista Iberoamericana. Instituto Internacional de Literatura Iberoamericana. Patrocinada por la Univ. de Pittsburgh. Pittsburgh, Pa.

IUP/HJ Hispanic Journal. Indiana Univ. of Pennsylvania, Dept. of Foreign Languages. Indiana.

LARR Latin American Research Review. Univ. of North Carolina Press *for the* Latin American Studies Assn. Chapel Hill.

LNB/L Lotería. Lotería Nacional de Beneficencia. Panamá.

NOSALF/IA Ibero Americana. Scandinavian Assn. for Research on Latin America (NOSALF). Stockholm.

OAS/LE La Educación. Organization of American States, Dept. of Educational Affairs. Washington.

PAIGH/H Revista de Historia de América. Instituto Panamericano de Geografía e Historia, Comisión de Historia. México.

RIB Revista Interamericana de Bibliografía/Inter-American Review of

Bibliography. Organization of American States. Washington.

SP Socialismo y Participación. Ediciones Socialismo y Participación. Lima.

SUR Sur. Buenos Aires.

UB/BA Boletín Americanista. Univ. de Barcelona, Facultad de Geografía e Historia, Depto. de Historia de América. Barcelona, Spain.

UBN/R Revista de la Biblioteca Nacional. Ministerio de Educación y Cultura. Montevideo.

UC/AT Atenea. Univ. de Concepción. Concepción, Chile.

UCA/S Sapientia. Univ. Católica Argentina Santa María de los Buenos Aires, Facultad de Filosofía. Buenos Aires.

UCLV/I Islas. Univ. Central de las Villas. Santa Clara, Cuba.

UCR/RF Revista de Filosofía de la Universidad de Costa Rica. San José.

UEN/LS Lateinamerika Studien. Univ. Erlangen-Nürnberg, Sektion Lateinamerika. Nürnberg, FRG.

UN/IV Ideas y Valores. Univ. Nacional, Instituto de Filosofía y Letras. Bogotá.

UNAM/L Latinoamérica. Univ. Nacional Autónoma de México, Facultad de Filosofía y Letras, Centro de Estudios Latinoamericanos. México.

UNAM/RMCPS Revista Mexicana de Ciencias Políticas y Sociales. Univ. Autónoma Nacional de México, Facultad de Ciencias Políticas y Sociales. México.

UNCR/R Revista de Historia. Univ. Nacional de Costa Rica, Escuela de Historia. Heredia.

UND/RP The Review of Politics. Univ. of Notre Dame. Notre Dame, Ind.

UNESCO/CU Cultures. United Nations Educational, Scientific and Cultural Organization. Paris.

UNPHU/A Aula. Univ. Nacional Pedro Henríquez Ureña. Santo Domingo.

URSS/AL América Latina. Academia de Ciencias de la Unión de Repúblicas Soviéticas Socialista. Moscu.

USB/RVF Revista Venezolana de Filosofía. Univ. Simón Bolívar [and] Sociedad Venezolana de Filosofía. Caracas.

UTIEH/C Caravelle. Univ. de Toulouse, Institute d'Etudes hispaniques, hispano-américaines et luso-brésilennes. Toulouse, France.

UY/R Revista de la Universidad de Yucatán. Mérida, Mexico.

INDEXES

ABBREVIATIONS AND ACRONYMS

Except for journal acronyms which are listed at: a) the end of each major disciplinary section, (e.g., Art, Film, etc.); and b) after each serial title in the *Title List of Journals Indexed*, p. 665.

a.	annual
ABC	Argentina, Brazil, Chile
A.C.	antes de Cristo
ACAR	Associação de Crédito e Assistência Rural, Brazil
AD	Anno Domini
A.D.	Acción Democrática, Venezuela
ADESG	Associação dos Diplomados de Escola Superior de Guerra, Brazil
AGI	Archivo General de Indias, Sevilla
AGN	Archivo General de la Nación
AID	Agency for International Development
a.k.a.	also known as
Ala.	Alabama
ALALC	Asociación Latinoamericana de Libre Comercio
ALEC	*Atlas lingüístico etnográfico de Colombia*
ANAPO	Alianza Nacional Popular, Colombia
ANCARSE	Associação Nordestina de Crédito e Assistência Rural de Sergipe, Brazil
ANCOM	Andean Common Market
ANDI	Asociación Nacional de Industriales, Colombia
ANUC	Asociación Nacional de Usuarios Campesinos, Colombia
ANUIES	Asociación Nacional de Universidades e Institutos de Enseñanza Superior, Mexico
AP	Acción Popular
APRA	Alianza Popular Revolucionaria Americana
ARENA	Aliança Renovadora Nacional, Brazil
Ariz.	Arizona
Ark.	Arkansas
ASA	Association of Social Anthropologists of the Commonwealth, London
ASSEPLAN	Assessoria de Planejamente e Acompanhamento, Recife
Assn.	Association
Aufl.	Auflage (edition, edición)
AUFS	American Universities Field Staff Reports, Hanover, N.H.
Aug.	August, Augustan
aum.	aumentada
b.	born (nació)
BBE	Bibliografia Brasileira de Educação
b.c.	indicates dates obtained by radiocarbon methods
BC	Before Christ
bibl(s).	bibliography(ies)
BID	Banco Interamericano de Desarrollo
BNDE	Banco Nacional de Desenvolvimento Econômico, Brazil
BNH	Banco Nacional de Habitação, Brazil
BP	before present

b/w	black and white
C14	Carbon 14
ca.	*circa* (about)
CACM	Central American Common Market
CADE	Conferencia Anual de Ejecutivos de Empresas, Peru
CAEM	Centro de Altos Estudios Militares, Peru
Calif.	California
Cap.	Capítulo
CARC	Centro de Arte y Comunicación
CARICOM	Caribbean Common Market
CARIFTA	Caribbean Free Trade Association
CBD	central business district
CD	Christian Democrats, Chile
CDI	Conselho de Desenvolvimento Industrial
CEBRAP	Centro Brasileiro de Análise e Planejamento, São Paulo
CECORA	Centro de Cooperativas de la Reforma Agraria, Colombia
CEDAL	Centro de Estudios Democráticos de América Latina, Costa Rica
CEDE	Centro de Estudios sobre Desarrollo Económico, Univ. de los Andes, Bogotá
CEDEPLAR	Centro de Desenvolvimento e Planejamento Regional, Belo Horizonte
CEDES	Centro de Estudios de Estado y Sociedad, Buenos Aires; Centro de Estudos de Educação e Sociedade, São Paulo
CEDI	Centro Ecuménico de Documentos e Informação, São Paulo
CEDLA	Centro de Estudios y Documentación Latinoamericanos, Amsterdam
CEESTEM	Centro de Estudios Económicos y Sociales del Tercer Mundo, México
CELADE	Centro Latinoamericano de Demografía
CELADEC	Comisión Evangélica Latinoamericana de Educación Cristiana
CELAM	Consejo Episcopal Latinoamericano
CEMLA	Centro de Estudios Monetarios Latinoamericanos, Mexico
CENDES	Centro de Estudios del Desarrollo, Venezuela
CENIDIM	Centro Nacional de Información, Documentación e Investigación Musicales, Mexico
CENIET	Centro Nacional de Información y Estadísticas del Trabajo, Mexico
CEPADE	Centro Paraguayo de Estudios de Desarrollo Económico y Social
CEPA-SE	Comissão Estadual de Planejamento Agrícola, Sergipe
CEPAL	Comisión Económica para América Latina
CERES	Centro de Estudios de la Realidad Económica y Social, Bolivia
CES	constant elasticity of substitution
cf.	compare
CFI	Consejo Federal de Inversiones, Buenos Aires
CGE	Confederación General Económica, Argentina
CGTP	Confederación General de Trabajadores del Perú
chap(s).	chapter(s)
CHEAR	Council on Higher Education in the American Republics
Cía.	Compañía
CIA	Central Intelligence Agency
CIDA	Comité Interamericano de Desarrollo Agrícola
CIDE	Centro de Investigación y Desarrollo de la Educación, Chile
CIE	Centro de Investigaciones Económicas, Buenos Aires
CIEDLA	Centro Interdisciplinario de Estudios sobre el Desarrollo Latinoamericano, Buenos Aires
CIEDUR	Centro Interdisciplinario de Estudios sobre el Desarrollo, Uruguay, Montevideo
CIEPLAN	Corporación de Investigaciones Económicas para América Latina, Santiago
CIMI	Conselho Indigenista Missionário, Brazil

CINTERFOR	Centro Interamericano de Investigación y Documentación sobre Formación Profesional
CINVE	Centro de Investigaciones Económicas, Montevideo
CIP	Conselho Interministerial de Preços
CIPCA	Centro de Investigación y Promoción del Campesinado, Bolivia
CLACSO	Consejo Latinoamericano de Ciencias Sociales, Secretaría Ejecutiva, Buenos Aires
CLASC	Confederación Latinoamericana Sindical Cristiana
CLE	Comunidad Latinoamericana de Escritores, Mexico
cm	centimeter
CNI	Confederação Nacional da Industria, Brazil
Co.	Company
COB	Central Obrera Boliviana
COBAL	Companhia Brasileira de Alimentos
Col./col.	Collection, Colección, Coleção, color
Colo.	Colorado
COMCORDE	Comisión Coordinadora para el Desarrollo Económico, Uruguay
comp(s).	compiler(s), compilador(es)
CONCLAT	Congresso Nacional de Classe Trabalhadora, Brazil
CONDESE	Conselho de Desenvolvimento Econômico de Sergipe
Conn.	Connecticut
COPEI	Comité Organizador Pro-Elecciones Independientes, Venezuela
CORFO	Corporación de Fomento de la Producción, Chile
CORP	Corporación para el Fomento de Investigaciones Económicas, Colombia
Corp.	Corporation, Corporación
corr.	corregida
CP	Communist Party
CPDOC	Centro de Pesquisa e Documentação, Brazil
CRIC	Consejo Regional Indígena del Cauca, Colombia
CSUTCB	Confederación Sindical Unica de Trabajadores Campesinos de Bolivia
CTM	Confederación de Trabajadores de México
CUNY	City University of New York
CVG	Corporación Venezolana de Guayana
d.	died (murió)
DANE	Departamento Nacional de Estadística, Colombia
DC	developed country; Demócratas Cristianos, Chile
d.C	después de Cristo
Dec./déc.	December, décembre
Del.	Delaware
dept.	department
depto.	departamento
DESCO	Centro de Estudios y Promoción del Desarrollo, Lima
Dez./dez.	Dezember, dezembre
dic.	diciembre, dicembre
disc.	discography
DNOCS	Departamento Nacional de Obras Contra as Sécas, Brazil
doc.	document, documento
Dr.	Doctor
Dra.	Doctora
DRAE	*Diccionario de la Real Academia Española*
ECLA	Economic Commission for Latin America
ECOSOC	UN Department of Economic and Social Affairs
ed./éd.(s)	edition(s), édition(s), edición(es), editor(s), redactor(es), director(es)
EDEME	Editora Emprendimentos Educacionais, Florianópolis

Edo.	Estado
EEC	European Economic Community
EFTA	European Free Trade Association
e.g.	*exempio gratia* (for example)
ELN	Ejército de Liberación Nacional, Colombia
ENDEF	Estudo Nacional da Despesa Familiar, Brazil
ESG	Escola Superior de Guerra, Brazil
estr.	estrenado
et al.	*et alia* (and others)
ETENE	Escritório Técnico de Estudios Econômicos do Nordeste, Brazil
ETEPE	Escritório Técnico de Planejamento, Brazil
EUDEBA	Editorial Universitaria de Buenos Aires
EWG	Europaische Wirtschaftsgemeinschaft. *See* EEC.
facsim(s).	facsimile(s)
FAO	Food and Agriculture Organization of the United Nations
FDR	Frente Democrático Revolucionario, El Salvador
Feb./feb.	February, Februar, febrero, febbraio
FEDECAFE	Federación Nacional de Cafeteros, Colombia
fev./fév.	fevreiro, février
ff.	following
FGTS	Fundo do Garantia do Tempo de Serviço, Brazil
FGV	Fundação Getúlio Vargas
FIEL	Fundación de Investigaciones Económicas Latinoamericanas, Argentina
film.	filmography
fl.	flourished
Fla.	Florida
FLACSO	Facultad Latinoamericana de Ciencias Sociales
FMI	Fondo Monetario Internacional
FMLN	Frente Farabundo Martí de Liberación Nacional, El Salvador
fold.	folded
fol(s).	folio(s)
FRG	Federal Republic of Germany
FSLN	Frente Sandinista de Revolución Nacional, Nicaragua
ft.	foot, feet
FUAR	Frente Unido de Acción Revolucionaria, Colombia
FUNAI	Fundação Nacional do Indio, Brazil
FUNARTE	Fundação Nacional de Arte, Brazil
Ga.	Georgia
GAO	General Accounting Office, Washington
GATT	General Agreement on Tariffs and Trade
GDP	gross domestic product
GDR	German Democratic Republic
GEIDA	Grupo Executivo de Irrigação para o Desenvolvimento Agrícola, Brazil
gen.	gennaio
Gen.	General
GMT	Greenwich Meridian Time
GPA	grade point average
GPO	Government Printing Office, Washington
h.	hijo
ha.	hectares, hectáreas
HLAS	*Handbook of Latin American Studies*
HMAI	*Handbook of Middle American Indians*
Hnos.	hermanos
HRAF	Human Relations Area Files, Human Relations Area Files, Inc., New Haven, Conn.

IBBD	Instituto Brasileiro de Bibliografia e Documentação
IBGE	Instituto Brasileiro de Geografia e Estatística, Rio de Janeiro
IBRD	International Bank of Reconstruction and Development
ICA	Instituto Colombiano Agropecuario
ICAIC	Instituto Cubano de Arte e Industria Cinematográfica
ICCE	Instituto Colombiano de Construcción Escolar
ICE	International Cultural Exchange
ICSS	Instituto Colombiano de Seguridad Social
ICT	Instituto de Crédito Territorial, Colombia
id.	*idem* (the same as previously mentioned or given)
IDB	Inter-American Development Bank
i.e.	*id est* (that is)
IEL	Instituto Euvaldo Lodi, Brazil
IEP	Instituto de Estudios Peruanos
IERAC	Instituto Ecuatoriano de Reforma Agraria y Colonización
IFAD	International Fund for Agricultural Development
IICA	Instituto Interamericano de Ciencias Agrícolas, San José
III	Instituto Indigenista Interamericana, Mexico
IIN	Instituto Indigenista Nacional, Guatemala
ill.	illustration(s)
Ill.	Illinois
ILO	International Labour Organization, Geneva
IMES	Instituto Mexicano de Estudios Sociales
IMF	International Monetary Fund, Washington
Impr.	Imprenta, Imprimerie
in.	inches
INAH	Instituto Nacional de Antropología e Historia, Mexico
INBA	Instituto Nacional de Bellas Artes, Mexico
Inc.	Incorporated
INCORA	Instituto Colombiano de Reforma Agraria
Ind.	Indiana
INEP	Instituto Nacional de Estudios Pedagógicos, Brazil
INI	Instituto Nacional Indigenista, Mexico
INIT	Instituto Nacional de Industria Turística, Cuba
INPES/IPEA	Instituto de Planejamento Econômico e Social, Instituto de Pesquisas, Brazil
INTAL	Instituto para la Integración de América Latina
IPA	Instituto de Pastoral Andina, Univ. de San Antonio de Abad, Seminario de Antropología, Cusco, Peru
IPEA	Instituto de Pesquisas Econômico-Social Aplicadas, Brazil
IPES/GB	Instituto de Pesquisas e Estudos Sociais, Guanabara, Brazil
IPHAN	Instituto de Patrimônio Histórico e Artístico Nacional, Brazil
ir.	irregular
IS	Internacional Socialista
ITT	International Telephone and Telegraph
Jan./jan.	January, Januar, janeiro, janvier
JLP	Jamaican Labour Party
Jr.	Junior, Júnior
JUC	Juventud Universitaria Católica, Brazil
JUCEPLAN	Junta Central de Planificación, Cuba
Kan.	Kansas
km	kilometers, kilómetres
Ky.	Kentucky
La.	Louisiana
LASA	Latin American Studies Association
LDC(s)	less developed country(ies)

LP	long-playing record
Ltd(a).	Limited, Limitada
m	meters, metros
m.	murió (died)
M	mille, mil, thousand
M.A.	Master of Arts
MAPU	Movimiento de Acción Popular Unitario, Chile
MARI	Middle American Research Institute, Tulane University, New Orleans
Mass.	Massachusetts
MCC	Mercado Común Centro-Americano
Md.	Maryland
MDB	Movimiento Democrático Brasileiro
MDC	more developed countries
MEC	Ministério de Educação e Cultura, Brazil
Mich.	Michigan
mimeo	mimeographed, mimeografiado
min.	minutes, minutos
Minn.	Minnesota
MIR	Movimiento de Izquierda Revolucionaria, Chile
Miss.	Mississippi
MIT	Massachusetts Institute of Technology
ml	milliliter
MLN	Movimiento de Liberación Nacional
mm.	millimeter
MNC	multinational corporation
MNR	Movimiento Nacionalista Revolucionario, Bolivia
Mo.	Missouri
MOBRAL	Movimento Brasileiro de Alfabetização, Brazil
MOIR	Movimiento Obrero Independiente y Revolucionario, Colombia
Mont.	Montana
MRL	Movimiento Revolucionario Liberal, Colombia
ms.	manuscript
M.S.	Master of Science
msl	mean sea level
n.	nació (born)
NBER	National Bureau of Economic Research, Cambridge, Massachusetts
N.C.	North Carolina
N.D.	North Dakota
NE	Northeast
Neb.	Nebraska
neubearb.	neubearbeitet (revised, corregida)
Nev.	Nevada
n.f.	neue Folge
N.H.	New Hampshire
NIEO	New International Economic Order
NIH	National Institutes of Health, Washington
N.J.	New Jersey
N.M.	New Mexico
no(s).	number(s), número(s)
NOIE	Nuevo Orden Económico Internacional
NOSALF	Scandinavian Committee for Research in Latin America
Nov./nov.	November, noviembre, novembre, novembro
NSF	National Science Foundation
NW	Northwest
N.Y.	New York

OAB	Ordem dos Advogados do Brasil
OAS	Organization of American States
Oct./oct.	October, octubre, octobre
ODEPLAN	Oficina de Planificación Nacional, Chile
OEA	Organización de los Estados Americanos
OIT	*See* ILO.
Okla.	Oklahoma
Okt.	Oktober
op.	opus
OPANAL	Organismo para la Proscripción de las Armas Nucleares en América Latina
OPEC	Organization of Petroleum Exporting Countries
OPEP	Organización de Países Exportadores de Petróleo
OPIC	Overseas Investment Corporation
Or.	Oregon
OREALC	Oficina Regional de Educación para América Latina y el Caribe
ORIT	Organización Regional Interamericana del Trabajo
ott.	ottobre
out.	outubre
p.	page(s)
Pa.	Pennsylvania
PAN	Partido Acción Nacional, Mexico
PC	Partido Comunista
PCCLAS	Pacific Coast Council on Latin American Studies
PCN	Partido de Conciliación Nacional, El Salvador
PCP	Partido Comunista del Perú
PCR	Partido Comunista Revolucionario, Chile and Argentina
PCV	Partido Comunista de Venezuela
PDC	Partido Demócrata Cristiano, Chile
PDS	Partido Democrático Social, Brazil
PDT	Partido Democrático Trabalhista, Brazil
PEMEX	Petróleos Mexicanos
PETROBRAS	Petróleo Brasileiro
PIMES	Programa Integrado de Mestrado em Economia e Sociologia, Brazil
PIP	Partido Independiente de Puerto Rico
PLANAVE	Engenharia e Planejamento Limitada, Brazil
PLANO	Planejamento e Assesoria Limitada, Brazil
PLN	Partido Liberación Nacional, Costa Rica
PMDB	Partido Movimento Democrático Brasileiro
PNAD	Pesquisa Nacional por Amuestra Domiciliar, Brazil
PNM	People's National Movement, Trinidad and Tobago
PNP	People's National Party, Jamaica
pop.	population
port(s).	portrait(s)
PPP	purchasing power parities
PRD	Partido Revolucionario Dominicano
PREALC	Programa Regional del Empleo para América Latina y el Caribe, Organización Internacional del Trabajo, Santiago
PRI	Partido Revolucionario Institucional, Mexico
PROABRIL	Centro de Projetos Industriais, Brazil
Prof.	Professor(a)
PRONAPA	Programa Nacional de Pesquisas Arqueológicas, Brazil
prov.	province, provincia
PS	Partido Socialista, Chile
PSD	Partido Social Democrático, Brazil
pseud.	pseudonym, pseudónimo

PT	Partido dos Trabalhadores, Brazil
pt(s).	part(s), parte(s)
PTB	Partido Trabalhista Brasileiro
pub.	published, publisher
PUC	Pontificia Universidad Católica, Rio de Janeiro
PURSC	Partido Unido de la Revolución Socialista de Cuba
q.	quarterly
rev.	revisada, revista, revised
R.I.	Rhode Island
s.a.	semiannual
SALALM	Seminar on the Acquisition of Latin American Library Materials
SATB	soprano, alto, tenor, bass
sd.	sound
s.d.	*sine datum* (no date, sin fecha)
S.D.	South Dakota
SDR	special drawing rights
SE	Southeast
SELA	Sistema Económico Latinoamericano
SENAC	Serviço Nacional de Aprendizagem Comercial, Rio de Janeiro
SENAI	Serviço Nacional de Aprendizagem Industrial, São Paulo
SEP	Secretaría de Educación Pública, Mexico
SEPLA	Seminario Permanente sobre Latinoamérica, Mexico
Sept./sept.	September, septiembre, septembre
SES	socioeconomic status
SESI	Serviço Social de Industria, Brazil
set.	setembre, settembre
SI	Socialist International
SIECA	Secretaría Permanente del Tratado General de Integración Centroamericana
SIL	Summer Institute of Linguistics (Instituto Lingüístico de Verano)
SINAMOS	Sistema Nacional de Apoyo a la Movilización Social, Peru
S.J.	Society of Jesus
s.l.	*sine loco* (place of publication unknown)
s.n.	*sine nomine* (publisher unknown)
SNA	Sociedad Nacional de Agricultura, Chile
SPP	Secretaría de Programación y Presupuesto, Mexico
SPVEA	Superintendência do Plano de Valorização Econômica de Amazônia, Brazil
sq.	square
SSRC	Social Sciences Research Council, New York
SUDAM	Superintendência de Desenvolvimento da Amazônia, Brazil
SUDENE	Superintendência de Desenvolvimento do Nordeste, Brazil
SUFRAME	Superintendência da Zona Franca de Manaus, Brazil
SUNY	State University of New York
SW	Southwest
t.	tomo(s), tome(s)
TAT	Thematic Apperception Test
TB	tuberculosis
Tenn.	Tennessee
Tex.	Texas
TG	transformational generative
TL	Thermoluminescent
TNE	transnational enterprise
TNP	Tratado de No Proliferación
trans.	translator
UCA	Universidad Centroamericana José Simeón Cañas, San Salvador
UCLA	University of California, Los Angeles

UDN	União Democrática Nacional, Brazil
UK	United Kingdom
UN	United Nations
UNAM	Universidad Nacional Autónoma de México
UNCTAD	United Nations Conference on Trade and Development
UNDP	United Nations Development Programme
UNEAC	Unión de Escritores y Artistas de Cuba
UNESCO	United Nations Educational, Scientific and Cultural Organization
UNI/UNIND	União das Nações Indígenas
Univ(s).	university(ies), universidad(es), universidade(s), université(s), universität(s), universitá(s)
uniw.	uniwersytet
Unltd.	Unlimited
UP	Unidad Popular, Chile
URD	Unidad Revolucionaria Democrática
URSS	Unión de Repúblicas Soviéticas Socialistas
US	United States
USAID	*See* AID.
USIA	United States Information Agency, Washington
USSR	Union of Soviet Socialist Republics
UTM	Universal Transverse Mercator
v.	volume(s), volumen (volúmenes)
Va.	Virginia
viz.	*videlicet*, that is, namely
vol(s).	volume(s), volumen (volúmenes)
vs.	versus
Vt.	Vermont
W.Va.	West Virginia
Wash.	Washington
Wis.	Wisconsin
Wyo.	Wyoming
yr(s).	year(s)

TITLE LIST OF JOURNALS INDEXED

Journals that have been included in the *Handbook* as individual items are listed alphabetically by title in the *Author Index*, p. 717.

Actualidades. Consejo Nacional de la Cultura, Centro de Estudios Latinoamericanos Rómulo Gallegos. Caracas. (CNC/A)

Alfa. Univ. de São Paulo, Faculdade de Filosofia, Ciências e Letras. Marília, Brazil. (FFCLM/A)

Allpanchis. Instituto de Pastoral Andina. Cusco, Peru. (IPA/A)

América Indígena. Instituto Indigenista Interamericano. México. (III/AI)

América Latina. Academia de Ciencias de la Unión de Repúblicas Soviéticas Socialistas. Moscú. (URSS/AL)

American Anthropologist. American Anthropological Assn. Washington. (AAA/AA)

American Antiquity. Society for American Archaeology. Menasha, Wis. (SAA/AA)

American Ethnologist. American Ethnological Society. Washington. (AES/AE)

American Historical Review. American Historical Assn. Washington. (AHA/R)

American Jewish Archives. Cincinnati, Ohio. (AJA)

American Jewish Yearbook. American Jewish Committee. New York.

The Americas. Academy of American Franciscan History. Washington. (AAFH/TAM)

Anales de Antropología e Historia. Instituto Nacional de Antropología e Historia, Secretaría de Educación Pública. México. (INAH/A)

Anales de la Sociedad Rural Argentina. Buenos Aires. (SRA/A)

Anales del Instituto de Investigaciones Estéticas. Univ. Nacional Autónoma de México. México. (IIE/A)

Annales de demographie historique. Société de démographie historique. Paris.

Annales: économies, sociétés, civilisations. Centre national de la recherche scientifique *avec le concours de la* VIᵉ Section de l'Ecole pratique des hautes études. Paris. (AESC)

Anthropologica. Pontificia Univ. Católica del Perú, Depto. de Antropología. Lima.

Antropología: Cuadernos de Investigación. Pontificia Univ. Católica del Ecuador. Quito.

Antropología Ecuatoriana. Casa de la Cultura Ecuatoriana. Quito.

Anuario Colombiano de Historia Social y de la Cultura. Univ. Nacional de Colombia, Facultad de Ciencias Humanas, Depto. de Historia. Bogotá. (UNC/ACHSC)

Anuario de Estudios Americanos. Consejo Superior de Investigaciones Científicas [and] Univ. de Sevilla, Escuela de Estudios Hispano-Americanos. Sevilla, Spain. (EEHA/AEA)

Anuario de Estudios Atlánticos. Patronato de la Casa de Colón. Madrid.

Anuario de Letras. Univ. Nacional Autónoma de México, Facultad de Filosofía y Letras. México. (UNAM/AL)

Anuario Histórico Jurídico Ecuatoriano. Corp. de Estudios y Publicaciones. Quito.

Araucaria de Chile. Peralta Ediciones. Pamplona, Spain.

Archeologia. A. Fanton. Paris. (ARCHEO)

Archivo Ibero-Americano. Los Padres Franciscanos. Madrid. (PF/AIA)

Archivo Iberoamericana de Historia de la Medicina. Consejo Superior de Investigaciones Científicas, Instituto Arnaldo de Villanova. Madrid. (IAV/AIHM)

Archivum Historicum Societatis Iesu. Institutum Scriptorum de Historia S.I. Rome. (AHSI)

Areíto. Areíto, Inc. New York. (AR)

Argos. Univ. Simón Bolívar, División de Ciencias Sociales y Humanidades. Caracas.

Arizona Quarterly. Univ. of Arizona. Tucson. (UA/AQ)

Art. Univ. Federal da Bahia, Escola de Música e Artes Cênicas. Salvador.

Art History. Routledge & K. Paul. London.

Artes de México. México. (ARMEX)

Atenea. Univ. de Concepción. Concepción, Chile. (UC/AT)

Aula. Univ. Nacional Pedro Henríquez Ureña. Santo Domingo. (UNPHU/A)

Belizean Studies. Belizean Institute of Social Research and Action [and] St. John's College. Belize City. (BISRA/BS)

Bibliotheca Americana. Coral Cables, Fla.

Boletim. Sociedade Brasileira de Musicologia. São Paulo. (SBM/B)

Boletín Americanista. Univ. de Barcelona, Facultad de Geografía e Historia, Depto. de Historia de América. Barcelona, Spain. (UB/BA)

Boletín Cultural y Bibliográfico. Banco de la República, Biblioteca Luis-Angel Arango. Bogotá. (CBR/BCB)

Boletín de Historia y Antigüedades. Academia Colombiana de Historia. Bogotá. (ACH/BHA)

Boletín de Investigación del Movimiento Obrero. Univ. Autónoma de Puebla, Instituto de Ciencias, Centro de Investigaciones Históricas del Movimiento Obrero. Puebla, Mexico.

Boletín de la Academia Chilena de la Historia. Santiago. (ACH/B)

Boletín de la Academia Hondureña de la Lengua. Tegucigalpa. (AHL/B)

Boletín de la Academia Nacional de Historia. Quito. (EANH/B)

Boletín de la Academia Nacional de la Historia. Caracas. (VANH/B)

Boletín de Lima. Editorial Los Pinos. Lima.

Boletín del Instituto de Historia Argentina y Americana Emilio Ravignani. Univ. Nacional de Buenos Aires. Buenos Aires. (IHAAER/B)

Boletín del Instituto Riva-Agüero. Pontificia Univ. Católica del Perú. Lima. (IRA/B)

Boletín del Museo del Hombre Dominicano. Santo Domingo. (MHD/B)

Boletín Nicaragüense de Bibliografía y Documentación. Banco Central de Nicaragua, Biblioteca. Managua. (BNBD)

Bulletin de la Sociéte d'histoire de la Guadeloupe. Archives départamentales *avec le concours du* Conseil général de la Guadeloupe. Basse-Terre. (SHG/B)

Bulletin de l'Institut français d'études andines. Lima. (IFEA/B)

Bulletin d'information des études féministes.

Centre d'Etudes féministes, Univ. de Provence. Aix en Provence, France.

Bulletin du Centre d'histoire des espaces atlantiques. Talence, France.

Bulletin of Hispanic Studies. Institute of Hispanic Studies. Liverpool, England.

Bulletin of Latin American Research. Oxford Microfilm Publications. Oxford, England.

Cahiers des Amériques latines. Paris. (CDAL)

Canadian Journal of History. Univ. of Saskatechwan. Saskatoon.

Caravelle. Univ. de Toulouse, Institut d'Etudes hispaniques, hispano-américaines et luso-brésiliennes. Toulouse, France. (UTIEH/C)

Caribbean Quarterly. Univ. of the West Indies. Mona, Jamaica. (UWI/CQ)

Caribbean Review. Caribbean Review, Inc. Miami, Fla. (CRI/CR)

Casa de las Américas. Instituto Cubano del Libro. La Habana. (CDLA)

Catholic Historical Review. American Catholic Historical Assn., Catholic Univ. of America Press. Washington. (ACHA/CHR)

The Centennial Review of Arts and Sciences. Michigan State Univ., College of Arts and Sciences. East Lansing. (MSU/CR)

Chungará. Univ. del Norte, Depto. de Antropología. Arica, Chile. (UN/C)

Cineaste. New York.

CLA Journal. College Language Assn. Morgan State College. Baltimore, Md. (CLA/J)

Clave. Revista ilustrada de música. São Paulo.

El Comercio. Lima. (EC)

Comparative Studies in Society and History. Society for the Comparative Study of Society and History. The Hague. (CSSH)

Contemporáry Review. London.

Conjonction. Institut français d'Haïti. Port-au-Prince. (IFH/C)

Criterio. Editorial Criterio. Buenos Aires. (CRIT)

Cuadernos Americanos. México. (CAM)

Cuadernos de Comunicación Alternativa. Centro de Integración de Medios de Comunicación Alternativa (CIMCA). La Paz.

Cuadernos de Historia. Univ. de Chile, Facultad de Humanidades y Educación, Depto. de Ciencias Históricas. Santiago. (UC/CH)

Cuadernos de Historia Regional. Univ. de Luján, Depto. de Ciencias Sociales. Luján, Argentina.

Cuadernos Hispanoamericanos. Instituto de Cultura Hispánica. Madrid. (CH)

Cuban Studies/Estudios Cubanos. Univ. of Pittsburgh, Univ. Center for International Studies, Center for Latin American Studies. Pittsburgh, Pa. (UP/CSEC)

Cultura. Banco Central del Ecuador. Quito. (BCE/C)

Cultura. Ministerio de Educación. San Salvador. (ESME/C)

Cultures. United Nations Educational, Scientific, and Cultural Organization. Paris. (UNESCO/CU)

Current Anthropology. Univ. of Chicago. Chicago, Ill. (UC/CA)

Dados. Instituto Universitário de Pesquisas do Rio de Janeiro. Rio de Janeiro. (IUP/D)

Del Caribe. Casa del Caribe. Santiago de Cuba.

Diálogos. El Colegio de México. México. (CM/D)

Discurso Literario. Oklahoma State Univ. Stillwater.

Dress. Costume Society of America. New York.

Eco. Librería Bucholz. Bogotá. (ECO)

Economy and Society. Routledge, Kegan & Paul. London.

La Educación. Organization of American States, Dept. of Educational Affairs. Washington. (OAS/LE)

Encuentro. Univ. Centroamericana, Instituto Histórico. Managua. (UCA/E)

Enlace. New York.

Estudios de Ciencias y Letras. Instituto de Filosofía, Ciencias y Letras. Montevideo. (IFCL/E)

Estudios de Cultura Náhuatl. Univ. Nacional Autónoma de México, Instituto de Historia, Seminario de Cultura Náhuatl. México. (UNAM/ECN)

Estudios de Literatura Argentina. Univ. de Buenos Aires, Facultad de Filosofía y Letras, Instituto de Literatura Argentina Ricardo Rojas. Buenos Aires.

Estudios Latinoamericanos. Polska Akademia Nauk, Instutut Historii. Warszara. (PAN/EL)

Estudios Paraguayos. Univ. Católica Nuestra Señora de la Asunción. Asunción. (UCNSA/EP)

Estudios Públicos. Centro de Estudios Públicos. Santiago.

Estudios Sociales. Corp. de Promoción Universitaria. Santiago. (CPU/ES)

Estudios Sociales Centroamericanos. Consejo Superior de Univs. Centroamericanas, Confederación Universitaria Centroamericana, Programa Centroamericano de Ciencias Sociales. San José. (CSUCA/ESC)

Estudos Econômicos. Univ. de São Paulo, Instituto de Pesquisas Econômicas. São Paulo. (IPE/EE)

Ethnographisch-Archäologische Zeitschrift. Deutscher Verlag Wissenschaften. East Berlin. (EAZ)

Ethnohistory. American Society for Ethnohistory. Buffalo, N.Y.

Ethnologia Polona. Zaklad Etnografii Instytutu Historii Kultury Materialnej Pan. Pazná, Poland.

Ethnologica Helvetica. Berne, Switzerland.

Ethnology. Univ. of Pittsburgh. Pittsburgh, Pa. (UP/E)

Ethnomusicology. Wesleyan Univ. for the Society for Ethnomusicology. Middletown, Conn. (SE/E)

Fénix. Biblioteca Nacional. Lima. (FENIX)

Film Quarterly. Univ. of California. Berkeley.

Florida Historical Quarterly. Florida Historical Society. Jacksonville. (FHS/FHQ)

Folklore Americano. Instituto Panamericano de Geografía e Historia, Comisión de Historia, Comité de Folklore. México. (IPGH/FA)

Fragmentos. Centro de Estudios Latinoamericanos Rómulo Gallegos, Depto. de Investigaciones. Caracas.

French Review. American Assn. of Teachers of French. Champaign, Ill.

Gaceta de Cuba. Unión de Escritores y Artistas de Cuba. La Habana. (UEAC/GC)

Heterofonía. México. (HET)

HISLA. Centro Latinoamericano de Historia Económica y Social. Lima. (HISLA)

Hispamérica. Revista de literatura. Takoma Park, Md. (HISPA)

Hispania. American Assn. of Teachers of Spanish and Portuguese, Univ. of Cincinnati. Cincinnati, Ohio. (AATSP/H)

Hispanic American Historical Review. Duke Univ. Press for the Conference on Latin American History, American Historical Assn. Durham, N.C. (HAHR)

Hispanic Journal. Indiana Univ. of Pennsylvania, Dept. of Foreign Languages. Indiana. (IUP/HJ)

Hispanic Linguistics. Univ. of Pittsburgh. Pittsburgh, Pa.

Hispanic Review. Univ. of Pennsylvania, Dept. of Romance Languages. Philadelphia. (HR)

Hispanófila. Univ. of North Carolina. Chapel Hill. (HISP)

Histoire, économie et société. Paris.

Historia. Univ. Católica de Chile, Instituto de Historia. Santiago. (UCCIH/H)

Historia. Univ. Estadual Paulista. São Paulo.

Historia Boliviana. La Paz.

Historia Mexicana. El Colegio de México. México. (CM/HM)

Historia y Cultura. Museo Nacional de Historia. Lima. (PMNH/HC)

Historia y Cultura. Sociedad Boliviana de Historia [and] Editorial Don Bosco. La Paz. (SBH/HC)

Historia y Cultura. Univ. Boliviana Mayor de San Andrés, Instituto de Estudios Bolivianos, Sección Cultura. La Paz. (UB/HC)

Historia y Geografía. Museo Nacional de Historia y Geografía. Santo Domingo.

The Historian. Phi Alpha Theta, National Honor Society in History. Univ. of Pennsylvania. University Park. (PAT/TH)

Historias. Instituto Nacional de Antropología e Historia, Dirección de Estudios Históricos. México.

Histórica. Pontificia Univ. Católica del Perú, Depto. de Humanidades. Lima. (PUCP/H)

The Historical Journal. Cambridge Univ. Press. Cambridge, England.

Historical Reflections/Reflexiones historiques. Univ. of Waterloo. Waterloo, Canada.

Historiografía y Bibliografía Americanista. Escuela de Estudios Hispano-Americanos de Sevilla. Sevilla, Spain. (EEHA/HBA)

History of Agriculture. International Assn. for the History of Agriculture. Kalyani, India.

History of European Ideas. Pergamon Press. Oxford, England.

History Workshop. Ruskin College. Oxford, England.

L'Homme. La Sorbonne, L'Ecole pratique des hautes études. Paris (EPHE/H)

Ibero Americana. Scandinavian Assn. for Research on Latin America. Stockholm. (NOSALF/IA)

Ibero-Amerikanisches Archiv. Ibero-Amerikanisches Institut. Berlin, FRG. (IAA)

Iberoromania. Max Niemeyer Verlag. Tübingen, FRG.

Ideas y Valores. Univ. Nacional, Instituto de Filosofía y Letras. Bogotá. (UN/IV)

Ideologies & Literature. Univ. of Minnesota, Institute for the Study of Ideologies and Literature. Minneapolis. (IL)

Index on Censorship. Writers & Scholars International. London. (INDEX)

Indiana. Beiträge zur Volker-und Sprachenkunde, Archäologie und Anthropologie des Indianischen Amerika. Ibero-Amerikanisches Institut. Berlin, FRG. (IAI/I)

Inter-American Economic Affairs. Washington. (IAMEA)

Inter-American Music Review. Published by Robert Stevenson. Los Angeles, Calif. (IAMR)

Interface Journal of New Music Research. The Hague.

The International History Review. Univ. of Toronto. Toronto, Canada.

International Review of History and Political Science. Review Publications. Meerut, India.

Investigaciones y Ensayos. Academia Nacional de la Historia. Buenos Aires. (ANH/IE)

Islas. Univ. Central de las Villas. Santa Clara, Cuba. (UCLV/I)

Jahrbuch für Geschichte von Staat, Wirtschaft und Gesellschaft Lateinamerikas. Köln, FRG. (JGSWGL)

Jamaica Journal. Institute of Jamaica. Kingston. (IJ/JJ)

The Jamaican Historical Review. Jamaican Historical Society. Kingston. (JHS/R)

Jazz Journal International. Billboard, Ltd. London.

Jewish Social Studies. Conference on Jewish Social Studies. New York.

Journal de la Sociétés des américanistes. Paris. (SA/J)

Journal of Anthropological Research. Univ. of New Mexico, Dept. of Anthropology. Albuquerque. (UNM/JAR)

The Journal of Caribbean History. Univ. of the West Indies, Dept. of History [and] Caribbean Univ. Press. St. Lawrence, Barbados. (UWI/JCH)

A Journal of Church and State. Baylor Univ., J.J. Dawson Studies in Church and State. Waco, Tex. (BU/JCS)

The Journal of Developing Areas. Western Illinois Univ. Press. Macomb. (JDA)

Journal of Economic History. New York Univ., Graduate School of Business Administration *for the* Economic History Assn. Rensselaer. (EHA/J)

Journal of Ethnic Studies. Western Washington Univ. Bellingham.

Journal of European Economic History. Banco di Roma. Rome.

Journal of Family History. National Council on Family Relations. Minneapolis, Minn. (NCFR/JFH)

Journal of Inter-American Studies and World Affairs. Institute of Interamerican Studies, Univ. of Miami. Coral Gables, Fla. (UM/JIAS)

The Journal of Interdisciplinary History. Massachusetts Institute of Technology Press. Cambridge. (JIH)

Journal of Latin American Lore. Univ. of California, Latin American Center. Los Angeles. (UCLA/JLAL)

Journal of Latin American Studies. Centers or institutes of Latin American studies at the univs. of Cambridge, Glasgow, Liverpool, London, and Oxford. Cambridge Univ. Press. Cambridge, England. (JLAS)

The Journal of Peasant Studies. Frank Cass & Co. London. (JPS)

Journal of Popular Culture. Bowling Green State Univ. Bowling Green, Ohio.

Journal of the West. Manhattan, Kan. (JW)

Jumpcut. Berkeley, Calif.

Káñina. Univ. de Costa Rica. San José.

Kentucky Romance Quarterly. Univ. of Kentucky. Lexington. (UK/KRQ)

Lading Meizhou Congkan. Latin American review. Beijing.

Language. Journal of the Linguistics Society of America. Waverly Press, Inc. Baltimore, Md. (LSA/L)

Language and Society. Cambridge Univ. Press. Cambridge, England

Lantérnu. Centraal Historisch Archief. Willemstad, Curaçao.

Lateinamerika Studien. Univ. Erlangen-Nürnberg, Sektion Lateinamerika. Nürnberg, FRG. (UEN/LS)

Latin American Literary Review. Carnegie-Mellon Univ., Dept. of Modern Languages. Pittsburgh, Pa. (LALR)

Latin American Music Review. Univ. of Texas. Austin. (LAMR)

Latin American Perspectives. Univ. of California. Riverside. (LAP)

Latin American Research Review. Univ. of North Carolina Press *for the* Latin American Studies Assn. Chapel Hill. (LARR)

Latin American Theatre Review. Univ. of Kansas, Center for Latin American Studies. Lawrence. (UK/LATR)

Latinoamérica. Univ. Nacional Autónoma de México, Facultad de Filosofía y Letras, Centro de Estudios Latinoamericanos. México. (UNAM/L)

Letras de Guatemala. Univ. de San Carlos de Guatemala, Facultad de Humanidades, Instituto de Estudios de la Literatura Nacional. Guatemala.

Linden Lane Magazine. Princeton, N.J.

Lingua. North-Holland Publishing Co. Amsterdam. (LINGUA)

Linguistics. Mouton. The Hague. (LING)

Lotería. Lotería Nacional de Beneficencia. Panamá. (LNB/L)

Luso-Brazilian Review. Univ. of Wisconsin Press. Madison. (UW/LBR)

Mesoamérica. Centro de Investigaciones Regionales de Mesoamérica. Antigua, Guatemala. (CIRMA/M)

Mester. Univ. of California, Dept. of Spanish and Portuguese. Los Angeles. (UCLA/M)

Mexican Studies/Estudios Mexicanos. Univ. of California Press. Berkeley.

Migraciones Internacionales en las Américas. Centro de Estudios de Migración: Centro de Estudios de Pastoral y Asistencia Migratoria. Caracas.

The Minnesota Review. New York.
Miscelánea Antropológica Ecuatoriana.
Museos del Banco Central del Ecuador.
Guayaquil.
Modern Language Notes. Johns Hopkins
Univ. Press. Baltimore, Md. (MLN)
Mountain Research and Development.
United Nations Univ., Tokyo [and] International Mountain Society, Boulder, Colo.

New Mexico Historical Review. Univ.
of New Mexico [and] Historical Society of
New Mexico. Albuquerque. (UNM/
NMHR)
New Scholar. Univ. of California, Committee on Hispanic Civilization [and] Center
for Chicano Studies. Santa Barbara.
(UCSB/NS)
Nicaráuac. Ministerio de Cultura. Managua.
(NMC/N)
Nieuwe West-Indische Gids. Martins Nijhoff.
The Hague. (NWIG)
Nouvelles questions féministes. Editions
Tierce. Paris.
NS NorthSouth NordSud NorteSur NorteSul.
Canadian Assn. of Latin American Studies,
Univ. of Ottawa. Ottawa. (NS)
Nuestra Historia. Fundación Nuestra Historia. Buenos Aires. (FNH/NH)
Nueva Historia. Asociación de Historiadores
Chilenos; World Univ. Service; [and] Univ.
of London, Institute of Latin American
Studies. London.
Nueva Revista de Filología Hispánica. El
Colegio de México [and] Univ. of Texas.

Orbis. Centre international de dialectologie
générale. Louvain, Belgium. (CIDG/O)

La Palabra y el Hombre. Univ. Veracruzana.
Xalapa, Mexico. (UV/PH)
El Palacio. School of American Research,
Museum of New Mexico [and] the Archaeological Society of New Mexico. Santa Fe.
(SAR/P)
Past and Present. London. (PP)
Pauta. Univ. Autónoma Metropolitana.
México.
El Pez y la Serpiente. Editorial Unión.
Managua.
Política, Economía y Sociedad. Fundación

para el Estudio de los Problemas Argentinos. Buenos Aires.
The Political Quarterly. London. (PQ)
Proceedings of the Rocky Mountain Council
on Latin American Studies Conference.
Las Cruces, N.M.
Prueba. Escuela de Comunicación Social,
Univ. Central de Venezuela. Caracas.
Publications of the Modern Language Association of America. New York. (PMLA)
Punto de Partida. Univ. Nacional Autónoma
de México, Dirección General de Difusión
Cultural. México. (UNAM/PP)

Reflexão. Pontificia Univ. Católica de
Campinas, Instituto de Filosofia e
Teologia.
Relaciones. El Colegio de Michoacán.
Zamora, Mexico. (CM/RE)
Relações Humanas. Instituto de Relações Sociais e Industrias. São Paulo. (IRESI/RH)
Representations. Berkeley, Calif.
Review. Center for Inter-American Relations.
New York. (REVIEW)
The Review of Politics. Univ. of Notre
Dame. Notre Dame, Ind. (UND/RP)
Revista Andina. Centro Bartolomé de las
Casas. Cusco, Peru. (CBC/RA)
Revista Brasileira de História. Associação
Nacional dos Professores Universitários de
História (ANPUH). São Paulo.
Revista Brasileira de Lingüística. Sociedad
Brasileira para Professores de Lingüística.
São Paulo. (SBPL/RBL)
Revista Brasileira de Política Internacional.
Instituto Brasileiro de Relações Internacionais. Rio de Janeiro. (ICA/RCA)
Revista Canadiense de Estudios Hispánicos.
Asociación Canadiense de Hispanistas,
Univ. de Toronto. Toronto. (UT/RCEH)
Revista Chilena de Historia y Geografía. Sociedad Chilena de Historia y Geografía.
Santiago. (SCHG/R)
Revista Chilena de Literatura. Univ. de
Chile, Depto. de Literatura. Santiago.
(UC/RCL)
Revista Colombiana de Antropología. Ministerio de Educación Nacional, Instituto
Colombiano de Antropología. Bogotá.
(ICA/RCA)
Revista da Academia Rio-Grandense de
Letras. Porto Alegre.
Revista de Ciencias Sociales. Univ. de Puerto

Rico, Colegio de Ciencias Sociales. Río Piedras. (UPR/RCS)

Revista de Crítica Literaria Latinoamericana. Latinoamericana Editores. Lima. (RCLL)

Revista de Economía y Estadística. Univ. Nacional de Córdoba, Facultad de Ciencias Económicas. Córdoba, Argentina. (UNC/REE)

Revista de Estudios Extremeños. Diputación de Badajoz, Institución de Servicios Culturales. Badajoz, Spain. (DB/REE)

Revista de Estudios Hispánicos. Univ. de Alabama, Dept. of Romance Languages, Office of International Studies and Programs. University. (UA/REH)

Revista de Filología Española. Consejo Superior de Investigaciones Científicas, Patronato Menéndez Pelayo, Instituto Miguel de Cervantes. Madrid. (CSIC/RFE)

Revista de Filosofía de la Universidad de Costa Rica. San José. (UCR/RF)

Revista de História. Univ. de São Paulo, Faculdade de Filosofia, Letras e Ciências Humanas, Depto. de História. São Paulo. (USP/RH)

Revista de Historia. Univ. Nacional de Costa Rica, Escuela de Historia. Heredia. (UNCR/R)

Revista de Historia de América. Instituto Panamericano de Geografía e Historia, Comisión de Historia. México. (PAIGH/H)

Revista de Historia de América y Argentina. Univ. Nacional de Cuyo, Facultad de Filosofía y Letras, Instituto de Historia. Mendoza, Argentina. (UNC/RHAA)

Revista de Historia de las Ideas. Instituto Panamericano de Geografía e Historia [and] Editorial Casa de la Cultura Ecuatoriana. Quito. (IPGH/RHI)

Revista de Historia del Derecho. Instituto de Investigaciones de Historia del Derecho. Buenos Aires.

Revista de Historia Militar. Servicio Histórico Militar. Madrid. (SHM/RHM)

Revista de Indias. Instituto Gonzalo Fernández de Oviedo [and] Consejo Superior de Investigaciones Científicas. Madrid. (IFGO/RI)

Revista de la Academia Colombiana de Ciencias Exactas, Físicas y Naturales. Bogotá. (ACCEFN/R)

Revista de la Biblioteca Nacional. Ministerio de Educación y Cultura. Montevideo. (UBN/R)

Revista de la Biblioteca Nacional José Martí. La Habana. (BNJM/R)

Revista de la Junta de Estudios Históricos de Mendoza. Mendoza, Argentina. (JEHM/R)

Revista de la Universidad Complutense. Madrid. (RUC)

Revista de la Universidad de México. México. (UNAM/RUM)

Revista de la Universidad de Yucatán. Mérida, Mexico. (UY/R)

Revista de la Universidad Nacional de La Plata. La Plata, Argentina. (UNLP/R)

Revista de Letras. Univ. Estadual Paulista. São Paulo.

Revista de Occidente. Madrid. (RO)

Revista de Teatro. Sociedade Brasileira de Autores Teatrais. Rio de Janeiro. (SBAT/RT)

Revista del Archivo Nacional de Historia, Sección del Azuay. Casa de la Cultura Ecuatoriana. Cuenca.

Revista del Instituto de Cultura Puertorriqueña. San Juan. (ICP/R)

Revista del Instituto de Historia del Derecho Ricardo Levene. Buenos Aires.

Revista del Instituto de Historia Eclesiástica Ecuatoriana. Pontificia Univ. Católica del Ecuador. Quito.

Revista del Instituto de Investigación Musicológica Carlos Vega. Univ. Católica. Buenos Aires.

Revista del Museo Nacional. Casa de la Cultura del Perú, Museo Nacional de la Cultura Peruana. Lima. (PEMN/R)

Revista del Pensamiento Centroamericano. Consejo Superior de la Empresa Privada (COSEP). Managua. (RPC)

Revista do Arquivo Municipal. Prefeitura do Município de São Paulo, Depto. Municipal de Cultura. São Paulo. (AM/R)

Revista do Instituto de Estudos Brasileiros. Univ. de São Paulo. São Paulo. (USP/RIEB)

Revista do Instituto Histórico e Geográfica Brasileiro. Rio de Janeiro. (IHAAER/B)

Revista Española de Lingüística. Sociedad Española de Lingüística. Madrid.

Revista Iberoamericana. Instituto Internacional de Literatura Iberoamericana; patrocinado por la Univ. de Pittsburgh. Pittsburgh, Pa. (IILI/RI)

Revista Inidef. Instituto Interamericano de Etnomusicología y Folclor. Caracas. (INIDEF)

Revista Interamericana de Bibliografía/Inter-American Review of Bibliography. Organization of American States. Washington. (RIB)

Revista Interamericana de Bibliotecología. Univ. de Antioquia, Escuela Interamericana de Bibliotecología. Medellín, Colombia.

Revista Latinoamericana de Filosofía. Centro de Investigaciones Filosóficas. Buenos Aires. (CIF/RLF)

Revista Mexicana de Ciencias Políticas y Sociales. Univ. Autónoma Nacional de México, Facultad de Ciencias Políticas y Sociales. México. (UNAM/RMCPS)

Revista Musical Chilena. Univ. de Chile, Facultad de Artes. Santiago. (UC/RMC)

Revista Musical de Venezuela. Instituto Latinoamericano de Investigaciones y Estudios Musicales Vicente Emilio Sojo, Consejo Nacional de la Cultura (CONAC). (RMV)

Revista Nacional de Cultura. Consejo Nacional de Cultura. Caracas. (CONAC/RNC)

Revista Paraguaya de Sociología. Centro Paraguayo de Estudios Sociológicos. Asunción. (CPES/RPS)

Revista Peruana de Cultura. Comisión Nacional de Cultura. Lima. (CNC/RPC)

Revista Portuguesa de Filosofía. Braga.

Revista/Review Interamericana. Univ. Interamericana. San Germán, P.R. (RRI)

Revista Venezolana de Filosofía. Univ. Simón Bolívar [and] Sociedad Venezolana de Filosofía. Caracas. (USB/RVF)

Revolución y Cultura. Ministerio de Cultura. La Habana. (RYC)

Revue de la Société haïtienne d'histoire et de géographie. Port-au-Prince. (SHHG/R)

Revue d'histoire française d'Outre-mer. Société de l'histoire des colonies françaises. Paris.

Revue d'histoire moderne et contemporaine. Paris.

Revue historique. Presses universitaires de France. Paris. (PUF/RH)

Rivista Geografica Italiana. Società di Studi Geografici e Coloniali. Firenze, Italy. (SSG/RGI)

Romance Notes. Univ. of North Carolina, Dept. of Romance Languages. Chapel Hill. (UNC/RN)

Romanistisches Jahrbuch. Univ. Hamburg, Romanisches Seminar, Ibero-Amerikanisches Forschungsinstitut. Hamburg, FRG. (UH/RJ)

Runa. Univ. de Buenos Aires, Facultad de Filosofía y Letras, Instituto de Antropología. Buenos Aires. (UBAIA/R)

Santiago. Univ. de Oriente. Santiago de Cuba.

Sapientia. Univ. Católica Argentina Santa María de los Buenos Aires, Facultad de Filosofía. Buenos Aires. (UCA/S)

Signs. Univ. of Chicago Press. Chicago, Ill. (UC/S)

Screen. Society for Education in Film and Television. London.

Siglo XIX. Univ. Autónoma de Nuevo León, Facultad de Filosofía y Letras. Monterrey, Mexico.

Sing Out! New York.

Slavery and Abolition. Frank Cass. London.

Social and Economic Studies. Univ. of the West Indies, Institute of Social and Economic Research. Mona, Jamaica. (UWI/SES)

Social Sciences. Union of the Soviet Socialist Republics Academy of Sciences, Section of the Social Sciences. Moscow. (USSR/SS)

Socialismo y Participación. Ediciones Socialismo y Participación. Lima. (SP)

Soundboard. Guitar Foundation of America. Riverside, Calif.

South Eastern Latin Americanist. Southeastern Conference on Latin American Studies. Clemson Univ. Clemson, S.C. (SECOLAS/SELA)

Southwestern Historical Quarterly. Texas State Historical Assn. Austin. (TSHA/SHQ)

Studies in Comparative International Development. Georgia Institute for Technology. Atlanta. (GIT/SCID)

Studies in Latin American Popular Culture. New Mexico State Univ., Dept. of Modern Languages. Albuquerque.

Studies in Social Sciences. West Georgia College. Carrollton.

Suplemento Antropológico. Univ. Católica de Nuestra Señora de la Asunción, Centro de Estudios Antropológicos. Asunción. (UCNSA/SA)

Sur. Buenos Aires. (SUR)

Temas Americanistas. Cátedra de Historia de América, Univ. de Sevilla. Sevilla, Spain.

Les Temps modernes. Paris. (TM)

Thesaurus. Instituto Caro y Cuervo. Bogotá. (ICC/T)

Third Woman. Indiana Univ., Chicano-
Riqueño Studies. Bloomington.
Third World Quarterly. Third World Foun-
dation, New Zealand House. London.
(TWF/TWQ)
Todo es Historia. Buenos Aires.
La Torre. Univ. de Puerto Rico. Río Piedras.
(UPR/LT)
Tricontinental. Organization for the Soli-
darity of the Peoples of Africa, Asia, and
Latin America, Executive Secretariat.
Havana. (OSPAAAL/T)

Universidad. Univ. Nacional del Litoral.
Santa Fe, Argentina. (UNL/U)
Universidade Estadual Paulista. São Paulo.
Universitas Humanistica. Pontificia Univ.
Javeriana, Facultad de Filosofía y Letras.
Bogotá. (PUJ/UH)

Vanderbilt University Studies in Anthropology. Nashville, Tenn.

Vanity Fair. Conde Nast Publications. New
York.
Veritas. Pontifícia Univ. Católica do Rio
Grande do Sul. Porto Alegre. (PUC/V)
Vida Hispánica. Assn. of the Teachers of
Spanish and Portuguese. Wolverhampton,
U.K. (ATSP/VH)
Vuelta. México. (VUELTA)

William and Mary Quarterly. Institute of
Early American History and Culture.
Williamsburg, Va.
The World of Music. Bärenreiter Kassal.
Basel, Switzerland.
World Literature Today. Univ. of Oklahoma.
Norman. (WLT)

Zeitschrift für Ethnologie. Deutschen Ge-
sellschaft für Völkerkunde. Braunscchweig,
FRG. (DGV/ZE)
Zeitschrift für Romanische Philologie.
Tübingen, FRG. (ZRP)

SUBJECT INDEX

Bibliography and General Works (1–250)
Art (251–950)
Film (951-1500)
History (1501–4500)

Language (4501–5000)
Literature (5001–7000)
Music (7001–7500)
Philosophy (7501–8000)

Abipón (indigenous group), 1720.
Abolition of Slavery. Brazil, 3464, 3500, 3517.
  Caribbean Area, 2454, 2456, 2488, 2507.
  Congresses, 2456. Cuba, 2483, 2485, 2547.
  Curaçao, 2450. Guadeloupe, 2512, 2542.
  Haiti, 2460, 2461, 2463, 2545. Jamaica,
  2492. Laws and Legislation, 2463. Martini-
  que, 2506, 2542. Saint Martin, 2535. West
  Indies, 2543.
Absatz, Alicia, 5018.
Acculturation. Andean Region, 1664, 2627.
  Araucano, 1611. Haiti, 2446. Japanese,
  1941. Latin America, 1695, 1872. Mexico,
  5204, 7132. in Music, 7132. Tzutuhil,
  1556. Viceroyalty of Peru, 1689, 1711,
  1768.
Achúgar, Hugo, 5908, 5983.
Acos, Peru (city). History, 3052.
Acosta, Cecilio, 5123a, 5128, 5137.
Acosta, Joaquín, 2685.
Adellach, Alberto, 6123.
Adomián, Lan, 7137, 7141.
Advertising. Mexico, 2050.
Aeronautics. Argentina, 3309.
Agazzi, Paolo, 983.
Age. Chile, 2794.
Agramonte, Emilio, 7124.
Agrarian Reform. Congresses, 1889. Costa
  Rica, 2308. Dictionaries, 4579. Haiti, 2462.
  History, 1889, 2133. Latin America, 1884,
  3022, 4579. Laws and Legislation, 2131,
  2137, 3020. Mexico, 1889, 2039, 2040,
  2067, 2087, 2118, 2119, 2131, 2133, 2135,
  2136, 2137, 2139, 2145, 2146, 2149, 2184,
  2202. Peru, 3020, 3034, 3078. Viceroyalty
  of New Spain, 1981.
Agricultural Industries. Brazil, 3497. History,
  1870. Latin America, 1870. Paraguay, 3333.
Agricultural Laborers. Mexico, 1909, 2095,
  2137.

Agriculture. Alto Perú, 2780. Andean Region,
  1652. Argentina, 3230, 3310. Bibliography,
  10. Bolivia, 10. Brazil, 1620, 3403, 3406,
  3411. Colombia, 2972. Cuba, 2483, 2546.
  Dictionaries, 1616. Ecuador, 3013. History,
  1870, 2064. Inca, 1616. Latin America,
  1870. Mexico, 1904, 1960, 2046, 2064,
  2073, 2084, 2087, 2116, 2185. Nicaragua,
  2280. South America, 2847. Surinam,
  2459. Venezuela, 2921. Viceroyalty of New
  Granada, 2665. Viceroyalty of New Spain,
  1961, 1971, 1993. Viceroyalty of Peru,
  1646, 2737.
Aguilera Malta, Demetrio, 5490.
Aguirre, Isadora, 6085.
Agustín, José, 5010, 5237.
Agustini, Delmira, 5915.
Air Pilots. Argentina, 3208.
Alagoas, Brazil (state). Literature, 6378.
Alajuela, Costa Rica (prov.). History, 2282.
Alausí, Ecuador (city). History, 1676.
Alberdi, Juan Bautista, 3203, 3281, 3291,
  7649, 7660.
Alcohol and Alcoholism. Venezuela, 2653.
Alegría, Ciro, 5497, 5512.
Aleijandinho. See Lisboa, Antônio Francisco.
Alemán, Miguel, 2134, 2138, 2174.
Alencar, José de, 6330, 6405.
Alezedo, José Bernardo, 7153.
Alfaro, Eloy, 1628, 3001, 3006, 3014.
Allende Gossens, Salvador, 3159.
Almeida, Manuel Antônio de, 6395.
Almeida Júnior, Belmiro Barbosa de, 450.
Alta Verapaz, Guatemala (dept.). History,
  1564.
Altagracia, Venezuela (city). Literature, 5515.
Alvarado, Salvador, 2124, 2126, 2127, 2133.
Alvarado de Ricor, Elsie, 5331.
Alvarenga, Oneyda Paoliello, 7082.
Alvarez, Carlos, 1042.

Alvarez, Santiago, 1061, 1070.
Alzate, Antonio de, 1931.
Amado, Jorge, 5648, 6429.
Amazonas, Brazil (state). Literature, 6385.
American Revolution (1776–1783), 5071.
Anarchism and Anarchists. Argentina, 3200.
  Brazil, 3460. Latin America, 1883.
Anchieta, José de, 3424.
Andacollo, Chile (city). Music, 7023.
Andonaegui, José de, 2613.
Andonaegui Family, 2613.
Andrade, Carlos Drummond de, 5648, 6428.
Andrade, Joaquim Pedro de, 1008, 1010, 1020.
Andrade, Jorge, 6338, 6342.
Andrade, Mário de, 426, 1010, 6415, 6417.
Andrade, Oswald de, 6371, 6379, 6418.
Antartic Region. History, 3304.
Anthropology. Europe, 5038. Guatemala,
  7094.
Antigua, Guatemala (city). Art, 353. History,
  2246.
Antín, Manuel, 978.
Antín, Miguel, 967.
Antioquia, Colombia (dept.). History, 2666,
  2878, 2965, 2967, 2983, 2985.
Anti-positivism. Mexico, 7550.
Antofagasta, Chile (prov.). History, 3164,
  3179.
Antônio, João, 5010.
Aparicio, Carlos Hugo, 5656.
Apulezo Mendoza, Plinio, 5483.
Aquino, Anastasio, 2275.
Arabs. in the Audiencia of Quito, 2698. in
  Caribbean Area, 2368.
Arana Castro, Francisco Javier, 2256.
Arango, Gonzalo, 5904.
Araucano (indigenous group), 1587, 1597,
  1611, 1612, 1648, 1657, 1668, 1702, 1764,
  1765, 1769.
Araújo, Emanoel, 452.
Arawak (indigenous group), 2392, 7008.
Arbeláez, Fernando, 5922.
Arbeleche, Jorge, 5908.
Arbenz, Jacobo, 2256.
Arce, Aniceto, 3087.
Archaeological Sites. See Excavations.
Archaeology. Jamaica, 2392.
Architects. Brazil, 3400. Uruguay, 3351.
Architecture. Andean Region, 1652. Argen-
  tina, 367. Bibliography, 486. Brazil, 431,
  484, 485, 486, 487, 491, 492, 510. Chile,
  3120. Colombia, 371. Cuba, 357. Ecuador,
  383. Mexico, 392, 395, 403. Peru, 417.
  Venezuela, 370, 411.
Archives. Archives de la Martinique, 34. Ar-

chives nationales (France), 40. Archivo
Centro-América (Guatemala), 5057. Archivo de Don Bernardo O'Higgins (Chile),
3152. Archivo General de Indias (Spain),
1910, 2233, 2400, 2650, 2816. Archivo
General de la Nación (Mexico), 1900. Archivo General de la Nación (Venezuela),
2629. Archivo General de Notarias (Mexico), 56, 57. Archivo General Francisco de
Miranda (Venezuela), 2649. Archivo Histórico de Miraflores (Venezuela), 2901. Archivo Nacional de Chile, 2970. Archivo
Nacional de Historia (Ecuador), 2617, 2877.
Archivo Nacional de la Nación (Argentina),
2826. Archivo Técnico de la Dirección de
Monumentos Prehispánicos del INAH
(Mexico), 61. Audiencia de Guadalajara,
1921. Australia, 42. Bibliography, 2105,
2339. Brazil, 2895. Caribbean Area, 42, 68.
Casa de Santander (Colombia), 2931. Cata-
logs, 31, 35, 36, 56, 57, 1887, 1997, 2339,
2351, 2352, 2755, 2816, 2877. Central
America, 68. Ecuador, 35, 36. Europe, 42,
2105. France, 40, 2339, 2449. Guadeloupe,
2440. Guatemala, 39. Lesser Antilles, 34.
Mexico, 31, 1887, 1915, 1997, 2139. Pan-
ama, 41. Peru, 2755. Surinam, 2351, 2352.
Uruguay, 2807. Venezuela, 33.
Arcila Robledo, Gregorio, 2964.
Arco, Gustavo, 5422.
Ardissone, Elena, 7663.
Arenas, Reinaldo, 5017.
Arequipa, Peru (dept.). History, 1598, 1646,
  2729, 2737, 3025, 3037, 3038.
Arévalo, Andrés, 1734.
Argentina and Brazil Relations, 3206, 3227,
  3261.
Argentina and Paraguay Relations, 3338,
  3339.
Argentina and Spain Relations, 5689.
Argentina and Union of the Soviet Socialist
  Republics Relations, 3229.
Argentina and United Kingdom Relations,
  2837, 2890, 3214, 3233, 3236, 3240, 3242,
  3292.
Argentina Sono Film, 970.
Arguedas, José María, 5003, 5493, 5496,
  5498, 5504, 5512, 7528.
Arias, Arturo, 1071.
Arias Madrid, Harmodio, 2312.
Arica, Chile (city). Music, 7099.
Arista, Mariano, 2097.
Arlt, Roberto, 5020, 5661, 5961.
Armenteros y Henao, Diego de, 1629.
Armijo, Manuel, 2077.

Barranquilla, Colombia (city). Literature, 5484.
Barrenchea y Albis, Juan de, 5093.
Barreto, Bruno, 1028.
Barreto, Lima, 6350.
Barreto, Tobias, 7629.
Barrios, Justo Rufino, 2311.
Barrios Amorín, Javier, 3360.
Barthes, Roland, 5251.
Basadre, Jorge, 3053, 3065.
Basave, Agustín, 7543.
Bascopé Aspiazú, René, 5526.
Baskets. Guatemala, 294.
Basques. in Chile, 3130. in Mexico, 1886, 1954.
Bass, Alan, 6571.
Bassoco, Antonio, 1954.
Bassols, Narciso, 2168.
Bastidas, Rodrigo de, 2634.
Batista da Costa, João, 446.
Batista y Zaldívar, Fulgencio, 2580, 2607.
Battle of Carreras, 2519.
Battle of Palo Alto, Texas, 2097.
Battle of Rivas (1856), 2282, 2294.
Bautista Aguirre, Juan, 5098.
Bautista Araujo, Juan, 2903.
Bautista Mentasti, Angel, 970.
Bauza, Mario, 7024.
Bay of Pigs Invasion (1961), 5403.
Belgrano, Manuel, 2889.
Belief and Customs. Borderlands, 2171. Brazil, 3407. Chile, 5832. El Salvador, 5306. in Literature, 5306, 5832. Peru, 1598. Viceroyalty of New Spain, 1563. Viceroyalty of Peru, 2751.
Belize and Caribbean Area Studies, 2517.
Bell, Lindolf, 6522.
Belli, Gioconda, 5918.
Bello, Andrés, 1863a, 3111, 3146, 5117, 5121, 5122, 5125, 5126, 5126a, 5132, 5141, 5141a, 5142, 5155, 5157, 5158, 7580, 7581, 7582, 7584, 7587, 7591, 7592, 7593, 7594.
Benalcázar, Sebastián de, 2687, 2699.
Benalcázar Family, 2699.
Benedetti, Mario, 6101.
Benedictines. Brazil, 3396, 3422.
Benzoni, Girolamo, 1800.
Bermudes, Pedro, 7096.
Betances, Ramón Emeterio, 2487, 2539.
Betancourt, Rómulo, 2898, 2899.
Betancur, Cayetano, 7599.
Bezerra, Alcides, 7637.
Biagini, Hugo E., 7663.
Bibliography. Andean Region, 18. Argentina, 18, 2816. Brazil, 21, 3437. Caribbean Area,

4, 22, 42. Guatemala, 55. Honduras, 6. Jamaica, 3. Latin America, 2339. Lesser Antilles, 34, 2325. Mexico, 14, 45. Nicaragua, 12. Panama, 15. Paraguay, 9. Peru, 45. Surinam, 2325. Uruguay, 7, 8. Venezuela, 33.
Bierce, Ambrose, 6555.
Bilingualism. Equatorial Guinea, 4533. Paraguay, 4503. Peru, 4512. Policies, 4503, 4512. United States, 4511.
Biography. Argentina, 2800, 3243, 3319, 5676. Barbados, 2396. Brazil, 51, 3453. Caribbean Area, 52. Chile, 2791, 3168. Colombia, 2687. Cuba, 2572, 2586, 5412. Dominican Republic, 2363, 2371. Ecuador, 2998. Guatemala, 2307, 5282. Honduras, 2317. Latin America, 2882, 5022, 7010, 7019. Latin Americanists, 64. Mexico, 47. Nicaragua, 2287. Panama, 2255. Paraguay, 3335, 3346. Peru, 3059. Río de la Plata, 2823. Study and Teaching, 5160. United States, 64. Venezuela, 2655, 2657, 2870, 2924, 5160. West Indies, 2331.
Bioy Casares, Adolfo, 5684, 6570.
Bishops. Catalogs, 2650. Costa Rica, 2300. Latin America, 1861, 1866. Nicaragua, 2253. Venezuela, 2650. Viceroyalty of New Spain, 1987.
Blacks. Brazil, 430, 496, 1031, 1757, 3369, 3374, 3447, 3491, 6154, 6282, 6315, 6544. Caribbean Area, 2360, 5044, 5445. Cuba, 2372. in Film, 1031. Haiti, 2424, 2429, 2432, 2561. Jamaica, 2517a, 2554. Latin America, 1775 5540. Laws and Legislation, 2360, 2517a. in Literature, 5044, 5445, 5476, 5540, 6154, 6282, 6315, 6544. Martinique, 2506, 2522. Nicaragua, 1534. Panama, 2218. Peru, 3034. Policies, 2828. Río de la Plata, 2828. Trinidad and Tobago, 2493. Venezuela, 2630, 2632.
Blanco, Andrés Eloy, 2900, 5931.
Blanco, Enrique, 2555.
Blanco, Lucio, 2184.
Bó, Armando, 975.
Boal, Augusto, 6342, 6343.
Bobadilla, Emilio, 7570.
Boero, Felipe, 7018.
Bogotá, Colombia (city). History, 2929, 2986. Language, 4541.
Bohento Chavero, Héctor, 7022.
Bohórquez, Pedro, 1759.
Bolívar, Simón, 388, 1865a, 1866b, 2514, 2529, 2844–2862, 2869, 2871, 2879, 2881, 2883, 2884, 5158, 7067, 7575.
Bolivia and United States Relations, 3104.
Bolton, Herbert Eugene, 2036.

Bombal, María Luisa, 5580, 5581, 5586, 5589.
Bonfioli, Higino, 988.
Bonifaz Ascásubi, Neptalí, 36.
Books and Book Dealers. Barbados, 44. Brazil, 500. Chile, 3111. History, 32. Latin America, 32. Paraguay, 5695. Spanish Colonies, 1832. Viceroyalty of Peru, 2748, 2758.
Borah, Woodrow Wilson, 1796.
Borba Filho, Hermilo, 6334.
Borderlands (region). History, 2013, 2023, 2036, 2042, 2130, 3307.
Borea Odría, Alberto, 3058.
Borge, Tomás, 2265, 5918.
Borges, Jorge Luis, 5004, 5014, 5017, 5033, 5636, 5640, 5642, 5652, 5685, 5894, 5927, 6566, 6570.
Borges, Miguel, 985.
Bosch, Juan, 2609, 5466.
Botany. Audiencia of Quito, 2695. Bibliography, 2660. Colombia, 2938. Guatemala, 2251. Viceroyalty of New Granada, 2660, 2667, 2671, 2673.
Boundaries. Brazil, 1635. Viceroyalty of Peru, 1708, 1764, 1765.
Boundary Disputes. Argentina/Chile, 3131, 3161. Colombia/Venezuela, 2918. Dominican Republic/Haiti, 2578. Ecuador/Peru, 3000. Honduras/El Salvador, 5307. Mexico/United States, 2129.
Boyacá, Colombia (dept.). Art, 371.
Braga, Henriqueta Rosa Fernandes, 7045.
Braga, Sônia, 1023.
Braithwaite, Edward Kamau, 6519.
Braun, Gustavo Henrique von, 3502.
Brazil and Argentina Relations, 3206, 3227, 3261.
Brazil and Europe Relations, 3465.
Brazil and Federal Republic of Germany Relations, 3465, 3496, 3515.
Brazil and Italy Relations, 3386, 3520.
Brazil and Portugal Relations, 3395.
Brazil and Río de la Plata Relations, 3446.
Brazil and South America Relations, 3519.
Brazil and Spain Relations, 3494.
Brazil and United States Relations, 3526.
Brazil and Uruguay Relations, 3356.
Bribrí (indigenous group), 13.
British. in Argentina, 3260.
Brodt, Manuel Pereira, 3531.
Brushwood, John S., 5917.
Bryce Echnique, Alfredo, 5546.
Bucaram, Asaad, 3003.
Bucaramanga, Colombia (city). History, 1790a.
Buddhism. in Literature, 5467.

Buenos Aires, Argentina (city). History, 2804, 2822, 2829, 2831, 2832, 2833, 2837, 3237, 3279, 3287, 3315, 3324. Literature, 5129, 5147a, 5621, 5659, 5662, 6080, 6566.
Buenos Aires, Argentina (prov.). History, 3196, 3231, 3253.
Buero Vallejo, Antonio, 6101.
Bunge, Alejandro, 3306.
Bunge, Carlos Octavio, 7658.
Bunge, Mario, 7662.
Buñuel, Luis, 1080.
Burgos, Julia de, 5898, 6527.
Business. Argentina, 3222. Mexico, 2158. Viceroyalty of New Spain, 1961.
Butler, Tubal Uriah Buzz, 2591.

Caballero y Góngora, Antonio, 2670, 2684.
Cabello Valboa, Miguel, 5087.
Cabezas, Omar, 5338, 5918.
Cabrera, Lydia, 6524.
Cabrera Infante, Guillermo, 5027, 5332, 5430, 6524.
Cacao. Ecuador, 2991, 2993, 2995.
Cáceres, Eduardo, 7117.
Caciques. Araucano, 1600. Ecuador, 1602, 1651, 1662. Guatemala, 1574. Venezuela, 1661. Viceroyalty of Peru, 1677.
Cadenas, Rafael, 5964.
Cádiz, Spain (city). History, 1847.
Caetano, João, 6339.
Cajamarca, Peru (dept.). History, 1615, 3077.
Cajar Escala, José A., 5340.
Calchaqui (indigenous group), 1759.
Caldas, Colombia (dept.). History, 2659, 2682, 2968.
Calendrics. Aztec, 1533, 1573a, 1581. Inca, 1642, 1772. Mesoamerica, 1559, 1565. Viceroyalty of New Spain, 1572.
Cali, Colombia (city). Literature, 6074.
Callado, Antônio, 437, 6397.
Callahuaya (indigenous groups), 1722.
Callao, Peru (city). History, 2728.
Calles, Plutarco Elías, 2133, 2149, 2157, 2173, 2175.
Calmon, Antônio, 1028.
Camagüey, Cuba (prov.). History, 2524.
Camargo, Sérgio de, 455.
Camargo y Cavallero, Juan, 1964.
Cambaceres, Eugenio, 5124, 5150.
Campesinos. See Peasants.
Campos, Augusto de, 6522.
Campos, Julieta, 5215.
Campos de São José, Brazil (city). Literature, 6211.

Rica, 5279. Guadeloupe, 2512. Peru, 2885.
Río de la Plata, 2800. Viceroyalty of Peru,
2722, 2750. West Indies, 2331.
Cluzeau-Mortet, Luis, 7163.
Coahuila, Mexico (state). History, 2015.
Cobija, Bolivia (city). History, 3097.
Cobo Borda, J.G., 5892.
Coca. Alto Perú, 2776. Andean Region, 1654,
1714. Congresses, 1714. History, 1685.
Inca, 1697. Latin America, 1685.
Coca (indigenous group), 1507.
Cocama (indigenous group), 1770.
Cocamilla (indigenous group), 1750.
Cochabamba, Bolivia (city). Music, 7042.
Cochabamba, Bolivia (dept.). Bibliography,
10.
Codices. Borgia, 1566. Catalogs, 1518.
Ixtlilxochitl, 1559. Magliabecciano, 1501.
Mesoamerica, 1501, 1509, 1528, 1542.
Mexico, 1518. Tudela, 1573a. Vindobonen-
sis, 1509.
Codina, Iverna, 5646.
Coffee Industry and Trade. Brazil, 3485,
3493, 3513, 3521, 3529, 3530, 3534. Co-
lombia, 2928. Costa Rica, 2254, 2302.
Puerto Rico, 2490. Venezuela, 2896.
Coins and Coinage. Brazil, 3418. Latin Amer-
ica, 2861. Viceroyalty of Peru, 2626.
Colán, Luis de, 1716.
Coliman-Hall, Marie-Thérèse, 6484.
Collagua (indigenous group), 382.
Colombia and Panama Relations, 2266.
Colombia and United States Relations, 2971.
Colombia and Venezuela Relations, 2901.
Colón, Panama (city). History, 2273.
Colonial Administration. Alto Perú, 2768.
Audiencia of Caracas, 2646. Audiencia of
Guadalajara, 1921. Audiencia of Quito,
2696, 2705. Borderlands, 2021, 2035. Bra-
zil, 3376, 3425. Caribbean Area, 2525.
Chile, 1624. Cuba, 2442, 2443, 2444. Ecua-
dor, 2688. Florida, 2467. Latin America,
1695, 1816, 1828, 1841, 1849, 2624. Laws
and Legislation, 1830, 1852, 1900, 1921,
2104, 2243, 2624, 2666, 2705. Mexico,
2104. Peru, 1606, 2689. Policy, 1955, 2611,
2828. Río de la Plata, 2828, 2832, 2834,
2838, 2840. Spanish Colonies, 1839, 1840.
Surinam, 2611. Trinidad and Tobago, 2395,
2491. Venezuela, 2634, 2641, 2642, 2643,
2644, 2645, 2646a, 2654. Viceroyalty of
New Granada, 2666, 2669. Viceroyalty of
New Spain, 1900, 1905, 1910, 1920a, 1927,
1952, 1953, 1955, 1955a, 1972, 1983, 1985,
1985a, 1986, 1994, 1995, 1998, 2034, 2240,

2243, 2244. Viceroyalty of Peru, 1622,
1670, 1671, 2618, 2727, 2736, 2738, 2740,
2747. Viceroyalty of Río de la Plata, 2835.
West Indies, 1806.
Colonial Architecture. Andean Region, 377a.
Argentina, 364, 366. Bibliography, 377a.
Brazil, 439, 441. Colombia, 368, 371. Cuba,
357. Ecuador, 376. Guadeloupe, 2337.
Guatemala, 353, 355, 358. Haiti, 2419.
Mexico, 315, 316, 317, 321, 322, 323, 324,
331, 332, 334, 339, 352. New Spain, 328,
341. Peru, 382, 384. Río de la Plata, 2814.
Colonial Art. Asian Influence, 329. Brazil,
430, 432, 436, 442, 505. Congresses, 313.
Latin America, 313. Mexico, 329, 348.
Paraguay, 362.
Colonial History. Alto Perú, 2774. Belize,
1539. Bibliography, 17, 33, 1866a, 2690.
Brazil, 17, 3388, 3506. Central America,
2225, 2234. Chile, 2784, 2792, 2795. Ecua-
dor, 2690, 2719. Guadeloupe, 2415. Guate-
mala, 2237, 2240, 2242. Honduras, 2233.
Latin America, 1866a, 2449. Laws and Leg-
islation, 2240. Martinique, 2409, 2415.
Panama, 41. Paraguay, 2802. Río de la
Plata, 2804, 2811. Surinam, 2354, 2457,
2458. Venezuela, 2628, 2629, 2630, 2631.
Viceroyalty of New Granada, 2668. Vice-
royalty of New Spain, 1900, 1953, 1964.
Viceroyalty of Peru, 1668, 2753. Virgin Is-
lands, 2374. West Indies, 2403, 2436.
Colonization. Araucano, 1600, 1702. Brazil,
3395. Caribbean Area, 2402. Chile, 1600.
Ecuador, 1688. Florida, 2474. French
Guyana, 3395. Guadeloupe, 2452. Guate-
mala, 2229. Jamaica, 2392. Latin America,
1685, 1827, 7502. Laws and Legislation,
2112. Louisiana, 2476. Mexico, 2112.
Southern Cone, 1592. Viceroyalty of New
Granada, 2659, 2669. Viceroyalty of New
Spain, 1916. Viceroyalty of Peru, 1726.
Columbus, Christopher, 1811, 1842, 1845,
1851, 1854, 1860, 5069.
Comanche (indigenous group), 2021.
Comic Books and Strips. History, 5001.
Comitán de Domínguez, Mexico (city). History, 1906.
Commerce. Argentina, 3237, 3260. Argen-
tina/United Kingdom, 3240. Audiencia of
Quito, 2711, 2712, 2713. Brazil, 501, 3380,
3394, 3395, 3496. California, 1897. Carib-
bean Area, 2390, 2525. Central America,
48. Chile, 3137. Cuba, 2443, 2444. Ecuador, 2867, 2993. Germany, 3496. Haiti,
2597. History, 501, 1847, 3380. Latin

America, 1813, 1847, 1868. Latin America/United States, 1817. Laws and Legislation, 3026. Mexico, 1960, 2087, 2100. Panama/Spain, 1812. Paraguay, 3333. Policy, 2444, 2867, 2894. Portuguese Colonies, 3394. Río de la Plata, 2811, 2830, 2833, 2894. Río de la Plata/Portugal, 2804. Spain/Spanish Colonies, 1849, 1850, 1865b. Spanish Colonies, 1858. Study and Teaching, 1813, 1924. Surinam, 2459. United Kingdom, 3260. Venezuela, 2638, 2639, 2658. Viceroyalty of New Spain, 1924, 1948, 1954, 1991. Viceroyalty of New Spain/East Asia, 1810. Viceroyalty of New Spain/Japan, 2000. Viceroyalty of New Spain/Philippines, 1928. Viceroyalty of New Spain/United Kingdom, 1992. Viceroyalty of Peru, 1671, 1698, 1716, 2617a, 2729, 2738. West Indies, 2397, 2416, 2464.

Communication. Brazil, 499.

Communism and Communist Parties. Argentina, 3217. Brazil, 3476, 3504. Chile, 3116. Colombia, 2980. Cuba, 2329, 2584. El Salvador, 2274. History, 2125. Mexico, 2125, 2128. Peru, 3071. Venezuela, 2901, 2917.

Community Development. Brazil, 3379. Peru, 3020.

Comparative Literature. Argentine/Brazilian, 5648. Congresses, 5900. Latin American/Russian, 5046. Mesoamerican/Central American, 5107.

Composers. Argentina, 7039. Chile, 7107, 7114. Costa Rica, 7097. Dictionaries, 7010. Ecuador, 7127, 7128. Latin America, 7004, 7009.

Computer Science. Latin America, 5. Mexico, 2194.

Concha, Andrés de, 326.

Conde de Tolosa (ship), 1805.

Confederación Perú-Boliviana. *See* Perú-Bolivian Confederation (1836–1839).

Conflict. Cuba, 2557a. Mexico, 2188. Viceroyalty of New Spain, 1985.

Confraternities. Argentina, 1882. Brazil, 1882, 3416. Costa Rica, 2221. in Literature, 5264. Panama, 5264. Viceroyalty of Peru, 1665.

Conibo (indigenous group), 1770.

Conquistadors. Chile, 2794.

Conselheiro, Antonio, 6565.

Conservatism. Colombia, 2943, 2944.

Constitutional History. Alto Perú, 2862. Argentina, 3281. Brazil, 3472. Central Amer-

ica, 2225. Guyana, 2576. Honduras, 2272. Mexico, 2085. Panama, 2266. Puerto Rico, 2608.

Contact. Araucano, 1657. Shuar, 1684. Transoceanic, 1815.

Cookery. History, 1890. Latin America, 1853. Mexico, 1890.

Copper Industry and Trade. Guatemala, 299.

Cordero, Roque, 7018.

Córdoba, Argentina (prov.). History, 3235.

Córdoba, Colombia (dept.). History, 2972.

Córdoba, Mexico (city). History, 2116.

Córdova, José María, 2878.

Córdova, Salvador, 2965.

Cornejo, Sergio, 7117.

Corporate State. Argentina, 3205.

Correia, José Celso Martinez, 1017.

Corrientes, Argentina (prov.). History, 3210.

Cortázar, Julio, 5003, 5004, 5006, 5332, 5637, 5667, 5688.

Cortázar, Octavio, 1059.

Cortés, Hernán, 1511, 2003, 2007.

Cortés Castro, León, 2267.

Cosmology. Andean Region, 1700. Araucano, 1611. Aztec, 5091. Inca, 1642. in Literature, 5091. Maya, 1549. Nahua, 1549.

Cossío, Juan, 5140.

Costa, João Batista da. *See* Batista da Costa, João.

Costa, João Zeferino da, 448.

Costa, Júlia da, 6421.

Costa Rican Civil War, 2257.

Costumbrismo. Bolivia, 5525. Chile, 6083. Costa Rica, 5327. Cuba, 5111. El Salvador, 5304. Guatemala, 5123.

Costume and Adornment. Audiencia of Charcas, 2772. Aztec, 1503. Brazil, 475. Guatemala, 293. Martinique, 298. Maya, 296. Mexico, 295, 303. Viceroyalty of Peru, 1621.

Cotacachi, Ecuador (city). History, 1748.

Cotapos, Acario, 7112.

Cote Lamus, E., 5922.

Cotton Industry and Trade. Brazil, 3490. Peru, 3067. Viceroyalty of Peru, 1977.

Coups d'Etat. Argentina, 3270a. Bolivia, 5523. Brazil, 3536. Chile, 3132, 5565. Colombia, 2987. Dominican Republic, 2609. El Salvador, 2268. Guatemala, 2313. Venezuela, 2912, 2919.

Courts. Cuba, 2600. Guatemala, 2240. Guyana, 2334. History, 2629. Martinique, 2522. Río de la Plata, 2826. Trinidad, 2491. Venezuela, 2629.

Crafts. Brazil, 435.

Credit. Mexico, 2116.
Creole Dialects. Caribbean Area, 4642, 4650, 4658, 4661, 6463. Colombia, 4649. Dictionaries, 4655, 4656. Discourse Analysis, 4638. Etymology, 4643. Grammar, 4639, 4661. Guadeloupe, 4647, 4655. Haiti, 4639, 4651, 4656, 4659. Influence of African Languages, 4640, 4643. Influence of Portuguese Language, 4649, 4650. Jamaica, 4638, 4654. in Literature, 6463, 6480. Martinique, 4646, 6485. Nicaragua, 4640. Panama, 4645, 4648. Puerto Rico, 4576. Study and Teaching, 4651. Surinam, 4641. Terms and Phrases, 4656.
Crime and Criminals. Argentina, 3272. Audiencia of Guadalajara, 1945. Brazil, 3456. Caribbean Area, 2521. Chile, 3156. Colombia, 2981. Cuba, 2537, 2546, 5400. Dictionaries, 4581. Dominican Republic, 2555. Guyana, 2334. Mexico, 2109, 2195, 5996. Venezuela, 2635, 2640. Viceroyalty of New Granada, 2679. Viceroyalty of New Spain, 1932. Viceroyalty of Peru, 1749, 2732.
Criollismo. Argentina, 5653. Guatemala, 5294, 5317.
Cristero Rebellion (Mexico, 1926–1929), 2145, 2163, 2177.
Cruz Martínez, Luis, 3148.
Cuadra, Pablo Antonio, 5933, 5962.
Cuba and Chile Relations, 3109.
Cuba and United States Relations, 2364, 2379, 2515, 2595, 5413.
Cuban Revolution (1959), 2557a, 2565, 2572, 2575, 2600, 2610, 5151, 5377, 5431, 5442, 5451, 5454.
Cuenca, Ecuador (city). Art, 377. Congresses, 3017. History, 1609, 2614, 2617, 2688, 3017.
Cuernavaca, Mexico (city). Art, 322. History, 1506.
Cuervo, Rufino José, 5165.
Cuesta, Jorge, 5711, 5923, 5932, 5956, 5960.
Cuevas, José Luis, 391, 402.
Culhuacán, 1570.
Cultural Identity. Argentina, 5665. Chile, 7106. Costa Rica, 5313. Cuba, 2335. Haiti, 2561. History, 1867. Latin America, 1775, 1803, 1867, 5016, 5038, 5042. Martinique, 6485. Mexico, 7548. Peru, 3076. Puerto Rico, 5460. Venezuela, 5148.
Cultural Policy. Brazil, 434. Cuba, 5448.
Culture. Andean Region, 5511. Argentina, 3215, 5662, 7665. Brazil, 3475, 3518, 6220, 7629. Caribbean Area, 79. Central Amer-

ica, 5106. Chile, 3146. Colombia, 2988. Cuba, 2389. Dominican Republic, 2332. Guadaloupe, 6478. Haiti, 6487. History, 1808, 2072, 2166, 3518, 6220, 7522. Latin America, 1808, 5039, 7522, 7534. Mexico, 2067, 2072, 2166, 7551. Nicaragua, 5977. Paraguay, 5695. Periodicals, 79, 2377. Peru, 3035. Philosophy, 7534, 7629, 7665. Puerto Rico, 2365, 2377. Saramaka, 2457. Venezuela, 2911. West Indies, 2403, 2435.
Cuna (indigenous group), 2283.
Cunha, Brasílio Itiberê da, 7062.
Cunha, Euclides da, 6362.
Curaçao and France Relations, 2450.
Curiepe, Venezuela (city). History, 2630, 2632.
Curitiba, Brazil (city). Literature, 6219. Music, 7066.
Cusi Yupanqui, Tito. See Titu Cussi Yupanqui, Diego de Castro.
Cuzco, Peru (city). Art, 372, 374, 381. History, 372, 374, 1599, 1774, 2736.
Cuzco, Peru (dept.). History, 2726, 2731, 3061, 3089.
Cuzzani, Agustín, 6050, 6123.

Dalma, Juan, 7656.
Dalton, Roque, 5983, 5987.
Damas, Léon-Gontran, 6488, 6489.
Dance. Andean Region, 1588, 7118. Brazil, 475, 7044, 7074. Cuba, 7125. Guatemala, 7094. Mexico, 7138. Peru, 7150. Theory, 7138.
Darío, Rubén, 5894, 5897, 5905, 5907, 5934, 5938, 5946, 5947, 5968.
Dartigenave, Philippe Sudre, 2570.
Daule, Ecuador (city). History, 1651.
Dávila Orejón Gastón, Francisco, 2643.
Debret, Jean Baptiste, 445.
Decorative Arts. Brazil, 511.
Deforestation. See Forests and Forestry.
Deities. Aztec, 1573a. Nahua, 1959.
Délano, Pablo, 7117.
Delfino, Augusto Mario, 5658.
Delgado, Antonio, 5225.
Demarigny, Claude, 6109.
Democracy. Brazil, 3432. Chile, 3134.
Demography. Andean Region, 2616. Audiencia of Quito, 1672. Caribbean Area, 2517b. Chile, 2788. Ecuador, 3012. Guadeloupe, 2426, 2489. Guatemala, 2252. Hispaniola, 2407. Latin America, 1872. Martinique, 2409. Mexico, 1904. Nicaragua, 2280. Río

de la Plata, 2811. Venezuela, 2925. Viceroyalty of New Spain, 1969, 2020, 2223. Viceroyalty of Peru, 1694, 2726.

Denevi, Marco, 6570.

Dependency. Argentina, 3229, 3262. Chile, 3137. Haiti, 2520, 2597. Latin America, 960. Paraguay, 3338.

DeRidder, Francis, 2493.

Derrida, Jacques, 6571.

Dessalles, Pierre, 2503.

Detective Mystery Stories. Brazil, 6124. Cuba, 5464.

Devrieux-déhoux, Lilliane, 6484.

Di Benedetto, Antonio, 5646.

Di Cavalcanti, Emiliano, 456a.

Dialectology. Argentina, 4516. Bibliography, 4540. Brazil, 4604, 4605, 4608. Caribbean Area, 4546, 4553, 4559. Central America, 4535. Chile, 4544. Colombia, 4541, 4543. Congresses, 4553. Colorado, 4555. Dictionaries, 4544, 4551, 4555. Dominican Republic, 4553. Equatorial Guinea, 4533. Guatemala, 4551. Honduras, 4534, 4557. Jamaica, 4654. Latin America, 4524, 4538, 4540. Mexico, 4519, 4521, 4536, 4539, 4547, 4550. Mixtec, 1540. New Mexico, 4555. Paraguay, 4531. Peru, 4525. Puerto Rico, 4520, 4529, 4548. Río de la Plata, 4530. Spain, 4512, 4538. Venezuela, 4532.

Díaz, Grégor, 6051.

Díaz, Jorge, 6085.

Díaz, Porfirio, 2039, 2046, 2047, 2048, 2049, 2051, 2065, 2067, 2068, 2075, 2084, 2087, 2089, 2090, 2092, 2098, 2106, 2112, 2126, 6064.

Díaz, Sergio, 7117.

Díaz del Castillo, Bernal, 5070, 7025.

Díaz del Castillo, Diego, 5110.

Díaz Grullón, Virgilio, 5466.

Díaz Mirón, Salvador, 5118.

Dictator Novels. Chile, 5574. Dominican Republic, 5404. Nicaragua, 5303.

Dictators. Guatemala, 2259, 2311.

Dictionaries. Acronyms, 4561. Afro-Americanisms, 4657. Americanisms, 4563, 4584. Antillanisms, 4575. Architecture, 4615. Argentina, 2880. Argentinisms, 4588. Atheism, 4567. Aymara/Spanish, 1595. Aztec/Spanish-Spanish/Aztec, 4564. Brazil, 51, 3453, 4609. Caribbean Area, 52. City Planning, 4615. Colombia, 2945. Commerce, 4568, 4621, 4622. Communication, 4585. Computers, 4583, 4619. Creole, 4657. Criminology, 4581. Cubanisms, 4588. Education, 4629. English/Portuguese, 4619, 4621. English/Portuguese-Portuguese/English, 4625, 4628. English/Spanish, 4583. Etymology, 4620. Florida, 4582. Journalism, 4614. Latin America, 4565, 4566, 4571, 4611. Latin Americanists, 64. Mexico, 47, 4575. Mineralogy, 4574, 4628. Nahuatl/English, 1508. Nahuatl, 4575. Natural History, 4565. Pachuco, 4572. Political Science, 4589, 4627. Portuguese/ Spanish, 4611. Puerto Rico, 4576. Quechua, 1616. Quechua/ Spanish, 4586. Real Academia Española, 4560. Religion, 4623. Slang, 4571, 4609, 4625. Social Science, 4585. Social Work, 4562, 4617. Spanish, 4569, 4570. Spanish/English, 4568. Synonyms and Antonyms, 4580. Telecommunications, 4619. Terms and Phrases, 4624. West Indies, 2331. Yoruba/Portuguese, 4618.

Diegues, Carlos, 1008, 1009, 1019, 1022.

Diez de Medina, Fernando Tadeo, 1691.

Diplomatic History. Argentina, 3241. Bolivia, 3104, 3340. Brazil, 3494. Chile, 3124. Cuba, 5422, 5547. Florida, 2469. France, 40. Haiti, 2528. Latin America, 40, 2859a. Mexico, 2120. Paraguay, 3337, 3339, 3340. Peru, 5547. Río de la Plata, 2841. United Kingdom, 3124. Uruguay, 3362. West Indies, 2445.

Discourse Analysis. Latin America, 4505.

Discovery and Exploration. Alto Perú, 2774. Borderlands, 2026, 2468. California, 2011. Falkland Islands, 2815. Florida, 2472. Latin America, 1837, 1842, 1845, 1851, 1854, 1860, 5099, 5104, 5757. in Literature, 5757. Mexico, 1951. Peru, 2735. North America, 5099, 5104. Río de la Plata, 2836. Spanish, 5757. Viceroyalty of New Spain, 2026.

Diseases. Caribbean Area, 2358. Colombia, 2942. Guatemala, 2238, 2279. History, 1892, 1937. Honduras, 2232. Latin America, 1823. Mexico, 1892. Uruguay, 3352. Viceroyalty of New Spain, 1913, 1937, 1966, 1968. West Indies, 2387.

Dissertations. Haiti, 6481.

Divorce. Viceroyalty of Peru, 2743, 2753a.

Dobles, Julieta, 5925.

Documentaries. Cuba, 1047. Dominican Republic, 1070. Haiti, 1067. Mexico, 1079, 1090. Nicaragua, 1098.

Domínguez Camargo, Hernando, 5076, 5077.

Dominican Republic and Haiti Relations, 2519.

Ethics. Argentina, 7650. Caribbean Area, 7578. Chile, 3167. Latin America, 7515.
Ethnic Groups and Ethnicity. Alto Perú, 2773. Andean Region, 1654, 1699. Audiencia of Quito, 1672. Bolivia, 1713a. Chile, 3151. Ecuador, 1603. Haiti, 2369. Policy, 1728. Study and Teaching, 1914. Viceroyalty of New Spain, 1914. Viceroyalty of Peru, 1728, 2757.
Ethnography. Alto Perú, 2773. Andean Region, 1586, 1682, 1712, 1735. Bolivia, 1724. Brazil, 1636. Chile, 1739. Ecuador, 1639, 1704. Guatemala, 1564, 2229. Peru, 1750, 1760. South America, 1742. Viceroyalty of Peru, 1657, 1696, 1701, 1711, 1723.
Ethnohistory. Bibliography, 1551, 1604. Study and Teaching, 1597, 1718.
Ethnology. Wayãpi, 1630.
Ethnomusicology. Brazil, 7046. Congresses, 7006. Latin America, 7006.
Evitar, Colombia (city). Music, 7121.
Excavations. Brazil, 490. Cacaxtla, 266. Copán (Honduras), 1527. Izapa (Mexico), 274. Mexico, 271. Palenque (Mexico), 268. Paraguay, 363.
Exiled Authors. Argentina, 5665. Chile, 5891. Paraguay, 5690.
Existentialism. in Literature, 5837, 5852. Nicaragua, 5837.
Expeditions. Amazônia, 3404. Bibliography, 2660. Guatemala, 2251. Mesoamerica, 1512. Río de la Plata, 2796a. South America, 1742. Viceroyalty of New Granada, 2660. Viceroyalty of Peru, 2700.
Expressionism. Brazil, 487.

Fabela, Isidoro, 2151.
Fabrega, Virginia, 5745.
Fabrés Costa, Antonio, 400.
Facio, Rodrigo, 2277.
Fajardo, Puerto Rico (city). History, 2601.
Falkland Islands. Bibliography, 3249. History, 3249, 3292, 3293, 3304, 3314, 3318. Literature, 5603.
Falkland/Malvinas War, 3208, 3214, 3233, 3241, 3246, 3299, 3309, 3314.
Fallas, Carlos Luis, 5316, 5339.
Family and Family Relations. Bibliography, 1779. Brazil, 3529, 6316, 6329. Chile, 2788. Haiti, 2561. Latin America, 1778, 1779, 1786. Laws and Legislation, 1949, 2825, 2826. in Literature, 6012, 6316, 6329. Mexico, 1886, 1909, 1930. Peru, 3034. Río de la Plata, 2824, 2825, 2826. Study and Teach-

ing, 1786. Viceroyalty of New Spain, 1940a, 1948, 1949, 1956, 1993, 1995, 2001, 2020.
Fang, Chen-Kong, 457.
Fantastic Art. Mexico, 404.
Fantastic Literature. Argentina, 5637. Brazil, 6138, 6172. Latin America, 5011.
Faria, Reginaldo, 999.
Farrapos Revolution (1835–1845), 3455, 3514.
Farré, Luis, 7655.
Faubert, Ida, 6483.
Federal Government. Mexico, 2081, 2198.
Federal War (1859–1863), 2923.
Feijóo de Sosa, Miguel, 2755.
Félix, María, 6011.
Feminism. Brazil, 6287. Cuba, 5405. Guatemala, 5713, 5868. Latin America, 5013, 5028, 5035, 5737, 5915, 6527. in Literature, 5028, 5193, 5405, 5502, 5558, 5563, 5713, 5737, 5868, 5915, 5919, 6072, 6287, 6527. Mexico, 5193. Peru, 5502. Spain, 6527. Venezuela, 5558, 5563.
Fernandes, Gaspar, 7096.
Fernández, Emilio, 1077.
Fernández, Justino, 339.
Fernández, Macedonio, 5655, 7646.
Fernández Cañizález, Victór, 5331.
Fernández de Agüero y Echave, Juan Manuel, 5079.
Fernández de Oviedo y Valdés, Gonzalo, 1799, 2245, 7025.
Fernández de San Vicente, Agustín, 2055.
Fernández del Castillo, Francisco, 1832.
Fernández Violante, Marcela, 1085.
Ferrari, Osvaldo, 5644.
Ferrari, Rosario S. de, 2291.
Ferreira, Alexandre Rodrigues, 3404.
Ferreira, Wilson, 3350.
Ferretti, Aurelio, 6123.
Ferrez, Marc, 480, 481.
Festivals. Brazil, 7072. Congresses, 287. Latin America, 287. Mexico, 287. Viceroyalty of Peru, 1668.
Fierro, Enrique, 5908.
Fiestas. See Festivals.
Figueiredo, Euclides, 3457, 3458.
Figueroa, Gabriel, 1077.
Film. Bibliography, 38, 952, 961, 1021. Congresses, 995. Cuba, 407. Festivals, 953, 955, 957, 962, 963. Finance, 969. History, 954, 969, 979, 980, 990, 993, 996, 1001, 1002, 1003, 1020, 1021, 1025, 1041, 1056, 1067, 1069, 1075, 1083, 1084, 1086, 1090, 1092, 1105, 1106. Laws and Legislation, 1083,

Medicine. Hispaniola, 2406.
Mediza, Alberto, 5908.
Meireles, Cecília, 6413.
Mella, Julio Antonio, 2592.
Mello, João Ramiro, 985.
Melo, João Cabral de, 6420.
Melo, Pedro Américo de Figueiredo e, 444, 449.
Mendanha, Joaquim José, 7074.
Méndez Ballester, Manuel, 6075.
Mendonça, Paulo, 999.
Mendoza, Argentina (prov.). History, 2814, 2894, 3270, 3300. Literature, 5646.
Mendoza, María Luisa, 5263.
Menéndez, Jesús, 2579, 5399.
Menéndez Pidal, Ramón, 5122.
Menezes, Batuque de Bruno, 6423.
Merchant Marines. Peru, 3026.
Merchants. Argentina, 3237. Costa Rica, 2309. Cuba, 2483. Viceroyalty of Peru, 2744. Viceroyalty of Río de la Plata, 2812. West Indies, 2397.
Mérida, Venezuela (city). History, 2651, 2654.
Mérida, Venezuela (state). History, 1661, 2636.
Metaphysics. Mexico, 7543.
Mexican Revolution (1910–1920), 2063, 2064, 2065, 2068, 2080, 2114, 2118, 2124, 2127, 2129, 2130, 2135, 2136, 2139, 2143, 2144, 2145, 2147, 2149, 2153, 2154, 2158, 2161, 2162, 2163, 2165, 2169, 2171, 2175, 2176, 2178, 2187, 2188, 2192, 2195, 2197, 2202, 2208, 2211, 2213, 5174, 5176, 5180, 7550, 7610. Study and Teaching, 2186.
Mexicans. in the United States, 2078.
México, Mexico (city). Art, 315, 394. Bibliography, 14. History, 14, 1557, 1885, 1905, 1913, 1929, 1931, 1956, 1965a, 1995a, 2002, 2098, 2106, 2190, 2191. Language, 4519, 4539, 4547, 4550, 4558. Literature, 5169, 5189, 5192, 5197, 5202, 5207, 5210, 5217, 6550.
México, Mexico (state). History, 2081.
Mexico and Europe Relations, 2061, 2062.
Mexico and France Relations, 1888.
Mexico and Germany Relations, 2082.
Mexico and Spain Relations, 2188.
Mexico and United Kingdom Relations, 2176.
Mexico and United States Relations, 2057, 2062, 2092, 2107, 2110, 2120, 2129, 2130, 2138, 2142a, 2151, 2156, 2169, 2170, 2175, 2176, 2180, 2199, 2201, 2204, 2206.
Meyer, Augusto, 6386.

Michoacán, Mexico (state). History, 1577, 1961, 1980, 2004, 2137, 2148.
Middle Classes. Argentina, 3287, 3310. Chile, 3139, 3160, 3177. Cuba, 5401. Ecuador, 5542. Mexico, 5223.
Middleton, Christopher, 6572.
Mier, Adolfo, 2941.
Mier Noriega y Guerra, José Servando Teresa de, 1975, 5071.
Milano del Bosch, María, 7026.
Military. Chile, 1739. Colombia, 2934. Latin America, 72. Peru, 3058, 3073. Policy, 1843. Spain, 1843. Venezuela, 2897, 2919.
Military Government. Bolivia, 5523. Brazil, 3523. Colombia, 2987, 2989. El Salvador, 2268. Venezuela, 2897, 2922.
Military History. Argentina, 3221, 3234, 3241, 3271, 3283, 3286, 3299, 3307, 3309. Bibliography, 3234. Borderlands, 2009, 2129. Brazil, 3206, 3400, 3425, 3431, 3447, 3457, 3466, 3480, 3481, 3482, 3502, 3512, 3523, 6142. Chile, 3125, 3132, 3142, 3159, 3162. Colombia, 2973. Congresses, 1835. Costa Rica, 2282. Cuba, 2441, 2444, 2565, 2586. Dominican Republic, 2363, 2519, 2555. Ecuador, 2874, 3004. El Salvador, 2268. Florida, 2479. Guadeloupe, 2481. Guatemala, 2307. Haiti, 2437, 2496, 2519. Honduras, 2293. Latin America, 72, 1799, 1835, 1836, 1838, 1865a. Mexico, 2054, 2077, 2097, 2139, 2157, 2158, 2174, 2175. Peru, 3036, 3058, 3059, 3073. Surinam, 2518. United Kingdom, 3299. Uruguay, 3358. Venezuela, 2648, 2656. Viceroyalty of New Granada, 2677, 2873. Viceroyalty of New Spain, 1929, 1933, 1995, 1995a, 2019, 2034, 2244. Viceroyalty of Peru, 1764, 2619, 2728. Viceroyalty of Río de la Plata, 2812, 2837. West Indies, 2428, 2656.
Military Police. Brazil, 3367.
Mill, Stuart, 7580.
Milla, José, 5123.
Millán, Gonzalo, 5747.
Minas Gerais, Brazil (state). Art, 431, 442, 498. Film, 988, 1001. History, 3367, 3426. Literature, 6130, 6233. Music, 7059, 7078.
Minerals and Mining Industry. Alto Perú, 2765, 2766, 2767, 2771, 2778. Argentina, 3300. Audiencia of Quito, 2691, 2718. Bolivia, 3087, 3094, 3099. Brazil, 3410, 3411, 3423, 3426. Chile, 3145. History, 1792, 1899, 3426. Honduras, 5299. Latin America, 1792, 1825. Laws and Legislation, 1899, 3300. in Literature, 5299. Mexico,

2115, 2118. Nicaragua, 5268. Peru, 3054. Pipil, 1545. Puerto Rico, 2596. Viceroyalty of Peru, 2737, 2753a.
Social Conflict. Argentina, 3269. Bolivia, 3102. Brazil, 6129. Chile, 3171. Colombia, 2957, 2958. Costa Rica, 2306. Ecuador, 3005. Honduras, 5300. Mexico, 1898. Peru, 3069. Río de la Plata, 2824. Venezuela, 5995.
Social History. Andean Region, 1675, 1681, 1735, 2616, 2759. Argentina, 3216, 3232, 3327. Audiencia of Quito, 2710. Aztec, 1580. Borderlands, 2017, 2171. Brazil, 425, 3370, 3450, 6220. Caribbean Area, 2324, 2390, 2451a, 2503. Central America, 2225. Chile, 2791, 3133. Colombia, 2929, 2933, 2937, 2948, 2988. Congresses, 1902, 2933. Cuba, 2389, 2441, 2547. Dominican Republic, 2367, 2385. Guadeloupe, 2359, 2440. Guyana, 2386. Haiti, 2480. Hispaniola, 2400. Inca, 1586, 1681. Intendency of Guadalajara, 1973. Jamaica, 2336. Latin America, 1627, 1879, 5113. Martinique, 2410. Mexico, 1890, 1902, 1909, 2037, 2041, 2046, 2067, 2083, 2090, 2146, 2147, 2175. Panama, 2219. Paraguay, 3345. Periodicals, 2377. Peru, 3027, 3057, 3067, 3076. Policy, 2146. Puerto Rico, 2375, 2377, 2380, 2533. Research, 2324. Río de la Plata, 2811. Saint Lucia, 6516. Study and Teaching, 1804, 1914, 2324. Trinidad and Tobago, 2395. Venezuela, 2646a, 2911. Viceroyalty of New Granada, 2661, 2662, 2664, 2665, 2668. Viceroyalty of New Spain, 1914, 1918a, 1963, 1982, 1999, 2005. Viceroyalty of Peru, 2737, 2753a. West Indies, 2435.
Social Policy. Chile, 3108. History, 3108.
Social Sciences. Bibliography, 50, 77. Honduras, 2223. Latin America, 50, 77. Periodicals, 50. Uruguay, 75.
Social Structure. Amazonia, 1834. Andean Region, 1590, 3021, 7118. Araucano, 1597. Aztec, 1568, 1571, 1960. Brazil, 3410. Chibcha, 1729. Chile, 3134. Guadeloupe, 2466. Hispaniola, 2407. History, 1590, 1799, 1808, 1834. Inca, 1717. Latin America, 60, 1793, 1799, 1808, 5528. Maya, 1525. Mexico, 1960, 2084. Peru, 1687. Puerto Rico, 5469. Río de la Plata, 2805, 2831. South America, 2842. Southern Cone, 1638. Trinidad and Tobago, 2569. Uruguay, 75. Venezuela, 2896. Viceroyalty of New Spain, 2025. Viceroyalty of Peru, 1665, 1751.

Socialism and Socialist Parties. Argentina, 3226, 3229, 3244, 3274, 5660. Brazil, 7639. Caribbean Area, 2345. Cuba, 2584, 6090. Dominican Republic, 7567. Ecuador, 2997, 3018. Guadeloupe, 2563, 2564. History, 1873, 2108. Latin America, 1873. in Literature, 5660, 6090. Mexico, 2108, 2118, 2125. Peru, 3029.
Sociolinguistics. Brazil, 4614, 4631, 4635. Caribbean Area, 4660. Congresses, 4511. Equatorial Guinea, 4533. Latin America, 4505, 4515. Martinique, 4646. Panama, 4645, 4648. Portuguese, 4511. Spanish, 4511, 4512.
Sociology. Argentina, 3255, 5638. Brazil, 3376. Chile, 5928. Colombia, 2934. Costa Rica, 2300. in Literature, 5459, 5928. Panama, 5340. Puerto Rico, 5459.
Soffia, José Antonio, 2970.
Sola y Ros, Francisco de, 2709.
Solana, Fernando, 1070.
Solás, Humberto, 1052.
Soldiers. Chile, 3148, 3159.
Solentiname, Nicaragua (community). History, 2261.
Solís, Daniel, 1073.
Solís y Valenzuela, Pedro de, 5050, 5080.
Solórzano, Carlos, 6070.
Somoza Debayle, Anastasio, 2297.
Somoza Debayle, Luis, 2297.
Songs. Brazil, 7047a. Ecuador, 7127. Venezuela, 7172.
Sonora, Mexico (state). History, 2029.
Sonqo, Peru (city). History, 1584.
Sonthonax, Léger Félicité, 2461.
Soro, Enrique, 7111.
Soto, Marco Aurelio, 2315.
Soto, Pedro Juan, 5471, 5472.
Sound Recording Industry. Brazil, 7049.
South America and Brazil Relations, 3519.
South America and Chile Relations, 3131.
Spain and France Relations, 2472.
Spain and Portugal Relations, 2820, 2893.
Spain and Spanish Colonies Relations, 1798, 1830, 1839, 1840, 1863b.
Spain and United Kingdom Relations, 2012.
Spain and United States Relations, 2469.
Spaniards. in Argentina, 3237. in the Dominican Republic, 2391. in Mexico, 2106, 2141, 2182, 2188, 2193, 5204.
Spanish. in Brazil, 3436.
Spanish American War (1898), 7085.
Spanish Civil War, 2141, 2584, 5204, 5506.
Spanish Colonies and East Asia Relations, 1856.

5045, 5070, 5215, 5254, 5291, 5304, 5421,
5449, 5502, 5528, 5534, 5558, 5563, 5580,
5582, 5789, 5832, 5858, 5879, 5885, 5886,
5919, 5925, 6069, 6125, 6135, 6155, 6167,
6278, 6311, 6372, 6402, 6484, 6491, 6525,
6527, 6543, 6559, 6563. Martinique, 2522,
6492. Mexico, 1885, 2164, 2177, 2956,
5254. Nicaragua, 2297. Ona, 1607. Peru,
3023, 5502, 5789. Portugal, 6372. Puerto
Rico, 2551. Río de la Plata, 2823. Spain,
6372, 6527. Surinam, 2508. Venezuela,
5563. Viceroyalty of New Spain, 1541,
1576, 1934, 1936, 1949. Viceroyalty of
Peru, 1651, 1659, 2730, 2733, 2743.
Wood, Patricio, 1059.
Wood, Salvador, 1059.
World War II, 3457.
Writing. Inca, 1705, 1717. Nahuatl, 1504,
1544, 1546, 1570. Pipil, 1545. Quechua,
1641.
Wulfes, Alexandre, 1006.

Xochimilco, Mexico (city). History, 1983.

Yagua (indigenous group), 1738.
Yáñez, Agustín, 5218, 5229, 5235, 5244,
5247, 5254.
Yaqui (indigenous group), 2071.
Youths. Argentina, 3211. Central America,

2298. Cuba, 2580, 2581. in Literature,
5612.
Yraeta, Francisco Ignacio de, 1948.
Yrigoyen, Hipólito, 3186, 3219, 3235, 3270a.
Yucatán, Mexico (state). Art, 270, 305, 317.
Film, 1087. History, 1898, 1981, 2068,
2073, 2076, 2124, 2126, 2127, 2382. Lan-
guage, 4521, 4522, 4536. Literature, 5138.
Yupanqui, Atahualpa, 7022.

Zacarías Tallet, José, 5425.
Zacatecas, Mexico (city). History, 1974.
Zaldúa, Francisco Javier, 2940.
Zamora, Mexico (city). History, 1894.
Zamora, Pedro, 2192.
Zanini, Mário, 454.
Zapata, Emiliano, 2136, 2139.
Zapata, Luis, 5213.
Zapotec (indigenous group), 1502.
Zárate, Agustín de, 5063.
Zaruma, Ecuador (city). History, 2691.
Zavalita, Carlos Eduardo, 5546.
Zea, Leopoldo, 7545, 7549.
Zeballo, Estanislao S., 3206a.
Zeno Gandía, Manuel, 5471.
Zepeda, Eraclio, 5753, 5916.
Zipoli, Domenico, 7037.
Zoology. Viceroyalty of New Granada, 2673.
Zorrilla de San Martín, Juan, 5164, 7641.

AUTHOR INDEX

Colegio Mayor del Rosario. Archivo, 369
Colindres O., Ramiro, 5307
College of the Virgin Islands, 6514
Collier, Simon, 3122
Colmenares, Germán, 2663–2664, 2937
Colmenter V., Felipe S., 2903
Colón, Adolfo, 5427
Coloquio de Antropología e Historia Regionales, *3rd, Zamora, Mexico, 1981,* 1889
Coloquio sobre la Cuentística de Onelio Jorge Cardoso, *La Habana, 1981,* 5428
Colson, R.F., 3448
Comas, Juan, 1814
O Comércio e suas profissões: imagens, Brasil, 1500/1946, 501
Cometta Manzoni, Aida, 7611
Comisión de Historia de la Columna 19 "José Tey," 2565
Comisión de Investigación Histórica de la Campaña de *1856–1857,* 2282
Comisión Nacional para la Defensa del Idioma Español, *Mexico,* 4528
Comissiong, Barbara, 4
La Compañía de comercio de Francisco Ignacio de Yraeta, *1767–1797,* 1948
Comparato, Frank E., 1512, 1527, 1575
Compilación de crónicas, relatos y descripciones de Cuenca y su provincia, 1609
Compton, Merlin D., 5494
Concolorcorvo. *See* Carrió de la Vandera, Alonso.
Concurso Estadual de Dramaturgia, *2nd, Florianópolis, Brazil, 1982,* 6317
Concurso Sérgio Porto, *6th, Goiânia, Brazil, 1983,* 6213
Condarco Morales, Ramiro, 3087
Conde, Teresa del, 397
Condo, Pedro, 5748
Conference of Caribbean Historians, *14th, San Juan, 1983,* 2566
Conference of the Association of Caribbean Studies, *4th, Havana, 1982,* 6513
Conference of the Association of Caribbean University and Research Libraries, *13th, Caracas, 1982,* 27
Conference of the Association of Caribbean University and Research Libraries, *17th, St. Croix, 1986,* 28
Conference on Critical Approaches to West Indian Literature, *Saint Thomas, V.I., 1981,* 6514
Conflictos y no-creencia en América Latina: hacia una superación a la luz de Puebla, 7512
Confluencia: literatura argentina por

brasileños, literatura brasileña por argentinos, 5648
Congreso Cultural de Verano del CCP y la Universidad de Miami, *2nd, Miami, 1982,* 5135
Congreso de Municipalidades de Venezuela, *1st, Caracas, 1911,* 2904
Congreso Interamericano de Etnomusicología y Folklore, *1st, Caracas, 1983,* 7006
Congreso Internacional de Filosofía Latinoamericana, *1st, Bogotá, 1980,* 7512a
Congreso Internacional de Filosofía Latinoamericana, *2nd, Bogotá, 1982,* 7512b
Conjunto, 6068
Connell-Smith, Gordon, 2567
Conniff, Michael L., 2218
Conquista y colonización en México, 1916
Conrad, Geoffrey W., 1519
Conrad, Robert Edgar, 3369
Consumer markets in Central America, 48
Consumer markets in Latin America, 49
Conte Porras, Jorge, 2219
Contemporary women authors of Latin America, 5008
Contents of Periodicals on Latin America, 50
Contín Aybar, Néstor, 5429
Cony, Carlos Heitor, 3449
Corcuera de Mancera, Sonia, 1890
Cordero de Espinosa, Susana, 5136
Cornejo, José, 7513
Cornejo A., Manuel, 67
Cornejo Polar, Antonio, 5009, 5495–5496, 5551
Corona, Eduardo, 492
Coronel Urtecho, José, 5975
Corradine Angulo, Alberto, 368
Corral, Wilfrido H., 5322
Correa, Miguel, 5390
Correa Bustamante, Francisco José, 7127
Corregido, Dolores Juliano, 1611
Correia-Alfonso, John, 1815
Cortázar, Connie, 2055
Cortázar, Julio, 5600, 5649–5650, 6534
Cortés, Alfonso, 5717
Cortés, Santo Rodolfo, 1816
Cortés Bargalló, Luis, 5790a
Cortés Conde, Roberto, 3218
Corti, Francisco, 360
Cortina, Alfredo, 2905
Corvalán, Graziella, 4503
Corvington, Georges, 2568
Corzano, Néstor, 5545
Coselino, Luis Alberto, 5791

Cosmos, Angel, 7137
Cossío, María Eugenia, 5221
Cossío Woodward, Miguel, 5391
Costa, Cacilda Teixcira da, 432, 462
Costa, Eduardo Alves da, 6256
Costa, Emilia Viotti da, 3450
Costa, Eunice R. Ribeiro, 486, 4615
Costa, Iraci del Nero da, 3410
Costa, Luiz Fernando Macedo, 496
Costa, René de, 5937
Costa, Rovílio, 3435
Costa, Vanda Maria Ribeiro, 3518
Costa Filho, Odylo, 6169
Costales, Alfredo, 1684, 1743, 2994
Costales, Piedad, 1684, 1743, 2994
Costantini, Humberto, 5792, 6554
Cotler, Julio, 3032
Cotrim, Alvaro, 444, 447
Cotrim, Lupe, 6257
Counselo, Jorge Miguel, 967, 969
Coutinho, Afrânio, 6230, 6357
Coutinho, Edilberto, 6170, 6286, 6391, 6411
Coutinho, Eduardo de Faria, 6230
Coutinho, Wilson, 463
Couturier, Edith B., 1949
Covantes, Hugo, 390
Coyer, Gabriel François, 2806
Craig, Ann L., 2131
Craton, Michael, 2327, 2497
Crawford, Leslie, 3354
Crawford de Roberts, Lois, 2995
Crawley, Eduardo, 3219
Crema, Antonio, 5559
Crespo, Horacio, 1902
Crespo Paniagua, Renato, 5998–5999
La Crisis de 1890, 3220
Critical issues in West Indian literature: selected papers from West Indian literature conferences, *1981–1983*, 6515
Cronologia cinematográfica brasileira, *1898–1930*, 996
Cronología militar argentina, *1806–1980*, 3221
Crow, Mary, 6525
Crumley de Pérez, Laura Lee. *See* Pérez, Laura Lee Crumley de.
Crusader vignettes, 6516
Cruz, Adelina Maria Alves Novaes, 3470
Cruz, Juana Inés de la, *Sor. See* Juana Inés de la Cruz, *Sor.*
Cruz, Ramón E., 2272
Cruz, Víctor de la, 5723
Cruz Reyes, Víctor C., 2232
Csicsery, George, 997
Cuadernos Americanos, 2132

Cuadernos de la Facultad de Humanidades, 2328
Cuadra, Manolo, 5281
Cuadra, Pablo Antonio, 5323–5324, 5793, 5897, 5976–5977, 6000
Cuadra Mejía, Alerto, 5794
Cuadros Silva-Santisteban, Gustavo, 3033
Cuban and North American Marxism, 7568
Cuban Center for Translation and Interpretation (ESTI), 2589
Cuban Studies/Estudios Cubanos, 2329
Cubitt, David J., 74, 2867
Cuche, Denys, 3034
Cuchí Coll, Isabel, 5898
Cudjoe, Selwyn Reginald, 2569
Cuéllar, Margarito, 5752
Cuenca Esteban, Javier, 1817
Cuentas Ormachea, Enrique, 7150
Cuentos limeños, 1950–1980: antología y estudio preliminar, 5546
Cuentos populares de Guatemala, 5282
Cuervo Hewitt, Julia, 5430
Cuesta, Jorge, 5707
La Cuestión de la tierra, 2133
Cuevas, Alexander, 2273
Cuevas, José Luis, 391
A Cultura nacional e a presença do MASP, 502
Culturas precolombinas: Chancay, 276
Culturas precolombinas: Paracas, 277
Cummings, Joseph, 6500
Cummins, Victoria Hennessey, 1950
Cumplido, Francisco, 3123
Cúneo, Dardo, 3222, 5651
Cunha, Antônio Geraldo da, 4616
Cunha, Liberato Vieira da, 6214
Cunha, Marlei, 6318
Curruhuinca-Roux, 1612
Cusi Yupanqui, Tito. *See* Titu Cussi Yupanqui, Diego de Castro.
Cussen, Anthony, 7582
Cuvi, Pablo, 6001
Cuza Malé, Belkis, 5431
Cuzco, Perú (*city*). Cabildo, 2736
Cypess, Sandra Messinger, 6069

Daget, Michèle, 2449
Daget, Serge, 2330, 2449
Daher, Luiz Carlos, 487
Dahlgren, Barbara, 1520
Dallal, Alberto, 5172, 7138
Dalton, Roque, 2274, 5795–5796, 6002
D'Altroy, Terence, 1614
Dambreville, Claude, 6443

Estudio socio-económico y cultural de Salta, 3232
Estudios del Reino de Guatemala: homenaje al profesor S.D. Markman, 2234
Estudios sobre la ciudad iberoamericana, 1783
Estudo de filologia e lingüística: em homenagem a Isaac Nicolau Salum, 4600
Etchecopar, Máximo, 7653
Etchepareborda, Roberto, 3233–3234, 3270a
Etna, Max, 2337
Ettmüller, Wolfgang, 3132
Etzel, Eduardo, 430
Evolução física de Salvador, 3397
Ewell, Judith, 2911
El Exilio español en México, 1939–1982, 2141
Exposición de artesanías tradicionales de la Argentina, 307
Exposición: la música en el arte precolombino: 30 de septiembre al 30 de diciembre, 1982, 7104
Eyzaguirre, Jaime, 2783, 3133

Fabre, Camille, 2512
Facchin, Emyr Carlos, 6133
Facio, Rodrigo, 2277
Facio, Sara, 3028
Fagundes, Morivalde Calvet, 3455
Fáinberg, Lev, 1620
Falcon, Francisco José Calazans, 3398, 3512
Falcón, Jorge, 7612
Falcón, Rafael, 5436, 6075
Fall, Yoro K., 1822
Fallas Monge, Carlos Luis, 2278
Fallope, Josette, 2513
Fals Borda, Orlando, 2668, 2941
Fang, Chen-Kong, 457
Faria, Alvaro Alves de, 6260
Farias, Elson, 6261
Farias, Roberto, 999
Farrell, Gerardo T., 7517
Farriss, Nancy Marguerite, 1525
Faury, Mára Lúcia, 6358
Fausto, Boris, 3456, 3467
Febres Cordero G., Julio, 2637
Federico González Suárez: la polémica sobre el Estado laico, 2999
Feinmann, José Pablo, 5654
Feldman, Lawrence H., 39
Feliciano Mendoza, Ester, 6413
Félix, Domingos, 6304
Felker, William L., 5057
Femenias, Blenda, 1621

Femmes de Amérique, 1784
Fernandes, Francisco Assis Martins, 3399
Fernandes, Millôr, 6262
Fernandes, Rofran, 3508
Fernández, Alejandro, 310
Fernández, Alicia, 32
Fernández, Ariel, 5014
Fernández, David W., 1622
Fernández, Gonzalo, 3134
Fernández, Guillermo, 5720
Fernández, Jesse, 413
Fernández, José B., 5437
Fernández, Justino, 393
Fernández, Macedonio, 6523
Fernández, Manuel A., 3135
Fernández, Martha, 326
Fernández, Miguel Angel, 5779
Fernández, Roberto G., 5437
Fernández, Teodosio, 6076
Fernández Baeza, Mario, 3136
Fernández de Lizardi, José Joaquín, 5096
Fernández del Castillo, Francisco, 1832
Fernández Fragoso, Víctor, 5807
Fernández Hall Haroldo, Francisco, 5287
Fernández Llerena, Raúl, 3037–3038
Fernández López, Manuel, 2889
Fernández Martínez, Montserrat, 2696
Fernández Moreno, Baldomero, 5721
Fernández Moreno, César, 5721
Fernández Morera, Darío, 5900
Fernández Olmos, Margarite, 5008
Fernández Retamar, Roberto, 5438–5439, 5940, 7569
Fernicola, Anna, 45
Ferrando, Roberto, 5099
Ferrari, Américo, 3039, 5655
Ferrari, Juan Carlos, 6010
Ferraz, Leda Maria Figueiredo, 485
Ferreira, Carlos, 971
Ferreira, Francisco de Paula, 4617
Ferreira, Sônia Maria Fernandes, 6263
Ferrer Benimeli, José A., 2854
Ferreras, Ramón Alberto, 2338, 2574
Ferrero, Roberto A., 3235
Ferrez, Gilberto, 480–481, 488, 3400
Ferris, Elizabeth G., 2142
Ferrol, Orlando, 4644
Festival Internacional de Poesía, 2nd, Morelia, Mexico, 1983, 5722
Festival Internacional de Teatro, 5th, Caracas, 1981, 6077
Festival Internacional de Teatro, 6th, Caracas, 1983, 6078
Fialdini, Rômulo, 489

Langagne, Eduardo, 5827
Lange, Francisco Curt, 7031, 7059–7060
Langer, Erick D., 1649
Lannot, Jorge O., 3317
Lapa, José Roberto do Amaral, 1875, 3380
Lapointe, Marie, 2076
Lara, Cecília de, 6395
Lara, Darío, 3002
Lara, Juan Jacobo de, 5453
Lara, Luis Fernando, 4528
Lara Figueroa, Celso A. 5282
Larousse encyclopedia of music based on *La musique: les hommes, les instruments, les ouevres*, 7011
Larrazábal Henríquez, Osvaldo, 5148, 5948
Larre Borges, Ana Inés, 5699, 7644
Larrea, Juan, 5021, 5981
Lasarte, Pedro, 5072
Lascano, Marcelo Ramón, 3263
Lassegue, Juan Bautista, 2752
Lastra, Pedro, 5073
Late Lowland Maya civilization: classic to postclassic, 257
Latin America and the literature of exile: a comparative view of the 20th-century European refugee writers in the New World, 5022
Latin American Literary Review, 5486
Latin American Newsletters, Ltd., 62
Latin American Theatre Review, 6089
Latin American oil companies and the politics of energy, 1876
Latouche, Eugène Bruneau. *See* Bruneau-Latouche, Eugène.
Lauer, Mirko, 5703
Laurenza, Roque Javier, 5907
Lauriete, Gérard, 4647
Lausent, I., 3052
Lavallé, Bernard, 1650, 2701, 2753–2753a
Lavandera, Beatriz R., 4505
Laviana Cuetos, María Luisa, 1711, 2702–2705
Lavrin, Asunción, 1962–1963
Lazzaro, Luis Aaron, 7629
Lazzarotto, Danilo, 3474
Le Riverend, Julio, 2523
Leal, Cláudio Murilo, 6270
Leal, Ildefonso, 2872
Leal, Luis, 1543, 5232
Leal, Rine, 6090
Leal, Wills, 1016
Leante, César, 5454
Lecaros Villavisencio, Fernando, 3053
Lecompte, Janet, 2077
Ledesma Izquieta, Genaro, 5549

Ledezma, Minelia de, 4594
Ledford-Miller, Linda, 4608
Lee, Wesley Duke, 462
Leenhardt, Jacques, 7521
LeGrand, Catherine, 2957–2958
Leiby, John S., 1964
Leinhoff, Dieter, 7096
Leitão, José Maria, 6185
Leite, A. Roberto de Paula, 6396
Leite, Ascendino, 6431
Leite, Lígia Chiappini Moraes, 437, 6397
Lemaitre, Eduardo, 2674, 2959
Lémann Cazabón, Juan, 7107
Lemmon, Alfred E., 7094
Lemoine, Ernesto, 2086
Lemos, Carlos A.C., 433, 492
Leñero, Estela, 6023–6025
Leñero, Vicente, 5188–5190
Lenz-Volland, Birgit, 1651
León, Arnaldo de, 2078
Leon, Fernando Ponce de, 482
León, Luis A., 1609
León, Nicolás, 2079
León García, Ricardo, 2137
León-Portilla, Miguel, 1544–1546, 1570, 1899, 2024, 5107
León Sánchez, José, 5292
Leonard, Thomas M., 2292
Lepkowski, Tadeusz, 2524
Lerche, Peter, 1652
Lerner, Elisa, 6052
Lértora Mendoza, Celina Ana, 7658–7659
Lesage, Julia, 1055
Lessa, Orígenes, 6138
Letras de la Audiencia de Quito: período jesuítico, 5098
Levine, Robert M., 3475
Levine, Suzanne Jill, 5589, 6553
Lewaw, I. Bar. *See* Bar-Lewaw, I.
Lewis, Colin M., 1787
Lewis, Robert E., 1965
Leyva Medina, Nelson, 2873
Lezama Lima, José, 5727
Liberman, Arnoldo, 5665
Los Liberales amarillos en la caricatura venezolana, 2915
El Libro de oro de Santander, 2960
El Libro jubilar de Pedro Henríquez Ureña, 5455
Libros de la hacienda pública en Nueva Segovia, 1551–1577, y Caracas, *1581–1597*, 2644
Libros de la Real Hacienda en la última década del siglo XVI, 2645

Melo, Lélia Erbolato, 4636a
Melo Neto, João Cabral de, 6276
Memorias de la lucha contra la tiranía, 2588
Memorias políticas y económicas del Consulado de Veracruz, *1796–1822*, 1972
Mencía, Mario, 2589
Mencos Franco, Agustín, 2244
Mendes, Claudinei Magno Magre, 3415
Mendes, Evelyse Maria Freira, 7631
Mendes, Luís Antônio Martins, 6277
Méndez, Francisco, 5294
Méndez, José Luis, 5459
Méndez Beltrán, Luz María, 1668, 3149
Méndez de Penedo, Lucrecia, 5953
Méndez-Faith, Teresa, 5694
Méndez Robles, Esilda, 2266
Mendonça, André Luiz Dumortout de, 4622
Mendonça, Antônio Sérgio Lima, 6418
Mendonça, Marcos Carneiro de, 3394
Mendonça, Rubens de, 3383
Mendoza Meléndez, Eduardo Néstor, 3059
Meneghetti, Cristina, 5840
Menéndez, Rómulo Félix, 3271
Menéndez Valdés, José, 1973
Meneses, Teodoro L., 5102
Meneses, Vidaluz, 5841
Menezes, Holdemar Oliveira de, 6190, 6224
Menezes, Mary Noel, 1669
Menotti, Emilia Edda, 3192
Menotti del Picchia, 464
Mensajes presidenciales, 2295
Menton, Seymour, 5026
Mentz, Brígida von, 2082–2083
Meo Zilio, Giovanni, 4507
Mera, Juan León, 3004
Merino Montero, Luis, 7109–7112
Merlande, Jacques Adélaïde. *See* Adélaïde-Merlande, Jacques.
Merlino, Rodolfo, 18
Merquior, José Guilherme, 6365
Merrim, Stephanie, 5027
Mertens, Hans-Günther, 2084
Mesa, José de, 377a-378, 3106
Mesa Gisbert, Carlos D., 981
Mesoamérica, 2223
Mestre Varela, Gema, 4527
Métellus, Jean, 6449
Methol Ferré, Alberto, 7624
Métral, Antoine, 2528
Mettas, Jean, 2449
Mexican art of the 1970s: images of displacement, 398
Mexico. Archivo General de la Nación, 1900
Mexico. Congreso Constituyente, 2085
Mexico. Congreso de Chilpancingo, 2086

Der mexikanische Silberberghau: 16. und l. Hälfte des 17. Jahrhunderts, 1974
Meyer, Claus, 440
Meyer, Doris, 5008
Meyer, Eugenia, 2080
Meyer, Jean A., 2175
Meyer, Lorenzo, 2110, 2176
Meyer, Michael C., 2027
Meyn, Marianne, 5460
Meza, Luis Antonio, 7152
Micciollo, Henri, 1064
Míccolis, Leila, 6287
Michaels, Albert L., 1057
Michel, Bayard, 6470
Mier, José M. de, 2869
Mier Noriega y Guerra, José Servando Teresa de, 1975
Mieses, Juan Carlos, 5842
Mieses Burgos, Franklin, 5728
Miguel, Brother, 6506
Mihovilovich, Juan, 5577
Mijares, Augusto, 2856
1.000 [i.e. Mil] títulos de autores brasileiros de filosofia, 7632
Mila, Luis, 369
Milanca Guzmán, Mario, 7169–7170
Mileo, Diego, 6036
Miles, Sara, 5987
Millar Corbacho, René, 2758
Miller, Barbara, 2177
Miller, Beth, 5502, 5954
Miller, Linda Ledford. *See* Ledford-Miller, Linda.
Miller, Mary Ellen, 258a
Miller, Robert Ryal, 1901
Miller, Rory, 3060
Miller, Sara, 1976
Miller, Simon, 2087
Miller, Virginia E., 259
Milliet, Sérgio, 6366
Millones, Luis, 1670
Milón Duarte, Luis. *See* Duarte, Luis Milón.
Minas e indios del Perú, siglos XVI–XVIII, 2771
Minchom, Martin, 1671–1672, 2707
Minera, Otto, 6027
Miño Grijalva, Manuel, 1673–1674, 1976a-1977, 2695
Miranda, Francisco de, 2649
Miranda, Julio E., 1105
Miranda Netto, Antônio Garcia de, 7065
Mirelman, Victor A., 3272
Mires, Fernando, 7618
Miró, Rodrigo, 5075, 5055
Miró Domínguez, Aurora, 4561

Widmer, Ernst, 7075, 7084
Wiemers, Eugene L., Jr., 2116
Wiencek, Henry, 254
Wijk, H.L. van. *See* Van Wijk, H.L.
Wilkerson, S. Jeffrey K., 1578
Wilkie, Everett C., Jr., 2479
Wilkie, James W., 1796, 1884
Willeke, Venâncio, 3392
Willemsen, Glenn Frank Walter, 2611
Williams, Raymond L., 5489
Williman, José Claudio h., 3366
Wilmot, Swithin, 2554
Wilson, Fiona, 3080
Wilson, Jams, 2318
Wilson, Lofton, 45
Winer, Víctor, 6004
Winford, Donald, 4660–4661
Winning, Hasso von. *See* von Winning, Hasso.
Wirth, John D., 1876
Wise, David O., 5511
Wobeser, Gisela von, 2006
Wojski, Zygmunt, 4559
Wolff, Egon, 6019
Woll, Allen L., 966
Woman who has sprouted wings: poems by contemporary Latin American women poets, 6525
Wong, Oscar, 5753
Wood, A.J.R. Russell. *See* Russell-Wood, A.J.R.
Wood, Richard E., 4515
Wood, Robert D., 1575, 1768, 2627
Woodward, Ralph Lee, 68
Woodyard, George, 6122
Woolley, Stan, 7024
World armies, 72
World Literature Today, 5262
Wortman, Miles, 1779
Wright, Thomas C., 1861, 1868a, 3182
Wunder, Gerd, 3183
Wynter, Sylvia, 2412
Wyrobisz, Andrzej, 314, 1862

Xavier, Alberto, 492
Xavier, Ismail, 1033

Yale University. Library, 45
Ycaza, Patricio, 3018
Ycaza Tigerino, Julio César, 7539
La Yerba mate y Misiones, 3326
Yerovi, Nicolas, 5819
Young, Dolly, 5263

Yudice, George, 5926
Yurkievich, Saúl, 5649, 5688, 5927
Yuste López, Carmen, 1928

Zagury, Eliane, 6386
Zalazar, Daniel E., 5161–5162, 7666–7667
Zaldívar Guerra, Sergio, 351
Zamora, Elías, 1579, 2252
Zamora, R., 285
Zanini, Walter, 432
Zantwijk, Rudolf A.M. van, 1580–1581
Zapata, Luis, 5211
Zapata Olivella, Juan, 5540
Zapater, Horacio, 1769
Zapatero, Juan Manuel, 2686
Zarama, José Rafael, 2687
Zarzar, Alonso, 1770
Zavadiker, Ricardo A., 7025
Zavala, Iris M., 5968
Zavala, Lorenzo de, 2117
Zavala, Silvio Arturo, 352, 1863, 2003, 2007–2008, 7558
Zavala Cataño, Víctor, 6058
Zavaleta, Carlos Eduardo, 5512
Zawisza, Leszek M., 2926
Zayas de Lima, Perla, 6123
Zayas Micheli, Luis O., 5477
Zea, Leopoldo, 7530, 7540–7541
Zea Flores, Carlos Enrique, 358
Zeceña Navas, Porfirio, 5314
Zeitlin, Maurice, 3184
Zeitz, Eileen M., 5045
Zemskov, 5046
Zenarruza, Jorge G.C., 2840
Zepeda, Eraclio, 5754
Zevi, Fauto, 495
Zilberman, Regina, 6437
Zílio, Carlos, 437
Zimmerman, Marc, 5986
Zimra, Clarisse, 6492
Ziólkowski, Mariusz S., 1771–1772
Zito Lema, Vicente, 5883
Zubatsky, David S., 73
Zuberbühler, Ricardo F., 3327
Zubizarreta, Carlos, 3346
Zubritski, Yuri, 1773
Zuccherino, Ricardo Miguel, 3328
Zuidema, R. Tom, 1774
Zuleta, Emilia de, 5689
Zuleta Alvarez, Enrique, 7578, 7668
Zúñiga, Neptalí, 2721
Zúñiga C., Edgar, 2253
Zúnigo Díaz, Francisco, 5315
Zurita, Raúl, 5884, 5928